African American Religious Thought

African American Religious Thought

An Anthology

Cornel West

Eddie S. Glaude Jr.

Editors

Westminster John Knox Press

LOUISVILLE • LONDON

Book design by Sharon Adams
Cover design by Eric Handel/LMNOP

First edition
Published by Westminster John Knox Press
Louisville, Kentucky

Permissions acknowledgments are on pages 1051–1054 and constitute a continuation of this copyright page.

This book is printed on acid-free paper that meets the American National Standards Institute Z39.48 standard. ♾

PRINTED IN THE UNITED STATES OF AMERICA

03 04 05 06 07 08 09 10 11 12 — 10 9 8 7 6 5 4 3 2 1

Library of Congress Cataloging-in-Publication Data

African American religious thought : an anthology / Cornel West, Eddie S. Glaude, Jr., editors.—1st ed.
    p. cm.
Includes bibliographical references.
ISBN 0-664-22459-8 (alk. paper)
1. African Americans—Religion.   I. West, Cornel.   II. Glaude, Eddie S., 1968–

BR563.N4A364 2004
230'.089'96073—dc21   2003053468

To the memory of James Melvin Washington,
Towering Intellectual and Prophetic Voice,
whose Wisdom continues to guide our journey

Contents

Introduction

Towards New Visions and New Approaches in African American Religious Studies

Cornel West and Eddie S. Glaude Jr.

African American religious studies has reached a crossroads. Such a moment was inevitable. As the field continues to grow and as scholars continue to produce a range of work on the subject, new theoretical and methodological questions are bound to arise. What then is this crossroads? In some ways, the field struggles to emerge from a certain set of theological reflections that have dominated it since its inception. To be sure, the works of James Cone and others brought the preoccupations of more traditional scholarship in the field into a new milieu in which new sorts of questions could be asked and black religious experiences could be examined differently. Cone's efforts to translate (with the skill of a brilliant systematic theologian) the insights of the prophetic black church tradition into an idiom of Black Power resulted in the formation of a new discourse—one that contained a number of different trajectories as to how African American religious studies could be configured and as to how black ministers might substantively intervene and minimize the suffering in black communities.

One notices these concerns in Gayraud Wilmore's definition of African American religious studies. He writes:

African American Religious Studies refers to the investigation, analysis and ordering of a wide variety of data related to the religions of persons of African descent for the purpose of authenticating and enriching personal faith and preparing clergy and laity for the ministry in the Black Church and community, understood in terms of competent and faithful leadership in worship, education, and corporate action in behalf of God's mission of liberation for all people.[1]

This definition reflects Wilmore's effort (1) to resist narrow functionalist accounts of black religion, which fail to take seriously the way black individuals think about God, and (2) to insist on the practical relevance of the field in efforts to fight against various forms of oppression. For Wilmore, the sorts of distinctions that make possible the dispassionate treatment of religion as "an object of inquiry" simply do not hold for African American religion. As he writes, "the best religious scholarship in the black academy is, perforce, 'believing scholarship,' accepting all the risks that such a position entails."[2] The realities of white supremacy and the role of black religion in resisting those realities make it difficult, in his view, to engage in "armchair theorizing" about African American religious practices. As such, the training of pastors becomes a critical component shaping courses of African American religious studies. So, for Wilmore, despite his commitment to interdisciplinary approaches to the subject matter, theological commitments and practical relevance are central to what scholars of African American religion do.

What we have set out to do in this massive undertaking is offer a new direction for the field. We do not hold the view that theological education frames the entire enterprise of African American religious studies. It is simply one crucial yet distinct part of a differentiated field of inquiry. In some ways, through our selection of essays for the book, we have attempted to answer the question: Where do we go from here? The extraordinary efforts of scholars in the field up to now have provided us with the requisite tools to engage in the kind of experimentation or tinkering requisite for the moment.

We hold the view that African American religious studies, in part, addresses the various ways the moral languages of black religious expression and their complex relation to the ethical and political aspects of culture inform African American life in particular and American life in general. In our view, it is not necessarily the case "that all other dimensions of the black community should find their expression as aspects of the religious experience of black folks."[3] It simply follows from the claim that

1. Gayraud Wilmore, "General Introduction," *African American Religious Studies: An Interdisciplinary Anthology*, ed. Gayraud Wilmore (Durham, N.C.: Duke University Press, 1989), xii–xiii.

2. Ibid., xii.

3. Charles Long, "Assessment and New Departures for a Study of Black Religion in the United States," in Wilmore's *African American Religious Studies*, 38.

black religious experience stands at the center of black life that the institutions, practices, and values singled out by the words "black religion"
help us gain insight into the doings and sufferings of these peculiarly modern people. We need not reduce the complexity of the beliefs, choices, and
actions of African Americans to expressions of black religion, nor should
we overextend the reach of the phrase.

The words "black religion" serve as a conceptual shortcut to manage
a number of different practices, beliefs, choices, values, events, and institutions that compose black life in the United States. Such a view requires
of scholars in the field—as it does in religious studies in general—a careful and systematic examination of the analytic value of the term "religion"
in our analysis of black culture. As we understand it, then, African American religious studies critically engages, among other matters, the way
"black religion" is understood—extending the analysis, as it were, beyond
an assessment of the place of black religion and its institutions in American society to a more critical analysis of the discursive and ritualistic formations that question traditional scholarly categories and open up new
sites for investigation. As one can see, we are not so worried about "armchair theorizing." In fact, we are calling for more careful "meta" reflection on the central category of our field, including its complex relations
to sophisticated conceptions of class, gender, sexual orientation, race, and
empire.

Historical periodization is important in this regard, and we maintain
that five significant historical moments ought to inform our inquiry into
African American religious life.[4] The first stage can be viewed as "African
American Religion as the Problem of Slavery." This period lasted roughly
from the mid-eighteenth century to 1863, from the Great Revivals to the
Emancipation Proclamation. During this period, African Americans
forged a distinctive Christian outlook in response to the institution of
slavery. The first African American religious denominations were formed
in the North. And we can begin to see the complex relationship between
black religious expression and a developing national black politics.

The second stage can be viewed as "African American Religion
and the Problem(s) of Emancipation." This stage, which lasted from
1864 to 1903, covers African American religious life from the period of

4. This periodization is based on Cornel West's account in *Prophesy Deliverance!* See chap.
4, this volume. *Prophesy Deliverance! An Afro-American Revolutionary Christianity* (Philadelphia:
Westminster Press, 1982), 101–5. Anniversary edition, with a new preface by the author,
Louisville, Ky.: Westminster John Knox Press, 2002.

Reconstruction and what Rayford Logan described as the nadir of black history to the publication of Du Bois's *Souls of Black Folk*. During this period, we see the failed attempts at a genuine multiracial democracy during Reconstruction and the sedimentation of Jim and Jane Crow throughout the South. This time was one of intense institutional terror against blacks in which the racist institutions of the United States rendered the vast majority of African Americans politically powerless, economically vulnerable, and socially degraded. We also see the resurgence of a distinctive black religious language urging a return to Africa, and the formation of Black Baptist Conventions. W.E.B. Du Bois's *Souls of Black Folk* offers an account of black religion in "Of the Faith of Our Fathers" and, in some ways, ushers in the treatment of African American religion as an "object of inquiry."

The third stage can be dated from 1903 to 1954, from the publication of *Souls of Black Folk* to the Supreme Court decision of *Brown v. Board of Education*. This stage can be viewed as "African American Religion, the City, and the Challenge to Racism." During this period, the Great Migration, international migration, and the urbanization of a large segment of the black population transformed black communities in cities and throughout the North. The appearance of twentieth-century black religious phenomena like Daddy Grace and Father Divine, Black Jews, the Moorish Science Temple, the Nation of Islam, Black Pentecostalism, and the civil religion of the Garvey movement also signaled a plurality of black religious expression that would affect the form and content of black political discourse. We also see the continued development of African American religious studies. Works include master's theses at the University of Chicago; classics such as Carter G. Woodson's *History of the Negro Church*, 1921; Benjamin E. Mays and Joseph Nicholson's *The Negro's Church*, 1933; Arthur Fauset's *Black Gods of the Metropolis*, 1944; and the profound work of Howard Thurman, all of which were produced within the rising tide of resistance to white supremacy in the United States.

The fourth stage can be seen as "African American Religion and the Black Freedom Struggle," and it dates from 1954, the *Brown v. Board of Education* decision, to 1969 and the publication of James Cone's *Black Theology and Black Power*. During this phase, we see the importance of the Civil Rights movement, with the prophetic leadership of Dr. Martin Luther King Jr. and the institutional strength of black churches, in efforts to break down the walls of segregation. One also notices the complex relationship between the religious dimensions of the Civil Rights movement and the

Black Power phase, and the significance of Malcolm X and the politics of black nationalism to the struggle for black studies and the emergence of black theology.

The fifth stage, from 1969 to the present, can be viewed as "The Golden Age of African American Religious Studies." Scholars of African American religion in this period include Albert Raboteau, John Blassingame, Sterling Stuckey, Eugene Genovese, Lawrence Levine, Joseph R. Washington, Evelyn Brooks Higginbotham, and others. Black theologians also produced an extensive body of literature that served as a basis for a vibrant and creative set of reflections about the basic premises of African American religious studies. During this phase, revisions of Cone's conception of theology are offered. Gender and class critiques become paramount. The work of Jacquelyn Grant, Delores Williams, Katie Cannon, and others are important in this regard. We also begin to see the critical insights of cultural studies impacting the study of African American religion. Essentialist conceptions of race and the racial politics of the Black Power era are criticized. Theological interests stand alongside other approaches to the subject, and African American religious studies begins to emerge from under the rubric of black theology and a singular Christian preoccupation.

Each of these five historical moments must be understood against the backdrop of (1) the implosion of Europe and the development of modernist discourses and their impact on religious life, (2) the emergence of the United States as a world power, and (3) the decolonization of the Third World. These historical coordinates, we believe, situate African American religious studies within a larger set of historical processes that certainly impact the life world of African Americans—holding off any tendency to ghettoize black strivings.

Three categories can help us organize the current state of the field in light of these historical moments: (a) black religious history, (b) black theology, and (c) the sociology of black religion. *Black religious history* involves accounts of the development of black religious institutions and the communities of the faithful that sustain them. This particular subfield is quite differentiated in that the published works range from general surveys to regional and local studies (church, denominational, and mission histories). Interesting historiographical debates have also emerged as scholars reflect on what can be called "orthodox" accounts of the interwar history of mainline black denominations. The vibrancy of this area of study is reflected in the Afro-American Religious History

Documentary Project, directed by Albert Raboteau of Princeton University and David Wills of Amherst College.[5]

Black theology emerged in the context of the black freedom struggle as a series of intense (academic) reflections about the relation between the historical experiences of black people in the United States and their faith in God. Its emergence coincides with the "golden era" of the study of black religion. Here the experiences of living in a white supremacist culture were explored in order to shed light on the essential meanings of black religious conviction and to underscore the importance of social context for theological reflection. Because black theologians reject what they take to be white interpretations of the gospel, we include under this category black biblical studies in which interpreters of the Bible developed techniques of interpretation informed by black experiences.[6]

Gayraud S. Wilmore and James Cone edited a documentary history of the subfield entitled *Black Theology: A Documentary History, 1966–1979.* Wilmore also published an influential historical survey of African American religious history, *Black Religion and Black Radicalism: An Interpretation of the Religious History of Afro-American People.* In many ways, this work provided the historical backdrop for the black theological project. James Cone remains the central figure in this area. Through various engagements with his work, at least two different approaches have emerged: narrativist theologians who take up the issue of social context but emphasize the importance of stories or narrative and, for some, the framework of Afrocentrism; and black womanist theologians and historians who unsettle the neat story of black theology by introducing the experiences of black women not simply in relation to a racist culture but a sexist one as well.[7]

5. David Wills and Randall K. Burkett, "Afro-American Religious History, 1919–1939: Bibliographic Essay and Resource Guide" (unpublished work); David Wills, "Bibliographical Essay: African-American Religious History," *Evangelical Studies Bulletin* 11, no. 1 (spring 1994): 6. Ethel L. Williams and Clifton E. Brown, *Afro-American Religious Studies: A Comprehensive Bibliography with Locations in American Libraries* (Metuchen, N.J.: Scarecrow Press, 1979); Michael W. Harris, "African American Religious History in the 1980s: A Critical Review," *Religious Studies Review* 20, no. 4 (October 1994): 263–75; *African-American Religion: Interpretative Essays in History and Culture,* ed. Timothy Fulop and Albert Raboteau (New York: Routledge, 1997); *African American Christianity: Essays in History,* ed. Paul E. Johnson (Berkeley: University of California Press, 1994).

6. We are thinking about the work of Vincent L. Wimbush and Cane Hope Felder's edited volume, *Stony the Road We Trod* (Minneapolis: Fortress Press, 1991).

7. For foundational texts in these areas, see Dwight Hopkins and George Cummings, eds., *Cut Loose Your Stammering Tongue: Black Theology in the Slave Narrative* (Maryknoll, N.Y.: Orbis, 1991), 2d ed. (Louisville, Ky.: Westminster John Knox Press, 2003); Dwight Hopkins, *Shoes That Fit Our Feet: Sources for a Constructive Black Theology* (Maryknoll, N.Y.: Orbis, 1994);

Since the beginning of black theology, the claims of black theologians have sparked intense and widespread debates. The theoretical works of William R. Jones, Charles Long, Cecil Cone, and others pushed the basic assumptions of James Cone's black theological project.[8] The scope of the debate extended across the discipline from the kinds of historical accounts informing black theology to questions about the organic relation between black theology and actual black churches. As Victor Anderson notes in his book, *Beyond Ontological Blackness: An Essay on African American Religious and Cultural Criticism*:

> most criticisms centered around the relation of black theology to black churches. Early critics asked how black theology could be a theology of the black churches if it fundamentally disentangles itself from the creed and confessions, as well as the liturgical practices that structure the black churches. . . . Others asked, in what sense could black theology be black since its theological method was derived from white theologians, notably Karl Barth and Paul Tillich?[9]

Still, others criticized the work for its lack of attention to class and its complicity in patriarchy. These debates in and around black theology constitute a discursive formation, because the arguments and counterarguments refer to the same object, share a similar style, and support a strategy, a common institutional or political pattern.[10] In this vein the discursive

---

Julian Kunnie, *Models of Black Theology: Issues in Class, Culture, and Gender* (Valley Forge, Pa.: Trinity Press, 1994); Riggins R. Earl, *Dark Symbols, Obscure Signs: God, Self, and Community in the Slave Mind* (Maryknoll, N.Y.: Orbis, 1993); and Peter J. Paris, *The Spirituality of African Peoples: The Search for a Common Moral Discourse* (Minneapolis: Fortress, 1995). See also Katie Cannon, *Black Womanist Ethics* (Atlanta: Scholars Press, 1988); Jacquelyn Grant, *White Women's Christ and Black Women's Jesus* (Atlanta: Scholars Press, 1989); Emilie M. Townes, ed., *Troubling in My Soul: Womanist Perspectives on Evil and Suffering* (Maryknoll, N.Y.: Orbis, 1993).

8. William R. Jones, *Is God a White Racist? A Preamble to Black Theology* (Boston: Beacon Press, 1998); Charles Long, *Significations: Signs, Symbols, and Images in the Interpretation of Religion* (Philadelphia: Fortress, 1986); Cecil Cone, *The Identity Crisis in Black Theology* (Nashville: AMEC, 1975). Also see Dwight Hopkins's recent edited volume, *Black Faith and Public Talk: Critical Essays on James Cone's* Black Theology and Black Power (Maryknoll, N.Y.: Orbis, 1999).

9. Victor Anderson, *Beyond Ontological Blackness: An Essay on African American Religious and Cultural Criticism* (New York: Continuum, 1995), 90.

10. M. Cousins and A. Hussain, *Michel Foucault* (London: Macmillan, 1984), 84–85.

practice of black theology (and the sheer volume of the published works that compose it) produces meaning about what constitutes the field of African American religious studies.

The sociology of black religion has always been given some attention in African American religious studies, stemming from the assumption that black religious and secular life are so intertwined that no reasonable distinction between the two can be made if we are to understand the complex workings of these folk. This assumption informs the early scholarly works in the field. From Du Bois's *Souls of Black Folk* and Woodson's *History of the Negro Church* to Mays and Nicholson's *The Negro's Church*, the study of black religion functioned, on one level, as a synecdoche for talking about the whole of black America. Other works also explored the role and function of black religious institutions in black society. Examples of this literature include Fauset's *Black Gods of the Metropolis*, E. Franklin Frazier's *The Negro Church* (1964), and C. Eric Lincoln's edited volume, *The Black Experience in Religion* (1974), as well as his *Race, Religion, and the Continuing American Dilemma* (1984) and the coauthored work with Lawrence H. Mamiya, *The Black Church in the African American Experience* (1990). The sociology of black religion involves then (at uneven levels of subtlety) politics, cultural criticism, and the study of a variety of black institutions that intersected with black religion.

With this historical periodization and these three extant categories in mind, this volume aims to broaden our conception of the field and to take seriously the importance of interdisciplinary approaches to African American religious practices. History, theology, and what can be called cultural criticism remain constitutive subareas of the field. One of our major tasks is to urge that we think about these areas within a broader framework that is not reducible to theological claims.

For us, the subject matter of African American religious studies includes the experiences of people of African descent shaped in the environment of the "New World" and understood with religious languages that interpret and evaluate those experiences to effectively transform them. The New World constitutes the place of encounter between various cultures—the primal scene where Africa and the West meet, and new peoples emerge in the aftermath of the violence that followed this fateful encounter. The New World, then, is the site of displacement, appropriation, and creolization as people adjust and adapt to the new environs and to the operations of power that define some as free persons and others as slaves and slave owners.

This encounter occurs against the backdrop of European modernity. Transformations in the political, economic, social, and cultural spheres in

Europe unleashed with the Reformation and consolidated by the nineteenth century changed how individuals and groups understood themselves, others, and the world around them. The emergence of secular forms of political power and an industrialized capitalist order, the decline of ecclesiastical authority and traditional social arrangements, and the sedimentation of a new way of producing and classifying knowledge provided "modern subjects" with a distinctive set of tools to make their world. The underside of these developments, however, consisted in the trafficking of black bodies, the subordination of women, and the emergence of new class formations.

African American religious studies begins with the assumption that it is a New World phenomenon, shaped by the complex variation of European modernity which evolved as American culture, and the intricate transactions between marginalized Africans and the American culture in which these people were both participants and victims.[11] African American religious studies as it developed in the United States, then, examines how these peculiar, black modern subjects came to terms with their status as slaves, struggled for dignity and freedom, and how they imagined a future for their children in the context of a democratic experiment in which, ideally, individuals were accorded dignity irrespective of their background, freedom was considered a natural right, *and* black people were held as chattel.

Of course, these intricate transactions employed the tools of the Old and New World. Africans brought with them the languages, beliefs, and practices of particular forms of life, which gave the ideas of democracy a different sound (a blue note perhaps) and aided in the construction of new institutions responsive to the needs of everyday life under the limiting conditions of slavery.[12] This statement is not to suggest a fixed conception of African culture in which New World articulations by people of African descent are understood as simply African. We want to acknowledge that wherever people of African descent are, Africa speaks—even, at times, with new words and inflections. To be sure, Africa was present, as Stuart Hall notes,

> in the everyday life of the slave quarters, in the languages and patois of the plantation, in names and words, often disconnected from their taxonomies, in the secret syntactical structures through which these languages were spoken, in the stories and tales told to children, in

11. West, *Prophesy Deliverance!* 22.
12. Sidney Mintz and Richard Price, *The Birth of African American Culture: An Anthropological Perspective* (Boston: Beacon Press, 1992).

religious practice and beliefs in the spiritual life, the arts, crafts, music and rhythms of slave and post-emancipation society.[13]

A central question in African American religious studies is how do we account for this African presence? How do we understand its power in the religious imagination of African Americans, its influence on the form and content of black religious expression, and its centrality to a conception of black identity forged in the struggle for freedom in the New World? These questions must be examined in light of the fact that black moderns created something new in the face of prevailing circumstances that can be described best as absurd.

One of the most important languages used to make sense of the absurd circumstances of slavery was that of Christianity. From about the mid-eighteenth century to the early nineteenth century, many African Americans converted to Christianity and found a way of interpreting their situation and hoping against hope that one day they would be free. The evangelical traditions of Baptists and Methodists were particularly appealing to the slaves, because of their emphasis on individual experience, the ecstatic nature of their worship services, and the belief that all were equal before God. African Americans found, then, in the Christian gospel as it was preached during the Great Revivals, liberating possibilities in their personal experiences of conversion, in the family resemblance of evangelical worship services with practices of an African past, and in a vocabulary that enabled the slave to escape the psychic effects of slavery. They were no longer extensions of a white master's will. Instead, many Christian slaves came to see themselves as a unique—even chosen—people with a different moral sense about them, capable of distinguishing intuitively the wrongness of slavery and racial discrimination and the rightness of their common complaint, because of their distinctive relationship to God. This connection with God allowed them to step outside of the master-slave relationship, which defined them as a means to the master's ends, and to see themselves as self-determining agents.

Theological, existential, and political considerations followed from this particular view. African Americans had to reconcile their conception of God with the reality of their suffering. As such, the problem of evil loomed large as a distinctive theological outlook was forged amid the bru-

13. Stuart Hall, "Cultural Identity and Diaspora," in *Colonial Discourse and Post-Colonial Theory: A Reader* (New York: Columbia University Press, 1994), 398.

tal realities of antebellum America. How are we to think about God, the gospel, Jesus, and slavery? J.W.C. Pennington's sermon in 1845 captures best what's at stake in this question and the unique theology that emerged from its answer:

> If you stand commended to the guidance of the Word of God, you are bound to know its position in reference to certain overt acts that crowd the land with curses. Take the last and greatest of the curses that I named above. I mean slavery. Is the word of God silent on this subject? I, for one, desire to know. My repentance, my faith, my hope, my love, and my perseverance all, all, I conceal it not, I repeat it, all turn upon this point. If I am deceived here—if the word of God does sanction slavery, I want another book, another repentance, another faith, and another hope![14]

So, in some ways, the distinctive theology of black Christianity stood as a loud rebuke of white Christianity. The adjectives matter here. For God, the gospel, and Jesus are all adapted to and understood within the context of the evil of white supremacy.

Existentially, this black Christian outlook informed how African Americans understood themselves, others, and the world around them. The personal experiences of conversion enabled otherwise degraded individuals to see themselves as worthwhile and precious in God's sight. This sense of self-worth was fortified by the religious rhetorics used in the construction of a communal identity. African Americans, through biblical analogy, came to see themselves as the children of God, linking as it were the freedom of the Israelites with their own eventual liberation. This religious symbology, however, did not yield a facile optimism. A tragicomic sensibility—in a blues-shaped idiom—informed the way African Americans imagined possibility for themselves and their children. They understood the limiting conditions of the world of action and drew on the power of their faith to confront candidly individual and collective experiences of evil with little expectation of ridding the world of all evil. A blues ethos

14. *A Two Years' Absence or a Farewell Sermon, preached in the Fifth Congregational Church, by J.W.C. Pennington*, Nov. 2, 1845 (Hartford, Conn., 1845). Also quoted in Hortense Spillers, "Moving On Down the Line: Variations on the African American Sermon," in Dominick La-Capra, *The Bounds of Race: Perspectives on Hegemony and Resistance* (Ithaca, N.Y.: Cornell University Press, 1991).

informed their beliefs, choices, and actions as they engaged an environment shot through with sin and impinging daily upon their lives.

African American Christianity provided then, to some extent, a political language to engage American slavery and racism. To be sure, the religious symbology used in the construction of a national black community
stood as a form of critique of American society for betraying its ideals as
well as a means for positive self-identification. America was supposed to
be the "shining city on the hill," the home of the "New Israelites." African
Americans, however, often figured America as Egypt and its slaveholding
citizens as Pharaoh. This figural rereading of America emerged out of the
black church, historically the most important institution in black America.

The "black church" (whether the invisible institution of the South or the
black churches and denominations of the North) was the principle site of
public engagement for African Americans. Here black individuals could participate directly in deliberation about their circumstances without public
humiliation from white Americans. (At least, this was the case for black men,
given the patriarchal assumptions informing the organization of black public space. Most women were relegated to subordinate positions in the private
domain.) The church also housed numerous activities, from schools to social
functions. Indeed, this institution gave birth to black civil society, provided
a leadership class in black ministers, and as Du Bois noted in *Souls of Black
Folk*, was "peculiarly the expression of the inner ethical life of a people in a
sense seldom true elsewhere."[15] Not only did the church serve as a site for
deliberation and social activity, it also—if Du Bois is right—provided social
and institutional moorings for the ethical utterances of black America.

Yet and still, African American Christianity and its institutional expression remained ambivalently connected to white America. In fact, to tell
the story of its development is, in some significant sense, to tell the history of American religion. Both are intimately—to borrow a usage from
James Baldwin—connected, and to study one without the other is to lose
sight of how race fundamentally shapes America's political and cultural
landscape. The ambivalence marks the "in but not of" status of African
Americans: the fact that the vocabularies acquired from the discourses of
democracy and Christianity were shadowed by the specter of slavery and
white supremacy. As such, the appropriation of Christianity was both
enabling and an accommodation in its political outlook, making possible
a critical insurgent politics as well as containing the more radical possi-

---

15. W.E.B. Du Bois, "Faith of Our Fathers," in *Souls of Black Folk* (New York: Library of
America, 1986), 499.

bilities of that politics. Hortense Spillers captures this ambivalence with her question: "Is it too much to say that the African could not *but* have become a Christian in the sociopolitical context of the United States, as a *strategy* for giving his or her historical ground and [humanity] here?"[16]

African American religious studies examines the complex and overlapping relationship between black religious discourses and the American ideology, and their relation to discourses of race, gender, class, and other values that continue to challenge our democratic ideals. What is the relationship of black religious traditions and black politics? How has this relationship changed as the political and social realities of America have changed? Each of the questions should be examined, we maintain, without recourse to easy either-or accounts of the relationship between black religion and politics that force one to say definitively that African American Christianity was either revolutionary in content or accommodationist in its political outlook. We suggest instead that a thick historicist sensibility ought to inform how we understand the connection between black religion and politics, and the various understandings that connection make possible for effective action in the present.

We have organized this book, in some ways, to tell a story about what black agents have done and made in light of the historical conditions that give their beliefs, choices, and actions meaning. Attention is given to the various fissures that disrupt monolithic conceptions of African American religious life. Gender, class, sexual orientation, and empire complicate the kind of story that can be told. Through interpretations of African American history—or better, in efforts to understand the different ways African Americans have attempted to solve crises—scholars of African American religion seek to comprehend what informs our contemporary setting, and better equip us to respond to the challenges confronting black communities and the country in general. In this sense, the historical work is, in a significant way, ethical work: a way of transforming prevailing realities that we view as bad by telling thick stories that provide us with the tools to engage in intelligently guided experimentation to make life better for ourselves and for future generations. In short, we hold the view that African American religious studies at its best tries to make theoretically explicit what is implicit in history, to describe and demystify cultural and social practices and offer solutions to urgent problems besetting African Americans.[17]

---

16. Spillers, "Moving On Down the Line," in her book *Black, White, and in Color: Essays on American Literature and Culture* (Chicago: University of Chicago Press, 2003), 263.
17. West, *Prophesy Deliverance!* 22.

❧❧❧❧❧❧❧❧

With the historical periodization we have offered and the three categories of history, theology, and cultural criticism as our guide, we have organized the book into eight sections. Parts 1 and 2 frame the more historical sections with theoretical reflections about African American religion. Part 1 introduces the reader to some of the classic formulations in the field. Here the student can acquire a sense of the general themes and different ideological approaches that have, in some ways, defined the study of African American religion.

Part 2 represents the various ways scholars have thought about the field at a certain level of abstraction. One can get a sense, for example, of the different assumptions informing sociological reflections on black religion in Orlando Patterson's essay and the pioneering work of C. Eric Lincoln. Students should also see the distinctive approaches to the study of African American religion evidenced in the essays of Cornel West and Charles Long, with West drawing on the pragmatist tradition and Long using a phenomenological approach. Evelyn Brooks Higginbotham and David Wills offer historical accounts that take seriously the impact of gender and race on the kind of story that can be told about African American religious history in particular and American religious history in general. Students should think about parts 1 and 2 together, and note the threads of continuity and discontinuity between the classic and more recent accounts of African American religion.[18]

The remaining parts of the book follow the historical periodization we have suggested. Part 3 addresses slavery. Part 4 concerns itself with postemancipation. The essays in part 5 take up the issues of migration and religious plurality. Part 6 addresses the significance of African American religion and the black freedom struggle. The essays in part 7 should be read in relation to part 6: they concern themselves with the discourse of black theology and its critics. Part 8 suggests, to some extent, the impact of cultural studies on the field and offers examples of different venues for scholarly work in and around African American religion. The selection of essays in each of these sections reflects our attempt to capture the inter-

---

18. We also urge that these essays be read alongside the other classical literature in religious studies (e.g., the works of Max Weber, Emile Durkheim, Sigmund Freud, Rudolph Otto, Mary Douglas, Mircea Eliade, William James, Mary Daly, and Clifford Geertz) to (1) demonstrate the extent to which scholars of African American religion are in conversation with more general theoretical reflections on religion and (2) to illustrate how the specific histories of people of African descent "color" their thinking about religion broadly understood.

disciplinary character of the field and to resist a kind of theological reductionism. We have included in each part essays on the gendered dimensions of African American religion. We reject an additive approach to questions of gender. As such, we decided not to separate the essays into a distinct section, because we believe gender to be constitutive of any approach to the subject matter.

In the end, each part takes up some of the issues we have briefly explored in this introduction. As a whole, the essays demonstrate the following points about African American religious studies:

1. African American religious studies begins with the assumption that it is a New World phenomenon, shaped by the complex variation of European modernity that evolved as American culture, and the intricate transactions between marginalized Africans and the American culture in which these people were both participants and victims.
2. This field addresses the various ways in which the axiological and existential languages of black religious expression and their complex relation to the ethical, political, and economic aspects of culture inform African American life in particular and American life in general.
3. African American religious studies critically engages the way "black religion" is understood—extending the analysis beyond an assessment of the place of black religion and its institutions in American society to a more critical analysis of the discursive and ritualistic formations that question traditional scholarly categories and open up new sites for investigation.
4. The discipline examines the complex and overlapping relationship between black religious discourses and the American ideology, and their relation to discourses of race, gender, class, and other values that continue to challenge our democratic ideals.

Hopefully, each of these formulations can aid in the continued development of new visions and approaches to the study of African American religion.

Personal Acknowledgments

Such an ambitious undertaking could not be the result of just the two of us. Many people have contributed to the completion of this project. Without Angela Jackson's extraordinary vision and courage the book would have never materialized. We are truly indebted to her. We also want to thank Mary Ann Rodriquez, whose diligence and organization stream-lined the process of acquiring permissions. We are also grateful to Stephanie Egnotovich, our editor. Her excitement for the project pushed us to complete the book. We are especially thankful to Kijan Bloomfield and Lauren Flinn, our two undergraduate assistants at Bowdoin College. And we must mention the support of our families, the sustaining force behind our work: Marie and Langston; Zeytun and Clifton.

Finally, we want to thank all of those scholars and activists, particularly the late James M. Washington, who have labored over the years to make the field of African American religion so vibrant and vital. This is our small contribution to what has been and will continue to be a labor of love.

Part 1

Prehistory of African American Religious Studies

Chapter 1

Of the Faith of the Fathers

W.E.B. Du Bois

It was out in the country, far from home, far from my foster home, on a dark Sunday night. The road wandered from our rambling log-house up the stony bed of a creek, past wheat and corn, until we could hear dimly across the fields a rhythmic cadence of song,—soft, thrilling, powerful, that swelled and died sorrowfully in our ears. I was a country school-teacher then, fresh from the East, and had never seen a Southern Negro revival. To be sure, we in Berkshire were not perhaps as stiff and formal as they in Suffolk of olden time; yet we were very quiet and subdued, and I know not what would have happened those clear Sabbath mornings had someone punctuated the sermon with a wild scream, or interrupted the long prayer with a loud Amen! And so most striking to me, as I approached the village and the little plain church perched aloft, was the air of intense excitement that possessed that mass of black folk. A sort of suppressed terror hung in the air and seemed to seize us,—a pythian madness, a demonic possession, that lent terrible reality to song and word. The black and massive form of the preacher swayed and quivered as the words crowded to his lips and flew at us in singular eloquence. The people moaned and fluttered, and then the gaunt-cheeked brown woman beside me suddenly leaped straight into the air and shrieked like a lost soul, while round about came wail and groan and outcry, and a scene of human passion such as I had never conceived before.

Those who have not thus witnessed the frenzy of a Negro revival in the untouched backwoods of the South can but dimly realize the religious feeling of the slave; as described, such scenes appear grotesque and funny, but as seen they are awful. Three things characterized this religion of the slave,—the Preacher, the Music, and the Frenzy. The Preacher is the most unique personality developed by the Negro on American soil. A leader, a politician, an orator, a "boss," an intriguer, an idealist,—all these he is, and ever, too, the centre of a group of men, now twenty, now a thousand in number. The combination of a certain adroitness with deep-seated earnestness, of tact with consummate ability, gave him his preëminence, and helps him maintain it. The type, of course, varies according to time and place, from the West Indies in the sixteenth century to New England in the nineteenth, and from the Mississippi bottoms to cities like New Orleans or New York.

The Music of Negro religion is that plaintive rhythmic melody, with its touching minor cadences, which, despite caricature and defilement, still remains the most original and beautiful expression of human life and longing yet born on American soil. Sprung from the African forests, where its counterpart can still be heard, it was adapted, changed, and intensified by the tragic soul-life of the slave, until, under the stress of law and whip, it became the one true expression of a people's sorrow, despair, and hope.

Finally the Frenzy or "Shouting," when the Spirit of the Lord passed by, and, seizing the devotee, made him mad with supernatural joy, was the last essential of Negro religion and the one more devoutly believed in than all the rest. It varied in expression from the silent rapt countenance or the low murmur and moan to the mad abandon of physical fervor,—the stamping, shrieking, and shouting, the rushing to and fro and wild waving of arms, the weeping and laughing, the vision and the trance. All this is nothing new in the world, but old as religion, as Delphi and Endor. And so firm a hold did it have on the Negro, that many generations firmly believed that without this visible manifestation of the God there could be no true communion with the Invisible.

These were the characteristics of Negro religious life as developed up to the time of Emancipation. Since under the peculiar circumstances of the black man's environment they were the one expression of his higher life, they are of deep interest to the student of his development, both socially and psychologically. Numerous are the attractive lines of inquiry that here group themselves. What did slavery mean to the African savage? What was his attitude toward the World and Life? What seemed to him good and evil,—God and Devil? Whither went his longings and strivings, and wherefore were his heart-burnings and disappointments? Answers to such questions can come only from a study of Negro religion as a development, through its gradual changes from the heathenism of the Gold Coast to the institutional Negro church of Chicago.

Moreover, the religious growth of millions of men, even though they be slaves, cannot be without potent influence upon their contemporaries. The Methodists and Baptists of America owe much of their condition to the silent but potent influence of their millions of Negro converts. Especially is this noticeable in the South, where theology and religious philosophy are on this account a long way behind the North, and where the religion of the poor whites is a plain copy of Negro thought and methods. The mass of "gospel" hymns which has swept through American churches and well-nigh ruined our sense of song consists largely of debased imitations of Negro melodies made by ears that caught the jingle but not the music, the body but not the soul, of the Jubilee songs. It is thus clear that the study of Negro religion is not only a vital part of the history of the Negro in America, but no uninteresting part of American history.

The Negro church of to-day is the social centre of Negro life in the United States, and the most characteristic expression of African character. Take a typical church in a small Virginian town: it is the "First Baptist"—a roomy brick edifice seating five hundred or more persons, tastefully finished in Georgia pine, with a carpet, a small organ, and stained-glass windows. Underneath is a large assembly room with benches. This building is the central club-house of a community of a thousand or more Negroes. Various organizations meet here,—the church proper, the Sunday-school, two or three insurance societies, women's societies, secret societies, and mass meetings of various kinds. Entertainments, suppers, and lectures are held beside the five or six regular weekly religious services. Considerable sums of money are collected and expended here, employment is found for the idle, strangers are introduced, news is disseminated and charity distributed. At the same time this social, intellectual, and economic centre is a religious centre of great power. Depravity, Sin, Redemption, Heaven, Hell, and Damnation are preached twice a Sunday with much fervor, and revivals take place every year after the crops are laid by; and few indeed of the community have the hardihood to withstand conversion. Back of this more formal religion, the Church often stands as a real conserver of morals, a strengthener of family life, and the final authority on what is Good and Right.

Thus one can see in the Negro church to-day, reproduced in microcosm, all that great world from which the Negro is cut off by color-prejudice and social condition. In the great city churches the same tendency is noticeable and in many respects emphasized. A great church like the Bethel of Philadelphia has over eleven hundred members, an edifice seating fifteen hundred persons and valued at one hundred thousand dollars, an annual budget of five thousand dollars, and a government consisting of a pastor with several assisting local preachers, an executive and legislative board, financial boards and tax collectors; general church meetings for making laws; subdivided groups led by class leaders, a company of militia, and twenty-four auxiliary societies. The activity of a church like this is immense and far-reaching, and the bishops who preside over these organizations throughout the land are among the most powerful Negro rulers in the world.

Such churches are really governments of men, and consequently a little investigation reveals the curious fact that, in the South, at least, practically every American Negro is a church member. Some, to be sure, are not regularly enrolled, and a few do not habitually attend services; but, practically, a proscribed people must have a social centre, and that centre for this people is the Negro church. The census of 1890 showed nearly twenty-four thousand Negro churches in the country, with a total enrolled membership of over two and a half millions, or ten actual church members to every twenty-eight persons, and in some Southern States one in every two persons. Besides these there is the large number who, while not enrolled as members, attend and take part in many of the activities of the church. There is an organized Negro church for every sixty black families in the nation, and in some States for every forty families, owning, on an average, a thousand dollars' worth of property each, or nearly twenty-six million dollars in all.

Such, then, is the large development of the Negro church since Emancipation. The question now is, What have been the successive steps of this social history and what are the present tendencies? First, we must realize that no such institution as the Negro church could rear itself without definite historical foundations. These foundations we can find if we remember that the social history of the Negro did not start in America. He was brought from a definite social environment,—the polygamous clan life under the headship of the chief and the potent influence of the priest. His religion was nature-worship, with profound belief in invisible surrounding influences, good and bad, and his worship was through incantation and sacrifice. The first rude change in this life was the slave ship and the West Indian sugar-fields. The plantation organization replaced the clan and tribe, and the white master replaced the chief with far greater and more despotic powers. Forced and long-continued toil became the rule of life, the old ties of blood relationship and kinship disappeared, and instead of the family appeared a new polygamy and polyandry, which, in some cases, almost reached promiscuity. It was a terrific social revolution, and yet some traces were retained of the former group life, and the chief remaining institution was the Priest or Medicine-man. He early appeared on the plantation and found his function as the healer of the sick, the interpreter of the Unknown, the comforter of the sorrowing, the supernatural avenger of wrong, and the one who rudely but picturesquely expressed the longing, disappointment, and resentment of a stolen and oppressed people. Thus, as bard, physician, judge, and priest, within the narrow limits allowed by the slave system, rose the Negro preacher, and under him the first Afro-American institution, the Negro church. This church was not at first by any means Christian nor definitely organized; rather it was an adaptation and mingling of heathen rites among the members of each plantation, and roughly designated as Voodooism. Association with the masters, missionary effort and motives of expediency gave these rites an early veneer of Christianity, and after the lapse of many generations the Negro church became Christian.

Two characteristic things must be noticed in regard to this church. First, it became almost entirely Baptist and Methodist in faith; secondly, as a social institution it antedated by many decades the monogamic Negro home. From the very circumstances of its beginning, the church was confined to the plantation, and consisted primarily of a series of disconnected units; although, later on, some freedom of movement was allowed, still this geographical limitation was always important and was one cause of the spread of the decentralized and democratic Baptist faith among the slaves. At the same time, the visible rite of baptism appealed strongly to their mystic temperament. To-day the Baptist Church is still largest in membership among Negroes, and has a million and a half communicants. Next in popularity came the churches organized in connection with the white neighboring churches, chiefly Baptist and Methodist, with a few Episcopalian and others. The Methodists still form the second greatest denomination, with nearly a million members. The faith of these two leading denominations was more suited to the slave church from the prominence they gave to religious feeling and fervor. The Negro membership in other denominations has always been small and relatively unimportant, although the Episcopalians and Presbyterians are gaining among the more intelligent classes to-day, and the Catholic Church is making headway in certain sections. After Emancipation, and still earlier in the North, the Negro churches largely severed such affiliations as they had had with the white churches, either by choice or by compulsion. The Baptist churches became independent, but the Methodists were compelled early to unite for purposes of episcopal government. This gave rise to the great African Methodist Church, the greatest Negro organization in the world, to the Zion Church and the Colored Methodist, and to the black conferences and churches in this and other denominations.

The second fact noted, namely, that the Negro church antedates the Negro home, leads to an explanation of much that is paradoxical in this communistic institution and in the morals of its members. But especially it leads us to regard this institution as peculiarly the expression of the inner ethical life of a people in a sense seldom true elsewhere. Let us turn, then, from the outer physical development of the church to the more important inner ethical life of the people who compose it. The Negro has already been pointed out many times as a religious animal,—a being of that deep emotional nature which turns instinctively toward the supernatural. Endowed with a rich tropical imagination and a keen, delicate appreciation of Nature, the transplanted African lived in a world animate with gods and devils, elves and witches; full of strange influences,—of Good to be implored, of Evil to be propitiated. Slavery, then, was to him the dark triumph of Evil over him. All the hateful powers of the Underworld were striving against him, and a spirit of revolt and revenge filled his heart. He called up all the resources of heathenism to aid,—exorcism and witchcraft, the mysterious Obi worship with its barbarous rites, spells, and blood-sacrifice even, now and then, of human victims. Weird midnight orgies and mystic conjurations were invoked, the witch-woman and the voodoo-priest became the centre of Negro group life, and that vein of vague superstition which characterizes the unlettered Negro even to-day was deepened and strengthened.

In spite, however, of such success as that of the fierce Maroons, the Danish blacks, and others, the spirit of revolt gradually died away under the untiring energy and superior strength of the slave masters. By the middle of the eighteenth century the black slave had sunk, with hushed murmurs, to his place at the bottom of a new economic system, and was unconsciously ripe for a new philosophy of life. Nothing suited his condition then better than the doctrines of passive submission embodied in the newly learned Christianity. Slave masters early realized this, and cheerfully aided religious propaganda within certain bounds. The long system of repression and degradation of the Negro tended to emphasize the elements in his character which made him a valuable chattel: courtesy became humility, moral strength degenerated into submission, and the exquisite native appreciation of the beautiful became an infinite capacity for dumb suffering. The Negro, losing the joy of this world, eagerly seized upon the offered conceptions of the next; the avenging Spirit of the Lord enjoining patience in this world, under sorrow and tribulation until the Great Day when He should lead His dark children home,—this became his comforting dream. His preacher repeated the prophecy, and his bards sang,—

> "Children, we all shall be free
> When the Lord shall appear!"

This deep religious fatalism, painted so beautifully in "Uncle Tom," came soon to breed, as all fatalistic faiths will, the sensualist side by side with the martyr. Under the lax moral life of the plantation, where marriage was a farce, laziness a virtue, and property a theft, a religion of resignation and submission degenerated easily, in less strenuous minds, into a philosophy of indulgence and crime. Many of the worst characteristics of the Negro masses of to-day had their seed in this period of the slave's ethical growth. Here it was that the Home was ruined under the very shadow of the Church, white and black; here habits of shiftlessness took root, and sullen hopelessness replaced hopeful strife.

With the beginning of the abolition movement and the gradual growth of a class of free Negroes came a change. We often neglect the influence of the freedman before the war because of the paucity of his numbers and the small weight he had in the history of the nation. But we must not forget that his chief influence was internal,—was exerted on the black world; and that there he was the ethical and social leader. Huddled as he was in a few centres like Philadelphia, New York, and New Orleans, the masses of the freedmen sank into poverty and listlessness; but not all of them. The free Negro leader early arose and his chief characteristic was intense earnestness and deep feeling on the slavery question. Freedom became to him a real thing and not a dream. His religion became darker and more intense, and into his ethics crept a note of revenge, into his songs a day of reckoning close at hand. The "Coming of the Lord" swept this side of Death, and came to be a thing to be hoped for in this day. Through fugitive slaves and irrepressible discussion this desire for freedom seized the black millions still in bondage, and became their one ideal of life. The black bards caught new notes, and sometimes even dared to sing,—

> "O Freedom, O Freedom, O Freedom over me!
> Before I'll be a slave
> I'll be buried in my grave,
> And go home to my Lord
> And be free."

For fifty years Negro religion thus transformed itself and identified itself with the dream of Abolition, until that which was a radical fad in the white North and an anarchistic plot in the white South had become a religion to the black world. Thus, when Emancipation finally came, it seemed to the freedman a literal Coming of the Lord. His fervid imagination was stirred as never before, by the tramp of armies, the blood and dust of battle, and the wail and whirl of social upheaval. He stood dumb and motionless before the whirlwind: what had he to do with it? Was it not the Lord's doing, and marvellous in his eyes? Joyed and bewildered with what came, he stood awaiting new wonders till the inevitable Age of Reaction swept over the nation and brought the crisis of to-day.

It is difficult to explain clearly the present critical stage of Negro religion. First, we must remember that living as the blacks do in close contact with a great modern nation, and sharing, although imperfectly, the soul-life of that nation, they must necessarily be affected more or less directly by all the religious and ethical forces that are to-day moving the United States. These questions and movements are, however, overshadowed and dwarfed by the (to them) all-important question of their civil, political, and economic status. They must perpetually discuss the "Negro Problem,"—must live, move, and have their being in it, and interpret all else in its light or darkness. With this come, too, peculiar problems of their inner life,—of the status of women, the maintenance of Home, the training of children, the accumulation of wealth, and the prevention of crime. All this must mean a time of intense ethical ferment, of religious heart-searching and intellectual unrest. From the double life every American Negro must live, as a Negro and as an American, as swept on by the current of the nineteenth while yet struggling in the eddies of the fifteenth century,—from this must arise a painful self-consciousness, an almost morbid sense of personality and a moral hesitancy which is fatal to self-confidence. The worlds within and without the Veil of Color are changing, and changing rapidly, but not at the same rate, not in the same way; and this must produce a peculiar wrenching of the soul, a peculiar sense of doubt and bewilderment. Such a double life, with double thoughts, double duties, and double social classes, must give rise to double words and double ideals, and tempt the mind to pretence or to revolt, to hypocrisy or to radicalism.

In some such doubtful words and phrases can one perhaps most clearly picture the peculiar ethical paradox that faces the Negro of to-day and is tingeing and changing his religious life. Feeling that his rights and his dearest ideals are being trampled upon, that the public conscience is ever more deaf to his righteous appeal, and that all the reactionary forces of prejudice, greed, and revenge are daily gaining new strength and fresh allies, the Negro faces no enviable dilemma. Conscious of his impotence, and pessimistic, he often becomes bitter and vindictive; and his religion, instead of a worship, is a complaint and a curse, a wail rather than a hope, a sneer rather than a faith. On the other hand, another type of mind, shrewder and keener and more tortuous too, sees in the very strength of the anti-Negro movement its patent weaknesses, and with Jesuitic casuistry is deterred by no ethical considerations in the endeavor to turn this weakness to the black man's strength. Thus we have two great and hardly reconcilable streams of thought and ethical strivings; the danger of the one lies in anarchy, that of the other in hypocrisy. The one type of Negro stands almost ready to curse God and die, and the other is too often found a traitor to right and a coward before force; the one is wedded to ideals remote, whimsical, perhaps impossible of realization; the other forgets that life is more than meat and the body more than raiment. But, after all, is not this simply the writhing of the age translated into black,—the triumph of the Lie which to-day, with its false culture, faces the hideousness of the anarchist assassin?

To-day the two groups of Negroes, the one in the North, the other in the South, represent these divergent ethical tendencies, the first tending toward radicalism, the other toward hypocritical compromise. It is no idle regret with which the white South mourns the loss of the old-time Negro,—the frank, honest, simple old servant who stood for the earlier religious age of submission and humility. With all his laziness and lack of many elements of true manhood, he was at least open-hearted, faithful, and sincere. To-day he is gone, but who is to blame for his going? Is it not those very persons who mourn for him? Is it not the tendency, born of Reconstruction and Reaction, to found a society on lawlessness and deception, to tamper with the moral fibre of a naturally honest and straightforward people until the whites threaten to become ungovernable tyrants and the blacks criminals and hypocrites? Deception is the natural defence of the weak against the strong, and the South used it for many years against its conquerors; to-day it must be prepared to see its black proletariat turn that same two-edged weapon against itself. And how natural this is! The death of Denmark Vesey and Nat Turner proved long since to the Negro the present hopelessness of physical defence. Political defence is becoming less and less available, and economic defence is still only partially effective. But there is a patent defence at hand,—the defence of deception and flattery, of cajoling and lying. It is the same defence which the Jews of the Middle Age used and which left its stamp on their character for centuries. To-day the young Negro of the South who would succeed cannot be frank and outspoken, honest and self-assertive, but rather he is daily tempted to be silent and wary, politic and sly; he must flatter and be pleasant, endure petty insults with a smile, shut his eyes to wrong; in too many cases he sees positive personal advantage in deception and lying. His real thoughts, his real aspirations, must be guarded in whispers; he must not criticise, he must not complain. Patience, humility, and adroitness must, in these growing black youth, replace impulse, manliness, and courage. With this sacrifice there is an economic opening, and perhaps peace and some prosperity. Without this there is riot, migration, or crime. Nor is this situation peculiar to the Southern United States,— is it not rather the only method by which undeveloped races have gained the right to share modern culture? The price of culture is a Lie.

On the other hand, in the North the tendency is to emphasize the radicalism of the Negro. Driven from his birthright in the South by a situation at which every fibre of his more outspoken and assertive nature revolts, he finds himself in a land where he can scarcely earn a decent living amid the harsh competition and the color discrimination. At the same time, through schools and periodicals, discussions and lectures, he is intellectually quickened and awakened. The soul, long pent up and dwarfed, suddenly expands in new-found freedom. What wonder that every tendency is to excess,—radical complaint, radical remedies, bitter denunciation or angry silence. Some sink, some rise. The criminal and the sensualist leave the church for the gambling-hell and the brothel, and fill the slums of Chicago and Baltimore; the better classes segregate themselves from the group-life of both white and black, and form an aristocracy, cultured but pessimistic, whose bitter criticism stings while it points out no way of escape. They despise the submission and subserviency of the Southern Negroes, but offer no other means by which a poor and oppressed minority can exist side by side with its masters. Feeling deeply and keenly the tendencies and opportunities of the age in which they live, their souls are bitter at the fate which drops the Veil between; and the very fact that this bitterness is natural and justifiable only serves to intensify it and make it more maddening.

Between the two extreme types of ethical attitude which I have thus sought to make clear wavers the mass of the millions of Negroes, North and South; and their religious life and activity partake of this social conflict within their ranks. Their churches are differentiating,—now into groups of cold, fashionable devotees, in no way distinguishable from similar white groups save in color of skin; now into large social and business institutions catering to the desire for information and amusement of their members, warily avoiding unpleasant questions both within and without the black world, and preaching in effect if not in word: *Dum vivimus, vivamus.*

But back of this still broods silently the deep religious feeling of the real Negro heart, the stirring, unguided might of powerful human souls who have lost the guiding star of the past and are seeking in the great night a new religious ideal. Some day the Awakening will come, when the pent-up vigor of ten million souls shall sweep irresistibly toward the Goal, out of the Valley of the Shadow of Death, where all that makes life worth living—Liberty, Justice, and Right—is marked "For White People Only."

Chapter 2

Origins of the Church

Benjamin Elijah Mays and Joseph William Nicholson

T he distinctive social, economic and psychological influences at work in each of five different epochs of the history of the United States affected in various ways the Negro churches that originated at the time, and are still reflected in those of them that have survived. Consequently it is of importance to point out that among the 609 urban churches and the 185 rural churches that were studied in this investigation there are representatives of each epoch.

The Slavery Epoch

The first of these epochs was between the years 1750 and 1859. During this period racial consciousness was roused by the controversy over slavery. Slavery as an institution was challenged by its adversaries. Operators of the underground railway were busily engaged transporting slaves to freedom. On the other hand, those citizens with pro-slavery sentiments were busy maintaining the institution. This controversy found its way into the churches. The reactions of the southern religious bodies were decidedly pro-slavery. The Negroes in many of the predominantly white churches voluntarily withdrew or were forced out. And likewise the whites withdrew from churches which were predominantly Negro.

Approval or disapproval of the institution of slavery was expressed, not only in the local churches, but by denominations as well. Large denominations like the Methodist and the Presbyterian found themselves divided on the issue; their divided sympathies were definitely influenced by the geographical regions in which their people lived.

The seriousness of this controversy in the church is reflected in the origins of forty-one of the 609 urban and five of the 185 rural churches of this study. Interesting and outstanding examples of Negro church origins of this early epoch are reported in the following excerpts from local church histories.

The Oldest Church of this Study

The oldest urban church of this study was established in Philadelphia. About the founder and the church, the autobiography of Richard Allen states, "I was born in the year 1760, February 14th, a slave to Benjamin Chew, of Philadelphia." After spending some time away from Philadelphia, Richard Allen returned and purchased his freedom.

> February, 1786, I came to Philadelphia. Preaching was given out for me at five o'clock in the morning at St. George church. . . . I preached at different places in the city. . . . I soon saw a large field open in seeking and instructing my African brethren, who had been a long-forgotten people and few of them attended public worship. . . . I raised a society in 1786 for forty-two members. . . . We all belonged to St. George's church. . . . We felt ourselves much cramped; . . . We established prayer meetings and meetings of exhortation, and the Lord blessed our endeavors, and many souls were awakened; but the elder soon forbid us holding any such meetings; but we viewed the forlorn state of our colored brethren, and that they were destitute of a place of worship. They were considered a nuisance.
>
> *Forced from Knees During Prayer*—A number of us usually attended St. George's church in Fourth Street; and when the colored people began to get numerous in attending the church, they moved us from the seats we usually sat on, and placed us around the wall, and on Sabbath morning we went to church and the sexton stood at the door and told us to go in the gallery. He told us to go, and we would see where to sit. We expected to take the seats over the ones we formerly occupied below, not knowing any better. We took those seats. Meeting had begun, and they were nearly done singing, and just as we got to the seats, the elder said "Let us pray." We had not been long upon our knees before I heard a considerable scuffling and low talking, I raised my head up and saw one of the trustees, H—— M——, having hold of the Rev. Absalom Jones, pulling him up off his knees, and

saying, "You must get up—you must not kneel here." Mr. Jones replied, "Wait until prayer is over." Mr. H—— M—— said, "No, you must get up now or I will call for aid and force you away." Mr. Jones said, "Wait until prayer is over, and I will get up and trouble you no more." With that he beckoned to one of the other Trustees, Mr. L—— S—— to come to his assistance. He came to William White, to pull him up. By this time prayer was over, and we all went out of the church in a body, and they were no more plagued with us in the church. This raised a great excitement and inquiry among the citizens, in so much that I believe that they were ashamed of their conduct . . . we had subscribed largely towards finishing St. George's church, in building the gallery and laying the new floors, and just as the house was made comfortable, we were turned out from enjoying the comforts of worshipping therein.

The New Church—We then hired a store-room and held worship ourselves. Here we were pursued by threats of being disowned, and read publicly out of meeting if we did continue to worship in the place we had hired; but we believed the Lord would be our friend . . . Here was the beginning and rise of the first church of the denomination later known as the African Methodist Episcopal. Many of the colored people in other places were in a situation nearly like those of Philadelphia and Baltimore, which induced us, in April, 1816, to call a general meeting, by way of conference. Delegates from Baltimore and other places which met those of Philadelphia, and taking into consideration their grievances, and in order to secure the privileges, promote union and harmony among themselves, it was resolved: "That the people of Philadelphia, Baltimore, etc., etc., should become one body, under the name of African Methodist Episcopal Church."[1]

The first Negro Baptist church of this study was established in 1841, in Richmond, Virginia.

Until that year, the congregation was mixed. The 387 white members then retired to Broad and Twelfth Streets, and 1,708 colored members remained in the old church of worship.[2]

Many are under the impression that the old church was given to the colored members but they paid $6,500 for the building. . . . The Attorney General of the State, Hon. Sidney S. Baxter, gave his written opinion: "That it would be inexpedient to make any portion of the trustees people of color and that it might endanger the title to the property." This opinion and the refusal of the First Baptist Church (white) to transfer the property made the colored brethren warm. . . . It was transferred in 1849 to their trustees: David R. Crane, Robert H. Bosher (white), John S. Kinney, Jas. C. Ellis, and Wm. Lightfoot (colored).[3]

The second Negro Baptist church of this study in Richmond, Virginia, was established in the following way:

Of the original members of the church (2nd Baptist white), none were Negroes, owing, doubtless, to the circumstances under which the movement began. The slavery question, however, came up as early as December, 1821. It seems that shortly before that time, David Roper, the Acting Pastor, had sold a Negro and had been criticised therefor. He brought the matter before the church and asked whether, in its judgment, it was permissible for a Christian to own and sell slaves. . . . It was answered in the affirmative, but in language that makes it plain that the church could not and would not endorse promiscuous trading in Negroes. Fifty-three years later, the first Negro member was admitted. . . . Thereafter, Negroes were received freely into membership, though the minister would indicate that subsequent to the Nat. Turner insurrection the consent of the masters had to be given before a Negro could be baptized. From the first, the colored members constituted something of a problem. In 1826, the sexton, presumably a white man, was given authority as a deacon to watch over the Negroes of the church and was encouraged to hold special meetings for them.

After the great revival of 1831, when many Negroes were received, a committee of seven of the older colored members were appointed to the task formerly assigned to the sexton. It was frankly said that the white members could not exercise intelligently the necessary church discipline. The next year an effort was made to segregate the colored members. Later, when Doctor Jett succeeded in organizing the First African Church, a committee was appointed, to act with one from the First in supervising, as required by law, the preaching at the African Church. Encouragement was also given such of the Negroes as desired to join the new congregation. Finally, it became evident, that the best results were not being accomplished and a resolution was passed not to receive other colored members except in unusual cases. Mrs. M. O. Roper's Harriett and a worthy man, Richard Balentine, were later regarded as exceptions and were admitted. After much discussion, the Negro members were finally organized as the Second African Baptist Church, and, on February 1, 1846, forty-three males and fourteen females were dismissed.

The church stood sponsor for the Second African Baptist; but apparently did not have to assume any financial liability. Annually until the close of the war between the states, a committee of the church was in general charge of the Negro congregation, attended its services, and gave counsel. When freedom came to the colored members and they threw off the tie that bound them the Second African had 1,100 members. In 1866 the committee headed by Jackson B. Wood, made a final report that contained this interesting observation: " . . . in our opinion, the organization which was formerly adopted is the very best which can possibly be carried out for the good government of the colored churches as well as for their promotion in piety."[4]

A separate enterprise in 1848, was begun for the thoroughgoing evangelization of colored people in Charleston, S.C., under the auspices of Rev. John Badger and the session of the Second Presbyterian Church. . . . The enterprise began as a branch congregation of the Second Presbyterian Church; then became a missionary church in 1857 with only 47 members. In order definitely to apportion the minister's time and the use of the church building the white members drew up the following statement.

> We do hereby agree that the pastor of this church is to be selected always with a view to his suitableness for laboring most profitably among the colored people, and that for all times the services and labors of the minister shall ordinarily be so divided as to apportion the regular morning services to the whites especially, and the remaining regular service or services to the blacks especially; and we do further agree that the colored people shall always be allowed in these services designed peculiarly for their benefit the main floor of the building, excepting such seats on the right and left of the pulpit as may be appropriated to the whites.[5]

Also in Charleston, S.C., following the split of the Methodist Episcopal Church which resulted in the Methodist Episcopal Church, South, in 1844, the problems of bi-racial worship became articulate.

"This exclusion of the church from its work among colored people only increased its interest in them."[6] The "Old Church" became their champion. During the Civil War, the proximity of the battlefield caused white people to desert their churches, and flee from Charleston. Therefore, in churches where Negroes had occupied the galleries only, they occupied the body of the churches. But "When Andrew Johnson began the work of reconstruction the white pastors and congregations returned, and began to demand their churches from the colored people. They saw no necessity for the presence of the Yankee preachers in the city, and felt that white and colored members might worship according to the old regime."[7] Negroes, however did not return to worship in the galleries of the white churches. Instead they organized colored churches.

In the deep South, Negroes and whites had, as in other places, worshipped together. In the case of the First African Baptist Church of New Orleans, La., we find that they first began as a part of the white church in 1817. There were forty-eight members, including sixteen white and thirty-two Negroes. These Negroes shared the turbulent life of the white church for a number of years, and in 1827 an African church of about twenty members was organized. They had "A colored minister named Asa Goldsberry, who just before had been bound over by the authority of the city, or otherwise, to be silent six months under the penalty of a law against colored preachers." "However, during the time Elder Fletcher pastored the white Baptist church (1850) the Negro members of his church were organized into a church under the care of a white brother. This second Baptist church numbered sixty-two members and was received into the Mississippi River Association (white) in 1859 under the fostering care of the Coliseum Baptist Church (white)."[8] The second Baptist church became the First African church because the church at which Asa Goldsberry was pastor did not survive.

In Philadelphia, in 1809, thirteen persons were dismissed upon their request from the First Baptist Church (white) for the purpose of forming the First African Baptist Church.[9] In the same city in 1844 a group of people sought and received the authority of the Presbytery to organize the Lombard Street Central Presbyterian Church.[10]

The five rural churches of this epoch originated in a manner similar to the forty-one urban churches. The Antioch Baptist Church is an example of these rural churches. It was organized June 5, 1818, in what is now Montgomery County, Alabama. The ground and graveyard were the gift of a Mr. Billy Wright. The church was predominantly white until about 1849 when about forty Negroes were received through baptism. In 1850 about sixteen more Negroes were baptized into the church. About this time the whites turned this church over to Negroes; but the white pastor had charge, and the property was still held by the whites. In 1854 another church called Elem, about five miles away, received forty-eight Negroes. Elem and Antioch received about 104 Negroes in four years.

In the year 1855 seven colored deacons were ordained in Antioch by the Reverend A. T. M. Handy, the white pastor. The first Negro pastor of Antioch was installed sometime in the post-Civil-War epoch, presumably about 1882.

The Civil War Epoch

The Civil War epoch, between the years 1860 and 1865, brought to a crisis the long-continued controversy, evasion and feinting over the question of slavery. From as early as 1808, the national church bodies had attempted to keep themselves intact and to pass the question of slavery on to the annual conferences by general rulings which in practice were subject to local discretion.

Dr. Carter G. Woodson, in the *History of the Negro Church*, states that among the rules adopted by the Methodists in 1824, one "provided that all preachers should prudently enforce upon their members the necessity of teaching their slaves to read the word of God, and allow them time to attend the public worship of God on our regular days of divine service."

> Another rule provided that Negro preachers and official members should have all the privileges which are usual to others in the district and quarterly conferences where the usages of the country did not forbid it. . . .
>
> The Presbyterians had tried to evade the Negro question but it was again brought up in view of the cruelty practiced in the traffic of slaves during the first decade of the nineteenth century. The General Assembly was forced to take some action again in 1815. It then referred to its previous resolutions on the subject and expressed regret that slavery of Africans existed, hoping too that such measures might be taken as would secure religious education at least to the rising generation of slaves as a preparation for their emancipation at some time in the future.[11]

These vacillations only delayed and did not help the churches in ultimately avoiding the denominational splits which came in 1844 for the Methodists, in 1845 for the Baptists, and in 1861 for the Presbyterians.

The church in the South became literally a new church; and the Negro, except for having his name on the church record, was practically shut out. According to Woodson, the Negro in this period became more proscribed than ever. Free Negroes were expelled from many southern communities. Negroes were forbidden to hold meetings except under the watchful eye of the whites. In slave states, the majority of Negroes became a decidedly neglected mass during the reaction, although many were nominally members of churches. When, because of the insurrectionary movement led by certain blacks like Gabriel Prosser, Denmark Vesey, and Nat. Turner, it became unpopular to teach Negroes to read and the educated white persons were not willing to supply this lack of religious workers among the blacks, there was no longer hope for ordinary religious instruction. This reaction was unusually disastrous to the Negro preacher when it was noised abroad that Nat. Turner was a minister. The rumor attached to Negro ministers throughout the South the stigma of using preaching as a means to incite their race to insurrection.[12]

These factors caused this epoch to be one of crucial importance for the development of the Negro church. Sixteen of the 609 urban and twelve of the 185 rural churches of this study originated during this time. The grip of these circumstances on the church was not broken until some years after the formal emancipation of the slaves.

The Post-Civil-War Epoch

The post-Civil-War and Reconstruction epoch, 1866 to 1899, gave new life to Negro enterprises. The Negro entered into as many activities as were open to him. He was particularly active in politics and educational work, but preeminently he engaged in the development of his church.

The Negro churches of this time originated especially from the initiative of individuals, groups, splits or schisms, and as missions of other churches. A study of the church origins reveals that 223 of the 609 urban and 110 of the 185 rural churches originated during this period. Of the 223 urban churches, 12 per cent were splits; 10 per cent were missions of other churches; and 63 per cent were the result of the initiative of individuals and groups; and 15 per cent were traceable to several causes. Of the 110 rural churches, 82 per cent were the result of the initiative of individuals and groups; 2 per cent were missions; 12 per cent were splits; and 4 per cent were started by the withdrawal of Negroes from white churches.

The freedom which the Negro felt in this period is best revealed by the fact that of the 333 rural and urban churches of this study which originated then, 231, or 69 per cent., came into existence through the initiative of individuals and groups. Examples of churches organized in this manner may be selected from a large number representing many localities in the United States.

In 1891 a few Baptists who lived in Nicetown (Philadelphia, Pa.) had a desire for a place of worship. After years of feeble effort this church, with the help of another church, has since grown into a self-supporting organization.[13] A group of people in Cincinnati in 1878, under the leadership of a minister, started a Sunday school which later became Calvary Methodist Episcopal Church.[14] In 1880, upon the advice of an older minister, a young minister, Matthew Anderson, took charge of Gloucester Mission in Philadelphia. This church later became the self-supporting congregation called the Berean Presbyterian Church.[15] A church was organized in Philadelphia in 1886 by a former cement worker. This man came from Washington, D.C., and began preaching to friends. The church is the outgrowth of the encouragement and help of these friends.

A church in New Orleans, originated, in 1872, because its members, formerly of another church, wanted a different type of ministry. Also in New Orleans, in 1896, a minister started a church as the result of a revival.

"In the year 1889, in Richmond, Va., for reasons presumably best known to themselves, about eighteen or twenty members of Bethel A.M.E. Church of this city withdrew from said church and sought to establish a church of their own liking and control."[16] In Chicago, in 1882, a number of members of Olivet Baptist Church withdrew by letters for the purpose of organizing a church.[17] In Baltimore, in 1874, two men with their brethren withdrew with their letters from the Union Baptist Church and organized another church.[18]

The number of churches growing out of day-schools or attempts to furnish secular education for Negroes, usually on the part of whites, are few. The most notable of these is the First Congregational Church of Atlanta. In 1867 the teachers and workers in the Storr school, a Congregational enterprise, organized the church. The school building was used as the meeting-place for a long while. "It was a church based on fellowship and love and not race or color." Individuals interested in the founding of Atlanta University were among its first members.[19]

The origin of the Ebenezer Baptist Church of Orangeburg County, South Carolina, is an example of the rural church of this period. This church withdrew from the Bull Swamp Baptist Church about 1873, according to the lone eighty-three-year-old survivor, John McCleod. Mr. McCleod's story goes that during the years when the Negroes worshipped in the white church, they sat together in the rear. Reverend William Durham, the minister, would shake hands with the Negroes and give them a hearty welcome. He liked to hear the colored people sing, and often had them lead the singing. For a while there were only seven Negro members. But later, when about thirty-five new converts were baptized, a large number of Negroes also were included. White women were baptized first, white men second, then Negro women and last Negro men. They were all fellowshipped into the church. The whites first, and the Negroes last. Negroes continued to join the church; and at a later time, about 1873, when Reverend Durham built a new church, he suggested that the Negroes use the old one. Many of the Negroes left and joined the Canaan Methodist Episcopal Church (a Negro church) which was already established. The Negroes who remained Baptist began worshipping in a brush arbor. Their number gradually increased to about seventy-five. They later accepted the gift of the old white church. With the exception of this gift, the Negro church has remained practically self-sustaining. The only relationship now existing between Ebenezer and the Bull Swamp White Baptist is that occasionally the deacons of Ebenezer invite the white Bull Swamp pastor to preach for them.

The New Century Epoch

In the Reconstruction epoch, 1866 to 1899, the Negro entered vigorously upon his newly-gained freedom. During the first years of this period, the evidence tends to show, there was great activity in the fields of politics, education and religion. But as time passed, the vigor and consuming passion of Negroes for independent achievement apparently lessened, and the glamour of the earlier accomplishments waned.

The New Century epoch, 1900 to 1914, was therefore quite ordinary. In politics and in educational pursuits the Negro's interest was not expressed or reflected by striking movements. There were no exciting events, no clashes of loyalties; and as a result the history of this period is comparatively dull.[20] In the church likewise, there were no stirring changes, although there continued a solid and steady growth during these years.

There was no decrease in the number of churches originating (except in the rural area which declined from an average of 3.2 churches to 1.7 churches per year) and there was also no stimulated advance. The origins of the churches from 1900 to 1914 show that 140 of the 609 urban and 26 of the 185 rural churches were established. Of the 140 urban churches, 7 per cent. were missions, 4 per cent. were the result of the migration of

Negroes, 14 per cent were splits, and 75 per cent resulted from the initiative of individuals or groups and other causes such as beginnings from Sunday schools, revivals and prayer meetings. In the rural areas during this time 62 per cent of the 26 churches resulted from the initiative of individuals or groups, 26 per cent were splits, 1, or roughly 4 per cent from Sunday schools, 4 per cent were missions, and 4 per cent were withdrawals from white churches.

The Migration Epoch

The epoch from 1915 to 1930 was characterized by the marked migratory movement of Negroes in the United States. It consisted of the general movement of members of the Negro population from the rural to urban centers, and from the urban South to the urban North. The report on *Negro Problems in Cities*, T. J. Woofter, Jr., Director, and the *Negro Year Book 1931–32*, by Monroe Work, point out that the migratory movement brought changes in the attitude of the whites toward the Negro in the South; created or aggravated problems of health, recreation, and housing in the cities; and introduced new problems for skilled and unskilled labor in the entire country, but especially in the large northern cities.

This period, in which the mobility of the Negro population is so sharply defined, is directly reflected in the origins and development of Negro churches, especially in the North. During this period 189 of the 609 urban and 16 of the 185 rural churches originated. The facts reveal that 54.4 per cent of 189 urban and 63 per cent of the 16 rural churches resulted from the initiative of individuals and groups. Church schisms or splits contributed 31 per cent of the urban and 38 per cent of the rural churches.

Fourteen per cent of the urban churches were the direct result of the migration. However, a few examples may be given to show that indirectly the migratory movement also found expression in many of those church-origins labelled *initiative of individuals and groups*. In Detroit, Michigan, an unemployed Negro minister observed the large number of people who were crowding the churches in the early days of the migration, and used this fact as the basis for starting a church.

In Philadelphia a man anxious to preach started a church in a community to which Negroes had recently moved. He began preaching in a house, and later moved the church to a store-front.

The Negro denominational bodies have repeatedly taken advantage of the migration to establish churches. In Detroit, two of these denominations have divided the city into districts. A church is placed in each district by each denomination; because, as it was stated, it is necessary for the denomination to take care of its members living there.

A Colored Methodist Episcopal church was started in Philadelphia as a result of a family of Colored Methodist Episcopalians migrating to that city from the South. Likewise a family formerly of Alabama organized a church in Detroit, because they were not satisfied with worshipping in a white church. In the same city, a group of migrants from Georgia sent for their preacher and organized a church. In New Orleans, a group of twenty people and their pastor, who had migrated from the rural districts of Louisiana to New Orleans, kept their church organization intact.

A rather unique example of the migratory movement as a source of new churches is found in the Morris Chapel Baptist Church of Philadelphia. At the time the church was organized, most of the people, twenty out of twenty-six, were from Greenwood, S.C. They had been members of the Morris Chapel Baptist Church in Greenwood. And this name was given to the new church. For the first two months the church conducted only Sunday school. After this time Reverend A. B. Jordan, a native of Greenwood, S.C., and pastor of the Greenwood Baptist Church in West Philadelphia, was invited to organize them. Later on Morris Chapel Church called Reverend Jordan as pastor.

Church Splits or Schisms

As compared with other forms of organization, splitting is a rather late practice among Negro churches. All splits or divisions do not arise from disagreements, because 10 of the 99 divisions recorded in this study were not splits in the sense of a militant breaking of relations but the result of friendly withdrawals, often accompanied by the letters of the withdrawing members.

In one church in Philadelphia, twenty men desired to dominate the membership; and, finding it impossible to do so, they withdrew and organized another church. Also in Philadelphia, a preacher was sent by the conference to another church out of the city. He preferred to remain in Philadelphia, and refused the new appointment. A number of people of his last church helped him organize a new one. Some churches have broken their denominational ties because of what they claim to be the autocracy and oppression of their denominational authorities. This type of church is found in Chicago, Baltimore and Detroit. Excerpts from the histories of a Detroit church and a Chicago church are as follows:

The Detroit church is the outgrowth of the desire of a group of people to unite their religious and financial resources and means that they might through a centralized, inclusive effort, offer the finest privileges and the fullest possible opportunities to the whole community for the religious, social, educational, and recreational good of all. . . . There is no outside governing authority and no hampering ecclesiastical affiliation. It is a church of the people, by the people, and for the people.[21]

The other church in Chicago states that it was organized "For religious liberty and freedom of action."[22] This group seeking return of a minister whom they regarded as a worthy leader, and failing to receive what they termed to be a fair hearing of their plea, and feeling at the same time that their minister had been harshly treated, drew out, as the following statement will indicate, and organized independently.

So astounding was the disappointment to the church in not having their petition granted, that many of the officers resigned, and they were followed by several hundred members of the church. The crisis had to come as the result of the reaction of the inner growth of unrest and discontent, a protest against a local dominating autocratic, ecclesiastical authority. To crystallize this reaction and protest in some permanent form, twenty men and women formed a council to take under advisement the formation of a new church. . . . After a careful analysis of the situation and the questions at issue, the final conclusion as the result of a sound and conservative judgment, they assumed the responsibility.

The Significance of These Church Origins

The data presented tend to show that churches which originated from discrimination and a growing racial consciousness characterized the first two epochs from 1750 to 1865.[23] Churches which originated from the initiative of individuals or groups, that is, the desire of the Negro to manage and direct his own religious activities, are found in all the epochs, but are probably most characteristic of the third, from 1866 to 1899.[24] The number of churches resulting from schisms or splits began to grow during the new-century epoch, 1900 to 1914. Following 1915, the most noticeable factor contributing to Negro church origins appears to be the migratory movement of Negroes.[25] From the earliest epoch down to the present, there has been a scattering of churches that originated as missions of other churches; but these are not markedly more characteristic of any one period than of another.[26]

The characteristic forces underlying Negro church origins are thus seen to have been five: growing racial consciousness, individual initiative, splits and withdrawals, the migration, and missions of other churches.

The Negro church began as a means of separating an unwanted racial group from common public worship; that is, it had a social and psychological origin. It has survived because of the economic, sociological and psychological factors in the church and in its environment.

Notes

1. Allen, Richard, Bishop, *The Life, Experience, and Gospel Labors* (Philadelphia, Pa., A.M.E. Book Concern), pp. 1, 19, 20, 21, 22, 32.
2. Souvenir Program of the 50th Anniversary of Dedication of the Building (Richmond, Va., First African Baptist Church, 1928), pp. 1, 5.
3. Johnson, W. T., *Historical Reminiscences of the First Baptist Church* (Richmond, Va., Hastings Deeds No. 82A Richmond Chancelor), pp. 9, 11. Also pp. 328 ff.
4. Taken from the "Ideal" (Bound Volume) 1921–23 Volume 5 of the Second Baptist Church (white).
5. Blackburn, George A., D.D., Excerpts from the *Life and Work of John L. Giraden, D.D., LL.D.*
6. After the split in the Methodist Episcopal Church which resulted in the organization of the Methodist Episcopal Church, South, the northern group of Methodists had no churches in the South through which it could contact Negroes. The writer being quoted here refers to the northern group as "the church" and the "old church." Churches of the Methodist Episcopal Church, South, either segregated Negroes or excluded them from worship services. The attitude of the northern group was more favorable than the southern group toward Negroes. Therefore in the face of the southern policy and the absence of any contact with Negroes because of the denominational split the northern group or "the old church" quickened its efforts to reach and christianize the Negro in the South.
7. Centenary Souvenir: W. H. Lawrence, "A Sketch of the History of the Reorganization of the South Carolina Conference and of the Centenary Church, Charleston, S.C.," p. 1.
8. "A Brief History and 104th Anniversary Celebration of First African Baptist Church, New Orleans, La.," pp. 23 ff.
9. Brooks, Chas. H., *Official History of the First African Baptist Church* (Philadelphia, 1922), pp. 11–13.
10. Jones, Robert, *Fifty Years in the Lombard Street Central Presbyterian Church* (Philadelphia, 1894).
11. Pp. 124 and 125.
12. Woodson, C. G., *History of the Negro Church*, p. 131.
13. "Souvenir Program and Brief History—Second Baptist Church," North Philadelphia, Pa., 1926.

14. Official Anniversary Program of Calvary M. E. Church, Cincinnati, Ohio, 1927.
15. Fiftieth Anniversary Program, Berean Presbyterian Church, Philadelphia, 1930.
16. Henry, Peter J., "Legal History of Leigh Street Memorial M. E. Church," Richmond, Va., 1931.
17. Historical Sketch of Bethesda Baptist Church, Chicago, 1925.
18. "Constitution and Manual of the Macedonia Baptist Church," Baltimore, 1902.
19. Original records of the First Congregational Church (Negro), Atlanta, Ga.
20. Woodson, C. G., *op. cit.*, chapters ix and xi.
21. Metropolitan Community Church, Inc., Detroit.
22. The People's Community Church of Christ (James D. Bryant), 1927.
23. [Appendix appears in original volume.]
24. Ibid.
25. Ibid.
26. Ibid.

Chapter 3

The Negro Spiritual Speaks of Life and Death

Love

Howard Thurman

The Negro Spiritual Speaks of Life and Death

The mystery of life and death persists despite the exhaustless and exhaustive treatment it has been given in song and story, philosophy and science, in art and religion. The human spirit is so involved in the endless cycle of birth, of living and dying, that in some sense each man is an authority, a key interpreter of the meaning of the totality of the experience. The testimony of the individual, then, is always fresh if he is able to make himself articulate to his fellows. Even when he is not, there is the persistent conviction that in some profound sense he himself knows and understands. When the external circumstances of life are dramatic or unusual, causing the human spirit to make demands upon all the reaches of its resourcefulness in order to keep from being engulfed, then the value of its findings made articulate, has more than passing significance.

I have chosen, coincidentally with the suggestion of Dean Sperry,[1] to examine the Negro spirituals as a source of rich testimony concerning life and death, because in many ways they are the voice, sometimes strident, sometimes muted and weary, of a people for whom the cup of suffering overflowed in haunting overtones of majesty, beauty and power! For many years it has been a growing conviction with me that the clue to the meaning of the spirituals is to be found in religious experience and spiritual discernment. To be sure, the amazing rhythm and the peculiar, often weird 1-2-3-5-6-8 of the musical scale are always intriguing and challenging to the modern mind. The real significance of the songs, however, is revealed at a deeper level of experience, in the ebb and flow of the tides that feed the rivers of man's thinking and aspiring. Here, where the elemental and the formless struggle to a vast consciousness in the mind and spirit of the individual, shall we seek the needful understanding of the songs of these slave singers. The insights disclosed are not original in any personal or private sense. The unique factor of the inspiring revelation is that, in the presence of their naked demand upon the primary sources of meanings, even without highly specialized tools or skills, the universe responded to them with overwhelming power.

In an essay included in a little book of meditations on Negro Spirituals published under the title *Deep River*, I located three major sources of raw materials over which the slave placed the alchemy of his desiring and aspiring: the world of nature, the stuff of experience, and the Bible, the sacred book of the Christians who had enslaved him. It was from the latter two that the songs of life and death originate. An examination of some of the insights to be found here is at once the purpose and proposal of my lecture.

Death was a fact, inescapable, persistent. For the slave, it was extremely compelling because of the cheapness with which his life was regarded. The slave was a tool, a thing, a utility, a commodity, but he was not a *person*. He was faced constantly with the imminent threat of death, of which the terrible overseer was the symbol; and the awareness that he (the slave) was only chattel property, the dramatization. It is difficult for us, so far removed in time and mood from those agony-ridden days, to comprehend the subtle psychological factors that were at work in the relationship between slave and master. If a slave were killed, it was merely a property loss, a matter of bookkeeping. The notion of personality, of human beings as ends so basic to the genius of the Christian faith, had no authentic application in the relationship between slave and master. The social and religious climate were uncongenial to such an ethic. Of course, there were significant exceptions to the general rule—which exceptions, by the light they cast, revealed the great moral darkness by which the period was engulfed. The situation itself stripped death of dignity, making it stark and nasty, like the difference between tragedy and melodrama. Death by violence at the hand of nature may stun the mind and shock the spirit, but death at the hands of another human being makes for panic in the mind and outrages the spirit. To live constantly in such a climate makes the struggle for essential human dignity unbearably desperate. The human spirit is stripped to the literal substance of itself. The attitude toward death is profoundly influenced by the experience of life.

It is important then to examine this literature to see what is revealed here concerning the attitude toward death. How significant is death? Is it the worst of all possible things that can happen to an individual:

Oh Freedom! Oh Freedom!
Oh Freedom, I love thee!
And before I'll be a slave,
I'll be buried in my grave,
And go home to my Lord and be free.

Obvious indeed is it here that death is not regarded as life's worst offering. There are some things in life that are worse than death. A man is not compelled to accept life without reference to the conditions upon which the offering is made. Here is something more than a mere counsel of suicide. It is a primary disclosure of an elemental affirmation having to do directly, not only with the ultimate dignity of the human spirit, but also with the ultimate basis of self-respect. We are face to face with a gross conception of the immortality of man, gross because it is completely exhaustive in its desperation. A radical conception of the immortality of man is apparent because the human spirit has a final word over the effect of circumstances. It is the guarantee of the sense of alternative in human experience, upon which, in the last analysis, all notions of freedom finally rest. Here is a recognition of death as the one fixed option which can never be taken from man by any power, however great, or by any circumstance, however fateful. If death were not implicit in the fact of life in a time-space dimension, then in no true sense would there be any authentic options in human experience: This concept regards death merely as a private option, private because it involves the single individual as if he and he alone existed in all the universe; option, because, while it assumes the inevitability of death as a factor in life, it recognizes the element of time which brings the inevitable factor under some measure of control.

The fact that death can be reduced to a manageable unit in any sense, whatsoever, reveals something that is profoundly significant concerning its character. The significant revelation is in the fact that death, as an event, is spatial, time encompassed, if not actually time bound, and therefore partakes of the character of the episodic. Death not only affects man by involving him concretely in its fulfillment, but man seems to be aware that he is being affected by death in the experience itself. There is, therefore, an element of detachment for the human spirit, even in so crucial an experience. Death is an experience *in* life and a man, under some circumstances, may be regarded as a spectator *of*, as well as a participant *in*, the moment of his own death. The logic here is that man is both a space binder and a time binder.

The second attitude toward death that comes to our attention is one of resignation mixed with elements of fear and a manifestation of muted dread—this, despite the fact that there seems to have been a careful note of familiarity with the experiences of death. It is more difficult for us to imagine what life was like under a less complex order of living, than is our lot. We are all of us participants in the modern conspiracy to reduce immediate contact with death to zero except under the most extraordinary circumstances. We know that death is a commonplace in the experience of life and yet we keep it behind a curtain or locked in a closet, as it were. To us death is gruesome and aesthetically distasteful as a primary contact for ourselves and our children. For most of us, when members of our immediate families die, the death itself takes place in a hospital. Particularly is this true of urban dwellers. From the hospital, the deceased is carried to a place of preparation for burial, the mortuary. When we see the beloved one again, the body has been washed, embalmed, and dressed for burial. Our exposure to the facts involved, the silent intimacies in preparation for burial are almost entirely secondary, to say the least. The hospital and the mortuary have entered profoundly into the life of modern man, at this point. The result is that death has been largely alienated from the normal compass of daily experience. Our sense of personal loss may be great but our primary relationship with death under normal circumstances tends to be impersonal and detached. We shrink from direct personal contact with death. It is very difficult for us to handle the emotional upsets growing out of our experience with death when we are denied the natural moments of exhaustive reaction which are derivatives of the performance of last personal services for the dead. Therapeutic effects are missed. Tremendous emotional blocks are set up without release, making for devious forms of inner chaos, which cause us to limp through the years with our griefs unassuaged.

This was not the situation with the creators of the Spirituals. Their contact with the dead was immediate, inescapable, dramatic. The family or friends washed the body of the dead, the grave clothes were carefully and personally selected or especially made. The coffin itself was built by a familiar hand. It may have been a loving though crude device, or an expression of genuine, first-class craftsmanship. During all these processes, the body remained in the home—first wrapped in cooling sheets and then "laid out" for the time interval before burial. In the case of death from illness all of the final aspects of the experience were shared by those who had taken their turn "keeping watch." Every detail was etched in the mind and emotions against the background of the approaching end. The "death rattle" in the throat, the spasm of tense vibration in the body as the struggle for air increased in intensity, the sheer physical panic sometimes manifest—all these were a familiar part of the commonplace pattern of daily experience. Out of a full, rich knowledge of fact such a song as this was born:

> I want to die easy when I die.
> I want to die easy when I die.
> Shout salvation as I fly.
> I want to die easy when I die.

A quiet death without the seizure of panic, the silent closing of the door of earthly life, this is the simple human aspiration here.

As if to provide some measure of contrast, the age-old symbolism of the river of death appears in a song like this:

> Chilly water, chilly water.
> Hallelujah to that lamb.
> I know that water is chilly and cold,
> Hallelujah to that lamb.
> But I have Jesus in my soul,
> Hallelujah to that lamb.
> Satan's just like a snake in the grass
> Hallelujah to that lamb.
> He's watching for to bite you as you pass
> Hallelujah to that lamb.

In a bold and audacious introduction of still another type of symbolism which has all the graphic quality of the essentially original, revealing the intimate personal contact with death and the dying, this old, old song announces:

> Same train carry my mother;
> Same train be back tomorrer;
> Same train, same train
> Same train blowin' at the station,
> Same train be back tomorrer;
> Same train, same train.

There is a sense of the meaning of death as a form of frustration (for those who remain) with a dimension of realism rare and moving in this song:

You needn't mind my dying,
You needn't mind my dying,
You needn't mind my dying,
Jesus goin' to make up my dying bed.

In my dying room I know,
Somebody is going to cry.
All I ask you to do for me,
Just close my dying eyes.

In my dying room I know,
Somebody is going to mourn.
All I ask you to do for me,
Just give that bell a tone.

In the third place, death is regarded as release, as complete surcease from anxiety and care. This is to be distinguished from that which may come after death. We are thinking here of the significance of death regarded somewhat as a good in itself. The meaning of death in such a view is measured strictly against the background of immediate life experience. It is not a renunciation of life because its terms have been refused, but an exulting sigh of sheer release from a very wearying burden:

I know moon-rise, I know star-rise,
    I lay this body down.
I walk in the moon-light, I walk in the star-light,
    To lay this body down.
I walk in the graveyard, I walk through the graveyard,
    To lay this body down.
I lie in the grave and stretch out my arms,
    To lay this body down.

Man, the time binder, one with the shimmering glory of moonlight and starlight and yet housed in a simple space-binding body, is heir to all the buffetings of the fixed and immovable, yet he can lay the body down and stretch out his arms and be at one with moonrise and starlight.

The note of the transcendence of death is never lacking—whether it is viewed merely as release or as the door to a heaven of endless joys. We shall examine the place and significance of the concepts dealing with that which is beyond death at a later point in our discussion. But the great idea about death itself is that it is not the master of life. It may be inevitable, yes; gruesome, perhaps; releasing, yes; but triumphant, NEVER. With such an affirmation ringing in their ears, it became possible for them, slaves though they were, to stand anything that life could bring against them.

It is next in order to examine the attitude taken toward life, because the attitude toward death cannot be separated from the attitude toward life. Was life merely a "veil of soul-making"? Was it merely a vast anteroom to the great beyond? Was it regarded as an end in itself? Or was it a series of progressions, a pilgrimage, a meaningful sojourn?

There seem to be no songs dealing with the origin of life as such or the origin of the individual life in particular. Life was regarded essentially as the given—it was accepted as a fact without reflection as to cause or reason. They were content to let the mystery remain intact.

Given the fact of life, there is much which has to do with interpretations of its meanings, its point and even its validity. In the first place, life is regarded as an experience of evil, of frustration, of despair. There are at least two moods in evidence here—one mood has to do with an impersonal characteristic of life itself. Loneliness and discouragement—such is the way of life. One cannot escape—such experiences are inherent in the process itself. Hence:

> Let us cheer the weary traveler
> Let us cheer the weary traveler,
> Along the heavenly way.

This has some elements similar to the philosophy of unyielding despair developed by Bertrand Russell in his essay on Free Man's Worship.[2]

> Sometimes I feel like a motherless child,
> A long way from home.

Here again is another song which reflects the same temper.
There is also the familiar note in:

> Nobody knows the trouble I've seen,
> Nobody knows my sorrow.
> Nobody knows the trouble I've seen,
> Glory, Hallelujah!

All the reaches of despair are caught up and held in a trembling wail in:

I couldn't hear nobody pray,
Oh, I couldn't hear nobody pray.
Oh, way down yonder by myself,
And I couldn't hear nobody pray.

A climactic chord in the mood of the seventh chapter of Paul's letter to the Romans is to be found in:

O wretched man that I am!
O wretched man that I am!
Who will deliver poor me?
My heart is filled with sadness and pain,
Who will deliver poor me?

The solitariness of the human spirit, the intensely personal characteristic of all experience as distinguished from mere frustration or despair is evident in such a song as:

I've got to walk my lonesome valley,
I've got to walk it for myself.
Nobody else can walk it for me,
I've got to walk it for myself!

Here we are in the presence of an essential insight into all human experience. It seems, sometimes, that it is the solitariness of life that causes it to move with such intensity and power. In the last analysis all the great moments of profoundest meaning are solitary. We walk the ways of life together with our associates, our friends, our loved ones. How precious it is to lean upon another, to have a staggered sense of the everlasting arms felt in communion with a friend. But there are thresholds before which all must stop and no one may enter save God, and even He in disguise. I am alone but even in my aloneness I seem sometimes to be all that there is in life, and all that there is in life seems to be synthesized in me.

It is a matter of more than passing interest that this element of overwhelming poignancy is relieved somewhat by a clear note of triumph. Out of the fullness of a tremendous vitality the lowering clouds are highlighted by an overflowing of utter exuberance:

I feel like a motherless child;
I feel like a motherless child;

Glory hallelujah!
Sometimes my way is sad and lone,
When far away and lost from home;
Glory hallelujah!

The same note appears in a softer key, expressive of a quiet but sure confidence:

Soon-a-will be done with troubles of the world;
Soon-a-will be done with troubles of the world;
Going home to live with God.

Or again the quality of triumph is to be found in the total accent of the song:

All-a-my troubles will soon be over with,
All-a-my troubles will soon be over with,
All over this world.

The second mood suggested in the interpretation of life as an experience of evil, of frustration, of despair, has to do with a personal reaction to the vindictiveness and cruelty of one's fellows. The mood is set in a definite moral and ethical frame of reference which becomes a screening device for evaluating one's day-by-day human relations. It would be expected that these songs would point indirectly to be sure, but definitely, to the slaveowner. But for the most part, the songs are strangely silent here. Many indeed have been the speculations as to the reason for this unnatural omission. There are those who say we are dealing with children so limited in mentality that there is no margin of selfhood remaining for striking out, directly or indirectly, in a frenzy of studied fury against the slave owner. This is arrant nonsense as the vast number of slave insurrections all through this terrible period will certify. There are those who say that the religion was so simple, so naive, so completely otherworldly that no impression was made by the supra-immoral aspects of the environment; only a simple acceptance of one's fate. Any person who has talked with an ex-slave could hardly hold such a position. There seems to be a more comprehensive answer than any of these. The fact was that the slave owner was regarded as one outside the pale of moral and ethical responsibility. The level of high expectation of moral excellence for the master was practically *nihil*. Nothing could be expected from him but gross evil—he was in terms of morality—amoral. The truth seems to be that the slave owner as a class did not warrant a high estimate of ethical judgment. There is no more tragic result from this total experience than the fact that even at the present time such injunctions as "love your enemies," etc. are often taken for granted to mean the enemy within the group itself. The relationship between slave and master, as far as both the slave and master were concerned, was "out of bounds" in terms of moral responsibility. It seems clear, then, that the second mood has to do with those "we group" relationships of the slave and his fellow bondsmen.

Such is the meaning of:

> Down on me, down on me,
> Looks like everybody in the whole round world is down on me.
> Talk about me as much as you please,
> I'll talk about you when I get on my knees.
> Looks like everybody in the whole round world is down on *me*.

> Sometimes I'm up, sometimes I am down,
> Sometimes I'm almost on the ground.
> Looks like everybody in the whole round world is down on me.

To refer to the refrain of one other such song:

> Oh, this is a sin-trying world,
> This is a sin-trying world.

In the second place, life is regarded as a pilgrimage, a sojourn, while the true home of the spirit is beyond the vicissitudes of life with God! This is a familiar theme of the human spirit. We are dealing with a striking theory of time. Time is measured in terms of events, actions, therefore intentions and desires. All experience, then, is made up of a series of more or less intense meaning-units that may fall in such rapid succession that the interval between is less than any quantitative value. Within the scope of an event-series all of human life is bound. Freedom can only mean, in this sense, the possibility of release from the tyranny of succeeding intervals of events. The totality of life, then, in its existential aspects, is thus completely exhausted in time. Death in such a view means complete cessation of any sense of interval and therefore of any sense of events. In short, here death means either finality or complete absorption from time-space awareness. Whatever transpires beyond death, while it can be thought of only in terms of time-space intervals, is of another universe of discourse, another quality of being.

It is in order now to raise a question as to the relation between *before* and *after* in terms of death and life. There seems to be no real break between before and after. Any notion of the continuity of life that transcends the fact of death is significant because of the advantage that is given to the meaning of life. Even though it be true that death is a process moving toward fulfillment in a single climactic event; as contrasted with life, death seems ever to be a solitary event; while life does not seem to be a single event but a process. Even at birth, the process of life seems to be well under way, well advanced. In the light of man's conscious experience with life, death seems to be a moment for the release of potentials of which the individual is in some sense already aware. Life then becomes illustrative of a theory of time that is latitudinal or flowing. On the other hand, death is suggestive of a theory of time that is circular or wheel-like.

Life always includes movement, process, inner activity and some form of irritation. Something more is implicit than what is apparent in any cycle or series of cycles that sustain all manifestations. In such a view, life takes on a definite character of timelessness. There are no isolated, unrelated and, therefore, inconsequential events or moments. Every day is fraught with antecedents and consequences the logic of which is *inner relatedness* rather than *outer seeming*. Every day is a day of judgment and all life is lived under a continuous and inner scrutiny.

To think of life, then, as a pilgrimage means that not only is life characterized by an undertow of continuity but also that the individual has no alternative but to participate responsibly in that continuity. It is this concept rooted in the New Testament interpretation of the meaning of life that is to be found in many of the Spirituals. A few such songs have been mentioned in other connections. One of the great utterances of this character is:

Done made my vow to the Lord,
And I never will turn back,
I will go, I shall go,
To see what the end will be.

My strength, Good Lord, is almost gone,
I will go, I shall go,
To see what the end will be.
But you have told me to press on,

I will go, I shall go,
To see what the end will be.

The goal of the pilgrimage looms large by inference in some of the songs. The goal is not defined as such in many of them—but the fact of the goal pervades the temper with which the journey is undertaken or endured. There is something filled with breathless anticipation and great strength in these lines:

Wait a little while,
Then we'll sing a new song,
Wait a little while,
Then we'll sing a new song.

Sometimes I get a heavenly view,
Then we'll sing a new song,
And then my trials are so few,
Then we'll sing a new song.

There is no attempt to cast a false glow over the stark ruggedness of the journey. The facts of experience are seen for what they are—difficult, often even unyielding.

It is a mighty rocky road,
Most done travelling.
Mighty rocky road,
Most done travelling.
Mighty rocky road,
Bound to carry my soul to the Lord.

Hold out your light you heaven-bound soldier,
Let your light shine around the world.

Of the sheer will to carry on under the compelling aegis of a great commitment, what could be more accurately expressive than:

Stay in the field,
Stay in the field,
Until the war is ended.
Mine eyes are turned to the heavenly gate,

Till the war is ended.
I'll keep my way, or I'll be too late,
Till the war is ended.

Here is still another variation of the same basic theme:

Oh, my good Lord, show me the way.
Enter the chariot, travel along.

Noah sent out a morning dove,
Enter the chariot, travel along,
Which brought back a token of heavenly love,
Enter the chariot, travel along.

What, then, is the fundamental significance of all these interpretations of life and death? What are these songs trying to say? They express the profound conviction that God was not done with them, that God was not done with life. The consciousness that God had not exhausted His resources did not ever leave them. This is the secret of their ascendency over circumstances and the basis of their assurances concerning life and death. The awareness of the presence of a God who was personal, intimate and active was the central fact of life and around it all the details of life and destiny were integrated.

It must be borne in mind that there seems to be little place in their reckoning for the distinction between God and Jesus. In some of the songs the terms God and Jesus are used interchangeably—to illustrate:

Did you ever see such a man as God?
A little more faith in Jesus,
A preaching the Gospel to the poor,
A little more faith in Jesus.

For the most part, a very simple theory of the incarnation is ever present. The simpler assumptions of Christian orthodoxy are utilized. There was no elaborate scheme of separate office and function between God and Jesus and only a very rare reference to the Holy Spirit. Whether the song uses the term, Jesus, or the oft repeated Lord, or Saviour, or God, the same insistence is present—God is in them, in their souls, as they put it, and what is just as important, He is in the facts of their world. In short, God is active in history in a personal and primary manner. People who live under great pressures, grappling with tremendous imponderables which left to themselves they could not manage, have no surplus energy for metaphysical distinctions. Such distinctions, apart from the necessity of circumstances or urgency of spirit, belong to those upon whom the hold of the environment is relatively relaxed. Urgency forces a reach for the ultimate, which ultimate in the intensity of demand is incorporated in the warp and woof of immediacy.

It is the next in order to examine the large place given to the otherworldly emphasis in these songs. What is the meaning of Heaven, of the final Judgment? In such considerations we come to grips with the conception of immortality implicit and explicit in the songs, and the basis for it.

Again and again I have heard many people (including descendants of these singers) speak disparagingly of the otherworldly emphasis as purely a mechanism of escape and sheer retreat. The argument is that such an emphasis served as a kind of soporific, making for docility and submission. It is further charged that here we are dealing with a clever device by which these people were manipulated into a position which rendered them more completely defenseless than they would have been without it.

Such an argument must be examined. In the first place, the facts make clear that religion did serve to deepen the capacity of endurance and the absorption of suffering. It was a precious bane! What greater tribute could be paid to religious faith in general and to their religious faith in particular than this: It taught a people how to ride high to life, to look squarely in the face those facts that argue most dramatically against all hope and to use those facts as raw material out of which they fashioned a hope that the environment, with all of its cruelty, could not crush. With untutored hands—with a sure artistry and genius created out of a vast vitality, a concept of God was wrenched from the Sacred Book, the Bible, the chronicle of a people who had learned through great necessity the secret meaning of suffering. This total experience enabled them to reject annihilation and affirm a terrible right to live. The *center of focus* was beyond themselves in a God who was a companion to them in their miseries even as He enabled them to transcend their miseries. And this is good news! Under God the human spirit can triumph over the most radical frustrations! This is no ordinary achievement. In the presence of an infinite desperation held at white heat in the consciousness of a people, out of the very depth of life, an infinite energy took shape on their behalf.

> Oh rise, shine, for thy light is a coming.
> Oh rise, shine, for thy light is a coming.
> My Lord says he's coming by and by.

Do we wonder then that they sang:

> Oh religion is a fortune,
> I really do believe.
> Oh religion is a fortune,
> I really do believe!

In the second place, this religious emphasis did not paralyze action, it did not make for mere resignation. On the contrary, it gave the mind a new dimension of resourcefulness. I had a college classmate who cleared his throat just before responding to the question of his teacher. The clearing of the throat broke the impasse between his mind and his immediate environment so that he could have a sense of ascendency in his situation. It was in some such fashion as this that these religious songs functioned. (Of course, they did much more than this.) Once the impasse was broken, many things became possible to them. They could make their religion vehicular in terms of the particular urgencies of the moment. "Steal away to Jesus" became an important call to those who had ears to hear. In other words, far from paralyzing action, religion made for detachment from the environment so that they could live in the midst of the traffic of their situation with the independence of solitude. The pragmatic result for them was an awareness that against the darkness of their days, something warred, "a strange new courage." To them it was the work of God and who could say to them NAY?

We turn now to an examination of the place and significance of the notion of judgment. Taking their clue from the word picture given by Jesus in the Gospels, the Judgment was the climax of human history. This made a tremendous appeal to the imagination. The figure of Gabriel was added to the imagery of Jesus. There are many references to Gabriel:

> O get your trumpet Gabriel
> And come down on the sea.
> Now don't you sound your trumpet
> Till you get orders from me—
>
> I got a key to that Kingdom
> I got a key to that Kingdom
> And the world can't do me no harm.

To mention the refrain of one other song:

Gabriel, Gabriel, blow your trumpet!
My Lord says he's going to rain down fire.

Some of these songs are almost pure drama. Consider this very old hymn, no record of which is to be found in any of the available collections:

Oh, He's going to wake up the dead,
Going to wake up the dead,
God's going to wake up the dead.
One of these mornings bright and fair,
God's going to wake up the dead.

The judgment is personal *and* cosmic so that even the rocks and mountains, the stars, the sea, are all involved in so profound a process:

My Lord what a morning!
My Lord what a morning!
When the stars begin to fall.

You will hear the trumpet sound
To wake the nations underground,
Standing at my God's right hand,
When the stars begin to fall.

The matter of most crucial importance is this—a man is brought face to face with his own life—personal accountability is the keynote:

When the master calls me to Him
I'll be somewhere sleeping in my grave.
In that great day when he calls us to him
I'll be somewhere sleeping in my grave.

The deep intimacy between the soul and God is constantly suggested. Even the true name of the individual is known only to God. There are references to the fact that the designation, Child of God, is the only name that is necessary. This gnosis of the individual is an amazing example of the mystical element present in the slave's religious experience. The slave's answer to the use of terms of personal designation that are degrading is to be found in his private knowledge that his name is known only to the God of the entire universe. In the Judgment everybody will at last know who he is, a fact which he has known all along.

O' nobody knows who I am, who I am,
  Till the Judgment morning.

Judgment takes place in time. It is a moment when the inner significance of a man's deeds is revealed. God shall deal with each according to his history. It was with reference to the Judgment that life took on a subdued character. Everybody is judged. The Judge is impartial. There is distinct continuity between the life on earth and the Judgment. Excuses are of no avail. God, the Judge, knows the entire story.

O', He sees all you do,
He hears all you say.
My Lord's-a-writing all the time.

Judgment was not thought of as being immediately after death. There is a time element between death and final judgment. Life, death, judgment, this was the thought sequence. When the final judgment takes place there will be no more time. What takes place after judgment has a necessitous, mandatory character ascribed to it. Man can influence his judgment before death—after death everything is unalterable. This notion of the ultimate significance of life on earth is another aspect of the theory of time to which we have made reference. Here is a faithful following of the thought of the Gospels.

And yet there is more to be said concerning the idea of the Judgment. What does the concept say? Are we dealing with a matter of fact and of literal truth? If we are, then the symbolism of the Judgment is necessarily an essential symbolism. What is the literal truth seeking expression in this symbolism? It is this: The life of man is significantly capable of rising to the demands of maximum moral responsibility. That which is capable of a maximum moral responsibility functioning in the tiny compass of single events takes on the aspects of the beyond-event, hence beyond time, therefore eternal. The conclusion seems inescapable that man is interpreted as having only mortal manifestations, but even these mortal manifestations have immortal overtones. If this were not true then there would be no significance in the symbolic fact of judgment. The literal truth requires a symbolism that is completely vehicular or revelatory.

Finally, we turn to an examination of the place and significance of the fact of Heaven in the thinking of these early singers. Heaven was a place—it was not merely an idea in the mind. This must be held in mind, constantly. The thinking about it is spatial. It is the thinking of Jesus in the Fourth Gospel. "I go to prepare a place for you. If I go and prepare a place for you I shall

come again, and take you into myself that where I am there ye may be also."
"In my father's house are many mansions." These word pictures supplied a
concreteness to the fulfillment of all earth's aspirations and longings. The
songs are many, expressing highly descriptive language of this character:

> I haven't been to heaven
> But I've been told,
> The streets are pearl
> And the gates are gold;
> Not made with hands.

What a plaintive wistfulness is found here:

> In bright mansions above,
> In bright mansions above,
> Lord, I want to live up yonder;
> In bright mansions above.

Such an aspiration was in sharp contrast to dimly lighted cabins with
which they were familiar. Perfection, truth, beauty, even goodness are
again and again symbolized by light. This is universal.

Heaven was as intensely personal as the facts of their experience or as
the fact of the Judgment. Here at last was a place where the slave was
counted in. He had the dignity of personal registration.

> O write my name, O write my name,
> The angels in heaven are going to write my name.
> Yes, write my name with a golden pen,
> The angels in heaven are going to write my name.

Heaven is regarded as a dimension of self-extension in the sense of private possession:

> I want God's heaven to be mine, to be mine,
> Yes, I want God's heaven to be mine,

Who is there that can escape the irony and the triumph in:

> I got a robe,
> You got a robe,

All God's children got robes,
When we get to heaven
We're going to put on our robes,
We're going to shout all over God's heaven.

There will be no proscription, no segregation, no separateness, no slave-row, but complete freedom of movement—the most psychologically dramatic of all manifestations of freedom.

All of these songs and many others like them argue for an authentic belief in personal immortality. In large part it is a belief growing out of the necessities of life as they experienced it. Family ties are restored, friends and particularly loved ones are reunited. The most precious thing of all was the fact that personal identity was not lost but heightened. Heaven would not be heaven, it would have no meaning, if the fact of contrasting experiences was not always possible and evident. There was a great compulsion to know then a new and different life, which knowledge could only be real if the individual were able to recall how it once was with him. We are not surprised to find a great emphasis on reunion. There was nothing more heart-tearing in that far-off time of madness than the separation of families at the auction block. Wives were sold from their husbands to become breeders for profit, children were separated from their parents and from each other—in fact, from the beginning, the slave population was a company of displaced and dispossessed people. The possibility of ever seeing one's loved ones again was very remote. The conviction grew that this is the kind of universe that cannot deny ultimately the demands of love and longing. The issue of reuniting with loved ones turned finally on the hope of immortality and the issue of immortality turned on the fact of God. Therefore God would make it right and once again God became the answer.

This personal immortality carried with it also the idea of rest from labor, of being able to take a long sigh cushioned by a deep sense of peace. If time is regarded as having certain characteristics that are event transcending and the human spirit is not essentially time bound but a time binder, then the concept of personal survival of death follows automatically. For man is never completely involved in, nor absorbed by, experience. He is an experiencer with recollection and memory—so these songs insist. The logic of such a position is that man was not born *in* time, that he was not created by a time-space experience, but rather that man was born *into* time. Something of him enters all time-space relationships, even birth, completely and fully intact, and is not created by the time-space relationship. In short, the most significant thing about man is what

Eckhart calls the "uncreated element" in his soul. This was an assumed fact profoundly at work in the life and thought of the early slaves.

This much was certainly clear to them—the soul of man was immortal. It could go to heaven or hell, but it could not *die*. Most of the references to hell are by inference. Not to be with God was to be in hell but it did not mean not to *be*.

It is in order to raise the same question about heaven that was raised previously about the Judgment. Are we dealing here with a matter of literal truth? Or are we once again dealing with necessary symbolism growing out of literal truth? In other words, what is the intrinsic meaning attached to or to be drawn out of the concept of heaven? Is this mere drama or some crude art form? Certain facts are quite evident in the picture given. Heaven was specific! An orderly series of events was thought to take place. The human spirit rests—the fulfillment of the exhausted. A crown, a personal crown is given—a fulfillment for those who strive without the realization of their strivings. There is a room of one's own—the fulfillment of life in terms of the healing balm of privacy. There are mansions—the fulfillment of life in terms of living with a high quality of dignity. There are robes, slippers—the fulfillment of life in terms of the restoration of self-respect. The idea at the core of the literal truth in the concept of heaven is this— life is totally right, structurally dependable, good essentially as contrasted with the moral concepts of good and evil. It affirms that the contradictions of human experience are not ultimate. The profoundest desires of man are of God, and therefore they cannot be denied ultimately.

> Our ship is on the ocean but
> We'll anchor by and by.

To use the oft-repeated phrase of Augustine, "Thou hast made us for Thyself, and our souls are restless till they find their rest in thee."[3] There is an order, a moral order in which men participate, that gathers up into itself, dimensional fulfillment, limitless in its creativity and design. Whatever may be the pressures to which one is subjected, the snares, the buffetings, one must not for a moment think that there is not an ultimate value always at stake. It is this ultimate value at stake in all experience that is the final incentive to decency, to courage and hope. Human life, even the life of a slave must be lived worthily of so grand an undertaking. At every moment a crown was placed over his head that he must constantly grow tall enough to wear. Only of that which is possessed of infinite potentials can an infinite demand be required. The unfulfilled, the undeveloped only has a future; the fulfilled, the rounded out, the finished can only have a past. The human spirit participates in both past and future in what it regards as the *present* but it is independent of both.

We may dismiss, then, the symbolism of these songs as touching life and death if we understand the literal truth with which they have to do. The moment we accept the literal truth, we are once again faced with the urgency of a vehicular symbolism. The cycle is indeed vicious. To be led astray by the crassness, the materialistic character of the symbolism so that in the end we reject the literal truth is to deny life itself of its dignity and man the right or necessity of dimensional fulfillment. In such a view the present moment is all there is—man is no longer a time binder but becomes a prisoner in a tight world of momentary events—no more and no less. His tragedy would be that nothing beyond the moment could happen to him and all of his life could be encompassed within the boundary of a time-space fragment. For these slave singers such a view was completely unsatisfactory and it was therefore thoroughly and decisively rejected. And this is the miracle of their achievement causing them to take their place alongside the great creative religious thinkers of the human race. They made a worthless life, the life of chattel property, a mere thing, a body, *worth living!* They yielded with abiding enthusiasm to a view of life which included all the events of their experience without exhausting themselves in those experiences. To them this quality of life was insistent fact because of that which deep within them, they discovered of God, and his far-flung purposes. God was not through with them. And He was not, nor could He be, exhausted by any single experience or any series of experiences. To know Him was to live a life worthy of the loftiest meaning of life. Men in all ages and climes, slave or free, trained or untutored, who have sensed the same values, are their fellow-pilgrims who journey together with them in increasing self-realization in the quest for the city that hath foundations, whose Builder and Maker is God.

❧❧❧❧❧❧❧❧❧

Love

The religion of Jesus makes the love-ethic central. This is no ordinary achievement. It seems clear that Jesus started out with the simple teaching concerning love embodied in the timeless words of Israel: "Hear, O Israel: The Lord our God is one Lord: and thou shalt love the Lord thy

God with all thy heart, and with all thy soul, and with all thy might," and "thy neighbour as thyself." Once the neighbor is defined, then one's moral obligation is clear. In a memorable story Jesus defined the neighbor by telling of the Good Samaritan. With sure artistry and great power he depicted what happens when a man responds directly to human need across the barriers of class, race, and condition. Every man is potentially every other man's neighbor. Neighborliness is nonspatial; it is qualitative. A man must love his neighbor directly, clearly, permitting no barriers between.

This was not an easy position for Jesus to take within his own community. Opposition to his teaching increased as the days passed. A twofold demand was made upon him at all times: to love those of the household of Israel who became his enemies because they regarded him as a careless perverter of the truths of God; to love those beyond the household of Israel—the Samaritan, and even the Roman.

The former demand was deeply dramatized by the fact that Jesus did not consider himself as one who stood outside of Israel. If he had regarded himself as one who was starting a new religion, a new faith, then it would not have been hard to account for bitter opposition. With justice, the defenders of the faith could have opposed him because he would have been deliberately trying to destroy the very grounds of Judaism. But if it be true—as I think it is—that Jesus felt he was merely serving as a creative vehicle for the authentic genius of Israel, completely devoted to the will of God, then in order to love those of the household he must conquer his own pride. In their attitude he seemed to see the profoundest betrayal of the purpose of God. It is curious that as each looked on the other the accusations were identical.

In the second place, Jesus had to deal with the Samaritans in working out the application of his love-ethic. His solution of this bitter problem is found in the story of the Good Samaritan. There is also the very instructive account of the interview between Jesus and the Syrophoenician woman.

Opposition to the interpretation which Jesus was giving to the gospel of God had increased, and Jesus and his disciples withdrew from active work into temporary semiretirement around Tyre and Sidon. The woman broke into his retreat with an urgent request in behalf of her child. Jesus said to her, "It is not meet to take the children's bread, and cast it to dogs." This was more a probing query than an affirmation. It had in it all the deep frustration which he had experienced, and there flashed through it generations of religious exclusiveness to which he was heir. "What right has this woman of another race to make a claim upon me? What mockery is there here? Am I not humiliated enough in being misunderstood by my own kind? And here this woman dares to demand that which, in the very nature of the case, she cannot claim as her due."

Into the riotous thoughts that were surging in his mind her voice struck like a bolt of lightning: "Truth, Lord: yet the dogs eat of the crumbs which fall from their masters' table."

"Go—go, woman, go in peace; your faith hath saved you."

But this was not all. Jesus had to apply his love-ethic to the enemy—to the Roman, the ruler. This was the hardest task, because to tamper with the enemy was to court disaster. To hate him in any way that caused action was to invite the wrath of Rome. To love him was to be regarded as a traitor to Jesus' own people, to Israel, and therefore to God. It was upon the anvil of the Jewish community's relations with Rome that Jesus hammered out the vital content of his concept of love for one's enemy.

"The enemy" can very easily be divided into three groups. There is first the personal enemy, one who is in some sense a part of one's primary-group life. The relationship with such a person is grounded in more or less intimate, personal associations into which has entered conflict. Such conflict may have resulted from misunderstanding or from harsh words growing out of a hot temper and too much pride on either side to make amends. It may have come about because of an old family feud by which those who were never a part of the original rift are victimized. The strained relationship may have been due to the evil work of a vicious tongue. The point is that the enemy in this sense is one who at some time was a rather intimate part of one's world and was close enough to be taken into account in terms of intimacy.

To love such an enemy requires reconciliation, the will to re-establish a relationship. It involves confession of error and a seeking to be restored to one's former place. Doubtless it is this that Jesus had in mind in his charge: "If thou bring thy gift to the altar, and there rememberest that thy brother hath ought against thee; leave there thy gift before the altar, . . . and go be reconciled to thy brother and then come and offer thy gift."

It is with this kind of enemy that the disinherited find it easiest to deal. They accept with good grace the insistence of Jesus that they deal with the rifts in their own world. Here, they are at the center; they count specifically, and their wills are crucial. When one analyzes the preaching and the religious teachings in the churches of his country, he discovers that the term "enemy" usually has this rather restricted meaning. When the Negro accepts the teaching of love, it is this narrow interpretation which is uppermost. I grew up with this interpretation. I dare to say that, in the white churches in my little town, the youths were trained in the same narrow interpretation applied to white persons. Love those who have a natural claim upon you. To those who have no such claim, there is no responsibility.

The second kind of enemy comprises those persons who, by their activities, make it difficult for the group to live without shame and humiliation. It does not require much imagination to assume that to the sensitive son of Israel the taxgatherers were in that class. It was they who became the grasping hand of Roman authority, filching from Israel the taxes which helped to keep alive the oppression of the gentile ruler. They were Israelites who understood the psychology of the people, and therefore were always able to function with the kind of spiritual ruthlessness that would have been impossible for those who did not know the people intimately. They were despised; they were outcasts, because from the inside they had unlocked the door to the enemy. The situation was all the more difficult to bear because the tax collectors tended to be prosperous in contrast with the rest of the people. To be required to love such a person was the final insult. How could such a demand be made? One did not even associate with such creatures. To be seen in their company meant a complete loss of status and respect in the community. The taxgatherer had no soul; he had long since lost it. When Jesus became a friend to the tax collectors and secured one as his intimate companion, it was a spiritual triumph of such staggering proportions that after nineteen hundred years it defies rational explanation.

The argument for loving this second enemy was the fact that he too was a son of Abraham. He was one of them, unworthy though he was. Here was the so-called call of blood, which cannot be stilled. God required that Israel be one people, even as he was one.

All underprivileged people have to deal with this kind of enemy. There are always those who seem to be willing to put their special knowledge at the disposal of the dominant group to facilitate the tightening of the chains. They are given position, often prominence, and above all a guarantee of economic security and status. To love such people requires the uprooting of the bitterness of betrayal, the heartiest poison that grows in the human spirit. There must be some understanding of how such people become as they are. Is it because they are weak and must build their strength by feeding upon the misery of their fellows? Is it because they want power and, recognizing the fact that they can never compete within the group for a place of significance, are thus driven by some strange inner urge to get by cunning what they cannot secure by integrity? Is it because they resent the circumstances of their birth and fling their defiance into the teeth of life by making everything foul and unclean within the reach of their contact and power?

There is no simple or single answer. In every ghetto, in every dwelling place of the disinherited throughout the ages, these persons have appeared. To love them means to recognize some deep respect and reverence for their persons. But to love them does not mean to condone their way of life.

Jesus demonstrated that the only way to redeem them for the common cause was to penetrate their thick resistance to public opinion and esteem and lay bare the simple heart. This man is not just a tax collector; he is a son of God. Awaken that awareness in him and he will attack his betrayal as only he can—from the inside. It was out of this struggle and triumph that Jesus says: "Love your enemies, do good to them which hate you." Hence he called Matthew, the tax collector, to follow him.

The third type of enemy was exemplified by Rome. The elements at work here were both personal and impersonal; they were religious and political. To deal with Rome as a moral enemy required a spiritual recognition of the relationship with the empire. This was made even more precarious because of the development of the cult of emperor worship. But Rome was the political enemy. To love the Roman meant first to lift him out of the general classification of enemy. The Roman had to emerge as a person.

On the surface this would not be too difficult. The basic requirement was that the particular Roman be established in some primary, face-to-face relationship of gross equality. There had to be a moment when the Roman and the Jew emerged as neither Roman nor Jew, but as two human spirits that had found a mutual, though individual, validation. For the most part, such an experience would be impossible as long as either was functioning only within his own social context. The Roman, viewed against the background of his nation and its power, was endowed in the mind of the Jew with all the arrogance and power of the dominant group. It would matter not how much the individual wished to be regarded for himself alone or to be permitted to disassociate himself from all the entangling embarrassments of his birthright; the fact remained always present. He was a Roman and had to bear on his shoulders the full weight of that responsibility. If he tried to make common cause with the Jew, he was constantly under suspicion, and was never to be trusted and taken all the way into the confidence of the other.

Of course, the Jewish person was under the same handicap. It was almost impossible for him to emerge as a person; always in the background was the fact of difference and the disadvantage of status. If he wanted to know the Roman for himself, he ran the risk of being accused by his fellows of consorting with the enemy. If he persisted, it would be simply a matter of time before he would be regarded as an enemy and forced to take the consequences. The more he explained his motives, the deep ethical and spiritual urgency which forced the irregular behavior, the more hypocritical he would seem.

Once isolation from one's fellows has been achieved, one is at the mercy of doubts, fears, and confusion. One might say, "Suppose I have misread the will of God. Suppose I am really acting in this way because I do not have the courage to hate. Suppose those I am learning to love turn and rend me with added contempt and condescension. Then what? Does it mean that God has failed me? Does it mean that there is, at long last, no ultimate integrity in the ethical enterprise? Does it mean that the love ideal is so absolute that it vitiates something as frail and limited as human life—that thus it is an evil and not a good? 'My God, my God, why hast thou forsaken me?'"

Love of the enemy means that a fundamental attack must first be made on the enemy status. How can this be done? Does it mean merely ignoring the fact that he belongs to the enemy class? Hardly. For lack of a better term, an "unscrambling" process is required. Obviously a situation has to be set up in which it is possible for primary contacts to be multiplied. By this I do not mean contacts that are determined by status or by social distinctions. There are always primary contacts between the weak and the strong, the privileged and the underprivileged, but they are generally contacts within zones of agreement which leave the status of the individual intact. There is great intimacy between whites and Negroes, but it is usually between servant and served, between employer and employee. Once the status of each is frozen or fixed, contacts are merely truces between enemies—a kind of armistice for purposes of economic security. True, there are times when something great and dependable emerges, and the miracle takes place even though the status has remained, formally. But during such moments status is merely transcended; it is not broken down. If it is transcended over a time interval of sufficient duration, a permanent emergence takes place. But, in a very tragic sense, the ultimate fate of the relationship seems to be in the hands of the wider social context.

It is necessary, therefore, for the privileged and the underprivileged to work on the common environment for the purpose of providing normal experiences of fellowship. This is one very important reason for the insistence that segregation is a complete ethical and moral evil. Whatever it may do for those who dwell on either side of the wall, one thing is certain:

it poisons all normal contacts of those persons involved. The first step toward love is a common sharing of a sense of mutual worth and value. This cannot be discovered in a vacuum or in a series of artificial or hypothetical relationships. It has to be in a real situation, natural, free.

The experience of the common worship of God is such a moment. It is in this connection that American Christianity has betrayed the religion of Jesus almost beyond redemption. Churches have been established for the underprivileged, for the weak, for the poor, on the theory that they prefer to be among themselves. Churches have been established for the Chinese, the Japanese, the Korean, the Mexican, the Filipino, the Italian, and the Negro, with the same theory in mind. The result is that in the one place in which normal, free contacts might be most naturally established —in which the relations of the individual to his God should take priority over conditions of class, race, power, status, wealth, or the like—this place is one of the chief instruments for guaranteeing barriers.

It is in order to quote these paragraphs from a recently published book, *The Protestant Church and the Negro*, by Frank S. Loescher:

> There are approximately 8,000,000 Protestant Negroes. About 7,500,000 are in separate Negro denominations. Therefore, from the local church through the regional organizations to the national assemblies over 93 per cent of the Negroes are without association in work and worship with Christians of other races except in interdenominational organizations which involve a few of their leaders. The remaining 500,000 Negro Protestants—about 6 per cent—are in predominantly white denominations, and of these 500,000 Negroes in "white" churches, at least 99 per cent, judging by the surveys of six denominations, are in segregated congregations. They are in association with their white denominational brothers only in national assemblies, and, in some denominations, in regional, state, or more local jurisdictional meetings. There remains a handful of Negro members in local "white" churches. How many? Call it one-tenth of one per cent of all the Negro Protestant Christians in the United States—8,000 souls—the figure is probably much too large. Whatever the figure actually is, the number of white and Negro persons who ever gather together for worship under the auspices of Protestant Christianity is almost microscopic. And where interracial worship does occur, it is, for the most part, in communities where there are only a few Negro families and where, therefore, only a few Negro individuals are available to "white" churches.

That is the over-all picture, a picture which hardly reveals the Protestant church as a dynamic agency in the integration of American Negroes into American life. Negro membership appears to be confined to less than one per cent of the local "white" churches, usually churches in small communities where but a few Negroes live and have already experienced a high degree of integration by other community institutions—communities one might add where it is unsound to establish a Negro church since Negroes are in such small numbers. It is an even smaller percentage of white churches in which Negroes are reported to be participating freely, or are integrated.

The same pattern appears to be true for other colored minorities, that is, Japanese, Chinese, Indians, Mexicans, Puerto Ricans. Regarding the Mexicans and Puerto Ricans, for example, a director of home missions work in a great denomination says his experience leads him to believe that "generally there is little, if any, discrimination here though in a community which has a large Mexican population it is quite true that they have their own churches."[1]

The enormity of this sin cannot be easily grasped. The situation is so tragic that men of good will in all the specious classifications within our society find more cause for hope in the secular relations of life than in religion.

The religion of Jesus says to the disinherited: "Love your enemy. Take the initiative in seeking ways by which you can have the experience of a common sharing of mutual worth and value. It may be hazardous, but you must do it." For the Negro it means that he must see the individual white man in the context of a common humanity. The fact that a particular individual is white, and therefore may be regarded in some over-all sense as the racial enemy, must be faced; and opportunity must be provided, found, or created for freeing such an individual from his "white necessity." From this point on, the relationship becomes like any other primary one.

Once an attack is made on the enemy status and the individual has emerged, the underprivileged man must himself be status free. It may be argued that his sense of freedom must come first. Here I think the answer may be determined by the one who initiates the activity. But in either case love is possible only between two freed spirits. What one discovers in even a single experience in which barriers have been removed may become useful in building an over-all technique for loving one's enemy. There cannot be too great insistence on the point that we are here dealing with a discipline, a method, a technique, as over against some form of wishful thinking or simple desiring.

Once the mutual discovery is made that the privileged is a man and the underprivileged is a man, or that the Negro is a man and the white man is a man, then the normal desire to make this discovery inclusive of all brings one to grips with the necessity for working out a technique of implementation. The underprivileged man cannot get to know many people as he knows one individual, and yet he is in constant contact with many, in ways that deepen the conflict. Is there some skill which may be applied at a moment's notice that will make a difference even in the most casual relationships? Such a technique may be found in the attitude of respect for personality.

Preliminary to any discussion of the significance of this attitude, some urgent word of caution must be given. For the most part the relationship between the weak and the strong is basically amoral, or it is characterized by a facile use of the mood of "the exception." It is easy to say about a particular individual, "He is different," or, "He is exceptional," and to imply that the general rule or the general attitude does not apply.

This mood of exception operates in still another way. A whole group may be regarded as an exception, and thus one is relieved of any necessity to regard them as human beings. A Negro may say: "If a man is white, he may be automatically classified as one incapable of dealing with me as if he were a rational human being." Or it may be just the reverse. Such a mood, the mood of exception, operates in all sorts of ways. A Republican may say the same thing about a Socialist. The deadly consequences of this attitude are evident. On the same principle scapegoats are provided, upon whose helpless heads we pour our failures and our fears.

The attitude of respect for personality presupposes that all the individuals involved are within what may be called the ethical field. The privileged man must be regarded as being within the area in which ethical considerations are mandatory. If either privileged or underprivileged is out of bounds, the point has no validity.

It is important now to ask how Jesus used this attitude. How did he spell it out? One day a Roman captain came to him seeking help for his servant, for whom he had a profound attachment—a Roman citizen seeking help from a Jewish teacher! Deep was his anguish and distress; all other sources of help had failed. That which would have been expected in the attitude of the Roman growing out of the disjointed relationship between them and the Jews was conspicuously lacking here. The fact that he had come to Jesus was in itself evidence to warrant the conclusion that he had put aside the pride of race and status which would have caused him to regard himself as superior to Jesus. He placed his need directly and simply before

Jesus, saying, "Lord, my servant lieth at home sick of the palsy, grievously tormented." By implication he says, "It is my faith that speaks, that cries out. I am stripped bare of all pretense and false pride. The man in me appeals to the man in you." So great was his faith and his humility that when Jesus said that he would come to his home, the captain replied, "I am not worthy that thou shouldest come under my roof; but speak the word only, and my servant shall be healed."

It was the testimony of Jesus that he had found no such faith in all Israel. The Roman was confronted with an insistence that made it impossible for him to remain a Roman, or even a captain. He had to take his place alongside all the rest of humanity and mingle his desires with the longing of all the desperate people of all the ages. When this happened, it was possible at once for him to scale with Jesus any height of understanding, fellowship, and love. The final barrier between the strong and the weak, between ruler and ruled, disappeared.

In the casual relationships between the privileged and the underprivileged there may not be many occurrences of so dramatic a character. Naturally. The average underprivileged man is not a Jesus of Nazareth. The fact remains, however, that wherever a need is laid bare, those who stand in the presence of it can be confronted with the experience of universality that makes all class and race distinctions impertinent. During the great Vanport, Oregon, disaster, when rising waters left thousands homeless, many people of Portland who, prior to that time were sure of their "white supremacy," opened their homes to Negroes, Mexicans, and Japanese. The result was that they were all confronted with the experience of universality. They were no longer white, black, and brown. They were men, women, and children in the presence of the operation of impersonal Nature. Under the pressure they were the human family, and each stood in immediate candidacy for the profoundest fellowship, understanding, and love.

In many experiences of the last war this primary discovery was made. Since an army is a part of the pretensions of the modern state, the state's using it to perpetuate the system of segregation is mere stupidity. The multiplication of moments when citizens—in this instance soldiers—may be confronted with an experience of universality is simply staggering. Aside from all consideration of the issues of war and peace, here is a public activity of the state in which the raw material of democracy can be fashioned into an experience of that personality confirmation without which there can be no lasting health in the state. It is not merely coincidental that this same experience is that out of which the ethical premise of love can find fulfillment.

The concept of reverence for personality, then, is applicable between persons from whom, in the initial instance, the heavy weight of status has been sloughed off. Then what? Each person meets the other where he is and there treats him as if he were where he ought to be. Here we emerge into an area where love operates, revealing a universal characteristic unbounded by special or limited circumstances.

How did Jesus define it? One day a woman was brought to Jesus. She had been caught in the act of adultery. The spokesman for the group who brought her said she was caught red-handed and that according to the law she should be stoned to death. "What is your judgment?" was their searching question. To them the woman was not a woman, or even a person, but an adulteress, stripped of her essential dignity and worth. Said Jesus: "He that is without sin among you, let him first cast a stone." After that, he implied, any person may throw. The quiet words exploded the situation, and in the piercing glare each man saw himself in his literal substance. In that moment each was not a judge of another's deeds, but of his own. In the same glare the adulteress saw herself merely as a woman involved in the meshes of a struggle with her own elemental passion.

Jesus, always the gentleman, did not look at the woman as she stood before him. Instead, he looked on the ground, busied himself with his thoughts. What a moment, reaching beyond time into eternity!

Jesus waited. One by one the men crept away. The woman alone was left. Hearing no outcry, Jesus raised his eyes and beheld the woman. "Where are those thine accusers? Hath no man condemned thee?"

"No man, Lord."

"Neither do I condemn thee: go, and sin no more."

This is how Jesus demonstrated reverence for personality. He met the woman where she was, and he treated her as if she were already where she now willed to be. In dealing with her he "believed" her into the fulfillment of her possibilities. He stirred her confidence into activity. He placed a crown over her head which for the rest of her life she would keep trying to grow tall enough to wear.

> Free at last, free at last.
> Thank God Almighty, I'm free at last.

The crucial question is, Can this attitude, developed in the white heat of personal encounter, become characteristic of one's behavior even when the drama of immediacy is lacking? I think so. It has to be rooted in concrete experience. No amount of good feeling for people in general, no amount of simple desiring, is an adequate substitute. It is the act of inner authority, well within the reach of everyone. Obviously, then, merely preaching love of one's enemies or exhortations—however high and holy—cannot, in the last analysis, accomplish this result. At the center of the attitude is a core of painstaking discipline, made possible only by personal triumph. The ethical demand upon the more privileged and the underprivileged is the same.

There is another aspect of the problem which is crucial for the disinherited who is seeking in his love to overcome his hatred. The disinherited man has a sense of gross injury. He finds it well-nigh impossible to forgive, because his injury is often gratuitous. It is not for something that he has done, an action resulting from a deliberate violation of another. He is penalized for what he *is* in the eyes and the standards of another. Somehow he must free himself of the will to retaliation that keeps alive his hatred. Years ago I heard an American missionary to Arabia make a speech concerning the attitude of the people in that land toward the British. He said that he and an Arab friend were taking a boat ride down a certain river when a British yacht passed. With quiet fury the Arab friend said, "Damn the English."

"Why do you say that? They have done good service to your country in terms of health and so forth. I don't understand."

"I said, 'Damn the English,' because they think they are better than I am." Here was stark bitterness fed by the steady oozing of the will to resentment.

It is clear that before love can operate, there is the necessity for forgiveness of injury perpetuated against a person by a group. This is the issue for the disinherited. Once again the answer is not simple. Perhaps there is no answer that is completely satisfying from the point of view of rational reflection. Can the mouse forgive the cat for eating him? It does seem that Jesus dealt with every act of forgiveness as one who was convinced that there is in every act of injury an element that is irresponsible and irrational. No evil deed—and no good deed, either—was named by him as an expression of the total mind of the doer. Once, when someone addressed him as "Good Master," Jesus is quoted as having said, "Why callest thou me good? There is none good, but . . . God."

In Jesus' insistence that we should forgive seventy times seven, there seems to be the assumption that forgiveness is mandatory for three reasons. First, God forgives us again and again for what we do intentionally and unintentionally. There is present an element that is contingent upon our attitude. Forgiveness beyond this is interpreted as the work of divine grace. Second, no evil deed represents the full intent of the doer. Third, the evildoer does not go unpunished. Life is its own restraint. In the wide sweep of the ebb and flow of moral law our deeds track us down, and doer and deed meet. "Vengeance is mine; I will repay, saith the Lord." At the moment of injury or in the slow burning fires of resentment this may be poor comfort. This is the ultimate ground in which finally a profound, unrelieved injury is absorbed. When all other means have been exhausted, each in his own tongue whispers, "There *is* forgiveness with God."

What, then, is the word of the religion of Jesus to those who stand with their backs against the wall? There must be the clearest possible understanding of the anatomy of the issues facing them. They must recognize fear, deception, hatred, each for what it is. Once having done this, they must learn how to destroy these or to render themselves immune to their domination. In so great an undertaking it will become increasingly clear that the contradictions of life are not ultimate. The disinherited will know for themselves that there is a Spirit at work in life and in the hearts of men which is committed to overcoming the world. It is universal, knowing no age, no race, no culture, and no condition of men. For the privileged and underprivileged alike, if the individual puts at the disposal of the Spirit the needful dedication and discipline, he can live effectively in the chaos of the present the high destiny of a son of God.

Notes

The Negro Spiritual Speaks of Life and Death

1. Willard Sperry (1882–1954) was dean of Harvard Divinity School, 1922 to 1953.
2. Bertrand Russell (1872–1970), controversial English philosopher and political activist, published "The Free Man's Worship" [*The Independent Review* 1 (December 1903): 415–24] shortly after an experience of "mystical illumination" prompted him to embrace pacifism. "In action, in desire, we must submit perpetually to the tyranny of outside forces," Russell wrote in this famous essay, "but in aspiration, we are free, free from our fellow men, free from the petty planet on which our bodies impotently crawl, free even, while we live, from the tyranny of death. Let us learn then that energy of faith which enables us to live constantly in the vision of the good; and let us descend, in action, into the world of fact, with that vision always before us."
3. St. Augustine, Bishop of Hippo (354–430), established the intellectual foundations of the early Catholic Church in his major works, *Confessions* and *The City of God*. The quotation is from *Confessions*, Book 1, Chapter 1.

Love

1. pp. 76–78.

Chapter 4

The Negro Church and Assimilation

E. Franklin Frazier

The Walls Came Tumbling Down

We have studied the transformations which have occurred in the Negro church and in the religion of Negroes as the result of urbanization. We have seen how the migrations of Negroes to cities have tended to uproot the traditional organization of the Negro community and changed the outlook of Negroes. As the result of the social disorganization of Negro life there has been a reorganization of life on a different basis in order to meet the demands of the city. Life in the cities of the North has brought a larger measure of freedom from racial prejudice and discriminations which had characterized race relations in the South. This new freedom has enabled Negroes to enter more into the mainstream of American life. Since this new freedom has been due partly to broad changes in the economic and social organization of American life, the Negro in the South benefited from these changes. The success which Negroes have achieved in breaking down racial barriers has been due partly to their own efforts. They have carried on a constant struggle in the courts and they have influenced to some extent public opinion. As the mid-century drew to a close a distinguished white woman, who had been associated with their struggle, could look back at the success which Negroes had made in breaking through racial barriers and say in the words of the well-known Negro spiritual, 'the walls came tumbling down'.[1]

However, as the racial barriers are broken down and Negroes increasingly enter into the mainstream of American life, the traditional organization of Negro life is constantly being undermined. The so-called process of integration, which is only an initial stage in the assimilation of

Negroes into American society, does not have the same effect on all parts of the social structure of the Negro community. The extent and the nature of the participation of Negroes in the wider American community is determined first by their class position. Negroes in the Black Belt or rural counties in the South where they constitute 50 per cent or more of the population are still almost completely isolated from the main currents of American culture. Although lower-class Negroes in cities, who include those engaged in domestic and personal services and those employed as unskilled labourers, have more contacts with American life, they are still more or less confined to the Negro community. As Negro workers acquire skills and become members of labour unions, they begin to enter into the mainstream of American life. This is, of course, more characteristic of Negro workers in the North than of those in the South. Many Negroes in the North who are employed as white-collar workers and in technical and professional occupations enter even more fully into the main currents of American society. Not only does their work enable them to share more fully in American culture but they associate more freely with their white fellow workers than any other section of the Negro population.

The second factor and a factor of equal importance, which determines the nature and extent of the participation of Negroes in the wider American community, is their own institutional life. The system of racial segregation in the United States has resulted in an almost complete duplication of the institutions of the American community within the Negro community.[2] We shall begin by considering those institutions which embody the secular interests of Negroes. As Negroes have moved from the world of the folk, they have established insurance companies and banks which have a purely secular end. These institutions are becoming a part of the different associations of insurance companies and banks and they are subject to state supervision. Then there are many other kinds of business enterprises, many of which cater especially to the personal and other needs of Negroes, and thus supply services often refused by white establishments. Negroes are expected to patronize these various so-called 'Negro' businesses because of 'racial loyalty'. There is a National Negro Business League and numerous Negro chambers of commerce. Among the more successful Negro businesses should be included the Negro weekly newspapers which have circulations running into the hundreds of thousands.

Then there are certain cultural institutions among which are included the various secret fraternal organizations such as the Masons, Odd Fellows, and the Elks. In this group we would also include the various college

Greek letter societies for men and women. Although they would not qualify as institutions, there are numerous social clubs which may be considered along with the cultural institutions. The most important cultural institution is, of course, the Negro church. It embodies, as we have seen, the cultural traditions of Negroes to a far greater extent than any other institution.

As 'the walls of segregation tumble down', it is the institutions which embody the secular interests of Negroes which are being undermined more rapidly than those representing their cultural interests. As white establishments cater to the personal needs of Negroes there is less need for what is known as 'Negro' businesses to supply such services. Moreover, as the large corporations and other so-called white business enterprises employ Negroes in all capacities, there is less need for an association of people engaged in 'Negro' businesses. Likewise, as white newspapers carry more news concerning Negroes and employ Negro journalists, the Negro newspapers decline in circulation as the foreign language newspapers have done. Although schools are cultural institutions, the segregated Negro public schools and state colleges will become less important.

The situation is different in regard to the cultural institutions within the Negro community. There are some privately supported Negro educational institutions with deeply rooted traditions in Negro life that resist the trend towards the integration of the Negro. On the other hand, as Negro professors are increasingly taken on the faculties of so-called white colleges and universities and Negro students are admitted to such institutions, Negroes are joining the mainstream of American life. When one comes to the Negro church which is the most important cultural institution created by Negroes, one encounters the most important institutional barrier to integration and the assimilation of Negroes. White churches may open their doors to Negroes and a few Negro ministers may be invited to become pastors of white churches; the masses of Negroes continue, nevertheless, to attend the Negro churches and the Negro church as an institution continues to function as an important element in the organized social life of Negroes.

The Church is no Longer a Refuge

The strength of the Negro church as a barrier to the integration of Negroes into the main currents of American life should not be overestimated, especially since the process of integration has not progressed very far. Moreover, it is necessary to differentiate the situation in the North from that in the South. In the South the Negro has scarcely begun his struggle to participate in the secular and public institutions of the American community. On the other hand, in the border states and in the North there is much larger participation of Negroes in the secular and public institutions of the American community. In the South the lives of Negroes still revolve about the activities of the Negro community. Even where they gain entrance into labour unions, they are excluded from the 'social' activities of these organizations. In the North Negroes are included increasingly in the 'social' activities of the various labour unions. Nevertheless, in the North the proliferation of organizations which provide for the 'social' needs of Negroes indicates the extent to which Negroes are still outsiders, so to speak. Moreover, the ecological or spatial segregation of Negroes, which is often the result of impersonal economic and social forces rather than prejudice and discrimination, tends to maintain the separate institutions of the Negro community. The church is the most important of these institutions in which the masses of Negroes find a refuge within white society which treats them with condescension if not contempt.

But the Negro church can no longer serve as a refuge as it did in the past when the majority of Negroes lived in the South under a system of racial segregation and the majority of the Negroes in the South lived in rural areas. Willy-nilly Negroes are drawn into the complex social organization of the American community. This is necessary for mere survival. Recognizing the need for a more complex social organization to serve the needs of urbanized Negroes and at the same time taking cognizance of the fact that Negroes were still excluded from labour unions, a Negro sociologist proposed that the Negro church, being the largest organized unit of Negro life, incorporate some of the functions of the new forms of organized social life which are required in the city.[3] It is apparent, however, that this proposal was impractical since the Negro church could not perform the functions of the new types of associations necessary to life in the city.

It was inevitable that the Negro should be drawn into the organized forms of social life in the urban environment. As a consequence, the Negro church has lost much of its influence as an agency of social control. Its supervision over the marital and family life of Negroes has declined. The church has ceased to be the chief means of economic cooperation. New avenues have been opened to all kinds of business ventures in which secular ends and values are dominant. The church is no longer the main arena for political activities which was the case when Negroes were disfranchised in the South. Negro political leaders have to compete with the white political leaders in the 'machine' politics of the cities. In a word, the Negroes have been forced into competition with whites in most areas of social life and their church can no longer serve as a refuge within the American community.

We have seen how Negroes in the established denominational churches developed secular interests in order to deal with race prejudice and discriminations to which they are exposed when the 'walls of segregation come tumbling down'. We have seen how lower-class Negroes have reacted to the cold impersonal environment of the city and of the large denominational churches by joining the 'storefront' churches and the various cults. These all represented their reaction to the crumbling traditional organization of Negro life as Negroes are increasingly cast afloat in the main stream of American life where they are still outsiders.

The Gospel Singers

Although the lower strata in the Negro community do not participate to the same extent as the upper strata in the main currents of American life, they are nevertheless increasingly assimilating the manners and customs of American society. There is thus achieved a certain external conformity to the patterns of American culture.[4] They continue to be influenced in their thinking and especially in their feelings and sentiments by the social heritage of the Negro which is represented by the Spirituals and religious orientation towards the world contained in the Spirituals. The masses of Negroes may increasingly criticize the church and their ministers, but they cannot escape from their heritage. They may develop a more secular outlook on life and complain that the church and the ministers are not sufficiently concerned with the problems of the Negro race,[5] yet they find in their religious heritage an opportunity to satisfy their deepest emotional yearnings.

Out of the revolt of the lower strata against the church and the growing secularization of Negro religion there has come an accommodation between traditional Negro religion and the new outlook of Negroes in the new American environment. This accommodation is symbolized by the Gospel Singers. The songs which the Gospel Singers sing have been described as a compound of 'elements found in the old tabernacle songs, the Negro Spirituals and the blues'.[6] Since the Negro has become urbanized, there has been an amazing rise and spread of 'gospel singing'. This has been attributed, and correctly so, to the fact that, 'As Negro churches have become more European in decorum and programme, the great mass of less Europeanized Negroes began to look elsewhere for full vented religious expressions in music and preaching'.[7] The important fact is that although the Gospel Singers have gone outside the church for a congenial form of religious expression, they nevertheless remain in the church and are a part of the church. Recently when a Gospel Singer died and her funeral was held in a large Baptist church in the Nation's Capital, it was reported that 13,000 persons viewed her remains, a thousand persons jammed the church, and another thousand lined the sidewalks outside the church. Dozens of gospel-singing groups came from neighbouring areas and as far away as Pennsylvania and Illinois. The white owner of a broadcasting company flew from Ohio to attend the funeral. Between 150 and 200 cars accompanied the body to the cemetery.[8]

More important still for us here is the fact that the Gospel Singers symbolize something that is characteristic of Negro religion from the standpoint of assimilation. Some of the so-called advanced Negro churches resented these gospel singers and refused to permit them to sing within their churches. They have gradually become more tolerant and let down the bars as the Gospel Singers have acquired status and acceptance within the white world. Such well-known gospel singers as Mahalia Jackson, Rosetta Tharpe, and the Ward Sisters have been accepted as 'artists'. The Gospel Singer not only sings to the Negro world but sings to the white world. One of the famous Ward Sisters stated that the gospel singing is popular because '. . . it fills a vacuum in people's lives. For people who work hard and make little money it offers a promise that things will be better in the life to come'.[9] She was thinking, of course, of Negroes but the Gospel Singers sing to white America as well. This is indicated by their hold on the record industry and their popularity on radio and television programmes.

Gospel singing has, of course, become commercialized and that is another indication of the relation of Negro religious life to assimilation. It indicates in a sense the terms on which the Negro is being assimilated. Moreover, white men in the South are beginning to imitate the Negro Gospel Singers. And Negro gospel singing is often featured as a part of the programmes on television. Thus, the religious folk-songs of the Negro are becoming secularized despite the fact that the singing of them in secular entertainment is a concession to the so-called religious revival in the United States. The Gospel Singers, then, unlike the cults, do not represent a complete break with the religious traditions of the Negro. They represent or symbolize the attempt of the Negro to utilize his religious heritage in order to come to terms with changes in his own institutions as well as the problems of the world of which he is a part.

In a sense, therefore, the attempts of the Negro to resist segregation in the sit-down strikes in the South represent the same falling back upon his religious heritage in time of crisis. This movement on the part of Negro students in the South is supposed to be based upon the non-violent resistance movement of Gandhi.[10] Some of its intellectual leaders like the Reverend Martin Luther King may use Gandhi's non-violent resistance as an ideological justification of the movement, but Gandhism as a philosophy and a way of life is completely alien to the Negro and has nothing in common with the social heritage of the Negro. As Negro students go forth singing the Spirituals or the Gospel hymns when they engage in sit-down strikes or sing their Gospel songs in response to violence, they are behaving in accordance with the religious heritage of the Negro.

Then there is another aspect of this movement which needs to be considered in relation to the changes in the religion of the Negro. Because of the improvement in their economic conditions, an increasing number of Negro students are able to attend the colleges for Negroes in the South. They are being drawn from those strata in the Negro population closest to the rural background and who, therefore, are closest to the folk heritage of the Negro. Education, or more specially the opportunity to attend college, is the most important factor enabling Negroes to achieve middle-class status. Moreover, the leaders of this movement have seen something of the world because of their army or other experiences, or their parents have had similar experiences. In their revolt against the racial discrimination they must fall back upon the only vital social heritage that has meaning for them and that social heritage is the religious heritage represented by the Spirituals which are becoming secularized.

The Religion of the New Middle Class

We have already seen how the Negro church and Negro religion have been affected by the new class structure which is emerging among Negroes in cities, especially in the North. Here we are interested in the religious outlook of the new Negro middle class which has become important among Negroes during the past twenty years or so. It is this class whose outward appearance and standards of behaviour approximate most nearly the norms of the white American society. Moreover, Negroes who have achieved middle-class status participate more largely than any other element in American life. It is for this reason that we shall focus attention upon the new middle class in studying the changes in the religious life of Negroes as they are related to the assimilation of Negroes into American society.

The growing importance of the new middle class in the Negro community is due to the continual differentiation of the population along occupational lines. Therefore, the new middle class is composed almost entirely of those persons who derive their incomes from services rendered as white-collar workers and as professional men and women. Despite the dreams of Negro leaders, fostered by the National Negro Business League at the turn of the century, that Negroes would organize big industries and large financial undertakings, Negroes have not become captains of industry nor even managers of large corporations. So-called 'Negro' business continues to consist mainly of small retail stores catering to the personal needs of Negroes. There are a small number of insurance companies, small banks, and newspapers which constitute their larger business enterprises. The owners and managers of these enterprises constitute the upper layer of the middle class while the increasing number of Negroes in skilled occupations constitute its lowest stratum. For reasons which have been indicated, in the North and West about 25 per cent of the Negro population is able to maintain middle-class standards while in the South only about 12 per cent are in this position.

The new Negro middle class is a new phenomenon in the Negro community because it has a different economic base and a different social heritage from the relatively small middle class which had become differentiated from the masses of Negroes by the first decade of this century.[11] This older middle class was an 'aristocratic' *élite* in a sense because its social status and preeminence were based upon white ancestry and family and its behaviour was modelled after the genteel tradition of the Old South. The upper layer derived their incomes from land but the majority of the members of the '*élite*' were employed in a large variety of occupations including positions as trusted retainers in white families. The new middle class has a different occupational basis and occupation is one of the important factors in determining status.

Since the opening of the century there had been a faith among middle-class Negroes in 'Negro' business as a means of solving their social as well as economic problems. This faith was somewhat as follows: as Negroes became businessmen they would accumulate capital and give employment to Negroes and once Negroes possessed wealth, white men would respect them and accord them equality. The new middle class has accepted without the critical attitude which experience should have given them, the faith in 'Negro' business as a way to social and economic salvation.

Since the emergence of the new middle class involves the rise of the more ambitious and energetic elements among the masses of Negroes to middle-class status, this new class does not possess the genteel tradition of the older middle class. This new class is largely without social roots except the traditions of the Negro folk represented in the Spirituals. But as these Negroes rise to middle-class status they reject the folk heritage and seek to slough off any reminders of their folk inheritance. However, since their rise to the middle-class status has enabled them to marry into families with the genteel tradition of the old middle class, there is often a confusion of 'aristocratic' and folk values. It is for this reason that many middle-class Negroes exhibit in their manners and behaviour the characteristics of both a peasant and a gentleman. Among this new class there is much confusion as to standards of behaviour and beliefs. There is a constant striving to acquire money in order to engage in conspicuous consumption which provides the outward signs of status and conformity to white American standards. They all possess the same goal, which is acceptance into the white community and they all profess, at least, a desire to be integrated into the white community.

Integration for the majority of middle-class Negroes means the loss of racial identity or an escape from the lowly status of Negroes and the contempt of whites. With integration they began to remove as much as possible from the names of their various organizations anything that would identify them as Negroes. This even extended to their church organizations. The Colored Methodist Episcopal Church became the 'Christian' Methodist Episcopal Church. It is significant, however, that when the middle-class leaders in the African Methodist Episcopal Church attempted to take 'African' out of the name and substitute the word 'American', there was a revolt on the part of the masses who demanded that 'African' be retained. This incident is indicative of the general attitude of the middle class towards the African background of the Negro. While there is some outward profession of pride in African independence and identification with Africa, the middle class rejects identification with Africa and wants above all to be accepted as 'just Americans'. It was the new middle class which was rising to importance in the 1920s that was most bitterly opposed to the Garvey Movement which had as its goal the identification of Negroes with Africa and African interests.[12] Middle-class Negroes seize upon identification with Africa only as a means of compensating for their feeling of inferiority and improving their status in the eyes of American whites.

Despite the fact that middle-class Negroes conform to the standards of whites and accept without question the values of American society, they are still rejected by the white world. They feel this rejection more keenly than lower-class Negroes who participate less in the white man's world and conform to the standards of their own separate world. Moreover, because of their position, middle-class Negroes have an ambivalent attitude towards their identification as Negroes. On the one hand, they resent the slightest aspersion upon Negroes. When placed in competition with whites they have feelings of inadequacy and when they find themselves in close association with whites they have feelings of insecurity though they may clamour for integration into the white world.[13] They are status seekers in a double sense; they strive to keep up with the expectations of their class in the Negro community and they seek or hope to gain status in the white world. In order to maintain high standards of consumption often both husband and wife work but they constantly complain of the 'rat race' to maintain life as they would live it. They live frustrated lives despite their efforts to compensate for their feelings of inferiority and insecurity. They have little time for leisure and the enjoyment of what they call the 'cultural' things of life. As a matter of fact, they have little appreciation of music or art and they read very little since reading has not become a tradition in the new middle class.

Their ambiguous position in American society together with their recent rise to middle-class status are reflected in the religious behaviour and attitudes of middle-class Negroes. There is first a tendency for middle-class Negroes to sever their affiliation with the Baptist and Methodist churches and join the Presbyterian, Congregational, and Episcopal churches. The middle-class Negroes who continue their affiliation with the Baptist and Methodist churches choose those churches with intelligent ministers and a relatively large middle-class membership. As a consequence there is a solid core of the Negro middle class that continues to be affiliated with the Negro church. However, middle-class Negroes continue their affiliation with the Negro church for a number of reasons. Their families may have been associated with the churches and the churches which they have known since childhood provide a satisfying form of religious worship. Although many middle-class Negroes continue to be affiliated with the church, the church is no longer the centre of social life for them as for the lower class. They are members of professional and business associations and Greek letter fraternal organizations, though 'social' clubs constitute the vast majority of these other forms of organized social activities. Some are thus able to satisfy their striving for status outside the church. But for others it is necessary to leave the Baptist and Methodist churches and join the Presbyterian, Congregational, and Episcopal churches in order to satisfy the desire for status.

The striving for status and the searching for a means to escape from a frustrated existence is especially marked among the middle-class Negroes who cannot find a satisfactory life within the regular Negro church organization. This probably accounts for the fact that during the past two decades middle-class Negroes have been joining the Catholic church.[14] Sometimes they send their children to Catholic schools where they will receive a discipline not provided in the public schools for Negroes. Very often after joining the Catholic church with the expectation that they will escape from their status as Negroes, they find that they are still defined as Negroes by whites. Some middle-class Negroes in their seeking to find escape from the Negro identification have gone from the Catholic church to the Christian Science church and then to the Bahaist church. Moreover, there is a tendency among middle-class Negroes to be attracted to Moral Re-armament, hoping that they would find a group in which they could lose completely their identification as Negroes and escape from their feelings of inferiority and insecurity. A small intellectual fringe among middle-class Negroes have affiliated with the Unitarian church. But some of them may still attend more or less surreptitiously the Methodist and Baptist churches on Friday nights.

This type of dual church affiliation is more characteristic of Negro professional men who affiliate with churches mainly for social and professional reasons. Some professional Negroes affiliate with a church which their friends or middle-class Negroes attend, and at the same time affiliate with churches attended by the lower class who are their clients. They are representative of the growing number of middle-class Negroes who have a purely secular outlook on the world. Some of them express contempt for religion and do not attend church though they may pretend to have some church affiliation. Since they have neither an intellectual heritage nor a social philosophy except a crude opportunism which enables them to get by in the white man's world, they may turn to all forms of superstition. This is because they are still haunted by the fears and beliefs which are a part of their folk heritage. They are often interested in 'spiritual' and 'psychic' phenomena. Very often the real religious feelings and faith of middle-class Negroes are expressed in their obsession with poker and other forms of gambling.[15]

The religious behaviour and outlook of the middle-class Negroes are a reflection of their ambiguous position as Negroes rise to middle-class status and become increasingly integrated into the American community. To the extent that they are becoming really assimilated into American society, they are being beset by the religious dilemmas and doubts of the white middle-class Americans. On the other hand, for the masses of Negroes, the Negro church continues to be a refuge, though increasingly less of a refuge, in a hostile white world.

Notes

1. Joshua fit de battle of Jericho,
   Jericho, Jericho,
   Joshua fit de battle of Jericho,
   And de walls came tumbling down.

   Mary White Ovington, *The Walls Came Tumbling Down* (New York, 1947).
2. See Frazier, *The Negro in the United States*, Part 3, 'The Negro Community and Its Institutions'.
3. See the proposal of Dr. George E. Haynes of the Federal Council of Churches, quoted in Drake and Cayton, *Black Metropolis*, p. 683.
4. Cf. 'Racial Assimilation in Secondary Groups,' in Robert E. Park, *Race and Culture* (Glencoe, Ill., 1950), Chapter 16.
5. See Drake and Cayton, *op. cit.*, pp. 650–4, concerning the rebellion of the lower classes against the church.
6. Arna Bontemps, 'Rock, Church, Rock,' in Sylvester C. Watkins (ed.), *Anthology of American Negro Literature* (New York, 1944), p. 431.
7. Willis Laurence James, 'The Romance of the Negro Folk Cry in America,' *Phylon*, Vol. XVI (1955), p. 23.
8. See *Washington Afro-American*, 5 April, 1960, for featured article on front page concerning death and funeral of Thelma Greene, at which a member of the Robert Martin Singers of Chicago sang a solo, 'God Specializes,' causing a number of persons to faint and to be carried out by nurses.
9. Interview with Clara Mae Ward in Winston-Salem, who claims she is only gospel singer ever to have visited the Holy Land. 'Singing for Sinners,' *News Week*, Vol. 50 (2 September, 1957), p. 86.
10. See 'The Revolt of Negro Youth', *Ebony* (May, 1960).
11. E. Franklin Frazier, 'The Negro Middle Class and Desegregation,' *Social Problems*, Vol. IV (April 1957), pp. 291–301.
12. See Frazier, *The Negro in the United States*, pp. 528–31.
13. E. Franklin Frazier, *Black Bourgeoisie* (Glencoe, Ill., 1957), pp. 216 ff.
14. The recent increase during the past twenty years in the number, which remains relatively small, of lower-class Negroes in the Catholic church has been due to aid provided them during the *Depression years* and the better educational facilities, as compared with the public schools, provided them by the Catholic church.
15. See *Black Bourgeoisie*, pp. 209 ff.

Part 2

Theorizing African American Religion

Chapter 5

American Africans in Conflict: Alienation in an Insecure Culture

Cornel West

Modernity, Colonial Provinciality, Localism

The Age of Enlightenment, from 1688 to 1789—roughly from the Glorious Revolution in England to the tumultuous French Revolution—constitutes the emergence of European modernity.[1] This occurred within an embryonic capitalist global economy that supported absolutist monarchies. It throve, mostly because of black slavery in the western hemisphere and the exploitation of working men, women, and children in the rural household industry of western Europe. The most populous European country, France, was the chief industrial center. Holland, especially the vivacious city of Amsterdam, maintained its two-century dominance in commerce and shipping as the major financial center in Europe.

The basic features of early modern European culture were the increasing acceptance of the authority of science, the appearance of a new kind of pagan neoclassicism, and the subjectivist turn in philosophy. The intellectual defense and institutional support of the practices of scientists became more and more persuasive to the literate population. These practices were guided by an adherence to a new paradigm of knowledge, an experimental method that attempted to test hypotheses and yield objective conclusions by appealing to evidence and observation. The increasing acceptance of the authority of science resulted in assaults on the authority of the church and on its theology and religious practices.

This Enlightenment revolt against the prestige of the church was part of a search for models of uncensored criticism. It led to a recovery of classical antiquity and especially a deep appreciation and appropriation of the artistic and cultural heritage of ancient Greece. This classical revival—or

77

neoclassical movement in eighteenth-century Europe—was partly the result of a four-hundred-year European love affair with Greece and Rome. This affair began in the Early Renaissance (1300–1500), intensified in the High Renaissance (1500–1530), cooled in the Mannerist era (1530–1600), and appeared again in full force during the Baroque period (1600–1750). In short, early modern European culture promoted a new, modern type of paganism.

The emergence of European modernity also witnessed a subjectivist turn in philosophy. This quest, initiated by Descartes, gave first place to concepts of the subject, the ego, or the self, and preeminence to the notion of representative knowledge. The subject, ego, or self constituted the starting point for philosophical inquiry, and mental representations by the subject, ego, or self supplied the principal means for subjects to make contact with objects, ideas to copy things, or concepts to correspond to the external world. Philosophy became the queen of the emerging scientific disciplines within this new paradigm as a metadiscipline which provided objective and valid grounds for knowledge claims put forward in the newer disciplines, especially physics. This turn in philosophy granted science a monopoly on truth in the marketplace of ideas, to the dismay of both artists and theologians. As Hans-Georg Gadamer has noted in our own time, this monopoly on truth entails a prejudice against prejudice, a supposed transcendence of prejudice through objectivity.

Immanuel Kant deepened Descartes's subjectivism by erecting new formal foundations upon a transcendental subject which builds an objective world by means of a universal conceptual scheme. In one grand stroke, he thus legitimated Newtonian science, vindicated Protestant morality, and set art in a realm of its own. The ultimate consequence of this architectonic endeavor was to isolate early modern European culture into separate spheres of goodness, truth, and beauty—and morality, science, and art—reinforcing meanwhile the role of philosophy as a tribunal of pure reason for the claims of culture.

Between 1776 and 1782 texts appeared and events occurred that were representative of this early modern period. These included Adam Smith's *The Wealth of Nations* (1776), Edward Gibbon's *The History of the Decline and Fall of the Roman Empire* (1776), the American Revolution (1776), David Hume's *Dialogues Concerning Natural Religion* (1779), Gotthold Lessing's *Nathan the Wise* (1779), Immanuel Kant's *Critique of Pure Reason* (1781), and the first part of Jean Jacques Rousseau's *Confessions* (1781). In these are the intellectual agenda of the period: the rise of the bourgeois capitalist order, the struggle between Christianity and neoclassical paganism, the widening gaps between philosophy, ethics, and art, and the increasing alienation of the individual.

The end of this period was marked by the birth of the United States, the first new nation, through a colonial, not a social revolution. After a century and a half of the reconciling of self-imposed exile with a well-developed European social and political consciousness, the problem of provinciality had become central in the development of American culture.[2] It resulted primarily from the geographical displacement of European peoples from that European civilization whose superiority they openly acknowledged. Adding to this, an antagonism to the indigenous American peoples and an unwillingness to mingle with unchristian African slaves created an alienated, intensely self-conscious, and deeply anxiety-ridden society.

The first stage of American culture was thus saturated with colonial provinciality. The first Americans looked to their parent civilization for intellectual and cultural resources, applying these to very un-European conditions principally by means of crude imitation. The most provocative commentators on the problematic of provinciality in American culture have been Alexis de Tocqueville, George Santayana, and Van Wyck Brooks.[3] On de Tocqueville's view, American culture smothered intellectual life in pursuit of democracy and equality, thereby vitiating the aristocratic requisites for cultural vitality. To Santayana, the agonized conscience of Calvinism and the metaphysical comfort of transcendentalism weighted like a genteel incubus upon the American mind, partly explaining the odd American juxtaposition of intellectual conservatism with technological inventiveness. For Van Wyck Brooks, American vacillation between Puritan purity and vulgar materialism, echoing William James's "angelic impulses" and "predatory lusts," fragmented the intellectual tradition and generated an unrestrained quest for wealth.[4]

Colonial provinciality reached its zenith in the first major figure of the Genteel tradition, Jonathan Edwards. The most profound of European-American thinkers, he constructed his defense of Calvinism from a sophisticated blend of the empiricism of Locke, the determinism of Newton, and the idealism of Plato.

Edwards' valorizing of Newton bespoke his attitude toward the authority of science, an attitude close to that of his own lesser contemporary and rival, Cadwallader Colden.[5] Yet Edwards distinguished the domain of science from the special arena of religious knowledge, the intuitive realm where the sixth sense, that of the heart, reserved for the elect, reigns. His fierce struggle against the voluntaristic Arminians likewise defended complex versions of original sin and predestination familiar from European Calvinism.

The Enlightenment left a comparable European stamp on the area of political thought. Jefferson's doctrine of natural rights and theory of moral sentiments revealed his debts both to classical antiquity and to Locke, Shaftesbury, and Frances Hutchinson.[6] The anticlericalism of Thomas Paine, and its concomitant defense of the freedom of conscience and speech, further exemplified the critical spirit of the European Enlightenment in America. Lastly, the radical environmentalism of Benjamin Rush and his humanitarian advocacy of the abolition of slavery and the rehabilitation of criminals revealed an Enlightenment belief in the unlimited possibilities of individuals in society when guided by reason.

American culture during the provincial period culminated in the Calvinist pietism, Enlightenment rationalism, and liberal republicanism of William Ellery Channing.[7] The vernal American Schleiermacher, Channing is the pivotal figure of the Genteel tradition, in its transition from Calvinism to transcendentalism, at the turning point between the colonial provinciality and the postcolonial provinciality in American culture. His revolutionary humanitarianism, bordering on utopian socialism, condemned slavery, bigotry, and pagan worldliness. He proposed to overcome these through Christian pietism, moral use of scientific knowledge, and the perfection of human nature through self-realization in democratic communities.

Channing's humanitarianism unfortunately did not serve either as guide or as norm for American practice toward Africans during the provincial period. The non-Christianity and black skin color of the dark pagan peoples threatened the self-identity of Puritan colonists inextricably bound to Christianity.[8] Since the absence of or even novel interpretation of Christian beliefs could often bring about mistreatment or banishment, the growing idea of white supremacy legitimated still harsher treatment for Africans.

In *The Souls of Black Folk* (1903), W.E.B. Du Bois eloquently described a double consciousness in black Americans, a dual lens through which they saw themselves.[9] For Du Bois, the dialectic of black self-recognition oscillated between being *in* America but not *of* it, from being black natives to black aliens. Yet Du Bois overlooked the broader dialectic of being American yet feeling European, of being provincial but yearning for British cosmopolitanism, of being at once incompletely civilized and materially prosperous, a genteel Brahmin amid uncouth conditions. Black Americans labored rather under the burden of a triple crisis of self-recognition. Their cultural predicament was comprised of African appearance and unconscious cultural mores, involuntary displacement to America without American status, and American alienation from the European ethos complicated through domination by incompletely European Americans.

This predicament was qualitatively different from that of other Africans in the diaspora, in the Caribbean, Canada, and Central and South America. Africans in the United States confronted a dominant Protestant European population whose own self-identity suffered from an anxiety-ridden provinciality. The black American struggle for self-identity has always contributed constructively to the American struggle for self-identity, though the latter has only exacerbated and complicated it in return.

During the colonial provincial stage of American culture, Africans were worse than slaves; they were also denuded proto-Americans in search of identity, systematically stripped of their African heritage and effectively and intentionally excluded from American culture and its roots in European modernity. Their search for identity focused principally on indigenous African practices, rituals, religions, and world views they had somehow retained.[10]

The process of cultural syncretism which combined indigenous African practices and provincial American culture generated a unique variant of American life, one far removed from, yet still tied to, European modernity. Added ingredients in this were the distinctly antimodern values and sensibilities of the southern United States, the geographic cradle of black America.

The first stage of African practice in America was neither barbarian nor provincial. Africans valued human life and sustained in their alien environment a religious cosmology which gave meaning to human existence. And it was not provincial, because it worshiped neither at the altar of British nor at the altar of American cultural superiority. Black people were relatively uninformed about British culture and not yet fully American. More pointedly, they had not yet arrived at a synthetic Afro-American identity.

Heyday of Modernity, Postcolonial Provinciality, Christian Practices

The heyday of modernity, the golden age of the modern period, fell roughly between 1789 and 1871—that is, from the French Revolution to the unification of the German Empire. During it, early modern European culture took root and flowered in the authority of science, in modern paganism, and in the historicizing of philosophical subjectivism. The industrializing capitalist world order consolidated at this time, and nation-states emerged, both phenomena enjoying the confidence of the new bourgeoisie. The dominated classes—factory workers and the rural labor force—began to grumble, but since they had limited organization and vision, this yielded minimal results.

This was, above all, the German Age, and the year 1807 alone witnessed the completion of Hegel's *The Phenomenology of Spirit*, Goethe's *Faust*, Part I, and Beethoven's Fifth Symphony.

Yet despite the romantic reply to the bland universality, glib generality, and monotonous uniformity of the Enlightenment, the authority of science emerged with flying colors. Romanticism attacked scientific arrogance and pretense, yet the brunt of its assault fell not on science per se but rather on the crudely mechanistic model of Newton's popular imitators. The conceptions of the mind and the world characteristic of this model repelled the Romantics. Disgusted with superficial distinctions, they relegated the dissective power of the mind to the understanding *(Verstand)* and its integrative activities to reason *(Vernunft)*, replacing mechanistic models with organic ones.[11]

The Romantics venerated a reason very different from that of the Enlightenment, which appealed ultimately to the experimental method and aimed to keep the imagination at bay. Romantic reason, on the other hand, is the epitome of a free creative imagination transcending the limits of the world of sense.

The Romantic movement, the golden age of European modernity, conveyed a sense of novelty.[12] The French Revolution, which in one stroke replaced feudal institutions with bourgeois capitalism, embodied the possibilities of social reconstruction and revolutionary transformation. The European exploration of other cultures and societies likewise buttressed curiosity about the unknown and brought to light distinctive features of its own emerging constituent national cultures. Lastly, widespread technological innovation and the increase of wealth in the early stages of the Industrial Revolution reinforced belief in the capacity of humankind to master nature and enjoy its fruits.

With Napoleon, the Romantic dream of transforming the social order mellowed to temperate efforts at self-realization.[13] The fascination with exotic and primitive peoples illustrated by the popular myth of the noble savage persisted, yet it soon revealed the repressive imperialist regimes that often evolve in interaction with foreigners. The tremendous energies generated by the early Industrial Revolution continued, but alienations and the formation of new class antagonisms revealed unforeseen instabilities in bourgeois capitalism.

Hegel's historicizing of the subjectivism cast would-be academic philosophers into the social, political, and cultural struggles of the period. His grand project took, in some sense, however, the form of a Christian Christology gone mad. In place of Kant's presupposed subject of knowledge, Hegel put a transindividual subject that externalized itself in the world and progressively evolved within it in a dialectical fashion. This development can be discerned, of course, only by the most adroit philosopher, namely, Hegel himself. This development is simultaneously the freedom march of humankind and the progressive self-consciousness of that transindividual subject, what Hegel called the *Weltgeist*, or world spirit.

The year 1859 was momentous for cultural works that portrayed the central themes and concerns of the golden age: Darwin's *The Origin of the Species*, Mill's *On Liberty*, Marx's *Critique of Political Economy*, Wagner's *Tristan und Isolde*, George Eliot's *Adam Bede*, Dickens' *A Tale of Two Cities*, Meredith's *The Ordeal of Richard Feverel*, Tennyson's *The Idylls of the King*, FitzGerald's *Rubaiyat of Omar Khayyam*, and Turgenev's *A Nest of Gentlefolk*. The dominant themes and concerns in these are the historical and evolutionary character of human existence, the scope of freedom and democracy in the prevailing order, and the emerging sentiments of European nationalism and of racism and sexism.

European hegemony over the life of the mind proved to be a major preoccupation of American culture during its provincial period. American artists and writers strove consciously to establish an autonomous national culture no longer dependent on that of Europe. America ought to sing its own songs, write its own poems, novels, and philosophy. America must look deep down within itself without using the lens of the parent civilization to do so.

The most important product of this self-absorptive mood in America was Ralph Waldo Emerson. In his famous lecture of 1837, "The American Scholar," Emerson portrayed Europe as the symbol of the dead past. The present task of American thinkers was to liberate themselves from slavish dependence on Europe. His message of self-reliance was not merely a reflection of a democratic and intuitive philosophy or a Jeffersonian vision of the self-sufficient yeoman farmer, but an attack on the prevailing provincialism of America in his day. Of course, without the idealism of Plato, the natural law theory of the Stoics, and the romanticism of Coleridge and Carlyle, there was little of intellectual substance left to "the sage of Concord," save his energetic spirit, charismatic style, and piercing wit. The postcolonial agenda of American culture called for homespun originality and indigenous inventiveness, despite the eclecticism and pretense this might entail.

Eclecticism and pretentiousness mark the most significant literary products of the American renaissance, as seen in the major works of Edgar Allan Poe, James Fenimore Cooper, Walt Whitman, Nathaniel Hawthorne, Herman Melville, Emily Dickinson, and Henry David Thoreau.[14] It is not that the works are artistic failures, but rather that they are products of a culture under the grip of provincialism, of a culture proud yet not solidified, boastful but not self-confident, eager to flex its muscles without agile flexibility.

Edgar Allan Poe, for example, with his English childhood and Parisian sensibilities, cared neither to imitate English literary models nor to write an authentic American tale. Instead, he created fantasies in which European aristocracy roamed about in bone-chilling German castles. James Fenimore Cooper's mythology loomed too large and his debt to the Scottish Sir Walter Scott was too pronounced. Walt Whitman, the effervescent American Goethe, was penetrating and provocative but hardly profound, a master of rhythmic and colorful language never able to attain a natural or comfortable idiom of expression. Though Whitman was, without a doubt, the most influential American poet of the period, his songs of himself and his democratic vistas of America seem too fabricated —or simply fail to ring true at all.

Postcolonial American culture's preoccupation with breaking away from Europe was far removed from the situation among Africans in the United States at the time. The initial tenacity with which Africans held on to their indigenous practices and the reluctance of many southern white slaveholders to teach Christianity to the slaves limited the Christianizing process in the early period. Even the Great Awakening of the 1740s, which swept the country like a hurricane, failed to reach the masses of slaves. Only with the Great Western Revival at the turn of the nineteenth century did the Christianizing process gain a significant foothold among black people.[15]

The central questions at this juncture are: Why did large numbers of American black people become Christians? What features of Protestant Christianity persuaded them to become Christians?

The Baptist separatists and the Methodists, religious dissenters in American religious culture, gained the attention of the majority of slaves in the Christianizing process. The evangelical outlook of these denominations stressed individual experience, equality before God, and institutional autonomy. Baptism by immersion, practiced by the Baptists, may indeed have reminded slaves from Nigeria and Dahomey of African river cults, but this fails fully to explain the success of the Christianizing process among Africans.[16]

Black people became Christians for intellectual, existential, and political reasons. Christianity is, as Friedrich Nietzsche has taught us and liberation theologians remind us, a religion especially fitted to the oppressed. It looks at the world from the perspective of those below. The African slaves' search for identity could find historical purpose in the exodus of Israel out of slavery and personal meaning in the bold identification of Jesus Christ with the lowly and downtrodden. Christianity also is first and foremost a theodicy, a triumphant account of good over evil. The intellectual life of the African slaves in the United States—like that of all oppressed peoples—consisted primarily of reckoning with the dominant form of evil in their lives. The Christian emphasis on against-the-evidence hope for triumph over evil struck deep among many of them.

The existential appeal of Christianity to black people was the stress of Protestant evangelicalism on individual experience, and especially the conversion experience. The "holy dance" of Protestant evangelical conversion experiences closely resembled the "ring shout" of West African novitiate rites: both are religious forms of ecstatic bodily behavior in which everyday time is infused with meaning and value through unrestrained rejoicing.[17]

The conversion experience played a central role in the Christianizing process. It not only created deep bonds of fellowship and a reference point for self-assurance during times of doubt and distress; it also democratized and equalized the status of all before God. The conversion experience initiated a profoundly personal relationship with God, which gave slaves a special self-identity and self-esteem in stark contrast with the roles imposed upon them by American society.

The primary political appeal of the Methodists and especially of the Baptists for black people was their church polity and organizational form, free from hierarchical control, open and easy access to leadership roles, and relatively loose, uncomplicated requirements for membership. The adoption of the Baptist polity by a majority of Christian slaves marked a turning point in the Afro-American experience.

On the one hand, the major organization among black Americans, the Christian churches, followed a polity farthest removed from modern bureaucratic and hierarchical forms of organization.[18] In this sense, the organizational form of most Afro-American churches, charismatic and often autocratic in leadership, neither promoted nor encouraged widespread respect for and acquisition of bureaucratic skills requisite for accountable leadership and institutional longevity. In short, the Christian churches' organizational form imposed considerable constraints on the administrative capabilities and institutional capacities of black people.

On the other hand, this organizational form ensured autonomous control over the central institution in the Afro-American community, which set blacks in the United States apart from other Africans in the diaspora. Independent control over their churches promoted the proliferation of African styles and manners within the black Christian tradition and liturgy. It also produced community-minded political leaders, polished orators, and activist journalists and scholars. In fact, the unique variant of American life we call Afro-American culture germinated in the bosom of this Afro-Christianity, in the Afro-Christian church congregations.

Decline of Modernity, Industrial Provinciality, Inclusionary Practices

The decline of European modernity between 1871 and 1950—from the unification of the German Empire to the emergence of the United States as the unquestioned supreme world power—occurred within the political and socioeconomic contours of an increasingly crisis-ridden monopoly capitalist world economy. This yielded devastating world wars, holocaust-producing fascist regimes, and sharp reaction against repressive communist governments. The dominated classes in industrial nations—including victims of racist and sexist oppression—flexed their political muscles more in this period and embarked on various courses toward inclusion in and ineffective opposition to the liberal capitalist order. The proliferation of mass culture, especially luxury consumer goods, effected a prolonged entrée of significant segments of the dominated classes into the bourgeois world of educational and occupational opportunities, middlebrow culture, and comfortable living.

In this modernist period, it seemed as if, for the West, "things fell apart; the center could not hold," to revise William Butler Yeats, the greatest English poet of the period. For science, a crisis set in. János Bolyai, N. I. Lobachevski, Karl F. Gauss, and Bernhard Riemann had already called into question the omnipresence of Euclidean geometry by discovering three-dimensional space and thereby making possible new, non-Euclidean geometries. Einstein's theory of special relativity undermined the prevailing Newtonian physics. Niels Bohr and Werner Heisenberg promoted the indeterministic character of quantum phenomena, which subsequently threatened classical laws of logic such as the law of distribution. Kurt Gödel demonstrated the incompleteness of mathematics and L. E. J. Brouwer rejected two-value logic and the law of excluded middle, hence paving the way for intuitionist mathematics.

For modern paganism, despair also set in. This revealed itself most clearly in 1922. That year, the modernist year *par excellence*, witnessed within twelve months the appearance of the most profound and probing works in the history of the modern West. These included T. S. Eliot's *The Waste Land*, James Joyce's *Ulysses*, Hermann Hesse's *Siddhartha*, Osip Mandelstam's *Tristia*, Eugene O'Neill's *Anna Christie*, Bertolt Brecht's *Baal*, e. e. cummings' *The Enormous Room*, Sinclair Lewis' *Babbitt*, Jean Toomer's "Song of the Sun," Wallace Stevens' "The Comedian as the Letter C," Max Weber's *Economy and Society*, I. A. Richards' (with C. K. Ogden and James Wood) *Foundations of Aesthetics*, and Sigmund Freud's essay on jealousy, paranoia, and homosexuality. These were published in the same year that Mussolini's Blackshirts marched on Rome; and less than a year after Lenin and Trotsky's suppression of the Kronstadt rebellion, a suppression that soured the hopes of many sympathizers of the Russian Revolution.

In philosophy during the modernist period, major attacks were also made upon the primacy of the subject. Despite Hegel's historicizing of the subjectivist turn in philosophy, academic philosophers managed to overthrow Hegelianism and replace it either with analytical realism in Britain, neo-Kantianism in Germany, and phenomenology in France, themselves later attacked by structuralism, existentialism, and analytical behaviorism.

During the decline of European modernity the most precious ideals of science, politics, philosophy, and the arts were radically called into question. This period was thus well disposed toward apocalyptic, crisis-centered views of history which stressed shock, the violation of expected continuities, and a deep sense of futility. Lionel Trilling—with his Arnoldian outlook and tactful candor—suggests that the modernist element signifies nihilism, "a bitter line of hostility to civilization," "a disenchantment with culture itself."[19]

This modernist temper projects the sense of an abrupt break with all tradition, a radical disruption from the past which implies not so much a revolution but rather a devolution or dissolution. Virginia Woolf reflected this modernist temper when she wrote, "On or about December 1910 human character changed."[20]

The industrial provincial stage of American culture neither escaped nor engulfed the modernist temper.[21] New attempts appeared to extend the Genteel tradition—or provide metaphysical comfort for agonized consciences—in the form of highly sophisticated idealist philosophical systems, as in the works of Borden Parker Bowne, James Edwin Creighton, and, above all, Josiah Royce. The monumental literary achievement of the expatriate Henry James subjected the Genteel tradition to close scrutiny and detailed analysis, appraising it as a mere interesting habit of mind among a host of others. The Genteel tradition no longer survived as a holistic world view, but rather as a subterranean sensibility upon which to build anew.[22]

During the modernist period, industrial provincial American culture presented clear-cut alternatives to its artists: either indigenize or become European. This dilemma was illustrated most graphically by the two exemplary American literary artists of the era, the seminal Mark Twain and the supercilious T. S. Eliot. For Twain, the aim was neither to resort to the eclectic strategies of Whitman or Melville nor to imitate the models and manners of Europe. Rather, it was to create the first genuine American idiom in literature. Similar to his fellow colleague and critic Ezra Pound, Eliot did not imitate Europeans, but rather became one. Although he expatriated to London, he had Paris on his mind and wrote his mature poetry under the influence of French symbolists and the classical European tradition of Homer, Ovid, and Dante. In this sense, Eliot was no longer from St. Louis and Pound no longer from Idaho. Both rested outside the gravity of industrial provincial American culture, not simply because they removed themselves from it, but rather because they discarded it.

On the philosophical front, this either-or dilemma took the form of a choice between warmed-over idealism and indigenous pragmatism, between updating the Genteel tradition and promoting a new reformist orientation.[23] Just as a dialogue between the Twain and Eliot streams never materialized, so a debate between Royce and Dewey never occurred. Both streams avoided each other, partly because of the divergent roads they chose and possibly because of their fundamental incompatibility.

The either-or dilemma of industrial provincial American culture is found only in the trained and talented artists and intellectuals of the rising Afro-American petite bourgeoisie, such as Alexander Crummell, W.E.B. Du Bois, Jean Toomer, Henry Ossawa Tanner, Alain Locke, Richard Wright, Laura Wheeler Waring, and others. The almost exclusive priority of African practices in the United States in this period was to gain inclusion within the rapidly expanding American capitalist order. With the increase of xenophobic sentiments and movements, the escalation of crypto-fascist terror in the southern part of the United States, and the vast immigration of eastern and southern European laborers to urban centers in the northern section of the United States, achieving Afro-American inclusion within the mainstream of American society proved difficult.

Public discourse within the Afro-American community concerning this inclusion was shaped by the debate that took place between the early

W.E.B. Du Bois and Booker T. Washington—the two major spokesmen of the Afro-American petite bourgeoisie.[24] There were, of course, other interlocutors in the debate, including William Monroe Trotter of the Niagara Movement, Rev. James Bowen of the Methodist Episcopal clergy, and Rev. George Washington Woodbey of the Socialist Party, but the privileged positions and voices of Du Bois and Washington drowned them out.

For both Du Bois and Washington, the pressing issues were neither impractical ones such as the redistribution of wealth, a more humane mode of production, or opposition to American imperialism (in Puerto Rico and the Philippines) nor impertinent ones such as the undesirability of miscegenation or the removal of the Christian taint on Afro-American culture. Rather, these two petit bourgeois leaders directed their attention to the form and content of Afro-American inclusion in American society.

Both agreed on the form: nonviolent reform within the legal, political, and economic channels of American life. They differed on the content: Washington favored self-help initiatives in the economic sphere and promoted a slow agrarian proletarianization process tied to increased Afro-American property holdings and wealth acquisition, whereas Du Bois opted for upward social mobility in the social and political spheres and supported a protest movement that would achieve equal legal, social, and political status for Afro-Americans in American society. They violently clashed, not simply because of their divergent viewpoints but, more important, because their limited access to resources and talent forced them to struggle for power on overlapping terrain.

The Du Bois–Washington debate set the framework for inclusionary African practices in the United States in this century. The numerous black ideological battles between integrationism and nationalism, accommodationism and separatism are but versions and variations of the Du Bois–Washington debate.[25] For example, Marcus Garvey, the great Jamaican leader of the first mass movement among Africans in the United States, simply gave Washington's self-help orientation a nationalist slant and back-to-Africa twist; his personal admiration of Washington is indisputable.

The first minor attempt to burst out of the framework of the Du Bois–Washington debate was the socialist viewpoint set forth in the pages of *The Messenger,* edited by the Young Turks, Chandler Owen and A. Philip Randolph.[26] This perspective, which echoed George Washington Woodbey's position more than a decade earlier, not only called into question the procapitalist assumption circumscribing the Du Bois–Washington debate but also linked the enhancement of Afro-Americans to the radical elements of the labor movement. This valuable addition proved to be premature at the time, especially given the racist character of the labor movement. But in decades to come, this perspective proved to be portentous. Randolph's long and distinguished yet flawed career bears out the depths of his foresight. In short, he was the pioneer on the frontier of Afro-American labor relations.

A second minor attempt to step outside the confines of the Du Bois–Washington debate consisted of the African Blood Brotherhood's amalgam of revolutionary black nationalism and scientific socialism.[27] Its principal figures—Cyril Briggs, Richard B. Moore, W. A. Domingo, Harry Haywood—were the first African communists in the United States. Their major contribution was that they put imperialist issues on the agenda of the Afro-American liberation movement. Yet such issues— along with untimely revolutionary rhetoric—remained on the back burner for petit bourgeois intellectuals and entrepreneurs, proletarian preachers and parishioners in urban centers, and sharecroppers, tenants, and yeoman farmers in rural areas throughout Afro-America.

The major vehicles by which black progress occurred in this period were patronage relationships with white elites and bosses in city machines, organized protest and boycott efforts (usually church-based) against discrimination, labor shortages during the two world wars, participation in the progressive labor movement (especially in the unionization of industrial workers), and achievements in athletics and entertainment. These diverse means of Afro-American upward social mobility constituted ad hoc measures which presupposed political oppression, economic exploitation, and social degradation as the prevailing realities and posited inclusion within the American liberal capitalist order as the desirable goal. Such inclusionary measures signified the Afro-American encounter with the modern world on a significant scale for the first time; they revealed the difficulties presented by racist American society, the desperation of a bastard people in hostile circumstances, and the determination of Africans in the United States, despite limited organization and vision, to be free.

End of Modernity, Postindustrial Cosmopolitanism, Dispersive Practices

We live now three decades afer the end of European modernity. The very term "postmodernism" reflects fear of the future; it is a backward-looking term. We witness the nuclear and ideological stand-off between the capitalist (not necessarily free) United States and the communist (definitely unfree) Soviet Union, both imperialist powers suffering immense internal decay. The dominated classes in industrial and postindustrial nations have accelerated the speed of their inclusion within the liberal capitalist regimes, accompanied by widespread tranquilizing and depoliticizing by mass culture. Poor, developing nations have launched successful political, anticolonial revolutions, yet often lapse into a neocolonial dependence on developed capitalist countries. A few developing nations even have had successful social revolutions, though they usually fall into the neocolonial Soviet orbit.

The recent stirrings of postmodernism can be illustrated in the following ways:

First, the crisis in science which emerged in European modernism is now becoming a more widespread crisis in the authority of science, in many ways similar to the crisis in the authority of the church in the Age of Enlightenment. This rudimentary state of demythologizing science relegates scientific descriptions and theories of the self, world, and God alongside rather than above religious, artistic, and moral descriptions and theories of the self, world, and God. This demythologizing process is promoted (usually unintentionally) by major figures in the philosophy of science, such as N. R. Hanson, Michael Polanyi, Thomas Kuhn, Imre Lakatos, and, above all, Paul Feyerabend.[28] This process signifies a deep authority crisis in knowledge, a kind of demonopolizing of science on truth and reality in the marketplace of ideas. It raises the prospect of a possible plurality of epistemic authorities on truth and reality as well as a frightening full-blown relativism or laissez-faire policy regarding access to truth and reality.

Second, the despair of modern paganism during the European modernist period has degenerated into various forms of cynicism, fatalism, hedonism, and narcissism in the lowbrow, middlebrow, and highbrow cultures of postmodernism. These attitudes and sensibilities—recently studied by Ihab Hassan, Raymond Olderman, Christopher Lasch, Heinz Kohut, Jerome Klinkowitz, and others—can be glimpsed in mass consumer culture, in popular movies, in television programs, and through disco records.[29] Postmodernist sentiments also can be found in such literary works as Jorge Borges' *Labyrinths* (1964), William Burroughs' *Naked Lunch* (1962), Donald Barthelme's *Snow White* (1967), Ishmael Reed's *The Free-Lance Pallbearers* (1967), John Barth's *Lost in the Funhouse* (1968), Ronald Sukenick's *The Death of the Novel* (1969), Kurt Vonnegut, Jr.'s *Slaughterhouse-Five* (1969), Raymond Federman's *Double or Nothing* (1972), Thomas Pynchon's *Gravity's Rainbow* (1973), and Philip K. Dick's *A Scanner Darkly* (1977). This degeneration—in mass culture and sophisticated literary texts—reveals, to a certain extent, the dead end to which modern paganism has come: impotent irony, barren skepticism, and paralyzing self-parody.

Third, philosophical attacks on the primacy of the subject are deepened and extended in postmodernism. In short, postmodernism is an accentuation and acceleration of the major developments and processes in European modernism. It is a deepening of the decline of modernity, with little sense of what is to follow, if anything at all. It bears the birth pains of slow epoch transition, the ironic excesses of prolonged historical suspension, and the ecstatic anticipations of a new, though not necessarily better, era.

The postindustrial cosmopolitan stage of American culture—the prevailing situation with its avant-garde domesticated by absorption into the marketable mainstream, its artists as professors, academic critics as artists, and philosophers as technicians—witnesses the emergence of the United States as the cultural vanguard in postmodernism. For the first time, European audiences look to the United States for artistic and cultural leadership. This leadership is not simply a result of the hegemony of U.S. world power or its supreme nuclear capacity. More important is the fact that it is an effect of a nation that has steadily gained cultural self-confidence while other leading European countries flounder in either self-pity (Germany), self-defeat (England), or self-obsession (France).

The point is not so much that the United States has come of age, but rather that the United States has seized Western cultural leadership in a declining and decadent age.[30] Of course, the United States has no Jean-Paul Sartre or Martin Heidegger, no Samuel Beckett or even Gabriel García Márquez. Yet cultural leadership in the West no longer requires such stellar figures; productive academic figures now suffice.

In postindustrial cosmopolitan American culture, the either-or dilemma of the previous period evaporates. Taking their cues from William Faulkner—without the size of his canvas, the complexity of his vision, and the depths of his talent—postmodern American artists are able to learn from Europe without a feeling of inferiority and of digging deep into American life without a sense of provinciality. In philosophy, the choice is no longer between the last of the Genteel tradition and the reformist orientation—idealism or pragmatism, Royce or Dewey—or even between the reformist orientation and the new realism. The very framework of such a choice has been eclipsed by the linguistic turn in philosophy, with its analytical rigor and technical argumentation.[31] Philosophy in the United States is no longer an arena in which comprehensive world views are adopted and intellectual attitudes cultivated, but rather a professional field of study where intricate puzzlelike problems are solved, resolved, or dissolved.

The professionalization and specialization at work in postindustrial cosmopolitan American culture find their counterparts in the process of differentiation currently proceeding in the Afro-American experience. This differentiation generates dispersive practices among Afro-Americans; heretofore untouched intellectual territories, secular outlooks, business ventures, occupational positions, geographic locations, and even sexual experimentations are now being discovered and enacted by Afro-Americans. This differentiation—though an index of progress—has rendered the collective enhancement of Afro-Americans even more problematic.

The paradox of Afro-American history is that Afro-Americans fully enter the modern world precisely when the postmodern period commences; that Afro-Americans gain a foothold in the industrial order just as the postindustrial order begins; and that Afro-Americans procure skills, values, and mores efficacious for survival and sustenance in modernity as the decline of modernity sets in, deepens, and yearns to give birth to a new era and epoch. The Afro-American petite bourgeoisie make significant gains in such circumstances, but even they have a fragile economic position and vulnerable political status, and they experience cultural atrophy. At the same time, the Afro-American underclass and the poor working class exhibit the indelible traces of their oppression in modernity and their dispensability in postmodernity: relative political powerlessness and perennial socioeconomic depression, cultural deterioration reinforced by devastated families and prefabricated mass culture, and subversive subcultures dominated by drugs and handguns which surface as civil terrorism in black ghettos and American cities.

The postmodern period has rendered the framework of the Du Bois–Washington debate obsolete, but presently there is little theory and praxis to fill the void. Let it suffice to say that a noteworthy product of the dispersive practices of Afro-Americans in postindustrial cosmopolitan American culture is the advent of Afro-American philosophy.

Notes

1. This claim is based on a particular periodization of the development of the Western world persuasively argued in Ernest Cassirer's *The Philosophy of the Enlightenment*, trans. Fritz C. A. Koelin and James P. Pettegrove (1932); Ernst Troeltsch's *The Social Teaching of the Christian Churches*, trans. Olive Wyon (1931), Vol. 1, pp. 23–34, and his *Protestantism and Progress: A Historical Study of the Relation of Protestantism to the Modern World*, trans. W. Montgomery (1912); and Peter Gay's magisterial work, *The Enlightenment: An*

Interpretation (Alfred A. Knopf, 1966), Vol. 1. For the classic Marxist treatment of the Enlightenment, see Max Horkheimer and Theodor Adorno, *Dialectic of Enlightenment*, trans. John Cumming (Herder & Herder, 1972), especially pp. 3–42.

2. For a classic treatment of this problematic of provinciality in the beginnings of the United States, see Merle Curti, *The Growth of American Thought*, 2d ed. (Harper & Brothers, 1951), pp. 3–126. Note also Max Lerner, *America as a Civilization* (Simon & Schuster, 1957), pp. 3–73. My own theory of the development of American provinciality is based in part on the seminal treatment of American culture by Geoffrey Thurley, *The American Moment: American Poetry in the Mid-Century* (St. Martin's Press, 1978), especially pp. 3–32.

3. Alexis de Tocqueville, *Democracy in America* (Alfred A. Knopf, 1944), ed. Phillips Bradley, Vols. 1 and 2; George Santayana, *The Genteel Tradition*, ed. Douglas L. Wilson (Harvard University Press, 1967); Van Wyck Brooks, *America's Coming-of-Age* (1915). The best secondary literature on de Tocqueville's unsurpassed analysis of American culture remains the superb extended essays by John Stuart Mill which accompany the de Tocqueville volumes. For insightful interpretations of Santayana's work, especially his classic 1911 essay, "The Genteel Tradition in American Philosophy" originally given at the Philosophical Union of the University of California at Berkeley and first published in his *Winds of Doctrine* (1913), pp. 186–215, see Danforth Ross, "The Genteel Tradition: Its Characteristics and Its Origins," Ph.D. dissertation, University of Minnesota, 1954; Douglas L. Wilson, "Introductory," in *The Genteel Tradition*, pp. 1–25, and Morton White, *Science and Sentiment in America: Philosophical Thought from Jonathan Edwards to John Dewey* (Oxford University Press, 1972), pp. 241–246. The best recent books on the long and winding career of Van Wyck Brooks are James Hoopes, *Van Wyck Brooks: In Search of American Culture* (University of Massachusetts Press, 1977), and Raymond Nelson, *Van Wyck Brooks: A Writer's Life* (E. P. Dutton & Co., 1980).

4. William James's notions were put forward in his address to the Anti-Imperialist League in 1903. See the Report of the Fifth Annual Meeting of the New England Anti-Imperialist League, November 28, 1903, with excerpts in Ralph Barton Perry, *The Thought and Character of William James*, Briefer Version (Harvard University Press, 1948), pp. 246–247. For a theory of American culture based directly on James's notions, see Thayer, *Meaning and Action: A Critical History of Pragmatism*, pp. 437–445. For a fine dramatic simplification of this theory, see Philip Rahv's well-known essay, "Paleface and Redskin," in his *Image and Idea* (New Directions, 1957), pp. 1–6.

5. Herbert W. Schneider, *A History of American Philosophy*, 2d ed. (Columbia University Press, 1963), pp. 23–26; Joseph L. Blau, *Men and Movements in American Philosophy* (Prentice-Hall, 1952), pp. 27–35.

6. Garry Wills, *Inventing America: Jefferson's Declaration of Independence* (Doubleday & Co., 1978), esp. pp. 167–319.

7. Schneider, *A History of American Philosophy*, pp. 55–61; Blau, *Men and Movements in American Philosophy*, p. 114. See also Andrew Delbanco, *William Ellery Channing: An Essay on the Liberal Spirit in America* (Harvard University Press, 1981).

8. Winthrop Jordan, *White Over Black: American Attitudes Toward the Negro, 1550–1812* (W. W. Norton & Co., 1968), Pts. 1–3, esp. pp. 44–98, 179–265; Thomas F. Gossett, *Race: The History of an Idea in America* (Southern Methodist University Press, 1965), pp. 17–31.

9. W.E.B. Du Bois, *The Souls of Black Folk* (Fawcett Publications, 1961), pp. 16–17. The best secondary treatment of this classic text can be found in Arnold Rampersad, *The Art and Imagination of W.E.B. Du Bois* (Harvard University Press, 1976), pp. 68–90, and Robert B. Stepto, *From Behind the Veil: A Study of Afro-American Narrative* (University of Illinois Press, 1979), pp. 52–91.

10. The most important work on the retention of African practices among black people in the United States (and New World) remains Melville J. Herskovits' *The Myth of the Negro Past* (Beacon Press, 1958). For a superb recent treatment of this phenomenon, see Raboteau, *Slave Religion*, pp. 4–92.

11. M. H. Abrams, *The Mirror and the Lamp: Romantic Theory and the Critical Tradition* (Oxford University Press, 1953), Ch. VII, pp. 156–183, Ch. VIII, pp. 184–225. See also the influential essays by Harold Bloom, "The Internalization of Quest-Romance," in *Romanticism and Consciousness: Essays in Criticism*, ed. Harold Bloom (W. W. Norton & Co., 1970), pp. 3–24, and Harold Bloom, "'To Reason with a Later Reason': Romanticism and the Rational," in his *The Ringers in the Tower: Studies in Romantic Tradition* (University of Chicago Press, 1971), pp. 323–337.

12. Jacques Barzun, *Classic, Romantic and Modern* (Little, Brown & Co., 1961), pp. 1–17, 96–114.

13. Abrams, *Natural Supernaturalism*, pp. 11–140, 327–372, 411–462.

14. For the classic text on this subject, see F. O. Matthiessen, *The American Renaissance* (Oxford University Press, 1941). Other notable works include V. L. Parrington, *Main Currents in American Thought*, Vol. 2 (Harcourt, Brace and Co., 1954), pp. 427–465; D. H. Lawrence, *Studies in Classic American Literature* (1923); R. W. B. Lewis, *The American Adam: Innocence, Tragedy, and Tradition in the Nineteenth Century* (University of Chicago Press, 1955), especially the Prologue, pp. 1–10; Richard Chase, *The American Novel and Its Tradition* (New York, 1957), esp. pp. 1–22; and Ihab Hassan, *Radical Innocence: Studies in the Contemporary American Novel* (Princeton University Press, 1961), pp. 34–60. This American search for newness is captured by the words of the two major literary figures of the period: Ralph Waldo Emerson and Herman Melville. In his renowned essay "Circles," Emerson states that "I am only an experimenter. . . . I simply experiment, an endless seeker, with no past at my back" *(Selected Writings of Ralph Waldo Emerson*, ed. William H. Gilman, p. 304; New American Library, 1965). In his famous essay, "Hawthorne and His Mosses," Melville writes, "Let us boldly contemn all imitation, though it comes to us grateful and fragrant as the morning, and foster all originality, though at first, it be crabbed and ugly as our own pine knots" (Herman Melville, *Moby-Dick*, ed. Harrison Hayford and Hershel Parker, pp. 546, 550; W. W. Norton & Co., 1967).

15. Raboteau, *Slave Religion*, pp. 128–132. Note also Lawrence W. Levine, *Black Culture and Black Consciousness: Afro-American Folk Thought from Slavery to Freedom* (Oxford University Press, 1977), pp. 60–61.

16. Herskovits, *The Myth of the Negro Past*, pp. 232–235. The material conditions under which many Africans in the United States became Christians are worth noting: the structure of domination was that of a preindustrial form of slavery; a lower ratio of Africans to whites than that in Latin America facilitated more frequent and intense African-white interaction; and though only 4.5 percent of all Africans imported to the western hemisphere came to the United States and Canada, an incredibly high rate of natural increase

soon quadrupled this percentage figure. Therefore most converts (though not all, such as the poet Phyllis Wheatley) were American-born Africans struggling to make sense of and give meaning to life without an immediate relation to African customs and world views. For further elaboration on this matter, see Raboteau, *Slave Religion*, pp. 87–92.

17. Raboteau, *Slave Religion*, pp. 59–75.

18. This point is accented by E. Franklin Frazier, *The Negro Church in America* (Schocken Books, 1964), pp. 30–34. For a more dialectical treatment—which highlights the liberating and debilitating aspects of the Black Christian Churches—see Eugene D. Genovese, *Roll, Jordan, Roll: The World the Slaves Made* (Random House, 1974), pp. 159–284. See also the first-rate dissertation of James M. Washington which is a pioneering study of the separate Black Baptists, "The Origins and Emergence of Black Baptist Separatism, 1863–1897," Ph.D. dissertation, Yale University, 1979.

19. Lionel Trilling, *Beyond Culture: Essays in Literature and Learning* (Viking Press, 1965), p. 3. In a famous essay entitled "The Idea of the Modern," in *The Idea of the Modern in Literature and the Arts*, ed. Irving Howe (Horizon Press, 1967), Irving Howe writes, "Nihilism lies at the center of all we mean by modernist literature, both as subject and symptom, a demon overcome and a demon victorious" (p. 39). For a more affirmative view of modernism, see Peter Gay, *Freud, Jews and Other Germans: Masters and Victims in Modernist Culture* (Oxford University Press, 1978). The best general treatment of modernism is Malcolm Bradbury and James McFarlane (eds.), *Modernism: 1890–1930* (Middlesex: Penguin Books, 1976), and the classic Marxist perspective is put forward by Georg Lukács in his influential essay, "The Ideology of Modernism," in *Marxism and Human Liberation*, ed. E. San Juan, Jr. (Dell Press, 1973), pp. 277–307.

20. Virginia Woolf, "Mr. Bennett and Mrs. Brown," in *Collected Essays*, Vol. 1 (London: Hogarth Press, 1966), p. 321.

21. The major texts on the industrial provincial stage of American culture are Henry F. May, *The End of American Innocence: A Study of the First Years of Our Own Time, 1912–1917* (Alfred A. Knopf, 1957); Robert H. Wiebe, *The Search for Order, 1877–1920* (Hill & Wang, 1967); Samuel P. Hays, *The Response to Industrialism, 1885–1914* (University of Chicago Press, 1957); Chase, *The American Novel and Its Tradition*, pp. 117–236; Hassan, *Radical Innocence*, pp. 61–95; and the seminal essay by Herbert G. Gutman, "Work, Culture, and Society in Industrializing America, 1815–1919," in *Work, Culture, and Society in Industrializing America: Essays in America's Working Class and Social History* (Vintage Books, 1977), pp. 3–78.

22. Alfred Kazin, *On Native Grounds: An Interpretation of Modern American Prose Literature* (Doubleday & Co., 1956), p. ix.

23. This formulation follows Richard Rorty's brilliant contemporary remake of Santayana's essay, entitled "Professionalized Philosophy and Transcendentalist Culture," in *The Georgia Review*, 30th anniversary, Winter 1976, pp. 757–769. For a broader characterization of the pragmatist attack on idealism, see Morton White, *Social Thought in America: The Revolt Against Formalism* (Beacon Press, 1957). Note also Bruce Kuklick, *The Rise of American Philosophy: Cambridge, Massachusetts, 1860–1930* (Yale University Press, 1977), pp. 129–227, 233–401. Related treatments on the phenomenon of professionalism in American culture are Burton J. Bledstein, *The Culture of Professionalism: The Middle Class and the Development of Higher Education in America* (W. W. Norton & Co., 1976), especially pp. 80–128, 287–334, and David F. Noble, *America by Design: Science, Technology, and the Rise of Corporate Capitalism* (Alfred A. Knopf, 1977).

24. August Meier, *Negro Thought in America, 1880–1915: Racial Ideologies in the Age of Booker T. Washington* (University of Michigan Press, 1963), pp. 161–278; S. P. Fullinwider, *The Mind and Mood of Black America: 20th Century Thought* (Dorsey Press, 1969), pp. 47–71; Abby Arthur Johnson and Ronald Maberry Johnson, *Propaganda and Aesthetics: The Literary Politics of Afro-American Magazines in the Twentieth Century* (University of Massachusetts Press, 1979), pp. 1–63; and Julius Lester, "Du Bois and Washington," in his fine introduction to *The Seventh Son: The Thought and Writings of W.E.B. Du Bois*, ed. Julius Lester (Random House, 1971), Vol. 1, pp. 41–52.

25. This insight is but one of many in the superb essay by Harold Cruse, "Behind the Black Power Slogan," in his *Rebellion or Revolution?* (William Morrow & Co., 1969), pp. 193–260.

26. For actual reprints of articles from *The Messenger,* see *Voices of a Black Nation: Political Journalism in the Harlem Renaissance,* ed. Theodore G. Vincent (Ramparts Press, 1973), pp. 43–51, 113–122. Reliable treatments of Owen and Randolph can be found in Philip Foner, *American Socialism and Black Americans: From the Age of Jackson to World War II* (Greenwood Press, 1977), pp. 265–287; Johnson and Johnson, *Propaganda and Aesthetics,* pp. 57–63; and Henry Williams, *Black Response to the American Left: 1917–1929* (Princeton University Press, 1973), pp. 80–93. For a fuller examination of Randolph, see Jervis Anderson, *A. Philip Randolph: A Biographical Portrait* (Harcourt Brace Jovanovich, 1972).

27. Similarly, reproductions of articles from *The Crusader,* the periodical of the African Blood Brotherhood, are in *Voices of a Black Nation: Political Journalism in the Harlem Renaissance,* pp. 123–136. Detailed treatments of this fascinating group are difficult to find. The best ones I know are Harry Haywood, *Black Bolshevik: Autobiography of an Afro-American Communist* (Liberator Press, 1978), pp. 122–131; Foner, *American Socialism and Black Americans,* pp. 309–311; Mark Solomon, "Red and Black: Negroes and Communism," Ph.D. dissertation, Harvard University, pp. 79–84; and Mark Naison, "The Communist Party in Harlem, 1928–1936," Ph.D. dissertation, Columbia University, 1975, Chs. I and II.

28. N. R. Hanson, *Patterns of Discovery* (Cambridge University Press, 1958); Michael Polanyi, *Personal Knowledge: Towards a Post-Critical Philosophy* (University of Chicago Press, 1958); Thomas S. Kuhn, *The Structure of Scientific Revolutions,* 2d ed. (University of Chicago Press, 1970), and "Reflections on My Critics," in *Criticism and the Growth of Knowledge,* ed. Imre Lakatos and Alan Musgrave (Cambridge University Press, 1970), pp. 231–278. Imre Lakatos, "Falsification and the Methodology of Scientific Research Programmes," in *Criticism and the Growth of Knowledge,* pp. 91–196; Paul Feyerabend, *Against Method* (Schocken Books, 1975) and *Science in a Free Society* (Schocken Books, 1978). For serious critical responses to the demythologizing of science, see Israel Scheffler, *Science and Subjectivity* (Bobbs-Merrill Co., 1967) and "Vision and Revolution: A Postscript on Kuhn," in *Philosophy of Science,* Vol. 39, No. 3 (Sept. 1972), pp. 366–374; Larry Laudan, *Progress and Its Problems: Towards a Theory of Scientific Growth* (University of California Press, 1977); and Clark Glymour, *Theory and Evidence* (Princeton University Press, 1980).

29. Ihab Hassan, *The Literature of Silence: Henry Miller and Samuel Beckett* (Alfred A. Knopf, 1968); *The Dismemberment of Orpheus: Toward a Postmodern Literature* (Oxford University Press, 1971); *Paracriticisms: Seven Speculations of the Times* (University of Illinois Press, 1975); *The Right Promethean Fire: Imagination, Science and Cultural Change* (University

of Illinois Press, 1980); Raymond Olderman, *Beyond the Waste Land: A Study of the American Novel in the Nineteen-Sixties* (Yale University Press, 1972); Christopher Lasch, *The Culture of Narcissism* (W. W. Norton & Co., 1978); Heinz Kohut, *The Analysis of the Self* (International Universities Press, 1971); *The Restoration of the Self* (International Universities Press, 1977); *The Search for the Self: Selected Writings of Heinz Kohut, 1950–1978*, 2 vols., ed. Paul H. Ornstein (International Universities Press, 1978); Jerome Klinkowitz, *Literary Disruptions: The Making of a Post-Contemporary American Fiction*, 2d ed. (University of Illinois Press, 1981). Relevant Marxist responses to and analyses of postmodernism include Fredric Jameson, *Marxism and Form: Twentieth-Century Dialectical Theories of Literature* (Princeton University Press, 1971); *Fables of Aggression: Wyndham Lewis, the Modernist as Fascist* (University of California Press, 1979); *The Political Unconscious: Narrative as a Socially Symbolic Act* (Cornell University Press, 1981), and his insightful essay "Reification and Utopia in Mass Culture," *Social Text*, Winter 1979, pp. 130–148; Russell Jacoby, *Social Amnesia: A Critique of Conformist Psychology from Adler to Laing* (Beacon Press, 1975); and Stuart Ewen, *Captains of Consciousness: Advertising and the Social Roots of the Consumer Culture* (McGraw-Hill Book Co., 1976). For a critical, even polemic, treatment of postmodernism, see Gerald Graff, "The Myth of the Postmodernist Breakthrough," *Tri-Quarterly*, No. 26 (Winter 1973), pp. 383–417, and his controversial book *Literature Against Itself: Literary Ideas in Modern Society* (University of Chicago Press, 1979). Of course, the basis of scholarship on postmodernism and mass culture was laid by the pioneering work of Max Horkheimer and Theodor Adorno with their classic essay "The Culture Industry: Enlightenment as Mass Deception," in *Dialectic of Enlightenment*, pp. 120–167, and the writings of David Riesman in his (along with Nathan Glazer and Reuel Denney) *The Lonely Crowd: A Study of the Changing American Character*, abr. ed. (Yale University Press, 1961); *Individualism Reconsidered* (Doubleday & Co., 1955), esp. pp. 12–27, 126–163; and *Abundance for What? and Other Essays* (Doubleday & Co., 1964), pp. 103–367.

30. This leadership fulfills the prophecy of Thomas Mann, the major German modernist writer, who writes in the last paragraph of his famous 1938 lecture given on his coast-to-coast tour, "I believe, in fact, that for the duration of the present European dark age, the centre of Western culture will shift to America" (*The Coming Victory of Democracy*, trans. Agnes B. Meyer, pp. 66–67; Alfred A. Knopf, 1938). Note also William Barrett's words regarding the situation of American intellectuals in 1945, "We were probably the last American generation to go through this old rite of looking toward Europe for our culture . . . that older exclusive filial relation to Europe—the sense of Europe as a unique treasure on which Americans must depend—was on the way out" (*The Truants: Adventures Among the Intellectuals*, p. 130; Doubleday & Co., 1982).

31. Kuklick, *The Rise of American Philosophy*, pp. 565–572. See also Richard Rorty's "Introduction," in *The Linguistic Turn*, ed. Richard Rorty (University of Chicago Press, 1967), pp. 1–39. For a slightly different perspective, note my essay "Nietzsche's Prefiguration of Postmodern American Philosophy," *Boundary 2*, Vol. 9, No. 10 (Spring–Fall 1981), pp. 241–270.

Chapter 6

Authority, Alienation, and Social Death

Orlando Patterson

All power strives for authority. A. Geoffrey Woodhead, in his study of Thucydides and the nature of power, observes that "there remains a need for spiritual and moral support, a need to say that an action is 'right' . . . whatever the realpolitik behind the action."[1] In our examination of the property concept we saw that the master-slave relationship cannot be divorced from the distribution of power throughout the wider society in which both master and slave find themselves. Total power or property in the slave means exclusion of the claims and powers of others in him.

If the master sought to exclude as far as possible all other claims and powers in his slave, it nevertheless remains true that he needed both the recognition and the support of the nonslave members of his community for his assumption of sovereign power over another person. An isolated master faced grave risks. Plato, who knew what he was talking about on this issue, shrewdly pointed out that a slave owner within his community had nothing to fear from his slaves because the entire state was ready to defend each individual citizen. But if he and his immediate family with more than fifty slaves were transported to the middle of a desert where no freeman could come to his defense, that citizen would be in great fear for his own life and that of members of his family, and he would try to ingratiate himself with the slaves by making promises and offers of freedom.[2]

Actually, the situation was more complex than this, for the danger the master faced was not merely physical. In all slaveholding societies the slave posed grave moral and spiritual dangers. Most slave populations have been so small that they were rarely considered a serious political menace; their danger lay in their capacity to offend supernaturally. The master's task, then, had both a negative and a positive aspect. On the negative side, he had to defuse the potential physical and spiritual threat posed by his slave's presence. And on the positive side, he had to secure extracoercive support for his power. Both were achieved by acquiring the thing we call authority.

Authority as Symbolic Control

What was involved in the acquisition of authority? From the community at large, authority came with the institutionalization of the slave relationship. It was achieved by incorporating it into the normative order. As Siegfried Lauffer puts it, the power relationship (*Gewaltverhältnis*) that formed the basis of the slave relationship had to become a rights relationship (*Rechtsverhältnis*).[3] Those who were not directly involved with the relationship—though indirectly influenced by it—had to come to accept it not just grudgingly, but as the normal order of things (as did the non-slaveholding Greek, Roman, Hausa, or antebellum southern farmer). Nor was it only the nonslaveholding "freeman" whom the master wished to acknowledge his authority. The arrogance of power knows no bounds, for the master desired too that the slave recognize his authority, as well as his right to dominate him. To the extent that he did, to that degree was he able to walk fearlessly into the desert with his slave. And the truth is that many masters succeeded. As the history of the slaveholding peoples of the Sahara shows, many a master accompanied by his slave knew, for long periods of their lives, only each other and the desert.

Understanding how this happens is no easy matter. Most social scientists faced with the problem of authority are content to cite a few well-known passages from Weber—the acknowledged authority on the subject—then continue blithely with their analysis. There is too much that is unsatisfactory in Weber's analysis for us to take this course. He tells us that authority has three sources: law, charisma, and tradition.[4] Law, however, cannot be a source of authority, for it is merely that complex of rules which has the coercive power of the state behind it. As the Scandinavian and other modern jurists have pointed out, to define law as normative rules is to evade the crucial issue.[5] Law itself begs for the thing we call authority; and as every student of jurisprudence knows, one of the major sources of law, and of law's authority, is tradition. Nor does Weber's notion of charisma get us very far. By its very nature, this is an exceptional phenomenon. No doubt there was the occasional master who was genuinely charismatic, but in general masters were no more endowed with unusual personal qualities than other persons, including their slaves.

We are left only with tradition. Weber was on the right track here, but unfortunately was too vague. What does tradition mean? And why should the traditional automatically convey authority? By tradition Weber was obviously referring to the total complex of norms, values, ideas, and patterned behavior we call culture. I agree that somewhere in this vast universe of received human experience is to be found the source of authority; but where?

The answer, I think, has been provided by students of symbolic anthropology, beginning with Meyer Fortes' critique of Weber.[6] Fortes and other British anthropologists, especially Raymond Firth, have argued that symbols, both private and public, constitute a major instrument of power when used directly or indirectly. Herein lies the source of authority. Those who exercise power, if they are able to transform it into a "right," a norm, a usual part of the order of things, must first control (or at least be in a position to manipulate) appropriate symbolic instruments. They may do so by exploiting already existing symbols, or they may create new ones relevant to their needs.

The full mechanics of this process of symbol appropriation is beyond the scope of the present work; what I shall do is examine the nature of symbolic control in the case of the master-slave relationship. Symbolic processes, like so many other areas of human experience, have both an intellectual and a social aspect. On the intellectual level symbolic thought attempts to explain, in the language of symbols, a given area of actual experience. It is essentially mythic, similar in intellectual form to the validating concepts and beliefs of religion. The social aspect of symbolic behavior refers to the ritual processes by means of which symbolic ideas are acted out in terms of real human interactions. Such actions invariably are highly formalized and ceremonial. Where the experience being symbolized extends over a long period of time, there is a tendency for a clearly defined symbolic pattern to develop: critical stages in the developmental process, and especially the transition from one stage to the next, are given special ritual expression. The celebrated work of Arnold Van Gennep examined, for example, the various ritual expressions of the human life cycle among a variety of peoples.[7] Similar rites of passage may be found in lasting relationships—and slavery, as we shall see, is one such case.

A final theoretical point to note is the contribution of Victor Turner who, in his masterful treatise on the Ndembu and in later theoretical writings, developed the concept of the dominant symbol.[8] Mythic and ritual processes by nature are multivocal, ambiguous, diffuse, and sometimes downright incomprehensible. Within a given cultural domain, however, a dominant symbol—a major mythic theme, a key ritual act—stands out as pivotal. By its emergence it makes possible an internal interpretation of the symbolic process on both the intellectual and the social level.

Slavery, I intend to show in this chapter, is a highly symbolized domain of human experience. While all aspects of the relationship are symbolized, there is overwhelming concentration on the profound natal alienation of the slave. The reason for this is not hard to discern: it was the slave's isolation, his strangeness, that made him most valuable to the master; but it was this very strangeness that most threatened the community and that most exercised that "primacy of feeling and willing over thinking" which is at the core of the symbolic mind. On the cognitive or mythic level, one dominant theme emerges, which lends an unusually loaded meaning to the act of natal alienation: this is the social death of the slave. On the ritual level, the enslavement process is expressed in terms of well-defined rites of passage.

The Two Conceptions of Social Death

If the slave no longer belonged to a community, if he had no social existence outside of his master, then what was he? The initial response in almost all slaveholding societies was to define the slave as a socially dead person. Claude Meillassoux and his associates have most thoroughly explored this aspect of slavery. They reject the simplistic materialist view, which fails to take account of this problem—which indeed does not even recognize the existence of the problem.[9] From the structural viewpoint, Meillassoux argues, slavery must be seen as a process involving several transitional phases. The slave is violently uprooted from his milieu. He is desocialized and depersonalized. This process of social negation constitutes the first, essentially external, phase of enslavement. The next phase involves the introduction of the slave into the community of his master, but it involves the paradox of introducing him as a nonbeing. This explains the importance of law, custom, and ideology in the representation of the slave relation. Summarizing his own views and those of his associate Michel Izard, Meillassoux writes: "The captive always appears therefore as marked by an original, indelible defect which weighs endlessly upon his destiny. This is, in Izard's words, a kind of 'social death.' He can never be brought to life again as such since, in spite of some specious examples (themselves most instructive) of fictive rebirth, the slave will remain forever an unborn being (non-né)."[10]

There is much of value in this analysis, although it exaggerates to make the point. It goes astray, or at any rate is likely to mislead, mainly in its overemphasis of external sources and conquest as the initiating act of enslavement. It is simply not the case that "the condition of slavery never results from an internal process of social differentiation." Meillassoux is here drawing too narrowly on his field experience in West Africa, in much the same way that an earlier French theorist, Henri Lévy-Bruhl, was led to the same conclusion by generalizing from the single experience of Roman slavery.[11] Slavery among the primitive Goajiros of Venezuela, the large-scale slavery in Korea from the Koryŏ period to nearly the end of the Yi dynasty, and Russian slavery during the seventeenth and eighteenth centuries are three cases of slavery operating in different contexts and on very different scales as the result of a process of internal differentiation.

In almost all premodern slaveholding societies, at least some slaves were locally recruited. The problems these slaves posed were no different from those presented by the more dramatically disrupted captives. What was different, however, was the manner of their social death. I suggest that there were two ways in which social death was represented and culturally "explained," depending on the dominant early mode of recruiting slaves. Where the earliest and most dominant mode of recruitment was external, the cultural mode of representing social death was what I shall call *intrusive* and this was likely to continue even where, later, most slaves were internally recruited. The second way in which social death was represented may be called *extrusive*, and this too was determined by the earliest dominant means of recruiting slaves. It persisted even if, later, there was a shift to external sources.

In the intrusive mode of representing social death the slave was ritually incorporated as the permanent enemy on the inside—the "domestic enemy," as he was known in medieval Tuscany.[12] He did not and could not belong because he was the product of a hostile, alien culture. He stood, on the one hand, as a living affront to the local gods, an intruder in the sacred space (the cosmicized circle, as Mircea Eliade would say, that defined the community).[13] The views of the Bella Coola Indians of British Columbia and of the Nias of Indonesia are not only nearly identical, but typical of all peoples. The Bella Coola were fond of saying that "no slaves came to earth with the first people," and Thomas F. McIlwraith comments: "To the Bella Coola, who still consider a man's power in the land as dependent to a considerable extent on his ancestral myth, a slave's greatest misfortune lay in the fact that he had no ancestral home, and hence no rights. . . . A slave was a stranger in a strange land, unsupported by a chain of ancestors reaching back to the beginning of time."[14] Similarly Peter Suzuki reports that among the Nias "the slaves are not mentioned in any ancestral myth, have no place in the world-tree, thus lack religion and consequently, a place in the cosmos. They have no past nor future, living as they do, on the whims and mercy of their masters. They live on the fringes of the cosmos and are viewed as being almost on a par with animals."[15]

On the other hand, the slave was symbolic of the defeated enemy, the power of the local gods, and the superior honor of the community. Because of the association of the slave with the enemy in this mode of representing social death, we are not surprised to find that slavery was associated with the military, and that the terminology of slavery took on a military flavor in many such societies. Among the Kwakiutl Indians of the northwest coast of America, "a slave is designated by the expression 'q!aku q!ak'o,'" the basis of which is the root "q!ak," meaning "to cut off the head." U. P. Averkieva observes:

> The custom of cutting off the heads of slain enemies and carrying them away as a sort of trophy, which existed side by side with [the practice] of enslavement, bears witness to the fact that, whereas in the distant past an enemy [taken prisoner] had his head cut off, because, as yet, there was no place in society for a slave, he later began to be inducted into slavery.[16]

The Ashanti of West Africa, like the peoples of early Mesopotamia, referred to slaves as people of a foreign country. Indeed, *adonke*, the general term for slave in Ashanti, was the same term for all foreign northerners; and in the Third Dynasty of Ur the word for slave literally meant man or woman of the mountain, the area from which the earliest slaves came.[17]

The Greek word for slavery, *doulos*, is still an etymological mystery, but it is significant that in spite of the highly commercial nature of Greek slavery in classical times and the fact that from the sixth century B.C. on the vast majority of slaves were bought at slave markets rather than captured, the agent of the state responsible for the public regulation of slaves was the war archon.[18] The Roman experience was even more revealing. P.R.C. Weaver, in his discussion of the *servus vicarius*, tells us that the term "is derived, *as is much of the domestic terminology of Roman slavery*, from military usage and organization" (emphasis added). A common term for slave was "captivus."[19] Roman law fully represented the intrusive conception of the slave. The Roman captured by the enemy lost all claims as a Roman citizen, but if he escaped and found his way back home, the principle of *postliminium* applied: he was fully restored to his original status, subject to a few restrictions and occasionally to a redeemer's lien.[20] The idea of social death was also given direct legal expression in Roman law. The slave was *pro nullo*. We learn, too, from the comedies of Plautus and Terence that the slave was one who recognized no father and no fatherland.[21]

Hebrew slavery in law and practice, in both ancient and medieval times, was highly intrusive. Fellow Jews could be and were enslaved in biblical times, but the slave was conceived of as the quintessential enemy within. In Leviticus we read:

> And as for thy bondsmen, and thy bondsmaids, which thou shalt have of the nations that are round about you, of them all shall ye buy bondsmen and bondsmaids. Moreover of the children of the strangers that do sojourn among you, of them shall ye buy, and of their families that are with you, which they have begotten in your land; and they shall be your possession. And ye shall make them an inheritance for your children after you, to hold for a possession; of them shall ye take your bondsmen forever.[22]

The foreign slave according to Maimonides "is like land in regard to the acquisition of title," and one who was a minor "is like cattle, and one may acquire title to him by the modes whereby title to cattle . . . is acquired."[23]

Medieval Christendom from its very early days defined all pagans and infidels who resisted conversion as enemies who could justly be enslaved if taken in war. Like the Hebrews, the medieval Christian nations permitted the enslavement of fellow Christians and denied that the conversion of slaves obliged masters to manumit them.[24]

It is in Islamic religious and social thought that we find the purest expression of the intrusive conception of social death. The outsider was foreigner, enemy, and infidel, fit only for enslavement after the jihad, to be incorporated as the enemy within. Legally the Muslim is not permitted to enslave coreligionists, although, as we shall see, many ways were found to get around this injunction. As a cultural mode of representation, however, the image of the slave as the captured enemy and internalized outsider in a state of social death was firmly fixed in Islamic thought. The most frequent expression for female slaves in the Qoran is "that which your right hand possesses." The slave is primarily "a person taken captive in war, or carried off by force from a foreign hostile country, and being at the time of capture an unbeliever."[25] Ali Abd Elwahed argued forcefully that in contrast to the basically ethnic conception of the slave's distinctiveness found in western slave societies, both ancient and modern, the Islamic world's conception was based on religious differences. He admitted that there were strong traces of racism in both the political and legal thought of the Arabs, but insisted that in their "collective representations" slavery was the result of captivity occasioned by just wars against the infidel.[26] Similarly, M. G. Smith has emphasized this difference in the representation of slavery among Islamic and West Indian slavemasters.[27] More recently, Paul Lovejoy has called attention to the need to distinguish between ideology and practice in the interpretation of slavery among Islamic peoples.[28] Quite apart from the problem of confusing ideology with reality, an overemphasis on the religious content of the Islamic mode of representing the social death of the slave has tended to obscure the more important common element in the Western and Islamic representations: the fact that they are both intrusive.

In sharp contrast with the intrusive conception of death was the extrusive representation. Here the dominant image of the slave was that of an insider who had fallen, one who ceased to belong and had been expelled from normal participation in the community because of a failure to meet certain minimal legal or socioeconomic norms of behavior. The destitute were included in this group, for while they perhaps had committed no overt crime their failure to survive on their own was taken as a sign of innate incompetence and of divine disfavor. Typical of the extrusive representation of social death among primitives were the Goajiro of Venezuela, among whom slavery was essentially "a consequence of the violation of the code of social order."[29] Among advanced archaic civilizations the Aztecs, Egyptians, and Chinese were typical. The Aztecs, while they took many prisoners of war, used them mainly in their religious ceremonies or else resettled them. Slavery was viewed as being of internal origin, and the slave was someone who had fallen as a result of destitution or criminality.[30] In pharaonic Egypt the terminology of slavery contrasted strikingly with that of early Mesopotamia in that it did not refer to the slave as a foreigner. Egyptian terminology accurately reflected the internal source of slavery and the fact that it arose primarily from destitution. To the Egyptians this status amounted to social and legal death, as 'Abd al-Muhsin Bakīr clearly shows.[31] And it was into this status that captives who were enslaved were assimilated. Significantly, the Egyptian word for captive, literally translated, meant "living dead."[32] China throughout its long recorded history held firmly to an extrusive conception of slavery. The slave was conceived of as a criminal, and the prisoner of war, if enslaved, was legally and ideologically assimilated to the status of the internal criminal.[33]

In none of the above-mentioned societies do we find really large-scale slavery, so it may be wondered whether the extrusive mode of representing slavery applies only to social systems in which the institution did not attain marked structural significance. This, however, is not the case. There are two quite dramatic cases of advanced societies highly dependent on slavery in which the institution was intrusively represented: these are Korea during the Koryŏ and Yi dynasties, and Russia from the late seventeenth century to near the end of the eighteenth century.

Although it is not generally known even among scholars specializing in the study of slavery, both Korea and Russia relied heavily on slaves not only in their economic sectors but for the performance of administrative roles, and Korea at varying periods had slave populations that constituted more than 30 percent of its total population.[34]

In Korea during the Koryŏ period slavery had a "moral . . . connotation"; slaves were persons from whom heaven had withdrawn its favor. In 1300 King Chungnyŏl of Korea responded in alarm to a draft of a plan by a Chinese, Kno-li Chi-su, to reform the system of slavery. The king explained thus: "Our ancestors have instructed us that these servile elements are of a different race and therefore it is not possible for them to become common people—to oppose the instructions of our ancestors is to endanger our social order."[35] Five hundred years later the conception of the slave was much the same. Both Susan Shin and Edward W. Wagner, from their studies of the census data of the late seventeenth century, found that social mobility was "overwhelmingly downward" and that the slave who stood at the bottom of the hierarchy was essentially someone who had fallen there.[36]

In Russia we find another important slaveholding society with an extrusive conception of slavery. One of the earliest sets of laws dealing with slavery in Russia dates back to the second half of the twelfth century.[37] The law listed three ways in which persons became slaves and it is significant that they excluded capture at war. This exclusion has puzzled Russian historians, and all sorts of theories have been advanced to explain the presumed omission, the most widely accepted being that the clauses in question dealt only with cases where a person becomes a slave by his own action. This may be the correct explanation, but equally plausible is another: in the same way that the enslaved prisoner of war in imperial China was assimilated to the status of a person who had become a slave as the result of conviction for a capital offense, so in Kievan Russia the captive may well have been assimilated to the dominant extrusive conception of the slave as an internally fallen person.

Even more revealing is the controversy surrounding the connotation of the term "izgoi." The term referred to aliens and freedmen but, significantly, its primary meaning was "a man who has lost his former status and is in need of special protection." In this regard it applied as much to orphaned princes and bankrupt merchants as to destitute ex-slaves and aliens.[38] Thus we find the alien being assimilated to the status of the fallen insider rather than the other way around.

After its virtual disappearance during the early seventeenth century slavery began to expand again during the era of Peter the Great and continued doing so until Russia became one of the most important of the European slaveholding states, including those of the New World. It remained unique among the European slave systems, however, in maintaining a highly extrusive conception of slavery. As in imperial China, slavery was very closely tied to the penal system and the slave was conceived of as someone who had committed a capital offense. Not all criminals became slaves, but the *kátorshniki* and *poseléntsi* who were sentenced to a lifetime of hard labor and forced colonization were public slaves in every sense of the term. "Both were by their sentences deprived of all civil rights. In the eyes of the law they were nonpersons; their property was distributed to their heirs; their wives could remarry since all family relations had been annulled by the sentences."[39]

The extrusive conception of slavery applied equally to private slaves who served their masters in urban areas. Earlier we saw how the three monotheistic religions reinforced an intrusive conception of slavery. It is therefore highly significant that Russia was the only Christian state whose church did not help to define the slave as a converted infidel. The Orthodox church, according to Richard Hellie, "condoned, and in fact, encouraged, the enslavement of Orthodox by Orthodox," and it did not object to the enslavement of Orthodox Christians by members of other faiths.[40] This becomes all the more extraordinary when we realize that in Muscovy national consciousness was expressed mainly in religious terms: "the Orthodox Church played a central role in the rise and consolidation of the Muscovite state."[41]

With slavery retaining its highly extrusive character in Russia, the slave was never the enemy within but the internally fallen. Ideological elaboration of the difference between slave and free did not seek the aid of religion but defined the gulf in terms of what Hellie calls "simulated barriers." One of these barriers is most revealing. Slave owners invented genealogical "claims of foreign origin for their clan." They claimed to be foreigners of noble dynastic origins "reigning over another people."[42] Almost all of these claims were false, but it is remarkable that the Russian slaveholder, instead of defining his slave as the captured foreigner within his land, chose exactly the opposite course in defining himself as the foreigner of noble ancestry. This of course is consistent with an extrusive conception of slavery, where the slave is the insider who has fallen.

We may summarize the two modes of representing the social death that was slavery by saying that in the intrusive mode the slave was conceived of as someone who did not belong because he was an outsider, while in the extrusive mode the slave became an outsider because he did not (or no longer) belonged. In the former the slave was an external exile, an intruder; in the latter he was an internal exile, one who had been deprived of all claims of community. The one fell because he was the enemy, the other became the enemy because he had fallen. At one extreme, even when prisoners of war became the major source of slaves in China during the period of the Northern dynasties, the representation of the slave as the internally fallen, the criminal, persisted; at the other extreme, in dynastic Mesopotamia as late as the Third Dynasty of Ur, when the vast majority of slaves were internally recruited, the intrusive representation of the slave as the defeated enemy, the people "from the mountain," endured.

It is precisely this persistence of one conception of slavery during periods when we might normally expect the other which explains many otherwise puzzling aspects of the study and treatment of the subject of slavery. Let me illustrate with one important example. It is almost universally believed by European and American writers and readers of history that slavery was abolished in the northern part of Western Europe by the late Middle Ages. Yet in France, Spain, England, and the Netherlands a severe form of enslavement of Europeans by Europeans was to develop and flourish from the middle of the fifteenth century to well into the nineteenth. This was penal slavery, beginning with galley slavery and continuing with its replacement by the Bagnes, or penal slavery in public works. Both were slavery in every sense of the term. They developed as substitutes for the death penalty at a time when there was not a prison system in Europe to accommodate the huge number of persons found guilty of capital offenses. To be sure, the growing incidence of such offenses was largely a reflection of the increase in the number of acts legally so defined. Indeed, there is growing evidence that the legal redefinition of crime and the resulting increase in penal and public slavery was largely determined by the need to regulate labor.[43]

It is truly extraordinary that European scholars have either neglected this whole aspect of the subject or defined it as something other than slavery when they have recognized it. When we look for reasons, it is too easy to claim that there has been a conspiracy of silence, or worse, a deliberate attempt to distort the historical facts. My own feeling is that there has been a genuine failure to recognize the institution for what it was owing to the pervasiveness of the intrusive conception of slavery in the Western intellectual consciousness. The same framework may explain the neglect of modern Russian slavery by West European scholars. Galley slavery and slavery in the Bagnes are immediately recognizable to anyone who understands the institutions in extrusive terms. When the King of France issued a royal letter to his judicial authorities requesting them to provide for the galleys "all malefactors . . . who have merited the death penalty or corporeal punishment, and also those whom they could conscientiously declare to be incorrigible and of evil life and conduct,"[44] he was issuing a call for more public slaves in much the same way that an oriental or Russian monarch would have done. The only difference was that the oriental or Russian ruler would have known that he was requesting more slaves and felt no qualms about it, whereas the French king, with his intrusive view of slavery, either believed he was requesting some other category of labor or conveniently persuaded himself that he was.[45]

Liminal Incorporation

Although the slave might be socially dead, he remained nonetheless an element of society. So the problem arose: how was he to be incorporated? Religion explains how it is possible to relate to the dead who still live. It says little about how ordinary people should relate to the living who are dead. This is the final cultural dilemma posed by the problem of slavery. James H. Vaughan, in his analysis of slavery (*mafakur*) among the Margi of Nigeria, has addressed this problem with considerable insight.[46] He tells us that traditional Margi society was "in theory, a closed system, recognizing birth as the only method of recruitment." Any outsider was an intruder into this social space and must remain an alien; but, equally, the insider who committed some capital crime offended the gods and his ancestors and in so doing broke society's invisible boundaries and made himself an alien.

The population of slaves among the Margi comprised both types of aliens, although the dominant representation of their social death was intrusive. The rich diversity of groups surrounding the Margi make them particularly aware of their social space. As Vaughan observes: "They are sensitive to a unifying 'Marginess'—largely consensual—that distinguishes them from the numerous other societies around them," and slaves are those who have breached "the boundaries of this closed system." The institution of slavery "bestows a rational—even utilitarian—place upon the anomaly of the permanent resident alien, by giving him an institutional marginality." Furthermore:

> The outstanding general characteristic of *mafakur* is that all *mafa*, without regard to political position, private influence, or wealth, hold in common a status that in structural terms is fundamentally and irrevocably intermediate with regard to membership in Margi society. But it is equally apparent that, despite their marginal status, their roles are fully integrated into society.[47]

Thus slavery involved two contradictory principles, marginality and integration, and Margi society reconciled this contradiction by "formalizing the marginality." Hence Vaughan calls the institution "limbic" (I prefer the more common anthropological term "liminal") "for its members exist in the hem of society, in a limbo, neither enfranchised Margi nor true aliens." But the Margi also enslaved local offenders, and these too were assimilated to the same limbic or liminal status of the institutionalized outsider. The criminal "remained in the society: a part of it, yet apart from it. He was not [physically] expelled, for that would be less humiliating. . . . Rather, it was the loss of identity and normality that was so objectionable to the proud Margi."

Institutionalized marginality, the liminal state of social death, was the ultimate cultural outcome of the loss of natality as well as honor and power. It was in this too that the master's authority rested. For it was he who in a godlike manner mediated between the socially dead and the socially alive. Without the master, as the Tuareg insist, the slave does not exist. The slave came to obey him not only out of fear, but out of the basic need to exist as a quasi-person, however marginal and vicarious that existence might be.

There were other gains to the master, as well as to the other members of the community, in the slave's liminality. The marginal person, while a threat to the moral and social order, was often also essential for its survival. In cultural terms the very anomaly of the slave emphasized what was most important and stable, what was least anomalous in the local culture of the nonslave population. This was particularly true of small-scale, highly integrated societies with little class division among the nonslave population.

Theda Perdue makes this point in her discussion of the precontact phase of Cherokee slavery. Before they adopted the institution of plantation slavery from the whites, the Cherokees kept slaves; but they contributed nothing to the economic, political, or social life of their warfare-oriented communities. Why then were slaves kept? Perdue's explanation is that the traditional belief system of the Cherokees rigidly categorized the social and physical universe. As with all systems of categorization, however, there were many anomalies that simply did not fit. The Cherokee way of handling such exceptions was to emphasize them, on the principle that it was precisely what stood at the margins that emphasized the boundaries. The slave acquired the same cultural significance among them as the bear—a four-footed animal, which nonetheless had the human habit of standing on its hind legs and grasping with its two front paws—or the *Uktena*, the mythical beast, "which had the body of a snake, the antlers of a deer and the wings of a bird." Similarly the *atsi nahsa'i*, or slaves, were utterly anomalous; they had the shape of human beings but had no human essence whatever, since humanness was defined in terms of belonging to a clan. The slave, in not belonging, emphasized the significance of belonging; in being clanless, emphasized the clan as the only basis of belonging; in being deviant, "helped establish and strengthen group identity among the Cherokees."[48]

We get a fascinating glimpse of the symbolic significance of the liminal slave in a more complex social system fraught with conflict in the Anglo-Saxon epic, *Beowulf*.[49] Beowulf's world was one riddled with internal feuding and external warfare. It was also a social order with a highly developed class system, in which an aristocratic warrior class lived off the surplus generated by its servants. Slavery and the slave trade were an integral part of this world. Indeed, literally the first event we come across in the prologue is a reference to the Danish hero Shild, who "made slaves of soldiers from every land, crowds of captives he'd beaten into terror."

In addition to social division there was a fundamental cleavage in the moral order of the world of Beowulf, between the old paganism and the newly acquired and not yet fully integrated Christianity. In the poem this is expressed in terms of the conflict between the forces of good and those of evil. This is not a tidy organic world; evil and conflict are ever present and recognized as such:

> The world,
> And its long days full of labor, brings good
> And evil: all who remain here meet both.[50]

The role of the slave in Beowulf's last and greatest battle is replete with symbolic meaning. First, it is significant that it was a runaway slave, beaten by his master, who in searching for a place to hide found "the hidden path" to the sleeping dragon, "awoke him from his darkness and dreams and brought terror to his [Beowulf's] people."[51] There is thus a forceful juxtaposition of the most pronounced social conflict (that between master and brutalized slave), with the most deep-seated moral conflict (that between Christianity and the lurking forces of evil and paganism, symbolized by the hidden "heathen treasure" and the dragon that protects it).

> So mankind's enemy, the mighty beast
> Slept in those stone walls for hundreds
>   of years: a runaway slave roused it,
> Stole a jeweled cup and bought
> His master's forgiveness, begged for mercy
> And was pardoned when his delighted lord took the present
> He bore, turned it in his hands and stared
> At the ancient carvings. The cup brought peace
> To a slave, pleased his master, but stirred
> A dragon's anger.[52]

Not only is there a symbolic association of social and moral conflict, but in the role of the slave as guide to the dragon's evil world we find one of the most remarkable statements of the slave's liminal status. It is significant that the slave was not counted among the twelve men who went to the dragon's den. And there might be some hint of his anomalous nature in the fact that he was the *thirteenth* person. It was precisely because he was marginal, neither human nor inhuman, neither man nor beast, neither dead nor alive, the enemy within who was neither member nor true alien, that the slave could lead Beowulf and his men across the deadly margin that separated the social order above from the terror and chaos of the underground, between good and evil, between the sacred world of the Christian and the profane world of the pagan.

A consideration of the important role of the slave's liminality brings us to an important feature of slavery that is often misunderstood. Although the slave is socially a nonperson and exists in a marginal state of social death, he is not an outcaste. The point must be emphasized in view of the easy use often made of the caste concept in interpreting American slavery and its postemancipation consequences.[53]

With the noteworthy exception of temple slaves, enslaved persons are never relegated to the status of an outcaste group, nor are they ever stratified as one of several castes in any of the societies that have a complex hierarchy of castes. Before explaining why, let us look at the nature of the relationship between caste and slavery.

The *Ethnographic Atlas* classifies the 186 societies of the Murdock World Sample with respect to "caste stratification." The four groupings are societies where:

(1) Caste distinctions of any kind are absent or insignificant.
(2) There are one or more despised occupational groupings (whether smiths or leather workers or whatever else), distinguished from the general population, regarded as outcastes, and characterized by strict endogamy.
(3) There is ethnic stratification in which a superordinate caste withholds privileges from and refuses to intermarry with a subordinate caste (or castes), which it stigmatizes as ethnically alien (for example, as descended from a conquered and culturally inferior indigenous population, from former slaves, or from foreign immigrants of different race and/or culture).
(4) Complex caste stratification exists, in which occupational differentiation emphasizes hereditary ascription and endogamy to the near exclusion of achievable class status.

The main advantage of this classification is that it takes account of both the narrow and the wide definitions of caste. Many scholars would hold that the term "caste" strictly applies only to societies in category (4), confined mainly to India and the related societies of Southeast Asia.[54] Others, who hold to the more general interpretation of the caste concept, would include societies in category (2) along with (4) as legitimate cases.[55] My own position is closer to the second, with the important qualification that for me caste additionally connotes some notion of ritual purity and pollution as a means of maintaining social distance. The existence of "hereditary endogamous groups" that are "socially differentiated by prescribed behavior" is a necessary but not sufficient criterion for defining castes, for this description is true of almost all class systems. In the light of this definition it is clear that I do not accept category (3) of the *Ethnographic Atlas* grouping as containing genuine caste systems, since ethnic differentiation need not be reinforced by notions of ritual purity and pollution.

With these observations in mind we can now examine the relationship between the presence or absence of slavery and types of caste stratification. This is reported in Table 2.1. The table is highly significant ($p = 0.002$), although there is no strong overall relationship. Most slavehold-

Table 2.1   The relation of slavery to caste stratification, as delineated by the Murdock *Ethnographic Atlas*.

Presence or absence of slavery	Type of society			
	Caste absent	Occupational groupings	Ethnic stratification	Complex caste differentiation
Slavery absent:				
Number	114	6	1	4
Percent	66.3	3.5	0.6	2.3
Slavery present:				
Number	33	10	2	2
Percent	19.2	5.8	1.2	1.2

NOTE: Chi square = 14.17, with three degrees of freedom. Significance = 0.0027.

ing societies, we see, do not have castes of any kind. Yet slavery is not incompatible with the existence of castes. There is a weak overall relationship with slavery as the dependent variable: the moderately strong association with occupational castes is balanced by a rather weak relation with complex caste systems.

More important is what is revealed by the ethnographic data on those societies which have both slavery and caste. In none of them (the rare cases of temple slavery excepted) were slaves either outcastes or segregated as distinct castes. Typical of slaveholding societies with occupational castes were the Margi, the Somali, and the Koreans. The rich historical and anthropological data on these societies indicate that slaves were held to be distinct from the caste groups in question.[56] There was never any marriage, or even illicit sexual relations, between the outcaste group and ordinary persons, whereas such relations were common between "free" males and slave women. It is typical of the boundary-crossing capacity of slaves that among the Somali they were the only persons who could have sexual relations and marry with both ordinary "free" Somalis and the outcaste Sab group. Furthermore, the outcaste groups could never lose their caste status, nor did they want to, while in all these societies slaves could be manumitted and become "free" persons. Third, the outcaste groups were usually segregated. The Korean paekchŏng, for example, had a high degree of internal autonomy, living in their own communities as an organized outcaste group. Slaves were never segregated simply because they were slaves. Fourth, the outcaste groups all had a monopoly of certain occupations in which they specialized; slaves were never confined to particular jobs. In all premodern societies they performed virtually the entire range of occupations, and even in modern capitalistic slave systems recent studies have indicated that the range of their occupations was much wider than previously thought.[57] Perhaps the most important difference is that while slaves may have been held in contempt, they were never avoided or feared because it was felt that they were polluting. The Sab of Somalia and the paekchŏng of Korea, however, were avoided for this reason.[58]

It is not difficult to understand why slaves were never assimilated to the status of outcastes. Slavery, we have seen, was primarily a relation of personal domination. There was an almost perverse intimacy in the bond resulting from the power the master claimed over his slave. The slave's only life was through and for his master. Clearly, any notion of ritual avoidance and spatial segregation would entail a lessening of this bond. Second, the assimilation of the slave to the status of an occupationally specialized caste would undermine one of his major advantages—the fact that he was a natally alienated person who could be employed in any capacity precisely because he had no claims of birth. Slaves universally were only sexually exploited in their role as concubines, but also in their role as mother-surrogates and nursemaids. However great the human capacity for contradiction, it has never been possible for any group of masters to suckle at their slave's breast as infants, sow their wild oats with her as adolescents, then turn around as adults and claim that she was polluted.

Indeed, the comparative data indicate that in societies with highly developed notions of ritual pollution one of the main reasons for keeping slaves was that they were nonpolluting and thus a major means of circumventing pollution norms. Among the Maori, for instance, every free person had *tapu*, a complex set of prohibitions that were the laws of the gods. Breaking these severely endangered the individual, since he lost his *mana* (power) and became vulnerable to supernatural forces. According to Elsdon Best:

> The shadow of *tapu* lay over the Maori from birth until death, his very bones and their resting place remained *tapu* for all time. The higher the rank of a person the more *tapu* was he. It is interesting to note that slaves were held to be free from *tapu* and yet no explanation is given as to their condition of welfare and their survival, why they did not perish in such a defenseless condition.[59]

They did not perish, we now know, because as natally alienated persons they were socially dead. "Even though he [the slave] had once been a chief in another tribe," Raymond Firth tells us, "his capture removed him from the *mana* of the gods and in things spiritual he ceased to count." In this liminal state he could cross boundaries prohibited to other persons and could perform the vital task of preparing the master's food, which if done by a mortal would result in certain spiritual and possible physical death.[60]

For much the same reasons we find in Nepal that slaves, while "politically the most debased section of Nepalese society," were nonetheless sometimes selected from the higher castes. "Indeed, in order to perform the various duties imposed on domestic servants, to be permitted to cross the threshold of an owner's dwelling, it was imperative for the slave to enjoy a degree of ritual purity conferred only by membership in certain castes." Paradoxically, even Brahmins were enslaved without losing caste.[61]

A consideration of the relation of slavery to caste leads us back to where we began: the liminality of the slave is not just a powerful agent of authority for the master, but an important route to the usefulness of the slave for both his master and the community at large. The essence of caste relations and notions of ritual pollution is that they demarcate impassable boundaries. The essence of slavery is that the slave, in his social death, lives on the margin between community and chaos, life and death, the sacred and the secular. Already dead, he lives outside the mana of the gods and can cross the boundaries with social and supernatural impunity.

The Rituals and Marks of Enslavement

Symbolic ideas are usually given social expression in ritualized patterns. Let us look now at the ritual aspects of the natal alienation of the slave. For all but the most advanced slave systems the acquisition of a slave is a very special event in the master's household. Even where slaves number as much as a quarter of the total household, their acquisition may be a once-in-a-lifetime event for the members, especially if the pattern of slaveholding is highly skewed. It was common for people in the premodern world to give ritual expression to special events and when one of those events involved the incorporation of a person defined as socially dead, it is easy to recognize that the event should not proceed without ceremony. The ritual of enslavement incorporated one or more of four basic features: first, the symbolic rejection by the slave of his past and his former kinsmen; second, a change of name; third, the imposition of some visible mark of servitude; and last, the assumption of a new status in the household or economic organization of the master.

Many cultures obliged the new slave to make a symbolic gesture of rejecting his natal community, kinsmen, ancestral spirits, and gods—or, where the slave was of local origin, of rejecting his own kin group and ancestral spirits in favor of those of his master. The ceremony was often simple and brief, but it was always deeply humiliating, sometimes even traumatic, for the slave.

Among the cannibalistic Tupinamba of South America we find slavery in its most primitive form. Most captives were eventually eaten, but in the many years between capture and execution the captives lived as the slaves of their captor and were usually well treated. Before they entered their captor's village the captives were stripped, dressed as Tupinamba, and decorated with feather ornaments. They were led to the graves of persons who had recently died and forced to "renew" or cleanse the bodies. The captives then performed a vital ritual function. They were given the weapons and other belongings of the deceased to be used for a time, after which they were handed over to the rightful heirs. "The reason for this," according to Alfred Métraux, "was that touching the belongings of a dead relative was fraught with dangers, unless they were first defiled by a captive."[62] Being socially dead, the captives were able to move between the living and the dead without suffering the supernatural harm inevitably experienced by the socially alive in such boundary crossing. After this ritual the prisoners were taken to the village, where their captivity was celebrated in song and dance, the captives themselves being forced to participate and "to dance in front of the hut where the sacred rattles were kept."[63]

Among the more complex Germanic peoples of early medieval Europe, the new slave of local origin placed his head under his master's arm and a collar or strap was placed around his neck.[64] We find a variant of this in late Anglo-Saxon England, where a man who through poverty was forced to sell himself into slavery had to place his head between his new master's hands; a billhook or an oxgoad was then given him to symbolize his new condition. This led to a special way of referring to enslavement, as when a Northumbrian mistress spoke of "all those people whose heads she took in return for their food in the evil days."[65] The expression gives a clue to the meaning of the ceremony; a man's head is associated with his mind and will and it is these, in addition to his labor, that the master takes.

If we look instead at traditional Africa, we find some interesting parallels and differences. The objective of the rituals was the same: to give symbolic expression to the slave's social death and new status. But the emphasis was less on personal and spiritual labor and more on the social use of the slave incorporated as a permanent marginal into a network of affiliation after a ritual break with his old kin ties and ancestral protectors. The Imbangala of northwestern Angola are typical.[66] All slaves, whether acquired from outside of Kasenje or within its boundaries, were considered alien to local lineages. In a special rite of passage the slave was first "cleansed" of his natal ties, by means of a medicine that denuded him of ancestral protection. Significantly, however, the medicine also eliminated any memory among the master's lineage of the slave's ancestry, so the very act of separation paved the way for the possible assimilation of the slave's descendants. This was followed by a dangerous purgatorical period in which the new slave was spiritually exposed, lacking the protection of both former and prospective ancestral spirits. Finally, the slave was incorporated (though not adopted) into the master's lineage via a naming ceremony in which he became an "alien dependent," protected once again, but without the full complement of names that was the birthright of every true member of the lineage.

The initiating ritual varied regionally, although its symbolic and practical objectives remained the same. Among the Kwanyama of southwestern Angola the rite was called *elyakeko*, which literally meant "to tread upon something." The captive was taken by the parents of the warrior to the whetstone kept in all Kwanyama houses:

> The father takes the stone and holds it in his hand, while his wife pours water over the whetstone, water which the father forces the prisoner to drink. After this has been done, the prisoner's master takes the stone and beats the victim on the top of the cranium with it, "to prevent him from having thoughts of escape." As the stone is motionless by nature, the Kwanyama believe the person so treated comes to possess the same quality.[67]

Similarly, among the Tiv of central Nigeria, "the purchaser and the man's agnates split a chicken which was held to sever the slave from his kin, thus making it impossible for him to run away, 'for he would have no place' to go."[68] Some African groups like the Aboh offered sacrifice to special shrines, and feasted;[69] others, such as the Ila, assigned the new slave "a spirit associated with a deceased member of the patrilineal group" and in a communal ritual the ancestors were informed of the newly affiliated slave and their protection was sought.[70] The length of time for full adjustment to their new status varied with the kind of slave: it was usually easier for women, but occasionally the path was smoother for men (as among the Ila). Whatever the variations, in all African traditional societies the new-comer, unless he was a "trade slave" destined for resale, was forced to deny his natal kin ties and acquire certain fictive kin bonds to the master and his family. The exact meaning of his new ties will be examined later.

The initiating ceremony served much the same purpose among kin-based societies in other parts of the world. Among the Kachin of highland Burma, for example, the shaved head of the new slave was rubbed with ashes from the master's hearth prior to his incorporation into the master's clan.[71] Shorn of the memory of his past, the slave received the ashes of his master's ancestral spirits. As a final example, we may take the Toradja of the central Celebes.[72] As soon as he was brought into his master's house, the slave was given a meal made of the same kind of food his master nor-mally ate, "so that his life spirit will be tranquil." The meal was usually served on the cover of a pot that was meant to help the slave forget his former attachments. Next, a little basket of rice, eggs, ubi, and coconut was prepared and was turned above the head of the slave seven times to the left and seven times to the right. The basket was then placed on the slave's head and the master invoked as follows: "You, so-and-so, wherever your life spirit may have gone, to your relatives left behind, here is rice which I give to you; eat it so that he may settle down on you and you may have a long life." The slave ate the contents, after which a priestess usu-ally came and invoked long life for the new slave. The symbolism here is self-evident and needs no commentary. Once again it involved the loss of independent social existence—of the slave's "life spirit"—the placating of the lost spirits and protection against them, and the incorporation of the slave into the marginal existence of the permanent alien.

In large-scale slave systems where the slave became a unit of produc-tion outside the household economy we do not, of course, find such elab-orate initiating rituals of enslavement. The newcomer was usually handed over to a trusted older slave to be taught the necessary skills to survive in his new environment. This is not to say, however, that ritual did not play a part even here. For we know that even in the brutal capitalistic slave plantations of the modern Caribbean, slaves had a rich ritual life and found their own ways of incorporating the new recruit.[73] The same was very possibly true of slaves on the latifundia of ancient Rome, given the rich and intense religious life of the slave population. But if the slave was not incorporated privately by his master, there was still the need to incor-porate him publicly, to give ritual expression to his presence as a large and significant, and potentially dangerous, element in the body politic. We shall see later that in such large-scale systems this task was performed by the state religion.

The second major feature of the ritual of enslavement involved the changing of the slave's name. A man's name is, of course, more than simply a way of calling him. It is the verbal signal of his whole identity, his being-in-the-world as a distinct person. It also establishes and advertises his relation with kinsmen. In a great many societies a person's name has magical qualities; new names are often received upon initiation into adulthood and into cults and secret societies, and the victim's name looms large in witchcraft and sorcery practiced against him. As Ernst Cassirer observed: "The notion that name and essence bear a necessary and internal relation to each other, that the name does not merely denote but actually *is* the essence of its object, that the potency of the real thing is contained in the name—that is one of the fundamental assumptions of the mythmaking consciousness itself."[74] Thus it is understandable that in every slave society one of the first acts of the master has been to change the name of his new slave. One must reject any simplistic explanation that this was simply a result of the master's need to find a name that was more familiar, for we find the same tendency to change names when slaves come from the identical society or language group as their masters.

There are several reasons for the change of name. The changing of a name is almost universally a symbolic act of stripping a person of his former identity (note, for example, the tendency among modern peoples to assign a new formal identification, usually a number, to both prisoners of war and domestic convicts). The slave's former name died with his former self. The significance of the new name, however, varied from one kind of slave culture to another. Among most kin-based societies the slave took the clan name of his new master. This was the first act in the creation of fictive kin ties. The situation was different, however, among that small group of kin-based societies where the slave was not incorporated into the household economy but was exploited separately, in a protocapitalist sector, and in most of the advanced premodern slave systems. Here the new name was often a badge of inferiority and contempt. Sometimes the names were either peculiarly or characteristically servile. A Greek name in republican Rome, for example, often indicated slave status or ancestry, and many traditionally Roman names eventually became favorite slave names, cognomens such as Faustus, Felix, Fortunatus, and Primus.[75] In Russia masters and slaves used the same names to a greater degree, which is understandable in the light of the local origins of most slaves: nonetheless, certain names such as Kondratii and Matrona became typical slave names.[76] In other societies such as China, those of the ancient Near East and pharaonic Egypt, the absence of family names was the surest mark of slavery.[77] Much more humiliating, however, were those cases in which insult was added to injury by giving the slave a name that was ridiculous or even obscene. Among the Duala of the Cameroon, slaves were given such names as "Irritation"; and among the Aboh of Nigeria, there were names like "Bluebeard" and "Downcast."[78] The Nootka of the northwest coast of America, the Icelanders, and the Kachin of highland Burma are all typical of peoples who took special delight in giving to female slaves names that demeaned both their status and their sex.[79]

Much the same pattern existed in the Americas, where the assignation and use of names was an important focus of conflict between masters and slaves. In the U.S. South slaves were sometimes whipped for using the forenames of important whites. The pompous classical names preferred by many planters were resented by most slaves, except when they were reminiscent of African names. Slaves usually changed their surnames after manumission, although sometimes, for purposes of protection, they kept the names of their ex-masters if they were important persons. Apparently many slaves selected their own surnames, which they used among themselves.[80] In doing so they often took the names (or "entitles" as they called them) of distant ancestors or former masters, in a direct symbolic rejection of their present master. Herbert G. Gutman insists that most slaves had surnames, and that the choice of a different name involved, on the one hand, a rejection of the "intimacy" of the ties of paternalism claimed by the master and, on the other hand, "served to shape a social identity independent of slave ownership."[81] This has become a highly contentious subject, one that has generated more heat than the points at issue merit. My own reading of the literature, including slave narratives and interviews, suggests that while there were many variations both within and between regions, most slave surnames in the United States were those of the owners and changed with a change of owner. Nor can the fact that slaves had no legal claim to surnames be dismissed as irrelevant "legalism" any more than can the fact that they had no legal claim to their own persons or labor.

The situation in Latin America was similiar to that uncovered in South Carolina by Peter Wood: the masters chose the names, but during the colonial period often selected African names; later the African names were replaced by Spanish ones. Thus in Colombia:

> The Spanish usually retained the *bozales'* African tribal names, or their place of origin in Africa, as the blacks' surnames. Second-

generation slaves might retain this African surname but usually either had no surnames, took the surnames of their masters, or were designated *criollos* (born in America).[82]

A census taken in Colombia in 1759 showed that almost 40 percent of the slaves had only one name; 30 percent had the surname Criollo, and the remainder had African tribal or regional surnames such as Mina, Congo, Mandingo, and Caraba. Blacks "were more likely to assume their owners' surnames following manumission than while they remained in captivity."[83]

Much the same pattern existed in other parts of Latin America. In Mexico, for example:

> All African slaves . . . were given a first name and were identified by that name. The names most commonly used included Juan, Antón, Francisco, Diego, Sebastian, and Hernando for males, and Maria, Isabel, Magdalena, Ana, and Catalina for females. Some slaves had a last name as well (usually that of the master)—slaves who were given only a first name were often identified by the addition of their tribal or their national origin. . . . Other slaves, such as Juan Viejo (old man) and Juan Tuerto (one-eyed), had a nickname appended to the first name.[84]

The pattern of naming in the Caribbean also was very similar to that of Spanish America and colonial South Carolina. In Jamaica, African day-names and tribal names were either selected in their pure form or adapted as English names. During the nineteenth century these African names acquired pejorative meanings: Quashee, a day-name that originally meant "Sunday" in Akan, came to signify a stupid, lazy slave; and Cudjo, which was the Akan day-name for "Monday," came to mean a drunkard.[85] Even a change to purely English or Creole names did not involve any lessening of degradation: slaves were given either classical names such as Phoebe and Cyrus, or insulting nicknames. On Worthy Park estate, for example, they had such names as Beauty, Carefree, Monkey, Villain, and Strumpet. These names were certainly imposed on the slaves by their masters or overseers, for as Craton notes: "To a significant degree, all these single slave names were distressingly similar to those of the estate's cattle, so that it is almost possible to confuse one list with another in the Worthy Park ledgers."[86] Toward the end of the eighteenth century an increasing number of slaves acquired a surname and usually at the same time changed their forename. This was permitted after baptism and may well have been one of the major incentives for Christianization in Jamaica. Whatever the reason, by the time of abolition most slaves had two names, usually English, with the surname being that of respected whites on the plantation or in the area.[87] Where children acquired surnames, these were rarely given before their tenth year "and very often these names reflect those of the whites on the estates (even when they were not the fathers)."[88]

Finally there were the French Antilles. While naming practices there were similar in broad outline to those in the British Caribbean, there were a few noteworthy variations.[89] Slaves were given a new name on the slave ships during the passage from Africa, yet among themselves they used their African names. A few days after arriving on the plantation each slave was given a nickname, which became his official name and was the one used by the planters. Apparently slaves continued among themselves to use other names as their Christian names, with the planters' names becoming their surnames. This tendency was much greater among males than females, the women for the most part using the single name given by their masters.

The slaves had a third name, acquired after baptism—usually that of a saint. This name was rarely used by the slaves themselves and almost never by the masters. Its main role was to indicate baptismal status.

As for the names themselves, French masters too used names of classical figures and names from literature. The blacks themselves apparently preferred names from the military lexicon such as Alerte, Jolicoeur, Sanssouci, and Fanfaron. The nicknames or second names given by the masters referred either to some physical characteristic of the slave (Longs-Bras, Conquerico, Torticolis, Hautes-Fesses) or to their area of origin (Fantu, Mina, Senegal). In some instances the African day-name was used, as in the British Caribbean and colonial South Carolina, but the masters, being French, insisted on a translation, so that the slaves were called Mercredi, Vendredi, and so on.

There was the same tendency in the French Antilles for African first names to be replaced by Creole names with the passing of the eighteenth century. The slaves late in that century had more opportunities to choose their names because of the much higher proportion of absentee owners and the rapid turnover of overseers. When they had a choice, they almost never selected the names of their owners: instead they used the names of ancestors who had belonged to another master, or an area of Africa, or colonial heroes and theatrical and literary figures known to be abolitionists, or—most commonly—of saints.

The slave's name was only one of the badges of slavery. In every slave-holding society we find visible marks of servitude, some pointed, some more subtle. Where the slave was of a different race or color, this fact tended to become associated with slave status—and not only in the Americas. A black skin in almost all the Islamic societies, including parts of the Sudan, was and still is associated with slavery. True, there were white slaves; true, it was possible to be black and free, even of high status—but this did not mean that blackness was not associated with slavery.[90] Perceived racial differences between masters and slaves could be found in a significant number of other societies ranging from the Ethiopians, the Bemba, and even the Lozis of Africa, to the Gilyaks and Lolos of eastern Asia.

Another way slaves were identified was by the ornaments they were either obliged or forbidden to wear. Usually a special kind of clothing was specified among peoples like the Ashanti and Chinese, and among peoples such as the Ibos as well, certain forms of jewelry were forbidden. Tlingit slave women could not wear the lip plug favored by free women. Obvious racial distinctions made it unnecessary to enforce clothing prohibitions on the slaves of the Americas and other areas of the modern world, although there were such rules in some areas.[91] The Greeks did not require their slaves to wear special clothes, but apparently (as in America) the slaves' style of dress immediately revealed their status.[92] Rome is fascinating in this regard. The slave population blended easily into the larger proletariat, and the high rate of manumission meant that ethnicity was useless as a means of identifying slaves. A ready means of identification seemed desirable, however, and a special form of dress for slaves was contemplated. When someone pointed out that the proposal, if carried out, would lead slaves immediately to recognize their numerical strength, the idea was abandoned.[93]

The presence of tattoos also identified slaves. They were universal in the ancient Near East, although apparently removable.[94] Surprisingly few societies in the premodern world branded slaves and when they did, as in China, Hellenistic Egypt (where it was eventually forbidden by law), and Rome, only incorrigible runaways were marked. In late medieval and early modern Europe, however, branding of galley and other public slaves was the norm. In France, from the middle of the sixteenth century, persons condemned to galley slavery were first publicly whipped and then the letters GAL were burned into their shoulders. Between 1810 and 1832, when branding was abolished, all public slaves (especially those sent to the Bagnes) were branded with the letters TP (Travaux perpétuels).[95] The branding of public slaves was not abolished in Russia until 1863. The *kátorshniki* were branded in a particularly grisly manner: the letters KAT were punctured on their cheeks and forehead, and gunpowder was rubbed into the wounds.[96]

Throughout the Americas slaves were routinely branded as a form of identification right up to the second half of the eighteenth century. Thereafter, although branding became mainly a form of punishment used on runaways and insubordinate slaves, it did not disappear as a means of identification, even in the United States. As late as 1848 a Kentuckian master identified a runaway female slave by announcing that she was branded "on the breast something like L blotched."[97] And South Carolina not only allowed branding until 1833, but mutilated slave felons by cropping their ears.[98] Branding as a customary form of identification only began to decline in the Caribbean during the last decades of the eighteenth century under abolitionist and missionary pressure. The LP mark with which slaves were branded on their shoulders in Worthy Park during the eighteenth century is still used today as a means of identifying the estate's cattle.[99]

Latin America showed much the same pattern, except that branding of runaways as a form of identification continued until well into the nineteenth century and may even have increased in Cuba during the expansive years at the middle of the century. Occasionally the branding of slaves backfired. In the Minas Gerais area of Brazil, runaway slaves who formed *quilombos*, or Maroon communities, were branded F on their shoulders if and when recaptured. Among the slaves themselves, however, the F brand became "a badge of honor rather than of infamy," and recaptured slaves proudly displayed it to their more cautious but admiring fellow sufferers. When the masters learned of this they replaced branding with a more gruesome form of punishment: the Achilles tendon on one foot was severed.[100]

Sometimes it was the absence of marks that identified slaves, as among the Yorubas who forbade slaves to scar themselves with Yoruba tribal marks; at other times it was the presence of such tribal marks that immediately betrayed the slaves, as among the Ashanti, who did not tattoo themselves like the many neighboring peoples they captured and enslaved. And one could always tell a Mende slave woman by the fact that her hands were not black with dye, since only nonslave women had the leisure and prerogative to dye cloth.[101]

There is one form of identification that deserves special attention, since it is found in the great majority of slaveholding societies: this is the shorn or partly shorn head. In Africa we find the shorn head associated with slaves among peoples as varied as the Ila and the Somali. In China, in highland Burma, among the primitive Germanic peoples, the nineteenth-century Russians, the Indians of the northwest coast, and several of the South American and Caribbean tribes, the heads of slaves were shorn (in the ancient Near East so was the pubic hair of female slaves). In India and pharaonic Egypt slaves wore their hair shorn except for a pigtail dangling from the crown. The Mossi of West Africa were unusual in that the head of the slave was periodically shaved by the master considering selling him, and the practice strongly influenced his final decision on the matter. According to A. A. Dim Delobsom: "Depending on where the hair starts to grow, whether well back on the head, at the forehead, or near the ears, the interpretation varies as to how the slave is to be regarded: as a dangerous being; as a lucky or unlucky influence on the family owning him."[102] Numerous other examples could be cited. The shaving of the slave's head was clearly a highly significant symbolic act. Of all the parts of the body, hair has the most mystical associations.[103] On the private or individual level, there is hardly a culture in which hair is not, for males, a symbol of power, manliness, freedom, and even rebellion; and for women, the crowning expression of feminine beauty. The shorn head is, conversely, symbolic of castration—loss of manliness, power, and "freedom." Even in modern societies we tend to shave the head of prisoners, although the deep symbolic meaning is usually camouflaged with overt hygienic explanations.

On the public or social level, the shorn head in premodern societies usually signified something more: it was a common symbol of transition, especially in the case of mourning the dead. The association between death, slavery, and the shorn head was made explicit for us by the Callinago Caribs of the Lesser Antilles, many of whom were wiped out by the Spaniards soon after their conquest of the islands. Raymond Breton, who visited them in the middle of the seventeenth century, wrote as follows:

> The women cut their hair upon the death of their husbands, and husbands cut their hair upon the death of their wives. The children cut their hair upon the death of their father or mother. The hair is cut for the period of a year. *The slaves have their hair cut all the time and are never allowed to let it grow. They have their hair cut to the neck which means that they are in mourning* (emphasis added).[104]

It is not unreasonable to conclude that the shorn head of the slave was one aspect of a stark symbolic statement: the man who was enslaved was in a permanent condition of liminality and must forever mourn his own social death.

How then do we explain the absence of the shorn head in the large-scale slave systems of the Americas? The answer, I feel, is highly revealing of the symbolic role of hair not only in slave relations but in race relations as well. First, there is the obvious fact that the masters were white and the slaves black—a somatic difference that obviated the need for the more common badges of slavery. Contrary to the common view, it was not so much color differences as differences in hair type that become critical as a mark of service in the Americas.

Color, despite its initially dramatic impact, is in fact a rather weak basis of ranked differences in interracial societies.[105] There are several reasons. For one thing, the range of color differences among whites and among blacks is greater than is normally thought. Dark Europeans, especially Latins, are not far removed from many Africans who come from areas other than the classic West African "jet-black" zone. The differences diminish even more when we take into account the permanent suntan acquired by most whites working in the tropics. Furthermore, the color differences are quickly blurred by miscegenation, which diminishes the significance of color much faster than is usually imagined. Very soon, therefore, in all slave societies of the Americas, there were numbers of slaves who were in fact lighter than many European masters: the probability that the mulatto slave offspring of an African mother and a very blond Cornish or Irish father was lighter than the average dark Welsh overseer was significantly above zero. Within a couple of generations the symbolic role of color as a distinctive badge of slavery had been greatly muted—though, of course, not eliminated.

Variations in hair were another matter. Differences between whites and blacks were sharper in this quality than in color and persisted for much longer with miscegenation. Hair type rapidly became the real symbolic badge of slavery, although like many powerful symbols it was disguised, in this case by the linguistic device of using the term "black," which nominally threw the emphasis to color. No one who has grown up in a multiracial society, however, is unaware of the fact that hair difference is what carries the real symbolic potency.[106] In the Americas, then, blacks' hair was not shorn because, very much like the Ashanti situation where the slaves came with a readymade badge (their tribal taboos), leaving the hair as it was served as a powerful badge of status. Shaving it would have muted the distinction.

Significantly, in those mixed-blood slaves where the hair type was European, we find a reversion to the premodern tendency of resentment of the slave's long hair on the part of the masters, not to mention excessive pride on the part of the slave. A telling instance of this comes from nineteenth-century Barbados. In 1835 the governor issued an order to the effect that all slaves convicted of crimes "shall have their hair cut off, and their heads washed, for the better promotion of cleanliness." This was a new practice, coming less than four years before the complete abolition of slavery. The governor, following European practice, no doubt introduced the order for genuinely hygienic purposes. However, it provided masters and, more frequently, mistresses with a golden opportunity to put "uppity" mixed female slaves in their place—as we learn from a September 1836 entry in the journal of John Colthurst, special magistrate of Barbados:

> Speaking of the practice of shaving the heads of apprentices, a young quadroon woman who had conducted herself very improperly to her mistress was brought up about a fortnight before my arrival in the island, and convicted by my predecessor of insubordination, and sentenced to labour on the tread mill for fourteen days, and her head (as a matter of course) to be shaved. This was accordingly done, and on the expiration of her punishment, she was sent home to her mistress, in all respects tamed and amenable, until she found she was laughed at by her fellow servants for the loss of her hair which, like all others of her particular complexion, is usually extremely beautiful, and of wavy and glossy black, and in the utmost profusion and great length. To replace her hair, she purchased false curls, and exhibited a beautiful front. Ere long, however, the circumstance of the original shaving of her head, and which she of course laid all to her mistress' account, created another quarrel, for which she was again brought up before me, in full curl. The charge was proven and another punishment was the consequence—solitary confinement for six days. If this woman's head had not been shaved in the first instance, it is clear there would not have been any necessity of a second application to the Special Magistrate. Therefore my objection to punishments of degrading nature, for it appeared in evidence upon this trial that whenever she put her hand to her head, after her return home from her first punishment, and found it bald, she flew into a rage, and swore she would be revenged.[107]

No doubt the female slaves of ancient Mesopotamia must have flown into similar though silent and repressed rages when they felt their shorn pubic hair, as did the male slaves of all the premodern slaveholding systems when they felt their bald or half-shorn heads. In the Americas the master class thought it achieved the same objective by making African hair the badge of servility. With mixed-race mulatto slaves they may well have succeeded; but with those who retained their African features the degree of symbolic success was questionable. As the shrewd magistrate Colthurst commented: "The negro laments over the loss of his lamb's wool much more than any fashionable young man in England would, having lost the most exquisite crop of hair in the world."[108] Unfortunately it was the mulattoes who were to define the symbolic meaning of hair in postemancipation and modern Caribbean societies. But that is another story.[109]

Fictive Kinship

I have several times referred to the practice of incorporating the slave as a fictive kinsman of his master in kin-based societies, and even in many of the more complex premodern systems. It is time to clarify exactly what this means. On the surface the relationship appears to be a straightforward adoption. All over the world we find the master being addressed as "father" and the slave as "son" or "daughter," and in matrilineal societies we find the term for the social father being used (that is, the term for "mother's brother," while slaves are referred to by the master as "sister's son"). This fictive kin relation extends also to other members of the master's family.

It would be a great mistake, however, to confuse these fictive kin ties with the claims and obligations of real kinship or with those involving genuine adoption. Some anthropologists are rather careless about making this distinction.[110] Relations, we are told, are always warm and intimate; it is difficult to detect any difference between the "adopted" slave and other young members of the family. No wonder some interpreters have concluded that slavery does not exist in these traditional societies, or that the traditional patterns of servitude are best called something else.

In order to avoid confusion it is best that we distinguish between two kinds of fictive kinship, what I shall call adoptive and, following Meyer Fortes, "quasi-filial."[111] Fictive kin ties that are adoptive involve genuine assimilation by the adopted person of all the claims, privileges, powers, and obligations of the status he or she has been ascribed. Fictive kin ties that are quasi-filial are essentially expressive: they use the language of kinship as a means of expressing an authority relation between master and slave, and a state of loyalty to the kinsmen of the master. In no slaveholding society, not even the most primitive, is there not a careful distinction drawn between the genuinely adopted outsider (who by virtue of this act immediately ceases to be an outsider) and the quasi-filial slave (who is nonetheless encouraged to use fictive kin expressions in addressing the master and other members of his family).

Thus among the pre-European Cherokees, for instance, a captive who was not tortured and put to death was either adopted or enslaved and there was no confusion on the matter. Persons adopted were "accorded the same privileges . . . as . . . those whose membership derived from birth."[112] Of the Tallensi slaves of West Africa, Fortes wrote: "Homeless and kinless, they must be endowed with a new social personality and given a definite place in the community. But the bond of actual paternity cannot be fabricated; the fiction is a makeshift and always remains so."[113]

At best, the slave was either viewed as an illegitimate quasi-kinsman or as a permanent minor who never grew up. He might be "of the lineage," but as the Imbangala of Angola illustrate, he was never *in* it.[114] Among the Ashanti, children of slaves remained slaves "forever" in spite of the adoption of the master's clan name, and while such children were preferred for political purposes (and well treated), their slave origins were never forgotten. They were laughed at in private, and people referred to them as having a "left-handed" clan affiliation. Old family slaves who became too familiar were put in their place, as several Ashanti proverbs indicate. For example: "If you play with your dog, you must expect it to lick your mouth."[115]

The Imuhag group of Tuaregs is instructive in this respect. We find here the standard pattern of fictive kin assimilation and the slave's adoption of the master's clan name. However, a slave's status as a fictive daughter did not get in the way of the master's taking her as his concubine or even his wife. Furthermore, the social distance between free and slave was great, in spite of the fictive kin bond. Masters in general distrusted their slaves, both male and female.[116] Female slaves were frequently accused of witchcraft, and we know from the anthropological psychology of witchcraft that such accusations invariably reflect an underlying fear and distrust of the accused.[117]

Even where there was considerable intermarriage between slave and free, in this way replacing fictive kinship with real, the assimilation of the slave was still not assured. As Polly Hill points out, the assimilation of *gandu* slaves (those on special slave farms) into the Nigerian Hausa society "was probably quite limited owing to the breakup of most *gandu* estates by the time the grandsons had reached marriageable age, if not before."[118]

One of the problems with many anthropological accounts of slavery in kin-based societies is that the emphasis on the structural aspects of social life often leads to a neglect of the purely human dimension. This is a serious drawback when it comes to understanding the real meaning of slavery, especially for slaves. Precisely because economic and class differences between masters and slaves were often not marked, the interpersonal and psychological dimensions of powerlessness became all the more important. It was deeply humiliating to be a slave in a kin-based society, and the indignity was no less because unaccompanied by class differentiation. Indeed, it may have hurt a good deal more. The latifundia slave could at least explain his degradation in terms of the economic parasitism and exploitation of his master. The slave in the kin-based society had no such external explanations. His degradation sprang from something presumably innate to his very being. And the degradation heaped upon him came in little ways, sometimes minor, sometimes cutting, but with the cumulative effect of a piranha assault.

Occasionally an anthropologist gives us a rare glimpse of this aspect of exploitation in a kin-based society. In his fine study of the Cubeo Indians of the northwestern Amazon, Irving Goldman records the following incident in the life of a servant girl who had been "adopted":

> The little girl, about nine, was addressed as "daughter" but held the status in the household of a servant. She took on the heaviest chores and was almost never free to play. Her lowly status was truly stigmatized by her lack of possessions. She was the only child among the Cubeo whom I have ever seen unadorned. . . . The children in the household enjoyed beating her as a way of teasing her, rather than wickedly. She took their pinchings and cuffings good-naturedly, on the whole, and had learned to pretend not to notice. Once, in the presence of the headman, her "father," the children were overdoing their teasing. She looked imploringly at the headman. Finally, she caught his eye and he said to her, "It is all right for you to run away." He saw no need to reprimand his own children.[119]

The distinction between adoptive and quasi-filial kinship helps us to understand why it is that even in the highly capitalistic slave systems of the Americas it was still possible to find the master-slave relationship expressed in "kinship" terms. Indeed, quasi-filial kinship became embroiled in the ongoing covert struggle for authority and dignity between masters and slaves, and it was often difficult to distinguish between genuine expression of affection, sheer duplicity, and psychological manipulation.

Two examples will illustrate. In the U.S. South the masters encouraged children to see them as the "Big Pappy," always benevolent, kind, and indulgent. Strict discipline was left to, and expected from, the slave child's parents. The slave children grew up making unfavorable comparisons between real parental authority and the quasi-filial paternalism of the master. The resulting erosion of the paternal bond was, of course, reinforced by the mortifying subjection of the slave parents to punishment before their children. As Genovese concludes: "If the tendency to worship the master and scorn the parents did not take a greater toll than it apparently did, the credit belongs to the slave parents, whose love for their children went a long way toward offsetting the ravages inherent in this scenario."[120]

We find quite a different scenario in Jamaica. In the absence of a cohesive master-class culture, relations between masters and slaves either lacked authority or were on the verge of losing it. Slaves, even here, employed quasi-filial kin terms, but often in sardonic ways, with their aggressive intent only lightly veiled. When the popular gothic novelist Monk Lewis, an absentee slave owner from England, toured his plantations in the early nineteenth century, he was overwhelmed by the reception from the slaves:

> In particular, the women called me by every name they could think of. "My son! my love! my husband! my father! You no me massa, you my tat" [father], said one old woman.[121]

Lewis might have been temporarily overwhelmed, but he was hardly deceived, as he later noted. Nor were any but the most naive of the masters who were so addressed. The use of quasi-filial kin terms not as an expression of loyalty or of subordination, but as a thinly disguised form of sarcasm signaled the failure of authority in this most brutal of slave systems.

Religion and Symbolism

The social death of the slave and his peculiar mode of reincarnation on the margin of his master's society was reinforced by the religious institutions of kin-based societies. As we have seen, the slave was usually forced to reject his own gods and ancestral spirits and to worship those of his master. Even so, he was frequently excluded from community-wide ritual practices: while it was all right for him to worship his master's ancestral spirits, he was not allowed to participate in cults that were associated with political power and office.

Among more advanced slaveholding systems religion played an even greater role in the ritual process of incorporating the slave to his marginal status. Most ritual activities became the specialized preserve of religious institutions. And in both its structural and ritual aspects religion reflected the more centralized nature of political power.[122] In the same way that the state had to develop a specialized set of laws to deal with the secular problems of the slave, so the state cult needed to develop a more specialized set of rules and beliefs to represent the condition of slavery.

Religion never played the important role in the development of Greek slavery that it did among the Roman, Islamic, or many Christian peoples. The practice of having the slave worship at the Greek family hearth continued well into the classical period. This hardly met the religious needs of the slaves any more than it would have sufficed for their masters. But slaves again were largely excluded from the extrahousehold religious cults of their masters. What is more, restraints were placed on their attempts to develop their own cults. The religious isolation and confinement of their slaves hardly bothered the Greek masters, for they did not care for any form of incorporation of slaves into the Greek community. Franz Bömer, one of the leading authorities on the religious lives of slaves in antiquity, tells us:

> The fact is that Greek slaves, and not only those from Delphi but from everywhere . . . wander like creatures who are dumb, like human bodies without face or profile, without individuality or self-consciousness, and most important, without a noticeable expression of any religious life, be it collective or personal. . . . The slaves of the Greeks are diametrically opposed to the religious wealth and vivaciousness of the slaves in Rome, who, in fact, could even convince foreign slaves to forget the gods of their native lands and accept Roman ways. Roman religion was stronger in the world of the little man.[123]

The contrast may be a little overdrawn, but the basic point is certainly correct. Roman slaves had more freedom in every part of their lives than Greek slaves. The Greek *polis* was an ethnically exclusive unit, whereas Rome was, from relatively early on, an ethnically and politically open system. It was not just slaves who were excluded from the Greek community, but all foreigners.

There were three respects, however, in which Greek religion aided in the adjustment of the slave to his social death. Along with women, slaves were allowed to participate in the state cult of Eleusis. The second important representation of slavery in Greek religion was the saturnalia-type festivals associated with a variety of cults. During these festivities (the oldest being the Cronia ritual) there was a reversal of roles in which slaves ate, drank, and played with their masters.[124] The late British anthropologist Max Gluckman has suggested that such rites of reversal both vented feelings of tension in conflict-ridden relationships and reaffirmed the rightness of the established order: "The acceptance of the established order as right and good, and even sacred, seems to allow unbridled license, even rituals of rebellion, for the order itself keeps this rebellion within bounds. Hence to act the conflicts, whether directly or by inversion or in other symbolical forms, emphasizes the social cohesion within which the conflicts exist."[125] It may be speculated that these rituals of reversal involved not just a means of releasing the tension inherent in the master-slave relationship, and thereby maintaining order, but emphasized the social death of the slave and his total alienation from Greek life. By playing the master, the slave came to realize, however fleetingly, what it was really like to be not just a free man, but more, a truly free man—that is to say, a Greek. When the playing was over and the roles were reversed to normal, the slave would know then with the sinking feeling of the morning after that socially and politically he was dead. The master, in his turn, learned from the role reversal not compassion for his slave, but the bliss it was to be free and Greek. The Cronia, then, was really a death and resurrection ritual: for the master, it was an affirmation of the life principle and freedom; for the slave, it was a confirmation of his living death, powerlessness, and degradation.

The third, perhaps most important, way in which Greek religion related to the condition of slavery was by sacred manumission. I am concerned here only with the role of religion in its legitimization. Sacred manumission was the technique of selling the slave to a god who, by not exercising his proprietary powers, allowed the slave to behave like a free man. The interesting thing about this practice is how secular it actually was. Religion was brought in as a means of legitimizing the manumission transaction only where formal legal mechanisms were absent. Where (as in Athens) legal mechanisms existed, we find no trace of sacred manumission. Bömer demolishes the traditional view that Apollo was a defender of slaves and the great symbol of Greek humanity. The idea of finding freedom in servitude to a god remained alien to Greek thought. The slave who was sold to Apollo was not given his freedom by the god; he merely acquired a de facto freedom by virtue of the fact that the god did not exercise his proprietary powers. This was a neat way of solving the problem created by the naturalistic theory of slavery. If the slave was by nature fit for nothing else, how could he become free? If he was socially dead, how could he be made socially alive? It was not possible. Thus selling the slave to a god salvaged the idea of his slaveness and the permanence of his servile status. Apollo was no defender of slaves, no oasis of universal humanity in the desert of Greek chauvinistic tyranny; on the contrary, he was the ideological salvation of the most inhuman product of the Greek mind—the Aristotelian notion of innate slavishness. Bömer's brilliant exposure of this false pretender to the sacred throne of humanism deserves to be quoted at length:

> The light that surrounded Apollo was cold and hard, and this coldness and hardness characterized his essence. He was no "divine friend of man" who could console the unlucky, the wounded and the homeless. These people found help later from Asclepius and Sarapis, and often consciously turned away from Apollo. This ruthless aspect, not the humane one, of the Delphic god revealed itself simultaneously in the enslavement of small groups . . . and in the Delphic form of sacral manumission.[126]

A fascinating aspect of Apollo is the fact that this god, who became the very embodiment of the "Hellenic Spirit," was of non-Greek origin. This has intrigued and puzzled students of Greek religion, especially the fact that the god was in all likelihood of barbaric, Asiatic origins. The main support for the Asiatic origin of Apollo, W.K.C. Guthrie tells us, is "the fact that at most of his great cult-centers in the mainland of Greece he appears as an intruder."[127] That the most Greek of Greek gods should be of barbaric origin offers ample room for speculation; equally tantalizing is the thought that there may be some connection between the intruder status of this god in the realm of the supernatural and the significance of his social role in the life of the vast number of intrusive slaves who were so essential to the socioeconomic fabric of Greek civilization.

Rome was different, and the slaves' religious life a great deal better. Not that Roman masters were any less cruel; they may have been even more brutal. Rather, Rome had a culture that was far more inclusive, with institutions that were incomparably more flexible, and in no area more so than religion. In primitive Rome and even as late as midrepublic times, slaves participated in the religion of the household, especially in the Lares cult. Originally the head of the cult was the paterfamilias. But as the latifundia replaced the household farm, the master withdrew from this role. By Cato's day the slave villicus or overseer directed the cult. With urbanization and the further growth of the latifundia, toward the end of the republic the Lares cult became increasingly attractive to slaves and freedmen.[128] The saturnalia and matronalia (festivals in honor of Mars and Hera originally celebrated by married women) were also important ritual supports for the slaveholding system from early times, the former quite possibly influenced by Greek traditions.[129]

As the gesellschaft principle of social organization replaced the gemeinschaft principle in Roman life, ritual specialization increased further. The slave-oriented cults, however, could only initiate the new slaves into the slave sector. There remained the urgent need to incorporate the slave and still more, his descendants, into the wider community. Several kinds of religious organizations were adapted to meet both the specific ritual needs of the slaves and the wider superstructural problem of somehow representing the slave system in supernatural terms.

There were, first, the interclass cults. In Jupiter, Juno, and especially Silvanus, we find originally Roman deities who were associated by the slaves with eastern counterparts with which they were more familiar. Many of the cults were of foreign origin—a good number of them brought to Rome by the slaves themselves. Most notable was Mithras, famous for the rapidity with which it attained popularity and the equality of master and slave in the performance of ritual practices.[130]

In the institution of the collegia, which constituted the organizational aspect of worship, the slave found not only a church but "a social club, a craft guild, and a funeral society";[131] and in holding one of the many offices, he or she experienced some vicarious sense of importance. The names of some of these colleges are very revealing. In the light of what we have said about slavery as a state of social death, it is not unreasonable to suppose that when the members of one college called themselves "comrades in death," they were referring not solely to their coming physical death.[132]

Finally, there was the role religion played in relating the slave and slavery to the wider sociopolitical order. Here it was the state cults that were critical. According to Bömer, during the republican era Jupiter Libertas had a special appeal to slaves because of the association of the god with freedom, but the evidence is slender and controversial.[133] Of much greater interest was the phenomenon of emperor worship and the extraordinary role of the slaves and ex-slaves in the imperial cults. The earliest of these, the Augustan Lares, was in fact a revival of the dying Lares cult to which the emperor added his own imprint. Keith Hopkins argues that this cult had been started by ex-slaves, Augustus simply institutionalizing the informal local celebrations into a state cult devoted partly to his worship.

"The cult provided rich ex-slaves, as organizers of the cult, with a prestigious and public outlet for social display. And it allowed emperor worship to flourish at street level."[134] It was not long, however, before emperor worship was accepted at all levels of society. It was a major legitimizing force among slaves for the simple reason that the emperor's cult introduced into Roman law the alien principle of asylum for slaves. The granting of the right of appeal to Caesar's statue was one of the few ways in which the state intervened between master and slave. The state was, of course, sensitive to this intrusion on the authority of the master, and in practice very few slaves attempted such an appeal. But in enhancing the authority of the emperor in the eyes of all, including even the meanest of slaves, the legitimacy of the system as a whole was reinforced. What the master lost in individual authority, the slave system as a whole gained, embodied as it was in the divine protective power of the deified emperor.[135] Still, as Moses Finley has pointed out: "In so one-sided a relationship, in a world in which there was little hope of material success for the majority of the free population (let alone the slaves), and in which the earthly power was now pretty close to despotism, fear rather than love was often the dominating emotion behind worship, at best fear and love together. Religion became increasingly centered on salvation in the next world, whereas it had once been chiefly concerned with life in this one."[136]

Among the religions of salvation, Christianity was to emerge slowly, then dramatically, over the next three hundred years as the religion par excellence, one that could forge a moral order which appealed to and united emperor and subject, master and slave.[137] A discussion of the means by which it achieved this is beyond the scope of the present work. It is generally accepted that Christianity found many of its earliest converts among the slave populations of the Roman Empire, although the fact is surprisingly difficult to authenticate.[138] What is certain, however, is that the slave experience was a major source of the metaphors that informed the symbolic structure of Christianity.[139]

The most cursory examination of "the three terms which are the keywords" of the Apostle Paul's theology (according to J. G. Davies) immediately reveals the extraordinary role of the slave experience as a metaphoric source. These key words are redemption, justification, and reconciliation.[140] Redemption quite literally means release from enslavement. Through Christ the believer is emancipated from sin. Justification means that the believer has been judged and found not guilty, in much the same manner as the slave who has received the most perfect of manumissions, the restoration of his natality with the legal fiction that he had been wrongfully enslaved. "Reconciliation or Atonement means the bringing together of those who have been separated," in much the same way that the manumitted slave is reborn as a member of a community. Paul in fact went so far as to use the idea of adoption to describe the relationship between redeemed man and God. "Redeemed, justified, reconciled, man is elevated from the status of slave to that of son, and becomes 'an heir through God' of the promised salvation."[141]

What Ambrosio Donini calls "the myth of salvation" became the unifying master concept of organized Christianity, and it is most powerfully evoked in the dominant symbol of the religion, that of the death and resurrection of Christ.[142] Man fell into spiritual slavery because of his original sin. Slavery, which on the level of secular symbolism was social death, became on the level of sacred symbolism spiritual death. When, however, we question what Christ's crucifixion meant, we find two fundamentally different symbolic interpretations. One explanation, which has profoundly conservative spiritual and social implications, held that Christ saved his followers by paying with his own life for the sin that led to their spiritual enslavement. The sinner, strictly speaking, was not emancipated, but died anew in Christ, who became his new master. Spiritual freedom was divine enslavement. Here was a confluence of two old ideas: the Near Eastern and Delphic notion of freedom through sale to a god, and the Judaic idea of the suffering servant and sacrificial lamb. It was not a very tidy symbolic statement, and it accounts in part for the occasional impenetrability of Paul's theology. He had this interpretation in mind, for example, when he made remarks such as the following: "The death that he died, he died unto sin once: but the life that he liveth, he liveth unto God."[143]

There was a far more satisfactory and at the same time more liberating symbolic interpretation of the crucifixion. The slave, it will be recalled, was someone who by choosing physical life had given up his freedom. Although he could, of course, have kept his freedom and died, man lacked the courage to make such a choice. Jesus, "his savior," by his death made this choice for him. It is this feature that was completely new in the religious behavior and death of Jesus. What it meant in symbolic terms was that Jesus did not redeem mankind by making mankind his slave in the manner of the old pagan religions. Rather, he annulled the condition of slavery in which man existed by returning to the original point of enslavement and, on behalf of the sinner about to fall, gave his own life so that the sinner might live and be free.

It is remarkable that Paul held also to this radically different interpretation of the crucifixion. The contradiction was directly paralleled by the well-known ethical contradiction of his theology. As Maurice Goguel has pointed out, Paul had two irreconcilable religious ethics.[144] One was the pre-Christian and essentially Judaic ethic of law and judgment, in which obedience to divine law, and judgment according to one's social and religious actions, were of the essence. The other was the ethic of the justified man. In this ethic Christ's death redeemed mankind of the burden of sin; the believer, through faith, was immediately emancipated. The first ethic corresponded to the conservative use of the slave metaphor; the second to the more liberal conception of slavery and emancipation. Paul tried to hold both these positions at the same time and thereby placed the believer, as Goguel points out, in the impossible position of one "who must struggle to realize in fact what he is in principle."[145] And he asks: "How can we now speak of a judgment for those who are in Christ, and therefore cannot be subject to condemnation?"[146]

The answer was to abandon the liberal view of emancipation and to canonize the essentially pre-Christian interpretation of salvation as reenslavement to a god, in the triumph of the conception of the believer as the slave of God and of Christianity as a theological transmutation of the order of slavery. Whatever other factors explain Christianity's conquest of the Roman world, there seems little doubt that the extraordinary way in which its dominant symbolic statements and meanings are informed by the experience of slavery was a major contributing factor. For the same reason too, Christianity was to provide institutional support and religious authority for the advanced slave systems of medieval Europe and of the modern Americas.

Christianity was not alone among the major world religions in legitimizing slavery. Earlier we noted the contradiction in Islam between the rationalization of slavery as a means of converting the unbeliever and the continuing enslavement of the converted. We find the same contradiction in Judaism and Christianity. The slave, in the city of the Christian God, was declared an insider, an integral part of the brotherhood of man in the service of God; but the slave, in the city of man, remained the archetypical outsider, the eternal enemy within, in a formalized state of marginality.

At first sight the contradiction is not obvious. Indeed, the opposite seems to be the case: the exclusion of the slave on the secular level was symbolically compensated for by his inclusion in the sacred community. The contradiction between marginality and integration, which slavery created, was apparently resolved by relegating each to a separate domain of cultural existence. But this theological solution on the part of a monotheistic slaveholder class works only where there is hegemonic imposition of a rigid dualism in the socioreligious ideology. This was exactly what happened in medieval Christendom under the conservative spell of Saint Augustine.[147] But Judaism and Islam were too this-worldly and too strongly monistic for such an interpretation to be taken seriously.[148] And the rise of Protestantism dealt a death blow to the neat symbolic compromise of the Middle Ages. Augustinian dualism lingered in the symbolic representation of Latin American slavery: hence the apparent anomaly that has baffled so many Anglo-American historians, that of a Catholic church stoutly declaring slavery a sin, yet condoning the institution to the point where it was itself among the largest of slaveholders.[149]

The Anglican masters of the Caribbean avoided the problem altogether by abandoning religion or making a mockery of it, both for themselves and for their slaves—clergymen in nineteenth-century Jamaica being "the most finished debauchers in the land."[150] As Richard S. Dunn has pointed out, the refusal of the English planters in the West Indies to convert their slaves to Christianity, in contrast with contemporary Latin masters, "can largely be explained by Protestant versus Catholic conversion techniques."[151] Protestantism by its very nature demanded the liberating conception of the crucifixion, with its emphasis on personal choice and freedom. Realizing this, the West Indian masters did everything possible to keep their slaves in ignorance of their creed—giving in only when, a few decades prior to abolition, they found their policy to be too easy a target in the propaganda war of the abolitionists.

How then do we account for the Protestant slave South where, during the late eighteenth and the nineteenth centuries, both masters and slaves were highly religious? It is clear that the special version of Protestantism that triumphed in the South and the peculiar socioeconomic features of the system together explain its unusual course of development.

Until nearly the end of the eighteenth century the U.S. South did not differ markedly from other Protestant slave systems. Masters were generally hostile to the conversion of their slaves, fearing—like their Caribbean counterparts—that the nature of their creed with its emphasis on instruction in the gospels, personal choice, and spiritual liberation would, if adopted by their slaves, undermine the masters' authority. As late as 1782 slaves in Georgia were still being whipped savagely for preaching,[152] and while Albert Raboteau may have overstated the case in claiming that "the majority of slaves . . . remained only minimally touched by Christianity by the second decade of the nineteenth century," he was not far wrong.[153]

Two major developments explain the remarkable change that took place during the nineteenth century. One was the great religious awakening that culminated in the religious conversion of the South from classical Protestantism to revivalist fundamentalism.[154] The second was the emergence in the South between 1790 and 1830 of a full-fledged slave system, a total commitment to the institution as an essential feature of the region's socioeconomic order, and the realization that if slavery was to function effectively the system had to be reformed. In Genovese's words, "whereas previously many slaveholders had feared slaves with religion, now they feared slaves without religion even more. They came to see Christianity primarily as a means of social control. . . . The religious history of the period formed part of the great thrust to reform slavery as a way of life and to make it bearable for slaves."[155]

Fundamentalist Protestantism was peculiarly suited to such a reform. Its emphasis on conversion as a sudden spiritual transformation rather than the result of reflection and instruction; its oral rather than literary missionary techniques; its other-worldliness, especially its insistence on salvation as a purely spiritual change, the rewards of which are to be achieved in the hereafter; its emphasis on piety and obedience, and on the sinfulness of the world and the flesh; made it a creed that the masters could confidently regard as a support for, rather than a subversion of, their authority.[156]

Nevertheless, it would be simplistic to interpret the role of religion in the slave South solely in terms of an opiate for the masses, a device used by the master class as an agent of social control. In the final analysis it was indeed just that, and there is abundant evidence that the master class cynically devised a "theology of slavery" in a crude attempt to rationalize the system. But as recent studies have shown, slaves quickly recognized the crude ideological strategy of their masters. Olli Alho's detailed analyses of the slave narratives "indicate that the carefully constructed theology of slavery built up by the whites became in many plantations nothing more than a joke" among the slaves.[157]

The slaves found in fundamentalist Christianity paths to the satisfaction of their own needs, creating the strong commitment to Christianity that has persisted to this day. In so doing they created an institutional base that provided release and relief from the agonies of thralldom, and even offered some room for a sense of dignity before God and before each other. Having said all this, I must emphasize that the religion they experienced was the same as that of their masters in all its essential doctrinal and cultic aspects; that while the spirituals they sang may have had a double meaning with secular implications, it is grossly distorting of the historical facts to claim that they were covertly revolutionary in their intent; and, most important of all, it is irresponsible to deny that however well religion may have served the slaves, in the final analysis it did entail a form of accommodation to the system.

In all of this I am in complete agreement with Genovese's penetrating interpretation of the role of religion in the slave South.[158] Where I differ from him, and from others such as Lawrence W. Levine[159] and Albert J. Raboteau who with equal skill and persuasion have emphasized the creative and positive side of religion for the slave, is in my interpretation of the specific means by which fundamentalist Christianity became at one and the same time a spiritual and social salvation for the slaves and an institutional support for the order of slavery.

To appreciate where we differ it is necessary to return to the nature of Christianity and to specify the peculiar doctrinal features of fundamentalism. Pauline Christianity, as we saw, was theologically dualistic, containing an ethic of judgment and an ethic of the justified person that were in constant tension with each other. These two ethics in turn were symbolically expressed in two contrasting interpretations of Jesus' crucifixion. Roman Catholicism resolved the tension by eliminating what I call the liberating pole of Pauline dualism, emphasizing the ethic of judgment and obedience; classic Protestantism resolved it by eliminating the conservative pole and by strongly reviving the ethic of the justified person.

What then is distinctive in fundamentalism? My answer is that it restored *both* poles and returned fully to Pauline dualism with all its contained tension and its contextual shifting from one ethical and symbolic pole to the other. If we do not understand this distinctive doctrinal feature of fundamentalism, we cannot fully appreciate how the religion could have spiritually sustained both slaves and masters as well as the system as a whole. We will also fail to comprehend the symbolic life of the slaves themselves.

If we next seek the major doctrinal and symbolic components of slave religion, we find that the fundamentalism of the slaves was, like that of all southerners, essentially Pauline in its overwhelming preoccupation with Christ and the crucifixion and in its ethical and symbolic dualism, its paradoxical tension between the ethic of judgment and the ethic of the redeemed sinner. Further, it is precisely this dualism that explains the apparent paradox that the religion of the slaves, doctrinally one with that of their masters, nonetheless allowed for the spiritual support of both groups and of the system as a whole.

Jesus and his crucifixion dominate the theology of the slaves and not, as recent scholars have claimed, the Israelites and Exodus story.[160] Not only is the theme of the crucified Christ explicitly central and dominant, but even when figures from the Old Testament are referred to (including Moses), closer examination reveals that the allusion is really to Jesus. Although Alho does not make the connection to Pauline theology, it is striking that his most important finding concerns the dualistic conception of Jesus in the religion of the slaves—that of Jesus as Messiah King and Jesus as comforting savior. He concludes his interpretation with a reference to an insightful contemporary observer: "The difference between the two main identities of Jesus reminds one of what T. W. Higginson wrote in his camp diary about the religious behavior of his black soldiers; softness, patience, and meekness on the one hand, hardness, energy, and daring on the other, seems to be reflected in the dualistic way in which the spirituals picture the figure and roles of Jesus."[161]

We can now explain how fundamentalism, a single religion, performed the contradictory roles it did in the slave South. Both masters and slaves adhered to Pauline ethical dualism, with its sustained "eschatological dissonance."[162] And in exactly the same way that Paul and the early Christians shifted from one pole of their doctrinal dualism to another as occasion and context demanded, so did the masters and their slaves. Thus the masters, among themselves, could find both spiritual and personal dignity and salvation in the ethic of the justified and redeemed sinner. The crucified Jesus as redeemer and liberator from enslavement to sin supported a proud, free group of people with a highly developed sense of their own dignity and worth. Similarly, the slaves in the silence of their souls and among themselves *with their own preachers,* could find salvation and dignity in this same interpretation of the crucified Lord. When the theologian Olin P. Moyd insists that "redemption is the root and core motif of black theology" and that it means essentially liberation from sin and confederation within the fellowship of black worshippers, it is, I suspect, to this end of the Pauline dualism that he is referring.[163]

As with the masters, the slave dualism had another pole. This is the ethic of law, judgment, and obedience, the ethic that found symbolic expression in the other Jesus, the more Judaic Messiah King who judges, who demands obedience, and who punishes the wicked and rewards the righteous. This is the Jesus who saves not by annulling slavery but by divine enslavement. To live with this Jesus demands, as Goguel tells us, watchfulness, obedience, and stoic acceptance.

Both masters and slaves held also to this conception of Jesus and, like Paul and the early Christians, shifted to this symbolic code in dealing with, and coming to terms with, all authority relations—not only the one between master and slave but, among the masters between male and female, upper class and working class, parent and child, and among the slaves between parent and child. In this way fundamentalism, by reverting to Pauline dualism, provided the slave South with the perfect creed, one much more subtle in its support for the system than most of the masters thought. The crude theology of slavery that the masters tried unsuccessfully to preach in the plantation mission was really quite unnecessary. Nor was it necessary for master and slave to have two separate religions. Christianity, after Paul, had already constructed an extraordinarily shrewd creed with a built-in flexibility that made it possible for emperor and slave to worship the same god without threatening the system, but also without denying all dignity to the oppressed.

In the U.S. South there developed the last and most perfectly articulated slave culture since the fall of the Roman Empire. The religion that had begun in and was fashioned by the Roman slave order was to play the identical role eighteen hundred years later in the slave system that was to be Rome's closest cultural counterpart in the modern world. History did not repeat itself; it merely lingered.

Notes

1. *Thucydides on the Nature of Power* (Cambridge, Mass.: Harvard University Press, 1970), pp. 153–154.
2. *The Republic*, 9:578 in Benjamin Jowett, ed. and trans., *The Dialogues of Plato* (New York: Random House, 1937), vol. 1, pp. 836–837.
3. Siegfried Lauffer, "Die Sklaverei in der griechisch-römischen Welt," in *Rapports* II, Eleventh International Congress of Historical Sciences, Stockholm, August 21–28, 1960 (Uppsala: Almquist and Wiksell, 1960), p. 76.
4. Max Weber, *Basic Concepts in Sociology*, trans. H. P. Secher (Secaucus, N.J.: Citadel Press, 1972), pp. 81–83. For a detailed analysis of Weber's use of this concept see Reinhardt Bendix, *Max Weber: An Intellectual Portrait* (London: Methuen & Co., 1966), pt. 3.
5. G.B.J. Hughes, *Jurisprudence* (London: Butterworth & Co., 1955), pp. 161–166. Hans Kelsen states the issue bluntly: "Law is a coercive order." "The Pure Theory of Law," in M. P. Golding, ed., *The Nature of Law* (New York: Random House, 1966), p. 112.
6. After criticizing Weber, Fortes points to the role "played by ceremony and ritual in the confirmation of status." Drawing on the seminal work of Everett Hughes, he notes that all statuses require a "mandate from society" (Hughes's term) and adds that "ritual mobilizes incontrovertible authority behind the granting of office and status and this guarantees its legitimacy and imposes accountability for its proper exercise." "Ritual and Office in Tribal Society," in Max Gluckman, ed., *Essays on the Ritual of Social Relations* (Manchester: Manchester University Press, 1962), p. 86.
7. *The Rites of Passage*, trans. M. B. Vizdeom and G. L. Caffee (London: Routledge & Kegan Paul, 1960). For a critical assessment of this work see Max Gluckman, "Les rites de passage," in Gluckman, *Essays on the Ritual of Social Relations*, pp. 1–52.

8. Victor Turner, *The Forest of Symbols* (Ithaca, N.Y.: Cornell University Press, 1967), pp. 30–32, esp. chap. 4. For a more general and theoretical statement see his "Symbolic Studies," *Annual Review of Anthropology* 4 (1975): 145–161.

9. Claude Meillassoux, *L'esclavage en Afrique précoloniale* (Paris: François Maspero, 1975), esp. pp. 11–26.

10. Ibid., pp. 20–21.

11. See Henri Lévy-Bruhl, "Théorie de l'esclavage," in M. I. Finley, ed., *Slavery in Classical Antiquity* (Cambridge: W. Heffer and Sons, 1960), pp. 151–169.

12. Iris Origo, "'The Domestic Enemy': The Eastern Slaves in Tuscany in the Fourteenth and Fifteenth Centuries," *Speculum* 30 (1955): 321–366.

13. See Mircea Eliade, *The Sacred and the Profane* (New York: Harvest Books, 1959), pp. 20–65.

14. *Bella Coola Indians* (Toronto: University of Toronto Press, 1948), vol. 1, p. 159.

15. *The Religious System and Culture of Nias, Indonesia* (The Hague: Uitgeverij Excelsior, 1959), p. 45.

16. *Slavery among the Indians of North America* (Moscow: U.S.S.R. Academy of Sciences, 1941), p. 80.

17. On Ashanti, see Robert S. Rattray, *Ashanti Law and Constitution* (Oxford: Clarendon Press, 1929), p. 29. On Ur see Bernard J. Siegel, *Slavery during the Third Dynasty of Ur,* Memoirs of the American Anthropological Association, no. 66 (1947), pp. 1–54. Siegel, after examining the available data, asserts, "We can thus conclude that the earliest notion of 'slave' was incorporated with the idea of 'foreigner,'" pp. 8–9. This linguistic usage persisted even when the vast majority of slaves were recruited from impoverished families. On the sources of slaves see pp. 9–27.

18. On the words used for "slaves" and their sources see William L. Westermann, *The Slave Systems of Greek and Roman Antiquity* (Philadelphia: American Philosophical Society, 1955), pp. 5–12. Also M. I. Finley, "Was Greek Civilization Based on Slavery?" in Finley, *Slavery in Classical Antiquity*, p. 146.

19. P.R.C. Weaver, "Vicarius and Vicarianus in the Familia Caesaris," *Journal of Roman Studies* 54 (1964): 118.

20. W. W. Buckland, *The Roman Law of Slavery* (Cambridge: Cambridge University Press, 1908), pp. 291–312.

21. See Peter P. Spranger, *Historische Untersuchungen zu den Sklavenfiguren des Plautus und Terenz* (Wiesbaden: Akademie Mainz, 1961), p. 65.

22. Lev. 25:44–46.

23. Maimonides, *The Code: Book Twelve, The Book of Acquisition*, ed. Isaac Klein (New Haven: Yale University Press, 1951), p. 809, and on the laws concerning heathen slaves, pp. 264–282.

24. See Maurice Keen, *The Laws of War in the Late Middle Ages* (London: Routledge & Kegan Paul, 1965), p. 137; and David Brion Davis, *The Problem of Slavery in Western Culture* (Ithaca, N.Y.: Cornell University Press, 1966), pp. 48, 100–101.

25. Robert Roberts, *The Social Laws of the Qorân* (London: Williams & Norgate, 1925), p. 54.

26. Ali Abd Elwahed, *Contribution à une théorie sociologique de l'esclavage* (Paris: Mechelinck, 1931), pp. 139, 166–167.

27. "Slavery and Emancipation in Two Societies," in M. G. Smith, ed., *The Plural Society in the British West Indies* (Berkeley: University of California Press, 1965), pp. 116–161.

28. "Conceptions of Slavery in the Nineteenth Century Sokoto Caliphate," paper presented at the Conference on the Ideology of Slavery in Africa, York University, Toronto, April 3–4, 1980.

29. Virginia Gutierrez de Pineda, *Organización social en la Guajira* (Bogota: Instituto Etnologico Nacional, 1950): 112.

30. Carlos Bosch Garcia, *La esclavitud prehispánica entre los Aztecas* (Mexico City: Colegio de Mexico, Centro de Estudios Históricos, 1944), p. 22.

31. *Slavery in Pharaonic Egypt* (Cairo: L'Institut français d'archéologie orientale, 1952), chap. 2.

32. Helmut Wiesdorf, *Bergleute und Hüttenmänner im Altertum bis zum Ausgang der römischen Republik: Ihre wirtschaftliche, soziale, und juristische Lage* (Berlin: Akademie-Verlag, 1952), p. 63.

33. E. G. Pulleyblank, "The Origins and Nature of Chattel Slavery in China," *Journal of the Economic and Social History of the Orient* 1 (1958): 204–211.

34. On Korea during the Koryŏ period, the major study in English is Ellen S. Unruh, "Slavery in Medieval Korea" (Ph.D. diss., Columbia University, 1978). Two useful general histories that deal with slavery during this period are Han Woo-Keun, *History of Korea* (Seoul: Eul-Yoo Publishing Co., 1970); and Takashi Hatada, *A History of Korea* (Santa Barbara, Calif.: ABC-Clio Press, 1969). On the Yi dynasty the major relevant studies in English are Susan S. Shin, "Land Tenure and the Agrarian Economy in Yi Dynasty Korea: 1600–1800" (Ph.D. diss., Harvard University, 1973); John Somerville, "Success and Failure in Eighteenth Century Ulsan: A Study in Social Mobility" (Ph.D. diss., Harvard University, 1974); and Edward W. Wagner, "Social Stratification in Seventeenth-Century Korea: Some Observations from a 1663 Seoul Census Register," in *Occasional Papers on Korea* 1 (1974): 36–54. Other works, including several in Korean (translated for the author) are cited in later references.

    On Russian slavery the most important work in English is that of Richard Hellie, *Slavery in Russia, 1450–1725* (Chicago: University of Chicago Press, 1984); see also his "Recent Soviet Historiography on Medieval and Early Modern Russian Slavery," *Russian Review* 35 (1976): 1–32. Of special interest are two other works: George Vernadsky, "Three Notes on the Social History of Kievan Russia," *Slavonic Review* 22 (1944): 81–92; and (although it is based entirely on secondary sources) J. Thorsten Sellin, *Slavery and the Penal System* (New York: Elsevier, 1976).

35. Cited in Herbert Passin, "The Paekchŏng of Korea," *Monumenta Nipponica* 12 (1956–1957): 31.

36. In addition to the works by Shin and Wagner cited above see Susan S. Shin, "The Social Structure of Kŭmhwa County in the Late Seventeenth Century," in *Occasional Papers on Korea* 1 (1914): 9–35.

37. Vernadsky, "Three Notes," pp. 81–82.

38. Ibid., pp. 88–92.

39. Sellin, *Slavery and the Penal System*, p. 121.

40. Hellie, *Slavery in Russia*, msp. XI-10.

41. Ibid., msp. X1–9.

42. Ibid., pp. X1-10–XI-11.

43. I draw heavily on several works in making these assertions, particularly Sellin, *Slavery and the Penal System*, and Michael R. Weissen, *Crime and Punishment in Early Modern Europe* (Sussex: Harvester Press, 1979). Sellin's work is itself largely an elaboration of

the thesis that "the demands of the labor market shaped the penal system and determined its transformation over the years, more or less unaffected by theories of punishment in vogue." This thesis had been developed in two earlier works, those of Georg Rusche and Otto Kirchheimer, *Punishment and Social Structure* (New York: Columbia University Press, 1939); and Gustav Radbruch, "Den Ursprung des Strafrechts aus dem Stande den Unfreien," reprinted in *Elegantiae juris criminalis* (Easel: Verlag für Recht und Gesellschaft, 1950). See also Sidney W. Mintz, "The Dignity of Honest Toil: A Review Article," *Comparative Studies in Society and History* 21 (1979): 558–566.

44. Cited in Sellin, *Slavery and the Penal System*, p. 41.

45. Not all contemporary penal reformers attempted to disguise the fact that the punishment they were calling for as a replacement for the death penalty was slavery, pure and simple. Thus the Milanese noble and penal reformer Cesare Beccaria in his influential tract, *Of Crime and Punishments*, stated bluntly that the alternative to the death penalty that he was advocating was "slavery for life." See Sellin, *Slavery and the Penal System*, pp. 65–69.

46. "Mafakur: A Limbic Institution of the Margi," in Suzanne Miers and Igor I. Kopytoff, eds., *Slavery in Africa* (Madison: University of Wisconsin Press, 1977), pp. 85–102.

47. Ibid., p. 100.

48. Theda Perdue, *Slavery and the Evolution of Cherokee Society, 1540–1866* (Knoxville: University of Tennessee Press, 1917), pp. 3–18.

49. Burton Raffel, ed. and trans., *Beowulf* (New York: New American Library, 1963). All citations are from this edition.

50. Ibid., lines 1060–62.

51. Ibid., lines 2210–11.

52. Ibid., lines 2279–87.

53. For the classic statement see John Dollard, *Caste and Class in a Southern Town* (New Haven: Yale University Press, 1937).

54. For one of the best statements of this view see Edmund R. Leach, *Aspects of Castes in South India, Ceylon, and North-West Pakistan* (Cambridge: Cambridge University Press, 1960).

55. Typical of this approach is James H. Vaughan who, "following anthropological usage," defines caste as "a hereditary endogamous group who are socially differentiated by prescribed behavior." See his "Caste Systems in the Western Sudan," in Arthur Tuden and Leonard Plotnicov, eds., *Social Stratification in Africa* (New York: Free Press, 1970), pp. 59–92. See also in the same volume Jacques Maquet, "Rwanda Castes," pp. 93–124.

56. On the Margi see Vaughan's two previously cited papers: "Mafakur: A Limbic Institution of the Margi," and "Caste Systems in the Western Sudan"; on the Somali see Enrico Cerulli, "Il diritto consuetudinario della Somalia settentrionale (Migiurtini)," *Somalia, scritti vari editi ed inediti* 2 (1959): 1–74. On Korea see Passin, "The Paekchŏng of Korea."

57. See Robert S. Starobin, *Industrial Slavery in the Old South* (New York: Oxford University Press, 1970); Claudia Dale Goldin, "The Economics of Urban Slavery, 1820–1860" (Ph.D. diss., University of Chicago, 1972); and Stanley L. Engerman, "A Reconsideration of Southern Economic Growth, 1770–1860," in *Agricultural History* 49 (1975): 343–361. On Jamaica see Barry Higman, *Slave Population and Economy in Jamaica, 1807–1834* (Cambridge: Cambridge University Press, 1976), chaps. 2–4, 10.

58. While the vast majority of outcaste groups were despised, a few were not, among them the *enkyagu* of the Margi.

59. *The Maori*, Memoirs of the Polynesian Society, no. 5 (1924), p. 251.

60. Raymond Firth, *Primitive Economics of the New Zealand Maori* (Wellington, N.Z.: R. E. Owen, Government Printer, 1959), p. 214.

61. Lionel Caplan, "Power and Status in South Asian Slavery," in James L. Watson, ed., *Asian and African Systems of Slavery* (Oxford: Basil Blackwell, 1980), pp. 177–180.

62. "The Tupinamba," in Julian H. Steward, ed., *Handbook of the South American Indians* (Washington, D.C.: Government Printing Office, 1948), vol. 3, p. 120.

63. Ibid.

64. A. M. Wergeland, *Slavery in Germanic Society during the Middle Ages* (Chicago: University of Chicago Press, 1916), p. 16.

65. H.R.P. Finberg, *The Agrarian History of England and Wales* (Cambridge: Cambridge University Press, 1972), p. 507.

66. J. C. Miller, "Imbangala Lineage Slavery," in Miens and Kopytoff, *Slavery in Africa*, pp. 205–233.

67. Carlos Estermann, *The Ethnography of Southwestern Angola* (New York: Africana Publishing Co., 1976), pp. 128–129.

68. Laura Bohannan and Paul Bohannan, *The Tiv of Central Nigeria* (London: Ethnographic Survey of Africa, 1953), pt. 8, pp. 45–46.

69. K. Nwachukwu-Ogedengbe, "Slavery in Nineteenth Century Aboh (Nigeria)," in Miers and Kopytoff, *Slavery in Africa*, p. 141.

70. Arthur Tuden, "Slavery and Social Stratification among the Ila of Central Africa," in Tuden and Plotnicov, *Social Stratification in Africa*, p. 52.

71. Edmund R. Leach, *Political Systems of Highland Burma* (London: Bell, 1954), p. 304.

72. N. Adriani and Albert C. Kruyt, *De Bare'e Sprekende Toradjas van Midden-Celebes* [The Bare'e-speaking Toradja of Central Celebes] (Amsterdam: Nood-Hollandsche Uitgevers Maatschappij, 1951), vol. 2, p. 142.

73. On Jamaica see Orlando Patterson, *The Sociology of Slavery: Jamaica, 1655–1838* (Rutherford, N.J.: Fairleigh Dickinson University Press, 1969), chap. 6. On the U.S. South see Eugene D. Genovese, *Roll, Jordan, Roll* (New York: Pantheon, 1974), esp. bk. 2. See also the detailed discussion of the slaves' cultural life in Charles W. Joyner, "Slave Folklife on the Waccaman Neck: Antebellum Black Culture in the South Carolina Low Country" (Ph.D. diss., University of Pennsylvania, 1977), chap. 3.

74. *Language and Myth* (New York: Dover Publications, 1953), p. 3.

75. There were, however, many peculiarly servile names, the best-known being perhaps "Rufio." This and other names suggest the national origins of the slaves, but as Gordon, Solin, and others have pointed out, it is dangerous to draw conclusions about the ethnic origins of Roman slaves on the basis of the available distribution of ethnic names. Slaves were often named for the place of purchase, which tells us nothing about their origin—a good case in point being the common slave name "Corinthus." Greek or hellenized names were often taken for cultural reasons. In an exceptional case a captive was allowed to keep his original name, the most famous example being Spartacus. Whatever the new name, the overwhelming tendency was for the slave's master or superior to select it. Principally for this reason slave names "do not often take the form of nicknames derived from physical characteristics." See Mary L. Gordon, "The Nationality of Slaves under the Early Roman Empire," in Finley, *Slavery in Classical Antiquity*, pp. 171–211; Lily Ross Taylor, "Freedman and Freeborn in the Epitaphs of Imperial Rome," *American Journal of Philology* 82 (1961): 113–132; and, more recently, Heikki

Solin, *Beiträge zur Kenntnis den griechischen Personennamen in Rom* (Helsinki: Societas Scientiarum Fennica, 1971).

76. Hellie, *Slavery in Russia*, mspp. XI-19–XI-27.

77. On the ancient Near East see Isaac Mendelsohn, *Slavery in the Ancient Near East* (Oxford: Oxford University Press, 1949), p. 31; on China see Pulleyblank, "The Origins and Nature of Chattel Slavery in China," p. 217; on Egypt see Bakir, *Slavery in Pharaonic Egypt*, pp. 103–107, 114.

78. Ralph A. Austen, "Slavery among the Coastal Middlemen: The Duala of the Cameroon," in Miens and Kopytoff, *Slavery in Africa*, p. 312. See also K. Nwachukwu-Ogedengbe, "Slavery in Nineteenth Century Aboh (Nigeria)," in the same volume, p. 140.

79. Edward Sapin and Morris Swadesh, *Native Accounts of Nootka Ethnography* (Bloomington: Indiana University Research Center in Anthropology, Folklore, and Linguistics, 1955), p. 177. When a Nootka slave escaped or was ransomed, a potlatch was given for him and he was assigned a new name. Carl O. Williams, *Thraldom in Ancient Iceland* (Chicago: University of Chicago Press, 1937), pp. 35–36.

80. Genovese, *Roll, Jordan, Roll*, pp. 443–450. See also Newbell N. Puckett, "American Negro Names," *Journal of Negro History* 23 (1938): 35–48. On the significance of name-changing upon emancipation see Ira Berlin, *Slaves without Masters* (New York: Vintage Books, 1976), pp. 51–52. On the struggle to retain African names in colonial South Carolina, the linguistic compromises worked out between masters and slaves (especially in the use of African day-names), and the ultimate disappearance of African names with the Americanization of the slave population see Peter H. Wood, *Black Majority: Negroes in Colonial South Carolina* (New York: Alfred A. Knopf, 1974), pp. 181–186. For an enslaved African's account of his reactions with each new master see Olaudah Equiano, *The Interesting Narrative of the Life of Olauda Equiano, or Gustavus Vasa, The African, Written by Himself* (Norwich, England: Printed and Sold by the Author, 1794), pp. 62, 87.

81. *The Black Family in Slavery and Freedom* (New York: Pantheon, 1976), pp. 230–256.

82. William F. Sharp, *Slavery on the Spanish Frontier: The Colombian Chocó, 1680–1810* (Norman: University of Oklahoma Press, 1976), p. 114.

83. Ibid., pp. 114–115.

84. Colin A. Palmer, *Slaves of the White God; Blacks in Mexico, 1570–1650* (Cambridge, Mass.: Harvard University Press, 1976), p. 39.

85. David De Camp, "African Day-Names in Jamaica," *Language* 43 (1967): 139–149. See also Patterson, *The Sociology of Slavery*, pp. 174–181.

86. Michael Craton, *Searching for the Invisible Man: Slaves and Plantation Life in Jamaica* (Cambridge, Mass.: Harvard University Press, 1978), p. 157.

87. Ibid., p. 158.

88. Higman, *Slave Population and Economy in Jamaica*, p. 173.

89. My discussion here of the French Antilles relies heavily on Gabriel Debien, *Les esclaves aux Antilles françaises, XVIIe–XVIIIe siècles* (Basse-Terre, Fort-de-France: Société d'histoire de la Guadeloupe et Société d'histoire de la Martinique, 1974), pp. 71–73.

90. See Bernard Lewis, "The African Diaspora and the Civilization of Islam," in Martin L. Kilson and Robert I. Rotberg, eds., *The African Diaspora* (Cambridge, Mass.: Harvard University Press, 1976), pp. 37–56.

91. During the eighteenth century the South Carolina masters attempted to regulate slave

clothing by law, but the attempt was abandoned because of a lack of interest of the masters in its enforcement. For a detailed discussion of the limited symbolic role of costume in the slave culture of South Carolina see Joyner, "Slave Folklife," pp. 206–219. Joyner found no evidence to support Genovese's claim that slaves preferred the color red. Over time the rough cotton "osnaburgs" became identified as "nigger cloth." American slaves, too, soon developed peculiar styles of dressing. See Genovese, *Roll, Jordan, Roll*, pp. 550–561. In Mauritius slaves were not permitted to wear shoes. The colonists declared that doing so "was tantamount to proclaiming their emancipation" (Burton Benedict, "Slavery and Indenture in Mauritius and Seychelles," in Watson, *Asian and African Systems of Slavery*, p. 141).

92. For further discussion see Victor Ehrenberg, *The People of Aristophanes* (New York: Schocken Books, 1962), p. 184.

93. We do not know when this incident, referred to by Seneca, occurred. See Seneca, *On Mercy* (Cambridge, Mass.: Harvard University Press, Loeb Classical Library, 1970), 1.24.1. Plautus also refers to the slaves' different style of dress although, of course, the setting is supposedly Greece. Plautus, *Amphitryo*, 114, in Plautus, *The Rope and Other Plays*, ed. and trans. E. F. Watling (New York: Penguin Books, 1964), p. 232.

94. There is still some controversy concerning exactly what the *abbuttum* or Babylonian slave-mark was, though it is certain that it was a mark of degradation. For a discussion of the subject see G. R. Driver and John C. Miles, eds., *The Babylonian Laws* (Oxford: Clarendon Press, 1960), vol. 1, pp. 306–309, 422–423.

95. Sellin, *Slavery and the Penal System*, pp. 49–50.

96. Ibid., p. 120.

97. Cited in Kenneth Stampp, *The Peculiar Institution* (London: Eyre & Spottiswoode, 1964), p. 185.

98. Ibid., p. 205.

99. Craton, *Searching for the Invisible Man*, p. 198.

100. C. R. Boxer, *The Golden Age of Brazil, 1695–1750* (Berkeley: University of California Press, 1969), p. 172.

101. Kenneth Little, "The Mende Farming Household," *Sociological Review* 40 (1948): 38.

102. A. A. Dim Delobsom, *L'empire du Mogho-Naba: Coutumes des Mossi de la Haute-Volta* (Paris: Domat-Montchrestien, 1943), p. 64.

103. On the psychoanalysis of hair and hairdressing see Charles Berg, *The Unconscious Significance of Hair* (London: Allen & Unwin, 1951). For a sympathetic critique of this work and a useful statement of the anthropological symbolism of hair see F. R. Leach, "Magical Hair," in John Middleton, ed., *Myth and Cosmos* (Garden City, N.Y.: Natural History Press, 1967), pp. 77–108. For a general study of hair and hair symbolism see Wendy Cooper, *Hair: Sex, Society, and Symbolism* (London: Aldus Books, 1971). And for a useful review of the anthropological literature on hair as private asset and public symbol see Raymond Firth, *Symbols: Public and Private* (Ithaca, N.Y.: Cornell University Press, 1973), pp. 262–298. As important as the content in hair symbolism is the structural principle that hair shaving always implies a transitional status.

104. Raymond Breton, "Father Raymond Breton's Observation of the Island Carib: A Compilation of Ethnographic Notes Taken from Breton's Carib-French Dictionary Published in 1665," trans. and ed. Marshall McKusick and Pierre Verin (New Haven: HRAF, 1957?), p. 42 (manuscript). See also Raymond Breton and Armand de la Paix, "Relations de l'Ile de la Guadeloupe," in Joseph Rennard, ed., *Les Caraibes, La Guadeloupe*

1635–1656 (Paris: Librairie Generale et Internationale, 1929), pp. 45–74; Irving Rouse, "The Carib," in Steward, *Handbook of the South American Indians*, vol. 4, pp. 552–553.

105. There is a vast literature on this subject. For a good overview see the papers collected in Magnus Mörner, ed., *Race and Class in Latin America* (New York: Columbia University Press, 1970). See also Charles Wagley, "On the Concept of Social Race in the Americas," *Actas del XXXIII Congreso Internacional de Americanistas* 1 (1959): 403–417; and Carl N. Degler, *Neither Black nor White: Slavery and Race Relations in Brazil and the United States* (New York: Macmillan Co., 1971). For an excellent study of the complexities of race, class, and color in a Caribbean slave society see Verena Martinez-Alier, *Marriage, Class, and Colour in Nineteenth-Century Cuba* (Cambridge: Cambridge University Press, 1974). For an interesting but flawed theory of the role of somatic perception in the development of race relations during and after slavery see Harry Hoetink, *The Two Variants of Caribbean Race Relations* (London: Oxford University Press, 1967). See also David Lowenthal, *West Indian Societies* (New York: Oxford University Press, 1972), esp. chap. 7; Florestan Fernandes, "Slaveholding Society in Brazil," in Vera Rubin and Arthur Tuden, eds., *Comparative Perspectives on Slavery in New World Plantation Societies* (New York: New York Academy of Sciences, 1977), pp. 311–342; and Leslie B. Rout, Jr., *The African Experience in Spanish America* (New York: Cambridge University Press, 1976), esp. chaps. 5 and 12.

106. For a discussion of the social psychology of hair and hair color, and the priority status of "good hair" over "good color," see the work of the Jamaican sociologist Fernando Henriques, *Family and Colour in Jamaica* (London: MacGibbon & Kee, 1968), esp. chaps. 1, 2, 13, and 14. As Henriques observes: "A dark person with good hair and features ranks above a fair person with bad [that is, African-type] hair and features" (p. 55).

107. Woodville K. Marshall, ed., *The Colthurst Journal: Journal of a Special Magistrate in the Islands of Barbados and St. Vincent, July 1835–September 1838* (Millwood, N.Y.: K.T.O. Press, 1977), p. 100. Resentment of the beautiful curls of some mulatto women also existed in South Africa.

108. Ibid.

109. See Rex M. Nettleford, *Identity, Race, and Protest in Jamaica* (N.Y.: William Morrow and Co., 1972), esp. chaps. 1, 3, and 5. On Trinidad see Bridget Brereton, *Race Relations in Colonial Trinidad, 1870–1900* (Cambridge: Cambridge University Press, 1979), and for the modern period Selwyn D. Ryan, *Race and Nationalism in Trinidad and Tobago* (Toronto: University of Toronto Press, 1972).

110. See, for example, James B. Christensen, *Double Descent among the Fanti* (New Haven: Human Relations Area Files, 1954), p. 96; and J. S. Harris, "Some Aspects of Slavery in Southeastern Nigeria," *Journal of Negro History* 27 (1942): 96.

111. Meyer Fortes, *The Web of Kinship among the Tallensi* (London: Oxford University Press, 1949), p. 25.

112. Perdue, *Slavery and the Evolution of Cherokee Society*, p. 11.

113. Meyer Fortes, *The Dynamics of Clanship among the Tallensi* (London: Oxford University Press, 1945), p. 52.

114. J. C. Miller, "Imbangala Lineage Slavery," in Miers and Kopytoff, *Slavery in Africa*, p. 213.

115. Rattray, *Ashanti Law and Constitution*, pp. 40–41.

116. André Bourgeot, "Rapports esclavagistes et conditions d'affranchissement chez les Imuhag," in Meillassoux, *L'esclavage en Afrique précoloniale*, pp. 85, 90.

117. On the psychology of witchcraft in West Africa see M. J. Field, *Search for Security: An Ethnopsychiatric Study of Rural Ghana* (London: Faber & Faber, 1960). See also the classic paper of S. F. Nadel on the subject, "Witchcraft in Four African Societies: An Essay in Comparison," *American Anthropologist* 54 (1952): 18–29.

118. *Rural Hausa: A Village and a Setting* (Cambridge: Cambridge University Press, 1972), p. 42.

119. *The Cubeo: Indians of the Northwestern Amazon* (Urbana: University of Illinois Press, 1963), Illinois Studies in Anthropology, no. 2, p. 130.

120. *Roll, Jordan, Roll,* p. 514.

121. *Journal of a West Indian Proprietor, Kept during a Residence in the Island of Jamaica* (London: 1834), p. 240.

122. For the classic statement of this view see Max Weber, *The Sociology of Religion,* trans. Ephraim Fischoff (Boston: Beacon Press, 1964), esp. chaps. 1, 3, and 14. See in particular Weber's discussion of the means by which Rome, like China and other Far Eastern states, developed "more inclusive associations, especially of the political variety," while retaining the power and significance of familial religious organizations and ancestral gods (pp. 15–16). See also Robert N. Bellah, *Beyond Belief* (New York: Harper & Row, 1970), chap. 2.

123. *Untersuchungen über die Religion der Sklaven in Griechenland und Rom* (Wiesbaden: Akademie Mainz, 1960), vol. 2, p. 144.

124. Ibid., vol. 3, pp. 173–195.

125. *Custom and Conflict in Africa* (Oxford: Basil Blackwell, 1955), p. 125; also chap. 5.

126. Bömer, *Untersuchungen über die Religion der Sklaven,* vol. 3, p. 44.

127. W.K.C. Guthrie, *The Greeks and Their Gods* (Boston: Beacon Press, 1950), p. 84; also chap. 7.

128. Bömer, *Untersuchungen über die Religion der Sklaven,* vol. 1, pp. 32–86.

129. For a good discussion of the saturnalia see E. O. James, *Seasonal Feasts and Festivals* (London: Thames & Hudson, 1961), pp. 175–177.

130. Bömer, *Untersuchungen über die Religion der Sklaven,* vol. 1, pp. 87–98.

131. R. H. Barrow, *Slavery in the Roman Empire* (London: Methuen & Co., 1928), p. 164.

132. Ibid., p. 168.

133. Bömer, *Untersuchungen über die Religion der Sklaven,* vol. 1, pp. 110–171.

134. *Conquerors and Slaves* (Cambridge: Cambridge University Press, 1978), pp. 212–213. See also Robert E. A. Palmer, *Roman Religion and Roman Empire: Five Essays* (Philadelphia: University of Pennsylvania Press, 1974), pp. 114–120.

135. Hopkins, *Conquerors and Slaves,* chap. 5.

136. *Aspects of Antiquity* (New York: Viking Press, 1969), p. 207.

137. For the classic analysis of the religions of salvation see Weber, *The Sociology of Religion,* chaps. 9–12.

138. Early Christianity, as Weber pointed out, was essentially a religion of urban artisans "both slave and free" (ibid., p. 95). See also Ernst Troeltsch, *The Social Teachings of the Christian Churches,* vol. 1 (London: Macmillan & Co., 1931); A. D. Nock, *Early Gentile Christianity and Its Hellenistic Background* (New York: Harper Torchbooks, 1957); Philip Carrington, *The Early Christian Church,* vol. 1 (Cambridge: Cambridge University Press, 1957). For a good recent treatment of Constantine's conversion and its consequences see J.H.W.G. Liebeschuetz, *Continuity and Change in Roman Religion* (Oxford: Clarendon Press, 1979), pp. 277–308.

139. See Ambrogio Donini, "The Myth of Salvation in Ancient Slave Society," *Science and Society* 15 (1951): 57–60. For a review of slavery in Christian thought see Davis, *The Problem of Slavery*, esp. chaps. 3 and 4.

140. J. G. Davies, "Christianity: The Early Church," in R. C. Zaehner, ed., *The Concise Encyclopedia of Living Faiths* (Boston: Beacon Press, 1959), p. 56.

141. Ibid., pp. 55–58.

142. For one of the best-known statements of the view that Christianity is primarily a religion built on the response to Jesus' crucifixion see John Knox, *The Death of Christ* (London: Collins, 1967). See also Christopher F. Evans, *Resurrection and the New Testament* (Naperville, Ill.: Alec R. Allenson, 1970).

143. Rom. 6:10.

144. Undoubtedly the most probing modern analysis of Paul's ethical dualism is Maurice Goguel's *The Primitive Church*, trans. H. C. Snape (London: Allen & Unwin, 1964), pp. 425–455.

145. Ibid., p. 428.

146. Ibid., p. 449.

147. On the chronic dualism of Saint Augustine see Karl Jaspers' brilliant critique in his *Plato and Augustine* (New York: Harvest Books, 1957), esp. pp. 109–119. Still valuable is J. N. Figgis, *The Political Aspects of St. Augustine's City of God* (London: Longmans, 1921). See my own interpretation in Orlando Patterson, *Ethnic Chauvinism: The Reactionary Impulse* (New York: Stein & Day, 1977), pp. 231–241.

148. See Weber, *The Sociology of Religion*, esp. chaps. 9 and 10.

149. We need not become involved here with the spent debate on the role of the Catholic church in Latin American slavery. See Davis, *The Problem of Slavery*, pp. 223–261; also Rout, *The African Experience in Spanish America*, chap. 5; Boxer, *The Golden Age of Brazil*, chaps. 5–7; and Palmer, *Slaves of the White God*, chap. 4, esp. the cases cited on pp. 113–114.

150. See William Lou Mathieson, *British Slavery and Its Abolition* (London: Longmans, 1926), pp. 109–114; Elsa V. Goveía, *Slave Society in the British Leeward Islands at the End of the Eighteenth Century* (New Haven: Yale University Press, 1965), pp. 263–310; and Patterson, *The Sociology of Slavery*, pp. 33–51. Although formally Catholic, the situation in the French Caribbean was more like that of the British islands. See Debien, *Les esclaves aux Antilles françaises*, pp. 249–295.

151. *Sugar and Slaves: The Rise of the Planter Class in the English West Indies, 1624–1713* (Chapel Hill: University of North Carolina Press, 1972), p. 249.

152. Albert J. Raboteau, *Slave Religion* (New York: Oxford University Press, 1980), p. 141.

153. Ibid., p. 149.

154. See John B. Boles, *The Great Revival, 1787–1805* (Lexington: University Press of Kentucky, 1972); also his *Religion in Antebellum Kentucky* (Lexington: University Press of Kentucky, 1976). On the ways in which Christian conscience was reconciled to bondage see H. Sheldon Smith, *In His Image, But—* (Durham, N.C.: Duke University Press, 1972).

155. Genovese, *Roll, Jordan, Roll*, p. 186.

156. See Edgar T. Thompson, "God and the Southern Plantation System," in S. S. Hill, ed., *Religion and the Solid South* (Nashville, Tenn.: Abingdon Press, 1972), pp. 51–91; and James L. Peacock, "The Southern Protestant Ethic Disease," in J. K. Morland, ed., *The Not So Solid South* (Athens: University of Georgia Press, 1971).

157. *The Religion of the Slaves* (Helsinki: Finnish Academy of Science and Letters, 1976), p. 139.
158. Genovese, *Roll, Jordan, Roll*, bk. 2, pt. 1.
159. Lawrence W. Levine, *Black Culture and Black Consciousness* (New York: Oxford University Press, 1978), chaps. 1 and 3.
160. See Levine, *Black Culture and Black Consciousness*, p. 33; and Raboteau, *Slave Religion*, p. 250. Alho's careful study of the spirituals and slave narratives does not support the view that the Exodus myth or identification with the children of Israel were the dominant themes in the religious beliefs of slaves. See Alho, *The Religion of the Slaves*, pp. 75–76.
161. Alho, *The Religion of the Slaves*, p. 79.
162. Goguel, *The Primitive Church*, pp. 454–455.
163. *Redemption in Black Theology* (Valley Forge, Pa.: Judson Press, 1979).

Chapter 7

The Racial Factor in the Shaping
of Religion in America

C. Eric Lincoln

The African Antecedents

When Zedekiah, the last King of Judah, delivered Jeremiah up to the nervous rabble of his decaying establishment, those so-called princes, too cowardly to murder the prophet outright, dumped him into an abandoned well and waited for nature to take its course. Tradition has it that Ebedmelech the African rescued Jeremiah and was rewarded by God's promise that in the impending destruction of Jerusalem and the Babylonian captivity he, Ebedmelech, would not be delivered into the hands of strangers (Jeremiah 38:1–13; 39:15–18).[1] There is another tradition that six centuries later another African, whose name was Simon, helped Jesus struggle up Mount Calvary under the burden of the cross (Mark 15:21),* which was to become the symbol of a New Jerusalem. Somewhere between Jeremiah and Jesus, between God's promise to Ebedmelech and Simon's travail on the way to Golgotha, Jewish nationhood reached its nadir, and Christian tradition began its remarkable ascendancy. The ramifications of that tradition are with us now, two thousand years later. At stake is the religious commitment and the religious identity of millions of Blackamericans whose identification with white American Christianity is distorted by the unfortunate history of racial dissonance within the organized structures of the faith. In consequence, many black Christians sensitive to the more subtle implications of a religion often construed as a legacy of their bondage are determined to reclaim that ancient biblical heritage

---

*There is a heretical tradition that Simon the African was crucified instead of Jesus.

156

which avoids the embarrassments of brotherly denigration in America, and reestablish their connection with the faith at its inception.

For those uncomfortable with more recent and less sanguine exposures to the faith, Pentecost takes on new meaning. For among those "devout men from every nation under heaven" (Acts 2:5) who heard Peter proclaim the promise to them and to their children (Acts 2:39) were men from Africa (Acts 2:10). But as if to underscore divine intention that *black*[2] Africa (which first touched the destiny of Israel when Abraham came out of Ur and settled in Egypt, and continued through all the centuries thereafter) should be a direct and unequivocal heir to that promise, after Pentecost, the divine imperative came to the evangelist Philip, directing him toward a rendezvous which made inequitable the inclusion of black Africans among the charter members of the faith. "Take the desert road that leads toward Gaza," Philip was told. Waiting for him on that road with a copy of the Book of Isaiah in his hand was an African nobleman, treasurer to Her Majesty Candace, Queen of Ethiopia. He invited Philip to join him in his chariot, received the good news from his lips, and accepted baptism at his hand (Acts 8:26–39), all of which symbolizes from the beginning the African involvement in the new faith that was to spread throughout the world.

This must be reckoned a momentous event in the history of Christianity, but whether it has probable significance for the present mood of black American Christians needs closer examination. At minimum, there is the indisputable fact that Christianity experienced an early and fruitful establishment in North Africa, in Egypt, and in Ethiopia; and that the church in Africa gave back to the Church Universal an extraordinary interest on its investment. During the three hundred years from the third through the fifth century, when the church wrestled with its most critical theological formulations, of the eighteen or twenty most prominent leaders, no fewer than nine were African: Clement, Origen, Tertullian, Cyprian, Dionysius, Athanasius, Didymus, Augustine, and Cyril. Cyprian and Augustine were the great intellectuals who worked out the basic political and theological doctrines of the Western church. How ironic it is that so much light should come from an allegedly "dark continent," and that it should eventuate in a civilization called the Christian West. Or that in time the Christian West, goaded by an insatiable economic self-interest, would turn again to Africa, not to bless her, but to suck her blood. But such are the inexplicables of human history. Neither the light of reason nor the illumination of the spirit is a sure hedge to the predaciousness that seems ever the corollary of power, irrespective of race, geography, or nationality. As fate would have it, the men who caught men (or bought them), and the men who were caught (or bought), were destined to play out their respective generations against the backdrop of the faith they were to share in a new world. But it was to be a world informed by latter-day apostles whose understanding of that faith was clouded by an incipient racism, a degraded economics, and an illusion of manifest destiny.

I have said that Africa knew the Hebrew nation in its infancy, from Abraham even; and the civilizations of Africa were ancient even then. Still, it is sometimes necessary to remind Christians in the West that Egypt is in Africa, and that Egyptians are Africans, despite the desperate efforts of our race-conscious latter-day historians to deny Africa a place of significance in the history of civilization. More than that, the Egyptians themselves are racial hybrids, representing a fusion of black peoples from the south with lighter-skinned races from the north. Even today the most casual observer is impressed by the strong physical resemblance between contemporary Egyptians and the so-called Negroid Africans of the sub-Sahara regions. As a case in point, the late Egyptian President Anwar Sadat would have been comfortably inconspicuous in any black church gathering until he prostrated himself for prayer. But the racial composition of the Egyptian people is for our present purposes somewhat beside the point, except that the peculiar convergence of events which brought Africans and American Christianity into a strange concubinage for three and a half centuries made it imperative to deny the African's role in the development of Egyptian civilization, in keeping with the conventional fiction of black cultural insignificance. This perspective has been promoted by practically all Western scholarship through a concerted pedagogical effort to separate Egypt as a cultural entity from the rest of Africa. But Egypt *was* and *is* African, and is quite likely to remain so, and the black experience in Egypt is hardly a matter of speculation wherever intellectual objectivity can be mustered.

One wonders why most Western historians have put themselves to such pains. The Blacks who were brought to America as slaves came from the coastal states of West Africa for the most part, not from Egypt. But the black presence in Egypt was established long before the white man came to Africa, whether to conquer, as did the Greeks and the Romans, or to deal in flesh, as did most of the rest of Western Europe. Despite the frustration it poses for scholars with such compelling needs to deny, or to reduce to insignificance, the black African's capacity for cultural relevance, the data of history simply refuse to be silent. In the final analysis, relevance itself is a matter of perspective. Perspective is an aspect of culture, and culture is by definition committed to values deriving from its own body of experience. One may redact the data of history in the interest of an alternative *theory*, but one cannot redact the facts of history and create an alternative *reality*. Whatever *was*, was indeed; and whatever *is*, is incontrovertible, a self-evident principle, it would seem. It is not our present task to seek to validate the relevance of the black experience in Egypt. My commitment is to another aspect of history which begins with the desecration of black Africa by the world's most advanced and enlightened white cultures, all of whose values were anchored in Christian perspectives. More particularly, our concern is America, where those perspectives continue to produce conflict between black and white Christians to this day. But we must begin with Africa, the motherland of the Black Diaspora, from which the sea captains of Europe and America took, in the course of four centuries, unnumbered tons of gold, uncounted shiploads of ivory, and millions upon millions of black men and women. To the plunderers, Africa was the "Gold Coast," the "Ivory Coast," the "Slave Coast." But it was never a community of people deserving Christian recognition and concern.

From 638, the Christian influence in Africa declined before the vast hegemony of Islam. In consequence, history was compelled to wait for Prince Henry the Navigator, that half-English, half-Portuguese Grand Master of the Order of Christ, to open up the so-called dark continent for Christ and commerce; and to see the slave trade established in medieval Europe fifty years before Columbus would discover a new Europe, where slavery was to become the major instrument of economic and social aggrandizement[3] for almost three centuries. But Portuguese Christianity was not alone in introducing black slavery to Europe, for, under Enrique III of Castile, gold and slaves from Africa were marketed in Seville in the last decade of the fifteenth century, and although good Queen Isabella, that canny and daring patron of Columbus, sought unsuccessfully to kill the practice before it was well rooted, she failed. She failed because the prevailing sentiment of the church was that it was better for a "heathen" to have his body bound and his soul free, than vice versa. So, by 1501, it was possible and profitable for the Spanish Crown to issue an edict permitting not only "freshly caught" Africans but those born in Christianity as well to be sold in America. At first the notion seemed to be that Christianized Blacks could better convert the Indians, although it was never quite clear why "savages" and "heathens" should promise greater success in the conversion enterprise than Christians boasting the spiritual seasoning of centuries. Perhaps the fact that slaves from Guinea brought four times as much in the American market as Indian slaves was not altogether irrelevant.

Impressed by the Spanish success, by the end of the fifteenth century Portugal had developed a voracious parasitism which she was to continue to indulge until she was dislodged by the freedom struggles that convulsed Africa after our most recent world war, leaving only the oppressive regime of the white South Africans to await some final Armageddon of liberation. With Africa as an inexhaustible source of supply for free black labor, Portugal contracted with Spain in the early days of the slave trade to provide the Spaniards with slaves for markets Spain had developed in the New World. By this arrangement the Portuguese hoped to maintain a monopoly on her very profitable procurements from the villages and towns of West Africa. But the neighboring states of Western Europe were not to be denied their share in this commerce, and the Portuguese monopoly was soon broken by Spanish, English, French, Dutch, and American competition. In the New World, labor was short and the market was aggressive. As a result, there were 500,000 slaves in the American colonies by the time of the Revolution—an embarrassing statistic patently inconsonant with the brave rhetoric of the Founding Fathers and the moral principles of an avowedly Christian nation.

Since no records were kept, we have no way of knowing how many, if any, of the slaves brought into the English colonies were Christian, although there were substantial numbers of black Christians with the Spanish adventurers in South and Central America, in Mexico, and in the Spanish settlements in Florida from the very beginning of the Spanish explorations in the New World. Some of them were slaves, some were not. Black Pedro Alonzo was captain of Columbus's flagship, the *Niña*. Another Black whose name was Estevanico, who with Cabeza de Vaca explored parts of Mexico and the Southwest, led an expedition into what is now New Mexico and Arizona, where he discovered the Zuni Indians. Estevanico is said to have planted the first wheat crop in America, in 1539. In the slave trade itself, the Catholic Portuguese and Spaniards were generally anxious to see their slaves baptized; the Anglo-Saxon Protestants were not. The Catholics, it seemed, gave a first consideration, however perfunctory, to the demands of the church. We are told that the Portuguese

> sold the performers of heathen rites and gave the proceeds to the poor. The numbers were so great that the slaver depended on the missionary to complete his cargo. Merolla sold a slave for a flask of wine for the sacraments. Even if Negroes had been baptized, the [Catholic] missionary saw no sin in enslaving them. In reality, however, baptism encouraged and sanctioned slavery for it made the

Negro a Christian and a man *nolens volens*, while the Christian slave trade was a beneficent agency to bring black barbarians into Christian civilization. Only, let not the slave be sold to heretics, for then he would be doubly damned.[4]

This was representative Catholicism at work in the slave trade: a bow toward Rome and on with the business at hand, being careful only to have no dealing with the heathen Mohammedans lest the poor souls, already damned for being black, be damned again for falling into the ways of Islam. The Protestants ignored Rome and bowed instead to an incipient racism which, ere long, would develop a ponderous psychology of justification that would burden both church and society in the West for generations. The Englishman considered *himself* first, above all. And when he contemplated his own perfection, he saw the alleged heathenism of the Africans as but one aspect of a generalized disparity. They were beings apart. They were not merely black, they were black *and* heathen. Historian Winthrop Jordan declares:

> Heathenism was from the Anglo-Saxon's point of view not so much a specifically religious defect, but was one manifestation of a general refusal to measure up to proper standards, as a failure to be English. . . . Being Christian was not merely a matter of subscribing to certain doctrines; it was a quality inherent in oneself and one's society. It was interconnected with all the other attributes of normal and proper men.[5]

It was all a matter of the black man's depraved condition. Since he was not an Englishman, his importance and his place in the Englishman's scheme of things was predetermined. From such a perspective the Anglo-Saxon could scarcely be expected to develop a warm appreciation of the African's humanity, his native religion, or his capacity to benefit from Christian instruction.

If the Anglo-Saxon's racial and cultural arrogance had been less consummate, it is possible that he could have learned something from the African which might have given him cause for reflection. The Africans he dismissed arbitrarily as heathens did, as a matter of fact, believe in one supreme God. Above the intermediary gods and spirits which so distressed the white man was always the One God who was the giver and sustainer of life. What the white man dismissed as African ancestor worship was a highly sophisticated expression of family integrity and continuity,

an observation strangely and unaccountably lost on a people so irrevoca-
bly committed to the institutionalization of family relationships as were
the English. What is more, the African moral codes were consistent with
the notion of One God of all people, a notion which has not always been
honored in the breech in the West. The slave trader saw none of this. He
understood less than he saw, and cared about less than he understood.
After all, "the English errand in Africa was not [the search for] a new or
perfect community, but a business trip."[6] The great civilizations the
Africans had raised at Ghana, at Mele, at Jenné, Songhay, and Timbuktu,
their art, their religion, their culture meant nothing to the men who came
bringing Bibles, trinkets, and chains.

As slavery went, the English were probably no worse than the worst and
certainly no better than the best, and the line that separated the one from
the other is scarcely discernible from any perspective of human responsibility. Whether Anglo-Saxon, Spaniard, or Dane, Portuguese, Dutch, or
American, the men who wasted Africa, decimated her towns and villages,
corrupted her politics, destroyed her economy, and hauled her people away
wholesale to distant lands where those who survived were reduced to submission and servility. It is not a question of whether the Anglo-Saxon was
better or worse. What is important is that America is the place where white
Christians and Blacks still confront each other in the continuing conflicts
of culture, morality, and religion we call the American dilemma.

Chained neck to neck, wrist to wrist, and ankle to ankle, and shipped
off into a new kind of Babylonian captivity in Christian America, the
Africans left their gods but not their God. Muslim and heathen alike, and
possibly some Christians as well, chained body to body between decks
four feet high; if they survived the darkness, the filth, the horror, and the
degradation of the "middle passage," they would arrive by and by in the
land of the American Christians: the Congregationalists, the Presbyterians, the Roman Catholics, the Quakers, the Lutherans, the Baptists, the
Methodists, and, of course, the Anglicans—once removed. There they
would eventually meet the white man's God.

The Gospel through the Windows

There was a fleeting moment in our history when some denominations
sought to commit their churches to do what our Founding Fathers had
elected not to do; namely, to give de facto recognition to the principle that
all men stand before God equal in their nakedness and need. But in the
end the churches failed to rescue what the statesmen decided to overlook.

Bigotry seeped through the restraints of the faith to join the undertow already sucking at the political foundations of the new nation. Black Christians, despairing of the peculiar spiritual mentality which confined them to the back pews and "nigger heavens" in the white churches, eventually withdrew and founded independent communions.

If there had been no racism in America, there would be no racial churches. As it is, we have white churches and black churches; white denominations and black denominations; American Christianity and black religion. Although there was no concerted effort at black conversion until the early eighteenth century, American Christianity was even then in a quandary about what to do about black Christians. The problem became acute once the number of Blacks who opted for Christ began to grow. The minutes of the Presbyterian Synod of South Carolina and Georgia meeting in 1834 disclose the vexations typically faced by the white churches:

> The gospel, as things are now, can never be preached to the two classes successfully in conjunction. The galleries or the back seats on the lower floors of white churches are generally appropriated to the Negroes, when it can be done without inconvenience to the whites. When it cannot be done conveniently, the Negroes must catch the gospel as it escapes through the doors and windows.[7]

It was evident that the black worshipper wanted somewhat more than the white man's convenience would allow, for "when the Negro worshipper gained conscious self-respect he grew tired of the back pews and upper galleries of the white churches, and sought places of worship more compatible with his sense of freedom and dignity."[8] However, the only place in which a black Christian was able to worship with dignity was in a black church. But black churches were considered dangerous to established white interests, and in every Southern state they were forbidden, suppressed, or severely regulated by law until the Civil War settled for all time the black Christian's right to independent worship. Even under the most benign circumstances, the black-church-within-the-white-church arrangement had never been a completely satisfying arrangement for either Blacks or whites. The peculiar conditions imposed upon Blacks to protect the white man's sense of uniqueness humiliated the one and posed a continuing moral contradiction for the other. This was no less true in the highly selective sermons preached for the Blacks than in the segregated arrangements for their worship. But the black Christians were no more blind to the abuse of the faith than to the abuse of themselves as human beings and fellow Christians. Accordingly, when the chasm of credibility could no longer be bridged by patience and humility, they determined to be free of what they could not accept. The remarks of ex-slave Lunsford Lane are revealing:

> There was one kind-hearted clergyman I used often to hear; he was very popular among the colored people. But after he had preached a sermon to us in which he urged from the Bible that it was the will of heaven . . . that we should be slaves, and our masters our owners, Many of us left him, considering like the doubting disciple of old, "This is a hard saying; Who can hear it?"[9]

There were many Blacks who, like Lunsford Lane, could not be reconciled to their status in the white church, and since they often found the doctrine preached to them there to be without comfort, their spiritual unrest must have increased with each occasion for doubt. They had their own thoughts about their bodies and their souls and their destinies, but it was extremely impolitic not to accept the white man's arrangements, for the white man represented the sum total of temporal power within the universe of the black experience in America. So in the white man's church they sat wherever his pleasure indicated they should, and waited. They stifled the urge to scream and to shout and to raise their arms to heaven; and they strangled the sobs and the moans that welled up inside and made their bodies shake and tremble like leaves in a storm. Only their tears could not be stayed—tears of sorrow and distress, so often mistaken for tears of joy for having the privilege of confronting God in the presence of the slavemaster.

With Fear and Trembling . . . as unto Christ

Often, when the white man's worship service was over, the black man's might truly begin, for neither his heart nor his private membership was in the white church, where he was scorned and demeaned. There was that *other* church, that *invisible institution* which met in the swamps and the bayous, and which joined all black believers in a common experience at a single level of human and spiritual recognition. Deep in the woods and safely out of sight of the critical, disapproving eyes of the master and the overseer, the shouts rolled up—and out. The agony so long suppressed burdened the air with sobs and screams and rhythmic moans. God's praises were sung. His mercy enjoined. His justice invoked. There in the Invisible Church the black Christian met God on his own terms and in his own way without the white intermediary. That invisible communion was the beginning of the Black Church, the seminal institution which spans most of the history of the black experience. It offers the most accessible key to the complexity and the genius of the black subculture, and it reflects both a vision of the tragedy and an aspect of hope of the continuing American dilemma.

Perhaps more than any other people since the Israelites were enslaved in Egypt, the Blackamerican has been shaped and characterized by the unique place religion has occupied in his personal life and in the common destiny of the race. His American experience is inseparable from his religious heritage because for much of that history there was little else to offer meaning to existence, or to fall back upon for strength to confront the exigencies of his distressed condition.

But Christianity in America had already been accommodated to black pacification and control in the interest of the most abominable institution ever to challenge Christian morality. In consequence, that version of Christianity urged upon the slaves bore no "good news" beyond a legacy of toil, and no hope for rescue this side of Jordan. It was a religion that called them to work and to die for the doubtful aggrandizement of self-appointed Christian masters whose calculated manipulation of the faith was intended to so confuse the slave as to make his dehumanization seem reasonable and inevitable. Was not the African the accursed son of Ham? *(Albeit he was not a Hebrew!)* Was not his blackness a sign of his degradation at *God's* hand? *(Although he was made in God's own image!)* And did not the Apostle Paul admonish the slave who wanted to join his fellowship of Christians that he must first return to his master, thereby proving for all times that there was no incompatibility between the faith and human bondage? Unrequited toil was the inevitable lot, the God-ordained lot, the *proper* lot of the black man and his progeny forever. It was the penalty for his sins, even as his blackness was the sign of his depravity. And this by divine decree. He must labor in the fields for his earthly master whom God had set over him, "from can-to-can't," i.e., from "can see to can't see"—from daylight until dark, all of his life, and for all time. He must not complain, for all that he was or ever would be depended upon his white master. *It was God's will!* To run away would be to commit an unforgivable sin—the theft of his master's God-given property, viz., himself! To kill himself would be to destroy property not his own. A slave who committed suicide could receive no rites of the church, and was destined to burn in hell forever. But if he bore his lot with love and patience, being at all times loyal and obedient to the masters set over him in this world, he would be properly rewarded in the world to come. *It was God's will,* and it was the white man's Christian duty, indeed, the white man's burden, to see that will fulfilled.

> Servants, be obedient to them that are your masters . . . with fear and trembling . . . as unto Christ. . . . Remember, God required this of you. . . . There is something so becoming and engaging in the modest, cheerful, good natured behavior that a little work done in that manner seems better done. . . . It also gains the goodwill and love of those you belong to. . . . Besides . . . your murmuring and grumbling is against God who hath placed you in their service.[10]

Such were the teachings of the white man's church as they were offered to the African who found himself involuntarily resident in America.

In the South

Those who laid claim to the black man's body, his labor, his children born and unborn, were Christians, and the strange claims these white Christians made upon their fellow Christians who were black were supported by a system of law anxious to accommodate the claims of property but insensitive to the claims of persons who happened to be black. This unfortunate priority of interests might well have been predicted in the larger context of the developing American self-perception. There was a world to be won, an empire to be built, and the notion that the Africans were provided by a benign providence to be the instruments of the white man's destiny seemed increasingly logical and circumspect. Empire building requires prodigious quantities of cheap labor. Slave labor seemed indispensable, and *African* slave labor appeared to be ideal. Indian slaves had proved to be impractical, indenture too clumsy, and the flood-tide of Eastern and Southern European immigration was far into a future yet to be created.* Into the furnace of expediency the Africans were thrust, and the question of their claims as persons was dismissed as academic and irrelevant.

---

*The high mortality rate among Indians confined in slavery was exacerbated by the relative ease (and frequency) with which they vanished into the familiar forests—and home. Some whites were enslaved through illegal extensions of indenture contracts and by other questionable stratagems. However, the prospect of trouble with the Crown made such practices hazardous. No such impediments stood in the way of African slavery.

Sooner or later the question of black humanity would have to be dealt with, of course, but for the moment it was simply not an issue of compelling significance. It could wait. In the meantime, the once tentative notions about the black man's "difference" would develop into inflexible ideologies, with all of the fervor and assurance that vested interests could muster. Both God and reason would be called to bear witness as the rationalizations of moral justification took on the encrustations of immutable truth. Peter Kalm, a Swedish observer traveling in America in 1748, struck by the indifference of the Americans concerning the spiritual condition of the Africans they enslaved, reported that the whites

> are partly led by the conceit of its being shameful, to have a spiritual brother or sister among so despicable a people, partly thinking that they would not be able to keep their Negroes so meanly afterwards; and partly through fear of the Negroes growing too proud, on seeing themselves upon a level with their masters in religious matters.[11]

The notion of sharing a brotherhood in Christ with Africans, in this world or any other, was certainly not a popular one. A typical response to so incredible a suggestion was said to have been: "What, such as they? What, those black dogs be made Christians? What, shall they be like us?" "Is it possible," one distraught Christian lady wanted to know, "that any of my slaves could go to heaven, and must I see them there?"[12]

In the South the essential factor at work was a racial tribalism which militated against sharing a common experience with Blacks as equals under any circumstances, religious or otherwise. Social distance must not be breeched by the ordinary amenities of common worship. Three hundred years later the churches of America would still be in scandalous agitation over the same issue. There would be kneel-ins and lockouts, and black caucuses and demands for reparations, and a variety of other forms of behavior which, in a Christian democracy, must have appeared to be bizarre to the most tolerant of observers. But the precedents were in place even before the issues were born. A convocation of Anglican ministers meeting at Oxford, Maryland, in 1731 revealed a sad lack of interest in the spiritual well-being of black people. Here is the record:

> Mr. Fletcher said his parishioners were generally so brutish that they would not suffer their Negroes to be instructed, catechized, or baptized. . . .

Mr. Airey finds the people of his parish very inclined to have their Negroes instructed, but they will not be at any pains and trouble of it. . . .

Mr. Manadier has often pressed on his people their obligation to instruct their Negroes, but yet they are very remiss and neglectful.

Mr. Nicholas says . . . he has from the pulpit and in conversation been Instant with his Parishioners to instruct their Negroes, in order to their being made Christians; but that the best answer he can get, even from the best people is that they are very sorry, and lament that they cannot comply with it.

Mr. Cox has urged the necessity of instructing the Negroes, but 'tho his Parishioners allow it to be a good thing, yet they generally excuse themselves as thinking it to be impractical.[13]

Father John Carroll, a distinguished Catholic clergyman, and later Archbishop of Baltimore and signatory to the Declaration of Independence, was sensitive to the fact that the Blacks were "'kept so constantly at work' that their spiritual nurture was neglected, with the result that they were 'very dull in faith and depraved in morals.'" But the sensitivity of the good bishop, like that of many of his Protestant counterparts, was apparently dulled by self-interest, for despite their dullness and depravity he owned, and presumably "kept constantly at work," several of these poor creatures himself.

If the experiences of these clergymen were typical of the colonial spirit, and the evidence suggests this to be the case, then the popular notion of that day that American slavery was preeminently, or even initially, an altruistic endeavor to save the heathen Africans from the consequences of black sin would hardly stand critical review. It is true that the Catholics in America were themselves suppressed, which ought to have made them more sensitive to the plight of the Blacks. But American Catholicism has traditionally been preoccupied with other interests, and the plight of black people in or outside the church has apparently never been an item of high priority for American Catholics. The Catholic Church had less spiritual impact upon the black experience during the developing years of the Republic than any other major communion with the exception of Judaism. But while both Catholics and Jews were themselves suspect in the eyes of the Protestant establishment, and neither communion was prepared to contribute to its own jeopardy by identifying with the interests of black people, the Jews became in time the principal advocates and participants in the black struggle for freedom.

The Anglicans were the "established" church in the five Southern colonies, but the institutional weakness of Anglicanism during the colonial period, coupled with the vested interests of its controlling factions, made that church an unlikely haven for the black dispossessed. Anglicanism was the preferred bracelet of the Southern aristocracy, which is to say the planter class. The Bishop of London could (and did) issue whatever pronouncements he thought wise, but the real control of the parish churches was in the hands of the vestrymen, who in most cases turned out to be the principal slaveholders. The strong sentiment for Christianizing the slaves which emerged in eighteenth-century England was simply not shared in America, where the principal issues had already congealed in terms of race rather than circumstance. Hence, the English suggestion that Blacks not only be allowed to become "brothers in Christ" to the colonists but be encouraged to become free men through hard work and faithful service only showed how vast the gap was between English and American thinking. To the English, slavery was a matter of happenstance—of fortune; and fortune could be changed if one could manage the cultural requirements of English civilization, of which Christianity was a cardinal example. But to the Americans it was a matter of race, and race was immutable and forever.

In the North

The situation in New England was dishearteningly similar in effect to that prevailing in the South. In 1701 the Society for the Propagation of the Gospel began sending missionaries from England to bring the faith to the Blacks. This was almost a hundred years after the Africans were introduced to Jamestown in 1619. Blacks arrived in Boston in 1638, and while life in Puritan New England was never as harsh as it was in the Anglican South, for one whose face was black—whether Christian, pagan, infidel, slave, or free—life was a struggle beyond imagination, and dignity was an anticipation for some other world. For most of the colonial period Christianity was effectively reserved for the elite, and its benefits were preempted by the elect. But in the context of prevailing circumstances men who were black were neither elite nor elect. They were the legion of the accursed and the damned. They were Africans. They had been separated from the roots of their ancient religions and forbidden to practice their alleged paganism in Christian America. They were damned, not by God, but by those same Christians who welcomed their bodies but denied their souls, and who turned them away from their churches. Like their brothers in the South, the Puritans chose to believe that Blacks and Indians were inferior beings who were a part of a divine inheritance God had set aside for them and their benefit! In that light, it is hardly astonishing that so little was done to minister to the Blacks' spiritual requirements when the existence of those requirements was not generally recognized. As late as 1680, Governor Bradstreet could inform the British Committee of Trade and Plantations that of the Blacks in Massachusetts there had been none baptized there as far as he knew.[14] History will forgive the governor for being incompletely informed about an event which was indeed rare—having occurred only once. But there was in fact a black woman in the household of a Reverend Stoughton of Dorchester who, "being well approved . . . for sound knowledge and true godliness," was baptized and admitted to the church in 1641.[15]

But the souls of black men and women in Puritan New England were not at a premium, to say the least. As a matter of fact, whether or not Blacks *had* souls was a popular subject of sporting debate among the most learned divines and theologians of the day. Dean Berkeley of Rhode Island let it be known in 1731 that his parishioners "consider the Blacks as creatures of another species, who [had] no right to be admitted to the sacraments. . . . Such," he added, was "the main obstacle to the conversion of those poor people."[16] Cotton Mather, in a celebrated work called *The Negro Christianized*, published in 1743, defended the black man's soul with consuming passion, and even suggested (blasphemy of blasphemies) that the Blacks just might be "the Elect of God" sent among the Puritans by Divine Providence! But Dr. Mather's arguments may well have derived from other interests. Whatever he may have thought about Blacks being elect, he urged the conversion of Blacks as a matter of great practical benefit to the masters. Enraptured by the possibilities inherent in black conversion, he exclaimed:

> Oh that our neighbors would consider the incomparable Benefits that would follow upon your Endeavors to Christianize your Negroes. . . . Oh the consolation that will belong to you! . . . Your Negroes are immediately raised unto an astonishing felicity. . . . They are become amiable spectacles such as the Angels of God would repair to the windows of heaven to look down upon. Tho' they remain your servants, yet they become the children of God. Tho'

they are to enjoy no Earthly Goods, but the small allowance that your Justice and Bounty shall see proper for them. . . . Tho' they are your vassals, and must with a profound subject wait upon you, yet the Angels of God now take them under their Guardianship. Oh what you have done for them. Happy Masters . . . it will not be long before you and they come . . . together in the Heavenly City . . . and [you] hear them forever blessing the gracious God for the Day when He first made them your servants.[17]

But Mather's arguments fell mostly on deaf ears. The Society for the Propagation of the Gospel in Foreign Parts, after a very meager harvest in its efforts to bring the Indians to Christ, eventually turned its attention to the Blacks. But the Puritans were more wary of the Anglican-based SPG than they were of whatever devils might be resident in the soul-less Africans among them. They kept the Blacks away from the missionaries, with telling results. The records of the society reveal that in 1729 their agent in Boston, one Dr. Cutler, harvested only one black convert, a slave. Twenty-one years later, in 1750, he could boast of having baptized "five Negro children, one of whom was a slave," during the seven months preceding his report. The society's laborers in neighboring Connecticut fared little better. The Reverend Samuel Seabury of New London noted in his report of November 12, 1739, that in the latter half of that year he had added to Christ's meager company of Blacks in America one mulatto servant and one Negro child.[18]

The Logic of Exclusion

We may safely conclude, then, that for the first hundred years of the American experiment the Christian church took no more official notice of black people than did the British Crown. Indeed, not as much, for as they were units of production to be bought and sold, the Crown had a vast economic stake in the granting of charters for the procurement and sale of Blacks in the interest of an uninterrupted labor supply for its growing dominions in America and the West Indies.

The interests of the church in America were more exclusive. At first the church was content merely to ignore whatever spiritual needs or potentials the African might have, despite the fact that an important rationale for slavery was that it was designed to provide for the moral and spiritual uplift of the benighted Africans. Later, when the economic blessings of slavery became more evident, the Christian slavemasters would hold themselves to be the very instruments of the divine plan for bringing the savage African to Christ, albeit via the slave block. He was the white man's burden, to be sure, but since he would reap great spiritual benefit from his lowly but disciplined sojourn among God's elect, his presence was to be tolerated as a Christian duty. Nonetheless, for the better part of a century the active proselytizing of these involuntary servants the settlers had brought among themselves with such solicitude was everywhere discouraged; and the penalties for instructing them in the Christian religion were severe enough to dampen the ardor of spiritual outreach for most Christian ministers who may have been troubled by the summary exclusion of Blacks from the churches. In consequence, it did come to pass that for all black people the American commonwealth so proudly conceived as a free, Christian nation was curiously un-Christian and demonstrably unfree as well.

Virginia and Massachusetts were the principal centers of the early colonial establishment, but as we have seen, lack of interest in the Christianization of Blacks was quite general. For the most part, the exclusion of Blacks from Christian concern was seldom a matter requiring comment or explanation. From the beginning, the Anglo-Americans considered the Blacks among them as beings of a lower order who, if they were human at all, were not human in the same sense that white men were human. Hence, neither the blessings of liberty nor the comforts of heaven were considered to have any reference to Blacks. It was simply understood that "men" meant *white* men, whether the context was social, political, religious, or general. In short, the American mind-set was such as to effectively exclude Blacks from any frame of reference dealing with what could be considered normative human interests or relations.

In those colonies where slaves were considered indispensable to the plantation economy, the economic investment in human bodies was enormous, and the planters were suspicious of any tampering with their property rights. "Talk to a planter about the soul of a Negro," commented a writer in a popular colonial journal, "and he'll be apt to tell you that the body of one Negro may be worth 20 pounds, but the souls of a hundred of them would not yield him one farthing."[19] There was also much concern that the religious enterprise required *time* for worship, and for being instructed or catechized and that time would be lost to production. In America, the maxim that time is money and that money requires no apology has a long history and a popular application. Sunday was the day the slaves were expected to devote to raising their own food and recouping their strength as best they could against the inevitability of the week ahead. The slave system was geared to the premise that black labor was a perishable commodity, and that its extraction should be at a steady, continuous rate, to be interfered with only under the most compelling circumstances. "Negroes . . . were bought for the purpose of performing labor. What fact could be more obvious and natural, or less demanding of explanation?"[20] In a system which routinely expected a slave mother to be back at her plow the same day she "dropped" (i.e., gave birth to) a child, "church-time," including time spent at instruction, prayer, or other religious endeavors, was thought of as time squandered at the master's expense.

But the main objection to the spiritual enlightenment of the Blacks derived from the fear that a slave who became a Christian might somehow claim freedom on that account. This was in itself enough to discourage absolutely any attempt at their conversion in the plantation country, although in New England, where full political rights could be held only by church members, the opportunities for Blacks to become Christians were hardly more favorable. The threat implied in social equality was a factor of consequence in both North and South. It was thought that the Blacks would become "uppity" or "impudent" by reason of their association with whites in religious services, and they would "not so readily keep their places" thereafter if they were admitted to fellowship with whites. Long before Crispus Attucks ran away from slavery to become the first American to die for this country's independence, the Corporation of Harvard College was bitterly protesting the seating of a Negro even in the gallery of the First Parish Church in Cambridge.

Aside from motives deriving from economic interest and conceit, there was also a real fear that slaves meeting under cover of religious worship would plot insurrection or revolt. These apprehensions proved to be well founded, for in the decades following the American Revolution, when it became clear to the black patriots that their political rights were totally unaffected by their patriotism or their valor, they were not reluctant to use whatever cover or pretext was available to strike more directly for their freedom. Indeed, having been bereft of all rights whatever by those for whose independence they had struggled, it was a sad revelation to learn that the cause of American independence for which they had fought was not a cause which recognized the right of freedom for anyone who happened to be black. Although information concerning insurrections, escape, sabotage, gentricide, and the like was commonly suppressed in the effort to avoid contagion, no segment of the slave era was free from the concerted acts of black people resisting their subjugation.

So it was that from the beginning the American Nation under God showed no serious concern for either the spiritual or the political needs of the black wards fetched from Africa. Left to their own resources, the vast majority of Blacks practiced whatever fragments of African religions they could remember, modified by the singular exigencies of life on the plantation. Most religious practices were secret, for while the slavemaster reserved Christianity for himself and his kind, he had no sympathy and less appreciation for other religions he did not understand or care to learn about. The "heathen rituals" of the Africans were generally dismissed as childish superstitions much given to the gibberish and frenzy indicative of a low order of intelligence which required continuous and white control. In consequence, all expressions of African religion were forbidden; and whenever possible, Africans with the same tribal or language affiliation were split up and sold off to widely separated plantations.

Opening the Doors

When the Society for the Propagation of the Gospel launched its campaign to have Blacks conditionally admitted to the select circle of American Christendom, it did so under the shadow of colonial legislation that had been passed by Maryland in 1664 and by Virginia in 1667 guaranteeing that a slave's status was unaffected by the circumstance of baptism. By 1706, four additional colonies had made a similar determination, and these laws were then given religious sanction by an edict from the Bishop of London in 1727. The edict assured the planters that conversion "does not make the least alteration in Civil property . . . but continues Persons in the same state as it found them. . . ."[21] The society's missionary activities were in some respects a curious turn of history, for the African involvement in Christianity was centuries old long before the English had given up some pagan practices very similar to those from which they now decided the Africans ought to be rescued. But, as we have already observed, the most difficult obstacle faced by the SPG was the white resistance to sharing the faith with Blacks. This antipathy was deeply embedded in custom and convention and fortified by law. As early as 1715, a North Carolina law provided a heavy fine "if any master or owner of Negroes, or slaves . . . shall permit or suffer any Negro or Negroes to build . . . on their lands . . . any house under pretense of meeting-house upon account of worship . . . and shall not suppress or hinder them. . . ." In 1800 a law in South Carolina made it illegal for "any number of slaves, free Negroes, mulattoes or mestizoes, even in the company of white persons to . . . assemble for the purpose of . . . religious worship, either before the rising of the sun, or the going down of the same."[22]

In North Carolina no slave or free Black could legally preach or exhort "in any prayer meeting or other association for worship where slaves of different families were collected together."[23] Other laws required the presence of whites—from five or six to a majority—at any meeting or worship service Blacks could attend. Some of the harsher proscriptions were in response to the slave insurrections of Toussaint L'Ouverture in Haiti, and Nat Turner and Denmark Vesey in Virginia, but the determination to limit and to direct the black religious experience was well established a hundred years before there was a major black resurrection to agitate the planters. There were other reasons born of more subtle imaginings, for, in America, Christianity was considered as unconditionally the white man's exclusive entitlement as any of the other cultural ensigns put forward as distinguishing the Anglo-Saxon heritage.

The Great Awakening

It was not until the first Great Awakening, that tumultuous series of outdoor revivals and camp meetings that swept the country around 1740, that the Christian religion became reasonably accessible to the black masses. The cold, impersonal churches of Puritan New England, where dispassionate, abstract theological arguments were offered from the lofty pulpits in lieu of preaching, had little appeal to Blacks, whose doctrinal views were anchored in a cheerless reality no learned argument could alleviate. In the South, the staid formalism of the Episcopal Church with its Latin liturgy and esoteric symbolism was hardly more attractive or comforting. The black condition demanded a God with *feelings*, a God the distressed could talk to! Only when it moved out of the established churches and into the groves and brush arbors, leaving behind the private pews, the nigger heavens, and the other demeaning trappings of class and race, did the white man's religion begin to take on real significance for black people. Fiery exhorters—some of whom were black—who could *"preach the Bible real,"* supported by fervent singing and praying and testifying, gave the Black Diaspora a perspective on the faith that bore promise of true spiritual utility.

In New England, despite the salubrious spirit of the Awakening, there was no immediate rush among Blacks to become Christians merely because the more onerous barriers to the faith had been temporarily relaxed. Normative Christian nurture still required a cultus, a fellowship, which in turn implied church membership, a status not easily attained by either the poor or the black. Despite the ardent efforts of the Society for the Propagation of the Gospel, if there was hungering and thirsting for the white man's religion, that yearning was scarcely reflected in the pews of the churches by the close of the Revolutionary War. The Reverend Samuel Hopkins of Newport attributed the absence of the Blacks to "the deepest prejudices against the Christian religion."[24]

The story was quite different in the South, where the Methodists and Baptists had gathered thousands of Blacks into their churches before the end of the eighteenth century.[25] When the Methodist Church was formally organized in 1784, fully one-fifth of its membership was black; and by the turn of the century, Blacks in the Methodist and Baptist churches were numbered in the tens of thousands. Presbyterians were a distant third, with smaller numbers of Blacks scattered among the other major denominations.

But that is not the whole story. The Episcopal Church, dominant in the states where Blacks were most populous, failed altogether to attract a significant black constituency. The Presbyterians and the Quakers, both more benign denominations in their attitudes toward Blacks, had little more success than the Congregationalists of New England, who considered themselves the principal friends of the Blacks.

The Great Awakening aroused in thousands of Americans, white and black, a new spiritual consciousness which culminated, in many cases, in church affiliation—mainly with Baptists and Methodists. Popular theory advanced to account for the black attraction to the faith at this peculiar moment in American history suggests that while New England Calvinism was too cold and reasoned for the African mind, Catholicism and Episcopalianism were "too symbolic and ritualistic," the Quakers "too meditative" and "too reflective." The burden of this argument, of course, rests upon the conventional presupposition that black people are "exuberant" and "emotional" *by nature*, impatient with symbolism and abstraction, and not much given to reflection. But, from the beginning, conventional Western perception conceived the African world as essentially a world of the senses, not a world of the mind. The practical effects of this condition explained the African's spiritual retardation and postponed his significant religious investment. The Great Awakening, with its spiritual boisterousness, uncomplicated preaching, and vivid stories, coupled with the opportunity for substantial personal participation through singing, praying, and testifying, struck a responsive chord in the African he had never before experienced in America. All this was thought to replicate to some degree traditional African religion, while elevating the African experience to increasingly higher planes of spiritual involvement. A major objection to this theory is that it strains too hard at the gnat of African emotionalism while overlooking the obvious: what the Africans found in the camp meetings of the Great Awakening was *acceptance and involvement as human beings*. However tentative his reception, and however transitory the occasion, the camp meetings became a sanctuary to which the African could escape for an interlude of peace and dignity from the humdrum horror of slavery. Under the brush arbors, the black slave was a servant among servants and a seeker among seekers, all terrified, sanctified, and exultant together. It was the only moment in his life that his color and his station were not the absolute conditioners of his humanity.

The camp meetings were a serious deviation from conventional norms of religious behavior, and the practices of the Great Awakening came under fire from the traditionalists of the day. The behavior of the Blacks was particularly cited as evidence of the alleged degenerate nature of revivalism. A prominent New England minister complained:

> So great has been the enthusiasm created by Wesley and Whitefield and Tennant . . . the very Servants and Slaves pretend to extraordinary inspiration, and under veil thereof cherish their idle dispositions, and in lieu of minding their respective businesses run rambling about to utter enthusiastic nonsense.[26]

Whether it was the religious style of the Great Awakening or the relaxation of social constraints that was decisive for black involvement, that involvement was furthered by the suspension of conventional procedures which required converts to go through a period of instruction before full admission to Christian fellowship. Because most white Christians held firmly to the belief that Blacks were incapable of receiving instruction, and incapable of fulfilling the moral obligations which were a part of that instruction, the practical result was to keep Blacks out of the churches because of these alleged inadequacies. In New England, where church membership and citizenship were closely linked, this linkage alone was effective in the exclusion of Blacks from the churches. In the South, the worrisome problem of the legal status of Christian slaves was a formidable deterrent to black evangelization, as was the great fear that social distance between Blacks and whites would be jeopardized. As it turned out, the Great Awakening not only was the wedge which opened the faith to the Blacks; it was also the first serious breach in the forbidding fortress of religious formalism which contributed to the effective maintenance of barriers between social classes as well as to the racial-caste arrangement.

But the most notable accomplishment of the Awakening was the legitimation of the spiritual quest at the level of felt need rather than at the level of privilege, so that the common man of whatever race was provided a less cumbersome access to the faith.

By the time Thomas Jefferson came to draft the Declaration of Independence, black Christians were a substantial segment of the church. The overwhelming majority of them were slaves, for they remained slaves after conversion, just as they remained slaves after the War for Independence had raised their hopes and claimed their blood. For all that, religion did make a difference in their lives, and it has continued to modify the black experience and its impingement upon America ever since.

Attracted by the informality and the excitement of the Awakening, Blacks accepted Christianity not so much because they could give vent to their alleged natural exuberance or native fervor but because it was suddenly available on terms they could live with. The rules which had kept them on the plantations and out of the churches were relaxed momentarily in the informality of the brush arbors, and the opportunities to enter into new kinds of relationships with other human beings were at least tentatively present. The consequences of the black religious involvement were both immediate and far-reaching. First of all, the argument about the African's spiritual and moral capacity was made moot by the fact that thousands of Blacks accepted Christianity and were received as Christians. This was a *fait accompli*. Impossible as it was, it *was*. Second, while the religious test of the Awakening was based on religious experience rather than theological understanding, the acquisition of some modicum of instruction and information was inevitable in the process of Christian worship and fellowship. Third, any kind of Christian association, even that of master and slave, modified relationships to some degree and raised implicit questions in the minds of all parties about the morality of the slave system. Finally, Christianity provided an organizational and moral base for self-liberation which in time the Blacks were certain to exploit.

It is a reasonable conclusion, then, that despite distortions and limitations, sharing the same religion provided opportunities for the socialization of Blacks and for the humanization of the whites who held them in thrall. Few slaves, torn away as they were from their previous cultures, found anything to fill the cultural vacuum in the day-to-day existence which marked the slave system. The societies and tribal orders to which they belonged in Africa could not be replicated under the slavocracy in America. The drums were forbidden; the familiar languages were forbidden, as were the ancient rituals and ceremonies providing for identity and community. The established policy of separating slaves with a common tribal or language background was everywhere enforced. As a result, not only were the ties of cultural continuity with the motherland summarily severed by commercial deportation, but the opportunities for reasonable reconstruction after resettlement were effectively eliminated. The slave plantation had no room and less sympathy for an African counterpart of the Little Italys, or the barrios, or the Chinatowns which were later to become features of American ethnic pluralism. Instead, every effort was made to preclude the possibility of the Africans ever having effective cultural communion with each other, not to mention acceptance in the general American community. The vast majority of the slaves were confined to the fields from daylight until dark, and their participation in the culture of America was hardly any different from what it would have been had they remained in Africa. Whatever they may have remembered of their previous religious experiences could scarcely be replicated in the remote corners of the plantation, and could do little to enhance their life of bondage in America.

In spite of the dismal prospects for the religious needs of the Africans during their first hundred years in America, Christianity played a major part in the development of the new black subculture, for once it gained a foothold on the plantation, it became a meaningful substitute for many of the lost institutions which had been so important to tribal life in Africa. Common worship, communal singing, a common ritual, and common beliefs broke down the barriers of language and custom and brought men and women of many different tribal affiliations together in religious associations. Further, it is reasonable to assume that, despite the fact that white Christians could not seem to overcome the felt need to hold other Christians in bondage, Christian conscience regarding the practice was probably never completely at ease. In the long run, the very long run, perhaps, it is a reasonable speculation that the incongruity of enslaving one's brothers and sisters in Christ might have touched even the most unregenerate "masters," and that abominable "peculiar institution" would in time have capitulated to the ethics of the same faith in which it sought its justification. Indeed, had the Great Awakening occurred a hundred years earlier, slavery as an institution might not have survived the Revolution, for once Blacks became Christians in large numbers, the problem of justification and maintenance was exacerbated, and the system may well have fallen under its own weight in time. This is not to overlook the fact that some Blacks were undoubtedly more securely accommodated to their condition through religious involvement, for, as we have seen, the critical doctrines of the faith were not immune to distortion and manipulation. But the accommodation of some to a system of oppression is also a powerful factor in the determination of others to be free. In any case, religion became the primary occasion for a more humane contact with whites, and in consequence it was the most important instrument of black socialization. At minimum, their acceptance as Christians, however conditional, was an implied admission that they had souls and were persons of worth and responsibility, and therefore entitled to some recognition beyond that of mere brutes and chattels.

But American Christianity never did imply a presumption of racial equality for Blacks, whether social, political, or spiritual. Nor did it concede to them the mature sense of moral accountability all white Christians were presumed to have. Morally, the black Christian was simply expected to do the best he could with his limited capacity. God and society would forgive him his failures so long as he kept the place assigned him in the sociopolitical structure.

Since the white man's religion was not an effective shelter from the incidental effects of his secular inclinations, the black man's hopes for relief from pariahism through conversion to Christianity were quite vain. There is no record that conversion brought liberty to a single slave throughout the long history of slavery in America. But there seems to be substantial evidence that over the long run Christianity tends to reduce its disharmonies by grinding its ad hoc distortions of convenience into eventual conformation. If this is true, it is interesting to speculate that had the slaves identified themselves completely with the religion of the slavemaster and become adepts in the faith, neither the South nor the nation could thereafter have controlled the forces and counterforces that would have been loosed in contention for the truth. But truth, for all its magnificence, can be a long, long time in coming.

Black Religion and Its Cultus

If the matter had ended with fulfillment of the white man's intentions, the development of black religion would have been quite different. Unquestionably, three centuries or so of American religion have left their mark. There are black Christians who still yearn to have their blackness washed away at the magic fountain they were taught to believe flowed exclusively from the mysterious inner sanctum of the White Church. This is a lingering testimony about an era when the message of the faith was indistinguishable from the agenda of its sponsors. But the fact that black

Christians were expected to accept uncritically the American version of the faith, and that they ran the risk of being humiliated by it, and of being spiritually stifled by its selective theology, could not, and did not, insure an abject spiritual underclass. For, despite the major role assigned religion in slave management, there was always a significant community of black Christians who had the grace and the spiritual acuity necessary to salvage value from the basic truths that underlay so much dross. Undoubtedly, both elements were inevitable features of the developing black experience, and the Black Church which finally emerged from that experience was destined to be racked by the differing perceptions of honest men and women in search of an expression of the faith which would transcend the vagaries of human manipulation, whatever their source.

Since religion required a *cultus*, i.e., a collectivity in communion with itself, there was no room in the White Church for the black Christians who needed to be persons as well as believers. In consequence, even in the face of the formidable odds that would seek to suppress it, control it, or laugh it to scorn, the Black Church was as inevitable as religion itself. It was a unique institution, destined to leave an unmistakable mark on the religious and cultural history of America, for, from the very beginning, at least some discerned in the revived faith a beacon of freedom. As early as 1773, a black group in Boston petitioned the Massachusetts legislature that all slaves be freed on the grounds that obedience to God was not a viable option under slavery.

Such black revolutionaries as Nat Turner and Gabriel Prosser were devout Christians, but they saw their own enslavement as inconsistent with the freedom they believed the Christian life required. In 1800, in the course of his plans to liberate black Virginia, Prosser is said to have ordered his men to spare the Quakers and the Methodists (who were at the time considered anti-slavery). On the other hand, thirty-one years later, Nat Turner ravaged the Virginia countryside with a band of followers who cut down anything white on sight—men, women, and children. Turner is said to have had a vision during which he was told: "The serpent is loosed. Christ has laid down the Yoke. You must take it up again."[27] Before he and his men were finally routed, Nat Turner's retribution took the lives of sixty-one of his white brothers in Christ who had tormented him and his fellow black Christians with slavery. There were many revolts and minor insurrections which were not publicized for fear that the contagion of freedom would spread, but thousands who did not revolt liberated themselves by running away. Much of the strategy for escape via the Underground Railroad was contrived under cover of religious gatherings, and critical to the impulse for freedom was the notion that true religion and slavery were somehow inconsistent and incompatible. If a man cannot serve two masters, then it is clear that God must be preferable.

A countertheme in the deep faith which underscores black religion to this day is expressed in the absolute assurance that God will take care of his own. "Leaving it to God" has often been interpreted as a form of passivity which has at times slowed or impeded the black will to freedom. As a result, there is a substantial history of criticism of the Black Church's alleged willingness to let God do for them what Blacks should do for themselves. There is substance to this censure, but there is also a history of circumstances which accounts for it. Part of the problem derived from the slave's understanding of God and the meaning of faith. The God of black religion is inevitably the God of the Old Testament. He is an ever-present, *here-right-now God;* and more than that he is a *fighting God*, a spiritual Paladin. Coupled with the warrior-God there is often the notion that true faith is the recognition of absolute contingency, i.e., the denial that man can of himself accomplish anything, and the unwillingness to compete with God, whose work and whose prerogative it is to deliver his own. It is still traditional among rural Blacks to cease all human activity when there is thunder or lightning or other indications that "the Lord is doing his work." The notion is that when God is at work, man's proper response is to be respectful and silent and out of the way. For those who laid the foundations of the Black Church, such an attitude was certainly not seen as the avoidance of self-help: it was the epitome of faith in a God who *needed* no help. Vengeance is mine, saith the Lord. One does not usurp that prerogative on impulse.

The misconceptions about black Christian passivity are of a piece with the misconceptions about black styles of worship. Ultimately, these misconceptions derive in both instances from differences in how God is perceived. Certainly a hero God "you can talk to" requires no symbolism and no esoterica. He is approachable, directly. Similarly, an all-powerful avenging God who is *here-right-now-and-ready-for-battle* may only require man to get out of the way so that he can act. Black religion embraces both notions of man's responsibility to work with God to accomplish his freedom, and man's responsibility to have consummate faith that God can handle the situation by himself. It must also be remembered that under slavery all members of the society were degraded by the system, and every human being was a potential enemy—a fact painfully illustrated by those slaves who turned out to be informers. There was no one to rely on with absolute confidence *except* God. This is the same unquestioning faith, born of dereliction and nurtured in the protracted agony of slavery, which, with the spirit of self-liberation, made black survival possible. Both readings of the faith were necessary, for in the absence of a strong religious conviction stabilized between extremes, the black experience in the context of American history would almost certainly have produced a different rendering.

Sources of the Black Experience in Religion

What were the sources of the religious experience of Blacks in America? There were at least two, and these were in conflict. The most obvious and the only official source of religious indoctrination for the slaves was the white preachers and exhorters who shared as a matter of course the prevailing presumptions of the slaveowners. The other source, which came to be called the Invisible Church, represented the slaves' effort to meet God on their own. Of the first source, historian Kenneth Stampp has said:

> Through religious instruction the bondsmen learned that slavery had divine sanction, that insolence was as much an offense against God as against the temporal master . . . servants should obey their masters . . . eternal salvation would be the reward for faithful service. . . .[28]

Professor Stampp is too modest. The essence of that version of Christianity taught to black people began with the injunction "Servants, obey your master," and concluded with the warning: "He that knoweth the will of the master and doeth it not will be beaten with many stripes." But between the order and the threat was an elaborately conceived, universally promulgated theological doctrine which made the wisdom of God the agent and the reason for the black man's fall from grace into slavery. Black Christians were given to understand that slavery was God's will and his enactment. It was a consequence of black people's peculiar sinfulness and depravity that they should suffer, and that white men should be the agents of providential justice set over them. The proper response, indeed the only acceptable response, was complete submission, joyful acceptance, loyalty, and patience forever. Or, as black convention has it: "Sing and pray, live on hay; there'll be pie in the sky bye and bye when you die!" Such a doctrine was said to have been highly successful in teaching certain slaves "respect and obedience to their superiors"; it made them "more pleasant and profitable servants," and "aided the discipline of a plantation in a wonderful manner." So impressed were they with the salutary effects such a rendition of the faith had on their slaves that a distinguished group of

South Carolinians published a pamphlet extolling "the practical working and wholesome effects of religious instruction when properly and judiciously imparted to our Negro peasantry."[29]

But the Negro peasantry wasn't necessarily buying all that was being sold. The black slave came early to the conclusion that religion as taught by the slavemasters or their representatives was not concerned with his salvation. The fact was that the religion he was offered was designed primarily to reduce the inherent hazards of slavekeeping to manageable proportions. By being made to function as a divine imperative in an enterprise that was patently Mephistophelian, it could insure the margin of security which extended slavekeeping long past its logical demise. In sum, it was a religious conspiracy designed to keep black people accommodated to an economic system in which they were compelled to be the uncompensated instruments of white Christian enrichment. In perpetuity. It was a sinister and presumptive enterprise, but one that has proven effective enough to blight three hundred and fifty years of Christian civilization in America. The consequences are everywhere apparent in the continuing American dilemma where the dehumanization of Christians by Christians with an eye for profit, or a yen for status, remains an accepted feature of the American scene. So blatant a strategy, even when attributed to the politics of God, was seen by the black slave for what it was from the very beginning. And it was rejected even then.

In 1787 two events of great historical significance took place in Philadelphia, the City of Brotherly Love. They were in stark contrast to each other in spirit and in their implications for the future of America. The delegates to the Philadelphia Convention gave their approval to the United States Constitution; and a little band of black Christians led by Richard Allen were pulled from their knees while praying in a segregated gallery in St. George's Methodist Episcopal Church.

In contrast to the Declaration of Independence, the construction of the Constitution provided little occasion for oratorical rhetoric. The men who gathered at Philadelphia for the Constitutional Convention were hard, practical men bent on preserving the prerogatives they had wrung from history, and intent on fully exploiting the incalculable promise of the new nation they were about to design. There were philosophers among them; and dreamers. But with the exception of a deist or two, they were men for whom Christianity in general, and Protestant Christianity in particular, represented the spiritual scaffolding upon which this nation under God should properly take form. Nonetheless, the suppression of liberty and the want of justice already in their midst were carefully ignored.

In the succeeding two hundred years of American history the spiritual and political energy spent in first trying to justify and then finally trying to undo what the Founding Fathers accomplished in their awesome moment of power has been of a magnitude unrivaled by any other interest. The price America has had to pay in dollars and in lives, in lost self-respect, and in human genius switched off to the low road of human perversity and hatred can be measured in terms of the present state of the nation's enduring racial dilemma. The Constitution, sadly profaned by three clauses protecting slavery, went on to become the law of the land. And Richard Allen and his intrepid band of black Christians went on to make a different kind of history by institutionalizing the Black Church in America.

The extraordinary genius of the Christian religion is exemplified in the fact that it has always managed to survive its distortions. For two thousand years the faith has been compromised by countless schisms and isms without succumbing to any of them. Popes, priests, preachers and parishioners, governments, and private interests have sought from the earliest times to subvert the authority and prestige of the church to private ends. None has enjoyed lasting success. Hence, the strategy of the slavocracy to use Christianity as the clinch pin for the institutionalization of slavery and caste in America was ultimately doomed to failure, although the failure of the strategy cannot be credited to renouncements of it, early or late. It is not that there have been no prophetic voices in the American church, but at the critical junctures of American history those voices have always been muted by the racism with which we are afflicted. Hence, the tragedy by American religion is that it succumbed so early and so completely to the fetish of racism, so clearly in contradiction to the principles by which Christianity claims to be informed.

Capitulation to racial idolatry made God himself, not the African slaves, the principal adversary, for whatever the strategies man may devise to distrain the flesh, only God's lien may lie against the soul. The distraint of the African's body and the labor derived from its possession is a historical *fait accompli*. But the strategy of American Christianity failed in its effort to make black Christians a class of spiritual subordinates in concert. For, in accepting Christianity in America, the Africans were not necessarily accepting American Christianity. The God they addressed and the faith they knew transcended the American experience. If the white man's religion sacrificed its moral and spiritual validity to the Baal of white supremacy, the Black Church was born of the firm conviction that the racial Baal was a no-god.

Notes

1. All biblical quotes are from the King James version.
2. Cf. Frederick Perry Noble, *The Redemption of Africa* (Chicago: Fleming H. Revell, 1899), Vol. 1, p. 7. Says Noble: "In the Egyptians we have a dark race originating from the mingling of black and white races. If these blacks were Negroes or like Negroes— and the best authorities regard this as the case . . . the civilization of Egypt is only less Negro than [Caucasian]." Obviously, the present writer accepts the dictum of the best authorities.
3. Saunders Redding, *They Came in Chains* (Philadelphia: Lippincott, 1950).
4. Noble, pp. 134–5.
5. Winthrop D. Jordan, *White Over Black* (Chapel Hill: University of North Carolina Press, 1968), p. 24.
6. Ibid., p. 27.
7. W.E.B. Du Bois, ed., "The Negro Church," p. 27.
8. Kelly Miller, *Radicals and Conservatives and Other Essays on the Negro for America* (New York: Saborken Books, 1968), p. 193.
9. Du Bois, *The Negro Church*, p. 30.
10. Gilbert Osofsky, *The Burden of Race* (New York: Harper & Row, 1967), p. 40.
11. Jordan, p. 183.
12. H. Shelton Smith, *In His Image, But . . .* (Durham: Duke University Press, 1972), p. 11.
13. Jordan, p. 186.
14. Lorenzo J. Greene, *The Negro In Colonial New England* (New York: Atheneum, 1968), p. 257.
15. Jordan, p. 93.
16. Ibid., p. 260.
17. Osofsky, p. 35.
18. Greene, pp. 271–2.
19. Ibid., pp. 259, 260.
20. Jordan, p. 179.
21. Greene, p. 261.
22. Du Bois, p. 11.
23. Ibid., p. 22.
24. Greene, p. 288.
25. Smith, p. 53. See also Carter G. Woodson and Charles H. Wesley, *The Negro in Our History* (Washington, D.C.: Associated Publishers, 1922), for a discussion of the failure of the Catholics, Episcopalians, Quakers, and Presbyterians to attract substantial numbers of black converts.
26. Greene, p. 276.
27. Benjamin Brawley, *A Social History of the American Negro* (London: Collier-Macmillan, 1970), pp. 140 ff.
28. Kenneth M. Stampp, *The Peculiar Institution* (New York: Alfred A. Knopf, 1956), p. 158.
29. Ibid., p. 159.

Chapter 8

The Black Church

A Gender Perspective

Evelyn Brooks Higginbotham

As I look about me today in this veiled world of mine, despite the noisier and more spectacular advance of my brothers, I instinctively feel and know that it is the five million women of my race who really count. Black women (and women whose grandmothers were black) are . . . the main pillars of those social settlements which we call churches; and they have with small doubt raised three-fourths of our church property.

W.E.B. Du Bois, *Darkwater* (1918)

Much has been written about the importance of the black church in the social and political life of black people. Much less has been written about black women's importance in the life of the church. This book is a study of women in the black church between 1880 and 1920—a period that has come to be known simultaneously as the "woman's era" and the "nadir" in American race relations. I argue that women were crucial to broadening the public arm of the church and making it the most powerful institution of racial self-help in the African American community. During these years, the church served as the most effective vehicle by which men and women alike, pushed down by racism and poverty, regrouped and rallied against emotional and physical defeat.

In some instances, church women contested racist ideology and institutions through demands for anti-lynching legislation and an end to segregation laws. They expressed their discontent with both racial and gender discrimination and demanded equal rights for blacks and women—advocating voting rights or equal employment and educational opportunities. Black women even drew upon the Bible, the most respected source within their community, to fight for women's rights in the church and society at large. During the late nineteenth century they developed a distinct discourse of resistance, a feminist theology. More often, however, their efforts represented not dramatic protest but everyday forms of resistance to oppression and demoralization. Largely through the fund-raising efforts of women, the black church built schools, provided clothes and food to poor people, established old folks' homes and orphanages, and made available a host of needed social welfare services.

This study attempts to rescue women from invisibility as historical actors in the drama of black empowerment. Since women have traditionally constituted the majority of every black denomination, I present the black church not as the exclusive product of a male ministry but as the product and process of male and female interaction. In offering a corrective to the near exclusion of women in most studies of the black church, my book departs from the more recent and positive discussion of exceptional women, the early women preachers.[1] Research on women preachers, while of great value, does not capture the more representative role of the majority of women church members. If taken alone, such discussion continues to render women's role as marginal. Left obscured is the interrelation between the rising black churches in the late nineteenth and early twentieth centuries and the indefatigable efforts of black women's organizations. Left unheard are women's voices within the public discourse of racial and gender self-determination. In short, the focus on the ministry fails to capture adequately the gender dimension of the church's racial mission. Ultimately, my study provides a vantage point for viewing the interplay of race, gender, and class consciousness, for it presents the church, like the black community it mirrors, as a social space of unifying and conflicting discourses.

I have focused my attention on the movement that brought into existence the National Baptist Convention, U.S.A., Inc. This movement represented and continues to represent the largest group—religious or secular—of black Americans. To persons not versed in church history, the term "convention" might bring to mind an annual meeting or tangential association. In the history of black Baptists, however, "convention" has almost the same meaning as "denomination." The black Baptist convention is distinct from that of white Baptists and emerged only because otherwise autonomous black Baptist churches voluntarily and freely came together.[2] Their collective association, beginning first at the state level and eventually embracing a national constituency, effected an unprecedented arena for public discussion and mobilization of resources on the part of African Americans.

Although conventions did not originate with late nineteenth-century black Baptists, their profound importance rests in their deployment as vehicles of black identity and empowerment. Ironically, it was the issue of slavery in 1844 that divided white Baptists into northern and southern conventions.[3] The close of the Civil War did not heal the rift among white Baptists, but it did give black Baptists the opportunity to forge a national unity and identity of their own. The decision to form a black national convention was motivated by discriminatory policies on the part of white Baptists, as well as by the growing support among African Americans in general for racial self-determination.[4]

James Melvin Washington's *Frustrated Fellowship: The Black Baptist Quest for Social Power* (1985) remains the most comprehensive discussion of the racial tensions that spurred the evolution of the black Baptist movement. Washington and others have described its separatist, indeed nationalist character as informed by philosophies of racial self-help and racial self-determination. But in chronicling the events that led to the development of the black Baptist church as a potent national force, they have focused overwhelmingly on the contributions of outstanding ministers within male-dominated state and national conventions.[5]

Black Baptist churchmen certainly recognized the importance of women's active support for the denomination's efforts toward racial self-help and self-reliance. Yet male-biased traditions and rules of decorum sought to mute women's voices and accentuate their subordinate status vis-à-vis men. Thus tainted by the values of the larger American society, the black church sought to provide men with full manhood rights, while offering women a separate and unequal status. As we will see, however complex the black Baptist women's own ideas were concerning separate roles for men and women—or the appropriate sexual division of labor— they would not lightly accept their own subordination in the struggle of their people.

The Black Church during the Nadir

The nationalist consciousness of the black Baptist church came of age during the years of heightened racism that followed Reconstruction. In 1880, when black Baptists took the first step toward creating a permanent national structure, the halcyon days of voting and political ferment among southern blacks had given way to growing disillusionment.[6] By 1890, it had become preeminently clear that the black community would have to devise its own strategies of social and political advancement. In that year

Mississippi adopted a disfranchisement plan that served as a model to the rest of the South. Disfranchisement formed part of the larger process of "depoliticalization": literacy tests, poll taxes, and other state election laws, along with social and psychological sanctions such as economic reprisal, violence, and threats of violence, affected the mass removal of blacks from the nation's political life. Political institutions and representative government became simply inaccessible and unaccountable to American citizens who happened to be black.[7]

Black men lost more than the ballot on election day. They lost many other rights, which theoretically the constitution and federal civil rights laws protected: the right to hold public office, sit on juries, allocate tax dollars for schools and other social services, protect their women and themselves from insult and victimization, and share in other basic human and citizenship rights. Black women, like all American women, had never shared political equality with their men. Once black men were denied the suffrage, however, black women became ever more powerless and vulnerable to southern racial hostility.[8]

As southern state after state during the 1880s and 1890s set in motion a barrage of discriminatory laws that routinized the separate and inferior status of blacks, violence and intimidation solidified the "Negro's place" in the New South. Between 1884 and 1900 more than 2,500 lynchings of blacks were recorded. American race relations reached an all-time low—the "nadir," as Rayford Logan termed the disquieting times.[9] Jim Crow, as segregation was called, quickly pervaded every part of life and made itself felt even in death. In employment, housing, places of amusement, public transportation, schools, hospitals, and cemeteries, segregation daily produced and reproduced racial identities, power, and disempowerment. During the "nadir," black communities turned increasingly inward. They struggled without the aid or protection of the federal government; worse yet, they suffered its policies of betrayal. In 1883 the Supreme Court had declared unconstitutional the federal Civil Rights Act of 1875, a law prohibiting racial discrimination in places of public accommodation. In 1896 the Court announced its sanction of the "separate but equal" doctrine.[10]

Powerless to avert the mounting tide of racist public opinion, black people struggled to maintain family and community cohesiveness in an environment that sought to tear both asunder. African Americans, looking now to themselves to educate the masses of their people, care for the needy, facilitate economic development, and address political concerns, tapped their greatest strength from the tradition of their churches.[11] From the early days of slavery, the black church had constituted the backbone of the black community. Truly African American in its origins, it provided a spiritual cohesiveness that permitted its people to absorb, interpret, and practice the Christian faith—to make it their own. As the "invisible institution" of the slaves, the church had long promoted a sense of individual and collective worth and perpetuated a belief in human dignity that countered the racist preachings of the master class.[12] In the decades following Reconstruction, the church's autonomy and financial strength made it the most logical institution for the pursuit of racial self-help. It functioned not only as the house of worship but as an agency of social control, forum of discussion and debate, promoter of education and economic cooperation, and arena for the development and assertion of leadership.

Recognizing its diverse roles, E. Franklin Frazier termed the black church a veritable "nation within a nation."[13] At the individual level, but especially when collectively joined in association, black churches represented not an escapist and other-worldly orientation but the only viable bastion of a community under assault. If for many of its members the black church remained a focus for the perpetuation of community identity, for many of its leaders it became the vehicle for consolidating every existing strength into a concerted campaign for racial self-reliance. Those who sought to make the church the flagship of black dignity espoused strong race-conscious views concerning the preservation of the black community, and, just as important, they sought to shape the community so that preservation could become progress.

Race consciousness reached its apogee with the creation of the National Baptist Convention, U.S.A. in 1895. Determined to create a forum through which black people could voice their spiritual, economic, political, and social concerns, the convention's leaders equated racial self-determination with black denominational hegemony. These ideas were not unique to the black Baptist church. The African Methodist Episcopal Church had emerged as a separate denomination during the dawning years of the nineteenth century.[14] By the late nineteenth and early twentieth centuries all the black denominations had established community institutions and advanced the philosophy of racial self-help. But it was in the black Baptist church where this philosophy found its largest following.

Black Baptists constituted the most numerically significant attempt to counter the debilitating intent and effects of American racial exclusivism, and thus their story broadly characterizes the black church and black community. The National Baptist Convention, which existed apart from the powerful white Northern Baptist Convention and Southern Baptist Convention, constituted the largest and most representative sample of the black churchgoing population. In 1906 it had 2,261,607 members, while the second largest denominational membership, African Methodist Episcopal, had only 494,777. The National Baptist Convention included 61.4 percent of all black church members in the United States.[15] By 1916 National Baptists numbered 2,938,579. The convention was larger than any other black religious group and larger than either of the two major white Baptist groups, namely, the Northern Baptist Convention with 1,232,135 or the Southern Baptist Convention with 2,708,870.[16] The numerical power of the black Baptist convention appears even more dramatic when compared against the other white denominations. In 1916 it ranked as the third largest religious body in the United States—trailing only the Roman Catholic and Methodist Episcopal churches.

The great majority of the convention's members, like the great majority of blacks themselves, lived in the South and in areas with populations under 25,000. But its leaders hailed from towns and cities, and thus the bulk of its programs were there. The convention's urban presence steadily increased as blacks began to migrate in larger and larger numbers to southern and northern cities. In 1906 the National Baptist Convention constituted the largest denomination, black or white, in Atlanta, Memphis, and Richmond. By 1916 it took the lead in Birmingham and Nashville, while continuing to dominate in Memphis and Richmond. In Louisville, Washington, D.C., and New Orleans, it was second only to the Catholic church, while its numbers grew exponentially in Philadelphia, Pittsburgh, and Chicago.[17] By sheer size alone, the black Baptist church formed a microcosm of the black population in America and included men and women from all social classes and geographic regions.

The Black Church as Public Sphere

By law, blacks were denied access to public space, such as parks, libraries, restaurants, meeting halls, and other public accommodations. In time the black church—open to both secular and religious groups in the community—came to signify public space. It housed a diversity of programs including schools, circulating libraries, concerts, restaurants, insurance companies, vocational training, athletic clubs—all catering to a population much broader than the membership of individual churches. The church served as meeting hall for virtually every large gathering. It held political rallies, clubwomen's conferences, and school graduations. It was the one space truly accessible to the black community, and it was this characteristic that led W.E.B. Du Bois, long before E. Franklin Frazier, to identify the black church as a multiple site—at once being a place of worship, theater, publishing house, school, and lodge.[18]

The church also functioned as a discursive, critical arena—a public sphere in which values and issues were aired, debated, and disseminated throughout the larger black community. The black Baptist convention movement facilitated the sharing and distribution of information through periodic statewide and national meetings, where thousands gathered and discussed issues of civic concern. Since black women constituted two-thirds of this movement, they had a crucial role in the formation of public sentiment and in the expression of a black collective will. Particularly through women's efforts, black communities with very limited income raised funds sufficient to build and sustain churches, schools, and social welfare services. At times in concert and at times in conflict with their men, black women initiated race-conscious programs of self-help.

The very nationalist discourse that unified black men and women betrayed inherent gender conflict. As a deliberative arena, the National Baptist Convention sought to speak for both men and women, but it did not encourage expression from men and women as equals. The convention's masculine bias was evident in its institutional structures and discourses. Positions of authority and power were monopolized by men. Thus women sought to develop their own voice and pursue their own interests, which at times overlapped and at other times contested the men's. Rising gender consciousness was part of a complex of ideas that informed black Baptist denominational work as a whole.

In 1900 women succeeded in forming an alternate sphere of deliberation within the larger denominational context of the National Baptist Convention. The Woman's Convention, defined as an auxiliary to the NBC, summoned a sisterhood more than one million strong and culminated nearly three decades of work by women's organizations at the local and state levels. Through their convention, black women shared knowledge of their state and local activities. They governed their own members, initiated their own agenda, elected their own leaders, and developed criteria that won respect and emulation from other women. In 1909 the convention boasted of having established the first school for black women that black women themselves owned. Through their school and their national convention, black Baptist women challenged many of the real and symbolic barriers that others—white Americans in general and even black men—sought to impose upon them in the church and larger society.[19] Rather than diminishing racial solidarity, rising gender consciousness made possible the effective drive toward a national black Baptist identity.

Through a racial and gender-based movement, black women confronted and influenced their social and political milieu, and they did so through the mediating influence of the church. According to Peter Berger and Richard Neuhaus, "mediating structures" constitute part of the public realm. They stand between private citizens and the large, impersonal institutions of public life, such as the government, and produce meaningful value systems as well as concrete mechanisms for ordering people's lives and addressing needs.[20] More effectively than any other institution, the church stood between individual blacks, on the one hand, and the state with its racially alienating institutions, on the other. The church's ability to sustain numerous newspapers, schools, social welfare services, jobs, and recreational facilities mitigated the dominant society's denial of these resources to black communities. And it was primarily the fund-raising activity of black women that undergirded the church's mediating function.

In characterizing the black church as a public sphere, my analysis moves in a different direction from such conceptual models as "civil religion" or "public religion." The concept of civil religion, made popular and controversial by Robert N. Bellah, calls attention to the character and role of religious symbolism in American political life. It locates religious symbols outside the confines of the church and asserts their life and meaning in expressions of patriotism, the general understanding and articulation of American national identity, and in public rituals and ceremonies such as holidays and presidential inaugurations.[21] Instead, my book stresses the public character and role of the black church. This is no small difference. The religious symbolism of the nation's public life—its collective thanksgivings and civic piety—held problematic and contradictory meanings for African Americans.[22] Frederick Douglass conveyed this point eloquently before a crowd of white Americans on the Fourth of July in 1852. Contrasting their celebration of liberty with the enslavement of his own people, Douglass called the Independence Day festivities "sacrilegious" and proceeded with his jeremiad: "Your prayers and hymns, your sermons and thanksgivings, with all your religious parade and solemnity, are to Him [God], mere bombast, fraud, deception, impiety, and hypocrisy."[23]

For African Americans, long excluded from political institutions and denied presence, even relevance, in the dominant society's myths about its heritage and national community, the church itself became the domain for the expression, celebration, and pursuit of a black collective will and identity. At issue here is the public dimension of the black church, not the religious dimension of the public realm. The question is not how religious symbols and values were promoted in American politics, but how public space, both physical and discursive, was interpolated within black religious institutions. Indeed, scholars of African American religion do not tend to utilize the concept of civil religion. For example, James Melvin Washington inverts Sidney Mead's usage of Chesterton's phrase—the "nation with the soul of a church"—by describing black Baptists as having a "church with the soul of a nation."[24]

In the closed society of Jim Crow, the church afforded African Americans an interstitial space in which to critique and contest white America's racial domination. In addition, the church offered black women a forum through which to articulate a public discourse critical of women's subordination. A gender perspective on the black church facilitates understanding the church's public dimension, since, in emphasizing discursive interaction between men and women, such a perspective more accurately portrays the church's extensive activities and influence at the grassroots level. I describe the black church not as the embodiment of ministerial authority or of any individual's private interests and pronouncements, but as a social space for discussion of public concerns. During the late nineteenth and early twentieth centuries, the church came to represent a deliberative arena, whose character derived from the collective nature of the church itself, namely, as a body of many diverse members, and from race-conscious feelings of nationalism.[25]

My analysis of the black church finds conceptual utility in the scholarly literature that has been inspired by Jürgen Habermas's formulation of the "public sphere." Habermas identified the public sphere as a historically situated and institutionalized discursive realm. It mediated between private citizens (civil society) and the state and afforded an arena for the rational formation and functioning of information, in other words, public opinion. In the collective effort to arrive at a "common good," public opinion emerged, Habermas posited, as "the tasks of criticism and control which a public body of citizens informally—and, in periodic elections, formally as well—practices vis-à-vis the ruling structure organized in the form of a state."[26] Thus separate and independent of the state and also the market economy, the public sphere operated as a realm where all citizens interacted in reasoned discourse, even in criticism of governmental authority.

Critics of Habermas question his idealization of the liberal or bourgeois public sphere, and they especially criticize his failure to explore more fully competing, non-bourgeois publics.[27] They pluralize the "public sphere" concept in order to represent, at specific historical moments, a number of groups and interests that stand in oppositional relationship within societies stratified along racial, class, and gender lines. These numerous "publics" may overlap, but more often conflict—becoming oppositional or "counter-publics."[28] While these scholars focus upon neither the black church, nor black women, their critiques of Habermas are especially illuminating for asserting a variety of public arenas in which people participate.

When E. Franklin Frazier termed the black church a "nation within a nation," he conveyed the meaning of a "counter-public sphere." Frazier's metaphor of the black church as nation suggests a public distinct from and in conflict with the dominant white society and its racist institutional structures. The church-sponsored press played an instrumental role in the dissemination of a black oppositional discourse and in the creation of a black collective will. As black literacy rose from a mere 5 percent in 1860 to 70 percent in 1910, the church served as a major site of print production in black communities. Penelope Bullock's study of the black periodical press notes that churches, particularly the Baptist, A.M.E., and A.M.E. Zion churches, took the lead in the publication of general magazines in the post-Reconstruction era. For example, the anti-lynching newspaper *The Free Speech and Headlight* of Memphis, which was made famous by Ida B. Wells, was a black Baptist–owned newspaper.[29] Black Baptist state conventions, men's and women's, figured prominently in newspaper publication during the late nineteenth century. In 1900 black Baptists at the local and state levels published forty-three newspapers, the great majority of which were located in the South.[30] This role of the church cannot be overstated, since there were no black newspapers with massive national distribution; nor were the ideas and activities of blacks considered newsworthy to the white press except in the most derogatory and repressive way.

The role of publishing was vital to the creation of a black civic vision. The *National Baptist Magazine*, publication of the National Baptist Convention, defined its scope as "devoted to the interests of the Negro Race in general."[31] The magazine featured articles and editorials on a variety of subjects, including black history, lynching, presidential elections, industrial education, and segregation on railroads. The publishing board of the National Baptist Convention reported a circulation of more than 13 million issues of various tracts and booklets between 1900 and 1903. The press published religious materials, but it also conceived of its mission as "moulding the doctrines and opinions and shaping the destiny of the future church and race." The National Baptist Convention unquestioningly viewed itself as a public in opposition to white America, and it referred to the importance of its press in this context: "The Negro Baptists of this country . . . must discuss, produce or provide literature capable of keeping the identity and increasing race pride of the rising generation or they must be entirely overshadowed by the dominant race of this country."[32]

The formation of the National Baptist Convention, U.S.A. and its auxiliary women's convention afforded black men and women social space in which to critique openly the United States government, its laws, and its institutions. In fact, the level of public discussion caused one of the leaders of the Woman's Convention to come under government surveillance.[33] There were also subtle, perhaps more far-reaching political implications. The Baptist convention offered black men and women a structure for electing representatives, debating issues, and exercising many rights that white society denied them. Benjamin Mays and Joseph Nicholson, pointing to this surrogate political role, stated that the "local churches, associations, conventions, and conferences become the Negro's Democratic and Republican Conventions, his Legislature and his Senate and House of Representatives."[34] Through their conventions, African Americans refuted notions of their inability or unreadiness for equal political participation. Among women, this understanding heightened support of women's suffrage. The political rhetoric espoused at black women's annual meetings included the demand not only for voting rights, but for full inclusion in American public life.

The black church constituted a public that stood in opposition to the dominant white public, and yet as the case of women illustrates, it did not form a monolith. Nor did it reveal values completely independent of white America. A gender perspective on the church lends clarity to this matter, since it locates different sites in which black women both embraced and contested the dominant values and norms of northern white Baptists, white women, and even black men. For example, during the 1880s and 1890s southern black and northern white Baptist women worked in a cooperative fashion rare for the times.[35] Their cooperation was not based upon identical motives and interests, but it indicated that divergent motives did not preclude mutual goals. Together, black and white women spread the Gospel, supported one another's organizations, financed black education, and alleviated the plight of the poor. The women's movement in the black Baptist church imagined itself both as part of the black community and as part of an evangelical sisterhood that cut across racial lines.[36] That black women voiced the race-conscious interests and agenda of the male-dominated movement precluded neither interracial cooperation with white women nor conflict with black men.

Church Women's Multiple Consciousness

During the late nineteenth and early twentieth centuries, laws and changing social attitudes were chipping away at barriers to women's right to property, to education, to the professions, and even to suffrage in the western states of Wyoming in 1890 and in 1896 in Utah, Colorado, and Idaho.[37] During the latter decades of the nineteenth century white and black women joined in religious associations and secular clubs to bring about social reform. They fought for temperance, educational opportunity, suffrage, and a variety of gender-related issues. "To be alive at such an epoch is a privilege, to be a woman then is sublime," proclaimed the black educator and feminist Anna J. Cooper during the heady times of the "woman's era."[38] Cooper's exhilaration expressed nothing less than the black Baptist women's rising expectations.

The years between 1890 and 1920 witnessed significant strides for women. The number of all women with professional degrees rose by 226 percent.[39] Hazel Carby notes the increase of black women writers during the decade of the nineties. Anna J. Cooper published her feminist critique *A Voice from the South* (1892); other publications included Ida B. Wells, *On Lynchings* (1892) and Gertrude Mossell, *The Work* of *the Afro-American Woman* (1894). Black women established their literary presence in novels: Amelia E. Johnson's *Clarence and Corinne* (1890) and *The Hazely Family* (1894); Emma Dunham Kelley's *Megda* (1891); Frances Ellen Watkins Harper's *Iola Leroy* (1892); and Victoria Earle's *Aunt Lindy* (1893). Moreover, black women's writings drew attention and praise in the burgeoning field of journalism, as was reflected by the chapter devoted to them in I. Garland Penn's *The Afro-American Press and Its Editors* (1890).[40]

The cynical era of Jim Crow and the optimistic woman's era stood entangled one with the other—their imbrication giving shape to the black Baptist women's nationalist, yet feminist appeal. The complexity of the racial and gender meanings of the age suggests both the multiple consciousness and multiple positioning of black women, and also the complexity of the black church itself—an institution overwhelmingly female in membership. The church, like the black community, cannot be viewed solely through the lens of race. A gender perspective on the black church reminds us that the history of African Americans cannot be excluded from the important effort to identify and study social relations between men and women.

The history of black Baptist women discloses not only the gender dimension of the church's racial mission, but its class dimension as well.[41]

The leadership of the women's convention movement formed part of an emergent class of school administrators, journalists, businesswomen, and reformers who served an all-black community. This educated female elite, frequently consisting of teachers or wives of ministers associated with educational institutions, promoted middle-class ideals among the masses of blacks in the belief that such ideals ensured the dual goals of racial self-help and respect from white America. Especially in the roles of missionary and teacher, black church women were conveyers of culture and vital contributors to the fostering of middle-class ideals and aspirations in the black community. Duty-bound to teach the value of religion, education, and hard work, the women of the black Baptist church adhered to a politics of respectability that equated public behavior with individual self-respect and with the advancement of African Americans as a group. They felt certain that "respectable" behavior in public would earn their people a measure of esteem from white America, and hence they strove to win the black lower class's psychological allegiance to temperance, industriousness, thrift, refined manners, and Victorian sexual morals.

On the one hand, the politics of respectability rallied poor working-class blacks to the cause of racial self-help, by inspiring them to save, sacrifice, and pool their scant resources for the support of black-owned institutions. Whether through white-imposed segregation or black-preferred separatism, the black community's support of its middle class surely accounted for the development and growth of black-owned institutions, including those of the Baptist church. On the other hand, the effort to forge a community that would command whites' respect revealed class tensions among blacks themselves. The zealous efforts of black women's religious organizations to transform certain behavioral patterns of their people disavowed and opposed the culture of the "folk"—the expressive culture of many poor, uneducated, and "unassimilated" black men and women dispersed throughout the rural South or newly huddled in urban centers.[42]

The Baptist women's preoccupation with respectability reflected a bourgeois vision that vacillated between an attack on the failure of America to live up to its liberal ideals of equality and justice and an attack on the values and lifestyle of those blacks who transgressed white middle-class propriety. Thus the women's pronouncements appeared to swing from radical to conservative. They revealed their conservatism when they attributed institutional racism to the "negative" public behavior of their people—as if rejection of "gaudy" colors in dress, snuff dipping, baseball games on Sunday, and other forms of "improper" decorum could eradicate the pervasive racial barriers that surrounded black Americans. The

Baptist women never conceded that rejection of white middle-class values by poor blacks afforded survival strategies, in fact spaces of resistance, albeit different from their own. Equally important, while the female leaders of the black Baptist church sought to broaden women's job opportunities and religious responsibilities, they revealed their conservatism in their unquestioning acceptance of man's sole right to the clergy.

Legacy of Resistance

Despite the limits of their movement, black Baptist women left an impressive record of protest against the racist and sexist proscriptions of their day. Eugene Genovese has written that "the living history of the Church has been primarily a history of submission to class stratification and the powers that be, but there has remained, despite all attempts at extirpation, a legacy of resistance that could appeal to certain parts of the New Testament and especially to the prophetic parts of the Old."[43] Exposing the black church's public dimension does not invalidate the centrality of its spiritual dimension in the private lives of black people or in the life of the black community. However, my interpretation of the church and black church women stresses the imbrication of the social and the spiritual within a context akin, but not identical, to what C. Eric Lincoln and Lawrence Mamiya call the "dialectical model of the black church." For Lincoln and Mamiya, this model postulates the black church to be in "dynamic tension" within a series of dialectical polarities: priestly versus prophetic functions; other-worldly versus this-worldly; particularism versus universalism; privatistic versus communal; charismatic versus bureaucratic; and accommodation versus resistance.[44]

I characterize the church as a dialogic model rather than dialectical, recognizing "dynamic tension" in a multiplicity of protean and concurrent meanings and intentions more so than in a series of discrete polarities. Multiple discourses—sometimes conflicting, sometimes unifying—are articulated between men and women, and within each of these two groups as well. The black church constitutes a complex body of shifting cultural, ideological, and political significations. It represents a "heteroglot" conception in the Bakhtinian sense of a multiplicity of meanings and intentions that interact and condition each other.[45] Such multiplicity transcends polarity—thus tending to blur the spiritual and secular, the eschatological and political, and the private and public. The black church represented the realm where individual souls communed intimately with God and where African Americans as a people freely discussed, debated, and devised an agenda for their common good. At the same time that church values and symbols ordered the epistemological and ontological understandings of each individual and gave meaning to the private sphere of family—both as conjugal household and as "household of faith"— church values and symbols helped to spawn the largest number of voluntary associations in the black community. It follows logically, then, that the church would introduce black women to public life. The church connected black women's spirituality integrally with social activism.

Although women's historians tend to focus overwhelmingly on the secular club movement, especially the National Association of Colored Women, as exemplary of black women's activism, clubwomen themselves readily admitted to the precedent of church work in fostering both "woman's consciousness" and a racial understanding of the "common good." Fannie Barrier Williams, a founding member and leader of the National Association of Colored Women, acknowledged in 1900: "The training which first enabled colored women to organize and successfully carry on club work was originally obtained in church work. These churches have been and still are the great preparatory schools in which the primary lessons of social order, mutual trustfulness and united effort have been taught. . . . The meaning of unity of effort for the common good, the development of social sympathies grew into woman's consciousness through the privileges of church work."[46]

The club movement among black women owed its very existence to the groundwork of organizational skill and leadership training gained through women's church societies. Missionary societies had early on brought together women with little knowledge of each other and created bonds of sisterly cooperation at the city and state levels. Not only Baptists but black Methodists, Presbyterians, and women in other denominations came together in associations that transformed unknown and unconfident women into leaders and agents of social service and racial self-help in their communities. For black Baptist women during the 1880s, the formation of state societies nurtured skills of networking and fund-raising. For more than a decade before the founding of the National Association of Colored Women, church-related societies had introduced mothers' training schools and social service programs, many of which were later adopted into the programs of the secular women's clubs.

More than mere precursors to secular reform and women's rights activism,[47] black women's religious organizations undergirded and formed an identifiable part of what is erroneously assumed to be "secular." The black Baptist women's convention thrust itself into the mainstream of

Progressive reform, and conversely such clubs as those constituting the secular-oriented National Association of Colored Women included church work as integral and salient to their purpose. This complexity precludes attempts to bifurcate black women's activities neatly into dichotomous categories such as religious versus secular, private versus public, or accommodation versus resistance.

Even such quotidian activities as women's fund raising, teaching in Sabbath schools, ministering to the sick, or conducting mothers' training schools embraced a politically subversive character within southern society. In many respects, the most profound challenge to Jim Crow laws, crop liens, disfranchisement, the dearth of black public schools, and the heinous brutality of lynching rested in the silent, everyday struggle of black people to build stable families, get an education, worship together in their churches, and "work the system," as Eric Hobsbawm terms it, "to their minimum disadvantage."[48] Arguments over the accommodationist versus liberating thrust of the black church miss the range as well as the fluid interaction of political and ideological meanings represented within the church's domain. Equally important, the artificiality of such a dichotomy precludes appreciation of the church's role in the "prosaic and constant struggle" of black people for survival and empowerment.[49] Edward Wheeler persuasively argues for the paradoxical implications of social uplift and accommodation: "Accommodation, which of course had a submissive tone, also had a subversive quality. On the one hand, uplift meant accommodation and surrender to the concepts, principles, and ideals of the dominant society. On the other, uplift was a denial of what white society meant by accommodation, for it spoke of a possibility to move beyond the limits prescribed by the dominant society."[50]

In the 1909 Atlanta University study of social betterment activities among African Americans, Du Bois attributed the greater part of such activities to the black church and specifically to church women.[51] In the final analysis the women's movement in the black Baptist church may be likened more to Harriet Tubman's repeated, surreptitious efforts to lead slaves step by step away from bondage than to Nat Turner's apocalyptic, revolutionary surge. Women's efforts were valiant attempts to navigate their people through the stifling and dangerous obstacle course of American racism. Committed to the causes of racial self-help and advancement, the convention movement among black Baptist women contributed greatly to the church's tremendous influence in both the spiritual and secular life of black communities. But the women's movement did something more. It gave to black women an individual and group pride that resisted ideologies and institutions upholding gender subordination. The movement gave them the collective strength and determination to continue their struggle for the rights of blacks and the rights of women.

Notes

1. See Jualynne Dodson, "Nineteenth-Century A.M.E. Preaching Women: Cutting Edge of Women's Inclusion in Church Polity," in Hilah F. Thomas and Rosemary Skinner Keller, eds., *Women in New Worlds: Historical Perspectives on the Wesleyan Tradition*, vol. 1 (Nashville: Abingdon Press, 1981), 276–292; Jean McMahon Humez, ed., *Gifts of Power: The Writings of Rebecca Jackson, Black Visionary and Shaker Eldress* (Amherst: University of Massachusetts Press, 1981), 1–50; William L. Andrews, ed., *Sisters of the Spirit: Three Black Women's Autobiographies of the Nineteenth Century* (Bloomington: Indiana University Press, 1986), 25–234.
2. C. Eric Lincoln and Lawrence H. Mamiya, *The Black Church in the African American Experience* (Durham, N.C.: Duke University Press, 1990), 25–26; Leroy Fitts, *A History of Black Baptists* (Nashville: Broadman Press, 1985), 64–79; Joseph H. Jackson, *A Story of Christian Activism: The History of the National Baptist Convention, U.S.A., Inc.* (Nashville: Townsend Press, 1980), 23–27.
3. Winthrop S. Hudson, *Religion in America: An Historical Account of the Development of American Religious Life*, 2nd ed. (New York: Charles Scribner's Sons, 1973), 202–203; Sydney E. Ahlstrom, *A Religious History of the American People* (New Haven: Yale University Press, 1972), 719–725.
4. See James Melvin Washington, *Frustrated Fellowship: The Black Baptist Quest for Social Power* (Macon, Ga.: Mercer University Press, 1985), 22–45.
5. Sandy D. Martin draws some attention to women's organized involvement in foreign mission support during the formative years of the National Baptist Foreign Mission Convention, but his discussion is brief. Most scholarly works on the black Baptist church identify a few individual women by name, but they fail to discuss women as a group and as significant contributors to the church's historic role. See Sandy D. Martin, *Black Baptists and African Missions: The Origins of a Movement, 1880–1915* (Macon, Ga.: Mercer University Press, 1989), 129–134; Washington, *Frustrated Fellowship*, 139; Jackson, *Story of Christian Activism*, 87–90, 135–145; Fitts, *History of Black Baptists*, 121–134; Lewis G. Jordan, *Negro Baptist History* (Nashville: Sunday School Publishing Board, National Baptist Convention, 1930); Owen D. Pelt and Ralph Lee Smith, *The Story of the National Baptists* (New York: Vantage Press, 1960).
6. The Baptist Foreign Mission Convention was founded in 1880. It was one of three organizations to merge in the formation of the National Baptist Convention, U.S.A. in 1895. Because of this, the NBC uses the 1880 date as its founding date. For a history of this convention, see Martin, *Black Baptists and African Missions*, 56–106.
7. Joel Williamson, *A Rage for Order: Black/White Relations in the American South since Emancipation* (New York: Oxford University Press, 1986), 171.
8. For a discussion of women during the Reconstruction and post-Reconstruction period, see Jacqueline Jones, *Labor of Love, Labor of Sorrow: Black Women, Work, and the Family from Slavery to the Present* (New York: Random House, 1985), chap. 2.

9. Rayford W. Logan, *The Negro in American Life and Thought: The Nadir, 1877–1901* (New York: Dial Press, 1954); Logan, *The Betrayal of the Negro: From Rutherford B. Hayes to Woodrow Wilson* (New York: Collier Books, 1965), 292–302; Neil R. McMillen, *Dark Journey: Black Mississippians in the Age of Jim Crow* (Urbana: University of Illinois Press, 1989), 197–253; Williamson, *Rage for Order,* 117–151.

10. In a series of cases between 1876 and 1896, the Supreme Court moved in a conservative direction, which culminated with the Plessy case and the euphemistic doctrine of "separate but equal." *United States v. Cruikshank,* 92 U.S. 542 (1876); *Civil Rights Cases,* 109 U.S. 3 (1883); *Plessy v. Ferguson,* 163 U.S. 537 (1896). See Derrick A. Bell, Jr., *Race, Racism, and American Law,* 2nd ed. (Boston: Little, Brown, 1980), 34–38, 83–91.

11. Early scholars of black history called attention to the importance of the home mission and educational work of the black church during the decades that followed the demise of Reconstruction. They especially emphasized the church's racial self-help efforts in response to diminishing civil and political rights. See William Edward Burghardt Du Bois, ed., *The Negro Church* (Atlanta: Atlanta University Press, 1903), 111–152; Carter G. Woodson, *History of the Negro Church* (Washington, D.C.: Associated Publishers, 1921), chaps. 4, 5.

12. The most comprehensive studies of slave religion are Albert J. Raboteau, *Slave Religion: The "Invisible Institution" in the Antebellum South* (New York: Oxford University Press, 1978), and Mechal Sobel, *Trabelin' On: The Slave Journey to an Afro-Baptist Faith* (Westport, Conn.: Greenwood Press, 1979). See also Eugene D. Genovese, *Roll, Jordan, Roll: The World the Slaveholders Made* (New York: Random House, Pantheon Books, 1974), 232–284.

13. E. Franklin Frazier, *The Negro Church* (New York: Schocken Books, 1964), chap. 3.

14. Gary Nash, *Forging Freedom: The Formation of Philadelphia's Black Community, 1720–1840* (Cambridge, Mass.: Harvard University Press, 1989), 227–233, 259–267; Gayraud Wilmore, *Black Religion and Black Radicalism: An Interpretation of the Religious History of Afro-American People,* 2nd ed. (Maryknoll, N.Y.: Orbis Books, 1989), 78–89; Lincoln and Mamiya, *Black Church in the African American Experience,* 47–75.

15. The figure for black Baptists in 1906 represents the number of Baptists under the National Baptist Convention and does not reflect those black Baptists who are listed under the Northern Baptist Convention, or those found among the Primitive Baptists, Two Seed Baptists, and Freewill Baptists. When all these groups are considered, black Baptists numbered 2,354,789 in 1906. I have also distinguished the A.M.E. church from such black Methodist groups as the A.M.E. Zion and the Colored Methodist Episcopal. The entire black Methodist population in 1906 was 1,182,131. See U.S. Department of Commerce and Labor, Bureau of the Census, *Special Reports: Religious Bodies, 1906,* vol. 1 (Washington, D.C.: Government Printing Office, 1910), 137–139; Sobel, *Trabelin' On,* 182.

16. For statistics of religious denominations, see Bureau of the Census, *Religious Bodies, 1906,* vol. 1, 137–139; Bureau of the Census, *Religious Bodies, 1916,* Part I (Washington, D.C.: Government Printing Office, 1919), 40.

17. For statistics on black Baptists, see Bureau of the Census, *Religious Bodies, 1916,* vol. 1, 121, 123–128. For a survey of the black population's predominantly rural and southern character during this period, see U.S. Department of Commerce, Bureau of the Census, *Negro Population, 1790–1915* (Washington, D.C.: Government Printing Office, 1918), 88–94.

18. Philip S. Foner, ed., *W.E.B. Du Bois Speaks, 1890–1919* (New York: Pathfinder Press, 1970), 97.

19. A wealth of materials related to the Woman's Convention, Auxiliary to the National Baptist Convention is found in the papers of Nannie Helen Burroughs, former corresponding secretary and president of the organization and also founder and president of the National Training School for Women and Girls. See Nannie Helen Burroughs Papers, Library of Congress.

20. Berger and Neuhaus are not concerned with historical perspective, nor do they see the church as the only such structure. Their concern is with mediating structures in the contemporary welfare state. They observe: "Not only are religious institutions significant 'players' in the public realm, but they are singularly important to the way people order their lives and values at the most local and concrete levels of their existence." They go on to note that the black community cannot be understood from a historical perspective without looking at the role of the black church. Peter L. Berger and Richard John Neuhaus, *To Empower People: The Role of Mediating Structures in Public Policy* (Washington, D.C.: American Enterprise Institute for Public Policy Research, 1977), 26–28.

21. For differing interpretations of "civil religion," see essays in Donald G. Jones and Russell E. Richey, eds., *American Civil Religion* (San Francisco: Harper and Row, 1974), especially chaps. 1, 2, 6, 7, 10; Robert N. Bellah and Phillip B. Hammond, *Varieties of Civil Religion* (San Francisco: Harper and Row, 1980), 3–23.

22. See the discussion of "mythic patterns of national mission" and the idea of national community in the form of covenant in John F. Wilson, *Public Religion in American Culture* (Philadelphia: Temple University Press, 1979), 34–39.

23. Frederick Douglass, "The Meaning of the Fourth of July to the Negro, 1852," in Philip E. Foner, ed., *The Life and Writings of Frederick Douglass*, vol. 2 (New York: International Publishers, 1950), 192; also see an analysis of Frederick Douglass's millennialist vision in David W. Blight, *Frederick Douglass' Civil War: Keeping Faith in Jubilee* (Baton Rouge: Louisiana State University Press, 1989), 101–121.

24. See Sidney B. Mead's usage of Gilbert Chesterton's phrase in his discussion of civil religion. Sidney B. Mead, "The 'Nation with the Soul of a Church,'" in Jones and Richey, eds., *American Civil Religion*, 45. However, the black scholar Charles Long writes from the point of view of African Americans: "The distinction between civil religion and church religion is not one that would loom very large for us." See Charles H. Long, "Civil Rights—Civil Religion: Visible People and Invisible Religion," in ibid., 211–221, especially 216; and Washington, *Frustrated Fellowship*, 135–157.

25. Benedict Anderson defines nation as "an imagined political community—and imagined as both inherently limited and sovereign." For black Baptists, the "imagined community" was racially bounded and its sovereignty was perceived as free of white control—hence black denominational hegemony. See Benedict Anderson, *Imagined Communities: Reflections on the Origin and Spread of Nationalism* (London: Verso, 1983), 14–16.

26. Jürgen Habermas, "The Public Sphere: An Encyclopedia Article (1964)," *New German Critique*, 1 (Fall 1974): 49–55; Habermas, *The Structural Transformation of the Public Sphere: An Inquiry into a Category of Bourgeois Society*, trans. by Thomas Burger with the assistance of Frederick Lawrence (Cambridge, Mass.: MIT Press, 1989), especially chap. 2. For differing interpretations that draw upon Habermas in discussing the role of religion in the public sphere, see Robert Wuthnow, *The Restructuring of American Religion* (Princeton, N.J.: Princeton University Press, 1988), chap. 4; Wuthnow, *The Struggle for*

America's Soul: Evangelicals, Liberals, and Secularism (Grand Rapids, Mich.: William B. Eerdmans, 1989), 10–15; and Jose Casanova, "Private and Public Religions," *Social Research*, 59 (Spring 1992): 17–57.

27. Critics of Habermas do not share his assessment of the breakdown and decline of the public sphere itself, nor do they agree with him when he attributes decline to the historical emergence of competing interest groups (the non-bourgeois strata) and the resultant diminution of the state's accountability to its citizenry. In contradistinction to Habermas, Nancy Fraser submits that "in stratified societies, arrangements that accommodate contestation among a plurality of competing publics better promote the ideal of participatory parity than does a single, comprehensive, overarching public." Nancy Fraser, "Rethinking the Public Sphere: A Contribution to the Critique of Actually Existing Democracy," *Social Text*, 25/26 (1990): 56–80.

28. They are responding to Habermas's discussion of the emergence of the public sphere as a distinct phase of bourgeois social formation in late seventeenth and eighteenth-century Europe. His critics note instead a multiplicity of competing publics, which existed then and continue to exist now based on racial, ethnic, class, and gender interests. For treatment of various types of counter-publics, see ibid., 61–68; John Keane, *Public Life and Late Capitalism: Toward a Socialist Theory of Democracy* (New York: Cambridge University Press, 1984), 92–94; Rita Felski, *Beyond Feminist Aesthetics: Feminist Literature and Social Change* (Cambridge, Mass.: Harvard University Press, 1989), 154–182.

29. *The Free Speech and Headlight* was published by the Reverend Taylor Nightingale, pastor of the Beale Street Baptist Church, although Ida Wells was its editor and chiefly responsible for voicing its social message. Wells does not figure as a participant of the women's movement of the black Baptist church, since she was a member of the A.M.E. Church and was active with the organized women's movement of that denomination. See Samuel Shannon, "Tennessee," in Henry Lewis Suggs, ed., *The Black Press in the South, 1865–1979* (Westport, Conn.: Greenwood Press, 1983), 325.

30. For example, black Baptist newspapers are discussed for the states of Alabama, Arkansas, Florida, and Missouri in Suggs, ed., *The Black Press in the South*, 30, 34, 38, 70–71, 103, 105, 212–214; also see National Baptist Convention, *Journal of the Twentieth Annual Session of the National Baptist Convention, Held in Richmond, Virginia, September 12–17, 1900* (Nashville: National Baptist Publishing Board, 1900), 191; Du Bois, ed., *Negro Church*, 121.

31. For discussion of the *National Baptist Magazine*, see Penelope L. Bullock, *The Afro-American Periodical Press, 1838–1909* (Baton Rouge: Louisiana State University Press, 1981), 73–76.

32. This statement can be found in the combined report for 1901 and 1902 of the National Baptist Convention, U.S.A., which is printed in Du Bois, ed., *Negro Church*, 115.

33. In 1917 the Department of War monitored the activities and mail of Nannie Helen Burroughs, corresponding secretary of the Woman's Convention, for remarks in condemnation of Woodrow Wilson. Records of the War Department, General and Special Staffs, Military Intelligence Division, "Black Radicals (Church of God)," from Record Group 165, National Archives.

34. Benjamin E. Mays and Joseph W. Nicholson, *The Negro's Church* (New York, 1933; rpt. New York: Arno Press and the *New York Times*, 1969), 9.

35. The most extensive holdings of northern white Baptist women are the records of the Woman's American Baptist Home Mission Society and the Women's Baptist Home

Mission Society, which are located in the American Baptist Archives Center in Valley Forge, Pennsylvania, and the American Baptist—Samuel Colgate Historical Library, Rochester, New York. Materials are also housed at the Franklin Trask Library in Andover-Newton Theological Seminary in Massachusetts.

36. The women's movement in the black Baptist church reflected a trend found in all the denominations in the late nineteenth century. Studies of white women's societies include Lois A. Boyd and R. Douglas Brackenridge, *Presbyterian Women in America: Two Centuries of a Quest for Status* (Westport, Conn.: Greenwood Press, 1983); Virginia Lieson Brereton and Christa Ressmeyer Klein, "American Women in Ministry: A History of Protestant Beginning Points," in Rosemary Ruether and Eleanor McLaughlin, eds., *Women of Spirit: Female Leadership in the Jewish and Christian Traditions* (New York: Simon and Schuster, 1979), chap. 11; Ruether and Rosemary Skinner Keller, *Women and Religion in America: The Nineteenth Century* (San Francisco: Harper and Row, 1981), 243–293.

37. Suzanne Lebsock, "Women and American Politics, 1880–1920," in Louise A. Tilly and Patricia Gurin, eds., *Women, Politics, and Change* (New York: Russell Sage Foundation, 1990), 35–59.

38. Anna J. Cooper, *A Voice from the South* (Xenia, Ohio, 1892; rpt. New York: Negro Universities Press, 1969), 143.

39. For black women's educational and social reform activities, see Dorothy Salem, *To Better Her World: Black Women in Organized Reform, 1890–1920*, 7–103; vol. 14 in Darlene Clark Hine, ed., *Black Women in United States History: From Colonial Tmes to the Present* (Brooklyn: Carlson Press, 1990); Bettina Aptheker, "Black Women's Quest in the Professions," in Aptheker, *Woman's Legacy: Essays on Race, Sex, and Class in American History* (Amherst: University of Massachusetts Press, 1982), 89–110; Cynthia Neverdon-Morton, *Afro-American Women of the South and the Advancement of the Race, 1895–1925* (Knoxville: University of Tennessee Press, 1989), 78–103; Jacqueline Rouse, *Lugenia Burns Hope: Black Southern Reformer* (Athens: University of Georgia Press, 1989), 41–85. Also see for white women, Lynn D. Gordon, *Gender and Higher Education in the Progressive Era* (New Haven: Yale University Press, 1990); Rosalind Rosenberg, *Beyond Separate Spheres: Intellectual Roots of Modern Feminism* (New Haven: Yale University Press, 1982); Robyn Muncy, *Creating a Female Dominion in American Reform, 1890–1935* (New York: Oxford University Press, 1991).

40. Hazel V. Carby, *Reconstructing Womanhood: The Emergence of the Afro-American Woman Novelist* (New York: Oxford University Press, 1987), 96–115; I. Garland Penn, *The Afro-American Press and Its Editors* (Springfield, Mass.: Willey, 1891), 366–427.

41. See E. Franklin Frazier's recognition of the middle-class orientation of the National Baptist Convention in Frazier, *Black Bourgeoisie* (New York: Macmillan, 1957), 89.

42. Houston Baker, in his discussion of the black vernacular, characterizes the "quotidian sounds of black every day life" as both a defiant and entrancing voice. Similarly, John Langston Gwaltney calls the "folk" culture of today's cities "core black culture," which is "more than ad hoc synchronic adaptive survival." Gwaltney links its values and epistemology to a long peasant tradition. See John Langston Gwaltney, *Drylongso: A Self-Portrait of Black America* (New York: Random House, 1980), xxv–xxvii; also Houston Baker, Jr., *Afro-American Poetics: Revisions of Harlem and the Black Aesthetic* (Madison: University of Wisconsin Press, 1988), 95–107; Baker, *Blues, Ideology, and Afro-American Literature: A Vernacular Theory* (Chicago: University of Chicago Press, 1984), 11–43.

43. Genovese, *Roll, Jordan, Roll*, 163.

44. Lincoln and Mamiya, *Black Church in the African American Experience*, 10–16.

45. The Russian linguist and critic Mikhail Bakhtin discusses "dialogism" and "heteroglossia" in specific regard to his theory of language: "Everything means, is understood, as part of a greater whole—there is a constant interaction between meanings, all of which have the potential of conditioning others." See M. M. Bakhtin, *The Dialogic Imagination: Four Essays*, ed. Michael Holquist and trans. Caryl Emerson and Michael Holquist (Austin: University of Texas Press, 1981), 293, 352, 426.

46. See Fannie Barrier Williams, "The Club Movement among Colored Women of America," in Booker T. Washington, N. B. Wood, and Fannie Barrier Williams, *A New Negro for a New Century* (Chicago: American Publishing House, 1900), 383.

47. For discussion of black and white women's church work as a forerunner to secular reform, see Ann Firor Scott, *The Southern Lady: From Pedestal to Politics, 1830–1930* (Chicago: University of Chicago Press, 1970), 141; Jean Friedman, *The Enclosed Garden: Women and Community in the Evangelical South, 1830–1900* (Chapel Hill: University of North Carolina Press, 1985), 111, 113, 115–126; Jacquelyn Dowd Hall, *Revolt against Chivalry: Jessie Daniel Ames and the Women's Campaign against Lynching* (New York: Columbia University Press, 1979), 70–77; Kathleen C. Berkeley, "'Colored Ladies also Contributed': Black Women's Activities from Benevolence to Social Welfare, 1866–1896," in Walter J. Fraser, Jr., R. Frank Saunders, Jr., and John L. Wakelyn, eds., *The Web of Southern Social Relations: Women, Family, and Education* (Athens: University of Georgia Press, 1985), 181–185.

48. Eric Hobsbawm, "Peasants and Politics," *Journal of Peasant Studies*, 1 (1973): 12, 16.

49. James Scott uses the phrase "prosaic and constant struggle" in his study of everyday forms of resistance in a Malaysian community. See James Scott, *Weapons of the Weak: Everyday Forms of Peasant Resistance* (New Haven: Yale University Press, 1985), 301.

50. Edward L. Wheeler, *Uplifting the Race: The Black Minister in the New South, 1865–1902* (Lanham, Md.: University Press of America, 1986), xvii.

51. W. E. Burghardt Du Bois, ed., *Efforts for Social Betterment among Negro Americans* (Atlanta: Atlanta University Press, 1909), 16, 22.

Chapter 9

The Central Themes
of American Religious History

Pluralism, Puritanism, and the Encounter of Black and White

David W. Wills

What is the religious history of the United States *about?* One answer, of course, is that it is about the same things as the history of religion everywhere—the human quest for the sacred, perhaps, and its expression in doctrine, practice, and community. The question as it is asked here, however, aims at what is distinctive or at least characteristic about the story of religion in America. It is a question about the central themes that do or should provide the plot lines for American religious history. The answer to this question, if one is to judge from most of the existing literature, is that there are two such themes—(1) pluralism and toleration and (2) Puritanism and collective purpose. The contention of this essay is that there is a third: the encounter of black and white.

Pluralism and Toleration vs. Puritanism
and Collective Purpose

The most common way of telling the tale of the United States' religious past is to center it on the theme of pluralism and toleration—the existence of religious variety in America and the degree to which it has (or has not) been tolerated and even affirmed. Typically, this version of our religious past tends toward some kind of American triumphalism: the United States has successfully solved the problem of religious diversity, a problem that elsewhere in the world has occasioned persistent repression and/or enduring intercommunal violence. This emphasis on success in the area of religion is often linked, moreover, with a generally triumphalist view of American institutions. The liberalism that has guided our practice of religious liberty is seen to have expressed itself in our political and social life as well.

Not all pluralism and toleration versions of our religious past are identical, however, nor equally upbeat in their assessment of the American experiment. They in fact vary considerably, mostly depending on the point at which genuine pluralism and toleration are seen to have been institutionalized in American life. According to the popular culture's cult of Thanksgiving and some of the older, more filiopietistic histories of the colonial period, religious liberty was established at the center of our religious life as soon as the Pilgrims landed at Plymouth Rock. Those who know anything of the history of religious establishments in the thirteen colonies, most especially in New England, know that this is a fantasy. More commonly, therefore, it is the adoption of the Constitution, above all the passage of the First Amendment, which is seen as the crucial landmark in the emergence of a normative religious pluralism in America. In this account, the colonial period was a time of struggle against repressive old-world establishmentarianism, but in our moment of birth as a nation we broke free of that past into an era when diversity was embraced and liberty made the religious law of the land.

Still other versions of the pluralism and toleration tale, however, suggest that the constitutional separation of church and state was merely a stage on the way to a genuine pluralism that had not yet arrived in the early national period. After all, religious establishments were still possible at the state level and they endured, in however attenuated form, in Connecticut until 1818 and in Massachusetts until 1833. Elsewhere, moreover, legal barriers sometimes remained to Catholic and to Jewish participation in political office-holding and everywhere a kind of normative WASPness prevailed. On this account, it was only in the late nineteenth and early twentieth centuries, as wave after wave of immigration eroded the Protestant predominance, that true religious diversity emerged as both fact and norm in American life. Writing of the post–World War I era, surveyors of American religious history who follow this line typically speak of "a post-Protestant America" or a new "age of religious pluralism."

Others, however, are persuaded that not even the twenties saw the real triumph of pluralism and toleration in the United States. The unhappy fate of Catholic Al Smith's 1928 presidential campaign is, according to this view, a vivid symbol of the persistence of exclusionary religious prejudice—and power. Only in the 1960s, it is sometimes proposed, was the full promise of our constitutional religious liberty realized. A Catholic at last occupied the White House, and in a decade of profound cultural upheaval, the hard crust of a repressive Protestantism was broken through and a thousand flowers of religion, both Eastern and Western, were allowed to bloom. Even this version, however, is prematurely celebratory for some. They suggest that while America in the 1960s may for a moment have repented of its past sins of intolerance, there has been a good deal of backsliding since. We are therefore still pilgrims on the path to the pluralist promised land. But perhaps it is just around the next cultural corner.

If those who stress the pluralism and toleration theme may be said to vary primarily in their optimism about when the American experiment in religious liberty was—or will be—fully realized, interpreters of our past who emphasize Puritanism may be classified according to their degree of pessimism about when the Puritan legacy either was—or will be—fully dissipated. Generally they agree that in its origins the American experiment was not so much an experiment in religious liberty as an attempt at a holy commonwealth. Whatever their sins of oppression against religious dissenters, this account suggests, the Puritans had an admirable sense of common purpose that stands in favorable contrast to the prevailing privatism and individualism of much of our subsequent history—including our religious history. Before they had even set foot in Massachusetts, the Puritans were advised by Governor John Winthrop that if they wished to succeed in building their "city upon a hill," they "must be knit together in this work as one man . . . as members of the same body." Puritanism, however, together with its strong sense of collective purpose, was destined to go downhill in America from this promising beginning. According to the gloomiest accounts, Puritanism scarcely outlived the generation that brought it to the New World. The settlers' children and their children's children went from Puritan to Yankee, as crass commercialism dissolved religious bonds and individual material goals supplanted common spiritual purpose.

Not all such accounts, however, are this pessimistic. Some contend that the Puritan legacy endured through the eighteenth century, decisively shaping the public-spirited patriotic zeal of the revolutionary years, the constitutional era's quest for "a more perfect union," and the new nation's sense of its historic mission. Only in the early nineteenth century, these interpreters suggest, was the Puritan legacy at last dissipated, as an orgy of revivalist religion, political democracy, and economic and geographical expansion set the country on its incurably individualist way. Still others, moreover, claim that even these accounts underestimate Puritanism's durability in American religion, especially in shaping our most deeply shared views of national destiny. Did not the Civil War, they ask, especially on the northern side, involve a great renewal of a broadly Puritan sense of collective purpose, enunciated with unsurpassed eloquence by Lincoln? Only later, they suggest, with the collapse of Calvinist orthodoxy as an intellectually respectable tradition and the more or less complete immersion of the country in the "great barbecue" of postwar economic development and the nascent culture of consumption, did the Puritan era in American culture finally come to a close.

It is a curious feature of the history of American Puritanism, however, that its demise seems to be announced afresh in every generation. For some, it was only the antibourgeois cultural revolt of the 1920s that at last broke the iron grip of Puritanism on the American spirit. Others, however, found in the extraordinary revival of scholarly interest in and appreciation for Puritanism in the 1930s the neo-Puritan spirit of much Protestant neo-orthodoxy and in the corporatist ethos of the New Deal signs that the Puritan impulse was not yet played out. Some thought the end came only in the 1960s. Sydney Ahlstrom, for example, at the conclusion of his massive *Religious History of the American People* (New Haven: Yale University Press, 1972), suggested that the Puritan Age in Anglo-American religious history lasted from the reign of Queen Elizabeth I to the decade that began with the election of John F. Kennedy. Others think the end is still not yet upon us, though presumably, sometime in the aftermath of the Reagan era, we can expect to hear again that the Puritan era in American cultural and religious history is, at long last, over.

For all their differences of tone and emphasis, the pluralism and toleration version of our religious past and the Puritanism and collective purpose way of telling the story have much in common. Indeed, it is relatively easy to combine them by seeing them as two sides of the same story: Puritanism's loss is pluralism and toleration's gain. The purpose of this essay, however, is not to resolve the question of which of these two interpretations is more adequate or how they might be combined. It is rather to suggest that whether together or alone these two ways of understanding our religious past are inadequate to one of the central realities of our history—the encounter of black and white.

The Southern Theme:
The Encounter of Black and White

One of the easiest and most vivid ways to see what is left out by the two prevailing accounts of our religious past is to ask—literally—where in the colonial era they begin their stories. New England is clearly the primary locus of early American Puritanism, and Puritan-centered stories of American religious history characteristically spend a great deal of time on the founding and initial development of the Massachusetts and Connecticut colonies. The religious and political ideas of such Puritan leaders as John Winthrop, John Cotton, Thomas Hooker, and Thomas Shepard are traced out in meticulous detail and the workings of the Puritan family, church, and polity analyzed with great care. In this sometimes stony New England soil, it is suggested, lie our deepest religious and cultural roots.

The pluralism and toleration story, however, more characteristically begins in the middle colonies of New York, New Jersey, and Pennsylvania. Granted, there is an important chapter of this story which also occurs in New England—the chapter centering on Roger Williams and Anne Hutchinson. But the pluralistic and tolerant Rhode Island colony clearly lies at the margin of the New England story, whereas the normative diversity of Pennsylvania (and West Jersey) and the moral *de facto* pluralism of New York (and East Jersey) constitute the very center of the religious history of the middle colonies. The contrast is further reinforced if one compares the remarkable ethnic homogeneity of colonial New England to the English, Scottish, Scotch-Irish, Dutch, and German mixture of the Middle Atlantic area. For those to whom the story of American religion centers on the positive embracing of diversity, that story is best seen to begin in the middle colonies.

What, then, about the Southern colonies? Where do they fit in either of the prevailing stories? Attempts have been made to win the interpretive game, as it were, two-to-one, by assimilating the southern story into that of one of the other two sections. It has sometimes been suggested, for example, that the dominant ethos of both early southern Anglicanism and southern dissent was, in the broadest sense, Puritan, and that the religious history of these colonies may therefore be subsumed rather easily under the New England story. Since colonial southern Protestantism is generally regarded as a less potent cultural force than the northern version, it can be argued that it makes sense to study Puritanism primarily in its intense New England form rather than in its somewhat diffuse southern version. Knowing, for example, that the son of Boston's John Cotton went to Charles Town, South Carolina, to serve as a Congregationalist pastor, helps us to be aware of the Puritan presence in the South, but it is still the father and not the son who is of primary interest to us.

Attempts have also been made, however, to interpret the early religious history of the South as essentially another phase in the history of pluralism and toleration. Indeed, on occasion it has been proposed that the South itself is the real heartland for this theme. In such accounts, the middle colonies tend to disappear altogether, and a cosmopolitan, tolerant,

Jeffersonian South is contrasted to a parochial, intolerant, Puritan North. That Virginia and Virginians should have played such an important role in the institutionalization of religious liberty in the constitutional era (e.g., through the state's adoption of the separationist Statute on Religious Liberty in 1785 and James Madison's shaping of the First Amendment a few years later) is here presented as the predictable flowering of a southern sensibility that has made its peace with religious diversity in a way that the northern conscience had not. America, it is suggested, began in Virginia.

If this is true, however, it seems odd to leave entirely out of account in defining the central themes of America's religious history the extraordinary black presence in Virginia and elsewhere in the South. Once the slave labor system had become established in the late seventeenth century, there was a rapid increase in the southern colonies' black population, so much so that in the eighteenth century parts of the Chesapeake area and all of the Carolina low country were characterized by a black majority. Under these circumstances, it seems highly questionable to characterize colonial southern religion solely on the basis of the religion of white Southerners—or to see as its central theme either the presence of diluted Puritanism or the triumph of a benign pluralism.

Is it not more plausible to see as the central theme of religion in the colonial South the encounter of black and white? This is, in a sense, a negative theme. It is the story of a distance, a gap. The Puritan colonies contained many dissenters and even more of what might be called the lukewarm. In the middle colonies, English and German Protestants sometimes had trouble understanding one another—literally—and there were in this region numerous other frontiers of religious difference and misunderstanding as well. But nowhere in colonial America was there a cultural or religious chasm comparable to that which separated black and white southerners. In part, of course, it was simply a matter of sheer cultural difference. Most of the Africans who were brought to the English colonies had not been Christians in their homeland and did not become such in the New World. Numerically significant Christianization of the slave population only began after 1760 and did not really come to full tide until 1830, by which time most American blacks were native born. While some blacks at the time of their capture and enslavement were Muslims, the vast majority were adherents of some form of African traditional religion—and it is presumably as such that they lived and died in America. For the most part, then, they did not speak the same religious language as white Southerners.

The distance between black and white in the colonial South was, however, far more than just a difference in religious or cultural tradition, and therefore not a gap that could have been closed, had the attempt been made, simply by acknowledging and accepting diversity. Since the encounter of black and white occurred within the context of a slave system that broadly and consistently subordinated blacks to whites, the previously existing cultural gap was transformed into a gap that involved power as well as meaning—and above all the relationship between the two. The world that had to be made sense of, by African Americans and European Americans alike, was a world that included the brutal reality of racial slavery. Given the vast difference in religious standpoint and the utter disparity in power with which their encounter began, it is scarcely surprising that black and white then and now have found it difficult to tell a shared, religiously meaningful story about their common fate.

It is this problematic encounter of black and white—which tests the limits of all our views of pluralism and undermines every attempt to formulate a sense of collective purpose—that is the Southern theme in American religious history. This is not to say, of course, that it is only a Southern theme; just as one can see the footprints of the Puritans in both the Middle Atlantic region and in the South and can hear the voice of toleration throughout the colonies, so one can also find the encounter of black and white in New England and the middle colonies. But just as the Puritan theme in our religious history initially comes to sharpest focus in New England, and the story of pluralism and toleration first takes center stage in the middle colonies, so the encounter of black and white is rooted most deeply in the colonial South. And just as we have to learn that black history is not to be thought of as only "black history" while white history is considered "American history," so we must come to see that southern history is no less "American history" than the history of New England or of the Mid-Atlantic states. The Southern theme in our religious history is equally as important as the other two and it is only by taking these three themes together, in all their complex interaction, that we can begin to move toward an adequate understanding of our religious past—and present.

Black and White from the Evangelical Awakening to the Present

If the encounter of black and white is one of the main themes of our religious history, what are the main stages in the development of this theme? If pluralism and toleration seem almost continuously to be on the increase in our history and Puritanism seems ever to be in decline, what is to be said of the encounter of black and white? Simply put, it is the story of a persisting and seemingly intractable gap or distance. Recurrent and some-times heroic efforts have been made to overcome this gap, but in the end it seems always to endure. The story of these efforts—and their failure—can be sketched here only in its broadest outline, concentrating on the eighteenth- and nineteenth-century encounter of blacks and whites in the context of evangelical Protestantism and their twentieth-century meeting in a religious milieu importantly shaped by ecumenical Protestantism and by cultural pluralism. The full story, of course, is as rich and compli-cated—and as subject to various interpretations—as the stories of Puri-tanism or pluralism and toleration.

It was Protestant evangelicalism that in part of the eighteenth and most of the nineteenth century played a central role both in defining the accept-able limits of pluralism and in mediating the legacy of Puritanism in American religious life. It was also in the context of evangelicalism that blacks and whites were for the first time drawn together religiously in sig-nificant numbers. No doubt before the evangelical awakenings of the mid-eighteenth century, blacks and whites in the South (and elsewhere) had begun to exchange folk beliefs and practices of a religious or quasi-religious sort, an important phenomenon that historians are only beginning to take sufficiently seriously. But it was only with the rise of evangelicalism that a biracial religious movement appeared in organized, public form. Particu-larly among the Baptists and the Methodists, who became the numerically preponderant Protestants during the evangelical era, there was a very con-siderable number of black converts; in some places they outnumbered white Baptists and Methodists. Testifying publicly about their conver-sions, taking part in church discipline, serving as exhorters and sometimes as pastors—even, on occasion, of predominantly white congregations—black Baptists and Methodists participated in the evangelical movement in a way they had participated in no previous colonial religious movement. Full mutuality and equality had scarcely been achieved, but the gap between black and white did seem to be narrowing.

Soon, however, the gap reappeared, this time in the very heart of evan-gelicalism itself. Early evangelicalism had attracted blacks in part because of its antislavery tendency, most marked among the Methodists. With the end of the social ferment of the revolutionary period, however, and the rapid movement of evangelicalism from the margins to the very center of Southern society, white evangelicals reconsidered the meaning of Amer-ican slavery and for the most part came to accept it. Meanwhile black evangelicals, eager for autonomy in administering their own affairs, dis-covered that when it came to questions of the exercise of leadership or control over property, white power was the almost invariable rule of ecclesiastical as well as civil order. The result of these developments—which undermined the sharing of both meaning and power—was racial schism. Black Methodists, under the leadership of such men as Richard Allen and James Varick, withdrew in large numbers to form their own independent denominations, most importantly the African Methodist Episcopal Church (1816) and the African Methodist Episcopal Zion Church (1821). (Black Baptists in 1840 organized the American Baptist Missionary Convention, the first in a series of black Baptist conventions that culminated decades later—in 1895—with the formation of the largest of all the black churches, the National Baptists Convention, U.S.A.) In the South, in a violation of religious liberty that tellers of the pluralism and toleration tale frequently overlook, slaves were often prevented by law from either joining these Northern-based denominations or forming comparable institutions of their own. But through song and story and informal networks, they maintained an Afro-American evangelical tradition sharply at odds with the slavery-affirming religion of their masters.

With the coming of the Civil War and more especially the era of Reconstruction, it momentarily seemed once again that the distance between black and white might be narrowed. Crucial here, of course, was the end of slavery—and the reinterpretation of what the meaning of American slavery had all along been. Among black evangelicals, slavery had long been regarded as an offense against God, a great wickedness for which all whites—North and South alike—could one day expect to feel the wrath of a just God. Some even speculated that God might both work that judgment and set the captives free by sowing violent conflict among the whites, a prophecy that the events of the Civil War years seemed to vindicate. It was essentially this interpretation of slavery and its end that Lincoln advanced in his second inaugural address, a speech that went further than any previous presidential statement toward creating a community of interpretation between black and white Americans. In the ensuing Reconstruction era, moreover, it initially seemed that this retelling of the nation's racial past might be matched with new opportunities for black participation—and the exercise of power—in the church and state alike. Unprecedented biracial efforts were made, often within the framework of evangelical Protestant ideas and institutions, both to foster religious collaboration and create a racially inclusive polity.

Soon, however, it became clear that the gap between black and white would not be closed, even in this the very heyday of evangelical influence. Southern white evangelicals proved unable to respond positively to emancipation and their northern counterparts had trouble overcoming paternalism, or sustaining long-term interest in the black struggle. The freedmen themselves, eager to take full control of their own religious lives, for the most part broke their ties to the evangelical churches of white Southerners and either joined the existing Afro-American denominations or helped launch such new black churches as the Colored Methodist Episcopal Church (1870). Their collaboration with Northern white evangelicals, especially in the field of education, was in some cases more enduring, but even here there was mounting stress, often centering on the question of black versus white control. By the end of the century, when blacks experienced increased disenfranchisement, segregation, and economic oppression, white evangelicals—whether Northern or Southern—made little protest. The distance between blacks and whites seemed as wide as it had ever been.

In the twentieth century, the main moment in which the gap between black and white in American religious life seemed to be closing was no doubt the Civil Rights era of the 1950s and '60s. The crumbling of the Southern system of segregation, under the combined onslaught of popular protest and federal power, seemed to represent the collapse of the great dividing wall between the races and, with blacks and whites marching together behind Martin Luther King, Jr., and even President Johnson declaring, "We Shall Overcome," an unprecedented day of biracial mutuality and understanding seemed at hand. This moment, though importantly shaped by the tradition of black evangelicalism, was primarily the product of religious and cultural forces other than evangelicalism. Among these two may be singled out ecumenical Protestantism and cultural pluralism.

Much of the prestige and social influence enjoyed by evangelicalism in the nineteenth century was assumed by ecumenical Protestantism in the twentieth. When it first took organizational form as the Federal Council of Churches in 1908, ecumenical Protestantism showed little interest in the gap between blacks and whites. Gradually, however, in part in response to the pressures from blacks within its own ranks, ecumenical Protestantism became increasingly concerned with race relations. In 1946, the Federal Council of Churches endorsed "a non-segregated church and a non-segregated society" and thereafter ecumenical Protestantism moved slowly but steadily along the path that led eventually to its active support of the Civil Rights movement of the 1960s.

Ecumenical Protestantism was scarcely capable on its own, however, of shaping the twentieth century encounter of black and white, even in its religious dimension. The term "cultural pluralism," which became current only during this period, does not refer simply to the empirical fact of cultural and religious variety, but rather to a movement to take from these facts a norm; to contend that America should understand itself precisely as a multicultural nation, a nation where people could have particular and varying cultural identities without forfeiting their status as full Americans. Normative pluralism, however, is never without its boundaries, and as the idea of cultural pluralism was applied to American religion, it came to mean that a religiously respectable American could be a Protestant, a Catholic, or a Jew—a formulation brilliantly analyzed by Will Herberg, in his mid-1950s classic, *Protestant-Catholic-Jew*. Ecumenical Protestantism, then, came to function as a kind of senior partner in a triple religious establishment with Catholicism and Judaism. By the time of the Civil Rights movement, Catholics and Jews were important and necessary allies for ecumenical Protestantism in its efforts to close the gap between blacks and whites.

At the height of the Civil Rights movement, to many that gap seemed ready to close. Soon, however, as the Civil Rights movement turned into the black power movement and a white backlash against black progress eclipsed white support for it, the gap seemed once again to widen, even within the world of the "triple establishment" itself. Ecumenical Protestantism's own black leaders proved surprisingly receptive to the newly emergent and highly polemical "black theology," as well as to militant demands that the churches both pay sizable "reparation" for their historic complicity in American racism and make room for a new degree of autonomous black power in the running of their own affairs. Black Catholics—a group that had grown steadily since the 1930s—became more insistent that the Roman Catholic church show greater respect for Afro-American patterns of piety, and make more room for black leadership. How could their church be truly catholic, some asked, if it insisted on canceling out their blackness rather than embracing it? Blacks and Jews meanwhile became involved in bitter recriminations over allegations of "Jewish racism" and "black anti-Semitism." What had gone wrong?

Both the prevailing sense of collective purpose and the dominant view of pluralism, it might be said, had been tested against the realities of the encounter of black and white and found wanting. Ecumenical Protestant supporters of the Civil Rights movement, bearers in many ways of the Puritan vision of the American "city on a hill," often wanted to believe that racial injustice in America consisted mostly in Southern racial segregation, and that a federally legislated end to that evil represented the final triumph of collective religious and moral purpose over recalcitrant regional wickedness. But in the light of the burning ghettoes, it became clear that it would take a good deal more than civil rights legislation to provide a happy ending for the story of American race relations. Meanwhile, religious pluralists who saw support for civil rights as an unproblematic extension of interfaith goodwill among Protestants, Catholics, and Jews discovered to their surprise that black America could not so easily be fitted into the prevailing—and rather comfortable—framework of religious pluralism and tolerations. The Nation of Islam was a homegrown religion that diverged in many ways from patterns of belief and practice common among Muslims in most parts of the world. But the pressure within black religious life of a powerful movement preaching Allah's imminent judgment on a Satanic America and calling for a "return" to the pure teachings of Islam made clear the limitations of the "Protestant-Catholic-Jew" definition of American pluralism.

Since the late 1960s, there has been a clear retreat from a direct facing of the gap between black and white as it was then so strikingly revealed. Laments for the loss of community in America and calls for a renewal of collective purpose are once more issued and debated with little or no mention of the realities of race. Religious pluralism in the United States is analyzed and celebrated with little acknowledgement that the polarities of race in our history are not quite the same thing as the varieties of our religion. Acknowledged or not, however, the gap between the races—a gap involving both the interpretation of the American experience and the degree of empowerment within it—remains one of the foundational realities of our national religious life. And however much members of both races might sometimes wish it were otherwise, the painful encounter of black and white is likely to remain in the future what it has been in the past—one of the crucial, central themes in the religious history of the United States.

Selected Bibliography for Further Reading

Harris, Michael W. "African American Religious History in the 1980s: A Critical Review." *Religious Studies Review* 20:4 (October 1994): 263–75.

Lincoln, C. Eric. *Race, Religion, and the Continuing American Dilemma.* New York: Hill & Wang, 1984.

Raboteau, Albert J., and David W. Wills. "Retelling Carter Woodson's Story: Archival Sources for Afro-American Church History." *Journal of American History* 77 (1990): 183–99.

Sernett, Milton C., ed. *Afro-American Religious History: A Documentary Witness.* Durham, NC: Duke University Press, 1985.

Wilmore, Gayraud S., ed. *African American Religious Studies: An Interdisciplinary Anthology.* Durham, NC: Duke University Press, 1989.

Chapter 10

Assessment and New Departures for a Study of Black Religion in the United States of America

Charles H. Long

Assessment

Though the present interest in the study of Black religion in the United States within the theological community must be seen within the context of the programmatic theological statements of Professor James Cone, his work does not constitute the beginnings of the study of Black religion in the United States by Black scholars within the theological tradition.

Prior to the work of Cone several works dealing with some aspect of Black religion published by Black scholars appeared. I refer to W.E.B. DuBois's *The Negro Church* (1903), Carter G. Woodson's *The History of the Negro Church* (1921), Benjamin Mays and Joseph Nicholson's *The Negro's Church* (1933), Mays's *The Negro's God* (1938), and E. Franklin Frazier's *The Negro Church in America* (1955). In addition, two dissertations from the University of Chicago were Carleton L. Lee's *Patterns of Leadership Among Negroes* (1950), and Miles Mark Fisher's *Negro Slave Songs in the United States* (1953). Even closer in time are C. Eric Lincoln's *The Black Muslims in America* (1961) and Joseph Washington's *Black Religion* (1964). On the specifically theological level the works of Howard Thurman have for some time set forth a distinctively new interpretation of Black religious experience.

If Cone's work does not constitute an absolutely new beginning, it does represent a shift that might form a watershed in the study of Black religion. From the work of Cone one is able to set forth a basis from which we might assess the works prior to his time and to plot new and different trends in the study of Black religion.

Professor Cone's book, *Black Theology and Black Power* (1969), is unique in several ways. He is not, however, the first one to make the point that

Jesus or God might be Black; a long line of Blacks have asserted this slogan, from Bishop William McNeal Turner to Marcus Garvey. Cone is distinctive in that his understanding of the Blackness of the godhead is carried on within the context of a systematic apologetic theology that argues from within the theological tradition for its cogency. This work should be seen as part of the civil rights movement and of the change of context from civil rights integrationism to Black Power. I quote from the first section of this work, where Cone says, "If, as I believe, Black Power is the most important development in American life in this century, there is need to begin to analyze it from a theological perspective. In this work an effort is made to investigate the concept of Black Power, placing primary emphasis on its relationship to Christianity, the Church and contemporary American theology." (p. 1)

He continues, "It is my thesis, however, that Black Power, even in its most radical expression, is not an antithesis to Christianity; nor is it a heretical idea to be tolerated with painful forbearance. It is, rather, Christ's central message to twentieth-century America. And unless the empirical denominational church makes a determined effort to capture the man Jesus through a total identification with the suffering poor as expressed in Black Power, that church will become exactly what Christ is not." (p. 2)

Even this emphasis is not new. The same kind of overtone is present in the works of C. Eric Lincoln and Joseph Washington, and of course, these particular phrases remind us of the work of Howard Thurman, *Jesus and the Disinherited* first published in 1949. In this work Thurman stated, "The significance of the religion of Jesus to people who stand with their backs against the wall has always seemed to me to be crucial. It is one emphasis which has been lacking—except where it has been part of a very unfortunate corruption of the missionary impulse, which is, in a sense, the very heartbeat of the Christian religion. The basic fact is that Christianity as it was born in the mind of this Jewish thinker and teacher appears as a technique of survival for the oppressed." (p. 29)

So the theme of Blackness and the oppressed in Cone's work is not novel. As I said before, the distinctiveness of his work is in the sustained systematic exposition, but there is yet another distinction: Cone, though acknowledging the oppression, mounted a theological critique of the oppressors from the stance of Power! To be sure, the power, as far as the text is concerned, is present in its rhetorical style, its open accusation, its prophetic pronouncements. It issued a challenge—a challenge to Black and white churchmen, and a challenge to American theology, and, for that matter, all Christian theology.

It was a book published by the right person at the right time and in the right place. It caught up with some of the themes of previous Black scholars of religion from the sociological and Christian ethics perspectives as well as the theological trends that were emerging within social ethics. It formed a continuity and a discontinuity with that milieu; it made clear a place on which to stand and thus it became a pointer, and if not a culmination, a hiatus. Its culmination lies in the theological statements that summarize the protest for justice in the history of Black scholarship in religion, its hiatus in the self-conscious theological assertiveness. If *Black Theology and Black Power* makes a clarion call and if its appearance on the scene was one of audacity, Cone's work of 1970, *A Black Theology of Liberation*, is a different kind of theological work. Its style is different; it sets about to fill in the blank spaces created by his previous work. It moves more carefully through the theological method and defines itself as part and parcel of a theology of liberation. Its more sober tone reminds one that additional theological work remains to be done and Cone sets forth those elements that must be dealt with within the complete corpus of a Black Theology of liberation.

In the meanwhile, the Fund for Theological Education had shifted resources to the support of doctoral studies in religion for Black students; the Society for the Study of Black Religion was organized and out of this ferment critical analyses and discussion of Cone's work and the rediscovery of other works published previous to Cone's *Black Theology* were brought to bear on the discussion. So, coincidentally and causally related to these two works, we are able to see the formation of a new discourse that brings older works into a new milieu and points to trends in other directions—directions stemming from this new discourse.

Major critical and alternate statements on the definition of Black Theology were contributed by Major Jones and Deotis Roberts. The most trenchant critique of Black Theology is probably that of William Jones's *Is God a White Racist? A Preamble to Black Theology* (1973). This work by Jones raises the essential issue of theodicy. Put simply it is this question: Is suffering, Black suffering, crucial for the Black theologian? To regard liberation as the summum bonum and sine qua non necessitates the opposite, suffering as oppression, as an aspect of the *summum malum*. The precondition for Black liberation as the objective for Black Theology is the prior affirmation of Black suffering as oppressive.

This is a crucial argument for it raises questions concerning not simply the enterprise of Black Theology, but of the Christian structure of existence itself; it forces one to ask whether the structure of Christian existence is capable of defining or expressing freedom for those who suffer.

While theologians were discussing Blackness within the context of theologizing, Gayraud Wilmore put out a kind of theological history of the Black Church. In his *Black Religion and Black Radicalism* (1972), Wilmore traced the history of the Black Church and its leaders as they responded to the various historical manifestations of racism in America. Though churches and church leaders took different stances during different periods, one is able to see a thread of continuity in the manner in which, in every case, the two structures of survival and protest constituted a kind of baseline around which these stances were taken. Again I see a skeletal structure in this work that should lead and has led in some quarters to more detailed historical studies of the Black Church. In part the works of James Washington and Albert Raboteau are already filling in some of the flesh of this sturdy skeleton erected by Wilmore.

A special word must be said about C. Eric Lincoln. The publication of his *Black Muslims in America* was a signal that something new was going to happen in the religious life of Black Americans. Lincoln has always been ahead of everyone else. He has a peculiar intellectual intuition about matters of this kind. Not only has he written extensively on the sociology of Black religion and the Black Church, giving us a reassessment of E. Franklin Frazier, and an excellent book of readings on *The Black Experience in Religion* (1974), he has encouraged and presided over the publication of several volumes which might not have seen the light of day apart from his confidence and faith in the authors. Not only for his own works but equally for this task and his hand in the works of others do we owe him a special thanks. This kind of genius is as much needed as the great intellectual ideas and to find both of these in one person is much more than one would expect.

With the mention of Lincoln, let me move on to another phase by way of a comment based upon his edited work, *The Black Experience in Religion*. If we examine this text we see that it covers a very wide range of materials and interpretations: articles on the Black Church, preachers and preaching, Black theology, Black sects and cults, and on Caribbean and African religions. From this work it is clear that Eric Lincoln has not confined the Black experience to the Christian churches in North America, nor is the attention to the Black churches in North America limited to a theological interpretation of their histories. "Black experiences" seems to constitute a world system, or a potentially world system, of communication and soteriological meaning. This was already a leitmotif in his work on the Black Muslims, for he saw the existence of Black Muslims at once as a protest against American racism and the expression of an alternate system of world communication. One may come at this point in another way if one looks at the activities and the work just put out by Gayraud Wilmore and James Cone. In their *Black Theology, A Documentary History, 1966–1979* (1979), the authors document the history of this movement and provide critical comments regarding Black Theology over this period of time, but they also include in this volume those meanings of Black Theology as a theology of liberation and thus the conversation and dialogue of Black Theology and theologians with Africans, Europeans, and Latin Americans extends the range of this soteriological communication.

A crucial issue will, in my opinion, emerge at this point. Is theology in any of its manifestations capable of sustaining this conversation or will it be sustained at another level that grows out of a more difficult conversation—a conversation that is an attempt to communicate the religious elements of one's cultural experience to another? To put it bluntly, how long will Jürgen Moltmann and Paul Holmer be able to maintain themselves in this conversation, or, if they are able to do so, will they prevent other Africans or Latin Americans from speaking? How continuous is the discussion with variant structures of liberation theology and how much will the cultural-historical experience form a discontinuity?

One of the themes running through a great deal of the interpretations of Black Theology and Black religion is the assertion that the Black community did not and does not make distinctions between the secular and the sacred and that it follows from this assertion that the Black Church is and has been the locus of the Black community. If this is so, then it means that the church is the locus of the expression of Black cultural life. Politics, art, business, and all other dimensions of the Black community should thus find their expression as aspects of the religious experience of Black folks. To test out this assertion Black scholars in religion should be conversant with works that deal with the wider ranges of Black experience. To some extent the society has a few members who were not trained in theological schools, but only a few. Only one of two sociologists of religion, no anthropologist of religion, poet, novelist, political scientist, or economist is among us. We must do the best we can to become conversant with them through their writings.

Harold Cruse, in his wonderful tour de force book of 1967 *The Crisis of the Negro Intellectual,* had asserted that only Blacks in America could make a cultural revolution and he called upon the Black intellectuals to develop what he called a Black cultural methodology. By this he meant a critical and creative hermeneutic that was capable of taking a stance within the American and Western tradition affirmatively and critically. It would involve not simply criticism of racial oppression but an identification within that culture while at the same time undercutting the very stance of one's authenticity with that tradition in status quo.

In another vein Cruse was stating in our times the issue that Du Bois raised in *Souls of Black Folk* (1903) as the double consciousness. But before I can give this discussion solidity, I must interject some other literature. First of all, there is a body of literature that deals with us explicitly and contingently, a body of scholarly works by Blacks and others that bear on our situation. These exist in contrast to a body of general American texts—texts that tell the American story, the American ideology, George Washington, the founding fathers, Thanksgiving, the Fourth of July, etc., etc., etc. In one way or other we were all educated in this mode so I don't need to go any further. We should, however, be aware of the internal critiques of myth-history. As far as history is concerned, let me mention only a few works: first, Francis Jennings's *The Invasion of America: Indians, Colonialism, and the Cant of Conquest* (1975), *Savagism and Civility* (1978) by Bernard Sheehan, and *Sons of the Fathers* (1976) by Catherine Albanese. Studies of this kind form a critique of the early American tradition and open the possibility for another mode of interpretation of American experience in terms of the new data and methods. These works should be read alongside the works of Vine Deloria. On Mexico I would recommend Jacques LaFaye's *Quetzalcóatl and Guadalupe* (1978). I think that these should be decisive for any critical cultural methodology that undertakes the analysis of the nature and reality of the world of the colonized during the colonial period. Millions of people were in fact colonized during the period of late Western expansion, but the progeny of these colonizers, at least at this time, did not have an imperialism over the methods and theories regarding the realities of persons and cultures during this period. As far as a philosophical critique is concerned, I would recommend the work of David Brion Davis, especially his *The Problem of Slavery in an Age of Revolution* (1975).

Closer to home there are a host of works by Black novelists, historians, anthropologists, sociologists, political scientists, etc. John Hope Franklin's editions of Black biographies from University of California Press include James Weldon Johnson, William Wells Brown, Ida B. Wells, T. Thomas Fortune, and Henry Ossawa Tanner. And even closer there are the works of John Lovell, Jr., and Eileen Southern on Black music or A. Leon Higginbotham's study of Blacks and the legal process. Works of this kind will help us make sense of the claim of a pattern of experience and expression within the Black community.

But there is another body of literature that is in one sense as close and in another sense quite distant from our work. It is close because it purports to deal with many of the same issues that face us and distant because it does not arise out of the primordium of cultural passions that generates our work. Therefore, while these works are exceedingly competent in terms of the questions that they pose and resolve, the very questions are structures of the alienation. I am speaking here of works such as Eugene Genovese's *Roll, Jordan, Roll* (1974), and Lawrence Levine's *Black Culture and Black Consciousness* (1977).

Eugene Genovese's *Roll, Jordan, Roll* is part of an oeuvre that includes *The Political Economy of Slavery* (1967) and the subtitle of *Roll, Jordan, Roll* is "The World the Slaves Made." This is in a dialectical relationship with the former work. It is an extremely valuable text and continues a line of interpretation from Newbell Niles Puckett's *The Magic and Folk Beliefs of the Southern Negro* (1969) through Kenneth Stampp's *The Peculiar Institution* (1956) to *Time on the Cross* by Robert Fogel and Stanley Engerman (1974).

Genovese's method carries strong overtones of the dialectic of Hegel and Marx and in carrying through this method he makes a major revision of the religion of the slaves. The problem with this text is hermeneutical. What is his stance before our history? What is most lacking is any possibility for the discussion of the experience of slavery and of the slave in the terms of a transcendent meaning of freedom. The dialectic of master-slave allows only for the discussion of the meaning of freedom and obligation within the structure of paternalism. The meaning of the religion of the slaves is too closely tied to and reduced to the structures of the economy. Though admitting the formation of a new consciousness, it remains rooted in the structures of materiality and transcendent meanings are projections of this rootedness. The subtlety of Du Bois's delineation of the double consciousness that tended to undercut its own formation is not an element of this analysis.

Levine's work, though bearing the title *Black Culture and Black Consciousness*, misses the point in the same manner—lack of participation as hermeneutical issue: the issue of living in and thinking about. Let me state what I have in mind at this point by reference to Du Bois's notion of the double consciousness. In one sense it is the issue of objectivity and subjectivity. The true rendering of Black experience and expression is not a privileged position for Black scholars. At the same time there is room for and necessity for historical and humanistic studies that combine the "thinking about," with the lived in participation. This methodological issue will become increasingly important in the work of Black scholars.

Let me give an example of what I have in mind by using Hegel's master/slave dialectic from this point of view:

> Even when the slave, ex-slave, or colonized person becomes aware of the autonomy and independence of his consciousness, he finds that, because of the economic, political and linguistic hegemony of the master, there is not space for the legitimate expression for such a human form. The desire for an authentic place for the expression of this reality is the source of the revolutionary tendencies in these religions. But on the level of human consciousness religions of the oppressed create in another manner. The hegemony of the oppressors is understood as a myth—myth in two major senses, as true and as fictive. It is true as a structure with which one must deal in a day-by-day manner if one is to persevere, but it is fictive as far as any ontological significance is concerned.
>
> But such a procedure does not define a simple dichotomy, for the day-to-day existence is in fact his labor—labor from which his autonomy arises; therefore his own autonomy takes on a fictive character. The truth of his existence must necessarily involve not only the change of this consciousness but the realization of the true and fictive consciousness of the oppressor. This drama is carried out again and again in the religions of the oppressed. But the basic structure of such meanings approximates the myth, for only the consciousness as myth can express the full range of this dialectical mode of being.
>
> The oppressed must deal with both the fictive truth of his status as expressed by the oppressor, i.e., his second creation, and the discovery of his own autonomy and truth—his first creation. The locus for this structure is the mythic consciousness which dehistorizes the relationship for the sake of creating a new form of humanity—a form of humanity which is no longer based on the master-slave dialectic. The utopian and eschatological dimensions of the religions of the oppressed stem from this modality.
>
> The oppressive element in the religions of the oppressed is the negation of the image of the oppressor and the discovery of the first creation. It is thus the negation that is found in community and seeks its expression in more authentic forms of community, those forms of community which are based upon the first creation, the original authenticity of all persons which precedes the master-slave dichotomy. There is thus a primordial structure to his consciousness, for

in seeking a new beginning in the future it must perforce imagine an original beginning. (Long, 1976, pp. 411–2)

Leonard Barret's discussion of the Cumina-Pukkumina in C. Eric Lincoln's *The Black Experience in Religion* expresses the meaning of this dialectical mode of consciousness at the level of ritual action, and his analysis might well carry over into some aspects of religious worship on the North American continent and allow us to rethink the impact of the Great Awakening on the slaves and other Black persons.

More congruent to, but offering a different methodological stance than either Genovese or Levine, is Roger Bastide's *African Religions of Brazil* (1978). In this work Bastide employs an intensive participant-observant *verstehen* method in accumulating his data. He was actually initiated into *candomble*, and this initiation was more than and deeper than that cute kind of story often related by anthropologists at cocktail parties. It was an expression of what he called a crisis of consciousness on a personal level and on the level of his scholarly discipline, comparative sociology; it raised the issue of the very raison d'être for study. It may be the case that such intimacy allowed for better understanding, but, what is more important, it prepared him to understand the dialectical modality of consciousness that while present in the *candomble* was at the same time an experience of modernity—that *candomble* and himself were struggling with similar problems. This is a masterful work by one who stands outside a tradition to study it in context.

What can one make of these various studies, presenting us with new data and new methods in light of the programmatic structures of Black Theology? First of all, though Black Theology is the most sustained protestant movement in Black religious thought, it has not picked up or fully exploited the social-ethical emphases of former Black religious thinkers and therefore has not made full use of a particular tradition in Black religious thought.

In connection with this point Black Theology, though making one of its resources the Black Christian institutional churches, had made hardly any inroads within these churches. The Black churches have not seen fit to affirm or to critically evaluate the project of Black Theology.

Neither Black Theology nor attendant works dealing with Black religion and Black culture have developed a general interpretative framework in which their interpretation makes for a distinctively new evaluation of religion and culture. (See Howard Dodson, "Needed: A New Perspective on Black History," 1981.) Is it possible for new works about Blacks to stay within the same framework that just a few years ago thrived on their exclusion? Responses to these questions lead to the next section of this paper.

Departures

We should wish to know, for example, how it would be possible to tolerate, and to justify, the sufferings and annihilation of so many peoples who suffer and are annihilated for the simple reason that their geographical situation sets them in the pathway of history; that they are neighbors of empires in a state of permanent expansion. How to justify for example, the fact that southwestern Europe had to suffer for centuries—and hence to renounce any impulse toward a higher historical existence, toward spiritual creation on a universal plane—invaders and later of the Ottoman empire? And in our day, when historical pressure no longer allows any escape, how can man tolerate the catastrophies and horrors of history—if beyond them he can glimpse no sign, no trans-historical meaning; if they are only blind play of economic, social, or political forces, or, even worse, only the result of "liberties" that a minority takes and exercises directly on the stage of universal history? (Eliade, p. 151)

The Negro is sort of a seventh son, born with a veil, and gifted with second-sight in this American world—a world which yields him no true self-consciousness, but only lets him see himself through the revelation of the other world. It is a peculiar sensation, this double consciousness, this sense of always looking at one's self through the eyes of the others, of measuring one's soul by the tape of a world that looks on in amused contempt and pity. One feels this two-ness—as American, as Negro; two souls, two thoughts, two unreconciled strivings; two warring ideals in one dark body, whose dogged strength alone keeps it from being torn asunder. The history of the American Negro is the history of this strife—this longing to attain self-conscious manhood, to merge this double self into a better truer self. In this merging he wishes neither of the older selves to be lost. He would not Africanize America, for America has too much to teach the world and Africa. He would not bleach his Negro soul in a flood of white Americanism, for he knows that Negro blood has a message for the world. . . . (Du Bois, pp. 3–4)

These two epigraphs form the context for this section. They are from the pens of two very dissimilar, from a conventional point of view, scholars. Eliade is the Rumanian-American émigré historian of religions, and the quotation comes at the end of his work *Cosmos and History* (1959) in the section entitled, "The Terror of History." W.E.B. Du Bois is the Black American scholar, leader, agitator, and historian; his quotation is taken from the very first section of the chapter entitled, "Of Our Spiritual Strivings," in his *Souls of Black Folk.*

There are, however, in the face of these dissimilarities several commonalities. Both of the statements are from a genre of literature that falls between scholarship and autobiography. They represent hermeneutical probings in which the stance and point of view espoused reveal a lived experience as the source of the probing. Both deal with human time as that temporal order that is the increment of imperialism and world systems that order through military, economic, and political power, such that they smother the time and histories of all who come into contact with them. Eliade raises the question of the philosophical justification of this kind of power in the terms of the apologia for it, and Du Bois's statement represents an assessment of the possibility of freedom once this power has effected its purpose. Both are interpretations of religion.

The bifurcation of the world that is coincidental to enslavement and conquest produces not only differing rhythms of the temporal sequences but also different meanings of the manifestation of world, the epistemologies for knowing it, and the practical activities for deciphering the meanings of cultural destinies. Invariably a normative meaning of history is supported and justified by the ideologies of conquest. And these ideologies are not simply the crass and crude slogans of blood and soil or manifest destiny. In the period of late Western expansion these philosophical ideologies were, more often than not, part and parcel of the enunciation of a universal humanism, making claims as it did for the essential status of all human beings. This is as true for the French philosophers, Montesquieu, Montaigne, Rousseau, as it is for the German philosophers from Kant to Hegel, and the English empiricists.

These philosophical ideologies must be seen as sometimes forming the foundation for, and at other times serving as the correlate of, the modern university disciplines that undertook the task of studying, classifying, and understanding the lives and cultures of those who had to undergo the histories of the conquerors, or in Eliade's term, the "terror" of their histories. What is remarkable on the epistemological level in these early new social sciences (and we might say almost to the present) is the fact that they hardly make mention of the contact situation itself, the fact of mutual discovery of the two cultures in the situation of colonialism—what Francis Jennings has called mutual discoveries. This is even more remarkable when we observe that one of the basic ingredients within the philosophical and cultural meaning of the conquerors is the evaluation of history. By history in this sense, I don't mean that valuation of temporality that is a pervasive characteristic of human existence. I mean a particular and peculiar interpretation and point of view regarding time, justified in many instances through recourse to progress, civilizing missions, and Christian theologies; it finds its supporters among the technological positivists of the left and the right.

Those who are forced to undergo this history are not subjected simply to economic and political exploitation; they are simultaneously forced to undergo an evacuation of their cultural meaning and the possibility for cultural creativity and stability. This evacuation of cultural meaning forced by the conqueror is matched by the presentation of the conquered people and culture as "problems of knowledge" in a special sense. They are "problems of knowledge" not so much in the conventional sense, but classified as special categories of this kind of problem. The taxonomies used to describe them allow them to become normal special problems, or normal exotic problems, and thus disciplinary structures need not fear their disappearance, for they were created by and for the disciplines and tend to exist as eternal intellectual problems. One of the most general and pervasive structures of this kind of problem revolves around the distinction primitive/civilized. (See my article "Primitive/Civilized: The Locus of a Problem," *History of Religions* 19, no. 6 [November 1980].) I show how meanings regarding a European discourse on wild men, women, and the insane, became the normative language for the discussion of the new geographies and cultures discovered by the Europeans from the fifteenth century to the present. This language still pervades many of our common disciplinary fields, and it is one of those forms of cultural language that has defined explicity and adumbrated a range of meanings and interpretative schema concerning Blacks in the United States. Critical and precise hermeneutical attention must be given to this level of our cultural and disciplinary languages as part of the creativity of Black scholarship if this scholarship is ever to form a new framework of interpretation. In this connection I have found that some of the philosophical positions set forth by Jacques Derrida are quite congruent with Du Bois's notion of a double consciousness. Especially in his program of deconstruction do I see a meaning of radical critique and creativity. I am pleased to find that younger scholars such as Cornel West at Union Seminary are of the same opinion.

Another area pertinent to this topic has to do with the general interpretation of American culture itself. If this culture is continually understood simply as the culture of Europeans who came to a virgin land all subsequent interpretations will tend to be wrong-headed. I have experimented with the most general categorization of American culture as an aboriginal-Euro-African culture.

In making this assertion or operating with this presupposition, I am trying to mitigate the notion that Euro-Americans serve as the reality principle for American culture and that others are not real until contact has been made with the Euro-Americans. All are real, but in differing modes. To decipher this meaning methodologically, I have had recourse to models from structural linguistics, where I employ the meanings of synchrony, diachrony, and silence as basic elements for a total language.

At another level, attention should be directed towards a comparative history of the religions of the oppressed. Vittorio Lanternari's work of this title *(Religions of the Oppressed*, 1963) is suggestive but its heavy-handed Marxism suffocates any genuine religious interpretation. Given the general context of oppression, what mode of consciousness emerges, what epistemological resources are created, and what meanings of world are actual and possible?

One of the problems of Black Theology is that none of its protagonists have attempted to delineate the meaning of power in our present situation. Power is assumed to be an eternal neutral category that can be had or grasped by the group or person lucky or militant enough to handle it. Power is a pervasive dimension of human existence but its constellation, locus, and influence is contextually situated. Paul Tillich's essay on the "End of the Protestant Era," in his *The Protestant Era* (1948) should complement W.E.B. Du Bois's statement of the twentieth century and the "rising tide of color." What is the meaning of power at the end of the protestant era? Do the oppressed slaver for the old capitalist protestant power or has a new locus and formation of power appeared to them? These are crucial issues and since religion is also a concern about power, its origins and its forms, such questions cannot be avoided.

My own work at this point has been at the level of what I call ideograms, (to borrow a term from Rudolf Otto). I have been concerned to pay close attention to the concrete expressions from this level to conceptualization in either the theological or philosophical mode, I have developed the liminal ideogram, a meaning that emerges from concreteness but is not yet a

234 *Charles H. Long*

concept. The ideogram allows for religious experience to adumbrate other dimensions of human existence in a preconceptual form raising the wider issues of reality, world, epistemology etc. Conceptual structures arising from these ideograms ought then to be constructive and critical. At the present time I am working with the passivity of power, the opaqueness of reality, the percussive nature of existence, and the rhythms of time.

The study of Black religion cannot be provincialized. Africans were brought to the New World as part and parcel of an international system of trade and communication; the meanings of the cultures of the former, colonized in the modern world, carry the same implications. Religious forms and expressions are the sources of new worlds of meaning; the study and understanding of Black religion has much to contribute to our future.

References

Albanese, Catherine. *Sons of the Fathers*. Philadelphia: Temple University Press, 1976.
Bastide, Roger. *African Religions of Brazil*. Baltimore: Johns Hopkins University Press, 1978.
Cone, James. *Black Theology and Black Power*. New York: Seabury Press, 1969.
———. *A Black Theology of Liberation*. Philadelphia and New York: Lippincott, 1970.
Cruse, Harold. *The Crisis of the Negro Intellectual*. New York: William Morrow, 1967.
Dodson, Howard. "Needed: A New Perspective on Black History," *National Endowment for the Humanities*, 2, no. 1 (February 1981): 1, 2.
Du Bois, W.E.B., *The Negro Church*. Atlanta: Atlanta University Press, 1903.
———. *Souls of Black Folk*. Chicago: A. C. McClurg & Co., 1903. Reprint. New York: Fawcett Publications, 1961.
Eliade, Mircea. *Cosmos and History*. New York: Harper Torch Books, Harper & Row, 1959.
Fisher, Miles Mark. *Negro Slave Songs in the United States*. New York: Citadel Press, 1963.
Frazier, E. Franklin. *The Negro Church in America*. 1955. Reprint. Liverpool: University of Liverpool Press, 1963.
Fogel, Robert and Stanley Engerman. *Time on the Cross*. Boston: Little, Brown, 1974.
Genovese, Eugene D. *The Political Economy of Slavery*. New York: Random House, 1967.
———. *Roll, Jordan, Roll*. New York: Random House, 1974.
Higginbotham, A. Leon, Jr. *In the Matter of Color*. New York: Oxford University Press, 1978.
Jennings, Francis. *The Invasion of America: Indians, Colonialism, and the Cant of Conquest*. Chapel Hill: University of North Carolina Press, 1975.
Jones, William. *Is God a White Racist? A Preamble to Black Theology*. Garden City, New York: Doubleday/Anchor, 1973.
LaFaye, Jacques. *Quetzalcóatl and Guadalupe*. Chicago: University of Chicago Press, 1978.
Lanternari, Vittoria. *Religions of the Oppressed*. New York: Alfred A. Knopf, 1963.
Lee, Carleton L. *Patterns of Leadership Among Negroes*. Ph.D. diss., University of Chicago Press, 1950.
Levine, Lawrence. *Black Culture and Black Consciousness*, New York: Oxford University Press, 1977.
Lincoln, C. Eric. *The Black Muslims in America*. Boston: Beacon Press, 1961.

————.*The World the Slaveholders Made.* New York: Random House, 1969.

————, ed., *The Black Experience in Religion.* Garden City, N.Y.: Doubleday/Anchor, 1974.

Long, Charles H., "Oppression in Religion, and the Religions of the Oppressed," *Harvard Theological Review,* 69, no. 3–4 (1976): 391–412.

————. "Primitive/Civilized: The Locus of a Problem," *History of Religions,* 19, no. 6 (November 1980).

Lovell, John, Jr., *Black Song, the Forge and the Flame.* New York: Collier-Macmillan, 1972.

Mays, Benjamin B. and Joseph W. Nicholson. *The Negro's Church.* New York: Institute of Social and Religious Research, 1933.

————. *The Negro's God.* Boston: Chapman & Grimes, Inc., 1938.

Phillips, Ulrich B. *American Negro Slavery.* Baton Rouge: Louisiana State University Press, 1966.

————. *The Slave Economy of the Old South.* Baton Rouge: Louisiana State University Press, 1968.

Puckett, Newbell Niles. *The Magic and Folk Beliefs of the Southern Negro.* New York: Dover Publications Inc., 1969.

Stampp, Kenneth. *The Peculiar Institution.* New York: Vintage Books, 1956.

Thurman, Howard. *Jesus and the Disinherited.* Nashville, Tenn.: Abingdon Press, 1949.

Tillich, Paul. *The Protestant Era.* Chicago: University of Chicago Press, 1948.

Wilmore, Gayraud. *Black Religion and Black Radicalism.* New York: Doubleday, 1972.

Wilmore, Gayraud and James Cone. *Black Theology, A Documentary History, 1966–1979.* Maryknoll, N.Y.: Orbis Books, 1979.

Woodson, Carter G. *The History of the Negro Church.* 1921. Reprint. Washington, D.C.: Associated Publishers, 1945.

Part 3

Slavery and a Black Religious Imagination

Chapter 11

Death of the Gods

Albert J. Raboteau

Let us rejoice in and adore the wonders of God's infinite love in bringing us from a land semblant of darkness itself, and where the divine light of revelation (being obscured) is in darkness. Here the knowledge of the true God and eternal life are made manifest; but there was nothing in us to recommend us to God . . .

Phyllis Wheatley

I had always been told from the time I was a small child that I was a Negro of African stock. That it was no disgrace to be a Negro and had it not been for the white folks who brought us over here from Africa as slaves, we would never have been here and would have been much better off.

"Aunt" Adeline, former slave

In one of her earliest poems Phyllis Wheatley reflected upon her religious heritage:

'Twas mercy brought me from my *Pagan* land,
Taught my benighted soul to understand
That there's a God, that there's a *Saviour* too . . .[1]

According to B. B. Thatcher, in his *Memoir of Phillis Wheatley*, the black poet remembered nothing of her African past with the exception of one ritual, "her mother's custom of *pouring out water before the sun at his rising.*" Thatcher remarks that this "no doubt, was a custom of the tribe to which she belonged, and was one of their religious rites."[2] There were other slaves, however, who remembered far more of their African past than

239

Phyllis Wheatley did and who held a different view of their forced migration from their native lands.

Charles Ball, in the narrative of his life under slavery, recounted a slave funeral at which he assisted:

> I assisted her and her husband to inter the infant . . . and its father buried with it, a small bow and several arrows; a little bag of parched meal; a miniature canoe, about a foot long, and a little paddle, (with which he said it would cross the ocean to his own country) a small stick, with an iron nail, sharpened and fastened into one end of it; and a piece of white muslin, with several curious and strange figures painted on it in blue and red, by which, he said, his relations and countrymen would know the infant to be his son, and would receive it accordingly, on its arrival amongst them . . . He cut a lock of hair from his head, threw it upon the dead infant, and closed the grave with his own hands. He then told us the God of his country was looking at him, and was pleased with what he had done.[3]

According to Ball, the father of the dead infant was a "native of a country far in the interior of Africa" who claimed to have been a "priest in his own nation."[4] Of the native Africans among the slaves, Ball states:

> They are universally of opinion, and this opinion is founded in their religion, that after death they shall return to their own country, and rejoin their former companions and friends, in some happy region. . . .[5]

African-born slave Chloe Spear, brought as a child to Boston, like Phyllis Wheatley, "wished for *death;* supposing that when she died, she would return to her country and friends." This belief was derived, according to her biographer, "from a superstitious tradition of her ancestors, who, she said, supposed that the first infant born in a family after the decease of a member, was the same individual come back again."[6]

Nor did all slaves agree that embracing the Christian gospel meant accepting enslavement as a "providential mercy," as European traveler Fredrika Bremer learned from a conversation with a "Lucumi" slave on a Florida plantation around 1850:

> 'You have come hither from Africa?' He replied, Yes; that he had been smuggled hither from Cuba many years ago. He was now overseer

on a plantation, and was very well off. He was a Christian and seemed pleased to be so. He spoke very sensibly and cheerfully, and had a good, open countenance.

'You do not wish to return to Africa?' said I. 'Oh yes, Missis; oh yes, that I do:' replied he; 'there I should be still better off.' 'But people often kill one another there,' remonstrated I. 'Oh but nobody troubles themselves about that. And there are a great many good people who live there at peace.' 'But look here, my friend,' said Colonel Mac I., who is a strong Calvinist; 'if you had remained in Africa, you would not have become a Christian as you are now, and then the devil, in the end, would have had you!' The negro laughed, looked down, shook his head . . . and at length exclaimed, again looking up with an expression of humor and inventive acuteness, 'Now, Massa, look'ee here! The Gospel is now being preached over the whole of Africa, and if I had remained there, what was to hinder me from being one who heard it as well there as here?' To this there was no reply to be made, and the . . . negro had the last word.[7]

Some slaves, like the ancestor of Leonard Haynes, rejected Christianity. Recounting a family tradition, Haynes states: "My grandfather of three generations came over from the Gold Coast of Africa and was sold to a Mr. Haynes in Georgia. My grandfather was an African priest. This fact made him hostile to Christian preachers and to the religion of the Christians. Hence, he refused to join with the other slaves in their religious gatherings. . . ."[8]

There were, moreover, a few Muslim slaves from Africa who continued, as best they could, to observe the customs of Islam. "Muh gran come from Africa," remarked Rosa Grant of Possum Point, Georgia. "Huh membuh when I wuz a chile seein muh gran Ryna pray. Ebry mawnin at sun-up she kneel on duh flo in uh ruhm an bow obuh an tech uh head tuh duh flo tree time. Den she say a prayuh. I dohn membuh jis wut she say, but one wud she say use tuh make us chillun laugh. I membuh it was 'ashanegad.' Wen she finish prayin she say 'Ameen, ameen, ameen.'" Similarly, Katie Brown of Sapelo Island, Georgia, was a descendant of Belali Mahomet, a Muslim slave and driver. ". . . Belali an he wife Phoebe pray on duh bead," Katie recounted. "Dey wuz bery puhticluh bout duh time dey pray and dey bery regluh bout duh hour. Wen duh sun come up, wen it straight obuh head an wen it set, das duh time dey pray. Dey bow tuh duh sun and hab lill mat tuh kneel on. Duh beads is on a long string. Belali he pull bead an he say, 'Belambi, Hakabara, Mahamadu.' Phoebe she say,

'Ameen, Ameen.'" Charles Lyell visiting Hopeton Plantation on St. Simons Island, Georgia, before 1845, encountered "Old Tom," head driver for the plantation, a Foulah who had remained a strict Muslim, though his children and grandchildren had "exchanged the Koran for the Bible." Omar ibn Said, a slave in North Carolina, wrote an autobiographical fragment in Arabic script in 1831 in which he recalled:

> Before I came to the Christian country, my religion was the religion of Mohammed, the Apostle of God—may God have mercy upon him and give him peace! I walked to the mosque before day-break, washed my face and head and hands and feet. I prayed at noon, prayed in the afternoon, prayed at sunset, prayed in the evening. I gave alms every year. . . . I went on pilgrimage to Mecca. . . . When I left my country I was thirty-seven years old; I have been in the country of the Christians twenty-four years.

During those twenty-four years Omar had converted to Christianity:

> When I was a Mohammadan I prayed thus: 'Thanks be to God, Lord of all worlds, the merciful the gracious, Lord of the day of Judgement, thee we serve, on thee we call for help. Direct us in the right way, the way of those on whom thou hast had mercy, with whom thou hast not been angry and who walk not in error. Amen.'—But now I pray 'Our Father' . . . in the words of our Lord Jesus the Messiah.[9]

According to the Reverend Charles Colcock Jones, "The Mohammedan Africans remaining of the old stock of importations, although accustomed to hear the Gospel preached, have been known to accommodate Christianity to Mohammedanism. 'God,' say they, 'is Allah, and Jesus Christ is Mohammed—the religion is the same, but different countries have different names.'" Some religious customs observed by the slaves seemed to combine African and Christian elements. For example, on the Sea Islands, as Rachel Anderson recalled, at harvest time: "We hab a big feas. All night we shouts an in duh mawnin right at sunrise we pray an bow low tuh duh sun." Alex Anderson described the practice of river baptisms: "Duh preachuh and duh candidates goes down in duh watuh. Den duh preachuh make a prayuh tuh duh ribbuh and duh ribbuh washes duh sin away."[10]

Despite these countervailing examples, it seems that in the United States the experience of Phyllis Wheatley, if not her theological explanation of it, has been the rule rather than the exception. Under British North American slavery, it seems that the African religious heritage was lost. Especially does this appear so when black religion in the United States is compared with the cults of Brazil and the Caribbean. In *candomblé, vaudou, santeria,* and *shango* "the acceptance of Christianity by the African slaves, and its transmission to their descendants, has by no means meant the disappearance of African beliefs or patterns of worship," but to a large extent has led to their continuity in a new "unified system of belief and ritual."[11] Why was the same not true of slaves in the United States? Two conflicting answers have been proposed: one is that African retentions in the United States were negligible because the African was almost totally stripped of his culture by the process of enslavement, and the other, that the slave system did not destroy the slaves' African culture and a considerable number of Africanisms continue to define Afro-American culture in the United States. The foremost advocate of the former position is E. Franklin Frazier; of the latter, Melville J. Herskovits.[12]

The Debate

Herskovits' most complete and most careful statement of his thesis is *The Myth of the Negro Past.* The myth that Herskovits was intent on destroying was the belief that the American Negro had no past except a history of primitive savagery in Africa from which he had been delivered by contact with European civilization in America. For Herskovits the destruction of this myth was not simply a matter of detached scholarship. It also had important practical ramifications in the struggle against racism. To deny that the black American had a culture and history of significance and sophistication in Africa and to suggest that African culture was not advanced enough to endure contact with superior European culture was to imply that Negroes were an inferior people. Furthermore, Herskovits thought it important to recognize the historical relevance of African retentions in order to evaluate cultural differences between white and black Americans in scientific rather than racist terms. Discrepancies between white and black values and behavior were due not to "culture lag," i.e., backwardness on the part of the blacks but to a different cultural background whose roots lay in Africa.[13]

As an anthropologist, Herskovits was interested particularly in the study of culture contact and acculturation. To the debate over African retentions he brought an amazingly broad perspective, informed by extensive field work in Dahomey, Dutch Guiana, Haiti, Trinidad, and, to a lesser degree, Brazil. He studied the "New World Negro" in the light of his research in the slaving area of West Africa where a large number of Afro-Americans originated. In discussing the culture of black people in the United States he insisted that the situation of North American Negroes be placed on a spectrum or continuum with other Afro-American societies. The scale of African retentions stretches from Dutch Guiana with the strongest and most integral examples of African culture, at one end, to the United States with the weakest and most fragmentary evidence of African influence, at the other. Herskovits thought it important to view the United States in comparison with other areas of the hemisphere where Africanisms are apparent in order to discover clues to more subtly disguised African patterns of culture in the United States.[14]

In contrast to Haiti and Brazil, African retentions in the United States cannot be ascribed with any certainty to definite areas of West Africa such as Nigeria or Dahomey. Herskovits compensates for this difficulty by defining West Africa as a single-culture area with an overall similarity and unity despite local differences. He suggests a "base line" of West African culture to serve as a measure for determining Africanisms in the United States; furthermore, within the general culture of West Africa there is a focus, and this focus is religion. Throughout New World Negro cultures the strongest Africanisms are to be found in religion.[15] Herskovits divided the myth of the Negro past into five statements, or submyths, and then proceeded to rebut each statement.

The first myth is: "Negroes are naturally of childlike character, and adjust easily to the most unsatisfactory social situations, which they accept readily and even happily. . . ." On the contrary, Herskovits argues, Africans and Afro-Americans are neither childlike nor naive, but have developed a sophisticated worldview. A mark of the sophistication of their worldview has been a refusal to interpret life in terms of a simplistic dichotomy between good and evil. This worldview has allowed them to "adapt to everyday situations of all sorts." Besides, blacks were not content with slavery. Slaves resisted individually and rebelled collectively from the earliest days of slavery in Hispaniola.[16]

The second myth states: "Only the poorer stock of Africa was enslaved, the more intelligent members of the African community raided having been clever enough to elude the slaver's nets." Herskovits answers that the slave trade was not selective of the dregs of African society. There were instances when troublesome rivals who belonged to royal or priestly ranks were sold into slavery by wary rulers attempting to safeguard their thrones. When priests of the water cult in the coastal area of Dahomey, for example, proved intransigent, the conquering king of Abomey solved the problem by selling them into slavery.[17]

"Since," according to the third myth, "the Negroes were brought from all parts of the African continent, spoke diverse languages, represented greatly differing bodies of custom, and, as a matter of policy, were distributed in the New World so as to lose tribal identity, no least common denominator of understanding or behavior could have possibly been worked out by them." Not so, contends Herskovits, since the majority of slaves came from the "areas lying in the coastal belt of West Africa and the Congo." He denies that a large number of slaves were brought from more than two or three hundred miles inland. Within this central slaving area there were two main language groups, Sudanic and Bantu. Within each group distinct dialects had a great deal of similarity in basic structure. Moreover, resemblances between the two large groups do exist. Finally, the slaving regions represented a unified cultural area. Therefore, the separation of tribes during slavery did not create an insurmountable "barrier to the retention of African customs in generalized form, or of their underlying sanctions and values." Slaves from differing tribes had a basis for communication when they "learned words from the language of their masters and poured these into African speech molds."[18] Herskovits goes on to make an even stronger assertion: just as European words were translated into African speech patterns, so European culture was translated into African value and behavior systems. Therefore, "the reasons most often advanced to account for the suppression of Africanisms in the New World turned out to be factors that encouraged their retention."[19] This is an extremely important contention, which will be examined later.

"Even granting," goes myth number four, "enough Negroes of a given tribe had had the opportunity to live together, and that they had the will and ability to continue their customary modes of behavior, the cultures of Africa were so savage and relatively so low in the scale of human civilization that the apparent superiority of European customs as observed in the behavior of their masters would have caused and actually did cause them to give up such aboriginal traditions as they may otherwise have desired to preserve." This belief is based upon a biased ethnology and a simplistic understanding of acculturative process. The culture of West Africa was neither savage nor low and was not automatically overwhelmed by contact with supposedly superior European culture. Africa was an active partner in the acculturative relationship, states Herskovits. However, in the United States, Herskovits admits, African religious behavior had to be reinterpreted "in light of a new theology." Two factors determined the degree of reinterpretation necessary. The first was the intensity of the exposure of slaves to European culture, as determined by the ratio of blacks to whites. The smaller the number of slaves, the more complete was the control of the master; the tighter the supervision, the more intense was the pressure to acculturate. A second factor influenced the slaves to reinterpret African behavior: traditional African openness to the "new and foreign." This characteristic African acceptance was particularly manifest in religion, where "both conquered and conquerors often took over the gods of their opponents." The resilience of slaves' attitudes toward new gods frequently led to "slightly modified African sanctions supporting forms of a given institution that are almost entirely European." In other words, a "principle of disregard for outer form while retaining inner values" is "characteristic of Africans everywhere" and is "the most important single factor making for an understanding of the acculturative situation."[20]

The fifth and final myth is: "The Negro is thus a man without a past." Herskovits asserts that the Negro does indeed have a past, a cultural history which makes him a distinctive participant on the American scene, as distinctive as the Swedish, German, or Irish immigrant. In brief, "the civilizations of Africa, like those of Europe, have contributed to American culture as we know it today."[21]

It is necessary in analyzing Herskovits' thesis and the evidence he adduces in its support to remember that he is attacking a myth. Demythologizers often run the risk of erring on the side of overstatement. This is a fault of which Herskovits is not innocent. Perhaps none took him to task for it more forcefully than the black sociologist E. Franklin Frazier, the foremost spokesman for a position diametrically opposed to Herskovits'. While admitting the existence of African retentions in Latin America and the Caribbean, Frazier denies that African culture was able to survive the conditions of slavery to any significant extent in the United States. He admits that a few individual slaves remembered something of their background in Africa. However, exceptions prove the rule: African traditions and practices did not take root and survive in the United States.

> These isolated instances only tend to show how difficult it was for slaves, who had retained a memory of their African background, to find a congenial milieu in which to perpetuate the old way of life. . . .

The slaves, it seems, had only a vague knowledge of the African background of their parents. . . .[22]

It is Frazier's position that the process of enslavement and the passing of earlier generations born in Africa destroyed the culture of the slaves. The vacuum thus created was filled by Christianity, which became the new bond of social cohesion. The new worldview which gave meaning to life was Christianity, articulated in the images and stories of the Bible, as accepted by the slaves and celebrated in their spirituals.[23]

Deculturation began, according to Frazier, on the other side of the Atlantic, before the Africans even set foot on the slave ships. The fact that many slaves were captured in intertribal warfare and the demands of the plantation work force ensured that a large percentage of the slave population was young and male. And young males "are poor bearers of the cultural heritage of a people." In the coastal barracoons slaves were mixed together without regard for kinship or tribal ties. The trauma of the Middle Passage further isolated slaves from countrymen who spoke the same language or observed the same traditions.[24]

On this side of the Atlantic the size of the plantation where the slave ended his journey was a significant factor in either allowing for or reducing African cultural retentions. On the larger plantations, where the black population was much larger than the white, there was less opportunity for contact and so the process of acculturation was slow. But, Frazier contends, the majority of slaves in the United States were situated on smaller plantations and farms: "In some of the Upland cotton regions of Alabama, Mississippi, Louisiana, and Arkansas the median number of slaves per holding did not reach twenty, while in regions of general agriculture based mainly upon slave labor in Kentucky, Maryland, Missouri, North Carolina, South Carolina, and Tennessee the median number of slave holdings were even smaller."[25] The process of "seasoning" ("breaking in") new slaves required the prohibition of African languages. "Salt-water" (African-born) Negroes were looked down upon by slaves already used to the ways of plantation America, and social pressure was exerted upon them to learn new customs.[26] Slaves were under continual surveillance and control. On the small farms the slaves worked with their white owners; on larger plantations they toiled under the eye of the driver and overseer. Gatherings of five or more slaves without the presence of a white observer were universally forbidden. In addition, the mobility of the slave population and the destruction of familial stability due to the internal slave trade made social cohesion an impossibility. Therefore, Frazier concludes, "It is impossible to establish any continuity between African religious practices and the Negro church in the United States."[27] Here the "Negroes were plunged into an alien civilization in which whatever remained of their religious myths and cults had no meaning whatever." African memories were forgotten, African patterns of behavior and attitudes toward the world lost their meaning. Slaves had to develop "new habits and attitudes" in order "to meet new situations."[28]

Frazier takes Herskovits to task for basing his assertions on flimsy evidence. Herskovits had not been able "to refer African survival in the United States to a specific tribe or a definite area." When he argues that the spirit of African belief is preserved under the adoption of European religious forms, Frazier counters that this simply means that the "existence of such survivals cannot be validated on scientific grounds." A case in point is Herskovits' attempt to explain the popularity of the Baptist church among black Americans by reference to water cults in Africa. The Baptists successfully proselytized Negroes, says Frazier, not because they practiced baptism by immersion but because they were energetic proselytizers with strong appeal for lower classes.[29]

Frazier admits that in the "magic and folk beliefs of the rural Negroes in the United States, some African elements have probably been retained." However, he hastens to add, it is a very difficult task to separate African from European folk belief. And as the Afro-Americans "have emerged from the world of the folk" the majority "have sloughed off completely the African heritage."[30]

The debate has been a lasting one. The positions represented by Herskovits and Frazier have continued in one form or another to inform a variety of discussion on black history and culture, including the fields of music, folklore, language, and art. There are those who deny that there is any difference between white and black Americans except color. There are those who ground black identity and black pride upon a reclamation of historical continuity with the African past. There are those who identify black rebellion with the survival of African culture. The ideological conflicts between separatists and integrationists have involved judgments about the survival of African culture in the United States. Commentators on black religious life have been subject to ideological pressures to take a stand in the Herskovits-Frazier debate, understanding that wider implications would derive from their conclusions. Given the implications and emotions involved in the issues, it is a difficult but, for that reason, all the more necessary task to evaluate the evidence with care and open-mindedness, to be aware of one's own preconceptions and not to draw hasty conclusions.

Cases in Point: Baptism by Immersion
and Spirit Possession

The weakest part of Herskovits' argument is his contention that he has found African retentions in the institutional form and theology of certain types of black churches. He is more convincing when he speaks of "patterns of motor behavior" and folk belief, but here, too, he weakens his credibility by overstatement.

Herskovits begins his chapter on "Africanisms in Religious Life" with the following statement:

> Underlying the life of the American Negro is a deep religious bent that is but the manifestation here of a similar drive that, everywhere in Negro societies, makes the supernatural a major focus of interest. The tenability of this position is apparent when it is considered how in an age marked by skepticism, the Negro has held fast to belief. Religion is vital, meaningful, and understandable to the Negro of this country because . . . it is not removed from life, but has been deeply integrated into the daily round. It is because of this, indeed, that everywhere compensation in terms of the supernatural is so immediately acceptable to this underprivileged folk, and causes them, in contrast to other underprivileged groups elsewhere in the world, to turn to religion rather than to political action or other outlets for their frustration.[31]

Arthur Huff Fauset's critique of this generalization is significant, especially because it has been widely held that black people are somehow "naturally" religious. Fauset denies statistically that Afro-Americans are greater churchgoers than other Americans.[32] As to the importance of the church in the black community, it is a fact explained by the intransigence of white racism which relegated black control to one social institution, the church. There is no proof that religion as a compensatory force among the underprivileged has been more widespread among the black poor than it has been among the oppressed of other ethnic backgrounds. Besides, religion has also functioned as a spur to resistance, self-assertion, and rebellion in black history. Finally, when given the chance, as for example during the period of Reconstruction, blacks have turned readily to political action. Herskovits' generalization about the "religious bent characteristic of Negroes everywhere" reveals a characteristic problem in his method: How is such an assertion to be proved, disproved, or even taken?

As an impressionistic remark it has a certain validity. Religion *has* played a central role in Afro-American culture in the United States. But it is a different matter to ground the "scientific" hypothesis that religion forms the focus of black culture in both the New World and in Africa on the observation that black people have a "religious bent." The sweeping generalization only seems to weaken credibility concerning particular examples.

Turning to specific institutional characteristics of the black churches, Herskovits found Africanisms in the worship of "shouting" churches. Listening to the radio broadcasts of black church services he concluded that "spirit possession by the Holy Ghost" inspired "motor behavior that is not European but African."[33] The rhythmic hand-clapping and antiphonal participation of the congregation in the sermon, and the theological view in which "God, Jesus, and the Holy Ghost are all concerned with the immediate fate of those who worship them," strike Herskovits as "deviations from the practices and beliefs of white Baptists." The *immediacy* of God in the services he heard, the manner in which "the Holy Ghost visits with the minister, taking messages to God from those in need of help," seemed to Herskovits to reflect the African heritage of the worshippers.[34] The theological example is not convincing. A sense of the immediacy of God, of his involvement in daily life is not a deviation from the beliefs of white Baptists or indeed of many other Christians. The role of the Holy Spirit as a messenger seems to be a sermonic conceit that is not foreign to Christian belief.[35] Hand-clapping and congregational response would not be in the least surprising to white holiness and pentecostal church members, nor would "spirit possession."

Perhaps the most frequently attacked example of a specific African survival cited by Herskovits is baptism by immersion which he links to water cults in Nigeria and Dahomey. The strong appeal of the Baptist denomination for Negroes was due partially to the West African religious background, where water cults are extremely important. The Baptists' insistence on immersion was an attractive rite to Africans familiar with water cults because the concept of baptism is one "that any African would find readily understandable." In Africa, Dutch Guiana, and Haiti, possession by water spirits drives the possessed devotee to hurl himself bodily into a stream, pond, or river. Similarly in the baptismal service of rural black Baptists the spirit occasionally falls upon the new Christian emerging from the water, causing him to shout. Therefore, baptism through "the transmutation of belief and behavior under acculturation . . . furnished one of the least difficult transitions to a new form of belief."[36] There are two objections that can be made to Herskovits' comments on baptism by immersion. While Herskovits embraces the principle "that the acculturative process in each locality is to be analyzed in terms of the peculiarities of its own historic past and its own socio-economic present," he violates this principle too frequently by glossing over significant differences.[37] Because he views the whole of Afro-America as a spectrum or continuum, he sometimes blurs important distinctions and argues from an example in one area to an invalid application in another. The applicability of his analogy that just as spirit possession occurs in the water cults in Africa, so is shouting associated with baptism in the United States breaks down upon careful examination. The African devotee is possessed by the god who has replaced his personality and who impels him into the water, the god's own element, whereas the tradition which lies behind baptism by immersion is Judeo-Christian and the descent of the Spirit on this occasion has the warrant of Scripture: " . . . he will baptize with the Holy Spirit."[38]

The second criticism, made by every critic of Herskovits, is that the appeal of the Baptist denomination for Afro-Americans did not derive from their African background but from the attraction of evangelical religion to the slaves. To be fair to Herskovits, it is necessary to point out that he lists several other reasons for the spread of the Baptist denomination among black people: the energy of the Baptist evangelists, the personal emotional appeal of revivalism, the ease with which a Baptist congregation could be founded, the opportunity for even the unlearned to preach. Herskovits clearly saw the African water cults as only part of the explanation.

Furthermore, there is a crucial aspect of Herskovits' argument which often goes ignored in the discussion of slave acculturation: the suggestion that at least some African religious concepts and behavior were not totally dissimilar to certain beliefs and practices characteristic of evangelical Protestantism. Perhaps the religious heritage of American Protestants and the African religious background were not completely antithetical. Culture contact was not in every case culture conflict with either Africa or Europe emerging victorious. The acculturative process was broader and more complex than simple retention or destruction of Africanism. Elements of African behavior and belief could have been modified by contact with European culture and could have merged with it in a new syncretistic form. Conversely, European traits could have been shaped and reinterpreted by the slaves in the light of their African past. On the one hand, the similarity of some traits may make it very difficult or even impossible to separate what is African from what is European in origin; on the other hand, this very commonality might have served to reinforce certain African elements while others withered under severe prohibition and attack. That some elements of African religion survived in the United States not as separate enclaves free of white influence but as aspects hidden under or blended with similar European forms is a thesis worth considering in more detail, especially since there are strong arguments for its validity in the areas of music, folklore, and language. There were two areas of commonality between African and European religion where mutual reinterpretation and syncretism possibly occurred: ecstatic behavior and magical folk-belief.

Ecstatic behavior, in the form of spirit possession, is, as we have seen, central to the liturgy of West African peoples and their descendants in many parts of the New World. Commonly, the rites of worship consist in drumming the rhythms of the gods, singing their songs, creating a setting so that they will come down and "ride" their devotees in states of possession. The possessed takes on the personality of the god, dancing his steps, speaking his words, bearing his emblems, acting out his character in facial expression and bodily gesture.

In the United States slaves and their descendants were not possessed by the gods of their fathers but they did engage in a type of ecstatic behavior called shouting. Is there a relationship between the phenomenon of shouting in black revivalistic churches in the United States and spirit possession in West Africa, South America, and the Caribbean?

Shouting was a common, if sensational, occurrence at the frontier camp meetings. While several accounts of these meetings stressed the slaves' peculiar propensity for shouting, white revivalists also shouted and jerked, barked and laughed a holy laughter as well.[39] Herskovits theorizes that it was the influence of the black participants in the camp meetings that accounted for the pattern of ecstatic behavior which emerged. In support of this contention, he refers to a description by Frederick Morgan Davenport which contrasts ecstatic behavior at a revival in Northern Ireland with one in Kentucky. The account states:

> I wish in closing to call attention to the difference in type of the automatisms of Kentucky and Ulster. In Kentucky the motor automatism, the voluntary muscles in violent action, were the prevailing type, although there were many of the sensory. On the other hand, in Ulster the sensory automatisms, trance, vision, the physical disability and the sinking of muscular energy were the prevailing types, although there were many of the motor. I do not mean that I can explain it.[40]

Davenport and Frazier explained the difference in behavior as a matter of chance. Herskovits thought the difference was due to the influence of the slaves upon the white revivalists in Kentucky. He states that "the tradition of violent possession associated with these meetings is far more African than European, and hence there is reason to hold that, in part at least, it was inspired in the whites by this contact with Negroes."[41] Herskovits supported his contention by referring to the difference between black and white revival services in the twentieth century as described by Hortense Powdermaker in *After Freedom*. At Negro revivals the participants were more active than were white congregations; "greater rhythm and spontaneity" were characteristic of the black revivalists; the black preacher's sermon was more melodic and regular, less halting than the white minister's; black congregations moved less convulsively and more smoothly than their white counterparts. Powdermaker attributed these motor differences to social conditioning, "the repression caused by the interracial situation" which "finds relief in unrestrained religious behavior." Herskovits held that the differences between white and black congregations "in the manifestation of ecstasy and hysteria" served to "underscore the differences between the worship characteristic of the cultures from which the ancestors of these two groups were derived."[42]

Although ecstatic behavior in response to the revivalist preaching of the camp meetings was an experience common to slaves and slaveholders on the frontier of late eighteenth- and early nineteenth-century America, the special responsiveness of the slaves to revivals was noted by several witnesses. One observer remarked: "By no class is a camp meeting hailed with more unmixed delight than by the poor slaves."[43] In 1807 Jesse Lee, a Georgia evangelist, noted: "The first day of the meeting, we had a gentle and comfortable moving of the spirit of the Lord among us; and at night it was much more powerful than before, and the meeting was kept up all night without intermission. However, before day the white people retired, and the meeting was continued by the black people."[44] John Leland noted in 1790 that slaves in Virginia "commonly are more noisy in time of preaching than the whites, and are more subject to bodily exercise, and if they meet with an encouragement in these things, they grow extravagant." In the camp meeting the slaves met with encouragement. The proclivity of the slaves for "bodily exercises" was not due to any innate emotionalism; nor was it totally due to the need of an oppressed class to release pent-up tension. Rather, the slaves tended to express religious emotion in certain patterned types of bodily movement influenced by the African heritage of dance.[45]

Slaves and ex-slaves sought and welcomed the presence of the Spirit, which moved worshipers to shout and dance not only during the special "seasons of revival" but also during regular church services (whenever allowed). Frederick Law Olmsted visited a black church in New Orleans where he experienced firsthand the power of evangelical preaching to arouse ecstatic behavior.

> As soon as I had taken my seat, my attention was attracted by an old negro near me, whom I supposed for some time to be suffering under some nervous complaint; he trembled, his teeth chattered, and his face, at intervals, was convulsed. He soon began to respond aloud to the sentiments of the preacher, in such words as these: "Oh, yes!" and similar expressions could be heard from all parts of the house whenever the speaker's voice was unusually solemn or his language and manner eloquent or excited.
>
> Sometimes the outcries and responses were not confined to ejaculations of this kind, but shouts, and groans, terrific shrieks, and indescribable expressions of ecstasy—of pleasure or agony—even stamping, jumping, and clapping of hands were added. . . . I was once surprised to find my own muscles all stretched, as if ready for a struggle—my face glowing, and my feet stamping—having been infected unconsciously. . . . I could not, when my mind reverted to itself, find any connection or meaning in the phrases of the speaker that remained in my memory; and I have no doubt it was his "action" rather than his sentiments, that had given rise to the excitement of the congregation.[46]

After attempting to capture the strong rhythm of the preacher's sermon with each beat marked by the antiphonal response of the congregation, Olmsted went on to describe the effect of the service on one of the worshipers.

> The preacher was drawing his sermon to a close . . . when a small old woman, perfectly black, among those in the gallery, suddenly rose, and began dancing and clapping her hands; at first with a slow and measured movement, and then with increasing rapidity, at the same time beginning to shout "ha! ha!" The women about her arose also, and tried to hold her. . . . The woman was still shouting and dancing, her head thrown back and rolling from one side to the other. Gradually her shout became indistinct, she threw her arms wildly about

instead of clapping her hands, fell back into the arms of her companions, then threw herself forward and embraced those before her, then tossed herself from side to side, gasping, and finally sunk to the floor, where she remained . . . kicking, as if acting a death struggle.[47]

To what extent, if any, did a tradition of African spirit possession influence such ecstatic behavior? There are two issues involved in comparing African spirit possession with the religious behavior of slaves and their descendants in American "shouting" churches. As Erika Bourguignon has succinctly stated:

> What is generally spoken of as "spirit possession" actually involves two distinct aspects, two distinct levels of ethnographic "fact": an observable behavior pattern and a system of cultural beliefs and interpretations. These, however, in turn structure expectations and therefore behavior.[48]

In other words, though not separated in fact, there are two aspects which should be distinguished for the sake of clarity in discussion: the faith context in which the possession experience occurs and the patterned style of outward response by which the ecstatic experience is manifest.

On the level of theological interpretation and meaning, African spirit possession differs significantly from the shouting experience found in the revivalist tradition of American evangelicalism. In the central possession cults of the Yoruba and Fon peoples, the devotees are possessed by a god—in the cults of Haiti and Brazil, by several gods in succession—whose personality displaces that of the human medium. The advice, commands, gestures, and identity of the god are transmitted through the possessed. Personality traits of the god are expressed in the patterned action of the possessed devotee who makes the god present to the cult community. It is believed that the possessed "has been invaded by a supernatural being and is thus temporarily beyond self-control, his ego being subordinated to that of the [divine] intruder."[49] The devotee becomes the carrier of the god, taking up the god's emblems, wearing his sacred colors, tasting his favorite food and drink. Comparing Haitian vaudouists with Spiritual Baptists (Shakers) from St. Vincent, Erika Bourguignon distinguishes between African and Protestant forms of spirit possession. "While the Haitian," she states, "impersonates specific, well-delineated anthropomorphic entities, with complex personalities and a great range of possible activities, the Vincentian does not." She adds that the "Haitian trancer sings and dances, smokes, drinks and eats," and sometimes "may climb a tree or dive into water" while possessed. "Most importantly, while the Haitian interacts with others during his possession trance, with spirits possessing people and with other human beings, the Vincentian does not." Instead, the Vincentian's attention "is drawn inward to his interaction with the Spirit." Though the Vincentian trancers "participate in a common experience," they do not interact with each other as the Haitians do "from the standpoint of a personal transformation." The "manner of operation" in both experiences, Bourguignon concludes, "is distinct in its formal and in its ideological features."[50] While Bourguignon is specifically comparing Haitian to Vincentian types of spirit possession, her differentiation is applicable to the North American possession experience as well. The context of belief shapes the possession experience and determines the manner in which the experience is interpreted. While there may be similar effects—ego enhancement and catharsis, to name only two—on this level of faith event, there are major differences between spirit possession as it occurs in African and Latin American cults, on the one hand, and the ecstatic shouting experience of United States revivalism, on the other. There is a discontinuity, then, between the African heritage of spirit possession and the black shouting tradition in the United States. The African gods with their myriad characteristics, personalities, and myths do not "mount" their enthusiasts amid the dances, songs, and drum rhythms of worship in the United States. Instead it is the Holy Spirit who fills the converted sinner with a happiness and power that drives him to shout, sing, and sometimes dance.

A different possession belief was held by the slave in North America. One explication of this belief was given by an ex-slave preacher and recorded in *God Struck Me Dead:*

> The old meeting house caught on fire. The spirit was there. Every heart was beating in unison as we turned our minds to God to tell Him of our sorrows here below. God saw our need and came to us. I used to wonder what made people shout but now I don't. There is a joy on the inside and it wells up so strong that we can't keep still. It is fire in the bones. Any time that fire touches a man, he will jump.[51]

It is in the context of action, the patterns of motor behavior preceding and following the ecstatic experience, that there may be continuity between African and American forms of spirit possession. While the rhythms of the drums, so important in African and Latin American cults, were by and large forbidden to the slave in the United States, hand-clapping, foot-tapping, rhythmic preaching, hyperventilation, antiphonal (call and response) singing, and dancing are styles of behavior associated with possession both in Africa and in this country.

The strong emphasis on rhythmic preaching, singing, moving, and dancing in the religious behavior of the American slaves has long been noted by observers. Ex-slave Robert Anderson described the patterns of religious expression which he saw in his youth during slavery:

> The colored people . . . have a peculiar music of their own, which is largely a process of rhythm, rather than written music. Their music is largely, or was . . . a sort of rhythmical chant. It had to do largely with religion and the words adopted to their quaint melodies were largely of a religious nature. The stories of the Bible were placed into words that would fit the music already used by the colored people. While singing these songs, the singers and the entire congregation kept time to the music by the swaying of their bodies or by the patting of the foot or hand. Practically all of their songs were accompanied by a motion of some kind . . . the weird and mysterious music of the religious ceremonies moved old and young alike in a frenzy of religious fervor. . . . We also had religious dances, which were expressions of the weird, the fantastic, the mysterious, that was felt in all our religious ceremonies.[52]

It appears from early accounts that the African tradition of "danced religion" retained a strong hold on the religious behavior of the slaves. Rev. Morgan Godwin, who arrived to minister to Marston Parish in York County, Virginia, in 1665, later wrote of the religious dancing of the slaves:

> . . . nothing is more barbarous and contrary to Christianity, than their . . . *Idolotrous Dances*, and *Revels*; in which they usually spend the *Sunday* . . . And here, that I may not be thought too rashly to impute Idolatry to their *Dances*; my conjecture is raised upon this ground . . . for that they use their Dances as a *means* to *procure Rain*; Some of them having been known to beg this liberty upon the Week Days, in order thereunto . . .[53]

During the seventeenth and much of the eighteenth century there was a great deal of indifference, reluctance, and hostility to the conversion of the slaves. (Not until the successive waves of religious revival known as the Great Awakening began in the 1740s did incidents of slave conversion occur in any sizable numbers.) In the face of this religious indifference some forms of African religious behavior seem to have continued. Rev. John Sharpe complained in 1712 that even Christianized slaves in New York "are buried in the Common by those of their country and complexion without the office; on the contrary the Heathenish rites are performed at the grave by their countrymen. . . ."[54] And Alexander Hewatt noted in 1779 that in South Carolina "the negroes of that country, a few only excepted, are to this day as great strangers to Christianity, and as much under the influence of Pagan darkness, idolatry, and superstition, as they were at their first arrival from Africa. . . ." He was particularly disturbed that Sundays and "Holidays are days of idleness . . . in which the slaves assemble together in alarming crowds for the purposes of dancing, feasting and merriment."[55] Later Methodist, Presbyterian, and Baptist revivalists condemned these secular forms of amusement and taught the slaves that conversion required their abandonment. While evangelical missionaries prohibited dancing as sinful, they afforded the slaves a morally sanctioned context for a sacralized type of dancing in the emotionally charged setting of the revival. In 1845 Sir Charles Lyell commented on the way in which slaves, though converted to Christianity, continued to dance.

> Of dancing and music, the Negroes are passionately fond. On the Hopeton plantation violins have been silenced by the Methodist missionaries. . . . At the Methodist prayer-meetings, they are permitted to move round rapidly in a ring, in which manoeuvre, I am told, they sometimes contrive to take enough exercise to serve as a substitute for the dance, it being, in fact, a kind of spiritual boulanger. . . .[56]

The unusual religious behavior of slaves at camp meetings aroused the disapproval of some Christian evangelists. In a work entitled *Methodist Error or Friendly Advice to Those Methodists Who Indulge in Extravagant Religious Emotions and Bodily Exercises* (1819), John Watson complained about the style of musical behavior of black revivalists in the Philadelphia Conference:

> Here ought to be considered too, a most exceptionable error, which has the tolerance at least of the rulers of our camp meetings. In the *blacks'* quarter, the coloured people get together, and sing for hours together, short scraps of disjointed affirmations, pledges, or prayers, lengthened out with long repetitious *choruses*. These are all sung in the

merry chorus-manner of the southern harvest field, or husking-frolic method, of the slave blacks; and also very greatly like the Indian dances. With every word so sung, they have a sinking of one or other leg of the body alternately; producing an audible sound of the feet at every step, and as manifest as the steps of actual negro dancing in Virginia &c. If some, in the meantime sit, they strike the sounds alternately on each thigh . . . the evil is only occasionally condemned and the example has already visibly affected the religious manners of some whites. From this cause, I have known in some camp meetings from 50 to 60 people crowd into one tent, after the public devotions had closed, and there continue the whole night, singing tune after tune, . . . scarce one of which were in our hymn books. Some of these from their nature, (having very long repetition choruses and short scraps of matter) are actually composed as sung and are almost endless.[57]

Besides shedding some light on "the original religious songs of blacks—as distinguished from the standard Protestant hymns that they sang—"[58] the account above is significant because it tends to support the argument that black patterns of behavior influenced white revivalists at the camp meetings.

Religious dancing and shouting were by no means confined to camp meetings. Olmsted remarked on the regular religious worship of the slaves on one plantation:

On most of the large rice plantations which I have seen in this vicinity, there is a small chapel, which the negroes call their prayer-house. The owner of one of these told me that, having furnished the prayer-house with seats having a back-rail, his negroes petitioned him to remove it, because it did not leave them *room enough to pray*. It was explained to me that it is their custom, in social worship, to work themselves up to a great pitch of excitement, in which they yell and cry aloud, and, finally shriek and leap up, clapping their hands and dancing, as it is done at heathen festivals. The back-rail they found to seriously impede this exercise.[59]

The religious dance most frequently described was the ring shout of the slaves in the Sea Islands. The ring shout, musicologists agree, is a particularly strong example of African-influenced dance style in the United States. Frazier and others have relegated the ring shout to the Sea Islands, where they admit Africanisms were strong, but there is evidence that the ring shout was a widespread and deeply ingrained practice among slaves in other areas as well. The following passage from A.M.E. Bishop Daniel Alexander Payne's autobiography indicates that he had met with the ring shout in many places a little over a decade after slavery:

> About this time [1878] I attended a "bush meeting." . . . After the sermon they formed a ring, and with coats off sung, clapped their hands and stamped their feet in a most ridiculous and heathenish way. I requested the pastor to go and stop their dancing. At his request they stopped their dancing and clapping of hands, but remained singing and rocking their bodies to and fro. This they did for about fifteen minutes. I then went, and taking their leader by the arm requested him to desist and to sit down and sing in a rational manner. I told him also that it was a heathenish way to worship and disgraceful to themselves, the race, and the Christian name. In that instance they broke up their ring; but would not sit down, and walked sullenly away. After the sermon in the afternoon, having another opportunity of speaking alone to this young leader of the singing and clapping ring, he said: "Sinners won't get converted unless there is a ring." Said I: "You might sing till you fell down dead, and you would fail to convert a single sinner, because nothing but the Spirit of God and the word of God can convert sinners." He replied: "The Spirit of God works upon people in different ways. At camp-meeting there must be a ring here, a ring there, a ring over yonder, or sinners will not get converted." This was his idea, and it is also that of many others. These "Bands" I have had to encounter in many places. . . . To the most thoughtful . . . I usually succeeded in making the "Band" disgusting; but by the ignorant masses . . . it was regarded as the essence of religion.[60]

In the exchange between Payne and the "Band" leader it is significant that the latter found the ring shout necessary for conversion and for the working of the Spirit.

Payne goes on to describe the "ring" of the "Bands," also known as "Fist and Heel Worshippers."

> He who could sing loudest and longest led the "Band," having his loins girded and a handkerchief in hand with which he kept time, while his feet resounded on the floor like the drumsticks of a bass drum. In some cases it was the custom to begin these dances after

every night service and keep it up till midnight, sometimes singing
and dancing alternately—a short prayer and a long dance. Someone
has even called it the "Voudoo Dance." I have remonstrated with a
number of pastors for permitting these practices, which vary somewhat in different localities, but have been invariably met with the
response that he could not succeed in restraining them, and an
attempt to compel them to cease would simply drive them away from
our Church. . . . And what is more deplorable, some of our most popular and powerful preachers labor systematically to perpetuate this
fanaticism. Such preachers never rest till they create an excitement
that consists in shouting, jumping and dancing.[61]

It seems, then, from Payne's account, as well as those of others, that dancing was a crucial part of worship for some slaves and ex-slaves. The label
"Voodoo Dance," which Payne records, was not entirely a misnomer.
There are close parallels between the style of dancing observed in African
and Caribbean cult worship and the style of the American "ring shout."
Folklorists John and Alan Lomax who recorded a ring shout in Louisiana
in 1934 enumerated the parallels.

We have seen "shouts" in Louisiana, in Texas, in Georgia and the
Bahamas; we have seen vaudou dancing in Haiti; we have read accounts
of similar rites in works upon Negro life in other parts of the Western
hemisphere. All share basic similarities: (1) the song is "danced" with
the whole body, with hands, feet, belly, and hips; (2) the worship is,
basically, a dancing-singing phenomenon; (3) the dancers always move
counter-clockwise around the ring; (4) the song has the leader-chorus
form, with much repetition, with a focus on rhythm rather than on
melody, that is, with a form that invites and ultimately enforces cooperative group activity; (5) the song continues to be repeated from sometimes more than an hour, steadily increasing in intensity and gradually
accelerating, until a sort of mass hypnosis ensues. . . . This shout pattern is demonstrably West African in origin.[62]

George E. Simpson has described the dancing of the Revivalist cult in
Jamaica in terms that bear striking resemblance to the American ring
shout.

Halfway through the service the leader may begin to circle counter-
clockwise the altar, or a table inside the church, or the "seal" in the

yard outside the church. The officers and leading members of the church, often up to twenty people, fall in behind him as all of them "labor in the spirit." . . . This "spiritual" dancing is believed to increase the religious understanding of the participants.[63]

There are a number of detailed descriptions of the technique of the ring shout in which African style dance patterns can be noted. W. F. Allen reprinted an account of the shout on the Sea Islands from the *Nation* (May 30, 1867):

> . . . the true "shout" takes place on Sundays or on "praise"-nights through the week, and either in the praise-house or in some cabin in which a regular religious meeting has been held. Very likely more than half the population of the plantation is gathered together. . . . But the benches are pushed back to the wall when the formal meeting is over, and old and young men and women . . . boys . . . young girls barefooted, all stand up in the middle of the floor, and when the 'sperichil' is struck, begin first walking and by-and-by shuffling round, one after the other, in a ring. The foot is hardly taken from the floor, and the progression is mainly due to a jerking, hitching motion, which agitates the entire shouter, and soon brings out streams of perspiration. Sometimes they dance silently, sometimes as they shuffle they sing the chorus of the spiritual, and sometimes the song itself is also sung by the dancers. But most frequently a band, composed of some of the best singers and of tired shouters, stand at the side of the room to "base" the others, singing the body of the song and clapping their hands together or on the knees. Song and dance alike are extremely energetic, and often, when the shout lasts into the middle of the night, the monotonous thud, thud, thud of the feet prevents sleep within half a mile of the praise-house. . . . It is not unlikely that this remarkable religious ceremony is a relic of some African dance. . . . Dancing in the usual way is regarded with great horror by the people of Fort Royal, but they enter with infinite zest into the movements of the "shout."[64]

As Harold Courlander wrote: "circular movement, shuffling steps and stamping, postures and gestures, the manner of standing, the way the arms are held out for balance or pressed against the sides, the movements of the shoulder, all are African in conception and derivation."[65] It has even been suggested by Lorenzo Dow Turner that the very word "shout" derives from *saut*, a term used by West African Muslims to denote "dancing or moving around the Kaaba."[66]

The ring form of religious dancing occurred on occasions other than revivals and praise meetings. Funerals, for example, were occasions for dancing and sometimes drumming, at least in the Sea Islands. Rachel Anderson, an elderly Georgia coast resident, recalled: "Use tuh alluz beat duh drums at fewnuls. Right attuh duh pusson die, dey beat um tuh tell duh uddahs bout duh fewnul. . . . On duh way tuh duh grabe dey beat duh drum as dey is mahchin long. Wen duh body is put in duh grabe, ebrybody shout roun duh grabe in a succle, singin an prayin."[67] And another old Georgian, Ben Sullivan, stated: "Dey go in a long pruhcession tuh duh buryin' groun. Den dey dance roun in a ring an dey motion wid duh hans. Dey sing duh body tuh duh grabe and den dey let it down an den dey succle roun in duh dance."[68]

In the ring shout and allied patterns of ecstatic behavior, the African heritage of dance found expression in the evangelical religion of the American slaves. To be sure, there are significant differences between the kind of spirit possession found in West Africa and in the shouting experience of American revivalism. Different theological meanings are expressed and experienced in each. But similar patterns of response—rhythmic clapping, ring-dancing, styles of singing, all of which result in or from the state-of-possession trance—reveal the slaves' African religious background. The shout is a convincing example of Herskovits' theory of reinterpretation of African traditions; for the situation of the camp-meeting revival, where enthusiastic and ecstatic religious behavior was encouraged, presented a congenial setting for slaves to merge African patterns of response with Christian interpretations of the experience of spirit possession, an experience shared by both blacks and whites. The Protestant revivalist tradition, accepted by the slaves and their descendants in the United States, proved in this instance to be amenable to the influence of African styles of behavior. Despite the prohibition of dancing as heathenish and sinful, the slaves were able to reinterpret and "sanctify" their African tradition of dance in the "shout."[69] While the North American slaves danced under the impulse of the Spirit of a "new" God, they danced in ways their fathers in Africa would have recognized.

Moreover, the argument, mentioned above, between Bishop Payne and the leader of the ring-shout band hints at a deeper level of reinterpretation. If, as Payne claims, the "ignorant masses" (read "less acculturated") regarded the ring shout "as the essence of religion," and if the shout leader's contention that "without a ring sinners won't get converted" was representative of general belief, the "holy dance" of the shout may very well have been a two-way bridge connecting the core of West African religions—possession by the gods—to the core of evangelical Protestantism—experience of conversion. There are also hints that the process of conversion may have been related in the slaves' minds to the African-style period of initiation into the cults of the gods. Slaves customarily spoke of the period of seeking conversion as "mourning" and thought of it as a time when the sinner should go apart, alone, to a quiet place to struggle with his sins. This period and place of retirement resemble the novitiate of West African and Caribbean cults in two details. Fugitive slave Henry Brown recalled that when his sister "became anxious to have her soul converted" she "shaved the hair from her head, as many of the slaves thought they could not be converted without doing this," a custom similar to initiation rites in Brazil, Trinidad, and West Africa. The other similarity may be noted in Samuel Lawton's description of a practice followed in the Sea Islands which resembled the use of cloth bands in the "mourning ground" ceremony of Spiritual Baptists in Trinidad: "Seekers may sometimes be identified by a white cloth or string tied around the head. This is a signal that they are seekin' and all others are to 'leave 'em alon.'"[70]

Ring shouts were also called "running sperichils," a term which suggests a connection with a broader and more inclusive category of religious expression, the Afro-American spirituals. There were several kinds of spirituals—shouts, anthems, and jubilees—serving different occasions and reflecting different moods. Styles ranged from the exciting tempo and rhythmic stamp of the shout to the slow, drawn-out "sorrow songs" which usually come to mind when the spirituals are mentioned. While the lyrics and themes of the spirituals were drawn from Biblical verses and Christian hymns, and although the music and melodies were strongly influenced by the sacred and secular songs of white Americans, the style in which the slaves sang the spirituals was African.

Frequently, musically literate observers despaired of adequately conveying the style and sounds of the spirituals they had heard. One who tried was Lucy McKim Garrison, who in 1862 wrote of the difficulties involved in her task:

> It is difficult to express the entire character of these Negro ballads by mere musical notes and signs. The odd turns made in the throat, and the curious rhythmic effect produced by single voices chiming in at different irregular intervals, seem almost as impossible to place on the score as the singing of birds or the tones of an Aeolian harp.[71]

A later compiler of spirituals complained of a similar problem: "Tones are frequently employed which we have no musical character to represent. Such, for example, is that which I have indicated as nearly as possible by the flat seventh. . . ."[72]

The singing style of the slaves, which was influenced by their African heritage, was characterized by a strong emphasis on call and response, polyrhythms, syncopation, ornamentation, slides from one note to another, and repetition. Other stylistic features included body movement, hand-clapping, foot-tapping, and heterophony. This African style of song performance could not be reduced to musical notations, which explains why printed versions do not capture the peculiar flavor of the slave songs, which were consistently labeled "wild," "strangely fascinating," of "peculiar quality," and "barbaric" by white observers.

Despite the African style of singing, the spirituals, like the "running spirituals" or ring shout, were performed in praise of the Christian God. The names and words of the African gods were replaced by Biblical figures and Christian imagery. African style and European hymnody met and became in the spiritual a new, Afro-American song to express the joys and sorrows of the religion which the slaves had made their own.[73]

Another area of religious behavior in which European traditions of slaveholders and African traditions of slaves proved consonant with one another was that of folk belief, the realm of magic, "hoodoo," and "conjure."

Folk Belief: From *Vaudou* to Conjuring

No discussion of Africanisms in the religious life of black Americans could be complete without reference to voodoo. However, when speaking of voodoo in the United States, as opposed to *vaudou* in Haiti, an important distinction must be made between voodoo as an organized cult and voodoo as a system of magic. Voodoo as a cult flourished until the late nineteenth century, particularly in New Orleans, though it was not confined to that area. From the early days of French Louisiana, the voodoo cult was associated with slaves imported from the French West Indies. Voodoo originated in the religion of Africans, but the most immediate catalyst to the growth of the cult in Louisiana was the emigration of slaves and free blacks from the island of Saint-Domingue at the time of the Haitian Revolution.

Initially the cult and the magical system of voodoo formed an integral whole, but gradually voodoo as an institutionalized cult of ritual worship disintegrated, while its tradition of "root work" persisted in folk beliefs widespread among slaves and their descendants down to the present day. Voodoo priests—and more commonly, priestesses—presided over the cult while building a large clientele for various charms and gris-gris. New Orleans became known as the capital of "root work," and voodoo, or hoodoo, came to be a synonym for conjuring and conjurers apart from the cultic context of its African-Haitian origins.[74]

By all accounts, voodoo in New Orleans was centered upon worship of a snake god. Drumming, dancing, singing, possession, animal sacrifice, eating, and drinking were customary at the ceremonies in Louisiana, as in Haiti and West Africa. In Dahomey the god Damballa (Da) was envisioned as a snake and as the rainbow, principle of fluidity and governor of men's destinies. Particularly in the coastal kingdoms of Arada and Ouidah, conquered by Dahomey in 1724–1727, the cult of the snake god Dangbe was strong. The captives from the Dahomean campaigns against Arada and Ouidah provided a supply of slaves for the West Indian market of the French traders.[75] Louisiana bought her first slaves from the islands of Martinique, Guadeloupe, and Saint-Domingue as early as 1716, when five hundred were imported, followed by three thousand more during the next year. Slaves from the French West Indies continued to enter Louisiana until later prohibitions hindered importation. A decree of the Spanish governor Galvez in 1782 forbade further importation of slaves from the island of Martinique because "these negroes are too much given to voodooism and make the lives of the citizens unsafe." In 1792 slaves from Saint-Domingue were also banned, though some were allowed to enter when their masters were granted asylum at the outbreak of the Haitian Revolution. In 1803 the United States acquired Louisiana and the ban on West Indian slaves was lifted. The largest influx of emigrants from Haiti occurred in 1809, when planters who had fled to Cuba to escape the revolution in Saint-Domingue were forced to emigrate again by France's declaration of war against Spain. It is estimated that New Orleans at that time received about two thousand slaves and an equal number of free people of color. Together with the earlier slave population of Arada or of Dahomean origin this group of Haitian refugees continued to observe the African tradition of *vaudou*.[76]

The few rather sensational accounts of voodoo services in New Orleans give the impression that voodoo was a monolithic snake cult, but there are hints that other *vodun* of the Dahomean pantheon survived besides Damballa, who was known as Damballa Wedo or Li Grand Zombi. One of Robert Tallant's informants, Josephine Green, recalled her mother's account of the time she saw the famous voodoo queen Marie Laveau:

> My ma seen her. . . . It was back before the war what they had her wit' the Northerners. My ma heard a noise on Frenchman Street where she lived at and she start to go outside. Her pa say, "Where you goin'? Stay in the house!" She say, "Marie Laveau is comin' and I gotta see her." She went outside and here come Marie Laveau wit' a big crowd of people followin' her. . . . All the people wit' her was hollerin' and screamin', "We is goin' to see Papa Limba! We is goin' to see Papa Limba!" My grandpa go runnin' after my ma then, yellin at her, "You come on in here Eunice! Don't you know Papa Limba is the devil?" But after that my ma find out Papa Limba meant St. Peter, and her pa was jest foolin' her.[77]

Papa Limba is Legba, who in Haiti, as noted above, is frequently identified with St. Peter. The role of St. Peter-Legba is revealed in part of an old voodoo song remembered by another of Tallant's informants, Mary Ellis. The song went:

> St. Peter, St. Peter, open the door,
> I'm callin' you, come to me!
> St. Peter, St. Peter, open the door. . . .[78]

Mary Ellis also recounted that "Marie Laveau used to call St. Peter somethin' like 'Laba.' She called St. Michael 'Daniel Blanc,' and St. Anthony 'Yon Sue.'" (Agasu?)[79] In her novel *An Angel by Brevet* (1904), Helen Pitkin described several voodoo meetings which, though "written in the form of fiction," were, she claimed, "accurate, being an exact reproduction of what she herself" saw or heard from her servants. In the service there are songs to Liba (St. Peter), Blanc Dani (St. Michael), and Vert Agoussou.[80] (In Dahomey, Agoussou is a god of special significance to the royal line.) Moreover, if Courlander is correct, the vodun Ogun Feraille "survived until recent times in Louisiana as Joe Feraille."[81] It seems, therefore, that along with Damballa Wedo, identified as Blanc Dani, at least Legba, Agoussou, and perhaps Ogun Feraille, were remembered and worshiped in New Orleans in the nineteenth century. As in Haiti, African gods were syncretized with Catholic saints and were associated with certain colors. It is possible that other gods existed in the voodoo pantheon which were not reported by extant sources, and that the outside observers who left accounts saw only the tip of the iceberg of voodoo belief and practice.

The voodoo cult in New Orleans came under the sway of a succession of strong leaders who traded their powers of magic for profit and prestige. By means of charms, amulets, and potions they claimed to predict the future and manipulate the present. Under the strong leadership of priestesses such as Sanite Dede and especially the two Marie Laveaus, mother and daughter, voodoo enjoyed a great deal of influence among the black and white citizens of New Orleans throughout most of the nineteenth century. The long reign of the two Maries stretched from 1830 to the 1880s and included a system of domestic spies among the servant class to keep Marie informed of important secrets. An annual voodoo celebration was held (on St. John's Eve) at Bayou St. John or on the banks of Lake Pontchartrain and the press was occasionally invited.[82]

Behind or apart from all these public aspects were the authentic and secret rituals of the voodoo cult, of which very little in the way of description has endured. There are no accounts of New Orleans voodoo services in the eighteenth century, only two of voodoo worship in the early nineteenth century, and one for the late nineteenth century. Apart from newspaper reports which "exposed" the sensational aspects of public voodoo "shows," these three accounts form the basis for almost all descriptions of voodoo worship in New Orleans.[83] Each account mentions the presence of a snake representing the god Li Grand Zombi; drumming, singing, dancing; possession, which usually begins when the priestess comes into contact with the snake god; oracular statements by the possessed priestess and priest; possession of the devotees; the pouring of rum or other liquors as a libation to the god; the spewing of liquor from the mouth of the priest as a form of blessing; Catholic syncretistic elements such as candles, an altar, prayers to the Virgin. All of these elements are characteristic of the Haitian's Afro-Catholic synthesis as well.

By the twentieth century, although voodoo as a cult had been transformed into something different, it had not, however, vanished totally. In the 1930s Zora Neal Hurston underwent initiation into a voodoo cult in New Orleans at the hands of a priest named Turner who claimed to have received his *connaisance* from Marie Laveau herself.[84] It is apparent, however, that the rich pantheon and complex theology of Haitian *vaudou* did not survive in New Orleans voodoo; the panoply of gods was attenuated and the rites of worship corrupted.

The initial popularity of voodoo as an organized cult in New Orleans was in part due to the city's cosmopolitan and permissive atmosphere which lasted even after the American purchase.[85] It would be a mistake, however, to think that the voodoo cult existed only in New Orleans. Mary Owen stated that voodoo dances occurred in Missouri in the late nineteenth century. However, she offers no description of voodoo ritual, and most of her article is concerned with voodoo as magic, or, as it was called, hoodoo.[86]

Hoodoo (also known as "conjure" or root work) was a system of magic, divination, and herbalism widespread among the slaves. Since New Orleans was looked upon as the prestigious center of conjuring,[87] the term "voodoo" was extended to conjuring and conjurers throughout the United States regardless of the term's original reference to African-Haitian cults. Hoodoo became the name for a whole area of folklore, the realm of signs, powers, and conjuring. Because magical beliefs and folk superstitions reveal close similarities and parallels worldwide, it is difficult to separate the folk beliefs and practices of African origin from those of European origin. This very similarity, however, may have resulted in a mutual reinforcement and a common interchange of folk beliefs between slave and master. There are, at any rate, a number of hoodoo beliefs which are demonstrably African in origin. These beliefs can be seen, in some cases, to be vestiges of African beliefs removed from their fully intelligible theological and ritual contexts but still remembered. Or, as Herskovits phrased it, "minutiae can persist after the broader lines of ritual procedure and their underlying rationalizations have been lost."[88]

The movement from *vaudou* to hoodoo can serve perhaps as a paradigm of the larger history of African religion in the United States. The way in which bits of African faith and practice persisted in folk beliefs and customs, though their original meaning had been lost, is evident in the following account from the New Orleans *Times-Democrat* of August 5, 1888. During a thunderstorm elderly Tante Dolores anxiously searched the house for some object. Not finding it, she ran to the yard. According to the article,

> Hither and thither she ran in rapid quest, until at last she stumbled upon the object of her search, no less a thing than an axe for chopping wood . . . a bright expression of joy irradiated her face.

Seizing the ax and raising it over her head, "she made pass after pass in the very face of the rushing current, as if chopping some invisible thing in twain." When the wind suddenly abated she returned to the house in triumph, stating that it never failed her if she "jest got there in time enough."[89]

A similar custom among Mississippi black folk was noted by Puckett:

> . . . foreign to European thought is the Southern Negro custom of going out into the yard and chopping up the ground with an ax when a storm threatens. This is supposed to "cut de storm in two" and so stop it. Others stick a spade in the ground to split the cloud, or simply place an ax in the corner of the house.[90]

The use of the ax as an antidote to the storm is significant, since the sacred emblem of the West African god of thunder and lightning, Shango, is an ax; but equally significant is the fact that the African theological background has disappeared and what remains is a folk custom. There is perhaps a trace of the thunder-stones hurled by Shango in the belief, as told to Puckett by an old "conjure doctor" in Mississippi, that "the Indian arrowheads often found in the locality were not made by man at all, but were fashioned by God out of thunder and lightning."[91] It was also a common saying in New Orleans "that when it thunders, *Le Bon Dieu* is roiling his stones."[92]

As seen previously, equestrian imagery is commonly used in Africa and Latin America to describe the relationship between a god and the devotee he mounts and rides in possession. The onset of possession in voodoo rituals in New Orleans was called, according to Castellanos, *monter voudou.*[93] A relic of this imagery can be seen in the term used by blacks in Mississippi for conjurers—"horses."[94]

In Africa and Latin America the seat of possession is often thought to be the head of the devotee. Thus, in Haiti, the *loa* of a deceased person must be removed from the corpse's head. The conjurer in late-nineteenth-century Missouri was said to be one that was "strong in the head."[95] In Africa a charm was regarded as having a spirit of its own and as having taboos which its user had to observe if it were to work. Mary Owen, speaking of a charm owned by Aunt Mymee, remarked that occasionally this "luck ball," worn under the right arm, was given a drink of whiskey. Mymee's charm was called "Lil Mymee," perhaps reflecting a multiple or complex soul concept, similar to the African notion that one's guardian soul has to be fed to keep it strong.[96]

The use of charms and counter charms, to harm or to ward off harm, is an essential trait of conjuring. Materials of great power for "fixing" or conjuring someone are hair and nail clippings, a piece of clothing or personal object belonging to the victim, dirt from a person's footprint, and, especially, grave dirt. Powders, roots, and herbs of various sorts are used to cause or to cure illness, since sudden sickness, physical and mental, is often viewed as the result of being "fixed" by someone who bears ill-will toward the sufferer. This view of misfortune reflects the traditional African perception of illness.

A continuation of African belief may lie behind the statement of Mississippi black folk that the spirit of a tree can speak to men. Indeed, it is not only trees that have spirits; everything does. Ruth Bass writes that an old Mississippi conjurer asked her, "What is in the jimson-weed that cures asthma if it isn't the spirit of the weed? What is that in the buckeye that can drive off rheumatism unless it's spirit?" She adds that he assured her that everything has spirit. To prove this, he said he could take her to a certain spring that was haunted by the ghost of a bucket, and he asked her: "Now if that bucket didn't have a spirit, where did its ghost come from?"[97]

The belief that a person's spirit wanders while the body sleeps was also a part of the lore of African black folk. "Pepul's sperrits wander at night an' effen dey's woke too sudden like de sperrit is likely tuh be left out walkin'."[98] For this reason, it was dangerous to sweep dirt out of the door after sunset lest you sweep out someone's spirit.[99]

African belief in the special power of twins, and of the person born next after twins, lasted in the United States. Loudell Snow interviewed a present-day voodoo practitioner, who explained to her one theory of how she came by her powers.

I had two brothers, they twins. And I were born behind the twins. Some people believe that twins have the gift, one of 'em. Some people say that I have the gift because I were born behind two twins. But I don't know. I always had the *urge* that I cure anything! I've always felt like that.[100]

While a fully developed cult of the ancestors did not persist in the United States, certain African funerary customs did remain. In Mississippi, for example, it was believed that the spirits of the dead roam on Halloween—a Western belief—but dinners were cooked for these spirits. Ruth Bass reported that "two persons must cook the supper, without speaking and without using salt in any form. . . . This food is served on the table with necessary plates and spoons and left all night. Sometime during the night the essence or spirit of the food is eaten by the . . . hungry spirits."[101] Similarly, in the Sea Islands, there were those "sut put a dish uh food out on the poach fuh the spirit, but some of em take cooked food tuh the grave an leave it theah fuh the spirit."[102] The African custom of decorating a grave with the personal belongings of the deceased was also common in the rural South. Cups, saucers, bottles, pipes, and other effects were left for the spirit of the deceased; frequently these items were broken or cracked in order to free their spirits and thereby enable them to follow the deceased.[103] Another reason for placing the personal belongings of the deceased on his grave was to "lay the spirit." Sarah Washington, an informant for the Georgia Writers' Project study, *Drums and Shadows*, speculated: "I dohn guess yuh be bodduh much by duh spirits ef yuh gib em a good fewnul an put duh tings wut belong tuh em on top uh duh grave," because the spirits don't have to come back for them. After her former master had died, one of the ex-slaves on Frances Butler Leigh's plantation placed a basin, water, and several towels on his grave, explaining, "If massa's spirit come, I want him see dat old Nanny not forget how he call every morning for water for wash his hands. . . ." Frances Butler Leigh records this incident as a mark of respect and affection shown by the former slave for her old master. It might be interpreted as well as an attempt to allay the ghost of the former master once and for all, so that Nanny need not be bothered with him ever again.[104]

Among the black folk of the United States, the West Indies, and West Africa it is commonly held that the crossroads are places of peculiar power for the exercise of evil magic. Another belief common to all three areas is the notion that a chicken with frizzy feathers can scratch up any harmful charms planted in its owner's yard.[105]

Belief in the power of witches to leave their bodies at night and ride their victims was common among black Americans, West Indians, and Africans. It was thought that salt or red pepper sprinkled on the skin of the absent witch would prevent her from reentering her body.[106]

Many Afro-American witchcraft beliefs are European in origin. As such, they are a prime example of an area where there is a fusion of African and European folklore. The capacity of folk beliefs from different peoples to parallel and mutually influence one another makes the enterprise of separating one from another not only difficult but also artificial and speculative. Here, perhaps, is a fitting place to end the search for Africanisms in black religion in the United States.

The resolution of the Herskovits-Frazier debate lies in recognizing the true aspects of both positions. It is not a debate with a winner and a loser, for using differing perspectives, both are right. Herskovits was right in demolishing the myth of the Negro past, in suggesting topics for future research, and in demonstrating the mutual influence of cultures in the acculturative process. His theory of reinterpretation as a factor in cultural contact is an advance over the notion that a people's beliefs, values, and behavioral patterns simply disappeared in the face of systematic oppression. He did succeed in demonstrating that elements of African culture survived slavery in the United States. It is true that he sometimes overstated his case. But it is also true that critics have caricatured his position and failed to appreciate some of his subtler arguments.

On the other hand, Frazier was also right. He was right in challenging excesses in Herskovits' argument, in posing the question of African survivals in terms of significance or meaning and in keeping sight of the real differences between Afro-American cultures in the United States and elsewhere in the hemisphere. If he tended to undervalue instances of African survivals in the United States, he did maintain that the new situation was important in influencing slaves to develop a new worldview and a new culture. While it is true that Africa influenced black culture in the United States, including black religion, it is also true that African theology and African ritual did not endure to the extent that they did in Cuba, Haiti, and Brazil. In the United States the gods of Africa died.

Why the gods died, why African theology and ritual did not survive here as elsewhere in the New World are questions which impinge on the developing field of study known as comparative slavery, an area which involves ethnography, sociology, economics, demography, and history. A great deal of comparative study remains to be done from the perspectives of all these disciplines. Until such study is more advanced than it is at the present time, only tentative conclusions can be reached about the discrepancy between African retentions in Latin America and the United States.

Hemispheric Perspectives: Differing Contexts

Why have African gods and rituals been able to survive so vigorously in several countries but not in the United States? To answer this question a number of reasons have been suggested. One explanation is that Catholicism was more conducive to the survival of African religion than was Protestantism. Though this explanation is only partial, it has some validity. As noted previously, certain customs of Catholicism proved to be supportive of some practices of African religions among the slaves of the French, Spanish, and Portuguese colonies. In Haiti, Cuba, and Brazil, Catholic devotion to the Blessed Virgin and to the saints offered a rich context for syncretism with the gods of Africa. The use of sacramentals (blessed objects), such as statues, pictures, candles, incense, holy water, rosaries, vestments, and relics, in Catholic ritual was more akin to the spirit of African piety than the sparseness of Puritan America, which held such objects to be idolatrous. Holy days, processions, saints' feasts, days of fast and abstinence were all recognizable to the African who had observed the sacred days, festivals, and food taboos of his gods.

Moreover, the Catholic Church, in Brazil and Cuba, presented the slaves with an institutional mechanism for the preservation of African religion in the organization of religious fraternities. To the extent that religious brotherhoods were organized around groups of slaves from the same or neighboring geographical areas of Africa, they offered an opportunity for regroupment and allowed the slaves and freedmen to preserve particular African customs and, to a limited degree, languages. They also provided a structure for cult organization and a covert setting for syncretisms of African and Catholic devotions. Herbert S. Klein, investigating the brotherhoods in Cuba, reveals their role in preserving African customs:

> . . . the African cofradias [confraternities] played a vital role in the social life of both slaves and freedmen, with their own saints and special functions in various holy marches and carnivals. Usually organized along lines of regional African origins, with its members coming from the same *nacion* . . . these associations were both of a religious and strongly benevolent nature. . . . In the great religious processions the Negro cabildos played an increasingly important part. Although outright African fetishes were quickly prohibited from display, the local saints and virgins showed so much influence of African mythology and even of African costume that these displays often tended to perpetuate pre-New World patterns and beliefs.[107]

The nature, then, of Catholic piety with its veneration of saints, use of sacramentals, and organization of religious fraternities among the slaves offered a supportive context for the continuity of African religious elements in recognizable form. In contrast, American Evangelical Protestantism, with its emphasis on biblical preaching, inward conversion, and credible accounts of the signs of grace, was not as conducive to syncretism with African theology and ritual. The contrast between Catholic America and Protestant America as an explanation for African retentions must not be pressed too far, for in Jamaica, for example, Cumina, Pocomania, and Revival groups represent clear syntheses of Protestant and African religions (with some additions from Catholicism). In more subtle form the

Spiritual Baptists, or Shouters, of Trinidad also prove the ability of Afro-Americans to continue some African-style customs along with a fundamentalistic Protestantism. Conversely, Afro-Americans in Louisiana were able to preserve only a vestige of the African pantheons and rituals (as far as can be determined), despite the presence of Catholicism during the periods of French and Spanish rule. Even the attenuated voodoo cult in Louisiana owed its strength to the influx of refugees from Saint-Domingue (now Haiti). It appears that factors other than religious differences must be taken into account.

Demographic factors also determined differences in degrees of African retention in Latin and British America. As both Frazier and Herskovits observed, the ratio of blacks to whites was much greater on the plantations of Latin America than it was on the plantations of the United States. In the tropics large plantations were worked by huge gangs of slaves, but in the United States the large plantation with hundreds of slaves was relatively rare. In the American South, where average slave population was comparatively small, contact between whites and blacks was more frequent than was usual in French, Spanish, and Portuguese colonies or, for that matter, in the British West Indies. Herskovits, using data from U.B. Phillips, summarized this distinction in the following statement:

> In the earliest days, the number of slaves in the U.S. in proportion to their masters was extremely small, and though as time went on thousands and tens of thousands of slaves were brought to satisfy the demands of the southern plantations, nonetheless the Negroes lived in constant association with whites to a degree not found anywhere else in the New World.[108]

As a matter of fact, in the Sea Islands, where the opposite conditions prevailed—a large slave population isolated from contact with white culture—the strongest incidence of African retentions in the United States were found. In comparison with slaves of the Piedmont area, the coastal and Sea Island blacks were far less acculturated to white America until fairly recent times.[109]

In addition, Curtin's census injects a further demographic factor into the discussion of differences between the slave population in the United States and tropical America. The distribution of Africans imported into New World slavery was not uniform throughout the hemisphere. Once again, the United States was unique. Of the total number of 9,566,000 African slaves imported into America from the beginning of the trade to

1861, only about 427,000 went to England's colonies on the North American continent and to the United States. (The figure includes 28,000 imported by French and Spanish Louisiana.) Thus the United States and Canada imported only 4½ percent of the total number of Africans imported into the New World.[110] A clearer picture of this inconsistent distribution emerges when importation figures are linked with the geographical areas of the importing colonies. Using Curtin's figures, C. Vann Woodward states that:

> The islands of the Greater Antilles . . . with an area roughly one third that of Texas, imported nearly six times the slaves landed in the entire territory of the United States. Of these islands, Saint Domingue . . . by 1794, had imported 864,000 or more than twice the total number of the United States. Jamaica had taken in 748,000 by the end of the legal trade in 1808, and Cuba which continued to import Africans for another half century or more, received 702,000. In fact, Cuba took in more after 1808 than the United States received in all.[111]

Brazil, roughly comparable in size to the continental United States plus Alaska, imported approximately 3,647,000 slaves, eight and a half times the number that the United States received. Thus, comparatively speaking, "the United States was only a marginal recipient of slaves from Africa."[112]

The amazing and as yet unexplained demographic fact, however, is the rate of natural increase of the U.S. slave population. By the time of emancipation in 1865 the number of slaves in the United States had grown to above four million, a figure ten times the number imported from abroad. In contrast, Saint-Domingue, which had imported 864,000 Africans, had by the end of the slave trade and of slavery in 1794 a slave population of 480,000. In 1834 emancipation freed 781,000 slaves in the British West Indies, but 1,665,000 had been imported during the centuries of slavery. Jamaica's freedmen numbered 311,000, though 748,000 Africans had been brought in as slaves. By the end of slavery in the Dutch colonies there was a freed slave population no larger than 20 percent of an estimated half million that had been imported.

Another method of demonstrating the uniqueness of the growth rate of the U.S. slave population is to make a comparison of modern racial statistics. Allowing for the problems involved in the procedure—such as the difficulty in identifying race—it appears that by the mid-twentieth century North America held 31.1 percent of the New World population of African descent, despite the fact that North America accounted for only

4½ percent of the total figure for Africans imported. In comparison, the Caribbean Islands, which had imported 43 percent, accounted for only 20 percent of the Afro-American population by mid-century; and Cuba, with 7.3 percent of the imports held 3 percent of the New World Negro population. Brazil, which had imported the largest number, comprising 38.1 percent, contained 36.6 percent by mid-century.[113]

If Afro-Brazilians had increased at the rate of the U.S. Negro population, they would have totaled 127,645,000 by the mid-twentieth century, twice the number of Afro-Americans estimated for the whole Western hemisphere. Instead the figure was 27,529,000. At the U.S. rate of increase, Afro-Cubans would have numbered 24,570,000 by mid-century rather than the actual 1,224,000.[114]

Thus the slave population of the British continental colonies and the United States had a rate of natural increase unique in the hemisphere. In Brazil and the West Indies the mortality rate of slaves for long periods of slavery exceeded the birth rate by wide margins. Why was this so? Planters in Brazil and the West Indies during some periods of the Atlantic slave trade found it more economical to supply their demand for slaves by importation rather than by encouraging them to reproduce. The cheapness of supply led them to regard slave reproduction with indifference if not hostility. According to Woodward, "Brazilian planters took no pains to balance the sexes among slaves and imported three or four times as many males as females."[115] In the United States the ratio of female to male slaves was nearer parity. The high mortality rate of slaves in Latin America also was due to decimation by tropical diseases, which, of course, were less rampant in more temperate climes. It must be admitted, however, that the reasons so far suggested do not explain adequately the completely atypical growth of the slave population in the United States.

Thus the bulk of the slave population in North America was native-born. In the United States the influx of Africans and of African cultural influence was far less extensive than in the Caribbean and in Brazil. In North America a relatively small number of Africans found themselves enslaved amid a rapidly increasing native-born population whose memories of the African past grew fainter with each passing generation.

The character of the religious milieu, the average number of slaves on plantations, and the number of Africans in the slave population were all factors in the survival or loss of African culture. In the United States all these factors tended to inhibit the survival of African culture and religion. It was not possible to maintain the rites of worship, the priesthood, or the "national" identities which were the vehicles and supports for African theology and cult organization. Nevertheless, even as the gods of Africa gave way to the God of Christianity, the African heritage of singing, dancing, spirit possession, and magic continued to influence Afro-American spirituals, ring shouts, and folk beliefs. That this was so is evidence of the slaves' ability not only to adapt to new contexts but to do so creatively.

Notes

1. *The Poems of Phillis Wheatley*, edited by Julian D. Mason, Jr. (Chapel Hill: University of North Carolina Press, 1966), p. 7.
2. Benjamin Bussey Thatcher, *Memoir of Phillis Wheatley* (Boston, 1834; New York, 1834), p. 13.
3. Charles Ball, *Fifty Years in Chains* (New York: Dover Publications, 1970), p. 265; reprint of *Slavery in the United States; A Narrative of the Life and Adventures of Charles Ball, A Black Man* (New York, 1837).
4. Ball, *Fifty Years*, p. 263.
5. Ibid., p. 219. Ball also describes the native Africans as "revengeful, and unforgiving," as well as feeling "indignant at the servitude that imposed upon them."
6. *Memoir of Mrs. Chloe Spear: A Native of Africa* . . . (Boston, 1832), p. 17.
7. Fredrika Bremer, *The Homes of the New World*, 2 vols. (New York, 1853), 2: 484–85.
8. Leonard L. Haynes, Jr., *The Negro Community Within American Protestantism, 1619–1844* (Boston: Christopher Publishing House, 1953), pp. 32–33.
9. *Drums and Shadows*, Georgia Writers' Project, Works Projects Administration, reprint (Garden City, N.Y.: Doubleday, Anchor Books, 1972), pp. 136–37, 154; Charles Lyell, *A Second Visit to the United States of America*, 2 vols. (New York, 1850), 1: 266; "Autobiography of Omar ibn Said, Slave in North Carolina, 1831," *American Historical Review*, Vol. 30, pp. 787–95, especially pp. 793–94; for more information on Bilali and Old Tom, see Lydia Parrish, *Slave Songs of the Georgia Sea Islands* (New York: Creative Age Press, 1942), pp. 24–27.
10. Charles Colcock Jones, *The Religious Instruction of the Negroes in the United States* (Savannah, Ga., 1842); p. 125; *Drums and Shadows*, p. 134.
11. Octavio Da Costa Eduardo, pp. 46, 123.
12. For Herskovits' views, see *The Myth of the Negro Past* (Boston: Beacon Press, 1958); for Frazier's position, see *The Negro Church in America* (New York: Schocken Books, 1964), pp. 1–19, *The Negro Family in the United States* (Chicago: University of Chicago Press, 1966), pp. 3–16, and *The Negro in the United States*, rev. ed. (New York: Macmillan, 1957), pp. 3–13. Other important comments on the debate can be found in *Afro-American Anthropology; Contemporary Perspectives*, edited by Norman E. Whitten, Jr. and John F. Szwed (New York: The Free Press, Macmillan, 1970). Also useful is Thomas Richard Frazier, "Analysis of Social Scientific Writing on American Negro Religion," 1967 Columbia University Ph.D. dissertation. A cogent attack on Herskovits' methodology is M. G. Smith's article, "The African Heritage in the Caribbean," in *Caribbean Studies: A Symposium*, edited by Vera Rubin (Seattle: University of Washington Press, 1957), pp. 34–46. Smith's attack is followed by a defense of Herskovits by George E. Simpson and Peter B. Hammond on pp. 46–53 of the same volume.
13. Herskovits, *Myth*, pp. xxviii–xxix, 20–32.

14. Ibid., pp. 6–9, 15–17.
15. Ibid., pp. 53–87, 122.
16. Ibid., pp. 86–105, 293.
17. Ibid., pp. 105–9, 293–94. The queen mother of the Dahomean king Glele was sold into slavery in Brazil during Glele's minority by his uncle, the regent. Upon Glele's accession he tried to find his mother, unsuccessfully.
18. Ibid., pp. 77–81, 294–96. Support for Herskovits' assertion that African speech patterns underlay the pidgin English of the slaves is presented by J. L. Dillard, *Black English: Its History and Usage in the United States* (New York: Random House, Vintage Books, 1973), pp. 39–138.
19. Herskovits, *Myth*, p. 296.
20. Ibid., pp. 141–42, 296–98.
21. Ibid., pp. 298–99. I have taken pains to outline Herskovits' position because I agree with Daniel Crowther that it is important "to direct attention to what Herskovits actually wrote, rather than to the sometimes naive, sometimes malicious misinterpretations of his position in secondary or tertiary sources" (quoted by Whitten and Szwed, p. 38).
22. Frazier, *Negro Family*, p. 7.
23. Frazier, *Negro Church*, pp. 1–16.
24. Ibid., pp. 1–2.
25. Ibid., pp. 2–3.
26. Frazier, *Negro Family*, pp. 7–8.
27. Frazier, *Negro Church*, p. 6.
28. Frazier, *Negro in the U.S.*, p. 3.
29. Ibid., p. 14.
30. Ibid., p. 21.
31. Herskovits, *Myth*, p. 207.
32. Arthur Huff Fauset, *Black Gods of the Metropolis* (Philadelphia: University of Pennsylvania Press, 1944), pp. 98–106.
33. Herskovits, *Myth*, p. xxiv.
34. Ibid.
35. The New Testament speaks of the Holy Spirit as a comforter and advocate, e.g., John 14:26.
36. Herskovits, *Myth*, pp. 232–35.
37. Ibid., p. 17.
38. Mark 1:8. I will return to the issue of spirit possession below. Here I only wish to stress the difference in the theologies reflecting the experience of possession by water spirits and baptism by the Holy Spirit.
39. See Charles A. Johnson, *The Frontier Camp Meeting* (Dallas, Texas: Southern Methodist University Press, 1955), pp. 56–62, and the description by Barton W. Stone of the scene at the Cane Ridge Meeting of 1801 quoted by Sidney Ahlstrom in *A Religious History of the American People* (New Haven: Yale University Press, 1972), pp. 434–35.
40. Frederick Morgan Davenport, *Primitive Traits in Religious Revivals* (New York: Macmillan, 1917), pp. 92–93, cited by Herskovits, *Myth*, pp. 230–31.
41. Herskovits, *Myth*, p. 231.
42. Hortense Powdermaker, *After Freedom* (New York: Atheneum, 1969), pp. 259–60; Herskovits, *Myth*, pp. 227–28.
43. John D. Long, *Pictures of Slavery in Church and State* (Philadelphia, 1857), p. 159.

280 Albert J. Raboteau

44. Cited by Ulrich Bonnell Phillips, *American Negro Slavery* (Baton Rouge: Louisiana State University Press, 1966), pp. 316–17.

45. John Leland, *The Virginia Chronicle* (1790), p. 13, cited by Herbert S. Klein, *Slavery in the Americas, A Comparative Study of Virginia and Cuba* (Chicago: The University of Chicago Press, 1967), p. 120. For an extended description of black participation in a nineteenth-century camp meeting, see Fredrika Bremer, *Homes of the New World*, 1: 306–17.

46. Frederick Law Olmsted, *The Cotton Kingdom*, 2 vols. (New York, 1861), 1: 310–11. For a modern analysis of this old tradition of preaching style, see Bruce Rosenberg, *The Art of the American Folk Preacher* (New York: Oxford University Press, 1970).

47. Olmsted, *Cotton Kingdom*, 1: 312–13. I am not claiming that this style of preaching or ecstatic response was unique to black Christians in nineteenth-century America.

48. Erika Bourguignon, "Ritual Dissociation and Possession Belief in Caribbean Negro Religion," in *Afro-American Anthropology*, edited by Whitten and Szwed, p. 88.

49. K. Stewart, cited by I. M. Lewis, *Ecstatic Religion* (Baltimore, Md.: Penguin Books, 1971), p. 65.

50. Bourguignon, pp. 91–92.

51. *God Struck Me Dead: Religious Conversion Experiences and Autobiographies of Negro Ex-Slaves* (Social Science Source Documents No. 2, Fisk University Social Science Institute, Nashville, Tenn., 1945, mimeographed copy), p. 153.

52. Robert Anderson, *From Slavery to Affluence: Memoirs of Robert Anderson, Ex-Slave*, edited by Daisy Anderson Leonard (Steamboat Springs, Colo.: The Steamboat Pilot, 1927), pp. 24–26, 31.

53. Morgan Godwin, *The Negro's and Indian's Advocate* (London, 1680), cited by Dean J. Epstein, "African Music in British and French America," *The Musical Quarterly*, Vol. 59, No. 1 (1973), pp. 79–80.

54. John Sharpe, "Proposals for Erecting a School, Library and Chapel at New York," New York Historical Society, *Collections* (1880), p. 341, cited by Epstein, p. 80.

55. Alexander Hewatt, *An Historical Account of the Rise and Progress of the Colonies of South Carolina and Georgia* (London, 1779), 2:100, 103, cited by Epstein, p. 81.

56. Sir Charles Lyell, *A Second Visit to the United States*, 1: 269–70.

57. John F. Watson, *Methodist Error . . .* (Trenton, N.J., 1819), pp. 28–31, cited by Eileen Southern, ed., *Readings in Black American Music* (New York: W. W. Norton & Co., 1971), pp. 62–64; see also Don Yoder, *Pennsylvania Spirituals* (Lancaster: Pennsylvania Folklore Society, 1961), pp. 27–28.

58. Southern, *Readings*, p. 62.

59. Frederick Law Olmsted, *A Journey in the Seaboard Slave States* (New York, 1856), p. 449.

60. Daniel Alexander Payne, *Recollections of Seventy Years*, 1st publ. 1886 (New York: Arno Press and The New York Times, 1969), pp. 253–55.

61. Ibid., pp. 254–56.

62. John A. Lomax and Alan Lomax, *Folk Song U.S.A.* (New York: Duell, Sloan & Pearce, 1947), p. 335.

63. George E. Simpson, cited by Harold Courlander, *Negro Folk Music U.S.A.* (New York: Columbia University Press, 1963), p. 196; see Chapter 2, p. 37, for Simpson's description of "laboring in the spirit." Courlander comments: "The Jamaican revivalists have overlaid and disguised the African elements in their worship, and hold themselves aloof from the so-called African cults such as the Cumina. Nevertheless, they form a bridge

between the ring shout in the United States and the openly acknowledged African-style cult activities of the West Indies and, of course, Africa itself," pp. 196–97.

64. [William Francis Allen, Charles Pickard Ware, Lucy McKim Garrison], eds., *Slave Songs of the United States*, 1st publ. 1867 (New York: Peter Smith, 1951), pp. xii–xiv; see also, for more detailed descriptions of the ring shout, W. F. Allen, "The Negro Dialect," *Nation*, 1 (December 14, 1865): 744–45, reprinted in Bruce Jackson, ed., *The Negro and His Folklore in Nineteenth-Century Periodicals* (Austin: University of Texas Press, 1967), p. 79; and H. G. Spaulding, "Under the Palmetto," *Continental Monthly*, 4 (August 1863): 188–203, reprinted in Bernard Katz, ed., *The Social Implications of Early Negro Music in the United States* (New York: Arno Press and The New York Times, 1969), pp. 4–8; and Thomas Wentworth Higginson, *Army Life in a Black Regiment*, 1st publ. 1869 (Boston: Beacon Press, 1962), p. 17.

65. Courlander, *Negro Folk Music*, pp. 195–96; see also Eileen Southern, *The Music of Black Americans: A History* (New York: W. W. Norton & Co., 1971), pp. 161–62.

66. Lorenzo Dow Turner, *Africanisms in the Gullah Dialect*, reprint (New York: Arno Press and The New York Times, 1969), p. 202. The Kaaba is "the small stone building at Mecca which is the chief object of pilgrimage of Mohammedans." *Sauwata*, derived from Arabic, means to run until exhausted.

67. *Drums and Shadows*, p. 133.

68. Ibid., p. 171. There were also variations of the ring shout called Rocking Daniel, Flower Dance, and Down to the Mire, used in religious settings, described by Davenport, pp. 54–55, and by Courlander, p. 201.

69. "The shout is a fusion of two seemingly irreconcilable attitudes toward religious behavior. In most of Africa, dance, like singing and drumming, is an integral part of supplication. . . . In the Euro-Christian tradition, however, dancing in church is generally regarded as a profane act. The ring-shout in the United States provides a scheme which reconciles both principles. The circular movement, shuffling steps, and stamping conform to African traditions of supplication, while by definition this activity is not recognized as a 'dance.' However, if one violates the compromise by going too far, he has committed an irreverent act" (Courlander, p. 195). To cross one's feet is to dance and would violate decorum.

70. Charles Stearn, *Narrative of Henry Box Brown* (Boston, 1849), pp. 17–18; Samuel Miller Lawton, "The Religious Life of South Carolina Coastal and Sea Island Negroes," Ph.D. dissertation, George Peabody College for Teachers, 1939, pp. 143–44; Higginson, pp. 205–206.

71. Letter to *Dwight's Journal of Music* (November 8, 1862), reprinted in Katz, p. 10.

72. Cited by Southern, *Music of Black Americans*, p. 200.

73. Ibid., pp. 172–224; Marshall Sterns, *The Story of Jazz* (New York: New American Library, Mentor, 1958), pp. 92–103. The specific debate over African vs. European origins for the Negro spirituals has used up even more ink and paper than the discussion over Africanisms in American culture generally. There is no need to review here the huge amount of literature on the spirituals. For a recent treatment of this issue, with references to the literature, see Part 1 of John Lovell's *Black Song: The Forge and the Flame* (New York: Macmillan, 1972). On the subject of early collections of Negro spirituals, reference has already been made to Katz; Higginson; and Allen, McKim, and Ware. See also Southern's collection of *Readings in Black American Music*, which reprints accounts of slave song, as does Bruce Jackson's *Negro and His Folklore*. See also

an important article by Alan Lomax, "The Homogeneity of African-Afro-American Musical Style," in *Afro-American Anthropology*, edited by Whitten and Szwed, pp. 181–201 in which Lomax applies cantometrics (a technique invented by him and Victor Grauer for measuring traits of song performance) to compare African and Afro-American styles of singing. Disagreeing with those who find little African influence in Afro-American spirituals, Lomax says that "Cantometric analysis points conclusively in another direction—that the main traditions of Afro-American song, especially those of the old-time congregational spiritual—are derived from the main African song style model. European song style did influence the African tradition in America in regard to melodic form and, of course, textual content. In most other respects, Afro-American song has hewed to the main dynamic line of the principal African tradition" (p. 197).

74. The fullest published account of the history of voodoo is Robert Tallant's *Voodoo in New Orleans* (London: Collier-Macmillan, 1962), which draws upon most of the earlier sources. I am indebted to an unpublished seminar paper done for the Yale History Department by Charles Hegler, who compared voodoo in New Orleans to *vaudou* in Haiti. For an encyclopedic treatment of hoodoo belief and practice, see Newbell Niles Puckett, *The Magic and Folk Beliefs of the Southern Negro*, 1st publ. as *Folk Beliefs of the Southern Negro* (Chapel Hill: University of North Carolina Press, 1926; New York: Dover, 1969); and Henry M. Hyatt, ed., *Hoodoo-Conjuration-Witchcraft-Rootwork* (Washington, D.C.: American University Bookstore, 1970); see also Jackson, especially his appendices, where he lists nineteenth-century periodical articles on Negro folklore; and the "Ethnology and Folklore" column which appeared frequently in issues of the *Southern Workman* from 1894 to 1900.

75. A. B. Ellis, "On Vodu-Worship," *The Popular Science Monthly*, 38 (November 1890–April 1891): 651–58.

76. Tallant, pp. 19–22; Lyle Saxon, Edward Dreyer, and Robert Tallant, compilers, *Gumbo Ya-Ya* (Cambridge, Mass.: Riverside Press, 1945; New York: Johnson Reprints Corporation, 1969, p. 225).

77. Tallant, p. 67.

78. Tallant, p. 111. In Haiti and Africa, *Legba*, the messenger between man and gods, enables divine-human communication to take place and receives the first praise and offerings at the liturgical rites. In this sense, he opens the way.

79. Ibid. Puckett notes, "in New Orleans a red ribbon was worn about the neck in honor of 'Monsieur Agoussou' . . . which demon especially loved that color" (Puckett, p. 221).

80. Helen Pitkin, *An Angel by Brevet* (Philadelphia, 1904), pp. 6, 182–212; cited by Puckett, pp. 192–96.

81. Courlander, *The Drum and the Hoe*, p. 321.

82. Tallant, pp. 44–105; George W. Cable, "Creole Slave Songs," *The Century Magazine*, 31 (April 1886): 807–28, reprinted in Katz, pp. 47–68.

83. Hegler, pp. 13–14; the three accounts are J. W. Buel, *Metropolitan Life Unveiled*, an anonymous account entitled *Souvenirs de l'America* and C. D. Warner, *Studies in the South and West*. Buel and Warner are quoted at length by Tallant, as is the anonymous account by Henry Castellanos in *New Orleans As It Was* (New Orleans, 1895), pp. 91–96.

84. Zora Neale Hurston, *Mules and Men*, 1st publ. 1935 (New York and Evanston, Ill.: Harper & Row, 1970), pp. 239–60; see also Herskovits' comments on Hurston's initiation experience in *Myth*, pp. 245–49.

85. The unique ambience of New Orleans is demonstrated by such institutions as the Mardi Gras Carnival and the Place Congo, a square in the city, where slaves were permitted to gather on Sunday afternoons to dance, sing, and drum. Place Congo was in existence until approximately 1843. For a description of Place Congo and the dances performed there, see Cable, "The Dance in Place Congo," *The Century Magazine*, 31 (February 1886): 517–32, reprinted in Katz, pp. 32–47.

86. Mary A. Owen, "Among the Voodoos," *Proceedings of the International Folk-Lore Congress*, 1891 (London, 1892), p. 240.

87. It was not uncommon for conjurers throughout the South to advertise themselves as New Orleans–trained.

88. Herskovits, *Myth*, p. 249.

89. Cited in *Gumbo Ya-Ya*, p. 250.

90. Puckett, p. 320.

91. Ibid., p. 315.

92. *Gumbo Ya-Ya*, p. 557.

93. Castellanos, p. 94.

94. Puckett, p. 201.

95. Mary Owen, p. 230.

96. Cited by Puckett, pp. 232–34.

97. Ruth Bass, "Mojo," *Scribner's Magazine*, 87 (1930): 83–90, reprinted in *Mother Wit from the Laughing Barrel: Readings in the Interpretation of Afro-American Folklore*, edited by Alan Dundes (Englewood Cliffs, N.J.: Prentice-Hall, 1973), pp. 385–86.

98. Ibid., pp. 386–87.

99. Ibid.; see also Edward L. Pierce, "The Freedmen at Port Royal," *Atlantic Monthly*, 12 (September 1863): 303.

100. Loudell F. Snow, "I Was Born Just Exactly with the Gift," *Journal of American Folklore*, 86 (July–September 1973): 277.

101. Ruth Bass, "Little Man," in Dundes, p. 394.

102. *Drums and Shadows*, p. 184.

103. Bass, "Little Man," p. 395; Puckett, pp. 104–7; Susan Showers, "A Weddin' and a Buryin' in the Black Belt," *New England Magazine*, 18 (1898): 478–83.

104. *Drums and Shadows*, p. 128; Frances Butler Leigh, *Ten Years on a Georgia Plantation Since the War* (London, 1883), p. 77.

105. Puckett, pp. 257, 319, 381; *Drums and Shadows*, pp. 117, 121, 178; Herskovits, *Myth*, p. 237.

106. The victim of a hag or witch "may gain possession of the tormentor's skin and sprinkle it with pepper and salt, so that it cannot be used." The *Southern Workman* printed a story "of a hag who finds her skin on the doorstep thus doctored, and after trying it on several times and finding it smarts and burns, she dances wildly about crying 'O Skinny, Skinny, Skinny, don't you know me?'" "Hags and Their Ways," *Southern Workman*, 23 (February 1894): 27.

107. Klein, p. 101; an analogous New World example of the amenability of Catholicism to syncretism with "pagan" beliefs is the Virgin of Guadalupe, whose shrine was built on the site of the most important shrine to Tonantzin, Aztec goddess and mother of the gods.

108. Herskovits, *Myth*, p. 120.

109. Guion G. Johnson, *A Social History of the Sea Islands*, p. 127; see Herskovits, *Myth*, p. 117.
110. Curtin, *Atlantic Slave Trade*, pp. 88–89; C. Vann Woodward, "Southern Slaves in the World of Thomas Malthus," in his collection of essays *American Counterpoint* (Boston: Little, Brown & Co., 1971), p. 82.
111. Woodward, pp. 83–84.
112. Curtin, cited by Woodward, p. 82.
113. Woodward, pp. 84–86.
114. Ibid., pp. 87–89. It should also be noted that "the phenomenal rate of increase among Afro-Americans in the South" occurred "against the background of an unparalleled rate of increase among the white population of the United States as a whole . . ." (p. 89).
115. Ibid., p. 102.

Chapter 12

The Christian Tradition

Black Conversion and White Sensibility

Religious Foundations of the Black Nation

Eugene Genovese

The Christian Tradition

In this secular, not to say cynical, age few tasks present greater difficulty than that of compelling the well educated to take religious matters seriously. Yet, for all except the most recent phase of the history of a minority of the world's peoples, religion has been embedded in the core of human life, material as well as spiritual. Bishop Berkeley spoke a simple truth: "Whatever the world thinks, he who hath not much meditated upon God, the human mind, and the *summum bonum* may possibly make a thriving earthworm, but will most indubitably make a sorry patriot and a sorry statesman."[1]

The philosophical problem of religion, its truth and falsehood, represents a domain only partially separate from that of politics.[2] Since religion expresses the antagonisms between the life of the individual and that of society and between the life of civil society and that of political society, it cannot escape being profoundly political.[3] The truth of religion comes from its symbolic rendering of man's moral experience; it proceeds intuitively and imaginatively. Its falsehood comes from its attempt to substitute itself for science and to pretend that its poetic statements are information about reality. In either case, religion makes statements about man in his world—about his moral and social relationships—even when it makes statements about his relationship to God. Even when a man's adherence to a religion is purely formal or ritualistic, essential elements of his politics are thereby exposed, for participation in rites normally means participation in social acts that precede, rather than follow, individual emotional response. He enters, usually as a child, into a pattern of socially directed behavior that conditions his subsequent emotional development and that, from the beginning, presupposes a community and a sense of common interest.[4] For good reason the whites of the Old South tried to shape the religious life of their slaves, and the slaves overtly, covertly, and even intuitively fought to shape it themselves.

The religion of Afro-American slaves, like all religion, grew as a way of ordering the world and of providing a vantage point from which to judge it. Like all religion it laid down a basis for moral conduct and an explanation for the existence of evil and injustice. The religion of the slaves manifested many African "traits" and exhibited greater continuity with African ideas than has generally been appreciated. But it reflected a different reality in a vastly different land and in the end emerged as something new. If black religion in America today still echoes Africa and expresses something of the common fate of black people on four continents, it has remained nonetheless a distinct product of the American slave experience. It could not have been other. But the religion of the slaves became Christian and unfolded as a special chapter in the general history of the Christian religions.

The notion of Christianity as pre-eminently a religion of slaves arose long before Nietzsche's polemics, which nonetheless must be credited with imparting to it special force and clarity. "The Christian faith, from the beginning," Nietzsche insists, "is sacrifice: the sacrifice of all freedom, all pride, all self-confidence of spirit; it is at the same time subjection, self-derision, and self-mutilation."[5] This cruel religion of painful subjection, he continues, softened the slaves by drawing the hatred from their souls, and without hatred there could be no revolt.[6] Africans eventually provided their own version of this interpretation of Christianity's political role. According to their widespread saying: "At first we had the land and you had the Bible. Now we have the Bible and you have the land."

The Nietzschean view of Christianity contains an element of truth, but remains a one-sided and therefore superficial judgment upon a religion that carried the ideas of spiritual equality and of the freedom of the will and soul across Europe and the world. Christianity has been a powerful conservative force, but it has been other things as well, even for slaves. Certainly, as Ernst Troeltsch suggests, its political conservatism—its willingness to render unto Caesar the things which are Caesar's—appeared as a powerful tendency from its beginnings in a patriarchal family based on strict submission of women to men, and worked its way out in slave and seigneurial society.[7] Certainly, Karl Kautsky has a point when he argues that ancient slaves obeyed their masters out of fear, whereas Christianity raised the spineless obedience of the slaves to a moral duty incumbent even upon free men.[8] However true, these strictures constitute only one side of that process we know as the history of the Christian religion. To see only that side is to surrender all chance to understand the contribution of Afro-American Christianity to the survival and mobilization of black America.

Early Christianity and the historical Jesus need not be interpreted as politically revolutionary, in either a social or a national-liberation sense, as some radical critics have tried to do.[9] The living history of the Church has been primarily a history of submission to class stratification and the powers that be, but there has remained, despite all attempts at extirpation, a legacy of resistance that could appeal to certain parts of the New Testament and especially to the prophetic parts of the Old. The gods must surely enjoy their joke. Christianity's greatest bequest to Western civilization lies in its doctrines of spiritual freedom and equality before God—those flaming ideas that Nietzsche and so many others have worked so hard to drown in contempt—but this bequest, these doctrines, negated and continue to negate the brilliant accomplishment of the Church in establishing and consolidating the principle of social order. Social order has always rested on a delicate reconciliation of the claims of society and those of the individual, but Christianity's courageous recognition that the antagonism must remain irreconcilable in this world has always tempted the wrath of those with apocalyptic visions and murderous commitment to the Kingdom of God on Earth.

Christianity did not spread as a cry from the hearts of slaves but, as Ambrosio Donini so suggestively argues, from the totality of slave society at the beginning of its disintegration.[10] Individual suffering by itself could not point away from the world toward a spiritual reconciliation beyond; only a widespread sense of being trapped in a world of general insecurity and disorder could do so. For this reason alone, in that day as in this, an ideology, to triumph, must appeal across class lines even while it justifies the hegemony of that particular class which has the wherewithal to rule.

From its beginnings Christianity has precariously balanced submission to authority against the courage of the individual will. In a special way, fraught with consequences for the oppressed of that time and after, it has not been able to maintain this balance without great violence, for it has never been able to impose permanent restraint on the socially subversive impulses of the will. But, for an impressively long epoch, it did influence the channels through which those impulses worked themselves out.

Even Troeltsch, who vigorously defends the ethical-religious against the social interpretation of the Jesus legend, admits that Jesus addressed himself primarily to the poor and oppressed and that the rich were not won to the Christian banner until the second century—that is, after the impact of Paul's crusade.[11] Whatever the historical Jesus may have preached, the fact remains that Mark, in his account of Barabbas, refers not to *an* insurrection but to *the* insurrection; that Jesus on the eve of his arrest tells his disciples to sell their cloaks and buy swords; that all the Gospels agree on his having entered Jerusalem to the politically seditious popular cry of *Hosannah;* that the Anabaptists had good reason to love and Luther good reason to hate the Book of James—"this revolutionary pamphlet," as Archibald Robertson calls it.[12] Whatever interpretation one chooses to put on the words that burn the pages of the Book of Matthew, it is easy to see how they could spur some men and women to radical action: "And ye shall be hated of all men for my name's sake: but he that endureth to the end shall be saved" (10:22). "Think not that I am come to send peace on earth: I came not to send peace, but a sword" (10:34). "And from the days of John the Baptist until now the kingdom of heaven suffereth violence, and the violent take it by force" (11:12). And with or without the specific sanction of the Gospels, Christianity offered to the oppressed and the despised the image of God crucified by power, greed, and malice and yet in the end resurrected, triumphant, and redeeming the faithful. However much Christianity taught submission to slavery, it also carried a message of foreboding to the master class and of resistance to the enslaved.

Christianity, even as expressed in the ostensibly conservative formulations of Paul, preached the dignity and worth of the individual and therefore threatened to stimulate defiance to authority, even as it preached submission. For no class was this message more vital than for slaves. The doctrine, "Render therefore unto Caesar the things which are Caesar's; and unto God the things that are God's," is deceptively two-edged. If it calls for political submission to the powers that be, it also calls for militant defense of the freedom of the spirit and the autonomy of the personality. But the master-slave relationship rests, psychologically as well as ideologically, on the transformation of the will of the slave into an extension of the will of the master. Thus, no matter how obedient—how Uncle Tomish—Christianity made a slave, it also drove deep into his soul an awareness of the moral limits of submission, for it placed a master above his own master and thereby dissolved the moral and ideological ground on which the very principle of absolute human lordship must rest. It was much more than malice that drove so many Southern masters to whip slaves for praying to God for this or that and to demand that they address all grievances and wishes to their earthly masters.[13]

Troeltsch finds it "most remarkable" that radical individualism should appear, in however conservative a form, in Paul himself. Pondering the sociopolitical conservatism of Paul in relation to the Christian doctrine of individual freedom, Troeltsch comments that the doctrine of submission contained within it much less love than resignation and contempt for existing institutions. The Christian utopia always carried radical political implications even in its more conservative, accommodationist, and other-worldly forms. It was, however, as Gramsci says, a gigantic attempt in mythological form to reconcile the actual contradictions of life in this world. When it proclaimed a single nature, endowed by God, for every man, it also proclaimed all men brothers. But in so doing, despite every attempt to separate the Kingdom of God from the kingdoms of man, it illuminated the chasm that separated the equality of men before God from the grim inequality of man before man.[14]

Christianity, like other religions, grew out of and based its strength upon the collective. In early tribal religions, African as well as European, God is at once a supreme member of the family—a veritable *paterfamilias*—and an independent force above the family who embodies its ideal life and symbolizes its unity.[15] The essentially tribal idea of God, however modified, never wholly departs from the sophisticated religions of civilized society. Afro-American slaves, drawing on both Euro-Christianity and their own African past, combined the two and in the process created a religion of their own while contributing to the shape of Christianity as a whole.

The genius of Christianity has appeared nowhere so impressively as in its struggle to reconcile freedom with order, the individual personality with the demands of society. From the consolidation of the Roman Catholic Church, with its central idea from Saint Cyprian—far less arrogant and far more humane than it might appear to Americans—"Outside the Church there is no salvation," to the heroic effort of the Puritans to build their City on a Hill, the Christian churches have fought to embody an acceptance of the dignity and sanctity of the human personality in submission to a collective discipline that alone can guarantee the freedom of the individual in a world haunted by the evil inherent in the nature of man. Those who are purified are so for His sake and through their unity in Him. Thus Troeltsch: "Absolute individualism and universalism . . . require each other. For individualism only becomes absolute through the ethical surrender of the individual to God, and being filled with God; and, on the other hand, in possession of the Absolute, individual differences merge into an unlimited love. . . ."[16]

The religious tradition to which the Afro-American slaves fell heir and to which they contributed more than has yet been generally recognized by no means unambiguously inspired docility and blind submission. Many of the white preachers to the slaves sought to sterilize the message, but they were condemned to eventual defeat. Too many carriers of the Word were themselves black men who interpreted in their own way. The Word transmitted itself, for some slaves and free Negroes in touch with slaves could read the Bible and counter the special pleading of the white preachers. And the black community in slavery, oppressed and degraded as it was, summoned up too much spirit and inner resourcefulness to be denied. In their own way the slaves demonstrated that, whatever the full truth or falsity of Christianity, it spoke for all humanity when it proclaimed the freedom and inviolability of the human soul.

Christianity as a religion of salvation that had arisen from and that had internalized a particular form of class relations, including and especially relations of lordship and bondage, impressed itself even upon its dissidents and transmitted to them the idealization of those very social relations which dissent had meant to challenge. As Ambrosio Donini writes: "In all the mystery religions, from that of Dionysus to that of Christ, the relationship between the faithful and the savior is seen as a relationship between a 'slave' . . . and his lord [*padrone*]."[17] In all precapitalist class societies man has had a lord and has sought a savior, who quite naturally has been cast in the image of the lord himself. The egalitarian doctrines associated with the Cargo Cults of Melanesia strikingly identified the expected "cargo" with the achievements of the European masters who were to be displaced. By making the cargo (the products of European technical and material superiority) an object of worship, the natives declared for their own freedom and for equality with the whites, but they sometimes came close to expecting the cargo as a gift from those same whites. Donini's words receive striking support from the slaves of the Old South as well, for some could think of no better way to refer to God than as "de Big Massa."[18]

The revolutionary danger point to the ruling classes came from the millennialist movements where the authority and legitimacy of lordship had been badly shaken—when submission to an earthly lord receded in society and could therefore recede in spiritual consciousness. Christianity could offer Roman slaves solace, a sense of personal worth, and even some hope of personal deliverance in this world through emancipation or amelioration of treatment, but it could offer no sense of the possibilities of liberation as a class.[19] That sense could only emerge among Christian slaves whose very enslavement was imbedded in a world of bourgeois social relations and bourgeois consciousness. But by then Christianity, in its several post-Reformation forms, had undergone profound transformations.

The general significance of the rise of Christianity among black slaves in the United States must be assessed as part of the centuries-long development of Christianity as a whole and therefore of the development of the civilization within which Christianity became the dominant religion. However much the rise of Christianity in the ancient world had been prepared, in Troeltsch's words, "by the destruction of national religions, which was the natural result of the loss of national independence,"[20] the fateful splits occasioned by the Reformation closed the circle and reconstructed Christianity as a series of discrete national religions even within the Roman Catholic sphere—one need only reflect on the French Church since the time of Philip the Fair and especially since the time of Napoleon. The Afro-American slaves of the United States, in contradistinction to those in Brazil, Cuba, or Saint-Domingue, inherited Protestant Christianity. Even this diluted and perverted Protestantism lent itself, in various subtle but discernible ways, to the creation of a protonational black consciousness. . . .

⚜⚜⚜⚜⚜⚜⚜

Black Conversion and White Sensibility

The processes by which and the rate at which black slaves converted to Christianity remain unclear. Edmund Ruffin thought that Africans had rarely become Christians in Virginia and that conversion came with the first generation born into slavery.[1] Since those early slaves, African-born and American-born alike, began to see some element of safety in conversion, if only because it gave them stronger claims to the sympathy of their masters, the spiritual significance of their conversion cannot readily be assessed. Even in cases of conversions of convenience, however, religious sincerity played a role, for the protection it sought rested on a spiritual doctrine of equality before God and the recognition of every man's "human claims upon other men."[2]

A pioneer historian of the conversion problem has argued that during the colonial period most of the slaves retained much of their African religious beliefs and lived and died strangers to Christianity.[3] In its own terms, this judgment may be correct, but it can nonetheless prove mis-leading. From the moment the Africans lost the social basis of their reli-gious community life, their religion itself had to disintegrate as a coherent system of belief. From the moment they arrived in America and began to toil as slaves, they could not help absorbing the religion of the master class. But, the conditions of their new social life forced them to combine their African inheritance with the dominant power they confronted and to shape a religion of their own. In time they would produce a religion—or perhaps it would be better to say a sensibility on which a religious sys-tem could be built—that would help shape the mainstream of American Christianity and yet retain its special aspect as a black cultural expression.

In terms recognizable to the white America in which the black devel-opment was lodged, the mass of the slaves apparently became Christians during the late eighteenth and early nineteenth centuries. By the last ante-bellum decade blacks constituted a large proportion of those attending Christian services. Northern abolitionists, for self-serving reasons but also because they rarely took pains to acquaint themselves with the actual life of the slaves, made themselves ridiculous by pointing to low figures for black church membership. The figures, unreliable as they are, in fact suggested large enough totals to lead W.E.B. Du Bois and other scholars to estimate that about one of every six adult slaves considered himself or herself attached to a Christian sect. Most southern whites did not hold formal church membership either, nor even attend services regularly. More often than not, those who did consider themselves staunch Chris-tians did not join a church until late in life. In the rural, quasi-frontier slave states good Christians went to the services that were available and had lit-tle opportunity to join the church that most suited their theological pref-erence. Black professions and actual church membership must be evaluated in this wider social context and cannot provide a suitable mea-sure of concern and commitment.

Little is known about the religious beliefs of the slaves during the sev-enteenth or most of the eighteenth century. Whites paid scant attention to them and did little to convert the slaves to Christianity. The white atti-tude grew initially out of fear as well as out of a cultural distance that bred indifference. Although during the seventeenth century the law clearly stated that baptism would not imply emancipation, slaveholders through-out the British and even French colonies continued to fear that Christian slaves would be declared free.[4] Under the circumstances whites believed, and some historians have continued to believe, either that the slaves wal-lowed in "superstition"—a word that Sidney Mintz has properly defined as "the other man's religion"—or, even more absurdly, that they had no spiritual life at all. Probably, the slaves retained their traditional African beliefs, but the coherence of traditional African religion must have steadily disintegrated under the several pressures of life in a new environment and under a new regimentation.

Thus, it is necessary to follow Luther P. Jackson's suggestion and to begin the story with 1760, when black conversion to Christianity started to assume noticeable proportions. Jackson divided the history of black Christianity in Virginia into three periods: 1750–1790, 1790–1830, and 1830–1860.[5] During the first period, 1750–1790, colonial religion took a popular turn, exhibiting an awakened consciousness and mass enthusiasm. Blacks responded to the roughhewn frontier preaching and were, for the most part, welcomed as participants. No few blacks appeared as preachers and acquired followings among both blacks and whites. The Baptists and Methodists who carried much of the new religious drive often expressed hostility toward slavery and a hope that it would vanish. Throughout the Upper South the spirit of the revivals manifested itself in a demand, often backed by administrative measures within the churches, for humane treatment of slaves and for recognition that they were brothers in Christ.[6] The inclusion of blacks and indeed the religious Awakening itself did not, however, extend much below Virginia; South Carolina, even then, stood as a bulwark of conservatism in religion as in most else.[7]

During the second period, 1790–1830, antislavery feelings in the churches began to dissolve under pressure from the slaveholders, who naturally dominated institutions based on participatory democracy within a slaveholding society. Simultaneously, enthusiasm for enlisting black brethren also waned, although something of a struggle went on.[8]

A great burst of proselytizing among the slaves followed the Nat Turner revolt. Whereas previously many slaveholders had feared slaves with religion—and the example of Turner himself confirmed their fears—now they feared slaves without religion even more. They came to see Christianity primarily as a means of social control. Hence the apparent contradictions of the period: a decline of antislavery sentiment in the southern churches; laws against black preachers; laws against teaching slaves to read and write; encouragement of oral instruction of slaves in the Christian faith; and campaigns to encourage more humane treatment of slaves. The religious history of the period formed part of the great thrust to reform slavery as a way of life and to make it bearable for the slaves.

They ordered things differently in South Carolina—as always. Unencumbered by a colonial past mired in religious enthusiasm and secure under the steady guidance of a cohesive low-country aristocracy, South Carolina proceeded slowly in the religious instruction of its slaves, much as it proceeded slowly in everything except proslavery extremism. Before the insurrectionary plot of 1822 the planters generally opposed religious instruction of the slaves. In part this hostility derived from a suspicion that many ministers and preachers held antislavery views.[9] William W. Freehling, our best authority, has even suggested that the ministry did not become safely proslavery until about 1840.[10] After the Denmark Vesey plot, however, despite the momentary hysteria over the alleged role of the churches in encouraging slave insubordination, South Carolina's great planter aristocracy began going to church, or rather began making sure that the slaves were going. As was to happen in Virginia a decade later, once faced with an insurrection of slaves who displayed religious inclinations, the slaveholders sobered up. If the slaves were going to get religion, then religion had to be made safe for slaveholders.

This progress of slaveholder sensitivity to the spiritual needs of the slaves called forth its echo within the churches. The clergy faced a choice. Should it follow the example of the Quakers or of other small groups and take high ground against slavery?[11] If so, it would be rendered, perhaps with no small amount of violence, irrelevant to the lives of the slaves. Or should it place the souls of the slaves above all material considerations and render unto Caesar the things which are Caesar's? The troublemakers were dealt with, and the deed was done. Step by step, the several churches embraced the proslavery argument. They won the trust of the masters and freed themselves to preach the gospel to the slaves. The Reverend Edward Thomas's view may stand for that of many others:

> I have some hope, too, of being able to effect some spiritual good among the Blacks, who abound in this Parish [St. John's Berkeley, South Carolina], and many of whose owners are quite willing that they should receive religious instruction from their Parish minister. If our Northern brethren would let our domestic institutions alone, the poor negroes would fare much better as to their souls; but the abolition measures have excited such a spirit of jealousy and suspicion that some Planters will not listen to the introduction of religion on their places.[12]

With a few notable exceptions, each denomination made its own accommodation in due time, and the schism of northern and southern branches merely strengthened a *fait accompli*. Thus, the General Assembly of the

Presbyterian Church declared in 1861 that the slave system had generally proven "kindly and benevolent" and had provided "real effective discipline" to a people who could not be elevated in any other way. Slavery, it concluded, was the black man's "normal condition."[13]

The soul-searching struggles in the eastern and border states did not recapitulate themselves in the western cotton states despite occasional mutterings. The turbulent slaveholders who conquered the Old Southwest in the 1820s and 1830s came to religion slowly and could hardly have been expected to try to bring their slaves on any faster. But they also had fewer fears. Indifference, not hostility, created the greatest obstacle to those who would convert the slaves. The slaveholders of Alabama never mounted a notable campaign against religious instruction. Those of Mississippi gave support early to the principle. And those of Arkansas and Louisiana, despite carping from the *Planters' Banner*, slowly overcame their own indifference and undertook the task. By 1850, Fredrika Bremer could report that although religious instruction in the western states moved slowly, a general advance was occurring.[14]

The rhythm of advance differed in the older and newer slave states but manifested the same tendency, although at different historical moments. After 1831, however, the southern slaveholders began to move in tandem. The unfolding unity on this special question reflected a growing sectional unity on the larger question of slavery itself, and it received considerable support from within the churches. As the churches overcame their qualms about slavery and either grudgingly accepted the facts of life or warmly embraced the proslavery argument, they put themselves in a position to proselytize among the slaves with the blessings and active support of the masters. In 1845, the flower of the South Carolina planter aristocracy assumed the lead in sponsoring the efforts of proslavery clergymen to bring their version of the gospel to the slaves.[15] The conscientious work of a Presbyterian minister, C. C. Jones of Georgia, provided the most famous instance. His book, *Religious Instruction of the Negroes*, and his pamphlet, *Suggestions for the Religious Instruction of the Negroes*, gained wide circulation, as did other such writings. Ministers like the Reverend William Capers in North Carolina prepared their ground carefully and sought, by patient effort, to convince the planters that "the novel experiment was a safe and judicious one."[16] Generally, they succeeded.

A few small scruples did have to be overcome along the way, even apart from the big one of slavery itself. Had the clergy been Roman Catholic, life might have been easier. But it was hard for Protestants, who had a clear idea of the role of mass literacy and use of the vernacular in their movement's great Reformation, to swallow the laws against teaching slaves to read and write. Still, how could they argue with South Carolina's Whitemarsh B. Seabrook, who sensibly pointed out that anyone who wanted slaves to read the entire Bible belonged in a lunatic asylum?[17] The answer conformed to necessity. It would be purely oral instruction. Nothing was lost save their own historic tradition—a small matter, despite pretensions, for any conservative movement.

As the slaveholders themselves became more self-consciously religious during the late antebellum period, they increasingly paid white preachers to conduct services for their slaves. If preachers could not come, or even if they could, the slaveholders would preach to the slaves themselves, and their wives would conduct Sunday school for the children or Bible readings for the adults. Governor Hammond of South Carolina insisted that those slaves who wished could attend plantation or town services at least once a month and that in the sparsely settled South whites fared no better. Plantation records throughout the South bear him out, and the testimony of ex-slaves contains little to raise suspicions.[18]

In the South Carolina low country many—some insist the great majority—of the slaveholders built chapels or "praise-houses" on their plantations, and the practice spread to the western cotton belt, at least among the larger planters. These efforts, along with the insistence on taking some of the house slaves to the white family's church, did not always evoke enthusiasm among the slaves.[19] The slave narratives contain numerous complaints of having been forced to attend service against their will. To make matters worse, when a master got religion he might do as William Wells Brown's master did: end all that Sunday frolic and foolishness and see to it that his slaves kept their minds on the Good Lord.[20]

Masters did not normally force their slaves to adopt their own denomination. The slaves preferred to become Baptists or Methodists, and even Roman Catholic planters were known to let them have their way. In South Carolina, for example, a large portion of the low-country planters remained Episcopalian throughout the antebellum period, but many of their slaves became Baptists. In some cases coercion did occur, as the postwar exodus of so many blacks from other denominations into the ranks of the Baptists and Methodists suggests.[21] But in most cases, a plantation had to take whatever preacher came through the area regardless of his sect.

The slaveholders' motives combined self-interest with a genuine concern for the spiritual welfare of their slaves and indeed of themselves. Many slaveholders came to believe that religion served them well as a means of control; others, who remained skeptical or held a contrary opinion, nevertheless would not deprive the slaves of preaching. Some had the good sense to know that if the slaves were listening to a reliable white preacher, they could not—not that moment, at any rate—be off in the woods listening to some suspect black exhorter. R.F.W. Allston, South Carolina's great planter, built a prayer house for his slaves and reported them "attentive to religious instruction, and greatly improved in intelligence and morals, in domestic relations, etc. . . . Indeed, the degree of intelligence which as a class they are acquiring is worthy of deep consideration."[22] The Alabama Baptist Association at its annual meeting in 1850 called for greater efforts to instruct the slaves: "Intelligent masters with the light of experience before them will regard the communication of sound religious instruction as the truest economy and the most efficient police and as tending to the greatest utility, with regard to every interest involved."[23] And Thomas Affleck included the following instructions to overseers in his *Cotton Plantation Record and Account Book*, which sold widely in the cotton states:

> You will find that an hour devoted every Sabbath morning to their moral and religious instruction would prove a great aid to you in bringing about a better state of things amongst the Negroes. It has been thoroughly tried, and with the most satisfactory results, in many parts of the South. As a matter of mere interest it has proved to be advisable, to say nothing of it as a point of duty. The effect upon their general good behavior, their cleanliness and good conduct on the Sabbath is such as alone to recommend it to the Planter and Overseer.[24]

These remarks, which echoed across the South with increasing force after 1831, revealed the place of religious instruction in the development of the proslavery argument. They formed part of the swelling demand to make slavery safer for the masters by making it more tolerable for the slaves—a demand that implicitly deepened the South's commitment to slavery as a permanent social order.[25]

The strategy of using religion as a method of social control could never have served its purpose had it been only that. The success of the political strategy for attention to the slaves' religious life paradoxically required a considerable degree of genuine Christian concern by the masters, for it depended upon the slaves' perception of a degree of sincere white interest in their welfare. The slaves did not often accept professions of white sincerity at face value; on the contrary, they seized the opportunity to turn even white preaching into a weapon of their own. White preaching could have a degree of conservative political effectiveness only when the slaves could accept the sincerity of the gesture.

Fortunately for the regime, the religious feelings of the masters were deepening during the nineteenth century, and their efforts for the slaves were taking on a stronger moral tone. There is no other way of reading the slaveholders' private diaries, journals, and letters. George De Berniere Hooper of Alabama referred to the death of a slave as the loss not only of a "friend" but of a "Brother in Christ." "I verily believe," he wrote to his wife, "that God has a high place prepared for them." John Rogers of Charleston, South Carolina, believing himself near the end, addressed his children: "I wish you also to give all the indulgence you possibly can to the negroes in going to Church, and making them repeat their questions, for this reason that if neglected we will have to answer for the loss of their souls. . . ." Everard Green Baker penned a prayer in his diary: "Oh my God enable me to live as a Christian should live to be a faithful husband, a kind father and master and an exemplary Christian, that I may set my family such an example as will be agreeable in the eyes of my Maker, and that I may be spared to rear my children in the fear and nurture of the Lord." Baker went to considerable trouble to swap land strips with his neighbors so that his slaves would have an easier time getting to church. Ebenezer Jones of Tennessee wrote to his children:

> Dear son and daughter may you ever mind
> And to your slaves be always very kind
> You soon with them on a level must meet
> When Christ doth call you to his judgment seat
> Christ will not ask if folks are black or white
> But judge the deeds and pass a sentence right
> The earth is not a place for our abode
> Prepare, prepare to meet a righteous God.[26]

The slaves could not remain insensible to such attitudes. Rather, as in so many other ways, they turned them to advantage. They used them as a yardstick with which to measure their masters and to strengthen their sense of themselves. John Brown, an ex-slave from Talladega, Alabama, whose master had taught his slaves to read and write, recalled:

> Sunday was a great day around the plantation. The fields was for-
> gotten, the light chores was hurried through, and everybody got

ready for the church meeting. It was out of the doors, in the yard fronting the big lot where the Browns all lived. Master John's wife would start the meeting with a prayer and then would come the singing—the old timey songs. But white folks on the next plantation would lick their slaves for trying to do like we did. No praying there, and no singing.[27]

The complexity of the masters' attitudes appears in such reports as that of Elige Davison, an ex-slave from Virginia. His master's religious sincerity expressed itself in his willingness to ignore the law and to teach his slaves to read the Bible. It did not, however, prevent his regularly breaking up slave families by sale.[28]

No matter how often such anomalies occurred, the masters' religious conversion more often than not benefitted the slaves, even if only slightly. In rare and extreme cases, such as those of John Rogers of Kentucky and James Harvey Greenlee of North Carolina, it led them to conclude that proper religious instruction would prepare the slaves for freedom. There can be no question of the depth of feeling expressed by Greenlee in his diary:

> Explained them there nature, the great importance of studying and practicing the truths they contain, that they should try to understand, for they gave information of things that belong to there future happiness, & point them to Jesus, as the great attoning sacrifice for man accepted of the Father as our surity and answered the demands of the Holy Law of God which we had violated—opened up the way by which God can be reconsiled to man, admitted through his righteousness to his favor, and adopted as his children. Lord grant that they may be made wise unto salvation, receive Christ as their Lord & portion and serve him with their whole heart. May we who have charge of them feel it is our indispensable duty to instruct them tho they are in a degraded and dependent condition . . . ever bearing in mind that their souls are as precious in the sight of him with whom we have to do, as tho they were as free as we are, or as white as the fairest son of Adam.[29]

Continued indifference, rather than hostility, explained the lack of religious instruction on most plantations where it was absent, but outright hostility never completely disappeared. Instructions such as those of a Louisiana sugar planter to his overseers in 1861 grew less frequent as time went on, but still appeared: "He must not allow preaching of any sort on the place nor allow the Negroes to go off the place to hear any kind of exhortation."[30] This hostility had several sources: in a few cases, a fanatical racist rejection of the idea that blacks could have souls or profit from any religious message; in most cases, a grave suspicion that religion, even in the anesthetized form of customary white preaching, undermined the social order of slavery. The critics may not have been wrong; the gains to the whites always accompanied risks. The Christian message, no matter how censored, took its toll on whites and blacks alike. The passionately pro-Confederate Eliza Frances Andrews wrote in 1865: "I don't think there ought to be any distinction of classes or races in religion. We all have too little 'gentility' in the sight of God for that."[31]

Throughout the nineteenth century, quite apart from the implications of the religious message of a Nat Turner, slaves drew their own conclusions from the most apparently innocuous preaching. In 1807 a Baptist church in Kentucky had to exclude a black woman because, on becoming a Christian, she denounced slavery. She had acquired the crazy idea that no Christian should hold slaves.[32] In the 1830s a slave girl who had repeatedly rebuked her mistress for running off to parties on Saturday night when she ought to have been preparing for the Sabbath, finally lost patience and tried to kill several whites.[33] In 1856, an old slave in Georgia sent his young master a touching acknowledgment for a gift of some tobacco: "Do, Missis, write and give him tousand tanks. Tell him *I can do nothing for him, but the Lord can do everything for him*; and I pray the Lord to bless him and make him a good Christian."[34] Missus and Young Massa took the message, as it was probably intended, as evidence of warm affection. They do not appear to have noticed the simple assumption of spiritual equality—indeed of the old slave's superiority—that it contained.

These recurring themes kept some slaveholders nervous to the end. They had company. Ruling classes have usually had to worry about the other side of the control mechanism inherent in the Christian religion. In 1811, an overseer in Virginia who had visited the British Isles wrote to his employer and put the debate in a larger perspective that deserves notice, whatever we think of his evaluations:

> As to the instructing and enlightening of Negroes whether it would be an advantage or a disadvantage to them I really can form no opinion, numerous indeed are the arguments used against it. I am clearly of opinion that it would be of great advantage to them while young by employing their minds in that manner & keeping them in proper subjection, and it certainly would be a means of keeping them from

vicious habits which they imbibe while young, but what effect it would have upon them afterwards, I am unable to judge. In some counties in England where I visited where the Servants are totally ignorant the farmers there use the same arguments against instructing & enlightening them as are used here against the negroes. I have heard some of them assert that they never knew one of them that was educated turn out well. But in Scotland where almost all of them are educated more or less and numbers of them pretty well informed I presume that there are not more obedient, industrious & faithful servants any where. . . .[35]

❧❦❧❦❧❦❧❦

Religious Foundations of the Black Nation

The slaves' Christianity cannot be understood as a façade behind which the countryside practiced pagan rites or wallowed in something called superstition. Nor, alternatively, can the beliefs and practices of the folk be understood as having corrupted the slaves' Christianity. Folk belief, including the belief in magic, constituted a vital element in the making of the slaves' own version of Christianity, and does not appear to have introduced any greater distortion into a supposedly pure Christianity than did those folk beliefs of ancient, medieval, or even modern Europe which steadily helped shape the formation of the high religion.

Even when the churches resolutely fought popular "superstition," they had to absorb much of it either by direct appropriation or by bending formal doctrine to provide the spiritual elements that made folk belief attractive. Thus, however harshly the sophisticated urban black ministers waged war on what they considered the pagan residues of their flock, they could not easily convince the conjurers or their supporters of any unchristian doing, nor could they avoid shaping their own doctrine in such a way as to answer the questions that the resort to magic posed.

The folk dynamic in the historical development of Afro-American Christianity saved the slaves from the disaster that some historians erroneously think they suffered—that of being suspended between a lost African culture and a forbidden European one. It enabled them to retain enough of Africa to help them create an appropriate form for the new content they were forging and to contribute to the mainstream of American national culture while shaping an autonomous identity. Their religion simultaneously helped build an "American" Christianity both directly and as a counterpoint and laid the foundation for a "black" Christianity of their own. That is, it made possible a universal statement because it made possible a national statement. But, for blacks, the national statement expressed a duality as something both black and American, not in the mechanical sense of being an ethnic component in a pluralistic society, but in the dialectical sense of simultaneously being itself and the other, both separately and together, and of developing as a religion within a religion in a nation within a nation.

Black religion had to be more than slave religion, not only or even mainly because many of its most articulate and sophisticated spokesmen were southern free Negroes and northerners who lived outside slave society, but because the racial basis of slavery laid the foundations for a black identity that crossed class lines and demanded protonational identification. The horror of American racism, as if to prove Hegel right about "the cunning of Reason," forced the slaves out of themselves—forced them to glimpse the possibilities of nationality rather than class. Had it not been so, they would have been condemned to the fate of the slaves of the ancient world; they would have remained a pathetic and disorganized mass at the bottom of a single social scale, with no possibility of building an autonomous culture or rising above the role of historical witness to the crime of ultimate class oppression. The Moorish black nationalists of the 1930s knew what they were talking about when they said, "Before you have a God you must have a nationality."[1] What they could not see was just how far the slaves had gone toward establishing both.

The origins of black Christian religion in the slave quarters—the roots of an embryonic national religion in the consciousness of the slave class—embodied two contradictions, the transcendence of which has yet to be effected. First, Christianity bound master and slave together in universal communion while it contributed to their separation into antagonistic peoples. Second, it imparted to the slaves, and through them to black America, a collective strength that rested on a politically dangerous kind of individualism.

In entering into Christian fellowship with each other the slaves set themselves apart from the whites by creating a distinctive style, sensibility, and theology. In the hands of militants and revolutionaries, the sense of being a people apart could lead to a belief that whites were the antichrist, but the universality of the Christian religion, embedded in an intimate, paternalistic plantation world, militated against such an interpretation and rendered it an idiosyncratic footnote. For the slaves, whites lived under God and were brothers in Christ. In its positive aspects, this sense of racial brotherhood gave the slaves a measuring rod with which to hold slaveowners to a standard of behavior appropriate to their own professions of Christian faith. By its very nature it forbade slaves to accept the idea that they had no right to judge their masters; it made judgment a duty. In thus being compelled to see some masters as "good" and some as "bad," the slaves had to take conservative ground and admit that a man did not necessarily stop being a Christian by holding slaves, although they did not take this concession to mean that slavery itself could be a proper order for a Christian society. This compromise strengthened their resistance to dehumanization, for it curbed the self-destructive tendency toward hatred. It left them free to hate slavery but not necessarily their individual masters. It left them free to love their masters as fellow sinners before God and yet to judge their relative merits as Christians and human beings. W.E.B. Du Bois could therefore express admiration for their profoundly Christian ability to love their enemies and yet defend them against the notion that in so doing they surrendered their manhood or accepted their masters' worldview.[2]

Thus, slave parents could teach their children to pray before going to bed:

> Now I lay me down to sleep,
> I pray de Lord my soul to keep,
> If I should die befo' I wake,
> I pray de Lord my soul to take.
>> Bless pappy, bless mammy,
>> Bless marster, bless missie,
>> And bless me, Amen![3]

Thus, a body servant could write a member of his master's family about the death of his young master in battle: "Dear Master Richard, You sent me word some time ago to write this morning. I will now try to give you an account of my feelings toward my young master who is now dead." He expressed sorrow that he was not there at the end to comfort him and drew from his young master's death a meaning for himself. "Master Richard, I say to you it is good to be religious. . . . I believe it as much as I ever believed anything in my life, that he is at rest. My heart believes it. I desire to be a better Christian. I want to go to Heaven. . . . My earnest desire is to be at rest after this life."[4] Thus, masters and slaves turned to each other for solace in times of grief with no sense of doing anything odd. When Pierce Butler, Fanny Kemble's ex-husband, died, their distraught daughter took comfort from an old woman who had been a slave on their Georgia plantation: "Missus, don't cry; it vex de Lord. I had t'irteen children, and I ain't got one left to put even a coal in my pipe, and if I did not trust de Lord Jesus what would become of me?"[5] It would be hard to hammer a revolutionary commitment out of such a spirit and even harder to raise a cry for holy war, but the generous legacy it bequeathed would provide enormous compensation for a people who had to survive and who never lost faith in a future built on human brotherhood.

If the contradictory nature of the slaves' religion as part of American Christianity and yet as a faith apart lessened revolutionary inclinations, the contradiction between its individual and its collective aspects proved even more fateful. The religion practiced in the quarters gave the slaves the one thing they absolutely had to have if they were to resist being transformed into the Sambos they had been programmed to become. It fired them with a sense of their own worth before God and man. It enabled them to prove to themselves, and to a world that never ceased to need reminding, that no man's will can become that of another unless he himself wills it—that the ideal of slavery cannot be realized, no matter how badly the body is broken and the spirit tormented.

The spiritual emancipation of the individual therefore constituted the decisive task of religion and the necessary foundation for black collectivity. But communion as a people, under so pressing a demand, reinforced that tendency toward atomization of the quarters which it was combatting. At the very moment that it was helping to create a sense of solidarity through mutual respect and love for each other, it was strengthening an extreme doctrine of the equality of individuals. The slaves desperately needed that doctrine to confront their masters, but they were whole men and women, not a jumble of abstractions; they could not easily assert their claims against the authority of their masters without asserting them against the claims of each other. The Reverend Henry H. Mitchell tells us: "The black preacher is not an army officer ordering men to their death. Rather he is a crucial witness declaring how men ought to *live*."[6] But, he adds, the tendency inherent in this role is to strengthen the individual at the expense of collective political assertion.

These contradictions propelled black religion forward to the creation of collective identity and pride. The black variant of Christianity laid the foundations of protonational consciousness and at the same time stretched a universalist offer of forgiveness and ultimate reconciliation to white America; and it gave the individual slave the wherewithal to hold himself intact and to love his brothers and sisters in the quarters, even as it blocked the emergence of political consciousness and a willingness to create a legitimate black authority. The synthesis that became black Christianity offered profound spiritual strength to a people at bay; but it also imparted a political weakness, which dictated, however necessarily and realistically, acceptance of the hegemony of the oppressor. It enabled the slaves to do battle against the slaveholders' ideology, but defensively within the system it opposed; offensively, it proved a poor instrument. The accomplishment soared heroically to great heights, but so did the price, which even now has not been fully paid.

Notes

The Christian Tradition

1. Quoted by R. H. Tawney, *Religion and the Rise of Capitalism* (Gloucester, Mass., 1962), title page.
2. For a trenchant discussion often quoted out of context by hostile critics, see Karl Marx and Frederick Engels, *On Religion* (Moscow, 1957), pp. 41–42.
3. See Balandier, *Political Anthropology*, pp. 100–101.
4. I have taken the liberty of following, even of paraphrasing, George Santayana's masterful *Reason in Religion*, Vol. III of *The Life of Reason* (New York, 1962), esp. pp. 12–15; see also E. E. Evans-Pritchard, *Theories of Primitive Religion* (Oxford, 1965).
5. Friedrich Nietzsche, "Beyond Good and Evil," *The Philosophy of Nietzsche* (New York, 1927), p. 432. For a good although not fully convincing critique, see Max Scheler, *Ressentiment* (trans. W. W. Holdheim and ed. Lewis Coser, New York, 1961), esp. Ch. 3.
6. Yet even Nietzsche found something to admire in Christianity—its ability to tame the masses. More interestingly, he regarded Christianity as a kind of plebeian revenge, born of envy, against the aristocracy. In his view it promoted dissembling and deception. The Christianity of the slaves in a way bears him out, but in a way very much removed from anything he could imagine.
7. Ernst Troeltsch, *The Social Teaching of the Christian Churches* (trans. Olive Wyon; 2 vols.; London, 1950), I, 295–296.
8. Karl Kautsky, *Foundations of Christianity* (trans. H. F. Mins; New York, 1953), pp. 355–356. Thus, Kautsky finds Christianity's primary role in the subjugation of the free urban masses of the empire rather than in any strengthening of lordship over the slaves themselves.
9. The most interesting attempt at such an interpretation by a Marxist is that of Archibald Robertson, *The Origins of Christianity* (2nd ed.; New York, 1962). But see also Clifford Geertz, "Religion as a Cultural System," in Michael Banton, ed., *Anthropological Approaches to the Study of Religion* (New York, 1966), pp. 1–46.
10. Donini, *Lineamenti di storia delle religioni*, pp. 196–199; Julien Freund, *The Sociology of Max Weber* (trans. Mary Ilford; New York, 1968), p. 202.
11. Troeltsch, *Social Teaching of the Christian Churches*, I, 39.
12. Robertson, *Origins of Christianity*, p. 182; also pp. 80 ff., 119, 183. Within the black liberation movement the boldest voice urging the revolutionary interpretation of the

historical Jesus has been that of Rev. Albert Cleage, for whom Jesus was the leader of a black (that is, nonwhite) Israel in a national liberation struggle against an allegedly white nation of Rome. The Rev. Mr. Cleage's emphases are suggestive: he hates Paul; lauds the Book of Mark; attacks the Book of John; and takes as major texts Matthew 10:34–36 ("I came not to send peace, but a sword") and Luke 11:23 ("He that is not with me is against me"). His national-racial interpretation aside—although it is absolutely essential from his own point of view—his reading of Christian history recapitulates that of a long line of Christian revolutionaries, including Thomas Münzer and one or two other lily-whites. See *The Black Messiah* (New York, 1969).

13. See, e.g., Rawick, ed., *S.C. Narr.*, III (4), 192; *Okla. Narr.*, VII (1), 78; WPA, *Drums and Shadows*, p. 180. For a remarkable Russian parallel see the speech of a landowner to his serfs as quoted in Hobsbawm, *Age of Revolution*, p. 149.

14. Troeltsch, *Social Teaching of the Christian Churches*, I, 82; and the cogent analysis of Antonio Gramsci, *Il Materialismo storico e la filosofia di Benedetto Croce* (6th ed.; Turin, 1955), pp. 91–98.

15. See the discussion of Georg Simmel, *Sociology of Religion* (trans. C. Rosenthal, New York, 1959), p. 44.

16. Troeltsch, *Social Teaching of the Christian Churches*, I, 57.

17. Donini, *Lineamenti di storia delle religioni*, p. 207.

18. For a discussion of these cults in depth see Peter Worsley, *The Trumpet Shall Sound: A Study of the "Cargo Cults" in Melanesia* (London, 1957); for their place in the history of such movements in general, see Vittorio Lanternari, *Religions of the Oppressed* (New York, 1963). On "de Big Massa," see esp. Botumel, *First Days Amongst the Contrabands*, pp. 104, 141, 154, 242.

19. On the general history of slavery as a problem for the Christian churches see D. B. Davis, *Problem of Slavery*. But see also the qualifications introduced into these generalizations by Mircea Eliade, "Paradise and Utopia: Mythical Geography and Eschatology," in Frank E. Manuel, ed., *Utopias and Utopian Thought* (Boston, 1966), pp. 260–280.

20. Troeltsch, *Social Teaching of the Christian Churches*, I, 43.

Black Conversion and White Sensibility

1. Scarborough, ed., *Diary of Edmund Ruffin*, Dec. 10, 1857 (I, 136–137).

2. I have quoted from Eric R. Wolf, *Sons of the Shaking Earth* (Chicago, 1964), who discusses the conversion of the Mexican Indians to the Catholicism of their Spanish conquerors (see p. 175). In later years white southerners switched from accusing the slaves of insincerity for reasons of protection to insincerity for reasons of frivolous social intercourse—a standard by which white church attendance might also be questioned. See Ingraham, *South-West*, II, 55–56; J. B. Sellers, *Slavery in Alabama*, p. 122.

3. Marcus W. Jernegan, "Slavery and Conversion in the American Colonies," *AHR*, XXI (April, 1916), 504–527. See also John Mitchell Justice, "The Work of the Society for the Propagation of the Gospel in Foreign Parts in North Carolina," unpubl. M.A. thesis, University of North Carolina, 1939.

4. These circumstances, as they obtained in Virginia, have been discussed in numerous works on the colonial period of American history. But for an interesting special case, discussed in hemispheric perspective, see William Renwick Riddell, "The Baptism of Slaves on Prince Edward Island," *JNH*, VI (July, 1921), 307–309. Some attention to the religious instruction of slaves was manifested in Virginia at least as early as the 1720s; see Tate, *Negro in Eighteenth-Century Williamsburg*, pp. 92–99, 117.

5. Luther P. Jackson, "Religious Development of the Negro in Virginia from 1760 to 1860," *JNH*, XVI (April, 1931), 168–239; also Parkinson, "Religious Instruction of Slaves," unpubl. M.A. thesis, University of North Carolina, 1948.
6. For evidence of demands for more humane treatment of slaves in the wake of the revivals, see Morton, *Robert Carter of Nomini Hall,* p. 241; George William Pilcher, "Samuel Davies and the Instruction of Negroes in Virginia," *VMBH,* LXXIV (July, 1966), 293–300; Guion Griffis Johnson, "The Camp Meeting in Ante-bellum North Carolina," *NCHR,* X (April, 1933), 106; and for a particular set of records showing the diverse administrative actions that might be taken, see the Hephzibah Church Books, 1819–1820, in the Merritt M. Shilig Memorial Collection, typescript at Louisiana State University.
7. Sirmans, *Colonial South Carolina,* pp. 77, 99–100, 231.
8. See, e.g., McColley, *Slavery and Jeffersonian Virginia,* p. 63.
9. In some parts of the South the suspicion was solidly grounded. See, e.g., Asa Earl Martin, *The Anti-slavery Movement on Kentucky Prior to 1831* (Louisville, Ky., 1918), pp. 84–87.
10. Freehling, *Prelude to Civil War,* pp. 336–337; also pp. 72–76. Cf. George Dangerfield, *The Era of Good Feelings* (New York, 1963), p. 224; Luther P. Jackson, "Religious Instruction of Negroes, 1830–1860, with Special Reference to South Carolina," *JNH,* XV (Jan., 1930), 72–114; Frank J. Klingberg, *An Appraisal of the Negro in Colonial South Carolina* (Washington, D.C., 1941).
11. See Claude R. Rickman, "Wesleyan Methodism in North Carolina," unpubl. M.A. thesis, University of North Carolina, 1952.
12. Rev. Edward Thomas to Rt. Rev. R. W. Whittingham, March 10, 1836, in the Whittingham papers.
13. Quoted in James H. Boykin, *North Carolina in 1861* (New York, 1961), p. 98.
14. J. B. Sellers, *Slavery in Alabama,* p. 294; Sydnor, *Slavery in Mississippi,* p. 55; Anson West, *History of Methodism in Alabama* (Nashville, Tenn., 1893), p. 719; J. G. Taylor, *Negro Slavery in Louisiana,* p. 149; Sitterson, *Sugar Country,* p. 101; Mooney, *Slavery in Tennessee,* pp. 96–97; Bremer, *Homes of the New World,* II, 434.
15. Jackson, "Religious Instruction of Negroes, 1830–1860," pp. 72–114.
16. J. H. Davie to Robert Davie.
17. Freehling, *Prelude to Civil War,* p. 135.
18. For J. H. Hammond's view of the frequency of religious services for slaves, see *The Proslavery Argument, as Maintained by the Most Distinguished Writers of the Southern States* (Charleston, S.C., 1852), p. 133, and *DBR,* VIII (Feb., 1850), p. 123; also C. C. Jones, *Religious Instruction,* p. 95; *ACPSS,* III (July, 1859), 201–204; Kemble, *Journal,* pp. 56–57; Wendell Holmes Stephenson, *Isaac Franklin: Slave Trader and Planter of the Old South, with Plantation Records* (University, La., 1938), p. 112. For a sampling of plantation manuscripts from different parts of the South see J. W. Witherspoon to Susan K. McDowall, Jan. 2, 1847, in the Witherspoon-McDowall Papers; Massenburg Farm Journal, March 15, 1840; Cornish Diary, 1843–1844; Hanson Diary, Dec. 16, 1860; Magruder Diary, April 11, 1846, March 3, 1856; Ervin Journal, 1848; Hilliard Diary, 1850; Hudson Diary, April 22, 1853; E. G. Baker Diary, Aug. 8, 1856; Magnolia Plantation Journal, Oct. 18, 1856, in the Warmoth Papers; Bayside Plantation Records, March 17, 1861; Minor Plantation Diary, Feb. 10, 1863.
   For a sample of the various activities of plantation mistresses in bringing religious instruction to the slaves see Magruder Diary, 1846 and 1856; Hanson Diary, Sept. 15,

1858, March 30, 1860; Broun Diary, Nov. 29, 1863; Clarissa E. (Leavitt) Town Diary, Feb. 1, 1853; Bethell Diary, Jan., 1845, Dec. 9, 1857, June 6, 1860; Eliza Clitherall Autobiography, ms. II, 2; and Wise, *End of an Era*, p. 37.

19. F. L. Riley, ed., "Diary of a Mississippi Planter," *Publications of the Mississippi Historical Society*, X (1909), 453; Chalmers Gaston Davidson, *The Last Foray, The South Carolina Planters of 1860: A Sociological Study* (Columbia, S.C., 1971), p. 83; C. P. Patterson, *Negro in Tennessee*, p. 146; *ACP*, II (Aug., 1854), 253–254.

20. *Narrative of William Wells Brown*, p. 12; cf. Col. John Hill Plantation Diary in the Edgefield (S.C.) Military Record, 1830.

21. W.E.B. Du Bois, "Reconstruction and Its Benefits," *AHR*, XV (July, 1910), 781–799; J. G. Taylor, *Negro Slavery in Louisiana*, p. 149; Heyward, *Seed from Madagascar*, p. 185; Davidson, *Last Foray*, pp. 85, 96; Rawick, ed., *Texas Narr.* IV (2), 60; Bondurant Reminiscences, typescript pp. 8–13.

22. Quoted in Phillips, "Radical Problems, Adjustments and Disturbances," in Chandler et al., eds., *South in the Building of the Nation*, IV, 210.

23. Quoted in C. S. Davis, *Cotton Kingdom in Alabama*, p. 89.

24. Copies of Affleck's book may be found in many collections of plantation manuscripts. These particular instructions were reprinted in *ACP*, II (Dec., 1854), 353–356.

25. See Jenkins, *Pro-slavery Thought*, pp. 13, 17. For a good general discussion of the ways in which religion was used for social control, see Eaton, *Growth of Southern Civilization*, p. 87.

26. George De Berniere Hooper to Caroline M. Hooper, May 13, 1853; John Rogers to "My Dear Children . . . ," April 5, 1842, in the Renwick Papers; E. G. Baker Diary, Sept. 4, 1859 (II, 48), also Dec. 30, 1855 (I, 37); Mooney, *Slavery in Tennessee*, p. 92.

27. Yetman, ed., *Life Under the "Peculiar Institution,"* pp. 45–46.

28. Ibid., p. 91.

29. Greenlee Diary, Dec. 31, 1848; also Rogers Journal, pp. 150–151.

30. Plantation Diary, 1861–1865, in the Minor Papers.

31. E. F. Andrews, *War-Time Journal of a Georgia Girl*, p. 72.

32. Walter Brownlow Posey, *The Baptist Church in the Lower Mississippi Valley, 1776–1845* (Lexington, Ky., 1957), p. 91.

33. Martineau, *Society in America*, II, 319.

34. As quoted in a letter from Mary Jones to Charles C. Jones, Jr., Dec. 22, 1856, in Myers, ed., *Children of Pride*, p. 277.

35. William McKean to James Dunlop, Dec. 2, 1811, in the McKean Letterbook.

Religious Foundations of the Black Nation

1. C. Eric Lincoln, *The Black Muslims in America* (Boston, 1961), p. 54.

2. Du Bois, *Gift of Black Folk*, esp. pp. 178, 188.

3. Rawick, ed., *S.C. Narr.*, III (4), 172.

4. Washington Wills to Richard Wills.

5. Leigh, *Ten Years*, p. 78.

6. H. H. Mitchell, *Black Preaching*, p. 203.

Chapter 13

Exodus

Theophus H. Smith

The tormented ones will want to discover (thus they have learned from Egypt) how they can powerfully conjure God to appear forthwith and help.

Martin Buber, *Kingship of God*[1]

In their reflections upon the meaning of the Emancipation Proclamation, Afro-American freed men and freed women and their folk theologians realized that a decisive event of biblical narrative had become an occurrence in their own historical experience. Lincoln's presidential order, following upon the cataclysm of civil war, demonstrated that the miraculous exodus of Hebrew slaves out of Egyptian bondage could become a mundane reality in contemporary terms. The implications of that lesson, reinforcing earlier apprehensions of divine providence and prophetic fulfillment, also promised future repetitions. The likelihood of ongoing recapitulations of biblical narrative became immediately accessible, even compelling, to the religious apprehension of thousands. Henceforth more than a minority of believers and converts would be convinced of the possibility that through prayer and expectation, through acts of obedience and righteousness, black folk could inherit divine promises of prosperity and freedom. Furthermore, an apparent precondition for such bestowals would appear to be their linkage to biblical models. That singular instance, the link between Lincoln's role in the emancipation and Moses' role in the Exodus, would distinguish itself as a kind of paradigm. In this manner a new development in the ancient tradition of biblical typology emerged in the collective psyche of a displaced people.

310 Theophus H. Smith

Typology is the hermeneutic (interpretive) tradition that links biblical types or figures to postbiblical persons, places, and events. Moreover, it is crucial for this hermeneutic that each particular dyad of a biblical "type" and its postbiblical "antitype" should be understood to represent a fulfillment of prophecy.[2] The origins of this tradition go back beyond the medieval period to the Christian Scriptures and the early church. Taken as a whole the two millennia have witnessed its formation into a uniquely Christian spirituality. Black religious figuralism also participates in that spiritual heritage. Nonetheless its adoption by Afro-Americans did not arise in a vacuum. Nor is it solely attributable to the pervasive influence of Puritan typology on all immigrant and relocated groups in United States cultural history. Puritan influence has been so compelling in that history that Werner Sollors has coined the term "typological ethnogenesis" to comprehend it. Sollors and other literary historians of Puritanism are convincing in the claim that disparate ethnic communities of whites, Jews, and peoples of color have inherited the Puritans' biblical figures for America. Just as they configured New England as "God's new Israel," as "Canaan" and as "Promised Land," in order to create their group identity as a New World "chosen people," so have other ethnic communities subsequently adopted and adapted that theological-political strategy.[3] Nonetheless a careful ethnographic investigation would reveal that each of them did so in distinctive ways, accommodating the Puritan hermeneutic to their antecedent traditions of spirituality.

For Afro-Americans the antecedent spirituality was distinctly extra-Christian. But one must do more than acknowledge the fact in passing. To take the West African sources of black American cultures seriously requires a structural or systematic incorporation of extra-Christian elements in our ethnographic investigations, and also (where relevant) in our theological formulations. In this chapter I attempt a structural treatment of black North American experience by stressing, on the one hand, the insistently ritual nature of black religion particularly as regards its appropriation of biblical typology. On the other hand I am careful to observe the bicultural character of black figural discourse. Maintaining a bicultural perspective ensures that the complexity of a culture and the density of its formations are displayed, rather than reducing black religion either to imputed African (ritual) elements alone or to conventionally Christian (theological) influences alone. In this connection one commentator has disclosed ritual elements operating in the figural theology of Puritan America.[4] Indeed, on this basis I will indicate some of the same incantatory dynamics in Puritanism that I find in black religious data. On the other hand I do not here apply the term 'conjuring culture' to Puritan American spiritual transformations in the New World; I reserve the term for African American transformations because of their more clearly articulated pharmacopeic, ritual, and magical orientations. The distinctively conjurational nature of black religion does not, I hasten to add, preclude a theological treatment of the tradition's Christian features as well.

The prominence of ritual in African and Afro-American cultures has been observed from a variety of disciplinary perspectives.[5] By ritual I mean social practices in which the creative impulse to pattern reality results in a repetitive structuring of human action. Ritual is a primal, and primary, mode of social interaction and performance. In operation it either precedes ideation, articulation of concepts, and symbolic expression (as in myth, poetry, or theatre) or subordinates these as means in its patterning of action. If we inquire to what end such processes aim, it appears that rituals are intended to be transformative more than representational. They are instrumental: focusing upon the "means to" rather than the "meanings of" transformed versions of reality.[6] So understood, rituals need not be limited to religious performances but can also include secular transformations. Neither need they be rigidly fixed by the invariant repetition of particular patterns, although continuity and conserving of similarities undergird their authoritative power to bond participants and induce their adherence. But in addition to invariant rituals, *homo ludens* (the human being as player) also improvises.[7] That is, we create supervisory modes or 'metapatterns' for altering the conventional patterning of our actions, while simultaneously observing the need for continuity and authority, in order to accommodate external contingencies and our own changing intentions in the structuring of reality. With respect to my subject in this chapter, a perennial source of emancipatory improvisations is the transformative process described by the anthropologist Victor Turner as *communitas:* the humanitarian bonding between persons in a community who intentionally dissolve class distinctions and conventional constraints in order to free each other for egalitarian relationships.[8]

Let us observe such improvisational play, with its communitarian intent, in the ritual strategies of black people in North America. Notable in this regard are ecstatic worship or spirit possession, on the one hand, and the folk tradition of conjure on the other. But by extension there are also aesthetic and political contexts in which ritual performances are featured. In the sections below I explore the ritual nature of black social and political figuration in the North American context, in a constructive effort that culminates in the presentation of an Afro-American repertory of biblically formed political configurations. In conclusion I also anticipate new developments in this black religious tradition of narrative reenactment—a tradition, I posit, which transforms the world through ritually improvised applications of biblical models.

God-Conjuring

In his literary theory Kenneth Burke also recognized ritual drama as the primal form of human action. Burke described ritual in metaphorical terms as the "hub" from which all other forms of distinctively human action radiate, like the spokes of a wheel. Human discourse, on this view, is best understood as "symbolic action" which retains genetic elements of its ritual origins.[9] It thereby conveys primal significations, as if continuing to function within a "ritual cosmos" (Zuesse) irrespective of changing contexts. Of course, some language users are more proficient in utilizing the power of discourse to recall and project ritual significations: poets and vocalists, preachers and orators, writers and dramatists. Their varied inducements to restore such a ritual cosmos are also an invitation to make the figurative efficacious; to participate in symbols not only cognitively, but so as to fulfill them on the scale of group actions and social dramas. "One must learn to enact the world differently. One must see every *thing* as *symbol*. It takes constant repetition and dramatization to achieve this ritual vision of life."[10]

In his 1961 study of "the new African Culture," Jahnheinz Jahn described black religions in similar terms. Jahn spoke of African and African American religions as traditions of "active worship" which "create" God, and which "install the divine being as such." Intriguingly, Jahn's language coincides with the conventional meaning of the word "conjure" as an act of the imagination: to conjure up a picture, image, or idea. "Analogously to the designation of an image," Jahn declares, "we may speak of the designation of divinity."[11] This formulation suggests that in worship a deity is conjured (summoned, evoked) in ways analogous to the imaging or imagining of a designated object. In conjunction with Jahn's notion of 'making' or inducing the deity, I retrieve Kenneth Burke's elucidation of incantation or the "incantatory": as a "device for inviting us to 'make ourselves over in the image of the imagery.'"[12] Burke's formulation suggests a reciprocal reference: to designate a deity is also to image or reimagine the self. Moreover, such reciprocity allows for an extension of incantatory dynamics beyond the primal context of ritual worship.

In its original context of ritual and worship, imaging or designating of the deity may be said to occur integrally within the primal experience of religious fascination, where the subject experiences terror or awe in the presence of the holy (Otto). But under the exigencies of historical experience the designation of deity may acquire some intention other than ritual or worship. From this perspective I propose the hypothesis that black North American experience features a development from designating or 'summoning' God in worship, to an intention to conjure God for freedom. The best places to verify such a development are writings in which religious expressions function rhetorically as ritual incantations—incantations that reciprocally summon God and, in Burke's phrase, "invite us to make ourselves over in the image of the imagery." The nineteenth-century "Ethiopian" texts of two black antislavery writers, David Walker and Robert Alexander Young, are ideal for this purpose. These writings are also remarkable in that they inaugurate black religious figuralism as a literary tradition—the literary-religious tradition of Ethiopianism.

Black literary expression is called Ethiopian when it depends for its rhetorical and prophetic force on Psalm 68.31 (King James Version): "Princes shall come out of Egypt; Ethiopia shall soon stretch out her hands to God." Albert Raboteau has described this text as "probably the most widely quoted verse in Afro-American religious history."[13] We will return to Ethiopia as a primary biblical figure in black religious tradition. More immediately it is helpful to observe, in early Ethiopianist texts, a displacement of conjuration from the sphere of ritual and worship to the existential sphere of human freedom. That displacement is evidently a *conditio sine qua non* for incantations like the following. First, in David Walker's *Appeal to the Coloured Citizens of the World* (1829) we read:

> Though our cruel oppressors and murderers, may (if possible) treat us more cruel, as Pharaoh did the Children of Israel, yet the God of the Ethiopians, has been pleased to hear our moans in consequence of oppression, and the day of our redemption from abject wretchedness draweth near, when we shall be enabled, in the most extended sense of the word, to stretch forth our hand to the Lord our God.[14]

This passage is notable for its *double* reference both to Exodus—"Pharaoh" and "the Children of Israel"—and to Ethiopia; indeed, Walker invokes "the God of the Ethiopians." This double use of biblical figures conveys as well the kind of incantatory reciprocity referred to in relation to Burke's expression "making ourselves over in the image of the imagery." For, reciprocally with the invocation of the God of the Ethiopians, the writer intends to remake Afro-Americans in the image of Hebrew slaves crying out under Egyptian bondage. Similar dynamics are evident in Robert Alexander Young's "Ethiopian Manifesto," which also appeared in 1829 and displays both the double reference to Exodus and Ethiopia and the reciprocal incantations of God and self.

> We tell you of a surety, the decree hath already passed the judgement seat of an undeviating God, wherein he hath said, "surely hath the cries of the black, a most persecuted people, ascended to my throne and craved my mercy; now, behold! I will stretch forth mine hand and gather them to the palm, that they become unto me a people, and I unto them their God."[15]

Here we may observe how a conjurational mode of spirituality is operative in the act of designating a deity. In the preceding passage a crucial element of such conjuration is that the "God of the Ethiopians" and an "undeviating God" are designated not only for the sake of worship—in order that "they become unto me a people, and I unto them their God"—but also for the sake of freedom, in that "the day of our redemption from abject wretchedness draweth near." The reference to freedom is crucial because it can be read not only as simple prophecy: that is, as a visionary prediction of the coming emancipation. Rather it is more profoundly understood as prophetic incantation: as religious expression intending to induce, summon, or conjure the divine for the realization of some emancipatory future. Again, such a "strategy of inducement" has been clearly described in Burke's literary theory:

> Neo-positivism has done much in revealing the secret commands and exhortations in words—as Edward M. Maisel, in *An Anatomy of Literature*, reveals in a quotation from Carnap, noting how the apparent historical creed: "There is only one race of superior men, say the race of Hottentots, and this race alone is worthy of ruling other races. Members of these other races are inferior," should be analytically translated as: "Members of the race of Hottentots! Unite and battle to dominate the other races!" The "facts" of the historical assertion here are but a strategy of inducement (apparently describing the scene for the action of a drama, they are themselves a dramatic act prodding to a further dramatic act).[16]

Two differences between strategies of inducement as presented by Burke and that which we find in Ethiopianism should be noted. First, the Walker and Young texts disclose an explicitly religious strategy, a strategy in which divine providence is invoked. The second difference follows from the first. The "secret commands and exhortations" of Walker and Young are designed not only for human readers but preeminently for that divine reader who has been designated as "undeviating" and who has been conjured as the "God of the Ethiopians." But there is a more significant dimension of Ethiopianism in these texts.

The strategic use of language here consists not only in the rhetoric of inducement or incantation but also in that of biblical figuralism. Thus the figure in Psalm 68.31—Ethiopia stretching out her hands to God—becomes prophetic with respect to the situation and destiny of black people in early nineteenth-century America: "when we shall be enabled, in the most extended sense of the word, to stretch forth our hand to the Lord our God" (Walker). Other variations are possible in the rhetorical use of this prophetic figure, as Young demonstrates by imagining or conjuring God seated on his throne and declaring: "Now, behold! I will stretch forth mine hand and gather them." In each instance it is the "God of the Ethiopians" who is designated, so that the biblical figure of Ethiopia is employed as an element (or prescriptively, as materia medica) within a strategy of inducement. Moreover, the figural identification of Ethiopia with 'all Africa' is juxtaposed with the God of the Bible in the phrase "God of the Ethiopians." Thus a symbol of Africa occurs in metonymic correlation with the deity of white Americans and signifies the conjoining and potential transformation of 'black' and 'white' religious traditions.

Finally, what is most consequential is that this God is designated for the purpose of human freedom. As the liberation theologian James Cone insists, it is the "God of the oppressed" who is invoked by the black freedom tradition.[17] Rather than move immediately to Cone's liberation theology, however, my task in this chapter requires that we remain at the pretheological level of religious ethnography. In this connection, the incantatory dimension in Ethiopianism can be construed as an effort to conjure-God-with-Scripture-for-freedom. By "stretching out their hands to God" in conversion, preaching, and ministry, the Ethiopianists imitate the Ethiopians of the prophecy in Psalm 68.31. This mimetic operation has its complement in the transformation of black American slaves who, by conversion, prayerful outcry, and longsuffering, become Mosaic slaves and thereby effectively induce God to grant them the same future of freedom as the Hebrew slaves were granted in the book of Exodus.

A final instance of black figural incantation in this brief review is the infamous "Address to the Slaves of the United States of America," delivered by Henry Highland Garnet in 1843. Garnet's speech explicitly incited slaves to revolt and violently overthrow their masters. It shared this feature with David Walker's *Appeal,* which explains why the text of Garnet's "Address" was appended to the 1848 publication of the *Appeal* by its promoters, and why both were banned in the South by their proslavery opponents. The Address employs only the Exodus figure, and the object of its incantatory inducements seems limited to the slaves as fellow human beings rather than also including the divine being. Despite such one-dimensionality Garnet's text employs other dynamics that claim our attention.

> You are not certain of heaven, because you suffer yourselves to remain in a state of slavery, where you cannot obey the commandments of the Sovereign of the universe. . . . The diabolical injustice by which your liberties are cloven down, *neither God, nor angels, or just men, command you to suffer for a single moment.* . . . You had better all die—DIE IMMEDIATELY, than live slaves and entail your wretchedness upon your posterity. If you would be free in this generation, here is your only hope. However much you and all of us may desire it, there is not much hope of redemption without the shedding of blood. If you must bleed, let it come all at once—rather DIE FREEMEN THAN LIVE TO BE SLAVES. It is impossible like the children of Israel, to make a grand exodus from the land of bondage. The Pharaohs are on both sides of the blood-red waters![18]

The strategy of inducement employed here involves the rather transparent tactic of arousing the slaves on the basis of their Christian piety and devotion. *If* you love God—the tactic asserts—whom you cannot fully obey and serve in your state of bondage, *then* you must murder your masters. Here we have, to say nothing more, a desperate inference. But more pertinent from an analytic perspective is Garnet's attempt to induce a higher degree of credibility and legitimacy for the inference by resorting to the figural elements of the biblical Exodus event: "It is impossible like the children of Israel to make a grand exodus from the land of bondage."

Two aspects of this reference to Exodus bear emphasizing. First, it is incantatory insofar as it engages its designated audience at the level of their spiritual and mimetic desire to be "like the children of Israel." In fact, we do well to read the passage as a 'counterspell.' It is Garnet's attempt to break or redirect the power which the Exodus figure wields over the slaves insofar as it induces them to wait for the same providential deliverance that attended the children of Israel. As the historian Timothy Smith has emphasized: "The Christian beliefs [the slaves] adopted enabled the African exiles to endure slavery precisely because these beliefs supported their moral revulsion toward it and promised eventual deliverance from it *without demanding that they risk their lives in immediate resistance.*"[19] But risking their lives for deliverance is precisely the disposition that Garnet, like Walker, sought to induce in his audience. In order to achieve that end he denied the literal correspondence between American slaves and Hebraic slaves, for such correspondence implies a providential destiny that supersedes violent resistance. This counterconjurational requirement leads to a second point of emphasis.

Like a master conjuror, Garnet did not simply deny the prophetic power or the providential efficacy of the Exodus figure. That blundering tactic would subvert his own basis of spiritual influence on his audience! Rather, he denied only the similarity of situations between ancient Egyptian bondage and American bondage. He pointed out that the case of American slavery presented a greater difficulty than its biblical precursor: "The Pharaohs are on both sides of the blood-red waters!" By such language Garnet used the figure to reject the figure. But despite this counterfigural intention his rhetoric implicitly confirmed the vitality and utility of a conjurational tradition that uses biblical figures for incantatory effect.

Before leaving Garnet's strategy of inducement, however, we have the opportunity to observe certain resonances between it and the statement by the Jewish philosopher Martin Buber. In the passage that prefaces this chapter, Buber noted the magical worldview of ancient Israel in the context of the Exodus narrative. Indeed, coincident with Zora Neale Hurston, Harry Hyatt, and some of their folk sources reviewed previously, Buber too represented conjuration as originally an Egyptian magical tradition. Referring to the Hebrew slaves in Egyptian bondage, Buber observed that "the tormented ones will want to discover (thus they have learned from Egypt) how they can powerfully conjure God to appear forthwith and help." However, he proceeds to speculate, Hebrew slaves failed in their efforts to conjure God. Rather they encountered a God who declared, in Buber's words, "You do not need to conjure Me, but you cannot conjure Me either." This speculative reconstruction of an ancient collective subjectivity is Buber's way, as he explains, of accounting for the eventual atrophy of overt or explicit efforts to conjure God in Israel's religious history. "What is here reported is, considered in terms of the history of religion, the 'demagicizing' of faith."[20] Without engaging that claim at either its ethnographic or its theological level of assertion (is it an orthodox retrojection onto the ancient past of later standards of progress or purity?), I am struck by its congruence with Henry Highland Garnet's evident forbearance. Is his failure explicitly to 'conjure God with scripture for freedom,' in contrast to his Ethiopianist peers, evidence of his advancement of, or alienation from, a vigorous and compelling tradition?

Ethnogenesis

To designate a deity, I have suggested, means also to image a self. But this reciprocity need not refer only to individual selfhood; it may also include corporate identity. Thus, when a community or people designates its patron god or deities it simultaneously constitutes or reconstitutes its collective identity. In figural Ethiopianism, accordingly, we see the interplay between emancipatory aspirations on the one hand and corporate formation on the other—a conjunction with theological dimensions that I cannot address here.[21] The aspect of corporate formation, however, is also the focus of a literary and ethnohistorical work previously mentioned, Werner Sollors's *Beyond Ethnicity: Consent and Descent in American Culture* (1986). A study in literary history and criticism in the field of ethnic American literatures, the book is most useful here for its development of the concept of "typological ethnogenesis." By this term Sollors means simply "the sense of peoplehood that emerged among Puritans and ethnic groups [who] drew on typology."[22] He then proceeds to document the ubiquitous figuration of peoplehood that employs biblical typology in ethnic America. We need not repeat Sollors's convincing survey here. It is sufficient to note his conclusion: "In post-Puritan America, white and black, business and labor, Jew and Gentile, could follow typological patterns and *become biblical antitypes.*"[23]

Sacred peoplehood through becoming a biblical antitype: that formula states the corporate interest of black America in biblical figuralism as manifested in Ethiopianism. The following three figures—Exodus, Ethiopia, and Egypt—are the major constituents of this typological ethnogenesis.

The Exodus Figure

Slaves prayed for the future day of deliverance to come, and they kept hope alive by incorporating as part of *their* mythic past the Old Testament exodus of Israel out of slavery. . . . The Christian slaves applied the Exodus story, whose end they knew, to their own experi-

ence of slavery which had not ended. . . . Exodus functioned as an
archetypal event for the slaves. The sacred history of God's liberation
of his people would be or was being repeated in the American South.
Albert J. Raboteau, *Slave Religion*[24]

In slave religion the figural vision of the emancipation as a type of biblical "Exodus" provides the paradigm for subsequent strategies and acts of
political imagination. The Exodus figure has informed Afro-American
political projects from the post-Reconstruction period to the recent civil
rights movement, in which a premier instance is Martin Luther King, Jr.'s,
leadership of the freedom movement. The figural dimension of King's
leadership has been nicely articulated by the historian Lerone Bennett, Jr.,
as consisting of two foci: "his original choice of himself as a symbolic
being . . . and the further fact that the movement was already based on the
solid rock of Negro religious tradition."[25] That the tradition was biblical
and typological explains both King's aptitude for, and success in, representing himself as a type of Moses. This representation had its climactic
expression in his final and prophetic speech, "I've been to the mountaintop!" There King envisioned himself as Moses on Mount Pisgah who
looks over into the Promised Land and affirms that, while he may not get
there, someday his people will.[26]

A noteworthy aspect of Exodus figuration in slave religion is the element
of inverting or improvising the conventional Puritan signification of the
figure. On the one hand, "white Christians had identified the journey
across the Atlantic to the New World as the exodus of a new Israel from
the bondage of Europe into the promised land of milk and honey." On the
other hand, "for the black Christian, as Vincent Harding has observed, the
imagery was reversed: the Middle Passage has brought his people to Egypt
land, where they suffered bondage under Pharaoh. White Christians saw
themselves as a new Israel; slaves identified themselves as the old."[27] The
slaves' inverse identification evinces an improvisational propensity: a
propensity not only for imitative appropriation but for variations and
transformations of the available Euro-Christian materials and resources.

Here a theological view leads to further ethnographic insight. In religious perspective the figure of Exodus signifies God's liberation of Israel
from Egyptian bondage by means of collective dependence on divine
providence—that is, without the need for autonomous acts of violence.
Thus the Mennonite theologian John Howard Yoder reminds us that
in the Exodus event the people of the Lord do not take up arms. Rather,
with an intensity that never recurs in subsequent biblical narrative, the

community was able to claim (in place of their own military capabilities) that "the Lord is a Warrior!" (from "The Song of Moses," Exodus 15.3).

> The exodus experience is of a piece with the ancient Hebrew vision of Holy War. The wars of JHWH were certainly lethal, but they were not rationally planned and pragmatically executed military operations; they were miracles. In some of them (and the Red Sea is such a case), the Israelites, according to the record, did not even use arms. The combatant was not a liberation front or terrorist commando but JHWH himself. . . . The Red Sea event is for the whole Old Testament the symbol of the confession that the Israelites do not lift a hand to save themselves.[28]

In mimetic correlation with biblical narrative, the emancipation of Afro-American slaves occurred also without massive slave insurrections or armed struggle. The divine supercession of human (pharaonic) resistance, by means of providential developments vis-à-vis the victims, constitutes an essential element of correspondence between Exodus and the emancipation. This level of figural correspondence would be altogether missing in such cases as John Brown's insurrection or Nat Turner's revolt, the more so had they succeeded on a vastly larger scale.

But Exodus figuration is not the only phenomenon of its kind in black culture. Related forms of religious figuralism operate as well in other political projects of the nineteenth and twentieth centuries, including black nationalist projects of revitalization. As we will see, those projects were spiritual-political in that they sought to transcend the prevailing structures of social oppression by using religious discourse to render the New World and the Old a locus of communitas (Turner)—of freedom, wholeness, and cultural creativity for black peoples.

The Ethiopia Figure

> Princes shall come out of Egypt; Ethiopia shall soon stretch out her hands to God.
>
> Psalm 68.31 (King James Version)

Probably eighteenth-century missionary interpretation bequeathed to black believers the use of "Ethiopia" as a symbol for all Africa and for black people everywhere. White Christians may also have first interpreted the verse as a prophecy of the mass conversion of black people to the faith. Finally, it also seems to be a product of European chauvinism to claim that

God's "providential design" ordained the slave trade in order to bring Christianity to Africa.[29] But gradually Afro-Americans cast the Christian fulfillment of the prophecy in their own perspective.

Generations of interpretation eventually developed into a literary-religious tradition called "Ethiopianism," which spanned the late eighteenth and early twentieth centuries, and engaged black communities on both the African and American continents. In Ethiopianism, Wilson Jeremiah Moses observes, Psalm 68.31 "came to be interpreted as a promise that Africa would 'soon' experience a dramatic political, industrial, and economic renaissance." This notion of African resurgence—resurgence against the background of the slave trade and Africa's nineteenth-century humiliation by European colonialism—included an accompanying vision of the decline of the West. "The rise in the fortunes of Africa and all her scattered children would be accompanied by God's judgement upon Europeans." We will return to this emphasis in the discussion of apocalyptic themes in black religious experience. It suffices at this time to recognize, with Wilson Jeremiah Moses, that through their quasi-religious interpretations nineteenth- and twentieth-century black nationalists have effectively "conjured" with Psalm 68.31.[30]

The Egypt Figure

It should be observed that Psalm 68.31 features both Egypt and Ethiopia as figures for prophetic fulfillment. The Ethiopia figure is explicitly situated in the conversion theme of the second half of the verse: "Ethiopia shall soon stretch out her hands to God." However, Ethiopianism as a social-political movement has also been energized by the first half of the prophecy regarding Egypt: "*Princes* shall came out of Egypt"—not slaves whether Hebrew or African! Here we must observe that the negative valuation of Egypt, which conventionally operates in Exodus figuration, is reversed in mature developments of Ethiopianism. For historically informed Ethiopianists ancient Egypt was understood to be a civilization of black rulers instead of a prison house of black slaves. An affirmation and even celebration of Egypt occurred, as Gayraud Wilmore points out, among black abolitionists and preachers of the nineteenth century and among black intellectuals after the First World War.[31] Indeed we may recognize the yearning for a Pan-African communitas in their bold, anti-structural identification with Egypt and Ethiopia as the two great monarchies of ancient Africa. In their countercultural figuration Egypt appears as a focus of ethnic pride and reclaimed heritage instead of (conventionally) the land of bondage and oppression. The celebrated wealth and stature of Egypt as one of the earliest human civilizations emerge in Ethiopianism through the retrieval of black people as leaders of culture and representatives of civilization.

In fact, in North America a resurgence of Egypt figuration is now occurring which inherits from Ethiopianism a tradition of Pan-African scholarship. This development promises to reverse the situation lamented earlier in this century by the Pan-Africanist scholar W.E.B. Du Bois, who described the historical amnesia afflicting black America in regard to the "mighty Negro past" of Egypt and Ethiopia. Here we may speculate that a new yearning for communitas is empowering the current figuration of Egypt in black America. Reclaiming Egypt and Ethiopia as the two pillars of a classical black heritage, today's Afro-American retrieves the historical ground, once again, in Du Bois's expression, to "be a co-worker in the kingdom of culture."[32] Rather than attempt to build a future black greatness in a historical vacuum, present-day Egypt figuralists struggle to expose the "destruction of black civilization," and the "myth of the Negro past." Moreover, they seek to reclaim their "stolen legacy" as the historical ground for present participation in the next age of great black civilizations.[33]

Repertory

By configuration I mean a distinctive pattern of social-political arrangements that typify a particular period in a culture's historical development. Of course, the term deliberately connotes the operative presence of an imaged or 'iconic' figure embedded in each configural phase. In this study the figures are predominantly biblical, of course, but it is evident that they may be derived from diverse sources in history and culture. Note also that, however providential the convergence of historical circumstance and biblical narrative, configurations are experientially and empirically grounded in the intensive patterning of communities upon figural models. That is, configurations are inseparable from the hermeneutic reflection on events conducted by an interpretive community. In this section I show how the operation of the Exodus figure in black American communities grounds social-political patterns and arrangements that constitute an Exodus configuration, how the Ethiopia figure forms Ethiopia configurations, and so on, with the Promised Land figure and other patterns.

Together these configurations constitute a catalogue or a repertory: a repertory of the Bible construed as a 'formulary' or 'conjure book'. Like a musical or dramatic repertory of selections, configurations constitute repeatable alternatives for social and political performances that are modeled on biblical narrative and figures. The following repertory consists of selected social dramas that may be occurring at any period in black historical experience. The potential for historical divergence from the Bible's narrative patterns is endless, of course, just as the Emancipation experience of the slaves differed in significant ways from the biblical Exodus. But it is the hermeneutic framework and its schematic congruence with biblical typology that make the notion of a repertory useful, and not a literal or even an allegorical fixation on exact correspondences between biblical history and black history. In any case, attempts to force exact and rigid correspondences remain uninformed by the ritual and improvisational dynamics of Afro-American spirituality. That spirituality is mimetic, not in the sense of literalistically imitating its models but by creatively transforming them at the same time it thoroughly appropriates them.

The Exodus Configuration

> Whenever the Judeo-Christian tradition has been accessible to oppressed peoples, this scenario of election, captivity and liberation has captured the imagination.
> Gayraud Wilmore, *Black Religion and Black Radicalism*[34]

In the Afro-American figural tradition it appears that all corporate liberation efforts can be configured, in the manner of ritual performances, as dramatic reenactments of Exodus, and their leaders envisioned as approximate types of Moses. We have already referred to the black freedom movement of the 1960s, and Dr. Martin Luther King's "Mosaic" leadership in it. But the freedom movement offers only the latest indication of the force of this figural principle. The earliest instance of the configuration antedates even the Emancipation-Exodus of the slaves in 1863. For we must recall that there were prior emancipation events of various northern states, as well as the termination of the slave trade in Britain and its New World colonies in 1807. The New York State emancipation of 1827, in which the celebrated orator and activist Sojourner Truth was freed, provides a case in point. It should also be recalled that, after the Civil War era, there occurred the Exodus events of the post-Reconstruction period extending through the late 1870s and the 1880s. These were not emancipations but migrations: the beginning of the mass migrations of black Americans out of the South that culminated in the great urban and northward migrations of the early twentieth century.

Indeed, participants and contemporary observers alike used the term "exodus" to describe the migrations.[35] The historian Herbert Aptheker tells us that already, during Reconstruction itself, black communities tended to move out of a state whenever radical legislators lost power. When Reconstruction in the South was finally terminated in 1877, numbers of black organizations and their leaders began planning both secretly and openly for mass relocation to the North. The first major move occurred in January 1879—the anniversary month of Lincoln's Emancipation Proclamation—starting from southern Louisiana. "Most of these men, women and children headed for Kansas—the land whence came John Brown."[36] Earlier in the 1870s Sojourner Truth had lobbied hard and long in Washington, and on lecture platforms around the country, for the United States government to set aside lands for black settlements in Kansas or "the West." She preferred Kansas to the missionary scheme of relocating blacks overseas to Liberia, and she expressed her views in the language of Exodus figuration:

> I have prayed so long that my people would go to Kansas, and that God would make straight the way before them. Yes, indeed, I think it is a good move for them. I believe as much in that move as I do in the moving of the children of Egypt [*sic*] going out of Canaan [*sic*]— just as much.[37]

In this manner Kansas was reconfigured as a specific locus of the American "Promised Land." This figural passion, which discovers or re-creates Exodus typologies wherever possible, derives from both existential and religious elements in Afro-American social experience. As W.E.B. Du Bois acknowledged, freedom itself has acquired a sacred or numinous quality in black culture. "Few men ever worshipped Freedom with half such unquestioning faith as did the American Negro for two centuries," Du Bois wrote a generation or more after Lincoln's executive order that freed the slaves. "Emancipation was the key to a promised land of sweeter beauty than ever stretched before the eyes of wearied Israelites."[38] But in addition to this visionary dimension there were also social-political and economic aspects of the post-Reconstruction exodus. The former slave and abolitionist Frederick Douglass recognized this clearly; he described the migrations "as an assertion of power by a people hitherto held in bitter contempt; [and] as an emphatic and stinging protest against high-handed, greedy and shameless injustice to the weak and defenseless." Moreover, Douglass employed a pharmacopeic metaphor in elaborating the social-economic dimension of the migration of black laborers: "[by] wisely using the Exodus example, they can easily exact better terms for their labor than ever before. Exodus is medicine, not food."[39]

Douglass's remarkable metaphor combines biblical figuralism with the curative orientation of African American conjure traditions. (His personal encounters with conjure lore are related in his autobiography, *Narrative of the Life of Frederick Douglass, An American Slave*, 1845.) Moreover, the use of the Exodus figure in a political context featuring sustained domination and exploitation of black workers in the "Reconstructed" South shows that black Americans, in the generation after Emancipation, still had recourse to Exodus strategies as a remedy or cure for oppression.

Before concluding this configuration we should observe the remarkable representation by black women of the patriarchal figure of Moses. I refer not only to Sojourner Truth in her political leadership during Reconstruction. It was Harriet Tubman who was called, during her own lifetime, "General Moses" and "the Moses of her people." Tubman earned this distinction by her performance as a liberator of hundreds of slaves on the underground railroad. This instance shows how even the working-class black woman, otherwise stereotyped as "the mule of the world" (Hurston),[40] is configured as a type of Moses by the troping virtuosity of black religious figuration.

The Ethiopia Configuration

Ethiopianism might have remained merely an escapist myth-system based upon Biblical proof-texts and confined to the circle of Negro church people had not a brilliant black scholar appeared on the scene in the 1870s and 1880s. . . . Their movement sprouted from the seed-bed of folk Ethiopianism. . . . His great contribution was toward the development of African "cultured nationalism."
St. Clair Drake, *The Redemption of Africa*[41]

In this passage St. Clair Drake has charted the transition from a specifically religious figuration of Psalm 68.31, "Princes shall come out of Egypt, Ethiopia shall soon stretch forth her hands to God" (King James Version), to its political impact in black nationalism. As we saw earlier, that Psalm was regarded as a prophecy of Africa 'stretching out her hands to God' through mass conversion to Christianity. Thus Ethiopianism had originally served to motivate black Christians in their own missionary efforts to "redeem" Africa by spreading the gospel and making converts there. That is, the tradition initially embodied a religious vision. Then arose a singular thinker who reconfigured Ethiopianism to promote, first, New World emigration back to Africa. Most radically however Edward Wilmot Blyden (1832–1912) extended Ethiopianism to create a post-Christian cultural nationalism. "When shorn of Christian beliefs about [Africa's] 'degeneration and 'redemption' through conversion to Christ, Ethiopianist thinking leads to a belief that the forces are latent within Africa itself to 'redeem' it."[42]

In contrast to Ethiopia figuration, Edwin S. Redkey has described the emigrationist and black nationalist periods of Ethiopianism as a "Black Exodus." The Exodus figure applies as well as Ethiopia because of the back to Africa motivation of black nationalism; a motivation that operated as late as the Garvey movement of the 1920s (the largest mass movement in black history). But this variation in figural terminology serves only to highlight the improvisational aspects of a configural repertory. In this repertory, the Exodus and Ethiopia figures alternate as if to increase the amplitude—the imaginative or iconic power—of correspondences between black experience and biblical narrative. Thus the "flexibility in the Black story"[43] allows for black nationalism to be configured alternately by Exodus and Ethiopia figuration. The same crossing of the Atlantic Ocean by which Africans were transported to the Americas is reversed by emigration. In such a reversal, the configural imagination can envision the return to Africa as a crossing of 'the Red Sea'—*back to Egypt!* But, as we saw earlier with respect to Egypt figuration, rather than a place of bondage Egypt is transvalued by black cultural nationalists as a positive representation of African greatness and potential destiny. By means of such improvisational transformation, a new Exodus is envisioned which leads out of captivity or exile in the New World.

Indeed, as we see in the conclusion, the New World as the site of exile or Diaspora is the most contemporary configuration of African American culture.

Americana

In this section I compare the African American uses of the Exodus figure with Puritan American antecedents in colonial New England. As already noted, biblical figuralism or typology is a Christian interpretive tradition that goes back to the early church and New Testament literature. It emerged as the authoritative way for Jewish Christians first, and Gentile Christians later, to read the Hebrew Scriptures prophetically: that is, by assigning Christian referents to sacred terms from the Jewish Scriptures.

Christ as a second Adam, as a second Moses or David, or John the Baptist as another Elijah, are all examples of such prophetic or figural fulfillment. Typology or figuralism can be defined as a hermeneutic or interpretive tradition in which a person or place, object or event, is connected to a second entity in such a way that the first signifies the second and the second fulfills or encompasses the first. Moreover, as Erich Auerbach insisted, biblical figuralism is distinguished from other symbol systems (especially allegory) in that its figures always refer to actual, historical entities. So radical and all-encompassing is this realistic reference that the Bible promises to absorb *both* cultural and individual histories by its figural frame of reference:

> All other scenes, issues, and ordinances . . . the history of all mankind, will be given their due place within its frame, will be subordinated to it. The Scripture stories . . . seek to subject us, and if we refuse to be subjected we are rebels . . . we are to fit our own life into its world, *feel ourselves to be elements in its structure* of universal history.[44]

The formation of individual believers by means of the same imitation of biblical types has been the traditional subject of the "lives of saints" or hagiographies. Such narratives focus on heroes of mimetic proficiency: those whose lives so conform to the models authorized in sacred texts that they themselves have become new exemplars in continuity with those texts.

The theologian James Wm. McClendon, Jr., has extended the hagiographic interest in exemplary lives with his innovative project in narrative studies, "biography as theology." The focal point for this project is the exemplary character of persons (not only canonically recognized saints but also ordinary persons) whose lives embody and display the theology of their community of reference. As models or exemplars they are human expressions or embodiments of their community's religious convictions. The term "exemplar" means a preeminent example, a model or pattern most worthy of imitation. The exemplary lives selected by McClendon for theological reflection include those of Dag Hammarskjøld and Martin Luther King, Jr. Speaking of the dominant images in these lives as "the key" to their biographies, McClendon illustrates how "the convergence of such images in a particular person helps to form his characteristic vision or outlook."[45] As we might expect, when discussing the "characteristic vision" of King it is the Exodus and Moses "images" that predominate.

King understands his work under the image of the Exodus; he is leading his people on a new crossing of the Red Sea; he is a Moses who
goes to the mountaintop, but who is not privileged to enter with his
people into the promised land. These are major images, and for
[King] there are others as well.[46]

This figural portrait of King is one example of McClendon's "biography
as theology," which programmatically treats individual lives and their
characteristic vision as informed by biblical images. By contrast, I treat
collective rather than individual character. (Elsewhere I have referred to
this distinction in terms of "ethnography as theology" in contrast to
"biography as theology."[47])

The prominence of the Exodus figure in the life of King is not a coin-
cidence; we have already seen that Exodus is a compelling figure for Afro-
American culture at large. The black theologian James Cone, for instance,
claims that "almost all blacks in America—past and present—have identified Egypt with America, Pharoah and the Egyptians with white slaveholders and subsequent racists, and blacks with the Israelite slaves."[48] In
this connection we may posit here a kind of continuum between biography and ethnography, similar to that which Sacvan Bercovitch observes
between biography and history in the social discourse of Puritan New
England. As Bercovitch remarks, the linking term in this continuum is
exemplum or "the exemplary."

For the seventeenth-century Puritan, *exemplum fidei* denoted a type
of Christ; and what he meant by type pertained equally to biography
and to history. . . . Biographically, the New Englander and the Israelites were correlative types of Christ; historically, the struggles of the
New England saints at that time, in this place . . . [were] the deeds
Christ was now performing through them in America.[49]

Because of their conviction that an individual life could constitute an
instance or "example for faith," Puritan histories of the colonies "read like
spiritual biographies of an elect land."[50] Since the groundbreaking work
of Perry Miller in early American studies there has come into being a substantial literature concerning the figural transformation of New England
into a type of biblical Israel. The present section briefly highlights this literature in order to locate black religious figuralism in a larger context
of North American figural discourse. But of course the primary focus is
an ethnography of black religious figuralism. In rendering connections

between these two figural traditions one need not insist on (nor alternatively deny) direct Puritan influences on black traditions of figural discourse. At any rate there is sufficient evidence to suggest the pervasive influence of typological thinking throughout North American history and culture. Sacvan Bercovitch's *Puritan Origins of the American Self* (1975), alongside Werner Sollors's examination of "typological ethnogenesis" in United States cultures, indicate a nearly universal influence of Puritan typology. Moreover Wilson Jeremiah Moses's work in black literary history corroborates specific instances of typological influences on Afro-American religion and culture. The "black jeremiad," for example, is a literary genre cognate with the so-called American jeremiad of Puritan tradition. Here however I only suggest a family resemblance between the African American and the mainstream Puritan American figural traditions, as a way of better understanding the mimetic aspects of Afro-American conjurational spirituality.

It is remarkable that the Exodus figure should be common to such dissimilar communities. The implications of the resemblance between the two traditions are more significant for this study than the question of historical sources and documented influence—an influence that awaits adequate investigation by historians. The lack of research, however, cannot be due to the marginality of black religious figuralism. On the contrary, the preliminary treatment given previously has already substantiated the centrality of biblical figures in black religious expression. Of course, as many observers have commented, the identification of Afro-American slaves with Israel's sufferings in the 'house of bondage' possessed more literal force than the same identification of white Americans. Again, Vincent Harding's comment about reversed (or inverse) images—America as "Promised Land" for the latter group, and America as "Egypt" for the former—illustrates one way to express the differing aspects of realism involved.[51]

Despite such contrasts in their use of biblical figures, by the mid-nineteenth century black Christians in North America had more in common with their white antagonists than with religious cultures anywhere else in the world. For, as reciprocally alienated but nonetheless proximate religious communities they shared the hermeneutics of figuralism generally, and the centrality of the Exodus figure in particular. On the basis of this hermeneutical and theological connection I judge, along with the historian David W. Wills, that "black religious leaders were also more involved than has been realized in appropriating, preserving, and defending the broadly Puritan tradition from which so much in American evangelism is derived."

Accordingly I proceed to display what Wills calls the "shared framework" between African American and Puritan American traditions, or what Paul Holmer called a common "grammar of faith."[52] I am specifically interested in a common *figural* grammar, but also in the differences between Puritan typology as one "mode of spiritual perception"[53] and Afro-American modes of spiritual perception.

In pursuing this matter of similarity and difference it is useful to hypothesize a conjurational or incantatory element operating in each Christian community.[54] Bercovitch provides a point of departure in his reference to the Puritans' extrapolations from the "spiritual sense" of Scripture—its *sensus spiritualis*. Going beyond orthodox exegeses of Scripture, the Puritans rendered their own experience as a coequal source of theological reflection. Their ostensible biblicism, Bercovitch argues, functioned as a mask which veiled or disguised their "inversion" of the traditional relationship between Scripture and experience.

> Early New England rhetoric is a titanic effort to secularize traditional images without abandoning the claims of exegesis. The clergy compensated for their extreme subjectivism in substance by an extreme orthodoxy in approach. . . . [They] instituted what might be called, for want of a better term, a rhetoric of inversion. . . . Discarding the difference between plural and singular, moving freely between historiography and spiritual biography, they inverted the notion of *exemplum fidei*, who stands for the elect community, into the notion of a church-state that is an elect Christian, *in imitatio Americae*.[55]

We may thus ascribe to Puritan typology an incantatory impulse, comparable in effect (however unconscious) to magical performances in the operation of spells or solemn invocations. The incantatory factor consists in the designation or 'invocation' of an entire people as a sacred image or icon. To refer again to Burke's useful expression, incantatory rhetoric functions "as a device for inviting us to 'make ourselves over in the image of the imagery.'" I propose that the figure of an "American Israel" was intended, defensively and iconographically, to reverse the European representation of America as a "howling wilderness" and of its colonists as the offscouring of the Old World among the native peoples or 'barbarians' of the New World.[56] Offensively, the iconic intent was to eclipse the representation of Old World cultures as preferential sites of divine activity in history, and to claim the New World instead as the contemporary focal point of God's redemptive activities.

On this view we may understand the Puritans' mimesis, in which New England appears as the biblical Israel, as a form of incantational self-representation. Indeed, one likely connection between Puritan and African American uses of the Israel figure resides in the incantatory element found in their respective preaching traditions. As the historian Donald G. Mathews observed, "the incantational preaching which New Light Baptists brought from New England was very much like the interaction between leader and worshipers in African religion."[57] Coincidentally, the incantatory style of such Baptist preachers may have inured that denominational tradition to generations of black converts during the course of successive encounters with Christianity, from the period of the Great Awakening in the eighteenth century to the great mass of conversions following the emancipation of 1865.

However, there is a toxic aspect of the Puritan typological tradition. As Bercovitch argues, the figure of "America" as "God's New Israel" (Cherry) has become a distorted and pernicious mythic symbol. The figure has come to symbolize a destiny that is familiarly invoked and, in the conventional sense 'conjured up,' by such mythic-symbolic constructs as "American dream," manifest destiny, "redeemer nation," and chosen peoplehood. "Only in the United States," Bercovitch claims, "has nationalism carried with it the Christian meaning of the sacred. Only America, of all national designations, has assumed the combined force of eschatology and chauvinism."[58] As Bercovitch also makes clear, this usurpation of sacred symbols did not occur accidentally. Rather, it was an extension of the Puritans' initial inversion of Scripture and experience. We may attribute America's figural excesses to the Yankee descendents of the Puritans, for whom "typology took on the hazy significance of metaphor, image, and symbol; what passed for the divine plan lost its strict grounding in Scripture; 'providence' itself was shaken loose from its religious framework to become part of the belief in human progress . . . [and] sacred history [translated] into a metaphor for limitless secular improvement."[59]

Bercovitch maintains, however, that these developments were not transformations of the typological heritage but essentially extensions and adaptations. For it was the Puritans themselves who had already transformed New England into an antitype of the biblical figures "Canaan" and "Israel." How could they have foreseen the future distortion of their labored exegeses? Had the 'genetic' or embryonic elements of their own distortion—their own errors of inversion—been made clear to them, could they have found the way to a more authentic figuralism? Bercovitch suggests that the Puritan fathers were incapable of heeding a number of contemporary efforts to warn them. One of the most vigorous alarms was sounded by Roger Williams (1603–1683). Writing at length to John Cotton from England, Williams castigated the colonists for their theocratic claims to the title of "New Israel." Insofar as such use was legitimate (that is, warranted by Scripture), he argued, the title applied to all "saints" or believers. But as colonists of America, or as citizens either of England or of New England, no one could claim separate distinction under the title. Furthermore, with regard to their conviction that a special providence was involved in establishing the preeminence of New England, and in vouchsafing there a continual fulfillment of prophecies, Williams remonstrated: "If this be not to pull *God* and *Christ* and *Spirit* out of Heaven, and subject them unto *naturall*, sinful, inconstant men, . . . let Heaven and Earth judge."[60]

With great acuity Williams's remarks expose the incantatory or magical element in Puritan typology: its impulse to compel "God and Christ and Spirit" out of Heaven and thus harness sacred energies for human enterprises. From the perspective of the present study the error of this attempt resides not in its imputedly manipulative character—which in any case can be otherwise construed (for example, as a synergism in which human agency participates or cooperates with divine providence).[61] Rather the problem resides in the repeated (if not inevitable) failure of civil society to configure itself genuinely as an antitype of a biblical figure. (Recall here Reinhold Niebuhr's thesis of Christian realism in *Moral Man and Immoral Society*.[62]) It may be existentially impossible for a collective to become an authentic biblical exemplar, an unambiguous example for faith. That was certainly the view of Roger Williams, who declared, without qualification and categorically: "*America* (as *Europe* and all nations) lyes dead in sin." To Williams's assertion of orthodoxy Bercovitch adds the clarification that as individual, anonymous, or generic Christians, "the Saints in New England, like all saints, belonged to the figural Israel. But *as New Englanders* they could no more arrogate that identity to themselves than could their neighbors, the Indians (Williams called *them* Americans), or the inhabitants of the Old World they had abandoned."[63]

Behind this typological insistence lies a theological distinction with consequences for the ethnographic comparison of Puritan American and African American typological traditions. It is the classical Western theological distinction between natural and supernatural existence. Natural existence in the classical view is inherently ambiguous; only the transcendence of temporal and material conditions will permit the manifestation of unambiguous life. This principle is found in various forms in the Christian gospels, but its most graphic articulation is found in St. Augustine's *The City of God* (413–426). Augustine insisted that the earthly church or people of God is inevitably mixed during its temporal existence. No matter how mightily a community strives for righteousness, it remains composed of two groups: people of the city of God, *civitas dei*, and people of the city of the devil, *civitas diaboli*. Never is it possible under the conditions of existence to separate the two, and so be able to declare that a living community fully constitutes an exemplar of the faith. In Roger Williams's more graphic terms: "Nature knows no difference between [people] . . . in blood, birth, bodies. . . . [Any land is] a ship at sea with many hundred souls . . . papists and protestants, Jews and Turks . . . whose weal and woe is common."[64]

Yet this view of reality, which recognizes the union of opposites in concrete experience, is also consistent with the conjurational worldview of African American folk tradition. That worldview has already been introduced with the concept of the world as a pharmacosm in which tonic and toxic aspects coinhere in the same phenomena. I will return to this issue as part of a philosophical treatment of wisdom perspectives in black culture and in the analysis of the biblical figure of Apocalypse. Here it is sufficient to posit a difference in worldview between the two traditions: a Puritan American tradition that projects its figural identity and destiny monolithically, as an unambiguous representation of biblical exemplars, and an African American tradition that is cognitively predisposed to view its reality (its tortuous past, blighted present, and foreseeable future) as simultaneously tonic and toxic.

Notes

1. Martin Buber, *Kingship of God*, 3rd ed., trans. Richard Scheimann (New York: Harper & Row, 1967), pp. 105–6.
2. Puritan theology in early America understood the type-antitype dyad to be prophetically or divinely constituted, "the God who predetermines history having lent it this power." As quoted by Ursula Brumm, *American Thought and Religious Typology* (New Brunswick, N.J.: Rutgers University Press, 1970), p. 23. On dyads and "figural prophecy" see the definitive study by Erich Auerbach, "Figura," in *Scenes from the Drama of European Literature*, ed. Wald Godzich and Jochen Schulte-Sasse (Minneapolis: University of Minnesota Press, 1984), pp. 29, 56, 72.
3. See Sacvan Bercovitch, *The Puritan Origins of the American Self* (New Haven: Yale University Press, 1975), and Conrad Cherry, ed., *God's New Israel: Religious Interpretations of American Destiny* (Englewood Cliffs, N.J.: Prentice-Hall, 1971). On "typological ethnogenesis" see Werner Sollors, *Beyond Ethnicity: Consent and Descent in American Culture* (New York: Oxford University Press, 1986), pp. 50, 57.

4. Sacvan Bercovitch, *The American Jeremiad* (Madison: The University of Wisconsin Press, 1978), pp. 132–76.
5. For example, see Evan M. Zuesse, *Ritual Cosmos: The Sanctification of Life in African Religions* (Athens: Ohio University Press, 1979). On the primacy of ritual as a "continuity" (Raboteau) between African and Afro-American cultures see Dona Richards, "The Implications of African-American Spirituality," in *African Culture: The Rhythms of Unity*, ed. Molefi Asante and Kariamu Asante (Westport, Conn.: Greenwood Press, 1985), p. 213.
6. These are the terms of John Middleton's distinction between the "magico-religious," and the mythological or cosmological, in *Magic, Witchcraft, and Curing*, ed. John Middleton (Garden City, N.Y.: The Natural History Press, 1967), p. ix.
7. See Johan Huizinga, *Homo Ludens: A Study of the Play Element in Culture*, trans. R.F.C. Hull (New York: Roy Publishing, 1950).
8. Victor Turner, *Dramas, Fields, and Metaphors: Symbolic Action in Human Society* (Ithaca, N.Y.: Cornell University Press, 1974), p. 274. Cf. also the treatment of *communitas* in his *The Ritual Process: Structure and Anti-Structure* (Ithaca, N.Y.: Cornell University Press, 1969), pp. 96–113.
9. Kenneth Burke, *The Philosophy of Literary Form: Studies in Symbolic Action* (New York: Vintage Books, 1957), p. 87.
10. Zuesse, *Ritual Cosmos*, p. 7.
11. Jahnheinz Jahn, *Muntu: The New African Culture* (New York: Grove Press, 1961), p. 219.
12. This is a formulation that Burke borrowed from John Crowe Ransom. Kenneth Burke, *The Philosophy of Literary Form: Studies in Symbolic Action* (New York: Vintage Books, 1957), p. 100.
13. Albert J. Raboteau, "The Black Experience in American Evangelicalism: The Meaning of Slavery," in *The Evangelical Tradition in America*, ed. Leonard Sweet (Macon, Ga.: Mercer University Press, 1984), p. 197.
14. David Walker, *David Walker's Appeal* (1829), ed. Charles M. Wiltse (New York: Hill & Wang, 1965), p. xiv.
15. Robert Alexander Young, "The Ethiopian Manifesto," in *A Documentary History of the Negro People of the United States*, ed. Herbert Aptheker (Secaucus, N.J.: Citadel Press, 1974), p. 91.
16. Burke, *The Philosophy of Literary Form*, p. 6.
17. James H. Cone, *God of the Oppressed* (New York: Seabury Press, 1975). This is perhaps the author's most definitive statement of black theology as a liberation theology that draws upon the indigenous sources of black religious experience and cultural productions—sermons, songs, and stories—as distinguished from academic or political formulations.
18. Henry Highland Garnet, "An Address to the Slaves of the United States of America," in *Black Nationalism in America*, ed. John H. Bracey, August Meier, and Elliott Rudwick (Indianapolis: Bobbs-Merrill, 1970), p. 71 ff. Alongside David Walker's "Appeal" this is the most provocative and incendiary antislavery statement in American history that features as well a powerful use of biblical (specifically Exodus) figuralism.
19. Timothy L. Smith, "Slavery and Theology: The Emergence of Black Christian Consciousness in 19th Century America," *Church History* 41 (1972): 498.
20. Buber, *Kingship of God*, p. 106.
21. In this connection the black theologian and pastor Olin P. Moyd has defined redemption in dual terms: not only liberation but also corporate formation. Within black Amer-

ican religious tradition, Moyd claims, "redemption has not been limited to liberation from oppression; it has also meant the divine process of being formed into a community where love and justice would prevail." By this dual emphasis Moyd intends to restore the full sense of the term as explicative of Afro-Christian faith. That full meaning has been reduced, on his view, in conventional theologies that limit redemption to salvation from sin and guilt. On the other hand the corporate or "confederation aspect" of the term has been neglected even by contemporary black theologians. Engaging in his own project of hermeneutic retrieval, therefore, Moyd wants to restore the "salvation-from-oppression dimension of redemption which has been neglected by Euro-American theologians" while reclaiming the element of corporate redemption found in "folk religious expressions which has been overlooked by Black theologians." Finally, Moyd suggests that this more adequate and wholistic sense of redemption has provided the theological rationale for moral action and ethical reflection in black religion and culture. Olin P. Moyd, *Redemption in Black Theology* (Valley Forge, Pa.: Judson Press, 1979), pp. 16, 33, 28.

22. Werner Sollors, *Beyond Ethnicity: Consent and Descent in American Culture* (New York: Oxford University Press, 1986), p. 42.

23. Ibid., p. 50; emphasis mine.

24. Albert J. Raboteau, *Slave Religion: The "Invisible Institution" in the Antebellum South* (New York: Oxford University Press, 1978), p. 311.

25. Bennett continues intriguingly: "What King did now—and it was a high achievement—was to turn the Negro's rooted faith in the church to social and political account by melding the image of Gandhi and the image of the Negro preacher and by overlaying all with Negro songs and symbols that bypassed cerebral centers and exploded in the well of the Negro psyche." Lerone Bennett, Jr., *What Manner of Man: A Biography of Martin Luther King* (Chicago: Johnson Publishing Co., 1964), p. 72.

26. Martin Luther King, Jr., "I See the Promised Land," in *A Testament of Hope: The Essential Writings of Martin Luther King, Jr.*, ed. James Melvin Washington (New York: HarperCollins Publishers, 1991), p. 286.

27. Raboteau, *Slave Religion*, p. 251. Raboteau cites the Harding comment as follows: Vincent Harding, "The Uses of Afro-American Past," In *The Religious Situation*, ed. Donald R. Cutter (Boston: Beacon Press, 1969), pp. 829–40. On Afro-American "symbolic reversals" see Lucius T. Outlaw, "Language and Consciousness: Towards a Hermeneutic of Black Culture," *Cultural Hermeneutics* 1 (1974): 403f.

28. John Howard Yoder, "Exodus and Exile: The Two Faces of Liberation," *Cross Currents* (Fall 1975): 299 f. Yoder's own reflections on corporate formation follow: "Peoplehood is not the product of liberation; peoplehood with a history and a trust in the God who has led the fathers is prior to liberation. This has implications for contemporary thinking. . . ." Ibid., p. 303.

29. St. Clair Drake, *The Redemption of Africa and Black Religion* (Chicago: Third World Press, 1970), p. 41.

30. Wilson Jeremiah Moses, "The Poetics of Ethiopianism: W.E.B. Du Bois and Literary Black Nationalism," *American Literature: A Journal of Literary History, Criticism, and Bibliography* XLVII:3 (November 1975): 412, 414. Moses, *Black Messiahs and Uncle Toms: Social and Literary Manipulations of a Religious Myth* (University Park: Pennsylvania State University Press, 1982), p. 160.

31. Gayraud S. Wilmore, *Black Religion and Black Radicalism: An Interpretation of the Religious History of Afro-American People* (Maryknoll, N.Y.: Orbis Books, 1983), p. 121.

32. Significantly linking black creative "powers" to the two major black monarchies of antiquity, Du Bois lamented that "these powers of body and mind have in the past been strangely wasted, dispersed, or forgotten. The shadow of a mighty Negro past flits through the tale of Ethiopia the Shadowy and Egypt the Sphinx. Throughout history, the powers of single black men flash here and there like falling stars, and die. . . ." W.E.B. Du Bois, "Of Our Spiritual Strivings," *The Souls of Black Folk* (New York: New American Library, 1969), p. 46.

33. Cf. Chancellor Williams, *The Destruction of Black Civilization: Great Issues of a Race from 4500 B.C. to 2000 A.D.* (Chicago: Third World Press, 1974), and Melville Herskovits, *The Myth of the Negro Past* (Boston: Beacon Press, 1958), and George G. M. James, *Stolen Legacy* (San Francisco: Julian Richardson & Associates, 1976).

34. Wilmore, *Black Religion and Black Radicalism*, p. 37.

35. Herbert Aptheker, ed., *A Documentary History of the Negro People in the United States*, vol. 2, *From the Reconstruction Era to 1910*, 5th ed. (New York: Citadel Press, 1951), p. 713.

36. Ibid.

37. Arthur H. Fauset, *Sojourner Truth: God's Faithful Pilgrim* (1938; reprint, New York: Russel Co., 1971), p. 175.

38. W.E.B. Du Bois, *The Souls of Black Folk* (New York: New American Library, 1969), p. 47.

39. Aptheker, *A Documentary History*, pp. 725–26. Aptheker's citation locates the Douglass excerpt in an address delivered before the American Social Science Association, September 12, 1879, and published in Boston in the *Journal of Social Science* XI (May 1880): 1–35.

40. The full passage reads, in folk dialect: "Honey, de white man is de ruler of everything as fur as Ah been able tuh find out. Maybe it's some place way off in de ocean where de black man is in power, but we don't know nothin' but what we see. So de white man throw down de load and tell de nigger man tuh pick it up. He pick it up because he have to, but he don't tote it. He hand it to his womenfolks. *De nigger woman is de mule uh de world* so fur as Ah can see." Zora Neale Hurston, *Their Eyes Were Watching God* (1937; reprint, New York: Harper & Row, 1990), p. 14. Emphasis mine. On the black woman as the (related) biblical figure of "Hagar-in-the-wilderness," see Delores S. Williams, *Sisters in the Wilderness: The Challenge of Womanist God-Talk* (Maryknoll, N.Y.: Orbis Books, 1993), pp. 22–29, 117–19, 196–98.

41. Drake, *The Redemption of Africa*, pp. 54, 61 f.

42. Ibid., p. 71.

43. Harold Dean Trulear, "The Lord Will Make a Way Somehow: Black Worship and the Afro-American Story," *The Journal of the Interdenominational Theological Center* XIII:1 (Fall 1985): 101. Cf. also James Cone, "The Story Context of Black Theology," *Theology Today* XXXII:2 (July 1975): 145.

44. Erich Auerbach, *Mimesis: The Representation of Reality in Western Literature*, trans. William Trask (Garden City, N.Y.: Anchor Press/Doubleday, 1952), p. 14 f. Cf. Auerbach, "Figura," pp. 11–76.

45. James Wm. McClendon, Jr., *Biography as Theology: How Life Stories Can Remake Today's Theology* (Nashville, Abingdon Press, 1974), p. 90.

46. Ibid., p. 93.

47. See my treatment of "ethnography as a source of theology" in Theophus H. Smith, "The Biblical Shape of Black Experience: An Essay in Philosophical Theology," pp. 27–35. Ph.D. dissertation, Graduate Theological Union, 1987.

48. James H. Cone, *For My People: Black Theology and the Black Church* (Maryknoll, N.Y.: Orbis Books, 1984), p. 63.
49. Bercovitch, *The Puritan Origins*, p. 35 f.
50. Ibid., p. 114.
51. Harding, "The Uses of the Afro-American Past," pp. 829–40.
52. In contrast to the range of cross-cultural studies in anthropology and ethnography, Wills attests that "there has been relatively little attention, within the context of American religious history, to the encounter of blacks and whites. This encounter has indeed often not been thought of as a central theme in our nation's *religious* history but it surely is. . . . Puritanism is studied so carefully largely because of its apparent impact on our collective sense of purpose and value. Studies of pluralism recurrently acknowledge that our pluralism has not characteristically involved sheer diversity but variety within a shared framework. It is precisely in the context of the encounter of blacks and whites, however, that our efforts to forge a common culture have been most severely tested." David W. Wills, *Black Apostles at Home and Abroad: Afro-Americans and the Christian Mission from the Revolution to Reconstruction*, ed. David W. Wills and Richard Newman (Boston: G. K. Hall, 1982), pp. ix, xi–xii. Paul L. Holmer, *The Grammar of Faith* (New York: Harper & Row, 1978).
53. This is Stephen Manning's expression in his essay "Scriptural Exegesis and the Literary Critic," in *Typology and Early American Literature*, ed. Sacvan Bercovitch (Amherst: University of Massachusetts Press, 1972), p. 58.
54. Cf. Jon Butler, *Awash in a Sea of Faith* (Cambridge, Mass.: Harvard University Press, 1990) on the prevalence of spiritualism in nineteenth-century American life. Although the theoretical basis for this hypothesis cannot be elaborated here, it is evident that it presupposes a rethinking of Puritan typology, and indeed the formation of American culture at large, from an Africanist or an African Americanist perspective.
55. Bercovitch, *The American Jeremiad*, p. 114 f.
56. Michael Wigglesworth, "God's Controversy with New England," in Cherry, *God's New Israel*, p. 44.
57. Donald G. Mathews, *Religion in the Old South*, in Chicago History of American Religion Series, ed. Martin E. Marty (Chicago: Chicago University Press, 1977), p. 191.
58. Bercovitch, *American Jeremiad*, p. 176. Cf. Bercovitch, *Puritan Origins*, p. 108, and Sollors, *Beyond Ethnicity*, pp. 42–50.
59. Bercovitch, *American Jeremiad*, p. 93 f.
60. Bercovitch, *Puritan Origins*, p. 110. Commenting on the intensity of Williams's theological censure, Bercovitch adds that he "debated with the baffled outrage of a man who just could not fathom his opponents' obstinacy. To some degree, we sense the same tone in the arguments of many others at home and abroad."
61. This perspective abandons the discredited view of magic as manipulative versus religion as petitionary or supplicative. As I indicate in the Introduction, one person's magic is another person's religion: that is, one's own manipulation can always be construed as supplicative and someone else's petition as manipulative. Hence the distinction collapses into ambiguity.
62. Reinhold Niebuhr, *Moral Man and Immoral Society* (New York: Scribner's, 1932).
63. Bercovitch, *Puritan Origins*, p. 110.
64. Ibid.

Chapter 14

Of the Black Church and the Making of a Black Public

Eddie S. Glaude Jr.

In his seminal work *The Negro Church in America*, E. Franklin Frazier declared that the black church in the United States was a nation within a nation. For Frazier, this phrase captured the role of the church in the lives of African Americans, how it circumscribed social activity and provided vocabularies for moral and ethical judgments. The black church was in fact the primary vehicle for the exercise of black agency, a place where the humanity of America's darker "citizens" was acknowledged and basic human aspirations for self-determination were achieved.

The role Frazier assigned the black church harkened back to 1849, when in describing black religious practices Martin Delany stated that "among our people generally, the church is the Alpha and Omega of all things. It is their only source of information—their only acknowledged public body—their state legislature ... their only acknowledged advisor."[1] Delany went on to criticize the black church in particular and Christianity in general for teaching what he perceived as subservience in the face of oppression. He wanted to break the hold that a certain reading of Christianity had on the minds and lives of African Americans: a naive pacifism or quietism when confronted with the evil of white supremacy. Yet Delany recognized within this institution the workings of black civil society. He acknowledged the importance and centrality of black religious practices, in spite of their obvious limitations, in the social and political lives of African Americans.

We can see the statelike function of the black church in Delany's characterization. Just as modern nation-states provide a lens through which their citizens can view themselves and others, the black church in the nineteenth century provided "vocabularies of agency" for its members and nonmembers, tools needed to make choices with regard to their fellows and environs. These vocabularies, ways of describing, evaluating, and acting, contributed to talk about what constituted justice, the good life, and communal flourishing, and as such provided the terms for social and political critique.

Drawing on these vocabularies, Theodore Wright in 1836 proclaimed that "the slave has a friend in heaven, though he may have none here." Wright, a black pastor of a Presbyterian church in New York City, went on to say:

> There the chains of the slave will be knocked off, and he shall enjoy the liberty of the sons of God. We know that the influence of prejudice, and the love of power and avarice will oppress us here, and exclude us from privileges, on account of our color; but we know it will not exclude us from heaven, for God is no respecter of persons. Though we must be despised here, we know that our Redeemer liveth. We trust in God, who is able to save all that come unto him. God speed you on! Go forward in his name, and you will prosper.[2]

Wright seemingly falls into the trap of a glib hope for a pie-in-the-sky heaven. But he draws on a fundamental precept of black Christianity, "God is no respecter of persons," and he locates God's transforming power—all are equal before his eyes—in the lives of black people: "I listen, and I think I hear the trumpet of jubilee sounding—I hear the voice of emancipation proclaiming to my down-trodden brethren, to stand up and be free!"[3]

Like the modern state, black churches also helped organize the resources of the life of the community through their institutional mechanisms and administration. We need only think of the numerous activities occurring under their roofs to get a sense of the churches' function in the lives of antebellum blacks. Schools, mutual aid societies, athletic clubs, libraries, insurance companies, and general social events were housed in black churches and captured by the churches' commitments to the Christian gospel as well as by the institutional arrangements of those commitments. Such activities aided in the construction of common ideological and cultural beliefs that were incorporated in the everyday doings and sufferings of its members and, to a great extent, its nonmembers.

As W.E.B. Du Bois noted in his classic text *Souls of Black Folk*, the black church stood as "peculiarly the expression of the inner ethical life of a people in a sense seldom true elsewhere."[4] That is to say, the black church was more than an institutional reflection of a community of the faithful. Rather, it embodied a basic reality: sustained black cultural solidarity in the context of a racist culture. Black Christians attended church not only to worship God but also to commune with similarly situated selves, "to share and expand together the rich heritage they have inherited,"[5] and to continue the development of a self-consciousness vital to potential problem-solving activity. In other words, black churches were not confined simply to their formal roles. Instead, their institutional boundaries were quite "elusive, porous, and mobile,"[6] such that the churches' sphere of influence extended well beyond their institutional walls to the public imaginings of antebellum black America.

Publics and the Black Church

But the analogy with the modern state only takes us so far. The church stood not only as the institutional organization of the community's resources and a kind of ideological and cultural common ground for everyday interaction or association among antebellum blacks. These institutions, as Evelyn Brooks Higginbotham rightly notes, were also "mediating structures,"[7] standing between black individuals and the racial state. As the U.S. nation-state, through its institutions, policies, conditions, and rules, as well as the social relations in which each of these were embedded, circumscribed the lives of black individuals and communities,[8] black religious institutions, through their ability to sustain numerous newspapers and other activities as well as their ability to render black experiences in the dramatic terms of the Bible, rearticulated the racial practices of the U.S. racial state and helped construct a collective identity.

These churches were organized publics consisting of "all those who [were] affected by the indirect consequences of transactions to such an extent that it [was] deemed necessary to have those consequences systematically cared for."[9] Black religious institutions were, to a large extent, the consequences of the efforts of members of the community to address their common ills. They resulted from the organization of publics for the protection of the interests shared by their members. The first edition of the African Methodist Episcopal discipline (1817), particularly the historical preface, suggests this point:

> We have deemed it expedient to have a form of Discipline, whereby we may guide our people in the fear of God, in the unity of the Spirit, and in the bonds of peace, and preserve us from that spiritual despo-

tism which we have so recently experienced—remembering, that we are not to Lord it over God's heritage, as greedy dogs, that can never have enough; but with long suffering, and bowels of compassion, to bear each other's burdens, and so fulfill the law of Christ.[10]

My description of black religious institutions as publics follows Higginbotham's brilliant analysis in *Righteous Discontent*. Higginbotham stresses "the public dimension of the black church, not the religious dimension of the public realm."[11] This reversal shifts the emphasis from the prevalence of religious symbols and values in the organization of our social lives and in our political languages to the different ways public spaces have been "interpolated within black religious institutions."[12] For example, in the preface to the AME discipline, the reality of race and its consequences were accounted for within the very effort to formulate rules and structure for the new church; the two went hand-in-hand. Such riffs (interpolating activity) on white Christianity (in this instance, white Methodism) and its complicity with slavery and white supremacy signaled a particular manner of engagement in public spaces in that black publicity always entailed the real possibility of personal humiliation or group sanction, since the organization of public spaces in the United States reflected the nation's racial attitudes. Black churches, then, were the sites for a public discourse critical of white supremacy and the American nation-state as well as the spaces for identity construction. Here African Americans engaged in public deliberation free of humiliation (at least by whites). They also spoke in a self-determining voice, defining a cultural identity through a particular idiom and style.

Unlike Higginbotham's, however, my understanding of publics draws on the work of John Dewey, not Jürgen Habermas. I am suspicious of Habermas's reliance on the Kantian picture of enlightened public opinion, and more inclined to favor beginning with what Dewey sees as characteristic forms of human action and their consequences. For Dewey, human beings, like all natural objects, exist in association with their kind. But unlike other objects, human beings act with intelligence, that is, they act in light of perceived consequences and efforts to control how those consequences might affect them.

The consequences of actions are thought of, in this view, in two ways: (1) those that affect only the individuals directly engaged in a particular transaction—these are private transactions—and (2) those with indirect consequences, that is, consequences affecting individuals not immediately concerned with the transaction. These are public only in the sense that the indirect consequences are "extensive, enduring, and serious."[13] A public, then, is formed when some association perceives a common interest in an effort to avoid some consequences and secure others; it "is created through an act of shared practical judgment."[14]

In this light, the actions of American whites in relation to African Americans had far-reaching consequences—extensive, enduring, and serious consequences indirectly affecting individuals not immediately concerned in the "transaction." Put simply, the existence of slavery and the reality of race affected all persons physically marked as black, slave or free! These realities led to the organization of African Americans, specifically those in the North who were "free," to deal with the indirect consequences of this associated activity. As such, publics were formed, particularly independent black churches, to respond to the conjoint action of white supremacists with state and ecclesiastical power.

I hasten to qualify this point. I do not want to image the independent black church movement as a complete reaction to white proscription. This would certainly obscure the more positive role it has had in the formation of black communities. I am merely suggesting that the cooperation among black individuals to address the common ills of their lives contributed to the construction of what would become a "national" community, for the conjoint activity of African Americans would not remain simply a reaction to white proscription. "Wherever there is conjoint activity whose consequences are appreciated as good by all singular persons who take part in it," John Dewey writes, "and where the realization of the good is such as to effect an energetic desire and effort to sustain it in being just because it is a good shared by all, there is in so far a community."[15]

With this formulation I am able to evade choosing between two related historiographical tendencies regarding the rise of independent black churches. The emphasis has been either on the story of white proscription, "the conscious exclusion from positions of power of black members in biracial congregations and denominations,"[16] or on the coming-of-age of black communities, that is, black communities becoming fully aware of themselves as distinctive collectivities with particular interests and needs (with separate churches as key components of their infrastructure). Both factors, in my view, are crucial to any adequate understanding of the role of black churches in the development of a national communal and political consciousness among antebellum blacks. We must keep track of both simultaneously, for without both factors at work in our interpretative activity we can lose sight of two important points.

First, if our focus remains only on white proscription, we tend to reduce the importance of the more proactive dimensions of black activism and community-building in the early nineteenth century. In one sense, this view can easily lead to the position that if racism ends, black communities and, in this case, specifically black churches, are no longer justified. Some such argument was made by William Whipper and members of the American Moral Reform Society in the mid-1830s. Here the idea that African Americans view as their responsibility the conservation, transmission, rectification, and expansion of the heritage of values they have received in order that succeeding generations may be assured of a better, more secure future gives way to a preoccupation with the practices of white racists and, in some cases, a facile form of humanism.

Second, if we focus only on a celebration of black cultural independence, then we have a tendency to reify the tools used only in attempts to solve specific social problems. That is, we fail to grasp that the functional adequacy of our concepts must be evaluated in the context of their particular situations. We tend to read too much in the deployment of the language of race and talk of national community. As a result, some theorists find the early nineteenth century filled with black ideologues of nationalism or racial essentialism—both odd descriptions in light of the historical context.

It remains important that we give a full account of the role of white discrimination in the formation of separate black churches, and some very good work has been done in this area.[17] Most of these accounts begin with the November 1787[18] incident in St. George's Methodist Episcopal Church in Philadelphia when several black members and local preachers were pulled from their knees during prayer and told to go to the seats designated for blacks. This incident precipitated the formation of the first two African congregations in the city in 1794, St. Thomas Episcopal Church and Bethel African Methodist Episcopal Church. Richard Allen, one of the key figures in this episode, would later help found the first *national* black denomination,[19] the African Methodist Episcopal Church. This moment, in some ways, is paradigmatic of the formation of separate African churches. We see similar incidents repeated throughout the major cities in the Northeast and along the Atlantic seaboard. As whites refused to share authority with their black members and continued to subject them to various forms of public humiliation (for example, refusing to christen black babies, serving blacks communion only after all whites were served, and denying blacks access to church burial grounds),[20] many African Americans sought to create institutions where they could worship and have fellowship without the burden of white Christian racism. Hence, they organized publics to secure consequences that enabled the possibility of the good life.

In New York City, for example, black Methodists, led by James Varick and Abraham Thompson, formed what came to be known as the African Methodist Episcopal Zion Church after continued conflict over the ordination of black preachers. In a letter to the bishops and preachers of the Philadelphia and New York Conferences, Varick and George Collins listed the major reasons for the formation of the new denomination; most important was the failure of the white church to extend the privileges necessary for black preachers to sustain a "ministry amongst our coloured brethren."[21]

Like the black Methodists, black Baptists faced the insult of white Christian proscription. In Boston, with the support of the predominantly white First and Second Baptist Churches, black Baptists organized the African Baptist Church in 1805 and appointed their pastor, the Reverend Thomas Paul, in 1806. Paul also helped organize the Abyssinian Baptist Church in New York City. Although these churches maintained active relations with white Baptist churches—and, in the case of the Boston congregation, joined the Boston Baptist Association in 1812—they nevertheless came into existence, for the most part, because of the prevalence of discriminatory practices. Elias Smith, a white Baptist minister, wrote of Paul in 1804, "When Thomas Paul came to Boston the Dr. [Samuel Stillman, a Baptist minister] told him it was Boston, and they did not mix colours."[22] This reality of white racial proscription and its consequences compelled African Americans to seek out a space for the free and autonomous worship of God and to secure an institutional setting for the social activity of solving problems confronting their community. To state the point baldly, God and community became by force of circumstance the objects of black Christian commitment in the early nineteenth century.

In one sense, my use of the conjunction *and* understates the extent to which faith in God and obligation to community were inextricably bound together in early nineteenth-century black America. Even as the infrastructures of newly emerging black communities began to settle in places such as Philadelphia and Boston, they were "always already" connected to an enduring and prophetic faith. Prior to the incident in St. George's Church, members of the black community in Philadelphia, with the leadership of Absalom Jones and Richard Allen, had formed a benevolent voluntary association called the Free African Society. Although written in the latter part of the eighteenth century, the society's preamble sheds light on the complex relation between faith and community among antebellum blacks generally.

Whereas Absalom Jones and Richard Allen, two men of the African race, who, for their religious life and conversation have obtained a good report among men, these persons, from a love to the people of their complexion who they beheld with sorrow, because of their irreligious and uncivilized state, often communed together upon this painful and important subject in order to form some kind of religious society, but there being too few to be found under the like concern, and those who were, differed in their religious sentiments; with those circumstances labored for some time, till it was proposed, after a serious communication of sentiments, that a society should be formed, without regard to religious tenets, provided the persons live an orderly and sober life, in order to support one another in sickness, and for the benefit of their widows and fatherless children.[23]

The "secular" aims of the society were framed by the religious faith of its members, however varied their denominational commitments. The organization not only hoped to provide social services and aid for "people of African descent," but the society also offered a moral or normative vision, based in its members' religious faith, for the community itself.[24]

This moral vision can be seen in the work of the African Union Society in Newport, Rhode Island, and similar organizations in Boston, New Haven, or Providence. In these organizations religious commitment and secular aims were rarely thought of separately. The Newport African Union Society, organized in 1780, "by the end of the decade sponsored a unified scheme of emigration with comparable organizations in Boston, Providence and Philadelphia."[25] The society also held religious services in the homes of its members. These societies passed resolutions to regulate the moral behavior of their members, visiting them regularly that they might increase in grace and knowledge and every Christian virtue. They also provided basic services for members and nonmembers. Because most white communities denied African Americans access to cemeteries, many societies owned their own cemetery properties. Some, like the Free African Society in Philadelphia, petitioned the city to designate land for a black cemetery. This social focus stood alongside the religious faith of the membership. Both provided the terms for the moral sense of community and established what Gayraud Wilmore describes as "a pattern of religious commitment that had a double focus: free and autonomous worship in the Afro-American tradition, and the solidarity and social welfare of the black community."[26]

David Walker's address in December 1828 before the General Colored Association in Boston brilliantly exploited this double focus. Walker understood the need for "forming societies, opening, extending, and keeping up correspondences" as a means "to ameliorate our miserable condition,"[27] for the violence of America's racist culture necessitated conjoint action. As Walker put it: "Do not two hundred and eight years of very intolerable sufferings teach us the actual necessity of a general union among us? Do we not know indeed, the horrid dilemma into which we are, and from which, we must exert ourselves, to be extricated?"[28]

The reality or evil of racist violence required faith in God and ourselves. Walker wrote: "It is our duty to try every scheme that we think will have a tendency to facilitate our salvation, and leave the final result to that God, who holds the destinies of people in the hollow of his hand, and who ever has, and will, repay every nation according to its works."[29] Here Walker simultaneously warns white America of its impending judgment and urges black America to action, for God's judgment of nations extends not only to acts of evil but also to submissiveness in the face of evils. African Americans must extricate themselves from their oppression—no one else. Even as some white Americans argue on their behalf, Walker maintained, "we should cooperate with them, as far as we are able by uniting and cultivating a spirit of friendship and of love among us."[30] A crass form of individualism gives way to a communitarian ethic: our duty is not only to ourselves but to the well-being of the community and those like us. Only with this orientation and the will of God, Walker claimed, will the "dejected, degraded, and now enslaved children of Africa . . . take their stand among the nations of the earth."[31]

As the demographics of antebellum black communities changed—with inmigration, the abolition of slavery in the northern states between 1777 and 1818, and the rise of an indigenous black leadership class—the timbre and tone of black self-assertion changed. These communities, by the late 1820s, "resting on a settled infrastructure of numerous benevolent organizations, black churches, residential proximity, and a deep-seated ethos of mutual assistance,"[32] had organized themselves (as evidenced in Walker's address) to speak directly to their circumstances and to envision the good life for all African Americans. Localities attempted to connect with other local communities, and a national imagined community began to take form. Samuel Cornish, a Presbyterian minister in New York City and coeditor of *Freedom's Journal* and editor of its short-lived successor, *The Rights of All*, wrote feverishly in 1829 of such an effort:

> Our general agent whose duty it shall be to continue travelling from one extremity of our country to the other, forming associations com-

municating with our people and the public generally, on all subjects of interest, collecting monies, and delivering stated lectures on industry, frugality, enterprise, etc. thereby [might link] together, by one solid claim, the whole free population, so as to make them think and feel and act, as one solid body, devoted to education and improvement.[33]

Such remarks exhibited an energetic desire and effort to sustain the consequences of a certain conjoint activity because this activity constituted a good shared by all.

Independent black churches stood as the primary institutional representation of this maturation. Through its conception of God, black religious life and its institutions provided support in the face of uncertainty as well as the languages to resist dread and despair. These institutions "embodied an ecstatic celebration of human existence without affirming prevailing reality: rejoicing in the mere fact of being alive yet maintaining a critical disposition toward the way the world is."[34] Black religious life enabled its participants, through faith, to see beyond the opaqueness of their condition in order to create room for the exercise of agency.[35]

The worship ceremonies within most of these institutions—the liturgies, the singing and dancing—invented, maintained, and renewed senses of communal identification that celebrated, even reveled in the uniqueness of black people and their relation to God. We see this most clearly, I believe, in the uses of biblical imagery to explicate the condition of black people in the United States and in the world. Daniel Coker, speaking before an excited congregation on January 21, 1816, about the recent Supreme Court decision in Pennsylvania that freed Bethel Church from Methodist Episcopal control, likened the plight of African American Methodists to that of Jews in Babylon. "The Jews in Babylon were held against their will. So were our brethren," Coker preached. "Those Jews as above stated, had not equal privileges with the Babylonians, although they were governed by the same laws and suffered the same penalties. So our brethren were governed."[36]

This analogy with the Jews of the Old Testament occupied the religious and political imagination of antebellum blacks. The Exodus story, for example, provided a hermeneutic lens to account for their condition and to articulate a faith that God was active in history. The slaves sang:

> God did say to Moses one day,
> Say, Moses, go to Egypt land,

> And tell him to let my people go.
> Canaan land is the land for me,
> And let God's saints come in.

These lines collapsed the past with the present in order that a future might be imagined, for God's activity in history assured African Americans freedom if they comported to his will.

To be sure, black churches provided in the nineteenth century the standards of judgment by which forms of life were critically examined and found wanting. We can think of this as their prophetic dimension. This dimension extended, as I suggested earlier, well beyond the community of the faithful into the social and political domains. Indeed black religious life provided vocabularies for political argument: the images of Exodus, Psalms 68:31, the suffering servant, a grace-centered piety, a concern with human fallenness, rituals of conversion, a persistent focus on evil—all are preoccupations of black religious life and are, subsequently, tools in black political life.

In the South, this biblical language made possible a hope among slaves that God would deliver his chosen people once again and that the evil of slavery would be no more. This sustaining faith, however, evaded or deferred the critical question of the existence of evil: Why did God allow us to suffer? In the North, these vocabularies were tools in the active fight against slavery and racism, providing a language to envision a moral community beholden to certain precepts and a particular way of being in the world. In the case of the slave evangelical in the South, Albert Raboteau suggests, the essence of Christian life was principally liturgical—the ecstatic experience of God's presence, singing, dancing, and shouting were central—whereas the essence of Christian life in the North was ethical, with a stress on education and moral reform.[37] Both nevertheless presupposed a moral community, a certain kind of associated activity intent on securing certain consequences and sustaining them for future generations.

W.E.B. Du Bois and the Problem of Description

Raboteau's distinction helps elucidate the differences in the tone of black evangelical piety in the South and in the North. In some ways, he amends Du Bois's earlier characterization in *Souls of Black Folk*, in which "the inner ethical life" of the church is rendered in rather schematic terms. For Du Bois, Christianity reinforces the passive submission of the slave; it becomes, in light of the persistence of the slave's condition, a form of religious fatalism, and is only transformed with the emergence of a free class of blacks who identified with "the dream of Abolition, until that which was a radical fad in the white North and an anarchistic plot in the white South had become a religion to the black world."[38] In Du Bois's view, black religious life oscillated between a form of deep religious fatalism and a pragmatically driven social ethic, that is, an other-worldly escapism and a this-worldly sense of racial advocacy.

Raboteau's use of liturgy to describe the essence of Christianity in the black South avoids the temptation to characterize black slave piety as necessarily escapist. The context of the slave South constrained certain kinds of actions, particularly open rebellions against the peculiar institution. It does not follow, however, that accommodation to such a brutal context necessarily entailed an internal acceptance of oppression. Indeed, Christian slaves turned to their faith and to biblical narrative to assure themselves of possibility. The slave would sing:

> He delivered Daniel from de lion's den
> Jonah from de belly ob de whale,
> and de Hebrew children from the fiery furnace,
> and why not every man?

Their internal attitudes, as Raboteau puts it, must be distinguished from their external actions, for "the inner world of slaves was the fundamental battleground and there evangelical Christianity served as an important weapon in the slave's defense of his psychological, emotional, and moral freedom from white domination."[39] And if that freedom found its most successful and eloquent expression in the frenzy of black religious practice, then so be it!

We must not conclude, however, that such frenzied action failed to include an ethics. Even as the slaves drew on the story of Exodus to account for their condition and found in Moses' words to the Israelites, "Stand still and see the salvation of God," assurance of eventual freedom, they knew that God's deliverance depended on their actions—how they comported themselves to his will. Put simply, liturgies always entail an ethics: they presuppose a certain way of being in the world and seek to impart that to participants and their activity. Liturgies, of course, do much more than this. My only intention here is to collapse a dichotomy that only takes us so far in understanding black religious practices. The emphasis on ethics *or* liturgy, however useful the word may be in avoiding bad descriptions, obscures the fact that both play a central role in the

South and in the North,[40] that liturgies and other rituals—just as explicit forms of racial activism—articulated early conceptions of the moral community among northern blacks as well as southern.

Raboteau's subtle correction of Du Bois remains important, however, for Du Bois redeployed his use of fatalism and racial advocacy in his analysis of black religion in the post-Reconstruction era. After abolition waned and the "Age of Reaction" swept over the nation, Du Bois maintained, the role of black religion entered a critical stage. First, the close proximity with the values of American democracy, what Du Bois called the "soul-life of the nation," and the tremendous religious and ethical forces moving throughout the nation necessarily affected African Americans. This proximity was overshadowed by the reality of race and its consequences. Black folk, despite America's rapid development, continued to confront the "Negro problem." They had to "live, move and have their being in it, and interpret all else in its light and darkness."[41]

This preoccupation with the problem of race was compounded by the growing pains of the community, that is, problems of family, of the status of women, of the accumulation of wealth, and of developing responses to forms of social deviance. The combination of these concerns, Du Bois wrote, meant "a time of intense ethical ferment, of religious heart-searching and intellectual unrest." He went on to say: "From the double life every American Negro must live, as a Negro and as an American, as swept on by the current of the nineteenth while yet struggling in the eddies of the fifteenth century,—from this must arise a painful self-consciousness, an almost morbid sense of personality and a moral hesitancy which is fatal to self-confidence."[42] The rapidly changing world and the increasing complexity of the black community itself produced what Du Bois believed to be a wrenching of the soul and a sense of bewilderment. He wrote that "such a double life, with double thoughts, double duties, and double social classes, must give rise to double worlds and double ideals, and tempt the mind to pretence or to revolt, to hypocrisy or to radicalism."[43]

An ethical paradox, then, marked the lives of black folk, Christian or not, in the late nineteenth century. Forced to confront the persistence of racial violence, the psychic torment and physical threat, the continued infringement on their rights and ideals, and a public conscience deaf to righteous appeal, African Americans' faith wavered between a sneer, a wail, and mere casuistry. As Du Bois wrote: "The danger of the one lies in anarchy, that of the other in hypocrisy. The one type of Negro stands almost ready to curse God and die, and the other is too often found a traitor to right and coward before force; the one is wedded to ideals remote, whimsical, perhaps impossible of realization; the other forgets that life is more than meat and the body more than raiment."[44] Du Bois mapped this distinction onto the South and the North. Just as the piety of the slave yielded a deep religious fatalism and forms of escapism, the slave's religious commitments and circumstances produced a "culture of dissemblance" and a way of being in the world that nurtured submissiveness and passivity. The North, on the other hand, because of the difficulties of quasi-freedom, wallowed in "radical complaint, radical remedies, bitter denunciation or angry silence."[45]

Sometimes ideal types are useful. They help us organize a crowded conceptual terrain. They tidy things up for us. But, sometimes, ideal types can be too successful; they make things too neat for us. As such, we lose sight of the messiness of human action, the ambiguity that surrounds the moments that most concern us. Du Bois rightly noted that between his two ideal types "wavers the mass of the millions of Negroes," moving from pretence to revolt, from hypocrisy to radicalism and back again. Rigid either-or formulations rarely help us capture this kind of ambiguity and ambivalence. In short, religious feeling in the black South was not simply liturgical or hypocritical, nor was the piety of the North merely ethical or tending toward anarchy. Ambivalence (about America, about themselves), what Du Bois provocatively described as a double life, was definitive of the religious and social experience of antebellum blacks even before the late nineteenth century.

I prefer the phrase "structure of ambivalence"[46] to Du Bois's use of "double life." I am more inclined to think about the ambiguities and ambivalences surrounding African American life in the United States in ways that extend beyond the psychic torment of black individuals. Instead, my use of structures of ambivalence references ambivalence "as a set, with specific internal relations, at once interlocking and in tension." The phrase also refers to a quality of experience, something heartfelt that has the enduring effect of defining a particular moment or period. Adapting Raymond Williams's apt description of structures of feelings, structures of ambivalence can be thought of as "social experiences in solution."[47] As an analytic tool, then, the phrase helps account for the tortuous relation of African Americans to American culture: their lingering sense of being in but not of a nation ambivalent about its own identity.[48]

The relation of black Christianity to Christianity broadly speaking is a case in point. Black evangelicals had to come to terms with the fact that early Christian evangelicalism was, to some extent, complicitous with slavery and white supremacy. Many of its proponents assumed the inferiority of black people. Such beliefs and actions confronted black Christians with a basic dilemma: what meaning could Christianity have for them if the religion was, as it was assumed, a white man's religion? Moreover, black Christians, in reckoning with the dominant form of evil in their lives, had to ask why a just God allowed them to suffer. As African Americans attempted to respond to these heart-wrenching questions, they "developed a distinctive evangelical tradition in which they established meaning and identity for themselves as individuals and as a people."[49] They were Christian but with a difference. American but not quite. Ambivalence marked their relation to a tradition within which they were ensconced and in tension.

This leads me to the first half of the nineteenth century, a period of intense ethical ferment. During this period, African Americans etched in vague outline the parameters of black Christianity, denying "the doctrinal basis of slaveholding Christianity by refusing to believe that God had made them inferior to whites."[50] Moreover, these peculiar Christians elevated their experience to biblical drama, and since God works his wonders in human history, constructed a salvific history in which God was on their side. Daniel Coker in 1810 offered such an account in the appendix of *A Dialogue Between a Virginian and an African Minister.* He drew on 1 Peter 2:9–10: "But ye are a chosen generation, a royal priesthood, and an holy nation, a peculiar people; that ye should shew forth the praise of him who hath called you out of darkness into his marvellous light: which in time past were not a people, but are now the people of God: which had not obtained mercy, but now have obtained mercy."[51] Although Coker and other black Christians concerned themselves with free and autonomous worship, they knew that their efforts extended well beyond the desire for ecclesiastical freedom. Black people were chosen. They were a holy nation, a peculiar people, and God's mercy brought some of them out of the darkness into the light. Those who were free were charged, then, with the moral responsibility to uplift those who were still bound. Independent black churches institutionalized this sensibility, and new figures, forms, and conventions gave it voice.

David Walker's *Appeal*

David Walker's *Appeal to the Coloured Citizens of the World* (1829) stands as a critical indication that new ways of thinking and acting among antebellum northern blacks were forming in the late 1820s. Not only the content of the document but its form heralded a dramatic change in the nature of black public engagement in the North. Walker explicitly called for armed black resistance against the sinful institution of slavery (resistance sanctified by the grace of God) and prophesied America's fall and destruction unless the nation repented for this evil. Walker's *Appeal*, then, was a black jeremiad, that is, a rhetoric of indignation urgently challenging the nation to turn back to the ideals of its covenant. Walker wrote:

> Oh Americans! let me tell you, in the name of the Lord, it will be good for you, if you listen to the voice of the Holy Ghost, but if you do not; you are ruined!!! Some of you are good men; but the will of God must be done. Those avaricious and ungodly tyrants among you, I am awfully afraid will drag down the vengeance of God upon you. When God almighty commences his battle on the continent of America for the oppression of his people, tyrants will wish they never were born.[52]

Wilson Moses suggests that such uses of the jeremiad often represent an early expression of black nationalism, for within the rhetorical form African Americans like Walker "revealed a conception of themselves as a chosen people."[53] (Remember: "the oppression of his people.") Yet the black jeremiad grew out of an ambivalent relation with white evangelical Christianity in the sense that African American uses of the form simultaneously rejected white America and participated in one of the nation's most sacred traditions. The black jeremiad as a rhetorical form ought to be understood as a paradigm of the structure of ambivalence that constitutes African Americans' relation to American culture.

I am particularly interested in the different ways ideas of peoplehood and community obligation are constructed within the rhetoric. Walker, for example, imaged African Americans as a chosen people, but he went beyond the analogy to provide ways to forge a committed and intelligent solidarity to respond to the reality of racism and its consequences. Walker's *Appeal* not only prophesied God's wrath (its particular linkage with the American tradition of the jeremiad), it also proposed to awaken a spirit of inquiry and investigation among antebellum blacks, offered a radically different way of engaging in public deliberation—one grounded in the pain and suffering of experience—and appealed for the moral responsibility of self-determination (if freedom was truly to be acquired and enjoyed). Walker's use of the jeremiad not only urged the nation to turn from sin; he also exhorted African Americans to act intelligently for themselves.

Walker aimed to cultivate among a downtrodden people the ability to ask appropriate questions and to seek answers to them intelligently. The preamble to the *Appeal* states: "But against all accusations which may or can be preferred against me, I appeal to Heaven for my motive in writing—who knows that my object is, if possible, to awaken in the hearts of my afflicted, degraded and slumbering brethren, a spirit of inquiry and investigation respecting our miseries and wretchedness in this Republican Land of Liberty!!!"[54] A critical examination of the experiences of African Americans was necessary for articulating an intelligent course of action in light of the specific realities of race and its consequences. For Walker, blacks were to respond appropriately to what was going on around them in order to secure certain outcomes and avoid others. He aimed to instill in blacks what can be called critical intelligence: an intelligence that was the sum of impulses, habits, emotions, and discoveries that indicated what was desirable and undesirable in future possibilities and that worked ingeniously on behalf of an imagined good for people of African descent.[55]

The first task of the *Appeal*, then, was to make sense of the prevailing discourse of race, which dehumanized African peoples. Walker counted American slavery as one of the most brutal forms of bondage in human history. What distinguished American slavery from all other historical examples was the ideological justification of the institution, which argued that African peoples were not a part of the human family—that somehow these organisms stood between man and ape. Walker wrote:

> I call upon the professing Christian, I call upon the philanthropist, I call upon the very tyrant himself, to show me a page of history either sacred or profane, on which a verse can be found, which maintains, that the Egyptians heaped the insupportable insult upon the children of Israel, by telling them that they were not of the human family. Can the whites deny this charge? Have they not, after having reduced us to the deplorable condition of slaves under their feet, held us up as descending originally from the tribes of Monkeys or Orang-Outangs! O! my God! I appeal to every man of feeling—is not this insupportable? Is it not heaping the most gross insult upon our miseries, because they have got us under their feet and we cannot help ourselves? Oh! pity us we pray thee, Lord Jesus, Master.—Has Mr. Jefferson declared to the world, that we are inferior to the whites, both in the endowments of our bodies and our minds?[56]

Walker understood the need to challenge this notion head-on, and his invocation of Jefferson served to focus his efforts to assess the very peculiar arena within which African Americans were to exercise critical intelligence.

Thomas Jefferson's speculations on black inferiority in the *Notes on Virginia* signaled the beginnings of a significant shift in the racial sentiments of the new nation. The ideological fervor of the American Revolution, which led to widespread condemnation of the institution of slavery, was giving way to the calcification of racial categories. These categories helped define who belonged and who did not. The Naturalization Act of 1790, for example, aided in the effort to consolidate an American national identity as European immigrants were transformed (through national legislation) into free "white" persons. We also begin to see efforts to define the African American slave more clearly as a "living tool, property with a soul."[57] American national identity by the end of the eighteenth century, then, was fast becoming associated with whiteness. And by the time of Walker's *Appeal*, such racial attitudes had hardened, often drawing on Jefferson for their justification.

In 1784 Jefferson wrote that "the blacks whether originally a distinct race, or made distinct by time and circumstances, are inferior to whites both in body and mind." For Jefferson, African Americans had never "uttered a thought above the level of plain narration." He also refused to accept environmental accounts of the differences between the races. Citing the harshness of slavery in classical Greece and Rome, Jefferson maintained that ancient slaves "excelled in science, insomuch as to be usually employed as tutors to their masters," and those who had "were of the race of whites." The condition of slavery, then, was not the determining factor in the present status of African slaves. As Jefferson wrote, "It is not their condition, . . . but nature, which has produced the distinction."[58]

Despite the seeming certainty of this conclusion, Jefferson hesitated. He claimed that such an opinion had to be made with great diffidence. Jefferson realized that his conclusion could easily lead to the degradation of an entire race. So, he concluded that such matters had to be decided by scientific investigation, requiring, as Jefferson put it, "many observations, even where the subject may be submitted to the Anatomical knife, to Optical glasses, to analysis by fire, or by solvents. How much more then where it is a faculty, not a substance, we are examining; where it eludes the research of all senses; where the conditions of its existence are various and variously combined; where the effects of those which are present or absent bid defiance to calculation."[59] Until conclusive evidence could be marshaled, African American inferiority, Jefferson maintained, had to be held as only a "suspicion" rather than a factual proposition.

Walker refused to accept the grounds on which Jefferson and others argued for black inferiority, for the appeal to science or rational deliberation emptied the issue of its moral significance. African Americans could respond to Jefferson on logical grounds, and many did so, but, for Walker, the psychic and physical horror of the consequences of such ideas required a different kind of response: one grounded in the pain and suffering of African Americans. Peter Hinks in his wonderful text *To Awaken My Afflicted Brethren* describes this move as Walker's strategy of emotionalism. On one hand, Walker holds the view that "the hypothesis of black inferiority was first and foremost a moral abomination founded on a vicious racial hatred of blacks by whites and on a desire to make the exploitation of the labor of an already subject people more perfect."[60] The terror of black subordination and its emotional expression was deployed as a counter to the "rational" arguments of white racists. On the other hand, this strategy aimed to affirm the experience of African Americans—to give voice to the terror, Hinks maintains, in order to move black individuals from the psychic havoc an oppressive situation "wrought on them to some new posture of internal coherency and self-respect."[61]

"Emotionalism" is a bad description here. It lends itself perhaps too easily to the idea that Walker's *Appeal* was unreasonably emotive. It is better to read Walker's strategy as an attempt to offer African Americans a new way of engaging in public conversation. Walker refused to believe that public deliberation always proceeded as rational discussion among enlightened subjects, particularly when the discussion had such deadly consequences. For him, rational deliberation about the inferiority of African people was on its face an absurdity. How could one argue rationally with someone who claimed that one lacked reason? Walker's response was not to assume the irrationality of the claim and then proceed to enlighten his mistaken interlocutor. No. A reasonable and appropriate counter, Walker maintained, was an outpouring that called attention to the absurdity of the utterance. Such a response gave powerful voice to matters otherwise considered private and to the fact that African Americans were not dim-witted beasts of burden but rather human beings capable of genuine feeling and of discerning their own interests. As Walker wrote, "You are not astonished at my saying we hate you, for if we are men, we cannot but hate you, while you are treating us like dogs."[62]

Just as Walker rejected a certain way of engaging in public conversation about race, he empowered African Americans to draw on their experience when engaging in public deliberation. The simultaneous doings and sufferings of black folk, for Walker, ought to determine the manner in which they deliberate about their common ills. In other words, the pain and suffering of their experience ought to mark their point of entry in public conversation about matters of race and its consequences. Walker believed that any discussion about race required that the interlocutors confront the true terror the subject called forth, not only the physical pain but the psychic violence of slavery and racial discrimination, both of which, in his view, necessitated conjoint action among black individuals. Walker's *Appeal*, then, belligerently gave voice to a range of emotions and impulses, habits and discoveries that characterized a people experiencing the brutality of slavery and white proscription. Such experiences, he maintained, could be the only basis for argument against the likes of Jefferson (or Henry Clay) and the insidious power of the "American ideology."

Walker believed that one of the real tragedies of slavery and racial discrimination was the extent to which these practices cultivated habits of servility among African Americans. In some ways, the problem Walker confronted was not so much the failure of African Americans to strike the first blow for freedom but, rather, their submission to racial hierarchies and "their consequent belief that they owed all whites certain respectful duties, that they were prevented from perceiving themselves as entitled to freedom and personal empowerment, and thereby seizing it when it was before them."[63] Walker's *Appeal* concerned itself with personality and provocation: a desperate attempt to convince African Americans that they were self-determining agents and that white Americans were not the bearers of freedom (only God assumed this role), and that as agents they must act for themselves and take the responsibility for their lives and their futures.

William James wrote that habits were "the enormous fly-wheel of society, its most precious conservative force." Habits forestalled revolutions, prevented "the hardest and most repulsive walks of life from being deserted by those brought up to tread therein."[64] Habits sanctioned conduct. They reinforced traditional ways of doing things and provided what John Dewey called "the center of gravity in morality" in the sense that our actions are often justified through conformity with "ancestral habit."[65] Walker understood this. The brutality of slavery and life as a humiliated and degraded people left African Americans doubting their worth and dignity. The force of their circumstances cultivated a "death-like apathy" and a habit of "abject servility." Walker's account of the story of the slave woman who helped capture a band of sixty escaped slaves demonstrated the degree to which slavery savaged the black personality.[66] In his view, this woman could not act as a self-determining agent, for she failed to understand herself outside of her relation to white masters. Walker described such actions as a form of servile deceit, born in the entrails of an evil form of life that dehumanized and betrayed African peoples. Such circumstances highlighted "the force of degraded ignorance" and made customary "deceit among us."[67] He aimed to shift the center of gravity from that of abject servility to that of critical intelligence and action. African Americans could not begin to change their condition until "they could acknowledge and describe the conditions and system under which they existed,"[68] and such an effort, in Walker's view, did not "consist in protecting devils."[69]

Walker hoped through his demonization of white slaveholders and racists to provoke blacks to think of freedom apart from white people and to define themselves not by their standards but by the laws of God. He understood, however, that ridding ourselves of the habit of servility required much more. Walker, as Peter Hinks rightly notes, believed that every African American had to experience metanoia, a radical transformation of heart and disposition. Of course, God's presence would precipitate such an event, but Walker went even further. This conversion would begin only when blacks unleashed their anger and expressed in public rage. Walker wrote: "There is an unconquerable disposition in the breast of the blacks which, when it is fully awakened and put in motion, will be subdued, only with the destruction of the animal existence. Get the blacks started, and if you do not have a gang of tigers and lions to deal with, I am a deceiver of the blacks and of the whites."[70] This radical rage would lead to a transvaluation of values. No longer would African Americans define themselves by the standards of whites, and no longer would they "meanly submit to their murderous lashes." Instead, their experience would ground their public conversation; they would speak events unspoken regardless of the feelings of whites. It is important to note that Walker was not advocating a destructive expression of anger. Not at all. His intent was to shift the center of gravity in our morality to a place where our justification for action emanates not from custom or habit but from conscience or some principle of thought. If African Americans were not rageful about their conditions, Walker maintained, then they obviously had failed to analyze and understand the problems of race and its consequences. Expression of rage, then, began the process of purging blacks of the habit of servility (if I can express rage at my tormentor's action, I can rise up against him) and of clarifying the particulars of their miseries and wretchedness.

Walker recognized, however, the tremendous obstacles blocking the way to such a transformation in consciousness. Years of brutal subordination left many African Americans believing that their station in life was to serve white people. Moreover, many white Americans had seemingly lost their capacity to recognize the evil of their actions. As Walker noted, the "avaricious spirit [of white men] and the natural love in them, to be called masters . . . bring them to the resolve that they will keep us in ignorance and wretchedness as long as they possibly can."[71] Radical rage served only to jump-start action in light of the moral imperative to respond to the evil of white supremacy—an evil that often shook the foundations of Walker's faith: "I aver, that when I look over these United States of America, and the world, and see the ignorant deceptions and consequent wretchedness of my brethren, I am brought ofttimes solemnly to a stand, and in the midst of my reflections I exclaim to my God, 'Lord didst thou make us to be slaves to our brethren, the whites?'"[72] Here Walker confronted head-on the particular problem of evil facing African Americans: how to reconcile our present circumstances with our faith in a just God.

His answer drew on the distinctive evangelical tradition of black America and his faith in the capacity of blacks to confront their condition courageously: "When I reflect that God is just, and that millions of my wretched brethren would meet death with glory . . . in preference to a mean submission to the lash of tyrants, I am with streaming eyes, compelled to shrink back into nothingness before my Maker, and exclaim again, thy will be done, O Lord God Almighty."[73] Rage might precipitate a transvaluation of values, but only the will of God could secure the victory. For Walker, the two went hand-in-hand: African Americans could not wait for God to liberate them; they had to act for themselves. But such actions had to emanate from him:

> We believe that, for thy glory's sake,
> Thou wilt deliver us;
> But that thou may'st effect these things,
> Thy glory must be sought.[74]

The great sin of Walker's contemporaries, in his view, was their failure to act intelligently for themselves, and insofar as they failed to do this they failed to act on what God had promised them. Walker stated the point quite directly:

> If you commence, make sure work—do not trifle, for they will not trifle with you—they want us for their slaves, and think nothing of murdering us in order to subject us to that wretched condition— therefore, if there is an attempt made by us, kill or be killed. . . . Look upon your mother, wife and children, and answer God Almighty! and

believe this, that it is no more harm for you to kill a man, who is trying to kill you than it is for you to take a drink of water when thirsty;
in fact, the man who will stand still and let another man murder him,
is worse than an infidel.[75]

In short, Walker believed it was the duty of every black Christian to
fight (even if it meant death) against the scourge of slavery and racial discrimination because submission to such evils was tantamount to a sin
against God.

Walker's *Appeal* illustrates the inseparable linkage between black religious life and black political activity. He even dedicated a number of pages
to extolling the virtues of Bishop Richard Allen, the primary symbol of
the independent black church movement. Walker wrote of Allen "that he
[had] done more in a spiritual sense for his ignorant and wretched
brethren than any other man of colour, since the world began."[76] Like
Allen, he drew on the distinctive tradition of black Christianity and found
the vocabularies to exhort African Americans to freedom. He wrote:
"Though our cruel oppressors and murderers, may (if possible) treat us
more cruel [*sic*] as Pharaoh did the Children of Israel, yet the God of the
Ethiopians, has been pleased to hear our moans in consequence of oppression, and the day of our redemption from abject wretchedness draweth
near, when we shall be enabled, in the most extended sense of the word,
to stretch forth our hand to the Lord our God."[77] This is salvific history
at its best,[78] for the brutalities of African American life are read in relation to biblical narrative, and African Americans are made over in the
image of Hebrew slaves. Walker wrote: "How cunning slave-holders
think they are!!!—How much like the king of Egypt who, after he saw
plainly that God was determined to bring out his people, in spite of him
and his, as powerful as they were. He was willing that Moses, Aaron and
the Elders of Israel, but not all the people should go and serve the Lord.
But God deceived him as he will Christian Americans, unless they are very
cautious how they move."[79] American structures of oppression are understood in relation to the dispositions of a people who have constituted
themselves as a community of the faithful, the chosen people of God. This
sense of being chosen aided in the development of a national consciousness (a sense of being obligated to others who are similarly situated) and
a national mission (the effort to secure some consequences for us and
avoid others).

It also imposed certain constraints on the nature of black associated
activity. The conjoint action of African Americans (and its reliance on

black Christianity) had to offer a moral vision not only for the black nation but for those against whom they struggled. Violent resistance remained a last resort; it was inevitable only if white America failed to live up to the principles of its covenant. In the form of a typical jeremiad, Walker wrote:

> I say let us reason. . . . I speak Americans for your good. . . . And wo, wo, to you if we have to obtain our freedom by fighting. Throw away your fears and prejudices then, and enlighten us and treat us like men and we will like you more than we now hate you. . . . Treat us like men, and there is no danger but we will live in peace and happiness together. For we are not like you, hard-hearted, unmerciful, and unforgiving. . . . Treat us then like men, and we will be your friends. And there is no doubt in my mind, but that the whole of the past will be sunk into oblivion, and we yet, under God, will become a united and happy people.[80]

Walker called on white Americans to humble themselves before God and to live up to the nation's promise. His efforts to exhort African Americans to see their worth and dignity, his aims to provoke this wretched class to act intelligently for themselves remained, in spite of the venom of the *Appeal*, ambivalently tied to "the values of liberty and equality that actually formed the hope that was America."[81] As Walker put it, "This country is as much ours as it is the whites, whether they will admit it now or not, they will see and believe it by and by."[82] For him, African Americans, remade in the image of the Hebrew slaves crying for freedom in Egypt, called the nation back to its principles and in the process defined themselves as a distinct people who were distinctly American.

Notes

1. Delany went on to say that "prayer is a spiritual means used in conformity to the spiritual law, and can only be instrumental in attaining a spiritual end. Neither physical wants, nor temporal demands of man can be supplied by it" in this serial in *The North Star*, 16 February 1849, 2; 23 March 1849, 2; and 13 April 1849, 2.
2. Theodore Wright, "The Slave Has a Friend in Heaven, Though He May Have None Here," in *Proceedings of the New England Anti-Slavery Convention* (Boston: Isaac Knapp, 1836), 20–22; reprint, Philip S. Foner and Robert James Branham, eds., *Lift Every Voice: African American Oratory, 1787–1900* (Tuscaloosa: University of Alabama Press, 1998), 165.
3. Foner and Branham, *Lift Every Voice*, 165.
4. W.E.B. Du Bois, *Souls of Black Folk*, in *W.E.B. Du Bois Writings* (New York: Library of America, 1986), 499.

362 Eddie S. Glaude Jr.

5. Cornel West, "Subversive Joy and Revolutionary Patience in Black Christianity," in *Prophetic Fragments* (Grand Rapids and Trenton: Eerdmans and Africa World Press, 1988), 163.

6. Timothy Mitchell, "The Limits of the State: Beyond Statist Approaches and Their Critics," *American Political Science Review* 85 (March 1991): 81. My thinking in this regard is greatly influenced by the work of Wahneema Lubiano. See her "Black Nationalism and Black Common Sense," in *The House That Race Built: Black Americans, U.S. Terrain*, ed. Wahneema Lubiano (New York: Pantheon, 1997), 232–52.

7. Evelyn Brooks Higginbotham, *Righteous Discontent: The Women's Movement in the Black Baptist Church, 1880–1920* (Cambridge: Harvard University Press, 1993), 8. She draws on the work of Peter Berger and Richard Neuhaus, *To Empower People: The Role of Mediating Structures in Public Policy* (Washington, D.C.: American Enterprise Institute, 1977).

8. This is a shorthand version of Michael Omi and Howard Winant's definition of the racial state in *Racial Formation in the United States: From the 1960s to the 1990s*, 2d ed. (New York: Routledge, 1994), 83–84. They rely on the work of Bob Jessup, *The Capitalist State* (New York: New York University Press, 1982), and Theda Skocpol, "Bringing the State Back In: A Report on Current Comparative Research on the Relationship between States and Social Structures," *Items* 36, nos. 1–2 (1982).

9. Jo Ann Boydston, ed., *John Dewey: The Later Works, 1925–1953*, vol. 2, *1925–1927* (Carbondale: Southern Illinois University Press, 1984), 245–46.

10. *The Doctrines and Discipline of the African Methodist Episcopal Church* (Philadelphia, 1817), 14.

11. Higginbotham, *Righteous Discontent*, 9.

12. Ibid.

13. Boydston, *John Dewey*, 2:314.

14. Matthew Festenstein, *Pragmatism and Political Theory: From Dewey to Rorty* (Chicago: University of Chicago Press, 1997), 85.

15. Boydston, *John Dewey*, 2:328.

16. Will Gravely, "The Rise of African Churches in America (1786–1822): Reexamining the Contexts," in *African-American Religion: Interpretive Essays in History and Culture*, ed. Timothy E. Fulop and Albert J. Raboteau (New York: Routledge, 1997), 136.

17. I am thinking of the work of Albert Raboteau, Will Gravely, Timothy Smith, Lawrence Levine, and a number of other religious historians.

18. I should acknowledge that there is some controversy around this dating. The Gallery incident is now commonly dated sometime in 1792. Albert Raboteau's essay on Richard Allen in *A Fire in the Bones* (Boston: Beacon, 1995) uses the 1792 date. I have chosen to stay with November 1787 because AME church historians have retained this date.

19. I have emphasized *national* here because of the existence of the African Union Church. This denomination tended to be more regional, appearing in Delaware, Pennsylvania, the New York region, and some congregations in the South. But the AME church was the first *truly* national black denomination.

20. Gravely, "Rise of African Churches," 137. Also see John H. Cromwell, "The First Negro Churches in the District of Columbia," *Journal of Negro History* 7 (1922): 65; *"The Negro Pew": Being an Inquiry Concerning the Propriety of Distinctions in the House of God, on Account of Color* (Boston: Isaac Knapp, 1837); B. W. Arnett, ed., *Proceedings of the Semi-Centenary Celebration of the African Methodist Church of Cincinnati, Held in Allen Temple, February 8–10, 1874* (Cincinnati: H. Watkin, 1874).

21. Christopher Rush, *A Short Account of the Rise and Progress of the African American Methodist Episcopal Church in America* (New York, 1843), 60–73; reprint, Milton C. Sernett, ed., *African-American Religious History: A Documentary Witness* (Durham: Duke University Press, 1985), 151.

22. Gravely, "Rise of African Churches," 138; also see Mechal Sobel, *Trabelin' On: The Slave Journey of an Afro-Baptist Faith* (Westport, Conn.: Greenwood, 1979), 265–66.

23. Preamble of the Free African Society (Philadelphia, 1787); reprint, John Bracey, Jr., August Meier, and Elliott Rudwick, eds., *Black Nationalism in America* (Indianapolis: Bobbs-Merrill, 1970), 19–20.

24. This healthy tension between religious commitments and secular aims exposes perhaps an ambiguity in the term *community*. We can think of communities in a descriptive sense. We can describe a range of communities of individuals banded together to secure and avoid particular consequences. Criminal syndicates, gangs, corporate elites, white racists, nation-states can all be described as communities of sorts. But communities not only have a descriptive sense; they also have what John Dewey calls a normative sense. The term describes not only our associations but also the way we *should* associate. Of course, gangs and criminal syndicates are examples of, on one level, highly social behavior, but they are also highly antisocial in other ways, and it is precisely in our concern with the kind of associations we make and sustain that the moral or normative sense of *community* takes on added force.

25. Gravely, "Rise of African Churches," 139; see also Robert G. Sherer, "Negro Churches in Rhode Island before 1860," *Rhode Island History* 25 (January 1966): 9–25; Julien Rammelkamp, "The Providence Negro Community, 1820–1842," *Rhode Island History* 7 (January 1948): 20–33.

26. Gayraud Wilmore, "The Black Church Freedon Movement," in *Black Religion and Black Radicalism: An Interpretation of the Religious History of the Afro-American People*, 2d ed. (New York: Orbis, 1994), 74–98.

27. David Walker, "Address Delivered before the General Colored Association at Boston," *Freedom's Journal*, 19 December 1828; reprint, Bracey et al., *Black Nationalism*, 31.

28. Bracey et al., *Black Nationalism*, 31.

29. Ibid.

30. Ibid., 32.

31. Ibid., 33–34.

32. Peter Hinks, *To Awaken My Afflicted Brethren: David Walker and the Problem of Antebellum Slave Resistance* (University Park: Pennsylvania State University Press, 1997), 91.

33. Samuel Cornish, *The Rights of All*, 18 September 1829.

34. West, *Prophetic Fragments*, 163.

35. Here I am simply echoing the description of Charles Long. His essay "Perspectives for a Study of African-American Religion" remains a critical guidepost for work in African American religious studies. In some ways, we have yet to come close to what he called for in 1971. Reprinted in Fulop and Raboteau, *African-American Religion*, 21–36.

36. Daniel Coker's sermon is reprinted in Herbert Aptheker, ed., *A Documentary History of the Negro People of the United States* (New York: Citadel, 1969), 77.

37. Albert Raboteau, "The Black Experience in American Evangelicalism: The Meaning of Slavery," in *African-American Religion: Interpretive Essays in History and Culture*, ed. Timothy E. Fulop and Albert Raboteau (New York: Routledge, 1997), 99–102.

38. Du Bois, *Souls of Black Folk*, 501.

39. Raboteau, "Black Experience in American Evangelicalism," 100.

40. I do not want to suggest that Raboteau fails to recognize this point: he says very clearly that "other-worldly symbols reflected this-worldly concerns" (100). My only aim here is to lobby for the elimination of the distinction altogether.

41. Du Bois, *Souls of Black Folk*, 501–2.

42. Ibid., 502.

43. Ibid.

44. Ibid.

45. Ibid., 504.

46. I have adapted this phrase from Hortense Spillers, "Moving On Down the Line: Variations on the African-American Sermon," in *The Bounds of Race: Perspectives on Hegemony and Resistance*, ed. Dominick LaCapra (Ithaca: Cornell University Press, 1991), 39–71. She writes that "if by ambivalence we might mean the abeyance of closure, or break in the passage of syntagmatic movement from one more or less stable property to another, as in the radical disjunction between 'African' and 'American,' then ambivalence remains not only the privileged and arbitrary judgment of a postmodernist imperative, but also a strategy that names the cultural situation as a *wounding*" (54). I take Spillers's aim here to extend what can be considered an analytic term of postmodern theory in the direction of the particular experiences of African Americans. To avoid the need for such verbal gymnastics, I simply join Spillers's notion with that of Raymond Williams (a move I think she makes but never explicitly acknowledges). In *Marxism and Literature* (Oxford: Oxford University Press, 1977), Williams defines what he calls "structures of feelings." He writes: "We are talking about characteristic elements of impulse, restraint, and tone; specifically affective elements of consciousness and relationships: not feelings against thought, but thought as felt and feeling as thought: practical consciousness of a present kind, in a living and interrelating continuity. We are then defining these elements as a structure: as a set, with specific internal relations, at once interlocking and in tension. Yet we are also defining a social experience which is still in process, often indeed not yet recognized as social but taken to be private, idiosyncratic, and even isolating, but which in analysis has its emergent, connecting and dominant characteristics, indeed its specific hierarchies" (132). *Structures of ambivalence* means, for me, then, a social experience (that is still in process) characterized by a sense of wounding, of being in but not of a nation that structures the experiences of African Americans.

47. Williams, *Marxism and Literature*, 134.

48. This formulation attempts to include what Cornel West calls the triple crisis of self-recognition, that is, the cultural predicament that "was comprised of African appearance and unconscious mores, involuntary displacement to America without American status, and American alienation from the European ethos complicated through domination by incompletely European Americans." *Prophesy Deliverance! An Afro-American Revolutionary Christianity* (Philadelphia: Westminster, 1982), 31.

49. Raboteau, "The Black Experience in American Evangelicalism," 92.

50. Ibid., 95.

51. Daniel Coker, *A Dialogue between a Virginian and an African Minister* (Baltimore: Benjamin Edes for Joseph James, 1819); reprint, Dorothy Porter, ed., *Negro Protest Pamphlets* (New York: Arno, 1969).

52. *David Walker's Appeal to the Coloured Citizens of the World, but in Particular, and Very Expressly, to Those of the United States of America* (New York: Hill and Wang, 1965), 13.

53. Wilson Moses, "The Black Jeremiad and American Messianic Traditions," in *Black Messiahs and Uncle Toms: Social and Literary Manipulations of a Religious Myth*, rev. ed. (University Park: Pennsylvania State University, 1993), 30–31.
54. *Walker's Appeal*, 2.
55. I adapted the concept of critical intelligence from John Dewey.
56. *Walker's Appeal*, 10.
57. See Charles Mills's *Blackness Visible: Essays on Philosophy and Race* (Ithaca: Cornell University Press, 1998), 7.
58. Thomas Jefferson, *Notes on Virginia*, in *The Life and Selected Writings of Thomas Jefferson*, ed. Adrienne Koch and William Peden (New York, 1944), 138, 139. Also see Winthrop Jordan, *White over Black: American Attitudes Toward the Negro, 1550–1812* (New York: Norton, 1977), 438.
59. Jefferson, *Notes on Virginia*, 141–43; Jordan, *White over Black*, 438–39.
60. Hinks, *To Awaken*, 209–10; my reading of Walker is greatly influenced by Hinks, whose reading of *Walker's Appeal* is the single best interpretation of the document available.
61. Ibid., 211.
62. *Walker's Appeal*, 70n.
63. Hinks, *To Awaken*, 214–15.
64. Quoted in *The Public and Its Problems*, in Boydston, *John Dewey*, 2:335.
65. Jo Ann Boydston, ed., *John Dewey: The Later Works*, vol.7, *1932* (Carbondale: Southern Illinois University Press, 1985), 162.
66. *Walker's Appeal*, 23–27.
67. Ibid., 23.
68. Hinks, *To Awaken*, 224.
69. *Walker's Appeal*, 25.
70. Ibid.
71. Ibid., 61–62.
72. Ibid., 28.
73. Ibid.
74. Ibid., 74.
75. Ibid., 25–26.
76. Ibid., 59.
77. Ibid., xiv.
78. Walker writes of salvific history early on in the *Appeal:* "But has not the Lord an oppressed and suffering people among them? Does the Lord condescend to hear their cries and see their tears in consequence of oppression? Will he let the oppressors rest comfortably and happy always? Will he not cause the very children of the oppressors to rise up against them, and oftimes put them to death? 'God works in many ways his wonders to perform'" (3).
79. Ibid., 66.
80. Ibid., 69–70.
81. Hinks, *To Awaken*, 247.
82. *Walker's Appeal*, 55.

Chapter 15

"Doers of the Word"

Theorizing African-American Women Speakers and Writers in the Antebellum North

Carla L. Peterson

Throughout the nineteenth century a number of black women traveled in the northeastern, mid-Atlantic, and midwestern states, insisting on their right to preach the gospel, to lecture, and to write on such topics as religious evangelicism, abolitionism, moral reform, temperance, and women's rights. Adapting a verse from the Epistle of James to describe their self-appointed cultural mission, they thought of themselves as "doers of the word."[1] In invoking themselves as such, these women recognized the extent to which their efforts to "elevate the race" and achieve "racial uplift" lay not only in their engagement in specific political and social activities but also in their faith in the performative power of the word—both spoken and written. For these and other activists—Sojourner Truth, Maria Stewart, Jarena Lee, Nancy Prince, Mary Ann Shadd Cary, Frances Ellen Watkins Harper, Sarah Parker Remond, Harriet A. Jacobs, Harriet E. Wilson, and Charlotte Forten—speaking and writing constituted a form of doing, of social action continuous with their social, political, and cultural work.

Doers of the Word is an attempt to understand the cultural work of these black women activists. As such, it forms part of the recovery work currently being undertaken by literary critics and historians alike to rediscover and reinterpret the complexities of nineteenth-century African-American culture and in the process shed new light on our present historical moment. More specifically, it takes its place alongside such exemplary scholarship as Dorothy Sterling's *We Are Your Sisters*, Angela Davis's *Women, Race, and Class*, Hazel Carby's *Reconstructing Womanhood*, Joanne Braxton's *Black Women Writing Autobiography*, Claudia Tate's *Domestic Allegories of Political Desire*, and Frances Smith Foster's *Written by Herself*. Its point of departure lies in the premise that resistant "civil rights movements" are not a modern phenomenon but can be traced at least as far back as the early nineteenth century, and that investigations of African-American culture in the "free" North provide an important counterweight to the more numerous histories of Southern slavery, where power relations between blacks and whites took on a highly specific and codified configuration. In particular, the study seeks to recover from scholarly neglect the contributions made by black women to racial uplift efforts in the North from the antebellum era through Reconstruction, to analyze the role of gender (as well as class and religion) in the construction of ideologies of black cultural nationalism during this period. Its goal is to enlarge our historical understanding of nineteenth-century black resistance movements by supplementing the existing scholarship on Frederick Douglass, David Walker, Henry Highland Garnet, Martin Delany, and other male figures with an examination of the role of black women in these movements.[2]

To analyze the cultural production of these women, I emphasize at the outset the need to ground literary scholarship in historical specificity. I would argue that since so much of our history has yet to be recovered, we are not yet in a position to theorize in a totalizing fashion about black literary production, either by constructing a literary canon of masterpiece texts; by formulating a black aesthetic based on the cultural matrix of the blues, the vernacular, or folk expression; or, more narrowly, by insisting upon the existence of a transhistorical black feminist aesthetic. Such theorizing tends to elide historical difference and to underestimate the complexity of African-American experience, thus promoting notions of an essential or authentic racial blackness that misunderstands the ways in which African Americans have been marked not only by the social category of race but also by gender, class, religion, and region.

Historical specificity does not imply, however, a mere devotion to the accumulation and recording of facts for, as Abdul R. JanMohamed and David Lloyd have insisted, the "theoretical and archival work of minority culture must always be concurrent and mutually reinforcing," so that if "archival work is essential to the critical articulation of minority discourse, at the same time . . . theoretical reflection cannot be dispensed with."[3] Archival work enables us to recover the details of a particular period of African-American history—to apprehend the specific circumstances under which African Americans experienced daily life and to reconstruct the various modes of social action and cultural expression through which they sought to counter oppression and empower themselves and their communities. On the basis of such recovery work, we can then attempt to interpret the nature, meaning, and implications of such action and expression—in short, to theorize their significance. Theory is, finally, embedded in archival work from the start since "history" is recoverable only through written texts and artifacts that themselves require interpretation. History is always already constructed and enmeshed in theory.

I begin my study in the early 1830s at the moment when a substantial body of writing by black women first emerged; and I trace this writing through the Reconstruction period in order to examine these women's reactions to the ever-shifting political and social landscape of race and gender relations after the Civil War as well as their expectations of the widened roles they hoped to play in both their communities and the nation at large. To analyze their writings, I have needed to historicize notions of literature and broaden literary study into a larger field of cultural investigation. Indeed, the dominant trend in literary scholarship has been to privilege the slave narrative as *the* African-American literary form of the antebellum period, focusing in particular on Frederick Douglass's 1845 *Narrative* and Harriet Jacobs's 1861 *Incidents in the Life of a Slave Girl.* In such a reconstruction, the slave narrative becomes the metonym for nineteenth-century African-American literary production. As a result, literary criticism of the late twentieth century has come dangerously close to replicating the historical situation of the early nineteenth century in its valorization of those African-American texts produced under the direction of white sponsors for the consumption of a white readership, while marginalizing and even occluding those other forms of narrative writing produced specifically for the black community.

Rather than privilege any one literary form over others and reify early African-American texts into a monolithic literary canon or tradition, I have followed nineteenth-century African-American definitions of what constitutes a literary text. At the end of a chapter entitled "Afro-American Literature" in *The Work of the Afro-American Woman* (1894), Mrs. N. F. Mossell appended a list of publications that juxtaposes slave narratives to sociological texts, fiction, journalism, history, religious studies, poetry, and spiritual autobiographies.[4] This list includes—as does my own study—genres and texts that would be considered either "nonliterary" by modernist criteria, and thus more appropriate to the fields of history or sociology, or "minor" by historical standards, and thus unworthy of serious attention. Mossell's inclusions thus sharply underscore the political significance of modernist disciplinary/aesthetic exclusion: the erasure from scholarly investigation of "minority" texts considered insufficiently "important" or "beautiful" by dominant cultural standards. Further extending this reevaluation of the African-American literary text, I suggest that literary analysis can no longer merely focus on texts as pure objects but must examine how these were shaped both by a politics of publication (for example, access to mainstream publishing houses, self-publication, white abolitionist patronage) and by a politics of reception (for example, negotiation of multiple audiences, audience constraints).

Such revised notions of textuality have led me finally to question the validity of dividing historical event from literary account as separate objects of scholarly investigation, the one pertaining to fields within the social sciences, the other to literary criticism. In my work I seek to bridge the disciplines of history, literary criticism, and anthropology by building upon Foucault's interdisciplinary model of discourse. For Foucault, discourse is above all a practical strategy designed to overcome the distinction between idea and action in historical study. It represents, quite generally, a means of constituting and producing social knowledge. Following his own formulation, it is a field of knowledge "made up of the totality of all effective statements (whether spoken or written), in their dispersion as events and the occurrence that is proper to them."[5] Discourses, then, are not simply verbal utterances but are constituted by social practices that themselves include institutions, their sites and modes of operation, forms of subjectivity, and power relations, as well as their enunciation.

Working with such notions from an explicitly feminist perspective, my study seeks to define and analyze the discourse of Northern African-American women from approximately 1830 to 1880 as generated both from within their culture and as a response to the dominant discourses of racism and sexism. In so doing I remain fully aware of the constructed nature of my narrative, that my attempts at historical reconstruction are grounded, in Donna Haraway's terms, in a "partial perspective" offering "situated knowledges."[6] My "partial perspective" is revealed from the outset in the initial series of questions that I ask about these African-American women and their literary production: What empowered them to act, to speak out, and to write? From what particular site(s) did they carry out such activities? What are the different power relations embedded in the different modes of acting, speaking, and writing, and how did these black women negotiate these relations? How might one distinguish between their social action and its literary representation?

From my "situated" location, I have been struck first of all by the limitations of current theory and its vocabulary to analyze the cultural production of black women. If indeed "all the women are white, all the blacks are men, but some of us are brave," how can the "brave" be conceptualized and with what terminology?[7] To answer this question we need, on the one hand, to examine the working relationship between black men and women, to analyze the ways in which they were on many occasions mutually supportive in their racial uplift efforts yet antagonistic on others. On the other hand, we must also assess the degree to which, given their racial difference, communication was possible between black and white women, and to which, even in the absence of direct contact, these women might have shared similar cultural values. To talk about the "brave" remains a complex task, however, for the very use of the term opens onto indefiniteness and multiplicity rather than neat categorization, and points toward an idea of "selfhood" that can be articulated only with difficulty. Accompanied by neither noun nor adjective that would specify it, the term *brave* forces us to recognize the extent to which sociological categories have reified notions of subjectivity and to rethink the ways in which these might be utilized, in the process dismantling binary modes of thought and throwing traditional systems of difference into crisis. Following Nancy Hewitt, we might instead think of the subject as a *compound* "composed of elements that are chemically bonded to each other, the composition of each being transformed so that the original components can no longer be separated from each other."[8]

I suggest at the outset that the "brave" who form the subject of this book worked and wrote from positions of marginality, from social, psychological, and geographic sites that were peripheral to the dominant culture and, very often, to their own. This notion of marginality is, however, as problematic as that of the brave, for, if positions at the center tend to be fixed, such is not the case for locations on the periphery, which can move and slide along the circumference. Indeed, the black women I study repeatedly shifted approaches, strategies, and venues as they sought to achieve their goals of racial uplift. Furthermore, we must be wary of constructing a fixed binary that opposes and hierarchizes center and margins, for such positionings are conceptualized, to return to Haraway's terms, only from "partial" and "situated" perspectives. Finally, we must be careful not to fetishize positions on the margins as "pure" spaces of "radical openness and possibility" but must recognize that "margins have been both sites of repression and sites of resistance."[9] Indeed, margins are often uncomfortable places; as the lives of African-American women, past and present, exemplify, they can be sources of horrifying pain, generators of unspeakable terrors, particularly in their exploitation of the black female body.

African-American Local Place in the Antebellum North

How can we begin, then, to conceptualize African-American culture in the antebellum North? We have long recognized the ways in which dominated peoples have often found their national history distorted, hidden, or even abrogated by imperialist-colonial forces and have needed to disrupt hegemonic notions of history and their place in them in order to initiate historical reconstruction from their own perspective. The line "time broadens into space" by the Australian poet Les Murray further suggests the extent to which such peoples have not been able to take place for granted and how, in fact, conditions of colonization, both internal and external, have equally foregrounded the category of space.[10] In the process, geography becomes of central importance, and what Edward Said has asserted as paradigmatic for externally colonized peoples is equally pertinent to the history of African Americans:

> [What] radically distinguishes the imagination of anti-imperialism . . .
> is the primacy of the geographical in it. Imperialism after all is an act
> of geographical violence through which virtually every space in the
> world is explored, charted, and finally brought under control. For
> the native, the history of his/her colonial servitude is inaugurated by
> the loss to an outsider of the local place, whose concrete geographi-
> cal identity must thereafter be searched for and somehow restored . . .
> historically and abductively from the deprivations of the present.[11]

If the local place is initially recoverable only through the imagination, the natives' ultimate goal is, of course, its actual restoration.

For nineteenth-century African Americans, this local space was double. It was, on the one hand, that place in Africa, before the Middle Passage, from which they or their forebears had been kidnapped but to which they for the most part did not wish to return, except perhaps through imaginative speculation. On the other hand, it was also that place in the United States—South or North—which functioned as what Foucault has called a "disciplinary partitioning" within a "carceral continuum," an enclosed panoptic space by means of which the dominant U.S. culture marked the exclusion of African Americans (as well as other racial and ethnic minorities) in order to keep them under constant surveillance, discipline them, and produce "docile bodies."[12]

If, from the point of view of those in power, such a panoptic space was designed to subjugate and police the Other, from the point of view of this

Other it eventually came to constitute "home." Foucault's vision of modern disciplinary society is presented mainly from the perspective of those in positions of authority. My study asks whether it is possible to imagine a scenario whereby the incarcerated could escape, and perhaps even return, the gaze of their wardens; undo the dominant culture's definitions of such binary oppositions as order/disorder, normal/abnormal, harmless/dangerous; break down those boundaries separating the one from the Other; and in the process create a space that they could call home. In seeking to answer this question, I remain mindful of the fact that home is never natural or safe; it is always grounded in a material situation that is subject to change and involves a complicated working out of the relationship between personal identity, family, and community that challenges the very notion of these entities as "coherent, historically continuous, stable."[13]

The panoptic space allotted to nineteenth-century African Americans in the free North was anything but mechanistically organized. The vast majority lived in urban environments—cities like Philadelphia, Boston, New York, Salem, and Rochester—which, under pressure from emerging Jacksonian commercial and manufacturing capitalism, had been reduced to near chaos. Social and economic mobility, foreign immigration, religious upheavals all contributed to an unprecedented degree of transience and fragmentation within, and between, cities. While their African-American inhabitants constituted a distinct social entity determinedly seeking to re-create a local place for themselves, they nonetheless remained a heterogeneous and shifting group, as did their experiences; such diversity undermines any essentialist notions of blackness that we might be tempted to construct.

In analyzing this African-American population I identify four social spheres through which it carried out its activities: the domestic, ethnic community, ethnic public, and national public spheres.[14] The heterogeneity of the black community manifested itself in a number of ways, for example, in a division between freeborn and slave-born inhabitants, persons of Northern and Southern origins, dark- and light-skinned individuals. Such divisions tended ultimately to sort themselves out along class lines. The elite, exemplified by Sarah Parker Remond, Charlotte Forten, and even Frances Ellen Watkins Harper, was generally composed of a freeborn, Northern-rooted, and light-skinned population, who had achieved a high degree of literacy. Its men found steady employment as small business owners and craftsmen, or, less frequently, as professionals, principally ministers (Richard Allen, Daniel Payne), teachers (William Watkins), and doctors (William Wells Brown, Martin Delany); some were even independent businessmen (Paul Cuffe, James Forten, John Remond). As James Horton has shown, these men aspired—often unrealistically—to incorporate the dominant culture's ideology of true womanhood into its social code and thereby privatize its women. As the century progressed, this elite increasingly withdrew from participation in Baptist and Methodist religious practices in order to affiliate with the more sedate black Episcopalian and Presbyterian churches. In contrast, the black subaltern class, of which Sojourner Truth and Jarena Lee were members, was composed primarily of unskilled laborers, the men employed as sailors, waiters, or mechanics, the women as domestics and laundresses. Less literate, this group was rooted in oral and folk culture and formed the bedrock of Methodist and Baptist churches.[15]

While such internal stratification was real enough, African-American elite and subaltern classes nonetheless formed a loosely knit cultural group; as Gary Nash has noted, "the lines that separated [their] cultural expressions . . . were never tightly drawn."[16] In fact, these black urban communities represented what Stallybrass and White have called a "hybrid place" in which categories usually kept separate—high and low, native and foreign, polite and savage, sacred and profane—commingle and result in cultural forms perceived as grotesque by the dominant culture.[17] Hybridity may be evidenced in the very notion of a black elite; for while its members did achieve high social positions as well-respected leaders of their community, their economic and occupational status was often disproportionately lower. Furthermore, many religious and cultural practices, which were themselves adaptations of Africanisms to North American black urban life, could on occasion bring together elite and subaltern classes—the antiphonal choral singing of religious worship, variants of the John Kunering ritual and the Congo dance, the parades of kings and governors on election day, the preparation and consumption of stews and other foods.[18]

If the principles of hybridity upon which these black urban communities were based were inexplicable to the dominant culture in their disruption of fixed hierarchies and binary oppositions, to their own members they were readily comprehensible as necessary strategies for self-empowerment, community building, and the construction of home. African Americans needed to resist, and to adapt themselves, not only to the forces of white racism but also to a growing capitalist economy in which wealth was increasingly concentrated in the hands of a small number of manufacturers who controlled the wage labor of an urban workforce composed of native whites, European immigrants, and blacks. At the very bottom of this workforce, black men and women strove to transform their marginal status into a source of strength, to achieve social and economic autonomy by circumventing capitalist structures and holding on to precapitalist forms of behavior. Urban blacks thus sought to engage in skilled crafts and trades in which in-house production or self-employment would be possible, in the process offering service to the black community rather than a white clientele.[19] Outside of work, community members came together in voluntary benevolent associations—mutual aid societies, orphanages, almshouses—designed to succor those in need.[20] In the domestic sphere, finally, living arrangements reflected an adaptation of African family patterns; households were based not primarily on nuclear family structures but rather on larger domestic networks that often included nonkin members, for example, boarders who were gradually incorporated into the household and contributed to its maintenance.

Within this black urban population, however, the elite did separate itself out to some degree, working, speaking, and writing from within the ethnic public sphere—a set of broader institutions designed to provide intellectual and political leadership to the African-American population as a whole. Although these institutions were located primarily in the North, they were conceived as national since they were dedicated to the national interest of all African Americans. One such institution was black Masonry, founded in 1784 with the opening of Boston's African Lodge No. 459 under the direction of Prince Hall, who insisted that the Masonic principles of charity be extended among blacks to encompass both local community service and broader antislavery work.[21] Of equal importance was the church, in particular the African Methodist Episcopal (AME) Church formed as a separate black discipline by Richard Allen in 1816 as an outgrowth of the Free African Society that had been organized in 1787 after he and Absalom Jones quit Philadelphia's Saint George's Methodist Church in protest over its discriminatory practices.[22] In 1831 Richard Allen was also instrumental in initiating the convention movement through which African Americans came together annually to debate public civic issues of critical importance to their welfare—for example, the abolition of slavery, the petitioning for civil rights, the establishment of vocational and other schools, strategies to combat job discrimination, the desirability of emigration. Rivaling the convention movement was the American Moral Reform Society that brought together the New York and Philadelphia leadership between 1835 and 1842.[23]

At about the same time that the black leadership began organizing its annual conventions, William Lloyd Garrison's antislavery movement was gaining momentum. Integrated from the outset, it included black men like Charlotte Forten's uncle, Robert Purvis, and Shadd Cary's father, Abraham Shadd, both of whom took part in the formation of the American Anti-Slavery Society in December 1833. Black men were also active members of many of the society's affiliates, the Massachusetts, New York, and Pennsylvania Anti-Slavery Societies, for example; in addition, several women's auxiliaries, such as the Philadelphia and the Boston Female Anti-Slavery Societies, were also organized around these male societies. The existence of such affiliate groups gave impetus throughout the 1830s to the formation of all-black antislavery societies in many smaller communities, Rochester and Geneva, New York; Troy, Michigan; and Lexington, Massachusetts, for example; yet these never converged to form a separate national organization.[24] Finally, but by no means least important as a vehicle for self-representation, the African-American press was inaugurated with the publication of Samuel Cornish and John Russwurm's *Freedom's Journal* in 1827, followed, among others, by the *Colored American*, Douglass's *North Star*, *Frederick Douglass' Paper*, and *Douglass' Monthly*, Shadd Cary's *Provincial Freeman*, and, on the eve of the Civil War, the first black monthly magazine, Thomas Hamilton's *Anglo-African Magazine*, which was eventually superseded by the *Weekly Anglo-African*.

Returning to Foucault's notion of discourse, what must be emphasized here is the centrality of these institutions—in particular the national institutions—to the reproduction of African-American social, cultural, and literary knowledge in the nineteenth century. In his analysis of antebellum American society, Alexis de Tocqueville had already pointed to the great significance of "associations" in U.S. democratic life. Later twentieth-century critics such as Antonio Gramsci and Benedict Anderson have further underscored the importance of institutions in the struggle of subaltern classes to resist hegemonic control and of emerging nationalist movements to forge national consciousness. Although institutions are frequently viewed as cumbersome bureaucracies that stifle individual initiative and inhibit social change, they have often provided subordinated groups with a means to power: they create organized consent among their members by means of specific cultural, social, and intellectual activities; they work to promote the welfare of the population as a whole over that of specific individuals or groups; they encourage the careful planning of resistance strategies; they make public and thus more effective hitherto privately held sentiments. In particular, both de Tocqueville and Anderson emphasize the importance of the newspaper as an institution that connects people by articulating a sameness of purpose and providing a common means of

376   *Carla L. Peterson*

executing designs. Thus, the newspaper, and other cultural forms as well, helps create "imagined community." For, if it is impossible for each member of the nation to know all the other members, these vehicles now make possible that "in the minds of each lives the image of their communion," a communion "conceived as a deep horizontal comradeship."[25]

African-American Discourse in the Antebellum North

I would argue that nineteenth-century African-American literary production—both spoken and written—had its origins not only in the white abolitionist movement that underwrote the publication of slave narratives but also in the national institutions of the black elite that addressed a specifically black audience. Through these organizations, the elite worked to construct a program of "racial uplift" that sought to raise the masses to its own social and cultural level as well as to theorize issues of black nationality. It came to conceptualize local place in terms of both the black community itself and the nation as a whole, demanding equal civil and political rights for all African Americans. Some social historians have argued that this agenda was threatened from the outset by divisions within the black elite as well as by its social ideology that sought merely to replicate the values of the hegemony and assimilate into white middle-class culture.[26] Indeed, this racial uplift program encouraged the elite self-consciously to assert its social distance both from the "degraded" Northern subaltern class of unskilled and illiterate laborers and from Southern slaves, to articulate its aspirations to middle-class status by means of improved education and acceptance of Euro-American standards of civilization, and to proclaim its adherence to the dominant culture's ethic of hard work, self-help, and moral purity.

Yet to critique this ideology of racial uplift as bourgeois or conservative is to misunderstand the dynamics of social change under conditions of internal (or external) colonization. Frantz Fanon, for example, has written of the need for a "revolutionary elite who have come up from the people" to acknowledge its estrangement from the masses before joining with them to undertake their political education, "opening their minds, awakening them, and allowing the birth of their intelligence."[27] Moreover, not only did the black elite seek to uplift the subaltern class, it also recognized the imperative need for racial solidarity: "Identified with a people over whom weary ages of degradation have passed," wrote Watkins Harper in 1857, "whatever concerns them, as a race, concerns me."[28] Finally, if this elite's assimilationist ideology was on one level complicitous with the dominant culture, on another level it sought to subvert this culture, condemning its failure to uphold its stated ideals and asserting the African American's right to both political freedom and cultural distinctiveness. Indeed, W.E.B. Du Bois was later to characterize such racial uplift work as a "determined effort at self-realization and self-development despite environing opinion," and to argue that these early leaders had in fact inaugurated a new period in African-American history in which "the assertion of the manhood rights of the Negro by himself was the main reliance" and the single most important goal "ultimate assimilation *through* self-assertion, and on no other terms."[29]

Given the fact of internal colonization and of the irretrievable loss of local place in the Old World, these early African-American leaders were only too well aware of their deracination and of the consequent need to come to terms with their Americanness and incorporate it into their lives. We can again turn to Fanon for an acute analysis of the problematics of defining a national culture once the impossibility of returning to a utopic precolonized condition and of claiming an originary folk culture has been acknowledged: "We must not therefore be content with delving into the past of a people in order to find coherent elements which will counteract colonialism's attempts to falsify and harm. . . . A national culture is not a folklore, nor an abstract populism that believes it can discover the people's true nature. . . . A national culture is the whole body of efforts made by a people in the sphere of thought to describe, justify, and praise the action through which that people has created itself and keeps itself in existence."[30]

Such notions of cultural hybridity were already fully articulated in the writings of Maria Stewart. As early as 1831, she openly lamented the fall of "poor, despised Africa" once "the seat, if not the parent of science, . . . the resort of sages and legislators of other nations," praised the rise of American civilization, and urged its imitation by African Americans: "I see [the American people] thriving in arts, and sciences, and in polite literature. Their highest aim is to excel in political, moral, and religious improvement. . . . The Americans have practiced nothing but head-work these 200 years, and we have done their drudgery. And is it not high time for us to imitate their examples, and practice head-work too, and keep what we have got, and get what we can?" Yet at the same time her writings exude a strong revolutionary note as she repeatedly invoked the Old Testament rhetoric of prophecy to chastise America for its oppression of blacks, envisaging its destruction at the hands of God and predicting the resurrection of the African race as recorded in Psalm 68: "'Ethiopia shall again stretch forth her hands unto God.'"[31]

Literary production like that of Maria Stewart may thus be seen as an important part of the self-empowerment and community-building strategies of the African-American elite. Yet if black leaders strove through writing to implement the stated objective of *Freedom's Journal*—"We wish to plead our own cause"—they also discovered that writing gave rise to complex problems of commodification. Indeed, the very act of authorship could at times separate black writers from their broader community, constituting them as a distinct class that sought to speak not only for itself but also for the subaltern, and thereby working to some extent against community cohesiveness. Furthermore, these writers often found it difficult to depend on a black readership and patronage exclusively and were consequently obliged to write under the aegis of white sponsors and to accede to the inevitable constraining presence of a white audience that might be indifferent or even unsympathetic to their needs. Finally, African-American literary production was vastly complicated by the dominant culture's market economy, which sought to regulate the production and dissemination of literary texts. Although the history of African-American publication in the antebellum period is difficult to reconstruct, available information suggests that the primary venues for publishing were self-publication, publication by a white abolitionist press (in particular that of Garrison's *Liberator*), publication in Britain, and lastly, publication by mainstream U.S. houses that generally remained reluctant to place black authors on their lists.

Given this disruptive potential of writing, what kind of literary discourse could nineteenth-century African-American writers invent for themselves in their efforts to write racial uplift? One common eighteenth-century myth held that enslaved blacks were but "talking apes" whose ability to speak had become the very cause of their enslavement, in contrast to those left behind in the jungle who had "refrain[ed] from speaking in order to avoid being made slaves."[32] But nineteenth-century African-American literary discourse cannot be dismissed as a mere aping of the dominant discourse that inevitably leads to enslavement to the values of the hegemony. Neither was it simply a version of Foucauldian "counter-discourse" designed to counter the dominant discourse by maintaining while reversing and redeploying the terms, categories, and values of the hegemony.

Aware of the necessity of becoming "producers" rather than remaining "merely, as now, consumers,"[33] African-American writers constructed a productive discourse generated from within the community that borrows the vocabulary and categories of the dominant discourse only to dislocate them from their privileged position of authority and adapt them to the local place.[34] This discourse constitutes, then, a particular form of Stallybrass and White's cultural hybridity, one that, as Homi Bhabha has suggested in another context, effectively deconstructs the dichotomy embedded in the assumption that colonial power manifests itself either in "the noisy command of colonialist authority or the silent repression of native traditions." Indeed, while this African-American discourse appears merely to reiterate the dominant discourse, it in fact disrupts it and "challenges its boundaries" by inscribing both presence and absence in its texts. On the one hand, it introduces what Bhabha has called "denied knowledges" from the native culture into the dominant discourse so as to "estrange" the latter's "basis of . . . authority."[35] On the other hand, it may also configure a silence around the gaps that open up between the "inter/faces of the 'official language' of the text and the cultural difference brought to it" by native tradition.[36] Counteracting the text's tendency toward cultural complicity, such presences and absences work to subvert literary commodification; they constitute, in fact, imaginative re-creations of local place and function as cultural sites of resistance. As Henry Louis Gates has suggested, black texts embody a "black double-voicedness," or "signify," as they repeat texts of the Western literary tradition but with a "signal difference" that resides in the author's evocation of "black" cultural forms.[37] Finally, if such a hybrid discourse is designed to negotiate multiple audiences, it also suggests the possibility of African-American authors' address to an "imagined community" beyond their immediate readership, a community preoccupied with the central task of forging a political and cultural nationality.

The Social Spheres of African-American Women

Within this general context of nineteenth-century African-American discursive practices, how can black women's culture and writing be specified? We need first of all to locate the particular position(s) of black women within Northern urban communities—to examine the different spaces they inhabited, to look at how they crossed social and geographic boundaries and negotiated "private" and "public" spheres. In so doing we must emphasize spatial plurality by remaining attentive to the ways in which the categories of race, gender, class, and culture complicated the politics of location of nineteenth-century black women. From such a perspective of heterogeneity, general paradigms break down; the private-public dichotomy must be adapted to specific historical circumstance. As we shall see, the discourse of these black women constitutes a particular form of hybridity in its disruption not only of the discourse of the dominant culture but also of that of the black male elite.

Historians of the dominant culture have typically located nineteenth-century women within the "private" sphere as opposed to the "public," which remained the province of men. More recently, however, scholars have insisted that this private-public dichotomy is too reductive and needs to be reconceptualized. They point out, first of all, that the private sphere is everywhere infiltrated by the public. Women's duties as laborers in the household, as procreators, and as socializers of children are all carried out in the name of the public interest; they may more properly be termed "domestic" rather than "private." Moreover, in antebellum America the Southern slave household itself defied the ideology of separate spheres as it contained within it aspects of both productive and reproductive relations, regulating both the labor and sexual relations of master and slave classes.[38] Finally, black men in the North obviously could not participate in activities in the national public sphere to the same extent as men from the dominant culture given the limitations imposed on their civil and political rights. Such a constraint helped minimize although it did not eradicate the domestic-public dichotomy in Northern black communities.

Like white women, black women saw "domestic economy" as an empowering cultural model. Yet the domestic sphere of black society cannot be conceptualized in the same way as that of the dominant culture. Indeed, given the economic system that undergirded Northern black communities, as well as the demographic situation of black women—greater percentage than men, low fertility and birthrate—African-American familial life cannot be construed in the same terms as the white middle-class family.[39] We cannot make assumptions about the primacy of the nuclear family nor of women as wives and mothers; we need to think instead in terms of broader domestic networks, both kin and nonkin. In fact, almost all the women studied followed the "anomalous" pattern of late marriage or early widowhood and consequently bore no, or few, children. They were thus freed from many of the domestic obligations that burdened most women, black and white. But, ever aware of the importance of preserving the integrity of black family life and its domestic networks, these black women sought to make of the family a site of cultural resistance. They constitute striking examples of how, to quote Mina Caulfield, "families, generally under the leadership of women, have fought back, defending subsistence production as it becomes more precarious, cementing family bonds and building new networks of mutual support as the old ones come under attack, consolidating and developing cultures of resistance—cultures which, like the role of women and family life itself, have been devalued under imperialist ideology."[40] Thus, Stewart, Prince, and Watkins Harper insisted that black women dedicate themselves to proper household maintenance, child rearing, gardening, diet, and hygiene. Still other women, like Sarah Mapps Douglass, spoke out on issues of women's physiology and anatomy, underscoring the need for black women to care for their bodies.[41]

Furthermore, the activities of black women, like those of black men, extended beyond the family into the ethnic community sphere. Black women joined in female benevolent associations that coexisted alongside similar men's organizations in order to take care of others in the community and, in particular, of each other. They involved themselves in what we could call the politics of domestic economy, which provided a solid base for cooperative community action. Stewart, Prince, Watkins Harper, and Jacobs, for example, devoted themselves to moral reform activities, creating "asylums" to shelter destitute young women, organizing mutual aid societies to succor the needy, or participating in the free produce and temperance movements. Stewart and Forten joined literary societies—the former Boston's Afric-American Female Intelligence Society in 1832, the latter a Philadelphia women's society in 1858—designed to enhance the intellectual and moral quality of black women's lives.[42] Black men, who were themselves deeply engaged in moral reform work, encouraged these benevolent activities, which they saw as necessary to the success of racial uplift. This community sphere thus functioned as an intermediate sphere situated somewhere between the domestic/private and the public. It can be viewed as "public" as it is located outside the "home" and remains preoccupied with the welfare of the general population, but it is also "domestic" in that it represents an extension of the values of "home" into the community; and it is "private" insofar as it is able to remain hidden, abstracted from the gaze of the dominant culture. For nineteenth-century African Americans, this sphere was vital to the preservation of both the bodily integrity and the psychic security of families and individuals.

Finally, many of these black women—Truth, Lee, Stewart, Prince, and Watkins Harper, for example—entered the national public sphere as workers, principally domestics or seamstresses. In this unprotected public sphere, black women suffered indignities and assaults not experienced by their white counterparts. In an autobiographical essay, Remond enumerated the many different places from which black women (and men) were likely to be expelled on account of racial prejudice: "They are excluded from public hotels, . . . omnibus[es], . . . steam-boats . . . places of amusements."[43] As public workers, black women gained little prestige but did achieve economic independence as well as the geographic mobility and physical freedom that would enable them to take part in the public work of evangelicism, abolitionism, temperance, and women's rights. In the postbellum period such activity was expanded to include increased participation in the temperance and women's rights movements as well as vocal support for the Fifteenth Amendment, collaboration with the educational institutions of the Freedmen's Bureau, and, in the case of Truth, lobbying for the granting of western territory to the freed people.

Importantly, however, significant limits *were* placed on black women's activities beyond the community level, in the ethnic public sphere of black national institutions dominated by men of the elite. It is true that several of the women studied here did form close personal friendships with men of this elite who, impressed by the women's extraordinary talent, disregarded the cultural constraints imposed on women's public activities to act as their mentors. Thus, David Walker became Stewart's role model; after his death she praised him as one who "has distinguished himself in these modern days by acting wholly in the defense of African rights and liberty";[44] as bishop of the AME Church, Richard Allen offered Jarena Lee an unofficial preaching role in Philadelphia's churches; Martin Delany was instrumental in helping Shadd Cary shape her ideas concerning political nationhood; Charles Lenox Remond encouraged his sister Sarah's activities as an antislavery lecturer; and, finally, William Watkins proposed a framework of Christian social justice that would later be that of his niece Watkins Harper as well. Nevertheless, these women were officially excluded from those black national institutions mentioned earlier through which men of the elite came together to promote public civic debate on practical issues of racial uplift as well as those more theoretical considerations of black nationality.[45] For example, in the first several years of its existence women were denied membership in the American Moral Reform Society; moreover, women were neither allowed to attain leadership positions in the AME Church nor permitted to voice their opinions at the annual national conventions; finally, considerable opposition was mounted within the black community against Shadd Cary's editorship of the *Provincial Freeman*. In thus restricting the role of black women in the articulation of racial uplift programs, the black male leadership strove, in what it believed were the best interests of the community, to contain heterogeneity, silence difference, and gender blackness as male.

Black Women and Liminality

How, then, could black women enter into the arena of public civic debate? I suggest that they did so by "achieving" an additional "oppression," by consciously adopting a self-marginalization that became superimposed upon the already ascribed oppressions of race and gender and that paradoxically allowed empowerment.[46] In so doing, these women entered into a state of liminality defined, following Victor Turner, as that moment and place in which an individual, separated from society, comes to be "betwixt and between the positions assigned and arrayed by law, custom, convention and ceremonial," and in which the creation of *communitas* becomes possible: "*Communitas* emerges where social structure is not. . . . [I]t transgresses or dissolves the norms that govern structured and institutionalized relationships and is accompanied by experiences of unprecedented potency."[47] From the perspective of the black women studied in this book, these liminal spaces came to function, however temporarily, as their "center," offering them greater possibilities of self-expression as well as the potential to effect social change. Yet even in their marginal positions these women were not purely "outside of" but remained "a part of"; as such they were never fully free from, but remained in tension with, the fixed social and economic male-dominated hierarchies that structured Northern urban life.

For the older generation of women, Truth and Lee, for example, the liminal space they chose to enter was the clearing, the site of religious evangelical activities that had been unleashed by the Second Great Awakening and drew the powerless—women, blacks, rural folk, and all those dislocated by the economic upheaval of the Jacksonian market revolution—to religion as a source of power. In such places social hierarchies of race, class, and gender are overturned and deconstructed as the congregants merge in varying degrees of religious ecstasy with the Godhead. For the somewhat younger women, Stewart, Watkins Harper, Remond, and Shadd Cary, their liminal place became that of the public platform from which they lectured to "promiscuous assemblies," audiences composed of both men and women. As oratory was deemed to be a specifically masculine genre and public speaking an activity proper only to men, these women were charged with unsexing themselves through an unseemly exposure of the female body. White women—Frances Wright, Angelina Grimké, Abby Kelley, Lucretia Mott, to name a few—were also engaged in public lecturing during this period and were equally vulnerable to public scorn and hostility.[48] But these women generally found themselves cushioned by their race, class affiliation, family ties, and secure economic status. In contrast, public speaking often led to greater social and economic uncertainty for black women. In making the decision to engage in such activities, they often left their employment as teachers, seamstresses, or domestics to live on their own, separated from family and community; public lecturing became their chief means of livelihood, frequently rendering them dependent on the generosity of their audiences and hosts. Finally, for almost all the women studied, marginality was engendered by the act of travel in which the mere fact of geographic displacement (as with Lee) or the journey away from "home" to another location (the frontier of Canada for Shadd Cary, the swamps of the South Carolina Sea Islands for Forten) could open up new sites of empowerment or simply challenge the very notion of a stable home for African Americans.

It is important to note, however, that these women often entered the liminal space of *communitas* alone and could remain isolated within it despite the fact that their activities were designed to enhance community welfare. Indeed, these women did not always become part of the *communitas* but rather held an ambiguous insider/outsider status in relation to it. Moreover, if it was the absence of social structure that made *communitas* possible, it was its very existence that enabled black men to organize themselves in the ethnic public sphere. The elite's exclusion of black women from its national organizations, coupled with the women's lack of public power to create similar formal institutions, prevented black women leaders from joining together to form a national political community of their own in the antebellum period.

As Ann Boylan has noted, black women eagerly joined the broad racially mixed antislavery movement, participating "in many Female Anti-Slavery Societies, and in the three Anti-Slavery Conventions of American Women held between 1837 and 1839."[49] Furthermore, a number of the black women under study here were clearly cognizant of each other's cultural work, and their paths did sometimes cross. An 1854 article by Shadd Cary entitled "The Humbug of Reform" contains a reference to a speech given by Sojourner Truth.[50] Given Truth's widespread reputation, most of the other women probably also knew of her public activities; and Truth and Jacobs undoubtedly collaborated in their activities with the Freedmen's Bureau in Virginia during the Civil War. In addition, we know that Stewart and Prince both worshiped at the First African Baptist Church in Boston while Thomas Paul was still pastor there. Watkins Harper and Shadd Cary clearly knew of one another through the intermediary of William Still, met in the late 1850s and probably again in the 1890s at the foundation of the National Association of Colored Women. A mentor-protégé relationship brought Remond and Forten together from approximately 1854 to 1858. Finally, as a leading member of post-Reconstruction Washington D.C. black society, Forten, who by then had married the well-known Presbyterian minister Francis Grimké, was undoubtedly acquainted with Watkins Harper, Jacobs, and Shadd Cary. Watkins Harper mentions Forten in an essay written in the mid 1870s and corresponded with Francis Grimké during the 1890s; Grimké also wrote a moving tribute to Jacobs on the occasion of her death; finally, both Forten Grimké and Shadd Cary attended meetings of the Bethel Literary and Historical Association in the 1880s and 1890s.

As noted earlier, antebellum black women did come together in significant numbers to create their own local organizations—principally literary, antislavery, and mutual aid societies—designed to take care of family and community needs. It is impossible to underestimate the importance of such local associations in helping the development of black women's organizational skills, encouraging self and community empowerment, and validating practical work as an essential component of nation building. Yet in the final analysis the creation of a national network of black women leaders that would allow them as a group to enter into the arena of public civic debate and engage in sustained written production did not occur in the antebellum period. It was not until the Reconstruction period that black women joined the national organizations of black men and white women in significant numbers; and it was not until the early 1880s that they were able to create national organizations of their own that would come to function as their own "home places."

If such liminal spaces functioned as centers of empowerment, however, they also remained sites of oppression, separating the women from their "homes" and "native" communities, forcing an unfeminine exposure of the body, and thus further reminding them of their difference. Indeed, nineteenth-century black women were conceptualized by the dominant culture chiefly in bodily terms, in contrast to middle-class white women whose femininity, as defined by the cult of true womanhood, cohered around notions of the self-effacing body. According to this ideology, white women were to be hidden in the privacy of the domestic sphere, where they were encouraged to develop purity of mind and soul, impose complete emotional restraint on their physical movements through stringent rules of etiquette, and veil their already pale and delicate bodies in clothes that, following the sentimental ideal of transparency, would translate inner purity into outward form.[51] In contrast, the black woman's body was always envisioned as public and exposed. If in Europe this exposed body was caged and subjected to minute scientific inquiry, in the United States it was perceived, at least initially, as an uninhibited laboring body that was masculinized.[52] In descriptions in *Journey in the Seaboard Slave States*, for example, Frederick Law Olmsted emphasized the exposure of the female slave's body: "The dress of most of them was . . . reefed up . . . at the hips, so as to show their heavy legs, wrapped round with a piece of old blanket, in lieu of leggings or stockings. Most of them worked with bare arms, but wore strong shoes on the feet, and handkerchiefs on their heads." Olmsted further noted that no distinction appears to have been made between the "muscular" field work of male and female slaves: "The women . . . were engaged at exactly the same labor as the men; driving the carts, loading them with dirt, and dumping them upon the road; cuffing down trees, and drawing wood by hand, to lay across the miry places; hoeing, and shoveling."[53]

Intimately linked in the white imagination to this masculine labor of slave women were those more feminine forms of work—the reproductive labor of childbirth, the obligation to fulfill the sexual pleasure of slave masters, and the nurturing of the latter's children. In Fanny Kemble's *Journal*, descriptions of the bodily suffering of slave women repeatedly associate the vicissitudes of "hard field work" with those of childbearing, emphasizing in particular "the terrible hardships the women underwent in being thus driven to labor before they had recovered from childbearing"; and an 1861 report commissioned by the federal government and reprinted by Remond noted that "cases occurred where the negress was overtaken by the pains of labour, and gave birth to her child in the field." Much less sympathetic, but perhaps more typical, was Olmsted's conflation of labor and sexuality in his depiction of the sensuality of slave women engaged in field work: "Clumsy, awkward, gross, elephantine in all their movements; pouting, grinning, and leering at us; sly, sensual, and shameless, in all their expressions and demeanor; I never before had witnessed, I thought, anything more revolting."[54] Feminine attributes and functions of the black female body were thus commonly represented in degraded terms as abnormal excessive sexual activity; and, when superimposed on masculine ones, led to the creation of a complexly ambiguous portrait of the nineteenth-century black woman. As a result, the public exposure of black women cultural workers on the margins could only be perceived by the dominant culture, and by a segment of the black male elite as well, as a form of social disorder that confirmed notions of the black female body as unruly, grotesque, carnivalesque.[55] In her 1846 *Memoirs*, for example, Zilpha Elaw recounts a conversation with a minister's wife who "assuming the theologian, reprobated female preaching as . . . disorderly and improper."[56]

Such cultural constructions could quite possibly result in the transformation of the black female subject into an "abject creature" who internalizes the images of herself as dirty, disorderly, and grotesque.[57] Although the writings by, and about, the women studied in this book may at times suggest racial insecurity, they are much more frequently pervaded by portraits of a sick and debilitated body. Indeed, almost all these women were plagued throughout their lives by illnesses that often remained undiagnosed but whose symptoms were headaches, fevers, coughs, chills, cramps, or simply extreme fatigue. In such instances illness may quite possibly have occurred as a consequence of the bodily degradation to which these women were subjected or as a psychosomatic strategy for negotiating such degradation. In either case the black female body might well have functioned as what Elaine Scarry has called the "body in pain," whereby the powerless become voiceless bodies subject to pain and dominated by the bodiless voices of those in power. In her book Scarry enumerates different mechanisms through which the voiceless body of pain can be transformed into a bodiless voice of power: most generally, the human subject seeks to alleviate pain by giving it a place in the world through verbal articulation; in the Judeo-Christian tradition, God authorizes man to divest himself of his body and seek power through the making of material artifacts, including language; in Christian interpretations of death, finally, the resurrection of the soul privileges the verbal category over the material by endowing man with an immortal voice.[58] Similarly, for Kristeva, abjection may be spiritualized by means of the Christian ritual of communion in which "all corporeality is elevated, spiritualized, and sublimated"; but, most importantly, it is "the Word . . . [that] purifies from the abject."[59]

How, then, did nineteenth-century black women social activists conciliate these differing interpretations of the black female body as empowered, on the one hand, and disordered on the other? The need to negotiate between these two extremes was particularly urgent for black female public speakers who offered themselves so vulnerably to the public gaze. In her *Memoirs*, for example, Zilpha Elaw recollected with pain how "the people were collecting from every quarter, to gaze at the unexampled prodigy of a coloured female preacher. . . . I observed, with very painful emotions, the crowd outside, pointing with their fingers at me, and saying, 'that's her,' 'that's her.'"[60] Audience response to Watkins Harper's public lecturing was even more telling, however, in its grotesque evocation of the black woman speaker as variably masculine and painted:

"I don't know but that you would laugh if you were to hear some of the remarks which my lectures call forth," she wrote in a letter to William Still. "'She is a man,' again 'She is not colored, she is painted.'"[61] In this comment the black woman speaker is predictably masculinized, and she is also racialized as "painted." Yet the term "painted" also resexualizes her, and dangerously so, as an actress, and perhaps even a prostitute. In fact, these women lecturers needed in some sense to become actresses in order to negotiate their public exposure in front of "promiscuous assemblies"; and, as we shall see, their acting strategies ranged from deliberate attempts to call attention to the materiality of the black female body in both its productive and reproductive functions in order then to subvert the dominant culture's construction of it (Truth), to efforts to decorporealize the body from the outset and present the self as a disembodied voice (Watkins Harper).

I would argue that from their dislocated and liminal positions these black women ultimately turned to the *literary representation* of self-marginalization—to the writing of self, spirituality, and travel, the reprinting of public lectures, and the creation of fictional worlds—in an attempt to veil the body while continuing their racial uplift activities in the public sphere. In particular, they turned to writing in reaction to, and in tension with, their exclusion from black national institutions. Striving to achieve an empowering narrative authority, they hoped that their writing would both challenge the power of those institutions to which they had been barred access *and* compel these institutions to legitimate their social activism in the public sphere.

My study of African-American women in the nineteenth century is loosely organized around the liminal sites I identified earlier—religious evangelicism, travel, public speaking—as well as the writing of fiction. The discussion of each woman begins with an attempt to narrativize and interpret those important social and biographical facts that might help us better to appreciate her cultural production. It then turns to an analysis of the cultural production itself, whether the speech in its printed form which, although never ascertainable, often sustains the fiction of the actual social exchange, or the written text. Taken together, my analyses suggest the possibility of tracing significant shifts in the use of literary discourses and generic conventions.

I argue that these black women appropriated many different cultural discourses ranging from a reliance on Africanisms to the adoption of standard literary conventions in order to become producers rather than mere consumers of literary expression. In her role as an itinerant lecturer, Truth was not only a Christian "doer of the word" but also a participant in the African belief in *Nommo*, or the Word as the productive life force that brings about generation and change. In addition, Truth employed Africanisms, folk proverbs and sayings, and African-American idioms in her lectures, creating what the dominant culture regarded as a quaint idiosyncratic speech; in fact, however, Truth's speech constitutes a serious political discourse through which she sought to define the specific positionality of nineteenth-century black women.[62] To prophesy the future of both black and white races in America and the role of black women in its making, Lee and Stewart grounded their sermons and spiritual writings in biblical discourse—particularly that of the Old Testament Prophets and the New Testament book of Revelation—producing powerful texts that their readers and audiences, however, often interpreted as mere emotional outbursts filled with undecipherable meanings. Watkins Harper, Forten, and Jacobs appropriated the sentimental discourse that had entered and permeated white women's culture by way of the eighteenth-century European cult of sensibility in order to invoke figures of sentimentality—the African-American slave (man, woman, child, or family), the drunkard husband or father, the seduced woman, the child dying of hunger—that would excite the readers' compassion and move them not to emotional consumption but to productive action. Given the particular social and cultural construction of black women's lives, such writing differed in significant ways from that of black men in its ability to imagine cultural possibilities specifically engendered by women's space and women's work. Finally, in the postbellum period black women sought to take advantage of the expansion and institutionalization of literary culture; and in becoming increasingly involved in the already existing national organizations of black men and white women while gradually creating institutions of their own, they hoped to appropriate new forms of social discourse that would help them further their cultural work.

As these black women narrated their thoughts and experiences, the location and perspective of the narrating *I* in relation to that which is narrated gained particular importance as evidenced by their careful manipulation of point of view, thus demanding from us a critical consideration of genre. Indeed, for these women the question of genre was not so much a choice of literary convention as an epistemological issue: how to represent the relationship of the self to the self and the Other. The only woman unable to author her own life story, Truth was obliged to confide its telling to white women abolitionists whose ethnobiographies construct her as irrecoverably Other. In asserting their desire and ability to narrate their own life stories themselves, Lee, Prince, Jacobs, and Forten wrote spiritual and secular autobiographies as well as journals in which the *I* seeks to narrate itself from its own constructed point of view. In composing travel accounts and ethnographies, Prince and Shadd Cary sought to deflect the public's gaze from themselves in order to represent the Other. Finally, in turning to more explicitly fictional modes and techniques in the 1850s, Wilson, Watkins Harper, and Jacobs created fictionalized versions of both self and Other from multiple perspectives, thereby striving to escape the scrutiny of the dominant culture and achieve perspectives of omniscience denied them in their actual historical moment and place.

Notes

1. Olive Gilbert and Frances Titus, *Narrative of Sojourner Truth* (Boston: Published for the Author, 1878), 250.
2. Since both Mary Ann Shadd Cary and Frances Ellen Watkins Harper published under both their maiden and married names in the antebellum period, I refer to them as Shadd Cary and Watkins Harper. For a recent study of the role of black men in nineteenth-century black cultural nationalism, see Sterling Stuckey, *Slave Culture: Nationalist Theory and the Foundations of Black America* (New York: Oxford University Press, 1987).
3. Abdul R. JanMohamed and David Lloyd, "Introduction," *Cultural Critique* 6 (1986): 8.
4. N. F. Mossell, *The Work of the Afro-American Woman* (Philadelphia: George S. Ferguson Co., 1894), 64–66.
5. Michel Foucault, *The Archaeology of Knowledge* (London: Tavistock, 1972), 27.
6. Donna Haraway, "Situated Knowledges: The Science Question in Feminism and the Privilege of Partial Perspective," *Feminist Studies* 14 (Fall 1988): 575, 581.
7. The phrase derives, of course, from the title of the 1982 book edited by Gloria T. Hull, Patricia Bell Scott, and Barbara Smith (Old Westbury, N.Y.: Feminist Press).
8. Nancy A. Hewitt, "Compounding Differences," *Feminist Studies* 18 (Summer 1992): 318.
9. bell hooks, "Choosing the Margin as a Space of Radical Openness," in *Yearning: Race, Gender, and Cultural Politics* (Boston: South End Press, 1990), 151. See also William L. Andrews, *To Tell a Free Story* (Urbana: University of Illinois Press, 1986), 167–204, for a discussion of the "uses of marginality" by ex-slave narrators.
10. Quoted in Hill Ashcroft, Gareth Griffiths, and Helen Tiffin, *The Empire Writes Back* (London: Routledge, 1989), 34. For discussions of "internal colonization," see Robert Blauner, "Internal Colonialism and Ghetto Revolt," in *Black Society in the New World*, ed. Richard Frucht (New York: Random House, 1971), 365–81, and Gayatri Spivak, "Who Claims Alterity?" in *Remaking History*, ed. Barbara Kruger and Phil Mariani (Seattle: Bay Press, 1989), 274, 278.
11. Edward Said, "Yeats and Decolonization," in *Remaking History*, ed. Barbara Kruger and Phil Mariani (Seattle: Bay Press, 1989), 10–11, 13.
12. Michel Foucault, *Discipline and Punish: The Birth of the Prison*, trans. Alan Sheridan (New York: Vintage Books, 1979), 195–228.

13. Biddy Martin and Chandra Talpade Mohanty, "Feminist Politics: What's Home Got to Do with It?" in *Feminist Studies/Critical Studies*, ed. Teresa de Lauretis (Bloomington: Indiana University Press, 1986), 195.

14. My use of these terms is an amplification of the vocabulary employed by Margaret S. Boone, "The Uses of Traditional Concepts in the Development of New Urban Roles: Cuban Women in the United States," *A World of Women*, ed. Erika Bourguignon (New York: Praeger, 1980), 235–69.

15. Gary Nash, *Forging Freedom: The Formation of Philadelphia's Black Community, 1720–1840* (Cambridge, Mass.: Harvard University Press, 1988), 145–54, 248–53, 260–67; and James Oliver Horton, "Freedom's Yoke: Gender Conventions among Antebellum Free Blacks," *Feminist Studies* 12 (Spring 1986): esp. 69–72.

16. Nash, *Forging Freedom*, 222.

17. Peter Stallybrass and Allon White, *The Politics and Poetics of Transgression* (Ithaca, N.Y.: Cornell University Press, 1986), 27.

18. Nash, *Forging Freedom*, 222; for a full discussion of the continued presence of African-isms in the antebellum North, see Stuckey, *Slave Culture*; and William D. Piersen, *Black Yankees: The Development of an Afro-American Subculture in Eighteenth-Century New England* (Amherst: University of Massachusetts Press, 1988).

19. Nash, *Forging Freedom*, 216–17, 250–53.

20. Leonard Curry, *The Free Black in Urban America, 1800–1850* (Chicago: University of Chicago Press, 1981), 196–215.

21. James Oliver Horton and Lois F. Horton, *Black Bostonians: Family Life and Community Struggle in the Antebellum North* (New York: Holmes and Meier, 1979), 28–31.

22. Carol V. R. George, *Segregated Sabbaths: Richard Allen and the Emergence of Independent Black Churches, 1760–1840* (New York: Oxford University Press, 1973).

23. Howard H. Bell, *A Survey of the Negro Convention Movement, 1830–1861* (New York: Arno Press, 1969). On the American Moral Reform Society, see Julie Winch, *Philadelphia's Black Elite: Activism, Accommodation, and the Struggle for Autonomy, 1787–1848* (Philadelphia: Temple University Press, 1988), 108–29.

24. For an extensive discussion of black abolitionism, see Benjamin Quarles, *Black Abolitionists* (New York: Oxford University Press, 1969).

25. Alexis de Tocqueville, *Democracy in America*, 2 vols. (1835–40; New York: Vintage Books, 1945), 2:109–28; Antonio Gramsci, *Selections from Cultural Writings*, ed. David Forgacs and Geoffrey Nowell-Smith (Cambridge, Mass.: Harvard University Press, 1985), 20–23; Walter L. Adamson, *Hegemony and Revolution* (Berkeley: University of California Press, 1980), 215–22; Benedict Anderson, *Imagined Communities: Reflections on the Origin and Spread of Nationalism* (London: Verso, 1991), chap. 3; ibid., 6–7.

26. See Frederick Cooper, "Elevating the Race: The Social Thought of Black Leaders, 1827–50," *American Quarterly* 24 (December 1972): 604–25.

27. Frantz Fanon, *The Wretched of the Earth*, trans. Constance Farrington (New York: Grove Press, 1968), 200, 197.

28. Frances Ellen Watkins, "The Colored People in America," in *Poems on Miscellaneous Subjects* (Philadelphia: Merrihew & Thompson, 1857), 53.

29. W.E.B. Du Bois, *The Souls of Black Folk* (1903; New York: New American Library, 1969), 84, 86.

30. Fanon, *The Wretched of the Earth*, 233.

31. Maria Stewart, *Meditations from the Pen of Mrs. Maria W. Stewart* (Washington, D.C., 1879), 68, 28, 32, 68.
32. Hester Hastings, *Man and Beast in French Thought of the Eighteenth Century* (Baltimore: Johns Hopkins University Press, 1936), 111.
33. *North Star*, March 23, 1849.
34. I paraphrase here the discussion of colonial discourse from Homi K. Bhabha, "Signs Taken for Wonders: Questions of Ambivalence and Authority under a Tree Outside Delhi, May 1817," *Critical Inquiry* 12 (Autumn 1985): 154–56.
35. Ibid., 154, 160, 156.
36. I paraphrase here the discussion of the function of silences in postcolonial texts in Ashcroft, Griffiths, and Tiffin, *The Empire Writes Back*, 54–55.
37. Henry Louis Gates Jr., *The Signifying Monkey: A Theory of Afro-American Literary Criticism* (New York: Oxford University Press, 1988), 51.
38. For more extensive discussions of these points, see Linda K. Kerber, "Separate Spheres, Female Worlds, Woman's Place: The Rhetoric of Women's History," *Journal of American History* 75 (1988): 9–39; Joan Kelly, "The Social Relation of the Sexes," in *Women, History, and Theory* (Chicago: University of Chicago Press, 1984), 1–18; Elizabeth Fox-Genovese, *Within the Plantation Household* (Chapel Hill: University of North Carolina Press, 1988), 37–99.
39. Curry, *The Free Black in Urban America*, 8–12.
40. Mina Davis Caulfield, "Imperialism, the Family, and Cultures of Resistance," *Socialist Revolution* 2 (1974): 74.
41. Dorothy Sterling, *We Are Your Sisters: Black Women in the Nineteenth Century* (New York: Norton, 1984), 129.
42. See also Dorothy B. Porter, "The Organized Educational Activities of Negro Literary Societies, 1828–1846," *Journal of Negro Education* 5 (October 1936): 556–66; and Sterling, *We Are Your Sisters*, chaps. 9–11.
43. Sarah P. Remond, "Sarah P. Remond," in *Our Exemplars, Poor and Rich; or Biographical Sketches of Men and Women*, ed. Matthew Davenport Hill (London: Cassell, Petter, and Galpin, 1861), 281.
44. M. Stewart, *Meditations*, 67.
45. For other discussions of the exclusion of black women from organizations of the male elite in the antebellum period, see Horton, "Freedom's Yoke," 51–76; and Winch, *Philadelphia's Black Elite*, 121.
46. See Michelle Zimbalist Rosaldo, "Woman, Culture, and Society: A Theoretical Overview," in *Woman, Culture, and Society*, ed. Michelle Zimbalist Rosaldo and Louise Lamphere (Stanford, Calif.: Stanford University Press, 1974), 28–30, for the use of the terms "ascribed" and "achieved" in anthropological discourse.
47. Victor Turner, *The Ritual Process: Structure and Antistructure* (Ithaca, N.Y.: Cornell University Press, 1977), 44–45, 126–28.
48. For a more extensive discussion of white women orators in the antebellum period, see Lillian O'Connor, *Pioneer Women Orators: Rhetoric in the Ante-Bellum Reform Movement* (New York: Columbia University Press, 1954).
49. Ann Boylan, "Benevolence and Antislavery Activity among African American Women in New York and Boston, 1820–1840," in *The Abolitionist Sisterhood: Antislavery and Women's Political Culture*, ed. John Van Horne and Jean Fagan Yellin (Ithaca, N.Y.: Cornell University Press, 1994), 120.

50. Mary Ann Shadd, "The Humbug of Reform," *Provincial Freeman*, May 27, 1854.
51. I paraphrase here the discussions of Barbara Welter, "The Cult of True Womanhood: 1820–1860," *American Quarterly* 18 (Spring 1966): 152; and Karen Halttunen, *Confidence Men and Painted Women* (New Haven, Conn.: Yale University Press, 1982), 71–91, 97.
52. For a discussion of European perceptions of the black female body, see Sander L. Gilman, "Black Bodies, White Bodies: Toward an Iconography of Female Sexuality in Late Nineteenth-Century Art, Medicine, and Literature," *Critical Inquiry* 12 (Autumn 1985): 204–42.
53. Frederick Law Olmsted, *A Journey in the Seaboard Slave States* (1856; New York: Negro Universities Press, 1968), 432, 386–87.
54. Frances Anne Kemble, *Journal of a Residence on a Georgian Plantation in 1838–1839*, ed. John A. Scott (Athens: University of Georgia Press, 1984), 293; *The Negroes and Anglo-Africans as Freedmen and Soldiers*, ed. Sarah Parker Remond (London: Victoria Press, 1864), 12; Olmsted, *Journey in the Seaboard Slave States*, 388.
55. For a discussion of the female grotesque, see Mary Russo, "Female Grotesques: Carnival and Theory," in *Feminist Studies/Critical Studies*, ed. Teresa de Lauretis (Bloomington: Indiana University Press, 1986), 213–29.
56. Zilpha Elaw, *Memoirs of the Life, Religious Experience, Ministerial Travels, and Labours of Mrs. Elaw*, in *Sisters of the Spirit*, ed. William L. Andrews (Bloomington: Indiana University Press, 1986), 147.
57. Julia Kristeva, *Powers of Horror: An Essay on Abjection*, trans. Leon S. Roudiez (New York: Columbia University Press, 1982), 10.
58. Elaine Scarry, *The Body in Pain: The Making and Unmaking of the World* (New York: Oxford University Press, 1985), 233–34, 219.
59. Kristeva, *Powers of Horror*, 120, 23.
60. Elaw, *Memoirs*, 91.
61. Quoted in William Still, *The Underground Railroad* (Philadelphia: Porter and Coates, 1872), 772. White women speakers such as Frances Wright were equally vulnerable to the charge of masculinization.
62. The issue of Africanisms in nineteenth-century African-American cultural life is extremely complex and, to a certain extent, must remain speculative. Historians of slavery have determined that kidnapped slaves came generally from West African and Central African tribes. Although the tribes undoubtedly had their own specific cultural forms, Sterling Stuckey has suggested that the experiences of the Middle Passage and of slavery must be seen as "incubators of slave unity across cultural lines, cruelly revealing irreducible links from one ethnic group to the other"; furthermore: "What we know of slave culture in the South, and of that of blacks in the North during and following slavery, indicates that black culture was national in scope, the principal forms of cultural expression being essentially the same. This is attributable mainly to the similarity of the African regions from which blacks were taken and enslaved in North America, and to the patterns of culture shared more generally in Central and West Africa" (Stuckey, *Slave Culture*, 3, 82).

Part 4

Black Destiny and the End of the Nineteenth Century

Chapter 16

"Ethiopia Shall Soon Stretch Forth Her Hands"

Black Destiny in Nineteenth-Century America

Albert J. Raboteau

Suffering and Destiny

On Sunday, June 4, 1899, the Reverend Francis J. Grimke mounted his pulpit, looked out over his fashionable congregation, adjusted his spectacles, and began to preach the first of a three-part series of sermons. Grimke, a graduate of Princeton Theological Seminary (1878) and pastor of the Fifteenth Street Presbyterian Church in Washington, D.C., was no pulpit-pounding ex tempore preacher. His parishioners were used to the logical, intellectual, and somewhat dry style of his sermons. On this Sunday, especially, he wanted to calm, not arouse, emotion. Nevertheless, behind the measured phrases and calm tone, his feelings showed through. The text that morning was from Acts 7:57, the stoning of Stephen: "Then they cried with a loud voice, and stopped their ears, and ran upon him with one accord, and cast him out of the city, and stoned him." Grimke's topic was lynching.[1]

Between 1889 and 1899, 1,240 black men and women were lynched in the United States, mainly, but not exclusively, in the South. In 1898 alone, white mobs had seized and murdered 104 black people. The victims' names, when known, were tallied month by month by some black newspapers. Their alleged crimes, posted as well, ranged from murder, rape, and arson to theft, "talking back," and "no charge." Accounts of the death of one victim in particular attracted Grimke's notice. Two months earlier, Sam Hose, a black man accused of assault and murder, had been burned alive by a white mob in Newnan, just outside Atlanta, Georgia. According to the newspapers, local whites celebrated the atrocity as a festive occasion. Close to 2,000 citizens, eager to get to the lynching on time, purchased tickets for the short train ride from Atlanta to Newnan. Along the route, women on porch steps waved handkerchiefs at the passing cars. Hundreds arrived too late to watch Hose die, but they pressed on anyway to see the charred corpse and to collect some souvenir of the day's outing. It was April 28, 1899—a Sunday.[2]

Grimke was shocked less by the lynching than he was by the spectators' enjoyment of it. How could people who claimed to be Christian go out and, on the very day of the Lord, do such things? How could the American church "with 135,667 preachers and more than 2,000,000 church members" permit "this awful, black record of murder and lawlessness?" How could it be that at this late date, a whole generation after slavery, blacks were still "a weak and defenseless race" at the mercy of a "Negro-hating nation"?[3] Race relations, on the eve of a new century, were worsening, not improving. Disfranchisement eroded the small gains blacks had won during Reconstruction; unprotected by the federal government, southern blacks had no recourse under a system of laws enforced by local whites.

Confronting the situation of his race in 1899, Grimke, like generations of black pastors before, had to find some meaning, some message of hope in all this misfortune, lest his people despair. "I know that things cannot go on as they are going on now," he told them. "I place my hope not on government, not on political parties, but on faith in the power of the religion of Jesus Christ to conquer all prejudices, to break down all walls of separation, and to weld together men of all races in one great brotherhood."[4] Grimke's claim that the power of Christianity would solve the problem of racism was hopeful, but not naively optimistic. The facts of his own life did not support an easy or simplistic belief in Christian progress. Grimke had learned at an early age the perversity and intransigence of American prejudice. His mother was a slave; his father was his master. After his father died, Grimke's white half-brother attempted to enslave him despite the provisions of their father's will. At the age of ten, Francis Grimke became a runaway slave. Captured several years later, he almost died in a Charleston workhouse where his brother had him jailed as a fugitive. After release, he was sold to a Confederate army officer, whom he served for the duration of the war. Grimke did not find it easy to regard whites as brothers. Even in the church, within his own denomination, he had experienced the spirit of caste in acts of overt discrimination. If Christianity were to triumph, it would be in spite of the American church, which he castigated in print as "an apostate church, utterly unworthy of the name which it bears."[5]

Yet Grimke did not despair. He kept faith in the power of Christianity to change the world, and this belief was validated by other events in his life. After the war, he had been educated and assisted North through the generosity of whites. At Lincoln University and Princeton Seminary, he had been instructed and respected by white professors. Most surprising of all, he had met and formed close family ties with two of his father's sisters, his white aunts, Sarah and Angelina Grimke, of antislavery fame.[6] From Charleston jail to Princeton Seminary, from betrayed brother to beloved nephew, from slave to prominent cleric: the trajectory of Grimke's own life contradicted despair. He was hopeful, then, that the racial situation would, in time, improve, but his hope strained in tension with his alienation from the nation and the church. Hope and alienation echoed through his sermons like some dissonant chord:

> In spite of the shallowness and emptiness and glaring hypocrisy . . . of the church . . . I still believe that Christianity is in this land. Today it is like a little grain of mustard seed, but it has entered the soil, has germinated, and is springing up. It is like the little lump of leaven which the woman hid in three measures of meal: but it has begun to work, and will go on working, diffusing itself, until the whole is leavened. God has promised to give to his Son the heathen for his inheritance, and the uttermost parts of the earth for his possession: and in that promise this land is included. Christianity shall one day have sway even in Negro-hating America; the spirit which it inculcates . . . is sure, sooner or later, to prevail. I have, myself, here and there, seen its mighty transforming power. I have seen white men and women under its regenerating influence lose entirely the caste feeling. . . . Jesus Christ is yet to reign in this land. I will not see it, you will not see it, but it is coming all the same. In the growth of Christianity, true, real, genuine Christianity in this land, I see the promise of better things for us as a race.[7]

In 1899, most white Americans, and some blacks as well, would have rejected Grimke's sermon as bitter and intemperate. He had libeled the nation whose destiny it was to Christianize and democratize the world, an "obligation" already undertaken in the Philippines. Some blacks, like the majority of whites, would have regarded the ideal of racial harmony envisaged in his sermon as a misguided and impractical dream. Blacks had no future in this white man's country and should emigrate back to Africa. A few, very few, blacks would have criticized his slavish allegiance to Christianity. The true religious identity of the black race was either Islam or

Judaism. For that matter, there were those, as there always had been, who found any religion meaningless in the struggle for freedom. But in 1899 the majority of black Americans would have agreed with Grimke that the ultimate solution to the "Negro problem" was to be found in Christianity, a Christianity, to be sure, unlike that of white Americans. With Grimke, they would have believed that blacks someday would take their rightful places in America, but an America transformed from the one they knew. They believed that the solution lay off in the future and were uncertain about the date and method of its achievement. They also believed that the present and the future were shaped by God's providence, in which they were assigned a particular role. In short, they believed that they had a destiny, and in that destiny the suffering of blacks like Sam Hose, and all those who preceded him, had meaning. These beliefs formed a theological tradition developed over the century, and in reaffirming that tradition, Grimke and his congregation reaffirmed the meaning of their lives.

That blacks had a divinely appointed destiny, no black Christian in the nineteenth century denied. But what was it? Since its fulfillment was still to come, who could be certain of its features? By what right did anyone identify this or that event as God's plan for the race? Black spokesmen, mainly clerical but also lay, struggled with this quandary in sermons, speeches, tracts, convention minutes, history books, resolutions, and editorials, from the beginning of the nineteenth century to the end. They searched the Bible, God's word, for signs of his will for the race. To interpret historical events, they looked to the Bible for precedents (or paradigms) and for prophecies (or predictions). They found both in two texts that served as the classical loci for interpreting black history in the nineteenth century: the book of Exodus and Psalms 68:31.

As long as slavery preoccupied the attention of antebellum blacks, the archetypal myth of Exodus dominated their thinking about black destiny. When slavery ended, as it did in the North early in the century, and oppression continued, even worsened, as it did in the 1830s and 1850s, black Americans read their future in Psalms 68:31: "Princes shall come out of Egypt and Ethiopia shall soon stretch forth her hands unto God." I do not mean to suggest that these texts were contradictory. In black religious thought and ritual, they were complementary. The intensity of slaves' identification with Israel had blunted the sharp edge of the question of why God had permitted slavery: We are Israel; God frees Israel.[8] But the underlying question remained. It was, of course, a particular instance of the universal problem of evil: why does God permit the innocent to suffer? At certain times during the nineteenth century, the more basic question pushed to the fore of black thought with great urgency. As J. Sella Martin lamented in the August 26, 1865, issue of the *Christian Recorder*: "Has Providence so little care for human lives as to permit the sacrifice of over a million of them for the purpose of overthrowing the system of slavery, only that its victims may be treated worse than slaves after they are free?" Martin was disturbed by the denial of suffrage for the freedman (indeed, for black men in general). The pressure of events ineluctably moved black religious thought beyond Exodus toward Job. In response, black clergy and laity meditated upon Psalms 68:31 as well as on Exodus. In addition to linking the present with the mythic past, they joined it to a mythic future when "princes shall come out of Egypt and Ethiopia shall soon stretch forth her hands unto God," without doubt the most quoted verse in black religious history.

In the destiny of the black race, predicted in Psalms 68:31, African-American Christians thought they could read the meaning of black suffering. But they confronted an immediate problem: unlike the book of Exodus, whose narrative was clear and easy to interpret, the verse in Psalms was obscure. Yet its very obscurity extended its explanatory range. Consequently, nineteenth-century interpretations of Psalms 68:31 differed widely. They all, however, clustered around three major themes: "the African race," "the redemption of Africa," and "the mission of the darker races."

The African Race

All interpreters of the verse agreed that Egypt and Ethiopia referred to "the African race." In a kind of mythic geography, nineteenth-century black Americans identified Ethiopia and Egypt with their own African origins and looked to those ancient civilizations as exemplars of a glorious African past, surely as legitimate a fictive pedigree as white American claims of descent from Greco-Roman civilization. "Ancient history, as well as holy writ, informs us of the national greatness of our progenitors," boasted African Methodist minister William Miller, in a sermon delivered in 1810. A host of black preachers and historians throughout the century substantially agreed with his sketch of the black past: "The inhabitants of Africa are descended from the ancient inhabitants of Egypt, a people once famous for science of every description." Biblical, archaeological, and historical evidence was marshaled by black scholars to prove that descendants of Egypt and Ethiopia had nothing to fear from any invidious comparison with the descendants of Europe. The vaunted superiority of Anglo-Saxon civilization was merely the empty boast of ignorant men. According to black historians, the "Children of Ham were clearly the first to lead off in the march of civilization." From the Egyptians, the torch had passed to the Greeks, from them to the Romans, and from the Romans, finally, and belatedly, to the Europeans. While the Egyptians were establishing law and political institutions, the sons of Japhet, the Europeans, were still "a savage race of men," "inhabiting the rocks and caverns, a wretched prey to wild beast and to one another." Hosea Easton, a minister from Hartford, could not resist digging in the point: "I would here remark that it is a little singular that modern philosophers, the descendants of this race of savages, should claim for their race a superiority of intellect over those who, at that very time, were enjoying all the real benefits of civilized life."[9]

Nineteenth-century blacks needed to reclaim for themselves a civilized African past in order to refute the charge that they were inherently inferior, especially because they, by and large, assumed that modern Africans and African-Americans were less civilized than Anglo-Americans. Most would have reluctantly concurred with William Wells Brown, escaped slave, novelist, lecturer, and historian, who in 1863 wrote: "I admit that the condition of my race . . . at the present time cannot compare favorably with the Anglo-Saxon." The disability of the race, however, was due to the circumstances of enslavement and oppression forced upon it by whites. The historical evidence indicated that once the reverse had been the case. But Egypt and Ethiopia had fallen. What had happened? Grown prosperous, they had, according to William Miller, forgotten God and turned aside to idolatry. "Where nations have turned aside to idolatry they have lost their civilization," explained black historian George Washington Williams. Hosea Easton placed the blame upon war. Whatever the cause, the fall from former glory had been great. African-Americans, lamented Easton, are "the remnant of a once noble but now heathenish people," as different from their ancestors as they are from other races. Williams theorized that "the genuine African has gradually degenerated into the typical Negro," "the lowest strata" of the once great African race. According to Miller, God's wrath was so aroused by the idolatry of Africans and Ethiopians that he pronounced judgment upon them through his prophet Isaiah: "Like as my servant Isaiah hath walked naked and barefooted three years, for a sign and wonder upon Egypt and Ethiopia, so shall the king of Assyria lead the Egyptian prisoners and Ethiopian captives, young and old, naked and barefooted, even with their bodies uncovered; to the shame of Egypt" (Isaiah 20:3–4). "My brethren," exclaimed Miller to his free black congregation, "you have all seen this prophecy astonishingly fulfilled even to a very late period, upon the unhappy Africans." Miller seems to have been unique in seeing the slave trade as the literal enactment of Isaiah's prophecy, but all black interpreters linked the decline of African civilization with moral degradation.[10]

Yet if princes had once ruled wisely in Egypt and if Ethiopia had seen the birth of civilization, might not their descendants in America, now Christianized and civilized, restore their rightful dignity among the nations? Could this have been the meaning of slavery: the education, elevation, and regeneration of the descendants of idolatrous Egypt and fallen Ethiopia? A number of articulate black clergymen thought so.

The Redemption of Africa

As early as 1808, in one of the earliest black sermons extant, Absalom Jones, pastor of St. Thomas's African Episcopal Church in Philadelphia, offered this answer to the question, Why has God permitted slavery? "It has always been a mystery," he confessed, "why the impartial Father of the human race should have permitted the transportation of so many millions of our fellow creatures to this country, to endure all the miseries of slavery. . . . Perhaps his design was, that a knowledge of the gospel might be acquired by some of their descendants, in order that they might become qualified to be the messengers of it, to the land of their fathers." The reticence of "Perhaps his design was" no doubt was due in part to Jones's reluctance to presume that he or any man knew for certain God's will, but it also sprang from another troubling fact. As Jones and other black ministers well knew, the evangelization and civilization of blacks was the rationale used by Europeans, from the mid fifteenth century on, to justify enslaving Africans. In other words, this explanation came dangerously close to absolving whites of their guilt for slavery. The black clergy refused absolution by distinguishing God's will from his permission. God wills good; he only permits evil, and from it draws good. Although "God permitted these things to come to pass," William Miller preached, "it does not follow that the oppressors of Africa are less culpable for their savage treatment to the unoffending Africans." George Washington Williams echoed the sentiment two generations later: "God often permits evil on the ground of man's free agency but he does not commit evil. The Negro of this country can turn to his Saxon brothers and say, as Joseph said to his brethren who wickedly sold him, 'As for you, ye meant it unto evil, but God meant it unto good; that we, after learning your arts and sciences, might return to Egypt and deliver the rest of our brethren who are yet in the house of bondage.'"[11]

Few questioned why it was necessary for Africans to learn these arts and sciences at the price of so much suffering. God chastises those he chooses. Through suffering, God was purifying Ethiopia's sons in America in order to make them "a chosen generation, a royal priesthood, and an holy nation, a peculiar people." The will of God is hidden in mystery, as Job long ago learned: "Be still and know that I am God! Clouds and darkness are round about me; yet righteousness and judgement are the habitation of my throne. I do my will and pleasure in the heavens above, and in the earth beneath; it is my sovereign prerogative to bring good out of evil and cause the wrath of man to praise me, and the remainder of that wrath I will restrain."[12] These were not so much answers as they were genuflections before the mystery of divine providence. The benevolence of that providence was assured by events: the abolition of the African slave trade on January 1, 1808, the abolition of slavery in New York on July 4, 1827, the emancipation of the British West Indies in 1834, and finally emancipation in the United States in 1865. These were indices of "the goodness of God, and his wisdom in all things." They were divine pledges that the psalmist's prediction was being fulfilled in the elevation, education, and progress of the African race in America.[13]

The purpose of God, revealing itself in human history, was the redemption of the African race. Slavery was his means for achieving this end—good drawn out of evil. But this was not all that Psalms 68:31 meant. The redemption of the African race included the redemption of Africa itself. The sons of Ethiopia, now enlightened by the Christian gospel, would return to Africa and rekindle the flame of religion and civilization snuffed out by idolatry so long ago. This, too, was God's will. However, nineteenth-century black preachers who espoused this view, as did most, faced a problem: the American Colonization Society. Founded in 1816 as a benevolent reform society, the ACS proposed a solution to the problem of slavery: the emancipation and repatriation of slaves in Africa. While the black clergy favored the evangelization of Africa and the emigration of those blacks who wished to return to Africa, they feared and condemned the ACS for plotting to forcibly remove free blacks from the United States in order to squelch antislavery agitation. Instead of gradually eroding slavery, the ACS, in their view, was bent on preserving and strengthening it. In response to this threat, black leaders spoke out against colonization in pulpit, platform, and press. Increasingly, the self-referents of blacks changed from "African" and "sons of Ethiopia," to "free colored" and "American." Increasingly, black spokesmen elaborated on the contributions of blacks to America, their participation in her wars, their blood and sweat shed on her soil. "African-Americans are here to stay" was a leit-motif through most of the conventions, editorials, and resolutions of the nineteenth century, both before the Civil War and after.[14]

To be sure, there were blacks who encouraged emigration, always voluntary, and who actually chose to emigrate themselves. Paul Cuffe in the late eighteenth century and Daniel Coker in 1820 had led expeditions to Sierra Leone. Moreover, during especially bad times, such as the 1830s, the 1850s, and the 1870s, emigration seemed more and more attractive as the only escape from white oppression. Martin Delany, before the war, and Henry McNeal Turner, after, argued strenuously for the benefits of emigration. Only in Africa, Turner maintained, could blacks fully assert their manhood rights, which, as far as he could see, this Negro-hating country would never recognize.[15]

Emigration, then, would fulfill two purposes: the Christianization of Africans and the colonization of Africa by African-Americans. Daniel Coker articulated the mixed, and to our eyes, ambiguous, motives of the emigrationists in a letter he mailed back to Maryland in 1820. "Oh, what a work is this," he exclaims. "What darkness has covered the minds of the people." Anyone "who loves souls would weep over them, and be willing to suffer and die with them." In a striking phrase, he confesses, "my soul cleaves to Africa. . . . I expect to give my life to bleeding, groaning, dark, benighted Africa." Then, without skipping a beat, Coker shifts from missionary zeal to mercantile calculation: "If you ask my opinion as to coming out;—I say, let all that can, sell out and come, come and bring ventures, to trade, etc., and you may do much better than you can possibly do in America, and not work half so hard. . . . Bring . . . two hogsheads of good leaf tobacco, cheap calico, and cheap handkerchiefs, pins, knives and forks, pocket knives, etc., with these you may buy land, hire hands, or buy provisions. I say, come—the land is good."[16]

Nineteenth-century black Americans presumed, as we have seen, that Africa needed their help. The African, according to an article published in the *AME Church Review* in 1890, "has made few strides along the line of intelligence; his sight has long become dimmed to apprehend his Maker. He has declined in the scale of human intelligence. He gropes in darkness. He has wandered from the shining face of his God into gross ignorance. The twentieth century of his Redeemer's advent dawns upon him sunk in superstition, and worshipping the creature more than the Creator."[17]

Alexander Crummell, the chief American advocate in the later nineteenth century for the evangelization of Africa and himself a missionary to Liberia for twenty years, reminded African-Americans of their duty to assist the simple, childlike Africans to the higher level of civilization that blacks in America already possessed. Though Crummell praised the natural modesty and generosity of the native Africans as superior to the immorality and corruption of the English and Americans, it was clear that the African stood in sore need of the blessings of technological civilization. In this regard, Crummell and other proponents of African missions revealed a deep ambivalence about Africa. On the one hand, they presumed that Africans were backward pagans. On the other, they knew from bitter experience that white Americans were racist, imperialistic, and materialistic. Europeans were superior in civilization, Africans in natural religiosity.[18]

Without Christianity, however, the African's inclination toward religion remained unfulfilled, perverted by idolatry, or misguided into Islam. It was the proper mission of the African-American to bring the African to the gospel. Whites had no business in Africa. As Emmanuel K. Love observed before the Black Baptist Foreign Mission Convention in 1889, "There is no doubt in my mind that Africa is our field of operation and that [as] Moses was sent to deliver his brethren, and as the prophets were members of the race to whom they were sent, so I am convinced that God's purpose is to redeem Africa through us." "This work," he concluded, "is ours by appointment, by inheritance, and by choice." Europeans had failed to Christianize the "dark continent" despite previous attempts. African-Americans would succeed, according to J. Sella Martin, because they could withstand the hostile climate that decimated whites and, more important, because their skin color would arouse the confidence, not the distrust, of the natives. Edward Wilmot Blyden argued that history itself proved that God intended Africa for black missionaries. By allowing slavery, God converted them; by permitting racism, he directed them back; and by completely shutting up the vast interior of Africa from exploration, "until the time arrived for the emancipation of her children in the Western World," God had clearly singled out black people as his chosen instrument to redeem Africa.[19]

A few dissenting voices denied that the redemption of Africa was the divinely appointed destiny of black Americans. For example, T. Thomas Fortune, militant editor of the *New York Age*, complained: "The talk about the black people being brought to this country to prepare themselves to evangelize Africa is so much religious nonsense boiled down to a sycophantic platitude. The Lord who is eminently just, had no hand in their forcibly coming here, it was preeminently the work of the devil. Africa will have to be evangelized from *within,* not *from without.*"[20] Fortune had economics but not symbolism on his side of the argument. Black churches, in fact, were too poor to mount a large-scale African campaign, and attempts to work through the missionary boards of white denominations ran into racial difficulties. Nevertheless, the idea of African missions loomed large in the consciousness of black Christians from 1870 on. Their experience of oppression seemed to verify the contours of Turner and Blyden's racial map: Africa stood for opportunity and manhood, America for discrimination and emasculation. Few African-Americans actually ventured the trip, but symbolically the mission to redeem Africa confirmed their importance as a people. Reflecting this attitude, the logo of the influential AME journal, the *Christian Recorder,* was redesigned. After 1869, the plain title in bold type gave way to a picture of the globe, turned to the continent of Africa. Three sailing ships from America draw near the western coast of Africa. Rays of light shoot out from the "dark continent," and beneath the globe stretches the banner, "Ethiopia shall soon stretch forth her hands to God."

As they imagined the future of redeemed Africa, nineteenth-century black writers reversed old stereotypes about the dark continent. George Washington Williams, for example, depicted this idyllic scene: "The sabbath bells will summon from scattered cottages smiling populations, linked together by friendship, and happy in all the sweetness of domesticated charities. Thus the glory of her latter day shall be greater than at the beginning, and *Ethiopia shall stretch forth her hands unto God.*" Edward Blyden, in 1862, foresaw a less pastoral and more active future: "Africa will furnish a development of civilization which the world has never yet witnessed. Its great peculiarity will be its moral development." A generation earlier, Hosea Easton had placed Africa "in the front ranks of the church, when she marches into the millennial era." The progression from the fall of Africa, to the redemption of Africa, to the future of Africa particularized the salvation of mankind in the history of the "African race." Viewing history from the perspective of Psalms 68:31, black theologians in the nineteenth century had divined a salvation-history for their people. They did not stop there; a few took a step beyond.[21]

The Mission of the Darker Races

Consistently, black Americans condemned American Christianity as hypocritical and false. Slavery and race hatred blatantly violated the Christian law of love. The indictment of John Edward Bruce, a newspaper columnist, written in 1891, may serve as a summary of most of the charges elaborated over the century:

> [The] white church of America . . . preaches and perverts the Gospel, . . . by indirection and evasion denies the fatherhood of God and the brotherhood of man, . . . makes the Black man who loves Jesus feel his inferiority and that he is a degree or two lower than the white Christian and a *ward* rather than an equal before God. . . . Judgement is coming! The noisome pestilence that walketh in darkness will have no terrors for the Godly, but they will as surely overtake the great majority of the Negro-hating white Christians as that God is just. And He is just, for He intended that his holy religion should enfold in its broad mantle, in the perfect equality of Democracy, every human being on earth, for He is no respecter of persons. The white American Christian is. Therefore, his religion is a religion of lies and hypocrisy. Is this plain enough?[22]

Two points in Bruce's brief against white Christians merit elaboration: first, his prediction of divine retribution, and second, his implicit critique of civil religion.

A great deal of the criticism leveled against American Christianity by African-Americans took the form of an apocalyptic warning, articulated best by David Walker in 1830. "Unless, America repents and soon, God will tear up the very face of the earth!"[23] In Walker's *Appeal to the Coloured Citizens*, and in other black jeremiads as well, God appears as the Lord of History, the Ruler of Nations, who reveals his will in events of the day. In effect, the jeremiad did more than enable blacks to vent their righteous indignation; it placed black Christians in a stance of judgment over white Christians; it consolidated a position of moral superiority for the descendants of the African race. As we shall see shortly, black theologians, in the late nineteenth century, extended the doctrine of black moral superiority from a national to a global scale.

Nineteenth-century blacks accused the nation of betraying not only Christianity but democracy, the national faith recorded in the national scriptures (the Declaration of Independence and the Constitution) and celebrated on the national holy day (July 4th). Deep alienation from the religion of the republic prompted the First Annual Convention of the People of Colour to pass a resolution in 1831 urging blacks "throughout the United States" to "set apart the fourth day of July, as a day of humiliation, fasting and prayer—and to beseech Almighty God to interpose on our behalf, that the shackles of slavery may be broken, and our sacred rights obtained." In 1865, the Washington, D.C., correspondent of the *Christian Recorder* reported that the Fourth of July celebration at Union Bethel AME Church "was the first Fourth of July of the colored people."[24]

Thus African-Americans scorned the Christianity of whites and questioned the civil religion of the nation. Some were driven away from Christianity by the race prejudice of white Christians, but most did not reject the gospel or the principles of democracy. In their critiques of American Christianity, blacks implicitly and sometimes explicitly cast themselves as the models of true Christianity in America. As Levi Coppin, editor of the *AME Church Review*, remarked in 1890, African-Americans thought that "this question of civilization [was] by no means settled": "We are firmly of the opinion that the best expression of Christian civilization is yet to be seen, and who knows but that some of the very characteristics of the Negro that are discounted by the present civilization, are the very things needed for that higher and better which is yet to come." The characteristics of the Negro that Coppin had in mind had by this time become standard in black sermons: the list included patience, humility, meekness, peacefulness, long suffering, kindness, charitableness—in a word, Christ-likeness. Notice that these virtues characterized not just individuals but the race as a whole. The "natural religious temperament" of the African race had been molded by providence into the imitation of Christ. These were the virtues that had to replace the jingoism, imperialism, racism, and materialism of America if Christian civilization were to become a reality. Coppin only hinted at what others boldly stated. "It is my solemn belief, that if ever the world becomes Christianized . . . it will be through the means, under God of the *Blacks*, who are now held in wretchedness, and degradation, by the white *Christians* of the world," claimed David Walker. The fourth national Negro convention in 1834 purposely alluded to the early Christians when it proclaimed that "our very sighs and groans like the blood of martyrs will prove to have been the seed of the church." One overzealous AME minister narrowed the mission of the race to the clergy of his own denomination, who were "the instruments in the hands of God for the redemption of Africa, the subjugation of America, and for bringing the world unto God and his Christ." In a less grandiose and more poetic style, the American Moral Reform Society of 1837 spoke of black faces "as so many Bibles, that shall warn this guilty nation of her injustice."[25]

The mission of black Christians to be the leaven of true Christian civilization was elaborated in greatest detail by two black theologians of the late nineteenth century. Theophilus Gould Steward and James Theodore

Holly moved the interpretation of Psalms 68:31 to a new global perspective. Both men insisted that the psalmist had predicted a special role for the darker races in the millennial phase of history, the end time. Steward, a minister of the AME Church, concluded in 1888 that the evidence of Scripture and the signs of the times indicated the end of the present age was near. Western Christianity had nothing more to offer believers; it could no longer speak to them with authority. Indeed, an end to the militaristic and racist corruption of Christianity by the West had to come if the pagan nations were ever to have the true gospel preached to them. Fratricidal warfare among the "Christian nations" would end the present age and a new and final age of a raceless and peaceful Christianity would begin, in which the darker, non-Christian peoples of the world (Africans, Indians, Chinese) would hear and accept the pure gospel of Christ, undefiled by Anglo-Saxon prejudice. This new religious age, Steward speculated, might well be led by the Church of Abyssinia, a "hidden church in the wilderness," which "God has maintained for himself as a witness," down through the centuries. "Then the really righteous unobscured by the perverse civilization—a civilization which is called Christian, but which is essentially Saxon—shall shine forth as the sun, and this hidden church of the wilderness shall come forth to lead Africa's millions, as a part of that fullness of the Gentiles which is to come to welcome the universal Christ."[26]

James Theodore Holly also defined a universal role in the end time for the darker races. According to Holly, writing in 1884, the "divine plan of human redemption" unfolds in three historic periods or dispensations. The first dispensation belonged to the Semitic race, whose task it was to formulate, write down, and preserve the Holy Scriptures. The second, or Japhetic, phase coincided with the apostolic or evangelical period, the age of the Europeans, who had been commissioned to spread the gospel. The Hebrew dispensation ended with the destruction of the Temple in A.D. 70. The Japhetic phase would end in warfare, after which the millennium would commence. During this thousand-year reign of peace and justice, the Hamitic race would bring to completion the divine plan of human redemption only imperfectly realized by the Semitic and Japhetic races. To the sons of Ham, "the elect among nations," "the crowning work of the will of God is reserved for the millennial phase of Christianity when Ethiopia shall stretch out her hands directly unto God." The Semites preserved the word of God, the Japhites preached it; during this last and greatest dispensation, the Hamites would put the word of God into practice. In a striking reversal of the legend of Noah's curse of Canaan, Holly explained why:

The African race has been the servant of servants to their brethren of the other races during all the long and dreary ages of the Hebrew and Christian dispensations. And it is this service that they have so patiently rendered through blood and tears that shall finally obtain for them the noblest places of service in the Coming Kingdom. That what has been a curse to them under Gentile tyranny will become a blessing to them under the mild and beneficent reign of Christ, and thus will be realized the double but adverse significations of the Hebrew word *barak* . . . which signifies to "bless," and also "to curse." . . . The curse of Canaan, dooming him to be a servant of servants unto his brethren, which lowered him to a place of dishonor under the earthly governments of men, will turn to a blessing unto him and exalt him to the posts of honor under the heavenly government of God.[27]

Steward and Holly pushed the interpretation of Psalms 68:31 as far as it could go in explaining human history—all the way to the millennium. In the process, they shifted the understanding of black destiny from a particularistic to a universal role. Reflecting upon their experience of suffering as a people, black Americans in the nineteenth century fashioned a theology of history whose conclusions, clumsily summarized, were these: Those who oppress and enslave others, those who make war, those who spread "civilization" by conquest, those who degrade other races, those who corrupt Christianity by making it a clan religion, are destined to destroy one another. Their age will shortly end. A new age will soon begin. In this new age, it will be the destiny of those who were oppressed but did not oppress, those who were enslaved but did not enslave, those who were hated but did not hate, to realize the gospel on earth.

Both Holly and Steward expected the age of Japheth to end soon. A twentieth-century skeptic might point out that it did not end soon enough to save Sam Hose, much less Mack Parker or Emmett Till. The skeptic would, of course, be right, but also would have missed the point. "Princes shall come out of Egypt and Ethiopia shall soon stretch forth her hands unto God" was not so much a prophecy as it was a prayer.

Notes

1. Francis J. Grimke, *The Works of Francis J. Grimke*, ed. Carter G. Woodson, 4 vols. (Washington, D.C.: Associated Publishers 1942), 1:291.
2. Arthur F. Raper, *The Tragedy of Lynching* (Montclair, N.J.: Patterson, Smith, 1969), 480. The *Richmond Planet* to which Grimke refers kept a month-by-month total of lynchings during the 1890s (Grimke, *Works*, 1:296–97).

3. Grimke, *Works*, 1:268.
4. Ibid., 267.
5. Ibid., vii–xxii, 268.
6. Gerda Lerner, *The Grimke Sisters from South Carolina: Rebels against Slavery* (Boston: Houghton Mifflin, 1967), 358–66.
7. Grimke, *Works*, 1:269–70.
8. See Lawrence W. Levine, *Black Culture and Black Consciousness: Afro-American Folk Thought from Slavery to Freedom* (New York: Oxford University Press, 1977), 33–55; Albert J. Raboteau, *Slave Religion: The "Invisible Institution" in the Antebellum South* (New York: Oxford University Press, 1978), 243–64.
9. William Miller, *A Sermon on the Abolition of the Slave Trade: Delivered in the African Church, New York, on the First of January, 1810* (New York, 1810), 4; William P. Alexander, *History of the Colored Race in America* (1887; reprint, New York: Negro Universities Press, 1968), 8; Hosea Easton, *A Treatise on the Intellectual Character, and Civil and Political Condition of the Colored People of the United States* (Boston, 1837), 9–10.
10. William Wells Brown, *The Black Man: His Antecedents, His Genius, and His Achievements* (Boston, 1863), 32; Miller, *On the Abolition of the Slave Trade*, 5–6; George Washington Williams, *History of the Negro Race in America*, 2 vols. (New York, 1883), 1:109; Easton, *A Treatise*, 19–20.
11. Absalom Jones, *A Thanksgiving Sermon Preached January 1, 1808, in St. Thomas's, or the African Episcopal Church, Philadelphia: An Account of the Abolition of the African Slave Trade* (Philadelphia, 1808), 18; Miller, *On the Abolition of the Slave Trade*, 7–8; Williams, *History of the Negro Race*, 1:113–14.
12. Nathaniel Paul, *An Address, Delivered on the Celebration of the Abolition of Slavery in New York, July 5, 1827* (Albany, 1827), 10–11.
13. See the sermons of Jones, Miller, and Paul. The anniversaries of these occasions were observed down to Emancipation.
14. Leonard I. Sweet, *Black Images of America, 1784–1870* (New York: W. W. Norton, 1976), 35–68.
15. John H. Bracey, Jr., August Meier, and Elliott Rudwick, eds., *Black Nationalism in America* (Indianapolis: Bobbs-Merrill, 1970), 38–48. See Martin R. Delany, *The Condition, Elevation, Emigration, and Destiny of the Colored People of the United States, Politically Considered* (Philadelphia, 1852); and *Official Report of the Niger Valley Exploring Party* (New York, 1861); Henry McNeal Turner, "Essay: The American Negro and the Fatherland," in *Africa and the American Negro: Addresses and Proceedings of the Congress on Africa*, ed. J.W.E. Bowen (Atlanta, 1896), 195–98; see also Turner's writings and speeches collected in Edwin S. Redkey, ed., *Respect Black* (New York: Arno Press, 1971).
16. Daniel Coker, quoted in Bracey, Meier, and Rudwick, *Black Nationalism*, 46–47.
17. George B. Peabody, "The Hope of Africa," *AME Church Review*, 7, no. 1 (July 1890): 58–59. Peabody was identified as an African studying at Lincoln University!
18. Alexander Crummell, *Christian Recorder*, September 23, 1865; "The Obligation of American Black Men for the Redemption of Africa," *African Repository* 48, no. 6 (June 1872): 162–68; *The Future of Africa* (New York, 1862); *Africa and America* (Springfield, Mass., 1891).
19. Emmanuel K. Love, Baptist Foreign Mission Convention Minutes, 1889, 7–8, cited in James M. Washington, "The Origins and Emergence of Black Baptist Separatism, 1863–1897" (Ph.D. dissertation, Yale University, 1979), 159; J. Sella Martin, "A Speech

before the Paris Anti-Slavery Conference, August 27, 1867," reprinted in Carter G. Woodson, ed., *Negro Orators* (Washington, D.C.: Associated Publishers, 1925), 261; Edward W. Blyden, "The African Problem and the Method of Its Solution," *AME Church Review* 7, no. 2 (October 1890): 205, 213. See St. Claire Drake, *The Redemption of Africa and Black Religion* (Chicago: Third World Press, 1970).

20. T. Thomas Fortune, *Black and White: Land, Labor, and Politics in the South* (1884; reprint, Chicago: Johnson Publishing, 1970), 86–87.

21. Williams, *History of the Negro Race*, 1:114; Edward W. Blyden, *Liberia's Offering* (New York, 1862), 82–83; Easton, *A Treatise*, 20.

22. Peter Gilbert, ed., *Selected Writings of John Edward Bruce: Militant Black Journalist* (New York: Arno Press, 1971), 49.

23. David Walker, *Appeal to the Coloured Citizens of the World*, 3d ed. (Boston, 1830); reprinted in Herbert Aptheker, ed., *One Continual Cry* (New York: Humanities Press, 1965), 104.

24. *Minutes and Proceedings of the First Annual Convention of the People of Colour* . . . (Philadelphia, 1831), 10–11; *Christian Recorder,* July 15, 1865. See also Frederick Douglass, "Fifth of July Speech, Rochester, N.Y., 1852," frequently reprinted.

25. Levi J. Coppin, editorial, *AME Church Review* 7, no. 1 (July 1890): 102–3; Walker, *Appeal to the Coloured Citizens*, 81 n; *Minutes of the Fourth Annual Convention for the Improvement of the Free People of Colour . . . New York, June 2–12, 1834* (New York, 1834), 27–30; James Porter, "Afro-American Methodism as a Factor in the Progress of Our Race," *AME Church Review* 7, no. 3 (January 1891): 321; *Minutes and Proceedings of the First Annual Meeting of the American Reform Society* (Philadelphia, 1837), reprinted in Dorothy Porter; ed., *Early Negro Writing, 1760–1837* (Boston: Beacon Press, 1971), 203.

26. T. G. Steward, *The End of the World; Or, Clearing the Way for the Fullness of the Gentiles* (Philadelphia, 1888), 119, 127.

27. James Theodore Holly, "The Divine Plan of Human Redemption, In Its Ethnological Development," *AME Church Review* 1 (October 1884): 79–85. For an interesting analysis of the idea of blacks as a messianic people, see Wilson Jeremiah Moses, *Black Messiahs and Uncle Toms: Social and Literary Manipulations of a Religious Myth* (University Park: Pennsylvania State University Press, 1982).

Chapter 17

The Making of a Church
with the Soul of a Nation, 1880–1889

James Melvin Washington

It took sixteen years for the black Baptists to form a national denomination to replace the CABMC [Consolidated American Baptist Missionary Convention]. In the meantime two major national bodies[1] were organized in order to deal with certain persistent problems that eventually would be addressed by one body.

Predecessors of the 1895 Convention

The first of those two bodies, the Baptist Foreign Mission Convention of the United States (BFMC), was organized in Montgomery, Alabama, during December 1880, one year after the collapse of the CABMC. The American National Baptist Convention (ANBC) convened for the first time in St. Louis on 25–29 August 1886 for the purpose of devising means for the creation of a national black Baptist denomination. Formation of these two organizations amounted to an admission that the three regional conventions were inadequate substitutes for a national denomination. Moreover, many black Baptist leaders were determined to dispute the prevalent belief that they did not have the ability to form and manage a national body.

The Foreign Mission Movement. Although the creation of the BFMC in 1880 reflected a longstanding commitment of black Baptists to foreign missions, the story of the foreign mission movement is not germane to the story of the formation of a black national denomination.[2] Nonetheless, a closer look at the ideology of this convention illustrates its major contribution to the unification movement.

The BFMC operated on the assumption that it would conduct foreign mission work, mostly in West Africa, while local associations and state conventions, with the assistance of the ABHMS (American Baptist Home Mission Society), would meet the evangelistic and educational needs of their local communities. Although there were several state conventions that supported African missions, this division of labor generally worked quite well so long as the brethren limited themselves to traditional forms of evangelism. But increasing discrimination against blacks in areas such as education, public accommodations, and jobs mandated a broadening of the preachers' understanding of evangelism. Some leaders began to accept the idea that dependence on traditional views of evangelism in the face of the enormous problems of constituents was social irresponsibility. Most of them wanted to change the nation, not to escape from it.

These Baptist leaders believed that black problems were national in scope and needed a national solution. Although political reconstruction had come to an end, there were vestiges of the innovative social legislation of the national and state Reconstruction governments that offered legal deterrents to discrimination—at least on paper. Nevertheless, Jim Crow received a new lease on life when the United States Supreme Court nullified the civil rights gains of the 1870s in 1883. This decision, made in the twilight of black Reconstruction political gains, signaled that the federal government was willing to leave the resolution of black problems to state government. This proved to be disastrous for black people because most of the state governments by the mid-1880s had been "Redeemed" (or returned to the control of the legatees of slavocracy, the conservative Southern Democrats).

As John Hope Franklin has written, "Reconstruction" itself "was essentially a national, not a sectional or racial problem."[3] But the federal government experienced a failure of nerve. The termination of the Reconstruction experiment attendant on the famous 1877 Hayes-Tilden Compromise did not diminish the proportions of the black problem. Seemingly perpetual economic hardship, political instability, and the rise of an increasingly complex industrial society exacerbated the struggle to help freedmen overcome the deprivations engendered by slavery.

While one may not minimize the religious and social importance of a faith closely adhering to the teachings of the Bible, it is apparent that the black Baptist foreign mission movement nourished those biblicistic tendencies that helped black Baptist preachers to mollify the hardships of their parishioners. These preachers refused to believe that a God of justice placed blacks in America for no reason at all. Their theological justification for engaging in African missions was closely tied to their need to explain why blacks were enslaved. Emanuel Love, president of the BFMC in 1889, stated this belief more clearly than any of his predecessors.

> We have met to *think, talk, pray,* and *give* in order that the gospel may be given to Africa, the land of our fathers. There is no doubt in my mind that Africa is our field of operation, and that Moses was sent to deliver his brethren, and as the prophets were members of the race to whom they were sent, so I am convinced that God's purpose is to redeem Africa through us. The evils of slavery were turned to gracious account, conferring upon us the blessings of civilization, and in return placing the negro [*sic*] Christians of this great country under lasting obligation to the work of African evangelization. This work is ours by appointment, by inheritance, and by choice.[4]

Sentiments such as these enhanced black solidarity by nourishing a sense of self-confidence and purpose. Unlike some of the Yankee-minded leaders of the CABMC, the BFMC, consisting mainly of Southerners, was unprepared to relinquish its racial identity. It continuously rejected invitations to merge with the Northern white American Baptist Missionary Union (ABMU). It was quite explicit about why it rejected the ABMU's offer in 1886.

> We believe . . . that to continue our work as an organization will develop qualities and powers in us as a people that will not be developed if we go into another [white] organization.

It then accused the white Baptists of not really being seriously interested in evangelizing Africa.

> Now to give up our organization will be to throw a check upon our efforts, and to a large degree hinder the work of evangelizing Africa. There is no reason, to our mind, why we should cooperate, but many why we should not—we need experience, we need self-reliance, we need those blessings that come to those who discharge their duty to God and man.[5]

Despite these separatist sentiments the BFMC ran into the same difficulties that had also plagued the CABMC.[6] It repeatedly tried to district the country in order to raise more money for African missions. Moreover by 1886 a new black national organization arose, taking from and sharing many of its members with the BFMC.

The Unifying Role of the American Convention. The American National Baptist Convention (ANBC) was actually the most ambitious attempt to found a black Baptist national denomination since the demise of the CABMC. It mediated between the various factions of the black Baptist family and the powerful Northern white societies. The second article of its Constitution specified the ANBC's major objective.

> The object of this Convention shall be to consider the moral, intellectual and religious growth of the denomination, and to deliberate upon those great questions which characterize the Baptist churches. And further, to devise and consider the best methods possible for bringing us more closely together as a church and as a race.[7]

This deliberative body provided a much-needed intellectual outlet for many of the younger and more progressive brothers and sisters[8] who were graduating in large numbers from Northern-sponsored Southern black schools, such as Shaw University (Raleigh, North Carolina) and Wayland Theological Seminary (Richmond, Virginia). The annual minutes for this Convention overflow with papers that grappled with problems of Baptist polity and with social and ethical questions.

Perhaps the most important new factor in this convention was the rise of a new generation of leaders who were able to take control of this renewal of the movement toward unity. Between 1886 and 1890 the presidency of the ANBC was graced and energized by the dynamic leadership of William James Simmons, a 37-year-old minister from Kentucky who gratified conventioneers with his wit and clarity of mind. In fact Simmons was almost single-handedly responsible for calling the brethren together in the first place. As president of the black State University of Kentucky, editor of the popular newspaper, the *American Baptist* (Louisville, Kentucky),[9] and president and organizer of the National Negro Press Association, Simmons was in a strategic position to encourage the unification of the Baptists. According to Bishop Henry McNeal Turner of the African Methodist Episcopal Church, Simmons's biographer,[10] Simmons suggested a national convention of black Baptists in the 5 April issue of his newspaper. The meeting took place in August 1886. Simmons gave the denominational sermon, and was unanimously elected president of the Convention and chairman of its executive committee. Simmons's militant denominationalism contributed greatly to his rise to power among the black Baptists. Turner described him as a man whose motto was "God, my race and denomination." His contemporaries seemed to be dazed by the man's charm, energy, and administrative acumen. Ida B. Wells characterized him as "a big man, figuratively and physically."[11] Nevertheless, older leaders who had earned fame in the CABMC also contributed to the success of the new enterprise.

Fifty-five-year-old Richard DeBaptiste, former president of the CABMC, was elected statistician of the new group. He offered the first statistical analysis of the growth of black Baptists. It is difficult now to recapture the jubilation and surprise that greeted DeBaptiste's claim that there were 1,066,131 Afro-American Baptists who belonged to 9,061 congregations whose property was valued at nearly 1.5 million dollars. Moreover DeBaptiste claimed that there were more than 4,572 converts.[12] These statistics gave DeBaptiste a solid basis for raising the central issue that confronted the 1886 ANBC as well as most of its subsequent meetings: the problem of the adequacy of Baptist polity for the enormous social needs of Afro-Americans.

> While it is evident that our church polity is favorable to the most wonderful expansion in growth of numbers, and the maintenance of entire uniformity in all essential points of doctrinal belief, it remains for us to demonstrate that it is equally adapted to obtaining the largest results in efficiency of service in proportion to numbers, and of liberality of contributions in proportions to means.[13]

DeBaptiste's latter query provided the backdrop in the 1886 meeting for black Baptist leaders to grapple with the tendency to use Baptist polity to sanction localism. Two papers presented at the 1886 meeting addressed this problem. Solomon T. Clanton, an 1883 black graduate of Baptist Union Theological Seminary,[14] delivered a paper entitled "Co-operative Union or Separation." After arguing that "race confidence" in black leadership would be enhanced through the union of black Baptist forces, Clanton, a fervent integrationist, argued that black Baptist unification would lead to greater cooperation among Baptist missionary endeavors, regardless of race. Furthermore he was convinced that more cooperation and unity on the part of black Baptists would stand as a testimony against the "foul" charge that blacks could not be amalgamated into American society. Clanton declared that it was the will of God that black Baptist unity should ring from the Atlantic to the Pacific, from the Lakes to the Gulf. In this way, prejudice, which is the child of ignorance, will be removed, the color-line, which is an invention of Satan, will be wiped out and race recognition on the ground of merit alone, without social amalgamation, will be secured on terms worthy of immortal men.[15]

James T. White of Arkansas, in another paper entitled "Need of Colored Baptists of the South," argued that black Baptists should unify in order to launch an attack against ignorant Southern preachers. He contended that these men gave ammunition to the bishops of the African Methodist Church who, White declared, spread "the impression abroad that the Baptists are an ignorant class at best." He added, "It is an advantage to the Methodist church [*sic*] to appear wise, while, by blowing their own horn, they make us appear to be ignorant." White confessed that this accusation, which had some merit, was peculiarly applicable to the Southern brethren. Although he himself was born in the North he felt compelled to come to the defense of Southern black Baptists. White had the credentials for doing this. He had served as a state senator from Helena, Arkansas, for a number of years and for an even longer period served as pastor of the Centennial Church. He argued that the major missionary concern of black Baptists should still be in the South where a more intelligent pulpit and an affluent pew were much needed. Since he did not see any possibility of black people leaving the South in great numbers, he believed that the most "proficient means" of making Southern black people "more amiable and attractive" would be "to maintain fraternal intercourse with each other. How easy could that be done!"[16] Both of these papers revealed that a new surge of black Baptist denominational loyalty was afoot.

While calling for unity, some leaders, unlike Richard DeBaptiste, entertained the possibility that disunity was the natural bedfellow of Baptist polity. William Simmons dismissed this problem at the 1887 meeting as an attempt to belittle Baptist efficiency and progress:

If the Baptist churches had not been the churches of God, our enemies would have killed us long ago. It can stand apparently more worldly mismanagement and live than all the other bodies on earth. A Baptist split only produces another Baptist church. No one expects less, nor more. It can only increase the number of our churches.

While defending Baptist polity Simmons did not fail to prod uncooperative brethren. According to Simmons the black Baptist family "is the largest religious denomination among our race in the United States, and is without doubt larger than all of them put together, but for want of organization has not wielded the power belonging even to its numerical strength."[17] Yet Simmons realized that chastisement without subsequent action would do little to attack the problem of disunity. Between the August 1887 meeting of the ANBC and the April 1888 meeting of its executive board, Simmons, the chairman of the board, accepted an appointment from the ABHMS to be its District Secretary for the South. During this same period Simmons used his new office to rally black Baptists. According to Richard DeBaptiste he sought "to secure a unification of interests in the mission and educational work of the colored Baptists, and to promote a closer union of the general organization among us."[18] Simmons announced at the April Executive Board meeting that he had succeeded in getting the BFMC and the Baptist General Association of Western States and Territories to meet in conference with the officers of the ABHMS, who had already planned to meet with the ANBC. This "joint meeting" took place in Nashville, Tennessee, 18–26 September 1888.

The phrase "joint meeting" was a euphemism used to express the black Baptist desire for unification. Actually the brethren held separate business meetings, then later held a fellowship meeting where they harangued endlessly about the beauties of unification. The actual proposals for unification were drawn up by a committee consisting of the leaders of the several conventions. But the leaders at this 1888 Nashville meeting were unable to agree on a plan for forming a national black denomination. They were more concerned about forming alliances that would place them in a united position to solicit funds from the disunited Northern Baptist societies. They believed that those societies were unwilling to accept solicitations from a united black Baptist denomination, but were willing to assist united black Baptist societies with agendas and organizations similar to their own. In 1888 the ABMU was more prepared to do this than the ABHMS, which was still determined to monopolize domestic mission work.[19]

R. J. Adams and E. F. Merriam represented the white ABMU at the Nashville meeting. They consulted with a joint committee consisting of the leaders of the BFMC and the Baptist General Association of Western States and Territories (BGA) to devise a "plan for the unification of all colored Baptists in foreign missions work, including a method of cooperation with the American Baptist Missionary Union." Actually the executive boards of the BFMC and the BGA "had met and recommended the report of the Joint Committee for adoption by their respective bodies."[20] The Joint Committee's Report called for the organization of a new body to be called the American Baptist Foreign Mission Convention. All black Baptist foreign mission societies were to merge with this new convention, which would be the only liaison between the white ABMU and black Baptists.

The internal organization of this proposed convention was quite similar to the CABMC's 1872 districting plan. This was partly the result of the influence of Rufus Lewis Perry. Still corresponding secretary of the CABMC (which existed only on paper), Perry was elected president of a joint session of the two foreign mission bodies. No doubt Perry's link with past efforts to achieve unity encouraged the separatist sentiments held by most of the brethren. Despite the prior approval of the boards, the majority of the BFMC voted to table the plan so that the new foreign mission convention, which never came into existence, could consider the merits of affiliating with the white ABMU.

Although the joint assembly expressed its appreciation for the presence of the ABMU's representatives, it distrusted the ABMU's motives. This longstanding distrust was aggravated by another event. Many of the delegates were angry because some of their colleagues had been locked out of first-class coaches of the Nashville, Chattanooga and St. Louis Railway even though they had paid for first-class tickets. A year later at another meeting this issue would gain greater prominence in the official proceedings of the conventions. But the 1888 delegates merely settled for passing a resolution that condemned discrimination on this occasion.[21] Despite this distraction, the foreign mission bodies still had to meet with the American National Baptist Convention.

The ANBC held its meeting 22–24 September 1888. The meeting with the representatives of the ABHMS took place on 25 September. It was originally scheduled to last two days, but was shortened because of the spread of yellow fever throughout the South. Despite this unforeseen event the ANBC's plan to unify the black Baptists in 1888 was temporarily subverted by the foreign mission bodies' attempt to unite. The localist leaders of the foreign mission groups were unprepared to merge with the nationalists in the ANBC.

Nonetheless the localists were exposed to the powerful nationalistic denominationalists in the ANBC, who were deeply committed to forging a truly national black Baptist denomination. Only one speech spoke directly to the challenge that faced the Baptists. The luminous oratory of D. W. Wisher, pastor of New York City's Olivet Baptist Church, posed the central questions, attacked segregation, and then depicted how the "glories" of unity would elevate a downtrodden race.

The power of unity will raise us high above the level of the common. It will enable us to destroy all narrow-mindedness among ourselves, and like a stream rushing from a mountain, sweeping down all obstacles, it will sweep from our midst, among the other nations of the country, and break down all prejudice and race pride of them who acknowledge us not as their equals. It will lift up our denomination higher and higher, and show the world that our church, indeed, is the church of which it is said that the days of her widowhood are over, and she is coming forth, out of her chamber, as a bride, gloriously adorned in her wedding garments, prepared to meet her groom.[22]

Wisher then lifted up a powerful and unforgettable[23] series of images:

Unity we need, and unity we want, but let it not be a unity of errors, but a unity of truth. Let it not be like the waters of a stagnant pool, over which the purifying breath of heaven sweeps in vain. Let it not be the unity of darkness, like the cloud-covered midnight sky, where neither moon nor star appears, neither the unity of a forced conformity, such as is found in polar seas, where eternal winter has locked up the waves in fetters, but pray that our unity, as Evangelical Protestants, as Baptists, may be like a fountain flowing ever fresh and free from the rock, like the rainbow that combines the seven prismatic colors into one glorious arch of promise, spanning the heavens, like old ocean's unfettered flow, as its waves rush in all their majesty and might, "distinct as the billows, but one as the sea."[24]

Wisher pointed to racial needs as the primary reason for the unity of black Baptists. Most of the delegates apparently shared his views. They too yearned for greater cooperation and fellowship among the Baptists. But questions of the distribution of power were not allowed to be dismissed lightly. The only thing the 1888 union meeting could achieve was to agree to hold joint anniversaries in 1889. Given this political reality many had resigned themselves to dreaming and hoping for the fruition of that which could not be seen. More was required than talking and dreaming, however, if the ANBC was to achieve its goal of unifying the Afro-American Baptists. Many believed that a greater sense of racial solidarity was a prerequisite to forming a strong racial ecclesiastical bond. But they really did not know how to create a greater sense of race loyalty in a society that frowned on black solidarity, and among white denominational brethren who had a history of working against such unions.

Preludes to the 1895 Convention

The romantic attraction of racial solidarity among these peculiar Baptists strengthened as a result of an assault in 1889 on Emanuel King Love, the president of the BFMC. Then when the American Baptist Publication Society, responding to white pressure, reneged in 1890 on an agreement it had made with the major leaders of both the BFMC and the ANBC, black separatists found their cause célèbre.

The "Southern Outrage." On the surface the assault on Emanuel King Love and his entourage, who were headed for Indianapolis to attend the 1889 meeting of the black BFMC, was not an unusual event. It had become an infamous custom among some white Southerners to attack "niggers" whenever they were in the mood. The causes of these senseless assaults were many and varied. Racism was the major, but by no means the only, factor. Nevertheless, more and more white vigilante groups sought to enforce the unwritten laws of custom in the late 1880s. By 1890 the state legislatures of Georgia and Louisiana were able to reinstitute the apartheid "Black Codes" that had controlled the activities of antebellum free blacks, and, for a time, postwar emancipated blacks. Assaults against blacks were only one of the several infringements upon their human rights. Some blacks were quick to protest. Led by Harvey Johnson, pastor of the Union Baptist Church, black Baltimoreans organized the Brotherhood of Liberty to defend themselves against the tidal wave of discrimination, lynchings, and brutalities that plagued blacks in Maryland. August Meier reports that more than 350 leading black Georgians, including E. K. Love, met in 1888 to show solidarity in their support of pending education legislation and temperance, as well as their opposition to chain gangs, discrimination by common carriers, lynch law, disenfranchisement, and "inequities" in the jury system.[25]

Despite these protests the ideology of White Supremacy gained a new lease on life, and suborned white Americans to engage in greater infringements on First Amendment rights of blacks. Not even black ministers of the Gospel were exempt from the consequences of ignoring unwritten segregationist customs. Love was not the first black minister to be deprived of his right to ride anywhere he wanted on a common carrier. The Reverend Mr. William H. Heard of the A.M.E. Church, who became a bishop after 1908, also received such treatment. When an A.M.E. bishop was ejected from his first-class seat, T. Thomas Fortune, editor of the *New York Age*, denounced the Southern railroads for relegating upstanding black leaders to the smoking cars "where the vilest of impudent white scum resort to swear, to exhale rotten smoke and to expectorate pools of stinking excrementation of tobacco."[26]

The response from white authorities proved to be token rather than decisive. The Interstate Commerce Commission, established in 1887, was responsible for regulating the activities of railroads, including charting regulations regarding seating. In 1887, 1888, and 1889 the Commission responded to suits brought against the railroads by black men such as William Heard, W. H. Councill, a black school principal, and E. K. Love. In each instance the Commission upheld an 1882 federal court ruling that blacks who purchased first-class tickets had a right to first-class accommodations, even though it also upheld the doctrine of "separate but equal" facilities. The Commission's rulings were never enforced, however. In fact most of the Northern white newspapers ignored it.[27] Since the legal system failed them, black leaders turned to the political process. The reaction to the assault on the Love entourage illustrates how the largest group of black Christians responded to this new racial challenge.

The Baxley Incident. Emanuel Love, pastor of the First African Baptist Church of Savannah and editor of the *Weekly Sentinel,* was approached by an agent of the East Tennessee, Virginia and Georgia Rail Road[28] to persuade his delegates to travel over this road. According to Love, the agent assured him that his delegates could get first-class accommodations through to Indianapolis. Love subsequently published an article to this effect in the *Georgia Baptist,* and urged all of the Georgia delegates to the black Foreign Mission Convention to patronize this line. By prior arrangement the delegates from Brunswick, Georgia, agreed to meet Love in Jesup on Monday, 9 September 1889. Love, G. M. Spratling and John Williams, Deacon J. H. Brown, Mrs. Janie Garnet, and others purchased tickets for seating in the first-class car. The delegates assumed that the ticket agent had enough blacks to fill a first-class car so that segregated seating could be arranged as custom demanded. But the train only had one first-class car and one smoking car. Since Love and most of his entourage had first-class tickets and were avid opponents of smoking and drinking, sitting in the smoking car was unthinkable.

As soon as the train was under way, Pastor Love went through the two cars saluting his comrades, including a black Methodist presiding elder. He then noticed that the white conductors and passengers began to whisper among themselves. A black workman warned him that trouble was ahead. Love immediately retraced his steps in order to warn his friends that danger was imminent. But he was too late.

Someone telegraphed ahead that Love, a well-known black preacher, and his group had taken seats among the white people. When they reached Baxley, Georgia, fifty or more men, armed with clubs, pieces of iron, and pistols, rushed into the car and brutally assaulted the "well-dressed" black delegates. Some of the delegates defended themselves. But most of them, including Love, had to flee for their lives. Mrs. Janie Garnet, a graduate of Atlanta University and a Brunswick schoolteacher, screamed from fright. One of the ruffians "put a cocked pistol to her breast and said, "You G-d D—d heffer, if you don't hush your mouth and get out of here, I will blow your G-d D—d brains out."[29] She fainted. After being treated for bruises and broken bones, most of the delegates, including Love, proceeded to Indianapolis to attend the national meetings.

This assault on influential black religious leaders was viewed by the denominational press and the black newspapers as an unusual instance of white Southern brutality and lawlessness. Most of the secular white-owned newspapers either ignored the incident or played down its significance. The incident angered most of the middle-class-minded national leaders of the black Baptists. It reminded them that no black person, regardless of social status, was immune from becoming the victim of white "ruffians." Furthermore it tested the effectiveness of their ties to the Republican Party. Love and his comrades, in a letter to the editor of the Philadelphia *National Baptist*, raised the salient questions in this regard.

> We look to God and ask what are we to do? What is the use of appealing to the Government? Our sufferings and inhuman outrages are known. The crimes are not committed in a corner—the men were not masked. The Government [has] known our condition. The Government protects its citizens abroad[.] It does seem that the glory of American citizenship means no glory for us. What are we to do?[30]

This last question was the primary one confronting the other delegates when their colleagues from Georgia arrived in Indianapolis.

The 1889 Indianapolis Meetings. Since the Northern white ABMU and its domestic counterpart, the ABHMS, had met with the black Convention the previous year, it was the American Baptist Publication Society's turn in 1889. The BFMC held its meeting, 12–14 September, while the ANBC met 15–18 September. Thus the meetings lasted one week, beginning and ending on a Thursday. The delegates then met in special session with the officers of the Publication Society on 18–19 September. These meetings, according to prior planning, were supposed to focus on celebrating the twenty-fifth anniversary of the Publication Society's work with freedmen. But the Love assault hovered over the proceedings like a cloud. One eyewitness expressed the regnant mood of the delegates:

> When our brethren saw with their own eyes these unmistakable evidences of oppression, knowing these delegates from the State of Georgia as distinguished far and near as peaceable, honest, well educated, temperate gentlemen, and realizing that things were coming to a terrible pass when our ministers of the gospel find it unsafe for their lives and persons to visit our annual gatherings to assist in their humble way in solving the problems of America, strong men were moved to copious tears.[31]

Despite the assault Love was in the chair to gavel the meeting of the Foreign Mission Convention to order on Thursday 12 September, just three days after he and his companions were attacked. The minutes of this gathering are unrevealing about the tension that filled the sanctuary of the Second Colored Church as bruised President Love chaired the opening exercises. With typical but obvious indifference to his own physical wounds, Love greeted the delegates, and with deep pathos declared,

> Though you may have met Apolyon on many battlefields since we were together last, and though you may have received severe wounds and have been greatly discouraged at times, let me earnestly hope that the Holy Spirit has revived your souls and that you are greatly encouraged on your pilgrim journey.[32]

The implied reference to the troubles of his delegation is graphic but still concealed. His strange silence throughout the remainder of the proceedings is unbelievable. Surely he said something in his own behalf. Again, the minutes are unrevealing. Nonetheless, even if he failed to speak up in his own behalf,[33] the more aggressive members of the Convention were not to be silenced. George Boling of Kentucky early in the proceedings interrupted routine business to ask whether or not the Committee on Resolutions would bring his resolution concerning the Love assault to the attention of the members of the Convention. President Love would have none of this, however. His Convention would be run according to its stated agenda. He did not allow Boling's resolution to come before the Convention until Sunday 15 September, as previously agreed. Given the delegates' anger it might have seemed wise not to consider the matter until later in the proceedings lest this issue eclipse the unification plan. The chair had little reason, however, to fear that this would have happened since Boling's resolution joined the issue of black Baptist unification with the need for black political solidarity.

Boling's resolution went beyond mere protest. He called for black Baptist solidarity on all fronts. He spoke the mind of many of the delegates as he declared that the attacks on the Love entourage had convinced them that "the time has come for us as heralds of the cross of Christ to teach our people the necessity of joining common cause." He proposed that solidarity could be shown by sending out a circular letter that would call on all Afro-Americans to contribute money to assist the victims of the assault in a suit against the railroad.[34] He also implied that black Baptist unity was a prerequisite to racial unity.

The Convention discussed Boling's resolution but did not act. After all it was meeting on the Lord's Day. Business of such a distasteful nature would not be allowed to dampen the movement of the Spirit. Nevertheless Harvey Johnson (whose separatist ideology will figure in later discussions) preached the 11 A.M. sermon. It was not his custom to dodge an opportunity to defend the race and call for race unity.

Johnson was the chief spokesman for the aggressive members of the Foreign Mission Convention who would not allow the Love Assault matter to fade away. Johnson insisted on the Monday following the Sunday debate over the Boling resolution that the clerk of the Convention read a communication from the prestigious First African Baptist Church of Savannah. The telegram stated that Love's congregation would voluntarily defray all expenses needed to prosecute the assailants. Johnson then urged the members of the Convention who endorsed the telegram to stand and sing the doxology. According to Solomon T. Clanton, the recording secretary, "This was enthusiastically sung by the great Convention."[35] The Convention also voted to ask the President of the United States to set aside a day of fasting and prayer in behalf of oppressed black Southerners. It then held a very brief meeting on Monday 16 September before it adjourned in order for its members to attend the ANBC. This convention then opened its deliberations once the BFMC adjourned.

The purpose of these sequential meetings, as has already been noted, was to formulate plans for the eventual unification of all national black Baptist forces. But the serious political divisions within the BFMC once again forestalled unification. These divisions are evident in the different positions that each convention took regarding the Love Assault.

The ANBC delegates were seemingly more inclined to make the Love Assault a cause célèbre than the more cautious, conservative, and older Foreign Missioners. Mostly Southern in origin and in numbers, the black BFMC apparently had more to lose than to gain in making a national issue of the affair; most of its members had to live in the deep South.[36] The ANBC was caught in the same dilemma, but its leadership came primarily from the border states and from the Southeastern seaboard states, Virginia and Maryland in particular, where racial pressures were less intense.

The ANBC responded to the Love Assault by passing a series of resolutions that had a stronger political bent than the one resolution passed by the BFMC. The ANBC's resolutions in effect condemned the assault and called upon President Benjamin Harrison to take appropriate action against the lawlessness of white Southerners. These resolutions were passed on the last day of the meetings after the ANBC delegates had waited in vain for the BFMC brethren to take action.

James A. Taylor of Virginia moved that a committee of five be appointed "to frame a memorial to present to the President of the United States, and Dr. [William James] Simmons [president of the ANBC] be chairman."[37] The motion passed, and Simmons appointed Walter Henderson Brooks of Washington, D.C., Harrison N. Boney of Alabama, Emanuel M. Brawley of Tennessee, and James A. Taylor of Virginia to the committee. All of these men were known to be outspoken black separatists. Their separatist sentiments were reflected in the tone and recommendations contained in their important resolutions.

Walter Henderson Brooks, pastor of the old Nineteenth Street Baptist Church, still smarting from confrontations with the ABHMS over its control of Wayland Theological Seminary in Richmond,[38] presented the committee's proposed resolutions to be submitted to the President of the United States. Brooks reported that the committee felt that the major blame for the Love Assault should be placed on the managers of the railroad because the railroad had the responsibility of protecting its passengers. They believed that the railroad was especially at fault if, as it had been rumored, its employees took part in the "Baxley ambush." The committee pointed out that something should be done to curb railroads that advertised as if they did not discriminate against blacks, but still catered to local segregationists' customs and laws that ignored the rights of black people. They suggested that any railroad that did not abide by federal civil rights should be prosecuted by the Interstate Commerce Commission.[39]

These resolutions reflected the belief of the ANBC delegates that black Baptists should go beyond the pious recommendation of the BFMC that the President of the United States should call for the nation to set aside the third Sunday in October as a day of prayer and fasting in behalf of the colored people of the United States. Although they concurred with the Foreign Mission brethren, the committee felt that this new display of racial hatred demanded a political solution. Therefore they asked the ANBC to endorse a resolution calling on President Benjamin Harrison "to recommend to the United States Congress an appropriation of $100,000,000 to aid the colored people in leaving the South." The amount was changed to $50 million by the time the committee gathered later in the year in the offices of the *Washington Bee* (District of Columbia) to explain its recent action to the black press. But the basic proposal remained intact. The committee had reached the conclusion, and the Convention concurred, that the South was hostile territory for black people, especially if "decent" and law-abiding black folk were not protected by the very law they sought to obey. The resolutions also called on white ministers to show leadership by counseling their people against brutality aimed at blacks. But given the history of indifference on the part of most white ministers, the black elders declared that this was a needful but vain hope.

As if grasping desperately for a long-range solution to the problem of racial hatred, they also advised young black men to take their families or themselves West where they could, in the words of Horace Greeley, "obtain lands and recognition and grow up with the country." They employed an Old Testament analogy to give biblical credentials to this prophetic advice to black young people. They declared, "The exodus of the Israelites from Egypt will be a small sized excursion compared to the move there will be [from] the South."[40] Before offering resolutions dealing with other denominational concerns of less importance, Brooks felt obliged to explain why a national black religious body should take the leadership in giving much needed political advice:

> Our political leaders are few, and even those we have cannot reach the people; therefore, it becomes our duty to speak out upon all questions that affect our people socially, economically, as well as religiously.

"God has always, in all ages," he added, "instructed and ruled the people through his own chosen and called men."[41] The Convention adopted all of the Committee's resolutions.

Although the minutes of the BGA are not extant, we know that this group, which met in Indianapolis along with the other black Baptist groups, also took action. It sent a telegram to President Harrison denouncing the Love Assault, and called on the president to take appropriate action. O. L. Pruden, assistant presidential secretary, telegraphed a reply informing the delegates that the president had referred the matter "to the Attorney-General for attention."[42] How the government finally dealt with this event is unclear.

Furthermore it was unclear whether or not this incident would deepen the racial chasm between black and white Baptists.[43] Several months passed before Baptists knew where they stood with Northern white Baptist leaders in regard to the resurgence of Jim Crow. They already knew where they stood with the Southern Baptists. Black bitterness about the complicity of white Southern Baptists still lingered. Robert A. McGuinn, black general missionary in Maryland, reflected the views of most black leaders when he stated that white Southern Baptists during slavery had "taught one-half the Gospel; they practiced one-fourth. Twenty-five years cannot remove it."[44]

The ABHMS, on the other hand, had not improved its popularity largely because its executive secretary, Henry Lyman Morehouse, responded angrily to the movement among black Southerners to gain control of its schools in the South. Morehouse attacked the separatist ideology that, he felt, encouraged black leaders to follow this path. While speaking before the 1888 black delegates in Nashville, he decried the dominance of the race spirit. He declared that his society had engaged in a "vast expenditure of energy" and money in behalf of "the black man in America" because it wanted blacks to "arise to the full stature of American and Christian manhood." He believed that after twenty-five years since emancipation the black man "should be a man with sympathies as broad as those of any other human being." He charged that "we hear much about the Negro in America. I want to hear more about America in the Negro—the American spirit of lively interest in all mankind. Let the American spirit be dominant over the race spirit."[45] These words fell on deaf ears, however. Blacks ignored hypocritical white leaders who preached that black people should practice Christian charity while they themselves resisted the call to share denominational wealth and power.

Black Baptist leaders also did not know where they stood with the American Baptist Publication Society. We have already seen how the black brethren rebuffed the ecumenical advances of the ABMU and the ABHMS in 1888. But how would they relate to the Publication Society? The separatist mood of the 1888 delegates convinced their leaders that organic union with white Baptists was untenable.

Having learned this lesson, black Baptist leaders proceeded to negotiate cooperative ventures with the Publication Society. But separatist
rhetoric, widely publicized in black minutes and newspapers, created
more problems than black Baptist leaders had expected. They discovered
that some of the leaders of the Publication Society could not summon
enough moral courage to challenge white supremacy. Indeed, the Society's own precarious economic structure made it just as determined in the
1880s to maintain a monopoly over publishing Baptist evangelistic literature as the ABHMS was determined in the 1860s and 1870s to control
the evangelization of the freedmen. Conflict came swiftly as the surge of
independence among a new generation of smart and aggressive young
black leaders encountered the tough and determined hegemony of the
Publication Society.

Notes

1. A black national Baptist Education Convention was organized 20–21 September 1892 in Savannah, Georgia. But its influence in the events that led to the creation of the National Baptist Convention was minimal.
2. The 1880 date for the origin of the National Baptist Convention resulted from contin-uing the custom of claiming the date of origin to be the date of the founding of the old-est constituent body of the merging organizations. The founders of the CABMC did this in 1866. Another reason why twentieth-century black National Baptists have given a central role to the foreign mission movement is largely because its first historian, Lewis Garnett Jordan, longtime executive secretary of the Foreign Mission Board of the incor-porated National Baptist Convention, simply listed the founding of the BFMC in 1880 as the date for the origin of the National Baptist Convention. There is no evidence that the organizers of the 1895 Convention held this view. Without being uncharitable it should be noted that Jordan left much evidence to support the claim that he was obsessed with the desire of the aged to be remembered. See *Atlanta Constitution*, 26 September 1895; and *Seventh Annual Report of Historian and General Missionary . . . of the National Baptist Convention, U.S. [Inc.]*, 1932, 28. The history of the black Baptist foreign mission movement still remains largely unrecorded. But important explorations into this immense enterprise have been made by Sandy Dwayne Martin, "Growth of Christian Missionary Interest in West Africa Among Southeastern Baptists, 1880–1915" (Ph.D. dissertation, Columbia University, 1981).
3. Franklin, *From Slavery to Freedom* (New York: Alfred A. Knopf, 1967) 301.
4. BFMC *Minutes*, 1889, 7–8.
5. BFMC *Minutes*, 1886, 32.
6. Ibid., 30–31.
7. ANBC *Minutes*, 1886, 13.
8. Women played a prominent role in these deliberations. Although they were not per-mitted to preach, they gave lectures on such topics as "Woman's Place in the Work of the Denomination." One woman, Miss Lucy Wilmot Smith of Louisville, Kentucky,

was even elected Historian of the Convention. See ANBC *Journal and Lectures*, 1887, 45–58, 65–67. The new role of women constitutes more evidence for the broad spirit of William Simmons. Ida B. Wells, the first famous black female journalist, said of Simmons, "In every way he could, Dr. Simmons encouraged me to be a newspaper woman, and whatever fame I achieved in the line I owe in large measure to his influence and encouragement" (Alfreda M. Duster, ed., *Crusade for Justice: The Autobiography of Ida B. Wells*, John Hope Franklin, series ed., *Negro American Biographies and Autobiographies* [Chicago: The University of Chicago Press, 1970] 32). The work of Evelyn Brooks on the history of the women's rights movement within the black Baptist family adds much to our understanding of these dynamics. See her two published articles: "Nannie Burroughs and the Education of Black Women" in Sharon Harley and Rosalyn Terborg-Penn, eds., *The Afro-American Woman: Struggles and Images* (Port Washington NY: Kennikate Press, 1978) 97–108, 131–33; and "The Feminist Theology of the Black Baptist Church, 1880–1900" in Amy Swerdlow and Hanna Lessinger, eds., *Class, Race, and Sex: The Dynamics of Control* (Boston: G. K. Hall, 1983) 31–59.

9. I have not been able to locate copies of this newspaper.

10. Turner shared a deep interest in politics with Simmons. Both had earned national reputations as a result of their involvement in Reconstruction politics. Turner was a Georgia legislator and postmaster, while Simmons worked on the county level in Florida before migrating to Kentucky. Both men were "race men" par excellence. See Turner's biographical sketch in Simmons, ed., *Men of Mark, Eminent, Progressive, and Rising* (Cleveland: George M. Rewell, 1887; reprint, New York: Arno Press, 1968) 5–19.

11. Ibid., 15; Duster, *Crusade for Justice*, 31.

12. It is impossible to establish the accuracy of DeBaptiste's figures since black Baptist data were gathered in haphazard fashion. The figures do seem to be plausible, however. DeBaptiste's rather crude but sensible method was simply to compare the statistics in his own compilation of association and convention minutes with those of the widely respected *American Baptist Year Book*. He was able to gather minutes that the editors of the *Year Book* never dreamed existed or were unable to secure. There were literally several hundreds of them. DeBaptiste counted 311. The *American Baptist Year Book* people often confused black Southern associations with white ones because the adjectives African, Colored or Negro were often not used by black Baptist groups. DeBaptiste's figures doubled the standard figure of 500,000 which the *Year Book* usually listed as the total number of black Baptists in the United States.

13. ANBC *Minutes*, 1886, 63, 67.

14. This seminary was located in Morgan Park, Illinois, and was the forerunner of the University of Chicago Divinity School. Other leaders of the ANBC also received their professional training at Baptist Union during the 1880s, including Charles Lewis Fisher, W. C. Jordan, and Robert J. Semple. See ANBC *Journal and Lectures*, 1887, 66.

15. ANBC *Minutes*, 1886, 77.

16. Ibid., 80.

17. ANBC *Journal and Lectures*, 1887, 12.

18. ANBC *Journal, Sermons and Lectures*, 1888, 64.

19. The white Southern Baptist Convention was not resting on its tradition of discrimination toward black Baptists in the South. According to one historian, it "had some type of ministry to the Negroes during 1882 and 1884 in at least eleven states." See John Edward Hughes, "A History of the Southern Baptist Convention's Ministry to the

Negro: 1845–1904" (Th.D. dissertation, Southern Baptist Theological Seminary, 1971) 155. By the 1880s both the Northern and Southern white Baptists had reached an undeclared agreement that black missionaries were better at evangelizing their own than were white missionaries. Although they did retain some white missionaries the majority of their labor force consisted of local or itinerant black preachers and a few laypersons. They also appointed state missionaries to coordinate and develop the work on this level. These missionaries usually worked with the cooperation of all the black Southern state conventions and a few of the white ones. The major outline of the Southern Baptist work in this regard is told in Hughes's dissertation. The Northern ABHMS's side of the story is told in several places. The black Baptist side of this story has yet to be told.

20. *National Baptist* (Philadelphia), 4 October 1888.

21. ANBC, *Journal, Sermons and Lectures*, 1888, 27, 47.

22. Ibid., 99.

23. This address was so well received that part of it was reprinted later at a crucial period in the history of the movement to unify. See *National Baptist Magazine* 1 (January 1894): 27–29. By 1900 Wisher had fallen out with his New York Baptist brethren and joined the African Methodist Episcopal Church. Ironically, he blamed his troubles on Baptist polity. Black Baptist leaders dismissed this. See *National Baptist Magazine* 7 (March 1901): 243. Wilson Jeremiah Moses's studies of black cultural nationalism during this period provide helpful insights about the context of these sentiments. See Wilson Jeremiah Moses, *The Golden Age of Black Nationalism, 1850–1925* (Hamden CT: Archon Books, 1978); and his *Black Messiahs and Uncle Toms: Social and Literary Manipulations of a Religious Myth* (University Park: Pennsylvania State University Press, 1982).

24. ANBC *Journal, Sermons and Lectures*, 1888, 99–100.

25. August Meier, *Negro Thought in America, 1880–1915: Racial Ideologies in the Age of Booker T. Washington* (Ann Arbor: University of Michigan Press, 1963) 70. Howard N. Rabinowitz (*Race Relations in the Urban South, 1865–1890* [New York: Oxford University Press, 1978]) provides an excellent general analysis of the impact of Southern urbanization upon race relations in the New South. Joel Williamson (*The Crucible of Race: Black-White Relations in the American South* [New York: Oxford University Press, 1984]) offers the most prodigious study of race relations during this era.

26. Quoted in Meier, *Negro Thought in America*, 71.

27. See Rayford W. Logan, *The Betrayal of the Negro* (London: Collier-Macmillan, 1965) 191.

28. This railroad line was having troubles of its own that had resulted from the expansion and consolidation of various smaller lines. See C. Vann Woodward, *Origins of the New South, 1877–1913* (Baton Rouge: Louisiana State University Press, 1971) 121–23.

29. *National Baptist* (Philadelphia), 10 October 1889.

30. Ibid. Also see *Baptist Home Mission Monthly* 11 (November 1889): 295–96, and the *Indianapolis Journal*, 12–14 September 1889.

31. *Washington Bee* (District of Columbia), 9 November 1889.

32. BFMC *Minutes*, 1889, 7.

33. Love was usually an outspoken defender of the race. His earnest desire to empathize with his Southern white neighbors, while bolstered by the ethics of Christian pacifism, appeared to placate racism when chastisement seemed more in order. See his *A Sermon on Lynch Law and Raping: Preached by Rev. E. K. Love, D. D., at 1st African Baptist Church, Savannah, Ga. . . . November 5th, 1893* (Augusta GA: Georgia Baptist Print, 1894) 3.

34. Ibid., 17.
35. Ibid., 28.
36. One black reporter described the sentiments of the Southern brethren vis-à-vis the more militant ones. Some believed that "the only way the colored man can save himself from being kicked to death is to kick back." Others were more conservative, and feared that measures of a nature too aggressive would aggravate the present difficulties and endanger the lives of the delegates when they returned home. See *Washington Bee* (District of Columbia), 21 September 1889.
37. ANBC *Journal*, 1889, 19.
38. James M. McPherson, *The Abolitionist Legacy: From Reconstruction to the NAACP* (Princeton: Princeton University Press, 1975) 285–86; and Adolph H. Grundman, "Northern Baptists and the Founding of Virginia Union University: The Perils of Paternalism," *Journal of Negro History* 63 (January 1978): 26–41.
39. Apparently the black Baptist brethren misunderstood the self-imposed limitation of the Interstate Commerce Commission's powers. Citing *U.S. vs. Buntin* (1882), the Commission refused to undermine racial segregation on railroad coaches. See Meier, *Negro Thought in America*, 72.
40. *Washington Bee* (District of Columbia), 9 November 1889.
41. ANBC *Journal*, 1889, 19.
42. BFMC Minutes, 1889, 29.
43. Nevertheless the prestigious white Philadelphia Baptist Ministers' Conference did send a telegram to the BFMC denouncing the incident. See ibid., 29–30.
44. Robert A. McGuinn, *The Race Problem in the Churches* (Baltimore: J. F. Weishampel, 1890) 53.
45. Quoted in Edward M. Brawley, ed., *The Negro Baptist Pulpit: A Collection of Sermons and Papers on Baptist Doctrine and Missionary and Educational Work by Colored Baptist Ministers* (Philadelphia: American Baptist Publication Society, 1890; reprint, Freeport NY: Books for Libraries Press, 1971) 299.

Chapter 18

Negotiating and Transforming the Public Sphere

African American Political Life in the Transition from Slavery to Freedom

Elsa Barkley Brown

On April 15, 1880, Margaret Osborne, Jane Green, Susan Washington, Molly Branch, Susan Gray, Mary A. Soach and "over two hundred other prominent sisters of the church" petitioned the Richmond, Virginia, First African Baptist Church's business meeting to allow women to vote on the pastor:

> We the sisters of the church feeling that we are interested in the welfare of the same and also working hard to finish the house and have been working by night and day ... We know you have adopted a law in the church that the business must be done by the male members. We don't desire to alter that law, nor do we desire to have anything to do with the business of the church, we only ask to have a vote in electing or dismissing him. We whose names are attached to this petition ask you to grant us this privilege.[1]

The circumstances surrounding these women's petition suggest the kinds of changes taking place internally in late-nineteenth and early-twentieth century black Richmond and other southern black communities. In the immediate post–Civil War era women had voted in mass meetings and Republican Party conventions held at First African, thus contradicting gender-based assumptions within the larger society about politics, political engagement and appropriate forms of political behavior. Now, women sitting in the same church were petitioning for the right to vote in an internal community institution, couching the petition in terms designed to minimize the request and avoid a challenge to men's authority and position.

435

Scholars' assumptions of an unbroken line of exclusion of African American women from formal political associations in the late-nineteenth century have obscured fundamental changes in the political understandings within African American communities in the transition from slavery to freedom. Women in First African and in other areas were seeking in the late-nineteenth century not a new authority but rather a lost authority, one they now often sought to justify on a distinctively female basis. As these women petitioned for their rights within the church and as other women formed voluntary associations in turn-of-the-century Richmond they were not, as often depicted in the scholarly literature, emerging into the political arena through such actions. Rather these women were attempting to retain space they traditionally had held in the immediate post-emancipation period. This essay explores the processes of public discourse within Richmond and other southern black communities and the factors which led to increasingly more clearly gendered and class spaces within those communities to understand why women by the 1880s and 1890s needed to create their own pulpits from which to speak—to restore their voices to the community. This exploration suggests how the ideas, process, meanings and practice of freedom changed within late-nineteenth-century southern African American communities and what the implications of those changes may be for our visions of freedom and for the possibilities of African American community in the late-twentieth century.

After emancipation, African American men, women and children, as part of black communities throughout the South struggled to define on their own terms the meaning of freedom and in the process to construct communities of struggle. Much of the literature on Reconstruction portrays freed African Americans as rapidly and readily adopting a gendered private-public dichotomy.[2] Much of the literature on the nineteenth-century public sphere constructs a masculine liberal bourgeois public with a female counterpublic.[3] This essay, focusing on the civic geography of post–Civil War black Richmond suggests the problematic of applying such generalizations to African American life in the late-nineteenth-century South. In the immediate post-emancipation era black Richmonders enacted their understandings of democratic political discourse through mass meetings attended and participated in (including voting) by men, women and children and through mass participation in Republican Party conventions. They carried these notions of political participation into the state Capitol engaging from the gallery in the debates on the constitutional convention floor.

Central to African Americans' construction of a fully democratic notion of political discourse was the church as a foundation of the black public sphere.[4] In the post-slavery era, church buildings also served as meeting halls and auditoriums as well as educational and recreational facilities, employment and social service bureaus and bulletin boards. First African, especially, with a seating capacity of nearly 4000, was the site of large political gatherings. Schools such as Richmond Theological Seminary and Richmond Colored High and Normal School held their annual commencement exercises at First African Baptist, allowing these events to become community celebrations. Other groups, such as the Temperance Union, were regularly granted the church for their meetings or rallies. As a political space occupied by men, women and children, literate and non-literate, ex-slave and formerly free, church members and nonmembers, the availability and use of First African for mass meetings enabled the construction of political concerns in democratic space. This is not to suggest that official versions and spokespersons were not produced, but these official versions were the product of a fairly egalitarian discourse and, therefore, represented the conditions of black Richmonders of differing classes, ages and genders. Within black Richmonders' construction of the public sphere, the forms of discourse varied from the prayer to the stump speech to the testimonies regarding outrages against freedpeople to shouted interventions from the galleries into the debates on the legislative floor. By the very nature of their participation—the inclusion of women and children, the engagement through prayer, the disregard of formal rules for speakers and audience, the engagement from the galleries in the formal legislative sessions—Afro-Richmonders challenged liberal bourgeois notions of rational discourse. Many white observers considered their unorthodox political engagements to be signs of their unfamiliarity and perhaps unreadiness for politics.[5]

In the decades following emancipation, as black Richmonders struggled to achieve even a measured amount of freedom, the black public sphere emerged as more fractured and perhaps less democratic at the end of the nineteenth century, yet even then it retained strong elements of a democratic agenda. This essay examines the changing constructions of political space and community discourse in the post-emancipation era.

Envisioning Freedom

In April 1865, when Union troops marched into Richmond, jubilant African American men, women and children poured into the streets and crowded into their churches to dance, kiss, hug, pray, sing and shout. They assembled in First African, Third Street African Methodist, Ebenezer and Second African not merely because of the need to thank God for their deliverance but also because the churches were the only institutional spaces, and in the case of First African certainly the largest space, owned by African Americans themselves.[6] As the process of reconstruction unfolded, black Richmonders continued to meet regularly in their churches, now not merely to rejoice. If Afro-Richmonders had thought freedom would accompany emancipation, the events of the first few weeks and months of Union occupation quickly disabused them of such ideas. Throughout the summer and fall of 1865 black Richmonders reported numerous violations of their rights. Among them were pass and curfew regulations designed to curtail black mobility and force African American men and women out of the city to labor in the rural areas. Pass and curfew violators (800 in the first week of June) were detained in bullpens—one for women and children, a separate one for men—away from and often unknown to family members. Black Richmonders also detailed numerous incidents of disrespectful treatment, verbal abuse, physical assault and torture. "Many poor women" told "tales of their frights and robberies"; vendors told of goods destroyed by military police. Private homes were not immune to the intrusions of civilian and military white men. One couple was confronted by soldiers, one of whom stood over them in bed "threatening to blow out their brains if they moved" while others "pillage[d] the house of money, watches, underclothing, etc."[7] Many spoke of the sexual abuse of black women: "gobbling up of the most likely looking negro women, thrown into the cells, robbed and ravished at the will of the guard." Men and women in the vicinity of the jail testified "to hearing women scream frightfully almost every night."[8]

The regular meetings in the African churches, originally ones of jubilation, quickly became the basis for constructing a discourse about freedom and organizing large-scale mass protest. On June 10, 1865, over 3000 assembled at First African to hear the report of the investigating committee which had conducted hearings and gathered the evidence and depositions necessary to present black Richmonders' case directly to Governor Francis H. Pierpoint and to the "chief head of all authority," the President of the United States. The protest memorial drawn up during the meeting was ratified at meetings in each of the other churches and money was raised through church collections to send six representatives (one from each church in Richmond and one from First Baptist, Manchester) to Washington. On Friday, June 16, these delegates delivered the mass meeting's protest directly to President Andrew Johnson:[9] "Mr. President: We have been appointed a committee by a public meeting of the colored people of Richmond, Va., to make known . . . the wrongs, as we conceive them to be, by which we are sorely oppressed." In their memorial, as in their meetings, black Richmonders recounted not merely the abuses but they also used their individual stories to construct a collective history and to combat the idea of being "idle negroes" unprepared for freedom.[10]

> We represent a population of more than 20,000 colored people, including Richmond and Manchester, . . . more than 6,000 of our people are members in good standing of Christian churches, and nearly our whole population constantly attend divine services. Among us there are at least 2,000 men who are worth $200 to $500; 200 who have property valued at from $1,000 to $5,000, and a number who are worth from $5,000 to $20,000. . . .
>
> The law of Slavery severely punished those who taught us to read and write, but, not withstanding this, 3,000 of us can read, and at least 2,000 can read and write, and a large number of us are engaged in useful and profitable employment on our own account.

The community they described was one based in a collective ethos; it was not merely their industry but also their responsibility which was the basis on which they claimed their rights:

> None of our people are in the alms-house, and when we were slaves the aged and infirm who were turned away from the homes of hard masters, who had been enriched by their toil, our benevolent societies supported while they lived, and buried when they died, and comparatively few of us have found it necessary to ask for Government rations, which have been so bountifully bestowed upon the unrepentant Rebels of Richmond.

They reminded Johnson of the efforts black men and women in Richmond had taken to support the Union forces against the Confederacy:

> During the whole of the Slaveholders' Rebellion we have been true and loyal to the United States Government; . . . We have given aid and comfort to the soldiers of Freedom (for which several of our people, of both sexes, have been severely punished by stripes and imprisonment). We have been their pilots and their scouts, and have safely conducted them through many perilous adventures.

They declared themselves the loyal citizens of the United States, those the federal government should be supporting. And finally they invoked the religious destiny that emancipation had reaffirmed, reminding the President of a "motto once inscribed over the portals of an Egyptian temple, *'Know all ye who exercise power, that God hates injustice!'*"[11]

Mindful of others' versions of their history, standing and entitlements, black Richmonders also moved to have their own story widely circulated. When local white newspapers refused to publish their account, they had it published in the *New York Tribune*.[12] Throughout 1865 and 1866 black Richmonders continued to meet regularly in mass meetings where men, women and children collectively participated in constructing and announcing their own story of community and freedom.[13] The story told in those mass meetings, published in northern white newspapers, carried in protest to Union officials, was also carried into the streets as black Richmonders inserted themselves in the preexisting national political traditions and at the same time widened those traditions. John O'Brien has noted that in the immediate aftermath of emancipation, black Richmonders developed their own political calendar, celebrating four civic holidays: January 1; George Washington's birthday; April 3 (emancipation day); and July 4.[14] White Richmonders were horrified as they watched former slaves claim civic holidays and traditions they believed to be the historical possession of white Americans and occupy spaces, like Capitol Square, which had formerly been reserved for white residents.[15]

The underlying values and assumptions that would pervade much of black people's political struggles in the city were forged in slavery and war and in the weeks following emancipation. Military regulations which limited black mobility and made finding and reunifying family members even more difficult placed the economic interests of white men and women above the material and social interests of African Americans. The bullpens, which detained many away from their families, and the raids on black homes, which made all space public and subject to the interests of the state, obliterated any possible distinctions between public and private spheres. Demanding passes and evidence of employment denied black Richmonders the right to act and to be treated not as economic units and/or property but as social beings and family members. The difficulty of finding decent housing at affordable prices further impeded freedpeople's efforts to bring their families together. All of these obstacles to and expectations of family life were part of what Eric Foner speaks of as the "'politicization' of every day life."[16]

These political issues underpinned Afro-Richmonders' petition to Johnson and would continue to underpin their political struggles in late-nineteenth-century Richmond. Even as they fashioned individual stories into a collective history, black Richmonders could and did differ on the means by which they might secure freedom—vigorously debating issues such as the necessity of confiscation.[17] But they also understood freedom as a collective struggle. When they entered the formal political arena through Republican party politics in 1867 this understanding was the foundation for their initial engagement with issues of suffrage and democracy. As Julie Saville has observed for South Carolina, freedpeople in Richmond "were not so much converted to the Republican party as they were prepared to convert the Republican party to themselves."[18] The post–Civil War southern black public sphere was forged in jubilation and struggle as African American men, women and children claimed their own history and set forth their own political ideals.

All the resources of black Richmonders became elements in their political struggles. The *Richmond Whig*, intending to ridicule the inappropriateness of freedpeople's behaviors and assumptions, highlighted the politicized nature of all aspects of black life during Reconstruction; the freedpeople's "mass meetings, committee meetings, and meetings of the different societies all have political significance. The superstitions of the colored people are availed on, and religion and Radicalism are all jumbled together. Every night they have meetings and musterings, harangues and sermons, singing and praying—all looking to political results."[19] Similarly the *Richmond Dispatch* reported an 1867 Republican meeting which began with "Harris, colored" offering "the most remarkable" prayer "we have ever heard. It was frequently interrupted by laughter and manifestations of applause":

> Oh, Lord God, bless our enemies—bless President Johnson. We would not even have him sent to hell. Come, oh come, good Lord, and touch his heart even while I am talking with you here to-night. [Amen.] Show him the error of his ways. Have mercy upon our 'Moses,' [Sarcastic. Great laughter and amens.] who, like Esau, has sold his birthright for a morsel of pottage—took us in the wilderness and left us there. Come down upon him, oh Lord, with thy blessing. God bless us in our meeting to-night, and help us in what we do. God forbid that we should choose any Conservative that has the spirit of the devil in his heart, and whose feet take hold on hell. God bless our friend—true and tried—Mr. Hunnicut, who has stood a great many sorrows and I think he can stand a great many more. [Laughter.] Bless our judge, Mr. Underwood, who is down here among us, and don't let anything harm a hair of his head.[20]

What the *Whig* and the *Dispatch* captured was a political culture in which the wide range of institutional and noninstitutional resources of individuals and the community as a whole became the basis for defining, claiming and securing freedom in post-emancipation Richmond. The church provided more than physical space, financial resources and a communication network: it also provided a cultural base that validated emotion and experience as ways of knowing, and drew on a collective call and response, encouraging the active participation of all.[21]

Virginia's rejection of the Fourteenth Amendment brought the state under the Reconstruction Act of 1867; a constitutional convention became prerequisite for full restoration to the Union. Black men, enfranchised for the delegate selection and ratification ballots, were to have their first opportunity to engage in the political parties and legislative chambers of the state. The struggles in which they had engaged in the two years since emancipation influenced the manner of black Richmonders' initial participation in the formal political arena of conventions and voting. On August 1, 1867, the day the Republican state convention opened in Richmond to adopt a platform for the upcoming state constitutional convention, thousands of African American men, women and children absented themselves from their employment and joined the delegates at the convention site, First African Baptist Church.[22] Tobacco factories, lacking a major portion of their workers, were forced to close for the day.

This pattern persisted whenever a major issue came before the state and city Republican conventions held during the summer and fall of 1867, or the state constitutional convention which convened in Richmond from December 1867 to March 1868. A *New York Times* reporter estimated that "the entire colored population of Richmond" attended the October 1867 local Republican convention where delegates to the state constitutional convention were nominated. Noting that female domestic servants were a large portion of those in attendance, the correspondent reported: "as usual on such occasions, families which employ servants were forced to cook their own dinners, or content themselves with a cold lunch. Not only had Sambo gone to the Convention, but Dinah was there also."[23]

These men and women did not absent themselves from work just to be onlookers at the proceedings, but to be active participants. They assumed as equal a right to be present and participate as the delegates themselves, a fact they made abundantly clear at the August 1867 Republican state convention. Having begun to arrive four hours before the opening session, African American men and women had filled the meeting place long before the delegates arrived. Having showed up to speak for themselves, they did not assume delegates had priority—in discussion or in seating. Disgusted at the scene, as well as unable to find a seat, the conservative white Republican delegates removed to the Capitol Square to convene an outdoor session. That was quite acceptable to the several thousand additional African American men and women who, unable to squeeze into the church, were now still able to participate in the important discussions and to vote down the proposals of the conservative faction.[24]

Black men, women and children were also active participants throughout the state constitutional convention. A *New York Times* reporter commented on the tendency for the galleries to be crowded "with the 'unprivileged,' and altogether black." At issue was not just these men and women's presence but also their behavior. White women, for example, certainly on occasion sat in the convention's gallery as visitors silently observing the proceedings; these African Americans, however, participated from the gallery, loudly engaging in the debates. At points of heated controversy, black delegates turned to the crowds as they made their addresses on the convention floor, obviously soliciting and relying upon mass participation. Outside the convention hours, mass meetings were held to discuss and vote on the major issues. At these gatherings vote was either by voice or rising and men, women and children voted. These meetings were not mock assemblies; they were important gatherings at which the community made plans for freedom. The most radical black Republican faction argued that the major convention issues should actually be settled at these mass meetings with delegates merely casting the community's vote on the convention floor. Though this did not occur, black delegates were no doubt influenced by both the mass meetings and the African American presence in the galleries, both of which included women.[25]

Black Richmonders were operating in two separate political arenas: an internal one and an external one. While these arenas were related, they each proceeded from different assumptions, had different purposes, and therefore operated according to different rules. Within the internal political process women were enfranchised and participated in all public forums—the parades, rallies, mass meetings and the conventions themselves.[26] Richmond was not atypical in this regard.[27]

It was the state constitutional convention, however, which would decide African American women's and men's status in the political process external to the African American community. When the Virginia convention began its deliberation regarding the franchise, Thomas Bayne, a black delegate from Norfolk, argued the inherent link between freedom and suffrage, and contended that those who opposed universal suffrage were actually opposing the freedom of African American people. In rejoinder, E. L. Gibson, a Conservative white delegate, enunciated several principles of republican representative government. Contending that "a man might be free and still not have the right to vote," Gibson explained the fallacy of assuming that this civil right was an inherent corollary to freedom: if the right were inherent then it would belong to both sexes and to all from "the first moment of existence" and to foreigners immediately. This was "an absurdity too egregious to be contemplated."[28] And yet, this "absurd" notion of political rights was what was in practice in the Richmond black community—males and females voted without regard to age, the thousands of rural migrants who came into Richmond suffered no waiting period but immediately possessed the full rights of the community. What was absurd to Gibson and most white men—Republican or Democrat—was obviously quite rational to many black Richmonders. Two very different conceptions of freedom and public participation in the political process were in place.

In the end only men obtained the legal franchise. The impact of this decision is neither inconsequential nor fully definitive. African American women were by law excluded from the formal political arena external to their community. Yet this does not mean that they were not active in that arena; witness Richmond women's participation in the Republican and the constitutional conventions. Southern black men and women debated the issue of women's suffrage in both the external and internal political arenas. In Nansemond County, Virginia, for example, the mass meetings resolved that women should be granted the legal franchise; in Richmond, while a number of participants in a mass meeting supported female suffrage, the majority opinion swung against it.[29] But the meaning of that decision was not as straightforward as it may seem. The debate as to whether women should be given the vote in the external political arena occurred in internal political arena mass meetings where women participated and voted not just before and during, *but also after* the negative decision regarding legal enfranchisement. This maintained the status quo in the external community; ironically enough, the status quo in the internal community was maintained as well—women continued to have the vote. African American men and women clearly operated within two distinct political systems.

Focusing on formal disfranchisement obscures women's continued participation in the external political arena. In Richmond and throughout the South exclusion from legal enfranchisement did not prevent African

American women from shaping the vote and the political decisions. Throughout the late 1860s and 1870s women continued to participate in political meetings in large numbers and to organize political societies. Some like the Rising Daughters of Liberty and the Daughters of the Union Victory in Richmond or the United Daughters of Liberty organized by coal miners' wives living outside Manchester had all-female memberships. Others, like the 2000-member National Political Aid Society, the Union League of Richmond and the Union Equal Rights League of Manchester had male and female members. Even though white Republicans made efforts to exclude them from further participation in political meetings by the late 1860s, African American women in Virginia, South Carolina, Louisiana and elsewhere were still attending these meetings in the 1870s.

Women's presence at these meetings was anything but passive. In the violent political atmosphere of the last years of Reconstruction, they had an especially important and dangerous role. In South Carolina, for example, while the men participated in the meeting, the women guarded the guns—thus serving in part as the protectors of the meeting. For those women and men who lived in outlying areas of Richmond and attended outdoor meetings, political participation was a particularly dangerous matter, a fact they clearly recognized. Meetings were guarded by posted sentinels with guns who questioned the intent of any suspicious people, usually white men, coming to the meeting. A reporter for the *Richmond Daily Dispatch* described one such encounter when he attempted to cover a political meeting of fifty women and twenty-five men.[30]

Women as well as men took election day off from work and went to the polls. Fraud, intimidation and violence became the order of election days. White newspapers and politicians threatened loss of jobs, homes and lives. Afro-Richmonders countered with a group presence. Often even those living within the city and short distances from the polling places went early, even the night before, and camped out at the polls, hoping that their early presence would require the acceptance of their vote and that the group presence would provide protection from violence and intimidation. In the highly charged political atmosphere of late-nineteenth-century Richmond it was no small matter for these women and men to participate in political meetings and show up at the election sites. The reasons for the group presence at the polls were varied. African American women in Virginia, Mississippi, South Carolina and elsewhere understood themselves to have a vital stake in African American men's franchise. The fact that only men had been granted the vote did not at all mean that only men should exercise the vote. Women throughout the South initiated sanctions against men who voted Democratic; some went along to the polls to insure a properly cast ballot. As increasing white fraud made black men's voting more difficult, early arrival at the polls was partly intended to counter such efforts.

Although election days in Richmond were not as violent as they were elsewhere throughout Virginia and other parts of the South, guns were used to intimidate and defraud. It is also probable that in Richmond, as elsewhere throughout the South, when black men went to camp out overnight at the polls, households feared leaving women and children unprotected at home. Thus the women's presence, just as the group presence of the men, may have been a sign of the need for collective protection. If Richmond women were at all like their sisters in South Carolina and Danville, they may have carried weapons with them—to protect themselves and/or help protect the male voters.[31] Women and children's presence reflects their excitement about the franchise but also their understanding of the dangers involved in voting. The necessity for a group presence at the polls reinforced the sense of collective enfranchisement. Women's presence at the polls was both a negative sanction and a positive expression of the degree to which they understood the men's franchise to be a new political opportunity for themselves as well as their children.

In the dangerous political atmosphere of the late-nineteenth century, the vote took on a sacred and collective character. Black men and women in Richmond, as throughout the South, initiated sanctions against those black men perceived as violating the collective good by supporting the Conservative forces. Black Democrats were subject to the severest exclusion: disciplined within or quite often expelled from their churches and mutual benefit societies; denied board and lodging with black families. Additionally, mobs jeered, jostled and sometimes beat black Democrats or rescued those who were arrested for such acts. Women were often reported to be in the forefront of this activity. Similarly, black women were said to have "exercised a positive influence upon some men who were inclined to hesitate or be indifferent" during the early 1880s Readjuster campaigns.[32]

All of this suggests that African American women and men understood the vote as a collective, not an individual possession; and furthermore, that African American women, unable to cast a separate vote, viewed African American men's vote as equally theirs. They believed that franchise should be cast in the best interest of both. This is not the nineteenth-century patriarchal notion that men voted on behalf of their wives and children. By that assumption women had no individual wills; rather men operated in women's best interest because women were assumed to have no right of input. African American women assumed the political rights that came with being a member of the community even though they were denied the political rights they thought should come with being citizens of the state.

To justify their political participation Richmond and other southern black women in the immediate post–Civil War period did not need to rely on arguments of superior female morality or public motherhood. Their own cultural, economic and political traditions provided rationale enough. An understanding of collective autonomy was the basis on which African Americans reconstructed families, developed communal institutions, constructed schools and engaged in formal politics after emancipation. The participation of women and children in the external and internal political arenas was part of a larger political worldview of ex-slaves and free men and women, a worldview fundamentally shaped by an understanding that freedom, in reality, would accrue to each of them individually only when it was acquired by all of them collectively. Such a worldview contrasted sharply with the "possessive individualism" of liberal democracy.[33] This sense of suffrage as a collective, not an individual possession was the foundation for much of African American women's political activities in the post–Civil War era.[34] Within these understandings the boundary lines between men's and women's political behavior were less clearly drawn and active participation in the political arenas—internal or external—seldom required a retreat into womanhood or manhood as its justification.

Even in the organization of militia units, post-emancipation black Richmonders, at least for a time, rejected the liberal bourgeois ideal of a solely male civic domain. By 1886 black men had organized three militia companies. By the late 1870s black women had also organized a militia company, although apparently only for ceremonial purposes; it reportedly was active only before and during emancipation celebrations. Its members conducted preparatory drills on Broad Street, one of Richmond's main thoroughfares. Frank Anthony, the man who prepared and drilled the women's company, demanded military precision and observance of regular military commands.[35] Unlike the men participating in the militias, who came from working-class, artisan, business and professional backgrounds, the women were probably working-class. Although they served no self-defense role, their drilling in Richmond streets and marching in parades challenged ideas and assumptions about appropriate public behavior held by both white southerners and white Unionists. The women's unit not only challenged, as did the men's, the idea of black subservience, but also suggested wholly new forms and meanings of respectable female behavior. There is no evidence concerning how long this women's unit survived or the causes of its demise. We can speculate that, besides horrifying whites, such a unit may have also become unacceptable to a number of black Richmonders. Increasingly, concerns about respectable behavior were connected to the public behavior of the working class and of women. This black women's militia, however, suggests the fluidity of gender notions in the early years of emancipation. The brevity of its appearance suggests how questions of public behavior became integral within black Richmond, just as they had been within the larger society. Yet for a time the actions of these women declared that perhaps no area of political participation or public ceremony was strictly a male domain.

Renegotiating Public Life

The 1880 First African women's petition followed three contentious church meetings, some lasting until two or three o'clock in the morning, at which the congregants considered dismissing and/or excluding the pastor, the Reverend James H. Holmes. This discussion was initiated at an April fifth meeting where two women were charged with fighting about the pastor. The April sixth meeting considered charges of "unchristian conduct" on the part of Holmes; those men present voted to exclude Holmes. A meeting on April eleventh endorsed a protest signed by all but two of the deacons against the earlier proceedings. The protest charged the anti-Holmes faction with trying to "dispose of the deacons, take charge of prayer meetings, the Sunday school and revolutionize things generally." The discussions which ensued over the next two months split the congregation; the May and June church business meetings were "disorderly" and "boisterous." Holmes and the deacons called in the mayor, city court judge, and chief of police to support the pastor and the police to remove or arrest those members of the congregation designated as "rebellious." After the anti-Holmes faction was removed from the church, the June meeting expelled forty-six men for "rebelliously attempting to overthrow and seize upon the church government." It also excluded the two women initially charged, one for fighting and the other for tattling; exonerated Holmes "from all false" accusation; and thanked the civil officers who attended the meeting and restored order. Only after these actions did the church consider the women's petition which had been presented in the midst of the controversy more than two months earlier.[36]

First African's records do not adequately reveal the nature of gender relations within the church in the late 1860s and 1870s. We do know that the pre–Civil War, sex-segregated seating patterns were abandoned by Richmond black Baptist churches immediately after the Civil War and that by the late 1860s women "not only had a voice, but voted in the business meetings" of Ebenezer Baptist Church.[37] Women who voted in political meetings held in First African in the 1860s and 1870s may have carried this participation over to church business meetings. Often in the immediate post–Civil War period, business and political meetings were not clearly distinguishable.

The petition of the women of First African makes clear, however, that by the early 1880s, while women attended and apparently participated in church meetings, the men had "adopted a law in the church that the business must be done by the male members." Whether Margaret Osborne, Jane Green, and others thought that their voices and interests were being inadequately represented, even ignored by the deacons, or wanted to add their voices to those, including the deacons, who were struggling to retain Holmes and control of First African, these women understood that they would have to defend their own rights. The women argued their right to decide on the pastor, justifying their petition by both their work on behalf of the church and the importance of their economic support to the church's ongoing activities and to the pastor's salary. Not until after the matter of Holmes's exclusion was settled were the petitioners granted their request. Since they apparently remained within First African, the petitioners' organization probably indicates that they were not among those dissatisfied with Holmes. It does suggest, however, their dissatisfaction with church procedure and the place of women in church polity. Still, the petition was conservative and the women denied any intention to demand full voting rights in church matters. The petition was not taken as a challenge to church authority, as were the actions of the anti-Holmes faction. When brought up for a vote in the June meeting, the women's petition was adopted by a vote of 413 to 16.[38]

The women's petition and the vote in favor of it suggest the tenuous and ambiguous position that women had come to occupy both within First African and within the internal political arena more generally. They participated actively in church meetings but the authority for that participation and the question of limiting women's role resurfaced throughout the late-nineteenth century. In the 1890s the women of First African would again have to demand their rights, this time against challenges to their very presence at church meetings, when a deacon sought to prohibit women from even attending First African business meetings. The women protested and the church responded quickly by requiring the deacon to apologize to the women and assure them that they were welcome at the meetings. The degree of women's participation and decision-making powers, however, remained ambiguous.

In 1901–1902 during another crisis period in First African, a number of men sought to blame the problems on women. John Mitchell, Jr., a member of First African and editor of the *Richmond Planet*, cited the active participation of women ("ladies who knew nothing of the machinery at work or the deep laid plans on foot") and children ("Sunday School scholars from 8 years of age upward") in church affairs, suggesting that they did not comprehend the proceedings and had been easily misled or manipulated by male factions. Deacon J. C. Farley cited women's active participation in church meetings as the problem, reminding the congregation that "it was the rule of the church" that women were only allowed to vote on the pastor but had extended their participation far past that. And the new minister, the Reverend W. T. Johnson, admonished the women, saying that "the brethren could almost fight in the church meeting and when they went out they would shake hands and laugh and talk. But the sisters would talk about it going up Broad St. and everybody would know what they had done." First African women rejected these assessments of their church's problems. A significant number walked out rather than have their participation censured; those who remained reportedly refused to be silent but continually "talked out in the meeting." Sister Margaret Hewlett later sought out the editor of the *Richmond Planet* to voice her opposition to the men's denunciation of women's roles and to make clear that the women thought the church's problems lay in the male leadership, saying specifically "the deacons were the cause of all the trouble anyway."[39]

In the early 1890s the *Virginia Baptist* publicized its belief that women, in exceeding their proper places in the church by attempting to preach, and in the community by their "deplorable" efforts to "exercise the right of suffrage," would lose their "womanliness."[40] The complexity of gender relations within the African American community was such that at the same time First African was debating women's attendance at church meetings and the *Virginia Baptist* was advocating a severely restricted women's role, other women such as Alice Kemp were known throughout the community as the authors of prominent male ministers' sermons and women such as the Reverend Mrs. Carter were establishing their reputations as "soul-stirring" preachers. The *Richmond Planet* reported these women's activities without fanfare, as if they were commonplace. The debate over women's roles also had become commonplace. The Reverend Anthony Binga, pastor of First Baptist (Manchester), noted the debate in his sermon on

Church Polity; Binga supported women teaching Sunday School, participating in prayer-meetings and voting "on any subject pertaining to the interest of the church" including the pastor; but he interpreted the Bible as forbidding women "throwing off that modesty that should adorn her sex, and taking man's place in the pulpit." The subject received community-wide attention in June 1895 when Ebenezer Baptist Church staged a debate between the ministers of Second Baptist (Manchester) and Mount Carmel, judged by other ministers from Fourth Baptist, First African, First Baptist (Manchester) and others on the subject, "Resolved that a woman has every right and privilege that a man has in the christian church."[41]

The debates within First African and other churches over women's roles were part of a series of political struggles within black Richmond in the late-nineteenth and early-twentieth centuries. As formal political gains, initially secured, began to recede and economic promise became less certain and less surely tied to political advancement, the political struggles over relationships between the working-class and the newly emergent middle-class, between men and women, between literate and nonliterate, increasingly became issues among Afro-Richmonders. Briefly examining how the sites of public discourse changed and how discussions regarding qualifications for and nature of individual participation developed suggests the degree to which debates over space and relationships represented important changes in many black Richmonders' assumptions about freedom itself.

The authority of the church in personal and civil matters decreased over the late-nineteenth and early-twentieth centuries. The church quietly acknowledged these changes without directly confronting the issue of its changed authority. The use of civil authorities to resolve the church dispute, especially since individual members continued to face censure if they relied on civil rather than church sanctions in a dispute with another member, suggests the degree to which First African tried to maintain its traditional authority over its members while acknowledging the limitations of its powers. First African turned outside not only itself but also the black community by inviting the intervention of the mayor, police chief and judge.[42] The decreasing authority of the church, however, accompanied a shrinking sphere of influence and activity for the church and the development of secular institutions and structures to take over, compete for, or share functions traditionally connected to the church as institution and structure. The changing church axis suggests important developments in the structures, nature and understandings of community in black Richmond.

After the Reverend James Holmes and the deacons of First African survived the 1880 challenge to their leadership, one of their first actions was to establish a regulation that church business meetings be closed to all but members. They had argued that it was outside agitators who had instigated and sustained the disorder and opposition. While this reflects concerns about internal church business, the closing off of the church was reflected in other central ways which potentially had more far-reaching consequences, and suggests the particularization of interests, concerns and functions of internal community institutions, and the changed nature of internal community politics. Having completed, at considerable expense, their new edifice, First African worried about avoiding damage and excess wear and tear. In November 1882 the church adopted regulations designed to eliminate the crowds of people attending weddings in the church by requiring guest lists and tickets, and to deny entirely the use of the main auditorium with the largest capacity for "programmes, closing of public schools, political meetings or feasts." In February 1883 when the Acme Lyceum requested use of the main auditorium for a lecture by Frederick Douglass, the church, following its new regulations, refused to grant the request, although it did offer as substitute the use of its smaller lecture room. That same year it denied the use of the church for the Colored High and Normal closing. The paucity of facilities available to black Richmonders meant that these activities now had to be held in much smaller facilities and the possibilities for the large mass meetings which First African had previously hosted were now reduced. Political meetings and other activities moved to other, smaller church sites or to some of the new halls being erected by some of the societies and businessmen. The latter, however, were more expensive to obtain since their rental was a major source of revenue for the group or individual owner; it also often particularized the meeting or occasion to a specific segment of the community. Without the large facility of First African, graduations and school closings could no longer be the traditional community-wide mass celebrations. Denied the use of First African and barred from the Richmond Theatre where the white high school students had their graduation, the 1883 Colored High and Normal graduation class held their exercises in a small classroom where very few could attend.[43]

First African did not initiate and was not singly responsible for the changing nature of Republican Party participation, but its actions reinforced the narrower sense of party politics that white Republicans had already tried to enforce. Disturbed at black influence over Republican meetings, beginning in 1870 white Republican officials had taken steps to limit popular participation and influence in party deliberations. First they moved the party conventions from First African to the United States courtroom, a facility which held many fewer people and was removed from the black community; then they closed the gallery, thus allowing none but official delegates to attend and participate. In such a setting they were able to adopt a more conservative platform. Black Republicans had continued, however, to hold mass meetings, often when dissatisfied with the official Republican deliberations. When they were dissatisfied with Republican nominees for municipal office that came from the 1870 closed party convention, for example, black Republicans agreed to convene their own sessions and make their own nominations.[44]

In increasingly delimiting the church's use, distinguishing more clearly between sacred and secular activities as when it began to disallow certain kinds of entertainments in its facilities or on its behalf, and attempting to reserve the church for what was now designated as the "sacred," First African contributed to the increasing segmentation of black Richmond.[45] With the loss of the largest-capacity structure some black Richmonders recognized the need to reestablish a community space. Edward A. Randolph, founder and first editor of the *Richmond Planet*, used Acme Literary Association meetings to argue regularly throughout 1883 and 1884 for the construction of a hall, a public meeting place within the community. His call was reinforced when the Choral Association was denied use of the Richmond Theatre and had to have its production in a small mutual benefit society hall, an inadequate facility for such a production. The construction of a large auditorium on the top floor of the Grand Fountain, United Order of True Reformers' bank and office building when it opened in 1890 was an effort to provide that space. It could hold larger gatherings than the other halls and most churches but still had only a small percentage of the seating capacity of First African.[46] A mass meeting on the scale common in the 1860s and 1870s could be held only outside the community and the facilities for such were often closed to African Americans.

As political meetings moved to private halls rather than church buildings, they became less mass meetings not only in the numerical sense; they also became more gatherings of an exclusive group of party regulars. This signaled not only a change in the role of the church but also a change in the nature of politics in black Richmond. The emerging format gave business and professional men, especially, greater control over the formal political process. First African's prohibitions against mass meetings, school closings, and other programs did not last long; the need and desire of members and other Afro-Richmonders for a space which could truly contain a community-wide activity eventually led members to ignore their prohibition. But instituting the prohibition had not only significantly affected community activities in the early 1880s; it also meant that, even after strict enforcement was curtailed, decisions about using the church for graduation exercises, political meetings and other activities were now subjects of debate. Afro-Richmonders could no longer assume the church as a community meeting place; instead they had to argue such. The church remained an important community institution, but it increasingly shared power with both civil authorities and other community institutions such as mutual benefit and fraternal societies.

The efforts by white Republican officials to limit popular decision-making and the decreased accessibility of First African as a community-wide meeting place affected a politics which had been based in mass participation. Mass meetings were still held throughout the late-nineteenth century, but they were now less regular. These changes were exacerbated by the struggle to retain the vote and office-holding and the necessity, therefore, to counter various tactics of both white Republicans and Democrats. The fraudulent tactics employed to eliminate black voters, for example, led some black Republicans, like John Mitchell, who continued to argue against literacy qualifications for voting, in the 1890s to encourage nonliterate black men to abstain from voting. Difficulty with many of the election officials' questions and with the ballots could not only delay the line but also the nonliterate voter's rights and/or ballot would more likely be challenged. Mitchell thought it important to get those least likely to be challenged or disqualified, and most capable of correctly marking the ballots, through the lines first before polls closed on them. While Mitchell argued for a temporary change in practice—not perspective—regarding the right of all to vote, his and other prominent black Republicans' prioritizing of the literate voter significantly changed the makeup of the presumed electorate.

As the divisions between black and white Republicans became deeper in the 1890s, Mitchell and other black Republicans began to hold small Republican caucuses in selected homes, in essence attempting to control ward conventions by predetermining nominees and issues. The ward conventions themselves were often held in halls rather than the larger churches. The organization in 1898 of a Central Republican League which would oversee black Republican activities through sub-Leagues in all the city's wards reinforced the narrowing party politics framework. Republican Party decision-making was now more clearly limited to Party regulars; the mass of black voters and other election activists were expected to support these channels of decision-making.[47] These changes, consistent with democratic politics and republican representative government as practiced in the late-nineteenth-century United States, served to limit the power and influence of most black Richmonders in the electoral arena. If many black men abandoned electoral politics even before formal disfranchisement, it was in large measure due to the effectiveness of the extra-legal disfranchisement efforts of white men. The exclusion from real decision-making power within the Republican Party and, in this respect within the community, was also decisive.

The increasingly limited notion of political decision-makers which these changes encouraged is also evident in other ways. In 1896 during a factional dispute among black Republicans, John Mitchell challenged the decisions made in one meeting by noting that a substantial portion of those attending and participating were not even "legal voters," that is, they were women. Although he espoused feminine dress and comportment, Mitchell supported women's rights and championed Dr. Sarah G. Jones's success as a physician as evidence of women's equality. He also endorsed women's suffrage while advising black women to understand the racism of the white women's suffrage movement and not to align themselves with it. Despite these personal convictions, Mitchell could dismiss or minimize opposing factions by a reference to the participation of women, suggesting the ways in which the meanings and understandings of politics, of appropriate political actors and even of the ownership of the franchise had changed in the late-nineteenth century.[48]

Questions of qualifications for participation in the external political arena and internal community institutions were now frequent. During the conflictual 1901 business meeting at First African, for example, John Mitchell, Jr., questioned his opponents' right to participate even though they were all church members by pointing out their unfamiliarity with parliamentary procedure or their inelegant ways of speaking. The women, who were the targets of much of Mitchell's challenge, refused to accept these as criteria for their participation and even denigrated what he put forth as his formal qualifications by talking out when he got up to speak, saying derisively, "Don't he look pretty."[49] Questions of formal education had already affected the congregation in fundamental ways, most obviously in the late-nineteenth-century debate over song, a debate which represented a significant change in the basis of collective consciousness.

The antiphonal nature of the traditional church service at First African and many black churches reinforced a sense of community. The services included spontaneous verbal and nonverbal interaction between minister

and prayer, speaker and congregation, thus allowing for the active participation of everyone in the worship service. It was this cultural discourse that
was carried over into the political meetings. One important element that
bound the congregation together was song; as Lawrence Levine has noted,
through their collective song churchgoers "meld[ed] individual consciousness into the group consciousness."[50] However, the practice of lining hymns
which was basic to collective song was one which white visitors often
referred to when they described what they perceived as the unrefined black
church services. Some black churchgoers saw the elimination of this practice as part of the work of uplifting the religious style and uplifting the race.
But with the elimination of this practice, those unable to read and follow the
lyrics in a song book were now unable to participate, to be fully a part of the
community, the collective. It was the equivalent of being deprived of a voice,
all the more significant in an oral culture. Daniel Webster Davis, a member
of First African and pastor of Second Baptist (Manchester) as well as public
school teacher, suggested such in his poem, "De Linin' Ub De Hymns":

> Dar's a mighty row in Zion, an' de debbil's gittin' high,
> . . . .
> 'Twuz 'bout a berry leetle thing—de linin' ub a hymn.
> De young folks say 'tain't stylish to lin' um out no mo';
> Dat dey's got edikashun, an' dey wants us all to know
> Dey likes to hab dar singin'-books a-holin' fore dar eyes,
> An' sing de hymns right straight along 'to manshuns in de skies.'
> . . . .
> An' ef de ol' folks will kumplain 'cause dey is ol' an' blin',
> An' slabry's chain don' kep' dem back frum larnin' how to read—
> Dat de mus' take a corner seat, an' let de young folks lead.
> . . . .
> We don' edikate our boys an' gals, an' would do de same again;
> . . . .
> De sarmon's highfalutin', an' de church am mighty fin';
> . . . .
> De ol'-time groans an' shouts an' moans am passin' out ub sight—
> Edikashun changed all dat, an' we belebe it right,
> We should serb God wid 'telligence; fur dis one thing I plead:
> Jes' lebe a leetle place in church fur dem ez kin not read.[51]

The debates about women's roles in the church and in the more formal
political arenas, like the debate over lining the hymns, were part of wide-

spread discussions about the nature of community, of participation and of freedom.

The proliferation of scholarly works centered on the flowering of black women's political activity in the late-nineteenth and early-twentieth centuries[52] has perhaps left the impression that this was the inaugural moment or even height of black women's participation in politics. Overt or not, the suggestion seems to be that black women came to political prominence as (because) black men lost political power.[53] In much of this scholarship the reasons for black women's "emergence" are usually tied to external factors. For example, the development of black women's clubs in the late-nineteenth century and their important roles in the political struggles of the twentieth century most often have been seen by historians as the result of the increasing development of such entities in the larger society and as reaction to vitriolic attacks on the morality of black women. Such a perspective explains this important political force solely in terms of external dynamics, but external factors alone cannot account for this development.[54] The internal political arena, which in the immediate post–Civil War era was grounded in the notion of a collective voice which gave men, women and children a platform and allowed them all participation, came increasingly in the late-nineteenth century to be shaped by a narrowing notion of politics and appropriate political behavior.

While mass meetings continued to be held, the more regular forums for political discussions were literary societies, ward meetings, mutual benefit society and fraternal society meetings, women's clubs, labor organizations, newspapers, streetcorners, kitchens, washtubs and saloons. In the development of literary societies as a primary venue for public discussion, one can see the class and gender assumptions that by the turn-of-the-century came to be central to the political organization of black Richmond. While some, as the Langston Literary Association, had male members only, most of the literary societies founded in the 1880s and 1890s had middle-class and working-class men and women members. Despite the inclusive nature of the membership and often of the officers, the form of discussion which developed privileged middle-class males. Unlike mass meetings where many people might take the floor in planned and unplanned expositions and attendees might freely interrupt or talk back to speakers, thus allowing and building mass participation, literary forums announced discussion topics in advance; charged individual members, apparently almost always male, to prepare a paper on the subject; and designated specific, also male, members to reply.

The discussions that then ensued were open to all present but the structure privileged those familiar with the conventions of formal debate. Women, who served as officers and attended in large numbers, may have joined in the discussion but their official roles were designated as the cultural arm of the forum—reading poetry, singing songs, often with political content appropriate to the occasion. The questions under consideration at the meetings often betrayed the class bias of the forum. Even when the discussions centered on some aspect of working-class life and behavior, the conversation was conducted by middle-class men. The purpose of the forums, as articulated by the Acme Literary Society, suggested the passive observer/learner position that most were expected to take: to hold "discussions, lectures, and to consider questions of vital importance to our people, so that the masses of them may be drawn out to be entertained, enlightened, and instructed thereby."[55] Given the exclusionary nature of the discussion in these literary forums, even though welcoming a wide audience, it is understandable that far more working-class black men and women saw the Knights of Labor as their principal political vehicle in the late 1880s.[56]

In the changing circumstances of the late-nineteenth century, working-class men and women and middle-class women were increasingly disfranchised within the black community, just as middle-class black men were increasingly disfranchised in the larger society. Men and women, working-class and middle-class, at the turn-of-the-century were struggling to move back to a political authority they once had—internally and externally. As they did so they each often justified such authority along distinctively gendered and class-based lines.

African American men countered the image of themselves as uncivilized, beastly rapists—an image white southerners used to justify disfranchisement, segregation and violence—with efforts to demonstrate their own manhood and to define white males as uncivilized and savage.[57] While white Richmonders told stories of black barbarity, John Mitchell, Jr., inverted the tale. The *Richmond Planet*, for example, repeatedly focused on the sexual perversions of white men with cases of rape and incest and spoke of white men in terms designed to suggest their barbarism: "Southern white folks have gone to roasting Negroes, we presume the next step will be to eat them."[58] In the process of unmanning white males, however, Mitchell and others developed a narrative of endangered black women. Urban areas, once sites of opportunity for women, became sexually dangerous places for the unprotected female, easy prey to deceitful and barbarous white males.[59] Black men's political rights were essential so that they could do as men should—protect their communities, homes, families, women. The focus on manhood could, initially, be the venue for discussing domestic violence as well. For example, the Reverend Anthony Binga, sermonizing against physical abuse of one's wife, drew on the discourse of manhood: "I have never seen a man whip his wife. I mean a *man*. Everyone who wears a hat or a coat is not a *man*. I mean a *man*." And the members of First African took as a serious issue of concern the case of a husband who had infected his wife with syphilis.[60] Concurrent with the narrative of sexual danger in the city and the larger society was an implied corollary narrative of protection within one's own community. Thus the discourse on manhood could keep the concern with violence against women in the public discussion while at the same time setting the stage for issues of domestic abuse and other forms of intraracial violence, which could be evidence of the uncivility of black men, to be silenced as politically dangerous.

In drawing on the new narrative of endangered women, middle-class black women, increasingly disfranchised by the connections between manhood and citizenship in the new political discourse, turned the focus from themselves and on to the working class, enabling middle-class women to project themselves as the protectors of their less fortunate sisters. In this manner they reinserted themselves into a public political role.[61] Autonomous women's organizations, such as the Richmond Women's League (later the Richmond Mothers' Club) or women's divisions within other organizations such as the Standing Committee on Domestic Economy of the Hampton Negro Conference, developed to serve these functions. These associations promulgated class-specific ideas of respectability, in part justifying their public role through the need to impart such protective measures to working-class women. Specific constructions of womanhood, as manhood, thus became central to the arguments for political rights. Through discussions of manhood and womanhood, middle-class men and women constructed themselves as respectable and entitled, and sought to use such constructions to throw a mantle of protection over their working-class brothers and sisters. By increasingly claiming sexual violence as a women's issue, middle-class black women claimed a political/public space for themselves but they also contributed to an emerging tendency to divert issues of sexual violence to a lesser plane and to see them as the specific interest of women, not bound up in the general concerns and struggle for freedom. This set the stage for the masculine conception of liberation struggle which would emerge in the twentieth century.[62]

Collective History/Collective Memory

In July 1895 three black women—Mary Abernathy, Pokey Barnes and her mother, Mary Barnes—were convicted in Lunenberg County, Virginia, of murdering a white woman. When the women were moved to the state penitentiary in Richmond their case became a cause célèbre in the black community there. For over a year black men and women in Richmond struggled to keep the Lunenberg women from being hung or returned to Lunenberg County for a retrial, fearing that a return to Lunenberg would mean death, the women lynched at the hands of an angry white mob. The community succeeded, and the three women were eventually released.

The organization of black Richmonders in defense of these women partly illustrates the increasingly gendered nature of internal community politics. Men and women were portrayed as having decidedly different roles in the defense; one avenue of defense was to draw on ideas of motherhood in defending these three women; and the Lunenberg women's release called forth very particular discussions of respectability and womanhood. John Mitchell, Jr., portrayed himself as the militant defender of the women. Women, led by schoolteacher Rosa Dixon Bowser, organized the Richmond Women's League for the purposes of raising funds for the women's defense, visiting them in jail and supporting their husbands and families. Through her column in the *Woman's Era* and her participation in the National Federation of Afro-American Women, Bowser, as did Mitchell, brought the case to national attention. The front page stories in Mitchell's *Planet* emphasized the Lunenberg women as mothers, especially reporting on Mary Abernathy's pregnancy and the birth of her child in her jail cell. While the pictures and stories during the fourteen-month struggle for their release portrayed the women as simply clad, barefoot, farm women the announcement of Pokey Barnes's final victory was accompanied by a photograph of her now transformed into a true Victorian woman with elegant balloon-sleeved dress, a symbol of respectable womanhood. Later descriptions of Barnes, on speaking engagements, emphasized her dress: "a neat fitting, changeable silk gown and . . . a black felt hat, trimmed with black velvet and ostrich plumes." Mitchell emphasized the importance of this transformation: "The picture showing what Pokey Barnes looked like when brought to Richmond the first time and what she appears to-day will be a startling revelation to the public and will fill with amazement the conservative people everywhere when they realize what a terrible blunder the execution of this young woman would have been." He thus suggested that it was her ability to be a respectable woman (signified superficially by a class-based standard of dress) which was the justification for his and others' protection of her.[63]

But the year-long discussion of these women's fates (the front page of nearly every issue of the *Richmond Planet* from July 1895 through early fall 1896 was devoted to these cases and included pictures of the women and sketches of their cabins) occurred alongside stories about lynchings or near lynchings of black men. Importantly, therefore, when black Richmonders spoke of lynching in the late-nineteenth century, they had no reason to assume the victim as male. When a freed Pokey Barnes rode as "mascot" in the 1896 Jackson Ward election rally parade, the idea of Mitchell and other black men as defenders was reinforced. But also affirmed was the underlying understanding that violence, including state repression, was a real threat to African American women as much as men. This meant that the reconstruction of clearly delineated notions of womanhood and manhood as the basis for political activism remained relatively ambiguous in late-nineteenth-century black Richmond. But issues of class and gender were increasingly evident, as when Pokey Barnes and Mitchell accepted public speaking engagements—ones in which she was clearly expected to be the silent symbol of oppression and he the vocal proponent of resistance. Barnes, countering that assumption, set forth her own understandings of her role and qualifications, contradicting the class and gender assumptions of Mitchell and of those who invited them: "she said that she was not an educated lecturer and did not have any D.D.'s or M.D.'s to her name, but she was simply Pokey Barnes, c.s. (common sense)." Her two-hour lecture on her ordeal, while giving credit to Mitchell, established herself as not only victim but also heroine.[64]

The rescue of the Lunenberg women by black Richmonders brought women's struggles to the fore of black rights and reaffirmed violence against women as part of their collective history and struggle. At the same time black Richmonders struggled to create a new category of womanhood that would be respected and protected, and of middle-class womanhood and manhood that could protect.[65] The plight of the Lunenberg women reaffirmed the collective history of black men and women at the same time as it invigorated increasingly distinct political vehicles for middle-class black men and women.

Just as disfranchisement, segregation, lynching and other violence denied the privileges of masculinity to African American men; segregation, lynching, sexual violence and accusations of immorality denied the protections of womanhood to African American women. Increasingly black women relied on constructing not only a respectable womanhood but, in large measure, an invisible womanhood. Hoping that a desexualized persona might provide the protection to themselves and their communities that seemed otherwise unobtainable, many black women carefully covered up all public suggestions of sexuality, even of sexual abuse. In the process issues specific to black women were increasingly eliminated from public discussion and collective memory.[66] In the late-twentieth century therefore many African Americans have come to link a history of repression and racial violence exclusively to challenges to black masculinity and thus to establish a notion of freedom and black liberation which bifurcates public discussion and privileges men's history and experiences. In 1991 when Supreme Court justice nominee Clarence Thomas challenged his questioners by calling the Senate Judiciary Committee hearings a "high-tech lynching," black Americans were divided in their response. Some men and women supported his analysis; others opposed either Thomas's analogy or his right to, in using such, assume the mantle of black manhood that he had so often rejected. Few people, however, questioned the assumption basic to Thomas's analogy that lynching and other forms of violence had historically been a masculine experience. Similarly, when black people across the country responded to the video of Los Angeles policemen's brutal beating of Rodney King, a narrative of state repression against black men followed.[67] The masculine focus is most evident in the widespread public discussion of "endangered" black men. While appropriately focusing attention on the physical, economic and social violence which surrounds and engulfs many black men in the late-twentieth-century United States, much of this discussion trivializes, or ignores the violence of many black women's lives—as victims of rape and other forms of sexual abuse, murder, drugs and alcohol, poverty and the devastation of AIDS. Seldom are discussions of rape and domestic violence included in summits on black-on-black crime. The masculinization of race progress which this implies often has some black leaders, looking to ways to improve the lot of men, not only omitting women from the picture but often even accepting the violence against women. What else can explain how Mike Tyson, even before he was charged with the rape of an eighteen-year-old black woman, would have been projected by ministers of the National Baptist Convention as a role model for young black men? By what standards would a man who had already publicly acknowledged that he enjoyed brutalizing women have been put forward as a role model—unless rescuing black men from poverty and inner-city death at any price, including violence against women, was the standard by which the good of the race was being defined?

Such is the long-term consequence of political strategies developed in the late-nineteenth century to empower black men and black women. Understandable and necessary in their day, they served to maintain a democratic agenda even as black political life became more divided. Eventually, however, the experiences of men were remembered as central to African Americans' struggles but the experiences of women, including the physical violence—lynchings, rapes, sexual and other forms of physical abuse as employees in white homes, domestic abuse—as well as the economic and social violence which has so permeated the history of black women in the United States, were not as vividly and importantly retained in our memory. We give life and validity to our constructions of race, community and politics by giving those constructions a history. Those who construct masculine notions of blackness and race progress and who claim only some forms of violence as central to African American liberation struggles are claiming/remembering a particular history. African American collective memory in the late-twentieth century often appears partial, distorted and dismembered. The definitions and issues of political struggle which can come from that partial memory are limited. Before we can construct truly participatory discussions around a fully democratic agenda where the history and struggles of women and men are raised as issues of general interest necessary to the liberation of all, we have some powerful lot of rerembering to do.[68]

Notes

An earlier version of this paper was presented at "The Black Public Sphere in the Reagan-Bush Era Conference," Chicago Humanities Institute, University of Chicago in October 1993, where I benefitted from the comments of Kenneth Warren and the discussion of the conference participants. Thanks also to Carol A. Breckenridge and to two anonymous reviewers for their comments, and to Nataki H. Goodall for her critical eye and unflagging support. The writing of this essay was facilitated by a research leave from the University of Michigan and research fellowships at the W.E.B. Du Bois Institute for Afro-American Research, Harvard University; and the Virginia Center for the Humanities.

1. Petition of Mrs. Margaret Osborne, et al. To the deacons and members of the First Baptist Church, April 15, 1880, recorded in First African Baptist Church. Richmond City, Minutes, Book II, June 27, 1880 (microfilm), Archives, Virginia State Library and Archives, Richmond, Virginia (hereafter cited as FABC).

2. The idea of the immediate adoption of a gendered public-private dichotomy pervades much of the historical literature on post–Civil War black communities. It is most directly argued by Jacqueline Jones: "the vitality of the political process, tainted though it was by virulent racial prejudice and violence, provided black men with a public forum distinct from the private sphere inhabited by their womenfolk. Black men predominated

in this arena because, like other groups in nineteenth-century America, they believed that males alone were responsible for—and capable of—the serious business of politicking." *Labor of Love, Labor of Sorrow: Black Women, Work, and the Family from Slavery to the Present* (New York: Basic Books, 1985), 66. But it is also an accepted tenet of otherwise rigorous analyses such as Eric Foner, *Reconstruction: America's Unfinished Revolution 1863–1877* (New York: Harper and Row, 1988), esp. 87.

3. Many recent discussions of the public sphere among U.S. scholars have orbited around the work of Jürgen Habermas whose 1962 *Struktur wandel der Öffentlichkeit* was published in 1989 in English as *The Structural Transformation of the Public Sphere: An Inquiry into a Category of Bourgeois Society*, trans. Thomas Burger with assistance of Frederick Lawrence (Cambridge: MIT Press). See also, Jürgen Habermas, "The Public Sphere: An Encyclopedia Article (1964)," *New German Critique* 1 (Fall 1974): 49–55. Critics who have emphasized the masculine bias in the liberal bourgeois public sphere and posited a female counterpublic include Nancy Fraser, "Rethinking the Public Sphere: A Contribution to the Critique of Actually Existing Democracy," and Mary Ryan, "Gender and Public Access: Women's Politics in Nineteenth-Century America," both in *Habermas and the Public Sphere*, ed. Craig Calhoun (Cambridge: MIT Press, 1992), 109–142 and 259–289, respectively. See also Nancy Fraser, "What's Critical About Critical Theory? The Case of Habermas and Gender," in Nancy Fraser, *Unruly Practices: Power, Discourse, and Gender in Contemporary Social Theory* (Minneapolis: University of Minnesota Press, 1989); Mary Ryan, *Women in Public: Between Banners and Ballots, 1825–1880* (Baltimore: Johns Hopkins University Press, 1990); Joan B. Landes, *Women and the Public Sphere in the Age of the French Revolution* (Ithaca: Cornell University Press, 1988); Rita Felski, *Beyond Feminist Aesthetics: Feminist Literature and Social Change* (Cambridge: Harvard University Press, 1989), 154–182. Focusing on contemporary politics, Iris Marion Young offers a critique of an ideal public sphere in which the universal citizen is not only masculine but also white and bourgeois, *Justice and the Politics of Difference* (Princeton: Princeton University Press, 1990).

4. For a study that conceptualizes the history of the black church in relation to Habermas's theory of the public sphere, see Evelyn Brooks Higginbotham, *Righteous Discontent: The Women's Movement in the Black Baptist Church 1880–1920* (Cambridge: Harvard University Press, 1993), esp. 7–13. Higginbotham describes "the black church not as the embodiment of ministerial authority or of any individual's private interests and pronouncements, but as a social space for discussion of public concerns" (1993:10).

5. Similar negotiations and pronouncements occurred in other post-emancipation societies. For a discussion of the ways in which British colonial officers sought to impose ideas of a liberal democratic moral and political order, with its attendant gender relations, on former slaves in the West Indies and then pronounced these ex-slaves incapable of responsible citizenship when they failed to wholly adopt such, see Thomas C. Holt, "'The Essence of the Contract': The Articulation of Race, Gender, and Political Economy in British Emancipation Policy, 1838–1866," paper presented at "The Black Public Sphere in the Reagan-Bush Era Conference," Chicago Humanities Institute, The University of Chicago, October 1993 (cited with permission of Holt).

6. The question of ownership was one of the first issues Afro-Richmonders addressed, as antebellum law had required the titles be in the names of white male supervising committees although the black congregants had themselves bought and paid for the buildings. Through a series of struggles black churchgoers had by the end of 1866 obtained

titles to all of their church buildings. See *New York Tribune*, June 17, 1865; Peter Randolph, *From Slave Cabin to Pulpit* (Boston: Earle, 1893), 94–95; John Thomas O'Brien, Jr., "From Bondage to Citizenship: The Richmond Black Community, 1865–1867" (Ph.D. diss., University of Rochester, 1974), 273–275.

7. Statement of Jenny Scott, wife of Ned Scott, colored, June 8, 1865; Statement of Richard Adams, colored, June 8, 1865; Statement of Nelson E. Hamilton, June 9, 1865; Statement of Lewis Harris, June 9, 1865; Statement of Wm. Ferguson, June 9, 1865; Statement of Albert Brooks, colored, June 10, 1865; Statement of Thomas Lucas, colored, June 12, 1865; Statement of Washington Hutchinson, Summer 1865; Statement of Edward Davenport, n.d.; Statement of Bernard H. Roberts, n.d.; Statement of Albert Williams, n.d.; Statement of Thos. J. Wayer, n.d.; Statement of Harry R. Jones, n.d.; Statement of Wellington Booker, n.d.; Statement of Stephen Jones, n.d.; Statement of John Oliver of Mass., n.d.; Wm. M. Davis to Col. O. Brown, June 9, 1865, all in Records of the Assistant Commissioner for the State of Virginia, Bureau of Refugees, Freedmen and Abandoned Lands, 1865–1869, Record Group 105, M1048, reel 59, National Archives, Washington. D.C.; *New York Tribune*, June 12, 17, August 1, 8, 1865; *Richmond Times*, July 26, 1865; S.E.C. (Sarah Chase) to Mrs. May, May 25, 1865, in Henry L. Swint, ed., *Dear Ones at Home: Letters from Contraband Camps* (Nashville: Vanderbilt University Press, 1966), 159–160; Julia A. Wilbur in *The Pennsylvania Freedman's Bulletin*, I (August 1865), 52, quoted in John T. O'Brien, "Reconstruction in Richmond: White Restoration and Black Protest, April–June 1865," *Virginia Magazine of History and Biography*, 89, 3 (July 1981): 273, 275.

8. *New York Tribune*, August 1, 8, 1865. One of the most neglected areas of Reconstruction history and of African American history in general is that of violence against women. This has led to the still prevalent assumption that black women were less likely to be victims of racial violence and the generalization that this reflects the fact that black women were less threatening than black men. Historian W. Fitzhugh Brundage, for example, concludes that black women had "greater leeway" to "voice their opinions and anger without suffering extralegal violence themselves," *Lynching in the New South: Georgia and Virginia, 1880–1930* (Urbana: University of Illinois Press, 1993), 80–81, 322–323n. This reflects both the emphasis on lynching as the major form of racial violence, and the limited historical attention to the black women who were lynched (at least fifteen between 1889 and 1898; at least seventy-six between 1882 and 1927). Even those ostensibly attuned to issues of gender and sexuality still assume that "the greatest violence was reserved for black men"; see, for example, Martha Hodes, "The Sexualization of Reconstruction Politics: White Women and Black Men in the South after the Civil War," *Journal of the History of Sexuality* 3 (January 1993): 404. Yet the evidence from Richmond and elsewhere suggests that the extent of violence against black women is greater than previously recognized, even greater than reported at the time. One North Carolina man, Essic Harris, giving testimony to the Senate Committee investigating Ku Klux Klan terror, reported the rape of black women was so frequent as to be "an old saying by now." Essic Harris testimony, July 1, 1871, in U.S. Congress, *Testimony Taken by the Joint Select Committee to Inquire into the Condition of Affairs in the Late Insurrectionary States* Vol.: *North Carolina* (Washington: GPO, 1872), 100. Only recently have historians begun to uncover and analyze sexual violence against black women as an integral part of Reconstruction history. See, for example, the dissertation-in-progress by Hannah Rosen, University of Chicago, which examines the rapes connected with the 1866

Memphis race riot. See also Catherine Clinton, "Reconstructing Freedwomen," *Divided Houses: Gender and the Civil War*, eds. Catherine Clinton and Nina Silber (New York: Oxford University Press, 1992), chapter 17.

9. *New York Tribune*, June 12, 17, 1865.

10. The *Richmond Times* (May 24, 1865), in refusing to publish black Richmonders' statements of protest, reasoned that they were mistaken in believing that they were all oppressed by the military and civilian officials; only the "idle negroes" were targets of military restrictions and inspections. Throughout the early months of emancipation both white southerners and white Unionists defined freedpeople's mobility in search of family or better jobs and in expression of their new-found freedom as evidence of an unwillingness to work. Similarly, those who chose to vend goods on city streets rather than signing work contracts with white employers were seen as lazy or idle. See O'Brien, "From Bondage to Citizenship," 117–131; see also various communications among the military command reprinted in U.S. War Department, *The War of the Rebellion: A Compilation of the Official Records of the Union and Confederate Armies*, Series I, Volume XLV, Part III-*Correspondence, Etc.* (Washington: GPO, 1894), 835, 932–933, 1005–1006, 1091, 1094–1095, 1107–1108, 1131–1132.

11. *New York Tribune*, June 17, 1865.

12. Black Richmonders were countering the very different image of their community put forth not only by white southerners but also by Union officers. Major-General H. W. Halleck, for example, emphasized the goodwill between Rebel and Union soldiers, both "brave and honest men, although differing in opinion and action"; justified the military restrictions on African Americans; and reported a lack of marriage relationships among African Americans "and the consequent irresponsibility of the parents for the care and support of their offspring." He argued that "colored females," especially, needed legal restrictions, supervision and suitable punishments, because "being released from the restraints imposed by their former masters and mistresses, . . . naturally fall into dissolute habits." H. W. Halleck, Major-General, Commanding, Headquarters Military Division of the James, Richmond, Va. to Hon. E. M. Stanton, Secretary of War, June 26, 1865, in U.S. War Department, *The War of the Rebellion*, 1295–1297. Halleck was one of the Union officers who was reassigned to a different command as a result of the June protest.

13. O'Brien details these meetings in "From Bondage to Citizenship," chapters 6–9.

14. O'Brien, "From Bondage to Citizenship," 326.

15. See, for example, *Richmond Enquirer*, February 23, 1866; *Richmond Dispatch*, July 6, 1866; *Richmond Times*, July 6, 1866.

16. Foner, *Reconstruction*, 121.

17. *Richmond Dispatch*, April 19, 1867; *New York Times*, April 19, 1867.

18. Julie Saville, "A Measure of Freedom: From Slave to Wage Laborer in South Carolina, 1860–1868" (Ph.D diss., Yale University, 1986), 273.

19. *Richmond Whig*, April 1, 1867.

20. *Richmond Dispatch*, October 5, 1867.

21. Aldon Morris makes a similar argument regarding the church and the modern civil rights movement, emphasizing the ways in which the church served as a physical, financial and cultural resource, with its sermons, songs, testimonies and prayers becoming political resources in the mobilization of participants and in the construction and communication of political ideology. *The Origins of the Civil Rights Movement: Black Communities Organizing for Change* (New York: Free Press, 1984). See also Robin D. G.

Kelley, "'Comrades, Praise Gawd for Lenin and Them!': Ideology and Culture Among Black Communists in Alabama, 1930–1935," *Science and Society* 52, 1 (Spring 1988): 59–82; Brenda McCallum, "Songs of Work and Songs of Worship: Sanctifying Black Unionism in the Southern City of Steel," *New York Folklore*, 14, 1 & 2 (1988): 9–33. For an argument that eliminating emotions and aesthetics from acceptable forms of public discourse becomes a means to eliminate particular groups of people from active participation in public life, see Iris Marion Young, "Impartiality and the Civic Public: Some Implications of Feminist Critiques of Moral and Political Theory," in *Feminism as Critique: On the Politics of Gender*, eds. Seyla Benhabib and Drucilla Cornell (Minneapolis: University of Minnesota, 1987), 56–76.

22. The following discussion of collective enfranchisement as the basis for black women's political activism in the post–Civil War era is drawn from Elsa Barkley Brown, "To Catch the Vision of Freedom: Reconstructing Southern Black Women's Political History, 1865–1880," in *African American Women and the Vote, 1837–1965*, ed. Ann D. Gordon (Amherst: University of Massachusetts Press, 1997).

23. *Richmond Dispatch*, August 1, 2, September 30, October 9, 1867; *New York Times*, August 1, 2, 6, October 18, 1867. My discussion of these events follows closely Peter J. Rachleff, *Black Labor in the South: Richmond, Virginia, 1865–1890* (Philadelphia: Temple University Press, 1984), 45–46. See also Richard L. Morton, *The Negro in Virginia Politics, 1865–1902*, Publications of the University of Virginia Phelps-Stokes Fellowship Papers Number Four (Charlottesville: University of Virginia Press, 1919), 40–43. Similar reports issued from other areas throughout the South, causing one chronicler to report that "the Southern ballot-box" was as much "the vexation of housekeepers" as it was of farmers, businessmen, statesmen or others: "Elections were preceded by political meetings, often incendiary in character, which all one's servants must attend." Election day itself could also be a problem. As one Tennessean reported in 1867, "Negro women went [to the polls], too; my wife was her own cook and chambermaid." Myrta Lockett Avary, *Dixie After the War: An Exposition of Social Conditions Existing in the South, During the Twelve Years Succeeding the Fall of Richmond* (New York: Doubleday, Page and Co., 1906; reprint, New York: Negro Universities Press, 1969), 282–284. See also Susan Bradford Eppes for similar occurrences in Florida, *Through Some Eventful Years* ([1926] reprint ed., Gainesville: University of Florida Press, 1968).

24. *Richmond Dispatch*, August 1, 2, 1867; *New York Times*, August 2, 6, 1867; see also Rachleff, *Black Labor in the South*, 45; Morton, *Negro in Virginia Politics*, 40–43.

25. The October 1867 city Republican ward meetings and nominating convention adopted the practice common in the black community's mass meetings: a voice or standing vote which enfranchised men, women and children. See, for example, the October eighth Second Ward meeting for delegate selection: "All who favored Mr. Washburne were first requested to rise, and forty were found on the floor, including women." *Richmond Dispatch*, September 20, October 9, 1867; January 2, 4, 14, 23, 24, February 15, 25, April 3, 8, 25, 1868; *New York Times*, August 6, October 15, 18, 1867; January 11, 1868: Rachleff, *Black Labor in the South*, 45–49; Avary, *Dixie After the War*, 229–231, 254.

The issue of children's participation is an interesting one, suggestive of the means by which personal experience rather than societal norms shaped ex-slaves' vision of politics. A similarly telling example was in the initial proposal of the African National Congress that the new South African constitution set the voting age at fourteen, a testament to those young people, as those in Soweto, who experienced the ravages of apartheid and whose fight against it helped bring about the political negotiations to secure African political rights and self-determination.

26. Compare black women's active participation in Richmond's formal politics—internal and external—in the first decades after the Civil War to Michael McGerr's assessment that nineteenth-century "women were allowed into the male political realm only to play typical feminine roles—to cook, sew, and cheer for men and to symbolize virtue and beauty. Men denied women the central experiences of the popular style: not only the ballot but also the experience of mass mobilization." McGerr's analysis fails to acknowledge the racial basis of his study, i.e., it is an assessment of white women's political participation. Michael McGerr, "Political Style and Women's Power, 1830–1930," *Journal of American History* 77 (December 1990): 864–885, esp. 867. My analysis also differs substantially from Mary P. Ryan, *Women in Public*. Ryan gives only cursory attention to African Americans but finds black women's political expression in the Civil War and Reconstruction eras restricted "with particular severity" and "buried beneath the surface of the public sphere," see 146–147, 156, *passim*.

27. For women's participation in political parades in Louisville, Kentucky; Mobile, Alabama; and Charleston, South Carolina, see Herbert G. Gutman, *The Black Family in Slavery and Freedom*, 380; *Liberator*, July 21, 1865, and *New York Daily Tribune*, April 4, 1865, both reprinted in *The Trouble They Seen: Black People Tell the Story of Reconstruction*, ed. Dorothy Sterling (Garden City, New York: Doubleday, 1976), 2–4. In other areas of Virginia besides Richmond and in South Carolina and Louisiana men and women participated in the political meetings. See, for example, Vincent Harding, *There Is a River: The Black Struggle for Freedom in America* (New York: Harcourt Brace Jovanovich, 1981), 294–297; Rupert Sargent Holland, ed., *Letters and Diary of Laura M. Towne Written from the Sea Islands of South Carolina, 1862–1884* (Cambridge: Riverside Press, 1912; reprint ed., New York: Negro Universities Press, 1969), 183; Testimony of John H. Burch given before a Senate committee appointed to investigate the exodus of black men and women from Louisiana, Senate Report 693, 46th Congress, 2nd Session, part 2, 232–233 reprinted in *A Documentary History of the Negro People in the United States*, 2 vols., ed. Herbert Aptheker (New York: Citadel Press, 1951), 2: 721–722; Thomas Holt, *Black over White: Negro Political Leadership in South Carolina during Reconstruction* (Urbana: University of Illinois Press, 1977), 34–35. Graphic artists recognized the participation of women as a regular feature of parades, mass meetings, and conventions as evidenced by their illustrations. See "The Celebration of Emancipation Day in Charleston" from *Leslie's Illustrated Newspaper*, reprinted in Francis Butler Simkins and Robert Hilliard Woody, *South Carolina During Reconstruction* (Chapel Hill: University of North Carolina Press, 1932; reprint ed., Gloucester, Mass.: Peter Smith, 1966), facing 364; "Electioneering at the South," *Harper's Weekly*, July 25, 1868, reprinted in Foner, *Reconstruction*, fol. 386; "Colored People's Convention in Session" reprinted in Sterling, *The Trouble They Seen*, 65.

28. *New York Times*, January 11, 22, 1868; *The Debates and Proceedings of the Constitutional Convention of the State of Virginia, Assembled at the City of Richmond* (Richmond, 1868), 505–507, 524–527.

29. *Richmond Dispatch*, June 18, 1867; Rachleff, *Black Labor in the South*, 48.

30. Rachleff, *Black Labor in the South*, 31–32; *Richmond Daily Dispatch*, May 10, 1867; *New Nation*, November 22, 29, December 6, 1866; Holt, *Black over White*, 35; Avary, *Dixie after the War*.

31. Barkley Brown, "To Catch the Vision of Freedom"; *Richmond Enquirer,* October 22, 1867; *Richmond Whig,* October 19, 1867; Robert E. Martin, "Negro Disfranchisement in Virginia," *The Howard University Studies in the Social Sciences,* 1 (Washington, D.C.: 1938): 65–79; *Richmond Afro-American,* December 2, 1962; Mrs. Violet Keeling's testimony before Senate investigating committee, February 18, 1884, Senate Report No. 579, 48th Congress, 1st Session, reprinted in Aptheker, *Documentary History,* 2: 739–741.

32. Barkley Brown, "To Catch the Vision of Freedom"; Howard N. Rabinowitz, *Race Relations in the Urban South, 1865–1880* (New York: Oxford University Press, 1978), 222; Alrutheus Ambush Taylor, *The Negro in the Reconstruction of Virginia* (Washington, D.C.: The Association for the Study of Negro Life and History, 1926), 181, 269; Michael B. Chesson, "Richmond's Black Councilmen, 1871–96," in *Southern Black Leaders of the Reconstruction Era,* ed. Howard N. Rabinowitz (Urbana: University of Illinois Press, 1982), 219n; Peter J. Rachleff, "Black, White and Gray: Working-Class Activism in Richmond, Virginia, 1865–1890" (Ph.D. diss., University of Pittsburgh, 1981), 473, 488n; *Richmond Dispatch,* October 25, 26, 1872; September 14, 1874; Avary, *Dixie after the War,* 285–286, 347; Thomas J. Evans, Alexander Sands, N. A. Sturdivant et al., Richmond, to Major-General Schofield, October 31, 1867, reprinted in *Documents of the Constitutional Convention of the State of Virginia* (Richmond: Office of the *New Nation,* 1867), 22–23; John H. Gilmer to Gen. Schofield reprinted in *New York Times,* October 30, 1867; *New York Times,* November 3, 1867; Wendell P. Dabney, "Rough autobiographical sketch of his boyhood years," (typescript, n.d.), 98–99, microfilm copy in Wendell P. Dabney Papers, Cincinnati Historical Society, Cincinnati, Ohio; Proceedings before Military Commissioner, City of Richmond, 26 October 1867 in the case of Winston Jackson filed as G-423 1867 Letters Received, ser. 5068, 1st Reconstruction Military District, Records of the U.S. Army Continental Commands, Record Group 393, Pt. 1, National Archives [SS-1049] (bracketed numbers refer to files in the Freedmen and Southern Society Project, University of Maryland; I thank Leslie S. Rowland, project director, for facilitating my access to these files); George F. Bragg, Jr., Baltimore, Maryland, to Dr. Woodson, August 26, 1926, reprinted in "Communications," *Journal of Negro History* XI (1926), 677.

33. See Thomas C. Holt, "'An Empire over the Mind': Emancipation, Race, and Ideology in the British West Indies and the American South," in *Region, Race, and Reconstruction: Essays in Honor of C. Vann Woodward,* ed. J. Morgan Kousser and James M. McPherson (New York: Oxford University Press, 1982), 283–314; also David Montgomery, *The American Civil War and the Meanings of Freedom: An Inaugural Lecture delivered before the University of Oxford on 24 February 1987* (Oxford: Clarendon Press, 1987), 11–13.

34. This is not to suggest that African American women did not desire the vote nor that they did not often disagree with the actions taken by some black men. One should, however, be careful about imposing presentist notions of gender equality on these women. Clearly for them the question was not an abstract notion of individual gender equality but rather one of community. That such a vision might become over time a lead into a patriarchal conception of gender roles is not a reason to dismiss the equity of its inception.

35. Dabney, "Rough autobiographical sketch," 17–18.

36. FABC, II, April 5, 6, 11, May 3, June 27, 1880.

37. First African minutes for 1841–1859 and 1875–1930 are available at First African and on microfilm in Archives, Virginia State Library. The Civil War and immediate post-emancipation minutes apparently have not survived. Peter Randolph, who came to

Richmond from Massachusetts within weeks of emancipation and became the first black man elected pastor of Ebenezer Baptist, attributed both the change in seating patterns and the formal inclusion of women as voters in church business meetings to his own progressivism. Whether or not he initiated such measures, it is unlikely either change would have been effected without wide acceptance within the congregation. Randolph, *From Slave Cabin to Pulpit*, 89.

38. FABC, II, June 27, 1880.

39. FABC, III, November 7, 20, 1899; *Richmond Planet*, July 6, 20, August 10, 31, 1901, March 8, 15, 1902. Similar debates must have occurred in Ebenezer Baptist Church as well. In approving the conduct of business at Ebenezer, Mitchell noted that "only the male members were permitted to vote" on the appointment of a new pastor, *Richmond Planet*, September 14, 1901. These debates over gender roles within black churches occurred on congregational and denominational levels. For studies which examine these debates at the state and/or national level, see, for example, Higginbotham, *Righteous Discontent*; Glenda Gilmore, "Gender and Jim Crow: Women and the Politics of White Supremacy in North Carolina, 1896–1920" (Ph.D. diss., University of North Carolina, Chapel Hill, 1992); Cheryl Townsend Gilkes, "'Together and in Harness': Women's Traditions in the Sanctified Church," *Signs: Journal of Women in Culture and Society* 10 (Summer 1985): 678–699.

40. *Virginia Baptist* cited in *Woman's Era*, 1 (September 1894), 8.

41. *Richmond Planet*, July 26, 1890; June 8, 1895; September 17, 24, November 19, 1898; September 9, 1899; Anthony Binga, Jr., *Sermons on Several Occasions*, I (Richmond, 1889), 97–99. Both Kemp and Carter were Baptist. A few women also conducted services in the Methodist church. Evangelist Annie E. Brown, for example, conducted two weeks of revival services at Leigh Street Methodist Episcopal Church in 1900, *Richmond Planet*, April 28, 1900. Even when one "female preacher . . . took up station" outside a Manchester barbershop and preached against the male members, claiming they were "leading the young down to perdition," the *Planet's* Manchester correspondent did not denounce her right to preach but rather suggested that if she "is called to preach the gospel, and is sanctified, as some say, why not organize a church of sanctification," rather than stand on street corners issuing "broad and uncalled for" attacks upon other ministers, *Richmond Planet*, December 12, 1896.

42. In July 1880 a council representing nine Richmond black Baptist churches censured First African for having called the police. "The First African Baptist Church, Richmond, Virginia, to the Messengers & Churches in General Ecclesiastical Council Assembled," in FABC, II, following April 3, 1881 minutes. For late-nineteenth century disciplinary procedures with regard to members who got civil warrants against other members, see for example, FABC, II, January 7, October 6, 1884; February 3, 1890.

43. FABC, II, June 27, November 6, 1882; February 5, April 2, 1883. Wendell P. Dabney, a member of that 1883 graduating class, remembered the students as having met in early June and "determined not to go to any church. That we would go to the Richmond Theatre or no where." He calls this "the first school strike by Negro pupils on record in the United States!" First African had, however, already denied the use of its facilities because of its new regulation. There is some evidence that, subsequent to the students' action, other black churches may have supported the young people by denying their facilities as well. Dabney, "Rough autobiographical sketch of his boyhood years," 107–109; Wendell P. Dabney, *Maggie L. Walker and the I. O. of Saint Luke: The Woman and Her Work* (Cincinnati: Dabney Publishing Co., 1927), 32–33. *New York Globe*, June 23, 1883.

44. Rachleff, "Black, White, and Gray," 307–309.
45. See, for example, the discussion of the reconfiguration of leisure space, including the barring of cakewalks and other dancing from the church, in Elsa Barkley Brown and Gregg D. Kimball, "Mapping the Terrain of Black Richmond," *Journal of Urban History*.
46. *New York Globe*, October 1883–January 1884. Estimates of the True Reformers' auditorium's seating capacity range from 900 to 1500 to 2000. Nearly 4000 people had been able to attend the March 1867 mass meeting held in First African in support of the Federal Sherman Bill. With their new edifices erected in 1890, Sixth Mount Zion and Sharon Baptist Churches had seating capacity of 1400 and 1200 respectively; most churches seated far fewer, Rachleff, *Black Labor in the South*, 40; *Richmond Planet*, March 14, May 31, 1890.
47. For information on the Central Republican League, see *Richmond Planet*, August–September 1898; *Richmond Evening Leader*, August 6, 16, 24, 27, 30, September 1, 28, October 12, 1898; *Richmond Times*, August 3, September 3, 11, 1898; *Richmond Dispatch*, September 14, 1898.
48. *Richmond Planet*, January 26, 1895; October 17, 1896. Similarly, when black Republican men formed the Negro Protective Association in 1898 to organize to retain their vote and political influence, one of the most controversial discussions concerned whether to allow a women's auxiliary, the main purpose of which would be to raise monies for electoral activities. Because of heated opposition the proposal was abandoned. *Proceedings of the Negro Protective Association of Virginia, Held Tuesday, May 18th, 1897, in the True Reformers' Hall, Richmond, Va.*
49. *Richmond Planet*, July 6, 1901.
50. Lawrence Levine, *Black Culture and Black Consciousness: Afro-American Folk Thought from Slavery to Freedom* (New York: Oxford University Press, 1977).
51. Daniel Webster Davis, "De Linin' Ub De Hymns," '*Web Down Souf and Other Poems* (Cleveland: The Helman-Taylor Company, 1897), 54–56.
52. The scholarly emphasis on this latter period is not merely a reflection of available sources. It also reflects the conceptual paradigms that have guided the investigation of black women's politics: a focus on the national level, often with minimal attention to different patterns within the North and the South; the acceptance of what Suzanne Lebsock has called the "consensus . . . that for women the standard form of political participation" in the nineteenth century "was the voluntary association"; an emphasis on autonomous women's organizations; and a focus on excavating political (and feminist) texts. This scholarly emphasis has produced a number of insightful works about the period; among them are Higginbotham, *Righteous Discontent*; Gilmore, "Gender and Jim Crow"; Hazel V. Carby, *Reconstructing Womanhood: The Emergence of the Afro-American Woman Novelist* (New York: Oxford University Press, 1987); Claudia Tate, *Domestic Allegories of Political Desire: The Black Heroine's Text at the Turn of the Century* (New York: Oxford University Press, 1992). Quote is from Suzanne Lebsock, "Women and American Politics, 1880–1920," in *Women, Politics, and Change*, eds. Louise A. Tilly and Patricia Gurin (New York: Russell Sage Foundation, 1990), 36.
53. Seeing the 1880–1920 period as "the greatest political age for women (including black women)," Suzanne Lebsock raises the question "what does it signify" that such occurred at "the worst" age for black people; "an age of disfranchisement and increasing legal discrimination," "Women and American Politics," 59, 37. Glenda Gilmore, in an otherwise thoughtful and nuanced study, contends that black women in North Carolina gained political prominence at the turn-of-the-century as (because) black men vanished from

472 Elsa Barkley Brown

politics—either leaving the state altogether or sequestering themselves in a nonpolitical world, "Gender and Jim Crow," chapter 5. It is an idea, however, that is often unstated but implicit in much literature which imagines black women's turn-of-the-century club movement as their initial emergence into politics. Such a narrative contributes to the fiction that black women were safer in the Jim Crow South than were black men.

54. I am indebted to Stephanie J. Shaw for making the point that it was internal community dynamics more so than external factors which gave rise to the black women's clubs in the late-nineteenth century. See Stephanie J. Shaw, "Black Club Women and the Creation of the National Association of Colored Women," *Journal of Women's History* 3 (1991): 10–25. In the end, my analysis of what those internal factors were differs somewhat from Shaw's; she attributes their rise to migration and the resultant presence of a newly migrated group within the community in the 1890s, who sought to re-create in these communities the associational life they had left in their home communities.

55. *New York Globe*, 1883 and 1884, *passim*; Acme quote is June 23, 1883; *Richmond Planet*, July 26, 1890; January 12, 1895; 1890–1895, *passim*.

56. For a discussion of black Richmonders' participation in the Knights of Labor, see Rachleff, *Black Labor in the South*, chapters 7–12.

57. Efforts to demonstrate manhood increasingly took on class and status dimensions. For an example of this, see the discussion of black militias and the military ritual taken on by black fraternal orders such as the Knights of Pythias, in Barkley Brown and Kimball, "Mapping the Terrain."

58. See for example, *Richmond Planet*, June 11, 1891; February 24, September 22, 1900; February 16, 1901; October 25, November 1, December 20, 1902. Ida Wells-Barnett, in her struggle against the violence aimed at black women and black men, also challenged the links between white supremacy and manliness. For a discussion of Wells-Barnett's writings in this regard, see Gail Bederman, "'Civilization,' the Decline of Middle-Class Manliness, and Ida B. Wells' Antilynching Campaign (1892–94)," *Radical History Review* 52 (Winter 1992): 5–30. Similarly, Frances Ellen Watkins Harper and Anna Julia Cooper associated Anglo-Saxon "imperialism with unrestrained patriarchal power," depicting white males as bestial devourers "of lands and peoples." Hazel V. Carby, "'On the Threshold of Woman's Era': Lynching, Empire, and Sexuality in Black Feminist Theory," *Critical Inquiry* 12 (Autumn 1985): 265.

59. The idea of sexual danger had been a part of the Reconstruction-era discourse, as evidenced in the mass indignation meetings and testimonies. Then, however, it was constructed as a matter of general interest, part of the general discussion of repression of African Americans. Now a more clearly gendered discourse developed where violence against men was linked to state repression and the struggle against it to freedom, and violence against women became a matter of specific interest, increasingly eliminated from the general discussions.

60. First African also excluded men found to have physically abused their wives. Binga, "Duty of Husband to Wife," in Binga, *Sermons on Several Occasions*, I, 304–305 (emphasis in original): FABC, II, August 6, September 3, November 5, 1883, April 7, 1884. Ultimately the members of First African were at a loss as to how to deal with the sexually transmitted disease, but the persistence of the church's efforts to take it up suggest the degree to which some members considered this a serious issue.

61. It is important to note the constructed nature of this narrative. Suzanne Lebsock has taken the development of women's clubs with these concerns as possible evidence of the

increased instances of exploitation of women, "Women and American Politics," 45. I suggest that the exploitation is not increased or even of greater concern, but that the venues for expressing and acting on that concern and the ideology through which this happens—both the narrative of endangerment and the narrative of protection—are the new, changed phenomenon. While the emphasis on motherhood and womanly virtues which undergirded the ideology of middle-class women as protectors may resonate with much of the work on middle-class white women's political activism in this period, it is important to bear in mind two distinctions: African American women's prior history of inclusion, not exclusion, shaped their discourse of womanhood and their construction of gender roles; they did so not in concert with ideas in the larger society but in opposition as white Americans continued to deny African Americans the privileges of manhood or the protections of womanhood, reinforcing the commonality rather than the separateness of men's and women's roles.

62. James Oliver Horton and Lois E. Horton suggest that a masculine conception of liberation, based on violence as an emancipatory tool available principally to men, developed within African American political rhetoric in the North in the antebellum period. "Violence, Protest, and Identity: Black Manhood in Antebellum America," in James Oliver Horton, *Free People of Color: Inside the African American Community* (Washington, D.C.: Smithsonian Institution Press, 1993), chapter 4.

63. Abernathy's and the Barnes's trials, incarceration, retrials, and eventual releases can be followed in the *Richmond Planet*, July 1895–October 1896; *Richmond Times*, July 23, 1895; *Richmond Dispatch*, September 13–19, October 2, 23, November 8, 9, 12, 14, 16, 21, 23, 24, 27, 28, 1895; July 5, 1896. For Bowser's discussion of the formation of the Women's League to protect the Lunenberg women, see *Woman's Era*, October and November 1895; Charles Wesley, *History of the National Association of Colored Women*. The first photographs of the women in the *Planet* appear August 3, 1895. The first picture of "Mary Abernathy and Her Babe" was published February 15, 1896. The post-release photograph of Pokey Barnes and Mitchell's comment regarding it appeared June 27, 1896. For a description of Barnes' attire, see March 6, 1897. Discussions of the case can be found in Brundage, *Lynching in the New South*; and Samuel N. Pincus, *The Virginia Supreme Court, Blacks and the Law 1870–1902* (New York: Garland Publishing, 1990), chapter 11. Brundage emphasizes the role of Governor O'Ferrall, and Samuel Pincus emphasizes the legal maneuverings which prevented the women's certain lynching. While emphasizing the importance of Mitchell's stands against lynching, Ann Alexander dismisses the prolonged front page coverage of the Lunenberg case in the *Richmond Planet* as mere sensationalism. "Black Protest in the New South: John Mitchell, Jr. (1863–1929), and the *Richmond Planet*" (Ph.D. diss., Duke University, 1973), 152–153. Yet it is certain that it was the continuous efforts of black men and women in Richmond which created the climate of protection for Pokey Barnes, Mary Abernathy and Mary Barnes, keeping their cases in the public eye, encouraging government and judicial officials to intervene, and providing the financial resources necessary to acquire a team of prominent white men as defense attorneys and advocates for the Lunenberg women. Pamela Henry has pointed to the focus on motherhood as a central point of the *Planet*'s defensive strategy and suggested the futility of such a strategy in an era when black women were denied the protections of Victorian womanhood. Pamela J. Henry, "Crime Punishment and African American Women in the South, 1880–1940," paper for Research Seminar in African American Women's History, University of Michigan, Fall 1992 (cited by permission of

Henry). I am uncomfortably cognizant of the fact that my narrative also, for the most part, silences Mary Abernathy and Pokey and Mary Barnes. This reflects my primary interest in understanding what this case illuminates about black Richmond. Abernathy and the Barneses, their lives and their cases, are certainly worthy of investigation in their own right; Suzanne Lebsock is currently undertaking such a study.

64. *Richmond Planet*, March 6, 1897.

65. The narrative of class and gender, protectors and protected, was not uncontested. For example, the women of the Independent Order of Saint Luke offered a counternarrative which emphasized the possibilities of urban life not only for the middle-class but importantly the possibilities of urban life for single, working-class black women who, through their collective efforts, could be their own protectors. Still further, they suggested that women—working-class and middle-class—through their political and economic resources, could become men's protectors. Reinterpreting the standards for "race men" to require support for women's rights, they thus reinserted women's condition and rights as a barometer of freedom and progress. Some aspects of the Saint Lukes' ideas regarding the relationship between the well-being of women and the well-being of men and of the community as a whole are traced in Elsa Barkley Brown, "Womanist Consciousness: Maggie Lena Walker and the Independent Order of Saint Luke," *Signs: Journal of Women in Culture and Society* 14, 3 (Spring 1989): 610–633.

66. It is important to understand this desexualization of black women as not merely a middle-class phenomenon imposed on working-class women. Many working-class women resisted and forged their own notions of sexuality and respectability. But many working-class women also, independent of the middle-class and from their own experiences, embraced a desexualized image. Who better than a domestic worker faced with the sexual exploitation of her employer might hope that invisibility would provide protection? Histories which deal with respectability, sexuality, and politics in all its complexity in black women's lives have yet to be written. For beginning discussions, see Darlene Clark Hine, "Rape and the Culture of Dissemblance: Preliminary Thoughts on the Inner Lives of Black Midwestern Women," *Signs: Journal of Women in Culture and Society* 14 (Summer 1989): 919–920; Elsa Barkley Brown, "'What Has Happened Here': The Politics of Difference in Women's History and Feminist Politics," *Feminist Studies* 18 (Summer 1992): 295–312; Paula Giddings, "The Last Taboo," in *Race-ing Justice, En-gendering Power: Essays on Anita Hill, Clarence Thomas, and the Construction of Social Reality*, ed. Toni Morrison (New York: Pantheon Books, 1992), 441–463.

67. Bytches With Problems, "Wanted," is one effort by young black women to democratize the discussion of repressive violence; focusing on the often sexualized nature of police brutality against black women, they remind us that such is often less likely to be included in statistics or acknowledged in the public discussion. *The Bytches* (Noface Records, 1991).

68. Elsa Barkley Brown, "Imaging Lynching: African American Women, Communities of Struggle, and Collective Memory," in *African American Women Speak Out: Responses to Anita Hill–Clarence Thomas*, ed. Geneva Smitherman (Detroit: Wayne State University, 1995).

Part 5

The Interwar Period:
Migration, Urbanization,
and Black Religious Diversity

Chapter 19

Racial Christianity

S. P. Fullinwider

The Negro intellectuals and spokesmen were faced with the problem of choosing between two worldviews as the new century approached. In the realm of religion it was a choice between an "other-worldly" and a "this-worldly" faith. Is the Christian message one which asks man to submit patiently to the evils of this world secure in the knowledge that paradise awaits the true Christian in the next, or is it a message of reform—calculated to bring to mankind a society based on brotherly love? A great many forces (which can be subsumed under the general heading, "the secularization of thought") were at work in the world of the intellectual to shift religious thought into "this-worldly" channels.

Rational religion in America, child of a clandestine marriage between Calvinism and the Enlightenment, had weaned the intellectual away from the fundamentalistic faith through a succession of theological vagaries ranging from William Ellery Channing's Unitarianism to Horace Bushnell's social Christianity to Walter Rauschenbusch's Social Gospel. Transcendentalism, socialism, Higher Criticism and Social Darwinism had done their work in convincing theologians like Washington Gladden and Walter Rauschenbusch that man is at least potentially good, and that God is working through history eventually to create a kingdom of heaven on earth.

These forces were generally absent from the Negro's religion, and for two very good reasons: first, the overwhelming majority of Negro clergymen were destitute of extensive education; second, the Negro's religious institutions were under the imperious domination of conservative fundamentalist leaders whose power rested less on book learning than on intrigue. As late as 1930 investigators found that a paltry 20 percent of

477

urban Negro pastors (of all denominations) were college graduates. The corresponding figure for rural Negro churches was 3 percent. The majority of Negro churches had no educational standards for their ministries; anyone who felt "called" could usually be ordained. In the Baptist denomination (which accounted for two thirds of the churchgoing Negroes), freedom promoted the proliferation of untrained ministers—all that was needed to start a new church was the agreement of four laymen and three ordained ministers.[1]

But the Negro clergyman was not necessarily a man of small talent. On the contrary, the church was the one area in the Negro world where a man of talent might get ahead—it was the one institution not dominated by whites. The various denominations tended to become vast political arenas where power struggle and intrigue were as rife as was religious fervor. Somehow in the turmoil the more progressive minded got shoved aside. So, in Negro religion, the shift to "this-worldly" religion, when it occurred, was an isolated and sporadic thing. But it was important.[2]

Commitments to worldviews involve (beyond exposure to new ideas and calm deliberation on the alternatives) such factors as the cultural milieu, institutional pressures, and such attitudinal sets as are formed in the unconscious. With regard to the last-named factor, the handling and channeling of aggression must be taken into account as playing an important part in the process of choice. Admitting this, how is the historian to handle it? Probably only on the level of hypothesis.

The hypothesis of the present chapter is this: That the "Christ-like" image (stereotype) of the Negro was born out of the formation of ego-defense mechanisms contrived in the slave's unconscious to maintain self-respect during a time when the choice in handling aggression was either to repress it or to be destroyed. The slave's patience, humility, and good nature were necessary for his survival. Now, these were the very traits that the Christian religion set before the slave and the post-Emancipation generation as the ideal for which all men should strive—they were the traits of Christ, himself. It was not difficult, therefore, for the oppressed Negro to interpret his subservient behavior as being Christ-like. In fact, it was necessary for his self-esteem (ego-defenses) that he see himself as not servile; that he see himself, rather, as the realization of the Christian ideal. In time the Negro came to see himself as being Christ-like, and this self-image became (for him) a racial stereotype. As a stereotype it was an ideal self-image, and remained such even for many of those whose independence of the white world was sufficient to allow them alternate modes of behavior—alternatives to patience, humility, and good-natured forbearance.

As more Negroes gained relative independence, more were free to express their aggressions in ways other than sporadic outbursts of violence or in sullenness. For the independent Negro the Christ-like image was no longer needed as an ego-defense, but as a racial stereotype it continued its strong hold as an ideal and as a means of identifying with the race. The image was a source of self-esteem because it allowed the Negro to compare favorably the Christ-like Negro with the inhuman white man. The invidious comparison the image involved was also a first-rate way of channeling aggression. It was a particularly useful thing for the militant clergy: the invidious comparison allowed them to be racists and still be (as they thought) good Christians. Just as important, it was a way to rationalize a shift to a "this-worldly" religion. Though the vast majority of Negro clergymen stayed with their fundamentalism, an important few were pushed by their hatred of oppression into a "this-worldly" fight for civil rights. The Christ-like image of the Negro suggested a mission—a mission to make reforms in this world. So, the image that began its career as an ego-defense was turned into a weapon of militancy and became the core of a race ideology—a race-oriented religion. This chapter, then, is the story of a few religious leaders who could not tolerate the "other-worldliness" of the fundamentalist faith; who, because of their militancy, forged a "this-worldly" faith devoted to the Christian ideals of brotherhood, but based on racial antagonism.

It was this small band of religious militants that represented the Negro clergy in the Niagara Movement and the early NAACP just after the turn of the century. They were few in number (perhaps a dozen), but disproportionately influential in Negro intellectual and militant circles. Well-educated, articulate in the religious journals, they helped to formulate the ideology of the Negro mission and to bring it into the militant protest movements.

II

In the years following the Civil War and Reconstruction periods, the Negro clergy, like other race leaders of that period, accepted most of the pronouncements white men were making upon the state of their race. They idealized American civilization and contrasted it with African "savagery"; they proclaimed America's Christian virtues and hoped the Negro would one day live up to them, believing that the white man was waiting for the opportunity to welcome him into the full status of citizenship. This type of thinking was true even of those who considered themselves intrepid militants. Bishop Alexander Walters of the A.M.E. Zion Church, for example, esteemed himself as a staunch fighter for civil rights. Among a multitude of things, he attempted to organize the race leadership in the National Afro-American Council (1898), and tried in 1908 to lead the Negro voters out of the Republican party. In that same year, following Theodore Roosevelt's extremely biased handling of the race riots in Brownsville, Texas, Walters led a group of ministers in an indignant rejection of the President's offer to discuss the matter. But his was the voice of the conservative clergy, calling upon the Negro to get education and wealth in order to make himself fit to live in the white man's civilization; telling him that he must work for the possession of character if he was to command respect.[3]

The same rationale of Negro inferiority is seen in the words of another leading Negro clergyman, Bishop W. J. Gaines of the A.M.E. Church: "Oh! ye Southern whites! among whom we live, and with whom in the same soil we expect to lie at last, let your hand of love go out to your poor, struggling brother in black, who has toiled so long through the weary night of ignorance and servitude, and help to lift him to the same heights of knowledge and virtue upon which you so proudly stand." Gaines was just going along with the general content of thought of the conservative clergy (the overwhelming majority) when he called upon the "virtuous" white man to extend a helping hand to the suffering Negro and lift him to the heights of white civilization. No doubt he strongly believed in the superiority of the white man over the Negro. But deep down in his psyche, or wherever it is that stereotypes dwell, he held a strongly contradictory opinion—he was, in fact, a devotee of the Christ-like image of the Negro. "No race," he wrote in reference to slavery, "ever acted more like Jesus Christ, whose life was one long, patient non-resistance to wrong." Bishop Gaines was doing some sort of unconscious juggling act, at one moment holding aloft the superior virtue of the white man, at another comparing the Negro with Christ.[4]

One thing that helped the conservative clergy to avoid confronting the contradictions in their thought was their great faith that God is operating the world according to some great plan. They had the traditional argument of proslavery orators to confirm this idea—the argument that God had brought the Negro hither to Christianize him. Gaines sensed something of God's plan; he was beginning to perceive the "dawning light of the Divine purpose," as it even now "begins to reveal itself . . ." God intends, he said, to Christianize Africa through the agency of the Afro-American. For his part, Alexander Walters felt that God had brought the Negro to

America that the *white man* be given the chance to learn true Christian leadership, which he would then go on to exercise over the world. In any case, both believed the Negro American had a mission—of sorts.[5]

The clergy was still full of optimism and faith in God's intentions as the 19th century began to run its course. L. J. Coppin, editor of the A.M.E. Church *Review* (1888–96), and later bishop, like many others would never forget the joyous moment of his emancipation. Was he not a personal witness to God's benevolent intent? He was convinced that one day the meek would inherit the earth—being Christ-like would pay off: "Now, if the Christian type of civilization is to be in the end the prevailing power, then the people who are the receptacles of the true Christianity will be the dominant people." In keeping with the conservative faith, Coppin instructed his people to wait and be good—it was at best a passive role.[6]

This was a concept of nonresistance, of submission and hope. It called for the repression of all hostile and aggressive tendencies. These clergymen were not ignorant of the daily depredations with which they were confronted, but the easiest way to handle hostility is not to have it; the easiest way not to have it is to have no enemies.

By the way of summing up this type of religious expression—the thought which appears to have been a near-consensus among the Negro clergy of the 19th century—it will be well to look at the ideas of perhaps the greatest Negro preacher of the time.

The Rev. Charles T. Walker was a Georgia Baptist who achieved fame in the 1880s. Neither of the famous white evangelists, Sam Jones nor Dwight L. Moody, claims Walker's biographer, was able to draw larger crowds to the revival meetings held in Atlanta's Exposition Park. Nor did anyone have more power in determining the selection of Negro ministers for the pastorates of the state. Walker (the "Black Spurgeon") first gained his reputation in a way reminiscent of Booker T. Washington. For several hours, during a National Baptist Convention in 1886, several of the brethren had been holding forth in derogatory terms against the whites. Walker arose, his face flushed with anger, and for some time held forth on the *goodness* of the whites. The same thing happened again in 1889. Walker was a devout believer in the goodwill of the whites, and argued that friendship should be returned for friendship.[7]

Again, in Walker, we see the peculiar blindness to oppression that characterized the clerical mind. God had freed the Negro from slavery. God was seeing to it that the Negro was getting a Christian education, wealth, and advancement in the professions. In all these things Walker was optimistic because God is in His heaven. His solution to the racial problem harked back to the individual redemption theme preached by Charles G. Finney in the 1820s: "The crying need of the age is men and women with pure, heartfelt, practical religion." There was nothing of militancy in Walker's message: "In this," he said, "we would do well to copy the life of our Savior. . . . He was sympathetic, tenderhearted, liberal, kind and generous. He was meek and, therefore, called a lamb; He was compassionate and charitable; He was content in poverty, patient in His deep afflictions. . . ." Walker's message was passively to endure fate—there was no room in his religion for the expression of hostility and aggression.[8]

In his optimism, Walker could not contain his admiration for the white man. "It seems to me," he said, "to be a logical conclusion, if honesty, truthfulness, chastity, industry and economy made the Anglo-Saxon great, the cultivation and practice of the same graces will make the negro great, prosperous and happy." Note that the Christ-like virtues were withheld from the Anglo-Saxon. These were reserved for the Negro. Like his contemporaries, Walker held dear the story of the slave's loyalty during the Civil War. He loved to relate Atlanta newspaperman Henry W. Grady's statement of it: "I want no truer soul," he quoted Grady as saying, "than that which moved the trusty slave, who for four years, while my father fought with the armies that barred his freedom slept every night at my mother's chamber door . . . ready to lay down his humble life on the threshold." The invidious comparison of the races was a potential in Walker, but never more than that. Optimism and faith in God's rule kept it on that level. He compared his race's situation with the great saga of the Hebrews in Egypt. His race, too, was being civilized for its great mission of bringing light to Africa. One need not question the ways of God, at least Charles Walker never did.[9]

Such was the near-consensus reached by the older generation of clergy and held dear as generation followed generation. It was a consensus born out of slavery and reinforced by Emancipation—the supreme example of God's benevolent will.

But even as the conservative-minded fundamentalists held the reins of church government firmly in their hands, a younger generation was living through the systematic oppression being dealt out by the white man in post-Reconstruction America. In the late 1880s and the 1890s we begin to hear a few voices raised in opposition to the ruling consensus. The official organ of the A.M.E. Church, the *Christian Recorder*, stuck rigidly to orthodoxy, but editor Coppin of the A.M.E. Church *Review* now and then opened his pages to dissent. Examination shows two trends forming: rebellion against the white man, and a tendency to submit the tenets of fundamentalism to scrutiny.

One Rev. William Hannibal Thomas wrote in the October, 1888 issue of the *Review* that oppression was everywhere getting worse; that two centuries of submission and passivity had not worked. He called for "aggressive resistance" to replace compliancy, and implied that neither God nor the white man was going to help the Negro. He went further, asserting that this is not a moral universe at all, that "it is neither intellect nor religion that rules the world, but physical force—brute force, if you please. . . ." Thomas' ego-defenses were badly out of kilter—the mechanism for repressing aggression was not working at all well. "The Negro," he continued, "must lay aside humility . . . and manfully protect himself, his family and his fireside from the lecherous assaults of white invaders."[10]

Another contributor to the *Review*, R. R. Downs, dared to aim a blow at the time-honored tradition of the Negro's Christ-like role during the Civil War. "Now," he said, "Negro apologists, with their watery eyes, go sniffling over the country with a 'sorry-we-are-here-and-sorry-we-are-living' manner, basing their pusillanimous effort of speech-making on the Negro's 'faithfulness to old master's family during the war.'"[11]

Downs ended his article with an appeal for more manliness. This became a rising note. The Rev. S. Martin declared that true Christianity demands dignity for all. And the Rev. R. William Fickland warned that if the A.M.E. Church failed to lead the fight for civil rights, the progressive members of the church would leave it and carry on the fight from without.[12]

Meanwhile, the voices evincing a more liberal theology began to make themselves increasingly heard in the *Review*. The gradual shift was from an all-powerful God who had absolute control over history toward a benevolent but weak God who could do little of practical value for the Negro. In other words, some, at least, of the clergy were losing faith in God's ability to handle the situation. They needed a religion that was concerned with the here and now, that would not demand that they hold their hostilities in check on the theory that meekness would carry them into heaven. They were working toward a religion that demanded equality—civil rights.

In 1891 the Rev. A. W. Upshaw discussed biblical criticism and found that while the "higher" criticism was largely capricious, and therefore pernicious, much of the criticism had done a commendable work for religion in clearing up interpretations. At another time he had conceded that there was much in the Old Testament that seemed doubtful, and concluded that the "New Theology" of Lyman Abbott was right in believing that clear revelation progresses from Moses to John. The New Testament, he thought, is better on God than is the Old. Upshaw was expressing the tendency among some of the clergy to shift away from the concept of an awful, omnipotent God to the one of God as the loving Father of mankind. The Rev. S. B. Jones, a self-proclaimed evangelist, asked the question, "How Should We Present God?" Too often, he said, evangelists pictured God as a "demon ruling with an iron hand." Evangelists should put more emphasis on His loving, forbearing side: "Let us then, in our revivals, have more of the love, gentleness, forbearance and justice of God, for in no unmistakable language He says, 'Fury is not in me.'"[13]

While some were probing the bastions of revelation and the omnipotent God idea, others had the temerity to suggest that the church pay some attention to the Negro's problems in this world—social problems. In 1894, one C.O.H. Thomas, in replying to a previous article in the *Review*, took an advanced position. The offending article had declared that the clergy should not discuss politics with their congregations. Not a bit of it, said Thomas, politics is based on moral law—the domain of the minister—and "it is the duty of the church and ministry to promote political and social reforms. . . ." If the church should omit this vital function, he continued, it will commit suicide. Should the church give "everything over to the control of the dreaded Socialist or fiendish Anarchist, give to them all the vital questions of the day, and confine the pulpit to 'Children's Day,' 'Missionary Day,' 'Education Day' and other meetings; together with belabored and prolixed discussions of either end of eternity . . ." the common people will quickly find other leaders. The Rev. Henry L. Phillips pushed further in this direction in his comments on General Booth's *Darkest England and the Way out of It*. Booth compared London's slums unfavorably with Dante's hell and with "darkest Africa." Phillips accepted this comparison and went on to say that it was foolish to preach the Gospel to those who are starving. "Man's first business," he wrote, "is with this life. Christ's first miracles were for the body." It is the minister's duty to attempt to lift people from slum conditions and "surround them with a new atmosphere, and give them an upward push."[14]

These were all timid steps away from what was basically a slave religion—a religion of acceptance and submission. If one were to criticize them, one would have to admit that their relevance is in showing how *little* the most daring of the clergy were disposed to question orthodoxy. Yet, the examples cited do indicate the direction that deviation from orthodoxy was taking in the 1880s and 1890s. Some of the clergy were beginning to question the power of God to do what was needed for the Negro race; some were not so sure that a patient, submissive waiting for the favor of God and the white man was their cup of tea. The old slave religion was being questioned. It would take the combined efforts of a young intellectual and an old fire-eater to pick up these threads and weave them into open rebellion.

<h1 style="text-align:center">III</h1>

The two apostates from the slave religion were R. R. Wright, Jr., editor of the *Christian Recorder* (1909–36), and Reverdy C. Ransom, editor of the A.M.E. Church *Review* (1912–24). Together they succeeded in making God lovable but weak, and in taking the mission of making society better from His shoulders and giving it to the Negro. Together, they transformed Christianity from a God-centered religion to a race-centered one, and if few of the clergy cared to follow them there were others who did—W.E.B. Du Bois, for example.

Always Wright and Ransom were very close. Together, in 1900 they organized the Institutional Church and Social Settlement in the heart of Chicago's newly forming black belt on the South Side. This was the formative experience, for both of them—the struggle against poverty and crime among the low down. They had the help of Miss MacDowell of the Chicago University Settlements and of Jane Addams, whose Hull House was their model. They had the close friendship of Clarence Darrow; with him they negotiated a peace between striking stockyard workers and Negro strikebreakers—a peace which resulted in opening the stockyard unions to Negroes. They were close friends with Robert Ingersoll. Years later, Reverdy Ransom preached the eulogy at Ingersoll's funeral. That shocked and confounded the orthodoxy, but Ransom felt that Ingersoll, the atheist, was a better Christian than a good many of his clerical detractors. The experience at the Institutional Church in Chicago was basic for Wright and Ransom for another reason: for a period of four years they had to struggle against the orthodoxy simply to keep their church alive. The A.M.E. hierarchy opposed the operation from the beginning, and after a four-year fight Ransom and Wright had no alternative but to resign.[15]

That was just the beginning of Wright's career in the Chicago settlements. He went from the Institutional Church to the Frederick Douglass Center, and later founded the Trinity Mission in the heart of Chicago's slums. In December, 1905, we find him writing to Charles W. Chesnutt, the Negro author, concerning opportunities for opening a settlement house in Cleveland, Ohio. In the midst of all this Wright was in the process of getting an education. When he wrote the letter of 1905 to Chesnutt he was already a graduate of the University of Chicago, had studied in Berlin and Leipzig, and was working toward a Ph.D. in sociology at the University of Pennsylvania—a degree that he would get in 1912.[16]

Ostensibly, in 1905, Wright was working on a study of Negro migration from the rural South to Philadelphia—a study that was later published in 1912 as *The Negro in Pennsylvania*. Actually, he was rounding out a faith—a system of thought that flew directly in the face of A.M.E. orthodoxy. It was a totally "this-worldly" faith—the Kingdom of God must be made here on earth. "The teaching of Jesus on the Kingdom of God emphasizes," he later wrote, "the conversion of the social order: the making of the kingdoms of this world, the kingdom of our God." The Kingdom of God on earth would be based on the principle of brotherhood. Wright was calling for a moral revolution; more than that, he was calling for a social revolution: "It is revolutionary. It will change our industrial relations. It will change our politics. It will change our standards of morality." It was socialism—as he gladly admitted—but that, according to him, was the least of it. He called his program "Social Service"—but was far more interested in the moral aspects than in the industrial aspects of it. Socialism would come as a matter of course as man brought the reign of Christ to the world.[17]

Wright had to go through the painful process of throwing out his own boyhood beliefs before he could rebel against the orthodoxy prescribed by the A.M.E. Church establishment. His first beliefs came from a father who was a fundamentalist and the president of a Georgia industrial school. The story is told that once, when the senior Wright was yet a boy ("no bigger than a bar of soap"), the great General O. O. Howard asked him for a message to carry back to the boys of the North. "Tell 'em we're rising," replied Wright. Howard presumably carried out his end of the bargain, the boy carried out his. And President Wright, Sr., of the Georgia State Industrial College, was at least comfortably certain that his rise was due to his adherence to the fundamentals. Every morning in chapel he treated his students and professors to a large dose of those fundamentals. Every Sunday he taught the Bible. Once he found he had on his hands a professor who thought lightly of the Bible. Exit one highly trained Yale graduate from the premises.

If the experience of the Yale man is any guide, R. R. Wright, Jr., was not brought up innocent of the fundamentals. It seems equally unlikely that he escaped an early exposure to the Christ-like image. One of the extant speeches of the senior Wright is a talk on Lincoln—the Emancipator was attributed with "many of the traits for which colored people are noted . . . :" a sweetness of disposition, a great patience of the wrong, a forgiving nature, and a readiness "to wait for the slow process by which God accomplished great blessings for mankind." The fundamentals were the ideas of Booker T. Washington generously seasoned with "other-worldly" religion.[18]

Though the son was an apostate from the right, he always thought of his father's principles with a measure of affection. In April, 1914, for example, he related an instance when evangelist Billy Sunday was called upon by the University of Pennsylvania to quell an outbreak of suicides, and concluded: "Thus another valuable testimony from an unexpected source is given to 'the old time religion.'" On occasion, young Wright sounded very much like the famous Tuskegee president himself—calling for moral improvement by the race, economic self-help and education as the way out of the race mire. In September of 1914 he defended Washington's self-help ideas as one-half of the necessary program of emancipation. On one occasion, Wright even went to the extreme of hoping for help from the white southerner. "We must," he then declared, "prove worthy of the service these noble men and women render us." In Wright's defense it must be said that he expected help from only a few whites at most. After the year 1915 Wright never again lost touch with reality.[19]

The year 1915 marked the crisis in Wright's intellectual life. The last straw seems to have been a particularly brutal lynching he had read about. On the day following the lynching he wrote: "To-day is perhaps the darkest day in the life of the Negro race during the past fifty years." The white man had, he said, entirely deserted the Negro in both the North and the South. "We are lynched," he wrote in intense anger, "we are hanged, riddled with bullets and burned. Excursions are run to have the daughters and sons of 'respectable leading citizens' witness the barbecuing of a nigger. . . ." After the lynching his judgment of the white man grew exceedingly bitter: "The white man is selfish and the American white man is the most grasping breed of humanity ever made." Never again did Wright speak in the accents of his more patient father. Never again did he make gestures in the direction of the "other-worldly" religion of the church orthodoxy.[20]

The 1915 intellectual crisis served the purpose of severing Wright's ties with the old faith, but it did more—it galvanized him into becoming a militant. He continued to believe in and develop his prayerful faith in the eventual advent of an earthly kingdom of heaven based on human brotherhood—all of his experience as a settlement worker and student of sociology worked in this direction. But his developing militancy sent him off in another direction. Building on his belief in the Christ-like Negro, and on his disgust with the white man, he began to build a race-centered religion.

Wright's "this-worldy" religion—his "Social Service"—was well developed before his 1915 intellectual crisis: "And He only emphasized the Fatherhood of God as a basis for the teaching of the Brotherhood of Man," he wrote in 1914. It need only be said that he continued to develop this train of thought; continued to deemphasize the importance of God and to increase emphasis on the spirit of brotherhood, until his religion ultimately pushed God into the obscure background. In 1935 (Wright was by then a bishop) we find him telling the World Fellowship Conference that any religion which preaches brotherhood and social service is valid. His rejection of A.M.E. orthodoxy was complete.[21]

The new note that appeared in Wright's post-1915 thought is one of militancy. He began to urge that the Negro race form an interest group and enter into the political arena. He gleefully urged the speedup of wartime migration of Negroes from the South as a boon to pressure politics. He called for the formation of a Negro political party to control the votes of its race and to elect Negroes to Congress. Then the idea suggested itself to him that the vast Negro wartime migration would force the northern states to arm men of his race and organize them into militia units. The South would have to follow suit. His imagination was working overtime.[22]

In his new militancy, Wright began calling for a new kind of Negro—one who would fight for the right. The meek Negro was not going to inherit the earth after all. More than anything else the colored man needed self-respect. Wright decided that Jesus had come carrying a sword—a spiritual sword to combat evil. "A man who shuns a fight with evil, with a lawbreaker, or a robber or a corruptionist," he said, "is not a peaceful Christian but a sinful coward." The race must always remember that before a Christian peace can come, right must triumph.[23]

Militancy, race consciousness, and a sense of God's impotence all conspired to redirect Wright's thinking into a new channel. He drew upon the Christ-like image of the Negro to fashion a race-centered religion. The ideas were introduced in a 1916 editorial entitled, "African Methodism and the Second Century." The world, he wrote, is in need of a rejuvenated Christianity. Who will give it new ideals? Not the white man, because "The Anglo-Saxon and the Teuton have failed." The white man does not have the religious temperament—a point that Wright felt was proven by the fact that he has never created a great religion. The European mind, materialistic and selfish, has never understood Christ. The Negro, on the other hand, is of a poetic nature; he lives little on earth and much in heaven, and "he suffers too long, and is too kind to be a European." The Negro, he continued, is peaceful, loving and forgiving; it is up to him to instill new religious life in the world. "But what has this to do with the African Methodist Church's mission in the Second Century?" he asked. "This and only this: If European (and American) Christianty is to get back to Jesus, it will be because those people who understand the temperament of Jesus take it back." African Methodism will carry the Christian message of brotherhood to the white man; "she must be heard always proclaiming 'God our Father, Christ our Redeemer and Man our Brother.' This is her task for the second century." Wright had pushed God into the background and had given the mission of saving mankind to the colored race. It was a difficult role he had created for his race—the Negro was to be a patient, meek, Christ-like man and yet a militant fighter for the right. In fact, two incompatible elements were latent in Wright's formulation; one was aggression, the other was love; one was racism, the other was Christianity.[24]

When we turn to the ministry of Reverdy C. Ransom, Wright's older colleague at the Institutional Church, we find the tension between racism and Christianity becoming more overt, more pronounced. Ransom was torn between two concepts of Christianity: Christianity as an instrument of (possibly bloody) revolution, and Christianity as the means by which the Negro would save democracy and the white man's soul. At one time we find him speaking with the intensity of a Hebrew prophet, denouncing the ungodliness of the white man and proclaiming the necessity of shedding a little blood in the cause of freedom. The next moment we find him extolling the Negro's inherent meekness and the need to conquer through love. Ransom could not decide whether John Brown or Christ should set the example for Negro religion.

We meet him in 1906 at Harpers Ferry telling the assembled militants of the Niagara Movement how John Brown was commissioned by God to strike down slavery by appeal to the higher law. Brown was a man who knew what few dare to admit, that freedom demands the shedding of blood: "A new birth of freedom within a nation," Ransom intoned, "is always accompanied with great suffering and pain. How much greater, then, the travail through which humanity must pass to bring forth its last and highest birth, for which all preceding ages have worked and waited until now." This note rang pleasantly in Ransom's ears. "Every good gift, even eternal salvation," he wrote in 1916, "has been bought with blood." It was a recurring theme.[25]

A deep and abiding lack of admiration and affection for the white man had possession of Ransom and nourished his militancy. He had red hair.

It grated on his soul that he should have red hair. His boyhood companions derisively called him a "white man's nigger" because of it. He had a
sneaking suspicion that somewhere back in the line of his progenitors there
had been an Irishman. He stoutly denied that it could have been an Anglo-
Saxon: "One thing I know, there is little of the Anglo-Saxon in me."[26]

When the post-Reconstruction movement was begun in the South to
force the Negro race into a caste status, Ransom was a young man just
entering the ministry (1885). He watched and agonized throughout the
years that his race was jim-crowed and disfranchised. No romantic myth
hid the actual conditions in the South from his eyes; he saw no paternalistic aristocracy there waiting hopefully for the day when the Negro would
prove himself ready for citizenship. "Senator Tillman of South Carolina,"
Ransom knew, "fully represents the attitude of the Southern whites when
he declares that they do not intend to accord Negroes, under any conditions, political or any other kind of equality. . . ." He had no illusions about
white civilization being a high plateau of achievement to be aspired to by
the Negro. His critique of that civilization was withering. When the
Negro heavyweight, Jack Johnson, won the championship (1903), Ransom noted caustically that the real savagery occurred outside of the ring.
The betting, the feverish excitement, the garish advertising, and, when
Johnson won, the widespread spite shown against his race, all convinced
Ransom that in America civilization and Christianity are only skin deep;
that beneath them prowls the animal. He saw the animal prowling whenever he read of another lynching—there was evidence of the white man's
brutal nature. It was time, he said, for the Negro to treat the whites as the
whites were treating him—brutality should be "answered by a volley of
bullets." "I am unwillingly," he said, "but slowly, coming to the conclusion that the only way for the Negro . . . to win and hold the respect of
the white people is to mete out to them a white man's measure in all the
relations of life."[27]

That was one side of the coin—the side in Ransom that opted for John
Brown and bloody retaliation. But Ransom had another side that stood in
opposition to bloodletting—a side that found its satisfaction in benign
contemplation of the Christ-like nature of his race: "The Negroes are a
kind-hearted people. Their nature is flooded with all the warmth of oriental sunshine which for ages beat upon them." It gave him satisfaction to
describe the Negro's gift to America in terms that had none of the overtones of revolt: "By [the Negroes'] influence the heart of America has been
softened with more kindness, a sweeter spirit has filled its life and a
stronger wave of emotion has swept the whole range of its philanthropy

and religion." And, as often as he counseled militancy to his people he counseled the emulation of Christ: ". . . we need more and above all these, the spirit and power of the Lord Jesus; purity, temperance, truth, justice, meekness, faith, righteousness, love: against these prejudice, hatred, injustice, oppression, violence have no power." The two most important elements in Ransom's thought were, therefore, polar opposites, corresponding to the aggression that he felt, and to the Christian ideals that he believed in.[28]

Ransom's militancy ran deep and started early in life. He was expelled from Oberlin College for organizing a protest against segregated dining room seating arrangements. Then, at Wilberforce, he ran afoul of the Trinity, poked fun at Genesis, had the audacity to speak up for the science of geology; all this in spite of a stern resolve to keep his opinions to himself. For 15 years after graduation he worked quietly in the vineyards of the Lord. These particular vineyards happened to be the slums of Pittsburgh where, as he poked around the tenement flats and alleys, he learned something about squalor and human degradation. After that experience he lost interest in the wonders of heaven; there was too much wrong in this world.

In Chicago (1900–04) and again in New York City (1913–24) Ransom operated settlement houses in the heart of the black ghettos' worst slums, always with the church hierarchy in strong opposition. He got interested in city politics in 1907 when he went to the Republican mayor of New York and asked that Negroes be put on the police force. The mayor would not, but Tammany would—if its candidates were elected. Ransom helped Tammany win the election, and then watched the police force become integrated. After that he organized campaigns to switch the Negro vote in New York to the Democratic party, and in this again he had to fight the church hierarchy. It was perhaps inevitable that Ransom would get involved up to his ears in the militant protest movements.

In 1905 the A.M.E. hierarchy made the egregious error of sending the intractable minister to Boston, just when that city was becoming the storm center of agitation against Booker T. Washington's leadership of the American Negro. It would not have been like Ransom to remain aloof from the vilification of Washington; it would have been asking too much to expect the Washington forces to refrain from dragging their clerical tormentor through the mud. It was a first-rate brawl. Ransom became a leader of the Niagara Movement (1905–09) in its revolt against Washington's policies, and then a leading speaker of the organizing campaign of the NAACP. In 1913 he captured control of the A.M.E. Church *Review* and turned its guns on Washington and religious orthodoxy. His war was mainly waged on two fronts, against "other-worldly" religion and against the caste system. The religion he fashioned as a result became "this-worldly" and race-centered.

Twelve years of editorials in the A.M.E. Church *Review* (1912–24) constitute a record of Ransom's religious formulations. One tendency was to make Christianity a doctrine of brotherhood on earth. In the January, 1917, editorial, he made Christianity stand on brotherhood and love, the upholding of justice, unselfish service to the poor and the weak, and opposition to oppression. Ransom decreed, in other words, that Christianity is a religion of civil rights and social reform. This was clearly phrased in his definition of African Methodism a year earlier: "This denomination," he wrote, "has prospered marvelously, its chief inspiration being not its religious doctrines, not its polity, but its spirit of manhood and equality for which it has stood these hundred years." But this was not a "love thine enemies" doctrine, for by this time hatred of the white man had become a dominant force in his thought. In 1918 he editorialized that if the whites continued with their white supremacy, the Negro had better abandon the dream of brotherhood and become "incarnate devils."[29]

As rebelliousness and the spirit of hostility grew in Ransom's breast, his religious ideas tended increasingly to become race-centered until it was a racial Christianity that he was preaching. In this racial Christianity brotherhood remained the ideal, but only the Negro was Christian. The teachings of Christ, the salvation of mankind, the kingdom of heaven on earth, all these became the mission of the more-Christ-like Negro:

> As we face the present blight of the white man's civilization and the spiritual and social impotence of his Christianity, the spiritual leadership among men lies open and vacant for any people who will qualify to enter and ocupy it. . . .
>
> If Americans of African descent can survive the social, economic, and political inferno through which they are passing, may now we hope with their growing intelligence and strength, they will arise in a great crusade for Justice and Righteousness and take the moral and spiritual leadership of the black race throughout the world to rescue the Cross of Christ from infidel Christianity.[30]

Ransom and Wright had taken the Christ-like image of the Negro, had added a mission ideology, and made it the core of their religion. Their religion had an important influence in the councils of the Niagara Movement and the early NAACP; it penetrated the classrooms of the Negro universities and colleges, became sociological dogma taught to thousands of students from the turn of the century through the 1920s. It represented the transformation of the old slave religion into a religion of militancy—the overthrow of the slave psychology. As such, it was a step in the emancipation of the Negro mind. But it had channeled aggression into the realm of mythology and so was itself an intellectual prison. It was a strange brew: part Social Gospel in its emphasis on the brotherhood of man, part racism. It set the Negro up as the moral arbiter of American civilization.

Notes

1. See Benjamin E. Mays and Joseph W. Nicholson, *The Negro Church* (New York: Institute of Social and Religious Research, 1933), pp. 10, 238.
2. See E. Franklin Frazier, *The Negro Church in America* (New York: Schocken Books, Inc., 1963), p. 43; and Carter G. Woodson, *The History of the Negro Church* (Washington, D.C.: The Associated Publishers, 1921), pp. 244 ff.
3. Alexander Walters, *(Boston) Guardian*, February 29, 1908; Alexander Walters, *My Life and Work* (New York: Fleming H. Revell Co., 1917), pp. 125–31, 208.
4. W. J. Gaines, *The Negro and the White Man* (Philadelphia: A.M.E. Publishing House, 1897), pp. 70, 65.
5. *Ibid.*, p. 20; Walters, *My Life and Work, op. cit.*, pp. 244–45.
6. L. J. Coppin, A.M.E. Church *Review*, Vol. 7 (July, 1890), pp. 102–103.
7. Silas X. Floyd, *Life of Charles T. Walker* (no imprint, 1902), pp. 77–80.
8. Charles T. Walker, sermon, June 6, 1888, quoted in Silas X. Floyd, *Life of Charles T. Walker*, pp. 125–29; Charles T. Walker, "The Negro Problem: Its Scriptural Solution," (Augusta, Ga.: Chronicle Job Printing Co., 1893), pp. 6, 8, sermon delivered at the Tabernacle Baptist Church, Augusta, Ga., June 4, 1893.
9. Walker, "The Negro Problem," *ibid.*, p. 13; Charles T. Walker, *Forty Years of Freedom. The American Negro: His Hindrances and Progress* (Philadelphia: Christian Banner Printers, 1903), pp. 5, 3.
10. William Hannibal Thomas, "Till Another King Arose, Which Knew Not Joseph," A.M.E. Church *Review*, Vol. 5 (October, 1888), p. 337.
11. R. R. Downs, "The Negro Is Known," A.M.E. Church *Review*, Vol. 7 (April, 1891), p. 412.
12. S. Martin, "Education before the Christian Era," A.M.E. Church *Review*, Vol. 8 (October, 1891), p. 194; R. William Fickland, "The Church: Its Opportunities," *Christian Recorder*, Vol. 58 (August 4, 1910), p. 1.
13. A. W. Upshaw, "Biblical Criticism," A.M.E. Church *Review*, Vol. 8 (October, 1891), pp. 198–201; A. W. Upshaw, "Reason and Revelation," A.M.E. Church *Review*, vol. 5 (October, 1888), p. 328; S. B. Jones, "What Is the Best Way of Conducting Revivals in the A.M.E. Church?" A.M.E. Church *Review*, Vol. 8 (October, 1891), p. 221.
14. J. W. Smith, "Ministers and Politics," A.M.E. Church *Review*, Vol. 11 (July, 1894), pp. 181–84; C.O.H. Thomas, "Politics, Ministers and Religion," A.M.E. Church *Review*, Vol. 11 (October, 1894), pp. 277, 280; Henry L. Phillips, "General Booth's Darkest England and the Way out of It," A.M.E. Church *Review*, Vol. 7 (April, 1891), pp. 405, 407.

15. Reverdy C. Ransom, "Ingersoll the Humanitarian," A.M.E. Church *Review*, Vol. 38 (April, 1922), pp. 173–175; Reverdy C. Ransom, *Pilgrimage of Harriet Ransom's Son* (Nashville: A.M.E. Sunday School Union, *ca.* 1948), pp. 93–136.

16. R. R. Wright, Jr. to Charles W. Chesnutt, December 5, 1905, Chesnutt papers, Fisk University Library.

17. R. R. Wright, Jr., *Social Service* (Philadelphia: A.M.E. Book Concern, 1922), pp. 21–22, 27–28; Editorial, *Christian Recorder*, Vol. 62 (March 19, 1914), p. 4.

18. R. R. Wright, Sr., "A Negro's Tribute to Lincoln," quoted in Elizabeth Ross Haynes, *The Black Boy of Atlanta* (Boston: The House of Edinboro Publishers, 1952), pp. 136–37.

19. R. R. Wright, Jr., "A Testimony to Evangelism," *Christian Recorder*, Vol. 62 (April 9, 1914), p. 4; R. R. Wright, Jr., "Booker T. Washington and Segregation," *Christian Recorder*, Vol. 62 (September 24, 1914), p. 8; R. R. Wright, Jr., "The Students' Conference at Atlanta," *Christian Recorder*, Vol. 62 (July 23, 1914), p. 4.

20. R. R. Wright, Jr., "Behind the Dark Clouds," *Christian Recorder*, Vol. 62 (January 21, 1915), p. 8; R. R. Wright, Jr., "Unlynchable Facts," *Christian Recorder*, Vol. 64 (November 16, 1916), p. 4.

21. R. R. Wright, Jr., "The Scriptural Basis of Social Service: What Jesus Christ Taught," *Christian Recorder*, Vol. 62 (August 27, 1914), p. 4; R. R. Wright, Jr., "Overcoming Racial and Religious Prejudices," Charles F. Weller (ed), *World Fellowship: Addresses and Messages by Leading Spokesmen of All Faiths, Races, and Countries* (New York: Liveright Publishing Corp., 1935), p. 322.

22. R. R. Wright, Jr., "Should Negroes Come North?" *Christian Recorder*, Vol. 64 (August 31, 1916), p. 4; R. R. Wright, Jr., "A Negro Party," *Christian Recorder*, Vol. 64 (September 28, 1916), p. 4.

23. Wright, *Social Service*, *op. cit.*, pp. 23–24; R. R. Wright, Jr., "The Christian's Peace," *Christian Recorder*, vol. 64 (December 21, 1916), p. 4.

24. R. R. Wright, Jr., "African Methodism and the Second Century," *Christian Recorder*, Vol. 64 (April 13, 1916), p. 4.

25. Reverdy C. Ransom, "The Spirit of John Brown," *The Spirit of Freedom and Justice: Orations and Speeches* (Nashville: A.M.E. Sunday School Union, 1926), pp. 16, 25; Reverdy C. Ransom, editorial, A.M.E. Church *Review*, Vol. 33 (July, 1916), p. 38.

26. Ransom, *The Pilgrimage of Harriet Ransom's Son*, *op. cit.*, pp. 16–23.

27. Reverdy C. Ransom, "John Greenleaf Whittier," *The Spirit of Freedom and Justice* (Nashville: A.M.E. Sunday School Union, 1926), p. 37; Reverdy C. Ransom, "The Reno Prize Fight," *The Spirit of Freedom and Justice* (Nashville: A.M.E. Sunday School Union, 1926), pp. 124–25; Reverdy C. Ransom, "Lynching and American Public Opinion," *The Spirit of Freedom and Justice* (Nashville: A.M.E. Sunday School Union, 1926), p. 139.

28. Ransom, "John Greenleaf Whittier," *op. cit.*, p. 35; Reverdy C. Ransom, "Future Influence of Negro Scholarship in America," *The Spirit of Freedom and Justice* (Nashville: A.M.E. Sunday School Union, 1926), p. 165; Reverdy C. Ransom, editorial, A.M.E. Church *Review*, Vol. 33 (January, 1917), p. 158.

29. Ransom, editorial, January, 1917, *ibid.*, p. 158; Reverdy C. Ransom, editorial, A.M.E. Church *Review*, Vol. 33 (January, 1916), p. 206; Reverdy C. Ransom, editorial, A.M.E. Church *Review*, Vol. 34 (April, 1918), p. 265.

30. Reverdy C. Ransom, *The Negro: The Hope or the Despair of Christianity* (Boston: Ruth Hill, 1935), pp. 3, 2 of Introduction.

Chapter 20

Religious Diversification during the Era of Advanced Industrial Capitalism

Hans A. Baer and Merrill Singer

A frican-American religion underwent a rapid process of diversification in the early decades of the twentieth century, particularly with the appearance of a wide array of new Holiness, Pentecostal, Spiritual, Islamic, and Judaic sects. To a large extent the baseline for this diversification was the "Black rural church." As an ideal type, the Black rural church is embodied especially in the Black Baptist congregations but also in many of the Black Methodist congregations that existed and continue to exist in the countryside, towns, and even small cities of the South. The rural church was the "sentimental model" that the migrants hoped to participate in when they attended the large mainstream congregations in the cities of the North and South, Since they often felt marginal in the stratified mainstream congregations, a significant number of these lower-class migrants attempted to re-create the ethos of the rural church in storefronts and converted residential buildings. In many cases, services at first were held in the apartment or home of a self-proclaimed religious leader before his or her congregation grew large enough to financially support larger meeting quarters.

The migrants often established independent Baptist congregations or exclusively lower-class Baptist congregations that sooner or later became affiliated with one of the national Baptist denominations. Often, however, the migrants were attracted to the "new gods of the metropolis"—the charismatic prophets and messiahs of various emerging sectarian movements (Fauset 1971). Charismatic, and sometimes flamboyant, individuals such as W. D. Fard, Elijah Muhammed, Father Divine, Daddy Grace, Elder Michauex, Bishop Cherry, and Prophet Jones are among the better known of these religious figures, but countless minor "gods" captured the religious imagination of the migrants. One of these lesser "gods" is Reverend Bobby E. Lawson, the "Royal Elect Ruler" of God's Elect Kingdom of Eternal Life (a storefront in Flint, Michigan, whose "First Annual Kingdom Jubilee" Baer attended during the summer of 1979).

The Black Rural Church

At the turn of the century, over 90 percent of African Americans resided below the Mason-Dixon line. While many southern cities underwent relatively rapid industrialization and population growth following the Civil War, Blacks did not migrate to them in as great numbers as whites did. As Rose (1948: 64) notes, "The tradition persisted that Negroes could not operate machines, or at least that was the argument used to keep them out of the new occupations. Negroes lost out in many of the skilled occupations they had formerly held." In 1910 about 80 percent of southern Blacks lived in rural areas (Marks 1985). Consequently, the vast majority of religiously active Blacks were attending relatively small churches in the countryside, towns, and small cities of the South at the time the Great Migration began. Furthermore, nearly all Black rural churches were and continue to be found in the South.

In attempting to capture the ethos of the Black rural church as an ideal, the major part of this section discusses the denominational forms, the politico-religious organization, the religious and secular activities, and the role of the Black rural church within the castelike system of the South. While we describe Black rural churches as they existed prior to the civil rights movement, we will speak in the ethnographic present. The remainder of this section presents a postscript on the status of the Black rural church since the civil rights movement.

It is important to note, however, that the Black rural church was not a static institution during the first half of the twentieth century. Unfortunately, no one to date has conducted a detailed study of the changes that the Black rural church underwent during this period. Nevertheless, some general patterns have been recorded. The out-migration of African Americans from the rural South to the cities of both the North and the South had a significant impact on the Black rural church during the first half of the twentieth century. As a consequence, most Black churches in the countryside have not had regular or full-time ministers. While out-migration contributed to an increase of this pattern during the twentieth century, it was not uncommon in earlier times. Some churches merged in order to deal with the shortage of ministers, but many continued to function despite heavy losses in membership. According to Raper (1936: 362), "A few Negro churches in Greene (Georgia) have been disbanded since 1922 because of the virtual depopulation of certain areas in the western half of the county, and many of the churches still intact are so weakened that they do not have Sunday services and now raise for their once-a-month preacher but a fraction of what they raised before the exodus."

Despite the general pattern of out-migration, not all churches underwent a decline of membership during the first half of the twentieth century. In his survey of 483 Black rural churches, Felton (1952: 46) found that, from 1939 to 1949, 190 (39.3 percent) increased in membership whereas 57 (11.8 percent) remained stationary and 236 (48.9 percent) underwent a decline in membership. The revival appears to have undergone some decline in significance during the twentieth century. Mays and Nicholson (1933: 253) reported that in the early 1930s most ministers in their survey asserted that "the revival no longer causes large numbers of 'conversions.' It is now used largely for reviving the church membership."

Denominational Variation

Many of the smaller communities in the rural South exhibit both socio-economic and religious homogeneity. The frequency of such a pattern contributes to the assertion among many southerners "that if a Negro is not a Baptist someone has been tampering with him" (Dollard 1937: 225). Many of the Black Baptist churches in small southern communities are not affiliated with any of the national Baptist denominations. For example, Shrimp Creek (pseudonym), a village of some four hundred Blacks located about fifteen miles south of Savannah, has five "independent small wooden Baptist churches" (Ottenberg 1959: 8).

Even in small Black communities where denominational variation exists, its significance may be minimized. In some instances, Baptist and Methodist congregations in small Black communities share the same building on alternate Sundays. The pattern of informal ecumenism between the Baptists and Methodists is further illustrated by the common practice of attending other churches on Sundays when one's own congregation is not conducting a service.

Denominational affiliation is more pronounced in towns and small cities, where it often reflects social status. As Johnson (1941: 155–56) observes, "Much of the rivalry between churches of the same or different denominations, and the uneconomical multiplication of churches and cults, traces back to this ferment of competition for social position and prestige within the Negro community." Nevertheless, even in these communities the significance of denominational variation is also deemphasized. In Cottonville (pseudonym), a Mississippi town with six Black churches (two Baptist, one Methodist Episcopal, one A.M.E., one belonging to "a sect called the Christians," and one Church of God in Christ), "The unimportance of sectarianism is frequently stressed, both from the pulpit and in conversation among the laity. On fifth Sundays of the month an inter-denominational Sunday is held, in which all participate except the Church of God in Christ" (Powdermaker 1967: 233).

While a fair amount of cooperation and visiting occurs between Missionary Baptist and Methodist congregations, especially in the smaller communities, most Holiness, Pentecostal, and Primitive Baptist congregations hold themselves—and are held by others—at a distance from the conventional churches. In Cottonville, members of the Church of God in Christ, whose ecstatic rituals are considered excessive by the Baptists and Methodists, view themselves as being more spiritually minded than their detractors. On St. Simons Island off the Georgia coast during the late 1920s, "the initial handful of converts to 'holiness' did not originally intend either to renounce their memberships in the Baptist churches or to form a congregation or church of their own. But the Baptists objected to the shouting and dancing of the 'saints' in the midst of their otherwise decorous worship service, and the converts were forced out" (Goldsmith 1985: 93). In certain rural parts of the Upper South, Black Primitive or "Hard Shell" Baptists, who stress the predestination, foot washing, and extreme congregational autonomy, refrain from interaction not only with other religious groups but with secular organizations such as Masonic lodges (Sutton 1983).

Politico-Religious Organization

The common responses to the shortage of ministers in the countryside have been intermittent scheduling of Sunday services and greater lay control over church affairs. As Mays and Nicholson (1933: 252) found in their survey of Sunday services in rural churches, most do not conduct services every Sunday. Of the 185 congregations in their sample, 10.8 percent of them held one service per month, 61.1 percent two services, 7.5 percent three services, 16.8 percent four services, and 3.8 percent eight services. Rural church membership varies widely depending in large part on local economic opportunities. For example, Richardson (1947: 49–51) found that, whereas 89.7 percent of the Blacks (many of whom were small farm owners) in Northumberland County, Virginia, belonged to churches, only 10.0 percent of the Blacks in Mississippi County, Arkansas (a predominantly tenant area), did so.

In Shrimp Creek, each church conducts a regular communion service with its visiting minister once a month (Ottenberg 1959: 12). The five Baptist congregations are served by four ministers (all of whom pastor Savannah churches), with two of them being served by the same minister. Some of the ministers also serve other rural churches near Savannah. In addition to the pattern of city ministers intermittently visiting outlying congregations, many rural churches are served by circuit preachers who may live in the countryside themselves. For example, Rev. Louis Cole (1901–81), a Black Baptist preacher, for many years conducted services in the North Mississippi–West Tennessee area, visiting Gatewood Church every first Sunday, Mount Vernon every second Sunday, Mount Gilliam every third Sunday, and Lagoshen every fourth Sunday. "In addition, he visited many other churches as a guest, substitute or assistant—at revivals, weddings, funerals, baptizings, fund-raising programs and special annual services such as Mother's Day, Founder's Day, Men's Day, Children's Day, Appreciation Day, Homecoming Day" (Walker 1985: 51).

Due to the pattern of absentee ministry, lay leaders assume most of the responsibility for maintaining and operating the churches in the countryside. In Shrimp Creek, the deacons maintain control over the Baptist churches and, although ministers are selected by the congregation following guest sermons, exert considerable input in this decision (Ottenberg 1959). They also administer church finances, supervise collections, organize prayer services and various social activities, hold joint meetings with other churches, and act as "spiritual fathers" to those seeking a conversion experience or "vision" to join the church.

> Positions of church leadership are correlated with financial means, age, and sex. In Kent (pseudonym), a small Piedmont milltown, "status in the church is often equated with faithfulness of contribution—and to some extent with amount" (Lewis 1955: 114). Similarly, most of the deacons in Shrimp Creek are descendants of the older well-established families and, while far from being affluent, "fall roughly into the middle or upper range of the economic level of the community" (Ottenberg 1959: 11).

Active church members in Missionary Baptist and Methodist churches generally belong to one or more of several age-graded and/or sexually exclusive auxiliaries such as Sunday schools, usher boards, choirs, and choral clubs. In addition to these organizations, Missionary Baptist churches have all-male deacon boards and all-female missionary societies, and the Methodists have boards of trustees, stewards, stewardesses, and deaconesses as well as missionary societies. The usher board, which often has junior and senior branches, is "one of the most prevalent, most active and most popular of rural church organizations" (Richardson 1947: 104).

Although nearly all ministers in rural areas are male, women greatly outstrip men in membership, attendance, and active participation. In his observations of three Black churches—the Field's Street Methodist Episcopal, the Mount Prospect African Methodist Episcopal Zion, and the Union Baptist—as well as in nearby churches of the hinterland of Kent, Lewis found that,

> Despite the fact that nominal control and direction are in the hands of the men, women apparently contribute a larger share of the financial and moral support. Church politics is primarily a man's game, but the women wield great indirect power. In a recent, prolonged dispute in one of the churches, the women staged a coup and temporarily assumed authority as a means of forcing a truce between factions in the church (Lewis 1955: 106).

Women's auxiliaries also sponsor most of the church entertainments and "socials."

Religious and Social Events

In the typical rural Black church, "the monthly [or bi-monthly] preaching service is the all important activity" (Raper 1936: 364). Since rural people have more difficulty seeing friends and acquaintances during the week than do town or city dwellers, the preaching service permits members and visitors to reestablish social bonds and to share information and gossip. The clothing of the congregants manifests the social nature of this event. Women wear their finest dresses, hats, hose, and jewelry. Men generally wear suits, even on hot humid summer days, although some of the younger men and adolescent males may wear only dress shirts and ties.

The Sunday preaching service, regardless of whether it occurs in a Baptist or Methodist church, almost invariably includes certain ritual events such as prayer, hymn-singing, testifying, "penny" and regular collections, the sermon, and the benediction, but the exact sequence in which these occur varies considerably from congregation to congregation (See John-son [1934: 153–61], Powdermaker [1967: 249] and Ferris [1972] for accounts of services in rural Black Baptist congregations). In each instance, however, the sermon, which occurs in the latter half of the ser-vice, functions as the focal ritual event of the service. Whereas ritual events prior to it collectively serve as a prelude to the climactic sermon, which may last over an hour, events afterwards are anticlimactic. Follow-ing Gennep (1960), it can be argued that pre-sermon events separate wor-shippers from the profane world whereas post-sermon ritual events reincorporate them back into this world. Separation is best exemplified in the testimony session, during which various members, especially women, review recent hardships in their lives and express their joy in being able to discard them, at least temporarily, since they are in the process of enter-ing a sacred liminal period. More so than any other portion of the service, the sermon or "message" constitutes a liminal period during which the preacher may act out the journey to heaven or various members of the congregation become ecstatic or "shout."

> The sermons of the average rural minister are long and repetitious. Phrases are emphasized by gestures and vehement expression. The congregation responds constantly with shouts of approval and con-viction. It is expected that several persons, mostly women, will "get happy" and give expression to long hysterical seizures in the course of which they testify to their salvation, release some pent-up sorrow over deceased relatives, or bemoan a hard and hopeless life or the unjusti-fied slander of their character in the community. The most emotional parts of the sermons are those which make reference to troubles and offer homely solace or inspired promise of reward or punishment by God, as the situation warrants. (Johnson 1941: 143–44)

The sermon and associated events often last well over an hour. Reincor-poration is symbolized by generally having the regular collection, which may take up to a half hour or even more, after the sermon.

Next to the preaching service, the Sunday school is theoretically the most important regularly scheduled religious event in the Black rural church. Even on those Sundays when a minister preaches at the church, he does not generally supervise the Sunday school, and rarely attends. "If he arrives at the church before the Sunday school is over, it is not an uncommon sight to see him standing on the outside of the building visit-ing with men, waiting for the Sunday school to adjourn" (Felton 1952:

48). The Sunday school usually meets every week and consequently is run almost exclusively by laypeople. Attendance at the Sunday school is invariably less than at the preaching service and in many instances other religious and social events. In a survey of 105 rural Sunday schools in four southern counties, Richardson (1947: 108) found that "Six schools had but five members or less; twenty-six had between eleven and twenty members, and fifty-three . . . ranged between twenty and fifty members." The larger Sunday schools are age-graded into two or more classes. The principal teaching method includes reading, explaining, and commenting upon Biblical passages.

On those Sundays when the minister is absent, or during the week, church auxiliaries or even nonchurch groups, such as lodges, schools, and burial societies, conduct prayer meetings and special programs. According to Richardson (1947: 104), usher boards play an instrumental role in organizing "sings," to which groups from other churches are invited, as well as other recreational affairs. Women's auxiliaries periodically sponsor church entertainments such as chicken hunts, suppers, candy pulls, and fashion shows, which are attended not only by church members but also the larger community (Powdermaker 1967: 278–85). A major purpose of such events is the raising of funds for the church and for needy members.

Since many Black people were introduced to Christianity at the revivals of the Great Awakenings during antebellum times, it should not be surprising that traditionally the revival constitutes the high point of the annual ritual cycle. Churches generally conduct revivals in the late summer or early fall after the harvest. Revivals, which may last as long as two weeks, often function as a homecoming day when former inhabitants of the community who have moved to other rural areas or even faraway cities return to their place of origin. As Hamilton and Ellison (1930: 25) report, "The typical revivalist is a man of extravagant gifts and unrestrained emotions [who] speaks fluently and loudly" and is an adept singer of songs "arranged to tunes which have a rhythmic swing." As a consequence, ecstatic behavior in the form of "shouting" and dancing is much more common during revivals than during regular religious services. While the Holiness and Pentecostal revivals tend to be the most exuberant, even members of some of the more sedate Baptist and Methodist congregations "get happy" on these occasions (see Dollard [1937: 253–56] and Powdermaker [1967: 253–56] for detailed accounts of revivals).

Traditionally, many young people joined the church under the emotional excitement of the revival. In the Baptist churches, baptisms by immersion at the bank of a river may occur as an aftermath of the revival.

The converts wear white, shirtlike garments and white headpieces. While most of the baptized emerge out of the water calmly and matter-of-factly, some do so shouting for joy (see Dollard [1937: 236–39] for a detailed account of a baptism).

Funerals are extremely significant religious occasions that often prompt more ecstatic behavior than preaching services or even revivals (see Johnson [1934: 162–79] and Powdermaker [1967: 249–52] for detailed accounts of funerals). For many church members, a proper burial constitutes the most valued goal in their lives.

> The basic pattern combines these essential steps: return of corpse to the home the evening before the funeral; on the day of the funeral body and funeral party are driven to the church. . . . The corpse is borne into the church while the church bell tolls and the choir sings or the minister utters an incantation; a song is sung by the choir and audience; a scripture reading and/or prayer is delivered by assisting minister or prominent church member; obituary, acknowledgement of flowers, messages, and testimonies by friends and neighbors are delivered; a eulogy is rendered by the pastor; final view of the remains is taken by the audience; internment follows, with male volunteers filling the grave after final rites. (Lewis 1955: 109)

The Role of the Black Rural Church in the Southern Caste System

The role of the Black church as it functioned in the countryside and small town of the South prior to the civil rights era must be considered in the larger context of the castelike system within which it was embedded. As Hraba (1979: 268) observes, "The racial caste system that followed Emancipation meant the exclusion of cheap black labor from nearly all trades save agrarian labor and domestic service, the segregation and exclusion of blacks from decent education, and the almost complete exclusion of blacks from the political process in the South." The defeat of the Populist movement, with its fragile white-Black tenant alliance, in the 1890s heightened color-caste distinctions through an extension of Jim Crow laws and practices throughout the South. While many whites were economically little better off than the Black masses, the few social privileges accorded under the caste system served to provide them with a sense of superiority over Blacks. Conversely, many whites left the land for skilled and semiskilled jobs in the textile mills and even some unionized trades.

The 1910 census reveals that over half of the gainfully employed blacks were in agriculture. More than half of the remainder (one-fourth of the total) were in domestic occupations. Thus on the eve of World War I, the vast majority of black Americans were located in the South and engaged in the production of agricultural staples. The position of blacks not engaged in agriculture had deteriorated greatly. Five out of every six southern artisans in 1865 were black, but only one in 20 was black in 1900. (Geschwender 1978: 169–70)

Blacks also held menial jobs in the lumber industry, coal mining, railroad maintenance, and tobacco factories—most of which were rurally based operations. In the cities and towns, the vast majority of Black workers were concentrated in either domestic and personal service or in unskilled positions as porters, draymen, laundresses, and seamstresses (Baron 1971: 16). Similarly, Blacks were restricted to the most menial positions in the growing southern textile industry.

In contrast to the existence of a small Black middle class or petite bourgeoisie in the cities and, to a lesser degree, the smaller towns, socioeconomic differences among African Americans in the countryside were minimal. Despite marked racial inequalities in land tenure, the number of Black-owned farms doubled between 1890 and 1910 due to financial loans that Black farmers were able to obtain from Black-owned banks (Marable 1981: 52–68). Unfortunately, the decline of cotton prices as a result of the closing of transatlantic commerce upon the outbreak of World War I, the coming of the boll weevil, soil erosion, and a general worsening of race relations in the South translated into the beginning of the demise of the African-American land-owning class.

Changes in farm ownership were accompanied by changing patterns of tenancy. The number of Black tenants increased from 670,000 in 1910 to almost 700,000 in 1930 and then declined to approximately 500,000 in 1940. White tenants numbered less than 870,000 in 1910, increased to approximately 1,090,000 in 1930 and declined to 940,000 in 1940. The rate of increase in tenancy between 1910 and 1930 was less rapid for blacks than whites, just as the rate of decline between 1930 and 1940 was more rapid. Blacks made up over half the agricultural wage labor force in 1910, but accounted for less than half in both 1930 and 1940. They were driven out of cotton agriculture more rapidly than whites, regardless of status. (Geschwender 1978: 177)

Given a declining agricultural economy, Blacks became an easy target for white hostility. Coupled with the availability of jobs in northern industries created by World War I and the economic prosperity of the 1920s, these conditions propelled massive numbers of Blacks to leave the rural areas of the South. As a result of this migration, as well as later ones, the Black rural church underwent a tremendous decline in membership and resources.

As is the case for all religious groups in complex societies, the role of the Black rural church has been and continues to be multifaceted and paradoxical. The Black rural church constitutes the principal center of sociability and a major repository of the Black cultural ethos. As Johnson (1934: 150) comments, "it offers the medium for a community feeling, singing together, praying together, and indulging in the formal expressions of fellowship." Black rural churches provide not only a locus for the renewal of social bonds but also a mechanism for assisting members in times of financial need, emergency, and personal sorrow. In the past, they played a major role in community-based education, and they still make regular contributions to Baptist and Methodist higher education funds. Programs are periodically conducted to raise funds for college students belonging to the local congregation. Religious services, social events, and fund-raising are openly recognized as forms of entertainment and opportunities for relaxation. In contrast to the grim puritanical tone of many white evangelical churches, Black churchgoers unabashedly see no contradiction between their search for spirituality and having "fun" or a "good time." Although always conditioned by a strong sense of remaining within the bounds of respectability, Black church behavior contrasts with its white counterpart in its reigning cultural definition of religious propriety.

In assessing the role of the Black rural church within the context of the southern caste system, particularly prior to the civil rights movement, many scholars have argued that on balance it functioned as a cathartic mechanism and a "refuge in a hostile white world" (Frazier 1974: 50) that inadvertently maintained the status quo. Charles Johnson (1941: 169) contended that the Black rural church is a "conservative institution" whose "greatest value appears to be that of providing emotional relief for the fixed problems of a hard life." In a similar vein, Powdermaker (1967: 285) asserted that it "serves as an antidote, a palliative, and escape" which tends to "counteract the discontents that make for rebellion." Obviously the Black rural church served to alleviate many of the frustrations, anxieties, and fears emanating from economic exploitation and sociopolitical repression that Blacks experienced under the castelike structure of the South.

Following Gramsci, it may also be argued that the Black rural church constituted a hegemonic agency permitting the southern planter and merchant classes to dominate Black people. This is not to say that white elites directly controlled activities that occurred in Black churches in small towns and the countryside. In these settings, African Americans have exerted a considerable degree of autonomy over their religious affairs. It is often asserted that the "Black church" is one institution over which African Americans are in full control (Powdermaker 1967: 223; Hamilton 1972). In reality, however, Black control over churches in the rural South was restricted by the patronage system. As Myrdal (1962: 874) points out, "Poverty often makes the Negro church dependent upon white benefactors."

It was quite common for Black ministers and congregations to obtain building materials and financial resources from white patrons in constructing or maintaining their churches in small towns and the countryside. In his study of Old City, Plantation Town, and their neighboring Mississippi counties, Davis (1940: 37–38) found that Black ministers often initiated a "gift" relationship with influential whites and attempted to persuade them to assume a patriarchal stance toward the Black community. A wealthy white woman stated that a leading Black minister in Plantation Town had convinced the members of her social circle to make regular donations toward his salary. Officers of the women's auxiliaries in the four largest Black churches in Plantation Town solicited funds for their ministers' salaries and church building funds from upper- and middle-class white women and white storekeepers. Davis, Gardner, and Gardner report the case of the treasurer of a Black church and lodge near Old City who served as "patriarch-tenant-manager" over a local group of tenant farmers:

> He has persuaded his landlord to make "advances" to tenants in cash rather than in supplies, so that tenants might be able to meet their financial obligations to the church and lodge. The "advancing" of from $12 to $15 every two weeks to a tenant-family provided a steady cash income for these organizations. (Davis, Gardner, and Gardner 1965: 246)

The obvious price that Blacks paid for the patronage system was accommodation to the caste system. However, it is important to note that most Black rural churches probably received little or no support from white patrons. What kept these churches in check? According to Davis (1940: 56), any Black preacher in Plantation Town, Old City, and their hinterlands who attacked the caste system was "in acute danger of being driven out of the area, or whipped." Consequently, Black ministers took great caution not to say anything that could be construed by whites as a condemnation of existing race relations. For the most part, however, Black religious leaders and churchgoers probably rarely even conceived of the thought of challenging the status quo. As Femia (1981: 33) observes, "the exigencies of survival and day-to-day practicalities restrict mental (or ideological) development, and subordinate even the unwilling and rebellious to the logic and norms of the system."

In some instances, whites directly manipulated Black ministers and congregations in order to ensure Black subordination. For example, Davis (1940: 34) found that white planters and businessmen in Old City, Plantation Town, and their neighboring counties, with the collaboration of the Negro Business League, "attempted to use the Negro churches during the Great Migration to check the migration of Negroes." On the whole, such instances of direct pressure by whites upon Black ministers to maintain the caste system were the exception rather than the rule. In his examination of a large number of sermons delivered by Black preachers in the Old City area, Davis (1940: 46–48) recorded no instances of a Black preacher attacking the caste system or suggesting any need for economic change. When Blacks in Old City expressed outrage at the hanging of two Blacks accused of murder, a Black minister told his congregation that such sentiments were futile because "We ain't no more than a coon with a collar 'round his neck" (quoted in Davis 1940: 46). The minister of a large Black church in the Plantation Town vicinity compared the relationship between his members and God to that between the Black tenant and his white landlord.

The hegemonic role of Black religion in inculcating the symbols of the color-caste system of the Old South is poignantly illustrated by the annual religious pageant entitled "Heaven Is My Home," conducted by one of the leading Black churches in Old City during the 1930s (Davis 1940: 67–69). Sponsored by the Old City Garden Club, the pageant was performed before separate Black and white audiences. In 1934, about half of the annual income of the church came from the white-sponsored pageant.

The pageant represents the dogma of the spiritual and other-worldly Negro, and emphasizes both the humility and the native genius for song of the Negro actors. When the white sponsors had the Negro actors photographed by a newsreel company, they placed them in front of an ante-bellum plantation house, with a group of Negroes dressed in plantation clothes standing around them.

The Negroes themselves symbolized the "whiteness" of God and Heaven by placing white or yellow-skinned Negroes in the roles of St. Peter, and the attendant angels. The patriarchal relationship of white to Negroes, and the latter group's humility and social subservience were expressed in the climax of the pageant when an old Negro woman played the role of a "mammy." This role proved the favorite of the white audiences, and was regarded by Negro church leaders as the chief reasons for the financial success of the entertainment. The white newspaper in Old City stated that the Negro "mammy" was the chief attraction of the pageant, and emphasized the fact that she was a former slave. Sentiment for the old plantation relationship of Negroes to whites, and for the continuance of the subservient position of Negroes was organized around this figure. (Davis 1940: 68–69)

The near-totality of the Black rural church as a hegemonic institution under the castelike system is exemplified by a sermon entitled "The Poor-Rich and the Rich-Poor" recorded by Hortense Powdermaker. In this sermon, a leading Black minister in the Cottonville area told a parable about a rich woman who was given her cook's shanty when she went to heaven whereas her cook received a big house for her service to God on earth. Some might interpret the sermon as a subtle critique of the caste system; Powdermaker (1967: 443) argues that it "supports the *status quo* by telling the poor—i.e., the Negroes—that their reward will be in heaven, and that they are rich in their poverty if they worship God." Yet, no stratified society, even one as rigid as the castelike system of the Old South, has exercised pure dominance. Dominated groups somehow manage to offer resistance to ruling classes or to hegemonic agencies and customs that indirectly foster the ideas of the ruling classes. As opposed to the strong emphasis on eternal damnation characterizing many white fundamentalist or evangelical religious groups, African-American Christianity has always stressed the joys of the afterlife. As Powdermaker (1967: 246) notes, "Benevolent mercy rather than stern justice is the chief attribute of the Negro's God. . . . The accent has shifted from hell to heaven, from retribution to forgiveness, from fear to hope."

The Black Rural Church since the Civil Rights Movement

In his assertion that the "black church functioned as the institutional center of the modern civil rights movement," Morris (1984: 4) is by and large referring to the complex of Black urban churches in the South rather than to its rural counterpart. Most of the prominent Black ministers involved in the civil rights movement, such as Martin Luther King, Jr., and Ralph D. Abernathy of Montgomery, Fred Shuttlesworth of Birmingham, Kelly Miller Smith of Nashville, and Wyatt Tee Walker of Petersburg, Virginia, were leaders of urban congregations (Marable 1984: 71). The migration of Blacks to the large and medium-sized cities of the South made it possible for the Black urban churches to operate on a scale unattainable in the small cities, towns, and countryside. In contrast, as MacAdam (1982: 92) observes, "the rural church was, in most cases, organizationally weak and conservative in orientation. Both factors served to limit the effectiveness of the rural black church as an institutional vehicle of social change." Nonetheless, an unknown number of Black rural churches did play a supportive role in the civil rights movement, and some were among the many southern Black churches burned or bombed during the 1960s.

Since the early 1950s, little research has been done on Black rural churches. The civil rights movement of the late 1950s and early 1960s transformed many aspects of everyday life in the rural South and eliminated terror as a primary mode of social control. While rural Blacks have gained—at least in theory—certain civil rights, such as the legal right to vote, attend integrated public schools, and use public facilities, most of them continue to be subjected to economic exploitation, poverty, racial discrimination, and perhaps more so than before, structural unemployment. In many ways, Black rural churches have remained as they were around the turn of the century. In the case of Promised Land, South Carolina,

> Crossroads, Mt. Zion, and Jacob's Chapel were "the center of all the community" in the 1970s in much the same way as they had been for a century. Membership rates for all churches were high. Seventy-eight percent of the families at Promised Land attended church at least several times a month. . . .
>
> There was little realistic difference between being a Baptist or a Methodist at Promised Land. . . . Half the families divided their church loyalties between the two denominations, the result of marriages between Baptist and Methodist youths who, like their parents before them, refused to relinquish ties with a church that was second in importance only to their kinship bonds. Children from these households usually attended both churches alternative weeks. Methodist wives often helped serve dinner at Baptist homecomings and Baptist husbands were equally visible at Methodist events. (Bethel 1981: 263)

In a similar vein, Dougherty (1978: 34) reports that in Edge Crossing (pseudonym), a rural Black community in north central Florida, the three local Baptist churches are the places where Black people of all ages "come after relating with one another through the week in schools, homes, stores, shops, and work." Mt. Calvary Baptist Church holds services on the second and fourth Sundays of the month, St. Peter's on the third Sunday, and Oak Ridge on the first Sunday. On months with a fifth Sunday, the churches rotate responsibility for holding services.

The most extensive survey of Black churches since the 1950s was completed recently by a team directed by C. Eric Lincoln and Lawrence H. Mamiya. The rural phase of the project consisted of interviews with 363 clergy who are the pastors of 619 churches in certain "Black Belt" counties of the South. Ongoing migration of Blacks to urban areas has left the arrangement of the absentee pastorate intact. The development of interstate highways and improved roads since World War II "led to increased mobility by absentee pastors" (Lincoln and Mamiya 1990: 96). In contrast to Mays and Nicholson's (1933: 254) prediction that the "day of the professional evangelist" was drawing to a close, Lincoln and Mamiya learned that the revival continues to function as a major form of religious renewal. Of the 619 churches in their sample, 542 (87.9 percent) have at least one annual revival (Lincoln and Mamiya 1990: 107). Although many Baptist churches and the Church of God in Christ (Pentecostal) have a ban on women pastors, they permit women to be "evangelists," in which capacity they may preach at revivals or special religious meetings. As opposed to Felton's (1952) finding that only 12.8 percent of the churches in his sample were involved with the National Association for the Advancement of Colored People (NAACP), Lincoln and Mamiya (1990: 109) report that 50.1 percent of the rural churches in their sample are involved with civil rights organizations and activities. It is important to note, however, that the NAACP as well as various other moderate Black civil rights organizations are no longer regarded by white elites as a serious threat. At any rate, as Lincoln and Mamiya (1990: 113–14) so aptly assert, "Black rural churches became the first institutions to carry the hopes and dreams of an outcast people. If they were not always heroic institutions, they at least contributed to the survival of their people in the most extreme and violent circumstances."

Industrialization, Migration, and Urbanization: The Proletarianization of the Black Peasantry

At the beginning of the twentieth century, nine out of ten Blacks in the United States were living in the South, the vast majority in the rural areas.

For the most part, African Americans constituted a castelike stratum held in "debt peonage" (Silberman 1964: 46) by the quasi-feudal character of the rural economy. The Black codes and other restrictive Jim Crow laws were used to control Blacks and thereby provide a manageable and inexpensive labor force. Despite these oppressive conditions, African Americans inhabited a relatively stable society; and it was not until World War I, with Black migration primarily to the urban North but also to the cities of the South, that Blacks underwent a rapid process of proletarianization.

Several events provided the impetus for the northward relocation of what ultimately amounted to a half million Blacks during or shortly after World War I. As Cox (1976: 58) observes, "on the whole, the 'push' of the Negro population from the rural South has been greater than the inducements or 'pull' of the cities." Prior to World War I, the industrial North had relied primarily on European immigrants for a cheap labor supply. An annual average of more than 900,000 immigrants entered the United States from Europe during the period 1910–14, but the onset of the war reduced the annual flow to about 100,000 (Geschwender 1978: 172). At the same time, World War I stimulated the economy and increased the demand for labor, a demand in large part fulfilled by the migration of southern Blacks. In the South, the spread from Mexico of the boll weevil, as well as soil erosion and depletion, seriously cut into agricultural productivity. Other push factors included the severity of labor exploitation, the relocation of many agricultural endeavors in the West, and continued lynching and physical intimidation by terrorist organizations like the Ku Klux Klan. Despite the protests of southern businessmen and planters, anxious over the loss of their supply of cheap labor, African Americans began to look to the North as a land of opportunity.

> Migration out of the countryside started in 1915 and swept to a human tide by 1917. The major movement was to Northern cities, so that between 1910 and 1920 the black population increased in Chicago from 44,000 to 109,000; in New York from 92,000 to 152,000; in Detroit from 6,000 to 41,000; and in Philadelphia from 84,000 to 134,000. That decade there was a net increase of 322,000 in the number of Southern born blacks living in the North, exceeding the aggregate increase of the preceding 40 years. A secondary movement took place to Southern cities, especially those with shipbuilding and heavy industry. . . . (Baron 1976: 105)

After the war, African-American migration to the cities continued. The war's end opened the floodgates once more to European emigration, and the 1920s saw the swelling of antiforeigner hysteria, culminating in the passage of prohibitive immigration quota laws. Northern capitalists supported this legislation because a seemingly more compliant proletariat had been discovered in the rural South. While the North may have been presented by labor recruiters as the Promised Land, what most Blacks found in Detroit, Chicago, Gary, Pittsburgh, Newark, New York, and other cities was considerably less inspiring. In the South they had occupied the lowest rungs of a rigid caste system; in the North—although theoretically possessing more legal rights—Blacks (as well as to a lesser degree southern whites) came to occupy the lower echelon in a split labor market (Bonacich 1976). In this capacity, they were frequently used as "scabs" to break strikes and thwart labor-organizing drives. There were instances of cooperation between white workers and Black workers during the early decades of the century, but competition for scarce jobs more often than not translated into hostile relations and provoked racist sentiments among white workers. At times this conflict was translated into race riots in which angry whites invaded Black neighborhoods. It is important to note that "the riots did not grow out of the inherent racial prejudice of their participants, but rather developed directly from the friction caused by the ways in which black labor was put to use in the North" (Smith 1981: 343).

Analyses of racism (Reich 1971) show that it serves a number of vital functions for an expanding capitalist economy: it rationalizes lower-class living and working conditions; it divides the working class into competing sectors, thereby depressing wages and other benefits; and, because elements of the racist ideology are internalized by members of the pariah group, it keeps the most exploited segment of the working class dispirited and less openly rebellious. Faced with the choice between a minimal existence and starvation, African Americans were unwittingly used as strikebreakers at wages well below those won by white workers in their struggles with the capitalist class. Eventually an accommodation between Black and white workers became institutionalized: whites came to occupy the professions and the skilled technical and craft positions while Blacks were relegated by and large to semiskilled or unskilled occupations (or perpetual unemployment or underemployment) at the bottom of the labor hierarchy. In more recent decades some Blacks have been able to make occupational advances, but the dual labor market essentially remains intact.

The generalization of racism beyond the economic realm—into housing, education, and other areas—ensures its credibility and effectiveness in the marketplace. Black migrants to the cities were consequently herded into decaying ghettos and provided with substandard schools and social services. In the case of Chicago, perhaps the most segregated of northern cities, Blacks were systematically excluded from white sections of the city, drastically limited in their choice of jobs, and barred from many places of public accommodation. This discriminatory pattern developed in similar fashion throughout the urban North.

Although the flight of rural Blacks into the cities of the North and the South never ceased, the Great Depression of the 1930s slowed the pace considerably. During this desperate period in American history, urban Blacks were subjected to severe deprivation, with unemployment reaching devastating proportions and evictions commonplace in Black ghettos. In some sections of Chicago's South Side, Black unemployment stood at over 85 percent by 1931 (Gosnell 1937). In response to rising social unrest among various segments of the society, the federal government instituted various relief programs, with the Federal Emergency Relief Aid having the most impact on poor Blacks. Whereas approximately 22,000 Black families had been receiving welfare in 1931, a year later this figure jumped to 48,000 (Bontemps and Conroy 1966: 296). In 1933, 26.7 percent of urban Blacks were on relief, compared with 9.6 percent of white city dwellers (Walters 1970: 91).

World War II ushered in a massive new influx of Blacks to the cities. While the demand for labor in defense industries initiated this development, the technological innovations in agriculture spurred the heavy migrant flow after the war. During this period, capital-intensive production supplanted the traditional labor-intensive character of southern agriculture. Mechanical corn and cotton pickers, self-propelled combines, bulldozers, one-man hay balers, and other mechanical devices were introduced on a large scale. Furthermore, the increasing shift to cash crops such as soybeans, which require minimal hand labor, also served to eliminate the need for Black agricultural workers. In addition, many Black landowners were unable to compete with the better financed and more highly mechanized white-owned farms. During the 1940s just over 1.5 million Blacks moved northward. During the 1950s and 1960s still another 2.9 million Blacks migrated to the North (Sackey 1973: 42). By 1970 only 52 percent of African Americans were located in the South, and the majority of Blacks in the North and the South were situated in urban areas (Baron 1976). Through this process, African Americans were transformed from an agrarian peasantry into a diversified urban proletariat.

In the process, their religious forms changed as well. As the primary institution available for responding to external threat and challenge, as well as internal aspiration and expression, the African-American church was remade anew in the shadow of the Great Migration.

The Mainstream Churches and the Rise
of the Storefronts and "Gods of the Metropolis"

By the turn of the century, what had become the "mainline" or "mainstream" churches in the African-American community were well in place in the large and medium-sized cities of both the South and the North. In contrast to the relatively narrow range of denominational variation among Black rural churches, Black urban churches even at this time exhibited a fair degree of heterogeneity. As we will see in greater detail later, this heterogeneity became more pronounced during the period between the two world wars. Table 1 illustrates denominational variation among Black churches in Philadelphia, Atlanta, and Chicago around the turn of the century.

As in the larger society, denominational affiliation reflected class differences in the Black community. As Du Bois remarked at the beginning of the century,

Table 20.1   Denominational Variation among Black Churches in Selected Cities around the Turn of the Century

	Philadelphia[a]	Atlanta[b]	Chicago[c]
Episcopal	6	1	1
Presbyterian	3	1	2
Congregational	—	1	—
Christian	—	1	1
Roman Catholic	1	—	—
Adventist	—	—	1
Methodist Episcopal	6	4	2
Methodist Protestant	1	—	—
African Methodist Episcopal	14	14	9
African Methodist Episcopal Zion	3	—	1
Colored Methodist Episcopal	—	3	—
Union African Methodist Episcopal	1	—	—
Baptist	17	29	11
Total	52	54	28

SOURCE: Derived from Du Bois 1903.
[a]Census taken in 1897.
[b]Census taken in 1901–2.
[c]Census date unspecified.

At St. Thomas' (Episcopal) one looks for the well-to-do Philadelphians, largely descendants of favorite mulatto house servants, and
consequently well-bred and educated, but rather cold and reserved
to strangers or newcomers; at Central Presbyterian one sees the
older, simpler set of respectable Philadelphians with distinctly
Quaker characteristics—pleasant but conservative; at Bethel may be
seen the best of the great laboring class—steady, honest people, well
dressed and well fed, with church and family traditions; at Wesley will
be found the new arrivals, the sightseers and the strangers to the
city—hearty and easy-going people, who welcome all comers and ask
few questions; at Union Bethel one may look for the Virginia servant
girls and their young men; and so on throughout the city. Each
church forms its own social circle, and not many stray beyond its
bounds. (Du Bois 1903: 203–4)

Black congregations affiliated with white-controlled denominations
catered to elite African Americans. In turn-of-the-century Atlanta, most
members of the Black Congregational, Episcopal, and Presbyterian congregations "are at least high school graduates, and a large per cent is composed of business and professional men and women" (Du Bois 1903: 73). In
contrast, the Methodist and Baptist churches exhibited considerable class
variation, both from congregation to congregation and within congregations. In the case of Atlanta Methodists, "A great majority of the members
of the smaller churches are common laborers and are quite poor. The members of the larger churches are in moderate circumstances, and although
most of them are laborers, there is a fair per cent of artisans and business
men among them" (Du Bois 1903: 72). Although in general Baptists tended
to be of a somewhat lower socioeconomic status than Methodists, the Baptist churches "were included among the most influential and wealthy
churches of the city" (Du Bois 1903: 73). On the whole, most Black Baptist
churches catered primarily to working- and lower-class people.

The period between 1900 and World War I saw an increase in the size
of the existing Black churches as well as the establishment of new congregations affiliated with the mainstream denominations as a result of the
gradual but steady migration of rural Blacks to the cities. As Gottlieb
(1987: 201) observes, as elsewhere, "Black preachers [in Pittsburgh] were
important gatekeepers for southern blacks in helping them find jobs, providing food and shelter in church buildings during emergencies, and organizing social or recreational programs." Furthermore, schisms within the

older congregations, often initiated by working-class members who revolted against control by middle-class members, also often led to the creation of new congregations. In Chicago, "Most of the Baptist churches were offshoots of Olivet, the oldest and largest Negro Baptist church in the city, while the A.M.E. churches were generally founded by dissident parishioners from Quinn Chapel and Bethel Church" (Spear 1967: 91).

Even prior to World War I, some of the larger Black congregations attempted to cater to the material needs of southern migrants. The most notable example was the Institutional Church and Social Settlement of Chicago, established in 1900 by Reverdy Ransom, who was destined to become one of the leading bishops of the African Methodist Episcopal church:

> Institutional operated a day nursery, a kindergarten, a mothers' club, an employment bureau, a print shop, and a fully equipped gymnasium; it offered a complete slate of club activities and classes in sewing, cooking, and music; its Forum featured lectures by leading white and Negro figures; and its facilities were always available for concerts, meetings, and other civic functions. . . . The wide range of social activities was designed to attract lower-class Negroes without church affiliation and sophisticated Negroes who found Institutional's emphasis on the social gospel more appealing than the traditional preoccupation with sin and salvation. (Spear 1967: 95–96)

In part due to the rise of secular social welfare agencies and lack of adequate finances, this innovative congregation declined before the end of the World War I era. The social services offered by some of the other large Black churches were considerably more modest. Olivet Baptist Church in Chicago started a relief program for the unemployed in 1908 (Spear 1967: 92). Bethel A.M.E. was the first organization in Detroit to conduct an outreach program among Black people by creating a social service department in 1911, and adding labor and housing bureaus a few years later (Katzman 1973: 140).

Unconventional African-American sects proliferated after World War I, but some of these groups began to emerge before the war. "A black congregation that held services in a converted frame residence on Chene Street became the First Church of God in Michigan in 1884, although it did not acquire a clergyman until 1917" (Katzman 1973: 145). The Holiness Church of the Living God was formed in Detroit in August 1909 by Bishop J.B.C. Cummings (Katzman 1973: 146). In Chicago, the Holy

Nazarene Tabernacle Apostolic Church was founded in 1908 by Natties L. Thornton; the Church of Redemption of Souls, a Spiritualist congregation, was holding services on State Street by 1915 (Spear 1967: 96). In 1896 William S. Crowdy formed the Church of God and Saints, the first Black Judaic sect in the United States, in Lawrence, Kansas. The initial step toward the Islamization of Black religion occurred with the founding of the Moorish Science Temple by Noble Drew Ali in Newark in 1913 (Essien-Udom 1962).

The process of urbanization that accompanies capitalist expansion has repeatedly been demonstrated to have unsettling effects on rural migrants, not only in industrial societies but also in the Third World. Next to the family, the church—despite its accommodative dimensions— had been the most important institution among African Americans in the rural South. As Williams (1974: 9) observes, "The migration to cities created a social crisis, for it separated masses of Blacks from their rural life style and destroyed the social organization which gave meaning to their segregated rural Southern society." Many migrants apparently found more-or-less comfortable niches in the large, well-established Baptist and Methodist congregations of the urban North and South. Olivet Baptist Church in Chicago grew from about four thousand members in 1915 to nearly nine thousand in 1920 (Spear 1967: 177). Many new congregations affiliated with established denominations also sprang up during this period. A survey of five selected northern cities between 1916 and 1926 indicated a 151 percent increase in the number of Black Baptist churches and an 85 percent increase in the number of African Methodist Episcopal churches (Scheiner 1965: 99). Pilgrim, Progressive, Provident, Liberty, and Monumental Baptist churches were founded between 1916 and 1919 in Chicago and grew into relatively large congregations within a decade (Spear 1967: 178). In Cleveland, the number of Black churches increased from 17 a few years before the Great Migration to 44 by 1918, 78 by 1921, and over 140 by 1933 (Kusmer 1976: 207).

However, the older Baptist and Methodist churches in the African-American community simply did not have the resources necessary to meet the material needs of overwhelming numbers of poor migrants. Furthermore, many migrants who had enjoyed positions of leadership and responsibility in rural churches found themselves relegated to the sidelines of the large urban congregations. In addition to seeming more bureaucratic, impersonal, formal, and sedate than their counterparts in the South, the established congregations increasingly adapted themselves to the more secular concerns of a new Black middle class (Frazier 1974).

Lower-class migrants frequently found they were viewed with disdain by their more affluent northern-born communicants and threatened by their sophistication.

A common strategy adopted by the migrants to deal with this situation was to establish storefront and house churches. Many storefront churches called themselves "Baptist," but Spear (1967: 176) contends that in reality "they often closely resembled the Holiness churches in their uninhibited form of worship." Furthermore, many African-American migrants were attracted to the Holiness, Pentecostal, Spiritualist or Spiritual, Judaic, Islamic, and other sects such as the Father Divine Peace Mission movement, and the African Orthodox church, which emerged in tremendous profusion not only in the industrial North but also in many cities of the South. Arthur Paris (1982: 27–28) cautions us not to lump all of the groups that occupied storefronts and house churches with "the welter of other spiritualist, nationalist, or neo-African groups that also used commercial space." The term "storefront" refers to a physical trait shared by many religious groups rather than a sociological category per se. Many substantial Black Baptist and some Black Methodist churches of today started out as storefront churches.

In their survey of Black churches in twelve cities, Mays and Nicholson (1933: 313) found that 777 of a total of 2,104 church buildings that they surveyed were storefronts or converted residences. About half of the 777 storefront congregations were Baptists; many others were of the Holiness and Spiritual varieties. In reality, the percentage of storefront and house churches, at least in certain cities, may have been considerably higher. Also, Mays and Nicholson may very likely have missed many of these churches in their survey. In his survey of 278 Black congregations in Chicago, Sutherland (1930: 47) found that 178 (64.0 percent) of them conducted services "in a single room in a vacant store or in an apartment building or in temporary tent quarters." Whereas 65.9 percent of 133 Baptist congregations worshipped in such settings, only 12 out of the 35 A.M.E., A.M.E. Zion, and C.M.E. congregations did so (Sutherland 1930: 57). Drake and Cayton (1945: 633) found that in Bronzeville 66.4 percent of the "Holiness" congregations, 52.2 percent of the "miscellaneous" congregations, and 50.1 percent of the "Spiritualist" congregations were housed in storefronts. In his survey of 173 Black storefront churches in the "Central Area" of Cleveland, Blackwell (1949) discovered that 79 were Holiness/Pentecostal, 71 Baptist, 17 Spiritual, 5 Methodist, and 1 Presbyterian. Given the poverty of the newly arrived migrants, the storefront served as temporary quarters before the congregation grew to such a size that it could afford to purchase or rent a larger noncommercial structure, often a church building being vacated by a white congregation whose members were fleeing to the suburbs.

Following Wallace's (1956) concept of revitalization movements, Harrison (1971: 244) describes storefront churches as "deliberate, conscious, organized efforts of migrants to create a more satisfying mode of existence by refurbishing rural religious behavior to an urban environment." While storefront churches in the Black community attract many individuals, they originally emerged—even prior to the Great Migration—as a response to the needs of the rural migrants, and they still serve this function. As opposed to the anonymity of the large urban church, the storefront provides its members with a sense of belonging to a religious community in which the pastor knows them personally. Furthermore, the storefront church, as Frazier (1974: 59) observes, permits its members to worship with a "maximum of free religious expression" which generally includes shouting, holy dancing, and the singing of spirituals and other popular religious hymns.

In the midst of the social crisis faced by the migrants from the rural South, Black religion became even more diversified than it had been before. As Nelsen and Nelsen (1975: 43) observe, "The story of the urban church in the postwar years is largely an epic of established black Protestantism trying to meet a major crisis with limited material resources and, all too often, with limited imagination as well—and of a restless population first searching for renewal at the old familiar altars, then turning to the storefronts, the Father Divines, the Black Muslims in their quest for a religion that could make the new and strange burdens of urban life somehow tolerable." In the 1920s Harlem offered migrants houses of worship such as the Metaphysical Church of the Divine Investigation, Mt. Zion Pentecostal Church, St. Matthew's Church of the Divine Silence and Truth, Congregation of Beth B'Nai Abraham, the Temple of Luxor, Sanctified Sons of the Holy Ghost, and Live-Ever-Die-Never Church (Reid 1926; Osofsky 1965: 144). This process of diversification later would be accelerated by the insecurities induced by the Great Depression, which affected Blacks even more adversely than it did whites. According to Wilmore (1983: 162), "the Black community, by the end of the decade of the 1930s, was literally glutted with churches of every variety and description."

Tables 2 and 3 roughly indicate the diversification that occurred within African-American religion during the 1920s and 1930s. Of the many unconventional religious groups found in the Black urban neighborhoods, the Holiness, Pentecostal, and Spiritual churches were the main varieties.

Table 20.2   Congregations Belonging to Selected Religious Bodies in Twelve Cities

	7 Southern Cities		5 Northern Cities		All 12 Cities	
	No.	% of total sample	No.	% of total sample	No.	% of total sample
Religious Bodies						
Baptist	661	61.5	446	45.3	1,127	53.6
Methodist	209	20.0	160	16.3	369	17.5
Holiness/Pentecostal	95	8.8	244	23.7	339	16.1
Spiritual	36	3.3	78	7.6	114	5.4

SOURCE: Adapted from Mays and Nicholson (1933: 210–22).

Table 20.3   Black Congregations in Chicago: 1928 and 1938

Denomination or Sect	Number of Churches and Percentage of Total			
	1928		1938	
	No.	%	No.	%
Baptist	133	45.1	215	45.3
Black Methodist	35	11.9	42	8.9
White-controlled groups	22	7.4	27	5.6
Community Churches, Inc.	3	1.0	10	2.1
Holiness/Pentecostal	56	19.0	107	22.6
Spiritual	17	5.8	51	10.7
Others	29	9.8	23	4.8
Total	295	100.0	475	100.0

SOURCE: Adapted from Sutherland (1930) and Drake and Cayton (1945).

An examination of Table 2 reveals that Holiness, Pentecostal, and Spiritual congregations were more common in northern cities than in southern ones. Table 3 shows that, at least in Chicago, Holiness, Pentecostal, and Spiritual churches increased in both numbers and in percentages of the total number of Black churches between 1928 and 1938. Drake and Cayton (1945: 413) also found the "existence of a number of small denominations indigenous to Bronzeville and such all-Negro 'cults' as the African Orthodox church, the Christian Catholics, the Temple of Moorish Science, and numerous fly-by-night groups organized around enterprising but untrained preachers."

Lincoln and Mamiya (1990: 407) estimate that 80.6 percent of churchgoing African Americans belong to seven religious bodies—the National Baptist Convention, U.S.A.; the National Baptist Convention of America; the Progressive National Baptist Convention; the African Methodist Episcopal church; the African Methodist Episcopal Zion church; the Christian Methodist Episcopal church; and the Church of God in Christ. They estimate that 5.9 percent of churchgoing African Americans belong to "smaller black communions," 5.1 percent to "predominantly white Protestant groups," and 8.4 percent to the Roman Catholic church. In reality, the number of African Americans belonging to "smaller black communions"—a category that presumably includes conversionist sects other than COGIC (Church of God in Christ), messianic-nationalist sects, and thaumaturgical sects—may be greater than the figure reported by Lincoln and Mamiya in that membership statistics for many unconventional African-American groups go unreported. At any rate, Table 4 presents the reported membership figures for major Black religious bodies. There exists considerable variation in the last reported year for membership figures among these religious bodies. Furthermore, as tends to be the case for most religious bodies, the figures may be inflated. Unfortunately, membership figures for

Table 20.4   Membership of Major Black Religious Bodies

Religious Body	Year Reported	No. of Churches	Membership
National Baptist Convention, U.S.A.	1958	26,000	5,500,000
National Baptist Convention of America	1956	11,398	2,668,779
Progressive National Baptist Convention	1967	655	521,692
National Primitive Baptist Convention	1975	606	250,000
African Methodist Episcopal church	1981	6,200	2,210,000
African Methodist Episcopal Zion church	1987	6,060	1,220,260
Christian Methodist Episcopal church	1983	2,340	718,922
Church of God in Christ	1982	9,982	3,709,661
Church of God in Christ, International	1982	300	200,000

SOURCE: Adapted from Jacquet (1989: 238–45).

many unconventional Black religious bodies are either difficult to obtain or unavailable.

Types of African-American Religious Sects

To comprehend the nature of religious diversity in African-American religion, we utilize a typology of Black sectarianism (Baer and Singer 1981). In the process of conducting research on various relatively unknown religious groups in the Black community, we concluded that there was a need for a typology that systematically recognizes the diversity of Black religious groups while placing them in a shared context. We recognized that the content, structure, and variability of African-American religion derives primarily from three sources: (1) influences from African cultures; (2) influences from religious patterns in European-American culture; and (3) religious responses on the part of Blacks to cope with their minority status in American society. Our typology focuses upon the third source, largely because it appears to be the overriding factor that has shaped all Black religious groups in the United States. Yinger appears to concur with our assessment:

> . . . Negro sectarianism is a product of the same fundamental causes as sectarianism in general, but there are some special factors that have affected it. It can be understood only in the total context of the Negro's place in American society. (Yinger 1970: 324)

Our typology concerns only those religious movements and organizations composed primarily of Black members, in keeping with our view that African-American religion is largely a response to the racism and class stratification inherent in American society. Our typology does not include white-controlled religious organizations, such as the Catholic church, various mainstream Protestant denominations, the Seventh Day Adventists, and the Jehovah's Witnesses, which contain either predominantly Black congregations or have Black members scattered among various predominantly white congregations. There are, of course, many important questions that the presence of African Americans in such organizations raises. For example, why do Blacks join predominantly white congregations, or why do they establish congregations affiliated with white-controlled religious groups? Or how do Black congregations, such as the Black Catholic churches common in southern Louisiana and central Kentucky, adapt the content of white-controlled religious organizations to the African-American experience?

For our typology of African-American sectarianism, we chose two dimensions as axes. One axis considers the "strategies of social action" that Black religious groups adopt in addressing their structural position in American society. In this regard, the response of a particular group may be instrumental; that is, it may focus on the attainment of concrete goals aimed at improving the objective material and social status of its adherents, or it may be expressive in that it releases the emotional tensions resulting from social oppression. The second axis considers the general "attitudinal orientation" of the members of various religious groups to the cultural patterns of the larger society, or more specifically to those of the dominant or majority group. A particular religious body may incorporate a positive orientation; that is, it may accept the overall values and behavioral patterns of the larger society. Or it may adopt a negative orientation in that it rejects or is repulsed by them, at least conditionally.

Figure 1 illustrates this typology in the form of a four-cell matrix. Each cell represents a different type of religious sect. While much of the sociology of religion is devoted to making fine-grained distinctions between "sect" and "cult," we dispense with these in our discussion. Instead, we emphasize the sectarian nature of African-American religious groups in

Figure 20.1   Religious Responses to the Larger Society among African Americans

		Strategies of Social Action	
Attitudinal Orientation	Positive	thaumaturgical sects	mainstream denominations or established sects
	Negative	conversionist sects	messianic-nationalist sects

that they all exist unavoidably in a state of some tension with the larger society. This is so because the racial status of their adherents automatically insures both the experience of oppression, individually and/or collectively, and the resultant use of the religious group to respond in some fashion to this experience.

Mainstream Denominations

The established sects or mainstream denominations in the Black community are committed, at least in theory, to a reformist strategy of social activism that will enable African Americans to become better integrated into the political, economic, and social institutions of the larger society. Many of the congregations of this type continue to exhibit a strong expressive side in worship activities, but they are strongly committed to various instrumental activities, such as lending support to various protests, raising funds to fight discrimination, and sponsoring college scholarships. Members of the mainstream denominations or established sects tend to accept the cultural patterns of the larger society and want to share in the benefits of the "American Dream."

The mainstream denominations are drawn primarily from two religious movements. The first movement included groups of free Blacks who separated from predominantly white congregations prior to the Civil War, and the second consisted largely of former slaves who separated from the white Baptists after the Civil War. Mainstream congregations are found today in associations such as the National Baptist Convention, U.S.A.; the National Baptist Convention of America; the Progressive National Convention; the African Methodist Episcopal church; the African Methodist Episcopal Zion church; the Christian Methodist Episcopal church; and the Second Cumberland Presbyterian Church in the United States. Although many of the congregations in these organizations include working-class and lower-class members, their leadership and orientation are generally middle-class. These bodies constitute the "mainline" or "mainstream" churches in the African-American community in that their orientation is toward the Black middle class and they have achieved both social legitimacy and stability, but they experience a sectarian tension with the larger society.

Messianic-Nationalist Sects

Messianic-nationalism is a variant of African-American nationalism that combines religious belief with the ultimate objective of achieving some degree of political, social, cultural, and/or economic autonomy. Sects of this type are generally founded by charismatic individuals regarded by their followers as messiahs or "messengers" of God, if not God in human form, who will deliver Blacks from the oppressive yoke of white dominance. In many cases, the death of the messiah precipitates an internal leadership crisis, often followed by a splintering process within the group. Central to the ideology of the messianic-nationalist sect is the repudiation of "Negro" identity as an oppressive white creation and the substitution of a new ethnic identity predicated on a belief in the unique spiritual importance of Black people. Rhetorically, at least, messianic-nationalist sects reject both mainstream goals and values. Additional core features of messianic-nationalism include:

(1) belief in a glorious Black past and subsequent "fall" from grace;
(2) vocal opposition to and criticism of American society and whites in general;
(3) anticipation of divine retribution against the white oppressors;
(4) assertion of Black sovereignty through the development of various rituals and symbols, such as national flags, anthems, and dress, and a separatist economic base as well as, plus at least in some cases, an interest in territorial separation or emigrationism; and
(5) chiliastic and messianic expectations of a new golden age for Black people.

In its own way, each messianic-nationalist sect includes the pivotal features listed above. In one group emigration may be stressed while in another it may play but a minor role in group ideology. Generally, these sects turn to Islam, Judaism, Christianity, or even a combination of all three traditions for their beliefs and rituals. It must be stressed, however, that whatever their outward difference, the majority of messianic-nationalist sects are strikingly similar. Of the four types in our typology, they constitute the most radical protest to and departure from the institutions and conventions of the larger society.

The adoption of an Israelite identity as one form of messianic-nationalism seemed inevitable in that African Americans have historically compared their plight in American society to that of the biblical Hebrews in the Egypt of the pharaohs. Congregations calling themselves "Black Jews" appeared about 1915 in Washington, Philadelphia, New York, and smaller cities, although there is evidence of such groups even earlier.

The best-known messianic-nationalist sects, however, are those that adopt an Islamic orientation. The first of the Black Islamic or Muslim sects was the Moorish Science Temple founded by Noble Drew Ali in Newark around 1913. The process of Islamization in the Black community was in large part continued with the emergence in the early 1930s of the Nation of Islam, first under the leadership of W. D. Fard and later of Elijah Muhammed. The rapid growth of the Nation of Islam, in large part accelerated by the dynamic inspiration of Malcolm X during the 1960s, did not check schismatic tendencies, which led to the appearance of numerous splinter Black Muslim sects, including the Ahmadiyya Moslem movement of Chicago, the Hanafis of Washington, D.C., and the Ansaru Allah community of Brooklyn.

The last major wing of the messianic-nationalist movement remained within the Christian fold but modified certain Christian beliefs in its efforts to create a more satisfying Black identity. The most noteworthy of these groups is the African Orthodox church, which grew out of Marcus Garvey's massive Universal Negro Improvement Association under the tutelage of George Alexander McGuire, a former Episcopalian clergyman. This assemblage urged Blacks to forget the image of a white God and instead worship a Black Madonna and a Black Christ. A similar orientation developed in Albert B. Cleage's Shrine of the Black Madonna, headquartered in Detroit. Cleage, a minister in the United Church of Christ, attracted considerable attention in the 1960s with his pronouncements that Jesus was a Black revolutionary who came to free people of color from white oppression (Harding 1969).

Conversionist Sects

Conversionist sects characteristically adopt an expressive strategy of social action, emphasizing the importance of various behavioral patterns—such as shouting, ecstatic dancing, and glossolalia—as outward manifestations of "holiness" or "sanctification." Wilson notes the following about the conversionist sect:

> . . . Its reaction towards the outside world is to suggest the latter is corrupted because man is corrupt. This type of sect takes no interest in programs of social reform or in the political solution of social problems and may even be actively hostile towards them. (Wilson 1969: 364)

Conversionist sects tend to be "otherwordly" and apolitical in orientation and rely upon the willingness of the individual to undergo a process of conversion as the meaningful way to effect social transformation. It is this emphasis on personal change, rather than promotion of religious conversion per se, that is the hallmark of these groups. As defined by the conversionist sects, living a life of holiness requires adherence to a puritanical morality and avoidance of the carnal activities, such as drinking, smoking, dancing, gambling, theatergoing, and illicit sex. The focus of the conversionist sect is the worship service as well as the revival meeting.

Next to the established sects, the conversionist sects, which consist primarily of a multitude of small Baptist, Holiness, and Pentecostal organizations and congregations, appear to be the largest religious type in the Black community. Many of the congregations, particularly of the "storefront" type, that are found in great numbers in the commercial districts of Black neighborhoods are examples of the conversionist sect. A few of the many Black Holiness and Pentecostal organizations include associations such as the Church of God in Christ, Church of Christ (Holiness) U.S.A., Christ's Sanctified Holy Church (Holiness), the Apostolic Church of Jesus Christ, the Pentecostal Assemblies of the World, and the House of Prayer for All People (Simpson 1978: 259). In addition, one finds a countless number of Holiness and Pentecostal congregations in the African-American community that have no formal affiliations with larger associations.

The Holiness movement, which emerged during the period following the Civil War, was not specifically aimed at Black Americans (Washington 1973: 60). On the other hand, despite the close alliance between some of its adherents and the Ku Klux Klan, the Holiness movement did occasionally bring poor whites and Blacks together in interracial revivals. Some Blacks also established Holiness sects. One of these, the Church of God in Christ, later became a Pentecostal group after its founder was influenced by the Azusa Street Revival, which started in Los Angeles in 1905, and is presently the largest of the Holiness/Pentecostal groups in the Black community (Simpson 1978: 259–60). In contrast to the Holiness movement, the Pentecostal movement emphasized one form of ecstatic behavior over all others as a mark of sanctification, namely speaking in tongues, or glossolalia.

Wilson (1969: 372) notes that conversionist sects, if they manage to survive and grow, are prone to a process of "denominalization." Some of the larger conversionist groups, particularly the Church of God in Christ, are being transformed into established sects with a more temporal view of the world and the possibilities for social change. On the whole, however, the great majority of conversionist groups in the Black community continue to provide their adherents with an escapist response to the problems of racism and social inequality.

Thaumaturgical Sects

Thaumaturgical sects maintain that the most direct way to achieve socially desired ends—such as financial prosperity, prestige, love, and health—is by engaging in various magico-religious rituals or by acquiring esoteric knowledge that provides individuals with spiritual power over themselves and others.

> These sects define themselves in relation to the wider society by affirming that normal reality and causation can be suspended for the benefit of special and personal dispensations. They resist acceptance of the physical process of aging and death and come together to affirm a special exception from everyday realities which assures each individual and his loved ones of perpetual well-being in the next world. For the present, they procure immediate advantages by accomplishing miracles. (Wilson 1969: 368)

Thaumaturgical sects tend to hold the individual responsible for his or her present condition and stress the need to develop a positive frame of mind while at the same time overcoming negative attitudes. Thaumaturgical groups generally accept the cultural patterns, values, and beliefs of the larger society but attempt to change the means for obtaining the "good life." Because of their individualistic orientation, such groups are largely apolitical and express little interest in social reform. Members of thaumaturgical sects view themselves as open-minded and are very amenable to religious syncretism.

Of these four types, the thaumaturgical sect has been the most neglected by scholars, despite their prevalence in the African-American community. Most commonly representative of this type are those groups that refer to themselves as "Spiritual" churches (Baer 1984). Various scholars, including Hurston (1931), Mays and Nicholson (1933), Jones (1939), Fauset (1971), Drake and Cayton (1945), Frazier (1974), and Washington (1973), refer to these groups as "Spiritualist," but the term "Spiritualist" was contracted to "Spiritual" in most of these groups around the 1930s and 1940s. The Spiritual movement in the Black community blends elements from American Spiritualism, Roman Catholicism, Black

Protestantism, and Voodoo (or at least its diluted form generally termed "hoodoo") and various other religious traditions.

The historical development of the Spiritual movement remains obscure, but it seems to have emerged in various large cities, particularly Chicago, New Orleans, and Detroit, in the 1910s. As was also true of many of the conversionist and messianic-nationalist sects, the growth of the Spiritual churches was in large part related to the migration of African Americans from the rural South to the cities of both the North and the South. Most Spiritual churches are quite small and are situated in store-fronts and converted dwelling buildings, but some are housed in impressive edifices and cater to relatively affluent working-class and professional people. Most Spiritual churches maintain at least a loose affiliation with a larger association. Prior to the death in 1979 of its charismatic leader, Clarence Cobbs, the largest of these many associations, the Metropolitan Spiritual Churches of Christ, Incorporated, may have had as many as 125 congregations (Melton 1978, vol. 2: 106).

One of the newest and perhaps the best known of the Black thaumaturgical sects is the United Church and Science of Living Institute founded in 1966 by the Rev. Frederik Eikerenkoetter II (better known as "Rev. Ike"). Rev. Ike teaches that the lack of money is the root of all evil and urges his followers to rid themselves of attitudes of deferred rewards in an afterlife and to start believing in their own abilities of acquiring a slice of the "American Dream" (Gallatin 1979). Lesser-known thaumaturgical sects among Black Americans include groups such as the Antioch Association of Metaphysical Science, established in 1932 by Dr. Lewis Johnson in Detroit, and the Embassy of the Gheez-Americans headquartered in Long Eddy, New York (Melton 1978, vol. 2: 243).

Although Spiritual churches, due to their highly syncretistic nature, exhibit many of the features found in other Black religious groups, their emphasis on the manipulation of one's present condition through the use of various magico-religious rituals and the acquisition of esoteric knowledge differentiates them from the latter. The Spiritual religion concerns itself with the concrete problems of its adherents and clients by attempting to provide them with the spiritual means to acquire finances, success in locating employment, love, or the improvement of a strained relationship. In contrast to the common but probably exaggerated view that African-American religion is "otherworldly," Spiritual people are concerned primarily with discovering solutions to their difficulties in the here and now.

References

Baer, Hans A.
  1984   *The Black Spiritual Movement: A Religious Response to Racism.* Knoxville: Univ. of Tennessee Press.

Baer, Hans A., and Merrill Singer
  1981   "Toward a Typology of Black Sectarianism as a Response to Racial Stratification." *Anthropological Quarterly* 54: 1–14.

Baron, Harold M.
  1971   "The Demand for Black Labor: Historical Notes on the Political Economy of Racism." *Radical America* 5, no. 2: 1–46.
  1976   "The Demand for Black Labor." In *Racial Conflict, Discrimination and Power: Historical and Contemporary Studies,* ed. William Barclay, Krishna Kumar, and Ruth P. Simms, 190–202. New York: AMS.

Bethel, Elizabeth Rauh
  1981   *Promiseland: A Century of Life in a Negro Community.* Philadelphia: Temple Univ. Press.

Blackwell, James Edward
  1949   "A Comparative Study of Five Negro 'Store-front' Churches in Cleveland." M.A. thesis. Western Reserve Univ.

Bonacich, Edna
  1976   "Advanced Capitalism and Black/White Race Relations in the United States: A Split Labor Market Interpretation." *American Sociological Review* 41: 34–51.

Bontemps, Arna, and Jack Conroy
  1966   *Any Place But Here.* New York: Hill and Wang.

Cox, Oliver C.
  1976   *Race Relations: Elements and Dynamics.* Detroit: Wayne State Univ. Press.

Davis, Alison
  1940   "The Negro Church and Associations in the Lower South." Research Memorandum, Carnegie-Myrdal Study. New York.

Davis, Alison, Burleigh Gardner, and Mary Gardner
  1965   *Deep South: A Social Anthropological Study of Caste and Class.* Chicago: Univ. of Chicago Press.

Dollard, John
  1937   *Caste and Class in a Southern Town.* Garden City, N.Y.: Anchor.

Dougherty, Molly C.
  1978   *Becoming a Woman in Rural Black Culture.* New York: Holt, Winston, and Rinehart.

Drake, St. Clair, and Horace R. Cayton
  1945   *Black Metropolis.* New York: Harcourt, Brace.

Du Bois, W.E.B.
  1903   *The Negro Church in America.* Atlanta: Atlanta Univ. Press.

Essien-Udom, E. U.
  1962   *Black Nationalism: A Search for Identity in America.* Chicago: Univ. of Chicago Press.

Fauset, Arthur H.
  1971   *Black Gods of the Metropolis.* Philadelphia: Univ. of Pennsylvania Press.

Felton, Ralph Almon
  1952   *Go Down Moses: A Study of 21 Successful Negro Rural Pastors.* Madison, N.J.: Dept. of the Rural Church, Drew Theological Seminary.

Femia, Joseph
 1981   *Gramsci's Political Thought: Hegemony, Consciousness and the Revolutionary Process.* Oxford: Clarendon.
Ferris, William R., Jr.
 1972   "The Rose Hill Service." *Mississippi Folklore Register* 6: 37–55.
Frazier, E. Franklin
 1974   *The Negro Church in America.* New York: Schocken.
Gallatin, Martin V.
 1979   "Rev. Ike's Ministry: A Sociological Investigation of Religious Innovation." Ph.D. diss. New York Univ.
Gennep, Arnold van
 1960   *The Rites of Passage.* London: Routledge and Kegan Paul.
Geschwender, James A.
 1978   *Racial Stratification in America.* Dubuque, Iowa: Wm. C. Brown.
Goldsmith, Peter D.
 1985   "Healing and Denominationalism on the Georgia Coast." *Southern Quarterly* 23, no. 3: 83–102.
Gosnell, Harold
 1937   *Machine Politics: Chicago Model.* Chicago: Univ. of Chicago Press.
Gottlieb, Pete
 1987   *Making Their Way: Southern Blacks' Migration to Pittsburgh, 1916–1930.* Urbana: Univ. of Illinois Press.
Hamilton, Charles V.
 1972   *The Black Preacher in America.* New York: William Morrow.
Hamilton, C. Horace, and John M. Ellison
 1930   *The Negro Church in Rural Virginia.* Blacksburg: Virginia Agricultural Station, Virginia Polytechnic Institute.
Harding, Vincent
 1969   "Resistance and Religion among Ante-Bellum Negroes." In *The Making of Black America*, ed. August Meier and Elliot Rudwick. New York: Atheneum.
Harrison, Ira B.
 1971   "The Storefront Church as a Revitalization Movement." In *The Black Church in America*, ed. Nelsen, Yokley, and Nelsen, 240–50.
Hraba, Joseph
 1979   *American Ethnicity.* Itasca, Ill.: F. B. Peacock.
Hurston, Zora Neale
 1931   "Hoodoo in America." *Journal of American Folklore* 44: 317–417.
Jacquet, Constant H., Jr.
 1989   *Yearbook of American and Canadian Churches 1989.* Nashville, Tenn.: Abingdon.
Johnson, Charles S.
 1934   *Shadow of the Plantation.* Chicago: Univ. of Chicago Press.
 1941   *Growing Up in the Black Belt: Negro Youth in the Rural South.* Washington, D.C.: American Council on Education.
Jones, Raymond
 1939   "A Comparative Study of Religious Cult Behavior among Negroes with Special Reference to Emotional Conditioning Factors." *Howard University Studies in the Social Sciences* 2, no. 2.

Katzman, David M.
  1973   *Before the Ghetto: Black Detroit in the Nineteenth Century.* Urbana: Univ. of Illinois Press.
Kusmer, Kenneth L.
  1976   *A Ghetto Takes Shape: Black Cleveland, 1870–1930.* Urbana: Univ. of Illinois Press.
Lewis, Hylan
  1955   *Blackways of Kent.* Chapel Hill: Univ. of North Carolina Press.
Lincoln, C. Eric, and Lawrence H. Mamiya
  1990   *The Black Church in the African American Experience.* Durham, N.C.: Duke Univ. Press.
MacAdam, Doug
  1982   *Political Process and the Development of Black Insurgency. 1930–1970.* Chicago: Univ. of Chicago Press.
Marable, Manning
  1981   *Blackwater: Historical Studies in Race, Class Consciousness and Revolution.* Dayton, Ohio: Black Praxis.
Marks, Carole
  1985   "Black Labor Migration: 1910–1920." *Insurgent Sociologist* 12, no. 4: 5–24.
Mays, Benjamin E., and Joseph R. Nicholson
  1933   *The Negro Church.* New York: Institute of Social and Religious Research.
Melton, J. Gordon
  1978   *The Encyclopedia of American Religions* 1 and 2. Wilmington, N.C.: McGrath.
Morris, Aldon D.
  1984   *The Origins of the Civil Rights Movement: Black Communities Organizing for Change.* New York: Free Press.
Myrdal, Gunnar
  1962   *An American Dilemma: The Negro Problem and Modern Democracy.* New York: Harper & Row.
Nelsen, Hart M., and Anne Kusener Nelsen
  1975   *Black Church in the Sixties.* Lexington: Univ. Press of Kentucky.
Osofsky, Gilbert
  1965   *Harlem: The Making of a Ghetto: Negro New York, 1890–1930.* New York: Harper & Row.
Ottenberg, Simon
  1959   "Leadership and Change in a Coastal Georgia Negro Community." *Phylon* 20: 718.
Paris, Arthur E.
  1982   *Black Pentecostalism: Southern Religion in an Urban World.* Amherst: Univ. of Massachusetts Press.
Powdermaker, Hortense
  1967   *After Freedom.* New York: Schocken.
Raper, Arthur F.
  1936   *Preface to Peasantry: A Tale of Two Black Belt Counties.* Chapel Hill: Univ. of North Carolina Press.
Reich, Michael
  1971   "The Economics of Racism." In *The Capitalist System*, ed. Richard Edwards, et al., 313–21. Englewood Cliffs, N.J.: Prentice Hall.

Reid, Ira De A.
1926 "Let Us Prey." *Opportunity* 4: 274–78.
Richardson, Harry V.
1947 *Dark Glory: A Picture of the Church Among Negroes in the Rural Church*. New York: Friendship.
Rose, Arnold
1948 *The Negro in America*. New York: Harper & Row.
Sackey, Charles
1973 *The Political Economy of Urban Poverty*. New York: Norton.
Scheiner, Seth M.
1965 *Negro Mecca: A History of the Negro in New York City, 1865–1920*. New York: New York Univ. Press.
Silberman, Charles P.
1964 *Crisis in Black and White*. New York: Vintage.
Simpson, George Eaton
1978 *Black Religions in the New World*. New York: Columbia Univ. Press.
Smith, Joan
1981 *Social Issues and the Social Order: The Contradictions of Capitalism*. Cambridge, Mass.: Winthrop.
Spear, Allan H.
1967 *Black Chicago: The Making of a Negro Ghetto, 1890–1920*. Chicago: Univ. of Chicago Press.
Sutherland, Robert Lee
1930 "An Analysis of Negro Churches in Chicago." Doctoral diss. Univ. of Chicago Divinity School.
Sutton, Joel Brett.
1983 "Spirit and Polity in a Black Primitive Church." Ph.D. diss. Univ. of North Carolina.
Walker, James Perry
1985 "Rev. Louis Cole, Black Baptist Circuit Preacher, 1901–1981." *Southern Quarterly* 23, no. 3: 49–69.
Wallace, Anthony F. C.
1956 "Revitalization Movements." *American Anthropologist* 58: 264–81.
Walters, Raymond
1970 *Negroes and the Great Depression*. Westport, Conn.: Greenwood.
Washington, Joseph J., Jr.
1973 *Black Sects and Cults*. Garden City, N.Y.: Doubleday.
Williams, Melvin D.
1974 *Community in a Black Pentecostal Church*. Pittsburgh: Univ. of Pittsburgh Press.
Wilmore, Gayraud S.
1983 *Black Religion and Black Radicalism*. Maryknoll, N.Y.: Orbis.
Wilson, Bryan R.
1969 "A Typology of Sects." In *Sociology of Religion*, ed. Roland Robertson, 361–83. Baltimore: Penguin.
Yinger, J. Milton
1970 *The Scientific Study of Religion*. New York: Macmillan.

Chapter 21

Chosen Peoples of the Metropolis

Black Muslims, Black Jews, and Others

Wilson Jeremiah Moses

Black messianic mythology in the United States has obviously not been confined to the Christian community. The "Great Migration" of masses of black people to such urban centers as Chicago, Detroit, New York, and Philadelphia during the period of the World Wars was accompanied by the flourishing of numerous urban cults, whose working-class leadership rejected Christianity as the religion of the hypocritical slavemaster. The new religions were often stridently militant, and often preached a doctrine of black supremacy. In some cases, their members identified with Marcus Garvey and rejected their American identity. They refused to call themselves "Negroes," interpreting the word as a badge of shame. They adopted a messianic rhetoric and proclaimed that they were a chosen people with a favored place in history. They would rise to meet a future of unparalleled glory, while the Christian West sank into oblivion.

The many apparent similarities between Black Jews in the United States and the more widely known sect called the Black Muslims have been noted, or at least implied, by a number of students.[1] Between the Ethiopian varieties of Christianity and Judaism, similarities also exist. Indeed, some ties may exist between Falasha Jews in Ethiopia and Black Hebrews in the United States, some of whom have returned to the Holy Land, where they live in uneasy relationship with Israel. Ties certainly exist between the Black Jews and the so-called "Ethiopian Movement," which originated with the tour of Henry McNeal Turner through South Africa in the 1890s and spread by the 1930s to East Africa, West Africa, and the United States. Rastafarianism in the West Indies is akin to this same Ethiopian movement.[2] The fact that messianic religiosity among the black people of the United States has expressed itself in Jewish and

Islamic, as well as in Christian forms indicates underlying strains of similarity between Pan-Africanism, Pan-Islamism, and Zionism.

The fact that there are similarities between these admittedly diverse phenomena should not be misinterpreted as meaning that they are all the same phenomenon. Nonetheless, the points of comparison between the Nation of Islam and the Black Jews represent similar responses by black Americans to an environment that has frustrated the aspirations of both groups in similar ways. It is ironic that while Pan-Islamism and Zionism find themselves in bitter conflict in the Middle East, both religious systems have legitimate offspring in black America whose practitioners share much of the same ideology. The various sects of Black Muslims and Black Jews in America would bitterly deny that their religions are both expressions of the same phenomenon, mere social movements assuming a messianic rhetoric and religious trappings that are purely accidental or metaphorical expressions of temporal aspirations. Pan-Islamists and Zionists would make similarly bitter denials. All would probably be justified in doing so; but students of religion as well as students of nationalism have long recognized that religion and nationalism are similar phenomena.[3] It would seem possible to discuss the similarities between the aforementioned movements without perforce denying or approving the validity of any or overlooking their individuality.

There is reason to believe that the black Jews of Ethiopia may be able to trace their Jewishness back farther than can some European Jews. During the ninth century, obscure accounts by Jewish travelers (like Eldad Haddani) began referring to the existence of a lost tribe of black Jews in Abyssinia. Medieval accounts of Ethiopia, written by outsiders, are notoriously unreliable. Stories abound of men with their heads in the middle of their chests, one-footed men, cannibals (anthropophagi), and demi-god rulers like Prester John, the legendary Christian king. Nothing definite was known of these black Jews, or Falashas, by the outside world until James Bruce mentioned them in his *Travels to Discover the Sources of the Nile* (Edinburgh, 1790). During the mid-nineteenth century, a number of reports by missionaries and other investigators confirmed the existence of Falasha communities. In 1949, Wolf Leslau reawakened interest in the Falashas with an article in *Commentary* describing the findings of his research in progress, based upon travels to Ethiopia in 1947.[4] Leslau returned to Ethiopia for additional research work in 1950, and in 1951 he published *Falasha Anthology: The Black Jews of Ethiopia*. Leslau's work has made Falasha writings, originally set down in the Geez language, available to English readers for the first time.

The Falashas, who refer to themselves as *beta Israel* or simply as *Israel*, trace their ancestry—as do the Christian royal family of Ethiopia—to the fruits of a liaison between King Solomon and the Queen of Sheba. Their name is believed to derive from the Ethiopic word fälläsä, meaning "to emigrate," which may suggest an origin outside Ethiopia. Some Falashas believe that they became separated from the main body of Judaism at the time of the exodus from Egypt; others believe that they came to Ethiopia with the first or second Diaspora. No one is certain whether the Falashas were originally Jewish immigrants or an indigenous people converted to Judaism. Wolf Leslau suggests, in any case, that their form of Judaism is "very primitive" and "might date from a time when the Mishnah and Talmud were not yet compiled."[5] An American group called the Ethiopian Hebrews claims descent from the Falashas, but scholars are uncertain of their origins.

The Black Jews in the United States were first studied by Raymond Jones, who focused his attention on Bishop Plummer of Washington, D.C., organizer of the Church of God and Saints in Christ.[6] The members of this group identified themselves as the "lost tribe of Israel," asserting that the Biblical Hebrews were originally black. Arthur H. Fauset described a similar group in Philadelphia during the early forties. Under the leadership of Prophet Cherry, they were organized as the Church of God and known popularly as "Black Jews" or "Black Hebrews."[7] This group was notable for its disdain of swine flesh, keeping of the Sabbath, opposition to all pictures or "graven images," tithing of members, and contempt for Christianity, especially black storefront religion. The Church of God was open only to black people, the original inhabitants of the earth. The first white man was named Gehazi; he received his color as a result of a curse for his sinfulness. This was an adaptation of the American Protestant myths identifying the origins of the black race with the curse of Cain or Noah's curse of Canaan. Black Jews and Black Muslims alike have been angered by these myths and have countered with myths of their own.

There are apparently numerous uncharted groups of Black Jews throughout the United States. One is tempted to believe that its adherents have gravitated to black Jewish sects more because of an aversion for mainstream American Protestantism than because of attraction to the religious and ethnic traditions of white Jews. A central idea and common trait of black American Jewish separatist groups has been a belief that all black people are the chosen people of God and that Biblical Hebrews—or at least the more faithful among them—were black. Numerous elaborate rationalizations have been worked out in support of this position. The following, taken from a statement by Rabbi Wentworth A. Matthew, leader of the central congregation in Harlem, is illustrative:

> When Rebecca . . . after many years conceived, she brought forth twins, one red and hairy all over like a hairy garment, while the other was plain and smooth as the black man invariably is. The first, the red and hairy one, was called Esau; the plain and smooth brother was called Jacob. This same Jacob, by four wives, begot twelve sons. After twenty years his name was changed from Jacob to Israel, and automatically his sons became the sons of Israel.[8]

Howard Brotz has studied the Black Jews of Harlem, who refer to themselves as the Commandment Keepers and once refused an invitation for closer cooperation with their white counterparts. The Commandment Keepers refuse to be called Negroes, as do the Black Muslims; they conform strictly to Orthodox Jewish religious practices and observe all holidays. Like black Christians, they are fond of comparing the bondage of the Hebrews in Egypt with the plight of black people in America. The Black Jews of Harlem are aware of the existence of the Falasha Jews in Ethiopia. The organizer of the Harlem group was an officer of the Garvey movement named J. Arnold Ford, sometimes wrongly confused with W. D. Fard, the first prophet of the Nation of Islam. Ford emigrated to Ethiopia in 1930.[9]

Vying with Ford to assume the role of spiritual leader among black nationalists was one Noble Drew Ali, leader of the Moorish Science Temple of America. This group was founded around 1914 in Chicago, Illinois. It had a highly secret character and encouraged, as did the Black Jews, ideas of racial supremacy. Membership was open to all "Asiatics," that is to say, dark-skinned people. A number of members of the Moorish Science Temple were also Garveyites. With the decline of the movement, many of its adherents found their way into the Nation of Islam, which was organized by Elijah Muhammad during the 1930s.

Howard Brotz commented upon similarities in doctrine and political ideology between the Nation of Islam and the Commandment Keepers of Harlem. He was incorrect in attributing to them a common organizer in the person of J. Arnold Ford, whom he confused with W. D. Fard, but he was correct in attributing to both of them a messianic conception of black history in the United States, resulting in a chosen-people doctrine and religious black nationalism.[10]

Somewhat more is known of J. Arnold Ford than was available at the time of Brotz's mention of him. He was a native of Barbados, born around 1876, the son of an evangelical preacher. He arrived in the United States shortly after the First World War and identified with the Harlem branch of the UNIA shortly after its founding. In 1924, Ford was forced out of the Garvey organization, in which he had served as music director and choirmaster, and became affiliated with an organization known as the Moorish Zionist Temple. A year later he moved out of that group, taking the choir with him to form Beth B'nai congregation.

Despite an apparent conflict with Garvey, which may have resulted from Garvey's preference for the Christian strain in Ethiopianism, Ford continued to preach Garveyist ideas. His nationalism and his commitment to repatriation were evident in his decision of 1930 to travel to Ethiopia in response to an invitation from an Ethiopian diplomat. The official purpose of the visit was to represent his congregation at the coronation of Ras Tafari and to work for the founding of an Afro-American settlement in the area near Lake Tana. Ford was followed by a small number of other Black Jews, who joined him in establishing a small colony in Addis Ababa.

Ford died in Ethiopia in 1935, and this, of course, invalidates Brotz's conjecture that he was the same person as W. D. Fard, the Detroit peddler who inspired Elijah Poole to assume the name of Elijah Muhammad and establish the Nation of Islam. As late as 1976, Wallace Muhammad, who succeeded his father to leadership of the sect, asserted that Fard was still alive and that he could dial him on the telephone any time he desired.[11]

The group once known as the Nation of Islam, but now called the World Community of Al-Islam in the West, was once the most vigorous black separatist sect. It has undergone dramatic changes since the death of Elijah Muhammad in 1975. The reasons for these changes are shrouded in secrecy, but the old militant, black nationalistic rhetoric that characterized the Nation and all Black Muslim separatism since the First World War has apparently been modified almost out of existence. Under the leadership of Noble Drew Ali and Elijah Muhammad, however, the Black Muslims in America, like the Black Jews, associated themselves with a chosen-people doctrine and a theory of black supremacy. Mr. Muhammad once acknowledged "a very high opinion" of Noble Drew Ali, and indeed many of his teachings were in conformity with those of the Moorish Science Temple.

At the core of Black Islam until 1975 was religious mysticism calculated to counteract doctrines of white supremacy with which most followers were familiar. Whites were viewed as devils, a cursed race brought into existence by the machinations of the mad scientist, Yakub. Total isolation from a white race, doomed by its own sinfulness to oblivion, was the goal of the Nation of Islam. The Black Muslims, like the Black Jews, viewed black Christians with absolute contempt, and they were not particularly concerned about relations with whites of their own religious persuasions. They did not seek acceptance from other Muslims, because their chief concern was with a spiritual jihad against white supremacy, rather than with the authentication of their movement in the eyes of outsiders.

Since the death of Muhammad, the Black Muslims have become less concerned with traditional black nationalistic goals and have focused their efforts on collectivist capitalism. Whites have been invited to join and even to address the congregations. The official weekly newspaper was assuming a "third world" as opposed to a traditional black-nationalist stance even before the death of Muhammad. By the mid-1970s, it had supported such disparate movements as Pan-Africanism, Pan-Islamism, Puerto Rican nationalism, and international socialism. Mr. Muhammad's much-emphasized goal of an all-black homeland for Afro-Americans was being downplayed considerably. The Black Muslims seemed to be abandoning, at least temporarily, territorial black nationalism for a more broadly conceived and conventional variety of Pan-lslamism.[12]

It is not to be expected that the entire Black Muslim community would turn and march in unison down the path to integration at the command of its new leadership. Wallace Muhammad leads the community only by virtue of his father's name and a few legal documents. By attempting to convert the organization from a nationalistic expression of mystical messianism into a pure business enterprise, Mr. Muhammad has, in the eyes of many, stripped the community of its reason for being. The doctrine that "blackness" is a state of mind, and that anyone can be black so long as he or she is willing to fight against the forces of racial oppression, will hardly seem acceptable to the die-hard separatists in the community. Already there have been defectors, among them the charismatic Minister Farrakhan, one-time spokesman for the Nation.[13] Now known as Abdul Haleem, he has broken with the World Community of Al-Islam in the West and has begun to work to revive the Nation of Islam in accordance with the principles of Elijah Muhammad.[14]

In 1967 some 190 Black Jews from Chicago migrated to Liberia, where they attempted to set up kibbutzim in the hinterland. Within two years, half of them had returned to Chicago or found occupations off the kibbutz in Liberia. In 1969 about 40 of this group emigrated to Israel, where they demanded the right to entry under the law of return. Remarkably, some of the "Black Israelites" brought with them their own variety of black-supremacist Zionism. One was quoted as saying: "This is our country—not yours. We will not accept your law." A spokesman back in Chicago added: "We are Israelites claiming our land to establish a kingdom of God. . . . Israel will be a country run totally by black men."[15]

Prince Asiel Ben-Israel, international ambassador for the Original Hebrew Israelite Nation, believes that his group is "genetically connected with the seed of Israel." He contends that the Orthodox Jews "have sent down their wise men and their soothsayers and their astrologists to talk with us, and they know that we are the people. . . , the Messianic people whom the prophecies have foretold would return to the land." Unlike many black nationalists, they do not acknowledge the claims of Palestinian Arabs to the Holy Land—they cannot have a claim on the land, since they have no claim on being Hebrews. Indeed, the Arab nations are enemies of the black world, for they attempt to convert African nations to the Muslim faith. Arabs are not Africans, but Caucasians, cousins of the Israelis, who have usurped the Holy Land. Like the Christians, they spread dissension by converting black people away from the ancestral Hebrew faith.[16]

Prince Asiel Ben-Israel cites Genesis 15:13 to prove his claims: "Know of a surety that thy seed shall be a stranger in a land that is not theirs; and shall serve them; and they shall afflict them 400 years." He also cites the next verse, or his own version of it: "And afterwards I will bring them up out of that land of captivity into the land which I gave unto their fathers for everlasting possession." The manner in which he interprets these words reveals a common characteristic of messianic leaders, including white Zionists. Ben-Israel sees his people as the victims of particularly severe predicaments of a kind unknown to the rest of humanity. Black Americans fulfill the prophecy, says the Prince, because they are "the only people who have been sold and who went into slavery in ships . . . , the only ones who are not being represented on the international scene."[17] So much for the Biblical argument. By way of scholarly support, Ben-Israel cites the work of Father Joseph Williams, *Hebrewisms of West Africa*, which argues that the cultures of West Africa are Hebrew in origin. Ironically, a version of the "Hamitic hypothesis," a myth much scorned by most black nationalists in America, becomes a fundamental belief of this particular sect.

The Hamitic hypothesis was a creation of C. G. Seligman, who argued that all worthwhile culture had been brought to Africa by a mysterious Semitic group of his own invention, whom he named the Hamites. Seligman found it necessary to create this imaginary people because of his belief that Africans were incapable of creating culture. The hypothesis argued not only for the drift of Semitic culture, but implied that only those Africans who were descended from the Hamitic stock were capable of producing civilization. Those black peoples in Africa who had shown any signs of cultural progress, or any ability to dominate less advanced tribes, were really not true Negroes; they were Hamites, a black race of Semitic origin.[18] The Ethiopian Hebrew Nation's insistence that West African culture is Judaic betrays a contempt for indigenous African culture and leaves them with strange bedfellows.

As one might expect, the Ethiopian Hebrew Nation is out of step with the majority of Pan-Africanist groups. Indeed, Prince Ben-Israel came away from the Sixth Pan-African Congress, held in Dar es Salaam, June 1974, thoroughly disenchanted:

> I felt the Congress was a vanity for Africans from America; for again, I witnessed a people who was divided with everybody else's doctrines. Some brothers got up speaking about Marxism; I saw another group of Africans from America talking about the Chinese doctrine of socialism; and I saw a group who said they were the intellectuals. . . . But what was really hurting was when the conference was opened, and the president of an African government walked on the stage with a white secretary and told the conference that it wasn't about race, that it was about social issues.[19]

The African unity that Prince Ben-Israel conceives will occur, he believes, only when ideological unity has been achieved. So long as Africans continue "talking about scientific socialism, Marxism, capitalism—all the *isms* that have been imported into Africa that are not African, Africa can never be unified." The way to African redemption is, of course, through the Hebrew faith. "We in Jerusalem are the unifiers," says the Prince, "because we have a pure, truly African doctrine, first of all, before the whole world; for we are truly the saviors of the world."[20]

Prince Ben-Israel claims that during his travels on the continent, especially in the bush, he has encountered numerous people who "want to come right now up to Jerusalem and be instructed and be taught so that they can go back and redeem their people." He maintains that the Sinai peninsula and the Holy Land are parts of Africa, separated only by the man-made ditch which is the Suez Canal. Africa will be united only when the political fallacy that separates Israel from the rest of the black world is obliterated. Once Jerusalem has been delivered, the rest of Africa will be united under its rightful capital, with the Hebrew faith its proper creed.[21]

Clarke Jenkins, an independent, self-trained scholar in Detroit, has privately published a study called *The Black Hebrews*, in which he argues that:

> The BLACKS of America, Called Negroes, or Negroid, are the descendents of Jacob, of the Tribe of Judah, Benjamin and Levi; forming the other tribes of the nation of Israel, who are among ALL nations of the earth, and being persecuted like their BLACK BROTHERS are, everywhere.[22]

Jenkins argues his point from the Biblical fact that Adam was made of earth, which is always black or dark, but never white. Until the time of Moses, there is no mention made in the Bible of white people. The white race originated with the disease of leprosy, as described in Leviticus, chapter 13. Jesus was not of this white or leprous stock, but of the true line of God's black or chosen people:

> Scripture record [*sic*] men as having both saw and talked with JESUS; and all accounts recorded were that HE had BROWN REDDISH EYES, SHORT HAIR LIKE THE LAMBS WOOL, and in those days wearing only sandals, or barefooted; the account describing His feet were that they were dark and ashy; as if they were burnt in a BRASS OR COPPER smelting furnace.[23]

Jenkins' facile interpretation of Scripture is reminiscent of that of other Black Hebrews, and it also shares similarities with the doctrines of black Islamic sects. All such groups are concerned primarily with demonstrating that they are a chosen people and that their blackness symbolizes their elect status. Thus, the central doctrines of Hebrew and Muslim sects are essentially the same.

However, the fact that urban messianic movements share basic similarities in origin and ideology does not mean that a spirit of good fellowship exists among them. Hostilities between Hanafi Black Muslims and the Nation of Islam have led to bloodshed.[24] Black Jews in the United States have a history of schism and disunity. Both the Hebraic and the Islamic sects view storefront Christian nationalism with contempt; they view one another as lost sheep, who may have grasped the accidentals of the messianic vision but remain deluded on certain essential points. An example of this attitude can be seen very well in the Ansaru Allah Community of Brooklyn, New York, formerly known as the Nubian Islamic Hebrew Mission, a singularly eclectic sect.

The Ansars are readily identifiable by their white robes and turbans. They are conspicuous in the streets and subways of New York, where they distribute pamphlets, take up collections, and are ever eager to discuss their movement with interested black people. The masses of black people seem to respond positively to them, although there is little likelihood that the Ansars will soon amass the 144,000 dedicated members whose enlistment is seen as a precondition for the millennium. The community is presided over by an elderly patriarch, Shaykh Dau'wd. Occasionally, they are visited by the community's founder, Al Hajj Al lmam Isa Abd'Allah Muhammad Al Mahdi, usually referred to as Imam Isa. "Because he is the spiritual Head and Director of an INTERNATIONAL community, it is very rare that he is able to spend time with us." The Imam is accepted by his community as the great-grandson of Al Imam Muhammad Ahmad Al Mahdi, who led the jihad (or holy war) against British colonialism in the Sudan during the 1880s. The Mahdi is reputed to have said, "I'll have a descendant who will rise in the West, that my name will be heard there." The Ansars attach great significance to the fact that Imam Isa was born one hundred years after the Mahdi and that he organized the community in 1970, thirty years before the turn of the century. The Imam is believed to fulfill the prophecy of Revelation 14:1: "And I looked and lo, a Lamb stood on the Mount Zion, and with him an hundred and forty four thousand having his father's name written on their foreheads." The Imam's followers believe that he is this sacrificial lamb, destined to suffer for the sins of his people, the 144,000, who will be ushered into paradise in the year 2000.[25]

Ansars accept the Old Testament, the New Testament, and the Qur'an as divine revelations, and their publications are filled with quotations from all three. Their symbols represent the eclecticism of their belief and include the seal of Ibrahim, a six-point star within a crescent, the horns of which point upward. The symbol of the Moorish Science Temple is a five-point star within a crescent, with horns pointing right; and that of the Nation of Islam is a five-point star within a crescent, with horns pointing left. According to Ansar literature, both of these Muslim symbols, like the Jewish Shield of David, represent their respective sect's *partial* knowledge of the truth, for the true symbol of the chosen is a six-point star. Ansar iconography also makes use of the ankh, a cross with a loop at the top, which is an ancient Egyptian symbol. They carry the flag of the Mahdi, which bears a crescent transfixed by a spear.[26] They wear white robes in fulfillment of a prophecy:[27]

> And one of the Elders answered, saying unto me, what are these which are arrayed in white robes? and whence came they? And I said unto him, Sir, thou knowest. And he said unto me, These are they which came out of great tribulation, and have washed their robes, and made them white in the blood of the Lamb. (Revelation 7:13–14)

His eminence, Imam Isa, carries a staff, as does a Christian bishop. He is sometimes depicted with a halo surrounding his head and shoulders.

Ansars accept, as do other Black Muslims, the prohibition on eating pork. They accept a mythology common among black cultists that the swine is a cross between the rat, the cat, and the dog.[28] White people are lepers, hence the color of their skin. They are referred to as Amorites, or as Canaan and his offspring, driven to total savagery by the curse of Noah. They retreated in ancient times into the Caucasus mountains, where "they (mainly the women) had sexual intercourse with the jackal (the original dog), and, through this intercourse, the offspring that was brought forth was an ape-like man. This is also how and where venereal diseases came about."[29] Whites are referred to as "Mankind" (man's kind) or as the pale man "that has evolved out of the Black man, through leprosy, to the ape, and back to a kind of man (man's kind)." Their bestial origins, say the Ansars, can still be easily observed in the texture and the quantity of their hair. One Ansar pamphlet is profusely illustrated with pictures of white sideshow freaks, afflicted with extreme hirsutism.[30]

Despite the complexity of their religious ideology and their system of symbols, which draw upon materials from numerous doctrines, the Ansars' overriding loyalty is to Islam. They are Islamic Hebrews and guard their identity jealously. Their literature is full of contempt for the numerous other black sects that claim a messianic mission, as well as for the figures who have emerged in messianic roles in recent years. There is especial contempt for those groups who claim to be descendants of the original Israelites—Black Jews in the United States and persons claiming to be Falashas. They also reject the claim of Haile Selassie that he was descended from the Israelites. They accept the Ethiopian Falashas as descended from Israel, but they assert that Falashas are Muslims who never leave their Ethiopian sanctuaries.[31]

The Ansars consider themselves Nubians, and feel that it is a disgrace for a black man to allow himself to be referred to by any other name. All Nubians are Ishmaelites and, along with the Bedouins, constitute the only pure, unadulterated human stock on earth; they are the only direct and unadulterated descendants of Abraham and Noah. They must now assert their claims as the chosen people, by reclaiming their heritage which was stolen from them by other nations. They must return to Arabic, the original tongue of original man; although now that language is monopolized by the Arabs living under the five-point star, which symbolizes their corruption. The Ansars support their contentions with inventive interpretations of the Torah, the Gospel, and the Qur'an. They also have a startlingly sophisticated knowledge of scientific jargon, enough to completely exasperate anyone who foolishly attempts to debate the phylogeny of the swine. Imam Isa and his community seem to have some potential for increasing their numbers; they may even be able to muster their 144,000 and fill the vacuum left by the Nation of Islam's defection from its own brand of orthodoxy.

During the black studies renaissance of the late sixties, students of black nationalism focused more attention on the Black Muslims than on the Black Jews. The siege of B'nai B'rith headquarters in Washington, D.C., by Hanafi Muslims in 1977 and the hijacking of an Israeli airliner to Entebbe Airport in Uganda in 1976 have tended to fix some false associations in the public mind. There seems to have been a journalistic tendency to link the Pan-African movement and all black nationalism with anti-Jewish feeling.[32] The fact that Uganda, nominally a Muslim nation, was led at the time by a pseudo-Pan-Africanist, Idi Amin, led many to construe a link between Pan-Africanism and Pan-Islamism. The public imagination was further confused by a tendency to draw parallels between the plight of Uganda's Asians and that of Germany's Jews. Of course, there is not necessarily a link between Pan-Africanism and Pan-Islamism; the Pan-African movement has been predominantly Christian since its founding in the late eighteenth century. In the twentieth century, Pan-Africanism and black nationalism have taken on some Islamic forms, but they have also taken on Judaic forms. Indeed, those black nationalists who are presently most hostile to the Jewish state are not Moslems, but Black Hebrews.

The claims of some black nationalists that they are the chosen people of the Bible and that they should possess the Holy Land are no more bizarre than the designs that some Zionists formerly had on East Africa. The proposal to establish a Jewish homeland in East Africa originated with the British government, and led to bitter dispute among Jewish nationalists.[33] Of course, those who stood firm for Palestinian resettlement won out in the end; but one wonders what would have been the consequences if the state of Israel had been founded in Kenya or Uganda. Would East Africans, rather than Palestinian Arabs, see themselves as the principal foes of the Jewish state? Edward Wilmot Blyden, one of the founders of the Pan-African movement, saw blacks and Jews as kindred peoples. He linked his movement to Zionism and invited the Jewish people to come to Africa and help with the uplift of the continent.[34] It seems unlikely, however, that contemporary Pan-Africanists would consider the offer still valid.

Stateless nationalisms attempt to justify their territorial aspirations in terms of moral, legal, or historical arguments. As the pamphlet literature of the various black sects and cults illustrates, an active imagination can easily manufacture a rationale to support claims of title to various desirable lands. In the long run, however, the claims of a national group to Palestine, Ethiopia, Liberia, or any other territory have nothing to do with moral rightness, Biblical authority, historical argument, or anything other than force of arms. No one really believes that Ugandan Asians would have fared any better under Zionist nationalism than they did under black nationalism. Israel is no more and no less moral than most other nations of the world. It owes its existence to economic and military power, not to its real or imagined messianic mission or historical ties to the Israelites of the Old Testament.

Black messianic sects provide a rich and colorful rhetoric, but have so far failed to endow their adherents with anything resembling economic or military power. Their adaptations of the chosen-people myth are perhaps useful for counteracting the attempts of Western society to impress black people with a sense of inferiority, but they serve no other function than to replace one set of irrationalities with another. It should not be surprising that such myths are appealing to urban-ghetto blacks, however. The Judeo-Christian tradition and American civil religion are eminently messianic. Black messianism, in its urban cultic forms, originated in the black American masses' sense of alienation from the great myth of American moral and spiritual superiority. The chosen peoples of the metropolis counter their sense of exclusion with the rationalization that they are the truly chosen ones. Still, they are dependent on the old Judeo-Christian idea that oppression endows the oppressed with a morally superior status over the oppressors.[35]

The militant rhetoric of black messianic cults and the racist character of many of their beliefs should not be seen as peculiar to black nationalism. There are many precedents for Biblically based racism in American religion that predate the rise of the black cults. Messianic doctrines are usually hostile to outsiders and ruthless in their dealings with them, for messianic doctrines have certain aspects that are not pretty. Every religious doctrine teaches its adherents to think of themselves as superior to the outsider. The ugly similarities shared by all messianic movements are not the exclusive property of Africans, of Asians, of Europeans, nor of any religious group. The "chosen people" doctrine was certainly not invented in America's black ghettoes, and black messianism can hardly be described as singularly racist or bloodthirsty in comparison to other such movements throughout the world.

Notes

1. Brotz makes this comparison in *The Black Jews of Harlem*, pp. 12, 57, 58. This should be supplemented by Gerber, *The Heritage Seekrs*. Also see Fauset, *Black Gods*, p. 99; and J. R. Washington, Jr., *Black Sects and Cults*, p. 155. During the 1960s, the Black Muslims preferred to be referred to as the Nation of Islam, and most scholars respected their wishes. After the death of Elijah Muhammad in 1975, the Nation changed its name to the World Community of Al Islam in the West, a matter that was widely unnoticed due to the declining effectiveness of the organization's publicity and the drabness of its new leadership. For the sake of convenience, I refer to the organization by its best-known name—the Black Muslims.

2. For an introduction to the traditions of Ethiopianism, see Shepperson, "Ethiopianism and African Nationalism," pp. 9–18. Further discussion of the tradition is in Drake, *The Redemption of Africa and Black Religion*; Kenyatta, *Facing Mt. Kenya*; and Thwaite, *The Seething African Pot*. The influence of Ethiopianism on the Black Jews is discussed by Deanne Shapiro in "Factors in the Development of Black Judaism," in Lincoln, *The Black Experience in Religion*, pp. 254–72.

3. For example, see Kohn, *The Idea of Nationalism*. Kohn argues not only that nationalism and religion are related concepts, but that the very idea of nationalism grew out of the Jewish tradition: "Three essential traits of nationalism originated with the ancient Jews: the idea of the chosen people, the consciousness of national history, and national Messianism. The act by which Jews became a people at the same time a chosen people occurred at the beginning of Jewish history . . . [when] the people received the mission to live and to act in history according to God's will" (pp. 36–37).

4. Leslau, "The Black Jews of Ethiopia."

5. Leslau, *Falasha Anthology*, p. x.

6. Jones, *A Comparative Study of Religious Cult Behavior among Negroes*, p. 103. Cf. J. R. Washington, Jr., *Black Sects and Cults*, pp. 132–33. Washington follows after Clark, *The Small Sects in America*, p. 151, in attributing this group's founding to Prophet William S. Crowdy.

7. Fauset, *Black Gods*, pp. 31–40.

8. Quoted in Brotz, *Black Jews of Harlem*, p. 20.

9. Brotz, *Black Jews of Harlem*, pp. 11, 49, 57; Vincent, *Black Power and the Garvey Movement*, p. 222; J. R. Washington, Jr., *Black Sects and Cults*, p. 134; and Ottley, *New World A-Coming*, p. 144. Vincent says that Ford studied Judaism in Ethiopia; but the most authoritative source on Ford's Ethiopia years is W. R. Scott's *Going to the Promised Land*, which makes no mention of Ford's studying Judaism in Ethiopia, but does mention a meeting between him and Falasha scholar Taamarat Emanuel in Manhattan in 1928 or 1929.

10. Fauset, *Black Gods*, p. 48; and Vincent, *Black Power and the Garvey Movement*, pp. 134–35. Essien Udom, *Black Nationalism*, p. 47, mentions the drifting of Moorish templars into the Nation. Brotz, *Black Jews of Harlem*, p. 12, contains the mistake concerning the identicality of Ford and Fard.

11. W. R. Scott, *Going to the Promised Land*, pp. 4–6; K. J. King, "Some Notes on Arnold Ford and New World Black Attitudes to Ethiopia," pp. 81–87; and Shapiro, "Factors in the Development of Black Judaism," pp. 266–70. Wallace Muhammad, quoted in *Newsweek*, March 15, 1976, p. 33, says: "I can go to the telephone and dial his [W. D. Fard's] number anytime I want to."

12. *Newsweek*, March 15, 1976, p. 33, notes the abrupt shift in Muslim philosophy from the separation shared by Mr. Muhammad and Noble Drew Ali that was described in Essien Udom, *Black Nationalism*. The doctrine of Yakubism is outlined in Elijah Muhammad, *Message to the Blackman in America* (Chicago: Muhammad Mosque of Islam No. 2, 1965), pp. 110–22. The principal revisionist text is Wallace Dean Muhammad, *As the Light Shineth from the East* (Chicago: WDM Publishing Co., 1980).

13. The most accessible summary of the Black Muslims' abandonment of their central doctrine is in Pinkney, *Red, Black, and Green*.

14. Minister Farrakhan expressed his views in an interview in *First World* (Spring 1978): 11.

15. *Newsweek*, January 27, 1969; and October 18, 1971. The author visited the Black Hebrew community in Liberia during February 1980.

16. Fuller, "Original Hebrew Israelite Nation," pp. 62–85.

17. Ibid., p. 64.

18. Seligman, *Races of Africa*.

19. Fuller, "Original Hebrew Israelite Nation," p. 84.

20. Ibid., p. 83.

21. Ibid., pp. 67, 76, 79, 83.

22. Clarke Jenkins, *The Black Hebrews of the Seed of Abraham, Isaac, and Jacob, of the Tribe of Judah, Benjamin, and Levi, After 430 Years in America* (Detroit: The Author, 1969), p. 142.

23. Ibid., p. 113.

24. "Muslim Rivalry," *Christianity Today*, 17 (February 16, 1973): 53–54; and "Holy War?" *Newsweek*, February 5, 1973, p. 41.

25. *'Id with the Ansars*, an undated tabloid publication of the Ansaru Allah Community distributed in New York during the summer of 1978, contains a sampling of doctrine.

26. Isa Muhammad, *Our Symbol* (New York: Ansaru Allah Community, 1977). The six-point star represents the six members of man, including the head, arms, legs, and penis. The five-point start represents the incompleteness of woman, and is believed to be Satanic.

27. *'Id with the Ansars*, p. 3.

28. Al Hajj Imam Isa Abd'Allah Muhammad Al Mahdi, *Did the Hog Come for Mankind?* (New York: Ansaru Allah Community, n.d.)

29. Ibid., p. 7. Elijah Muhammad also makes much of the friendship between the white man and the dog in *Message to the Blackman*, pp. 119–20.

30. Ibid., pp. 7–12.

31. Al Hajj Imam Isa Abd'Allah Muhammad Al Mahdi, *The Tribe of Israel Is No More* (New York: Ansaru Allah Community, n.d.), contains arguments against veneration of Haile Selassie and other false prophets, and rejects the claims of black nationalists in the United States that they represent true Judaism or Islam.

32. Weisbord, *Ebony Kinship*.
33. The best summary of this aspect of the history of Zionism is Weisbord, *African Zion*.
34. Drachler, *Black Homeland/Black Diaspora*, p. 3, observes Blyden's interest; also see Edward W. Blyden, "The Jewish Question" (1898; reprinted in Lynch, *Black Spokesman*).
35. Elijah Muhammad, *Message to the Blackman*, pp. 133–34, attacks "The White Race's False Claim to be Divine Chosen People."

Chapter 22

Religious Ethos of the UNIA

Randall K. Burkett

Several insightful Black intellectuals contemporaneous with Marcus Garvey have at least alluded to the religious motifs which were to be found in the program and propaganda of the Universal Negro Improvement Association. One of the first of these was Claude McKay, one-time correspondent for the *Negro World*, who wrote an article for the April 1922 issue of the radical magazine, *Liberator*, in which he suggested that the essence of the appeal of this new "Negro Moses" was Garvey's imitation of one Alexander Bedward, a West Indian cultic leader who flourished in Jamaica between 1891 and the early 1920s. The Bedwardites constituted "a religious sect . . . purely native in its emotional and external features," which was "the true religion of thousands of natives." McKay hypothesized that perhaps "the notorious career of Bedward, the prophet, worked unconsciously upon Marcus Garvey's mind and made him work out his plans along similar spectacular lines."[1]

McKay's readers, familiar with Bedward's career, were aware, of course, that he had recently been placed in a Jamaican mental institution. He was committed for having prophesied that as the Black incarnation of Jesus Christ, he would on a given day be whisked off to heaven in a white throne, returning after three days to wreak destruction upon the (white) non-elect.[2] Presumably McKay's implication was that the same fate might be appropriate for Garvey, or at least that Garvey, like Bedward, was best understood as an impostor and a fraud.[3]

A more suggestive, if still cursory, analysis of the religious aspects of the Garvey movement was made in a brief article by E. Franklin Frazier published in 1926. Writing in the *Nation*, Frazier called for a "closer examination of the ideals and symbols which Garvey always held up for his followers," and suggested that precisely this symbolism was the basis of Garvey's unique appeal. He pointed specifically to resonant religious themes such as the "redemption of Africa," which Frazier saw as formally analogous to the syndicalists' myth of the general strike. The "redemption of Africa" had become for the UNIA a central motivating mythos, an equivalent to the idea of paradise which had been lost, but which was "always almost at hand." Formative events of the Judeo-Christian tradition were likewise re-symbolized:

> Garvey who was well acquainted with the tremendous influence of religion in the life of the Negro proved himself matchless in assimilating his own program to the religious experience of the Negro. Christmas, with its association of the lowly birth of Jesus, became symbolic of the Negro's birth among the nations of the world. Easter became the symbol of the resurrection of an oppressed and crucified race.[4]

Such "naive symbolism," as Frazier termed it, ought not to blind one to the power which the symbols possess in evincing commitment and devotion; nor need one conclude that Garvey was simply a "common swindler" capitalizing on the superstitions of a people for selfish gains, "when the evidence seems to place him among the so-called cranks who refuse to deal realistically with life."[5] Whether in spite of or because of his lack of realism, however, Garvey had achieved a dramatic goal: sustained grassroots support on a mass basis. As Frazier concluded, "He has the distinction of initiating the first real mass movement among American Negroes."[6]

It is not insignificant that whereas the editors of the *Negro World* relegated to the back pages of their paper a brief reply to the "Bedwardism" charge leveled by McKay, they reprinted the full text of Frazier's article and reserved their own corrective assessment of certain aspects of his critique to a subsequent editorial column.[7] Evidently Frazier's intuition concerning the importance both of the movement itself and of the religious elements within it was in much closer agreement with the UNIA's self-understanding than was McKay's perspective.

Unfortunately, no one developed the suggestions advanced by Frazier, by way of a systematic investigation into the religious framework around which the UNIA was organized. Instead, the typical application of the "religious" interpretation was made in a pejorative sense, the point being that Garvey's was but another in a long string of "escapist" or "utopian" cultic movements which have had the net effect in the Black community of siphoning off effective protest into an "other-worldly" and apolitical realm. James Weldon Johnson provided an example in his condescending description of the UNIA:

> The movement became more than a movement, it became a religion, its members became zealots. Meetings at Liberty Hall were conducted with an elaborate liturgy. The moment for the entry of the "Provisional President" into the auditorium was solemn; a hushed and expectant silence on the throng, the African Legion and Black Cross nurses flanking the long aisle and coming to attention, the band and audience joining in the hymn: "God Save our President," and Garvey, surrounded by his guard of honour from the Legion, marching majestically through the double line and mounting the rostrum; it was impressive if for no other reason than the way in which it impressed the throng.[8]

While such men as McKay, Frazier, and Johnson were thus aware of the presence of religious motifs within the UNIA, they were mostly content to use this knowledge as a club with which to attack Garvey. One suspects that for all of these men religion was basically understood as synonymous with "escapism," or as compensation in another world for material rewards denied in the present world.[9] Simply to conclude that Garveyism was a religion was therefore to go a long way towards discrediting it, or denying the need to take it seriously.[10] Where religion is viewed more broadly, however, as that universal phenomenon endemic to the human enterprise whereby one attempts to make sense of the world in face of the meaning-shattering events by which one is continually bombarded, a more careful examination of these "religious elements" within the UNIA appears to be justified. The question then becomes whether these are isolated and/or extrinsic elements, adopted only for their instrumental value, or whether they have a larger significance. If the latter is the case, then it will become important to see how these elements are woven into a coherent view of the world.

This chapter provides a careful descriptive analysis of the religious ethos of the UNIA, examining the structure and format of its meetings, noting the vocabulary with which members addressed issues, clarifying the role of chaplains within the organization, and elucidating the religio-political symbols of nationhood by which its purposes were embodied. This discussion should therefore provide a foundation for the "closer examination of the ideals and symbols" of the UNIA which was called for by Frazier a half century ago.

Typical UNIA Meetings

From the descriptive point of view alone, one can scarcely help being struck by the fact that meetings of the Universal Negro Improvement Association possessed many of the characteristics of a religious service. This was true of special rallies that were held in Madison Square Garden, of the regular Sunday evening meetings in Harlem's Liberty Hall, and of local division and chapter meetings that were held throughout the United States and the Caribbean. A typical example of the special rallies is one held in Madison Square Garden on March 16, 1924, on the occasion of the return to the United States of a delegation which the UNIA had sent to Europe and Africa "to Negotiate for the Repatriation of Negroes to a Homeland of Their Own in Africa."[11] More than ten thousand persons attended the evening program.

The festivities opened with a colorful procession of officers of the Association and a parade of units from the numerous auxiliary organizations of the UNIA, including the Black Cross Nurses, the Royal Guards, the Royal Engineering Corps, the Royal Medical Corps, and the Universal African Legion. During the procession, the officers sang "Shine on Eternal Light," one of the official opening hymns used by the Association. It had been written by the bandmaster of the UNIA, Rabbi Arnold J. Ford. Next, the audience joined in singing the first, third and fourth stanzas of Reginald Heber's century-old missionary hymn, "From Greenland's Icy Mountains," which was also used as an opening hymn.[12] The Chaplain-General offered a prayer, which was followed by an elaborate and carefully selected musical program. First the UNIA band played a march and the UNIA choir offered the "Gloria." There were three solos, followed by a quartet rendering of "Heaven," written by Black composer Harry T. Burleigh; and the musical presentation was capped by a stirring solo sung by Mme. Marie B. Houston. All of the numbers were explicitly religious in terms of theme, and although this was perhaps a more elaborate musical program than usual, the UNIA meetings at both national and local levels invariably featured outstanding musical talent.[13]

Sir William Sherrill, the Second Assistant President-General, delivered the first speech of the evening, elucidating the purpose of the UNIA. Another musical interlude introduced the high point of the evening: Marcus Garvey's address, "The Negro and the Future." Garvey's speeches were always carefully timed to achieve the maximum impact and were delivered in a fiery and dramatic style that left no member of the audience unmoved. His talk was followed by a brief sermonette by Rev. Dr. William H. Moses, a New York City Baptist minister whose subject for the evening was the familiar Biblical text, "Ethiopia Shall Soon Stretch Forth Her Hands unto God." The speeches were followed by a presentation of delegates and announcements, and the program was closed by the singing of the first verses of the African National Anthem and "The Star Spangled Banner"[14] and a benediction. The format of a religious service was followed even to the point of receiving an offering, which was the normal practice both at special rallies such as the one just described and at the regular Sunday evening meetings in the Harlem Liberty Hall.

While the massive rallies at Madison Square Garden were doubtless more elaborate in their planning and execution than the regular weekly programs at Liberty Hall, the spirit and tone of those weekly meetings were the same. A typical Sunday evening program is described in the following excerpt from a *Negro World* report:

> The meeting tonight opened with the customary religious service of congregational singing of anthem and prayer, followed by all repeating the Twenty-Third Psalm, after which the High Chancellor, the Rev. Dr. G. E. Stewart, the presiding officer, offered a special prayer for the safe return of the President-General. Then followed the musical program, the Liberty Choir and the Black Star Line Band performing their parts well. Mr. Samuels sang a baritone solo. Madame Fraser-Robinson was the soloist.[15]

The speakers for this particular evening included, in addition to Stewart, two other clergymen: William H. Ferris, a Harvard Divinity School alumnus and editor of the *Negro World*; and Frederick A. Toote, "Speaker in Convention" and one of the founders of the African Orthodox Church. Toote's speech was devoted almost wholly to the imminent return of Marcus Garvey, who was just concluding an extensive trip through the Caribbean on behalf of the UNIA. He closed with a "fervent appeal to all friends of the movement to help make the reception to be tendered to Mr. Garvey an unqualified success," and his appeal evidently did not go unanswered, as the paper reported:

> This brought a voluntary response of nearly everyone present, who came forward and made a liberal contribution toward the expenses of

the proposed welcome. Following this, the meeting closed, with everyone in a happy frame of mind, and elated over the glad tidings that had been heard.[16]

For a time Sunday morning programs were also held in the Harlem Liberty Hall, and these were evidently strictly worship services. On at least one occasion, the morning worship service was reported in the Pittsburgh *Courier's* regular weekly section "Among the Churches," which published summaries of sermons delivered in Harlem's most prestigious churches. Reporting on the program "At Liberty Hall" for Sunday, May 23, 1924, the *Courier* noted that an "overflowing crowd" was in attendance at the eleven o'clock service. The Reverend G. Emonei Carter presided, and Bishop George Alexander McGuire delivered the sermon based on a text from the book of Hebrews, chapter eleven.[17]

The meetings of local UNIA chapters and divisions across the country similarly reflected the tone of a religious service and followed a carefully ritualized pattern. The following item concerning the Los Angeles Division, dated January 30, 1923, is typical of the reports appearing weekly in "The News and Views of UNIA Divisions" section of the *Negro World*:

> The Los Angeles Division, No. 156, met in their hall, 1824 Central Avenue, with the president, Mr. D. J. Henderson. The meeting opened by singing "From Greenland['s] Icy Mountain," the motto being repeated by the chaplain. The front page of the *Negro World* was read by Mr. Henderson.
>
> Mr. J. J. Stafford, second vice-president was present as master of ceremonies. First on the program was a selection by the choir, next Rev. A. Brown, [on the] subject, "Love is the Greatest Thing." A paper [was read] by Mr. Hoxie stating what the editor of the "Los Angeles Times" (White) said: "That the great God who we serve is a Black Man," referring to the finding [recently of the] Egyptian King [Tut, who died], 3000 years ago. Mr. Hoxie said we, the Negroes that were brought to this country as slaves, never knew of anything, not until Marcus Garvey came. Go on, go on, Marcus Garvey, until victory shine upon the continent of Africa.[18]

Local UNIA meetings were normally held on Sunday evenings, though some divisions held morning services as well. Almost always, when a division was first founded, meetings were held in the church of a friendly (or at least a neutral) minister in the community, though each local organization was strongly encouraged by national headquarters to build its own "Liberty Hall" as quickly as possible. Often, as in the case of the Los Angeles Division, the prime mover on the UNIA's behalf was a prominent clergyman. In this instance it was the influential pastor of Tabernacle Baptist Church, the Reverend John Dawson Gordon, in whose church the Association held its meetings for over a year and a half.[19] Gordon soon became a national officer of the UNIA, and a large number of his congregation became active Garveyites.[20]

As was the case at the special rallies and in the Harlem Liberty Hall meetings, then, local UNIA meetings were characterized by hymn singing, prayers, and sermons by local clergymen. Special rituals were devised to give local groups a sense of identification with the national organization, such as public reading of the front page of the *Negro World*, which was always written by Marcus Garvey. A regular feature of the local meetings was the welcoming of new visitors and the introduction of prominent community leaders in the audience. The reports carried in the "News and Views" section of the *Negro World* invariably concluded with a listing of influential citizens who had attended the chapter or division meeting, and special prominence was given to testimonials of support from any clergymen present. In addition to these regular weekly features of local meetings, there were special ceremonies prescribed for unique events such as the "unveiling" of the charter of a new UNIA chapter or division, a practice not dissimilar from the dedication and consecration ceremonies found in many churches. Mortgage burning ceremonies were likewise held by local UNIA groups.

Vocabulary of the UNIA

There is another important sense in which the UNIA reflected a religious ethos, namely, in the language and the vocabulary on which the movement drew both to describe its own purposes and to evoke commitment and loyalty amongst its membership. Unquestionably the vocabulary of the UNIA was drawn from the religious realm, as can be attested by practically every issue of the *Negro World*.

Garvey himself provides a classic example in a speech he delivered in February 1921 at Liberty Hall. On that occasion he stated:

> I wish I could *convert* the world of Negroes overnight to the tremendous possibilities of the Universal Negro Improvement Association. It

pains me every every [*sic*] moment of the day when I see Negroes losing the grasp they should have on their own. You of Liberty Hall I must
ask you [*sic*] to *go out as missionaries* and *preach this doctrine* of the Universal Negro Improvement Association. Let all the world know that
this is the hour; this is the time *for our salvation*. Prayer alone will not
save us; sentiment alone will not save us. We have to work and work
and work *if we are to be saved* . . . the time is now to *preach the beatitude
of bread and butter*. I have contributed my bit to *preaching this doctrine*.[21]

The "doctrine" of the UNIA to which Garvey continually referred, and
which he here felicitously characterized as "the beatitude of bread and
butter," was a combination of faith in oneself, in one's race, and in God.
It included a political and an economic, as well as a specifically religious
program, though all were expressed in religious terminology. The most
widely touted element of Garvey's political program, for instance, was the
"Back to Africa" demand, which was most frequently described in terms
of the "Redemption of Africa." This theme has a venerable place in Black
American history,[22] and Garvey was by no means using the idea in ignorance of its past history.

Garvey's speeches and editorials were sermonic in style, containing
extensive use of Biblical references and religious imagery. Every address
was a call to commitment, determination, and sacrifice, with a not infre-
quent note of apocalypticism creeping in. Amy Jacques Garvey has
recorded in her biography of her husband that as a boy, young Marcus
learned his lessons in elocution by standing outside the opened windows
of churches in Kingston—churches in which the most outstanding
preachers of the day delivered their addresses.[23] Perhaps he learned more
than lessons in rhetoric while listening at those open windows.

Another example of the tendency of Garveyites to express political programs in a religious vocabulary is found in this excerpt from a revivalist-
style speech by the Reverend James W. H. Eason, who was the first
Chaplain-General of the UNIA, and later was named "Leader of American Negroes." Speaking on the topic, "The Significance of the Life
Pledge," he remarked,

A life pledge makes a man out and out, a man all round, who stands
four-square to every wind that blows. Play the man; the race demands
it. Africa expects every man to do his duty. Liberia is calling to you
for commercial development.

I want everyone in this building tonight to make a life pledge, come weal, come woe. I will count one in the uplift of my race; I will count one to glorify my God; I will count one to help put over the Liberian constructive loan. I will pledge my word, my money and my sacred honor to see to it that the Liberian constructive loan is a success, that the ideas of the provisional president may be advanced and spread abroad to the world.[24]

Such calls for "life pledges, " Garvey's "vision of a redeemed Africa," and his hope to "convert the world of Negroes" did not go unheeded. Indeed, numerous Garveyites have indicated that their decisions to join the UNIA were more than rhetorically analogous to a conversion experience. Some have provided descriptions of the process by which they were "grasped" and brought into the fold of Garvey's organization. One of these was William L. Sherrill, himself the son of a Methodist Episcopal minister in Hot Springs, Arkansas, who as early as 1922 accepted Garvey's call. Amy Jacques Garvey preserved the text of Sherrill's conversion experience as he recalled it many years after the event:

Here was I, a successful business man with a family, member of a church, a lodge, and fully insured to protect them. I did not have to join anything else. I subscribed to the anti-lynching campaign every time a Negro was lynched. I did not like to hear people talk about conditions of my people, as I had overcome many of them; let everybody else do likewise. I argued this way against the persuasion of friends.

One night on my way to a show, I saw a huge crowd outside a church. I went up and said, "What's going on in there?" A lady turned to me and said, "Man alive, don't you know that Marcus Garvey is in there talking? Yes, indeed, Garvey in person." "Shucks, " I said, "I may as well see what he looks like." I could not get near the windows, so I had to get a ticket for standing room only. I squeezed in, until I could get a good look at him; then suddenly he turned in my direction, and in a voice like thunder from Heaven he said, "Men and women, what are you here for? To live unto yourself, until your body manures the earth, or to live God's Purpose to the fullest?" He continued to complete his thought in that compelling, yet pleading voice for nearly an hour. I stood there like one in a trance, every sentence ringing in my ears, and finding an echo in my heart. When I walked out of that church, I was a different man—I knew my sacred obligations to my Creator, and my responsibilities to my fellow men, and so help me! I am still on the Garvey train.[25]

It was not only the magnetism of Garvey's personality that was capable of eliciting such total commitment to the movement. Richard Hilton Tobitt, for instance, an African Methodist Episcopal clergyman in Bermuda, felt the call of the UNIA when reading the *Negro World*. As he observed in a biographical essay some years later,

> It was while giving a public lecture in St. Paul's A.M.E. Church, Hamilton City, Bermuda, on the subject, "Is Education Necessary to the Negro?" that a copy of "The Negro World" was placed in my hands for the first time. . . . Having carefully analyzed the program of the UNIA as set forth by its founder, Marcus Garvey, and believing in the integrity of the man and the righteousness of the course he espoused, I caught his vision and became a ready disciple of Garveyism, which I discovered was the "Master Key" . . . to the correct solution of the vexed race problem of the world and a sane and practical exposition of true religion. Without delay, I set to work to organize the Bermuda Division of the UNIA . . . and "left the court of Pharaoh, choosing rather to suffer affliction with my people than to dwell in the land of Goshen."[26]

Such conversions often came at a high price. Tobitt, for instance, in his reference to the "Court of Pharaoh" was no doubt alluding to his disbarment from the ministry of the AME Church in Bermuda as a consequence of having joined the UNIA. In addition, government funds for the school over which he presided were withdrawn, the governor of the island declaring that Tobitt had clearly demonstrated by his action that he was "no longer a fit person to be entrusted with the education of children."[27]

Religious vocabulary was consistently used by Garveyites in their Sunday evening speeches in Liberty Hall. A typical headline in the *Negro World* for February 26, 1921, quoted William Ferris, who "Says Gospel Message of UNIA Has Swept Over the World Like a Tidal Wave, Giving Hope and Inspiration to the Negro Everywhere."[28] One A. S. Gray spoke to an audience in Oakland, California, on the "Righteousness of the UNIA."[29] Marcus Garvey called upon his followers to "act as living missionaries to convince others,"[30] and on another occasion referred to the UNIA as "the great ark of safety."[31] Such language persisted in the pages of the *Negro World* to the paper's very last issue. In an editorial by Mme.

M.L.T. De Mena, published in that issue on October 17, 1933, the paper's editor described "Garveyism as the guiding star of Ethiopia's restoration."

> The Sacred few, the noble few, the gallant few, who . . . from a burning heart and languishing soul . . . felt the true zealousness and sublimity of race consciousness, the fundamentality of nationhood, the infancy of a great commonwealth, operated and goevrned [*sic*] by Negroes in yonder fragrant Africa's sunny fields; yea a modern heaven and refuge, a substantial environment, a solace wherein all Negro generations will be called blessed. This is our abiding faith, the eternal creed, the renovated religion, that now appeals and aches within the breast of our hundred million Negroes under the ethics of the Universal Negro Improvement Association.[32]

The *Negro World* itself was referred to as the "Testament of the UNIA" because, according to one official, it "has been the greatest missionary in building up divisions and making converts to the cause outside of New York City."[33] Indeed, one could go so far as to say that the *Negro World* began to take on the quality of a sacred text. As earlier noted, part of the ritual of each Sunday evening program in the local "Liberty Halls" outside of New York City consisted in reading aloud the lead editorial which comprised the entire front page of each issue of the paper. The public reading of this editorial gave Garvey regular access to all UNIA members and insured that all would receive inspiration and information directly from their leader.[34]

Chaplains in the UNIA

The religious ethos of UNIA meetings, which was set by the formal structure of the regular programs and by the language used by its officials, was further reinforced by the presence of chaplains at both local and national levels. Each chapter or division was required by the UNIA constitution to select a chaplain, whose duty it was to attend to the spiritual concerns of the members. All chaplains were under the direction of the Chaplain-General, who was a member of the High Executive Council, the UNIA's ruling body.

By far the most able of the Chaplains-General was West Indian–born George Alexander McGuire, who was elected to the post at the first annual International Convention of the Negro Peoples of the World in August 1920. Under his leadership, the religio-political nationalism which was present in the UNIA from its earliest days was made ever more explicit and pervasive. One of his first deeds as Chaplain-General, for instance, was to compile the *Universal Negro Ritual*, published in 1921. The *Ritual* was modeled after the Book of Common Prayer on which McGuire was raised as a member of the Church of England and which he later used as a priest in the Protestant Episcopal Church.

All chaplains were obliged to follow and all members were encouraged to acquire and study the *Ritual*, which prescribed the standard order of service to be followed in UNIA meetings. The standard format, exemplified in the three services described earlier, opened with the hymn "From Greenland's Icy Mountains" and with one or more of the special prayers which McGuire compiled. These were to be followed by singing of either "O Africa Awaken" or "Shine on Eternal Light" (both hymns especially composed for the UNIA), prior to presentation of the featured events of the program. "These preliminaries," it was remarked on one occasion, "lend a religious air to the meeting, and the audience responds and participates with a fervor and zeal that is highly commendable."[35] The meeting closed with additional prayers and the African National Anthem.[36] As will be detailed in a later chapter, in addition to standardizing the order by which meetings were to proceed, McGuire included in the *Ritual* a baptism and a burial service for UNIA members. On occasion, marriages also took place under Association auspices. Clearly, in McGuire's conception, the UNIA was an all-embracing institution ministering to the spiritual needs of its members from the cradle to the grave.

Under McGuire's leadership the role of the chaplains was broadened and clarified, and efforts were made to upgrade the standards required of those who sought the post. At the time of his election as Chaplain-General, McGuire was able to effectuate changes in the UNIA constitution in order to accomplish these goals. One such revision concerned Section 63 of the Book of Laws, which henceforth required that all chaplains of local divisions or chapters "must be ordained ministers or have their first license."[37] The implementation of this section presumed, of course, the membership of at least one ordained clergyman in every UNIA division in the country as well as the willingness of each division to grant a significant leadership role to that person. McGuire may have encountered some resistance to this rule, as is suggested by the following notice made in the "Chaplain-General's Department" column in the *Negro World:*

The Chaplain-General hereby announces that in accordance with Section 63 that [*sic*] no Chaplains in the various Divisions will be recognized as qualified for such office unless they meet the requirements as laid down. Evidence must be sent to this office of the ordination of Chaplains to the ministry, or credentials of license as lay-readers or local preachers. *There can be no excuse for lack of qualification as His Grace the Chaplain-General is ready to issue a license to any layman who can pass a fair and reasonable examination in English and religious knowledge.*[38]

Opposition to the ordination requirement apparently persisted, and in the 1922 revision of the General Laws, the relevant section was made simply to read, "All Chaplains of the UNIA and ACL shall be intelligent persons versed in reading and interpretation of the Universal Ritual and the Scriptures."[39]

Another constitutional revision which McGuire discussed in the *Negro World*, and which required action by local UNIA chaplains, concerned the necessity of creating youth organizations in each UNIA division. The relevant section of the General Laws required "That in every Division of the UNIA, a juvenile branch be formed *and only teachings of spiritual and racial uplift be taught.*"[40] The Rules and Regulations for Juveniles, which were published as part of the *Constitution and Book of Laws*, indicate the type of training envisioned for children of UNIA members. A variety of classes were to be formed. The Infant Class included all children, ages one to seven, and they were to be taught the following:

Bible Class and Prayer. Doctrine of the UNIA and ACL. Facts about the Black Star Line Steamship Corporation, the Negro Factories Corporation, and History of Africa (in story book fashion).[41]

Children aged seven to thirteen composed the Number Two Class, and they were divided by sex for their program. For the girls this included:

Taught to make Souvenirs with cloth, needle and thread, for sale for Juvenile Department. Ritual of Universal Negro Improvement Association. Write Negro stories, taught Race pride and love. Taught Negro history and Etiquette and be given disciplinary training by the Legions.[42]

Boys received the same training, except that they were to make souvenirs from wood rather than by needle and thread.

The "Cadets" class consisted of youths aged thirteen to sixteen, who were required to study the *Ritual*, military training, flag signals, and

Negro history. Books specifically recommended for study included J. A. Rogers's *From Superman to Man*, Sydney H. Olivier's *White Capital and Colored Labor*, Hubert H. Harrison's *When Africa Awakes*, and the book *African Lure and Lyrics*. It was specified that the class was to be taught by a member of the Universal African Legions "who is acquainted with military tactics."[43]

Finally there was a Preparatory Nursing Class under the direction of the Black Cross Nurses, for girls aged fourteen to eighteen. Their responsibilities included: "Making uniforms for Juveniles; Negro History; Etiquette; Talk on latest topics of the day; Elementary Principles of Economy; Negro Story Writing; Hygiene and Domestic Science."[44]

A Lady Vice-President was placed in charge as superintendent of the Juvenile Department, and teachers were to be appointed by the division president. There is no indication as to how often classes were expected to meet, though it seems clear that the intent was to supplement rather than to replace the public education system. Coming out of the tradition of the Protestant Episcopal Church, in which confirmation classes and catechetical training were long established, McGuire was aware of the importance of providing a mechanism whereby Negro youths could regularly and from an early age be taught the spiritual and racial values of the organization. In all cases it was the responsibility of the chaplains to provide religious training for juveniles. Not surprisingly, on completion of the *Universal Negro Ritual* McGuire turned to the task of devising a *Universal Negro Catechism* for use in the juvenile branches to assist in this task.

Finally, in one of his columns in the *Negro World* for the "Chaplain-General's Department," McGuire set forth the model of chaplaincy to which he hoped all would aspire, and listed the duties of the office as he perceived them. They were:

a. To conduct Divine Service according to the Universal Negro Ritual on Sunday mornings or afternoons where it is the desire of the members of the Division to have such Sunday service.

b. To conduct the Ritual as prescribed in the Ritual Book in connection with Mass Meetings or Members' Meetings.

c. To instruct the members of the Juvenile Branch in his Division in the knowledge supplied in the Universal Negro Catechism.

d. To see that every member of his Division purchase the Universal Negro Ritual and the Universal Negro Catechism.

e. To visit the sick and afflicted members of his Division and report to the proper officers any case needing charity.

f. To govern his own life and conversation in such manner as may prove him worthy to be a moral and spiritual guide to his fellow members.[45]

In brief, McGuire hoped that the chaplains would function as spiritual leaders to members, inculcators of racial and moral values for the young, counselors and comforters to the sick and needy, and models of the moral and righteous life for the entire community. Their presence in each local chapter or division was meant to insure that the religious ethos established as normative by the national organization would be carefully followed in every UNIA gathering across the country.

Garveyite Regalia and the Paraphernalia of Nationhood

We have thus far examined the rituals, both implicitly and explicitly religious, to be found in meetings of the UNIA; described the language, drawn primarily from the religious realm, by which its programs were presented; and observed the role of the "religious virtuosi" (to borrow a term from Max Weber) who were specially designated to inculcate the values and norms of the Association. What remains to be noted, in this essentially descriptive discussion concerning the religious ethos of the Garvey movement, is the multitude of religio-political symbols of nationhood by which the UNIA fostered the idea of peoplehood and self-identity.

Nationhood was the perdurable motif around which much of the activity in the UNIA revolved. The constitution, first adopted in 1918 and amended in succeeding years, set forth the constituent elements of the nationhood motif in systematic fashion. The list of officers, for instance, included a President-General who was at the same time Provisional President of Africa (the chief administrative position, which Garvey held himself). Assistant Presidents-General also held the titles of "Titular Leader of American Negroes" or "Titular Leader of the West Indies, South and Central America." There were appointed Ministers of African Legions, of Education, and of Labor and Industries, as well as Ministers Plenipotentiary, who were designated as ambassadors "to all regular governments" and to the League of Nations.[46] In addition to enumerating these titles of officials modeled after that of a national government, the constitution also authorized a variety of agencies to perform quasi-governmental tasks. These included a Civil Service, which gave regular exams and offered limited positions to be filled by UNIA members in good standing; a Passports Bureau, which issued passports to facilitate travel of members from one branch to another; and a Bureau of Justice, to insure the rights of Negroes wherever they might reside throughout the world. Even taxes were levied: In addition to the one-dollar annual membership tax, there was a ten-cent-per-month levy as a "death tax," in exchange for which members were to receive free burial by the Association.[47]

Garvey took care to integrate religious imagery into his conceptualization of the "new nationality." The official motto of the UNIA was "One God! One Aim! One Destiny!" The motto was to be found emblazoned on the official banner, on UNIA stationery, and on the letterhead of the *Negro World*, and it was repeated at every meeting of the Association. The notion of a unified religious faith for all Black persons implied by the words "One God" was a perennial topic for discussion at International Conventions and was a theme to which Garvey frequently returned in his speeches. The official slogan, "Pro Deo, Pro Africa, Pro Justitia," was less widely used than the motto, although it also contained a God referent.

On the official letterhead of UNIA stationery was also printed the Biblical injunction from Acts 18:26, "He created of one blood all nations of man to dwell upon the face of the earth." To be sure, Garveyites were unabashed in proclaiming the goals of their organization as being the uplift of one particular racial group, but this was always presented in the context of a demand for respect of the rights of all mankind and a commitment finally to the brotherhood of man and the Fatherhood of God.

The most frequently cited Biblical passage by far, and the one which most often served as a text for sermon topics in Liberty Halls around the country, was the one from Psalms 68:31, "Princes shall come forth from Egypt; Ethiopia shall soon stretch forth her hand to God." This Biblical prophecy has been cited by Black churchmen in America at least since the eighteenth century, to specify God's special concern for men of African descent.[48] The concern for Africa that was so central to the UNIA, and the conviction that God was working in history through the instrumentality of the UNIA to create a nation, Africa, as a part of His larger purposes, rendered this verse from the Psalms uniquely appropriate to the Garvey movement. The meaning of the passage, as understood by Garveyites, was explicated in the *Universal Negro Catechism*:

Q. What prediction made in the 68th Psalm and the 31st verse is now being fulfilled?

A. "Princes shall come out of Egypt, Ethiopia shall soon stretch forth her hands unto God."

Q. What does this verse prove?

A. That Negroes will set up their own government in Africa, with rulers of their own race.[49]

Here was Biblical warrant and ultimate grounding for the Association's political program, and irrefragable evidence that the UNIA's work was indeed of God.

The Psalmist's prophecy concerning Ethiopia was also incorporated in the "Universal Ethiopian Anthem," another basic element in the UNIA's paraphernalia of nationhood. Written by Ben Burrell and UNIA Choirmaster Arnold J. Ford, it again illustrates the mixture of religious and political elements which was so characteristic of Garveyite rituals and symbols. The text of the hymn, which was officially adopted as the anthem "of the Negro race," is as follows:

> Ethiopia, thou land of our fathers,
> Thou land where the gods loved to be,
> As storm cloud at night sudden gathers
> Our armies come rushing to thee.
> We must in the fight be victorious,
> When swords are thrust outward to glean;
> For us will the Vict'ry be glorious
> When led by the red, black and green
>
> Chorus
>
> Advance, advance to victory!
> Let Africa be free!
> Advance to meet the foe
> With the might
> Of the red, the black, and the green.
>
> Ethiopia, the tyrant's falling
> Who smote thee upon thy knees;
> And thy children are lustily calling
> From over the distant seas.
> Jehovah the Great One has heard us,
> Has noted our sighs and our tears,
> With His spirit of love He has stirred us
> To be one through the coming years.

Chorus

O Jehovah, Thou God of the ages,
Grant unto our sons that lead
The wisdom Thou gav'st to Thy sages
When Israel was sore in need.
Thy voice thro' the dim past has spoken,
Ethiopia shall stretch forth her hand,
By Thee shall all fetters be broken
And Heav'n bless our dear Motherland.[50]

In sharp contrast to the much more familiar "Negro National Hymn," written by James Weldon Johnson some twenty years earlier, Ford's anthem was a call for military preparedness in anticipation of an inevitable conflagration which would be demanded before God's promise of freedom could be realized. Johnson's hymn, "Lift Every Voice and Sing," had breathed an air of determined hopefulness reflective of faith in the "harmonies of Liberty" which were working gradually but certainly toward a victory that was all but won. The God of whom Johnson had spoken was a benevolent if stern God, who has guided and is guiding the destiny of Black people to justice and to their promised land, to "the place for which our fathers sighed," which for Johnson was surely not Africa, but a just and truly democratic United States of America.[51] For Ford, however, it was Ethiopia which was the object of the people's affection, and it was the God of retribution, Jehovah, who would insure that just as He had long ago led His people, Israel, to freedom, so now would He work through the instrument of the Universal Negro Improvement Association to achieve the redemption of His people and of their homeland, Africa.

It should be evident from the foregoing that the religious ethos of the UNIA was pervasive, embracing nearly every facet of its organizational life. The religious elements we have described were not isolated or random occurrences, but are to be found everywhere one looks within the movement. And just as recent students of religion in America have insisted that the God-references, the ceremonial and the religious symbols of nationhood developed over the past two hundred years of this nation's existence cannot simply be dismissed as insignificant "ritualistic" expressions, but are "indicative of deep-seated values and commitments"[52] worthy of careful examination, so can it be argued that the rituals and symbols developed by the Universal Negro Improvement Association are constitutive of a coherent way of viewing the world which deserves to be taken seriously.

Notes

1. Claude McKay, "Garvey as a Negro Moses," *Liberator* 5 (April 1922), p. 8. In his autobiography *A Long Way*, pp. 55, 67, 87, McKay reports it was on the urging of his good friend, Hubert H. Harrison, that he started sending articles to Garvey's paper from Europe. Harrison was at the time an active Garvey supporter and columnist/editor for the *Negro World*.
2. Bedward had specified December 31, 1920, as the date of his ascension. On Bedward, see Leonard E. Barrett, *The Rastafarians: A Study in Messianic Cultism in Jamaica* (Rio Piedras, Puerto Rico, 1968), pp. 55–57; Martha Warren Beckwith, "Some Religious Cults in Jamaica," *American Journal of Psychology* 34 (1923), 32–45, esp. pp. 40–45; and Roscoe M. Pierson, "Alexander Bedward and the Jamaica Native Baptist Free Church," in Randall K. Burkett and Richard Newman, eds., *Black Apostles: Afro-American Clergy Confront the Twentieth Century* (Boston, 1978).
3. McKay, "Garvey as a Negro Moses," p. 8. McKay does temper his judgment of Garvey by remarking on the UNIA leader's "energetic and quick-witted mind." As McKay goes on in the article to make clear, the real basis of his objection to Garvey was the latter's persistent anti-union and anti-socialist economic program.
4. E. Franklin Frazier, "Garvey: A Mass Leader," *Nation* 123 (August 18, 1926), p. 148.
5. Ibid.
6. Ibid.
7. The *Negro World* reply to McKay is found in *NW* 12:16 (June 3, 1922), p. 12. Frazier's article was reprinted in *NW* 21:2 (August 21, 1926), p. 5, with an editorial reply in *NW* 21:3 (August 28, 1926), p. 4.
8. James Weldon Johnson, *Black Manhattan*, p. 255.
9. For a discussion of James W. Johnson's attitude towards religion generally, see the comments by Benjamin E. Mays in his book *The Negro's God as Reflected in His Literature* (New York, 1969), pp. 234–36. Frazier's negative assessment of the religion of the Negro, which he said has "cast a shadow over the entire intellectual life of Negroes and has been responsible for the so-called backwardness of American Negroes," was summarized in his influential essay *The Negro Church in America* (New York, 1963), p. 86. Stanford M. Lyman, in his recent study *The Black American in Sociological Thought* (New York, 1972), places Frazier's critique of the Negro church in the context of his sociological framework developed out of the Chicago school of sociology under the tutelage of Robert E. Park. See especially his discussion in ch. 2, pp. 55–67.
10. A similar association is made by August Meier in his *Negro Thought in America: 1880–1915* (Ann Arbor, 1966), where he concludes that "The escapist Utopian character of the Garvey movement as a response to economic deprivation is revealed in the fact that a large number of ex-Garveyites joined the Father Divine movement during the depression of the 1930s," p. 315, n. 39. Interpreters more sympathetic to Garvey have also been chary of calling attention to the religious elements for fear of lending credence to the earlier associated notion that Garveyism was simply "an oversized sect or cult, an escapist pseudo-religion of which Garvey was God while many of his followers

were only a cut above fools." Theodore G. Vincent, *Black Power and the Garvey Movement*, p. 1, *et passim*, is typical in this respect.

11. The text of the speech delivered by Marcus Garvey on this occasion is printed in *Philosophy and Opinions of Marcus Garvey* (henceforth *P&O*), ed. Amy Jacques Garvey (New York, 1969), II, 118–123. A copy of the evening program guide is preserved in Vol. 32 of the "Alexander Gumby Collection on the American Negro," housed in the Department of Special Collections, Columbia University. See also the account in the *New York Times*, March 17, 1924, p. 2.

12. For a more detailed discussion of Garvey's use of hymn, see chapter 3 of Randall Burkett, *The Religious Ethos of the UNIA*.

13. Amy Jacques Garvey, writing in her biographical study *Garvey and Garveyism* (London, 1970), observed concerning the place of music in the UNIA, "Our people love to sing; it is said they sang their way out of slavery, through their spirituals, which expressed their sorrow, and their firm belief that God was leading them, as He had led the children of Israel through the Wilderness, and Daniel out of the lion's den. So Garvey outlined a set of meaningful hymns, and [Ben] Burrell and [Arnold J.] Ford of the music department put them into proper verse and set them to music" (p. 47). Most of these hymns were published in Ford's *Universal Ethiopian Hymnal*, which is discussed below.

14. Garvey always insisted that the UNIA was not a subversive organization intent on the overthrow of the United States government, and inclusion in the program of "The Star Spangled Banner" was meant to underscore this point.

15. *NW* 10:22 (July 16, 1921), p. 1.

16. Ibid.

17. Pittsburgh *Courier*, May 31, 1924, p. 13.

18. *NW* 14:2 (February 24, 1923), p. 7.

19. Gayraud S. Wilmore's characterization of the Black church as "the NAACP on its knees" might thus just as accurately be applied to the UNIA during the early 1920s. See his *Black Religion and Black Radicalism* (Garden City, 1972), p. 197. The practice of allowing protest organizations to utilize facilities of Black churches as a forum for debate and a base of operations has a long history, extending from the anti-slavery period to the present day.

20. On occasion, when a minister was won over to the UNIA, his entire congregation would join the Association. See for example the statement of one R. H. Cosgrove of Natchez, Mississippi, who reported at an International Convention of the UNIA that "he pastored a little church of about 500 members, and everyone was a member of the association, as he was of the opinion that if he was to be a spiritual leader he should also be able to lead them in their temporal affairs. He attended the convention to see things for himself so that he could take back to the people who trusted him a true report of the work of the movement." *NW* 17:1 (August 18, 1924), p. 2.

21. *NW* 10:2 (February 19, 1921), p. 4. Emphasis added.

22. See St. Clair Drake, *The Redemption of Africa and Black Religion* (Chicago, 1970).

23. Amy Jacques Garvey, *Garvey and Garveyism*, p. 5.

24. *NW* 9:12 (November 6, 1920), p. 8. On Eason, see my *Black Redemption: Churchmen Speak for the Garvey Movement* (Philadelphia, 1978), chapter 3.

25. Amy Jacques Garvey, *Garvey and Garveyism*, p. 266. See also the biographical sketch of Sherrill in *NW* 15:5 (September 15, 1923), p. 4, and George Alexander McGuire's remarks in introducing Sherrill at the Fourth International Convention, *NW* 13:3 (September 2, 1922), p. 12.

26. *NW* 15:10 (October 20, 1923), p. 10.
27. Reported by William F. Elkins in "Marcus Garvey, the *Negro World*, and the British West Indies: 1919–1920," *Science and Society* 36 (Spring 1972), p. 71. All was not loss for Tobitt, however, for his conversion opened new horizons for the expression of his social and religious conscience. He was one of the signers of the famous "Declaration of Rights of the Negro Peoples of the World" in 1920, and was elected leader of the Eastern Province of the West Indies. He subsequently held numerous posts within the UNIA.
28. *NW* 10:2 (February 26, 1921), p. 3.
29. *NW* 13:18 (December 18, 1922), p. 8.
30. *NW* 10:2 (February 26, 1921), p. 4.
31. *NW* 30:22 (December 26, 1931), p. 1.
32. "Are We Discouraged?" *NW* 32:11 (October 17, 1933), p. 4.
33. *NW* 10:7 (April 2, 1921), p. 3. The speaker was George Alexander McGuire.
34. The point should not be pushed too far, however, so as to suggest that the *Negro World* literally replaced the Bible as the sacred text for UNIA members. An instructive comparison is available in the pattern followed in the Father Divine Peace Mission Movement, where, according to Arthur Huff Fauset, "The sacred text . . . is not the Bible, but the *New Day*, a weekly periodical issued by the organization. Followers invariably refer to this book [*sic*] rather than to the Bible when they wish to speak with authority." *Black Gods of the Metropolis* (Philadelphia, 1944), p. 60. Divine, who gained prominence in Harlem in the years shortly after the decline of the Garvey movement, appears here to have radicalized an idea found in more moderate form in the UNIA. Similarly, Divine seems to have taken to an extreme other journalistic ideas originated by Garvey: whereas the *Negro World* published verbatim texts of many speeches delivered at Liberty Hall and most of the speeches delivered elsewhere by Garvey, the *New Day* published verbatim transcripts of practically every word uttered by Father Divine at his famous banquet meetings. And whereas the *Negro World* contained a regular Spanish column and (briefly) a French column, due to the circulation of the paper in Latin America and French-speaking Africa and the Caribbean, the *New Day* regularly carried translations of Divine's speeches in French, Spanish, German, and Russian. It is significant that when the *Negro World* at last folded, on October 17, 1933, with publication of Vol. 32, No. 11, its presses and remaining supplies were purchased by none other than Father Divine, who published as a predecessor to the *New Day* his *World (Peace) Echo*. At least the first fifteen issues continued to number their papers with a dual system: Old Series, Vol. 32, No. 12 (following the *Negro World* numbering); New Series, Vol. 1, No. 1; etc. A careful study of the relationship between these two historically contiguous movements should be undertaken.
35. *NW* 8:18 (June 5, 1920), p. 2.
36. The text of the anthem is printed below.
37. *NW* 10:7 (April 2, 1921), p. 7.
38. Ibid. Emphasis added.
39. *Constitution and Book of Laws Made for the Government of the Universal Negro Improvement Association, Inc., and African Communities League, Inc., of the World* (New York, July 1918; Revised and amended August 1922). General Laws, Sec. 62, p. 57. Coincidentally or not, McGuire by this time had been ousted from the UNIA.

40. *NW* 10:7 (April 2, 1921), p. 7. Emphasis added. See also Sec. 61 of the revised 1922 edition of the *Constitution and Book of Laws*, p. 57.
41. Ibid., p. 85.
42. Ibid.
43. Ibid., p. 86.
44. Ibid.
45. *NW* 10:7 (April 2, 1921), p. 7.
46. *Constitution and Book of Laws*, p. 56.
47. Vincent, *Black Power*, p. 167, lists these and other of the "trappings of nationhood" fostered by the UNIA.
48. Absalom Jones and Richard Allen, in their brief encomium to whites who were working to improve the condition of slaves in the United States, concluded with the words, "May he, who hath arisen to plead our cause, and engaged you as volunteers in the service, add to your numbers until the princes shall come forth from Egypt, and Ethiopia stretch out her hand unto God." *A Narrative of the Proceedings of the Black People, During the Late Awful Calamity in Philadelphia, in the Year, 1793*, in Dorothy Porter, ed., *Negro Protest Pamphlets* (New York, 1969), p. 23. This is the first written evidence I have been able to discover concerning the use of this passage by Black churchmen.
49. The *Universal Negro Catechism*, written by George Alexander McGuire in 1921, is discussed elsewhere. The passage is quoted from p. 11.
50. The text of the Anthem may be found in *P&O*, II, pp. 140–41. The militancy evidenced by the anthem is typical both of the general mood of Harlem in the post-War period and also of the aggressiveness which especially in its earliest period was characteristic of Garveyite rhetoric. The circumstances of its writing are themselves indicative of the incidents which all too often were perpetrated on Black Americans and which they were increasingly unwilling to accept without resistance or retaliation. According to an article in the *Negro World*, the hymn was occasioned by the brutal slaying in 1919 of a young woman who had been working as a housemaid in New York City. The girl, aged 17, had been raped by the head of the household where she worked. When she reported to her mistress that she was pregnant as a result of the attack, the woman, a "Negro hater, " became enraged and threw her out of the house. Soon thereafter, according to the article, "she was found dead, her body horribly mutilated." William A. Stephenson, "The Universal Ethiopian Anthem and How It Came to Be Written," *NW* 15:2 (August 25, 1923), p. 2.
51. In his autobiography *Along This Way* (New York, 1961), pp. 154–56, Johnson described the circumstances of the song's composition, the score for which was composed by his brother J. Rosamond Johnson. The second stanza of "Lift Every Voice" seems to make clear that it is the new home in America which is the Negro's rightful heritage, as a result of his centuries of struggle here.
52. Bellah, "Civil Religion in America," p. 333.

Chapter 23

Marcus Garvey, Father Divine, and the Gender Politics of Race Difference and Race Neutrality

Beryl Satter

C. D. Austin's 1936 letter to Marcus Garvey was not the adoring missive Garvey might have expected. After briefly recounting his years of committed support for Garvey and the Universal Negro Improvement Association (UNIA), Austin came to his main point: that Father Divine was God and that Garvey would do well to recognize this fact. "'Garvey-ism' was the highest grace this so-called race had. . . . But to-day a greater than Garvey is here. [Y]ou were regarded as the world's most fearless leader in this present civilization before the coming of FATHER DIVINE. . . . Please try HIM out as 23,000,000 of us did, you need HIM as all the World does," Austin exhorted.

Garvey was not about to turn to Father Divine as his personal savior. Instead, Garvey pushed through a lengthy resolution at the UNIA's 1936 convention that condemned Father Divine in no uncertain terms. Father Divine's claim to be God was "blasphemy of the worst kind." Divine was a common swindler and under the control of scheming whites. Most seriously, Garvey accused Divine of "race suicide." According to the UNIA resolution, Divinites "separate themselves sexually from the bond of matrimony" and cease to "reproduce the species of the race by having children." Such a policy, the resolution declared, would lead to the "complete extermination of the Negro race in the United States in one generation. . . ."[1]

Garvey was right to focus on race suicide in this resolution, since the valuation of racial identity was one of the key differences that separated Garvey's movement from Divine's. Marcus Garvey was the Jamaican-born head of the UNIA, an organization that reached its peak of strength in the early 1920s and whose organizing principle could be summarized in the slogan "Race First." A faith in the importance of racial solidarity under-

lay the three goals of Garvey's UNIA: to arouse a unified race consciousness in all peoples of African descent, whether living in the United States,
the West Indies, or Africa; to strengthen this united black race by organizing black-owned and managed, large-scale business enterprises and
shipping lines; and finally, to create a black-governed nation in Africa that
would host the creation of a renewed black civilization and stand up for
the rights of black people everywhere.[2]

Father Divine, born George Baker, was an African American of obscure
origin who founded the most notorious new religion of Depression-
era America—the Harlem-based Peace Mission movement. If Garvey's
UNIA was premised on "Race First" and faith in national destiny, then
Divine's Peace Mission was premised on a belief in race neutrality and
faith in Father Divine as God. Father Divine was most well-known for his
ability, during the height of the Great Depression, to feed thousands daily
at his free, fifty-course Peace Mission banquets. The Peace Mission program was more clearly enacted, however, in the scores of racially integrated, sexually segregated, and celibate communes formed by Divinites
in the 1930s. Within these communes, which Peace Mission members
called "heavens," Divinites refused to recognize race, arguably the key
social division of modern America. In a dramatic reversal of the racial segregation characteristic of the larger society, black and white Divinites
worked and lived together in heavens, took care to mix the seating at Divinite banquets so as to alternate black and white diners, and refused to
acknowledge verbally the existence of racial difference.[3]

Why was Marcus Garvey so enraged over Divine's success, and what
role did the two men's contrasting views of race and sexuality play in this
feud? When discussing the tension between Garvey and Divine, scholars
of the UNIA and the Peace Mission point to the fact that large numbers
of Garveyites were among the thousands[4] joining Divine's Peace Mission.
Historians explain this crossover membership, and Garvey's extreme reaction to it, in terms of broad similarities between the UNIA and the Peace
Mission. Both movements centered around a charismatic leader, provided
concrete benefits to their members, promoted economic enterprise, and
encouraged political action. Although Garvey denounced as blasphemy
Divine's claims to be God, Garvey's own self-presentation as a "Black
Moses" and his suggestion that blacks think of God as dark skinned may
have eased the way for some black Americans to accept Father Divine as
God. Finally, Garvey and Divine's shared interest in New Thought, a popular early twentieth-century religious ideology that claimed one's thoughts
could literally create one's material reality, may also have facilitated the

transition for those who shifted allegiances from Garvey to Divine in the mid-1930s.[5]

I would argue, however, that one cannot fully understand either the internal trajectories of the two movements or the relationships between them unless the gender politics of the two organizations are carefully examined. The need for a gender analysis is clearly suggested by the specific histories, constituencies and ideologies of the Peace Mission and the UNIA. For example, according to both contemporary and scholarly accounts, anywhere from 75 to 90 percent of Divine's followers were African American women.[6] This predominance of women suggests that the Peace Mission should be analyzed as a black women's movement and its gender politics given particular attention. In contrast, although some women held high-ranking positions, Garvey's UNIA appears to have been a predominantly male organization. Yet the very intensity of the UNIA's masculinist cast—represented in everything from its official hierarchy, which placed UNIA women's organizations under the command of male presidents, to UNIA ritual, in which black men marched in costumes of warriors, judges, and kings—suggests that a particular gender vision was at the heart of UNIA politics.[7]

In the following pages I therefore examine the gender politics of the UNIA and the Peace Mission movement. I focus particularly on the connections between the racial ideologies of the UNIA and the Peace Mission, on the one hand, and the gender ideologies, gender organizations, and experience of women within the two movements, on the other. I argue that the opposing gender politics of the two movements can help illuminate the crossover in membership between the UNIA and the Peace Mission and, more importantly, can contribute to an understanding of the relationship between racial ideologies and the choices historically available to African American women.

Scholars of Marcus Garvey and Father Divine have not analyzed the relationship between these men's racial ideologies and the roles available to their female followers. Some scholarship has explored the history of women in the two movements and (to a lesser extent) the gender politics of the two movements. While Garvey scholars agree that UNIA publications promoted public roles for men and private roles for women, more recent scholarship has added complexity to the image of a sexist UNIA. Barbara Bair points out that the UNIA's calls for active, public roles for men and passive, private roles for women overturned white images of black men as feminine and black women as masculine and challenged the white double standard, which held that white women should be sheltered in the home while black women worked. Ula Taylor suggests that the UNIA emphasis on black women as men's helpmates did not imply that black women could not also be leaders. On the contrary, she argues that black women, who have historically viewed white racism rather than black men as their oppressor, have a long tradition of both supporting their husbands (and families) and assuming community leadership roles. Finally, UNIA scholars agree that despite the official paeans to black women as wives and mothers, the UNIA in fact offered women a wide variety of participatory roles and was one of the few organizations offering leadership positions to black women in the 1920s.[8]

Unlike Garvey's UNIA, Father Divine's Peace Mission movement was a predominantly female organization. However, no scholar of the Peace Mission has considered the overwhelming numerical predominance of black women in the movement as a sign that the Peace Mission should be analyzed primarily as a black women's movement. Instead, many Peace Mission scholars have noted women's participation in the movement only to emphasize women's fanaticism, ignorance, or sensual longings for Father Divine.[9] Jill Watts, author of the most recent book on Father Divine, is one of the few scholars to discuss Divine's female followers without reducing their interest in Divine to sexual or psychological aberrations. Watts argues that the communal and celibate Peace Mission lifestyle freed women from isolated housekeeping, traditional gender roles, and the dangers of childbearing. Watts also interprets Divine's protectiveness toward his women followers (for example, his calling up a storm to punish a man who put his wife in a mental hospital) and his self-description as both mother and father to his flock as symbolic support for "women's rights."[10]

In sum, scholarship on the UNIA and the Peace Mission shows the appeal as well as the drawbacks these organizations held for their women members. This essay focuses more specifically on the connections between the racial ideologies of the two movements and the positions of women within them. By contrasting the gender politics of Garvey's Race First UNIA with those of the Peace Mission, a predominantly black movement that explicitly denied racial difference, this essay highlights the ways that ideologies of race shape the forms of activism available to women. More specifically, it addresses the following questions about the UNIA and the Peace Mission movement. What was the relationship between Garvey's Race First philosophy and the place of black women within the UNIA? Did the drastic situation faced by African Americans during the Great Depression threaten Garvey's vision of black womanhood? Why might some African American women have rejected the role of UNIA race mother for that of celibate, race-neutral Peace Mission angel? Was joining the Peace Mission simply a desperate and culturally suicidal abandonment of black racial identity, black culture, and black men? Or might the Peace Mission ideology of race and gender transcendence have enabled the creation of a new form of African American political culture, expressing the hopes of the most marginalized members of depression-era Harlem? What can the UNIA and the Peace Mission tell us about the relationship between ideas of race purity or race neutrality, on the one hand, and polarized gender oppositions, nationalism, and cultural identity, on the other?

Race and Gender in Garvey's UNIA

The contrasting gender politics of the Peace Mission and the UNIA derived most directly from their leaders' opposed understandings of the roles of black race purity and race pride in the struggle against white racism. As early as 1921, Marcus Garvey became committed to race purity as the factor distinguishing the UNIA from other black organizations. His insistence upon the importance of race purity led him to praise the race purity ideals of the Ku Klux Klan, to attack his African American opponents as "nearly all Octoroons or Quadroons," and even to suggest that lighter-skinned blacks be consciously bred out of the racial pool.[11]

As a number of scholars have observed, ideologies of race purity have, historically, led to male control of women's bodies. Southern white race purity codes, for example, entailed a double form of male control of women's bodies; relying on a gender ideology that depicted white women as pure and black women as animalistic, white race purity ideas justified both the sequestering of white women and white men's sexual terrorism against black women.[12] A race purity ideal functioned differently for the UNIA—an organization that expressed the hopes of a people struggling for dignity and self-determination—than it did for ruling whites, who used an ideology of race purity to ensure the continuation of their economic and political dominance. Garvey's brand of race purity contained none of the threats to white women that white race purity held for black women. His lauding of the beauty of dark skin was a necessary and even revolutionary counter to centuries of white maligning of the physical appearance of African Americans. In this context, Garvey's call for race unity among the dispersed peoples of African descent was a bold and politically astute effort to unite the dispossessed in a struggle for inde-

pendence, as well as a courageous attempt to politicize and interna-
tionalize the awakening of black race consciousness characteristic of
the 1920s.[13]

Garvey's emphasis on race consciousness and race purity inevitably
molded the UNIA's proscriptions about gender. For example, race purity
advocates generally value women primarily as mothers of the race. UNIA
leaders clearly voiced this perspective. As one Garveyite official wrote, if
"you find any woman—especially a black woman—who does not want to
be a mother, you may rest assured she is not a true woman."[14] To ensure
that women's offspring were of the proper race, black women needed to
be maintained in the same sort of protective isolation that white men
apparently secured for their women. As another UNIA official explained,
black men must

> throw our protecting arms around our women . . . let us go back to
> the days of true manhood when women truly reverenced us . . . let us
> again place our women upon the pedestal from which they have been
> forced. . . .[15]

The UNIA was thus committed not to promoting the dignity and power
of black women in general but to protecting black women from racial
defilement and regaining black women's reverence and respect for the
black man. Many black women supported such a policy of chivalrous protection as a welcome alternative to their position as exploited workers who
were vulnerable to sexual harassment by white employers.[16] This does
not, however, negate the fact that so-called protection of women by men
involves control as well as benevolence.

The cultural meaning of motherhood in African American communities often had a different resonance than it did for white middle-class
Americans, and it is important to note that a lauding of motherhood does
not necessarily connote a limitation of women's personal autonomy or
political power. Although black mothers, like white mothers, have long
shouldered the primary responsibility for child raising, among African
Americans this has less often meant intensive and isolated child rearing
and more often meant women's willingness to engage in extradomestic,
income-producing activities in order to fund their children's educations.
This broader, more public and political understanding of African American motherhood is reflected in the tradition of "community mothers"—
often elderly women who function as "role models, power brokers, and
venerable elders" in black communities—who are respected less for the

quality of their private mothering than for their activist role in holding together the broader community.[17]

In some ways, the UNIA Race Mother ideal seemed to draw upon the African American community motherhood tradition. The UNIA had a woman's page entitled "Our Women and What They Think," which was intended to give women a voice in the otherwise male-dominated journal of the UNIA, *Negro World*. Edited by Garvey's wife, Amy Jacques Garvey, some "Our Women" articles asserted that black women's responsibilities were "not limited" to homemaking and childcare, but included "tackling the problems that confront the race," including working with men "in the office as well as on the platform." These articles clearly implied a vision of motherhood that entailed community activism as well as private domesticity.[18]

In many respects, however, the UNIA race mother diverged significantly from the community mother concept. While the community mother depended for her effectiveness on a base of autonomous black women's organizations, political organizations for UNIA women were not autonomous. Although each of the local UNIA divisions had both a man and a woman president, the "lady president" had authority over the women's section, while the male president had authority over the local division as a whole. In addition, a hierarchical sexual division of labor existed within the UNIA; men ran the UNIA businesses and represented the movement as statesmen and diplomats, while women provided clerical, cultural and civic support services. This system discouraged the sort of informal but powerful leadership exerted by community mothers.[19]

Finally, it is clear that the term *motherhood* had a far more biological meaning for Garveyites than *community motherhood* had traditionally connoted in African American communities. (After all, the community-leading "mother" was often an elderly woman.) UNIA ideology implied that marriage and child-care held a special significance for Garveyite women. According to *Negro World* articles, while Garveyite men were to uplift the race through aggressive engagement in business and commerce, Garveyite women were literally to produce a "better and stronger race" through the quality of their childcare. *Negro World* columnists repeatedly heralded this more biological form of race-building as "the greatest privilege that can come to any woman in this age, and to the Negro woman in particular."[20]

The UNIA glorified black men as soldiers, leaders, and rulers. As Barbara Bair points out, Garvey's ritual and verbal imagery consistently invoked visions of black men as kings, emperors, and popes. Garvey called himself the Provisional President of Africa, conferred orders such as the

Knight Commander of the Nile on his most devoted followers, and created a special militia, the African Legion, whose full-dress military uniforms drew large audiences at UNIA parades. The Black Cross Nurses, a UNIA women's organization that provided health counseling and services to their communities, were also a regular feature of UNIA parades, and a group of women in military uniform marched in at least one UNIA parade. This female participation does not lessen the fact that the most dramatic spectacle at UNIA parades was the uniformed male Garveyites.[21] The UNIA's identification of black men as the epitome of black humanity became even more emphatic during the Depression; in 1934 a journal entitled *Black Man* succeeded the UNIA's journal *Negro World*.

The implications of the UNIA's emphasis on martial and leadership roles for men and race motherhood roles for women were mixed for Garveyite women. On the one hand, a few prominent women achieved positions of great responsibility and influence within the UNIA despite the movement's official sanctioning of public roles for men and private roles for women. Furthermore, numerous lesser-known women learned important organizational skills by actively participating behind the scenes.[22] On the other hand, Garveyite women who tried to follow the New Negro Woman model of both creating a perfect home life and actively serving the UNIA inevitably found themselves exhausted by the multiple demands on their lives.

Amy Jacques Garvey epitomized their situation. Garvey expected her to be the perfect wife, while also serving as his secretary, legal adviser, fund-raiser, editor, and full-time propagandist. Jacques Garvey fulfilled these multiple roles until the birth of her two children in 1930 and 1933. Their births occurred during a period when Garvey was travelling frequently, desperately strapped for money, and entirely preoccupied with reviving the UNIA. Receiving little financial or practical aid from Garvey, Jacques Garvey dropped her political work altogether in order to feed, shelter, and educate her children. Looking back over her years with Garvey and the UNIA, Jacques Garvey noted bitterly, "What did he ever give in return? The value of a wife to him was like a gold coin—expendable, to get what he wanted, and hard enough to withstand rough usage in the process."[23]

Amy Jacques Garvey's experience indicates that without considerable financial and practical support from the race father, the UNIA race mother was more likely to find herself isolated and exhausted than active and empowered. She might even begin to feel that irresponsible black men, as much as white racism, were her primary obstacles. For example, women in a Jamaican division of the UNIA complained that they were fighting the battle for race uplift alone. Angry at black men whom they called cowards for their abandonment of race and family responsibility, these women invited men to a women's meeting to remind them of their "duty towards the women of their race."[24] Maymie Leona Turpeau De Mena, a high-ranking UNIA member who later stunned Garvey by publishing the Divinite paper *World Echo*, complained in 1924 that although women formed "the backbone and sinew of the UNIA," they have been "given to understand that they must remain in their place."[25] Jacques Garvey herself wrote angry editorials in the mid-1920s in which she attacked black men for their "lack of appreciation for their noble women. . . ." She wrote, "We are tired of hearing Negro men say, 'there is a better day coming,' while they do nothing to usher in the day."[26]

By the mid-1920s, Garveyite women were not the only people with complaints about Garvey's leadership and organization. Despite its initial growth, the UNIA soon began to weaken as a result of organizational infighting, governmental harassment, and business fraud and naiveté. Garvey was eventually jailed for mail fraud in 1925, and deported to Jamaica in 1927.[27]

After Garvey's deportation the leaderless and bankrupt American branches of the UNIA gradually declined. Factional disputes within UNIA locals as well as Garvey's own growing political distance from the needs and concerns of American blacks were deeply damaging. Most detrimental of all to the UNIA, however, was the declining economic strength of black Americans. As early as 1927, private welfare agencies reported unusually high levels of suffering and unemployment in Harlem and other black communities, and conditions only became more difficult when the Depression reached the rest of the nation in the 1930s. In this context of severe economic stress, the UNIA's faith in business enterprise and its push to sell stock for its shipping line became increasingly irrelevant to the working- and lower-middle-class blacks who had formerly provided the backbone of the UNIA.[28]

The Depression also undercut the gender strategy of the UNIA, which called for black women to cede public roles to their men in order to devote themselves to their offspring and so strengthen the race. The Depression had a particularly devastating impact on black men. In the 1920s, certain low-wage, dead-end service jobs had been reserved for African American men, but by the 1930s even these positions became scarce as desperate whites crossed the color line to compete for porter and janitorial jobs. White men were willing to take occupations formerly filled by black men, but neither black nor white men would take menial women's work, even in the worst years of the Depression. This meant that black women, like white women, could sometimes find jobs more quickly than either black or white men. The jobs were usually temporary, required grueling labor, and paid well below the minimum needed to survive.[29] Nevertheless, the fact that Depression-era black women found jobs at slightly higher rates than black men meant that by the 1930s the gender strategy of the UNIA no longer offered a viable alternative for most black Americans.

The very forces that undercut Garvey aided Divine; it is surely not coincidental that 1927—the year of Garvey's deportation and the first year in which private welfare agencies documented real suffering in Harlem—marked the year when newspapers first reported the growing popularity of a previously obscure black preacher who called himself Father Divine.[30] What were the race and gender strategies of the Peace Mission? How did these strategies fit the situation of the middle-aged, working-class African American women who constituted the vast majority of Divine's followers?[31]

Father Divine's 1930s Peace Mission Movement

One can begin to answer these questions by looking at the Peace Mission's analysis of race. From Divine's millenarian perspective, both the concept of race purity and the very existence of racial division had been transcended. In contrast to Garvey's wish to ensure Negro purity, Divine insisted that the very term *Negro* was false because it referred to no historical reality.[32] Divine claimed that race was a social construction. He explained, "there is no so-called blood of some special race. Blood is blood, Spirit is Spirit, Mind is Mind!"[33] Divine preached the unified descent of all peoples from God. He told his followers to "recognize only the lineage from whence you really came"—that is, the heavenly lineage encompassing all peoples ready to transcend their human natures. To claim this transcendent ancestry, all Divinites took new angelic names, such as Faithful Love or Glorious Illumination, upon joining the Peace Mission movement. As Divine explained, "Angelic Names . . . mean the Angelic Nature. Name means nature."[34]

Divinites stressed the importance of angelic names in part because of Divine's New Thought belief that to name something was to shape it in thought and so to create it. Calling oneself by an angelic name was therefore equivalent to becoming reborn as an angel. This belief that to speak of a thing was to create it had special application to Divine's thinking about race and racial strategy. It led to a crusade by Divinites against the use of racial and ethnic slurs; such vocabulary, Divine claimed, carried with it "the GERMS of SEGREGATION and DISCRIMINATION and the very GERM of LOWRATION by the saying of such terms unconsciously. . . ."[35] Divine carried this idea to the extreme in his preaching that the first and most significant step toward eradicating racism was avoiding words that referred to racial difference itself. As Divine explained,

> Thoughts are things! If we dwell upon them we will become to be partakers of them, automatically. Therefore we hardly use the word that is commonly known as race, creed, or color, among us.[36]

By using phrases such as the "'so-and-so' people" or "people of light complexion" in place of "Negro" or "Caucasian," Divine believed he was helping to rid the world of both racial differences and the structure of segregation and discrimination that such differences were used to justify.

Divine similarly downplayed the existence of gender difference. Divine referred to his followers as "so-called men" and "those who call themselves women."[37] When encouraging his followers to manifest in their behavior a new heavenly mind or spirit, he said, "Spirit and mind is [*sic*] the same as the principle of Mathematics, it is not confined to complexion, is it? Neither is it confined to sex, as far as male or female." He also downplayed his own gender. "GOD is your Father, your Mother, your Sister, and your Brother," he told his followers.[38] Divine's appearance seemed to suggest gender neutrality. An unusually small man who wore neat, tailored suits, Divine struck both his male and female followers as "cute" and "sweet."[39]

The resulting gender politics of the Peace Mission stood in stark contrast to those of the UNIA. The UNIA encouraged Garveyite women to see themselves primarily as mothers to the Negro race, and they had gained respect as wives and mothers at the cost of certain restrictions on their behavior. Divinite women rejected the identity of mother in favor of sister, the prefix commonly adopted by Divine's female followers. According to the Divinites, an "evangelical life" did not entail private devotion to husband and offspring in service to the race. Instead, it meant the immediate realization of an angelic—that is, communal, racially integrated, sex segregated, and celibate—lifestyle in service to God, or Father Divine.

Father Divine's insistence upon celibacy was not overtly linked to his analysis of race. It derived, first of all, from the premises of New Thought. Intrigued by the power of mind over matter, many New Thought authors advocated celibacy as the ultimate victory of the spiritual over the material. Father Divine's arguments for celibacy were indistinguishable from those offered by other New Thought leaders; like them, he insisted that sexual activity dissipated human energy; strengthened the "lower" rather than the "higher" nature, and was incompatible with the self-denial needed to achieve angelic status.[40] More crucially, however, the practice of celibacy among Divine's followers signified their millenarian perspective. Practices of sexual excess or abstinence are common in millenarian movements, whose members typically break religious or sexual taboos as a symbol of their distance from the corrupt past.[41]

Father Divine's insistence upon celibacy cannot, however, be understood entirely outside of a race context. To Garvey, the idea of a black man advocating celibacy was tantamount to race suicide; the salvation of African Americans required healthy and numerous black bodies.[42] Divine's answer to segregation and racism was to deny the body altogether—both the racialized and the sexualized body. In his millennial world of raceless and genderless angels, racial segregation could not possibly have a place.[43] It was Divine's firm belief that the human body had been transcended that enabled Divine's followers to battle segregation and to live in racially integrated groups; black and white together was the ultimate symbol that the human body itself no longer reigned.

Divine's rejection of the black sexualized body meshed perfectly with that same denial by white America. Because Divine's movement was sex segregated and celibate, it could be looked upon as a relatively nonthreatening curiosity by white outsiders.[44] The existence of large-scale, racially mixed communal living that was *not* celibate would likely have triggered white hysteria and even violence.[45] Although bound up with the claim that race difference did not exist, celibacy in Divine's movement ensured that at the most basic level race purity ideology remained unchallenged.

Divine's reasons for insisting on sex segregation and celibacy were not, however, identical to women's reasons for joining a movement with those tenets. Women's reasons for joining the Peace Mission were complex. While some joined because of severely demanding family and financial situations, others joined because of the appeal of living communally with other women.[46] The rejection of both men and conventional gender roles attracted many Divinite women.[47] Indeed, they sometimes extended that rejection farther than Divine himself intended. When encouraging his followers to disregard earthly divisions, Divine spoke almost exclusively of "races, creed and colors," rather than divisions between men and women.[48] But women heard what they wanted to hear in his words. For example, Divine told his followers, "Your bodies are pure from vice and from crime, because you have been Redeemed from all mankind." However, when arrested for voter registration disruption, Divinite women refused to ride in the same car with male prisoners, explaining that they could not because "Father has redeemed us from men."[49] This claim that God had redeemed them from men stood in stark contrast to the attitude of Garveyite women, who in the early 1920s carried banners in UNIA parades proclaiming "God Give Us Real Men!"[50]

Divinite women took new angelic names to assert publicly their new status as members of a community of "sisters and brothers." While most took names like Joyous Light or Happy Flower, many chose explicitly male angelic names, such as Joshua Love, Jasper Aaron, and Jonathan Mathew.[51] This is particularly significant given Father Divine's New Thought insistence that "Name means Nature." These women were rejecting not only their status as wives, but also as women.

The sex-segregated and female-dominated Peace Mission had little hierarchy, gendered or otherwise. There was simply Father Divine; his small group of black and white, male and female "secretaries"; and the numerous, loosely organized cooperative businesses and communes of the Divinite Kingdom. This apparent lack of hierarchy was only relative, given that all Divinites saw themselves as worshipers of the movement's ultimate leader, Father Divine. Nevertheless, Peace Mission "extensions" of the 1930s were quite varied and remarkably autonomous.[52] Equally telling, the Divinite paper, *The Spoken Word*, had no women's page. Instead, reports on the doings of sisters and brothers were featured throughout.

Divinite rituals drew upon and sanctified women's experiences. At Peace Mission banquets, Divine ritually ladeled the first portion of soup, cut the first piece of meat on every platter, and poured coffee from a large silver urn. Father Divine's symbolic opening of the banquet did not overturn gender roles; indeed, a specially trained staff of Divinite women usually served the remainder of the banquet meal. Nevertheless, Divine's opening ritual must have been especially powerful for black women domestics, who probably made up the majority of Peace Mission adherents. The sight of "God himself" performing their daily service activity elevated and sanctified their labors. Moreover, women could relax and enjoy a meticulous table setting that reflected an elegance usually seen only in the homes of white employers. Now they, as domestic workers, were not serving, they were being served.[53]

What effects did Peace Mission social organization—which included no hierarchy, no heterosexuality, no private property, and no privatized home and child care—have on Divinite women? On the whole, the Peace Mission seemed to free their energy and creativity. Despite the Depression-era context, African American women formed scores of Peace Mission extensions and businesses—communal living arrangements as well as restaurants, food stores, and dressmaking and clothing shops.[54] Divinite women also collectively owned, ran and supervised the Promised Land, the nearly seven hundred Peace Mission communal farms located on over two thousand acres of land in upstate New York.[55] Observers initially doubted the feasibility of the Promised Land project. "[T]hese fanatics are hardly endowed with that stability of temperament and self-discipline required to endure the hardships of an agricultural existence," a hostile white biographer of Divine noted in 1937. However, Divine's followers—mostly middle-aged black women who had spent their younger years in the rural South—knew how to work a farm. Three years later, newspapers respectfully described the now-thriving farms and their related enterprises.[56]

Besides creating successful urban and rural cooperatives during the midst of the Great Depression, Divinite women became increasingly involved in political action. By the mid-1930s, the Divinite newspaper *Spoken Word* contained a mix of radical political reporting (often lifted from such journals as the *New Masses* and the *New Republic*) and the verbatim words of Father Divine's speeches, which combined transcendent visions with calls for political education and action. Women read the *Spoken Word* as a holy text, and soon their banquet testimonials began to reflect diverse political visions. As a *New York World-Telegraph* reporter sarcastically noted,

> followers arose to give testimonials. These took on a political hue.... A lean woman gave testimony to the effect that she had sat for three weeks in the spectator's gallery in the U.S. Senate and had discovered that the country was governed by a pack of noodles. Another woman told of a paradise that took on a decided Marxist tinge as she described it. Still another saw that the hope of the country lay in a benevolence reminiscent of Tammany Hall.[57]

Simultaneously, Divine introduced more practical skills to his followers. In 1935 he suggested that they attend night school to become literate and so qualify for voter registration. In response, Divinite women flooded the night schools, making up 20 percent of the students in 1935. This marked the first time in ten years that any woman had attended night school classes at Harlem's Public School 89.[58] It appears that only the radical lifestyle change involved in communal Divinite living enabled significant numbers of Harlem women to attend adult education classes—a telling indication of the depth of the problems that had hitherto made adult education virtually impossible for Harlem women.[59]

Divinite women were soon putting their new political skills into practice. They formed the overwhelming majority of the close to three hundred Harlem Divinites who attempted en masse to register to vote in 1935.[60] Women undertook other actions as well. Divinite sisters enacted peaceful resistance to segregation by entering restaurants in racially mixed groups. They also participated in joint Communist-Divinite parades (where they mixed cries of "Father Divine is God!" with slogans like "Down with Fascism!").[61] Finally, women were prominent in Divine's Righteous Government, an organization within the Peace Mission dedicated to the political implementation of Divine's vision. Of the organization's six departments, women headed at least three (politics, education, and research).[62]

Peace Mission women created a distinctive Divinite culture. Commentators, for instance, frequently noted the power of the hot swing or boogie-woogie style music at Divinite banquets. Accompanying the orchestrated music was a women's choir, which sang about social wrongs, racial injustice, or love for Divine. As one observer reported, these songs were "no orthodox hymns. They are original, colorful, completely alive outpourings. Often they attain the very heights of folk art."[63]

Peace Mission women also expressed themselves through distinctive clothing and appearance. According to the *Spoken Word*, today's woman should have "a sturdy, husky . . . physical type of beauty, as in Russia, and not the Clara Bow, Jean Harlow type of flaming youth."[64] The type of clothing favored by Divinite women can be gleaned from scattered reports. While the men of the movement wore dark, neatly pressed suits, one *New York Times* article described Divinite women as "clad chiefly in brilliant red, light blue and vivid purple garments. . . ."[65] Their dress starkly contrasted with the official costumes of some Garveyite women. As Barbara Bair points out, male members of Garvey's African Legion wore elaborate, military-style costumes, while their sister organization, the Black Cross Nurses, wore loose dresses and capes suggestive of self-sacrificing nuns and nurses.[66]

One might think that the Peace Mission's refusal even to use the word *Negro*, much less promote the physical perpetuation of African Americans as a race, would be accompanied by a devastating erasure of black culture as a whole. Again, a comparison with Garvey's UNIA proves instructive.

Garvey valued black artistic expression, and his UNIA prompted a tremendous outpouring of black literary writings. UNIA poetry concentrated on the battle against racial injustice, the reawakening of Africa, and paeans to Garvey himself. The poems tended to maintain the trademark UNIA emphasis on Race Manhood, however, while depicting black women as queens, victims, virgins, or "Mothers of Men."[67] In his eagerness to promote self-respect in African Americans, Garvey encouraged the use of European poetic forms and scorned dialect poetry as degrading. He denigrated black folk culture, attacked the work of Harlem Renaissance authors, and viewed jazz and spirituals as impediments to racial progress.[68]

The cultural output of the Peace Mission similarly centered on opposition to racial injustice and hymns of praise to the movement's leader. Divinite songs and rituals did not emphasize Race Manhood, however. Instead, the 1930s Peace Mission accepted the experience of its black members as normative for the entire membership, black or white, and strongly stressed the value of black women's experience during the movement's central ritual occasions. In contrast to Garvey's contempt for jazz, Divine made an eclectic mix of popular and traditional music central to his ritual practice. He served the food and spoke the language of the black working class.[69] Divine validated the emotional testimonial style that had long been a means of expression for rural and urban African Americans and encouraged them to infuse their prayer with political content.

Later Years of the UNIA and the Peace Mission Movement

Living first in Jamaica and later in London, Garvey continued his efforts to rebuild the UNIA throughout the 1930s. His declining influence was painfully obvious, however. For example, when Garvey started his School of African Philosophy, a training course for UNIA leaders, in the mid-1930s, he published ads declaring "1,000 Students Wanted!!" The first session of the school, held in London in September 1937, attracted eleven students. By the time of Garvey's premature death in 1940, he was penniless and almost devoid of followers.[70]

During the final decade of his life, Garvey's politics became more mystical and more masculine. "It is *thought* that created the Universe. It is *thought* that will master the Universe," he wrote in 1937. Garvey had long been interested in New Thought, and in the 1920s he had drawn on New Thought rhetoric to encourage black men to persevere in business. Now he used New Thought ideas to argue that the real explanation for his movement's decline was the inner weakness of black men. "Mind is the thing that rules and the black man to-day falls below the level of a white man only because of the poverty of his mind," Garvey claimed. He also drew upon New Thought to support his arguments about the importance of racial separatism. Blacks suffered because they were captive to the denigrating thoughts and propaganda of an alien race, Garvey wrote. To be truly free, they needed to create their own thought environment or atmosphere. "Any race that accepts the thoughts of another race, automatically, becomes a slave of that other race. As men think, so they do react . . . ," he wrote in 1930.[71]

By the 1930s, Garvey increasingly spoke of a coming racial Armageddon that would bring a victory for blacks only when the "Negro makes himself a man" and forms a "great phalanx of noble fighting braves."[72] Given Garvey's commitment to the idea that mental images could make or break black people, it is not surprising that a considerable proportion of his 1930s journal *Black Man* consisted of poems he wrote with titles like "Go And Win!" "Win the Fray!" and "GET UP AND DO." These poems, replete with images of marching "He-Men," represented Garvey's final efforts to rouse a masculine, martial spirit in his readers.[73]

By the mid-1930s, Garvey apparently lost interest in the role of black women in racial uplift. His School of African Philosophy, which promised to train its students as UNIA leaders, diplomats, and entrepreneurs, included tips on how to deal with one's wife and family and seemed to assume a male audience. Yet Garvey's failure to delineate a specific role for black women seemed to allow at least some Garveyite women to assume that the UNIA leader whom the lessons promised to create could be female; of the School's initial eleven students, four were women.[74] Nevertheless, in one of Garvey's last comments on gender politics in 1934, he condemned blacks who used birth control. The resolution seemed to cast black women once again as "race mothers."[75] His attack on birth control seems of a piece with his praise of Hitler and Mussolini as self-made men and with his 1937 boast that "[w]e [in the UNIA] were the first Fascists."[76] Like the fascists, Garvey dreamed of a violent settlement of race problems. Black men would become warriors, and black women would produce the bodies needed in the coming race war.

If 1927 marked a turning point for Garvey and the UNIA, then the equivalent year for Divine's movement was 1936. That year, a number of events convinced outsiders that the Peace Mission was on the verge of becoming a radical political force: Divinites' rush to register to vote, their creation of a Righteous Government Platform to which all candidates hoping for the Divinite vote must conform, and their apparent alliance with the Communist Party. In response to this perceived political threat, U.S. government harassment of the Peace Mission intensified.[77] A series of sexual scandals, exposés, and defections further weakened Divine's movement. Finally, to escape paying reparations to a disgruntled former Divinite, Divine moved from Harlem to Philadelphia in 1942. This move left Divine, like Garvey, permanently separated from his base of support in New York City.[78]

Perhaps in response to these crises, Father Divine spent the years between 1937 and 1942 consolidating his authority over the Peace Mission movement. The *Spoken Word*, with its eclectic mix of Divine's banquet speeches; movement news; and radical local, national, and international political reporting, was replaced in late 1936 by the Divinite journal *New Day*. Typical issues of *New Day* contained approximately ninety pages of Divine's banquet speeches, ten pages of letters, and one page of world news.[79] In 1940 and 1941, Divine officially incorporated several of the movement's most active centers, began bringing all Peace Mission properties under centralized supervision, and instituted rules whereby no Peace Mission could be started without the permission of a parent church.[80]

By the mid-1940s, Peace Mission membership had declined dramatically.[81] This decline was possibly related to a number of factors, including the end of the Depression, Divine's self-imposed exile from Harlem, and Divinite dissatisfaction with the increasingly rigid nature of the movement. The Peace Mission's loss of members can also be explained in terms of the dynamics typical of millennial movements. The force driving such movements' rejection of mainstream social, political, and economic arrangements is a deeply felt protest against the injustices of mainstream society. Once these injustices are addressed directly by political movements, millennial faiths often find that their central appeal to their membership has been undercut. As Robert Weisbrot points out, the Double V campaign of the 1940s as well as the rise of the Civil Rights movement in the 1950s, both of which directly challenged segregation and other forms of deeply embedded white racism, may have severely undercut the appeal of Divine's movement.[82]

After a millenarian group begins to lose members, the message of its prophet tends to change. Instead of criticizing the evils of an oppressive social system, the prophet often begins to blame social ills on the evils of the oppressed people themselves. The prophet then preaches self-purification rather than confrontation as the means for bringing about the millennium. It is not surprising, then, that when the numbers of Divine's followers began to dwindle, he began to blame injustice on the imperfections of the oppressed.[83] African Americans "had committed the sin in setting up color in the first place," Divine now insisted. "They set it up in their consciousness and they would find it everywhere they went and *they* and no one else would be responsible."[84] This shift to self-blame echoed the attacks on black laziness leveled by Marcus Garvey in the 1930s when he too found himself the prophet of a dwindling movement.

Divine's political outlook shifted dramatically with the outbreak of World War II. He seemed to interpret the war as a contest between the racists and segregationists he abhorred, on the one hand, and the united, peaceful planet that he had long promoted, on the other. When the United States entered the war Divine therefore fiercely supported the war effort and did all he could to promote a fervent American nationalism among his followers.[85] Indeed, during the war years, the same Father Divine who had once stated that "I am none of your nationalities. You don't have to think I AM an American. . . . I AM none of them" now claimed that the only way to ensure world peace was by turning the world into a gigantic United States of America.[86] The United States, as the "amalgamation of all nations," was chosen as the site of the "Kingdom of GOD on earth," Divine insisted. Eventually all nations of the earth would fly the American flag and accept the Constitution, which Divine believed was divinely inspired, as their charter of government.[87] Instead of preaching the absence of race or gender divisions under the neutrality of African American–inflected religious practice, Divine instead preached the absence of national divisions under the neutrality of American global dominance. By the 1950s, Divine directed his most passionate tirades not against "RACISM and all MATERIALISM and every adverse and undesireable tendency," but against communists and unions, who Divine claimed were "inspired by atheism and Nazism and other isms that spell division, to undermine the foundations of our government, which we all revere!"[88]

As Divine became both increasingly nationalistic and anxious about the ideological purity of his followers, his understanding of celibacy (and with it, the position of Divinite women) changed dramatically. In the 1930s, Divine had embraced celibacy as a sign of the distance between those living as angels in Divine's millennial heavens and those who had not yet acknowledged Father Divine as God; but his comments on celibacy were few and far between. By the 1950s, celibacy as well as virginity took on increasing importance to Father Divine. He began to preach that if his followers remained celibate they would live forever.[89] His growing stress on virginity could be seen in the changing nature of three Divinite orders—the Rosebuds, the Lily-buds, and the Crusaders—first created between 1938 and 1941.

The most important of these orders was the Rosebuds, which was both a women's order and the official Divinite choir. In the mid-1940s, Divine praised the Rosebuds mainly for their skill at purchasing properties in "restricted" areas and as exemplars of economic independence.[90] By the 1950s, however, Divine seemed to value the Rosebuds primarily for their virginity. According to the Rosebuds' Creed, adopted by the early 1950s, the Rosebuds pledged to let their "every deed and action express virginity."[91]

The new emphasis on virginity had multiple meanings for the Divinites. On the one hand, Divine's insistence on virginity symbolized, as it always had, the boundaries between the elect and the unredeemed world. On the other hand, the aggressive virginity of Divine's new orders seemed linked to his belief in the millennial role of the United States. By the 1950s, Divine seemed to view the United States as a Peace Mission writ large. Just as Peace Mission members erased trouble-causing differences through both the inclusive strategy of interracial living and the exclusive strategy of repressing all potentially divisive physical desires, so too did they imagine the United States erasing difference through both the inclusive strategy of expanding to include all peoples and the exclusive strategy of battling the "ruthless ideology of Socialism and Communism." Divinites equated the words *virgin* and *virtuous*. The virgin righteousness of Divinites showed their kinship with the virgin righteousness of America itself.[92]

As the meaning of celibacy shifted under the weight of Divine's new nationalism, so too did Divine's emphasis on race neutrality take on a different meaning. Rather than stating that all race was a construction, Divine seemed particularly interested in denying the existence of the African race. Throughout the 1950s, for example, the *New Day* repeatedly published Divine's statement that "I do NOT represent races, creeds or colors, Therefore I AM NOT what you think or take me to be, I AM NOT a N____o and I AM NOT representing any such thing as the N____o or the C_____ race. . . . I AM a REAL, TRUE AMERICAN ONE HUNDRED PERCENT."[93]

Divine supported his One Hundred Percent Americanism by organizing his church in ways that brought it closer to mainstream white culture. Instead of challenging mainstream gender roles, for example, Divine's orders now approximated the gender norms of 1950s American culture. The Rosebuds pledged to remain "submissive, meek and sweet," while the male Crusaders pledged to be "active, effective, integral" members of Father Divine's movement.[94]

Divine also reshaped his own life and image according to more mainstream ideals. In 1946, he took a seventeen-year-old petite and blond-haired white Canadian woman as his second wife (his first wife, Peninnah, was a heavy-set, African American woman—both marriages were "purely spiritual").[95] It appears that Divine attempted to alter his photographic image in order to downplay his dark skin. According to one observer, by the 1950s Divine's followers insisted that his complexion was not dark. The observer reported that Divine's official photographers used "every known photographic technique" to lighten the shade of Divine's skin. The result could be seen in *New Day* photographs from the mid-1950s, in which the complexions of Father and Mother Divine appear to share a similar washed-out, off-white color, and in the color photographs of Divine currently on display at the Divine Tracy Hotel in Philadelphia, which give his complexion an orange cast.[96]

Divine's praise of all things American culminated in 1953 when he and his wife moved to Woodmont, an 1890s robber-baron estate located in Gladwyne, Pennsylvania. While heaven had formerly been located in a three-story Harlem collective, it was now an elegantly appointed mansion, which Divine described as "a home that is set apart for MOTHER DIVINE and MYSELF as though a private family. . . ."[97] Once installed in Woodmont, Divine seemed to believe that all was well in his own life, and so in America and in the world. "GOD IS ON THE THRONE NOW," he announced during his first week at Woodmont.[98] From this point on, Divine had little to say about the state of America or the world at large. Until his death in 1965, *New Day* editions mainly reprinted speeches by Mother Divine, along with letters and speeches written by Father Divine in the 1930s and 1940s.

Conclusion

A comparison of Divine's Peace Mission movement and Garvey's UNIA indicates that the very different racial ideologies of these movements profoundly affected their gender politics. Garvey's UNIA protested the race-caste system in America by urging blacks to unify as a race. In Garvey's view, the strength of this black race was dependent on the continued growth of a healthy and recognizably black population. The production of a healthy black population, in turn, could occur only if black women found the appropriate mates and devoted themselves to raising strong children. This left black men to provide for, defend, and rule the united black nation. Garvey's strategy ultimately put black manhood, as well as race, "first."

In contrast, Divine's 1930s Peace Mission protested the American race-caste system by denying race difference altogether and attempting to practice complete racial integration. In the context of a depression-era society predicated upon race hierarchy, however, large-scale enactments of racial transcendence would be tolerated only if accompanied by the rejection of sexuality. Divine's interest in celibacy may have had purely religious roots. Nevertheless, his choice of celibacy as the primary symbol of angelic living *was* crucial to his ability to create a racially integrated movement.

Both Garvey's Race First and Divine's race neutrality thus entailed control of women's sexuality. Garvey's UNIA channeled women's sexuality into the role of wife and mother, while Divine's Peace Mission forbade heterosexuality and even heterosociability. Garvey's gender strategy, however, assumed the existence of a steady male wage and was therefore a tolerable option for black women only during periods of relative economic well-being. As the UNIA crumbled during the Great Depression, thousands of African American women became followers of Father Divine and accepted his millennial race-neutral approach. They willingly accepted celibacy and sex segregation in exchange for the social, political, and economic opportunities offered by the Peace Mission movement.

Marcus Garvey felt that black culture would thrive only in the context of strong, patriarchal black families. Although he encouraged African American artistic production, Garvey nevertheless denigrated many aspects of black culture that struck him as too dreamy and undisciplined to contribute to the building of a great nation. One might assume a close tie between race pride and an assertive black culture, but the early years of the Peace Mission movement suggest that race purity ideology need not be a precondition for the assertion of a vibrant black culture. Divine's African American, working-class, female followers brought their tastes in food, music, and dress to the Peace Mission movement. These women formed the majority of Divine's followers in Harlem, and they largely shaped the purportedly race-neutral culture of the Peace Mission as a whole.

While Divine's movement peaked in the mid-1930s, these same years saw Garvey living in exile from his American base of support. Once the remaining American UNIA locals lost followers to Divine as well as to other political and religious leaders, Marcus Garvey ironically began to draw more heavily upon the same New Thought ideas that animated

Divine's speeches. While Divinites used New Thought ideas about the power of words and thought to deny the existence of race as well as gender difference, Garvey articulated a New Thought philosophy that was both more political and more vindictive. He used New Thought ideas about the power of influence to shore up his calls for a renewed black art, literature, and history to counter the "thoughts of a race that has made itself by assumption superior."[99] Garvey also took to heckling his readers repeatedly about the need to become more masculine and aggressive, as if this were a realistic alternative to organized political activism. Despite the economic pressures of the Great Depression, Garvey refused to modify his vision of gender roles within the UNIA; given the fact that the only UNIA resolution of the 1930s that was directed at women condemned birth control, it appears that Garvey continued to envision black women as mothers of the race.

If Garvey's continuing emphasis on women as reproducers reflects the drawbacks of a race-purity approach, the later history of the Peace Mission suggests the extreme instability of a formula of race neutrality as a method of opposing the American race-caste system. By the 1950s, Divine's denial of race had changed into a denial of the existence of racism and a consequent lauding of the United States as a racially just (rather than simply a multiracial) society. Divine's complacency about conditions in the United States increased after he moved into the Woodmont mansion and began to live out his own version of the paterfamilias experience. Instead of a neutrality in which a form of African American culture was the norm, Divine's increasing personal comfort as well as his increasing nationalism led him to promote a neutrality that drew upon the dominant white culture. Divine's movement shows that, although the denial of race difference in some ways counters the need to control women's reproduction and can therefore allow some innovation in social and economic arrangements, such a denial is not enough to counter other forces leading to a strict policing of women's bodies—in this case the force of nationalism. Divine's movement indicates how nationalism even without anxieties over reproducing the race can be imprisoning for women, since the purity claimed for the nation is too easily symbolized by the female virgin body.

The histories of Marcus Garvey's UNIA and Father Divine's Peace Mission movement demonstrate some of the pressures faced by African American organizations that attempt to challenge the racial status quo. In addition to the usual difficulties of organizing poor or culturally marginalized people, on the one hand, and the drain of constant governmental harassment, on the other, African American organizations face special stresses that result from their racialized identity in white America. Black organizations can find themselves in a double bind; while calls to race pride may unify African Americans politically, a slip from race pride to race purity can easily occur. Race purity, in turn, encourages protective attitudes toward women. These attitudes restrict women's behavior and are, in any case, extremely difficult to implement in the context of economic oppression that creates the need for antiracist organizing in the first place. At the same time, the rare black organization that attempts to claim the position of race neutrality, usually appropriated by European Americans, stands to lose the specificity of the culture it is fighting to strengthen. The gender politics of African American religious and political movements must not be overlooked; they throw into high relief the complex and confining links between nationalism, race consciousness, gender, and sexuality that continue to shape modern American politics and culture.

Notes

1. C. D. Austin's letter and the UNIA's condemnation of Father Divine are reprinted in Robert A. Hill, ed., *The Marcus Garvey and Universal Negro Improvement Association Papers*, vol. 7 (Berkeley, Calif., 1990), 707–8, 705.
2. See E. David Cronon, *Black Moses: The Story of Marcus Garvey and the Universal Negro Improvement Association* (Madison, Wis., 1974); Amy Jacques Garvey, *Garvey and Garveyism* (1963; New York, 1978); Judith Stein, *The World of Marcus Garvey: Race and Class in Modern Society* (Baton Rouge, La., 1986).
3. See Robert Weisbrot, *Father Divine and the Struggle for Racial Equality* (Urbana, Ill., 1983); Jill Watts, *God, Harlem, U.S.A.: The Father Divine Story* (Berkeley, Calif., 1992); Roma Barnes, "'Blessings Flowing Free': The Father Divine Peace Mission Movement in Harlem, New York City, 1932–1941" (Ph.D. diss., University of York, England, 1979); Charles Braden, *These Also Believe: A Study of Modern American Cults and Minority Religious Movements* (New York, 1949), 1–77.
4. Accurate membership statistics for both the UNIA and the Peace Mission are difficult to determine. In the 1920s, Garvey claimed a UNIA membership of six to eleven million, while in the 1930s Divine claimed to have twenty million followers worldwide. Historians estimate from fifty thousand to two hundred thousand active Garveyites in the mid-1920s, and from thirty thousand to fifty thousand Divinites in the 1930s. See Emory J. Tolbert, *The UNIA and Black Los Angeles: Ideology and Community in the American Garvey Movement* (Los Angeles, 1980), 7 n. 7; see Lawrence Levine, *The Unpredictable Past: Explorations in American Cultural History* (New York, 1993), 121; Watts, *God, Harlem, U.S.A.*, 142; Weisbrot, *Father Divine*, 69.
5. For comparisons of Garvey and Divine, see Weisbrot, *Father Divine*, 190–96; Watts, *God, Harlem, U.S.A.*, 115–18; Hill, *Papers*, vol. 7, 641 n. 9; Robert A. Hill and Barbara Bair, eds., *Marcus Garvey: Life and Lessons* (Berkeley, Calif., 1987), xxviii–xxx, xlix–l. Also see documents on Divine in Hill, *Papers*, vol. 7, 641, 704.
6. See Weisbrot, *Father Divine*, 59–60; Hubert Kelly, "Heaven Incorporated," *American Century* 121 (Jan. 1936): 106; "Kingdom Sings and Registers," *New York Sun*, 4 Nov.

1935. Some west coast Divinite heavens had a majority of white followers. See Charles P. LeWarne, "Vendovi Island: Father Divine's 'Peaceful Paradise of the Pacific,'" *Pacific Northwest Quarterly* (Jan. 1984): 2–12.

7. I am indebted to the work of Barbara Bair and Tera W. Hunter on the gender politics of the UNIA. See Barbara Bair, "Women and the Garvey Movement: The Politics of Difference" (paper presented at Rockefeller Humanities-in-Residence talk, Rutgers University, 1989); Tera W. Hunter, "Feminist Consciousness and Black Nationalism: Amy Jacques-Garvey and Women in the Universal Negro Improvement Association" (paper presented at Women's History Research Seminar, Yale University, 1983). Also see Barbara Bair, "True Women, Real Men: Gender, Ideology and Social Roles in the Garvey Movement," in Dorothy O. Helly and Susan M. Reverby, eds., *Gendered Domains: Rethinking Public and Private in Women's History* (Ithaca, N.Y., 1992), 154–66.

8. See Tony Martin, "Women in the Garvey Movement," and Honor Ford-Smith, "Women and the Garvey Movement in Jamaica," in Rupert Lewis and Patrick Bryan, eds., *Garvey: His Work and Impact* (Trenton, N.J., 1991), 73, 75, 78, 81; Bair, "True Women, Real Men," 156, 160; Ula Yvette Taylor, "The Veiled Garvey: The Life and Times of Amy Jacques Garvey" (Ph.D. diss., University of California Santa Barbara, Jan. 1992), 194, 214; Hunter, "Feminist Consciousness," 22–23.

9. For example, although Robert Weisbrot notes the preponderance of women in the Peace Mission, their gender becomes central to his analysis only when he remarks that women gazed at Divine with "sensual longing" or notes that "[s]ome of these women, black as well as white, appeared to experience sexual orgasms during their frenzied behavior at the banquets." See Weisbrot, *Father Divine*, 86. Among Divinite scholars only Sara Harris notes that male followers also gazed adoringly at Divine. See Sara Harris, *Father Divine* (New York, 1971), 339–40. Also see Barnes, "Blessings Flowing Free," 273.

10. Watts, *God, Harlem, U.S.A.*, 35, 42. Watts's sympathetic account of women in the Peace Movement still relegates their experiences to a few pages in an extensive study; she does not analyze Divine's movement as a black women's movement. Furthermore, Watts's consistently positive slant on the Peace Mission sometimes leads her to normalize what was clearly an extremely unconventional and socially challenging religious movement. For example, in addition to calling Divine an "articulate advocate of women's rights," Watts describes the typical Peace Mission heaven as a rehabilitation center that offered occupational therapy, job training, day care and support group therapy (42, 47, 106, 128). This 1980s vocabulary is misleading. Abandoning children to children's extensions where they were raised communally is not day care, absolute gender segregation and celibacy are hardly necessary in order to free women from the fear of childbirth (35), and calling up storms to avenge female mental hospital patients is not the standard definition of women's rights. Watts's image of a protherapy, pro–women's rights Father Divine certainly makes the movement seem less alien, but at the cost of misrepresenting the less socially acceptable aspects of Divinite behavior.

Watts's effort to portray Divine as a rational and consistent individual leads her to distort the erratic nature of Divine's political life. For example, although Father Divine joined his editorial staff in passionately attacking capitalism, encouraging his followers to be radicals, and allying himself with the Communist Party in the United States during the depression, and only turned to anti-Communism and strident American nationalism in the 1940s, Watts claims that the Father Divine of the 1930s held the same views as the Father Divine posthumously depicted by his 1970s and 1980s followers—as a man (or God) whose most passionately held political beliefs are support for capitalism and opposition to welfare. She creates this more consistent picture by attributing undated speeches by Divine that were published posthumously by his followers in the 1970s to Divine in the 1930s. For an example of Watts's anachronistic use of 1970s *New Day* reprints, see 209, nn. 50–56. For her efforts to portray Divine as a fervent procapitalist in the 1930s, see 100–101, 104–6, 119–20, 126, 128, 134–35. For an alternative view, see original *Spoken Word*, editions from 1935–36.

11. See Hill, *Papers*, vol. 1, lxxi, lxxx–lxxxi; Cronon, *Black Moses*, 111, 191–95; Jacques Garvey, *Garvey and Garveyism*, 176–78; Hill and Bair, *Marcus Garvey*, 204.

12. See Hazel Carby, *Reconstructing Womanhood: The Emergence of the Afro-American Woman Novelist* (New York, 1987), 20–39; Jacqueline Dowd Hall, "'The Mind That Burns in Each Body': Women, Rape, and Racial Violence," in Ann Snitow, Christine Stansell, and Sharon Thompson, *Powers of Desire* (New York, 1983), 328–49.

13. See Levine, *Unpredictable Past*, 107–36. In contrast, white calls for race unity functioned to convince working-class whites that nonwhites, rather than an exploitative economic system, were the source of their problems. Black race consciousness created political coalitions among the powerless internationally; white race consciousness sundered potential coalitions domestically among the powerless.

14. *Negro World*, 17 May 1924, cited in Bair, "Women and the Garvey Movement," 10. Garveyites frequently wrote of women not simply as mothers but as "Mothers of Men." See Bair, "Women and the Garvey Movement," n. 17, 28–29.

15. Percival Burrows, in *Negro World*, 9 June 1923, cited in Bair, "Women in the Garvey Movement," 10.

16. See Bair, "True Women, Real Men," 156. Articles in *Negro World* indicate that Garveyite women were angry only that UNIA men were not taking their responsibilities as chivalrous protectors seriously enough. For example, see "Ladies of Jamaica Division Lead Men in Constructive Efforts," *Negro World*, 7 Apr. 1923; "Respect and Protection of Our Women a Vital Question," *Negro World*, 23 Aug. 1924; "Listen Women!" *Negro World*, 9 Apr. 1927.

17. See Jacqueline Jones, *Labor of Love, Labor of Sorrow: Black Women, Work and the Family, from Slavery to the Present* (New York, 1986), 96–99; Cheryl Townsend Gilkes, "The Roles of Church and Community Mothers: Ambivalent American Sexism or Fragmented African Familyhood?" *Journal of Feminist Studies in Religion* 2 (spring 1986): 44; Eileen Boris, "The Power of Motherhood: Black and White Activist Women Redefine the 'Political,'" in Seth Koven and Sonya Michel, eds., *Mothers of a New World: Maternalist Politics and the Origins of the Welfare State* (New York, 1993), 213–45.

18. See "The Black Woman's Part in Race Leadership," *Negro World*, 19 Apr. 1924; "Women in the Home" and "The Kinf [*sic*] of Girl Men Like," *Negro World*, 9 Feb. 1924; "Emancipated Womanhood," *Negro World*, 15 Nov. 1924; Taylor, *The Veiled Garvey*, 222–24.

19. Bair, "Women and the Garvey Movement," 5–8; see Gilkes, "Ambivalent American Sexism."

20. See "Obligations of Motherhood," *Negro World*, 29 Mar. 1924; "Emancipated Womanhood," *Negro World*, 15 Nov. 1924. Also see Hunter, "Feminist Consciousness," 16, 18; Ford-Smith, "Jamaica," 73, 75, 78, 81.

21. See Hill, *Papers*, vol. 1, liii; Bair, "Women and the Garvey Movement," 7; photograph by James VanDerZee, "Garvey Women's Brigade, 1924," in Roger C. Birt, "For the

Record: James VanDerZee, Marcus Garvey and the UNIA Photographs," *Exposure* 27 (fall 1990): 11; Martin, "Women in the Garvey Movement," 70.

22. See Bair, "True Women, Real Men," 160–66; Martin, "Women in the Garvey Movement"; Ford-Smith, "Jamaica," 67–69, 77–82. UNIA women made an unsuccessful plea for more autonomy within the movement in 1922; see Bair, "True Women, Real Men," 160–61.

23. Jacques Garvey, *Garvey and Garveyism*, 169, 218–51; Taylor, "The Veiled Garvey," 301, 309, 329.

24. "Ladies of Jamaica Division Lead Men in Constructive Efforts," *Negro World*, 7 Apr. 1923.

25. M.L.T. De Mena, *Negro World*, 19 Apr. 1924, cited in Hunter, "Feminist Consciousness," 22–23.

26. "Listen Women!" *Negro World*, 9 Apr. 1927; *Negro World*, 24 Oct. 1925, cited in Gerda Lerner, ed., *Black Women in White America: A Documentary History* (New York, 1973), 579.

27. See Cronon, *Black Moses*, 75–134, 142–44; Stein, *World of Marcus Garvey*, 202, 206–7.

28. See Cheryl Lynn Greenberg, *"Or Does It Explode?" Black Harlem in the Great Depression* (New York, 1991), 13, 20–22, 28, 39–40; Levine, *Unpredictable Past*, 135; Hill, *Papers*, vol. 7, xliii–xlvii; Stein, *World of Marcus Garvey*, 255.

29. See Greenberg, *"Or Does It Explode?"* 66, 74, 77, 197.

30. Watts, *God, Harlem, U.S.A.*, 62.

31. Conditions for working-class African American women in 1930s Harlem were dire. During the Depression, the vast majority of African American women in Harlem were employed in domestic service. While unskilled black male workers earned between two dollars and six dollars per day, African American women employed as domestics were earning between four dollars and ten dollars per *week* for twelve- to fourteen-hour days. See Greenberg, *"Or Does It Explode?"* 45, 78, 80; Jones, *Labor of Love*, 154, 179, 199. Furthermore, although most black women worked outside of the home, many of the steps taken by Harlemites to stretch their limited incomes—such as taking in boarders and preparing their own food and clothing—were performed by women and thus added considerably to African American women's already oppressive work loads. See Greenberg, *"Or Does It Explode?"* 176, 180.

The multiple stresses placed on middle-aged, African American women in Harlem help explain why this group was particularly prepared to join a millenarian social movement like the Peace Mission. In addition, statistical evidence indicates that many of Divine's female followers had been part of the Great Migration of 1916–21. Migrants, immigrants, or colonized people are the populations most likely to join millenarian groups. See Barnes, "Blessings Flowing Free," 123–24; Yonina Talmon, "Pursuit of the Millennium: The Relation Between Religious and Social Change," *Archives Europeennes de Sociologie* 3 (1962): 133, 144–45, 149.

32. Divine explained that the term *Negro* was employed "for the specific purpose of bringing about a division among the people, and to belittle and lowrate those that were of a darker complexion, by calling them not AFRICAN by nature, neither an ETHIOPIAN, neither an EGYPTIAN, but by calling them something that they never were. Tell your Educators to search the Scripture, and also search the History, and see if there is a nation by the name of what they call the People in America" (*Spoken Word*, 30 Nov. 1935, 20). Also see *Spoken Word*, 4 Jan. 1936, 27.

33. See *Spoken Word*, 30 Mar. 1935, 10; *Spoken Word*, 16 Mar. 1935, 7.

34. *Spoken Word*, 26 Oct. 1935, 28; *Spoken Word*, 9 Nov. 1935, 29.

35. *New Day*, 24 Nov. 1945, 7.

36. *Spoken Word*, 4 Jan. 1936, 27. Divine's refusal to speak of (and thereby mentally create or strengthen) negative circumstances led to odd verbal practices within the group. For example, Divinites referred to Amsterdam Avenue as Amsterbliss, and used the greeting Peace instead of Hello because they did not want to speak of and so strengthen hell.

37. See Watts, *God, Harlem, U.S.A.*, 35.

38. *Spoken Word*, 30 Mar. 1935, 9; *Spoken Word*, 29 June 1935, 3; Barnes, "Blessings Flowing Free," 210 n. 82.

39. Arthur Hoff Fauset, *Black Gods of the Metropolis* (1944; New York, 1970), 65, 67; Robert Allerton Parker, *The Incredible Messiah: The Deification of Father Divine* (Boston, 1937), 120. Divinite women frequently spoke of Divine's "beautiful starry baby eyes," indicating that they saw him as baby as well as father. See "A Revelation," *Spoken Word*, 23 Nov. 1935, 15; Parker, *Incredible Messiah*, 129.

40. On New Thought arguments for celibacy, see Beryl Satter, "New Thought and the Era of Woman, 1875–1895" (Ph.D. diss., Yale University, 1992), 328–96. For Father Divine's arguments in favor of celibacy, see *Spoken Word*, 6 Apr. 1935, 3; 26 Oct. 1935, 27; 2 Nov. 1935, 5. Although Divine usually spoke of celibacy as a practice of godly self-denial, he sometimes addressed the issue in terms of population control. See *Spoken Word*, 6 Apr. 1935, 3; also see *Spoken Word*, 26 Oct. 1935, 18.

41. See Peter Worsley, *The Trumpet Shall Sound: A Study of "Cargo" Cults in Melanesia*, 2d augmented ed. (New York, 1968), 250–51; see *Spoken Word*, 29 Apr. 1935, 3.

42. See Marcus Garvey, "Big Conference of U.N.I.A, in Canada," in Hill, *Papers*, vol. 7, 705; Marcus Garvey, "What God Means to Us," in Hill, *Papers*, vol. 7, 107–8; Marcus Garvey, "Lessons from the School of African Philosophy," in Hill and Bair, *Marcus Garvey*, 234–37.

43. Divine's denial of the body did not extend to practices of self-mortification or to dietary restrictions. He encouraged his followers to eat heartily by making a fifty-course banquet the ritual center of his movement.

44. Even in light of the Divinite ban on sexual relations, white observers were still shocked by the level of intimacy that existed between Divine's black and white followers. For example, see John Hosher, *God in a Rolls-Royce: The Rise of Father Divine, Madman, Menace, or Messiah* (New York, 1936), 171; Braden, *These Also Believe*, 26.

45. Contemporary observers made this point. See Harris, *Father Divine* (New York, 1971), 98; Braden, *These Also Believe*, 20.

46. There is some evidence that the Peace Mission, with its insistence on sex-segregated living and repudiation of reproduction as a strategy of racial uplift, also drew lesbians seeking an alternative to the confines of family life. One 1937 denunciation of the Peace Mission movement claimed it was a lesbian haven. This exposé was highly unreliable. See Barnes, "Blessings Flowing Free," 212. On the other hand, Divine himself periodically warned his followers not to sleep in each other's rooms: "I do not want anyone [in] the Peace Mission movement . . . going into others' private rooms that you are not assigned to. . . . Some of you so-called sisters . . . will not stay away from others' rooms— from the other Rosebuds' rooms, other sisters' rooms . . ." (Harris, *Father Divine*, 338). A 1950s report on the movement notes that while there is no overt homosexuality in the movement, some must exist; "its practice is written all over the stances and the faces of

some followers." See Harris, *Father Divine*, 338. See also Barnes, "Blessings Flowing Free," 209.

47. Divine sanctioned unconventional work roles for women by choosing a young black woman, Flying Determination, as his personal pilot, and by appointing women to serve as Peace Mission chauffeurs. See photograph of Flying Determination in scrapbook, "Father Divine," Schomburg Center for Research in Black Culture, New York; see Braden, *These Also Believe*, 27.

The Divinites were proud of the fact that they ignored gender-coded work-roles. For example, an article in the *Spoken Word* reported on a newsreel in which, "Not only was FATHER seen digging with a pick but Faithful Mary had one too. Mother was seen expertly handling a shovel and doing other work usually considered to be a 'man's' work" (*Spoken Word*, 14 Feb. 1925).

48. For example, see *Spoken Word*, 30 Mar. 1935, 11.

49. *Spoken Word*, 29 June 1935, 3; "29 of Divine Flock Seized in Vote Row," *New York Times*, 7 Oct. 1936. Divine sometimes came very close to this formulation, however. In a speech in October 1935, he said that the person who was redeemed from "all lust and passion" would be "Redeemed from among men, If you are in the likeness of a woman you are Redeemed from among men—that is if you live an Evangelical life. . . ." See *Spoken Word*, 19 Oct. 1935, 12. In later years, Divine explicity warned his male and female followers not to ride together in buses. See *New Day*, 13 Aug. 1942, 110.

50. See Jacques Garvey, *Garvey and Garveyism*, 49; Bair, "Women and the Garvey Movement," 9.

51. Parker, *Incredible Messiah*, 157, 231–33; Harris, *Father Divine*, 59; *Spoken Word*, 4 Jan. 1936, 28; "Kingdom Sings and Registers," *New York Sun*, 4 Nov. 1935.

52. Although white journalists typically characterized Divine as the controlling boss of his "chain store heavens," evidence indicates that Peace Mission communes were surprisingly independent of one another. For example, see affidavits by Charles Calloway and John Lamb and a letter from John Lamb in Mother Divine, *Peace Mission Movement*, 78–81, 82–85, 110. For a detailed analysis of the economic structure of Divinite communes, see Braden, *These Also Believed*, 27–42. Also see Weisbrot, *Father Divine*, 122–31, and Kenneth E. Burnham, *God Comes to America: Father Divine and the Peace Mission Movement* (Boston, 1979), 9. On the political independence of Divinites, see Watts, *God, Harlem, U.S.A.*, 57, 125, 131; also see 111, 132.

53. See Barnes, "Blessings Flowing Free," chap. 1. One Divinite woman who identified with Divine's role as server explained, "It is a thing of infinite beauty to actually see Father Divine—God in action at the table *serving*. . . . He pours the coffee so beautifully. So much rhythm, just like music from a violin. . . ." See Parker, *Incredible Messiah*, 129. Also see Weisbrot, *Father Divine*, 180; Braden, *These Also Believe*, 3.

54. See Parker, *Incredible Messiah*, 145–50; *Spoken Word*, 9 Feb. 1935, 15; 18 May 1935, 6; 22 June 1935, 18; 4 Jan. 1936, 28. Also see "Divine's Restaurant Puzzles Magistrate," *New York Times*, 12 June 1935; Barnes, "Blessings Flowing Free," 284; Weisbrot, *Father Divine*, 123–25; and Braden, *These Also Believe*, 27–42.

55. See *Spoken Word*, 23 Nov. 1935, 7; Weisbrot, *Father Divine*, 125–31. On women as workers and managers of the Promised Land, see *Spoken Word*, 14 Feb. 1935; "Divine Pilot Arks Up 1936 Jordon," *New York Post*, 20 Aug. 1936; "Divine Scene at Olympics," *New York Sun*, 8 July 1937; and "Biggest Businessman in Harlem has Extended his Holdings to Heaven," *New York World-Telegraph*, 10 Sept. 1936.

Marcus Garvey, Father Divine, and Gender Politics   601

56. Parker, *Incredible Messiah*, 285–86; see "Father Divine's Movement Expands," *New York Times*, 2 July 1939; "Strike a Balance," *New York Post*, 28 June 1939.

57. "Father Divine's 'Heaven' Favors Reapportionment," *New York World-Telegraph*, 2 Mar. 1935.

58. Weisbrot, *Father Divine*, 96; Jones, *Labor of Love*, 193; Barnes, "Blessings Flowing Free," 461–62.

59. Harlem women who had migrated from the rural South may also have spurned adult education because in their experience education did not bring mobility. See Greenberg, *"Or Does It Explode?"* 18. Once they became Divinite Angels, however, previous experiences of discrimination would be discounted, since they now believed that their every desire could be fulfilled.

60. Barnes, "Blessings Flowing Free," 464; "Kingdom Sings and Registers," *New York Sun*, 4 Nov. 1935.

61. *Spoken Word*, 13 Apr. 1936; *Spoken Word*, 23 Nov. 1935, 1; Mark Naison, *Communists in Harlem During the Depression* (New York, 1983), 129.

62. Barnes, "Blessings Flowing Free," 459; *Spoken Word*, 31 Aug. 1935. As always in Peace Mission publications, no mention was made of the race of these women. It is likely, however, that at least some of the Righteous Government leaders were middle-class white women. On the effects of the Righteous Government crusade on Divinite women and men, see Barnes, "Blessings Flowing Free," 518, 521–32, 574 n. 13.

63. Harris, *Father Divine*, 328; also see Fauset, *Black Gods*, 105–6; Braden, *These Also Believed*, 72; Hosher, *God in a Rolls-Royce*, 127.

64. *Spoken Word*, 31 Aug. 1935, 7.

65. "Divine's 'Angels' Win Fight to Register," *New York Times*, 10 Oct. 1936. Also see Parker, *Incredible Messiah*, 166–67. Other observers confirmed that satiny reds, blues, and purples were the colors favored by Divinite women. One observer described Divinite Faithful Mary as "richly dressed in a white and purple satin affair. The white covered the upper part of her body and met the purple in a sharply zig-zag formation just above the waist." Hosher, *God in a Rolls-Royce*, 146. Another reporter described the dress of Divinite Sarah Moss, who wore a white straw hat; white skirt, shoes, and gloves; and a bright scarlet satin blouse. "Court Lifts Veil on Divine Garage," *New York Times*, 5 June 1936, 7. Divinite women liked to contrast fiery colors with whites. This practice seemed to embody the Divinite creed of racial integration and to echo on their bodies the Peace Mission pattern of seating black and white women next to each other at Divinite banquets. See photographs accompanying "Father Divine in Harlem," *Vanity Fair*, Jan. 1936, 39; photograph of Peninnah in Weisbrot, *Father Divine*, following 90.

66. Bair, "Women and the Garvey Movement," 7. See "Notice," *Negro World*, 28 Apr. 1923; David Levering Lewis, *When Harlem Was in Vogue* (New York, 1981), 39–40.

67. Tony Martin, *Literary Garveyism* (Dover, Mass., 1983), 45–46; Bair, "Women and the Garvey Movement," n. 17, 28–29.

68. Hill, *Papers*, vol. 7, l–liv.

69. See Weisbrot, *Father Divine*, 180, on the sparerib stews and pork commonly served at Peace Mission banquets. Divine spoke openly of his identification with his followers, "I AM the common people," he declared. He even claimed to make grammatical errors so that his followers "might understand ME: that I might be with them in their grammatical errors, and erroneousness; that I might lift them and they might lift me." See *Spoken Word*, 18 May 1935, 5; Burnham, *God Comes to America*, 29. Peace Mission

members in turn felt in Divine they had "A God Like Me." See *Spoken Word*, 23 Nov. 1935, 16.

70. See ad in *Black Man*, late Oct. 1935; Hill and Bair, *Marcus Garvey*, xlix; Stein, *World of Marcus Garvey*, 266.

71. Hill and Bair, *Marcus Garvey*, 275 (Garvey's italics), 149, 7.

72. *Black Man*, Jan. 1934, 14.

73. For example, see *Black Man*, Dec. 1933, 14; Jan. 1934, 14, 16; Mar.–Apr. 1934, front cover; Aug.–Sept. 1935, front cover; late Mar., 1936, front cover.

74. Hill and Bair, *Marcus Garvey*, xlix.

75. Amy Jacques Garvey had condemned birth control for blacks in the 1920s. She wrote that "birth control suits [white people] but not us; it is our duty to bear children, and care for those children so that our race may have good men and women through whom it can achieve honor and power." See *Negro World*, 9 Apr. 1927, 7. By the 1930s, however, Amy Jacques Garvey seemed disturbed by her observation that although "malnutrition was taking its toll" on poor Jamaicans, "the fecundity of the people was undiminished." This makes the timing of Garvey's condemnation particularly odd. See Jacques Garvey, *Garvey and Garveyism*, 217, 206. Also see "Negroes Decreasing, Whites Increasing in U.S.A.," *Black Man*, late Dec., 1935, 13; see Hill, *Papers*, vol. 7, 705.

76. Hill and Bair, *Marcus Garvey*, lvii–lviii. On the relationship between pronatalism and fascism, see Claudia Koonz, *Mothers in the Fatherland: Women, the Family and Nazi Politics* (New York, 1987); Victoria De Grazia, *How Fascism Ruled Women: Italy, 1922–45* (Berkeley, Calif., 1992).

77. See Weisbrot, *Father Divine*, 165; Barnes, "Blessings Flowing Free," 286, 216; "Court Lifts Veil on Divine Garage," *New York Times*, 5 June 1936, 7; Parker, *Incredible Messiah*, 273.

78. Weisbrot, *Father Divine*, 209–10. On Peace Mission sex scandals, see Watts, *God, Harlem, U.S.A.*, 144–52, 155. Millennial movements attract rebellious and nonconformist individuals and so are inherently unstable and inclined to fissions. Thus although external harassment took its toll on the movement, the splits from within were equally damaging. As Barnes points out, the Peace Mission was in many ways a family, and "[l]ike many another . . . family, the Peace Mission Movement could be suffocating and cruel." Former members described Peace Mission Heavens as ridden with jealousy and intrigue, and told of their own terrors that Divine, as God, would find and punish them if they dared to leave the movement. See Barnes, "Blessings Flowing Free," 229; Hadley Cantril, *The Psychology of Social Movements* (New York, 1941), 136–37.

79. See *New Day*, Dec. 8, 1936. This format varied little for the next twenty years. See also Watts, *God, Harlem, U.S.A.*, 160, 144.

80. See Braden, *These Also Believe*, 215; Weisbrot, *Father Divine*, 209–10; Watts, *God, Harlem, U.S.A.*, 161–63.

81. Harris, *Father Divine*, 15; see 14–17.

82. See Weisbrot, *Father Divine*, 211; Worsley, *Trumpet Shall Sound*, xxxvii–xxxviii, xlix, 232.

83. See Worsley, *Trumpet Shall Sound*, 232–33. Although Father Divine's belief in the creative power of thought always contained the potential of self-blame, this tendency had been muted during the 1930s heyday of his movement. At that time, Divine attributed even criminal behavior to the sufferings of people under unjust laws. In one 1935 banquet speech, Divine explained that "[e]ven cultured men at times, and others that are not cultured, resort to crime because of segregation, because of the dishonesty of Poli-

tics, and the dishonesty of the Laws. . . ." See *Spoken Word*, 7 Dec. 1935, 5–6. On another occasion, Divine explicitly sanctioned rebellion against unjust laws. "God is a law-breaker and a law-violator," he said. *Spoken Word*, 26 Oct. 1935, 12.

84. *New Day*, 13 July 1974, 17, cited in Watts, *God, Harlem, U.S.A.*, 88. After Father Divine's death in 1965 the *New Day* continued to publish selected reprints of his speeches. They cite the time and place that Divine gave the speech. Because Watts gives only the date of the *New Day* issues, it is not certain whether Divine made this statement after 1936. The tone of the comment fits Divine's increasingly punitive attitude in the 1940s and 1950s, however.

85. *New Day*, 22 July 1944, 44; see *New Day*, 13 Aug. 1942, cover; Braden, *These Also Believe*, 1, 18, 21.

86. Father Divine, speech originally delivered in 1932 and published in *New Day*, 1 Mar. 1975, cited in Watts, *God, Harlem, U.S.A.*, 88.

87. See Mother Divine, *Peace Mission Movement*, 35, 144, 149–50; see Father Divine's speech of 6 Oct. 1945 in *New Day*, 18 July 1987, 7.

88. See *New Day*, 22 July 1944, 7; Divine's sermon of 6 Feb. 1951 in *New Day*, 2 Dec. 1978, cited in Weisbrot, *Father Divine*, 212.

89. See Harris, *Father Divine*, 120; Mother Divine, *Peace Mission Movement*, 52.

90. The Rosebuds, Divine said in 1944, were "making an INDEPENDENT PEOPLE in the land! And as they LIVE their INDEPENDENCE and do not depend on individuals for anything . . . they will stand INDEPENDENTLY and do any and everything for themselves. . . ." *New Day*, 22 July 1944, 8; see *New Day*, 24 Nov. 1945.

91. The Rosebuds became Divine's primary, though not exclusive, exemplars of virginity. The Crusaders, a male order, similarly pledged to "live so that every thought, word and deed is virgin pure in its righteousness." The Lily-buds, an order for older women, were not required to be literal virgins. Nevertheless, their pledge promised that they had been "redeemed from the mortal, carnal life. . . ." See *New Day* Supplement, 15 Sept. 1956, 2a, s12; Burnham, *God Comes to America*, 84–96; Mother Divine, *Peace Mission Movement*, 32. On Divine's emphasis on virginity, see Harris, *Father Divine*, 236–37. It is not clear exactly when the Rosebuds' Creed, with its strong emphasis on virginity, was first proposed. The earliest reference I have found is in Harris, *Father Divine*, published in 1953.

92. The Rosebuds' uniform exemplified the merging of nationalism and virginity typical of Divine's later movement. In sharp contrast to the fiery colors and satiny textures adopted by Peace Mission women of the 1930s, the Rosebuds wore blue skirts, white blouses, red jackets with large Vs on the lapels (standing for Virgin, in some accounts, and Virtue and Victory, in others), and tiny red, white, and blue neckties. The use of the famous World War II V symbol to embody not only the predestined victory of the United States but also the virginity of Divine's red-white-and-blue-clad Sweets is a near-perfect exemplification of the merging of body and community symbolism typical of religious sects. The Rosebuds' victory over lower bodily impulses symbolically merged with a hoped-for American victory over "lower" nations. See photos in *New Day*, 11 Sept. 1954; Harris, *Father Divine*, 248–49; Watts, *God, Harlem, U.S.A.*, 161; Mother Divine, *Peace Mission Movement*, 32; see Mary Douglas, *Natural Symbols: Explorations in Cosmology* (New York, 1982). Numerous mainstream Americans shared Divine's obsession with virginity and anti-communism in the 1950s. See Elaine Tyler May, *Homeward Bound: American Families in the Cold War Era* (New York, 1988), 92–113.

93. Letter from Father Divine to Citizens Emergency Defense Conference, 4 Aug. 1953 in *New Day*, 11 Sept. 1954, *New Day*, 30 Apr. 1955, 17, and many other *New Day* issues.

94. See Burnham, *God Comes to America*, 86–96; Watts, *God, Harlem, U.S.A.*, 161. These similarities were somewhat superficial, however, since male and female Divinites, unlike mainstream Americans, continued to live separate, celibate lives.

95. Among Peace Mission members, only Father Divine could marry. Divinites interpreted Divine's marriage as "the Marriage of CHRIST to HIS Church" and stressed that the marriage was purely spiritual. Father Divine frequently referred to the new Mrs. Divine as his Spotless Virgin Bride. See Mother Divine, *Peace Mission Movement*, 53–58, 147.

96. See photographs of Father and Mother Divine in supplement, *New Day*, 11 Sept. 1954; see Harris, *Father Divine*, 182–83.

97. See *New Day*, 26 Sept. 1953, 6–7 and entire issue; see Mother Divine, *Peace Mission Movement*, 59, 80.

98. *New Day*, 26 Sept. 1953, 13.

99. Garvey, "African Fundamentalism," in Hill and Bair, *Marcus Garvey*, 7.

Chapter 24

Charles Manuel "Sweet Daddy" Grace

John O. Hodges

With the close of the First World War in 1919, blacks in the United States looked forward to enjoying the rights and privileges of all first-class citizens. But white Americans seemed equally determined that the fruits of liberty should be reserved for themselves and their heirs. Although the National Association for the Advancement of Colored People had scored some impressive victories for blacks in the courts, the organization was ill-equipped to address the deep spiritual yearning felt by blacks, especially those on the lower end of the economic scale. The mainline black denominations achieved some success but failed to speak to the total needs of black Americans. The time seemed ripe for Marcus Garvey and other charismatic leaders who attempted to address at once the economic and spiritual problems facing black Americans. One of the most significant of these messiahs was Charles M. Grace, better known to his followers as "Sweet Daddy."

Biography

Charles Manuel "Sweet Daddy" Grace, the charismatic and flamboyant founder and leader of the United House of Prayer for All People on the Rock of the Apostolic Faith, was born Marcelino Manoel de Graca on 25 January 1881 in Brava, Cape Verde Islands, a Portuguese territory off the West African coast. Of African and Portuguese ancestry, he was one of ten children born to Delomba and Emmanuel de Graca, a Portuguese stonecutter. Grace came to the United States around 1903 and worked, at various times, as a cook and grocer in New Bedford, Massachusetts, a Portuguese settlement. Some time after arriving in this country, he changed his name to Charles M. Grace and began his career as a holiness preacher. According to a niece, in a 1960 interview with Kays Gary of the *Charlotte Observer*, Grace had once been married and had had a son (who died at a young age). The marriage ended in divorce because the wife "didn't want a spiritual life." The wife, whom the niece declined to identify, was no doubt Jennie J. Lombard of New Bedford, whom Grace reportedly married on 2 February 1909.

Charles Grace established his first House of Prayer in West Wareham, Massachusetts, in 1924 and began preaching around 1925 in tents throughout the Southeast. The bishop, a title he assumed early in his ministry as head of the House of Prayer, quickly established a number of Houses along the eastern seaboard from as far south as Tampa to as far north as Buffalo. But the greatest number of Houses were established in the southeastern states of Georgia, North Carolina, and South Carolina. These Houses were almost always built in a blighted area of the city, giving some credence to the opinion held by a black minister in Charlotte, North Carolina, according to Rufus Wells, that Daddy Grace "took a rock no one else would use and made it the cornerstone of his church."

Grace and his followers seldom spoke of these establishments as churches and frowned on outsiders who insisted on doing so. They preferred the term "Houses of Prayer," based on Isaiah 56:7: "These I will bring to my holy mountain, and make them joyful in my house of prayer; their burnt offerings will be accepted on my altar; for my house shall be called a house of prayer for all peoples." The tendency in the organization to follow a literal interpretation of Scripture is seen here, as well as in the reference to the altar as the "holy mountain," a designation that holds to this day.

Daddy Grace, in establishing his religious empire, was beset by obstacles from every quarter. But each new setback, far from diminishing the bishop's power and authority, actually seemed to support the claim of his invincibility made by many of his followers. An elder in the Grace organization who had been a member of one of the first Houses of Prayer in Charlotte recounted the following incident to Rufus Wells of the *Washington Afro-American* in February 1960.

> Once when Sweet Daddy was on trial for preaching false doctrine, he said there would be a sign from heaven to prove that he was a spiritual man. While the court was in recess, a ball of fire came down from heaven and knocked a huge limb from a tree in the courtyard. Lots of people were standing in the yard, but no one was hurt. This was the sign he had predicted. The court dismissed the case against him.

To outsiders the incident was a mere chance occurrence, but to the faithful it was evidence of Grace's divine powers.

In 1934, Grace faced a Mann Act charge in Brooklyn, New York, for allegedly transporting a young woman across state lines for immoral purposes. The twenty-year-old woman, a pianist in the Grace organization, said they lived together as man and wife. After a three-day trial, Grace was found guilty and was sentenced to a year and a day in jail. After posting a $7,500 bond and appealing the case, he was acquitted. During the same year the government filed a lawsuit against him for tax evasion, beginning a series of such litigations against Grace and his organization. The government claimed that he owed back taxes in the amount of $15,000 for the years 1927–32, a period during which it was shown that he had paid only $41 in income tax. This suit was later dismissed, as Grace successfully argued that his "income" consisted of free-will donations to the church that were not taxable.

Later, in 1957, a most trying year for the now aging cleric, Grace was hauled into court on at least two occasions. Mrs. Louvenia Royster, a schoolteacher from Waycross, Georgia, filed a suit claiming she had married Grace on 26 September 1923 in New York City, when he was known as John H. Royster. This suit was dismissed, as Grace showed documents proving that he had been out of the country when the marriage was said to have taken place. In the second case, Grace was arrested on a charge of striking a fourteen-year-old girl at the House of Prayer in Richmond, Virginia. According to Wells, the girl claimed that she had resisted his efforts when it appeared that "he was trying to feel my legs, way up high." As in the previous cases, he was cleared of the charges. Through all of these trials, his followers remained faithful, claiming that Daddy could not sin. And in those cases involving women, it seemed as if the female members of his organization provided the greatest support.

The air of invincibility was carefully cultivated by Daddy Grace himself. With his long flowing hair, two-inch fingernails (painted red, white, and blue), cutaway coat, and chauffeured limousines, the bishop struck an impressive if not awesome figure. He was an unquestioned leader and enjoyed total control of the affairs of his organization. Although there was a General Council, this body served at the pleasure of the bishop and was clearly only advisory. Daddy Grace had the last word in all matters involving this organization. According to anthropologist Arthur Fauset in *Black Gods of the Metropolis*, Grace often boasted that he would not have a minister serve under him whom he considered smart enough to question his undisputed authority.

Although Grace established his first House of Prayer in West Wareham, not far from his home in New Bedford, he achieved his greatest success in Charlotte, North Carolina, a city in which the group today claims a membership that rivals that of the traditional denominational churches. This congregation, at least during the 1960s, occupied the largest single black church structure in the city. The first House in Charlotte began when Grace visited that city in 1926 and set up a tent located at 3rd and South Caldwell streets. Here Grace preached and baptized a number of converts in a small lake.

Some of the older members who remember Grace's first visit to Charlotte suggest that part of Grace's power and magnetism lay in the physical resemblance he bore, for some at least, to Jesus. The *Charlotte Observer* of 13 January 1960 carried the following testimony of one of the oldest members:

> I know he seemed different from any man; so one day I ask him, "ain't you Jesus?" And he said, "Look upon me and what you see then that is what I am." Then I came to know that while Jesus was dead, he was carrying Christ in him and he was the last prophet. There ain't going to be no more.

Grace, in fact, unlike his rival Father Divine, never claimed to be God. But it is also fair to say that he never attempted to dispel the impression of those of his followers who insisted that he occupied a station alongside the Trinity. The terms that Grace himself preferred were "God's representative" or "God's chief angel." He saw himself as undertaking a powerful mediating role, as is evidenced by an often-quoted passage, where he plays on the name as "Grace." He would admonish his followers, according to Arthur Fauset in *Black Gods of the Metropolis:* "Never mind about God. Salvation is by Grace. . . . Grace has given God a vacation, and since God is on His vacation, don't worry him. . . . If you sin against God, Grace can save you, but if you sin against Grace, God cannot save you."

The House of Prayer for All People, as its name implies, is open to all, regardless of race, color, or creed. Many of the first members of the organization were from lower-economic backgrounds. And though this particular group still accounts for the majority of the organization's membership, there is an ever increasing number of well-educated middle-class blacks. According to a recent issue of *Truth and Facts*, the membership today claims individuals from all economic levels, including doctors, lawyers, and teachers. Although there are some whites and members of other ethnic groups in the various Houses, the membership is predominantly black. Those whites who join tend to be young and liberal and are attracted to the organization's commitment to a worship service free of the bias and prejudice of the color bar so often associated with the mainline denominations.

The House of Prayer emphasizes conversion, sanctification, divine healing, and the gift of the Holy Spirit manifested through speaking in tongues and thus belongs to the group of churches commonly called Pentecostal. Like most of these churches, the House of Prayer is fundamentalist in its teachings. It stresses the inerrancy of biblical Scripture and prohibits drinking, profanity, adultery, fornication, and interfaith marriages. Although there is an unwritten dress code, it does not appear to be applied as strictly as in a number of the other holiness churches.

From God's White House, the organization's headquarters located at 601 M Street in the nation's capital, to the smaller missions, the "churches" exhibit a remarkable degree of uniformity, even to the point of the predominant color scheme of red, white, and blue that is found both inside and outside the structures. Services at each of the Houses are held nightly, beginning around 7:30 or 8:00 P.M., and throughout the day on Sundays. They are often spontaneous affairs, punctuated by singing, blaring trombones, ecstatic shouting, and testimonies to the healing powers of Grace or of one of his numerous products, which are sold at each of the services. Although there is preaching, it does not occupy center stage, as it does for example in the traditional Baptist church. Grace, in fact, was not considered a dynamic speaker.

The single most important event occurs each year during convocation, a kind of convention that attracts members from across the nation. These convocations are held in late summer and early fall in locations where there are Mother Houses with sufficient seating to accommodate the vast numbers who regularly attend. The appearance of the bishop (the title was assumed by Walter McCollough in 1962) near the end of the week is the central attraction. There are programs in his honor on Friday and Saturday evening; and on Sunday morning, there is a large baptism, followed by a parade through the neighborhood.

The House of Prayer's emphasis on fund-raising is clear and unmistakable, leading some to consider this aspect as a rite in itself. Indeed, the *General Council Laws of the United House of Prayer for All People* contains numerous references to the proper conduct of the members and pastors regarding the collection and disposition of funds. Various "laws" forbid the local pastor from handling money yet require him to be knowledgeable of "every penny raised and spent." Another law mandates that "each House must have representative a man besides the pastor to take note of everything and accompany the pastor at the time of checking." Further checks on the handling of funds are accomplished through the establishment of two important committees: a banking committee and a bills-paying committee. At least two of the members of the banking committee must go to deposit all funds before they are eventually sent to the headquarters in Washington. All bills are to be paid by check. Whereas the local pastors are bound by stringent rules of accountability, the bishop himself enjoys the widest latitude in all financial matters. Rule #40, often referred to as the Golden Rule, states: "All pastors must see to it that each member pays his convocation fee and substantial rallies put on for the upbuilding of the Kingdom of Heaven and this is to be put in the hands of our General Builder to build as he sees fit without bounds." One night per week, usually on Tuesday or Wednesday, the local pastor is permitted to keep for himself the money collected.

Much of the organization's revenue is raised through numerous clubs and groups that vie with each other in efforts to achieve the "victory," accorded to the individual or group that raises the largest sum of money. The financial report from the Charlotte Mother House for 7 February 1971 lists over thirty such groups, including the Elder Board, Grace Soldiers, Literature Club, String Band, Home Lovers, Female Scouts, Senior Queens, Female Royal Guards, Willing Workers, Soul Hunters, and Junior Nurses. Whatever other responsibilities these organizations have, their chief duty seems to be that of fund-raising.

Additional revenue is generated through the sale of a line of products bearing the leader's name, all of which carry rather fantastic claims. Grace soap and Grace cold cream can cleanse the body and promote healing; Grace writing paper is helpful in composing a good letter; and Grace coffee beans brew the best cup of coffee.

The most important of these products is *Grace Magazine*, a monthly reportedly published since the late 1920s. Inside the front cover of each issue is a picture of Daddy Grace with the caption: "Daddy Grace, the Last Prophet." The contents page includes the magazine's statement of purpose: "[T]o unfold the Hidden truth of the gospel; to Magnify the life of Christ; to Teach, to appreciate the Gift of God; to Testify of the Present Blessing Received by the Thousands, and Healing by the Millions." Testimonies regarding healing are a central emphasis of the magazine, taking up more than half of an average issue. The magazine not only serves as the official organ for proclaiming the healing powers of Grace and of the various products but also is believed to have healing powers itself. Interviews conducted with several of the older members of the Charlotte House disclosed that many in the organization, usually women, regularly wear pieces of the magazine on their bodies to ward off illness and ill fortune. One woman claimed that after applying a small piece of the magazine to a corn on her toe, the pain ceased and the corn went away. Another credited the magazine with healing a bone ailment, and still another wrote of the power of the magazine when used in conjunction with some other Grace product. She said:

> On June 15, 1944, I was doing some work in my garden, and a snake bit me. . . . I then took some of the Grace Hair Grower and put it on a piece of *Grace Magazine* and made a plaster and applied it to the place where I had been bitten and it was healed, and I am still well. I had faith in the God of Daddy Grace. I thank God for Sweet Daddy Grace and all the Grace products.

These statements, representative of the type of testimonies that can be found in each issue, point to the central role that divine healing occupies in the religion.

Before his death of a heart attack in Los Angeles on 12 January 1960, Charles Grace could claim a following of over three million in well over one hundred Houses and financial holdings estimated at over $25 million. But the House of Prayer itself seemed to be in great turmoil. The organization had lost not only its spiritual leader and "boyfriend to the world" but a skilled businessman and tactician who had been able to keep the government and other detractors at bay. The IRS greeted the news of his death with a tax suit of nearly $6 million on the Grace estate. Lawyers for the House of Prayer maintained that the properties did not belong to Grace personally but to the church and therefore should enjoy the tax-exempt status commonly afforded such property. Indeed, Grace left only $70,000 to his relatives; the rest was willed to the organization. After a lengthy court battle, U.S. District Court Judge George L. Hart, Jr., ordered, in March 1963, that assets of over $4.6 million be turned over to the House of Prayer.

The House of Prayer also had to contend with internal problems. The constitution, for example, did not clearly provide for a successor to Daddy Grace. There were several pretenders to the throne, each claiming in some way to have been appointed by Grace himself. Elder Walter McCollough, a native of Great Falls, South Carolina, and the owner of a dry cleaning establishment in Washington, prevailed after a long, bitter struggle that eventually had to be handled by the courts. The court ordered a new election between the major candidates when a group of dissident elders questioned the legitimacy of the first election and therefore McCollough's claim to leadership. Capturing 410 of the 462 delegates' votes, McCollough assumed his office on a permanent basis on 8 April 1962.

McCollough's greatest task still lay before him: he had to heal the wounds caused by the protracted legal battle as well as to justify his status as Daddy Grace's successor. This was no easy matter, as Grace had been considered the "Last Prophet," after whom there would be no other. To make as smooth a transition as possible and to dispel any impression that his actions were motivated by self-interest, McCollough for the first few years of his administration tried to keep the organizational structure as it had been under Grace's leadership. He considered himself Grace's son and, for a while, called himself "Sweet Daddy Grace" McCollough. A man of fair complexion, he allowed his hair and fingernails to grow, so that even casual observers could see a striking physical resemblance between the two men. Gradually, over a period of twenty-five years, he seems to have built the organization in his own image. The Grace products have now given way to McCollough shampoo, McCollough soap, and various other McCollough products, including *McCollough Magazine.* Moreover, as the official successor to Daddy Grace, McCollough assumed the title of bishop, which had been reserved exclusively for Daddy Grace. When several members of the Mother House in Charlotte were asked about the differences between McCollough and Grace, most of the respondents faithful to McCollough claimed that there is no essential difference, only that the work is now greater. They pointed to the number of new Houses that are cropping up throughout the nation in cities that heretofore had no Houses. A major reason for this expansion is that McCollough tells his followers that they should not live in a city where there is no House of Prayer. If one is not there, they should build one. These kinds of efforts have kept the organization vibrant and flourishing; today it is one of the largest of the independent Christian communities in the United States and is a major force in the spiritual lives of thousands of black Americans.

Appraisal

Despite bits of biographical information that can be found here and there, Bishop Charles Manuel Grace remains something of an enigma to us. This, of course, is owing largely to the bishop himself, who, it is reported, often spoke in riddles or parables when he felt pushed or pinned down on a fine point. Added to this are questions regarding his intellectual prowess. Some have claimed that Grace could speak several languages, whereas others insist just as vigorously that he had great problems reading and writing.

Grace never delved into the arcanae of theological or religious thought. His belief system, as he himself once suggested, was based on faith rather than religion. As God's intermediary, he promised his followers spiritual as well as material rewards that they could have in the present. Grace never emphasized the compensatory, otherworldly doctrines that Benjamin Mays and Joseph Nicholson found to characterize much of the preaching in the black church during the 1930s. For members of the House of Prayer, the Word was made flesh in the embodiment of Grace himself.

There are those, of course, who consider Grace to have been more of a businessman than a spiritual leader. They have fallen just short of agreeing with Joseph Washington's assessment: "The movement was a profit-making venture by a black entrepreneur who succeeded by manipulating spiritual hunger into a system of self-aggrandizement." Although Grace certainly lived comfortably, perhaps extravagantly, reports of his personal wealth are no doubt exaggerated. Most of the money seemed to have been ploughed back into the organization in the form of larger and better-appointed sanctuaries, apartment buildings, and other properties that belonged to the House of Prayer and not to Grace personally.

Mays and Nicholson, in their book *The Negro's Church* (1933), conclude, "It is characteristic of the Negro church that the Negro owns it and that it is largely the product of his hand and brain." The statement is perhaps even more relevant in regard to the House of Prayer, for the members not only own the titles to the various sanctuaries but the deeds as well. It had always been the policy of Grace (and now McCollough) to complete payment of the building before it was dedicated as a House of Prayer. Those members of the congregation who may not own their own homes can point with pride to their partial ownership in the House of Prayer.

The House of Prayer, which prides itself on being open to all, regardless of color or creed, may be vulnerable to charges of sexism. Although women in most of the Houses outnumber men two or three to one, they are forbidden (based on Scripture) from advancing in the church's hierarchy to positions of minister or elder. Although there appear to be no insurgent voices among the women at this time, one wonders how long this silence will continue in light of the protests by women in the mainline churches.

Survey of Criticism

There have not been many scholarly studies of Charles Grace or the United House of Prayer. The classic study remains Arthur H. Fauset's *Black Gods of the Metropolis*, in which he discusses four other black groups of the urban North in addition to the House of Prayer. Though Fauset's study was done over forty years ago, it still provides very useful information, since there have been few changes in ritual and organization. A more sustained treatment of the House of Prayer may be found in Albert Whiting's dissertation, "The United House of Prayer for All People: A Case Study of a Charismatic Sect." Whiting lived among the members of the Augusta, Georgia, House for a month in order to get a firsthand look at its religious practices. The study includes fascinating interviews with the members, but the effort to determine personality characteristics from such information is less successful. A more recent study is John W. Robinson's essay "A Song, a Shout, and a Prayer," which updates Fauset's materials and provides useful information on the transition from Grace to McCollough. There are also several news series that appeared shortly after Grace's death, in such dailies as the *Washington Post*, the *Afro-American*, and the *Charlotte Observer*. Of these, Phil Casey's seven-part series, appearing in March 1960, provides the most detailed data.

Further research on Bishop Charles Grace and the United House of Prayer is necessary to correct certain negative and unfounded generalizations, such as the view held by Sydney Ahlstrom in *A Religious History of the American People* (1972). He asserts that adherents are from "depressed elements of the black communities" with deep insecurities, anxieties, and psychic needs. It is questionable whether those individuals who join the House of Prayer differ radically from those who join the more orthodox groups. What appears to be the case is that the House of Prayer and similar organizations have been more imaginative and resourceful in addressing the full gamut of needs of their followers. There seems to be little doubt that the United House of Prayer will continue to flourish in its own right, not merely as an alternative to the mainline churches.

Bibliography

Studies about Charles Manuel "Sweet Daddy" Grace

Casey, Phil. "The Enigma of Daddy Grace." *Washington Post*, 6–13 March 1960.
Fauset, Arthur H. *Black Gods of the Metropolis: Negro Religious Cults in the Urban North.* Philadelphia: University of Pennsylvania Press, 1944.

Gary, Kays. "Spiritual Life Not for Wife, So Daddy's Marriage Ended." *Charlotte Observer,* 13 January 1960, p. 2A.

Gaultney, Judy. "House of Prayer Got Its Start in Downtown Tent." *Charlotte News.* 17 February 1979, p. 5A.

General Council Laws of the United House of Prayer for All People. Washington, D.C.: United House of Prayer, 1938.

LaFarge, John. "The Incredible Daddy Grace." *America* 103 (2 April 1960): 5.

McCollough, Walter. *The Truth and Facts: United House of Prayer.* Washington: House of Prayer, 1986.

MacDonald, Donald. "Daddy Grace Coming Sept. 7 to Dedicate His New Church." *Charlotte News,* 14 August 1954, section 2, p. 1.

Oberdorfer, Don. "Daddy Grace Profited by Being a Prophet." *Charlotte Observer,* 3–4 February 1960.

Robinson, John W. "A Song, a Shout, and a Prayer." In *The Black Experience in Religion,* edited by C. Eric Lincoln. Garden City, N.Y.: Doubleday, Anchor Books, 1974.

Washington, Joseph R., Jr. *Black Sects and Cults.* Garden City, N.Y.: Doubleday, 1972.

Wells, Rufus. "Secrets of Daddy Grace." *Washington Afro-American.* 12 February–5 March 1960, magazine section.

Whiting, Albert N. "The United House of Prayer for All People: A Case Study of a Charismatic Sect." Ph.D. diss., American University, 1952.

York, John. "The Spiritual Empire of Sweet Daddy Grace." *Charlotte Observer,* 20 February 1983, pp. 1E, 7E.

Chapter 25

The Black Roots of Pentecostalism

Iain MacRobert

In 1965, at a time when most white American Pentecostal authors had either written William Joseph Seymour and his black prayer group out of their movement's history or trivialized his central role, Walter Hollenweger recognized that:

> The Pentecostal experience of Los Angeles was neither the leading astray of the Church by demons . . . nor the eschatological pouring out of the Holy Spirit (as the Pentecostal movement itself claims) but an outburst of enthusiastic religion of a kind well-known and frequent in the history of Negro churches in America which derived its specifically Pentecostal features from Parham's theory that speaking with tongues is a necessary concomitant of the baptism of the Spirit.[1]

The historical origins of Pentecostalism in the United States lie primarily in the Wesleyan-Holiness, Keswick and Higher Life Movements, and in the black American church.[2] While the white influences on the early Pentecostal Movement have been recognized by Pentecostal historians, they have often disparaged and sometimes completely ignored the crucial influences of Afro-American Christianity. White pioneers and early leaders like Charles Fox Parham or Ambrose Jessup Tomlinson have been recognized—even eulogized—whereas Seymour, one of the most influential of the pioneers, has generally been marginalized and his important role even denied by the myth of no human leadership, and this in spite of the recognition accorded him by such diverse people as Frank Bartleman in the United States, Alexander A. Boddy in Britain, and G. R. Polman in the Netherlands.[3] Parham may have been accused of homosexuality and Tom-

616

linson of financial mismanagement and megalomania, but Seymour was less acceptable to most North American Pentecostal historians than either of them. They were white, he was black.

A more scholarly and rigorous historian, James R. Goff, continues to maintain that "Parham, more than Seymour, must be regarded the founder of the Pentecostal movement," because "it was Parham who first formulated the theological definition of Pentecostalism by linking tongues with the Holy Spirit baptism."[4] For Goff, glossolalia as the initial evidence of Spirit baptism is "the *sine qua non* of the experience" and "the central theological corpus which has always defined the movement."[5] To characterize Pentecostalism in terms of the evidence doctrine is, however, to accept a narrow, inadequate, white, North American definition which is belied, not only by Pentecostals in the two-thirds world, but also by some white classical Pentecostals in Britain, and by many black-majority Pentecostal churches both in Britain and in the United States itself.[6]

Because Pentecostalism is primarily found not on a theological proposition, but on a shared perception of human encounter with the divine, it has roots in many Christian traditions and in a diversity of cultures; but it is first and foremost an experiential rather than a cognitive movement. Goff maintains that "the primacy of theological formulation" labels Parham as chronologically the founder of Pentecostalism.[7] While doctrine was important to some early Pentecostals (though generally less so to black worshippers), all theological formulations were both secondary to their pneumatic experience and, to a greater or lesser extent, inadequate in their attempts to understand or explain the Pentecostal phenomena. The Pentecostal movement did not spread to fifty nations within two years of the Azusa Revival or grow to its current size of some 360 million adherents worldwide as a result of Pentecostal "theology" or Parham's evidence doctrine, although his understanding of tongues as *xenoglossa* did encourage early Pentecostal foreign missions.[8]

The particular attraction of Pentecostalism to people around the world and the ease with which it has been indigenized in non-Western societies lies in its black experiential roots which provide a substratum of enduring values and themes for the bulk of the Movement outside of white North America and Europe.

One historian who has taken Seymour's role seriously is the Methodist clergyman, Douglas J. Nelson. In 1981, Nelson completed his thesis—under Hollenweger's supervision—on "The Story of Bishop William J. Seymour and the Azusa Street Revival."[9] His historical and biographical research made Seymour's crucial role clear. Seymour, however, was not simply an American with a black skin. Nor was his socialization solely determined by his negative encounters with the aftermath of American slavery and enduring discrimination and racism. Seymour and the other black worshippers who brought to birth the Azusa Street revival and the world-wide Pentecostal Movement which flowed from it shared an understanding and practice of Christianity which had developed in the African diaspora out of a syncretism of West African primal religion and culture with Western Christianity in the crucible of New World slavery.

African Roots and the Black Leitmotif

Africans, brought as slaves to the Americas, did not arrive *tabula rasa* nor did forced acculturation totally eradicate their primal religious beliefs. On the contrary, both in Africa and in the Americas these pre-literate beliefs were transmitted from generation to generation by oral tradition and symbolism. In narratives—myths, legends, and folk tales—songs, parables, and other aphorisms, ritual, drama, dance, and the rhythms and tones of "talking" drums, African religious ideas were preserved to be syncretized with the Christianity of white America and thus produce a distinctively black form of Christianity. Albert J. Raboteau has well summarized this process:

> Shaped and modified by a new environment, elements of African folklore, music, language, and religion were transplanted to the New World by the African diaspora. . . . One of the most durable and adaptable constituents of the slave's culture, linking African past with American present, was his religion. It is important to realise, however, that in the Americas the religions of Africa have not been merely preserved as static "Africanisms" or as archaic "retentions" . . . African styles of worship, forms of ritual, systems of belief, and fundamental perspectives have remained vital on this side of the Atlantic, not because they were preserved in a "pure" orthodoxy but because they were transformed. Adaptability, based upon respect for spiritual power wherever it originated, accounted for the openness of African religions to syncretism with other religious traditions and for the continuity of a distinctively African religious consciousness.[10]

The primal religious beliefs brought from Africa with the diaspora included a powerful sense of the importance of community in establishing and maintaining both the personhood of individuals and an experiential relationship with the spirit world of ancestors and divinities. They inhabited a world in which the sacred and profane were integrated and the ability to tap into the *force vitale* by means of divination and spirit possession was considered essential to the welfare of the community, the wholeness of the individual, and the success of any major undertaking in the material world.[11]

To attune themselves to the power of the spirits, both in Africa and in the New World, they used rhythm and music. Polyrhythmic drumming, singing, dancing, and other motor behavior opened up the devotee to spirit possession. In Africa, these were understood as the spirits of the ancestors and divinities. In the Americas new understandings grew out of the pragmatic syncretism of their primal religion with Western Christianity. The possessing spirits of Africa became identified with the apostles, prophets, saints, angels, and Holy Spirit of the white missionaries but phenomenologically there was considerable continuity.[12]

In spite of missionary attempts to demythologize the perceptions of slaves, literacy brought them into contact with the world of the Bible which, like their own, was concerned with the relationship between the spiritual and the natural. The biblical accounts of miracles, healings, exorcisms, spiritual power, and the presence of the Holy Spirit in people's lives did not seem so different from their own experiential ancestral religion. Furthermore, their identification with the story of Israel's bondage in Egypt and their subsequent Exodus to the promised land meant that freedom was understood as more than liberation from the power and consequences of personal sin. An African concept of sin as antisocial activities was reflected in an understanding of the work of the devil as predominantly in the concrete realities of enslavement. The Lord of Hosts who delivered his people from Pharoah's oppression was the God of liberation from political and social evil.[13]

The adventism of evangelical revivalism was also particularly attractive to black Christians for it proclaimed an apocalyptic revolution to be inaugurated by the Second Coming of Christ. The high, the mighty, and the oppressor were to be put down, while the humble, the powerless, and the oppressed—the Saints—were to be exalted. This eschatological status-reversal was believed to be immanent. Thus the black church in the Americas embraced an inaugurated eschatology which was congruent with an African sense of the future which is so close that it has almost arrived. And if at any moment they were to put on their golden slippers "to walk the golden streets" it was because—in spite of their bondage and sub-human status—they were the children of God now! Others were inspired by the scriptures and their Christian faith to plan insurrections during Sunday services and other ostensibly religious gatherings.[14]

The revivalism of the late eighteenth and early nineteenth centuries attracted black people because it stressed an experiential conversion of the heart rather than an intellectual or catechetical religion. "The powerful emotionalism, ecstatic behavior, and congregational responses of the revival," writes Raboteau, "were amendable to the African religious heritage of the slaves, and forms of African dance and song remained in the shout and the spirituals of Afro-American converts to evangelical Protestantism." "In addition," continues Robateau, "the slaves' rich heritage of folk belief and folk expression was not destroyed but was augmented by conversion."[15]

Thus much of the primal religion of West Africa was syncretized with Western Christianity and, in particular, with those themes which were of primary importance to the survival and ultimately the liberation of an oppressed people. Certain leitmotifs which echo both their African origins and their sojourn in the "Egypt" of chattel slavery surface again and again in the black church of the Americas. An integrated holistic worldview, the immanence of the divine, belief in spirit possession, spirit healing and spirit power, the importance of dreams and trances, the extensive use of rhythm, certain types of motor behavior, antiphonal participation in worship, baptism (immersion) in water, and the centrality of community all had African antecedents and reemerged during the revivalist camp meetings of the eighteenth and nineteenth centuries where they also influenced whites.[16]

Other leitmotifs of white evangelical or biblical origin became particularly important in the black Christian community: the imminent Parousia, an inaugurated eschatology, and an "Exodus" theology which perceives freedom in sociopolitical as well as spiritual terms. These leitmotifs were expressed, not in systematic propositions but in the oral, narrative, sung, and danced liturgy and theology of the black Christian community.[17]

By the beginning of the twentieth century, many of the black churches in the United States—particularly in the North—had largely conformed to white, middle-class, conservative evangelicalism. Both the black and white Holiness people—who were mainly proletarian—were dissatisfied with the "deadness" and "worldliness" in many churches and looked for a world-wide revival as the harbinger of the imminent Second Advent of Christ. One such Holiness preacher was William J. Seymour.[18]

William Joseph Seymour and the Azusa Street Revival

Born in the South in 1870, the son of emancipated slaves, Seymour grew up in the midst of violent racism. Nelson writes that during his first twenty-four years of life:

> Seymour receives little or no formal schooling but works hard, educates himself . . . drinks in the invisible institution of black folk Christianity, learns to love the great Negro spirituals, has visions of God, and becomes an earnest student of unfulfilled scriptural prophecy.[19]

That invisible institution of black folk Christianity with its black leitmotif formed the cultural and religious basis for Seymour's subsequent role as the leader of the Azusa Street Revival.

Seymour was "seeking for interracial reconciliation" but was aware that this could only be brought about with the aid of divine power.[20] Leaving the interracial Methodist Episcopal Church, he joined another less bourgeois interracial group, the Evening Light Saints, who taught—in addition to holiness, divine healing, racial equality, and a kind of ecumenism—that a final great outpouring of the Spirit was about to take place before the end of world history. Their holiness doctrine, like that of the rest of the Holiness Movement, was based on a simplistic understanding of Wesley's teaching and stressed that a second crisis experience of entire sanctification should follow conversion. Some, following the teaching of Charles G. Finney, also stressed the social aspects of Wesley's teaching and defined sanctification as a willingness to become involved in social action as an outworking of personal faith and consecration.

After recovering from smallpox, which left him blind in one eye, Seymour was ordained by the Evening Light Saints and, during the summer of 1905, was serving as the pastor of a black Holiness church in Jackson, Mississippi. In October he received reports that glossolalia as an evidence of the power of the Holy Spirit was being experienced at the Bible School of Charles F. Parham in Houston, Texas. While outbursts of glossolalia have recurred again and again throughout the history of the Church from the day of Pentecost to the present, in 1901 Parham was responsible for the teaching that it is both the initial evidence of Spirit baptism and the ability "to preach in any language of the world."[21] While the former tenet has become widely, but by no means universally, accepted by Pentecostals, the latter, like his Anglo-Saxon Israel, antimedicine, and conditional immortality teaching, has been largely rejected.[22]

Seymour enrolled at Parham's Bible School. At nine o'clock each morning, he attended classes "segregated outside the classroom beside the door carefully left ajar by Parham" who "practices strict segregation."[23] Leaving Houston, Seymour travelled to the cosmopolitan city of Los Angeles to become pastor of a small black (Church of the Nazarene) Holiness mission on Santa Fe Street. At nightly meetings he preached on conversion, sanctification, divine healing, and the imminent Second Advent; and on Sunday morning he spoke on glossolalia as a sign accompanying Spirit baptism, and this in spite of the fact he had not yet spoken in tongues himself. Returning to the mission for the evening service he found the doors locked against him. He lived and worshipped in the home of Edward S. Lee and his wife and later with Richard and Ruth Asbury. Both couples were black. On Friday the sixth of April, Seymour and a small group began a ten-day fast. Three days later Lee asked Seymour to pray for his recovery from illness. After anointing and prayer Lee felt better and requested that Seymour pray for him to receive the Holy Spirit with the evidence of tongues. He was not disappointed.[24]

Later that night in the Asbury home, a group of black "sanctified wash women" were singing, praying, and testifying. As Seymour rose to preach on Acts 2:4, he recounted the events that had taken place earlier that evening but could preach no longer because as soon as he had completed his account of Lee's experience, Lee burst forth in tongues. Nelson describes what followed:

> The entire company was immediately swept to its knees as by some tremendous power. At least seven—and perhaps more—lifted their voices in an awesome harmony of strange new tongues. Jennie Evans Moore, falling to her knees from the piano seat, became the first woman thus to speak. Some rushed out to the front porch, yard, and street, shouting and speaking in tongues for all the neighborhood to hear. . . . Teenager Bud Traynor stood on the front porch prophesying and preaching. Jennie Evans Moore returned to the piano and began singing in her beautiful voice what was thought to be a series of six languages with interpretations.[25]

Within three days the original all-black group was receiving visits from whites as well as blacks to witness and experience glossolalia, trance, and healing. On the twelfth of April Seymour spoke in tongues himself.[26]

The revival rapidly outgrew the Asbury home and a rundown former African Methodist Episcopal chapel was leased at 312 Azusa Street.

Cleared of construction materials which had been stored there, sawdust was spread on the dirt floor and pews fabricated from odd chairs, nail kegs, and boxes with planks laid across them. The three services which were conducted each day often overlapped. Some meetings only attracted about a dozen people but within a month Sunday attendance had risen to 750 or 800 with a further four or five hundred, for whom there was no room, crowding outside.[27] Nelson declares that, "multitudes converged on Azusa including virtually every race, nationality, and social class on earth, for Los Angeles contained the world in miniature. . . . Never in history had any such group surged into the church of a black person."[28] Multiracial congregations were unusual. Black leadership of such congregations, while not unheard of, was extremely rare.

Spirit baptism was, for Seymour, more than a glossolalic episode. It was the power to draw all peoples into one Church without racial distinctions or barriers. Seymour's newspaper, *The Apostolic Faith* of September 1906, declared that "multitudes have come. God makes no difference in nationality. Ethiopians, Chinese, Indians, Mexicans, and other nationalities worship together."[29] Black witnesses to those events recalled that, "everybody went to the altar together. White and colored, no discrimination seemed to be among them."[30] "Everybody was just the same, it did not matter if you were black, white, green, or grizzly. There was a wonderful spirit. Germans and Jews, black and whites, ate together in the little cottage at the rear. Nobody ever thought of color."[31] White witnesses echoed the same theme: "The color line was washed away in the blood."[32] Visiting from England, the Church of England clergyman, Alexander A. Boddy, recorded that

> It was something very extraordinary, that white pastors from the South were eagerly prepared to go to Los Angeles to the Negroes, to have fellowship with them and to receive through their prayers and intercessions the blessings of the Spirit. And it was still more wonderful that these white pastors went back to the South and reported to the members of their congregations that they had been together with Negroes, that they had prayed in one Spirit and received the same blessings as they.[33]

Within five months of the birth of this Movement, thirty-eight missionaries had gone out from Azusa. In only two years it had spread to over fifty nations worldwide, but the radical challenge to racism was by this time being subverted and rejected by some arrogant and pusillanimous whites. Parham, who propagated the Anglo-Saxon Israel teaching of white supremacy and wrote for the notoriously racist Ku Klux Klan, was horrified at the desegregation and the adoption of black liturgy by whites which had taken place and castigated Azusa for having "blacks and whites mingling" and "laying across one another like hogs."[34] In 1912 he wrote:

> Men and women, whites and blacks, knelt together or fell across one another; frequently, a white woman, perhaps of wealth and culture, could be seen thrown back in the arms of a big "buck nigger," and held tightly thus as she shivered and shook in freak imitation of Pentecost. Horrible, awful shame![35]

Dissociation and Replication

In 1914 the white-dominated Assemblies of God was formed, thus ending, in the words of Vinson Synan, "a notable experiment in interracial church development."[36] Two years later, the "new issue" controversy over the baptismal formula and the nature of the Godhead resulted in the withdrawal of the "Jesus Name" Oneness Pentecostals and the further purging of black people and elements of the black leitmotif from the Assemblies of God. Thus, writes Robert Mapes Anderson, "the Assemblies became an all but 'lily white' denomination. . . . Since 1916, except for a few black faces here and there in urban congregations in the Northeast, the Assemblies has remained a white man's church."[37] The moralistic Oneness Pentecostals fared little better. The same desire for white "respectability," racial segregation, and the rejection of the black leitmotif tore them apart so that by 1924 there were separate white and black organizations. When the Pentecostal Fellowship of North America was set up in 1948 with the ostensible purpose of demonstrating to the world the fulfillment of Christ's prayer for Christian—in this case Pentecostal Christian—unity, only white organizations were invited to join. In 1965, having added a further nine organizations to the original eight, it was still exclusively white.[38]

What began in April 1906 as a black revival under Seymour's leadership incorporated the leitmotif of black Christianity in the Americas and Parham's distinctive doctrine of glossolalia as an evidence of Spirit baptism and the instrument of world evangelization. Almost immediately it became interracial and spread at a phenomenal rate, both in the United States and throughout the world. White Pentecostals in the United States, however, exploited doctrinal disagreements to dissociate themselves from their black brethren, to distance themselves from the black origins of the

Movement, and to purge it of its more obviously black and radical elements which, however, re-emerge again and again wherever Pentecostals of the African diaspora meet for worship.

In Britain, for example, the black Pentecostal congregations which have been established by settlers from the Caribbean from the early 1950s fall into three broad categories. Those which are part of the white-dominated, three-stage, Trinitarian organizations in the United States, like the Church of God (Cleveland) [known in Britain as the New Testament Church of God] and the Church of God of Prophecy, or the white-dominated, moralistic United Pentecostal Church, tend to be culturally ambivalent, and there is often considerable tension between white-defined fundamentalist "orthodoxy" and "orthopraxis" and the black leitmotif which can never be totally stifled. Other three-stage, Trinitarian, "Church of God"–type congregations have broken free from white headquarters in the United States and are significantly more "black" in their beliefs, liturgy, and practice. But the congregations which demonstrate the most overt commitment to the black leitmotif tend to be the Oneness groups with black headquarters in the United States or the Caribbean which pre-date the West Indian migrations of the late 1940s and early '50s.

These groups continue to pulsate most clearly with the liturgical characteristics of the Azusa Revival:[39] orality, narrativity, dance, and liturgical motor behavior with the extensive use of music and rhythm; an integrated and holistic worldview incorporating Spirit possession[40] and trances; the importance of dreams, healing and the need for spiritual power to change the material (and social) world; the importance of community and human relationships—including the abolition of the color line—if life and religion are to be worthwhile; freedom as a sociopolitical as well as a spiritual issue; the imminence of a revolutionary world order inaugurated by the Second Advent of Christ, which is already to some extent present in an inaugurated eschatology. These themes were all in evidence at Azusa as they had been in the church of the African diaspora in the United States, and they are replicated among black Pentecostals in Britain and in the two-thirds world where the overlay of white, North American "orthodoxy" is often quite superficial and in many situations—when the North Americans have gone home—totally absent. Parham's evidence doctrine, while of real importance to most white North American Pentecostals, some European Pentecostals, and a few mission churches, is largely irrelevant to most Pentecostals in the underdeveloped and developing nations and serves only as a redundant symbol of Pentecostal "orthodoxy" for most black Pentecostals in Britain.

Does It Matter?

"Directly or indirectly," writes Synan, "practically all of the Pentecostal groups in existence can trace their lineage to the Azusa Mission."[41] If this is true, then Seymour rather than Parham or Tomlinson is the most significant historical figure in the early Pentecostal Movement. But does it actually matter who the person primarily responsible was: Parham, who taught that glossolalia is the evidence of Spirit baptism and who advocated and practiced racial segregation; Tomlinson who forbade political involvement and led a racially divided church,[42] or Seymour who, as part of the African diaspora, believed in and lived out a Pentecostal experience with socially revolutionary implications? It matters to many black Pentecostals in the United States, Britain, and South Africa who have to confront the social, economic, and political sins of racism, discrimination, and apartheid.[43] It matters—though they may not realize it—for many white Pentecostals who in the denial of their Movement's roots perpetuate the racial arrogance and support for an oppressive sociopolitical and economic *status quo* which makes them the enemies of the Gospel to the poor. And it matters so that Pentecostalism does not become—or indeed remain—an individualistic ideology used by the powerful to control the powerless, or an alien ideology internalized by the powerless to control themselves, but returns to its original emphasis on God's pneumatic empowering of the powerless to be agents of transformation in both the Church and the wider society.

Notes

1. Walter J. Hollenweger, *The Pentecostals* (London: SCM Press, 1972), 23–24; originally in his ten-volume *Handbuch der Pfingstbewegung* (Geneva, 1965–67).
2. See Vinson Synan, *The Holiness-Pentecostal Movement in the United States* (Grand Rapids, Michigan: William B. Eerdmans, 1961), and Vinson Synan (Ed.), *Aspects of Pentecostal-Charismatic Origins* (Plainfield, NJ: Logos International, 1975).
3. Frank Bartleman, *Azusa Street* (Plainfield, NJ: Logos International, 1980 [originally 1925]), especially 46; A. A. Boddy in *Confidence* (September, 1912); G. R. Polman, letter to G. A. Wumkes, 27th February 1915.
4. James R. Goff, *Fields White Unto Harvest: Charles F. Parham and the Missionary Origins of Pentecostalism* (Fayetteville: University of Arkansas Press, 1988), 11.
5. Ibid.
6. The Elm Pentecostal Church in Britain, following the teaching of George Jeffreys, maintains that any of the gifts of the Spirit are evidence of Spirit baptism. While most of the black Pentecostal organizations have articles of faith—largely inherited from their white co-religionists—which state their belief in glossolalia as the initial evidence—in practice it is largely ignored and displaced by an implicitly inclusive charismatology.

7. Goff, 15.
8. Barrett's estimate of 360 million Pentecostals may be a little too high for the narrower definitions of Pentecostalism because it includes traditions which pre-date both Parham (1901) and Seymour (1906). David B. Barrett, "The Twentieth Century Pentecostal/ Charismatic Renewal in the Holy Spirit, with Its Goal of World Evangelization" in *International Bulletin of Missionary Research*, Vol. 12, no. 3 (July 1988).
9. Douglas J. Nelson, "For Such Time As This: The Story of Bishop William J. Seymour and the Azusa Street Revival" (unpublished Ph.D. dissertation, University of Birmingham, 1981).
10. Albert J. Raboteau, *Slave Religion: The Invisible Institution in the Antebellum South* (Oxford: Oxford University Press, 1978), 4–5.
11. Iain MacRobert, *The Black Roots and White Racism of Early Pentecostalism in the USA* (Bassingstoke: Macmillan Press, 1988), 9–14.
12. Ibid., 14–15.
13. Ibid., 15–18.
14. Ibid., 20–23, 33–36.
15. Raboteau, 149.
16. Melville J. Herskovitz, *The Myth of the Negro Past* (Boston: Beacon Press, 1958), 227–31.
17. MacRobert, *Black Roots*, 31–34.
18. Ibid., 38–42.
19. Nelson, 31, 153–8.
20. Ibid., 161.
21. Sarah E. Parham (Comp.), *The Life of Charles F. Parham: Founder of the Apostolic Faith Movement* (Joplin, Missouri: Tri-State Printing Co., 1930), 51–52.
22. On Parham's theories of racial supremacy, see: Charles Fox Parham, *A Voice Crying* in *the Wilderness* (Joplin, Missouri: Joplin Printing Co., 1944 [originally 1902]), 81–84, 92–100, 105–118; and Charles Fox Parham, *The Everlasting Gospel* (Baxter Springs, Kansas, 1942), 1–4.
23. Nelson, 35.
24. Ibid., 187–90; MacRobert, *Black Roots*, 51–52.
25. Nelson, 191.
26. Ibid., 191–92.
27. Ibid., 192–94, 196; *The Apostolic Faith*, Vol. 1, No. 1 (September 1906), 1, col. 1; Bartleman, 47–48.
28. Nelson, 196.
29. *The Apostolic Faith*, op. cit., 3, col. 2.
30. Quoted in Synan, *Aspects*, 133.
31. Quoted in Nelson, 234 n. 91.
32. Bartleman, p. 54.
33. *Confidence* (September 1912).
34. Parham, *Everlasting Gospel*, 1–3.
35. Charles Fox Parham, *Apostolic Faith*, Baxter Springs, Kansas (December 1912).
36. Synan, *Holiness-Pentecostal*, 153.
37. Robert Mapes Anderson, "A Social History of the Early Twentieth Century Pentecostal Movement" (Ph.D. thesis, Columbia University, 1969), 319–20; published in a revised form as *Vision of the Disinherited: The Making of American Pentecostalism* (New York: Oxford University Press, 1979).

38. Synan, *Holiness-Pentecostal*, 179–80.
39. Iain MacRobert, "Black Pentecostalism: Its Origins, Functions and Theology with special reference to a Midland Borough" (unpublished Ph.D. dissertation, University of Birmingham, 1989), 39.
40. Even Bartleman, a white Pentecostal pioneer, constantly refers to the baptism with, in or of the Holy Spirit as "possession." Bartleman, 72 ff.; see also Seymour in *The Apostolic Faith*, Vol. 1, No. 4 (December 1906), 1, col. 4.
41. Synan, *Holiness-Pentecostal*, 114.
42. A. J. Tomlinson, *Answering the Call of God*, 9–10, quoted in Lillie Duggar, *A. J. Tomlinson* (Cleveland, Tennessee: White Wing Publishing House, 1964), 21; A. J. Tomlinson, quoted in C. T. Davidson, *Upon This Rock* (Cleveland, Tennessee: White Wing Publishing House and Press, 1973), 437–38, 448, 518, 552–53, 594; "Minutes of 45th Assembly (1950)," quoted in *Church of God of Prophecy Business Guide* (Cleveland, Tennessee: White Wing Publishing House and Press, 1987), 45.
43. See, for example, Nico Horn, "The Experience of the Spirit in Apartheid South Africa," in *Azusa Theological Journal*, Vol. 1, No. 1, Durban, South Africa: Relevant Pentecostal Witness Publications (March 1990), 19–42.

Chapter 26

"Together and in Harness"

Women's Traditions in the Sanctified Church

Cheryl Townsend Gilkes

All human communities contain enterprising and historically aware members who struggle to maintain the cherished values, statuses, roles, activities, and organizations of earlier generations that serve to structure the group's presentation of self and, therefore, constitute tradition. Within the black community in the United States, women have been some of the most enterprising agents of tradition. Since sociologists have seriously neglected study of tradition, women, and black people, black women's traditions in community institutions represent the most underdeveloped topic of social inquiry.

Black women and men have perceived racial oppression to be the most pervasive source of their individual and group suffering, but it has not been the sole catalyst for their collective action. In addition to mounting organized responses to problems of political subordination, economic exploitation, and social exclusion, black people have constructed a historical community that has provided a context for traditions, distinctive ethnic identity, and group consciousness. When pressure to abandon tradition has come from outside the black community, maintaining tradition has become a matter of political resistance, even though this struggle may take place in parts of the community that typically avoid confrontation with the dominant culture. For example, religion and religious activity have been the most important spheres for the creation and maintenance of tradition. Black women have invested considerable amounts of time, energy, and economic resources in the growth and development of religious organizations.

Recognition of the variety of strong traditions that black women have established in the religious and secular affairs of their community has been obscured by sociologists' exclusive focus on family roles and on black women's deviation from patriarchal expectations in a sexist and racist society. The tendency to view black churches only as agencies of sociopolitical change led by black male pastors also obscures the central and critical roles of black women. Throughout all varieties of black religious activity, women represent from 75 to 90 percent of the participants; yet there is little documentation or analysis of their role in the development of this oldest and most autonomous aspect of black community life.[1] This article examines the place and importance of black women amid their traditions within one segment of the black religious experience, the Sanctified Church.

The Sanctified Church, a significant but misunderstood segment of a very pluralistic black church, comprises those independent denominations and congregations formed by black people in the post-Reconstruction South and their direct organizational descendents. In contrast to those Baptist and Methodist denominations organized before the Civil War, the Sanctified Church represents the black religious institutions that arose in response to and largely in conflict with postbellum changes in worship traditions within the black community. Although these congregations and denominations were part of the Holiness and Pentecostal movements of the late nineteenth and early twentieth centuries, the label "Sanctified Church" emerged within the black community to distinguish congregations of "the Saints" from those of other black Christians. This label not only acknowledges the sense of ethnic kinship and consciousness underlying the black religious experience but also designates the part of the black religious experience to which a Saint belongs without having to go through the sometimes dizzying maze of organizational histories involving at least twenty-five denominations.

The importance of the Sanctified Church lies in its relationship to black history, its normative impact on the larger black religious experience, and its respect for and positive redefinition of black women's historical experience. When black people were first making choices about their cultural strategies as free women and men, the Sanctified Church rejected a cultural and organizational model that uncritically imitated Euro-American patriarchy. In the face of cultural assaults that used the economic and sexual exploitation of black women as a rationale for their denigration, the Sanctified Church elevated black women to the status of visible heroines—spiritual and professional role models for their churches. At a time when Baptist and Methodist denominations relegated Christian education to the structural margins of their organizations, the Sanctified Church professionalized this activity, and women were able to use their roles as educators and the "educated" as a source of power and career opportunity. At a time when employment opportunities for black women were the worst possible, the Sanctified Church presented "professional" role models for black working women to emulate. Higher education and work were identified as legitimate means of upward mobility for black women, and they were encouraged to achieve economic power through white-collar employment. As a consequence, the women's growing economic power helped to maintain their collective autonomy and reinforced their heroic role in the church. Finally, taking their cue from the feminist infrastructure of the black women's racial uplift movement, churchwomen created an institutional basis for women's self-consciousness. The result was an alternative model of power and leadership within the most authoritarian and least democratic of formal organizations—the episcopally governed church. These religious organizations transformed the negative and contradictory experiences of black women into an aspect of community life that maintained tradition and fostered social and individual change.

Within the Sanctified Church, black women have created for themselves a variety of roles, careers, and organizations with great influence but with variable access to structural authority. Their activities and their consciousness represent a part of the black religious experience that underscores both the dynamic and unsettled nature of gender relations in the wider black community and the historical centrality of gender as a public issue within it. Although the women in the Sanctified Church have worked within structures that range from egalitarian to purely patriarchal, they have neither ceased nor relaxed their efforts to improve their status and opportunities within these organizations. In a variety of ways, their efforts are related to those of women in other black religious and secular organizations.

Women's experience in the Sanctified Church has been part of the larger historical role of black women, a role that emphasizes independence, self-reliance, strength, and autonomy and that contradicts the dominant culture's expectations and demands of women.[2] Like many of the black community's activities of the late nineteenth and early twentieth centuries, the rise of the Sanctified Church contained a gender-conscious response to the problems of racial oppression. Concern about the status and role of women was reflected in one among a number of cultural debates within the post-Reconstruction black community. In a response to black women's suffering and role demands in the context of violent racial oppression, the Sanctified Church took account of at least four specific aspects of their history when developing churchwomen's roles: the devaluation of black women by dominant culture, the education of black women and their recruitment as educators of "the Race" during the late nineteenth and early twentieth centuries, the "relative" economic independence of black women through sustained participation in the labor force, and the autonomous political organization of black women between 1892 and 1940.[3]

The rise of the Sanctified Church also occurred when "liberation of the race was the immediate goal of blacks, [and] the men attached great importance to the females' roles in the effort."[4] In 1896, black women formed the National Association of Colored Women after several years of autonomous organizing. Their efforts earned them W.E.B. Du Bois's admiration and praise as the "intellectual leadership of the Race."[5] The ethic sustaining their efforts supported women's leadership as a necessary part of the overall effort to benefit the community and the world. Clubwoman Josephine St. Pierre Ruffin stated this clearly in 1892: "Our women's movement is a woman's movement in that it is led and directed by women for the good of women and men, for the benefit of all humanity. . . . We want, we ask the active interest of our men; . . . we are not alienating or withdrawing, we are only coming to the front, willing to join any others in the same work."[6] "The Saints" carried this ethic and a positive perception of the role of the "Race woman" into their new denominational structures as they separated or were ejected from the more established Baptist and Methodist churches. Specific women's tradition reflected the high value placed on women's political and educational leadership.

Leaders of the early Sanctified Church were also responsive to the fact that the majority of job opportunities for black women were in domestic service and agricultural work. As black people migrated and the church became more urban, this consciousness generated a concern for the problems of black women as household domestics. As household workers, black women were subject to sexual exploitation by white men who assumed that all black women were morally loose and appreciated male advances. Many black parents saw the education of their daughters as a strategy to avoid such risks. As a result, white observers often criticized black parents' failure to discriminate against their daughters. These educated women were expected to play a role in elevating their sisters, and black women's gatherings were the settings of just such "uplifting" socialization. Church and community activities were organized around household domestics' "time off" as alternatives to the entertainments available in the world of "sinners." Churches encouraged both the educated and the uneducated to be "ladies." While not entirely feminist, these strategies fostered a high degree of woman consciousness within the black religious community.

The black women who responded to Holiness and Pentecostal preachers and evangelists represented the broad spectrum of Afro-American women. These women were as militantly pro-black, pro-woman, and pro-uplift as their Baptist and Methodist sisters were, and their political consciousness was fueled by spiritual zeal. They were somewhat more successful than Baptist and Methodist women in gaining access to the pulpit or lectern; in those churches where they failed, the "double pulpit" emerged as a compromise between the women's spiritual militance and biblical patriarchy. In some cases, Baptist and Methodist women defected to the Sanctified Church in order to exercise their gifts.

The militancy of organized women in the Sanctified Church led to the almost total divergence of women's leadership roles from that of the "pastor's wife." Such separation of marital role from leadership status came more slowly in black Baptist and Methodist churches than in the Sanctified Church, where women's opportunities for leadership became more and more diverse, offering a wide choice of religious careers. In those denominations in which women were unable to become elders, pastors, and bishops, they assumed the roles of church mothers, evangelists, missionaries, prayer band leaders, deaconesses, and, most important, "teachers"; these alternatives were also available in those denominations in which women were eligible for all leadership roles. Where churchwomen were officially "the second sex," they achieved quite powerful positions of influence and structural authority.

The various women's traditions existing within these churches are as much a response to the sociohistorical realities of black womanhood as to perceived biblical mandates and doctrines. One could almost argue that these traditions are more woman-centered than religious. Although all Protestants read the same King James Bible, the black interpretation of scripture had radically different organizational consequences than did the white male reading of the same texts. Whatever the degree of patriarchal control, black churches have been influenced in some way by the militancy of the women of the Sanctified Church.

"Women God Raised Up": The Elevation of Black Women

At the time when white Americans were calling black people a nation of "thieves, liars, and prostitutes,"[7] Sanctified Church members were calling each other "Saints." They perceived themselves to be set apart for sacred

634 Cheryl Townsend Gilkes

purposes; these men and women were confident that God "had raised them up" for a special calling. Regardless of the intensity of racial oppression, it was the responsibility of the "Saints" to do everything in their power to prevent whites from casting them down. Black women represented the overwhelming majority of "Saints" in need of elevation and protection from the physical and cultural assaults of white racism.

The church's resistance strategies have included the adoption of distinctive dress codes and the refusal to use first names in any public settings that could be interracial. Even cornerstones and signs listing church officers give only first initials and surnames. It is important to recognize that this tactic to achieve personhood applies to women as well as men: if male elders are listed with initials, church mothers are similarly listed. In church publications, elders, church mothers, and all others are also identified in this way. All this was (and still is) intended to prevent white racists from calling black Saints by their first names, a white practice used as a strategy to depersonalize and to devalue black people. Although largely overlooked as a tactic in cultural resistance, the Saints' use of initials rather than first names remains a very forceful answer to the daily irritations and abrasions of southern race relations. Accommodation to racism is, in the context of the preaching of the Sanctified Church, an accommodation to sin.

Although white people withheld ordinary titles of respect for blacks, such as Mr., Mrs., and Miss, they relaxed such overt racism when using the religious titles of fellow southern Protestants. In the Baptist and Methodist churches, such courtesies were often extended only to the black preacher. The Sanctified Church, however, saw as ministry those roles reserved exclusively for women and therefore included women when contemplating the problem of interracial protocol. This failure to exclude women from protocol is clear testimony to the woman consciousness of the Sanctified Church, a consciousness evident in the glowing terms used to describe both women's and men's activities in denominational newspapers and reports. If images of the Sanctified Church were derived solely from such reading, one could almost believe that the roles of mothers, evangelists, and missionaries were structurally equivalent to those of the male elders, bishops, and pastors. Unlike men in other churches, men in the Sanctified Church have not ignored or trivialized women's roles. Thus these women with their expanded roles, important careers, and influence have been perceived as "the women God raised up."

The Church of God in Christ (COGIC), largest denomination of the Sanctified Church, ostensibly does not permit the ordination of women, and churchwomen have never let the matter rest. While there is a widespread agreement to disagree within the church. Bishop O. T. Jones represented the quintessence of the truce when he wrote, "The proper place of women in the church is an age old debate and from all appearances it seems that it perhaps will be an eternal one—for most mortals at least."[8] Despite its sexism, the church became the structural paradigm for other denominations. Despite or because of women's exclusion from pulpits, the most powerful Women's Department of any black denomination arose within the COGIC.

The Women's Department is a characteristic feature of the Sanctified Church denominations. James Shopshire argues that a defining characteristic of the power structures of these churches is their control by "a board of bishops" and the prevalence of an independently organized "women's work . . . where female leaders assume much authority, but with deference and loyalty to the bishops." Although these churches adopt the terminology associated with episcopally governed churches, they reflect the Baptist roots of their leadership in a tendency toward a Presbyterian style of more or less sharing power between the laity and the clergy. As a result, "a person may be upwardly mobile . . . to regional and national positions of relative independence from local congregations."[9] This is especially true for Women's Departments, which offer career mobility for a wide range of women.

Women leaders include those called to the ministry and denied access to pastoral positions, women who prefer the role of evangelist to that of pastor, women who actually have charge of churches in the absence of a pastor, and women who are Spirit-filled religious activists and congregational leaders. The political skill of the early Women's Department of the COGIC was such that nearly all women's roles, including that of "laywoman," were eventually included in that denomination's official definition of the ministry. The term "layman" was not so included. Thus the avenues of social mobility for women in the church branched out and were officially recognized. The diversity of roles allowed women to exercise influence beyond their congregations, which laymen were not organized to do. Women's Departments today retain unparalleled power in matters of policy and practice for all laywomen and continue to provide ladders of career mobility. They communicate both to the women of the church and to the male leadership and, regardless of restrictions, determine the role models available to churchwomen. This means that the choice of heroines of the Women's Department, and thus of the church as a whole, reflects churchwomen's values and view of reality.

In order to contribute to the construction of those role models in the early days of the Sanctified Church, women needed to attend the regional and national conventions and convocations. For the black women of the late nineteenth and early twentieth centuries, such travel was full of risks, and Jim Crow laws made these undertakings all the more difficult. Since women played a large part in developing individual congregations, the church recognized as issues of common concern the problems of their travel and need for respect in public places. In order to counter the stereotypes used as rationales for the abuse of black women, Sanctified Church women were encouraged to "dress as becometh holiness." One early bishop was convinced that the sight of women of the COGIC dressed according to the dictates of the Women's Department would restrain the most ardent racists.

There was a decided contrast between the ecstatic style of worship of these churches and the formal style of dress. Women wore black or white uniformlike dresses, and evangelists and church mothers devised a uniform or "habit" called "the Saint" to wear in services and on trains. At regional or national meetings, the highest ranking woman—the district missionary, the district supervisor, or the national supervisor—determined the dress of all other women present and decided whether they wore white on a particular day. While this may seem a rather trivial matter, the problem of discipline was not, and clergymen were required to adhere to equally stringent dress codes.

Thus the women of the early COGIC and other Sanctified Church denominations achieved such a position of respect and autonomy that they defined the content of their own roles. Furthermore, church members could not advance ideologies of patriarchy that contradicted standards of holiness since "holiness" was the most important achieved status in these churches—and a status not humanly conferred. Biblical debate concerning women was confined to structural norms, not the nature, quality, or character of women per se. Denominations that ordained women to be elders and pastors argued about women becoming bishops: in others in which all roles were open, there was no controversy. However, the egalitarian denominations would not recognize a woman's call at as early an age as they would a man's.[10] Within the COGIC, the church was forced to argue that women were completely capable but that the COGIC did not recognize the feminist biblical argument.[11]

Since women evangelists or revivalists founded or "dug out" many churches, they could not be excluded from church histories: they were too important to the tradition of holiness and to church growth. When male church leaders identified in their spiritual biographies those preachers who effected their conversions, the revivalists were often women. Thus the personal and congregational accounts passed down in written records and oral tradition placed a high value on the contribution of women and men to the most important goal of the church—salvation and holiness.[12]

The extension of women's spiritual contributions into autonomous leadership networks and careers fostered the development of heroines and myth, the most important pillars of tradition. In a social setting that placed a primary value on spirituality, "the women God raised up" as "Mothers in Zion" could not be excluded simply for the sake of male domination. The many tensions created by the intrusion of patriarchal norms were eased by the fact that both men and women placed a high value on holiness, and women played a heroic role in upholding that value. Women's allusion to Deborah who "arose a mother in Israel" in their self-descriptions provided a legitimate counterideology to the patriarchal desires of churchmen.[13] Finally, elevation to clearly articulated roles of spiritual leadership guaranteed that female heroines were part of the culture of the church shared by both men and women.

"Women May Teach": Education as a Source of Power

Education has represented a supreme cultural value in the black church and community. The Sanctified Church arose during the height of the struggle for black education, which led to the expanded role of women as educators. The parents of church founders were slaves who had made their children's education a life's goal that was often not realized. Church officials' personal accounts of conversion echo laments over their own lack of education. Because the Sanctified Church became stereotyped as the sects and cults of illiterate black masses and disaffected urban migrants, both black and white observers failed to apprehend the high value these denominations placed on literacy and higher education. Thus it is important not to view their teaching ministries as a devalued area of female segregation. Male denominational leaders recruited educated women precisely because of their importance to the future.

The Sanctified Church's emphasis on biblical authority made learning "the Word" an important means for living a sanctified life. Educational goals therefore comprised general literacy, biblical literacy, advanced academic and professional achievement, and biblical expository skills, and these goals apparently ranked second in priority after salvation and holiness. The Saints were encouraged to acquire "the learning" without losing "the burning." Those able to teach biblical and general literacy skills and to provide appropriate spiritual role models were chosen as teachers.

The growth in women's roles as teachers resulted from a combination of male decisions and female enterprise. The male church organizers shared the larger cultural value of education, and their decisions to recruit female educators converged with the women's desires for important roles in their churches and with trends toward black women's education in the wider community. Recruitment occurred during that period in black history when the education of women was a conscious response to aspects of their oppression and when they were also being encouraged to act as educators of "the Race." Thus the deployment of women teachers in black education was carried out with almost total disregard for the dominant culture's norms; these women were not limited to teaching children or relegated to roles subordinate to men's. Black women capitalized on their leadership in church education. The early Women's Departments revolved around the Prayer and Bible Study Bands, which expanded the literacy skills of women collectively; these groups paralleled the clubs and seminar groups that were part of the early National Association of Colored Women. This collective self-education was reflected in the expansion of women's leadership roles in denominations and in the growth of the Women's Departments.

Although engaged in conflict with the larger black community over the importance of ecstatic worship, the Sanctified Church admired the same heroines in racial uplift and black education. The examples of prominent churchwomen such as Mary McLeod Bethune, Nannie Helen Burroughs, Ida B. Wells, and Mary Church Terrell prompted the founder of the COGIC, Bishop C. H. Mason, to recruit Mother Lizzie Woods Roberson, a Baptist teacher and academy matron, to be the first "overseer" of the women's work. Encouraged to travel in order to enlist and appoint women leaders, she also conducted revivals as an organizer. Another woman, Arenia C. Mallory, was hired as a teacher at Saints' Academy in Lexington, Mississippi. Church histories describe her as a protégée of Mary McLeod Bethune. After the death of the first principal of Saints' Academy, Mallory became head of the school, which then grew from a primary academy to an accredited junior college. For a while, she was the only black woman college president. As conflicts over theology, doctrine, biblical interpretation, and church polity fostered differentiation within the Sanctified Church, women's importance as educators and the high value placed on educated women were not diminished. When denominations argued about the ordination of women, those that chose to ordain preserved the teaching roles of evangelist and missionary.[14]

In addition to their role in developing attitudes about and organizations for formal education, Sanctified Church women were permitted to teach the Gospel. Teaching the Gospel involved setting forth biblical doctrine, church polity, and duties; conducting revivals; presenting teachings in the morning service in lieu of and in the style of a sermon; and "having charge of a church in the absence of the pastor."[15] The tasks of the teaching role differed very little from the task of the preaching role reserved for men. In some denominations, evangelists not only could have charge of churches but also, as in the case of Pentecostal Assemblies of the World, could serve communion and perform marriages. In some instances, the difference between women's and men's credentials was merely internal; for all practical and legal purposes, women evangelists were clergy. Often members of particular congregations have been hard-pressed to distinguish between men's preaching and women's teaching. One young woman I interviewed observed, "I went to the service and the elder preached. Then he invited the women to speak. They preached, and they were much better than the man."

In the COGIC, women developed their own standards for examining and promoting evangelists. While it is conceivable that a COGIC churchman may be ordained as an elder with very little preaching and administrative experience, the Women's Department sets radically different requirements for women aspiring to become national evangelists. In order to receive such a license, a woman must preach revival successfully in seven states.[16] COGIC churchwomen are strongly motivated to develop their gifts and to develop a national reputation as revivalists in order to receive approval from the Women's Department.

The most widely shared value in the total black religious experience is the high premium placed on good preaching, which is as important in the black church as good music—another area in which women are not restricted. In the COGIC, the women's system guarantees that their "teaching" skills are superior. The dynamic and effective teaching of these women stands in stark contrast to the official stance of the COGIC that women are not called to preach. The availability of women evangelists who are in theory skilled "teachers" but in reality excellent preachers allows the elder with minimal skills in the pulpit to provide good preaching for his congregation. Since black Baptist and Methodist denominations tend to call all evangelists "Reverend" and to call male pastors conducting revival away from their own churches "Evangelist," the uninitiated may believe that these women are preachers. In the formative days of the Sanctified Church, the role of evangelist was an alternative for those women in Baptist and Methodist denominations who were unable to exercise their gifts either from the pulpit or from the floor. Such women went "over" into the Sanctified Church. Contemporary changes among Baptists and Methodists have reversed this earlier trend.

Women's concentration in educational roles in the early Sanctified Church was not simply a form of female segregation; instead it was the basis for alternative structures of authority, career pathways, and spheres of influence. More important, those leaders and historical accounts that provide the church with normative legitimacy and modify the stereotype of its members as poor and illiterate credit the influence of women's educational work. Given the overall, sometimes exaggerated, respect and deference that the black community confers on educators, these women have legitimized the image of the "professional" woman throughout the church. As a result, women in the Sanctified Church have established a more differentiated model of social mobility and occupational aspiration than have the men.

"$10,000 in a Paper Bag": The Economic Limits of Subordination

In the black community, educated women work outside the home. Contrary to trends in the dominant culture, the higher the social class of black women, the greater their rate of labor force participation.[17] Organizers of the black Holiness and Pentecostal churches were children of freedwomen who worked for wages and thus were more sympathetic to the problems and stereotypes black women faced. These church leaders learned that it was working churchwomen who decided what proportion of their earnings would go to the church. However, black churchwomen did not wait for their pastors to discover their economic importance; they demonstrated their economic power collectively. After 1906, black congregations, conventions, and denominational convocations became acquainted with Women's Day, when women take charge of the program and turn over to the congregation, the convention, or the denomination the money they have raised. In one church I visited, this contribution was one-third of the church's budget for the year. While black congregations also hold Men's Days, men have rarely matched the contributions of the women. The fund-raising ability of women remains a traditional source of male-female rivalry in black churches.

The overwhelming female majorities in the early Sanctified Church meant that women's economic enterprise and labor force participation were essential for church growth and survival. Thus women's financial power was a major contradiction to the ethic of male domination and control. This contradiction was intensified by the dynamics of economic decision making in black families and black women's relatively greater economic independence.

Strong Women's Departments retained control over the disbursement and allocation of their funds. Women paid the expenses of their leaders and staff members, collected offerings for the evangelists and church mothers "teaching" in the churches and representing districts and congregations at national meetings, and provided benevolence for unemployed men, women, and their families. Sanctified Church women raised money for their pastors' and bishops' wives to travel to conventions and simply to have some funds of their own. These women believed in economic cooperation with men, not in economic dependence on them.

Black women have a history of handling financial matters efficiently. Early Women's Departments often assessed each member an equal amount of money to meet goals, one of several monetary practices that paralleled those of the clubs of the National Association of Colored Women. As their activities grew, Sanctified Church women adopted the practice of contributing money throughout the year and then presenting this collection at the end of Women's Day or of a convention. Such practices had their roots in benevolent and mutual aid associations, with the sacred and secular practices becoming mutually influential. In a sense, churchwomen extended their domestic economic practices to their households of racial uplift and their households of faith.

By 1951, the COGIC Women's Department had grown to such an extent that the women began meeting in a separate convention under the leadership of Lillian Brooks Coffey. Using the structure of state and district supervisors, Mother Coffey collected money prior to and during the convention and then presented it to the church at the end of the convention. She inaugurated this practice at a convention where she surprised the church by presenting Bishop Crouch with "thousands of dollars" in a paper bag.[18] The women's importance to the survival of congregations led some to the false belief that black women were better off economically than black men. Since women tithed faithfully and prominently, it was easy to perceive them as the most powerful economic segment of the black community. Such perceptions made the image of the matriarch so believable to black men.

Whatever their beliefs and ideologies concerning female subordination, men in the Sanctified Church ultimately have been confronted with the economic necessity of maintaining good relationships with their female members. At some point during the church year, it has been in the interest of the most sexist and domineering pastor to advocate financial support for the local, district, and national women's work. Like almost all black pastors, these men also have acknowledged the collective economic power of churchwomen on Women's Day—and they often have vacated their pulpits to do so. Finally, the collective economic power of women has been reinforced at the district, jurisdictional, and national levels when the superintendents and bishops receive the quarterly or annual "reports" from the Women's Department.

"The Women Stuck Together": Collective Autonomy

Women's economic power has limited attempts by bishops and pastors to impose themselves directly on the activities of women. Churchwomen have thus been free to discuss issues and problems that churchmen may not have wanted to hear. While the dynamics and degree of male domination of local congregations varies, black women, because of their autonomous organizations, occasionally remind their brethren, "If it wasn't for the women, you wouldn't have a church."

Although many denominations were formed between 1895 and 1950, those that survived and flourished were those with strong Women's Departments. Structures of female influence enabled denominations with charismatic male founders to grow after those founders died; other denominational movements with high visibility but no structures of female influence almost disappeared. The Women's Department of the COGIC was formed at approximately the same time that the denomination was reconstituted as Pentecostal in 1907 and after women's auxiliaries, missions, societies, and clubs had grown and developed in black Baptist and Methodist churches. The founder of the COGIC, divorced from a woman who was still living, could not remarry. His position as an unmarried head of a church was almost unique in black church history, a marked departure from the traditional pattern of a preacher married to a professional woman leader (usually a teacher). This historical "accident" generated the model of a nearly autonomous women's organization. Mason not only recruited Mother Roberson to head the women's work but also on her advice appointed women's overseers along the same jurisdictional and district lines as the male overseers who later became bishops. The title "overseer," a literal translation of the Greek word usually translated as "bishop," was used in the early days of the church for both men and women leaders in the church. Such usage implied that the founders of the COGIC and other denominations initially envisioned a church organized in parallel structures of both male and female overseers. This vision was closer to the dual-sex political systems characteristic of some West African societies than to the patriarchal episcopal polities of European origin.

The founding of the Sanctified Church coincided with the most extensive and energetic period of organizing by black women. In the 1890s, the Fire Baptized Holiness Church of God of the Americas was founded as an egalitarian denomination. The COGIC began as a Holiness church in 1895 toward the end of, but distinct from, the Church of God movement that established an interracial and egalitarian denomination. In the same year, black women began holding national conventions focused on the problems of "the Race" and of black women. Women were eligible for ordination in the A.M.E. Zion Church, the church of Harriet Tubman. During this period, they organized major women's auxiliaries among black Baptists and Methodists, and they formed the National Association of Colored Women, which assembled women across the boundaries of religion, class, and intensity of skin color. By 1907 and the beginning of the Pentecostal Movement, the black woman had a prominent image as Race woman, clubwoman, churchwoman, and educator in the black community. Black clubwomen and schoolteachers in the Sanctified Church were prepared to assume roles of leadership and possessed the skills to do so.

The period between 1895 and World War II was the era of "racial uplift." In addition to race relations, female employment, and the multiple problems of group advancement, black women made the "status of the ministry" a central concern of their national programs, first in the Colored Women's League and the Federation of Afro-American Women and, after the merger of these organizations, in the National Association of Colored Women.[19] Women in the Sanctified Church were committed to the cause of racial uplift. They retained their commitment to ecstatic worship, which black Baptists and Methodists were rejecting. They also retained an emphasis on women's interests, education, professionalism, and the cultivation of a black female image that contradicted the dominant culture's stereotypes.

Some of the organizational features of the Sanctified Church Women's Departments have since disappeared in the black women's clubs where they may have originated. One such example is the Women's Purity Class, where women still learn their "proper place" in their churches and homes. A Baptist clergywoman I interviewed who visited such a class remarked, "Those classes are interesting. One woman told me, 'The Bible says that I should be in subjection to my husband, but that's the *only* man!'" In these classes—as well as the meetings of the evangelists, missionaries, and church mothers; the Prayer and Bible Bands; the Sewing Circles; and the organizations of the Deacons' Wives, the Bishops' Wives, and the Pastors' Wives—women are able to develop a perspective on their position in their churches that includes important critiques of church politics and structure. In such settings, women learn the language of biblical feminism and maintain their collective autonomy, arguing that it is not "proper" for pastors "to teach . . . things that women should know."[20]

In structuring their activities, women in the Sanctified Church retained the features of organizations founded during the most intensive era of Afro-American feminism; the network of small groups they organized around churchwomen's specialized roles formed a feminist infrastructure within a patriarchal organization. Many women belonged to several of these groups, which provided multiple perspectives on women's roles in the form of direct statement and biblical allusions. When churchwomen showed their strength, it arose from these many networks and was described in biblical terms.

The role of the Women's Department in the COGIC during the crisis precipitated by the founder's death illustrates the importance of the women's infrastructure to the survival of the denomination. During that crisis, while the men were fighting constitutional battles in the courtrooms, the Women's Department continued to function under the leadership of Mother Anna Bailey. While sources are cryptic, the Women's Department seemed to exercise veto power over the direction of policy, structure, and choice of leaders. The women also participated in the election of the bishops, who in turn elected the presiding bishop. Finally, the church's newspaper took special note of Mother Bailey's approval of the final choice of the board.[21]

Writing later in an official church history, Lucille Cornelius emphasized the contribution of the Women's Department to the survival and integrity of the COGIC. She emphasized that "the women stuck together and held the church in harness until the brethren could find their identity in the form of leadership that we must have in this time."[22] The phrase "in harness," a biblical term meaning "prepared or organized for war," referred to the children of Israel leaving Egypt. The statement reflects some of the disdain that the well organized feel for the relatively disorganized; the women knew that they could do better. Cornelius's tone also suggests the frustration of many black women who, regardless of conflicts and inequities, were reluctant to abandon institutions they played a major role in building.

Churchwomen have advanced a public strategy of cooperation with men. While their oral tradition is militant, their written tradition is indulgent, eschewing overt conflict. Recently, church mothers were admonished to "remember . . . [that the pastors] are the Lord's people."[23] It seems that the biblical ethic of love and of church unity has reduced the temptation toward open rebellion. Yet these women are aware that other denominations have been founded by women more militant in opposing subordination. Examples of female leaders within the denomination heighten women's sense that entire congregations and perhaps the entire church could continue in the absence of male leadership. However, racial oppression serves to remind black women of the importance of unity. The tension generated by a hostile dominant culture encourages women to adopt a cooperative model of gender relations and to support male leadership that, as Cornelius wrote, is necessary "in this time."

Men in the early Sanctified Church were aware of the tension between women's leadership skills and the structural realities within their institutions. Although bishops and elders married evangelists and missionaries, historically a woman's marital status did not determine her access to leadership; only one of the four national supervisors of women was married to a man nationally prominent in the church. In a very few but significant cases where pastors died and were therefore "absent" from their churches, bishops did not appoint any other male leaders to replace them but left the widows, licensed evangelists, in charge. The COGIC discovered that such congregations were more efficiently managed.[24] Finally, while churchwomen today admonish their sisters to cooperate with pastors, many pastors head congregations that were "dug out" and managed by women until those women sent for a pastor.

In other denominations that do not restrict women, female evangelists have become elders or pastors through the prompting and encouragement of women's organizations. In the Church of the Living God, Christian Workers for Fellowship, for example, women recognized that the sacred traditions of the wider black community did not encourage women in ministry in the way they encouraged men.[25] Both churchwomen and clubwomen depended on their autonomous organizations to achieve positions of leadership.

The women's methods of leadership have evolved in direct contrast to the authoritarian style demanded by the nature of episcopal polity: hierarchical, individualistic, and dominating.[26] In comparison, women's leadership tends to be consensus oriented, collective, and more inclusive, involving larger numbers of people in decision making. Visible women leaders have been able to represent large organizations of women in both sacred and secular settings. Black churchwomen have thus transformed their autonomy into the form of power best described as influence and created a pluralist political structure in an episcopally governed church where pluralism was never intended.

The collectivism and autonomy of organized women has been the most significant historical factor in the survival of denominations within the Sanctified Church. In churches with structures derived from male positions, women's organizations with parallel structures maintain the visibility of female leaders. Finally, this collectivist orientation has also kept alive a cooperative model of gender relations and pluralist political practice in an elitist organization.

Beyond "This Time": Tradition, Cooperation, and Prospects for Change

Women's standing in the Sanctified Church presently ranges from subordination in the COGIC to equality with men in the Fire Baptized Holiness Church of God of the Americas and the Mount Calvary Holy Church of America. While access to authority is a problem for these churchwomen, they do not experience structural marginality, a major difficulty for women in white churches. According to Rosemary Ruether, churchwomen were marginalized because they "seldom controlled the processes of the cultural interpretation of their actions," which led to their exclusion from the myths and heroic accounts central to church tradition. Women's exclusion from leadership followed, except "in those areas where roles based on gifts of the Spirit were recognized."[27] Both men and women in the Sanctified Church attain leadership through their expression of gifts of the Spirit, which perhaps explains in part why marginality and exclusion do not characterize the type of subordination women experience in black Pentecostal and Holiness denominations. Where the processes of cultural interpretation have been external to the church, the entire Sanctified Church has suffered. Where the interpretive process was internal to the church, black women influenced and, in some cases, controlled that process.

The politics of sexism in the Sanctified Church are the politics of incomplete male domination, and the politics of feminism are the politics of cooperative protest, collective enterprise, and assertive autonomy. Therefore, strong and visible women's traditions are part of the total church culture that is passed on in the socialization of new members. Recruits and young people learn beliefs, values, and ways of thinking that depart from the dominant culture's notion of women's place in churches and other formal organizations. Church members also learn to admire the distinctive aspects of black women's experience and their historical role without accepting the negative images and stereotypes imposed by the dominant culture.

By writing symbolic accounts of women's participation in the extraordinary events that made the growth and development of these denominations possible, churchwomen continue to reinforce these heroic images. In American society, women have been permitted more expression of gifts of the Spirit, the most important aspect of these denominations' identities. Clearly, women must be included in the symbolic accounts or myths strengthening the norms of holiness that define the unique position of the Sanctified Church on the continuum of black religious experience.

The presence of prominent female heroines in holiness has prevented churchwomen from becoming alienated by their structural subordination in the Sanctified Church. The collective and self-conscious politics of female influence modify the politics and pain of male domination. Over time, black women in the Sanctified Church have drawn on the strength of their skills and historical experiences to create structural conditions tending toward equality. Yet even in denominations where women have full access to authority, some of which were formed in protest against discrimination, black women and men have not pursued a course of antagonism or separatism. Instead, a model of dual-career religious leadership has emerged. Where women church members have a higher status than their husbands ("Mr. and Rev.," or "Deacon and Elder," or "Mr. and Elder"), men express pride in their wives' achievements. Through a combination of heroic accounts, symbolic leaders, and an alternative organizational setting, black women have maintained a tradition of protest and cooperation—a dialectical tradition—within the Sanctified Church.

The Sanctified Church and its women's traditions are an important resource for the entire range of the black religious experience. Churchmen cannot ignore the written tradition of women's achievement, and they ignore the oral tradition of cooperative protest with great difficulty. In denominations that do not ordain women, female members point to their tremendous records of service and continue the conflict over their role in the church. If and when these denominations change their stance—and there are a variety of reasons to be pessimistic about this prospect—ordained women will have a greater impact than they now do as unordained evangelists. As has been the case in the area of music, the Sanctified Church continues to have normative impact on the larger black experience greater than would be expected from its actual number of members, and that number is growing.

A major problem exists concerning the values of churchmen, which range from a commitment to patriarchy, domination, and hierarchy to a belief in male-female cooperation and mutual influence. The history of the Sanctified Church demonstrates that both sets of values exist in the world of black men. In the Sanctified Church and beyond, many black men want to achieve the pure patriarchy they have never truly experienced. The functional necessity of women to the very survival of congregations, convocations, and denominations opposes such a tendency. James Tinney suggests that some black men absent themselves from churches precisely because of authoritarian male domination.[28] However, such male resistance to religious patriarchy is undermined by the dominant culture's persistent denigration of black women as matriarchs who are too assertive, powerful, and aggressive. Such labeling feeds a sexist backlash within the black community that encourages a rejection of the model of womanhood black women represent and deepens intragroup hostilities.[29]

Thus it has become fashionable since the civil rights movement to dismiss the achievements of black women in church, community, and society at large as a mere consequence of economic necessity. Unfortunately, many black men perceived the message of the 1960s to be, If you will be sexist, we white men won't be racist. Such ideological assaults led to attempts to enforce European or dominant culture patriarchy where it had been effectively resisted.

The disestablishment of sexism in the dominant culture remains a threat to many black males who perceive the traditional model of gender relations as a component of the goal of assimilation. In order to persist in this thinking, such men must reject as unseemly and inappropriate any institutional record that suggests a tradition of heroism by black women. They must refuse to transform their observations of women's church and community roles and of the historical records of the churches into an internalized norm of egalitarian gender relationships. The saving grace for black women in the Sanctified Church is that, even in a context of structural subordination, they do control the record books and therefore the written record of their role. As long as women are involved in this process of cultural interpretation, there exists a strong egalitarian potential within the Sanctified Church. Additionally, black women do have their allies among pastors who have never adopted or who have abolished the separate lectern or "double pulpit" and among sympathetic bishops who will ordain them to take a charge outside the church (e.g., military chaplaincies) or to begin new churches.

Racial oppression and its gender-specific racist ideologies still invade the black experience. Black women who do not conform to patriarchal traditions have been particularly victimized. Unless black women's image in the dominant culture changes radically, their struggles against racial oppression must proceed both inside and outside the black community; they will continue to be tied to internal struggles to maintain what power they now have in the face of embarrassed black male opposition, as well as to the external struggles with white racism. As long as racism limits opportunities for black men, black women will continue to express some ambivalence about competing with black men inside the black community and will also strive to avoid direct confrontation and overt conflict. As long as racism and patriarchy operate as combined forces in the oppression of black women and men, black women will not abandon those institutions that are responsive to the shared aspects of the problems. The history of formal and informal organization within the black community suggests that the cooperative and egalitarian model of male-female leadership would be the preferred outcome. Black women's traditions in the Sanctified Church yield great hope for the transformation of structures that alienate and trivialize women's experiences. In the meantime, black women will maintain their solidarity and organizational strength—"stuck together [holding] the church in harness"—until deliverance comes.

Notes

1. Teressa Hoover, "Black Women and the Churches: Triple Jeopardy," in *Black Theology: A Documentary History*, ed. Gayraud Wilmore and James Cone (Maryknoll, N.Y.: Orbis Books, 1979), pp. 377–88; James Tinney, "The Religious Experience of Black Men," in *The Black Male*, ed. Lawrence E. Gary (Beverly Hills, Calif.: Sage Publications, 1981), 269–76. See also Pearl Williams-Jones, "A Minority Report: Black Pentecostal Women," *Spirit: A Journal of Issues Incident to Black Pentecostalism*, 1, no. 2 (1977): 31–44.
2. Bonnie Thornton Dill, "The Dialectics of Black Womanhood," *Signs: Journal of Women in Culture and Society* 4, no. 3 (Spring 1979): 543–55.
3. On the dominant culture's devaluation of black women, see Bell Hooks, *Ain't I a Woman: Black Women and Feminism* (Boston: South End Press, 1981). On the role of black women in education, see Linda Perkins, "Black Women and Racial 'Uplift' Prior to Emancipation," in *The Black Woman Cross-culturally*, ed. Filomena Chioma Steady (Cambridge, Mass.: Schenkman Publishing Co., 1981), pp. 317–34; Angela Y. Davis, *Women, Race and Class* (New York: Random House, 1981); and Gerda Lerner, ed., *Black Women in White America: A Documentary History* (New York: Random House, 1971). On the "relative" economic independence of black women, see Dill; and Davis. On the political organization of black women, see Perkins; Davis; and Cheryl Townsend Gilkes, "Living and Working in a World of Trouble: The Emergent Career of the Black Woman Community Worker" (Ph.D. diss., Northeastern University, 1978).

4. Perkins, p. 321.

5. W.E.B. Du Bois, "Votes for Women," in *The Crisis Writings*, ed. Daniel Walden (1912; reprint, Greenwich, Conn.: Fawcett Publications, 1972), pp. 339–40, esp. p. 340.

6. Elizabeth Lindsey Davis, *Lifting as They Climb: A History of the National Association of Colored Women* (Washington, D.C.: Howard University, Moorland Spingarn Research Center, 1933), p. 19.

7. Ibid.

8. Charles H. Pleas, *Fifty Years of Achievement (History): Church of God in Christ* (Memphis, Tenn.: Church of God in Christ Publishing House, n.d.), p. 35.

9. James Shopshire, "A Socio-historical Characterization of the Black Pentecostal Movement in America" (Ph.D. diss., Northwestern University, 1975), pp. 144–45.

10. Church of the Living God, Christian Workers for Fellowship, *Glorious Heritage: The Golden Book—Documentary and History* (n.p.: Church of the Living God, Christian Workers for Fellowship, 1976).

11. Church of God in Christ (COGIC), *Official Manual with the Doctrines and Discipline of the Church of God in Christ* (Memphis, Tenn.: COGIC Publishing House, 1973).

12. Lucille Cornelius, *The Pioneer History of the Church of God in Christ* (Memphis, Tenn.: COGIC Publishing House, 1975); Church of the Living God; Pleas.

13. Judg. 5:7.

14. COGIC; Church of the Living God.

15. COGIC.

16. Women's Department, COGIC, *Women's Handbook* (Memphis, Tenn.: COGIC Publishing House, 1980).

17. Priscilla Douglas, "Black Working Women: Factors Affecting Labor Market Experience," Working Paper (Wellesley College, Center for Research on Women, 1980).

18. Cornelius (n. 12 above), p. 24. Oral tradition and interviews set the amount at a minimum of $10,000.

19. Elizabeth Lindsey Davis (n. 6 above).

20. Women's Department, COGIC (n. 16 above), p. 21.

21. Cornelius (n. 12 above), p. 27.

22. Ibid.

23. Women's Department, COGIC (n. 16 above), p. 21.

24. James Tinney, "Black Pentecostals: The Difference Is More Than Color," *Logos Journal* 10, no. 3 (1980): 16–19.

25. Church of the Living God (n. 10 above).

26. Jualynne Dodson, "Black Women as an Unknown Source of Organizational Change" (Providence, R.I., Society for the Scientific Study of Religion, 1982, mimeographed).

27. Rosemary Radford Ruether and Eleanor McLaughlin, eds., *Women of Spirit: Female Leadership in the Jewish and Christian Traditions* (New York: Simon & Schuster, 1979), pp. 16–17.

28. Tinney, "The Religious Experience of Black Men" (n. 1 above).

29. Dill (n. 2 above); Pauli Murray, "The Liberation of Black Women," in *Voices of the New Feminism*, ed. Mary L. Thompson (Boston: Beacon Press, 1970), and "Jim Crow and Jane Crow," in Lerner, ed. (n. 3 above), pp. 592–99; Hooks (n. 3 above).

Chapter 27

Reverend George Washington Woodbey

Early Twentieth-Century California Black Socialist

Philip S. Foner

In the *Ohio Socialist Bulletin* of February 1909 Reverend Richard Euell, a black minister of Milford, Ohio, published "A Plan to Reach the Negro." The Negro, he wrote, "belongs to the working class and must be taught class consciousness." Blacks could be more rapidly recruited into the party if Socialists would go to them in their churches and point out "the way to freedom and plenty." Most of them had no experience with any organization other than the church and could think of committing themselves to action only in religious terms. The Bible, even motion pictures about the "Passion Play," could be used effectively to imbue religion with radicalism and convince the black working class of the evils of the capitalist system and the virtues of Socialism.[1]

The first black Socialist to conduct the type of work Reverend Euell recommended was Reverend George Woodbey (sometimes spelled Woodby), and he had already been performing this function for the Socialist cause for several years before a "Plan to Reach the Negro" was published.

George Washington Woodbey, the leading Negro Socialist in the first decade of the 20th century, was born a slave in Johnson County, Tennessee, on October 5, 1854, the son of Charles and Rachel (Wagner) Woodbey. Of his early life nothing is known other than that he learned to read after freedom came, was self-educated, except for two terms in a common school, and that his life was one of "hard work and hard study carried on together." A fellow Socialist who knew him wrote: "He has worked in mines, factories, on the streets, and at everything which would supply food, clothing and shelter."

Woodbey was ordained a Baptist minister at Emporia, Kansas, in 1874. He was active in the Republican Party of Missouri and Kansas and was a leader in the Prohibition Party, and when he moved to Nebraska he became a prominent force in the prohibition movement in that state. In 1896 Woodbey ran for lieutenant governor and Congress on the Prohibition ticket in Nebraska.

That same year, he made his first acquaintance with the principles of Socialism when he read Edward Bellamy's *Looking Backwards,* and his interest was further aroused by copies of the *Appeal to Reason* which came into his hands. Although he subscribed to the *Appeal,* he did not join the Socialists. Instead, he joined the Populist Party, and in 1900, he supported William Jennings Bryan, the Democratic and Populist candidate for President. But he also heard Eugene V. Debs speaking during the presidential campaign and was so impressed that when the Democratic Party asked Woodbey to speak for Bryan, he agreed but delivered speeches which were geared more to the ideas advanced by Debs than those by the Democratic candidate. After several such speeches, the Democrats stopped scheduling dates for Woodbey's speeches, and the black minister came to the conclusion that his place was in the Socialist camp. He resigned his pulpit and announced to his friends that henceforth his life "would be consecrated to the Socialist movement." A Nebraska Socialist recalls:

> We remember him in the stirring days of the inception of the Socialist movement in Omaha. Night after night he spoke on the streets and in the parts of that city. Omaha had never had the crowds that attended Woodbey's meetings.[2]

Woodbey visited his mother in San Diego during the spring of 1902, and immediately made an impression on the comrades in Southern California. A dispatch to the *Los Angeles Socialist* on May 31, 1902, expresses this clearly:

> Socialism is on the boom here in this county and city. We have had Rev. G. W. Woodbey, the Colored Socialist orator of Nebraska with us for nearly a month during which time he has delivered 23 addresses and will speak again tonight, and then he will do some work in the country districts where he has been invited to speak. . . .
>
> Comrade Woodbey is great and is a favorite with all classes. He came here unannounced ostensibly to see his mother who resides here but as he says that he is "so anxious to be free," that he feels

impressed to work for the cause constantly. He has had very respectable audiences both on the streets and in the halls. He likes to speak on the street and it is the general verdict that he has done more good for the cause than any of our most eloquent speakers who have preceded him. He is full of resources and never repeats his speeches, but gives them something new every time. He requested me to state in my notes to the "Socialist" that he desires to visit Los Angeles later on if you folks can find a place for him. He makes no charges but depends entirely on passing the hat for his support. . . .[3]

Los Angeles did find a place for Woodbey, and he delivered a series of soap-box speeches and lectures in the leading hall. When after one of his speeches, Woodbey was denied admittance to the Southern Hotel and Northern Restaurant because of his color, the Los Angeles Socialist Party organized a successful boycott of the establishments and distributed leaflets reading:

We demand as trade unionists and socialists, that every wage-worker in Los Angeles bear well in mind these two places that depend on public patronage—the Northern Restaurant and the Southern Hotel—keep away from them. They draw the color line.[4]

Woodbey accepted an offer to become minister of the Mount Zion Baptist Church in San Diego and made his home in California for the next two decades. He was elected a member of the state executive board of the Socialist Party, and soon became widely known in the state as "The Great Negro Socialist Orator." In a Los Angeles debate with Archibald Huntley, Ph.D., where Woodbey took the affirmative of the topic, "Resolved that Socialism is the True Interpretation of Economic Conditions and that it is the Solution of the Labor Problem," he was listed as a "well-known Socialist Lecturer."[5]

An announcement that Woodbey would deliver a reply to Booker T. Washington's "Capitalist Argument for the Negro" packed Los Angeles' leading hall on May 1, 1903. He paid tribute to Washington "as a gentleman" and educator, but added: "He has all the ability necessary to make a good servant of capitalism by educating other servants for capitalism." Woodbey charged that whether consciously or not, Tuskegee Institute fulfilled the role of providing black workers to be pitted against white workers so as to bring about a general lowering of wage scales. What Washington failed to understand was that there was basically no unity between capitalists, white or black, and workers, white or black. "There is no race division industrially, but an ever-growing antagonism between the exploiting capitalists, black or white, and the exploited workers, black or white." In this "industrial struggle," the working class was bound to "ultimately triumph."

> And then the men of all races will share in the results of production according to their services in the process of production. This is Socialism and the only solution to the race problem.[6]

A frequent target of the police of San Diego, Los Angeles, San Francisco, and other California communities, Woodbey was in and out of jail several times between 1902 and 1908, and was hospitalized more than once as a result of police brutality. But he gave as well as received. When he was attacked and driven off a street corner in San Diego in July 1905 by Police Officer George H. Cooley, Woodbey led a group of protesters to the police station to lodge a complaint. There Cooley again attacked the black Socialist, "using at the same time oaths and language too mean and vile to print." Woodbey was literally thrown bodily out of the station house. He immediately brought charges against the police officer for assault and battery and informed his California comrades:

> In the days of chattel slavery the masters had a patrol force to keep the negroes in their place and protect the interests of the masters. Today the capitalists use the police for the same purpose.

But slaves had rebelled despite the patrols, and he was following that tradition by telling the police that they could not get away with their brutality against enemies of the capitalist system.

Although Woodbey's case against the police was prosecuted by the County Attorney, assisted by Job Harriman, California's leading Socialist attorney, and although all witnesses testified that the Negro Socialist's conduct had been "perfectly gentlemanly," and that he had a perfectly lawful right to be at the station house, the jury, composed of conservative property owners, took only fifteen minutes to find the defendant not guilty. Woodbey was furious and published the names of the jury men, calling upon all decent citizens to have nothing to do with them. He followed this up by returning immediately to the soap box in San Diego and held one of the biggest street corner meetings in the city up to this time. As he wrote:

The case has made more Socialists that I could possibly have made in many speeches. Had I not gone to the court with the matter the public would forever have contended that I was doubtless doing or saying something that I had no right to do or say. And when I complained I would have been told that if I had gone to the courts I would have got justice. Now, as it is, nothing of the kind can be said, and the responsibility is placed where it rightly belongs.

Many non-Socialists in San Diego, Woodbey noted, were learning the truth of the Socialist contention that "the police force are the watch dogs of capitalism."[7]

In more than one California city Woodbey was arrested and hauled off to jail for trying to sell copies of his Socialist booklets.[8] The writings made Woodbey's name known throughout the entire Party in the United States and even internationally.

Describing Woodbey as "the greatest living negro in America," a white Socialist noted that "his style is simple and his logic invincible. He knows the race question, and one of his most popular lectures relates to the settlement of this vexed question under Socialism." Woodbey's ability to explain Socialism in simple terms led to the demand that he "embody some of the things he has said to the thousands who have listened to his talks, in a written form. . . ." The response was the pamphlet *What To Do and How To Do It or Socialism vs. Capitalism.* A copy of a small edition, privately printed, fell into the hands of A. W. Ricker, a Socialist organizer in the West and South. While at the home of Socialist publisher Julius A. Wayland, in Girard, Kansas, he read it aloud to the Wayland family. "At the conclusion," Ricker wrote, "we decided that the book ought to be in the hands of the millions of American wage slaves, and we forthwith wrote to Rev. Mr. Woodbey for the right to bring it out."[9]

It was published as No. 40 of the widely distributed *Wayland's Monthly* in August 1903. Ricker gave it a send-off in the *Appeal to Reason,* writing:

The book in many respects is the equal of "Merrie England," and in the matter of its clear teaching of the class struggle, it is superior. It has been read by every negro in Girard, (Kansas), and has made Socialists of those who were susceptible of understanding after every other effort had failed to shake their unreasoning adherence to the republican party. A good supply should be ordered by every local in the land, there is no book in the language that will excel it in propaganda value, and we expect to see it pass through one edition after another, as soon as it is read by the comrades.[10]

Since Robert Blatchford's *Merrie England*, published in England in 1894 and in the United States in 1900, was considered one of the best of the Socialist educational publications, the tribute to Reverend Woodbey's pamphlet was well understood by readers of the *Appeal to Reason*.

Woodbey's forty-four-page booklet carried the touching dedication:

> This little book is dedicated to that class of citizens who desire to know what the Socialists want to do and how they propose to do it. By one who was once a chattel slave freed by the proclamation of Lincoln and wishes to be free from the slavery of capitalism.[11]

In his preface Reverend Woodbey acknowledged that there was "nothing original" in his little book, his aim being simply to make the subjects treated "as plain as possible to the reader." It was not directed to those who were already convinced of the superiority of Socialism over Capitalism, but to "meet the demands of that large and increasing class of persons who have not yet accepted Socialism, but would do so if they could see any possible way of putting it into practice." Within this framework, Reverend Woodbey's booklet is an effective piece of Socialist propaganda, and so highly thought of in Socialist circles that by 1908 it had been translated into three languages and gained for its author an international reputation.[12]

Basically, the booklet consisted of a dialogue between the author and his mother whom he has rejoined after nearly seventeen years of separation. She expresses her astonishment at having learned that her son had become a Socialist. "Have you given up the Bible and the ministry and gone into politics?" she asks. Her son attempts to convince his mother that it is precisely because of his devotion to the principles enunciated in the Bible that he became a Socialist, and that as the years passed, he became more and more convinced of the correctness of his decision. When his mother points out that among his comrades were a few who believed neither in God nor in the Bible, her son readily agrees, but reminds her that he found "a still larger number of unbelievers in the republican party before I left it some twenty years ago," and that other parties had their "equal portion" of nonbelievers. More important, while he believed in the Biblical account of God, the origin of the earth and man, and members of his Party did not, he and they were able to agree that "man is here, and the earth is here, and that it is the present home of the race, at least." They did not, to be sure, see eye-to-eye about the "here-after." Since Socialism was "a scheme for bettering things here first," he could be a "good Socialist" without surrendering his belief in God or the Bible. There was room in the Socialist Party for those who were interested only in what it could do for mankind in the present world and for those who, like himself, were "Socialists because they think that mankind is entitled to the best of everything in both this world and the next." Finally, his mother accepts the idea that under Socialism persons would be free to have "their own religion or none, just as they please, as long as they do not interfere with others."[13]

Having laid at rest his mother's anxiety and made her willing to listen to the fundamental principles of a movement which obviously had not destroyed her son's religious convictions, Reverend Woodbey proceeds to explain to her the evils of capitalist society and the way by which Socialism, gaining power through the ballot box, would set out to eliminate these evils. After he takes his mother through such subjects as rent, interest, and profits, all gained from labor's production, and value which is created only by labor but the fruits of which are appropriated entirely by the capitalists, she expresses bewilderment at the meaning of such words. Her son then illustrates what they mean in simple language and in terms of daily experience. Here, for example, is how he explained surplus value:

> Why didn't the slave have wealth at the close of the war? He worked hard.
> "Because his master got it," mother replied.
> "The wage worker's master got what he produced, too."
> "But wasn't he paid for his work?" asked mother.
> Yes, about seventeen cents on every dollar's worth of wealth he created. . . .

Under Socialism, he continues, the capitalist would have to turn over to the State a "large amount of capital created by labor" which he had taken from the worker while the latter, having been deprived of all he produced under capitalism, would have nothing to turn over. The very rich would have no reason to complain "since he and his children, who have done nothing but live off the labor of those who have nothing to turn over, are to be given an equal share of interest with those who have produced it all. So you see we Socialists are not such bad fellows as you thought. We propose to do good unto those who spitefully use us, and to those who curse us, by giving them an equal show with ourselves, provided that they will here-after do their share of the useful work."[14]

But his mother expresses concern that the capitalists will not yield peacefully to having the "land, factories, and means of production" turned over to the cooperative commonwealth by a Socialist Congress elected by the people, and that they would start a war to retain their holdings. Her son concedes that this would quite likely occur just as the slaveholders had refused to abide by Lincoln's electoral victory and precipitated a civil war. But the capitalists would never succeed in the war they would seek to stimulate, for the majority of the people had clearly become convinced that Socialism was the only solution to their problems, or else the Socialists could not have won their electoral victories. Hence, the capitalists would have no one to do the fighting for them:

> The slaveholder did not dare to arm the negro, on his side, without proclaiming emancipation, and to do that was to lose his cause; so with the capitalist, if he dares to offer all to the poor man who must fight his battles, he has lost his cause; and with this condition confronting the capitalist, there is no danger in taking over the entire industrial plant as soon as the Socialists can be elected and pass the necessary laws. And the Socialist party will go into power just as soon as the majority finds that the only way to secure to itself its entire product is to vote that ticket.[15]

Mother has only one question left about the transition from capitalism to Socialism: "Have the people a right to do this?" Her son reminds her of the Declaration of Independence which clearly affirmed the right of the people, when any form of government became destructive of the rights of life, liberty and the pursuit of happiness, "to alter and abolish it and institute a new government" which would be most likely to effect "their safety and happiness." On this the Socialists stand, the son declares firmly. Moreover, it was none other than Abraham Lincoln who, in his speech of January 12, 1840, in the House of Representatives, had said "just what the Socialist now say." He had then declared: "Any people anywhere being inclined and having the power have the right to rise up and shake off the existing government and form a new one that suits them better. . . ."[16]

His mother now fully satisfied, the son proceeds to describe how different departments of government—agriculture, transportation, distribution, intelligence, education, and health—will operate under Socialism providing for the needs of the people rather than under capitalism, for the profits of the capitalist. Occasionally, the mother interrupts the narrative with questions that bring answers that satisfy her. Thus, when she asks whether the workers who would own and operate the factories under Socialism "would know how to do the work," the answer reassures her:

> Why, the workers are the only ones who do know how to run a factory. The stockholders who own the concern know nothing about doing the work. If the girl who weaves in the factory should be told that Socialism is now established, and that henceforth she is to have shorter hours of labor, a beautiful sanitary place to work in, and an equal share of all the wealth of the nation, to be taken in any kind of thing she wants, do you think she would forget how to work? And if on the other hand, all she produces is to go to the girl who does nothing but own the stocks, then she can work right along. Seems to me, you might see the absurdity of that, mother. "I believe I do see, now," she said, after a moment's hesitation. Then apply that illustration about the girls, to all the workers, and you will get my meaning.[17]

As might be expected, Mother asks, "Like all other women, I want to know where we are to come in." Her son assures her that it was to the interest of "the women, more than the men, if possible, to be Socialists because they suffer more from capitalism than anyone else." For one thing, the Socialist platform demands "the absolute equality of the sexes before the law, and the repeal of the law that in any way discriminates against women." Then again, under Socialism each woman would, like each man, have her own independent income, and would become "an equal shareholder in the industries of the nation." Under such liberating conditions, a woman would have no need "to sell herself through a so-called marriage to someone she did not love, in order to get a living," and, for the first time in history, could marry only for love. Under capitalism, the working man was a slave, "and his wife is the slave of a slave." Socialism would liberate both, but since it would give women political equality and economic freedom, it would actually do more for women than ever for men.[18]

By now Mother has been converted, and the booklet ends with the comment: "Well, you have convinced me that I am about as much of a slave now as I was in the south, and I am ready to accept any way out of this drudgery, mother remarked as the conversation turned on other subjects."[19]

Here and there *What To Do and How To Do It* reflected Edward Bellamy's influence on Reverend Woodbey, and sections of the 1903 pamphlet are shortened versions of the 1887 *Looking Backward.*[20] In the main, however, the pamphlet revealed that the black minister had broken with Bellamy's utopianism. While Bellamy emphasized "equitable" distribution of wealth under Nationalism, Woodbey was convinced that the solution lay closer to Marx's maxim, "From each according to his abilities, to each according to his needs." Bellamy rejected the label "socialism" as dangerous and un-American.[21] But Woodbey welcomed it and believed its principles were in keeping with the best in the American tradition. Like many in the Socialist Party, Woodbey believed that with the capture of sufficient political offices through the ballot box, socialism could be rapidly achieved. But he was one of the very few in the Party in 1903 who took into account the danger that the capitalists would not sit by and calmly watch their control of society eliminated by legislative enactments, and instead would, like the slave owners in 1860, resort to violence to prevent the people's will from being carried into effect. To be sure, unlike Jack London, who, in his great 1908 novel *The Iron Heel,* predicted that the oligarchy of American capitalists would seize power from the Socialists and destroy the democratic process by violence, Woodbey was confident that the capitalists would fail.[22] Nevertheless, by even raising this issue in his pamphlet, Woodbey was in advance of nearly all Christian Socialists.

Early in *What To Do and How To Do It,* Reverend Woodbey assured his mother that he would at a future date tell her "more about what the Bible teaches on this subject" of Socialism.[23] He fulfilled his promise a year later with *The Bible and Socialism: A Conversation Between Two Preachers,* published in San Diego, California, by the author. The 96-page booklet was dedicated to "the Preachers and Members of the Churches, and all others who are interested in knowing what the Bible teaches on the question at issue between the Socialists and the Capitalists, by one who began preaching twenty-nine years ago, and still continues."[24]

As the sub-title indicates, *The Bible and Socialism* consists of a dialogue between Woodbey and another clergyman. The latter is a local pastor to whom Woodbey's mother has given a copy of the 1903 pamphlet and invited to her home to hear her son convince him that he was wrong in contending that "there is no Socialism in the Bible." When the skeptical pastor questions Woodbey about the Socialist claim that Karl Marx discovered the principles of Scientific Socialism and points out that this was centuries after the Bible was written, Woodbey notes, first, that no new idea is ever entirely new and is in some way based on what went before, and, second, that

Marx, the greatest philosopher of modern times, belonged to the same wonderful Hebrew race that gave to the world Moses, the Lawgiver, the kings and prophets, and Christ the Son of the Highest, with his apostles, who, together, gave us the Bible that, we claim, teaches Socialism. Doubtless Marx, like other young Hebrews, was made acquainted with the economic teachings of Moses, and all the rest of the Old Testament sages and prophets, whatever we find him believing in after life.

If we are able to show that the Bible opposes both rent, interest, and profits, and the exploiting of the poor, then it stands just where the Socialists do.[25]

After agreeing that Marx was not a Christian but noting that this was of no significance since Socialism had nothing to do with a man's religion or lack of it, Reverend Woodbey devotes the rest of his pamphlet to detailed references, quotations, and citations to convince the pastor that since the Bible—both the Old and New Testaments—did actually oppose "rent, interest, and profits, and the exploiting of the poor," it was a Socialist document with close affinity to such classics as *The Communist Manifesto*, *Capital* and other writings of Marx. As a Jew, Woodbey emphasizes, Marx was able to do "the greatly needed work of reasoning out from the standpoint of the philosopher, what his ancestors, the writers of the Old and New Testaments, had already done from a moral and religious standpoint."[26] This is not to say, he continues, that there is no difference between a Socialism based merely on a "moral and religious standpoint" and Scientific Socialism just as there was a fundamental difference between the Socialism advanced by Utopian reformers prior to Marx and that set forth by the father of Scientific Socialism. For Scientific Socialism was based on the class struggle which had dominated all history and dominated existing relationships in capitalist society. When the pastor asks Woodbey if the class struggle also exists in the church, there is the following discussion in which his mother joins:

Master and slave, before the war, all belonged to the same church. They met on Sunday and prayed together, and one church member sold the other the next day. So now, in many cases, master and wage slave belong to the same church, meet on Sunday and pray together, and the one turns the other off from even the pittance he allowed him to take out of his earnings as wages or sets him out of house and home for non-payment of rent, or under mortgage, the next day. All that, notwithstanding the Bible says love brother and the stranger as oneself.

It took the abolitionist, in and out of the church, to show the inconsistency of slavery and force a division, as the Socialists are now doing.

"Yes," said mother, "I belonged to one of that kind of churches, myself, before the war."[27]

Just as his mother was converted at the end of the 1903 pamphlet, so, too, the pastor by the close of *The Bible and Socialism.* He confesses he had learned little of economics while in college, and since he joined the ministry, he had been too busy to give more than a casual thought to the Bible's "economic teachings" and whether or not the churches adhered to them. But as a result of the "interesting evening conversations," he was a changed man:

> . . . being convinced that Socialism is but the carrying out of the economic teachings of the Bible, I shall endeavor to study it and lay it before my people to the best of my ability.[28]

There may have been little new for white religiously inclined Socialists in Woodbey's pamphlet since the Christian Socialists had already published a considerable body of literature demonstrating to their satisfaction that the Bible and Socialism were compatible. But to black church-goers much of what was in the pamphlet was new and certainly must have made an impressive impact. Moreover, while many Christian Socialists preached an emotional propaganda replete with Christian ethics, they tended to ignore the class struggle or to relate their biblical references to the contemporary scene. Not so Woodbey; he was a firm believer in the class struggle, had read Marx, and was not in the least reluctant to couple discussions of the Old and New Testaments with specific evils in twentieth-century American society.

Woodbey's third and last Socialist pamphlet was *The Distribution of Wealth*, published in 1910 at San Diego by the author. The sixty-eight-page booklet consists of a series of letters to J. Jones, a California rancher-friend of the author, in which Woodbey describes how the distribution of wealth created by productive labor would operate "after Socialism has overthrown the capitalist method of production." Pointing out in his preface that there was little in Socialist literature on how the future co-operative commonwealth would function, Woodbey, without the slightest hesitation, declared he would attempt to fill the gap. Affirming his right to do so, he noted:

> If the socialist movement is based upon truth, it cannot be destroyed by the utmost freedom of discussion, nor is the movement or the party necessarily in danger, because your views or mine are not at once adopted even should they be corrected. All I ask of the reader is a fair, honest consideration of what I have written.[29]

What he wrote is an interesting elaboration of how the different institutions under capitalism would operate in the new Socialist society. Some of this had already been set forth in his 1903 *What To Do and How To Do It*, but here he develops it further. In 1903, it will be recalled, Woodbey had conceded that the capitalists would resort to armed resistance to prevent the Socialist society from coming into being. Now, however, he appears to believe that while capitalists would resist the transition to Socialism with "tremendous opposition," it would not necessarily lead to war. Once socialism had proven its superiority over capitalism, even the capitalists and their children would acquiesce and decide to live under it. (A clear throw-back to *Looking Backward*.) He writes:

> Let us go back, for instance, to the slaveholder, by the way of illustration. He declared that he would go to war before he would permit himself and family to labor like the negro slave and live in poverty, rags and ignorance. He had been taught to believe that that was the necessary outgrowth of labor. And I submit that the condition of labor under chattel slavery was a poor school in which to teach the child of the master a desire to labor. So the capitalist of today and his children look upon the workers as he has them in the sweatshops, mines and factories of the country, putting in long hours for a bare existence, under the most unsanitary conditions, living in the worst of places, and eating of the worst of food; and, like his brother, the slaveholder, he is determined that he and his shall not be reduced to such straits. It has not yet dawned upon him that when the people who work own the industries in place of him, all of these disagreeable conditions will at once disappear. . . . It is my opinion that, notwithstanding the false education of the children of the wealthy, even they in the first generation will have so much of their distaste for labor taken away that we will have little or no trouble with them when the majority have changed conditions.[30]

Woodbey's rancher friend keeps asking whether people would work under socialism once the fear of poverty and unemployment were removed. Woodbey's answer is interesting:

> When chattel slavery prevailed, as we said, men thought that labor must continue to be always what it was then, and that because the slave sought to escape he wouldn't work for wages. So now the capitalist, and those who believe in capitalism, think that labor must continue always to be just what it is now; and as some people won't work under the new and better conditions.
>
> It is a wonder to me that men are so willing to work as they are under the present conditions. The fact is, the mind of the child is such that it accepts what it is taught now, and will do the same then.
>
> The boy that was born a slave thought that it was natural for him to be one, and the young master took it for granted that he was intended to be master. But the boy that is born free never thinks that any one ought to own him; nor does the youngster born at the same time with him think that he ought to own him. But instead, they both go to school often in the same class. They at once accept the conditions under which they were born. No, my friend, there is no danger of the children not at once accepting the new conditions under Socialism, and we have proved there will be so little loss through idlers, even in the first generation of old folks, that it will not be found worth bothering about. And as the old and infirm should of necessity be looked after with the best of everything from the very beginning, it will be found when the time comes that the thing to do will be to let every one work and be sure that we have abundance of everything for all, and then let everybody help themselves, wherever they may be, to what we have on hand, as we do with what the public now owns. Indeed, they can be better trusted then than now, with all fear of the future banished forever.[31]

It is perhaps significant that this is the only one of Woodbey's pamphlets which ends without the second party convinced of the truth of the author's arguments and converted to Socialism. Probably Woodbey himself realized that he had tackled a difficult subject, that his presentation was too tentative to be effective in total conversion. At any rate, he ended his last letter:

> Hoping that I have been able to make it clear to you that under Socialism it will be possible to equitably distribute the products of

industry and that you and your family will at once join the movement, I will close this somewhat lengthy correspondence by saying that I would be pleased to hear from you soon.

Yours for the cause of the Revolution.
G. W. Woodbey[32]

Reverend Woodbey was a delegate to the Socialist Party conventions of 1904 and 1908; indeed, he was the sole representative of the Negro people at these gatherings. At the 1904 convention Woodbey took the floor twice. On the first occasion, he expressed his opinion on the seating of A. T. Gridely of Indiana who was being challenged because he had accepted a position in the state government after passing a civil service examination. The question at issue was whether A. T. Gridely had violated the Socialist principle of not accepting a position under a capitalist government. Woodbey spoke in favor of seating A. T. Gridely, arguing that in Germany the Socialists boasted of the number of comrades in the army, and noting that certainly such Socialists were doing work for a capitalist government. "We all know," he continued, "that we work for capitalists when we work at all, and we would be pretty poor if we did not work for capitalists at all."[33] On the second occasion, he spoke up in favor of the Party National Secretary receiving a salary of $1,500 a year which he called "not a dollar too much."[34] But the failure of the convention to deal with the Negro question in the Party platform or of the delegates to discuss it once during the entire convention aroused no comment from the only black delegate.

At the 1908 convention, Woodbey took the floor four times. On one occasion, in a discussion of franchises held by private corporations, he advanced what for the Socialist Party was the bold position that the Socialists declare themselves "in favor as fast as they can get in possession in any locality, of taking everything without a cent, and forcing the issue as to whether there is to be compensation or not. (Applause). I take the ground that you have already paid for these franchises—already paid more than they are worth, and we are simply proposing to take possession of what we have already paid for."[35] On another occasion, Woodbey recommended that the National Committee elect its own executive committee from its own members, and on still another, he opposed a time limit being imposed before a Party member could be nominated for office on the Socialist ticket to ensure that he would not betray the movement. Woodbey argued that the danger of such persons "selling out" was just as great if they were members for years instead of months. "In my judgment, a man who understands its [the Party's] principles is not more liable to do it after he has been in the party six months than five years."[36]

The other occasion in which Woodbey spoke at the 1908 convention marked the only time during the two national gatherings that he commented on an issue related to the race question. That was when he took a firm stand, during the discussion of the immigration resolution, against Oriental exclusion and, indeed, exclusion of any immigrants. His speech, coming as it did from a California delegate, was a remarkable statement and certainly not calculated to win friends among Socialists in his state. But it was in keeping with the tradition of black Americans since the era of Reconstruction: in 1869, the Colored National Labor Union went on record against exclusion of Chinese immigration. Woodbey conceded that it was generally believed that all who lived on the Pacific coast were as "a unit" in opposing Oriental immigration. But he did not, though a delegate from California, share this view:

> I am in favor of throwing the entire world open to the inhabitants of the world. (Applause). There are no foreigners, and cannot be unless some person comes down from Mars, or Jupiter, or some place.
>
> I stand on the declaration of Thomas Paine when he said "The world is my country." (Applause). It would be a curious state of affairs for immigrants or descendants of immigrants from Europe themselves to get control of affairs in this country, and then say to the Oriental immigrants that they should not come here. So far as making this a mere matter of race, I disagree decidedly with the committee, that we need any kind of a committee to decide this matter from a scientific standpoint. We know what we think upon the question of race now as well as we would know two years from now or any other time.[37]

Woodbey scoffed at the idea that the entrance of Oriental immigrants would reduce the existing standard of living, arguing that regardless of immigration or no immigration, it was the "natural tendency of capitalism" to reduce the standard of living of the working class, and that if they could not get Oriental labor to do work more cheaply in the United States, they would export their production to the oriental countries where goods could be produced more cheaply than in this country.[38] Woodbey's prediction that American capitalists would export production to cheap labor countries of the Orient, was, as American workers today fully realize, to bear fruit.

Continuing, Woodbey spoke eloquently of the contradiction between immigration restriction and the principles of international Socialism. As he saw it, socialism was based "upon the Brotherhood of Man," and any stand in opposition to immigration would be "opposed to the very spirit of the Brotherhood of Man." Reminding the delegates that Socialists were organized in China and Japan as well as in other countries, he asked:

> Are the Socialists of this country to say to the Socialists of Germany, or the Socialists of Sweden, Norway, Japan, China, or any other country, that they are not to go anywhere on the face of the earth? It seems to me absurd to take that position. Therefore, I hope and move that any sort of restriction of immigration will be stricken out of the committee's resolution. (Applause.)[39]

It is unfortunate that while he had the floor, Woodbey did not attack delegates like Ernest Untermann and Victor Berger for the anti-Negro character of their arguments in favor of Oriental exclusion. Nevertheless, Woodbey's speech on the immigration resolution ranks high in Socialist literature even though it has been ignored by all students of the subject.[40]

Only once at either the 1904 or 1908 conventions did the delegates take notice of the fact that Woodbey was a black representative. That was when his name was placed in nomination as Debs' running-mate in the presidential election of 1908. Delegate Ellis Jones of Ohio presented his name to the convention in a brief but moving speech. "Comrades . . . the nomination that I want to make for our Vice-President . . . is a man who is well known in the movement for many years. The Socialist Party is a party that does not recognize race prejudice and in order that we may attest this to the world, I offer the name of Comrade Woodbey of California."[41] But Woodbey received only one vote—that of Jones.[42] The nomination went to Ben Hanford who had been Debs' running mate in 1904. Possibly had Debs, who did not attend the convention, wired the delegates that Woodbey's nomination would be a major contribution of American Socialism in the struggle against racism, the vote would have been different. But Debs did not believe that the Party should do anything special on the Negro question, and this view was shared by all at the convention except for the one delegate who nominated and voted for Woodbey. Since the fact that Woodbey was even placed in nomination has escaped the attention of every historian of the Socialist Party,[43] it is clear that the significance of the one vote he received has been generally overlooked.

Following the 1908 convention, Woodbey began a tour of Northern cities with fairly large black populations and delivered a series of soap-box speeches in favor of the Socialist ticket.⁴⁴ In addition, the National office of the Socialist Party circulated his four-page leaflet, *Why the Negro Should Vote the Socialist Ticket.* The author was described as a member of the State Executive Committee, Socialist Party of California, and formerly Pastor of African Church, in Omaha, Nebraska. Typical of Woodbey's propaganda technique, the leaflet consisted mainly of a speech, supposedly delivered by a Reverend Mr. Johnson, Pastor of the African Baptist Church, who had called his congregation together to explain why he had decided "to vote the Socialist ticket at the coming election."

The Socialist movement, he pointed out, sought to bring together all working people into a party of their own, so that through such a party "they may look after the interest of all who work regardless of race or color." Since Negroes were nearly all wage workers, it was clear that only such a party could really represent them. "All other parties have abandoned the negro, and if he wants an equal chance with everyone else, he can get it in no other way than by voting the Socialist ticket." No other party, including the Republicans, stood for eliminating poverty, and just as once, the elimination of slavery was crucial for the Negro, so today was the elimination of poverty. Socialism would create a society without poverty, a society in which the land, mines, factories, shops, railroads, etc., would be owned collectively, and the Negro "being a part of the public, will have an equal ownership in all that the public owns, and this will entitle him to an equal part in all the good things produced by the nation." In this future society, moreover, he would not have to abandon his belief in religion. On the contrary, by providing all with sufficient food to eat and decent places in which to live, Socialism would be fulfilling the fundamental ideas set down in the Bible.

Finally, Woodbey called for unity of white and black workers, urging them to "lay aside their prejudices and get together for their common good. We poor whites and blacks have fought each other long enough, and while we have fought, the capitalists have been taking everything from both of us." The Socialist movement was the embodiment of this unifying principle, for it was

part of a great world movement which includes all races and both sexes and has for its motto: "Workers of the world unite. You have nothing to lose but your chains; you have a world to win."⁴⁵

Woodbey's first published appeal directly to his people on behalf of the Socialist Party is an excellent illustration of the black minister's great abil-

ity to take a complex subject and simplify it so that even a political illiterate could understand it.

Woodbey expanded on several points in his leaflet in articles early in
1909 in the Chicago *Daily Socialist*. In "The New Emancipation," he
emphasized the common interests of black and white workers under capitalism, condemned black strikebreaking and the doctrine that Negroes
should seek to solve their problems by the accumulation of wealth. Even
if a few Negroes could become wealthy, the fact still remained that "their
brothers are getting poorer every day." What then was the answer?

> Give the negro along with others the full product of his labor by
> wrenching the industries out of the hands of the capitalist and putting
> them into the hands of the workers and what is known as the race
> problem will be settled forever. Socialism is only another one of those
> great world movements which is coming to bless mankind. The
> Socialist party is simply the instrument for bringing it about, and the
> negro and all other races regardless of former conditions are invited
> into its folds.[46]

In another article, "Socialist Agitation," Woodbey called for the use of
all forms of educational techniques to reach the black masses, "the press, the
pulpit, the rostrum and private conversation." Socialist agitators must
understand that they would face imprisonment and other forms of mal-
treatment, but this was to be expected when one sought to overthrow an evil
system. "For attempting to overthrow the slave system, Lincoln and Lovejoy were shot, John Brown was hung, while Garrison, Phillips and Fred
Douglass were mobbed." Naturally, Socialist agitators "are equally hated
and despised," and they faced constant distortion of what they stood for.

> Because the Socialists recognize the existence of a class struggle they
> are some times accused of stirring up class hatred. But, instead, they
> simply recognize the fact that capitalism, by its unequal distribution
> of wealth, has forced on us a class struggle, which the Socialists are
> organizing to put down and bring on the long talked of period of uni-
> versal brotherhood.[47]

When Woodbey advised Socialist agitators to expect to be persecuted,
he spoke from personal experience. At the time he was a delegate to the
1908 Socialist convention, he was out on bail, having been arrested in San
Francisco early in the year with thirty other Socialist speakers for defying

a ban against street-corner meetings. This was in the midst of the economic crisis following the Panic of 1907, and the Socialists were holding meetings to demand relief for the unemployed.

Even before the Wobblies made free-speech fights famous, Socialists had engaged in such battles and had used specific aspects of the strategy followed by the I.W.W. in their spectacular free-speech fights.[48] In the case of the 1908 San Francisco free-speech fight, the Socialists deliberately violated a city ordinance forbidding street meetings without police permits for all organizations except religious groups. When a speaker was arrested for speaking without a permit, his place was speedily filled on the soap box. Speaker after speaker, men and women, black and white, mounted the soap box, were arrested, and dragged off to the jail. Woodbey was one of the first to be dragged off and jailed. Along with his comrades he was released on bail.[49]

"The police can't stop us," Woodbey told a reporter during the 1908 convention. "They can and do arrest us when we speak, but they can't stem the tide that has been started no more than they can the ocean. The more they ill treat us, the more Socialists there are." Despite police opposition, the Socialists were determined to obtain relief for "the hordes of honest working men [in San Francisco] who are starving because they can't get the work they so earnestly desire."[50]

With the aid of liberals and labor groups, the Socialists were able to force the City Council of San Francisco to repeal the objectionable ordinance, and charges against Woodbey were dropped.[51] He continued to participate in free-speech fights, and in 1912 was a key figure in what was probably the most famous free-speech fight in American history—the free-speech fight in San Diego, California. San Diego was, of course, Woodbey's home town, and the place where he was the pastor of the Mt. Zion Church for several years until he was removed because, as one who knew him wrote, he "loosened up his flock with the Bible, then finished his sermon with an oration on Socialism."[52]

On January 8, 1912, the San Diego City Council passed an ordinance creating a "restricted" district, forty-nine blocks in the center of town, in which streetcorner meetings might not be held. Unlike ordinances in other cities banning street-speaking, that in San Diego made no exception for religious utterances. All street-speaking was banned in the so-called "congested district." The reason given was that the meetings blocked traffic, but it was clear that the real purpose was to suppress the I.W.W.'s effort "to educate the floating and out-of-work population to a true understanding of the interests of labor as a whole," as well as their determination to organize the workers in San Diego who were neglected by the A.F. of L. Among these neglected workers were the mill and lumber and laundry workers and streetcar conductors and motormen. This determination had infuriated John D. Spreckels, the millionaire sugar capitalist and owner of the streetcar franchise, and he and other employers had applied pressure on the Council to pass the ordinance. Certainly, San Diego had plenty of room for her traffic, and no one believed that this little town in Southern California would suffer a transportation crisis if streetcorner meetings continued.[53]

Two days before the ordinance was supposed to go into effect, the I.W.W. and the Socialists held a meeting in the center of the restricted district at which Woodbey was a leading speaker. The police broke up the meeting but did not intimidate the fighters for free speech. On January 8, 1912, the *San Diego Union* carried the following on its front page:

SOCIALISTS PROPOSE FIGHT
TO FINISH FOR FREE SPEECH

Following a near-riot Saturday night during a clash between the police department, on the one hand, and Socialists, Industrial Workers of the World on the other, the Socialists and I.W.W. members held a running street meeting last night at Fifth and H streets, but the meeting was orderly, and there was not any semblance of trouble.

During the meeting members of the organizations policed the sidewalks and kept them clear, so that the city police would have no objection to make. Among the speakers were Mrs. Laura Emerson, Messrs. Hubbard and Gordon for the Industrial Workers of the World, and George Washington Woodbey, Kaspar Bauer and Attorney E. F. Kirk for the Socialists.

The part played by the police in the affair of Saturday evening was denounced, but none of the speakers grew radical, It was announced that the fight for free speech will be waged with vigor, but in a dignified manner.

The police, aided by vigilantes, responded with more than vigor and in anything but a dignified manner. The brutality against the free-speech fighters in San Diego was so horrendous that after an investigation ordered by Governor Hiram Johnson, Colonel Harris Weinstock reported: "Your commissioner has visited Russia and while there, has heard many horrible tales of high-handed proceedings and outrageous treatment of innocent people at the hands of despotic and tyrannic Russian authorities. Your commissioner is frank to confess that when he became satisfied of the truth of the stories, as related by these unfortunate men (victims of police and vigilante brutality in San Diego), it was hard for him to believe that he was not still sojourning in Russia, conducting his investigation there, instead of in this alleged 'land of the free and home of the brave.'"[54]

Woodbey was several times the victim of brutal police assaults as he insisted on exercising his right-of-free-speech, and he filed charges of "Malicious and unofficial" conduct against the chief of police, captain of the detectives, and several policemen whom he accused of brutality.[55] As a leading figure in the Free Speech League, the organization which coordinated the free-speech fight, Woodbey was frequently threatened by vigilantes, and on one occasion, he barely escaped death. *The Citizen*, official organ of the Labor Unions of Southern California, reported in mid-April 1912:

> Rev. Woodbey, a negro preacher, has been threatened for his activity. A few nights ago he was taken to his home by a committee from the Free Speech League. As the party left the car at a corner near Woodbey's home an automobile was noticed in front of the house. Upon examination it was found to contain two armed men. Across the street another vigilante was stationed, and in the alley two more armed men were found. The strength of the committee with Woodbey probably saved his life, as members of the League challenged the vigilantes to do their dirty work. The preacher's house was patrolled by armed men from the League all night.[56]

The free-speech fight in "Barbarous San Diego" was still in full swing in late April 1912 when Woodbey left to attend the Socialist Party national convention in Chicago as a delegate from California. By the time he returned home, the struggle was still continuing and he did what he could to help the cause, faced with defeat as a result of the power of the police, vigilantes, and the state government. Wobblies continued to be clubbed and arrested, and there was little that could be done to prevent the wholesale violation of their civil rights. "They have the courts, the mails and funds," Laura Payne Emerson lamented.[57] It was not until 1914 that the right of the I.W.W. to hold street meetings was established. Although the ordinance still remained on the statute books, the police no longer interfered when Wobblies spoke at street corners in the forbidden district. On the invitation of the I.W.W., Reverend Woodbey was one of the regular speakers at such meetings.[58]

Woodbey's associations with the I.W.W. may not have pleased some California Socialists, and his role in the free-speech fights probably disturbed members of his congregation. But he was candidate for state treasurer on the Socialist ticket in 1914 and was still listed as Pastor of Mt. Zion Church in San Diego and member of the state executive board of the Socialist Party in *The Christian Socialist* of February 1915 which published two articles by the militant black Socialist minister. These, the last known writings of Reverend Woodbey on Socialism, were "What the Socialists Want" and "Why the Socialists Must Reach the Churches with Their Message." The first was in the form of a dialogue, a familiar Woodbey technique, between the minister (here called Parker) and George Stephenson, a black mail carrier. Stephenson asks to be told "in short, and the simplest way possible, just what it is you Socialists are trying to get any way," and Woodbey proceeds to enlighten him, pointing out the features of the Socialist society which he had presented in greater detail in his previous pamphlets. When the mail carrier leaves convinced that there was no way to answer the arguments in favor of Socialism, his teacher shouts after him: "Hold on a minute, we would solve the race problem of this and all other countries, by establishing the brotherhood of man which Christ taught."

In the second piece, Woodbey insisted that the Socialists would never succeed unless they won over "the millions of working people who belong to the various churches of the country," and proceeded to indicate how he did his part in this endeavor. His chief weapon was to play up the point that "the economic teaching of the Bible and of Socialism is the same, and that for that reason he (the church member) must accept Socialism in order to stand consistently by the teaching of his own religion." After having shown the church member that the Bible, "in every line of it," was "with the poor and against their oppressors," it was necessary to convince him that the solution for the ills of society was not charity which was at best "only a temporary relief," but the collective ownership and operation of the industries. The last point had to be reached slowly and step by step, but if the Socialist agitator keeps using the Bible as his authority, he will carry the church member along to that conclusion. The danger was that too many Socialists antagonized church members by linking anti-religion with Socialism. Hence, he advised against using agitators "who do not understand the Christian people, to carry this message, for the reason that they are sure to say something that will spoil the whole thing."

We know nothing of Reverend Woodbey after 1915. But we leave him at this point in his career still as confirmed a Socialist as ever. "I would not vote for my own wife on a platform which did not have the Socialist message in it," he told an audience in December 1914.[59]

Just how many blacks Woodbey converted by the method he outlined in his last Socialist writing is impossible to determine. But Hubert H. Harrison, a militant black Socialist in New York, said of Woodbey's work as a national Party organizer: "He has been very effective."[60] At least one prominent black Socialist attributed his conversion to Socialism to Reverend Woodbey. In the Chicago *Daily Socialist* of September 29, 1908, Reverend George W. Slater, Jr., Pastor, Zion Tabernacle in the Windy City, wrote:

> For years I have felt that there was something wrong with our government. A few weeks ago I heard Comrade Woodbey, a colored national organizer of the Socialist party, speaking on the streets in Chicago. He showed me plainly the trouble and the remedy. From that time on I have been an ardent supporter of the Socialist cause.

Notes

1. *Ohio Socialist Bulletin*, February 1909.
2. *Chicago Daily Socialist*, May 11, 1908; John Mather, *Who's Who of the Colored Race*, Chicago, 1921; A. W. Ricker in *Appeal to Reason*, October 31, 1903.
3. Reverend George W. Woodbey, *What To Do and How To Do It or Socialism vs. Capitalism*, *Wayland's Monthly*, No. 40, August 1903, p. 4; A. W. Ricker in *Appeal to Reason*, Oct. 31, 1903. Correspondence with the Omaha Public Library, the University of Nebraska Library, the Nebraska State Historical Society, and the United Methodist Historical Society at Nebraska Wesleyan University has failed to turn up any information on Reverend Woodbey in their files and his role as a Populist and Socialist in Nebraska.
3. *Los Angeles Socialist*, May 31, 1902.
4. *Los Angeles Socialist*, July 12, 1902.
5. Ibid., Dec. 17, 1904; *Common Sense*, Los Angeles, Oct. 27, 1906.
6. *Los Angeles Socialist*, May 2, 1903.
7. *Common Sense*, Los Angeles, August 1905.
8. Ibid., Oct. 8, 1904, March 7, April 11, 1908.
9. A. W. Ricker, *Appeal to Reason*, October 31, 1903.
10. Ibid. Robert Blatchford's *Merrie England*, published in London in 1894, was a book of 26 chapters and 210 pages in which the superiority of Socialism over Capitalism is brilliantly set forth in clear, plain language.
11. Woodbey, *op. cit.*, p. 3.
12. *Chicago Daily Socialist*, May 11, 1908.
13. Woodbey, *op. cit.*, pp. 5–7.
14. Ibid., pp. 15–19.
15. Ibid., p. 20.

16. Ibid., pp. 20–21.
17. Ibid., p. 24.
18. Ibid., pp. 37–38.
19. Ibid., p. 44.
20. Compare, for example, Woodbey's discussion of an international credit system under Socialism (pp. 36–37) with Bellamy's discussion of the same system in Chapter 8 of *Looking Backward*.
21. In a letter to William Dean Howells a few months after the publication of *Looking Backward*, Bellamy wrote that "the word socialist is one I could never well stomach. In the first place it is a foreign word in itself, and equal foreign in all its suggestions. . . . Whatever German and French reformers may choose to call themselves, socialist is not a good name for a party to succeed with in America. No such party can or ought to succeed which is not wholly and enthusiastically American and patriotic in spirit and suggestions." (Quoted in Arthur E. Morgan, *Edward Bellamy*, New York, 1941, p. 374.)
22. For a discussion of *The Iron Heel*, see Philip S. Foner, *Jack London: American Rebel*, New York, 1964, pp. 87–97.
23. Woodbey, *op. cit.*, p. 7.
24. G. W. Woodbey, *The Bible and Socialism: A Conversation Between Two Preachers*, San Diego, 1904, Preface.
25. Ibid., p. 7.
26. Ibid., pp. 69, 83, 90.
27. Ibid., p. 69.
28. Ibid., p. 96.
29. G. W. Woodbey, *The Distribution of Wealth*, San Diego, California, 1910, p. 7.
30. Ibid., pp. 41, 44–45.
31. Ibid., pp. 54–55.
32. Ibid., p. 68. Woodbey's fellow-California Socialist closed his letters, "Yours for the Revolution, Jack London."
33. *Proceedings of the National Convention of the Socialist Party Held at Chicago, Illinois, May 1 to 6, 1904*, Chicago, 1904, pp. 47–48.
34. Ibid., p. 182.
35. *Proceedings, National Convention of the Socialist Party, Held at Chicago, Illinois, May 10 to 17, 1908*, pp. 208–9.
36. Ibid., pp. 290–91.
37. Ibid., p. 106.
38 Ibid., pp. 106–7.
39. Ibid., pp. 107–8.
40. The most detailed discussion of the 1908 convention in relation to the immigration issue is Charles Leinenweber, "The American Socialist Party and 'New' Immigrants," *Science & Society*, vol. XXXXII, Winter, 1968, pp. 6–12. It does not even mention Woodbey's speech in opposition to the resolution calling for a study of the necessity for immigration restriction.
41. *Proceedings, National Convention . . . 1908*, p. 163.
42. Ibid., p. 164.
43. Neither Ira Kipnis nor Ray Ginger mention Woodbey's nomination in their discussion of the 1908 Convention.

44. New York *Evening Call*, Nov. 2, 1908.

45. Reverend G. W. Woodbey, "Why the Negro Should Vote the Socialist Ticket," four-page leaflet, undated, copy in Socialist Party Papers, Duke University Library.

46. G. W. Woodbey, "The New Emancipation," *Chicago Daily Socialist*, Jan. 18, 1909.

47. G. W. Woodbey, "Socialist Agitation," Ibid., Jan. 4, 1909.

48. Philip S. Foner, *History of the Labor Movement in the United States*, vol. IV, New York, 1965, p. 173.

49. San Francisco *Call*, San Francisco *Chronicle*, Feb. 1–8, 1908.

50. *Chicago Daily Socialist*, May 11, 1908.

51. San Francisco *Call*, June 12, 1908.

52. In a letter to the author, Harland B. Adams of San Diego summarized a conversation he had with Dennis V. Allen, a black San Diegan who in the years 1912 to 1916, as a postal clerk, delivered mail to the home of Reverend Woodbey. According to Mr. Allen, Reverend Woodbey lived at 12 Twenty-Ninth Street, San Diego. He described Woodbey as "a rather dark Negro, slender and about 5 feet 11 inches. Mrs. Woodbey was extremely stout, almost to the point that with her age and weight, it was difficult for her to get about. She was known by nearly everyone in the small Negro population of San Diego at that time as Mother Mary or Mother Woodbey. She was a devout Baptist Christian and regularly attended the Baptist Church at 29th and Clay, which still exists." The Woodbeys, Mr. Allen continued, owned the property where he lived, as well as the house next door which he rented to a Negro who was a veteran of the Civil War.

    According to Mr. Allen, he was in a group that drafted Reverend Woodbey as the pastor for the Mt. Zion Baptist Church, and was also part of the group which had him removed. Although extremely popular, and though he drew large crowds to his sermons, his dismissal "was a direct result of mixing too much Socialism with his Bible, and this the members of his church resented."

    Dennis V. Allen organized the San Diego Race Relations Society in 1924, and held the post of president for thirty-six years.

53. Foner, *op. cit.*, vol. IV, pp. 194–95.

54. Ibid., pp. 199–200.

55. San Diego *Union*, Feb. 22, 1912. The charges were ignored by the authorities.

56. *The Citizen* reprinted in *St. Louis Labor*, April 27, 1912. In her study, "The I.W.W. Free Speech Movement San Diego, 1912" (*Journal of San Diego History*, Winter, 1973, pp. 25–33), Rosalie Shanks does not once mention Reverend Woodbey.

57. *Industrial Worker*, Oct. 17, 1912.

58. *The Wooden Shoe* (Los Angeles), Jan. 22, 1914.

59. *California Social Democrat*, Dec. 12, 1914.

60. New York *Call*, Dec. 16, 1911.

Part 6

Black Religion and the 1960s

Chapter 28

From *The Luminous Darkness*

Howard Thurman

Despite all that has been said about the pattern of segregation in our society, it is my conviction that time is against it. In fact, much of the current effort to hold the line may be viewed as a back-against-the-wall endeavor. The more the world becomes a neighborhood in which time and space are approaching zero as a limit, the more urgent becomes the issue of neighborliness. Man can now circle the entire earth's surface in a matter of minutes. Communication is now instant! This means that the external symbols of segregation—the wall, the ghetto, the separate locale as a mandatory restriction binding upon groups of people because of race, color, creed, or national origin—cannot survive modern life. The emphasis here is upon the two words "external symbols." When I suggest that time is against the pattern of segregation, I am referring to the symbols. The walls are crumbling—this is one of the dramatic facts of our world. The fact itself is very frightening to many who have lived always behind the walls, within the walls, or beyond the walls. It is deeply disturbing also to those who have found the existence of the walls essential to their own peace, well-being, and security. Out of sight, out of mind—this can no longer be the case.

So much emphasis is placed upon the fact of the existence of the walls that the symbolic fact of the walls is ignored or is an unknown quantity. It must be remembered that segregation is a mood, a state of mind, and its external manifestation is external. The root of the evil, and evil it is, is in the human spirit. Laws which make segregation illegal may or may not attack the root of the evil. Their great function is to deny the binding character of the external symbol by giving it no legal standing. They alert the body politic to the variety of external manifestations of the mood, the state of mind, and declare that wherever such manifestations appear, they are not to stand. This is most important because it calls attention to that of which segregation is the manifestation. As such it becomes a tutor or a guide for the human spirit. The law cannot deal with the human spirit directly. This is not within its universe of discourse.

What happens when the external symbol is outlawed and the walls of segregation are razed to the ground is a concern of the law only at the point that safeguards are being erected against other external symbols. And this is of vast importance—though negative basically. The reaction of the human spirit that has lived under the pattern of segregation on both sides of the wall, when the wall is removed, is apt to be one of panic and profound mental and spiritual distress. When my family and I lived on the campus of Howard University, our front yard was enclosed by a picket fence along the outside of which was a sidewalk leading from the main walk of the campus to the street. We had a dog whose name was Beariemore. It was his chief-in-the-yard sport to lie upon the steps facing the direction of the main walk, watching for the appearance of a Western Union boy coming toward the fence on his bicycle. Beariemore would wait for him at the corner of the fence, bark him all the way, the full length of the yard, and send him on his way. Then he would return to his former waiting position. One day after a very heavy snowfall, there were snow-drifts four to five feet high in one corner of the yard. Beariemore began his game as usual. Only this time when he chased one of the boys he did not take the snowdrift into account. I heard him yelp as if he were in great pain. I ran to the door, thinking that someone had hurt him. He was all right except that when he found himself over the fence with no barrier between him and the Western Union boy, he panicked. People who are conditioned to living behind the walls and those whose emotional security is dependent upon the stability of the walls are apt to be seized by a sense of panic, not only if the walls are removed, but if their removal is imminent. Such a condition is spiritual.

At such a time the real task of making or building a decent society of equality will emerge. Since segregation is the manifestation of a state of mind and mood of the human spirit, in a situation of threat a new and more subtle manifestation of the mood may appear. The wall is in the mind and in the spirit.

The situation is apt to be aggravated by the fact that the wall has existed so long that it may no longer be regarded as a symbol but as the thing itself. Wherever this is the case, the removal of the wall is thought to be the riddance of segregation. When I was a college boy in Atlanta, our football team played a team of regular army men from a Negro regiment. At dinner in the evening before the game, the behavior of the soldiers was very crude and somewhat embarrassing. At the next chapel service, the dean of the college, in commenting on the behavior of the soldiers, said, "It is a long way from slavery to a sense of freedom and no former slave or former slaveowner can make it in fifty years."

The issue then is twofold. The walls that divide must be demolished. They must be cast down, destroyed, uprooted. This is beyond debate. There must be ceaseless and unrelenting pressure to that end, using all the resources of our common life. These barriers must be seen for what they are, a disease of our society, the enemy of human decency and humane respect. In many ways, they are so much a part of our landscape that they seem to belong to the landscape and as such are regarded as germane to the American way of life. The resistance against their reversal is so rooted that it has created a new term in the current vocabulary—backlash. As has been suggested earlier, the walls seem so permanent that to advocate their removal must be conditional: those who are the obvious sufferers because of their presence must prove themselves worthy of such action. In other words, the walls are sacrosanct and to tamper with them can be done only out of a mood of grace and compassion. In fine, the walls have an established right to be, even though what this right is, is never quite clear and he who would remove the walls must show cause. Their destruction is such a monumental undertaking and is calling for such huge costs in human lives, resources of money, time, and energy, that an everwidening weariness is apt to sweep over the land in the wake of the crumbling of the walls. And this is the danger. When the walls are down, it is then that the real work of building the healthy American society begins. The razing of the walls is prelude—important, critical, urgent, vital, but prelude nevertheless. About this there must be no mistake.

The removal of the walls is the first step in the attack on the mood of which they are a manifestation. Care must be exercised to see to it that new walls will not be built. One of the things that will make it easier to build new walls of segregation in the form of new kinds of discrimination is what has been aptly called the discrimination gap which is the huge burden of the American Negro. This aspect of the issue has been effectively described by Whitney Young, the executive director of the National Urban League, in his recent book *To Be Equal:* "For at this moment in history, if the United States honestly drops legal, practical, and subtle racial barriers to employment, housing, education, public accommodations, health and welfare facilities and services, the American Negro still will not achieve full equality in our lifetime." He goes on to say that "more than three centuries of abuse, humiliation, segregation, and bias have burdened the Negro with a handicap that will not automatically slip from his shoulders as discriminatory laws and practices are abandoned. The situation is much like that of two men running the mile in a track meet. One is well-equipped, wears track shoes and runs on cinders. The other is barefoot and runs in sand. Seeing that one runner is outdistancing the other with ease, you then put track shoes on the second fellow and place him on the cinder track also. Seconds later it should surprise no one to see that the second runner is still yards behind and will never catch up unless something else is done to even the contest."[1]

All the damage done by the existence of the walls must be repaired and healed. It is not a part of the work of this essay to suggest such a program. I know of no more comprehensive, clear, and creative blueprint to this end than is set forth in Whitney Young's book.

The other aspect of the issue has to do with the mood, the state of mind out of which discrimination and the response to discrimination come in the first instance. The issue is a moral and spiritual one and falls within the broad and specific scope of morality and religion. The point of departure for this final aspect of my discussion is to be found at the beginning of the essay where reference is made to the fact that Negroes and white persons are often excluded from each other's magnetic field of value. The first step in giving the kind of new orientation that will bring one into moral focus is the loss of fear. When the relationship between the groups is devoid of fear, then it becomes possible for them to relate to each other as human beings and have far more that unites them than divides them.

The burden of being black and the burden of being white is so heavy that it is rare in our society to experience oneself as a human being. It may be, I do not know, that to experience oneself as a human being is one with experiencing one's fellows as human beings. Precisely what does it mean to experience oneself as a human being? In the first place, it means that the individual must have a sense of kinship to life that transcends and goes beyond the immediate kinship of family or the organic kinship that binds him ethnically or "racially" or nationally. He has to feel that he belongs to his total environment. He has a sense of being an essential part of the structural relationship that exists between him and all other men, and between him, all other men, and the total external environment. As a human being, then, he belongs to life and the whole kingdom of life that includes all that lives and perhaps, also, all that has ever lived. In other words, he sees himself as a part of a continuing, breathing, living existence. To be a human being, then, is to be essentially alive in a living world.

> I like to feel that strange life beating up against me. I like to realize forms of life utterly unlike mine. When my own life feels small, and I am oppressed with it, I like to crush together, and see it in a picture, in an instant, a multitude of disconnected unlike phases of human life—a mediaeval monk with his string of beads pacing the quiet orchard, and looking up from the grass at his feet to the heavy fruit trees; little Malay boys playing naked on a shining sea-beach; a Hindu philosopher alone under his banyan tree, thinking, thinking, thinking, so that in the thought of God he may lose himself; a troop of Bacchanalians dressed in white, with crowns of vine-leaves, dancing along the Roman streets; a martyr on the night of his death looking through the narrow window to the sky, and feeling that already he has the wings that shall bear him up; an Epicurean discoursing at a Roman bath to a knot of his disciples on the nature of happiness; a Kaffir witch doctor, seeking for herbs by moonlight, while from the huts on the hillside come the sound of dogs barking, and the voices of women and children; a mother giving bread and milk to her children in little wooden basins and singing the evening song. I like to see it all: I feel it run through me—that life belongs to me; it makes my little life larger; it breaks down the narrow walls that shut me in.[2]

In a conversation with three Indian chiefs in one of the Canadian provinces, I was deeply impressed particularly by the reply of one of them to the query, "Are you a Canadian and then an Indian, or are you an Indian and then a Canadian?" His reply, as it came through the interpreter, was essentially this: "I come from some miles near the Arctic circle in the north country. I live with the snow, the ice, the sharp wind in the winter; with the streams, the flowing waters, the sun and the blossoms in summer. These flow into me and I flow into them. They keep me and I keep them. I am a part of them and they are a part of me. I am not sure what you mean when you say Indian or Canadian."[3]

What he is saying is that he has a sense of being a part of an extended life that belongs to him and to which he belongs. Instead of its spreading him out so that all the margins of the self fade and vanish away, it deepens and intensifies his essential sense of uniqueness without the devastation of a sense of being different. The same basic principle was manifested by an experience in Nigeria. At the close of a lecture before the Press

Club, I was invited to a small room for refreshments. I asked for a kind of soft drink called ginger beer. My host opened the bottle, poured a little on the floor as he said, "For my ancestors," and then he filled my glass.[4] In this concept of the extended family, as I saw it, there is a variation of the same theme. To experience oneself as a human being is to know a sense of kinship with one's total environment and to recognize that it is this structural relationship that makes it possible for one to experience himself as a human *being*. Being white or black becomes merely incidental and is of no basic significance. Does this seem far-fetched and speculative or unrealistic?

What is meant here can be most clearly understood if we look at the conditions that obtain when differences of race, culture, ethnic, or national origin are sloughed off, when the essential fact of being a human being in the world is brought sharply into focus. In times of disaster, when the only thing that is relevant is that a man is stripped of all superficial categories that separate and divide, one gets some notion of what it means just to be a human being in the world among other human beings who are all structurally bound together by a total environment. Flood, earthquakes, disaster know nothing of race or class. "God causes his sun to shine on the just and the unjust, his rain to fall on the evil and the good."

In our own country, when the national life is threatened, we make common cause in which for the moment everybody is counted in as an essential human being, possessed of certain resources that are needful for the survival of the common life. Despite the fact that this is an act of desperation and convenience, which act may be so interpreted by all, nevertheless the salutary effect obtains in the lives of those who are counted *in* merely because they are needed. As ironical as this is, nevertheless, the national registration during the last World War made an important impact on the life of Negroes, particularly in the South. A man who had been called "J. B." all his life and who knew no other name had to make a name for himself out of the initials. Think of what it meant to this man who had been regarded by his society as without name or significance to find himself suddenly on the receiving end of personal attention from the vast federal government. Now his name was known, his address duly noted, and his *intention* to be a consumer of certain goods such as meat, sugar, gasoline, and automobile tires was registered.[5] An entirely fresh dimension of personal awareness opened out before him. He began to experience himself as a human being. The fact that the new status was crisis-created must not obscure what was really at work here. The new experience did not know anything about a crisis situation.

But it is not only the situation of the collective crisis that creates a climate in which the individual human being emerges with an experience of himself as a human being. Here at last we come face to face with the original claim of religion and here I refer especially to the ethical insight brought into the stream of contemporary life by the Judaeo-Christian tradition.

It is most unfortunate that the trustees of this insight, namely the religious institutions, have failed singularly to witness to the insight. The impact upon the individual when he experiences himself as a human being is to regard himself as being of infinite worth. Such a sense of worth is not confined by narrow limits of the self so that worth may be determined by contrast with something or someone of less worth. No, this is a specious basis for ascertaining worth. Such a sense of worth is rooted in one's own consciousness which expands and expands until there is involved the totality of life itself. As important as is the clue to one's self-estimate, as found in the attitude of others in the environment, this is not now what is at issue. To experience oneself as a human being is to feel life moving through one and claiming one as a part of it. It is like the moment of insight into a new idea or an aspect of truth. What initially is grasped by the mind and held there for meaning begins slowly or suddenly to *hold* the mind as if the mind itself is being thought by a vaster and greater Mind. It is like the thing that happens when you are trying to explain something to a child and you finally succeed in doing so. Then the child says, "I see." In that moment you are no longer there in fact. The barrier that stood between the child's comprehension of the idea and the idea itself has been removed. There is a flowing together, as if the child and the idea were alone in all the universe!

The ultimate meaning of experience is felt in such a way that all of oneself is included. It is total, it is unified and unifying. It is not the experience of oneself as male or female, as black or white, as American or European. It is rather the experience of oneself as *being*. It is at such a time that one can hear the sound of the genuine in other human beings. This is to be able to identify with them. One man's response to the sound of the genuine in another man is to ascribe to the other man the same sense of infinite worth that one holds for oneself. When this happens, men are free to relate to each other as human beings—good, bad, mean, friendly, prejudiced, altruistic, but human beings. Whatever may be the nature of the shortcomings, they are seen from the view on the other side where the person lives whose shortcomings are being encountered.

This is the precious work of the imagination. There is an apt quotation in Russell Gordon Smith's *Fugitive Papers:* "On the seventh day, therefore, God could not rest. In the morning and the evening He busied Himself with terrible and beautiful concoctions and in the twilight of the seventh day He finished that which is of more import than the beasts of the earth and the fish of the sea and the lights of the firmament. And he called it Imagination because it was made in His own image; and those unto whom it is given shall see God."[6]

The place where the imagination shows its greatest power as the agent of God is in the miracle which it creates when one man, standing where he is, is able, while remaining there, to put himself in another man's place. Many years ago I was the overnight guest in the house of a friend. I was seated the next morning in the living room reading the morning paper. His little boy rode into the room in his kiddy car, stopped it in front of me, and said, "Mr. Thurman, will you please help me change my tire, I just had a blowout." I helped him jack up his car, take the old tire off, replace it with a spare, and then remove the jack. He sat in his car, stepped on the starter, but the motor would not start. He pulled out the choke; nothing happened. He got out of the car, opened each side of the hood, tinkered a little, then tried again with the same results. Then a strange thing happened. His shoulders became very stiff, a grim look swept over his tender countenance, and words flowed forth from his lips that were taken verbatim from his father under such circumstances. Still nothing happened. He got out of the car and came around to me. "Mr. Thurman, lend me your pencil." With my pencil in hand, he opened the gas tank of his car, put the pencil down into it, held it up to the light. "Ah, the tank is empty. No wonder it wouldn't start." He rushed out to the kitchen, came back with a glass of water, sat in his kiddy car, drank the water, started the motor, and rode out of the living room, through the dining room and into the kitchen.

This is the idea. A man can send his imagination forth to establish a beachhead in another man's spirit, and from that vantage point so to blend with the other's landscape that what he sees and feels is authentic—this is the great adventure in human relations. But this is not enough. The imagination must report its findings accurately without regard to prejudgments and private or collective fears. But this too is not enough. There must be both a spontaneous and a calculating response to such knowledge which will result in sharing of life and resources at their deepest level.

This is to experience oneself as a human being and to have that essential experience illumined and underscored by experiencing one's fellows as human beings. This is what every person seeks to have happen to himself. Every man lives under the necessity for being at home in his own house, as it were. He must not seem to himself to be alien to himself. This is the thing that happens when other human beings relate to him as if he were not a human being or less than a human being. It is possible for a man to declassify whole groups of people on the basis of certain criteria which he establishes or which he inherits. For instance, it may be to denigrate all people who come from a particular country, locale, or region, or all who speak a certain language, or all whose skin has pigmentation of any kind or a particular kind, or all who claim a different religious faith.

It may be that the experience of which we speak is not possible unless and until the individual sees himself as being contained or held by something so much more than he is that his life is brought into a focus of self-conscious meaning and value. Such an experience is possible only in the light of ultimate values and ultimate meanings. And this is what religion undertakes to guarantee; the extent to which Christianity is religious is the extent to which it would guarantee such an experience for the individual.

Once when I was very young, my grandmother, sensing the meaning of the constant threat under which I was living, told me about the message of one of the slave ministers on her plantation. Whatever he developed as his theme on the rare occasions when he was able to hold services for his fellow slaves, the climactic moment came in these exhilarating words: "You are not slaves; you are not *niggers* condemned forever to do your master's will—you are God's children." When those words were uttered a warm glow crept all through the very being of the slaves, and they felt the feeling of themselves run through them. Even at this far distance I can relive the pulsing tremor of raw energy that was released in me as I responded to her words. The sense of being permanently grounded in God gave to the people of that far-off time a way to experience themselves as human beings.

But this is one side of the coin. The community of believers must be involved in the same kind of experience. The normal reaction to experiencing oneself as a human being is to seek to experience other people as human beings. This does not have to be in the name of religion exclusively. Such a reaction is automatic unless there is some kind of intervention which short-circuits the process. The thing that determines the character of how one relates to one's fellows in any manner that has personal meaning in it is shaped by how the individual defines others. This is but another aspect of the issue as discussed earlier. The community of Christian believers is under the judgment of a command to love God, which is the response to the awareness that God cares or loves the individual and one must love one's neighbor as oneself.

There has emerged in the tradition of the Christian movement a secondary consideration, which is that the Christian must love especially those who are Christians. Here is a tie that binds all Christians as members of the Body of Christ. If this is the case, then to be a part of the Body of Christ is to share the love of all those who are a part of the Body of Christ. To spell it out: not only would a Baptist be under the demand to love all other Baptists and a Methodist to love all other Methodists, etc., but it would be binding upon each one who claimed to be a Christian, and therefore a part of the Body of Christ, to love all others who make such a claim. It would follow then that the Christian would be unique among other men in that the Christian is secure in the love of other Christians. Indeed at one time in the history of Christianity it was this that separated the Christian from the world. "Behold how the Christians love each other." The formula can be stated categorically: the Christian has a special sense of being loved by God because he accepts the idea that God loved him by giving His son for his redemption. His response to the redemptive giving of God is to love God. "I love him because he first loved me." All Christians are involved in this relationship with God, therefore all Christians must give love to one another as a part of the giving of love to God.

The tragedy is that even among those whose profession of faith subscribes completely to the above, the total relationship gives evidence of another kind. In fact, it is precisely accurate to say that the church, which is the institutional expression of the doctrine, has given little indication that being a member of the Body of Christ has any bearing on how one member relates to the other members. Granted it may be less evident among those who are a part of the same sectarian tradition. There is much to indicate that the further a particular group may be from the so-called mainstream of the convention of the doctrine, the more apt we may be to find the practice of love of all who belong to the household of faith. One of my earliest memories is of greeting people at our door who asked for my parents because they wanted to talk to them about religion. Two things I remember: they called themselves Russellites,[7] and despite the fact that they were white they made themselves at home in the living room. Nothing entered into what they did or what they said that drew the color line.

Until most recently, no one expected the white Christian to love the black Christian or the black Christian to love the white Christian. Historically in this country, the church has given the sweep of its moral force to the practice of segregation within its own community of believers. To the extent to which this has been done, the church has violated one of the central elements in its own commitment. It has dared to demonstrate that the commitment is not central, that it does not believe that Christians are bound to love one another.

The effect of its position with reference to Christians of other races is far-reaching. It is to be noted that the doctrine has to be accommodated and dealt with in a manner that will hold the doctrine secure and at the same time tolerate its profound violation. How is this accomplished? With reference to the Negro, the church has promulgated a doctrine that makes the Negro the object of its salvation while at the same time it denies him the status of a human being, thereby enhancing the difficulties he must face in his effort to experience himself as a human being. Time after weary time, the church has dishonored its Lord. When I asked Mr. Gandhi, "What is the greatest handicap that Jesus has in India?" instantly he replied, "Christianity." And this is what he meant.

The purpose here is not to indict but rather it is to lament the fact that such is the situation. The point must be clear that the commitment to love as it stands at the center of the Christian doctrine of God has not prevented the Christian from excluding Negroes from his Christian fellowship, nor has it prevented the Christian who is Negro from excluding white people from his Christian fellowship. To the extent that this is true, being Christian may not involve a person either in experiencing himself as a human being or in relating to others so as to experience them as human beings. The sad fact is that being Jewish, Catholic, or Protestant seems to make little difference in this regard.

If being Christian does not demand that all Christians love each other and thereby become deeply engaged in experiencing themselves as human beings, it would seem futile to expect that Christians as Christians would be concerned about the secular community in its gross practices of prejudice and discrimination. If a black Christian and a white Christian, in encounter, cannot reach out to each other in mutual realization because of that which they are experiencing in common, then there should be no surprise that the Christian institution has been powerless in the presence of the color bar in society. Rather it has reflected the presence of the color bar within its own institutional life.

On the other hand, if Christians practiced brotherhood among Christians, this would be one limited step in the direction of a new order among men. Think of what this would mean. Wherever one Christian met or dealt with another Christian, there would be a socially redemptive encounter. They would be like the Gulf Stream or the Japanese Current tempering and softening the climate in all directions. Indeed the Christian would be a leaven at all levels of the community and in public and private living. Of course, such a situation may lend itself to all kinds of exploitation and betrayals—but the Christian would be one of the bulwarks of integrity in human relations in an immoral society.

If the Christian limited his practice to other Christians, thereby guaranteeing that the church, wherever it existed, at whatever cost, would not tolerate segregation within its body, then there would be a kind of fierce logic in its position. It would be consistent within itself because it would practice brotherhood without regard to race, color, and all the other barriers. It would make for a kind of arrogance and bigotry toward those who were not fortunate or wise enough to put themselves in the way of being Christian. This would narrow the basis of the faith deliberately, while at the same time providing enough room for the outsider to come in and belong. But the church has historically tended to reject this alternative.

It is true and freely acknowledged that there are many changes afoot. Here and there through the years the Gospel has been at work despite the prohibition placed upon it by many denials. There is a power in the teaching which, when released, goes on to work its perfect work. Slowly there have emerged certain ingredients in the social climate that have had a softening effect. Much of this is due to the introduction of the teachings of Jesus and the Christian religious experience into society.

In recent time it has become increasingly a part of the public policy and private practice of the church to put itself squarely on the side of cleaning its own house of the evils that separate the brethren. It has become more and more aggressive in attacking the presence of those same evils wherever they are in our society. It is a prestige factor in the church to take a challenging position in the matter of the treatment of Negroes. Very often when I am visiting in a city, clergymen and laymen proudly announce that their particular church is "integrated," or they may complain that they are wide open in the welcome of Negroes but that Negroes do not come. One is glad to witness the changes that are taking place and may regard the changes as delayed reactions to the impact of the Gospel in the church itself. But the thought persists that this is the response of the church to the pressure of the secular community upon it, rather than the response of the church to the genius of the Gospel which it proclaims. Perhaps it is both. Even the church cannot be in the position of establishing the ground rules by which God works in the development of the good life for His children.

But why has the church been such a tragic witness to its own Gospel? It does seem to me at times that it is because the church is not sufficiently religious. By this I mean that it is not wide open to the Spirit of the living God. Its genius as an institution has to be sectarian in character. Perhaps there can be no such thing among men as the Church of God; it is the nature of institutionalism to be adjectival; some qualifying word must always precede the word "church." It has to be some *kind* of church, and this gives it its unique character and position.

This fact creates a terrible dilemma. How important is the limiting and defining character? It may be that the church as such is an abstraction which only becomes concrete when a peculiar pattern or style of worship, etiquette, or doctrine emerges to define the character and give context to the abstraction. Nothing is ultimately admissible that may threaten the institutional structure that gives to the Christian religion its form and substance. But suppose as a part of the form and substance of the church all believers must commit themselves to loving all men, believers and nonbelievers, as children of God and therefore members one of another? Then the tremendous resources of such a church would be at the disposal of the performing ethic. Under such a circumstance, the whole missionary-conversion process would be reversed—men would knock at the door of the church to find out what they need to do to become what, in evidence, the Christian is. The life that the church lives in the world would "bring the world to Christ." This surely means first of all to go ye into one's very own world, one's very own life, to go into every part of one's very own being and proclaim the good news that one can be free to experience oneself as a child of God and to experience all other men as children of God. Of such is a part of the miracle of Jesus. Men came to him with the searching question, What must I do? How may I? He made the life of God contagious!

The problem may not be so simple. It is too easy to say or to believe that the church has not been true to its own Gospel. The question that deserves probing is Why? Is it because of human frailty? Is it because man has not evolved to the point that he is sufficiently human to deal justly and to promote the common good? Is there some inherent limitation in the nature of man that works against his doing for himself and with and on behalf of others that which makes for harmony, wholeness, love? Is it because of what the church recognizes as original sin? If not, precisely from what is the believer saved by the death and resurrection of Christ? Are the roots of conflict deep into a long forgotten past?

Why is it that in many aspects of life that are regarded as secular one is apt to see more sharing, more of a tendency for human beings to experience themselves as human beings, than in those areas that are recognized as being religious? There seems to be more of a striving toward equality of treatment in many so-called secular institutions in our society than has characterized those institutions whose formal religious commitment demands that they practice the art of brotherhood. When I was in college, I heard two Negro men arguing on this very issue. We were on an all-day train ride in the third of the day coach designated for Negroes. Finally, one of the men, to clinch his point, said, "If I had committed a crime and was being tried in court, I would much rather have a jury made up of gamblers, race track men, pimps, than one made up of people who profess Christianity. I know I'd get much fairer treatment."

There is something out of line somewhere. Can it be that matters which have to do with human relations are not the legitimate concern of religion? Hardly. The fact cannot be ignored that generally our society does not expect the church to be any kind of guide in these matters. It seems to me that one of the really tremendous things that is happening before our very eyes is that the religious community is now being judged by the same standards of human relations as the secular institutions in our society. This means that the church is slowly winning the right to be regarded as an institution that has a stake in the earthly fate of mankind. It has always concerned itself with charity, with good works, with the meeting of the creature needs of man; it has always concerned itself with the preaching of a doctrine of salvation which addressed itself to the spiritual condition as far as the soul was concerned; but for some reason that has puzzled me all of my life, the religious community tended not to concern itself with the total needs of a man as a human being. And that, after all, is what matters most. Always it is a human being who hungers, who is sick, who is ignorant, who suffers. And he cannot be touched in any way that counts unless the word gets through to him that he is being experienced as a human being by the person for whom he is the object of good works.

Perhaps there is something inherent in the religious experience that always pulls back toward the personal center out of which the individual operates and the religious context that gives existential meaning to the experience itself. It is this latter frame of reference that creates the categories out of which the dogma of a particular faith comes. In this sense it may seem an unrealistic demand that religious experience be universal. If this is a true picture, then such notions or concepts as brotherhood, reverence for life, respect for personality, do not rightfully belong to the behavior pattern of the religious devotee. Such ideas would then invade the religious man's life from the wider context of his living, the areas of his life that are beyond and outside of the parochial and the sectarian character of his religious faith. I have often pondered the fact that men of different faiths may share common experiences which are outside of their specifically religious fellowship, and that on behalf of such demands they may make tremendous sacrifices, without feeling under any necessity to share the intimacy of their experience of God.

Or it may be in order to raise a question about the universality of an ethic which grows out of a sectarian or parochial religious experience. Could it be that we are face to face with an inherent weakness in religious experience, as such, that it is private, personal, and binding upon the individual only to the extent that he identifies himself with another and thereby becoming one with him at all the levels and all the ways that are significant? Here may be a clue, for wherever the Christian religious experience has made a difference in the one-to-one relationship of the believer, one sees this kind of private, personal identification at work. When I identify with a man, I become one with him and in him I see myself. I remember a quotation out of the past—the statement "know thyself" has been taken more mystically from the statement "thou hast seen thy brother, thou has seen thy God." This is the true meaning of the reference earlier about listening for the sound of the genuine in another. Such an experience cannot become a dogma—it has to remain experiential all the way. It is a probing process trying to find the opening into another. And it requires exposure, sustained exposure. One of the great obstacles to such exposure is the fact of segregation.

The religious experience as I have known it seems to swing wide the door, not merely into Life but into lives. I am confident that my own call to the religious vocation cannot be separated from the slowly emerging disclosure that my religious experience makes it possible for me to experience myself as a human being and thus keep a very real psychological distance between myself and the hostilities of my environment. Through the years it has driven me more and more to seek to make as a normal part of my relations with men the experiencing of them as human beings. When this happens love has essential materials with which to work. And contrary to the general religious teaching, men would not need to stretch themselves out of shape in order to love. On the contrary, a man comes into possession of himself more completely when he is *free* to love another.

I have dwelt at length upon the necessity that is laid upon the church and the Christian because the Christian Church is still one of the major centers of influence in the American community. Too, the Christian Church claims to be under the judgment of God as it fulfills itself in human history. But it must be remembered that what is true in any religion is to be found in that religion because it is true, it is not true because it is found in that religion. The ethical insight which makes for the most healthy and creative human relations is not the unique possession of any religion, however inspired it may be. It does not belong exclusively to any people or to any age. It has an ancient history, and it has been at work informing the quality of life and human relations longer than the records and the memories of man. Just as scattered through the earliest accounts of man's journey on this planet are flashes and shafts of light illuminating the meaning of man and his fellows, so in our times we find the widest variety of experiments pointing in the same direction and making manifest the same goals. Men are made for one another. In this grand discovery there is a disclosure of another dimension: this experience of one another is not enough. There is a meaning in life greater than, but informing, all the immediate meanings—and the name given to this meaning is religion, because it embodies, however faintly, a sense of the ultimate and the divine.

There is a spirit abroad in life of which the Judaeo-Christian ethic is but one expression. It is a spirit that makes for wholeness and for community; it finds its way into the quiet solitude of a Supreme Court justice when he ponders the constitutionality of an act of Congress which guarantees civil rights to all its citizens; it settles in the pools of light in the face of a little girl as with her frailty she challenges the hard, frightened heart of a police chief; it walks along the lonely road with the solitary protest marcher and settles over him with a benediction as he falls by the assassin's bullet fired from ambush; it kindles the fires of unity in the heart of Jewish Rabbi, Catholic Priest, and Protestant Minister as they join arms together, giving witness to their God on behalf of a brotherhood that transcends creed, race, sex, and religion; it makes a path to Walden Pond and ignites the flame of nonviolence in the mind of a Thoreau and burns through his liquid words from the Atlantic to the Pacific; it broods over the demonstrators for justice and brings comfort to the desolate and forgotten who have no memory of what it is to feel the rhythm of belonging to the race of men; it knows no country and its allies are to be found wherever the heart is kind and the collective will and the private endeavor seek to make justice where injustice abounds, to make peace where chaos is rampant, and to make the voice heard on behalf of the helpless and the weak. It is the voice of God and the voice of man; it is the meaning of all the strivings of the whole human race toward a world of friendly men underneath a friendly sky.

Notes

1. New York: McGraw-Hill Book Company, 1964, pp. 22–23. [Citation reprinted from the original.]
2. Olive Schreiner, *The Story of an African Farm* (London: Ernest Benn, Ltd., 1951 ed.), pp. 201–2. [Citation reprinted from the original.]
3. As one of the first projects of his "wider ministry," Thurman traveled to Vancouver in mid-October 1962 to meet with the Federation of Saskatchewan Indian Chiefs. According to Thurman, this encounter was the first between these Canadian Indian leaders and an African American public figure. For fuller accounts of the meeting, see *With Head and Heart*, 242–47; "Annual Report: The Wider Ministry, 1962–63"; and "Draft Report on Federation of Saskatchewan Indians." The latter two documents may be found in the Howard Thurman Papers (1984 Gift), Boston University, Department of Special Collections, B. U. Subject Files, Box 56, "Annual Report, 1962–63" and Box 65, "Federation of Saskatchewan," respectively.
4. In fall 1963, Thurman served as Visiting Lecturer in the Department of Religious Studies at the University of Ibadan near Lagos, Nigeria. For an extended treatment of his first and only trip to Africa, see *With Head and Heart*, 193–211.
5. During World War II all citizens of the United States were required to register with the federal government to receive ration coupons for certain foods and consumer goods in limited supply.
6. New York: Columbia University Press, 1930, p. 96. [Citation reprinted from the original.]
7. The "Russellites" was the former name—until 1931—of the Jehovah's Witnesses, founded by Charles Taze Russell (1852–1916) in 1872.

Chapter 29

Martin Luther King, Jr., and the African-American Social Gospel

Clayborne Carson

Most recent studies of Martin Luther King, Jr., emphasize the extent to which his ideas were rooted in African-American religious traditions. Departing from King's own autobiographical account and from earlier studies that stressed the importance of King's graduate studies at Crozer Theological Seminary and Boston University,[1] contemporary scholars have focused attention on King's African-American religious roots.[2] The Martin Luther King, Jr., Papers Project has contributed to this scholarly trend by documenting the King family's long-standing ties to Ebenezer Baptist Church and the social gospel ministries of his father and grandfather, both of whom were civil rights leaders as well as pastors.[3] The King project's research also suggests, however, that the current trend in scholarship may understate the extent to which King's African-American religious roots were inextricably intertwined with the European-American intellectual influences of his college years. The initial volumes of the project's fourteen-volume edition of King's papers have contributed to a new understanding of King's graduate school experiences, demonstrating that his academic writings, though flawed by serious instances of plagiarism, were often reliable expressions of his complex, evolving *Weltanschauung*.[4] Moreover, King's writings make clear that his roots in African-American religion did not necessarily separate him from European-American theological influences, because many of the black religious leaders who were his role models were themselves products of predominantly white seminaries and graduate schools. Rather than being torn between two mutually exclusive religious traditions, King's uniquely effective transracial leadership was based on his ability to combine elements of African-American and European-American religious traditions.

King was deeply influenced by his childhood immersion in African-American religious life, but his years at Crozer and Boston increased his ability to incorporate aspects of academic theology into his sermons and public speeches. His student papers demonstrate that he adopted European-American theological ideas that ultimately reinforced rather than undermined the African-American social gospel tradition epitomized by his father and grandfather. Although King's advanced training in theology set him apart from most African-American clergymen, the documentary evidence regarding his formative years suggests that his graduate studies engendered an increased appreciation for his African-American religious roots. From childhood, King had been uncomfortable with the emotionalism and scriptural literalism that he associated with traditional Baptist liturgy, but he was also familiar with innovative, politically active, and intellectually sophisticated African-American clergymen who had themselves been influenced by European-American theological scholarship. These clergymen served as role models for King as he mined theological scholarship for nuggets of insight that could enrich his preaching. As he sought to resolve religious doubts that had initially prevented him from accepting his calling, King looked upon European-American theological ideas not as alternatives to traditional black Baptist beliefs but as necessary correctives to those beliefs.

Tracing the evolution of his religious beliefs in a sketch written at Crozer entitled "An Autobiography of Religious Development," King recalled that an initial sense of religious estrangement had unexpectedly and abruptly become apparent at a Sunday morning revival meeting he attended at about the age of seven. A guest evangelist from Virginia had come to talk about salvation and to seek recruits for the church. Having grown up in the church, King had never given much thought to joining it formally, but the emotion of the revival and the decision of his sister to step forward prompted an impulsive decision to accept conversion. He reflected, "I had never given this matter a thought, and even at the time of [my] baptism I was unaware of what was taking place." King admitted that he "joined the church not out of any dynamic conviction, but out of a childhood desire to keep up with my sister." In the same sketch, he wrote that, although he accepted the teachings of his Sunday school teachers until he was about twelve,

> this uncritical attitude could not last long, for it was contrary to the very nature of my being. I had always been the questioning and precocious type. At the age of 13 I shocked my Sunday School class by

denying the bodily resurrection of Jesus. From the age of thirteen on doubts began to spring forth unrelentingly.[5]

King's recognition that he did not share some of the religious convictions of other family members might have been emotionally devastating, but his inalienable sense of belonging to the church led him toward reconciliation rather than continued rebellion. Although his convictions removed him from the kind of fundamentalist faith that placed great importance on emotionalism and a conversion experience, he never considered abandoning his inherited faith. His early doubts did not interfere with his intense involvement in church life, his love of church music, or his fascination with the art of preaching. His father, Martin Luther King, Sr., noted the way in which his son absorbed attitudes ("he loved church . . . the feeling for ceremonies and ritual, the passionate love of Baptist music") and skills ("a great speaker . . . and he sang, too, in a fine, clear voice") that would prepare him for a preaching career.[6] Letters written to his parents in his early adolescence reveal an intimate knowledge of the details of Baptist church life: congregational governance, ward meetings, church finances, and continual social events.[7]

Moreover, King was aware that the accomplishments of his father's generation of African-American religious leaders represented more than just emotional folk preaching and scriptural literalism. Despite theological differences, King attributed his decision to enter the ministry to the influence of a father who "set forth a noble example that I didn't [mind] following." King's father and grandfather were not only Baptist ministers but also pioneering exponents of a distinctively African-American version of social gospel Christianity. When King's grandfather, the Reverend A. D. Williams, arrived in Atlanta in 1893, social gospel activism was becoming increasingly common among both black and white urban clergymen. After taking over the pastorate of Atlanta's Ebenezer Baptist Church in March 1894, Williams built a large congregation through forceful preaching that addressed the everyday concerns of poor and working-class residents. Baptist denominational practices encouraged ministers such as Williams to retain the support of occasionally rebellious congregations through charismatic leadership that extended beyond purely spiritual matters. Having arrived in Atlanta on the eve of a major period of institutional development among African-American Baptists, Williams joined two thousand other delegates and visitors who met at Atlanta's Friendship Baptist Church in September 1895 to organize the National Baptist Convention, the largest black organization in the United States.

For the remainder of his life, Williams played a leading role in Baptist affairs, both at state and national levels. In addition, he took the lead in responding to W.E.B. Du Bois's call for civil rights activism by joining five hundred other black Georgians in February 1906 to form the Georgia Equal Rights League. In 1917, Williams became one of the founders of the Atlanta branch of the National Association for the Advancement of Colored People (NAACP). After becoming president of the local chapter in 1918, he mobilized newly enfranchised African-American women in a campaign to register black voters. He also led a successful drive to pressure white officials into providing improved educational facilities for black children. This effort resulted in the establishment of a black high school that Martin Luther King, Jr., later attended.

Martin Luther King, Sr., continued this tradition of social gospel activism after he married Williams's only daughter in 1926. Although his son would sometimes depict him as a conservative, King, Sr., identified himself as a social gospel preacher who believed that his ministry should be focused on the everyday needs of his congregation rather than otherworldly concerns. While a theology student at Morehouse College, King, Sr., had been exposed to the liberal theological ideas of C. D. Hubert, who headed the school's theology program. As the two ministers struggled to retain the loyalty of their congregations during the Great Depression, King recalled that Williams insisted, "Whosoever carries the word must make the word flesh." King explained that Williams used church funds to "make food available to the hungry and clothes to those without them. We kept children while mothers worked. The church bought and supplied medicines. Ebenezer tried to be an anchor as the storm rose."[8]

After taking over Ebenezer upon Williams's death in 1931, Martin Luther King, Sr., expanded the scope of his predecessor's politically engaged ministry. Early in 1935, he organized meetings to encourage blacks to register to vote and, despite resistance from more cautious clergymen and lay leaders, organized a march to City Hall. A year later he became chairman of the Committee on the Equalization of Teachers' Salaries, which was formed to protest against discriminatory policies that paid higher salaries to white teachers than to equally qualified blacks. In spite of receiving threatening hate letters, he played a leading role in the sustained struggle for pay equity.[9] King's firm insistence that the Christian church should participate in civil rights activities set him apart from politically conservative scriptural fundamentalists. In 1940, he revealed his commitment to social gospel Christianity in an address on "the true mission of the Church" delivered to the Atlanta Missionary Baptist Association:

Quite often we say the church has no place in politics, forgetting the words of the Lord, "The spirit of the Lord is upon me, because he hath [anointed] me to preach the Gospel to the poor; he hath sent me to heal the broken-hearted, to preach deliverance to the captives, and the recovering of sight to the blind, to set at liberty them that are bruised."

. . . God hasten the time when every minister will become a registered voter and a part of every movement for the betterment of our people. Again and again has it been said we cannot lead where we do not go, and we cannot teach what we do not know.

As ministers a great responsibility rests upon us as leaders. We can not expect our people to register and become citizens until we as leaders set the standard.[10]

In addition to seeing his father as both a social activist and a scriptural conservative, King, Jr., was also aware of many other models of politically engaged religious leadership. He admired the Reverend William Holmes Borders, who had built Wheat Street Baptist Church into Atlanta's largest black church and who possessed the academic credentials that King's own father lacked. Although both ministers had struggled from poverty to graduate from Morehouse College, Borders had also obtained a divinity degree from Garrett Theological Seminary and a master's degree from Northwestern before returning to Atlanta, where he taught religion at Morehouse and became an outspoken preacher at Wheat Street. According to biographer Taylor Branch, King and his friends studied "Borders' mannerisms, his organizational style, and above all the high-toned sermons in which he aroused his congregation without merely repeating the homilies of eternal life."[11]

After entering Morehouse College at the age of fifteen, King was profoundly influenced by the example of the college's president, Dr. Benjamin Elijah Mays, a family friend who was the kind of dedicated, intellectually sophisticated religious leader that King wished to emulate. Selected in 1940 to succeed John Hope as head of Morehouse, Mays was the first Morehouse president with a Ph.D. Although not a "Morehouse man" himself, Mays had internalized the Morehouse tradition calling for students to use their skills on behalf of the black community. An outstanding debater during his own undergraduate years, Mays often used his Tuesday morning talks to the student body as occasions to express his commitment to the social gospel and to challenge Morehouse students to struggle against segregation rather than accommodate to it. By the time

King entered college, Mays had returned from a trip to India as one of a growing number of African-American disciples of Mahatma Gandhi. King later described Mays as one of the "great influences" in his life.[12]

At Morehouse, King received his initial exposure to modern critical theology when he took a course on the Bible taught by another family acquaintance, Professor George D. Kelsey, a Morehouse graduate who had recently received his doctorate from Yale. In 1945 Kelsey had initiated an Annual Institute for the Training and Improvement of Baptist Ministers and had thereby gained the admiration of King, Sr., who described Kelsey as a teacher who "saw the pulpit as a place both for drama, in the old-fashioned, country Baptist sense, and for the articulation of philosophies that address the problems of society." Kelsey later remembered King, Jr., as an earnest student who took the subject matter of the course seriously. "I made it my business to present lectures on the most strenuous teaching of Jesus," Kelsey recalled. "It was precisely at this time that Martin's eyes lit up most and his face was graced with a smile."[13] Shortly after teaching King, Kelsey published an article arguing that "the problem of race is indeed America's greatest moral dilemma," giving King a phrase that he would use in his first book, *Stride toward Freedom* (1958).

In addition to Mays and Kelsey, King was also undoubtedly aware of many black religious leaders who combined academic erudition with a thorough grounding in African-American religious traditions. While at Crozer Seminary, King often debated theological and political issues with J. Pius Barbour, a family friend and Morehouse graduate, who had graduated from the seminary a decade before King's arrival. King was also familiar with the progressive ideas of Howard University president Mordecai Johnson, whose 1949 speech in Philadelphia recounting a trip to India stirred King's interest in Gandhian ideas. Howard Thurman, whose influential social gospel statement *Jesus and the Disinherited* appeared in 1949, was also a family friend of the Kings: he had attended Morehouse with King, Sr. When Thurman became Boston University's dean of the chapel, he developed a personal acquaintance with King, Jr., who was then attending the university.

Benefiting from this extensive exposure to proponents of African-American social gospel, King was able to perceive theological training as a means of reconciling his inclination to follow his father's calling with his desire for intellectual respectability. King's descriptions of his decision to enter the ministry reveal that he had accepted the social mission of the church even though he had not yet resolved his theological doubts. He realized that the Baptist religion he had absorbed during his youth had derived mainly from daily contact with church life rather than from theological reflection. Growing up in the church provided a substitute for orthodox theological convictions; born a Baptist, he never felt the need to affirm all the tenets of the denomination. In his "Autobiography of Religious Development," he explained: "Conversion for me was never an abrupt something. I have never experienced the so called 'crisis moment.' Religion has just been something that I grew up in. Conversion for me has been the gradual intaking of the noble ideals set forth in my family and my environment, and I must admit that this intaking has been largely unconscious."[14]

The consistency of King's basic religious and political convictions throughout his life suggest that his collegiate training was not a transformative experience but was rather a refinement of preexisting religious attitudes. Recognizing that a Ph.D. degree from a northern university would set him apart from most other Baptist ministers, he approached his graduate education with skepticism and perhaps even a touch of cynicism, self-consciously acquiring academic credentials that would add intellectual respectability to ingrained beliefs rooted in early religious experiences. King's rejection of scriptural literalism did not lead him away from the Baptist church but toward an increasing interest in liberal theology. His understanding that religious belief could be rooted in reason also enabled him to think more seriously about an idea he had previously rejected: becoming a minister.

The elder King had always wanted both of his sons to follow his career choice and eventually, perhaps, serve as pastors for the Ebenezer congregation. He listened to his wife's entreaties on the need for the children to make their own career choices, while hoping that his sons would make use of his connections among Baptists: "family ties, school and fraternal relationships, the so-called hometown connections that kept phones ringing and letters moving in consideration of help requested and granted, favors offered and accepted."[15] Despite being aware of their father's wishes, however, King, Jr., and his younger brother, A. D., were reluctant to conform to paternal expectations. The latter dropped out of Morehouse before finally deciding on a ministerial career, and the former spent his first three undergraduate years determined to become first a physician and then a lawyer—but not a minister like his father. Determined to assert his independence from his father and continuing to question aspects of his father's religious beliefs, King, Jr., nevertheless received a strong impetus toward becoming a preacher from his father's ever-present example.

A crucial period in King's deliberations about his career came during the summer of 1947, when he led religious services for his fellow student workers at a tobacco farm in Simsbury, Connecticut. Even before leaving Atlanta he had received his preaching license, and—more than he had during his 1944 stay in Simsbury—welcomed the opportunity to lead the weekly religious gatherings at the farm. After several weeks of deliberation, he telephoned his mother from Simsbury to tell her of his intention to become a minister. By the time he returned to Morehouse for his final year, he had pushed doubt out of his mind. His initial inclination to become a doctor or lawyer was overwhelmed by an "undying urge to serve God and humanity through the ministry." The decision was the culmination of his experiences. "My call to the ministry was neither dramatic nor spectacular," he later wrote in his application to seminary.

> It came neither by some miraculous vision nor by some blinding light experience on the road of life. Moreover, it was a response to an inner urge that gradually came upon me. This urge expressed itself in a desire to serve God and humanity, and the feeling that my talent and my commitment could best be expressed through the ministry. . . . During my senior year in college I finally decided to accept the challenge to enter the ministry. I came to see that God had placed a responsibility upon my shoulders and the more I tried to escape it the more frustrated I would become.[16]

Once the decision was made, King's friends recognized its inevitability, given his experiences, contacts, and abilities. Even at this early stage in his development as a preacher, his abilities as a pulpit orator were evident to those who heard him. Samuel DuBois Cook recalled that King delivered a "Senior Sermon" in the Morehouse Chapel a week before graduation. "He knew almost intuitively how to move an audience," Cook remembered. "He asserted that there are moral laws in the universe that we cannot violate with impunity, any more than we can violate the physical laws of the university with impunity."[17] King resolved to become a minister, but he continued to reject the anti-intellectualism that he associated with fundamentalism. His subsequent critical study of biblical texts and religious practices was driven by a desire to strengthen the rationale for a decision he had already made. He applied to several seminaries known to be academically rigorous and hospitable to liberal religious views, including Andover Newton in Massachusetts, Union in New York, and Crozer in Pennsylvania.

King's graduate school education should be viewed within the context of his struggle to synthesize his father's Christian practices and his own theological skepticism. Seen from this perspective, King's experiences at Crozer and Boston constituted neither a pilgrimage toward the social gospel views of his Crozer professors nor a movement toward the personalism of those at Boston. Instead, King eclectically drew upon the writings of academic theologians as he moved away from Christian liberalism toward a theological synthesis closer to aspects of his father's religious faith, particularly toward a conception of God as a source of support in times of personal need. Rather than becoming more liberal in college, he became increasingly skeptical of intellectualized conceptions of divinity. As King became increasingly aware of the limitations of liberal Christian thought, he acquired a renewed appreciation for his southern Baptist roots. His Crozer papers occasionally referred to his experiences in order to explain his theological preferences. He noted that his initial attraction to liberalism stemmed from its willingness to "answer new problems of cultural and social change," unlike its theological opponent, fundamentalism, which sought "to preserve the old faith in a changing milieu."[18] As he continued his studies, however, King found his initial attraction to liberal theology "going through a state of transition." His personal experience with "a vicious race problem" had made it "very difficult . . . to believe in the essential goodness of man"; on the other hand, he explained that "in noticing the gradual improvements of this same race problem I came to see some noble possibilities in human nature." While remaining wary of his father's conventional religious beliefs, King was becoming, he acknowledged, "a victim of eclecticism," seeking to "synthesize the best in liberal theology with the best in neo-orthodox theology."[19]

At Crozer, King was introduced to personalism, a philosophical school of thought that had developed in the late nineteenth century at Boston University and other American universities. After reviewing a text by Boston professor Edgar S. Brightman, a leading personalist theologian, King reported, in an essay for one of his classes, that he was "amazed to find that the conception of God is so complex and one about which opinions differ so widely." King conceded that he was still "quite confused as to which definition [of God] was the most adequate," but thought that Brightman's personalist theology held the greatest appeal.[20] Its emphasis on the reality of personal religious experience validated King's own religious experiences. King reaffirmed his belief that "every man, from the ordinary simplehearted believer to the philosophical intellectual giant, may find God through religious experience."[21] His reading of Brightman led him to discover his own spirituality:

How I long now for that religious experience which Dr. Brightman so cogently speaks of throughout his book. It seems to be an experience, the lack of which life becomes dull and meaningless. As I reflect on the matter, however, I do remember moments that I have been awe awakened; there have been times that I have been carried out of myself by something greater than myself and to that something I gave myself. Has this great something been God? Maybe after all I have been religious for a number of years, and am now only becoming aware of it.[22]

Brightman's explanation of religious experience convinced King that he could experience God's powerful presence in his own life without the benefit of a sudden religious conversion. Personalism validated the notion that experience rather than intellectual reflection should be the basis of religious belief. "It is through experience that we come to realize that some things are out of harmony with God's will," King wrote in another essay. "No theology is needed to tell us that love is the law of life and to disobey it means to suffer the consequences."[23] King's adoption of personalism as a theological orientation enabled him to reject abstract conceptions of God while continuing his search for cogency and intellectual sophistication.

By the time King entered Boston University, he was learning how to use his theological training to enrich his preaching and, in the process, return to his roots as a Baptist preacher. King's academic theological studies at Crozer had encouraged him to question many aspects of his religious heritage, but by his final year King had also become skeptical of many tenets of theological liberalism. The church of his parents and grandparents had imparted an understanding of God and of the purposes of Christian ministry that could not be displaced by theological sophistication. He later explained that his study of personalism at Crozer and Boston reinforced his beliefs rather than supplanted them. Personalism's "insistence that only personality—finite and infinite—is ultimately real strengthened me in two convictions: it gave me a metaphysical and philosophical grounding for the idea of a personal God, and it gave me a metaphysical basis for the dignity and worth of all human personality."[24]

At Boston, King expanded his criticism of theological liberalism by adopting many of the ideas of Reinhold Niebuhr. King applauded Niebuhr's rigorous analysis of "the fundamental weaknesses and inevitable sterility of the humanistic emphasis" of liberalism in the twentieth century.[25] He was also drawn to Niebuhr's economic and moral analysis of capitalism, such as the notion that modern industrial civilization was responsible for "appalling injustices," particularly the "concentration of power and resources in the hands of a relatively small wealthy class."[26] Injustices are inherent in human society, Niebuhr argued, because humans engaged in collective activity are essentially immoral, whereas individuals acting on their own possess a moral conscience. Niebuhr sought to resolve the tension between "moral man and immoral society" by reinterpreting the traditional Christian notion of *agape*, or divine love.[27] Agreeing with Niebuhr's analysis, King stated that *agape* may not be achievable in an immoral society but "remains a leaven in society, permeating the whole and giving texture and consistency to life."

King was particularly receptive to Niebuhr's criticism of love and justice as conceived in both liberal and orthodox theology. In orthodoxy, "individual perfection is too often made an end in itself," whereas liberalism "vainly seeks to overcome justice [through] purely moral and rational suasions." Liberalism, King wrote, "confuses the ideal itself with the realistic means which must be employed to coerce society into an approximation of that ideal." King agreed with Niebuhr's emphasis on making realistic moral choices and with his social analysis, but he believed that Niebuhr lacked an adequate explanation of how *agape* operates in human history: "He fails to see that the availability of the divine *Agape* is an essential [affirmation] of the Christian religion."[28]

Given the academic environment in which he attended graduate school, it is hardly surprising that King's theological writings did not explicitly draw upon the insights of African-American religion. Yet, although King's graduate school writings understated the degree to which his attitudes had been shaped by African-American religious writings, he was certainly aware of the publications of Kelsey and Mays and probably those of Thurman and Borders. Once accustomed to contrasting the religious emotionalism of his father's religion with the intellectual sophistication he saw in the writings of white academic theologians, King became aware during his graduate research that orthodox Christianity was not necessarily anti-intellectual.

Overall, King's theological development in seminary and graduate school reflected his lifelong tendency to incorporate the best elements of each alternative. As when choosing between capitalism and communism or between power politics and pacifism, King sought to synthesize alternative orientations: "An adequate understanding of man is found neither in the thesis of liberalism nor in the antithesis of neo-orthodoxy, but in a synthesis which reconciles the truths of both."[29] King described his graduate training as an attempt to bring together "the best in liberal theology with the best in neo-orthodox theology" in order to come to an understanding of man. His enormous respect for the writings of Reinhold Niebuhr derived from the pleasure he felt in finding a theological stance that synthesized faith and intellect. He probably heard echoes of his father's fundamentalism in Reinhold Niebuhr's neo-orthodoxy, which reaffirmed the limits of human perfectibility. Niebuhr provided an intellectual rationale for King's recognition of the limitations of liberal theology. As King wrote during these years, he had become "so enamored of the insights of liberalism that I almost fell into the trap of accepting uncritically everything it encompasses." After reading Niebuhr, King recalled becoming more aware of "the depths and strength of sin" and

> the complexity of man's social involvement and the glaring reality of collective evil. I realized that liberalism had been all too sentimental concerning human nature and that it leaned toward a false idealism. I also came to see that the superficial optimism of liberalism concerning human nature overlooked the fact that reason is darkened by sin. The more I thought about human nature, the more I saw how our tragic inclination for sin encourages us to rationalize our actions. Liberalism failed to show that reason by itself is little more than an instrument to justify man's defensive ways of thinking. Reason, devoid of the purifying power of faith, can never free itself from distortions and rationalizations.[30]

By the time he finished his course work, King had come to affirm some of the enduring values of his religious heritage, particularly conceptions of a divine goodness capable of acting in history. In one qualifying examination King declared that, despite modern society's moral relativism, God's judgment was final and eternal. "God has planted in the fiber of the universe certain eternal laws which forever confront every man. They are absolute and not relative. There is an eternal and absolute distinction between right and wrong." One indispensable answer to the theodicy question, King argued, was contained in the concept of the suffering servant, one of the "most noble" teachings of the Old Testament. "His suffering is not due to something that he has done, but it is *vicarious* and *redemptive*. Through his suffering knowledge of God is [spread] to the unbelieving Gentiles and those unbelievers seeing that this suffering servant is innocent will become conscious of their sins and repent and thereby be redeemed. The nation would be healed by his [wounds]." The death of Jesus Christ on the cross was the fulfillment of the prophecy of the suffering servant, but King argued that humanity should not wait on His saving grace. An individual's "faith and fellowship with God," King wrote, was the "ultimate solution to the problem of suffering."[31]

King's choice of a dissertation topic reflected an interest in the nature of God that derived both from his academic studies and from his preaching. In addition to writing several term papers on the topic, King wove the theme of theodicy into several sermons while at Boston, including one entitled "What Does It Mean to Believe in God?"[32] In his introduction to the dissertation King explained that the conception of God should be examined because of "the central place which it occupies in any religion" and because of "the ever present need to interpret and clarify the God-concept."[33]

By early 1953, when King enrolled in a course on dissertation writing at the beginning of his research, he was fairly certain about the conclusions he would reach in his dissertation. King recognized the limitations in the thinking of theologians Paul Tillich and Henry Nelson Wieman. "Both overstress one side of the divine life," he wrote, "while [minimizing] another basic aspect. Wieman [stresses] the goodness of God while minimizing his power. Tillich stresses the power of God while [minimizing] his goodness."[34] With his own beliefs still rooted in an African-American religious tradition that perceived God as a personal force interceding in history, King found Tillich's and Wieman's conceptions of divinity unworthy of worship. In the evaluative chapter, King expressed belief in a "living" God, not Tillich's "being-itself" or Wieman's "source of human good." "In God there is feeling and will, responsive to the deepest yearnings of the human heart; this God both evokes and answers prayer." Conceiving of such a God as a person was preferable to Tillich's and Wieman's use of abstract philosophical terms. "It would be better by far to admit that there are difficulties with an idea we know—such as personality—than to employ a term which is practically unknown to us in our experience." King concluded that Tillich and Wieman both set forth a God who is less than personal, despite their comments to the contrary suggesting that God was more than personal, unable to be defined by the concept of personality. "Both Tillich and Wieman reject the conception of a personal God, and with this goes a rejection of the rationality, goodness and love of God in the full sense of the words."[35]

Despite his disagreement with certain aspects of both men's conceptions of divinity, King appreciated their criticism of humanism. King approvingly noted that Tillich and Wieman both emphasized God's

immanence, or "the primacy of God over everything else in the universe."
"Such an emphasis," he argued, "sounds a much needed note in the face
of a supernaturalism that finds nature so irrational that the order of creation can no longer be discerned in it, and history so meaningless that it
all bears the 'minus sign' of alienation from God." In a characteristic effort
to reconcile two positions that were in dialectical tension, King extracted
what he considered positive aspects of their thought to create an eclectic
synthesis. Echoing his preliminary analysis of their positions, King
asserted that "both Tillich and Wieman are partially correct in what they
affirm and partially wrong in what they deny. Wieman is right in emphasizing the goodness of God, but wrong in minimizing his power. Likewise
Tillich is right in emphasizing the power of God, but wrong in minimizing his goodness."[36]

In the sermons King delivered while writing his dissertation, he
expressed his conception of God using more vivid language than his
stilted, derivative academic diction. He skillfully incorporated into his sermons those aspects of his theological training that affirmed his ties to the
religion of his parents and grandparents. His father later affirmed that his
son's roots in the African-American preaching tradition remained strong
even after years of graduate study. "M. L. was still a son of the Baptist
South, there'd never be any doubt about that."[37]

King's ability to blend these elements can be seen in his earliest known
recorded sermon, "Rediscovering Lost Values."[38] King delivered the sermon to a large Baptist church in Detroit in late February 1954, just days
after finishing his final comprehensive examination and a few weeks
before the graduate school approved his dissertation outline. In the
Detroit sermon, King told the familiar biblical story of Joseph and Mary,
who realized, while walking to Nazareth, that they had left Jesus behind
in Jerusalem. Just as Joseph and Mary had returned to rejoin Jesus, King
advised, society should rediscover the precious values that had become
lost in the rationalizations that guided behavior in the modern world. "If
we are to go forward," he said, "if we are to make this a better world in
which to live, we've got to go back. We've got to rediscover these precious
values that we've left behind." Despite the many technological advances
and material comforts of American society, King argued, humanity had
lost the spiritual compass provided by a deep and abiding faith in God.
"The real problem is that through our scientific genius we've made of the
world a neighborhood, but through our moral and spiritual genius we've
failed to make of it a brotherhood." King insisted that "*all* reality hinges
on moral foundations," that "this is a moral universe, and . . . there are

moral laws of the universe, just as abiding as the physical laws." Decrying
ethical relativism—"Now, I'm not trying to use a big word here"—King
expressed a belief in moral absolutes that evoked enthusiastic responses
from the congregation.

> I'm here to say to you this morning that some things are right and
> some things are wrong. *(Yes)* Eternally so, absolutely so. It's *wrong* to
> hate. *(Yes, That's right)* It always has been wrong and it always will be
> wrong! *(Amen)* It's wrong in America, it's wrong in Germany, it's
> wrong in Russia, it's wrong in China! *(Lord help him)* It was wrong in
> two thousand B.C., and it's wrong in nineteen-fifty-four A.D.! It always
> has been wrong, *(That's right)* and it always will be wrong! . . . Some
> things in this universe are absolute. The God of the universe has
> made it so.[39]

In King's view contemporary society had lost sight of this "mighty precious value," adopting instead "a pragmatic test for right and wrong." In
the modern world, he asserted, most people believed that "it's all right to
disobey the Ten Commandments, but just don't disobey the Eleventh,
Thou shall not get caught." The moral decay that King identified in modern culture could be recovered only by ethical living. "The thing that we
need in the world today is a group of men and women who will stand up
for right and be opposed to wrong, wherever it is."[40]

King argued that making ethical decisions was impossible without
rediscovering the precious value of faith in God. King charged that many
people, including those who attended church every Sunday, had lost their
faith in God. "We must remember that it's possible to affirm the existence
of God with your lips and deny his existence with your life." Returning to
the biblical parable, King asserted that "we had gone a whole day's journey, and then we came to see that we had unconsciously ushered God out
of the universe." The materialism of American consumer culture had
caused some to lose sight of God, and King cautioned that "automobiles
and subways, televisions and radios, dollars and cents can *never* be substitutes for God."[41]

King's sermon drew upon traditional African-American religious ideas,
particularly the notion of God acting in human history. Alluding to a verse
in Psalm 23 and to a familiar hymn, King concluded by affirming faith in
the God "who walks with us through the valley of the shadow of death,
and causes us to fear no evil," in the God "who has been our help in ages
past, and our hope for years to come, and our shelter in the time of storm,

and our eternal home."[42] King concluded with a rousing affirmation of God as an integral part of his life. "As a young man with most of my life ahead of me, I decided early to give my life to something eternal and absolute. Not to these little gods that are here today and gone tomorrow. But to God who is the same yesterday, today, and forever."[43]

Seen in the context of his preadult experiences, King's graduate school years enabled him to acquire academic credentials while retaining his basic religious beliefs. When he applied to Boston University's doctoral program, King had stressed his desire to enter the world of theological scholarship, stating that he was "desirous of teaching in a college or a school of religion."[44] At Crozer, King had initially been estranged from his roots, but by the time he entered Boston University he had rediscovered the liberating potential of his African-American Baptist heritage. Although he clearly wanted to base his religious beliefs on solid theological foundations, he left Boston as a preacher rather than as a scholar. Forging an eclectic synthesis from such diverse sources as personalism, theological liberalism, neo-orthodox theology, and the activist, Bible-centered religion of his heritage, King affirmed his abiding faith in a God who was both a comforting personal presence and a powerful spiritual force acting in history for righteousness. This faith would sustain him as the civil rights movement irreversibly transformed his life.

King's rapid rise to prominence resulted from his ability to combine the insights of European-American theological scholarship with those of African-American homiletics. Although his published descriptions of his "pilgrimage to non-violence" generally emphasized the impact of his academic training,[45] in more personal statements he acknowledged his black Baptist roots. "I am many things to many people," King acknowledged in 1965, "but in the quiet recesses of my heart, I am fundamentally a clergyman, a Baptist preacher. This is my being and my heritage for I am also the son of a Baptist preacher, the grandson of a Baptist preacher and the great-grandson of a Baptist preacher."[46] Rather than being torn between mutually exclusive cultural traditions, King's public, transracial ministry marked a convergence of theological scholarship and social gospel practice. Drawing upon a variety of intellectual and religious traditions to arouse and enlighten his listeners, King was profoundly affected by his experiences both as a preacher's son at Ebenezer and as a diligent student at Crozer Seminary and Boston University. King's theological education distinguished him from all but a few African-American preachers and temporarily separated him from his childhood environment, but theological studies ultimately led King to a deeper appreciation of traditional

African-American conceptions of God as a source of support, especially in times of personal crisis. Later in his career as a movement leader, King would reflect that when he had "been battered by the storms of persecution," he had gained strength and determination from

> the reality of a personal God. True, I have always believe[d] in the personality of God. But in the past the idea of a personal God was little more than a metaphysical category that I found theologically and philosophically satisfying. Now it is a living reality that has been validated in the experience of everyday life. God has been profoundly real to me in recent years.[47]

Notes

1. See, for example, Martin Luther King, Jr., *Stride toward Freedom: The Montgomery Story* (New York: Harper & Row, 1958), chapter 6; Kenneth L. Smith and Ira G. Zepp, Jr., *Search for the Beloved Community: The Thinking of Martin Luther King, Jr.* (Valley Forge, Pa.: Judson Press, 1974); and John J. Ansbro, *Martin Luther King, Jr.: The Making of a Mind* (Maryknoll, N.Y.: Orbis, 1982).
2. See, for example, James H. Cone, "Martin Luther King, Jr.: Black Theology—Black Church," *Theology Today* 40 (January 1984): 409–12; Lewis V. Baldwin, *There Is a Balm in Gilead: The Cultural Roots of Martin Luther King, Jr.* (Minneapolis: Fortress Press, 1991).
3. Clayborne Carson, Ralph E. Luker, and Penny A. Russell, eds., *The Papers of Martin Luther King, Jr.*, vol. 1, *Called to Serve, January 1929–June 1951* (Berkeley and Los Angeles: University of California Press, 1992).
4. See Clayborne Carson et al., "Martin Luther King, Jr., as Scholar: A Reexamination of His Theological Writings," *Journal of American History* 78 (June 1991): 93–105.
5. Martin Luther King, Jr., "Autobiography of Religious Development," in Carson et al., eds., *Papers of Martin Luther King, Jr.*, 1: 361. According to King's application to Crozer Theological Seminary, the date of his joining the church was May 1, 1936.
6. Martin Luther King, Sr., with Clayton Riley, *Daddy King: An Autobiography* (New York: William Morrow, 1980), 127.
7. See Carson et al., *Papers*, 1: 102–7.
8. Ibid., 89.
9. Ibid., 104.
10. Martin Luther King, Sr., "Moderator's Annual Address—1940," quoted in Carson et al., *Papers*, 1: 34. On the eve of the Montgomery bus boycott of 1955–56, King would use similar arguments in a speech to the Birmingham branch of the NAACP criticizing the apathy of church leaders on political issues. "'You must do more than pray and read the Bible,' to destroy segregation and second-class citizenship," the local newspaper reported him saying, "'you must do something about it.'" See "Apathy among Church Leaders Hit in Talk by Rev. M. L. King," *Birmingham World*, January 25, 1955. King would later deliver the speech, entitled "A Realistic Approach to Progress in Race Relations," on many occasions.

11. Taylor Branch, *Parting the Waters: America in the King Years, 1954–63* (New York: Simon and Schuster, 1988), 54, 64. See also James W. English, *The Prophet of Wheat Street* (Elgin, Ill.: David C. Cook, 1967).
12. King, Jr., *Stride toward Freedom*, 145.
13. Renee D. Turner, "Remembering the Young King," *Ebony*, January 1988. In this article Kelsey recalled that King took Kelsey's course "The Teachings of Jesus" in his sophomore year.
14. King, Jr., "Autobiography of Religious Development," *Papers*, 1: 361.
15. King, Sr., and Riley, *Daddy King*, 128.
16. Statement of Martin Luther King, Jr., August 7, 1959, written in response to a request by Joan Thatcher, publicity director of the Board of Education and Publication of the American Baptist Convention, Division of Christian Higher Education, July 30, 1959, Martin Luther King Collection, Mugar Library, Boston University; quoted in Mervyn Alonza Warren, "A Rhetorical Study of the Preaching of Dr. Martin Luther King, Jr., Pastor and Pulpit Orator" (Ph.D. dissertation, Michigan State University, 1966), 35–36. While at Crozer, King wrote: "My call to the ministry was not a miraculous or supernatural something, on the contrary it was an inner urge calling me to serve humanity. I guess the influence of my father also had a great deal to do with my going in the ministry. This is not to say that he ever spoke to me in terms of being a minister, but that my admiration for him was the great moving factor; he set forth a noble example that I didn't min[d] following. Today I differ a great deal with my father theologically, but that admiration for a real father still remains." King, Jr., "Autobiography of Religious Development," *Papers*, 1: 363.
17. Samuel DuBois Cook, quoted in Turner, "Remembering the Young King," 42.
18. Martin Luther King, Jr., "The Sources of Fundamentalism and Liberalism Considered Historically and Psychologically," in Carson et al., *Papers of Martin Luther King, Jr.*, 1: 240.
19. Martin Luther King, Jr., "How Modern Christians Should Think of Man," in Carson et al., *Papers of Martin Luther King, Jr.*, 1: 274.
20. Martin Luther King, Jr., "A Conception and Impression of Religion Drawn from Dr. Brightman's Book Entitled *A Philosophy of Religion*," in Carson et al., *Papers of Martin Luther King, Jr.*, 1: 410–11.
21. Martin Luther King, Jr., "The Place of Reason and Experience in Finding God," in Carson et al., *Papers of Martin Luther King, Jr.*, 1: 234.
22. King, Jr., "Conception and Impression of Religion," *Papers*, 1: 415–16.
23. King, Jr., "Place of Reason and Experience," *Papers*, 1: 234.
24. King, Jr., *Stride toward Freedom*, 100.
25. Martin Luther King, Jr., "Reinhold Niebuhr," April 2, 1952, in Carson et al., *Papers of Martin Luther King, Jr.*, vol. 2 (1994).
26. Martin Luther King, Jr., "Reinhold Niebuhr's Ethical Dualism," May 9, 1952, in Carson et al., *Papers of Martin Luther King, Jr.*, vol. 2 (1994).
27. Reinhold Niebuhr, *Moral Man and Immoral Society* (New York: Scribner, 1933).
28. King, Jr., "Niebuhr's Ethical Dualism," *Papers*, vol. 2 (1994).
29. Martin Luther King, Jr., *Strength to Love* (Philadelphia: Fortress Press, 1963), 149. In resolving the conflict between capitalism and Marxism, he wrote, "The Kingdom of God is neither the thesis of individual enterprise nor the antithesis of collective enterprise, but a synthesis which reconciles the truths of both."

30. King, Jr., "How Modern Christians," *Papers*, 1: 274. King later asserted that "Niebuhr's great contribution to contemporary theology is that he has refuted the false optimism characteristic of a great segment of Protestant liberalism, without falling into the anti-rationalism of the continental theologian Karl Barth, or the semi-fundamentalism of other dialectical theologians. Moreover, Niebuhr has extraordinary insight into human nature, especially the behavior of nations and social groups. He is keenly aware of the complexity of human motives and of the relations between morality and power. His theology is a persistent reminder of the reality of sin on every level of man's existence. These elements of Niebuhr's thinking helped me to recognize the illusions of a superficial optimism concerning human nature and the dangers of a false idealism. While I still believed in man's potential for good, Niebuhr made me realize his potential for evil as well. Moreover, Niebuhr helped me to recognize the complexity of man's social involvement and the glaring reality of collective evil." King. Jr., *Stride toward Freedom*, 99.

31. Martin Luther King, Jr., Qualifying Examination Answers, Theology of the Bible, November 2, 1953, in Carson et al., *Papers of Martin Luther King, Jr.*, vol. 2 (1994).

32. King gave this sermon at First United Baptist Church in Lowell, Massachusetts, on April 12, 1953.

33. Martin Luther King, Jr., "A Comparison of the Conceptions of God in the Thinking of Paul Tillich and Henry Nelson Wieman" (Ph.D. dissertation, Boston University, 1955), in Carson et al., *Papers of Martin Luther King, Jr.*, vol. 2 (1994).

34. King, Notes for "A Comparison of the Conceptions of God in the Thinking of Paul Tillich and Henry Nelson Wieman," February 4–May 22, 1953, Martin Luther King Papers, Mugar Library, Boston University, Box 107, Folder 28.

35. Martin Luther King, Jr., "A Comparison of the Conceptions," in Carson et al., *Papers of Martin Luther King, Jr.*, vol. 2 (1994).

36. Ibid.

37. King, Sr., and Riley, *Daddy King*, 147.

38. A tape recording of the sermon at Detroit's Second Baptist Church on February 28, 1954, was preserved by the church's historical committee. The tape recording served as the basis for the transcription of "Rediscovering Lost Values" that appears in Carson et al., *Papers of Martin Luther King, Jr.*, vol. 2 (1994).

39. King, "Rediscovering Lost Values," *Papers*, vol. 2 (1994). The congregation's responses, which are indicated in italics and parentheses, have been retained in this lengthy quotation, but omitted in other quotations from this sermon. They are preserved in the complete transcription.

40. Ibid.

41. Ibid.

42. King alluded to the hymn, "Oh God, Our Help in Ages Past."

43. King, "Rediscovering Lost Values," in Carson et al., *Papers of Martin Luther King, Jr.*, vol. 2 (1994).

44. Martin Luther King, Jr., "Fragment of Application to Boston University," in Carson et al., *Papers of Martin Luther King, Jr.*, 1: 390.

45. See, for example, King, Jr., *Stride toward Freedom*, chapter 6, and Martin Luther King, Jr., *Strength to Love* (Philadelphia: Fortress Press, 1963), chapter 15.

46. Martin Luther King, Jr., "The Un-Christian Christian," *Ebony* 20 (August 1965), 76.

47. King, Jr., *Strength to Love*, 155.

Chapter 30

The Religion of Black Power

Vincent Harding

For scholars and ordinary citizens standing near the edges of the latest stage of America's perennial racial crisis, certain conclusions are easy to come by, especially when they are formed against the glare of burning buildings, the staccato reports of weapons and a certain malaise verging on fear. To the observers who are at all concerned with what might be called religious phenomena, there is an especially deceptive set of circumstances and deductions surrounding the newest expression of Black Power as a force within the ancient struggle. For if movements are judged primarily by their public rhetoric and other obvious manifestations, it seems abrasively apparent that the time of singing, of preaching, and of nonviolent concern for the redemption of American society is rapidly passing, if not gone. More black love for whites evidently burns in every ghetto-shaped inferno. By certain standards, the religious elements of the struggle are to be studied only as historical manifestations from a recent and lamented past.

Such an interpretation of the present black moment is encouraged by the words of an anonymous spokesman for the current mood: "Man, the people are too busy getting ready to fight to bother with singing any more." When a song does burst forth it often proclaims.

> Too much love,
> Too much love,
> Nothing kills a nigger like
> Too much love [13:25].*

---

*Citations refer to reference and page number of works listed at the end of this chapter.

Even in the presence of such compelling testimony against the adequacy of the older, more comforting religious symbols, rituals, and words, it would be myopic to miss the central issues of human life and destiny which course through the current expression of blackness. Issues of anthropology, incarnation, the nature of the universe and of God, issues of hope and faith, questions of eschatology and of the nature of the kingdom, problems concerning love and its functions—all these and more are at stake in the present situation. That they are usually disguised, often submerged, and sometimes denied does not lessen the power of their reality. Indeed the inherent power of the issues may be heightened by such camouflaging pressures. (One may even conjecture that the current black mood is in surprising harmony with much of the American trend towards a secular religion or a religionless church which, though it often overreacts to older explicit orthodox formulations, is shaped unmistakably by the life of the streets.)

Black Power and the New Man

In spite of the tendency among Black Power advocates to repress any reference to the earlier Afro-American religious expressions—especially as they were found in the nonviolent movement—the most familiar word from the past remains available to set the stage for an exploration of the religious implication of the current themes. At a forum on Black Power in Atlanta during the fall of 1966, while discussing "love," a spokesman for Black Power was heard to say, "Martin King was trying to get us to love white folks before we learned to love ourselves, and that ain't no good."

When there is serious reflection upon these words, a meaningful examination of the religious elements of Black Power may properly begin, for here is an issue which, if not the heart of the affair, is certainly very near the center of things. In spite of some public images to the contrary, it is likely that no element is so constant in the gospel of Blackness—at least as it is encountered in its native communities—as the necessity of self-love. One writer tells much that is crucial to the story when she refers to "the inner power that comes with self-esteem, the power to develop to full stature as human beings" [4:29].

Healthy self-esteem has been seen in many traditions as a prerequisite to the establishment of community—whether with a spouse, a society, or a God. It has most often been the bedrock of love. It is surely this that comes through in the teaching of Jesus to love the neighbor as oneself.

Black Power is a calling for black self-love, but it is not an unambiguous summons. Its clearest implications on this level are suggested by John Oliver Killens, one of the major literary spokesmen for the movement, when he writes,

> [Black Power] does not teach hatred; it teaches love. But it teaches us that love, like charity, must begin at home; that it must begin with ourselves, our beautiful black selves. [11:36]

Stokely Carmichael has put this love in the context of the building of a black society "in which the spirit of community and humanistic love prevail" [2:8]. So in spite of "too much love" and in spite of the fact that Carmichael also admitted that the word was "suspect," no writer in the newest black state fails to refer to a need for this love among black people.

Such an emphasis grows partly out of historical necessity, for all who make it are actively aware of the crushing psychological effects American life has had on the self-image of black men and women. However it may also rise out of an intuitive recognition that a call to love cuts across the deepest grain of man's being when it is addressed to an individual who is without some clear ground of self-respect.

It is precisely at this point that the ambiguity of the new black love becomes most evident, especially as it is exemplified in the writing of Killens. In the essay cited above he goes on to say that the love taught by Black Power is

> so powerful that it will settle for nothing short of love in return. Therefore it does not advocate unrequited love, which is a sick bit under any guise or circumstance. Most black folk have no need to love those who would spit on them or practice genocide against them. . . . Profound love can only exist between equals. [11]

Killens' point of view represents much of the thinking on this subject in Black Power circles, and it is obviously a retort to what is understood to be nonviolence and to what is thought to be the teaching of Christian churches, especially black ones. However, it may be an overreaction, for, while one is eminently wise to realize that love flows out of self-esteem, one may be less than wise in demanding a predetermined response to black love. In a sense this is an interesting variation on one of the basic pitfalls of the rhetoric of nonviolence. For while the nonviolent movement promised that black love would bring predictable, favorable white responses, Killens says that, unless whites respond as they ought, love will stop. Much of the world's religion teaches that love demands nothing more than the freedom of the other to respond. Perhaps it takes the strongest love of all to continue in the path while realizing that such freedom can never be coerced.

Perhaps, however, it is even more pertinent to note that Killens speaks of love and hate as being totally irrelevant until black and white men are equals. This is the even stronger frame of mind in the ghettos today. Love for Black Power is, as Carmichael puts it, a love "within the black community, the only American community where men call each other 'brother' when they meet. We can build a community of love," he says, "only where we have the ability and power to do so among blacks" [2:8]. At this juncture white persons are simply not considered as valid objects of black love. Such love (or, more accurately, its outward appearance) has been forced from blacks for too long; now, as one of the movement's most sensitive authors puts it, for many of the present black generation,

> the white man no longer exists. He is not to be lived with and he is not to be destroyed. He is simply to be ignored. . . .

If whites consider this relegation to nonexistence as hatred, Julius Lester says, such an interpretation "is only a reflection of [their] own fears and anxieties. . . ." As for blacks, he says, "There is too much to do to waste time and energy hating white people" [13:24].

This powerful strand of Black Power thinking raises a long series of religiously oriented issues. First among many is the recurring issue regarding the control and direction of love. If it is assumed—as it surely must be—that black love must begin among black people and find its nurture there, can it be quarantined? What shall be said of a love that is willed towards some men and not towards others? Is this goal in any way related to the deadly disease that has afflicted so much of American life for so many generations?

An interim goal is now to make white men "invisible" while black men are brought into the light. Can it be brought off by blacks with any less poisoning of the spirit than occurred in whites who invented "tuning out"? If it is true that white men dream long dreams of the dark brothers they have rejected, what are the dreams in black beds? Such an exploration must also ask whether it is enough not to hate. Does our recent experience suggest that hatred might well be preferable to the creation of a new breed of nonexistent nonblack men?

The answers do not come with ease. Perhaps refusal to hate is enough to begin with when one considers the deep sources of human justification for black hatred and revenge against whites. Perhaps those who can rise out of such carefully poisoned wells of human experience with the strength not to hate their oppressors have made a major beginning, whatever their dreams may be. Of course, if anyone should dare to press on and raise the most disturbing religious issue of even loving enemies, there may be two initial responses. It must first be acknowledged that the American religious communities have offered no consistent examples of this love for enemies, especially in times of war. (Black people consider themselves at war, and they have imbibed more of American religion than they know.) Second it is essential that all questioners should examine the possibility that men may need the freedom to hate their enemies before love can become an authentic response. It may be that black freedom offers no less dangerous a path than any other variety.

Black Power and the New Community

In part, an answer to our questions must await the further development of the black pilgrimage in this hostile land. Now it is sufficient to note another major thrust of the Black Power movement that has deep religious moorings, a sharing in men's constant search for community. As black exiles search in an often alien world for the ground of their being, the movement is increasingly towards the building of community. Love is recognized as a necessary foundation for this structure—whatever its form.

There was a time when the vision of the community to be built was as large as America, but that is no longer the case. At least that seems no longer a task that black men can set themselves to. Julius Lester put it this way:

> At one time black people desperately wanted to be American, to communicate with whites, to live in the Beloved Community. Now that is irrelevant. They know that it can't be until whites want it to be, and it is obvious now that whites don't want it. [13:25]

Now black men must build their own beloved black community, Lester concludes. Does such a statement indicate a recoil from the religious search for the fully inclusive community, or is it a more sober and therefore a more faithful estimate of the world and of the power of race?

Those persons who think of such a withdrawal into blackness as a racist or nationalist retreat from universalism would likely find comfort in the thoughts of one of the Afro-American leaders who said, "The fact that we are Black is our ultimate reality. We were black before we were born" [8:3]. When one considers some of the basic "realities" of American life, there is a certain soundness in this view, and it is supplemented by Lester's call for black men to recognize and celebrate "those things uniquely theirs which separate them from the white man."

Those who see goals of black community as falling short of the goal of universal community must recognize the fact that black men in America have long been encouraged to disdain their community no less than themselves. Therefore, such a call may be the beginning of true corporate health and integrity for black people. It is surely a significant change from the major direction of Afro-American movement toward the larger society during the past generation, for that has been largely a movement away from the ghettos, away from the ground out of which we sprang. "Integration" has most often been the call to escape. (At least it was so interpreted until hard white rocks made clear the nature of its siren sounds.) Now a Karenga teaches that "Our purpose in life should be to leave the Black Community more beautiful than we inherited it" [8:27]. Now Carmichael and others like him plead with black college students to train themselves not to be siphoned out of the ghettos, but to pour themselves back into it. This direction of Black Power is one of its surest words of judgment upon the black churches of the Afro-American communities. It is the same judgment that the Nation of Islam and Malcolm X brought, for it speaks to congregations and pastors who usually have no more use for the black depths than their white Christian counterparts.

The call for communal identification among the black outcasts of America has had observable impact and will probably increase in force. It is the closest thing to a sense of religious vocation that some of the current black college and graduate students know. It is surely significant that one of them spoke in the image of John Donne's human land mass when he voiced the response of a growing proportion of his generation. In a recent article in *Ebony* magazine, Stanley Saunders, a Rhodes Scholar now in Yale's law school, confessed his former attempts to hide from his white friends the truth of his origins in the blackness of Watts. Saunders said this attempt was for him a means of gaining acceptance and assimilation into the American society. Now, with the coming of the new black consciousness, that has changed. He can say instead,

> If there is no future for the black ghetto, the future of all Negroes is diminished. What affects it, affects me, for I am a child of the ghetto.

When they do it to Watts, they do it to me, too. I'll never escape from the ghetto. I have staked my all on its future. Watts is my home. [17:36]

There is probably a message in these words for all who see the call for solidarity with the black community as a call away from universalism. For it is quite possible that the earlier liberal invitations to highly selected black men—calls into the Party or into the Church, or into some other wing of the idol of Integration—were really deceptive, or at least premature. Perhaps we were urged towards an identification with mankind-at-large (often meaning white mankind) before we had learned to identify with our black neighbors. It is likely that our humanity really begins in the black ghetto and cannot be rejected there for an easier, sentimental, white-oriented acceptance elsewhere. So it may be that the question of "who is my neighbor?" is answered for us.

Of paramount importance is the fact that these questions are being answered for persons in the ghettos who will never see Yale. Many of the burgeoning black-oriented groups—organized in varying degrees of structural sophistication—are manned primarily by young men who have been cast out of the restless bowels of a technological society. Now in their teens and early twenties, with little prospect of any meaningful work in the larger society as it now stands, these black youths have begun to find themselves as members of groups dedicated to the protection and development of the ghetto that has so long been their prison. The new vision that Black Power has brought to them may be one of the most important of all its consequences. These were the rejected stones of integration. They had neither the skills nor the graces demanded. They may well become the cornerstones of a renewed black community.

Such a transformation may suggest that if black men are ever to achieve to the larger universal calling, we must, like Paul, clearly apprehend the things which are a part of our own racial and cultural heritage. Perhaps we must be able to glory in that past as a gift of God before we will be prepared to count it as garbage for the sake of the new family of man [16]. For if we begin with a conception of our ancestral community as garbage, of our heritage as worthless, we shall be guilty of irresponsible escapism and not growth when we move to transcend them. Isn't it taught in some circles that Jesus of Nazareth had first to explore the most profound levels of his own culture—both physically and spiritually—before he was eligible to transcend it?

So Black Power holds a healthy possibility for the coming of true religious community. It suggests the destruction of ugly and ironic caste distinctions within the Afro-American community. It encourages the discovery of roots long buried and rejected. It insists that men be true to themselves. It calls a broken people to see its own black section of the mainland. It reveals the gifts of those who were once the scorned members of the black body. Karenga may therefore be most accurate when he writes, "Until Blacks develop themselves, they can do nothing for humanity" [8:2]. Obviously, what is being suggested is that men must not only love themselves in order to love their neighbor, but they must love their communities in order to love the world.

Actually, many sections of the world are already included in the concerns of Black Power, and one has the feeling that there is intimated in these concerns a universalism that is at least as broad as that known by most western religious traditions. Black Power calls for an identification between black people here and all the wretched nonwhites of the earth. (Some leaders, like Carmichael, now expand this to the poor and oppressed of every color.) This is certainly the meaning of Lester's statement that, while a black man must now live his life in the United States

> only within the framework of his own blackness [that] blackness links him with the Indians of Peru, the miner in Bolivia, the African and the freedom fighters of Vietnam. What they fight for is what the American black man fights for—the right to govern his own life. [13:25]

(Is it possible that a universalism based on suffering, struggle, and hope is more vital than some vague identification based on common links to a possible dead Creator-Father?)

Such breadth of concern for "the broken victims" in their struggle to be free is surely another of Black Power's judgments upon American religion, especially the faith of those persons who claim a great tradition of prophetic concern for social justice, and those who claim a master who came to set all broken victims free. For while such religious respectables stand silently or march weakly protesting, the devotees of Black Power identify themselves unambiguously with the oppressed and with the revolutions made by the oppressed. So if only by sheer numbers—the numbers of the earth's humiliated people—such identification actually brings Black Power into the orbit of a universality more authentic than the largely parochial sentiments of a "Judeo-Christian" western commitment.

Nor are the righteous delivered by pointing accurately to the fact that Black Power makes no effort to identify with the oppressors who, according to the teachings of many traditions, are also theoretically eligible for concern. The example of American religion has been poor (perhaps it will eventually prove poisonous), for its identification has been largely with the exploiters or with those who live comfortably because of the action of exploitation. Therefore black men may well sense a need to redress this imbalance, this "crookedness" that is prevalent throughout the western world—no matter how many times the *Messiah* is sung, which refers to making the crooked become straight (Isaiah 40:3–4, e.g.).

Perhaps, too, black rebels remember the example of Jesus, the focus of much of western religion. For while he evidently was filled with ultimate concern for both oppressed and oppressor, he reserved his sharpest words of judgment for the politico-religious leaders and oppressors within the Jewish community, and his death came outside the gates of respectability. Black Power may well suggest that religious concern for both sides does not mean neutrality in the face of injustice. Indeed, it reminds us that the world most often will not permit that questionable luxury even should it be desirable.

(This identification with the wretched of the earth is especially significant for the incipient struggle for leadership between Black Power adherents and the traditional spokesmen of the Negro masses—their ministers. For though there have been important exceptions, the public stance of most of the respectable pastors has been in accord with the dominant American attitudes towards modern, radical revolution. By and large, the black church hierarchy has been no more Christian than its white counterpart on such issues, except where the accident of race has forced it to certain stances. Should the sense of solidarity with the exploited peoples grow to major proportions in the Afro-American communities, it may well prove impossible for such religious leaders to hold on to their already shaky grounds.)

Black Messiahs and Marching Saints

The qualified universalism of Black Power is also streaked with vivid suggestions of Messianism at many points. Indeed, Afro-American intellectual history has long been filled with images of Black messiahs, either individually or en masse, rising up to deliver Black America from its bondage and White America from its lethal folly. Though the first event was always guaranteed the second did not necessarily follow from it in every case [9]. In our own century the theme was first voiced fully in the fascinating and significant movement led by Marcus Garvey. It was this audacious black genius who sent a Messianic promise to the black world from his cell in the Atlanta Federal Penitentiary. In 1925, Garvey said,

> If I die in Atlanta my work shall then only begin, but I shall live, in the physical or spiritual to see the day of Africa's glory. When I am dead wrap the mantle of the Red, Black, and Green around me, for in the new life I shall rise with God's grace and blessing to lead the millions up the heights of triumph with the colors that you well know. Look for me in the whirlwind or the storm, look for me all around you, for, with God's grace, I shall come and bring with me countless millions of black slaves who have died in America and the West Indies and the millions in Africa to aid you in the fight for Liberty, Freedom and Life [7:136–137].

There are still Afro-Americans in this country, the West Indies, and Africa who attribute every movement towards black liberation to the living, vibrant spirit of Marcus Garvey.

It was so, too, with Malcolm X, and after his death there came a resurgence of the Messianic theme. The visions of an anointed leader and a Messianic people have been most recently joined in the work of a black novelist, Ronald Fair. Writing in *Negro Digest* about the meaning of Black Power, Fair moved quickly to the issue of ultimate hope, and said,

> We are the ones who will right all the wrongs perpetrated against us and our ancestors and we are the ones who will save the world and bring a new day, a brilliantly alive society that swings and sings and rings out the world over for decency and honesty and sincerity and understanding and beauty and love. . . . [5:30, 94]

Again the chosen people are black and promise a new day out of the matrix of their sufferings. Fair was not specific about the means by which the newness would come, but he said, "we fight on and we spread the love we have been told we cannot feel for ourselves to each and every black man we meet."

Finally the novelist tied the Messianic people to its leader and invoked the revered name when he said,

> We look about us and wait because somewhere, somewhere in the tenements in Harlem, or from the west side of Chicago, or from Watts, there *will* be another Malcolm and this one won't be murdered.

As Ronald Fair read the moment, "every black man in this country is aware that our time has come" [5:94].

Now is the fullness of time in many black minds; and though traditional religion is often denied, the deeper symbols and myths are appropriated to express the sense of expectation that stirs within the black communities, focused now in the ideology of Black Power. As might be predicted, the black Messianic hope expands beyond America's shores, and this aspect of it was also expressed by Killens. He wrote,

> We black Americans are no longer a "minority" but a part of that vast majority of humanity yearning to be free and struggling with every ounce of their strength to throw off the blackman's burden and the yoke of white supremacy. We are a part of that fellowship of the disinherited which will surely inherit the earth in this century. [11:37]

The ambiguities of Fair's "fight" are largely discarded in Killens' vision of the way ahead. It is those who were forced to be meek (as some count meekness) who now enter into armed struggle to inherit the earth.

Another spokesman for Black Power is even less ambiguous, for Nathan Hare speaks of a "Black Judgment Day around the corner" for America. He envisions it as a possible "black *blitzkrieg* . . . making America a giant, mushrooming Watts, in which this country will either solve its problems or get the destruction it deserves" [10:01]. It is surely not presumptuous to suggest that elements of the same vision impel an H. Rap Brown to demand from the nation that it either "straighten up" or face the fire of judgment.

Within the heart of Black Power stands the perennial tension between a salvation leading to swinging and singing and love, and a day of destruction demanded by a just God. Throughout the history of black American radicalism run the themes of repentance and atonement or judgment [18:62–147]. Always there is the memory of bloodshed being connected to the remission of sins. But when the chosen, sinned-against people become both armed and anointed, when the saints march with guns, then the issues are mooted, and the day of the Lord is clouded indeed. For it may be that armed and marching black saints in Harlem are not likely to conceive of their task any differently than those who killed infidel Indians in New England, cut off unrepentant heads in old England, or now burn "suspected" children in Vietnam. Is it given to black men any more than to whites to be self-commissioned executors of Divine judgment on evildoers? Easy replies must not suffice, for what if the Divine Judge has retired from his bench, leaving all things in the hands of men? What then? Does evil for evil become mandatory?

Black Resurrection: The Power and the Glory

What are the means to be used in building new black men, new black communities and a renewed, black-oriented world? Already certain pathways have been suggested. The new men must come partly from a new vision of themselves. Indeed the image that has been constantly used in this century involves more than new self-image, it presumes resurrection. Ever since Marcus Garvey preached an Easter sermon on "The Resurrection of the Negro" in 1922, the theme has been constantly renewed. For Garvey, self-knowledge was a key to this resurrection.

On the occasion of his sermon he said, "We are about to live a new life—a risen life—a life of knowing ourselves" [6:88]. His central passage in the discourse was an anticipation of so much that was to come on the black scene that it merits another temporary movement back into the first quarter of the century. Continuing the crucial image of resurrection, Garvey said,

> I trust there will be a spiritual and material resurrection among Negroes everywhere; that you will lift yourselves from the doubts of the past; that you will lift yourselves from the slumbers of the past; that you will lift yourselves from the lethargy of the past, and strike out in this new life—in this resurrected life—to see things as they are. [6:90]

The theme was continued faithfully in the Nation of Islam where Elijah Muhammad constantly spoke of "dead, so-called Negroes" who needed to be resurrected to their true life as black men [14]. At the current juncture the same concept finds various expressions among those who seek to build new black men. Thus Ron Karenga insists that "We must not be so busy calling the Negro dead that we can't work out methods to resurrect him" [8:17]. One of the methods is obviously the love and concern that other black men show for the "dead" brother. Another, related path to new life is suggested by Carmichael who speaks of "the necessity to reclaim our history and our identity from the cultural terrorism and depredation of self-justifying white guilt" [3:639]. The process of teaching becomes crucial. History becomes a balm for healing and a hope for new beginnings.

The pages of recent black history are thus filled with testimonies of Afro-Americans who saw themselves as "dead" or "sick" before their contact with the healing and resurrecting power of black concern and black self-knowledge. One of Karenga's own disciples (and the word is used intentionally) recently wrote,

> I can remember myself before Maulana ["Great Leader," the title assumed by Karenga] showed me the "Path of Blackness." I was so sick no one but Maulana could have saved me. Running around with no identity, purpose or direction. Maulana gave me an alternative to this white system. . . . I say, "all praises due to Maulana." [8:iii]

Such dependence upon new or previously hidden knowledge for salvation is at least as old as Gnosticism and most of the mystery religions, and perhaps one also hardly needs to comment about the significance of love as a conqueror of death. Nevertheless it might be well to note that in a world where God's absence is more evident than his presence to large numbers of men, an individual's worth may no longer be sufficiently affirmed in terms of his worthiness before a Divine being. Or could one say that black love and resurrection are simply ways of speaking about and discovering incarnation where it is most needed today?

Some persons are nevertheless disturbed by what they consider a "glorification of blackness" in the healing process under discussion. In a significant sense, this is exactly what is involved with the relationship of Black Power to black and broken men who have been made ashamed of their blackness. It is indeed glorified; and a perceptive theological interpreter of this aspect of the issue offers a most helpful understanding of the action when he writes,

> The glorification of blackness implicit in the term Black Power is a conscious or unconscious effort to stake a claim for the Worth of those in our nation who are termed nonwhite. Essentially it is a clarification. The root meaning of the term "glorify" is to clarify, to make clear and plain and straight. [19:139]

Nor does Nathan Wright confine the issue to the human sphere with this highly suggestive description of black glorification. He goes on to say,

> All of life must be clarified in this sense. It must be given and seen in that dimension which sets it forth in terms of glory—now and forever. To see life as it truly is means to see it as God sees it, in its eternal

dimension, in the glory appropriate to its involvement with and in the life of God. [19:139–140]

If one follows this invaluable line of thought, it is obvious that Black Power has within it the possibility of setting black men in an entirely new light—the light of their Creator. They are called upon to see themselves as they were meant to be. This glorification has the potential of setting them at peace with themselves—and with the creative purposes of the universe; they no longer need to curse God and die. For their blackness is now—like the rest of their createdness—a sign of His love and not His anger.

At its best, such glorification sets black men at peace whether or not the white world recognizes the reality of their dark blessedness; such clarity makes it unnecessary for them to prove to whites the facts of that glory or even to demand that they be recognized. For men at peace with the universe are at once profoundly at peace with themselves and with all others who participate in that universe. Unfortunately, such a time is not yet with us, and black men have been forced to live in shameful dependency and self-negation for too long. So the process of resurrection may well be more like three generations than three days for some of the black dead. But it is also possible that the coming forth may be unlike the quiet stories of the Gospels and more like the volcanic eruptions of the Old Testament or the fire-framed bursting of the graves in the vision of John.

One difficult aspect of the rebuilding task urged by Black Power is the break with white leadership. This has long been a subject of furious discussion among blacks, and in this century it began when several Negro members of W.E.B. Du Bois' radical, black Niagara Movement refused in 1909 to join the newly created white-dominated National Association for the Advancement of Colored People [1: vol 2, 927]. In our own time the issue was perhaps raised most sharply by SNCC, partly as a result of its Mississippi Summer experience of 1964. Even before the experiment of bringing large numbers of whites into the state had begun, it was reported that some black staff members of the organization "felt that it would destroy everything which they had accomplished." According to Julius Lester's account, the objectors were convinced that

> Whites, no matter how well meaning, could not relate to the Negro community. A Negro would follow a white person to the courthouse, not because he'd been convinced he should register to vote, but simply because he had been trained to say Yes to whatever a white person wanted. [13:23]

Therefore it was determined that the resurrection of black people required decisive breaks with the old patterns of life, patterns of constant dependence on whites which had been begun in slavery and then encouraged ever since. By 1966, Stokely Carmichael had put the new dictum into words, using "psychological equality" as a synonym for black mental resurrection. He wrote, "The need for psychological equality is the reason why SNCC today believes that blacks must organize in the black community. Only black people can convey the revolutionary idea that black people are able to do things themselves" [2:6].

While this decision on the part of Black Power advocates has been one of the most difficult for well-intentioned whites to abide, there is much logic in its direction if one is primarily concerned with the building of men and communities which have been shattered, threatened, or used by forces with white faces. It is difficult for white men and women to be told to go and organize in white communities "where the racism really is," but such words are certainly worthy of serious consideration, especially if one's deepest concern is with the healing of shattered black egos more than with the bolstering of relatively intact white ones.

Even though the logic is powerful, the implications of the moment towards separation and the questions it raises are no less significant. How shall the black and white victims of American racism best find their healing before the last night settles in? What is the nature of the binding process and under what conditions shall it best take place? One wonders, for instance, if the restoration of broken, embittered spirits can take place apart from the presence—at some point—of the offending, denying, guilt-dominated brother. Or is it impossible for black men to build the necessary strength to love themselves—which must precede all else—except through studied alienation from their former oppressors, even the truly repentant ones? Perhaps an even more sobering and "practical" question is whether or not a white community without inner quietness will allow the black workers time and space to build a unique (and thereby threatening) set of structures and beings.

The models for guidance are difficult to discover, but it is evident that the ancient issue of means and ends is involved in the discussion, if one takes seriously the stated goals of some of the Black Power advocates. For instance, few members of the younger, enraged generation have any program of separate states or of Zionism on another continent. Therefore most seek to find some *modus vivendi* on the American scene. At the heart of the matter under discussion is the issue of how we can prepare black people to live with integrity on the scene of our former enslavement and our present estrangement. In examining this matter, Karenga says, "We're not for isolation but interdependence—but we can't become interdependent unless we have something to offer." In other words, he says, "We can live with whites interdependently once we have Black Power" [8:3]. So the summary response to the central question seems to be that it is only a temporary withdrawing of the black community into itself which will prepare it for interdependence, and therefore the end appears threatened by the seemingly unavoidable means.

(Somehow the black-white dilemma is often suggestive of an unhealthy and mutually destructive marriage which may require at least a period of separation for the mutual benefit of the two partners. At other times America seems to be the forever unfaithful lover of the Blues, the lover who is always lamented but never left—until the last, inevitably bloody scene. The same unclarity that marks the religious response to unhealthy love affairs and destructive marriages is likely present when one searches for guidance here. Is divorce preferable to the kitchen knife? But what would divorce mean?)

A question no less difficult arises in another step that Black Power takes towards the building of black men and the black community—the emphasis on self-defense. Speaking for his organization in 1966, Carmichael set the most obvious theme: "SNCC reaffirms the right of black men everywhere to defend themselves when threatened or attacked" [2:5]. Moving the idea from a right to an authentication of black freedom, Killens wrote, "Men are not free unless they affirm the right to defend themselves" [11:33]. But for those who would intelligently explore Black Power, even these explanations are insufficient. It was Killens who set out—largely by implication—the fuller and more profound psychological significance of self-defense for black men. He wrote in the same revealing article,

> We black folk have a deep need to defend ourselves. Indeed we have an obligation. We must teach the brutalizers how it feels to be brutalized. We must teach them that it hurts. They'll never know unless we teach them. [11:34]

The issues raised by this series of statements are worthy of thoughtful consideration, for they eventually move to a level of profound moment. On the surface they seem to be nothing more than an affirmation of the somewhat disreputable "American right" to self-defense. (A right, incidentally, which most Americans have no sound moral grounds for questioning when it suddenly appears among angry black men.)

In some ways this affirmation of self-defense is an obvious response to a situation in which black people find that neither separation, respect, nor love is forthcoming from the dominant portion of the society. On another, related level, it is a repetition of the earlier theme of judgment at the hands of the injured. As we have mentioned, in a world in which God is at least obscure, and where no one else seems a dependable agent of justice for black people, black men should stand firmly on their responsibility to do the necessary work. There is, however, an even more profound issue involved in what Killens describes so sensitively as "a deep need" for black men to defend themselves. What he seems to be implying is this: when men have long been forced to accept the wanton attacks of their oppressors, when they have had to stand by, and watch their women prostituted, it is crucial to their own sense of self-esteem that they affirm and be able to implement their affirmation of a right to strike back.

The basic human search for a definition of manhood is here set out in significant black lineaments. Does manhood indeed depend upon the capacity to defend one's life? Is this American shibboleth really the source of freedom for men? Is it possible that a man simply becomes a slave to another man's initiative when he feels obliged to answer his opponent on the opponent's terms? Is there perhaps a certain kind of bondage involved when men are so anxious about keeping themselves alive that they are ready to take the lives of others to prevent that occurrence? The question is really one of the image man was meant to reflect; what is it? Certain ways of looking at the world would suggest that such questions are pointless before they come from the lips. Other religious perspectives might suggest that manhood can be discussed, but only in terms of the capacity to create new grounds for response to danger, and in the act of bringing new life into being, rather than in the animal capacity to strike back.

In his characteristically vivid way, Karenga allows no circumventing of the issue. He writes, "If we fight we might be killed. But it is better to die as a man than to live like a slave" [8:19]. In the midst of a hostile, threatening environment the Zealot pathway is often chosen by those who are in honest search of their manhood, by those who seek to protect and avenge their oppressed community. Most persons who claim to be followers of the Man who introduced Zealots to a new way of response have chosen not to follow him at this point. And here is one of the most telling witnesses to the possibility that Black Power may be more fully bound to the traditions of the western Christian world than its proponents would ever dare believe.

Now, if it is possible that the fullest stature of man was found in one who honestly and sharply opposed his enemies but finally faced them with his cross, then Black Power may have chosen far less than the best available way. If it has chosen a bondage to death, the mistake is completely understandable. It is understandable not only because retaliatory violence is deeply etched into the American grain, but also because men who have been forced up against crosses all of their lives find it difficult to take one up when the choice is fully theirs. It is understandable, too, because western society now seems unable to offer any normative response to the question, "What is man?" Moreover it appears totally without courage to experiment with possibilities beyond the old, "heroic," destructive replies.

Perhaps one possibility yet stands in the future, and Black Power's immediate choice must not be counted as its last. For who knows where the inner quest will lead black men if they are honestly in search of true manhood, true community, and true humanity? Are there not grounds for hope wherever men are soberly and devotedly engaged in the quest for new light?

Old White Models and New Black Hopes

If the relationship of self-defense to the building of black manhood is crucial on the personal level, then it is likely that the kinds of power by the black community is the focal question on the broader scale. Not only is it crucial, but it faces us with another set of religious issues of considerable force. Initially one must ask: what is the power necessary to build the new black community? Perhaps Stokely Carmichael best summarized the normative Black Power response when he wrote,

> Almost from its beginning, SNCC sought to [build] a program aimed at winning political power for impoverished Southern blacks. We had to begin with politics because black Americans are a propertyless people in a country where property is valued above all. We had to work for power, because this country does not function by morality, love, and nonviolence, but by power. [2:5]

Political, economic and social power with a final recourse to armed self-defense are at the heart of the black search, even though Carmichael has since gone on to espouse aggressive guerrilla warfare. Ron Karenga, who feels the movement is not yet ready for such warfare, put the issues of power for the black community more colorfully, but no less directly when he said,

> Like it or not, we don't live in a spiritual or moral world and the white boys got enough H-bombs, missiles, T.V.'s, firehoses and dogs to prove it.

Therefore, he concluded, "we must move not spiritually but politically, i.e., with power" [8:19].

In some ways it is understandable to hear the avowed revolutionaries among Black Power forces refer to political, economic, and military realities as the ultimate forces in life. It is even more interesting to note that same direction in the forceful statement of an impressive group of black churchmen who wrote on the subject of black and white power in 1966. In the midst of the national furor over the newly discovered term, the churchmen published a full-page advertisement in the *New York Times* which said, in part, "The fundamental distortion facing us in the controversy about 'black power' is rooted in a gross imbalance of power and conscience between Negroes and white Americans." After setting out this basic introduction to their thesis, the statement continued,

> It is this distortion, mainly, which is responsible for the widespread though often inarticulate assumption that white people are justified in getting what they want through the use of power, but that Negro Americans must, either by nature or by circumstances, make their appeal only through conscience. As a result, the power of white men and the conscience of black men have both been corrupted. The power of white men is corrupted because it meets little meaningful resistance from Negroes to temper it and keep white men from aping God.

Tracing the corruption of the black conscience, the churchmen attributed it to a condition in which,

> having no power to implement the demands of conscience, the concern for justice is transmuted into a distorted form of love, which, in the absence of justice, becomes chaotic self-surrender. Powerlessness breeds a race of beggars. We are faced now with a situation where conscienceless power meets powerless conscience, threatening the very foundations of our nation. [15:187]

It was evident that the churchmen were convinced that "conscience," or "love" as they later referred to it, was "powerless" without the coercive forces of the society. They appeared no less disturbed than John Killens about "unrequited love," and in a sophisticated adumbration, the group simply gave religious expression to the political views of Carmichael, Karenga and a host of other black spokesmen. Though it is not fully stated they seem to be saying that the ultimate weapons necessary for the building of the new black community are those now monopolized by white power leaders. Blacks have to get their hands on some of these weapons and perhaps depend upon their own consciences to "temper" black uses of the same instruments whites had used for such destructive purposes. But when blacks begin getting their proper share of the power, it would appear that they might be less dependent upon the development of "conscience"—unless it was theirs in large supplies "by nature" rather than "by circumstance." How then would Black Power be tempered?

A question at least as compelling is this: Does the theological position implicit in the churchmen's statement carry a doctrine of two kingdoms with it? Do these leaders seek the Kingdom of the weaponless, defenseless, homeless King at certain times, and the Kingdom of the armed, propertied, politically powerful, American, white (soon to be technicolored) King at another time? Where do the kingdoms meet? Are the guidelines to the nature of human community as blurred as those for the nature of man? On issues of ultimate power, are the insights of Christian ministers only accidentally the same as Stokely Carmichael's and Ron Karenga's?

The implications of the churchmen's statement are numerous and provocative but it is important to supplement that statement with an even more theologically astute brief for Black Power by one of the individual senators, Nathan Wright. Dr. Wright, who is also chairman of the National Conference on Black Power, recently wrote of the image of God and its relationship to power among black men. He said,

> In religious terms, a God of power, of majesty and of might, who has made men to be in His own image and likeness, must will that His creation reflect in the immediacies of life His power, His majesty and His might. Black Power raises . . . the far too long overlooked need for power, if life is to become what in the mind of its Creator it is destined to be. [15:136]

In a fascinating way Karenga, one of the best trained and most thoughtful of the Black Power leaders, picks up the precise theme set down by Wright. In all likelihood he does it independently, so it is even more significant and illuminating that his definition of Black Power should also find its basis in a powerful deity. He writes, "God is God who moves in power; God is God who moves in change and creates something out of nothing. If you want to be God just think about that" [8:26]. (Karenga's last sentence is not random rhetoric. Evidently he has so imbibed the homocentric orientation of the American society that he upstages the

Mormons by telling men that they become Gods now by entering into Godlike action. Indeed, the emphasis on autonomous black action is another of the hallmarks of Black Power ideology, a hallmark that leaves little room for any dependence on what might be called grace—a hallmark that would stamp it as far more Protestant than one might desire.)

The difficulty with the analogy evoked by Wright and Karenga is its failure to recognize another aspect of the power of God within the biblical tradition. If Wright and the other black churchmen put any serious stock in the life and teachings of Jesus of Nazareth as the clearest possible window to the face of God, then one must at least examine another way of power. That is, one must see the power of God demonstrated in weakness and in humiliation. Is it not possible that the God who dies for his enemies, who rejects their terms and their weapons—and their kind of power—is also worthy of consideration as a model for the empowerment of the black community?

Though it is difficult to propound, it would appear that such a question may have some possible validity when one remembers some of the goals of Black Power. May not one properly ask if a new black community will be created by the appropriation of the old American weapons of power? More specifically, what of Karenga's insight into the nature of racism? He said at one point,

> Racist minds created racist institutions. Therefore you must move against racism, not institutions. For even if you tear down the institutions that same mind will build them up again. [8:14]

How does one "move against racism"? Surely not with "H-bombs, missiles, T.V.'s, firehoses . . . dogs" and all the other institutions of political power now possessed by "the white boy." And what of Stokely Carmichael's strangely religious metaphor: "For racism to die, a totally different America must be born" [2:61]? Will a black community in search of a new society really participate in the process of new birth by a reactionary fixation on all the kinds of power which have helped to corrupt the nation? How does new birth come?

Talk of weakness and death, quests for new birth, all tend to be at once sources of fascination and anathema for the current black breed. It is likely that the apparently contradictory references to such matters in their writings are largely unconscious, and that the conscious stance is one of opposition to Gods who die on crosses. As we have seen, black men have been chained to weakness for so long that any talk of voluntarily choosing a way that the society counts as weak is considered sheer madness.

Is this the scandal of the cross for the present black moment? Or is it all foolishness in the most irrelevant sense of the word? Perhaps Karenga was most true to himself and to the universe when he said, "We don't live in a spiritual or moral world." Somehow it sounds like the old black deacons who constantly joked behind the minister's back: "Praying is fine in a prayer meeting but it ain't no good in a bear meeting."

If the world is primarily a bear meeting, and if the only way to survive in such a gathering is by becoming a bear, then the way of Black Power is evident. (Even the preachers seem to agree with elements of Black Bear Power.) Nevertheless, in such a situation, the way of human beings remains cloudy.

Black Power and Religion: Beyond Implications

Reference to a black prayer meeting serves as a reminder that the discussion of religious issues in this essay has generally grown out of the intimations, suggestions, and tendencies one finds in the words and deeds of Black Power advocates. There has been almost no attempt to address the subject of the precise, institutionalized religious manifestations of Black Power, largely because such an attempt would be somewhat premature. It is evident, however, that if the ideology does institutionalize itself, a more clearly articulated religious message and ritual will likely develop, or rather a set of such phenomena will emerge.

Anticipation of this is present already throughout the black ghettos. Ever since the days of Garvey's African Orthodox Church, Black Nationalist groups have found religion to be one of their major modes of expression. The Nation of Islam's success is the best known indication of the power inherent in this direction. Recently—especially since Malcolm X's appearance on the national scene—there have been many Black Nationalist attempts to reestablish variations of African religious practices, and one can only speculate on the mutual transformations such attempts may bring about.

None of these developments should be surprising, of course. For instance, when the strongly nationalist Bandung Conference of Afro-Asian peoples gathered in 1955 a resolution was passed "to resurrect their old religions and cultures and modernize them. . . ." Similarly at the world conference of black writers, artists, and intellectuals held in Paris in the following year, one of the participants said that "the main and only resolution called for the rehabilitation of their ancient cultures and religions" [20:22]. These were significant international prefigurings of Black Power in America, and they probably suggest the way that the Afro-American movements will increasingly take.

Besides the plethora of Black Nationalist religious experiments in the ghettos of the land, it is likely that Karenga's West Coast organization, US, has so far articulated the most clearly structured and self-consciously religious manifestos of all the Black Power groups. It is representative of much of the movement's concerns both in its rather humanistic, secular (in the most recent religious sense of that word) orientation and in its obvious reaction to the black Christian churches. Thus Karenga teaches that "We must concern ourselves more with the plans for this life, rather than the next life which has its own problems. For the next life across Jordan is much further away than the grawl [*sic*] of dogs and policemen and the pains of hunger and disease" [8:26].

In spite of the familiar reference to Jordan, groups like Karenga's tend to believe that men live on only through the lives of their children, and there is among them a strong emphasis on the rebuilding of the shattered black home. In such a home the role of the woman follows almost strictly Pauline lines, and some female believers in Black Power find it difficult to adjust their western indoctrination of equality to the old-new emphasis on the supremacy of the black man.

The New Testament stream that flows through their doctrine of the relationship of husband to wife does not prevent Black Power groups from engaging in constant attacks on the Christian churches. For instance, Karenga—in keeping with many other similar leaders who preceded him—says that "Christians do good because they fear—we do good because we love. They do good because God says so—we do good . . . in response to need" [8].

The issue of religion is constantly before many of the young persons who are drawn back into the ghettos by the urgent logic of Black Power. As they return—from college or from prison—to struggle against what can be reasonably described as "principalities and powers" which seem anonymously but fiercely to control the life of their people, they find themselves often insufficient as autonomous sources of inner strength. They cannot return to the Christian churches they once knew, because these churches have so often appeared irrelevant to the real needs of the community and most often they are controlled by older men and women who seem unprepared for the competition from radical black youth. In here, strangely enough, a few black Christian churches have responded fully to the call of Black Power. In Detroit the pastor of one such congregation, the Reverend Albert B. Cleage, Jr., of the Central United Church of Christ, preaches of a black revolutionary Jesus who came to set the non-white peoples free. A Black Madonna is the focal point of worship, and the church has probably attracted more persons committed to Black Power than any other single institution still connected to the Christian churches.

Even when they cannot find such havens, there is nevertheless something in the black religious tradition that continues to attract many racially conscious young people. For instance, it is most moving and revealing to watch a group of them respond totally with clapping and dancing to the gospel songs that continue to shape the tradition that spawned them. They are at home for a time. Ideologies aside, this is still "Soul."

On what may or may not be another level of their being, some of the group also sense a strange sense of attraction to Jesus of Nazareth. They are convinced that an encounter with the historical Jesus would likely be a meeting with a revolutionary, but they have been turned off by the whiteness infused into this Jesus by the western Christian tradition. They are also able and often accurate catalogers of the unfaithfulness of the churches—black and white. Sometimes they consider these churches as irrelevant as white persons are. A few of the seekers turn to Judaism, but often meet the reality of the Jewish middleman in the ghettos and find it an obstacle to faith. Others move towards Islamic variations of belief, often giving up their western, Christian names. This is partly another declaration of independence from slavery and its postreconstruction variations, but it is in some situations simply part of the ancient practice of men taking on new names when they find new faiths.

In the light of their search for the lineaments of a new societal order, it is surely significant that some black groups have now moved towards various forms of communitarianism. In locations like Los Angeles and Philadelphia attempts are made to find this style of life in the urban context. In upper New York state real estate has been set aside for such an experiment; while in Brooklyn a group of some sixty men and women now plan for moving back to the south, to the land. Is it likely that such actions represent more than exercises in anguished flight? Is it possible that they are really a challenge to the two settings which have been most destructive to black life—the city and the south? Are they expressions of hope in the power of resurrected black lives to conquer even these ancient foes?

There is a sense of religious ferment on the path to Black Power, a sense that is not easy to document. Mixtures of old and new approaches to the essential issues of life are being attempted. Allah and other gods of Africa enter into competition with Yahweh, Jesus, and Buddha. It is a joyously difficult time, but part of the affirmation of Black Power is "We are a spiritual people." The institutional manifestations of that affirmation are still being tested. A people separated from their past now attempt to build bridges, create new realities, or search among the ruins for whatever remains of value there may be.

So Afro-Americans enter the experience that many peoples have known before them, peoples who in time of national crisis have turned to the gods they knew before the coming of Christian missionaries, seeking for what seemed a more solid ground. For should it be forgotten that such searches have taken place in this century no less significantly in Ireland and Germany than in Kenya and the Congo.

As for the possible results here, one can only begin to speculate, for instance, on the impact of some African religions on a Black Power movement that is still more western oriented and Protestant than it can possibly admit. Will these religions which seek unity and harmony with the forces of God in the universe transform an ideology that is still determined to change the world around it? Can one accept the Yoruba dreams and dress without falling sway to its worldview? Only the questions are available now.

Meanwhile, few adherents of Black Power deny their need for religious moorings and, though no clear pattern has yet emerged, it must be evident by now that for many persons this movement is likely to become as full a "church" as the earlier phase was for others. Not only does it begin to fill the need for personal commitment and a sense of fellowship with other similarly committed black persons; it also embodies impressive social concern, a call for ultimate justice, and a search to be present with the sufferers of the society. Gladly identifying with the oppressed beyond national borders, this church increasingly seeks to glorify at least that part of God which may reside in black folk.

In the midst of such developments, one central question cries out for an answer, the kind of answer that is perhaps to be found most fully in the insight of true religion. Though often articulated only in parts, if put into words by Black Power adherents, it would be, "How shall we deal with an enemy who has more power than we do, who has long controlled and destroyed our lives that are even now more fully dependent upon him than we dare confess?" Whatever religion arises from the heart of Black Power will need to address itself to such a dilemma with more honesty than most black religion has ever done before. (One of the generally unrecognized religious blessings of this movement is the honesty it has already forced into the black-white dialogue in America. It has not produced hate; it has rather revealed hate and called upon both whites and blacks to admit its sorrowful depths. There are, of course, large segments of the society who still fear this radical honesty, but it is likely that they also fear true religion.)

Epilogue: Martin Luther King and Black Power

No discussion of black religion in America today can ignore the immensely important figure of Martin Luther King, Jr. In spite of statements to the contrary, he remains an individual of critical importance for anyone who would gain insights into the black experience here. Therefore it is crucial to examine King's response to a movement that has seemed to push him off the stage. The encounter may well provide unexpected illumination for some summary views.

In his most recent work, *Where Do We Go From Here?* [12], King attempts an assessment of Black Power that is significant and revealing, not for its originality or its challenge, but for the basic weakness of his response to the realities evoked and addressed by the ideology. There is in one chapter a favorable interpretation of the "positive" aspects of Black Power as a psychological healing force. Then as King attempts to define the elements which will bring the "necessary" power to the black community, he refers to power as "the strength required to bring about social, political or economic changes," and identifies this power in many of the same ways as the churchmen and the leading Black Power advocates. When the words come from King, however, they bear somewhat more powerful implications. He writes,

> There is nothing essentially wrong with power. The problem is that in America power is unequally distributed. This has led Negro Americans in the past to seek their goals through love and moral suasion devoid of power and white Americans to seek their goals through power devoid of love and conscience. . . . It is precisely this collision of immoral power with powerless morality which constitutes the major crisis of our times. [12:37]

In religious (as well as political) terms, King's words constitute something of a crisis in themselves and raise many difficult issues. They tempt us, most importantly, to ask whether King was describing his own movement when he spoke of Negroes in the past who sought goals "through love and moral suasion" because no other way was available to them. If this identification is precise, then one must surely question the nature of such love and the motives of the moral susasion. And if the love was "powerless" why were there so many past references made to "the power of love and nonviolence"—references found even in King's current work?

Surely the talk of love and suasion that was a kind of last resort is not in keeping with the insights of the great teachers of nonviolence, who set out this way for men who were not cowards, who had other weapons available, but who chose to put them aside for the sake of a better way. King's statements cause one to ask if there was really a nonviolent movement at any point. Was "too much love" really the problem? Could it be that nonviolence was simply impossible for a people who had never had an opportunity to affirm their manhood or to choose violence as a way of response on a widespread scale? Perhaps the late, lamented nonviolent movement can really come only after the Malcolms, Stokelys, and Raps have offered another real choice to millions of black folk.

Even more significant for the present discussion is King's failure to deal clearly and precisely with the central black radical conviction concerning America. Its advocates believe (and they have a growing company of fellow believers) that this nation will not allow black men the freedom, opportunity, and restitution needful for meaningful lives without a total, violent disruption of the society. Like revolutionaries before them, they believe that the national fabric must be rent before white people will believe in the validity of black demands for life. Here is the price of three centuries of racism, they say. King does not really respond to this assumption. He warns against cynicism, but fails to set out in clarity his response to a situation in which even massive, disciplined nonviolent resistance will continue to meet increasingly violent (and/or sophisticated) repression.

Somehow the night of that terror seems too dark for King to enter. His only real attempt at an answer to the Black Power conviction is a vague statement of faith, but the object of the faith also remains vague. King writes,

> Our most fruitful course is to stand firm, move forward nonviolently, accept disappointments and cling to hope. Our determined refusal not to be stopped will eventually open the door to fulfillment. By recognizing the necessity of suffering in a righteous cause, we may achieve our humanity's full stature. To guard ourselves from bitterness, we need the vision to see in this generation's ordeals the opportunity to transfigure both ourselves and American society. [12:46–47]

There are missing links and false notes apparent in any religiously focused examination of this central statement. Nowhere is there any explanation of why King believes that the door "will eventually open." Is it faith in American goodness, in the power of a nonviolent movement that he hardly discusses, or faith in an abstract justice in the universe? (King's God often seems no less dead than anyone else's—at least if one judges life by appearance in the printed pages.) Without such clarification, his call could be dismissed as a Pollyanna voice attempting to challenge the whirlwind.

Even more important is his failure to discuss the possible reasons for an amorphous, variously motivated group of black people to suffer without retaliation the continued scorn and injury of people they consider at least fools and at most devils. When King referred to "powerless morality" and identified authentic power for black people with economic and political power, he was then likely obligated to ask who would be willing to live without such power once it became possible either to kill for it or to kill to protest its denial.

It would appear that, unless King is ready to face black men with the need to suffer without retaliation and also to live without the power he considered "necessary," much of his argument against violence falls apart. For the violence of revolutionaries comes not from "hatred," as he says, but from the insistence of the oppressed that they must have at least a proportionate share of the power which the oppressor insists upon keeping and defending by violent means. Leaders like Karenga say such power is absolutely necessary for black men. So does King. Black Power leaders are convinced that the country will not make such power available without armed struggle of one kind or another. What does a believer in religious nonviolence have to say to such a situation? Is it enough not to face it squarely? And if he does must King eventually choose between armed struggle and a powerless future for black people in the United States?

In a sense this dilemma is a reminder of how much the present black situation—especially in its religious dimensions—is a microcosmic expression of the main lines of the development of American Christian ethics in this century. Within the microcosm King stands for the liberal tradition, continuing to maintain faith in American goodness, in reason, in the ordered nature of the world. Such a stance seems to require his refusing to look directly into chaos, seems to demand that he fail to trace the deepest lineaments of the nation's racist core. In a sense King appears to hope that dark "principalities and powers" in massive array are only figments of overexercised religious imagination. In their place he substitutes an eloquent dream.

On the other hand stand the proponents of Black Power, like some dark blossoms of "realism" gone beyond control. They look with cynical but not dishonest eyes at the forces of evil in the society, at their depth and their extent. They see without flinching the possibility that power will not be shared voluntarily, that atonement cannot come without the shedding of blood, and they are determined that as little of the blood as possible will flow from them. They see the night and prepare men for its terror. They refuse to dream. But like much of the realist position, they also fail to acknowledge sufficiently (perhaps because of insensitivity on certain levels of their being) the reality of creative, healing forces in the situation. Somehow the power of resurrection is totally irrelevant to the struggles they outline, except in the most personal applications to individual "dead" black men.

Moved out of the metaphorical microcosm, these two perspectives are badly in need of each other for the mutual sharing and the possible mutual growth which may well be the nation's only visible hope in the racial crisis. The necessary, relentless determination of Black Power to look fully on the evil of American life must be informed by some hope even more solid than King's, some expectation of creative possibilities (even of Messiahs), some determination not to succumb to the enemy's disease. Even more soberly put, it may be that all who speak with any seriousness about addressing the profound social and psychological distortions brought by American racism must be prepared to experiment with totally new weapons, and be ready (how hard the words!) for complete defeat—at least as it is commonly counted.

For if racism rages as deep into American life as it appears and if violence is its closest brother, then a black revolution will no more solve the problem than a civil war did (even if Rap Brown gets his atomic bomb). So it may be most responsible to ask if it is more than despair to speak of a long, grueling battle with no victory—and no illusions—this side of the grave? Has it been important and necessary simply to learn that there are no large citizen armies of white deliverers? Was it not absolutely necessary that all trust in courts and troops and presidents be shattered? Is this part of a black coming of age, a coming which will eventually reveal that even the black God of the ghetto is dead?

Perhaps, though, he is not dead. Perhaps this new God has not lived long enough to die. Perhaps there is still a Beloved Community ahead. But if it is, it must be seen as the kingdom whose realization does not depend upon whether whites (or anyone else around) really want it or not. If it comes, it may come only for those who seek it for its own sake and for the sake of its Lord, recognizing that even if He is black, the final glory is not the glory of blackness, but a setting straight of all the broken men and communities of the earth. In some strange ways Black Power may be headed in that way, but it probably needs some new and stripped-down coming of Martin King's most fervent hopes to accompany its path.

On the other hand, if the night is already too dark for the way to be found, or if society should make it impossible for these two black tendencies to live and find each other, then there seems little to expect that is not apocalyptic. This has always been a religious implication of life, especially black life. It is certainly one of the deepest implications of a wishful liberalism and an inescapable possibility for a Black Power that finally accepts not America's weapons but also its ultimate definitions of manhood, power, majesty, and might.

Was it for this that we have come so painfully far together—and yet apart—in this strange land? Was it only for this? Is there no saving message from the drums of our homeland, or did all gods die at once?

References

1. Herbert Aptheker, ed. *A Documentary History of the Negro People in the United States*, 2 vol. (New York: Citadel Press, 1965).
2. Stokely Carmichael, "What We Want," *New York Review of Books* 7, no. 4 (22 September 1966).
3. Stokely Carmichael, "Towards Black Liberation," *Massachusetts Review* (Autumn 1966).
4. Anita Cornwell, "Symposium on Black Power," *Negro Digest* 16, no. 1 (November 1966).
5. Ronald Fair, "Symposium on Black Power," *Negro Digest* 16, no. 1 (November 1966).
6. Amy Jacques Garvey, ed. *Philosophy and Opinions of Marcus Garvey* (New York: Universal Publishing House, 1923).
7. Marcus Garvey, in Edmund D. Cronon, *Black Moses* (Madison, Wis.: University of Wisconsin Press, 1964).
8. Clyde Halisi and James Mtume, eds. *The Quotable Karenga* (Los Angeles: US, 1967).
9. Vincent Harding, "Religion and Resistance Among Antebellum Negroes, 1800–1860" in *Making of Black America*, August Meier and Elliot Rudwick, eds. (New York: Atheneum, 1972).
10. Nathan Hare, "Symposium on Black Power," *Negro Digest* 16, no. 1 (November 1966).
11. John Oliver Killens, "Symposium on Black Power," *Negro Digest* 16, no. 1 (November 1966).
12. Martin Luther King, Jr., *Where Do We Go from Here?* (New York: Harper & Row, 1967).
13. Julius Lester, "The Angry Children of Malcolm X," *Sing Out* 16, no. 5 (November 1966), an important and eloquent contribution to our understanding of the coming of Black Power.
14. Elijah Muhammad, *Message to the Black Man*.
15. National Committee of Negro Churchmen, "Black Power," in Nathan Wright, Jr., *Black Power and Urban Unrest* (New York: Hawthorne Books, 1967).

16. Philippians 3.
17. Stanley Saunders, "I'll Never Leave the Ghetto," *Ebony* 20, no. 10 (August 1967).
18. David Walker, *Appeal* (1829); reprint in Herbert Aptheker, ed., *One Continual Cry* (New York: Humanities Press, 1965).
19. Wright, *Black Power.*
20. Richard Wright, *White Man, Listen!* (Garden City, N.Y.: Anchor Books/Doubleday, 1964).

Chapter 31

Integrationism and Nationalism in African-American Intellectual History

James H. Cone

No one stated the dilemma that slavery and segregation created for Africans in the United States as sharply and poignantly as W.E.B. Du Bois. In his classic statement of the problem, he spoke of it as a "peculiar sensation," a "double-consciousness," "two souls, two thoughts, two unreconciled strivings; two warring ideals in one dark body, whose dogged strength alone keeps it from being torn asunder." The "twoness" that Du Bois was describing stemmed from being an African *in* America. "Here, then, is the dilemma," he wrote in "The Conservation of Races." "What, after all, am I? Am I an American or am I a Negro? Can I be both?"[1]

Integrationist thinkers may be defined as those who answer "Yes" to the question, "Can I be both?" They believe it is possible to achieve justice in the United States and to create wholesome relations with the white community. This optimism has been based upon the "American creed," the tradition of freedom and democracy as articulated in the Declaration of Independence and the Constitution, and is supported, they believe, by the Jewish and Christian Scriptures. The integrationist line of thought goes something like this: If whites really believe their political and religious documents, then they know that black people should not be enslaved and segregated but rather integrated into the mainstream of the society. After all, blacks are Americans, having arrived even before the Pilgrims. They have worked the land, obeyed the laws, paid their taxes, and defended America in every war. They built the nation as much as white people did. Therefore, the integrationists argue, it is the task of African-American leaders to prick the conscience of whites, showing the contradictions between their professed values and their actual treatment of blacks. Then whites will be embarrassed by their hypocrisy and will grant blacks the same freedom that they themselves enjoy.

On the other hand, nationalist thinkers have rejected the American side of their identity and affirmed the African side, saying, "No, we can't be both." They have contended that 244 years of slavery, followed by legal segregation, social degradation, political disfranchisement, and economic exploitation means that blacks will never be recognized as human beings in white society. America isn't for blacks; blacks can't be for America. The nationalists argue that blacks don't belong with whites, that whites are killing blacks, generation after generation. Blacks should, therefore, separate from America, either by returning to Africa or by going to some other place where they can create sociopolitical structures that are derived from their own history and culture.

Integrationism and nationalism represent the two broad streams of black thought in response to the problem of slavery and segregation in America. Of course, no black thinker has been a pure integrationist or a pure nationalist, but rather all black intellectuals have represented aspects of each, with emphasis moving in one direction or the other, usually at different periods of their lives. What emphasis any black thinker made was usually determined by his or her perspective on America, that is, whether he or she believed that blacks would soon be included in the mainstream of American life on a par with whites. When blacks have been optimistic about America—believing that they could achieve full equality through moral suasion and legal argument—they have been integrationists and have minimized their nationalist tendencies. On the other hand, despair about America—believing that genuine equality is impossible because whites have no moral conscience or any intention to apply the laws fairly—has always been the seedbed of nationalism. To understand Martin King's and Malcolm X's perspectives on America and their relation to each other, it is important to see them in the light of these two different but interdependent streams of black thought.

Integrationism Before Martin King

Integrationists have had many able advocates since the founding of the republic. Among them were the great abolitionist Frederick Douglass, many prominent black preachers, and representatives of the National Association for the Advancement of Colored People (NAACP), the National Urban League, and the Congress of Racial Equality (CORE).

Frederick Douglass was the outstanding advocate of integrationism during the nineteenth century. Born a slave, Douglass escaped from slavery and became an international figure with his powerful speeches and writings in defense of the full citizenship rights of blacks. For him the existence of slavery was a staggering contradiction of the principles of the Constitution and the concept of humanity.

Unlike the white abolitionist William Lloyd Garrison, who denied his allegiance to a Constitution ratified by slaveholders, Douglass embraced it as an "anti-slavery document" and then proceeded to quote it as supporting evidence for the abolition of slavery. The Constitution reads, "'We the people'; not we the white people," Douglass proclaimed; "and if Negroes are people, they are included in the benefits for which the Constitution of America was ordained and established."[2]

No one was as persuasive as Frederick Douglass in pointing out to whites the hypocrisy of extolling the "principles of political freedom and of natural justice" articulated in the Declaration of Independence while holding blacks as slaves. His well-known Independence Day speech in Rochester, New York, on the topic "What to the Slave Is the Fourth of July?" was calculated to cut deeply into the conscience of whites who thought of themselves as civilized. "To [the slave], your celebration is a sham," he proclaimed to a stunned white audience. "Your denunciation of tyrants, brass-fronted impudence; your shouts of liberty and equality, hollow mockery. . . . There is not a nation on the earth guilty of practices more shocking and bloody than are the people of the United States."[3]

Douglass's scathing words did not mean that he had given up on America and would accordingly seek separation from the land of his birth. He was offered an opportunity to stay in England where he was given many honors, but he rejected the idea. Douglass believed that blacks could find justice in the United States and safely intertwine their future with that of the white majority. He was severely critical of blacks and whites who proposed the colonization of blacks in Africa or some other place. "It's all nonsense to talk about the removal of eight million of the American people from their homes in America to Africa," he said, "The destiny of the colored Americans . . . is the destiny of America. We shall never leave you. . . . We are here. . . . To imagine that we should ever be eradicated is absurd and ridiculous. We can be modified, changed, assimilated, but never extinguished. . . . This is our country; and the question for the philosophers and statesmen of the land ought to be, What principle should dictate the policy of the nation toward us?"[4]

Although Douglass experienced many disappointments in his fight for justice, he never lost his love for America or his belief that blacks would soon achieve full freedom in the land of their birth. "I expect to see the colored people of this country enjoying the same freedom [as whites]," he said in 1865, "voting at the same ballot-box . . . , going to the same schools, attending the same churches, traveling the same street cars, in the same railroad cars, . . . proud of the same country, fighting the same foe, and enjoying the same peace, and all its advantages."[5]

Optimism about blacks achieving full citizenship rights in America has always been the hallmark of integrationism. This optimism has been based not only on the political ideals of America but also upon its claim to be founded on Christian principles. Blacks have believed that the Christian faith requires that whites treat them as equals before God. No group articulated this point with more religious conviction and fervor than black preachers.

According to black preachers, Christianity is a gospel of justice and love. Believers, therefore, must treat all people justly and lovingly—that is, as brothers and sisters. Why? Because God, the creator of all, is no respecter of persons. Out of one blood God has created all people. On the cross Jesus Christ died for all—whites and blacks alike. Our oneness in creation and redemption means that no Christian can condone slavery or segregation in the churches or the society. The integration of whites and blacks into one community, therefore, is the only option open for Christians.

As early as 1787, Richard Allen (an ex-slave and a Methodist minister) led a group of blacks out of St. George Methodist Church in Philadelphia, and in 1816 he founded the African Methodist Episcopal (AME) Church. He did this because he and his followers refused to accept segregation in the "Lord's house." A few years later, James Varick and other blacks in New York took similar action and organized the African Methodist Episcopal Zion (AMEZ) Church. Black Baptists also formed separate congregations.

Independent black churches were not separatist in the strict sense. They were not separating themselves from whites because they held a different doctrinal view of Christianity. Without exception, blacks used the same articles of faith and polity for their churches as the white denominations from which they separated. Separation, for blacks, meant that they were rejecting the *ethical* behavior of whites—they were rejecting racism that was based on the assumption that God created blacks inferior to whites. Blacks also wanted to prove that they had the capability to organize and to operate a denomination just like whites. In short, black Christians were bearing witness to their humanity, which they believed God created equal to that of whites. The motto of the AME Church reflected that conviction: "God our Father, Christ our Redeemer, Man our Brother." "When these sentiments are universal in theory and practice," the AME bishops said in 1896, "then the mission of the distinctive colored organization will cease."[6]

Not all black Christians chose the strategy of separation. Instead, some decided to stay in white denominations and use them as platforms from which to prick the conscience of whites regarding the demands of the gospel and to encourage blacks to strike a blow for freedom. "Liberty is a spirit sent out from God," proclaimed Henry Highland Garnet, a Presbyterian minister, "and like its great Author, is no respecter of persons."[7]

Following the Civil War, the great majority of black Christians joined black-led churches among the Methodists and Baptists. The independence of these churches enabled their pastors to become prominent leaders in the black struggle for integration in the society. Prominent Baptists included Adam Clayton Powell, Sr., and Jr., of the Abyssinian Baptist Church (New York), Martin Luther King, Sr., of Ebenezer Baptist Church (Atlanta), William Holmes Borders of the Wheat Street Baptist Church (Atlanta), and Vernon Johns of the Dexter Avenue Baptist Church (Montgomery). Reverdy C. Ransom, an AME minister, was a "pioneer black social gospeler." Other significant voices included Benjamin E. Mays, president of Morehouse College, and Howard Thurman, dean of Rankin Chapel and professor of theology at Howard University. All spoke out against segregation and racism in the white churches and the society, insisting that the integration of blacks and whites into one community was the demand of the Christian faith. In his book *Marching Blacks*, Adam Powell, Jr., accused white churches of turning Christianity into "churchianity," thereby distorting its essential message of "equality" and "brotherhood." "No one can say that Christianity has failed," he said. "It has never been tried."[8]

How can whites claim to be Christians and still hold blacks as slaves or segregate them in their churches and the society? That has been the great paradox for black Christians. Since whites attended their churches regularly, with an air of reverence for God, and studied the Bible conscientiously, blacks expected them to see the truth of the gospel and thereby accept them into their churches and the society as brothers and sisters. Many black Christians believed that it was only a matter of a little time before Jesus would reveal the gospel truth to whites and slavery and segregation would come tumbling down like the walls of Jericho. That was the basis of the optimism among black Christians.

Too much confidence in what God is going to do often creates an otherworldly perspective which encourages passivity in the face of injustice and suffering. That happened to the great majority of blacks from the time of the Civil War to the coming of Martin Luther King, Jr. The organized fight for justice was transferred from the churches to secular groups, commonly known as civil rights organizations, especially the NAACP, the National Urban League, and CORE. Each came into existence for the sole purpose of achieving full citizenship rights for African-Americans in every aspect of American society. They often have used different tactics and have worked in different areas, but the goal has been the same—the integration of blacks into the mainstream of American society so that color will no longer be a determining factor for success or failure in any human endeavor.

Founded by prominent whites and blacks in 1909, the NAACP was the first and has been the most influential civil rights organization. Branded as radical before the 1960s, it has been a strong advocate of integration, using the courts as the primary arena in which to protest segregation. The NAACP is best known for its successful argument before the United States Supreme Court against the doctrine of "separate but equal" schools for blacks and whites, claiming that such schools are inherently unequal and therefore unconstitutional. The 17 May 1954 school desegregation decision has often been called the beginning of the black freedom movement of the 1950s and 1960s.

One year after the founding of the NAACP, the National Urban League was organized. Less aggressive than the NAACP, the Urban League was founded "for the specific purpose of easing the transition of the Southern rural Negro into an urban way of life. It stated clearly that its role was to help these people, who were essentially rural agrarian serf-peasants, adjust to Northern city life." Using the techniques of persuasion and conciliation, the Urban League appealed to the "enlightened self-interest" of white business leaders "to ease the movement of Negroes into middle class status."[9]

A generation later, in 1942, the Congress of Racial Equality was founded in Chicago. The smallest and most radical of the three groups, CORE is best known for introducing the method of nonviolent direct action, staging sit-ins in restaurants and freedom rides on buses. This new dimension of the black struggle for equality had a profound effect on the civil rights movement in the 1950s and 1960s and particularly on Martin King.

Unlike the black churches, which had few white members and no white leaders, the civil rights organizations included whites in every level of their operations. For example, a white person has often served as the president of the NAACP, and each of the three organizations has had a significant number of whites serve on its board of directors. They claimed that the implementation of integration must apply to every aspect of the society, including their own organizations. The inclusion of whites also limited their independence and made them vulnerable to the nationalist critique that no black revolution can be successful as long as its leadership is dependent upon white support.

Black Nationalism Before Malcolm X

The roots of black nationalism go back to the seventeenth-century slave conspiracies, when Africans, longing for their homeland, banded together in a common struggle against slavery, because they knew that they were not created for servitude. In the absence of historical data, it is not possible to describe the precise ideology behind the early slave revolts. What we know for sure is that the Africans deeply abhorred slavery and were willing to take great risks to gain their freedom.

This nationalist spirit was given high visibility in the slave revolts led by Gabriel Prosser, Denmark Vesey, and Nat Turner during the first third of the nineteenth century. But it was also found in the rise of mutual-aid societies, in the birth and growth of black-led churches and conventions, and in black-led emigration schemes. Unity as a people, pride in African heritage, the creation of autonomous institutions, and the search for a territory to build a nation were the central ingredients which shaped the early development of the nationalist consciousness.

There have been many articulate voices and important movements of black nationalism throughout African-American history. Among them were David Walker and Martin Delany during the antebellum period and Henry McNeal Turner, Marcus Garvey, Noble Drew Ali, and Elijah Muhammad during the late nineteenth and early twentieth centuries.

The central claim of all black nationalists, past and present, is that black people are primarily Africans and not Americans. Unlike integrationists, nationalists do not define their significance and purpose as a people by appealing to the Declaration of Independence, the Constitution, Lincoln's Emancipation Proclamation, or even the white man's religion of Christianity. On the contrary, nationalists define their identity by their resistance to America and their determination to create a society based on their own African history and culture. The posture of rejecting America and accepting Africa is sometimes symbolized with such words as "African," "black," and "blackness." For example, Martin Delany, often called the father of black nationalism, boasted that there lived "none blacker" than himself. While Douglass, in typical integrationist style, said, "I thank God for making me a man simply," he reported that "Delany always thanks Him for making him a black man."[10]

The issue for nationalists was not only human slavery or oppression. It was also the oppression of *black* people by *white* people. Nothing aroused the fury of nationalists more than the racial factor in human exploitation. Their identity as black touched the very core of their being and affected their thoughts and feelings regarding everything, especially their relations with white people. Nationalists, unlike integrationists, could not separate their resentment of servitude from the racial identity of the people responsible for it. "White Americans [are] our *natural enemies*," wrote David Walker in his *Appeal* in 1829. "By treating us so cruel," we "see them acting more like devils than accountable men." According to Walker, "whites have always been an unjust, jealous, unmerciful, avaricious and blood-thirsty set of beings, always seeking after power and authority."[11]

Black nationalism was defined by a loss of hope in America. Its advocates did not believe that white people could ever imagine humanity in a way that would place black people on a par with them. "I am not in favor of caste, nor a separation of the brotherhood of mankind, and would as willingly live among white men as black, if I had an *equal possession and enjoyment* of privileges," Delany wrote in 1852 to the white abolitionist William Lloyd Garrison; he went on: "but [I] shall never be reconciled to live among them, subservient to their will—existing by mere *sufferance*, as we, the colored people, do, in this country. . . . I have no hopes in this country—no confidence in the American people."[12]

This difference in emotional orientation between nationalists and integrationists led to disagreement in their definition of freedom and their strategies for achieving it. For nationalists, freedom was not black people pleading for integration into white society; rather it was separation from white people so that blacks could govern themselves. For many nationalists, separation meant emigration from the United States to some place in Africa or Latin America. "Every people should be the originators of their own designs, the projector of their own schemes, and creators of the events that lead to their destiny—the consummation of their own desires," Delany wrote in his best-known work, *The Condition, Elevation, Emigration, and Destiny of the Colored People of the United States* (1852). "No people can be free who themselves do not constitute an essential part of the *ruling element* of the country in which they live," said Delany. "The liberty of no man is secure, who controls not his political destiny. . . . To suppose otherwise is that delusion which at once induces its victim, through a period of long suffering, patiently to submit to every species of wrong; trusting against probability, and hoping against all reasonable grounds of expectation, for the granting of privileges and enjoyment of rights, that will never be attained."[13]

The ebb and flow of black nationalism, during the nineteenth century and thereafter, was influenced by the decline and rise of black expectations of equality in the United States. When blacks felt that the achievement of equality was impossible, the nationalist sentiment among them always increased. Such was the case during the 1840s and 1850s, largely due to the Fugitive Slave Act (1850) and the Dred Scott decision (1857).

During the Civil War and the Reconstruction that followed it, black hopes soared and even Delany stopped talking about the emigration of blacks and began to participate in the political process in South Carolina, running for the office of lieutenant-governor.

Black expectations of achieving full citizenship rights, however, were short-lived. The infamous Hayes Compromise of 1877 led to the withdrawal of federal troops from the South, thereby allowing former white slaveholders to deal with their former slaves in any manner they chose. The destructive consequences for blacks were severe politically, economically, and psychologically. Accommodationism emerged as the dominant black philosophy, and Booker T. Washington became its most prominent advocate. Washington replaced Frederick Douglass as the chief spokesperson for blacks, and ministers were his most ardent supporters.

During the period of the "nadir" and the "long dark night" of black people's struggle for justice in America, Henry McNeal Turner, a bishop in the AME Church, and Marcus Garvey of the Universal Negro Improvement Association (UNIA) articulated nationalist perspectives that were more directly linked with the subsequent philosophy of Malcolm X. Like Malcolm's, their perspectives on America were derived from the bottom of the black experience. They spoke a language that was full of racial pride and denunciation of white America. It was intended to elevate the cultural and psychological well-being of downtrodden blacks burdened with low self-esteem in a society dominated by the violence of white hate groups and the sophisticated racism of the Social Darwinists.

A native of South Carolina, Turner grew up on the cotton fields with slaves and learned to read by his own efforts. He was a proud and fearless man, and his nationalism was deepened as he observed the continued exploitation of blacks by whites, North and South, during and following

Reconstruction. When the Supreme Court ruled in 1893 that the Civil Rights Act of 1875 was unconstitutional, Turner felt that that "barbarous decision" dissolved the allegiance of black people to the United States. "If the decision is correct," he wrote, "the United States Constitution is a dirty rag, a cheat, a libel, and ought to be spit upon by every negro in the land."[14]

The betrayal of Reconstruction, the "enactment of cruel and revolting laws," lynching and other atrocities, reenslavement through peonage, and political disfranchisement encouraged Turner to conclude that blacks would never achieve equality in the United States. He became an ardent advocate of emigration to Africa. "There is no more doubt in my mind," Turner said, "that we have ultimately to return to Africa than there is of the existence of God."[15]

Although Turner was elected a bishop in the AME Church, he was not the typical holder of that office. The more whites demeaned blackness as a mark of inferiority, the more Turner glorified it. At a time when black and white Christians identified God with European images and the AME Church leaders were debating whether to replace the word "African" in their name with "American," Turner shocked everyone with his declaration that "God is a Negro."[16]

Although Turner addressed his message to the sociopolitical problems of the black masses in the rural South, he did not create an organization to implement his African dream. That distinction fell to Marcus Garvey.

On 23 March 1916, one year after Turner's death, Marcus Garvey came to the United States from his native Jamaica. While Turner's base was the rural South, Garvey worked in the urban North, mainly in Harlem. While the geography was different, the people were essentially the same, being mostly immigrants from the South in search of the American dream of economic security, social advancement, and political justice. Instead they entered a nightmare of racism and poverty which they thought they had left behind in the South.

Garvey understood the pain of color discrimination because he experienced it personally and observed it in the lives of other blacks in Jamaica and also during his travels in Central America, Europe, and the United States. It seemed that everywhere he traveled blacks were being dominated by others. "Where is the black man's Government?" he asked. "Where is his King and his kingdom? Where is his President, his country, and his ambassador, his army, his navy, his men of big affairs?" Unable to find them, Garvey, with the self-assurance of a proud black man, then declared: "I will help to make them."[17]

Garvey knew that without racial pride no people could make leaders and build a nation that would command the respect of the world. This was particularly true of blacks who had been enslaved and segregated for three hundred years. In a world where blackness was a badge of degradation and shame, Garvey transformed it into a symbol of honor and distinction. "To be a Negro is no disgrace, but an honor, and we of the Universal Negro Improvement Association do not want to become white."[18] He made blacks feel that they were somebody and that they could do great things as a people. "Up, you mighty race," Garvey proclaimed, "you can accomplish what you will," and black people believed him.

As whites ruled Europe and America, Garvey was certain blacks should and would rule Africa. To implement his African dream, he organized the UNIA, first in Kingston, Jamaica, and later in New York. "Africa for the Africans" was the heart of his message. In 1920 Garvey called the first International Convention of Negro Peoples of the World, and 25,000 delegates from twenty-five countries met in New York City. A redeemed Africa, governed by a united black race proud of its history, was the theme which dominated Garvey's speeches. "Wake up Ethiopia! Wake up Africa!" he proclaimed. "Let us work towards the one glorious end of a free, redeemed and mighty nation. Let Africa be a bright star among the constellation of nations." "A race without authority and power is a race without respect."[19]

No one exceeded Garvey in his criticisms of the philosophy of integration, as represented by the members of the NAACP and other middle-class black leaders and intellectuals. He believed that any black organization that depended upon white philanthropy was detrimental to the cause of Africa's redemption and the uplifting of the black race. "No man will do as much for you as you will do for yourself."[20] By depending on whites, blacks were saying that they could not do it alone, thereby creating a sense of inferiority in themselves.

According to Garvey, integration is a self-defeating philosophy that is promoted by pseudo-black intellectuals and leaders. He accused integrationists of wanting to be white and completely ignoring the socioeconomic well-being of poor blacks at the bottom. W.E.B. Du Bois, then the editor of the NAACP's *Crisis* magazine, was one of Garvey's favorite targets of criticism. Garvey urged his followers that "we must never, even under the severest pressure, hate or dislike ourselves."[21] His criticism of the NAACP and Du Bois was very similar to Malcolm X's attack upon the same organization and its executive director, Roy Wilkins, during the 1960s. Black nationalists are defined by race confidence and solidarity, and they are often intemperate in their criticisms of black integrationists, for they believe integrationists compromise the self-respect and dignity of the race by wanting to mingle and marry white people—the enemy.

In 1920, Garvey's UNIA claimed a membership of four million and a year later six million, with nine hundred branches. While most scholars insist that the numbers were inflated, no one denies that Garvey organized the largest and most successful mass movement of blacks in the history of the United States. Garvey did what all black nationalists after him have merely dreamed of doing, and that is why they continue to study his life and message for direction and inspiration.

Concerned about Garvey's popularity, the government, with the help of black integrationist leaders, convicted him of mail fraud. Upon his imprisonment and deportation, black nationalism entered a period of decline. But the problems of oppression and identity which gave rise to it did not disappear.

In addition to Marcus Garvey's UNIA, two movements were important in defining the nationalism that influenced Malcolm X: the Moorish Science Temple founded by Noble Drew Ali in Newark, New Jersey, and the Nation of Islam—the "Black Muslims"—founded in Detroit in 1930 by the mysterious Wallace D. Fard and later headed by his disciple, Elijah Poole, a former Baptist minister from Sandersville, Georgia. Elijah Poole as Elijah Muhammad achieved his authority in the Black Muslim religion because he convinced Black Muslim believers, including Malcolm, that Allah came to North America "in the person of Wallace D. Fard," taught him for three and a half years, and then chose him as his Messenger.

Both movements rejected Christianity and white people and affirmed the religion of Islam and an African-Asian identity. Both movements were primarily religious, having less political emphasis than Garvey's UNIA. Although the Moorish Science Temple is still in existence, it was important mainly as a forerunner of the Nation of Islam. The Nation of Islam received many members from the Moorish Science Temple following the assassination of Noble Drew Ali.

The Nation of Islam was the most important influence on the life and thought of Malcolm X. Its importance for Malcolm was similar to the role of the black church in the life of Martin King. While Garvey influenced Malcolm's political consciousness, Elijah Muhammad defined his religious commitment. Elijah Muhammad was the sole and absolute authority in defining the doctrine and practice of the Nation of Islam. While affirming solidarity with worldwide Islam, he proclaimed distinctive doctrines. The most important and controversial one was his contention that whites were by nature evil. They were snakes who were incapable of doing right, devils who would soon be destroyed by God's righteous judgment. White people, therefore, were identified as the sole cause of black oppression.

In Black Muslim theology the almighty black God is the source of all good and power. To explain the origin of the evil of black oppression, Muhammad rejected the Christian recourse to divine mystery or God's permissive will, instead setting forth his own distinctive explanation, which focused on the myth of Yacob. Out of the weak individuals of the black race, Yacob, a renegade black scientist, created the white race, thereby causing all of the evil which has flowed from their hands: "The human beast—the serpent, the dragon, the devil, and Satan—all mean one and the same: the people or race known as the white or Caucasian race, sometimes called the European race. Since by nature they were created liars and murderers, they are the enemies of truth and righteousness, and the enemies of those who seek the truth."[22] This myth was important for Malcolm's view that the whites are evil by nature. The myth and its doctrinal development came exclusively from Elijah Muhammad.

The logical extension of this doctrine is that since black people are by nature good and divine, they must be separated from whites so they can avoid the latter's hour of total destruction. The solution to the problem of black oppression in America, therefore, is territorial separation, either by whites financing black people's return to Africa or by providing separate states in America.

Although the Nation of Islam and other nationalist movements (especially Garvey's) were the dominant influence in shaping Malcolm's life and thought, he was also indebted to the integrationist protest tradition. The same kind of cross current of nationalist and integrationist influences bore upon the career of Martin King, though he was indebted far less to the nationalist tradition. No sharp distinction can be drawn between the traditions, because representatives of both were fighting the same problems—the power of "white over black" and its psychological impact upon the self-esteem of its victims. Nationalists and integrationists were aware of the truth of each other's viewpoint, even though they did not always acknowledge it. Integrationists realized the danger of complete assimilation into American society. Like nationalists, they did not want to destroy the cultural and spiritual identity of blacks. That was perhaps the major reason why black churches and fraternal and sororal organizations remained separate from whites. Despite their repeated claim about 11:00 A.M. on Sunday morning being the most segregated hour of the week, black ministers in black denominations made no real efforts to integrate their churches. They knew that if they did, their power as blacks would have been greatly curtailed and their own cultural and spiritual identity destroyed. The advocates of integration, therefore, focused their energies primarily on the political and economic life of America. They believed that justice was possible if whites treated blacks as equals under the law.

Likewise, black nationalists realized the danger of complete isolation from the political and economic life of America. That was perhaps the major reason for the frequent shifts in their philosophy. Black nationalism was not primarily a Western, "rational" philosophy, but rather a black philosophy in search of its African roots. It was a cry for self-esteem, for the right to be recognized and accepted as human beings. Its advocates knew that blacks could not survive politically or economically in complete separation from others, especially whites in the United States. Neither could any other people (including whites) survive in isolation from the rest of the world. Everyone was interdependent. The black masses, therefore, did not follow nationalists because of their call for separation from America. Rather it was because of the nationalists' ability to speak to their "gut level" experience, that is, to express what it *felt* like to be black in white America.

Integrationists and nationalists complemented each other. Both philosophies were needed if America was going to come to terms with the truth of the black experience. Either philosophy alone was a half-truth and thus a distortion of the black reality in America. Integrationists were *practical*. They advocated what they thought could be achieved at a given time. They knew that justice demanded more. But why demand it if you can't get it? Why demand it if the demand itself blocks the achievement of other desirable and achievable goals? In their struggle for justice, they were careful not to arouse the genocidal instincts inherent in racism. Thus they chose goals and methods which many whites accepted as reasonable and just. The strengths and weaknesses of the integrationist view are reflected in the life and ministry of Martin King.

Nationalists were *desperate*. They spoke for that segment of the African-American community which was hurting the most. Thus, they often did not consider carefully the consequences of their words and actions. The suffering of the black poor was so great that practical or rational philosophies did not arouse their allegiance. They needed a philosophy that could speak to their existence as black people, living in a white society that did not recognize their humanity. They needed a philosophy that empowered them to "respect black" by being prepared to die for it. Overwhelmed by misery, the black poor cried out for relief, for a word or an act that would lift them to another realm of existence where they would be treated as human beings. In place of an American dream, nationalists gave the black poor an African dream. The strengths and the weaknesses of this perspective were reflected in the life and ministry of Malcolm X.

Martin King and Malcolm X were shaped by what Vincent Harding has called the "Great Tradition of Black Protest,"[23] a tradition that comprised many variations of nationalism and integrationism. Their perspectives on America were influenced by both, even though they placed primary emphasis on only one of them. Both integrationism and nationalism readied Martin and Malcolm for leadership in the black freedom movement of the 1950s and 1960s—with Martin proclaiming an American dream from the steps of the Lincoln Memorial and Malcolm reminding him of an American nightmare in the streets of Harlem.

Notes

1. W.E.B. Du Bois, *The Souls of Black Folk* (1903; reprint, New York: Fawcett Premier Book, 1968), pp. 16, 17; idem, "The Conservation of Races" (1897), in Julius Lester, ed., *The Seventh Son: The Thought and Writings of W.E.B. Du Bois* (New York: Vintage Book, 1971), vol. 1, p. 182.

2. Philip S. Foner, ed., *Frederick Douglass: Selections from His Writings* (New York: International Publishers, 1964), p. 57.

3. Ibid., pp. 52–53.

4. Cited in Lerone Bennett, Jr., *Pioneers in Protest* (Chicago: Johnson Publishing Co., 1968), pp. 208–9.

5. Foner, ed., *Frederick Douglass*, p. 44.

6. Cited in Peter J. Paris, *The Social Teaching of the Black Churches* (Philadelphia: Fortress Press, 1985), p. 25 n. 26.

7. Henry Highland Garnet, *An Address to the Slaves of the United States of America* (1843), reprinted with David Walker's *Appeal* (1829), in *Walker's Appeal & Garnet's Address to the Slaves of the United States of America* (New York: Arno Press/New York Times, 1969), p. 93.

8. Adam Clayton Powell, Jr., *Marching Blacks*, rev. ed. (New York: Dial Press, 1973), p. 194.

9. Kenneth B. Clark, "The Civil Rights Movement: Momentum and Organization," *Daedalus*, 95 (Winter 1966), p. 245.

10. Cited in Theodore Draper, *The Rediscovery of Black Nationalism* (New York: Viking Press, 1970), p. 22; for an interpretation of the origin of black nationalism, see August Meier, "The Emergence of Negro Nationalism," Parts I and II, *Midwest Journal*, vol. 45, Winter 1951 and Summer 1953, pp. 96–104 and 95–111.

11. *Walker's Appeal and Garnet's Address*, pp. 71, 73, 27–28; see also Sterling Stuckey, *The Ideological Origins of Black Nationalism* (Boston: Beacon Press, 1972), pp. 97, 99, 55–56.

12. Carter G. Woodson, ed., *The Mind of the Negro as Reflected in Letters Written during the Crisis, 1800–1860* (1926; reprint, New York: Russell & Russell, 1969), p. 293.

13. Martin Robison Delany, *The Condition, Elevation, Emigration, and Destiny of the Colored People of the United States* (1852; reprint, New York: Arno Press/New York Times, 1969), p. 209; see also John H. Bracey, Jr., August Meier, and Elliott Rudwick, eds., *Black Nationalism in America* (Indianapolis: Bobbs-Merrill Co., 1970), p. 89.

14. Henry McNeal Turner, "The Barbarous Decision of the Supreme Court" (1883), in Edwin S. Redkey, ed., *Respect Black: The Writings and Speeches of Henry McNeal Turner* (New York: Arno Press/New York Times, 1971), p. 63.

15. Ibid., p. 165; Edwin S. Redkey, *Black Exodus: Black Nationalist and Back-to-Africa Movements, 1890–1910* (New Haven: Yale University Press, 1969), p. 29.

16. Henry McNeal Turner, "God Is a Negro" (1898), in Redkey, ed., *Respect Black*, pp. 176–77.

17. Amy Jacques Garvey, ed., *Philosophy and Opinions of Marcus Garvey* (New York: Arno Press/New York Times, 1969), vol. 2, p. 126.

18. Ibid., pp. 325–26.

19. Ibid., vol. 1, pp. 5, 2.

20. Cited in E. David Cronon, *Black Moses: The Story of Marcus Garvey and the Negro Improvement Association* (Madison: University of Wisconsin Press, 1955), p. 173.

21. Garvey, ed., *Philosophy and Opinions*, vol. 2, p. 326.

22. Cited in Louis E. Lomax, *When the Word Is Given . . .* (New York: Signet Book, 1964), p. 56. The classic study on the Nation of Islam is C. Eric Lincoln, *The Black Muslims in America* (Boston: Beacon Press, 1961, Rev. ed., 1973). See also E. U. Essien-Udom, *Black Nationalism: The Search for an Identity in America* (Chicago: University of Chicago Press, 1962); James Baldwin, *The Fire Next Time* (New York: Dell, 1962). An early significant study is Erdmann Doane Beynon, "The Voodoo Cult Among Negro Migrants in Detroit," *American Journal of Sociology*, May 1938, pp. 894–907. See also Monroe Berger, "The Black Muslims," *Horizon*, Winter, 1964, pp. 48–65. The best source for the teaching of Elijah Muhammad is his *The Supreme Wisdom: The Solution to the So-Called Negroes' Problem* (Chicago: University of Islam, 1957); also his *Message to the Blackman* (Chicago: Muhammad's Temple No. 2).

23. Vincent Harding, *There Is a River: The Black Struggle for Freedom in America* (New York: Harcourt Brace Jovanovich, 1981), p. 83.

Part 7

Black Theology and Its Critics

Chapter 32

A Sense of Urgency

Albert B. Cleage Jr.

"Behold, the hour is at hand. . . ." (Matthew 26:45)

This morning's paper has an article listing all the Black Nationalist groups in the city, saying that for all or most of them the Shrine of the Black Madonna is their spiritual home.

There are a lot of different attitudes, different ideas, and different programs, it says, but all of them feel at home here. I think that is one of the reasons why, in Detroit, we move faster and farther and know where we're going in a more complete sense, because we do have this unity. We can come together here, knowing we're all for the Nation, and if we disagree on details, we still are brothers and we love one another.

As time passes, as the revolution in which we are all engaged develops, we have more and more a sense of tremendous urgency about the whole thing. If we look back to last year, there is in each of us a sense of urgency which we did not have then. We are much more impatient. We are much more given to being irritated at the man, at his efforts to sidetrack us and to talk us away from our objectives. We have a sense of urgency. We do want freedom, and we want it now.

This sense of urgency permeates everything that we do. We may not realize it, but it permeates every group that we're participating in. On the job you feel different than you used to feel. You are conscious of things that you never used to feel. You didn't used to mind so much when the man called you "boy." Now, if he calls you "boy," he's going to have to fight. He comes up just trying to be friendly, and he's made five mistakes before he's gotten through the first two sentences. And you don't say,

765

"Well, that's just the way white folks talk." You say, "That's the way white folks got to *stop* talking."

That's our tremendous sense of urgency. The way you feel is the way millions of black people are feeling from coast to coast. That's why things bubble up every once in a while. Then everybody runs around trying to explain why it happened. We're just on the verge all the time. It doesn't take anything special because we don't like it any time of day or night. So anything can cause us to do something because we don't like it, never did like it, and are never going to like it. We have a sense of urgency. We're irritated; we're aching to do something.

Even the policemen realize it. They know that when they start something now they're going to have to shoot somebody. They don't just stop you and say, "Come here, nigger, where are you going?" and think nothing's going to happen. Some of them still do it, but they know it's a different kind of situation.

It is this terrible sense of urgency that grips us all, gives a different direction to everything we do, the things we say, to our organizations, to our working together, to our programs. A terrible sense of urgency.

For some this sense of urgency is a sense of hope. There are black people who believe that this whole thing is going to be settled in just a little while. Not too many, but there are some. And they work with this terrible sense of urgency thinking that they're going to do what has to be done and get it over with. "Somehow, we're going to build a new world, and the white man's going to change." There is urgency and hope there.

For others there is the urgency of despair. They have a profound conviction that nothing really can be done, that we have come to the end of a long journey, and there is no hope at all.

So there is urgency and despair on the one hand and urgency and hope upon the other.

So even in this great moment of rebellion, of revolution, of change, we are a confused people because we have not yet decided what it is that is really important as we move forward. Most of us want to do those things that must be done. Most of us want freedom and we're willing to use any means necessary to get it. We agree on these things, but when is this new world coming? When are we to be free? When are we to have the things that belong to us? If we're to have them, then we want a timetable. If we're not to have them, then we want to get about the task of tearing up everything there is in sight.

We have tremendous decisions to make, and that is a part of our inner feeling of urgency and frustration. We're not quite sure.

I am reminded of the last days of Jesus, the Black Messiah who came to a Black Nation of people who were divided and didn't know which way to turn, just as we don't. He came to bring them together and to teach them that unity, love for each other, sacrifice, commitment and discipline were essential if they were to be free. His whole ministry was going about among a Black Nation preaching to them about the things that had to be done if they were to find freedom from oppression by a white nation, Rome. Everything he did was trying to bring a people together.

Remember it says he turned his face steadfastly toward Jerusalem. This was as his ministry reached its climax. It seemed that everything was going his way. Crowds of people gathered when he passed through villages because people wanted to hear what he was saying. He talked to them about the possibility of building a Nation. And they came out and gathered around. They climbed up on trees and buildings that they might hear him. They wanted to hear. But they were not yet ready for the sacrifice, the unity and the discipline necessary to build a Nation. They came together and screamed and cried out, "Hosannah! Hallelujah," and then they went home. The Nation had not yet been built because you don't build a Nation at a mass meeting. You may get the idea. You may get inspiration. You may get a feeling of strength from the brothers and sisters who are there. But you don't build a Nation at a mass meeting.

So Jesus, as he passed from town to town, from city to city, knew that these people who came together and shouted and screamed did not yet constitute a Nation. They were still divided; they were still individuals, each fighting for his own little prestige, for the things he wanted for himself. Listening to Jesus he might say to himself, "It's a wonderful dream, this dream of the Black Nation. But I don't want to get out on a limb and do the wrong thing and hurt myself." And he would drift away and go home.

So Jesus knew that a Nation had not come into being. And he said, "I will turn my face toward Jerusalem, because I must bring to a climax all these efforts, all these ideas, all these conflicting opinions, all of this individualism. I must find a way to dramatize what it means to build a Nation. I must make black people understand what it means to build a Nation." That is why he turned his face steadfastly toward Jerusalem.

When he came to Jerusalem, he had one simple task. He had twelve disciples who would follow him. He wanted them to understand what was happening and to be able to carry on after his crucifixion because for Jesus the crucifixion was not the end. For Jesus the Black Nation must last for a thousand years, for ten thousand years, for a million years. A man might die for the Nation, but the Nation must live.

Sometimes we forget that. You know, it takes courage to say, "I am willing to die," but you must then be able to say, "What am I willing to die for?" Jesus knew. He said, "I am willing to die. As an individual, I am willing to make this kind of a sacrifice that the Nation may live." We have to remember that today. You know all he went through. He brought the disciples together in the upper room, and they had the Last Supper. But we could just as easily call it the "First Supper" because it wasn't the end, it was the beginning. He brought them together, knowing that the end was at hand and that even there among their number were those who would betray him.

Always, in any movement, when any people undertake to build a Nation, there are betrayers in the midst of the closely knit group that stands at the heart and center. Jesus knew it, and he turned to the twelve and said, "You've walked with me, talked with me. You've eaten with me. I've given you everything I've got. And yet one of you will betray me." And they said, "Who is it; is it I, Lord?" And he looked at them, and he knew, "It's all of you. In one way or another, you will all betray me." He knew it, but he didn't hate them. They would betray him out of their human weakness.

He said, "Behold the hour is at hand." The disciples could easily have said, "Our leader is about to be destroyed. We should all die with him. We must make this the greatest destruction of people in the history of the world." Wouldn't that have been ridiculous? Then what would his death have meant? Jesus said, "The hour is at hand for *my* sacrifice." And he talked to the disciples in the Upper Room that they might understand and carry on the work of building the Nation. He talked to them at great length. He had a sense of the urgency of the moment. He knew how upset they were that things were not going as they wanted them to go, how they wanted to take power, how they wanted to strike out against Rome. He knew all of their feelings. But he talked to them. He tried to get them to understand the meaning of the simple little things. He broke the bread and said, "This is my body which is broken for you." He poured the wine and said, "This is my blood, which is shed for you." The willingness of the individual to sacrifice himself for the Nation.

And then he washed their feet. You may have laughed at foot-washing Baptists, but there is as much validity in washing the feet as there is in drinking the wine and eating the bread. Jesus did it. He washed their feet to symbolize that if you want to build a Nation, you've got to be willing to serve. He said, "I came forth to serve." Leadership is a kind of service. And you have to be humble to get down on your knees and wash your brother's feet. They said, "Oh, no, Lord. Don't do that; you're our leader."

And he said, "If I can't wash your feet, get up and go because you don't belong to me." He was trying to give them a last message about what it means to build a Nation: a group of people so bound together in love that they are willing to accept menial, subservient positions because in this way they serve the Nation. A people so bound together in love that they are willing to die that the Nation may not die.

He said, "The hour is at hand." And he was right. They betrayed him. Judas did it for money. We see that every day. Thousands of such betrayers are in our own city, paid by Congressional committees, paid by other agencies, paid by one force or another to destroy us. Black brothers betraying for thirty pieces of silver.

Then he asked Peter, James and John, "Come out and pray with me a while; I know that the end is at hand." They went out, and he was wrestling with himself to keep his sense of conviction, his willingness to die that the Nation might live. He prayed, and when he looked around they had gone to sleep. Betrayers just out of natural, human weakness. They couldn't stay awake, they were tired. You know how often you betray the Nation just because you're tired. Not because you're evil or vicious, not because the man got to you. You're just tired. You just don't have the energy, that's all. That's all Jesus was telling them, "I know how it is. You're tired." He didn't say they weren't tired. He was tired too. Try a little harder, then. If he's willing to die, you can at least try a little harder to stay awake.

Then a little later on, you remember Peter's denial. After Jesus had been arrested, Peter kind of followed along, and when the guards said, "I believe he's with him," Peter said, "I don't know him; never *saw* him." The same Peter who had said, "I'll die before I'll betray you, Lord. Maybe the rest of them, but not me!" And Jesus looked at him with compassion and said, "Before the cock crows, you will betray me three times." Just a human betrayal. What was Peter afraid of? If you'd come up to fight him, he would have fought. But they weren't fighting. It was just the situation. Maybe they would laugh at him, talk about him, "Oh, you're one of his followers!" You know how they do when you go some place and they ask, "What church do you belong to?" And you try to look the other way. They say, "You belong to Rev. Cleage's church?" You know what I'm talking about—that kind of betrayal. That is betrayal because if you stand for something, you stand for it any time, any place, with anybody. When they say, "Do you belong to Rev. Cleage's church," say, "No, I belong to *my* church—the Nation. Rev. Cleage just happens to belong to it, too."

We have a task with our sense of urgency. We have to get a long view. Now Rap Brown is doing a tremendous thing. I think we have to keep him alive just as long as we can. He is doing the same kind of thing Jesus did. He is making himself a symbol, and the man is going to have to destroy him. There's no question about it. We've got to give him all the support and help and protection we can. Not because we all have to believe that guerilla warfare in the street is the way, but because he keeps us conscious of one thing: the seriousness of the rebellion in which we are now engaged. We can easily forget it if he doesn't keep screaming. We can easily act like this rebellion is some kind of little plaything. But he keeps reminding us, "This is a fight for survival."

So God help H. Rap Brown! We need him. I don't care what he does to the white folks, whether they're scared, whether they like it or don't like it. *We* need him because he keeps us conscious of the seriousness of the rebellion that we're in. But we don't need *just* H. Rap Brown. The revolution is not *just* getting ready for guerilla warfare. This whole thing that we are engaged in, building a Nation, is not just preparing to all die in the streets. We have to be ready to die in the street if that becomes necessary. But until it does become necessary, there's a whole lot else that we've got to be doing.

There is a whole lot of foolish talk going on among Black Nationalists these days. So many college students come to me and say, "They're telling me that I ought to drop out of college, that college is the man's bag, that I don't need education. I'm losing touch with the people." I ask, "Who's been telling you this?" And they say, "Well, the fellas out there." I say, "Where are they, in some place drinking some beer? What are *they* doing?" They say, "Well, they're staying in touch with the masses." I say, "That's good. You let them stay in touch with the masses, and you stay in school and learn something." Because we need people who are ready to *do* something. We're getting ready right now to organize the community, but you know what we black people have to do? We have to call in Saul Alinsky for $100,000 to tell us how to organize. We need some boys in school learning something. We need people learning everything because we're not living for today. We're not revolting for today. We're not revolting just so we can be free, but so that our children, and our great-grand-children can be free. And that's not done in a day.

If we end up fighting in the streets, there has to be a remnant that remains because we're fighting for a Nation. We've got to preserve some part of the Black Nation. We have to see that a remnant remains because the Nation must go on. We are not fighting just for the happiness and satisfaction of struggle. I know you've held it all in for a long time. You've taken a whole lot of abuse. You can remember when the first little white kid called you "nigger," and you're still mad about it. But that does *not* mean that you can't use some kind of common sense when you fight. We're *not* going to all die in the street; we must have some who are left. And we've got to start preparing them.

We're building a Nation. And when you come forward here to join this church, you're coming into a Nation. And I don't think only about the next two or three years. We had a meeting the other night, and Brother Dowdell warned, "You know, Rev. Cleage can't live forever." I'm very conscious of that. We must start getting young men ready now. We are not like some other church that can pick up any rabble rouser and call him to come here, because he wouldn't know what to rabble rouse about. We have to train our own young men. We have to take some young Black Nationalists and militants and send them to school to learn how to pastor this church when I get too old to stand up here. We have to train people. That's a part of being a Nation: thinking about tomorrow and the day after tomorrow. We must plan for a thousand years.

We start out buying property right here in this neighborhood where we are. The Black Star Co-op is talking about buying a building in the next block to open a supermarket. It may be a little one to start, but a pretty good little one, though. And we'll buy other things as we go. We'll buy and we'll never sell. And in five hundred years, you can't come anywhere west of Woodward Avenue but we'll own it! That's a Nation. A Nation doesn't exist for today. The white man is building for a thousand years from now and we've been talking about satisfaction for today. We need businessmen. We need people who know what they're doing in all areas. We need to be putting something together that's going to last. We need to be bringing people together who are going to stay, who are not going to be split up by a little difference of opinion. We're building a Nation.

When you begin to think that every little child sitting here is an heir to what we're doing today, your perspective becomes different. You know you're going to do what's necessary to preserve him. He has to be preserved. You have to get all the freedom you can for him. You know, any fifty of us could be sacrificed today if by dying we could advance the Nation. But we have to keep constantly in mind that the *Nation* is the important thing. The little children yet unborn; the little children sitting here who will have children. We are concerned about *their* children. That's building a Nation. That's a perspective. That's why men are willing to die. No one would die willingly if his death was meaningless. He'd turn back, find a way out. But when you're building a Nation, your whole conception is different. And that's what we're trying to do.

We are going to have a lot of differences of opinion. It is not going to be easy. And we're growing so fast. We just don't know each other with so many people coming in so fast. But we're going to get acquainted if some Sunday morning we have to lock the door till we all get to know one another. You can't work in the Nation if you don't know each other. We've got to know whose child is running around so that we can talk to him. Our young people have to feel that this is their Nation because we're building for them.

The hour is at hand. And the hour is the hour of building a Black Nation. Some of us, if need be, must die. Anytime we forget that we must be willing to die, the Nation is through. Because anybody can oppress us if we're afraid to die. We have to have a basic commitment to build a Black Nation. And this we will build on the teachings of Jesus Christ, the Black Messiah.

That's why the Black Madonna is so important to us. The Black Madonna is a black woman standing there with a little black child in her arms. And in every generation, that's what we are fighting for—that little black child. We don't care whose child it is. He's *our* child, and that's what we're fighting for. Because he has to carry on the Nation, because you are not going to be here forever either! And we have to leave this nation in the hands of people who understand it and who are willing to die for it as we are willing to die for it. That little black baby is the whole thing we're fighting for, and we need so many things to make that fight meaningful in today's world.

We need to understand ways of fighting. We don't fully understand that yet. I was talking about this to one of our members, and she suggested the idea in the Old Testament of a wheel within a wheel. The Nation is the big wheel, and inside there has to be a whole lot of little wheels always turning. Wherever you are, you've got to be a Black Caucus. Do you understand that? If you're in a school and there are only four black teachers there, you four have got to get together. If the principal is no good, then you have to dedicate yourselves as a Black Caucus to getting rid of that principal. What I mean by no good is no good as far as black children are concerned. Our black lawyers have to become a Black Caucus to clean out Recorder's Court. They don't yet understand what their function is. It's not enough for them to earn a living. They have to become a Black Caucus. All the black lawyers have to stand together. They have to point out every bit of discrimination. They know what's happening in Recorder's Court, they know what the judges are doing. They have to put pressure on them so that they know what they have to do.

That's a wheel within a wheel. If you're in a factory, you have to get your brothers together in your department. When they have you training a white person to take your position and to promote over you, you have to stop it. But it takes a caucus to do that. You can't do it by yourself. We have to have a caucus everywhere. When they see three black folks anywhere, they have to know that there is a Black Caucus.

Some of you send your children away to college. You sweat, you want them to go to a good college, you want them to learn something. Well, the best way to make them learn something is to tell them when they go, "Find the Black Power Caucus on your campus and get in it right away. Make your college meaningful in the black revolution." Then they are not getting away from the struggle when they go to college. They are a part of it because they're bringing the college into the mainstream of our black revolution. Everywhere we are we have to be a Black Caucus. If you belong to some little inane social club, and they sit around and do nothing, you've got to be a Black Caucus in that club. Change it or tear it up!

The unemployed out in the street, each one feels by himself—put upon, miserable. We have to organize a caucus of unemployed to strike at the system that's oppressing them and keeping them down, that keeps them out in the street. You read the miserable statistics in the papers where the man has to admit that our unemployment is terrible. They need organization to be a Black Caucus of unemployed. We've got to do it. We need a Black Caucus of mothers receiving Aid to Dependent Children, of welfare people. All wheels within a wheel. Our Nation, and groups functioning everywhere, disciplined, organized, together because we love one another.

The church is the soul of the Nation. It has to be. All these little wheels are whirling within the Nation, all stemming from one common faith and commitment. We buy property, train leadership, build for our great-great-great-grandchildren. And our unity, our commitment, our dedication to the Black Nation are all symbolized in the sacrament of Holy Communion.

Maybe you have taken communion lightly. But the broken bread is the symbol that we are willing as individuals to sacrifice ourselves for the Nation. The wine is the symbol that we're willing to shed our blood for the Nation. So when we come together, it's as though we were around a table united, a people, a Nation. And we are saying in our participation, in the sacrament of Holy Communion, "I am a part of the Nation. I accept this sacrifice which the Black Messiah made as the symbolic sacrifice which I'm willing to make that the Nation may be built, that it may grow, that it may have power. I'm willing." This is why we come together with the sacrament of Holy Communion.

And this is what baptism is. When members come into the church, we baptize members who have not been baptized, as well as those who would like to be baptized again because they want to be baptized into the Nation. We baptize into the Nation in the Name of the Father, the Son and the Holy Spirit. This baptism is meaningful because you die to all your old Uncle Tom ways, the slave ways you used to have. And you are born again, you are resurrected in the newness of life into the Black Nation. And then you come and take the sacrament of Holy Communion. You are in the Nation. We are building it; some of us may die, but the remnant must live. And it is a wonderful thing to be a part of the struggle and know that no matter what happens anywhere in the world, this Black Nation will go on. We are committed to it. We believe in it.

Heavenly Father, we thank thee for the opportunity which is ours to come into thy house, to participate in this service of worship and this rededication of ourselves to thee and thy service. We believe that it is thy will and thy teaching that we undertake to build on earth thy kingdom. And that thy kingdom on earth is the Black Nation which we are building. We feel that we have thy support, thy strength, thy guidance in this task which we have accepted for ourselves. Be with us to give us strength when we are weak, to give us guidance when we are lost. Be with us to give us a sense of brotherhood when we feel torn apart by feelings of individualism. Bind us together. Make us brothers and sisters in this Nation. Unite us in love. This we ask in the name of the Black Messiah. Amen.

Chapter 33

Black Spirituals

A Theological Interpretation

James H. Cone

Contrary to popular opinion, the spirituals are not evidence that black people reconciled themselves with human slavery. On the contrary, they are black freedom songs that emphasize black liberation as consistent with divine revelation. For this reason, it is most appropriate for black people to sing them in this "new" age of Black Power. And if some people still regard the spirituals as inconsistent with Black Power and black theology, that is because they have been misguided and the songs misinterpreted. There is little evidence that black slaves accepted their servitude because they believed God willed their slavery. The opposite is the case. The spirituals speak of God's liberation of black people, his will to set right the oppression of black slaves despite the overwhelming power of white masters. . . .

And if "de God dat lived in Moses' time is jus de same today," then that God will vindicate the suffering of the righteous black and punish the unrighteous whites for their wrongdoings.

A large amount of scholarship has been devoted to the music and poetry of the black spiritual, but little has been written about its theology. Apparently most scholars assume that the value of the black spiritual lies in its artistic expression and not its theological content, which could be taken to mean that blacks can "sing and dance good" but cannot think. For example, almost everyone agrees with W.E.B. Du Bois's contention that "the Negro is primarily an artist"[1] and that his gift of music to America is unsurpassed. But what about the black person as a philosopher and theologian? Is it not possible that the thought of the spiritual is as profound as its music is creative, since without thought art is impossible? In this essay my purpose is to investigate the theological implications of the black spirituals, with special reference to the meaning of God, Jesus Christ, suffering, and eschatology.

I

No theological interpretation of the black spirituals is valid that ignores the cultural environment that created them, and understanding a culture means, in part, perceiving its history. Black history in America is a history of black servitude, a record of pain and sorrows, slave ships and auction blocks. It is the story of black life in chains and of what that meant for the souls and bodies of black people. This is the history that created the spirituals, and it must be recognized if we are to render a valid theological interpretation of these black songs.

The logical place to begin is 1619 when twenty black Africans were sold as indentured servants at Jamestown, Virginia. Actually there was nothing historically unusual about that event, since indentured servitude was already in existence, and many whites were victims. But in 1661 the significance of 1619 was clearly defined when Virginia legalized black slavery, declaring that people of African descent would be slaves for life. Maryland legalized black slavery two years later, and soon after all colonies followed suit. America became the land of the free for white people only, and for blacks she became a land of bondage.

Physical slavery was cruel. It meant working fifteen to twenty hours per day and being beaten unmercifully if one displayed the slightest fatigue. The auction block became a symbol of "brokenness" because no family ties were recognized. Husbands were separated from wives and children from parents. There were few laws protecting the slaves, since most whites believed that Africans were only partly human (three-fifths was the fraction fixed by the Fathers in 1787). Later, to put down any lingering doubts, the highest court of the land decreed that black people had no rights that white people were bound to respect. Slaves were property, as were animals and objects; their owners could dispose of them as they saw fit—provided they did not endanger the welfare of the society as a whole.

It has been said that not all masters were cruel, and perhaps there is some truth in the observation—particularly if it is made from a perspective that does not know the reality of the slave-experience. But from the black perspective, the phrase "good" master is an absurdity, a logical contradiction. To speak of "good" masters is like speaking of "good" racists and "good" murderers. Who in their right minds could make such nonsensical distinctions, except those who deal in historical abstractions? Certainly not the victims! Indeed, it may be argued that the so-called good masters were in fact the worst, if we consider the dehumanizing effect of mental servitude. At least those who were blatant in their physical abuse did not camouflage their savagery with Christian doctrine, and it may have been easier for black slaves to make the necessary value-distinctions so that they could regulate their lives according to black definitions. But "good" Christian masters could cover up their brutality by rationalizing it with Christian theology, making it difficult for slaves to recognize the demonic. Undoubtedly, white Christianity contributed to the phenomenon of "house niggers" (not all domestic servants were in this category), those blacks who internalized the masters' values, revealing information about insurrections planned by their brothers. The "good" masters convinced them that slavery was their lot ordained by God, and it was his will for blacks to be obedient to white people. After all, Ham was cursed, and St. Paul did admonish slaves to be obedient to their masters.

Initially, white masters did not permit their slaves to be Christianized. Christian baptism implied manumission, according to some; and there were too many biblical references to freedom. But white missionaries and preachers convinced slavemasters that Christianity made blacks "better" slaves—obedient and docile. As one slaveholder put it: "The deeper the piety of the slave, the more valuable he is in every respect."[2] White Christianity assisted in the internalization of white values in the minds of slaves, reconciling them to the condition of servitude. The Christianity taught to black slaves was a distorted interpretation of the gospel, geared to the ideological enforcement of white racism. Black resistance to slavery was interpreted as sin: revolt against the master was said to be revolt against God, and that could only mean eternal damnation. To be sure, Christianity offered freedom, but for slaves it was interpreted to mean freedom from sin, the lust and passion that made them disregard the interests of their masters. Such was the history that created the spirituals.

II

But the history that created the spirituals contains much more than what white people *did* to black people. Black history is also the record of black people's historical strivings, an account of their perceptions of their existence in an oppressive society. What whites did to blacks is secondary. The primary reality is what blacks did to whites in order to restrict the white assault on their humanity.

When white people enslaved Africans, their intention was to dehistoricize black existence, to foreclose the possibility of a future defined by the African heritage. White people demeaned the sacred tales of the black fathers, ridiculing their myths and defiling the sacred rites. Their intention was to define man according to European definitions so that their brutality against Africans could be characterized as civilizing the savages. But white Europeans did not succeed, and black history is the record of their failure. Black people did not stand by passively while white oppressors demoralized their being. Many rebelled—physically and mentally. Black history in America is the history of that rebellion.

Black rebellion in America did not begin with the Civil Rights movement and Martin Luther King, nor with Black Power and Stokely Carmichael or the Black Panther Party. Black resistance has roots stretching back to the auction blocks and the slave codes. It began when the first black person decided that death would be preferable to slavery. If white government officials could just realize this, then they might be able to understand the Black Panthers and other black revolutionaries. White people should know about Harriet Tubman and her liberation of more than three hundred black slaves. They should know about Henry Garnett and his urgent call for rebellion among the slaves. Black slaves were not passive, and black history is the record of their physical resistance against the condition of human bondage.

To understand the history of black resistance, it is also necessary to know the black spirituals. They are historical songs that speak about the rupture of black lives; they tell us about a people in the land of bondage and what they did to hold themselves together and to fight back. We are told that the people of Israel could not sing the Lord's song in a strange land. But, for blacks, their *Being* depended upon a song. Through song, they built new structures for existence in an alien land. The spirituals enabled blacks to retain a measure of African identity while living in the midst of American slavery, providing both the substance and the rhythm to cope with human servitude.

Much has been said about the compensatory and otherworldly ideas in the black spirituals. While I do not question the presence of that theme, there is, nevertheless, another train of thought running through these songs. And unless this emphasis is considered, it is possible that the spirituals cannot be understood. I am referring to the emphasis on freedom in this world, and the kinds of risks blacks were willing to take in order to attain it.

Oh Freedom! Oh Freedom!
Oh Freedom, I love thee!
And before I'll be a slave,
I'll be buried in my grave,
And go home to my Lord and be free.

The theme of freedom and activities it implied explains why slave-holders did not allow black slaves to worship and sing their songs unless authorized white people were present to proctor the meeting. And after the Nat Turner revolt, black preachers were declared illegal in most southern states. Black religious gatherings were often occasions for organizing resistance against the institution of slavery.

Black history is the stuff out of which the black spirituals were created. But the "stuff" of black history includes more than the bare historical facts of slavery. Black history is an experience, a soulful event. And to understand it is to know the Being of a people who had to "feel their way along the course of American slavery,"[3] enduring the stresses and strains of human servitude but not without a song. *Black history is a spiritual!*

III

The divine liberation of the oppressed from slavery is the central theological concept in the black spirituals. These songs show that black slaves did not believe that human servitude was reconcilable with their African past and their knowledge of the Christian gospel. They did not believe that God created Africans to be the slaves of Europeans. Accordingly they sang of a God who was involved in history—*their* history—making right what whites have made wrong. Just as God delivered Moses and the Children of Israel from Egyptian bondage, drowning Pharaoh and his army in the Red Sea, so also he will deliver black people from American slavery. It is this certainty that informs the thought of the black spirituals, enabling black slaves to sing:

Oh Mary, don't you weep, don't you moan,
Oh Mary, don't you weep, don't you moan,
Pharaoh's army got drownded,
Oh Mary, don't you weep.

The basic idea of the spirituals is that slavery contradicts God; it is a denial of His will. To be enslaved is to be declared *nobody*, and that form of existence contradicts God's creation of men to be his children. Because black people believed that they were God's children, they affirmed their *somebodiness*, refusing to reconcile their servitude with divine revelation. They rejected white distortions of the gospel, which emphasized the obedience of slaves to their masters. They contended that God willed their freedom and not their slavery. That is why the spirituals focus on biblical passages that stress God's involvement in the liberation of oppressed people. Black people sang about Joshua and the battle of Jericho, Moses leading the Israelites from bondage, Daniel in the lions' den, and the Hebrew children in the fiery furnace. Here the emphasis is on God's liberation of the weak from the oppression of the strong, the lowly and downtrodden from the proud and mighty. And blacks reasoned that if God could lock the lion's jaw for Daniel and could cool the fire for the Hebrew children, then he certainly could deliver black people from slavery.

> My Lord delivered Daniel
> Why can't He deliver me?

Contrary to popular opinion, the spirituals are not evidence that black people reconciled themselves with human slavery. On the contrary, they are black freedom songs which emphasize black liberation as consistent with divine revelation. For this reason it is most appropriate for black people to sing them in this "new" age of Black Power. And if some people still regard the spirituals as inconsistent with Black Power and black theology, that is because they have been misguided and the songs misinterpreted. There is little evidence that black slaves accepted their servitude because they believed God willed their slavery. The opposite is the case. The spirituals speak of God's liberation of black people, His will to set right the oppression of black slaves despite the overwhelming power of white masters. For blacks believed that there is an omnipotent, omnipresent, and omniscient power at work in the world, and that he is on the side of the oppressed and downtrodden. As evidence they pointed to the blind man who received his sight, the lame who walked, and Lazarus who was received into God's Kingdom while the rich man was rejected. And if "de God dat lived in Moses' time is jus' de same today" then that God will vindicate the suffering of the righteous blacks and punish the unrighteous whites for their wrongdoings.

IV

Some will argue, with Marx, that the very insistence upon *divine* activity is always evidence that people are helpless and passive. "Religion is the sign of the oppressed creature, the heart of the heartless world . . . the spirit of a spiritless situation. It is the *opium* of the people."[4] There were doubtless some black slaves who *literally* waited on God, expecting him to effect their liberation in response to their faithful passivity; but there is another side of the black experience to be weighed. When it is considered that Nat Turner, Denmark Vesey and Harriet Tubman may have been creators of some of the spirituals, that "Sinner, please don't let this harvest pass" probably referred to a slave resistance meeting,[5] that after 1831 over two thousand slaves escaped yearly,[6] and that black churches interpreted civil disobedience as consistent with religion, then it is most likely that many slaves recognized the need for their own participation in God's liberation. Indeed, many believed that the only hands that God had were their hands, and without the risk of escape or insurrection, slavery would never end. This may be the meaning of the song, "Singin' wid a sword in ma han'." The sword may be the symbol of the need of black slaves to strike a blow for freedom even though the odds were against them. Certainly the strict enforcement of the slave codes and the merciless beating of many slaves who sang spirituals tend to point in that direction.[7] What is certain is that Christianity did not dull the drive for liberation among all black slaves, and there is much evidence that slaves appropriated the gospel to their various styles of resistance.

Seeking to detract from the theological significance of the spirituals, some critics may point out that black slaves were literalists in their interpretation of the Scripture, and this probably accounts for their acceptance of the white masters' interpretation of the Bible. Of course, it is true that slaves were not biblical critics and were unaware of erudite white reflections on the origins of biblical writings. Like most of their contemporaries, they accepted the inerrancy of Scripture. But the critical point is that their very literalism supported a black gospel of earthly freedom. They were literal when they sang about Daniel in the lions' den, David and Goliath, and Samson and the Philistines. On the other hand, they dispensed with biblical literalism when white people began to use the curse of Ham and Paul as evidence that blacks ought to accept their slavery. As one ex-slave preacher put it:

When I starts preaching I couldn't read or write and had to preach what Master told me, and he say tell them niggers iffen they obeys the master they goes to Heaven: but I knowed there's something better for them, but daren't tell them 'cept on the sly. That I done lots. I tells 'em iffen they keeps praying, the Lord will set 'em free.[8]

Black slaves were not naive as is often supposed. They knew that slavery contradicted humanity and divinity, and that was why they cited biblical references that focused on the liberation of the oppressed. They believed that God would deliver them. As he once locked the lion's jaw for Daniel, he would paralyze the power of white masters.

> Who lock, who lock de lion,
> Who lock, de lion's Jaw?
> God, lock, God lock de lion's jaw.

The point is clear. God is the liberator, the deliverer of the weak from the injustice of the strong.

It is significant that theology proper blends imperceptibly into christology in the spirituals. No theological distinction is made between the Son and the Father. Jesus is understood as the King, the deliverer of men from unjust suffering. He is the comforter in time of trouble, the lily of the valley, and the bright morning star.

> He's King of Kings, and Lord of Lords,
> Jesus Christ, the first and last
>   No man works like him.

The death and resurrection of Jesus are particular focal points of the spirituals. The death of Jesus meant that the savior died on the cross for black slaves. His death was a symbol of their suffering, their trials and tribulation in an unfriendly world. When Jesus was nailed to the cross and the Romans pierced him in the side, he was not alone; blacks suffered and died with him. That was why they sang:

> Were you there when they crucified my Lord?
>   Were you there when they crucified my Lord?
> Oh! sometimes it causes me to tremble, tremble, tremble;
>   Were you there when they crucified my Lord?

Black slaves were there! Through the experience of being slaves, they encountered the theological significance of Jesus' death. With the crucifixion, Jesus makes an unqualified identification with the poor and helpless and takes their pain upon himself. They were there at the crucifixion because his death was for them.

And if Jesus was not alone in his suffering, they also were not alone in their slavery. Jesus is with them! Herein lies the meaning of the resurrection. It means that Jesus is not dead but is alive.

He rose, he rose from the dead,
An' de Lord shall bear my spirit hom'.

The resurrection is the divine guarantee that their lives are in the hands of him who conquered death, enabling men to do what is necessary to remain obedient to the Father, the creator and sustainer of life.

V

Though black slaves believed that the God of Jesus Christ was involved in the historical liberation of oppressed people from bondage, the continued existence of American slavery seemed to contradict that belief. If God was omnipotent and in control of human history, how could His goodness be reconciled with human servitude? If God had the power to deliver black people from the evil of slavery as he delivered Moses from Pharaoh's army, Daniel from the lions' den, and the Hebrew children from the fiery furnace, why then were black slaves still subject to the rule of white masters? Why are we still living in wretched conditions when God could end this evil thing with one righteous stroke?

These are hard questions, and they are still relevant today. In the history of theology and philosophy, these questions are the core of the "problem of evil": college and seminary professors have spent many hours debating them. But black slaves did not have the opportunity to investigate the problem of suffering in the luxury of a room with all the comforts of modern living. They encountered suffering in the cotton fields of Georgia, Arkansas, and Mississippi. Under the whip and pistol, they had to deal with the absurdities of human existence. Every time they opened their eyes and visualized the contradictions of their environment, they realized they were "rolling through an unfriendly world." How could a good and powerful God be reconciled with white masters and overseers? What explanation could the Holy One of Israel give for allowing the existence of an ungodly slave institution?

In order to understand the black slave's reaction to his enslavement, it is necessary to point out that his reflections on the problem of suffering were not "rational" in the classical Greek sense, with an emphasis on abstract and universal distinctions between good and evil, justice and injustice. The black slave had little time for reading books or sitting in the cool of the day, thinking about neat philosophical answers to the problem of evil. It was not only illegal to teach slaves to read, but most were forced to work from daybreak to nightfall, leaving no spare time for the art of theological and philosophical discourse. The black slave's investigation of the absurdities of human existence was concrete, and it was done within the context of the community of faith. No attempt was made to transcend the faith of the community by assuming a universal stance common to "all" men. In this sense, his reflection on human suffering was not unlike the biblical view of Yahweh's activity in human history. It was grounded in the historical realities of communal experience.

The classic examples in biblical history are found in the prophet Habakkuk and the sage Job. Both raised questions about the justice of God, but they were clearly questions for the faithful—not for philosophers. They took on significance only if one were a member of the community of faith. Habakkuk was concerned about the violence and the destruction of the land as witnessed in the army of the Chaldeans, while Job questioned the deuteronomic success formula. But in each case, the ultimate sovereignty of God was not denied. What was requested was a divine explanation so that the faithful could understand the ways of the Almighty. There was no philosophical resolution of the problem of evil. Suffering was a reality of life, and the believer must be able to take it upon himself without losing faith.

VI

In the spirituals, the slave's experience of suffering and despair defines for him the major issue in his view of the world. He does not really question the justice and goodness of God. He takes for granted God's righteousness and vindication of the poor and weak. Indeed, it is the point of departure for his faith. The slave has another concern, centered on the *faithfulness* of the community of believers in a world full of trouble. He wonders not whether God is just and right but whether the sadness and pain of the world will cause him to lose heart and thus fall prey to the ways of evil. He is concerned about the *togetherness* of the community of sufferers. Will the wretched of the earth be able to experience the harsh realities of despair and loneliness and take this pain upon themselves and not lose faith in the gospel of God? There was no attempt to evade the reality of suffering. Black slaves faced the reality of the world "ladened wid trouble, an' burden'd wid grief," but they believed that they could go to Jesus in secret and get relief. They appealed to Jesus not so much to remove the trouble (though that was included), but to keep them from "sinkin' down."

Significantly, the note of despair is usually intertwined with confidence and joy that "trouble don't last always." To be sure, the slave sings, "Sometimes I feel like a motherless child, a long way from home"; but because he is confident that Jesus is with him and has not left him completely alone, he can still add (in the same song!), "Glory Hallelujah!" The black slaves did not deny the experience of agony and loneliness in a world filled with trouble.

> Nobody knows the trouble I've seen,
> Nobody knows my sorrow.
> Nobody knows the trouble I've seen,
> Glory, Hallelujah!

The "Glory, Hallelujah!" is not a denial of trouble; it is an affirmation of faith. It says that despite the pain of being alone in an unfriendly world the black slave is confident that God has not really left him, and *trouble* is not the last word on human existence.

> Soon-a-will be done with the trouble of the world;
> Soon-a-will be done with the trouble of the world;
> Going home to live with God.

It appears that the slave is not concerned with the problem of evil per se, as if he intuitively knows that nothing will be solved through a debate of that problem. He deals with the world as it *is*, not as it might have been if God had acted "justly." He focuses on present realities of despair and loneliness that disrupt the community of faith. The faithful seems to have lost faith, and he experiences the agony of being alone in a world of hardship and pain. That is why he sings:

> I couldn't hear nobody pray.
> Oh I couldn't hear nobody pray.
> Oh way down yonder by myself
> And I couldn't hear nobody pray.

VII

Related to the problem of suffering was the future, the "not-yet" of black existence. How was it possible for black slaves to take seriously their pain and suffering in an unfriendly world and still believe that God was liberating them from earthly bondage? How could they really believe that God was just when they knew only injustice and oppression? The answer to these questions lies in the concept of heaven, which is the dominant idea in black religious experience as expressed in the black spirituals.

The concept of heaven in black religion has not been interpreted rightly. Most observers have defined the black religious experience exclusively in terms of slaves longing for heaven, as if that desire were unrelated to their earthly liberation. It has been said that the concept of heaven served as an opiate for black slaves, making for docility and submission. But to interpret black eschatology solely in terms of its outmoded cosmology fails to take seriously the culture and thought of a people seeking expression amidst the dehumanization of slavery. It is like discarding the Bible and its message as irrelevant because the biblical writers had a three-storied conception of the universe. While not all biblical and systematic theologians agree with Rudolf Bultmann's method of demythologization in his efforts to solve the problem of biblical mythology, most agree that he is correct in his insistence that the gospel message is not dependent on its pre-scientific world-picture. Is it not possible that the same analogy is true in regard to the heaven theme in the spirituals?

Let me admit, then, that the black slaves' picture of the world is not to be defended as a viable scientific analysis of reality: that their image of the Promised Land, where "the streets are pearl and the gates are gold," is not the best way of communicating to contemporary Black Power advocates with their stress on political liberation by any means necessary; that a "new" black theological language is needed if black religion is going to be involved in articulating the historical strivings of black people in America and the Third World; and that the language of heaven is a white concept given to black slaves in order to make them obedient and submissive. The question nevertheless remains: How was it possible for black people to endure the mental and physical stresses of slavery and still keep their humanity intact? I think the answer is found in black eschatology; and maybe what is needed is not a dismissal of the idea of heaven but a reinterpretation of this concept so that oppressed blacks today can develop styles of resistance not unlike those of their grandparents.

VIII

The place to begin is Miles Fisher's contention that the spirituals are primarily "historical documents." They tell us about the black movement for historical liberation, the attempt of black people to define their present history in the light of their promised future, not according to their past miseries. Fisher notes that heaven for early black slaves referred not only to a transcendent reality beyond time and space; it designated the earthly places that blacks regarded as lands of freedom. Heaven referred to Africa, Canada, and the states north of the Mason-Dixon line.[9] Frederick Douglass wrote about the double meaning of these songs:

> We were at times remarkably buoyant, singing hymns, and making joyous exclamations, almost as triumphant in their tone as if we had reached a land of freedom and safety. A keen observer might have detected in our repeated singing of
>
> > O Canaan, sweet Canaan,
> > I am bound for the land of Canaan,
>
> something more than a hope of reaching heaven. We meant to reach the *North*, and the North was our Canaan.[10]

But while it is true that heaven had its historical referents, not all black slaves could hope to make it to Africa, Canada, or even to the northern section of the United States. The failure of the American Colonization Society's experiments crushed the hopes of many black slaves who were expecting to return to their African homeland. And blacks also began to realize that the North was not as significantly different from the South as they had envisioned, particularly in view of the Fugitive Slave Act of 1850 and the Dred Scott decision in 1857. Black slaves began to realize that their historical freedom could not be assured as long as white racists controlled the governmental process of America. And so they found it necessary to develop a style of freedom that included but did not depend upon historical possibilities. What could freedom mean for black slaves who could never expect to participate in the determination of society's laws governing their lives? Must they continue to define freedom in terms of the possibility of escape and insurrection as if their humanity depended on their willingness to commit suicide? It was in response to this situation that the black concept of heaven developed.

For black slaves, who were condemned to carve out their existence in human captivity, heaven meant that the eternal God has made a decision about their humanity that could not be destroyed by white slavemasters. Whites could drive them, beat them, and even kill them; but they believed that God nevertheless had chosen black slaves as his own and that this election bestowed upon them a freedom to *be*, which could not be measured by what oppressors could do to the physical body. Whites may suppress black history and define Africans as savages, but the words of slavemasters do not have to be taken seriously when the oppressed know that they have a *somebodiness* that is guaranteed by the heavenly Father who alone is the ultimate sovereign of the universe. This is what heaven meant for black slaves.

The idea of heaven provided ways for black people to affirm their humanity when other people were attempting to define them as nonpersons. It enabled blacks to say yes to their right to be free by affirming God's eschatological freedom to be for the oppressed. That was what they meant when they sang about a "city called heaven."

> I am a poor pilgrim of sorrow
> I'm in this world alone.
> No hope in this world for tomorrow.
> I'm trying to make heaven my home.
> Sometimes I am tossed and driven.
> Sometimes I don't know where to roam.
> I've heard of a city called heaven.
> I've started to make it my home.

In the midst of economic and political disfranchisement, black slaves held themselves together and did not lose their spiritual composure because they believed that their worth transcended governmental decisions. That was why they looked forward to "walking in Jerusalem just like John" and longed for the "camp meeting in the Promised Land."

IX

Despite the ways that black eschatology might have been misused or the crude forms in which it was sometimes expressed, it nevertheless provides us today with the best theological foundation for enabling American theologians to develop a concept of the future that is related to black oppression. Black theologians have little patience with so-called political theologians of America who say that they are concerned about humanizing the world according to God's promised future but do not relate that future to the history and culture of that people who have been and are being dehumanized and dehistoricized by white overlords. With all the talk among American theologians about "hope theology," "humanistic messianism," "Marxist-Christian dialogue," and revolutionary theology, one would expect that such language could easily be related to black people and their thoughts on eschatology and divine liberation. But white

American theologians have been virtually silent on black liberation, pre-
ferring instead to do theology in the light of a modern liberalism that
assumes that black people want to integrate into the white way of life.
Such silence is inexcusable, and it is hard not to conclude that they are
enslaved by their own identity with the culture and history of white slavemasters. What they need is liberation, and this can only happen when they
face the reality of Black Power and what that means for the oppressed of
the land.

One of the effective starting points for that encounter with reality is the
body of black spirituals that came to maturity in the antebellum years. Far
from being poignant expressions of shattered humanity, they were affir-
mations of hope—hope that enabled black slaves to risk their lives for
earthly freedom because they knew they had a home "over yonder."

Notes

1. W.E.B. Du Bois, *The Gift of Black Folk* (1924; reprint, New York: Washington Square
   Press, 1970), p. 158.
2. Cited in Vincent Harding, "Religion and Resistance Among Antebellum Negroes,
   1800–1860," in *The Making of Black America*, vol. 1, ed. August Meier and Elliott Rudwick (New York: Atheneum, 1969), p. 181.
3. Comment by Guy Johnson of the University of North Carolina, cited in Sterling
   Stuckey, "Through the Prism of Folkore," in *Black and White in American Culture*, ed.
   J. Chametyky and S. Kaplan (Amherst: University of Massachusetts Press, 1969), p. 172.
4. Karl Marx and Friedrich Engels, *On Religion* (New York: Schocken Books, 1964), p. 42.
5. Miles Fisher, *Negro Slave Songs in the United States* (New York: Citadel Press, 1953),
   pp. 27–28, 66–67, 181–185.
6. Ibid., p. 108. It is important to note that Fisher is quoting the conservative estimate of
   a southern historian.
7. See ibid., chapter 4. Fisher notes that the spirituals were used to convene secret meetings among slaves, and the colony of Virginia prohibited them as early as 1676 (pp. 29,
   66 ff.). Most colonies joined Virginia in outlawing the secret meetings, but "neither out-
   lawry nor soldiery prevented [them] from hemispheric significance" (p. 67).
8. B. A. Botkin, ed. *Lay My Burden Down* (Chicago: University of Chicago Press, 1945),
   p. 26.
9. See *Negro Slave Songs*, chapters 1–4.
10. *Life and Times of Frederick Douglass* (1892; reprint, New York: Collier Books, 1962),
    p. 159.

Chapter 34

Slave Theology
in the "Invisible Institution"

Dwight N. Hopkins

My uncle, Ben, he could read de Bible, and he allus tell us some day us be free. And Massa Henry laugh, "Haw, haw, haw." And he say, "Hell, no, yous never be free. Yous ain't got sense 'nuf to make de livin', if yous was free." Den, he takes de Bible 'way from Uncle Ben and say it put de bad ideas in he head, but Uncle gits 'nother Bible and hides it, and Massa never finds out.

John Bates, ex-slave

The black church begins in slavery; thus slave religion provides the first source for a contemporary statement on black theology. The black church's unique tradition springs from the emerging theology of African American chattel. While white masters attempted to force their Christianity onto their black property, slaves worshiped God secretly. Out of these illegal and hidden religious practices, the "Invisible Institution," black Christianity and black theology arose. Though chained and illiterate, black people dared to *think* theologically by testifying to what the God of Moses had done for them. For example, recording the Christian substance of the spirituals—the novel religious songs created by blacks under slavery—Colonel Thomas Wentworth Higginson, a white officer in the Civil War, observed:

[The slaves'] memories are a vast bewildered chaos of Jewish history and biography; and most of the great events of the past, down to the period of the American Revolution, they instinctively attribute to Moses.[1]

Unfortunately, Higginson described these penetrating theological insights of the unlettered black bondservants as "bewildered chaos." He failed to appreciate the hermeneutical insights of the poor. For the slaves, Moses acted as a human instrument of divine liberation, because Yahweh had utilized him to emancipate the slaves. If Yahweh could do this against Pharaoh, then surely Yahweh had brought about all "the great events" of liberation movements, including the American Revolution against the British oppressors. Furthermore, because the black slaves identified themselves with the biblical Hebrew slaves and because Yahweh had continued to act in human history, black American bondsmen and bondswomen maintained hope and certainty for their own deliverance from the cauldron of white American chattel. Consequently this "bewildered chaos," in fact, marked the slaves' developing theological critique from the Bible's powerless voices.

An examination of slaves' lives and thought about God conveys several important factors in the religious lineage of the black church. For instance, slave theology consistently experienced God dwelling with those in bondage, personal and systemic. The black religious experience prevented any separation between the sacred and the secular, the church and the community. On the contrary, in the "Invisible Institution" black theology grew out of the community and the "church." As a result, *God* ruled with unquestioned omnipotence and realized release from total captivity. And *Jesus* assumed an intimate and kingly relationship with the poor black chattel. Slaves emphasized both the suffering human Jesus as well as Jesus' warrior ability to set the downtrodden free. Moreover, the slaves distinguished their *humanity* from the white slave master. For blacks, God and Jesus called them to use all means possible to pursue religiously a human status of equality.

Furthermore, in radical distinction to white Christianity, religious encounters in ex-slave narratives, autobiographies, and the spirituals suggest an alternative theological interpretation with at least two aspects. First, African American slaves pictured a political dimension in their theology. They saw a direct political power struggle between serving their God and serving the white slave master's god. In certain situations whites claimed to be God on earth and mandated black submissiveness to a white idolatry that contradicted the slaves' loyalty to God's ultimacy.

Second, slaves' religious thought accented an original cultural expression. Not only did the slaves wage a political battle for the supremacy of their liberator God, but they also chose to worship this God in their own language and idiom, and in the extraordinary clandestineness of their own black religious community. Thus God's self was manifested in the specific textures of an African American slave story.

Today's black theology, church, and community need to be thankful that God spared a few formerly enslaved African Americans to pass on this black theological tradition. In the words of an ex-slave, John Brown, who gave praises to God for the opportunity to tell it like it actually was, we read:

> Lord! have mercy! have um mercy! Lord you done spared a few un us to tell de tale um, um, um, bout how hit was um, um wid us poor folks in dem days um, um, um. We done pray for dis day to come of freedom.[2]

Before we look at specific examples of how slaves told their story about the coming of freedom (through the slaves' black theology expressed in their experiences with God, Jesus, and human purpose), we investigate and define the contours of the "Invisible Institution"—the religious organization that served as the backdrop for the slaves' black theology.

The Contours of the "Invisible Institution"

From the Slaves' Perspective

To tell the slaves' religious story as the first source for today's black theology, one has to acknowledge the convergence of a reinterpreted white Christianity with the remains of African religions under slavery. It was precisely in the "Invisible Institution" that slaves synthesized these two foundational God-encounters to form slave theology.

Though slaves did not have direct access to the specifics of their former African religious practices and beliefs, they did maintain some theological remains—religious Africanisms. Unfortunately, the European slave trade, the practice of mixing Africans from different villages, the prohibition by white people of the use of African languages, and the fading memories of succeeding slave progeny[3] all served to dampen the vibrancy of a coherent African theology in slave thought. Nevertheless, enslaved Africans brought religious ideas and forces of theological habit with them to the "New World."

These Africans in bondage were not ignorant theologically. On the contrary, it was their structural religious world-view of God, Jesus, and human action that sustained them against the racist assaults of European slavers and their descendants in the "New World." Yet despite the existence of the slaves' black theology, white people continued to brand enslaved Africans as biologically subhuman, culturally uncivilized, and religiously heathen. Note the following emphasis of a prominent white missionary to Africa:

I arrived at Bende to attempt anew the dredging and purifying of that ugly jungle pool of heathenism, with its ooze-life of shocking cruelty, reptilian passions and sprouting evil, spreading itself broad in the shadows amidst the most fruitful land on earth. . . . Thus Christianity views her domain-to-be, lifting herself high above the secret springs of paganism's turgid streams below.[4]

Here whites endow Africans with reptilian qualities of passion and an inherent theological anthropology of evil. Conversely, white theology and white Christianity were normative and by definition superior ("lifting herself high above"), hence by nature dominating ("Christianity views her domain-to-be"). For white missionaries, who accompanied European slave traders to Africa, African communities offered no points of convergence for Christianity and African traditional religions. Instead of seeking points of theological contact with African indigenous religions, white theology served as the religious justification for Christian colonialism and racist plundering of black lands ("the most fruitful land on earth").

But Africans, even as they were bound as booty for the "New World," survived and resisted by remembering and relying on their traditional religions. And it is this primordial religious reflex that was bequeathed to the future black slaves in the "Invisible Institution."

The African Contribution to Slave Theology

Enslaved Africans brought a distinct perception of God to North America. African traditional religions described their ultimate divinity as the High God. "God has nowhere or nowhen" speaks to the omnipresence and non-derivative status of the divinity.[5] Some even called God "the Almighty," denoting divine omnipotence. By unbounded power God can do all things in heaven and on earth. This power is also what enables human beings to achieve their goals. God is both transcendent and immanent in African traditional religions. And God's authority entails all of creation. As the first and last cause, God created all things and thus holds the ultimate and final power over the visible and invisible creations. Humanity is contingent, but God is absolute authority.[6]

Furthermore, African indigenous religions believe in a God who cares; some call God "the Compassionate One," others see "the God of pity," who rescues victims in need. God is kind and "looks after the case of the poor man." In fact, God is the main hope of the poor in society. As Guardian and Keeper, God is named "the Protector of the poor" by some

African traditional religions. They further specify that "there is a Saviour and only he can keep our lives."[7] As judge, God metes out justice, punishment, and retribution. Similarly, God displays protectiveness by avenging injustice. God is a divinity of partiality to the victim; God sides with the political powerlessness of society's injured.

In addition to these definite attributes of God, the theological framework shared by enslaved Africans in the "New World" also included a belief in theological anthropology—what it means to be God's created humanity.

African traditional religions shared a belief in a dynamic and interdependent relation between the individual and the community. The latter defined the former. Individualism proved anathema. To be human meant to stand in connection with the larger community of invisible ancestors and God and, of course, the visible community and family.

Africans recognize life as life-in-community. We can

> truly know ourselves if we remain true to our community, past and present. The concept of individual success or failure is secondary. . . . Our nature as beings-in-relation is a two-way relation: with God and with our fellow human-beings.[8]

African religions gave rise to a dynamic interplay between community and individual. Whatever happened to the communal gathering affected the individual, and whatever happened to the individual had an impact on the community. Such a theological view of humanity cuts across bourgeois notions of white Christianity's individualism and "me-first-ism." It seeks to forge a group solidarity and identity, beginning with God, proceeding through the ancestors to the community and immediate family, and continuing even to the unborn. One cannot be a human being unless one becomes a part of, feels a responsibility to, and serves the community. To preserve the community's well-being (through liberation) in African religions is to preserve the individual's well-being (through salvation). Thus salvation and liberation become a holistic individual-collective and personal-systemic ultimate concern.

In this theological anthropology African traditional religions also accent the role and importance of the ancestors. The ancestors are connections to the past religious traditions and practices. They are the glue to the sacredness of culture or way of life. Oftentimes one would have to placate the ancestors in order to reach the High God. So connectedness (or lack of connectedness) to those who hold religio-cultural deposits has grave implications regarding one's relation to the Divine. For my purposes, the cultural significance of the ancestors' role is the most relevant. The memory and presence of the ancestors helped preserve and teach the cultural heritage of the community. To be human-in-community necessitated a cultural dimension in African traditional religions.

Furthermore, enslaved Africans brought with them a sense of wholeness in the High God's relation to creation. Because God created all things, there was no separation between the sacred and secular, the church and the community.

> A sense of wholeness of the person is manifested in the African attitude to life. Just as there is no separation between the sacred and the secular in communal life, neither is there a separation between the soul and the body in a person. Spiritual needs are as important for the body as bodily needs are for the soul.[9]

One does not dichotomize God's sovereignty in any sphere. African traditional religions did not see the possibility of saving the spirit or the soul while the freedom of the body went unattended.[10]

Bush Arbor Theology

Enslaved Africans took the remnants of their traditional religious structures and meshed them together with their interpretation of the Bible. All this occurred in the "Invisible Institution," far away from the watchful eyes of white people. Only in their own cultural idiom and political space could black slaves truly worship God. Ex-slave Becky Ilsey describes the hidden nature of the "Invisible Institution" pre–Civil War: "'Fo de war when we'd have a meetin' at night, wuz mos' always 'way in de woods or de bushes some whar so de white folks couldn't hear."[11] Slaves would sneak off "twixt eight an' twelve at night"[12] to hold church. At times, slaves sought whatever shelter they could find for their sanctuary in order "to talk wid Jesus." They "used to go 'cross de fields nights to a old tobacco barn on de side of a hill."[13]

If they found no standing shelter they would construct a bush (or hush) arbor for their illegal prayer meetings. Ex-slave Arthur Greene remembers:

> Well-er talkin' 'bout de church in dem days, we po' colored people ain' had none lak you have now. We jes made er bush arbor by cuttin' bushes dat was full of green leaves an' puttin' 'em on top of four

poles reachin' from pole to pole. Den sometimes we'd have dem bushes put roun' to kiver de sides an' back from der bottom to der top. All us get together in dis arbor fer de meetin'.[14]

Other times slaves secretly gathered in an appointed cabin in the slave quarters. "Niggers have benches in dey house dat dey use when dey have prayer-meetin's."[15] Some ingeniously set up worship spots in the fields ("Dey hab big holes out in de fiel's dey git down in and pray."). Some developed regular praying grounds. "Us niggers used to have a prayin' ground down in the hollow," remembers Richard Carruthers. And Andrew Moss echoes: "Us colored folks had prayer grounds. My mammy's was a old twisted thick-rooted muscadine bush." And still others would simply "slip down the hill" to worship.[16]

In the "Invisible Institution," the slaves displayed a remarkable clarity concerning the cultural dimension of their theology. They knew that God spoke to them in their own medium. In fact, African American chattel could not worship God truthfully unless they "talked" with God through their black culture. Ex-slave Emily Dixon makes it plain:

> Us could go to de white folk's church [in a segregated section], but us wanted ter go whar us could sing all de way through, an' hum 'long, an' shout—yo' all know, jist turn loose lack.

In slave religious culture the liberating Spirit made one "jist turn loose lack." The Spirit fed the slaves and instructed them on how to communicate with God using their own indigenous resources. "We used to steal off to de woods and have church, like de Spirit moved us—sing and pray to our own liking and soul satisfaction," states Susan Rhodes. Her testimony exemplifies the slaves' need to be filled with the spirit to their *own* liking and soul satisfaction. And when they claimed their relation to God through the Spirit's pouring into their unique expressions, Rhodes resumes, "we sure did have good meetings, honey . . . like God said."[17]

Like their self-expression in the cultural sphere, slaves acknowledged that their religious worship and theological development meant a political fight to preserve the "Invisible Institution." White folks not only passed laws to prevent African American bondsmen and bondswomen from receiving unsupervised religious instructions, but they also sought to whip and kill slaves who met secretly to praise God. Thus the "Invisible Institution" symbolized both a cultural statement of slave theology and a liberated space in which slaves controlled the political power to develop their theology.

To fight white folks politically—to claim and worship in their own space of sacred power—blacks devised various stratagems to conceal the "Invisible Institution." Minnie Folkes remembers: "So to keep de soun' from goin' out, slaves would put a gra' big iron pot at de do'." Katie Blackwess Johnson concurs: "I would see them 'turn down the pots' to keep the folks at the big-house from hearin' them singin' and prayin'."[18] Yet the whites proved relentless in imposing their theology on the slaves and attempting to squash the bondservants' political struggle to "hold church." Whites sent out "patrollers" to make bed checks in the slave shacks and to comb the woods to stifle the "Invisible Institution." Consequently, slaves responded with "lookouts" as decoys to confuse the patrollers. West Turner testifies, "Well, dey made me de lookout boy, an' when de paddy-rollers [the patrollers] come down de lane past de church . . . well, sir, dey tell me to step out f'm de woods an' let 'em see me." The patrollers chased after Turner, who led them into a booby trap. Turner continues:

> Dem ole paddyrollers done rid plumb into a great line of grape vines dat de slaves had stretched 'cross de path. An' dese vines tripped up de horses an' throwed de ole paddyrollers off in de bushes.[19]

Turner's eyewitness account of the slaves' illegal church gatherings indicates a virtual political guerrilla warfare. Similarly, the picturesque story of former slave Rev. Ishrael Massie attests to the expression of slave religion in the "Invisible Institution" as hand-to-hand combat over who would have power to control the theology of the oppressed African Americans. Rev. Massie underscores this point:

> Lemme tell ya dis happenin' at a meetin'. Ole preacher would come in bringing . . . a long knot of lightwood. . . . When de paterrolers knock at de dow . . . dis preacher would run to de fiah place, git him a light an' take dat torch an' wave hit back an' fo'th so dat de pitch an' fiah would be flyin' every which a way in dese paterrolers faces— you know dat burnt 'em.[20]

Clearly part of the black preacher's pastoral duties included waging a physical war against white "principalities and powers" on earth.

To sum up, in the development of the political and cultural dimensions of the "Invisible Institution," the preacher and his or her following had no other choice but to steal away and "call on the name of the Lord" without fear of white power's lethal presence. Two factors brought this about:

the proscriptions of white Christian theology, and the slaves' faith in God's partiality to the poor.

White Christianity

White theology forced its domination upon black life by ruthlessly controlling and rendering slaves subservient to white humanity. First, the *practice* of white slave masters' Christianity restricted African Americans' access to an independent encounter with religion. For instance, in those cases where whites allowed blacks to attend church, slaves experienced segregation in seating. Samuel Walter Chilton recalls: "Colored folks had to set in de gallery. Dey [white Christians] didn' 'low dem to take part in service." Similarly Caroline Hunter's former slave master would not permit slaves to enter the church sanctuary. A white man would preach to them in the basement of the church building. And Mr. Beverly Jones confirms: "'Couse they wouldn' let us [slaves] have no services lessen a white man was present. Most times the white preacher preached. . . . That was the law at that time!"[21]

In addition to legal restrictions in worship, the everyday practice of white Christianity displayed no ethical difference between "Christian" whites and non-Christian whites. The white master of ex-slave Jack White was a "Mef'dis preacher" who whipped his blacks just as often and just as cruelly as other white people did. To intensify the pain and heinousness of the lashing, this preacher would "drap pitch an' tuppentine on dem [the slaves' welts] from a bu'nin' to'ch." Another white preacher intentionally put out any fires built by his slaves during the winter. As a result, his bondservants "et frozen meat and bread many times in cold weather." And maintaining the tradition of white Christianity's practical barbarity, this particular preacher soaked the raw whipping wounds of his slaves in a "salt bath."[22]

Summarizing the slaves' perspective of white Christianity's daily brutalities, former bondswoman Mrs. Joseph Smith offers this succinct and insightful conclusion:

> Those who were Christians [and] held slaves were the hardest masters. A card-player and drunkard wouldn't flog you half to death. Well, it is something like this—the Christians will oppress you more.[23]

Besides the practice of white slave masters' Christianity, white theology sought to control and make black people slaves to its *doctrinal propositions.* The uncivilized witness and ethics of whites were not simply aberrations from their faith claims about God. On the contrary, white folks literally practiced what they preached. Their *theology* itself propagated white control and black subservience as the normative expression of the Christian gospel.

The slave narratives overflow with white theological justifications for the "peculiar institution." First, the worship leader "always took his text from Ephesians, the white preacher did, the part what said, 'Obey your masters, be good servants.'" Hence whites employed the authority of the Bible in a self-serving and racist interpretation. Having adopted this Pauline epistle as a standard homily, slave masters further construed a catechism for their black human property. "We had a catechism to learn," narrates Sister Robinson. "This wuz it: 'Be nice to massa an' missus, don't tell lies, don't be mean, be obedient an' wuk hard.'" Coupling this religious instruction with the following white man's sermon renders even more clearly the intricacies of slave-master theology. Quoting a white preacher, ex-slave Jenny Proctor restates:

> Now I takes my text, which is, Nigger obey your master and your mistress, 'cause what you git from them here in this world am all you ever going to git, 'cause you just like the hogs and the other animals—when you dies you ain't no more, after you been throwed in that hole.[24]

What does this tell us about white theological beliefs regarding black religious humanity? Whites viewed slaves like other livestock ("hogs and the other animals"). Therefore God had created them and intended for them to work for their white masters with a cheerful and loyal countenance. Further, lacking any ultimate future of heavenly reward, slaves needed to rest content with the earthly constraints of bondage.

Finally, even if slave masters granted any possibility of slaves attaining the blessed repose of heaven, they had to beseech the white man as their Savior. For example, a slave master caught his slave praying and demanded that the slave explain to whom he offered supplications. The slave replied: "Oh Marster, I'se just prayin' to Jesus 'cause I wants to go to Heaven when I dies." Belligerently and arrogantly, the Marster replied, "You's my Negro. I get ye to Heaven."[25] Here we touch the heart of white Christianity and theology. The white man believed he filled the mediating and liberating role of Jesus Christ. As the anointed Jesus, the white man possessed omnipotent and salvific capabilities. For black chattel to reach God, then, whites forced African Americans to accept the status of the white race as divine mediator. However, black folks rejected these scurrilous and heretical faith claims.[26] Though physically bound, slaves nevertheless directly encountered the biblical God in their own theological creativity.

The Slaves' Black Theology

White theological proscriptions served as the negative incentive for slaves to pursue their independent religious thinking. On the positive side, blacks felt the powerful living presence of the Divine in the midst of their daily burdens and concentrated in the "Invisible Institution." These radical religious experiences colored their biblical interpretation, and thus they produced a theology of liberation. So far we have reviewed the various contours of the "Invisible Institution." Against that backdrop we can chart three manifestations of this liberation encounter with the slaves' black theological perspective on God, Jesus Christ, and humanity.

God

Exodus: God Heard Our Cries

African American bondsmen and bondswomen discovered their own predicament and deliverance in the story of the Old Testament Israelites, who also suffered bondage.

> All us had was church meetin's in arbors out in de woods. De preachers would exhort us dat us was de chillen o' Israel in de wilderness an' de Lord done sent us to take dis land o' milk and honey.[27]

And so they reached back into biblical times and appropriated Yahweh's promises and accomplishments for their contemporary dilemma. Paralleling the faith of the Israelites, ex-slave Henry Bibb wrote in his autobiography: "I never omitted to pray for deliverance. I had faith to believe that the Lord could see our wrongs and hear our cries."[28] Pursuing a theological journey from the Old Testament Yahweh to their current religious life with God, slaves directly experienced for themselves the mighty words of Yahweh: "I have surely seen the affliction of my people which are in Egypt and I have heard their cry. . . . And I am come down to deliver them" (Ex 3:1–8a). In this biblical paradigm American slaves discovered the *nature* of God as the One who sees the afflictions of the oppressed, hears their cries, and delivers them to freedom.

Despite white folks' prohibitions against learning to read the Bible and despite the apparent immortality of the slave system, black chattel persisted in a faith in the God of freedom. They combined remains from African traditional religions with the liberation message in the Bible and simply refused to accept white theology. John Bates fondly recalls: "My uncle, Ben, he could read de Bible, and he allus tell us some day us be free." Bates's statement signifies the slaves' unshakeable intellectual analysis and heartfelt belief that the *being* and *work* of God was liberation. Consequently, they incessantly prayed for deliverance.[29]

Indeed, for those in chains, God heard their cries.[30] God did not turn a deaf ear to such soul-wrenching supplications; neither did God ignore such "little ones" in distress. God displayed the *compassion* of a loving and caring parent with the inherent attribute of *agape*—an unflinching divine love for the poor. This knowledge of Yahweh-God's steadfast love empowered illiterate slave preachers to risk the pain of death in order to proclaim the word of God to a bush arbor "congregation."

An unidentified slave preacher remembers how he first began preaching by regurgitating the prescribed words of the slave master ("obeys the master"). Though lacking in literacy, this preacher nonetheless felt filled with God's Spirit, which moved him to contradict his previous sermon on subservience obliged by white theological doctrine ("I knowed there's something better for [the slaves]"). As a result, he felt compelled to proclaim the word of God "but daren't tell [the slaves] 'cept on the sly. That I done lots." Perhaps surreptitiously crowded deep in a damp ravine under the bright blackness of the midnight hour, this preacher in chains brought forth the good news to his brothers and sisters: "I tells 'em iffen they keeps praying, the Lord will set 'em free."[31] God hears and God frees.

More specifically, God freed the slaves in one decisive divine action—the Civil War. Various slave stories, accordingly, attribute the success of the Yankee forces over the Confederates to God's will. Charles Grandy typifies this sentiment.

> Den a gra' big star over in de east come right down almos' to de earth.
> I seed it myself. 'Twas sign o' war alright. Niggers got glad. All dem
> what could pray 'gin to pray more 'n ever. So glad God sendin' de war.[32]

Like the Old Testament Yahweh, who sent natural signs before freeing the Israelites, God disrupted the normal course of nature with a "gra' big star" coming from the east as a sign of war. And the poor became "so glad God sendin' de war." Clearly, for African American chattel, God's compassion and *agape* did not exclude a belligerent deed against the enemies of God's people. Consistent with the biblical narrative and reflecting out of their own story, slaves knew that divine pathos brought God to the defense of victims of injustice. Because of love, the Divinity resorts to a warlike nature. J. W. Lindsay believed "that perhaps God means to bring good out of this great war. God is a man of war, and Jehovah is his name."[33] The slaves, then, conjured up theological images of Jehovah with arms outstretched leading the victorious advance on the battlefield against the evil system of slavery.

Yet the slaves did not restrict the image of God the Warrior to the Civil War. They also linked this war notion against evil and bondage to a holistic concept of God's mercy as a balm for individual tribulations. In other words, God served the reliable role of black people's total deliverer, both in the systemic and in the personal realms. For instance, Ole Ant Sissy had suffered from paralysis for numerous years. But when she heard of the war's conclusion and the abolition of slavery, she "hobbled on out de do', an stood dere prayin' to Gawd fo' his Mercy." Theologically, bondsmen and bondswomen coupled corporate freedom with personal healing. Note how the Good News of victory through battle yields a cure for paralysis. "God is a momentary God" whose mercy can answer one's prayers in a mere moment.[34]

We Have a Just God

The slaves' prayerful beseeching of God for deliverance indicates that they believed fundamentally that God's nature was one of justice and liberation. In fact, such a faith kept hope alive for these poor chattel, who groaned under the heel of a stultifying existence. All around them stood white Christians, taunting them with the supposedly biblically based and inherent superiority of white skin over black. Moreover, whites apparently had the military and intellectual power to implement this heretical claim of theological racism. But divine justice radically subverted the priority of white-skinned privileges in the slaves' sacred world-view. More specifically, with solemn certainty and joyful delight, blacks sang: "We have a just God to plead-a our cause/We have a just God to plead-a our cause/We are the people of God./He sits in Heaven and he answers prayer."[35]

A just God brought righteousness in situations of conflict between the weak and the strong. For human property, righteousness corrected unjust relations and placed the Divinity squarely and unapologetically on the side of the oppressed. How could it be otherwise? Surely, since Yahweh heard their anguished cries and saw their cruel plight, Yahweh would "make things right." By bearing the innocent victims' burden, God stood with them and, furthermore, burst asunder systemic tentacles that literally choked the very lives of African American bondsmen and bondswomen. In an interview former slave James L. Bradley boldly declared: "God will help those who take part with the oppressed. Yes, blessed be His holy name! He will surely do it."[36] In a word, God sides with the downtrodden.

Conversely, God punishes the wicked. Understandably, the slaves believed in a theological formula of divine justice and righteousness in which the oppressor reaped the deserved condemnation. Black chattel underwent sadistic and savage treatment at the hands of fiendish white folks. Whites often gave slaves fifty to five hundred lashes and then poured salt, turpentine, or ground bricks into the fresh wounds. White males entered slave cabins and raped black women in the presence of their husbands. White males consistently "broke in" young black girls just arrived into puberty. Quite often slaves had their thumbs cut off for attempting to learn reading and writing. Slave traders purchased black women, snatched their children from their nursing breasts, and threw the babies on the side of the road to die. Death stalked the slaves like a bounty hunter dogging a fugitive. The slightest whim could set off the vicious nature of whites. In one instance a slave woman accidentally spilled gravy on the white dress of a slave mistress. The master took the black woman outdoors and cut her head off.[37]

Hence, for the enslaved, the justice and righteousness of God could only bring retribution for tormentors. Julia Brown concurs: "When he died we all said God got tired of Mister Jim being so mean and kilt him." But divine establishment of right relations entailed even more chastisement for the offender. "God has whipped some of 'em worse dan dey beat us."[38] Even more, satisfaction for sinful and vicious acts against society's weak did not cease with the slave masters. It resumed with and haunted their descendants. Drawing on all of his theological knowledge and religious experience, former slave the Rev. Ishrael Massie asserted: "God's gwine punish deir chillun's chillun, yas sur!"[39]

Similarly, slaves juxtaposed God's justice with the kingdom of God. In fact, they perceived institutional slavery as a struggle between two kingdoms—that of God and that of Satan. Not surprisingly, the white master was Satan's proxy and belonged to his domain. The fruits of the master's earthly labor, then, yielded a permanent dwelling in hell. "I ain' plannin' on meetin' him in heaven," says a slave about her master. The fact that "Marse was an' ole Methodist preacher" would not prevent his arrival in the flames of hell. Others claimed that their masters were so mean they "went past heaven."[40]

Not only did a biblical interpretation of divine sovereignty inform bondservants about the masters' demonic kingdom, white practice gave credence to such a belief. When white patrollers happened upon the secret worship services of the "Invisible Institution," they inevitably whipped slaves fresh from prayer. As white hands ferociously gripped bull-whips and broke the exposed skin of bent black backs, the patrollers mocked God and claimed: "Ef I ketch you heah agin servin' God, I'll beat you. You havn' time to serve God. We bought you to serve us." Based on black folks' reading of Christian scriptures, all who opposed God served Satan. And when one master arrogantly proclaimed, "The Lord rule Heaven, but [I] Jim Smith rule the earth," slaves knew to which kingdom they belonged.[41]

To belong to God's realm meant African American chattel professed themselves children of God, who promised that they, the meek, should inherit the earth. Like Israel, if God owned them in God's sacred domain, they held the deed to a land of milk and honey. For the God of deliverance would fulfill the divine promise to God's possessions. Under slavery the children of God secretly hoped for the day of Jubilee, the inbreaking of God's Kingdom on earth. In fact, when "the walls came tumbling down" with God's Civil War, former chattel could "jist turn loose lack" and speak the truth. If previously they practiced stealth and ambiguity in theological imagery, now they plainly proclaimed. While former white masters slithered into hiding at the sound of advancing cannon fire, former slaves joyously jumped for Jubilee. They cried out with a renewed spirit and an open, defiant chorus:

> Old massa run away
> And us darkies stay at home.
> It must be now dat Kingdom's comin'
> And de year of Jubilee.[42]

Finally, the issue of the black slaves' perception of God (kingdom-coming talk) in contrast to the white masters' faith is, in the most fundamental and profound sense, a theological debate about the nature of God. One ex-slave tells a story about a white minister who, more than likely, preached the standard "slaves obey your master" sermon to the blacks on the plantation. Uncle Silas, a 100-year-old slave, hobbled up to the front row and challenged the white preacher with a pointed inquiry: "Is us slaves gonna be free in Heaven?" The preacher abruptly halted his religious instructions and eyed Uncle Silas with vile contempt and a desire to kill him for questioning white theological doctrine. However, Uncle Silas did not budge and this time resumed the debate with a yell: "Is God gonna free us slaves when we git to Heaven?" The white preacher withdrew a hand-kerchief, mopped the sweat from his pale white brow and replied, "Jesus says come unto Me ye who are free fum sin an' I will give you salvation." Undaunted Uncle Silas rebutted: "Gonna give us freedom 'long wid salvation?" The preacher resumed his homily and Uncle Silas remained standing up front during the rest of the service.[43] Uncle Silas epitomizes the millions of blacks under slavery who refused to accept white people's notion of God, that is, that blacks were to serve whites and maybe receive some amorphous reward after death. On the one hand stood a white male, symbolizing theological degrees, recognized Christian ordination, patriarchy, racial privilege, economic power, and Satan. On the other stood Uncle Silas, poor, black, unlettered, and a child of God.

For Uncle Silas, and the slaves, the debate revolved around the nature of God's liberation, the nature of the in-breaking of God's kingdom. Above all, Yahweh brought freedom; without it personal salvation proved an opiate of the oppressed. Note that Uncle Silas does not deny the fruit of individual salvific power. What he wants to know and what he *demands* to know is whether or not individual release from sin intersected with the radical overthrow of a racist system of injustice. What does God have to say about that? From the vantage point of chattel, we have seen how God embodies the Exodus, realizes justice for the marginalized, and brings God's children into the Kingdom.

Jesus

Jesus Won't Die No More

In the above story the white preacher attempted to undermine the pressing theological queries of Uncle Silas by bastardizing Jesus' promise of salvation. Still, Uncle Silas remained undeterred and vigorously pressed the question of Jesus' salvation in relation to liberation. This surfaces the slaves' interpretation of Jesus' role in their overall theological construct.

Deeply rooted in the Old Testament Scriptures, black people linked Jesus to Israel's fate and, consequently, underscored the ultimate and decisive dimension of divine presence. The following spiritual confirms this assertion:

> Jesus said He wouldn't die no mo',
> Said He wouldn't die no mo',
> So my dear chillens don' yer fear,
> Said He wouldn't die no mo'.

De Lord tole Moses what ter do,
Said He wouldn't die no mo',
Lead de chillen ob Isr'el froo',
Said He wouldn' die no mo'.[44]

It is clear that slaves positioned Jesus in the time of Moses. "De Lord tole Moses what ter do" indicates that Jesus had become Moses' contemporary. Because bondservants anchored themselves in the great deliverance achievements of Yahweh and the story of the oppressed Israelites, their sense of divine time did not restrict itself to a linear progression of God's interaction in human affairs. In fact, far from being a whimsical interpretation of the Bible, black folks' retro-projection of Jesus to Moses' days reflects an authentic and faithful reading of scripture. The slaves correctly followed the instructions from the prologue of John's gospel, which didactically states: "In the beginning was the Word and the Word was with God." If the Word, who is Jesus, existed in the beginning of time, then surely Jesus had the ability and the power to exhort Moses during the latter's time.

However, the appearance of Jesus during Moses' time speaks about more than human time. In addition and more fundamentally, the above quoted spiritual pinpoints the divine time of *kairos*—the divine importance of Jesus' earthly mission of liberation. The constant refrain of Jesus never dying anymore underlines the momentous significance of Jesus' death and resurrection for humankind, particularly the prototype oppressed Israel. Why the heavy emphasis on "die no mo'"? Because Jesus defeated the kingdom of Satan and all the political forces of evil representative of the demonic in all realms. Jesus won't "die no mo'" because there is no need for a future divine intermediary to conquer the political demons of evil powers. For the black chattel, then, the liberating nature of Jesus dying meant a radical alteration witnessed by Jesus initiating the kingdom.

At the same time that we fathom the import of Jesus' death, we must be careful not to miss the slaves' conscious interplay between the liberation motif of poor oppressed Israel in the Old Testament and the liberation motif of Jesus in the New Testament. Positioning Jesus back with Moses did not mean that black folks made relative or negated the earth-shattering divide between the political power of Satan and that of Jesus realized by the latter's earthly appearance (in the New Testament). On the contrary, by stationing Jesus back with Moses, the entire Exodus event becomes a paradigmatic foreshadowing of the liberation consequences of Jesus' death and resurrection—the universal poor's grand exodus from poverty to freedom. The slaves were radically centered on Jesus.

In a sense, Israel's rough wilderness journey and ultimate victory in Canaan mirrored Jesus' cross-resurrection experience. The interweaving of the Israel story with Jesus not dying anymore points to the slaves' claim of such a theological parallel. The One Jesus, noted for a sacrificial emptying-suffering and resurrection-glorification, acted as the freedom Word in Israel's suffering and eventual "glorification." Placing Jesus during the time when Moses led the first cross-resurrection journey, the first covenant, prepares the slaves for and confirms the omnipotent, liberating, and irresistible grace of the cross-resurrection event, that is, the final covenant. Jesus had a hand in the movement of Israel; when Jesus died, Jesus would never "die no mo'" because the cross-resurrection event symbolized the finality of satanic powers' absolute rout. Moreover, the constant emphasis on "die no mo'" sounds a note of confidence, courage, and hope for the blacks in bondage—"So my dear chillens don' yer fear." There is no need to fear the earthly white power structure. Since Jesus, through Moses, led the exploited Israelite people to victory and finished off Satan with the Cross and Resurrection, no human advocates for the Devil could defeat Jesus' just cause of black people's struggle for liberation.

The ultimate goal of Jesus' liberation movement by necessity must lead to freedom because the very being of Jesus is freedom. The following famous slave spiritual defines this ontological character.

> Steal away, steal away,
> Steal away to Jesus,
> Steal away, steal away home,
> I hain't got long to stay here.

In this instance, slaves employed a double meaning as a communication code to deceive paranoid whites ever on the lookout for religiously inspired slave rebellions. Such disguised slave songs heralded a distinct slave language. Thus even in their culture, bondsmen and bondswomen spoke of Jesus in their own linguistic modality. Black folk related to one another in a religious cultural medium that befuddled the normative white English and circumvented standard (white) morphology. Accordingly, in certain instances "Steal Away" utilized Jesus to represent a secret prayer meeting of the "Invisible Institution." In other cases Jesus stood for passage on Harriet Tubman's Underground Railroad to Canada or up North. For the Rev. Nat Turner, a black Baptist preacher, "Steal Away to Jesus" symbolized the gathering of his prophetic band of Christian witnesses in preparation for armed struggle and guerrilla warfare against slavery.[45]

Regardless of the usage of "Jesus" in black slave English—whether a free space; or a meeting to strategize for freedom; or freedom in heaven, the land of milk and honey in the cultural language of African American chattel—the essential being of Jesus is freedom.

Jesus' Offices and Attributes

In addition to ascribing ultimate significance and liberation ontology to Jesus, slaves also experienced specific offices in Jesus in particular, the kingly and priestly offices.[46] King Jesus imaged a conquering hero, a valiant warrior defiantly and triumphantly situated upon his majestic stallion. Given the slaves' lowly and persecuted existence, nothing could better picture the kingly office than a mighty and royal warrior. Slaves, therefore, sang from the depths of hearts that yearned for the King to come upon his stead as the Liberator. "Ride on, King Jesus," cry out the lyrics of one spiritual, "Ride on, conquering King."[47] Another verse describes Jesus and Satan: "King Jesus ride a milk-white horse," whereas "Satan ride an iron-gray horse." The slaves made their Jesus theology explicit; the Warrior King fought Satan, king of another kingdom. Because Jesus brought the Good News of ultimate deliverance and revealed a being of liberation, King Satan stood for all that prevented freedom. For black chattel, King Satan's earthly domain was the slavery system, which would inevitably succumb to the Conquering King.

The kingly office linked directly to the priestly office of Jesus in another slave spiritual.

> King Jesus lit de candle by de waterside,
> To see de little chillun when dey truly baptize.
> Honor! Honor unto de dying Lamb.
>
> Oh, run along chillun, an be baptize
> Might pretty meetin' by de waterside.
> Honor! Honor! unto de dying Lamb.[48]

Here the Conquering King serves as pastor over the "Invisible Institution," "pretty meetin' by de waterside." In the office of priest Jesus officiates at the baptismal rituals, initiating the religious service by lighting the candles. Secretly gathered at a stream or brook around midnight, black chattel called on the Lord to preside over their ceremony of dying and rising again through the process of full immersion, that is, "when dey truly baptize." Quite fittingly, just as Jesus had died and risen again—and thus become a new person—the slaves wanted to experience that same manifestation of new life in the presence of the One who was born again so that they too might be free in the New Being of Jesus. Coupled with the ontological essence of Jesus, baptism in the presence of the priestly Jesus signified deliverance from the earthly snares of sin and oppression. Therefore, to become new a slave died and buried the old self of subservience and attachment to sin-slavery and raised up the new self from the baptismal waters into salvation-liberation before the Priest. To be in Jesus is to be in freedom.

One also has to grasp the significance of the "dying Lamb" metaphor in the spiritual. Jesus offered Jesus' self as the paradigmatic sacrifice on the altar for the welfare of all humankind by spilling blood and dying. Quite conscious of this theological and cosmological priestly function, slaves, accordingly, give "Honor! unto de dying Lamb," and they run along to partake of the results of the Lamb's death by plunging themselves in the baptismal waters. One honors the Lamb by imitation and by service. Hence, under the loving eye of the priestly Jesus, slave baptism marked both a religious ceremonial and theological rite of passage. Reflecting their correct grasp of the Christian Scriptures, the slaves knew that the blood of the Lamb washes one clean of all sin through the ritual of baptism and, at the same time, the dying Lamb shifts the new person forever into the domain of Jesus, hence a theological transformation.

Besides the kingly and priestly offices, slaves acknowledged certain personal attributes of Jesus in the role of friend, converter, and mother. Slaves deeply cherished friendship. Friendship did not simply hold a status of casual acquaintance; quite the opposite, it literally brought either life or death. For example, the religious rebellions led by Denmark Vesey and Gabriel Prosser against slavery were both imperilled and then betrayed by obsequious slaves subservient to white theological idolatry. The denial of friendship resulted in black men and women losing their lives in these aborted religious uprisings.[49] Understandably, slaves attributed the supreme title of friend to Jesus, the One who never would forsake you in trials and tribulations. Black folk sang with confidence:

> Old Satan is one busy ole man;
> He rolls dem blocks all in my way;
> But Jesus is my bosom friend;
> He rolls dem blocks away.[50]

There is some ambiguity about the nature of Satan's "blocks" in this particular spiritual. But one can understand that, because slaves labored in the cotton fields and sang these lines in the presence of the white master, they wanted to allow enough ambiguity in the words to keep Ole Massa from detecting their full meaning. Out of necessity slaves developed a deceptive linguistic culture of survival to subvert white discovery of genuine slave thought. But when this spiritual burst forth from the prayerful lips of black folk in the "Invisible Institution," their own sacred political and cultural space, Satan distinctly and most definitely denoted slavery and the evils of white people. For the slaves Jesus, the bosom friend, ceaselessly and consistently destroyed the "blocks" of the devilish slave system and thereby thwarted death and preserved black life.

In the second personal attribute, Jesus as Converter dynamically holds together individual and communal, sacred and secular salvation-liberation. When Jesus entered their lives for the first time, slaves sensed a profound turning away from sin and evil and a turning toward Jesus. Black folks named this process conversion, the movement toward the divine in Jesus. To partake of salvation, therefore, one underwent a conversion experience. Fannie Moore relates this testimony of her mother immediately after the elder's conversion engagement with Jesus:

> I'se saved. De Lord done tell me I'se saved. Now I know de Lord will show me de way, I ain't gwine to grieve no more. No matter how much you all done beat me and my chillen de Lord will show me de way. And some day we never be slaves.[51]

When Jesus converts a person, he or she no longer can live and see in the old manner. Jesus communicates directly and instructs the convert that past sins have been washed away and that the person has been set on a new path. This new direction of salvation, this new journey or way, provides certainty about future liberation and a radically new vision about upcoming events in both individual and collective life. The above conversion witness imparts such a definite faith in the new life that, with the Word of Jesus, even whippings and severe punishment cannot deter the proclamation of the hope of good news to come.

Certainly the conversion process first frees Fannie Moore's mother from grievance and heavy burdens. Indeed, her personal transformation gives her nothing but joy and hope in those things not yet seen but promised; Jesus frees her personally. But glad tidings do not restrict themselves to one individual. The mother rejoices not only because Jesus has given her strength to bear torment and distress, but also because, having met Jesus, she knows that "trouble won't last always"; that is, slavery will soon perish and all things will be made new in the Lord's time. She joins personal salvation with the future redemption of the entire black community; she links her own existential sacred release with the total deliverance of the community. Harking back to her African cosmological nexus between sacred and secular as well as accurately building from the biblical intertwining of religious and "non-religious," a convened slave cannot shout for joy unless that joy encompasses deliverance for oppressed humankind.

Resuming the story, Fannie Moore describes her mother in this manner: "My mammy just grin all over her black wrinkled face." Though her face is jet black, with all the consequent negative and deleterious implications conjured up under slavery, Mammy nonetheless experienced the future vision of earthly liberation granted to her by Jesus' grace in conversion. Not even the whip of the slave master prevented Mammy from rejoicing in the Lord always for what the Lord had done for her. Jesus set her on the straight and narrow way. And even when the cowhide lashes ripped the skin off of her back, she "just go back to de field a singin'." Neither the bullwhip nor the backbreaking labor could stop her melodious voice from rising to heaven. No doubt she sang with renewed theological clarity and energy such sentiments as: "I don't feel weary and noways tired" and "Good news, member, good news, And I hearde from heav'n today."[52]

The image of Jesus as mother, the third and last personal attribute, evolves in the following spiritual:

> I heard the voice of Jesus callin'
> Come unto me and live.
> Lie, lie down, weepin' one,
> Rest thy head on my breast,
> I come to Jesus as I was,
> Weary and lone and tired and sad,
> I finds in him a restin' place,
> And he has made me glad.[53]

Weighted down with aches and pains caused by forced labor (which yielded absolute profit for whites), black human property struggled to maintain some sense of physical relief and spiritual nourishment. No earthly force could provide an adequate "restin' place"; Jesus could. Slaves needed suckling and nurturing; Jesus bestowed both. Jesus, exhibiting maternal qualities, beckoned them to "rest thy head on my breast," a secure place where those in bondage could relax in the warmth and renewing milk of divine comfort. A mother's sustenance supplies all the physical, intellectual, and spiritual support required to fend off the "troubles of de world," so that Jesus' little children could survive the lethal snares of Satan on their journey down the straight and narrow path. Yes, conversion enabled one to turn away from the vicious entrapments of the sinful slavery system (for example, not succumb to the false omnipotence of white folks) and pursue the righteousness of a new way. But conversion did not completely remove one from the brutal realities of the white man's rawhide whip. Rather, to maintain a faithful and liberated mind, spirit, and body, one needed to lean on the Lord.

Thus Jesus extended outstretched arms and offered the manna of life: "Come unto me and live." A child of the Lord needed only to come to Jesus, just as any child would approach his or her loving parent for restoration and vivifying renewal. For the poor, all the world says No!, but Jesus calls the earth's downtrodden to lie in the cradle of divine arms. Jesus offers soothing solace and acceptance for the weary, tired, and sad. Summoned from the cotton, sugarcane, or tobacco fields after eighteen hours of work, whipped with one hundred stripes from a cat-o-nine tails, soul crushed when one's babies were sold to the highest bidder, repeatedly raped by white slave masters and their sons, who together forced entrance into black women's slave cabins,[54] intellectually assaulted by laws forbidding the teaching of reading and writing to slaves, and kicked into the "nigger box" for several weeks because white people wanted to "break them down," black chattel needed and craved the loving and salutary breast of Jesus, the Mother, who "made me glad."

Jesus' offices and attributes brought joy because slaves rightly perceived an incarnational divine purpose that not only privileged the lowly social location of poor blacks but also marshalled all of creation for their ultimate deliverance. Rev. Bentley, a black Baptist preacher, recounts a sermon he once gave to his co-bondservants before emancipation.

> I remember on one occasion, when the President of the United States came to Georgia . . . the president came in a grand, beautiful carriage and drove to the best house in the whole town. . . . But a cord was drawn around the house to keep us negroes and other poor folks from coming too near. . . . But the great gentlemen and the rich folks went freely up the steps and in through the door and shook hands with him.

Rev. Bentley draws from the depths of his slave theological knowledge and convictions in order to paint an accurate picture of Jesus' sole incarnational intent. On the one side, he distinguishes the president enveloped in all the amenities of opulence and eminent stature. The president of the United States, archetypal political figurehead, holds the reins of the white power structure. The president assumes his commander-in-chief status at the behest of the nation's wealthy. Boasting the best of white, slave-master Christianity, he struts about under the mantle of absolute prestige with a sense of authoritative erudition like a king before his subjects. He epitomizes the sacred bearer of white culture and language; he depicts the pinnacle of male dominance in society. The president surrounds himself with wealth and those of his ilk: a grand beautiful carriage, the best white house, and the company of the rich white folks.

On the other hand, Rev. Bentley indicates a theological divide symbolized by the "cord." The cord symbolizes slavery, a rope used to whip and hang blacks, a barrier to forcefully lock out the poor African Americans from the earth's riches, which they have labored to create. Unlike the rich white folks, blacks huddle at the bottom of the steps to the wealthy white house; they cannot "freely" enter anywhere. They have no grand carriage or fine horses, and they never shake the president's hand. They lack decent clothing, adequate food, and sufficient shelter. The cord serves to rope them in and press them to the plow like the harness around a mule's neck. The cord wraps around their mind and spirit to stunt their theological and emotional development. The cord hides and confines them in the dinginess of the slave quarters. They cannot be seen or heard; they cannot plead their cases before earthly "royalty." White people have given them the gift of slavery and a rope, not liberation.

Then Rev. Bentley resumes his sermon:

> Now, did Christ come in that way? Did he come only to the rich? . . . No! Blessed be the Lord! He came to the poor! He came to us, and for our sakes![55]

Indeed, from the viewpoint of those at the bottom of the steps, Jesus Christ incarnated Jesus' self in the condition of poverty. Was not Jesus born in a manger amid cow dung because the powerful "capitalist" owner of the inn refused admission to wealthless strangers like Mary and Joseph? Did not Jesus become homeless, forced to wander in the back alleys of this world, "no place to lay his head"? Jesus too had been hunted like a criminal and outcast by the bloodhounds and rulers of his day. Had not the official theologians and religious leaders mocked and scorned Jesus' scriptural interpretations? And finally, did Jesus not endure whipping and a bloodied body pierced by nails to a wooden cross like the black ones lynched from a sagging tree on white folks' plantations? Rev. Bentley preached a theology that resonated with his slave congregation. With rustic but sophisticated clarity he apprehended the divine self-emptying into the human Jesus among squalor ("He came to the poor!"), and he knew that Jesus with all of God's creation came "for our sakes." Jesus Christ materialized for the poor and intended liberation for the poor. Hence Jesus delivers the gospel of incarnational divine purpose for human freedom.

Humanity

Created in Freedom

Perceptions of God and Jesus paved the way for the slaves' notion of a God-given humanity; they knew they were created in freedom. White theology and white Christian ethical practices notwithstanding, black folk maintained they were not livestock but infused from inception with inherent human attributes fashioned by divine hands. Former slave Charlie Moses sums up this belief in theological anthropology: "God Almighty never meant for human beings to be like animals. Us niggers has a soul an' a heart an' a mine. We ain't like a dog or horse."[56] The omnipotence of divine creation decried white heretical faith claims and produced black people as God's possessions, fully equipped with necessary and sufficient qualities and resources to function in a liberated manner. Though enslaved, bondsmen and bondswomen believed that God brought them into this world with souls that allowed them to express their spirituality and religious experience with the Holy. Likewise, God gave them hearts to beat with the feelings and emotions that characterize human capabilities in situations of pathos and exhilaration. They were not callous labor items. And God provided them with "a mine" to think independently and rationally about theological phenomena in relation to their full hearts and spirit-filled souls.

A soul signified a space for the Spirit to enter and transform black chattels' servile pariah status. A heart offered a receptacle for the divine compassion for liberation. And a mind proved vital in systematizing the black-God encounter so that the slaves' struggle for liberation was not simply a spontaneous and random assault against the heights of white power, but a deliberate and cohesive sacred world-view marching with the Spirit's warmth and God's passion for justice. To know in one's mind the freedom of God's liberation movement likewise entailed the feeling of the spiritual warmth in one's conversion process from the grip of sinful racism and toward the straight and narrow path of righteousness. Moreover, to have this knowledge meant that one possessed the emotional capability and intellectual gift to contrast the former non-converted, enslaved self with a renewed zest for deliverance.

Black folk felt deeply about their God-given humanity; none yearned to be a "dog or horse"; they sought to be liberated persons. Once planted on free soil, James L. Bradley speaks the truth about his former slave colleagues: "How strange it is that anybody should believe any human being could be a slave, and yet be contented!" Bradley strikes at the heart of white theological anthropology. Whites believe that blacks want to be and enjoy being subservient to white power. This basic fallacy lies in white people interpreting themselves as normative for black human self-definition. This view posits, at worst, an inherent lowly status to black attempts to handle major theological issues of the heart, soul, and mind and, at best, showers empty, false praises on black theological endeavors that attempt to imitate and, thereby, hopefully become white. Contrary to white folks' notions of black humanity, Bradley responds with the true image of African American humanity endowed with divine virtues when he proclaims: "I was never acquainted with a slave, however well he was treated, who did not long to be free."[57]

Black people longed to be free because they possessed not an ingrained lowliness or willingness toward a white mind-set but an inherent and natural gravitation toward freedom. An irrepressible longing to be free engulfed black humanity. In his autobiography Henry Bibb describes this irresistible divine impulse: "It kindled a fire of liberty within my breast which has never yet been quenched." Thus in the very definition of black humanity, the yearning for liberation burned like a prairie fire, swift and wide. And nothing, neither white supremacy nor theological heresy, could put out this flame sparking slaves to achieve their God-intended full creativity. Bibb believes that the fire of resistance is part of his nature. Furthermore, he finds proofs of divine liberation for humankind in what he terms "the inevitable laws of nature's God." He concludes the necessity for black liberation from two divinely created sources: from the natural disposition of slaves (in contrast to their existential disposition) the heat of deliverance never wanes or subsides, even after attaining freedom; and from the tug of liberation manifest in God's creation of nature, whose laws display the foundational beauty of inevitable liberty unfettered by human constraints. Echoing the slaves' heart-soul-mind human paradigm, which whites named treason, Bibb concludes: "I could see that the All-wise Creator had made man a free, moral, intelligent and accountable being."[58]

This subversiveness in black chattels' paradigm of theological anthropology grew out of their use of the intellect from the poor's perspective.

They knew that humanity spells liberty. Hence slaves constantly had to struggle with unraveling the false theological consciousness existentially imposed by white definition (the slaves' temporary predicament) and the natural primordial gift from God (the slaves' created humanity). One can observe the slaves' wrestling with these two contradictory states of being in the theological testimony of ex-slave Thomas Likers.

> But as soon as I came to the age of maturity, and could think for myself, I came to the conclusion that God never meant me for a slave, [and] that I should be a fool if I didn't take my liberty if I got the chance.[59]

Once reaching religious intellectual maturity and thinking for himself without the forbidding noose of white religious catechism, homily, or doctrine, Likers discovered a whole new world of liberation, no doubt in the Bible, nature, and in himself. Like his fellow slaves' post-conversion, he perceived a three-part movement of human transformation. In part one the Divine had originally molded him out of nothing into freedom; in the second part, the white man had refashioned and skewed his given nature into the warped satanic system of slavery. But, upon reaching theological adulthood, Likers felt beckoned to participate with God (through Jesus Christ) in the re-creation of himself along the natural intent of unchained humanity. To act as God's copartner in the third phase of divinely inspired re-created humanity, Likers had to take his liberty through the resistance of politics and the culture of resistance.

Resistance of Politics

Through the grace of the ultimate paradigmatic New Humanity of Jesus Christ, attaining the fully re-created African American self required political resistance. In this regard slaves showed ingenuity, courage, and creativity. God called them to pursue a human life in opposition to unbridled white power. Accordingly, they devised means and mechanisms for combating slave forces of evil; they resisted individually and collectively for their free humanity. Individually, slaves ran away from plantation labor and overseer lashes. Such acts of defiance represented in microcosm slave insurrection by way of sporadic strikes, for African American chattel stood at the vortex of slavery's successful economic production. Likewise, uncompensated slave work built the infrastructure of the southern territory. Thus individual runaways launched continual sorties against the very underpinnings of white societal well-being when they refused to remain chattel—and instruments of production for white profit. Numerous slave interviews testify to black folks' assertion of humanity by speaking with their feet. Former slave Arthur Greene confirms these illegal departures from white plantations: "Lord, Lord! Yes indeed, plenty of slaves uster run away. Why dem woods was full o' 'em chile." Greene continues to describe a particular acquaintance of his who habited with nature to avoid reintroduction into slavery.

> I knowd one man dat took an' run away 'cause his master was so mean an' cruel. He lived in a cave in de groun' fer fifteen yeahs 'fo' Lee's surrender. He made himself a den under de groun'; he an' his wife, an' raised fifteen chillun down dar.[60]

In the wilderness one was immersed in God's manifestation of the divine laws of natural freedom. Above we discovered Henry Bibb's attestation of human freedom revealed to him in "inevitable laws of nature's God." The wilderness setting and nature tradition provided both a haven from white imposition of political power over black humanity as well as a communing with and reaffirmation of God's word of deliverance. Black people knew that Yahweh had brought the oppressed Israelite laborers out of Egypt into the wilderness on their way toward Canaan land. God had led them. And in this temporary sojourn of the Hebrew children Yahweh had provided manna from heaven. Apparently the biblical God also maintained and nourished the slave who dwelled in a cave for fifteen years. Not only did he survive off of the fruits of the wilderness, but God blessed him and his wife with their own lives and the lives of fifteen children. For them the wilderness experience supplied protection from ever present white eyes and assisted their free humanity with sustaining sustenance. Truly God could make a way out of no way for those who dared to claim their genuine humanity.

Dwelling in the woods, in a cave in the wilderness, individual contraband slaves, no doubt, sent their voices up to Jesus. One of their spirituals indicates this:

1. I sought . . . my Lord in de wilderness,
   [I seek my Lord] in de wilderness, in de wilderness;
   I sought . . . my Lord in de wilderness,
   For I'm a-going home.

2. I found . . . grace in the wilderness. . . .[61]

Why were the woods so full of runaways, slaves who defined their humanity as more than white folks' private property and no less than as free children of God? Because the One who offered freedom to oppressed humanity tarried there on the boundaries of society in opposition to the whitewashed columns of the slave masters' residences. Therefore African American bondservants sought to exist with the Lord Jesus, who had conquered Satan's evil hold on all humanity, in "de wilderness." Jesus' momentous victory empowered those who dared to reach out to receive the divine offer of liberation. In a word, slaves sought to bring to fruition the full potential of their humanity by making themselves available in the wilderness to Jesus' power to break burdensome yokes for deliverance. No wonder they shouted: "I found free grace in the wilderness." Wilderness grace freely offered by Jesus conveyed a calling and commission to realize African American freedom, free grace for human freedom.

Individual political resistance to the desecration of God's black humanity also showed in the slaves' tenacious acts of self-defense. Because God created them, slaves had faith that their very being contained deposits of divine presence, which compelled them to act in self-defense to preserve these infused life-sustaining deposits from the finger of God. In one example, an overseer severely lashed an old black woman for what he perceived as her slow plowing in the fields. In response, the slave woman took her work implement and defended herself. "The woman became sore [from the whipping] and took her hoe and chopped him right across his head, and, child, you should have seen how she chopped this man to a bloody death."

To attack slaves, then, equalled a demonic attack on their inherent Godness. One could not allow Satan's earthly devils to prevail over that which belonged to the kingdom of God. On the contrary, once converted to the path of God through Jesus, black chattel believed they were obligated to wage a battle against the evil forces that relentlessly and untiringly struggled to pull them back to the dominion of Satan's white representatives. In a similar situation, another overseer expressed his anger toward an Aunt Susie Ann and "beat her till the blood run off her on the ground." Aunt Susie feigned unconsciousness as she fell to the aggressor's feet, and after the white overseer had put away his whip Aunt Susie grabbed this weapon and "whips him till he couldn't stand up."[62] The slaves did not believe that God's children should suffer despoiling of their bodies— temples of God's creation—in order for them to clothe themselves again with the idolatrous raiments of sin. Therefore, black chattel had to draw an unyielding line of demarcation between their humanity, crafted by divinity, and a subservient self slaving beneath Satan's rule.

Nevertheless, from a practical standpoint, one black slave could not succeed against the monstrosity of the slavery institution. Nor was the African American definition of humanity limited to an individual's singular rebellious nature. In fact, the resistance of politics connected individual opposition to communal insurrectionary support; one person succeeded in achieving full humanity only when the community aided in the deliverance process. Individual black humanity was manifested fully in relation to and in the context of a larger African American communal humanity. "Runaways use to come to our house all de time," relates former slave Mollie Booker, "to git somepin to eat." No one person, no matter how self-reliant, could sustain himself or herself in an absolute condition of isolation from the protective eyes and ears of fellow slaves if he or she wished to succeed in political resistance.

In certain cases the shrewd "antennas" of one group of slaves detected trouble for another group. For example, Susan Broaddus worked in the white folks' Big House where she overheard the slave master exclaim: "Gonna sell 'em, I swear fo' Christ, I gonna sell 'em." But Broaddus could not read or write. Knowing of his house servant's illiteracy, the master spelled the name of the two slaves he intended to sell further south into a harder and more cruel life in slavery. Susan Broaddus made "believe I didn't even hear" as the master spoke the letters of the chattel to be sold. But she "was packin' dem letters up in my haid all de time" and the first opportunity she got, she hurried out to the slave quarters and unpacked those letters to her own father "an' say 'em to him jus' like Marsa say 'em." Immediately her father, who could read and spell, notified the two slaves in question. The next day the two "had run away. . . . Dey never could fin' dose two slaves. Was gone to free land!"[63]

Clearly, to get to free land individual slaves relied upon multifarious communal ingenuity and stratagems. However, in the individual-collective definition of African American humanity, the most organized and efficient black political resistance—short of the slaves' victory in the Civil War—was the Underground Railroad with Moses, known more familiarly as Harriet Tubman, leading the way. Harriet Tubman set out for freedom one day by walking off of her white master's plantation in Maryland. Yet God spoke with her in such a way that she believed her own liberated existence, after successfully reaching "up north," contained a void as long as the remainder of her former slave community languished under the whimsical whips of wicked whites "down south." Though she had tasted the fruit of freedom, the plight of her fellow oppressed humankind and the weight of their dilemma under the institution of slavery moved her to return to the land of "Egypt" under God's instruction to set God's people free. Hence, slaves throughout the South recognized the name of Moses, the captain of the Underground Railroad. For instance, former slave Robert Ellett describes the success of Moses in her elusive moving of slaves from bondage to freedom, from deformed life to full humanity, from Satan's domain to God's kingdom. "'Moses' would come around" and, relates Ellett, "she would run [slaves] away and get them over near the border line . . . the next night on what you call the 'Underground Railroad.'"[64] In sum, slaves employed both individual and collective courage to pursue their God-given free humanity through the resistance of politics against the wickedness of the slave masters.

The Culture of Resistance

The anthropological resistance of politics went hand-in-hand with African American theological notions of a culture of resistance. Since slaves understood their created being through the lens of liberation, they defined and forged an appropriate black way of life—a culture of resistance—that provided them with an ethic of survival in the grip of white supremacy. Three instances of this cultural ethic, this lifestyle of black human resistance, will suffice: 1) a taking-not-stealing practice; 2) a duality of survival; and 3) a discourse of solidarity.

Taking-Not-Stealing.   Slave masters and their paid Christian ministers constantly exhorted slaves against stealing their masters' livestock and, of course, against stealing away to freedom. White theologians preached against such survival activities on the slaves' part as the work of the Anti-Christ. Instead of obeying their earthly owners, African American chattel rebuffed such doctrinal maxims and differentiated between stealing and taking. They defined "stealing" as the illegal removal of a fellow bond-servant's private property and taking as the removal of that which they believed the master had wrongfully stolen from the slaves. One former slave sums up the consensus: "Chile, nigger had to steal, an' I know ma mommer didn't tell no lie." What compelled enchained African Americans to disobey one of the cardinal rules of white law and risk certain brutal punishment if not death? The necessity of sheer survival mandated that they had to preserve their lives, that is, their humanity, by removing the basic provisions of life from the master's till. "See ole Mars and Missus give us such little rations," comments Marrinda Jane Singleton, "led her slaves to stealin'." For slaves, authentic religion and a Christian way of life did not mechanically flow from an abstract white prescription of negativities regarding ethical commands. A perspective from below, a perspective of black human survival, identified and affirmed right and wrong in contrast to those white folks who held privilege and power in society and could thus pontificate, legislate, and propagate the moral axioms of an oppressor class. Furthermore, while white people ate well and wrote sermons and theology about how their black human property should do good and not succumb to ethical impurities, African American chattel suffered emaciated bodies. The slaves "didn't get nothing but fat meat and corn bread and molasses. And they got tired of that same old thing," says one ex-slave. Consequently, they had to "illegally" enter the hen-house to get chickens or the smokehouse to get hams or the vegetable patches to procure adequate nourishment. In a word, they had to define and develop a culture of resistance, a way of life to survive slavery's onslaught on their humanity. As one former slave asks: "That ain't stealin', is it?"[65]

Blacks claimed they learned their "stealing" or "taking" from the biggest rogue of all, the white master. Another ex-bondsman offers his theological, anthropological insight:

> All you hear now is 'bout de nigger stealin' from dese here po' white devils. De whole cause of stealin' an' crime is 'cause dey fo'ced the nigger to do hit in dem back days. . . . White folks certainly taught niggers to steal. If they had given them enough to eat dey wouldn' have no cause to steal.[66]

This former slave underscores the insidious ethical nature of whites by classifying them with Satan ("po' white devils"). Hence evil human beings, that is, white humanity, utilized coercion against the children of God; this resulted in the latter's devising a new survival ethic. Whites did not give blacks enough to eat; on the contrary, they intentionally starved African Americans, giving their slaves a "cause to steal."

In addition, because slaves were forbidden normal sustenance, they maintained a historical perspective and connection to their native origins that led them to a new ethical interpretation. They did not suffer historical amnesia about how whites emerged as the dominating social class in North America. Rather, they rebelled against white practices due to the blatant hypocrisy of white theological instructions about the ethics of black humanity.

> "Dey allus done tell us it am wrong to lie and steal," explained Josephine Howard of Texas, "but why did de white folks steal my

mammy and her mammy? Dey lives clost to some water, somewher over in Africy. . . . Dat de sinfulles' stealin' dey is."[67]

White folks did the first stealing, "de sinfulles' stealin' dey is." How could slave masters discourse about the right and wrong of human practices when they had forcefully taken Africans from their motherland and the protective and watchful eyes of their parents? In Africa blacks had lived in their own political kingdoms with indigenous cultural expressions and theological world-views. Having committed a grave anthropological sin—stealing a race of people from their God-given space on earth—white folks, in the slaves' opinion, would forever reap the whirlwind of their own original sin. Specifically, their black property would never submit to white theology as long as African Americans retained their own historical theological consciousness.

The white slave-master class was not unaware of the theological foundation to black differentiation between stealing and taking. Indeed, a white slave mistress unwittingly surmised the biblical basis for the slaves' "robbing our [whites'] store room, meat house, etc." when she commented that slaves "think it right to steal from us, to spoil us, as the Israelites did the Egyptians."[68] Even in their theological anthropology, black folk upheld a scriptural stance. Just as the Israelites struggled in a land of bondage and formulated their own ethical norms as Yahweh's possessions, poor blacks perceived their plight similarly. To take from a white pharaoh, then, resulted naturally from what Yahweh-God required of God's created offspring. To fall short of what the Divinity required would upset the slaves' theological grasp of their original intended purpose to be free. Hence they developed their culture of resistance, which included their taking-not-stealing practice. Sarah Fitzpatrick succinctly summarizes:

> Niggers didn't think dat stealin' wuz so bad in dem times. Fak' is dey didn't call it stealin', dey called it takin'. Dey sa, "I ain't takin' f'om nobody but ma' mistrus an' Marster, an' I'm doin' dat 'cause I'se hongry!"[69]

Duality of Survival.   To further preserve their humanity in their culture of survival black chattel engineered a way of life that dichotomized between a conscious false display of the slave self in the company of the white master and an authentic expression of the true African American self in the presence of fellow enslaved blacks. Slaves viewed their dire straits from the marginalized vantage of ill-equipped underdogs waging a religious and theological war against evil earthly powers. To successfully engage a well-fortified enemy and prove victorious in the long run, then, necessitated the shrewdest possible techniques in one's total way of life. Therefore, on a daily basis slaves cultivated an uncanny astuteness to show one carefully sculptured facade to the white folks in order literally to live another day.

For example, generally blacks regurgitated all the theological catechisms taught by white theologians and preachers. Blacks did their jobs in the fields and in the Big House just as white folks instructed them. Likewise, blacks executed a myriad of other orders forced upon them by slave masters and mistresses. However, this acceptance of the institution of slavery was the "slave" face performed to keep the white folks off balance so that black chattel could survive and plan further the next move in a long-range strategy to be free, to assume full humanity. In his autobiography ex-slave Henry Bibb testifies to this necessary duality: "The only weapon of self defense that I could use successfully was that of deception." Not only did one defend oneself by politically resisting with physical force, one also preserved one's God-given humanity by culturally utilizing an ethic of deception.

But such a culture of resistance does not necessarily indicate African American fear of whites. Rather, it suggests a sober assessment that the enemy of slave humanity was a formidable opponent, one to be taken very seriously. To avoid becoming "uppity" or "obnoxious" to white folks, blacks feigned acceptance of white anthropological normalcy. Former slave Lunsford Lane writes the following in his narrative:

> Ever after I entertained the first idea of being free, I had endeavored so to conduct myself as not to become obnoxious to the white inhabitants, knowing as I did their power, and their hostility to the colored people.[70]

Once attaining knowledge of their original liberated humanity created by the Divinity ("the first idea of being free"), they consciously conducted themselves in such a manner as to keep slave masters off balance in the black-white relationship on the plantation. They gave whites the appearance of complying submissiveness and good-natured cooperation, for the more whites believed they had total control of blacks, the more blacks received breathing space to chart their next secret move of resistance for freedom.

This duality of survival contained an "African American" face in addition to the "slave" face, the former signifying the true humanity of the bondservants. One gained privileged access into this real face in situations controlled by blacks. The "Invisible Institution" represented the premier example. Here African American life or humanity forged its unadulterated self with the attendance of God's Spirit. Here the full process of conversion positioned the slave forever along the path of deliverance. The "Invisible Institution," in a word, exemplified the raw African American human life. Assembled deep in the woods, with only an overturned pot for protection, African Americans found worship space in which to thrive by maintaining morale in situations that seemed hopeless; preserving mental sanity in the face of the irrational white world; holding on to a sense of definiteness in a world where slaves lacked control of their present and future; refueling their energy in a white world full of sorrow in order to face the next day; synthesizing memories of African religious structures and practices with reinterpreted Christian beliefs to build a unique African American theology under slavery; organizing and plotting slave political and cultural resistance; and praising God for the divine intent of liberation against a world where Marsa branded them with hot irons as white people's slaves. It was this African American face that slaves forever withheld from the slave masters. During an American Freedmen's Inquiry Commission interview in 1863, former slave Robert Smalls gives the interviewer a hint of this duality of survival:

Q. Do the masters know anything of the secret life of the colored people?
A. No, sir; one life they show their masters and another life they don't show.[71]

Slaves not only used craftiness to survive, they also employed a discourse of solidarity.

Discourse of Solidarity.   Ex-slave Rev. Ishrael Massie informs us about a cave that a runaway built in the woods during slavery time. Despite the fact that all the slaves, including Rev. Massie, "knew whar he [the fugitive] wuz," no one turned him in to his Massa. Massie explains why: "In dem days, ya kno', niggers didn't tell on each other."[72] Indeed, not to tell on each other proved a vital ethical discourse of solidarity and survival for African American humanity. To betray this slave's cave in the southern backwoods was tantamount to desecrating a place where God had revealed the inherent gift of freedom through the inevitable laws of nature. Fellow slaves, then, could not surrender the space in which a co-chattel had liberated himself or herself, responding to the free grace of deliverance offered by Jesus in the wilderness. Moreover, an escaped slave graphically symbolized the efficient success of blacks' politics of resistance and culture of politics. The longer the escapee survived, the more he or she gave fellow sufferers hope for ultimate freedom.

Furthermore, no adherent to a liberating theology, a religious experience constructed out of the poor's biblical interpretation, would fracture the religious individual-collective dynamic ("all us slaves knew whar he wuz"). They all knew of the fugitive's whereabouts. But they were likewise cognizant of their own tradition, which rightly perceived the freedom of the individual as immensely benefiting the potential or realized emancipation of the collective, and vice versa. Also, to break the discourse of solidarity ("didn't tell on each other") would be to submit to white folks' religious and theological instructions—"slaves obey your masters." Similarly, abdication to white theology would confirm blacks' actual allegiance to the kingdom of Satan—the peculiar institution of slavery. Then all that the "Invisible Institution" stood for would amount to nought. To the contrary, those words, "don't tell on each other," articulated bondservants' dogged refusal and life-and-death determination not to commit suicide of the self, that is, not to mimic white theology. A former slave from another plantation echoes the sacred vow: "You see we never tole on each other."[73] Though legally private property belonging to whites, slaves defiantly refused to tell on each other in order to uphold their natural African American humanity. God had created them and, to keep the faith in God's grace, they delved into all possible political and cultural resistance.

Conclusion

After successfully defeating the Confederacy in the Civil War, four million African Americans claimed their freedom. We saw how they attributed that historic accomplishment to God sending "de war" and to Jesus the Warrior and Liberator. Between 1619, when the initial group of Africans stolen from their homeland arrived in the "New World," and 1865, the conclusion of the Civil War, black chattel mixed the remnants of their African traditional religions with biblical Christianity. In particular, they illegally and secretly met and worshiped in the "Invisible Institution." Over two hundred years of surreptitious religious gatherings allowed them to create a coherent and dynamic theology, which, if today's African American church is to take itself seriously, cannot be ignored. How can contemporary black ecclesial gatherings continue to drift on and be tossed to and fro by the battering and deleterious waves of white theology without an authentic Christian rudder? How can the black church call itself church if it refuses systematically to study and learn from the profound experience of its slave foreparents with the Divine? Truly, over two hundred years of African American "God-talk" provides an abundant source for the development of a contemporary black theology.

But this chapter has only scratched the surface. We have discovered the beginnings of some of the key elements needed in the constructive task for today's black theology. For instance, we saw how slave theology verified the intimate link between the church and the community, a connection that does not pit the sacred against the secular, as in certain elements in Euro-American theology. Because God rules all of creation, slaves understood that the political and the cultural dimensions of life carried theological implications. Moreover, to segregate religion and leave the secular to the secularist is, in fact, to surrender black humanity to heretical faith assertions perpetrated by the demonic dimensions of white theology. We also discovered the emphasis on the communal nature of the "Invisible Institution." Drawing on their African traditional religions and the Bible, the Old Testament in particular, slaves could only comprehend total deliverance as including the individual and the community. Thus they did not fall prey to a white capitalist theological precept that glorifies individualism and private-property democracy. Today's black theology has to promote individuality and communalism, not individualism and selfish motivations.

Furthermore, the black theology of the "Invisible Institution" tells us about the importance of perseverance through cross-bearing. For over two centuries African Americans endured and resisted white Christian assaults on black humanity. Through prayer and proper supplication to God, with Jesus as the captain of their old ship of Zion, and through the Spirit's empowerment, black folks made it through to emancipation. Paraphrasing old slave wisdom, "God may not come when you call him, but he's right on time!"

Thus the slaves' religious story verifies a contemporary black theological emphasis on doing theology from the perspective of the black poor. To deny this theological privilege is to betray the African American church's Christian tradition. We only hear God's word of liberation and salvation from the position of God's hearing and freeing a marginalized community as that chosen community moves toward justice. Moreover, since God freely gives deliverance to those who have nothing to lose in this world, black theology today must discern the signs of the times in the political and cultural life of the black church and community. And so,

God's self is revealed in attempts to alter unjust power relations and in the linguistics, thought forms, and way of life of the have-nots.

Finally, slave religious experience based itself on the Bible. African Americans under white slavery glued themselves to a theology filled with the "let my people go" witness of Yahweh in the Old Testament and with Jesus the Liberator of the poor in the New Testament. It is this faith, this black theology, that powered them through over two centuries of white theological heresy and white supremacy. Therefore, when their penultimate judgment day arrived, we can appreciate the following account of a former slave regarding the Civil War's end:

> [When freedom came] we was dancin' an' prancin' an' yellin' wid a big barn fir jus' ablazin' an' de white folks not darin' to come outside de big house. Guess dey [the slaves] made 'em up [spirituals], 'cause purty soon ev'ybody fo' miles around was singin' freedom songs. One went like dis:
>
> > I's free, I's free, I's free at las'!
> > Thank God A'mighty, I's free at las'![74]

Notes

1. Thomas Wentworth Higginson, *Army Life in a Black Regiment* (New York: W. W. Norton, 1984; originally published 1869), p. 49. Higginson commanded "the first slave regiment mustered into the service of the United States during the . . . civil war" (p. 27).
2. Charles L. Perdue, Jr., et al., eds., *Weevils in the Wheat: Interviews with Virginia Ex-Slaves* (Bloomington, Ind., and London: Indiana University Press, 1980; originally published by the University Press of Virginia in 1976), p. 62.
3. For a review of the European trading in Africans and the implantation of Africans in the New World, see Vincent Harding, *There Is a River: The Black Struggle for Freedom in America* (New York: Harcourt Brace Jovanovich, 1981), chaps. 1–2; and John Hope Franklin, *From Slavery to Freedom: A History of Negro Americans* (New York: Alfred A. Knopf, 1980), chaps. 3–5.
4. Ogbu U. Kalu, "Church Presence in Africa: A Historical Analysis of the Evangelization Process," in *African Theology En Route*, ed. Kofi Appiah-Kubi and Sergio Torres (Maryknoll, N.Y.: Orbis Books, 1979), p. 18. This quotation comes from a white missionary at the beginning of the twentieth century. However, these theological views were held since the first European contact with Africa.
5. John S. Mbiti, *Concepts of God in Africa* (London: SPCK, 1970), p. 6. Also see Gwinyai H. Muzorewa, *The Origins and Development of African Theology* (Maryknoll, N.Y.: Orbis Books, 1985), p. 9.
6. Mbiti, pp. 8–21.
7. Mbiti, pp. 31–76. Also see Muzorewa, p. 10.
8. Mercy Amba Oduyoye, "The Value of African Religious Beliefs and Practices for Christian Theology," in Appiah-Kubi and Torres, p. 111. Also see Muzorewa, p. 17;

E. Thomas Lawson, *Religions of Africa* (New York: Harper & Row, 1985), p. 97; and Mbiti, *African Religions and Philosophy* (Garden City, N.Y.: Anchor Books, 1970), p. 141.

9. Oduyoye, p. 111.

10. For treatments of the African influence in slave religion, see Gayraud Wilmore, *Black Religion and Black Radicalism: An Interpretation of the Religious History of Afro-American People* (Maryknoll, N.Y.: Orbis Books, 1983), chap. 1; and Albert J. Raboteau, *Slave Religion: The "Invisible Institution" in the Antebellum South* (New York: Oxford University Press, 1980), chaps. 1 and 2.

11. Becky Ilsey, quoted in Lawrence Levine, *Black Culture and Black Consciousness: Afro-American Folk Thought from Slavery to Freedom* (New York: Oxford University Press, 1981), p. 41.

12. Archie Booker, quoted in Perdue, pp. 52–53.

13. Charles Grandy, quoted in Perdue, p. 119.

14. Arthur Greene, quoted in Perdue, pp. 124–25.

15. Levi Pollard, quoted in Perdue, p. 230.

16. Ex-slave quotations come from James Mellon, ed., *Bullwhip Days: The Slaves Remember, An Oral History* (New York: Weidenfeld & Nicolson, 1988), p. 190; and Norman R. Yetman, *Life Under the "Peculiar Institution": Selections from the Slave Narrative Collection* (New York: Holt, Rinehart and Winston, 1970), pp. 53, 231, 56.

17. Quotations are found in Mellon, pp. 186–87, 194–95. Other ex-slave references to the cultural dimension of the "Invisible Institution" can be found in Levine, pp. 41, 42; Perdue, p. 100 ("'Cause we wanted to serve God in our own way. You see, 'legion needs a little motion—specially if you gwine feel de spirret"), p. 322; Clifton H. Johnson, ed., *God Struck Me Dead: Religious Conversion Experiences and Autobiographies of Ex-Slaves* (Philadelphia: Pilgrim Press, 1969), p. 153; and Eugene D. Genovese, *Roll, Jordan, Roll: The World the Slaves Made* (New York: Pantheon Books/Random House, 1972), p. 214 ("White folks can't pray right to de black man's God. Can't nobody do it for you. You got to call on God yourself when de spirit tell you.").

18. Perdue, pp. 93, 161. Throughout the slave narratives one discovers this reference to the turned-over pot. Also see Yetman, p. 229.

19. West Turner, quoted in Perdue, p. 290.

20. Ishrael Massie, quoted in Perdue, p. 208.

21. Perdue, pp. 183, 230, 150, 71.

22. Yetman, p. 33; Mellon, pp. 196-97.

23. See John W. Blassingame, ed., *Slave Testimony: Two Centuries of Letters, Speeches, Interviews, and Autobiographies* (Baton Rouge, La.: Louisiana State University Press, 1977), p. 411.

24. B. A. Botkin, ed., *Lay My Burden Down: A Folk History of Slavery* (Chicago: University of Chicago Press, 1957), p. 91. References for quotations on white sermons and catechisms can be found in Perdue, pp. 241, 183; Harriet A. Jacobs, *Incidents in the Life of a Slave Girl, Written by Herself* (Cambridge, Mass.: Harvard University Press, 1987), pp. 68–69; and Frederick Douglass, *Life and Times of Frederick Douglass* (New York: Collier Books, 1973; the first condensed version originally published in 1845), p. 157.

25. Yetman, pp. 231–32. Also review Levine, pp. 41–42, 46; and Perdue, pp. 207, 290.

26. Other ex-slave narratives substantiate white theological hubris. See Botkin, pp. 25, 94; Yetman, pp. 180–81, 262.

27. Charles Davenport, quoted in Yetman, p. 75.

28. Henry Bibb, *Narrative of the Life and Adventures of Henry Bibb, An American Slave, Written by Himself* (Philadelphia, Penn.: Historic Publications, n.d.), p. 114. Bibb originally published his book in 1849.

29. For a sampling of slave accounts of praying for freedom, see Perdue, pp. 94, 115; Mellon, pp. 190, 196; Yetman, pp. 177, 308, 312; and Blassingame, pp. 661, 700.

30. Solomon Northup, *Twelve Years a Slave* (New York: Dover Publications, 1970; originally published in 1854), p. 68.

31. Botkin, p. 26.

32. Charles Grandy, quoted in Perdue, p. 115.

33. J. W. Lindsey, quoted in Blassingame, p. 404. Also note Horace Muse's comment, "No res' fer niggers 'till God he step in an' put a stop to de white folks meanness," in Perdue, p. 216.

34. The theological view of "momentary God" comes from a narrative in Botkin, p. 34. The reference to Ole Ant Sissy comes from Perdue, p. 127.

35. Miles Mark Fisher, *Negro Slave Songs in the United States* (Secaucus, N.J.: The Citadel Press, 1978), p. 54.

36. James L. Bradley, quoted in Blassingame, p. 690.

37. Blassingame, pp. 125–26.

38. Perdue, pp. 72, 33; Yetman, p. 48; and Botkin, p. 178.

39. Ishrael Massie, quoted in Perdue, p. 206. Also see another ex-bondsman's similar claim on pp. 80, 93–94.

40. Perdue, pp. 274, 1. Other references to the theology of the heaven-hell kingdoms can be found in Mellon, p. 178, and Botkin, p. 121. George White stated: "Dey ask me de other day if I thought any of de slaveholders was in heaven an' I told 'em no 'cause dey was too mean" (Perdue, p. 311).

41. Botkin, p. 163; Perdue, pp. 93–94.

42. Yetman, pp. 113–14. For a description of the slaves' image of Jubilee, see Fisher, p. 121. For the slaves' self-interpretation as the children of God, see Yetman, p. 205.

43. Perdue, p. 184.

44. Levine, p. 28.

45. Fisher, pp. 66 ff; and John Lovell, Jr., *Black Song: The Forge and the Flame* (New York: Paragon House Publishers, 1986), pp. 125, 191, 238, 379. For further examination of the theological and religious thought of Rev. Nat Turner, see Stephen B. Oates, *The Fires of Jubilee: Nat Turner's Fierce Rebellion* (New York: The New American Library, 1975). For Harriet Tubman's theology, review Sarah Bradford, *Harriet Tubman: The Moses of Her People* (Secaucus, N.J.: The Citadel Press, 1961).

46. The slaves considered all aspects of Jesus as prophetic in the sense of subverting white Christianity. Therefore I do not develop a specific section on Jesus' prophetic office.

47. Levine, p. 43; William F. Allen, Charles P. Ware, and Lucy M. Garrison, eds., *Slave Songs of the United States* (New York: Books for Libraries Press, 1971, originally published 1867), p. 11.

48. Fisher, pp. 16–17.

49. See Harding; Wilmore.

50. Jacobs, p. 70; Fisher, p. 48.

51. Yetman, p. 228.

52. Allen, Ware, and Garrison, pp. 70, 97.

53. Yetman, p. 225.

54. Former slave Phillip Ward recalls, "Marsa bringing his son . . . down to the cabin. They both took her [a black woman]—the father showing the son what it was all about" (Perdue, p. 301).
55. Rev. Bentley, quoted in Levine, p. 49.
56. Charles Moses, quoted in Mellon, p. 182.
57. James L. Bradley, quoted in Blassingame, p. 689.
58. Bibb, p. 17.
59. Thomas Likers, quoted in Blassingame, p. 395.
60. Arthur Greene, quoted in Perdue, pp. 125, 153.
61. Fisher, p. 74.
62. Botkin, p. 176. For the reference to the black woman plowing in the field, see Botkin, p. 175.
63. Perdue, pp. 55–56.
64. Robert Ellett, quoted in Perdue, p. 85. For fuller details on the theological significance of the Underground Railroad, see Bradford.
65. Yetman, p. 53. Other quotations can be found in Botkin, p. 26, and Perdue, pp. 245, 226.
66. Perdue, p. 124.
67. Genovese, p. 605.
68. Ibid., p. 602.
69. Sarah Fitzpatrick, quoted in Blassingame, p. 652.
70. Lunsford Lane, quoted in Gilbert Osofsky, ed., *Puttin' On Ole Massa: The Slave Narratives of Henry Bibb, William Wells Brown, and Solomon Northup* (New York: Harper & Row, 1969), p. 9. The quotation from Henry Bibb comes from Bibb, p. 17.
71. Robert Smalls, quoted in Blassingame, p. 377.
72. Ishrael Massie, quoted in Perdue, p. 210.
73. Mrs. Jennie Patterson, quoted in Perdue, p. 220.
74. Perdue, p. 128.

Chapter 35

Black Theology and the Black Woman

Jacquelyn Grant

Liberation theologies have arisen out of the contexts of the liberation struggles of Black Americans, Latin Americans, American women, Black South Africans and Asians. These theologies represent a departure from traditional Christian theology. As a collective critique, liberation theologies raise serious questions about the normative use of Scripture, tradition and experience in Christian theology. Liberation theologians assert that the reigning theologies of the West have been used to legitimate the established order. Those to whom the church has entrusted the task of interpreting the meaning of God's activity in the world have been too content to represent the ruling classes. For this reason, say the liberation theologians, theology has generally not spoken to those who are oppressed by the political establishment.

Ironically, the criticism that liberation theology makes against classical theology has been turned against liberation theology itself. Just as most European and American theologians have acquiesced in the oppression of the West, for which they have been taken to task by liberation theologians, some liberation theologians have acquiesced in one or more oppressive aspects of the liberation struggle itself. Where racism is rejected, sexism has been embraced. Where classism is called into question, racism and sexism have been tolerated. And where sexism is repudiated, racism and classism are often ignored.

Although there is a certain validity to the argument that any one analysis—race, class or sex—is not sufficiently universal to embrace the needs of oppressed peoples, these particular analyses, nonetheless, have all been well presented and are crucial for a comprehensive and authentic liberation theology. In order for liberation theology to be faithful to itself it must hear the critique coming to it from the perspective of the Black woman—perhaps the most oppressed of all the oppressed.

I am concerned in this essay with how the experience of the Black woman calls into question certain assumptions in Liberation Theology in general, and Black Theology in particular. In the Latin American context this has already been done by women such as Beatriz Melano Couch and Consuelo Urquiza. A few Latin American theologians have begun to respond. Beatriz Couch, for example, accepts the starting point of Latin American theologians, but criticizes them for their exclusivism with respect to race and sex. She says:

> . . . we in Latin America stress the importance of the starting point, the praxis, and the use of social science to analyze our political, historical situation. In this I am in full agreement with my male colleagues . . . with one qualitative difference. I stress the need to give importance to the different cultural forms that express oppression; to the ideology that divides people not only according to class, but to race and sex. Racism and sexism are oppressive ideologies which deserve a specific treatment in the theology of liberation.[1]

More recently, Consuelo Urquiza called for the unification of Hispanic-American women in struggling against their oppression in the church and society. In commenting on the contradiction in the Pauline Epistles which undergird the oppression of the Hispanic-American woman, Urquiza said: "At the present time all Christians will agree with Paul in the first part of [Galatians 3:28] about freedom and slavery that there should not be slaves. . . . However, the next part of this verse . . . has been ignored and the equality between man and woman is not accepted. They would rather skip that line and go to the epistle to Timothy [2:9–15]."[2] Women theologians of Latin background are beginning to do theology and to sensitize other women to the necessity of participating in decisions which affect their lives and the life of their communities. Latin American theology will gain from these inputs which women are making to the theological process.

Third World and Black women[3] in the United States will soon collaborate in an attack on another aspect of Liberation Theology—Feminist Theology. Black and Third World women have begun to articulate their differences and similarities with the Feminist Movement, which is dominated by White American women who until now have been the chief authors of Feminist Theology. It is my contention that the theological perspectives of Black and Third World women should reflect these differences and similarities with Feminist Theology. It is my purpose, however, to look critically at Black Theology as a Black woman in an effort to determine how adequate is its conception of liberation for the total Black community. Pauli Murray and Theressa Hoover have in their own ways challenged Black Theology. They have spoken for themselves.

I want to begin with the question: "Where are Black women in Black Theology?" They are, in fact, invisible in Black Theology and we need to know why this is the case. Because the Black church experience and Black experience in general are important sources for doing Black Theology, we need to look at the Black woman in relation to both in order to understand the way Black Theology has applied its conception of liberation. Finally, in view of the status of the Black woman vis-à-vis Black Theology, the Black Church and the Black experience, a challenge needs to be presented to Black Theology. This is how I propose to discuss this important question.

The Invisibility of Black Women in Black Theology

In examining Black Theology it is necessary to make one of two assumptions: (1) either Black women have no place in the enterprise, or (2) Black men are capable of speaking for us. Both of these assumptions are false and need to be discarded. They arise out of a male-dominated culture which restricts women to certain areas of the society. In such a culture, men are given the warrant to speak for women on all matters of significance. It is no accident that all of the recognized Black theologians are men. This is what might be expected given the status and power accorded the discipline of theology. Professional theology is done by those who are highly trained. It requires, moreover, mastery of that power most accepted in the definition of manhood, the power or ability to "reason." This is supposedly what opens the door to participation in logical, philosophical debates and discussions presupposing rigorous intellectual training, for most of history, outside the "woman's sphere." Whereas the nature of men has been defined in terms of reason and the intellect, that of women has to do with intuition and emotionalism. Women were limited to matters related to the home while men carried out the more important work, involving use of the rational faculties.[4] These distinctions were not as clear in the slave community.[5] Slaves and women were thought to share the characteristics of emotionality and irrationality. As we move further away from the slave culture, however, a dualism between Black men and women increasingly emerges. This means that Black males have gradually increased their power and participation in the male-dominated society, while Black females have continued to endure the stereotypes and oppressions of an earlier period.

When sexual dualism has fully run its course in the Black community (and I believe that it has), it will not be difficult to see why Black women are invisible in Black Theology. Just as White women formerly had no place in White Theology—except as the receptors of White men's theological interpretations—Black women have had no place in the development of Black Theology. By self-appointment, or by the sinecure of a male-dominated society, Black men have deemed it proper to speak for the entire Black community, male and female.

In a sense, Black men's acceptance of the patriarchal model is logical and to be expected. Black male slaves were unable to reap the benefits of patriarchy. Before emancipation they were not given the opportunity to serve as protector and provider for Black women and children, as White men were able to do for their women and children. Much of what was considered "manhood" had to do with how well one could perform these functions. It seems only natural that the post-emancipation Black men would view as primary importance the reclaiming of their property—their women and their children. Moreover, it is natural that Black men would claim their "natural" right to the "man's world." But it should be emphasized that this is logical and natural only if one has accepted without question the terms and values of patriarchy—the concept of male control and supremacy.

Black men must ask themselves a difficult question. How can a White society characterized by Black enslavement, colonialism, and imperialism provide the normative conception of women for Black society? How can the sphere of the woman, as defined by White men, be free from the evils and oppressions that are found in the White society? The important point is that in matters relative to the relationship between the sexes, Black men have accepted without question the patriarchal structures of the White society as normative for the Black community. How can a Black minister preach in a way which advocates St. Paul's dictum concerning women while ignoring or repudiating his dictum concerning slaves? Many Black women are enraged as they listen to "liberated" Black men speak about the "place of women" in words and phrases similar to those of the very White oppressors they condemn.

Black women have been invisible in theology because theological scholarship has not been a part of the woman's sphere. The first of the above two assumptions results, therefore, from the historical orientation of the dominant culture. The second follows from the first. If women have no place in theology it becomes the natural prerogative of men to monopolize theological concerns, including those relating specifically to women. Inasmuch as Black men have accepted the sexual dualisms of the dominant culture they presume to speak for Black women.

Before finally dismissing the two assumptions a pertinent question should be raised. Does the absence of Black women in the circles producing Black Theology necessarily mean that the resultant theology cannot be in the best interest of Black women? The answer is obvious. Feminist theologians during the past few years have shown how theology done by men in male-dominated cultures has served to undergird patriarchal structures in society.[6] If Black men have accepted those structures, is there any reason to believe that the theology written by Black men would be any more liberating of Black women than White Theology was for White women? It would seem that in view of the oppression that Black people have suffered, Black men would be particularly sensitive to the oppression of others.[7]

James Cone has stated that the task of Black Theology "is to analyze the nature of the gospel of Jesus Christ in the light of oppressed Black people so they will see the gospel as inseparable from their humiliated condition, bestowing on them the necessary power to break the chains of oppression. This means that it is a theology of and for the Black community, seeking to interpret the religious dimensions of the forces of liberation in that community."[8] What are the forces of liberation in the Black community and the Black Church? Are they to be exclusively defined by the struggle against racism? My answer to that question is No. There are oppressive realities in the Black community which are related to, but independent of, the fact of racism. Sexism is one such reality. Black men seek to liberate themselves from racial stereotypes and the conditions of oppression without giving due attention to the stereotypes and oppressions against women which parallel those against Blacks. Blacks fight to be free of the stereotype that all Blacks are dirty and ugly, or that Black represents evil and darkness.[9] The slogan "Black is Beautiful" was a counterattack on these stereotypes. The parallel for women is the history of women as "unclean" especially during menstruation and after childbirth. Because the model of beauty in the White male-dominated society is the "long-haired blonde," with all that goes along with that mystique, Black women have an additional problem with the Western idea of "ugliness," particularly as they encounter Black men who have adopted this White model of beauty. Similarly, the Christian teaching that woman is responsible for the fall of *mankind* and is, therefore, the source of evil has had a detrimental effect in the experience of Black women.

Like all oppressed peoples the self-image of Blacks has suffered damage. In addition they have not been in control of their own destiny. It is the goal of the Black liberation struggle to change radically the socioeconomic and political conditions of Black people by inculcating self-love, self-control, self-reliance, and political power. The concepts of self-love, self-control, self-reliance, and political participation certainly have broad significance for Black women, even though they were taught that, by virtue of their sex, they had to be completely dependent on *man;* yet while their historical situation reflected the need for dependence, the powerlessness of Black men made it necessary for them to seek those values for themselves.

Racism and sexism are interrelated just as all forms of oppression are interrelated. Sexism, however, has a reality and significance of its own because it represents that peculiar form of oppression suffered by Black women at the hands of Black men. It is important to examine this reality of sexism as it operated in both the Black community and the Black Church. We will consider first the Black Church and second the Black community to determine to what extent Black Theology has measured up to its defined task with respect to the liberation of Black women.[10]

The Black Church and the Black Woman

I can agree with Karl Barth as he describes the peculiar function of theology as the church's "subjecting herself to a self-test." "She [the church] faces herself with the question of truth, i.e., she measures her action, her language about God, against her existence as a Church."[11]

On the one hand, Black Theology must continue to criticize classical theology and the White Church. But on the other hand, Black Theology must subject the Black Church to a "self-test." The task of the church according to James Cone is threefold: (1) "It proclaims the reality of divine liberation. . . . It is not possible to receive the good news of freedom and also keep it to ourselves; it must be told to the whole world. . . ." (2) "It actively shares in the liberation struggle." (3) It "is a visible manifestation that the gospel is a reality. . . . If it [the church] lives according to the old order (as it usually has), then no one will believe its message."[12] It is clear that Black Theology must ask whether or not the Black Church is faithful to this task. Moreover, the language of the Black Church about God must be consistent with its action.[13] These requirements of the church's faithfulness in the struggle for liberation have not been met as far as the issue of women is concerned.

If the liberation of women is not proclaimed, the church's proclamation cannot be about divine liberation. If the church does not share in the liberation struggle of Black women, its liberation struggle is not authentic. If women are oppressed, the church cannot possibly be "a visible manifestation that the gospel is a reality"—for the gospel cannot be real in that context. One can see the contradictions between the church's language or proclamation of liberation and its action by looking both at the status of Black women in the church as laity and Black women in the ordained ministry of the church.

It is often said that women are the "backbone" of the church. On the surface this may appear to be a compliment, especially when one considers the function of the backbone in the human anatomy. Theressa Hoover prefers to use the term "glue" to describe the function of women in the Black Church. In any case, the telling portion of the word backbone is "back." It has become apparent to me that most of the ministers who use this term have reference to location rather than function. What they really mean is that women are in the "background" and should be kept there. They are merely support workers. This is borne out by my observation that in many churches women are consistently given responsibilities in the kitchen, while men are elected or appointed to the important boards and leadership positions. While decisions and policies may be discussed in the kitchen, they are certainly not made there. Recently I conducted a study in one conference of the African Methodist Episcopal Church which indicated that women are accorded greater participation on the decision-making boards of smaller rather than larger churches.[14] This political maneuver helps to keep women "in their place" in the denomination as well as in the local congregations. The conspiracy to keep women relegated to the background is also aided by the continuous psychological and political strategizing that keeps women from realizing their own potential power in the church. Not only are they rewarded for performance in "backbone" or supportive positions, but they are penalized for trying to move from the backbone to the head position—the leadership of the church. It is by considering the distinction between prescribed support positions and the policy-making, leadership positions that the oppression of Black women in the Black Church can be seen more clearly.

For the most part, men have monopolized the ministry as a profession. The ministry of women as fully ordained clergypersons has always been controversial. The Black church fathers were unable to see the injustices of their own practices, even when they paralleled the injustices in the White Church against which they rebelled.

In the early nineteenth century, the Rev. Richard Allen perceived that it was unjust for Blacks, free and slaves, to be relegated to the balcony and restricted to a special time to pray and kneel at the communion table; for this he should be praised. Yet because of his acceptance of the patriarchal system, Allen was unable to see the injustice in relegating women to one area of the church—the pews—by withholding ordination from women as he did in the case of Mrs. Jarena Lee.[15] Lee recorded Allen's response when she informed him of her call to "go preach the Gospel":

> He replied by asking in what sphere I wished to move in? I said, among the Methodists. He then replied, that a Mrs. Cook, a Methodist lady, had also some time before requested the same privilege; who it was believed, had done much good in the way of *exhortation*, and *holding prayer meetings;* and who had been permitted to do so by the *verbal license* of the preacher in charge at the time. But as to women preaching, he said that our Discipline knew nothing at all about it—that *it did not call* for women preachers.[16]

Because of this response Jarena Lee's preaching ministry was delayed for eight years. She was not unaware of the sexist injustice in Allen's response.

> Oh how careful ought we be, lest through our by-laws of church government and discipline, we bring into disrepute even the word of life. For as unseemly as it may appear nowadays for a women to preach, it should be remembered that nothing is impossible with God. And why should it be thought impossible, heterodox, or improper for a woman to preach, seeing the Saviour died for the woman as well as the man?[17]

Another "colored minister of the gospel," Elizabeth, was greatly troubled over her call to preach, or more accurately, over the response of men to her call to preach. She said:

> I often felt that I was unfit to assemble with the congregation with whom I had gathered. . . . I felt that I was despised on account of this gracious calling, and was looked upon as a speckled bird by the ministers to whom I looked for instruction . . . some [of the ministers] would cry out, "you are an enthusiast," and others said, "the Discipline did not allow of any such division of work."[18]

Sometime later when questioned about her authority to preach against slavery and her ordination status, she responded that she preached "not by the commission of men's hands: if the Lord had ordained me, I needed nothing better."[19] With this commitment to God rather than to a male-dominated church structure she led a fruitful ministry.

Mrs. Amanda Berry Smith, like Mrs. Jarena Lee, had to conduct her ministry outside the structure of the A.M.E. Church. Smith described herself as a "plain Christian woman" with "no money" and "no prominence."[20] But she was intrigued with the idea of attending the General Conference of 1872 in Nashville, Tennessee. Her inquiry into the cost of going to Nashville brought the following comments from some of the A.M.E. brethren:

> "I tell you, Sister, it will cost money to go down there; and if you ain't got plenty of it, it's no use to go"; . . . another said:
> "What does she want to go for?"
> "Woman preacher; they want to be ordained," was the reply.
> "I mean to fight that thing," said the other.
> "Yes, indeed, so will I," said another.[21]

The oppression of women in the ministry took many forms. In addition to not being granted ordination, the authenticity of "the call" of women was frequently put to the test. Lee, Elizabeth, and Smith spoke of the many souls they had brought to Christ through their preaching and singing in local Black congregations, as well as in White and mixed congregations. It was not until Bishop Richard Allen heard Jarena Lee preach that he was convinced that she was of the Spirit. He, however, still refused to ordain her. The "brethren," including some bishops of the 1872 General Conference of the A.M.E. Church, were convinced that Amanda Berry Smith was blessed with the Spirit of God after hearing her sing at a session held at Fisk University. Smith tells us that " . . . the Spirit of the Lord seemed to fall on all the people. The preachers got happy. . . ." This experience brought invitations for her to preach at several churches, but it did not bring an appointment to a local congregation as pastor or the right of ordination. She summed up the experience in this way: " . . . after that many of my brethren believed in me, especially as the question of ordination of women never was mooted in the Conference."[22]

Several Black denominations have since begun to ordain women.[23] But this matter of women preachers having the extra burden of proving their call to an extent not required of men still prevails in the Black Church today. A study in which I participated at Union Theological Seminary in New York City bears this out. Interviews with Black ministers of different denominations revealed that their prejudices against women, and espe-cially women in the ministry, resulted in unfair expectations and unjust treatment of women ministers whom they encountered.[24]

It is the unfair expectations placed upon women and blatant discrimi-nation that keeps them "in the pew" and "out of the pulpit." This matter of keeping women in the pew has been carried to ridiculous extremes. At the 1971 Annual Convocation of the National Conference of Black Churchmen,[25] held at the Liberty Baptist Church in Chicago, I was slightly amused when, as I approached the pulpit to place my cassette tape recorder near the speaker, Walter Fauntroy, as several brothers had already done, I was stopped by a man who informed me that I could not enter the pulpit area. When I asked why not, he directed me to the pas-tor who told me that women were not permitted in the pulpit, but that he would have a man place the recorder there for me. Although I could not believe that explanation a serious one, I agreed to have a man place it on the pulpit for me and returned to my seat in the sanctuary for the contin-uation of the convocation. The seriousness of the pastor's statement became clear to me later at that meeting when Mary Jane Patterson, a Presbyterian Church executive, was refused the right to speak from the pulpit.[26] This was clearly a case of sex discrimination in a Black church—keeping women "in the pew" and "out of the pulpit."

As far as the issue of women is concerned it is obvious that the Black Church described by C. Eric Lincoln has not fared much better than the Negro Church of E. Franklin Frazier.[27] The failure of the Black Church and Black Theology to proclaim explicitly the liberation of Black women indicates that they cannot claim to be agents of divine liberation. If the theology, like the church, has no word for Black women, its conception of liberation is inauthentic.

The Black Experience and the Black Woman

For the most part, Black church*men* have not dealt with the oppression of Black women in either the Black Church or the Black community. Fred-erick Douglass was one notable exception in the 19th century. His active advocacy for women's rights was a demonstration against the contradic-tion between preaching "justice for all" and practicing the continued oppression of women. He, therefore, "dared not claim a right [for him-self] which he would not concede to women."[28] These words describe the convictions of a man who was active both in the church and in the larger Black community. This is significant because there is usually a direct relationship between what goes on in the Black Church and the Black secular community.

The status of Black women in the community parallels that of Black women in the church. Black Theology considers the Black experience to be the context out of which its questions about God and human existence are formulated. This is assumed to be the context in which God's revelation is received and interpreted. Only from the perspective of the poor and the oppressed can theology be adequately done. Arising out of the Black Power Movement of the 1960s, Black Theology purports to take seriously the experience of the larger community's struggle for liberation. But if this is, indeed, the case, Black Theology must function in the secular community in the same way as it should function in the church community. It must serve as a "self-test" to see whether the rhetoric or proclamation of the Black community's struggle for liberation is consistent with its practices. How does the "self-test" principle operate among the poor and the oppressed? Certainly Black Theology has spoken to some of the forms of oppression which exist within the community of the oppressed. Many of the injustices it has attacked are the same as those which gave rise to the prophets of the Old Testament. But the fact that Black Theology does not include sexism specifically as one of those injustices is all too evident. It suggests that the theologians do not understand sexism to be one of the oppressive realities of the Black community. Silence on this specific issue can only mean conformity with the status quo. The most prominent Black theologian, James Cone, has recently broken this silence.

> The Black church, like all other churches, is a male dominated church. The difficulty that Black male ministers have in supporting the equality of women in the church and society stems partly from the lack of a clear liberation-criterion rooted in the gospel and in the present struggles of oppressed peoples. . . . It is truly amazing that many black male ministers, young and old, can hear the message of liberation in the gospel when related to racism but remain deaf to a similar message in the context of sexism. . . .[29]

It is difficult to understand how Black men manage to exclude the liberation of Black women from their interpretation of the liberating gospel. Any correct analysis of the poor and oppressed would reveal some interesting and inescapable facts about the situation of women within oppressed groups. Without succumbing to the long and fruitless debate of "who is more oppressed than whom?" I want to make some pointed suggestions to Black male theologians.

It would not be very difficult to argue that since Black women are the poorest of the poor, the most oppressed of the oppressed, their experience provides a most fruitful context for doing Black Theology. The research of Jacquelyne Jackson attests to the extreme deprivation of Black women. Jackson supports her claim with statistical data that "in comparison with black males and white males and females, black women yet constitute the most disadvantaged group in the US, as evidenced especially by their largely unenviable educational, occupational, employment and income levels, and availability of marital partners."[30] In other words, in spite of the "quite insignificant" educational advantage that Black women have over Black men, they have "had the greatest access to the worst jobs at the lowest earnings."[31] It is important to emphasize this fact in order to elevate to its rightful level a concern for the condition of Black women, not only in the world at large, but in the Black community and the Black Church. It is my contention that if Black Theology speaks of the Black community as if the special problems of Black women do not exist, it is no different from the White Theology it claims to reject precisely because of its inability to take account of the existence of Black people in its theological formulations.

It is instructive to note that the experience of Black women working in the Black Power movement further accented the problem of the oppression of women in the Black community. Because of their invisibility in the leadership of the movement they, like women of the church, provided the "support" segment of the movement. They filled the streets when numbers were needed for demonstrations. They stuffed the envelopes in the offices and performed other menial tasks. Kathleen Cleaver, in a *Black Scholar* interview, revealed some of the problems in the movement which caused her to become involved in women's liberation issues. While underscoring the crucial role played by women as Black Power activists, Kathleen Cleaver, nonetheless, acknowledged the presence of sex discrimination.

> I viewed myself as assisting everything that was done. . . . The form of assistance that women give in political movements to men is just as crucial as the leadership that men give to those movements. And this is something that is never recognized and never dealt with. *Because women are always relegated to assistance* and this is where I became interested in the liberation of women. Conflicts, constant conflicts came up, conflicts that would rise as a result of the fact that I was married to a member of the Central Committee and I was also

an officer in the Party. Things that I would have suggested myself would be implemented. But if I suggested them the suggestion might be rejected. If they were suggested by a man the suggestion would be implemented.

It seemed throughout the history of my working with the Party, I always had to struggle with this. The suggestion itself was never viewed objectively. *The fact that the suggestion came from a women gave it some lesser value.* And it seemed that it had something to do with the egos of the men involved. I know that the first demonstration that we had at the courthouse for Huey Newton I was very instrumental in organizing; the first time we went out on the soundtrucks, I was on the soundtrucks; the first leaflet we put out, I wrote; the first demonstration, I made up the pamphlets. And the members of that demonstration for the most part were women. I've noticed that throughout my dealings in the black movement in the United States, that the *most anxious, the most eager, the most active, the most quick to understand the problem and quick to move are women.*[32]

Cleaver exposed the fact that even when leadership was given to women, sexism lurked in the wings. As executive secretary of the Student Nonviolent Coordinating Committee (SNCC), Ruby Doris Robinson was described as the "heart beat of SNCC." Yet there were "the constant conflicts, the constant struggles that she was subjected to because she was a woman."[33]

Notwithstanding all the evidence to the contrary, some might want to argue that the central problem of Black women is related to their race and not their sex. Such an argument then presumes that the problem cannot be resolved apart from the Black struggle. I contend that as long as the Black struggle refuses to recognize and deal with its sexism, the idea that women will receive justice from that struggle alone will never work. It will not work because Black women will no longer allow Black men to ignore their unique problems and needs in the name of some distorted view of the "liberation of the total community." I would bring to the minds of the proponents of this argument the words of President Sekou Toure as he wrote about the role of African women in the revolution. He said, "if African women cannot possibly conduct their struggle in isolation from the struggle that our people wage for African liberation, African freedom, conversely, is not effective unless it brings about the liberation of African women."[34] Black men who have an investment in the patriarchal structure of White America and who intend to do Christian theology have yet to realize that if Jesus is liberator of the oppressed, all of the oppressed must be liberated. Perhaps the proponents of the argument that the cause of Black women must be subsumed under a larger cause should look to South African theologians Sabelo Ntwasa and Basil Moore. They affirm that "Black theology, as it struggles to formulate a theology of liberation relevant to South Africa, cannot afford to perpetuate any form of domination, not even male domination. If its liberation is not human enough to include the liberation of women, it will not be liberation."[35]

A Challenge to Black Theology

My central argument is this: Black Theology cannot continue to treat Black women as if they were invisible creatures who are on the outside looking into the Black experience, the Black Church, and the Black theological enterprise. It will have to deal with the community of believers in all aspects as integral parts of the whole community. Black Theology, therefore, must speak to the bishops who hide behind the statement, "Women don't want women pastors." It must speak to the pastors who say, "My church isn't ready for women preachers yet." It must teach the seminarians who feel that "women have no place in seminary." It must address the women in the church and community who are content and complacent with their oppression. It must challenge the educators who would reeducate the people on every issue except the issue of the dignity and equality of women.

Black women represent more than 50 percent of the Black community and more than 70 percent of the Black Church. How then can an authentic theology of liberation arise out of these communities without specifically addressing the liberation of the women in both places? Does the fact that certain questions are raised by Black women make them any less Black concerns? If, as I contend, the liberation of Black men and women is inseparable, then a radical split cannot be made between racism and sexism. Black women are oppressed by racism *and* sexism. It is therefore necessary that Black men and women be actively involved in combating both evils.

Only as Black women in greater numbers make their way from the background to the forefront will the true strength of the Black community be fully realized. There is already a heritage of strong Black women and men upon which a stronger nation can be built. There is a tradition which declares that God is at work in the experience of the Black woman. This tradition, in the context of the total Black experience, can provide data for the development of a wholistic Black Theology. Such a theology will repudiate the God of classical theology who is presented as an absolute Patriarch, a deserting father who created Black men and women and then "walked out" in the face of responsibility. Such a theology will look at the meaning of the total Jesus Christ Event; it will consider not only how God through Jesus Christ is related to the oppressed men, but to women as well. Such a theology will "allow" God through the Holy Spirit to work through persons without regard to race, sex, or class. This theology will exercise its prophetic function, and serve as a "self-test" in a church characterized by the sins of racism, sexism, and other forms of oppression. Until Black women theologians are fully participating in the theological enterprise, it is important to keep Black male theologians and Black leaders cognizant of their dereliction. They must be made aware of the fact that Black women are needed not only as Christian educators, but as theologians and church leaders. It is only when Black women and men share jointly the leadership in theology and in the church and community that the Black nation will become strong and liberated. Only then will there be the possibility that Black Theology can become a theology of divine liberation.

One final word for those who argue that the issues of racism and sexism are too complicated and should not be confused. I agree that the issues should not be "confused." But the elimination of both racism and sexism is so crucial for the liberation of Black persons that we cannot shrink from facing them together. Sojourner Truth tells us why this is so. In 1867 she spoke out on the issue of suffrage and what she said at that time is still relevant to us as we deal with the liberation of Black women today.

> I feel that if I have to answer for the deeds done in my body just as much as a man, I have a right to have just as much as a man. There is a great stir about colored men getting their rights, but not a word about the colored women; and if colored men get their rights, and not colored women theirs, you see the colored men will be masters over the women, and it will be just as bad as it was before. So I am for keeping the thing going while things are stirring: because if we wait till it is still, it will take a great while to get it going again. . . .[36]

Black women have to keep the issue of sexism "going" in the Black community, in the Black Church, and in Black Theology until it has been eliminated. To do otherwise means that they will be pushed aside until eternity. Therefore, with Sojourner Truth, I'm for "keeping things going while things are stirring. . . ."

Notes

1. Beatriz Melano Couch, remarks on the feminist panel of Theology in the Americas Conference in Detroit in August 1975, printed in *Theology in the Americas*, ed. Sergio Torres and John Eagleson (Maryknoll, N.Y.: Orbis Books, 1976), p. 375.

2. Consuelo Urquiza, "A Message from a Hispanic-American Woman," *The Fifth Commission: A Monitor for Third World Concerns* IV (June–July 1978), insert. The Fifth Commission is a commission of the National Council of the Churches of Christ in the USA (NCC), 475 Riverside Drive, New York, N.Y.

3. I agree with the Fifth Commission that "the Third World is not a geographical entity, but rather the world of oppressed peoples in their struggle for liberation." In this sense, Black women are included in the term "Third World." However, in order to accent the peculiar identity, problems, and needs of Black women in the First World or the Third World contexts, I choose to make the distinction between Black and other Third World women.

4. For a discussion of sexual dualisms in our society, see Rosemary Ruether, *New Woman/New Earth* (New York: Seabury Press, 1975), chap. 1; and *Liberation Theology* (New York: Paulist Press, 1972), pp. 16 ff. Also for a discussion of sexual (social) dualisms as related to the brain hemispheres, see Sheila Collins, *A Different Heaven and Earth* (Valley Forge: Judson Press, 1974), pp. 169–170.

5. Angela Davis, "Reflections on the Black Woman's Role in the Community of Slaves," *The Black Scholar*, vol. 4 no. 3 (December 1971), pp. 3–15. I do take issue with Davis's point, however. The Black community may have experienced "equality in inequality," but this was forced on them from the dominant or enslaving community. She does not deal with the inequality within the community itself.

6. See Sheila Collins, op. cit., Rosemary Ruether, op. cit., Letty Russell, *Human Liberation in the Feminist Perspective* (Philadelphia: Westminster Press, 1974); and Mary Daly, *Beyond God the Father* (Boston: Beacon Press, 1973).

7. Surely the factor of race would be absent, but one would have to do an in-depth analysis to determine the possible effect on the status of Black women.

8. James Cone, *A Black Theology of Liberation* (Philadelphia: J.B. Lippincott, 1970), p. 23.

9. Eulalio Baltazar discusses color symbolism (white is good; black is evil) as a reflection of racism in the White Theology which perpetuates it. *The Dark Center: A Process Theology of Blackness* (New York: Paulist Press, 1973).

10. One may want to argue that Black Theology is not concerned with sexism but with racism. I will argue in this essay that such a theology could speak only half the truth, if truth at all.

11. Karl Barth, *Church Dogmatics*, vol. 1, part 1, p. 2.

12. Cone, op. cit., pp. 230–232.

13. James Cone and Albert Cleage do make this observation of the contemporary Black Church and its response to the struggles against racism. See Cleage, *The Black Messiah* (New York: Sheed and Ward, 1969), passim; and Cone, op. cit., passim.

14. A study that I conducted in the Philadelphia Conference of the African Methodist Episcopal Church, May 1976. It also included sporadic samplings of churches in other conferences in the First Episcopal District. As for example, a church of 1,660 members (500 men and 1,160 women) had a trustee board of 8 men and 1 woman and a steward board of 13 men and 6 women. A church of 100 members (35 men and 65 women) had a trustee board of 5 men and 4 women and a steward board of 5 men and 4 women.

15. Jarena Lee, *The Life and Religious Experience of Jarena Lee: A Colored Lady Giving an Account of Her Call to Preach the Gospel* (Philadelphia, 1836), printed in Dorothy Porter, ed., *Early Negro Writing 1760–1837* (Boston: Beacon Press, 1971), pp. 494–514.

16. Ibid., p. 503 (italics added). Carol George in *Segregated Sabbaths* (New York: Oxford University Press, 1973), presents a very positive picture of the relationship between Jarena Lee and Bishop Richard Allen. She feels that by the time Lee approached Allen, he had "modified his views on woman's rights" (p. 129). She contends that since Allen was free from the Methodist Church he was able to "determine his own policy" with respect to women under the auspices of the A.M.E. Church. It should be noted that Bishop Allen accepted the Rev. Jarena Lee as a woman preacher and not as an ordained preacher with full rights and privileges thereof. Even Carol George admitted that Lee traveled with Bishop Allen only "as an unofficial member of their delegation to conference sessions in New York and Baltimore," "to attend," not to participate in them. I agree that this does represent progress in Bishop Allen's view as compared to Lee's first approach; on the second approach, he was at least encouraging. Then he began "to promote her interests" (p. 129)—But he did not ordain her.

17. Ibid.

18. "Elizabeth: A Colored Minister of the Gospel," printed in Bert James Loewenberg and Ruth Bogin, ed., *Black Women in Nineteenth-Century American Life* (University Park, Pa.: The Pennsylvania State University Press, 1976), p. 132. The denomination of Elizabeth is not known to this writer. Her parents were Methodists, but she was separated from her parents at the age of eleven. However, the master from which she gained her freedom was Presbyterian. Her autobiography was published by the Philadelphia Quakers.

19. Ibid., p. 133.

20. Amanda Berry Smith, *An Autobiography: The Story of the Lord's Dealings with Mrs. Amanda Berry Smith, the Colored Evangelist* (Chicago, 1893); printed in Loewenberg and Bogin, op. cit., p. 157.

21. Ibid.

22. Ibid., p. 159.

23. The African Methodist Episcopal Church started ordaining women in 1948, according to the Rev. William P. Foley of Bridgestreet A.M.E. Church in Brooklyn, New York. The first ordained woman was Martha J. Keys.

   The African Methodist Episcopal Zion Church ordained women as early as 1884. At that time, Mrs. Julia A. Foote was ordained Deacon in the New York Annual Conference. In 1894 Mrs. Mary J. Small was ordained Deacon and in 1898, she was ordained Elder. See David Henry Bradley, Sr., *A History of the A.M.E. Zion Church*, vol. (part) II, 1872–1968 (Nashville: The Parthenon Press, 1970), pp. 384, 393.

   The Christian Methodist Episcopal Church enacted legislation to ordain women in the 1970 General Conference. Since then approximately 75 women have been ordained. See the Rev. N. Charles Thomas, general secretary of the C.M.E. Church and director of the Department of Ministry, Memphis, Tennessee.

   Many Baptist churches still do not ordain women. Some churches in the Pentecostal tradition do not ordain women. However, in some other Pentecostal churches, women are founders, pastors, elders, and bishops.

   In the case of the A.M.E.Z. Church, where women were ordained as early as 1884, the important question would be, what happened to the women who were ordained? In addition, all of these churches (except for those which do give leadership to women) should answer the following questions: Have women been assigned to pastor "class A" churches? Have women been appointed as presiding elders? (There is currently one woman presiding elder in the A.M.E. Church.) Have women been elected to serve as bishop of any of these churches? Have women served as presidents of conventions?

24. Yolande Herron, Jacquelyn Grant, Gwendolyn Johnson, and Samuel Roberts, "Black Women and the Field Education Experience at Union Theological Seminary: Problems and Prospects" (New York: Union Theological Seminary, May 1978).

25. This organization continues to call itself the National Conference of Black Churchmen despite the protests of women members.

26. NCBC has since made the decision to examine the policies of its host institutions (churches) to avoid the reoccurrence of such incidents.

27. E. Franklin Frazier, *The Negro Church in America;* C. Eric Lincoln, *The Black Church Since Frazier* (New York: Schocken Books, 1974), passim.

28. Printed in Philip S. Foner, ed., *Frederick Douglass on Women's Rights* (Westport, Conn.: Greenwood Press), p. 51.

29. Cone, "Black Ecumenism and the Liberation Struggle," delivered at Yale University, February 16–17, 1978, and Quinn Chapel A.M.E. Church, May 22, 1978. In two other recent papers he has voiced concern on women's issues, relating them to the larger question of liberation. These papers are: "New Roles in the Ministry: A Theological Appraisal" and "Black Theology and the Black Church: Where Do We Go from Here?"

30. Jacquelyne Jackson, "But Where Are the Men?" *The Black Scholar,* op. cit., p. 30.

31. Ibid., p. 32.

32. Kathleen Cleaver was interviewed by Sister Julia Herve. Ibid., pp. 55–56.

33. Ibid., p. 55.

34. Sekou Toure, "The Role of Women in the Revolution," *The Black Scholar,* vol. 6, no. 6 (March 1975), p. 32.

35. Sabelo Ntwasa and Basil Moore, "The Concept of God in Black Theology," in *The Challenge of Black Theology in South Africa,* ed. Basil Moore (Atlanta, Ga.: John Knox Press, 1974), pp. 25–26.

36. Sojourner Truth, "Keeping the Things Going While Things Are Stirring," printed in Miriam Schneir, ed., *Feminism: The Essential Historical Writings* (New York: Random House, 1972), pp. 129–130.

Chapter 36

Divine Racism
The Unacknowledged Threshold Issue for Black Theology

James Cone
God, Champion of the Oppressed

William R. Jones

Divine Racism
The Unacknowledged Threshold Issue for Black Theology

Divine Racism
The Unacknowledged Threshold Issue for Black Theology

This chapter purports to show that the issue of divine racism has been illegitimately ignored by the current black theologians. I say "illegitimately" because the question has been avoided only by disregarding concrete and explicit features of their own thought. Since specific conclusions advanced by the black theologians are meaningful and valid only if they provide a convincing refutation of the charge of divine racism, the absence of an analysis and denial of the question "Is God a white racist?" constitutes a curious inconsistency and removes the necessary support the superstructure of their respective systems requires. I will show specifically that the issue of divine racism is implicit in the following propositions affirmed by the black theologians: black theology is a theology of liberation; the politics of God and blacks as God's chosen people are central themes in black theology; and black theology is committed to a total and comprehensive examination of the Christian tradition.

Divine Racism: Explicit and Implicit

The same argument cannot be used to demonstrate that the issue of divine racism is central for each black theologian. For most, it is necessary to proceed by way of inference, showing that an explicit concept, conclusion, or methodological position acknowledged by the black theologian presupposes the question of divine racism or its refutation. However, for one theologian, James Cone, the route of logical inference is not required, for the concept is explicitly asserted in a way that reveals its centrality. Cone declares: "Either God is identified with the oppressed to the point that their experience becomes his, or he is a god of racism."[1] And to remove all doubt regarding the meaning of "identification," he claims in a similar vein, "Black theology refuses to accept a God who is not identified totally with the goals of the black community. If God is not for us and against white people, then he is a murderer, and we had better kill him. The task of black theology is to kill Gods who do not belong to the black community."[2]

These statements clearly indicate that Cone is not only aware of the issue of divine racism, but even more important, he regards it as an unavoidable issue for black theology. Note that his analysis establishes two opposing options, which define the arena for black theological discussion and construction. There is the option of "a God of racism," one who is *against* or *indifferent to* black liberation. The second option is the logical and theological opposite: a God *for* black liberation. By defining the task of black theology as destroying Gods who are not for black liberation, Cone is maintaining that the black theologian must effectively refute the position of divine racism. In fact he appears to claim that the black theologian can defend the position that God is for black liberation, only by refuting the charge that He is a god of racism. His words also convey the meaning that this refutation is the crucial part of the black theologian's task. If the analysis of Cone here is correct, then his own definition of the purpose of black theology creates the exact critical apparatus and the rules of the game I will use to criticize his system.

It is not difficult to show that the theodicy issue is also central for the remaining black theologians, and these factors further establish its centrality for Cone. The starting point for this demonstration is the conclusion already established: suffering introduces the theodicy question. Thus the general issue of theodicy and the particular issue of divine racism are central because of the status the black theologians assign to black suffering. Theodicy and divine racism are controlling issues because black oppression and suffering are made the starting point for theological analysis.

It can now be established that black suffering is either explicitly or implicitly central for the contemporary black theologians. Here is an explicit reference from the theology of James Cone: "The point of departure for black theology is the question, How do we dare speak of God in a suffering world . . . in which blacks are humiliated because they are black? This question . . . occupies the central place in our theological perspective."[3]

A similar emphasis is present in J. Deotis Roberts' discussion of "The Black Man's God."

> I am taking the position that the problem of God presents itself to blacks in terms, not of the existence of God, but rather in terms of the moral attributes of God. . . . The Christian understanding of God must develop out of the black presence in a white racist society, and out of an experience of oppression endured for almost four centuries.[4]

What is not always explicit in the language of black theology may often lie implicit. For example, once "black liberation" is established as the primary goal or the rationale for black theology, black suffering becomes its necessary starting point. "Liberation" as defined by the black theologians means nothing if it does not mean release from the suffering that lies at the heart of oppression. To define liberation as the *summum bonum*, the highest good for blacks, is, at the same time, to make that suffering which is the core of oppression the essential ingredient of the *summum malum*, the ultimate evil.

Each of the black theologians regards his position as a theology of liberation, and this motif is usually proclaimed in the title of the work: *A Black Theology of Liberation, Liberation and Reconciliation: A Black Theology*. Even where "liberation" is absent from the title, it is soon discovered to be the black theologian's principal focus.

What is less obvious is that the issue of divine racism becomes an unavoidable issue in the context of any "black theology of liberation." To undertake the construction of a black theology of liberation requires the prior conclusion that black suffering is oppressive or negative. God disapproves of it; He does not demand that blacks should endure it. But suffering is multievidential;[5] it can express a relation of divine favor or disfavor. Consequently, the possibility of divine disfavor cannot be avoided.

By virtue of his task, the black theologian of liberation is committed to the view that black oppression is not evidence of divine disfavor. Accordingly, he is required to show—if he is to avoid the indictment of begging the question—that the general class of divine disfavor, of which divine racism is a subclass, does not accurately describe the black situation.

Other segments of the black theologian's thought force the issue of divine racism. It has already been established that ethnic suffering raises the question of divine racism. Accordingly it is necessary only to demonstrate that the black theologians describe black suffering as a variety of ethnic suffering. It will become clear that each affirms that black suffering is maldistributed, enormous, dehumanizing, and transgenerational. At this juncture, however, it is sufficient to note that to define the black situation as *oppressive* is actually to affirm the essentials of ethnic suffering; and the definition of the black situation as oppressive, we have seen, is the consequence of the black theologian's own definition of his task as a theology of liberation.

The Politics of God, and Blacks as God's Chosen People

There are other determining factors that oblige the black theologian to resolve the issue of divine racism at the outset of his theological construction, and these are factors common to his basic position. Each black theologian affirms the doctrine of the politics of God as an essential plank. Man must decide where God is working for human liberation in our midst and join Him in the struggle. The following statement from Cone is representative of this viewpoint: "Black theology merely tries to discern the activity of the Holy One as he effects his purpose in the liberation of man from the forces of oppression. We must make decisions about where God is at work so we can join him in his fight against evil."[6]

But given ethnic suffering and the multievidentiality of suffering, certain restrictions are placed on the theological employment of the politics of God. Without the prior refutation of the charge of divine racism, the black theologian begs the question if he affirms the politics of God. It goes without saying that Cone and others advocate joining God because they presuppose that He is on the side of blacks. This is to say that where God is active in human affairs He is engaged for the (a) good of (b) blacks—if not all of mankind. But ethnic suffering and the multievidentiality of suffering call both (a) and (b) into question. The excessive amount of black suffering and its enormity, both of which are admitted by calling the black situation oppressive, make it risky if not foolhardy to affirm that God is at work for the liberation of blacks. Must not the black theologian first explain how their plight came about in the first place in the face of God's alleged activity in their behalf? In sum, it is not possible to make the politics of God the second floor of the edifice of black theology without a foundational theodicy that decisively answers the charge of divine racism. The politics of God presupposes that God is not a white racist, without establishing it.

Much the same argument can be made regarding another favorite motif of black theology: blacks as God's "chosen people." To regard blacks as God's elect involves the prior conclusion that God is favorably inclined toward them. But this claim can be made only if the opposite relation, divine disfavor, has been effectively eliminated. And this, again, demands the refutation of divine racism as logically prior to any proposition about divine favor.

Divine Racism and a *de Novo* Theology

The precondition for constructing a black theology is the conviction that an unacknowledged white theology, a theology of racism and oppression, dominates the field. Black theology, then, by definition is committed to a theological development not only beyond this white theology but in conscious and fundamental opposition to it. My purpose now is to show that this understanding of black theology requires a *de novo* approach to theologizing and that within this context the issue of divine racism cannot be avoided.

The black theologians assign primacy to the black experience as the theological norm. It is argued, for instance, that theological reflection must begin with the questions and issues that are pressing upon the black mind and heart. In this way, the black experience determines the theological agenda; it selects the appropriate theological issues, and ranks them. Moreover, the answers must not only harmonize with the black experience, they must also hasten the actualization of the aspirations incarnate in the black hope.

Again, the black experience passes final judgment upon the functional and dysfunctional quality of the entire theological tradition. A theological concept is functional if and only if it advances black liberation or liberation-reconciliation. As Cone concludes, "The legitimacy of any language, religious or otherwise, is determined by its usability in the struggle for liberation."[7]

On the basis of the foregoing analysis—and here we arrive at the crucial point for the argument—the black theologian is committed to a total examination of the theological tradition. Once it is concluded that Christianity is infected with "Whitianity," once it is granted that a racist doctrine of the tradition has been perpetuated, the tradition must be scrutinized in the most radical and comprehensive manner. Like the rotten apples in the barrel of good apples, nothing prior to the examination can be regarded as sacrosanct for black theology—be it God, Jesus, or the Bible. Each and every category must be painstakingly inspected, and if it is found to be infected with the virus of racism or oppression, it must be cast aside.

The same point can be made from another perspective: Once the black theologian is convinced that a racist variety of Christian faith has continued, he must proceed, as it were, *de novo*, placing the entire tradition under a rigid theological ban. And this ban can be lifted only when each part proves its orthodoxy by showing its racist quotient to be minimal.

I question whether the black theologians have recognized the sweeping consequences of their presuppositions here. I also take the position that their appraisal has not been sufficiently comprehensive and radical. From my vantage point I see a fatal residue of the oppressor's worldview in some of their theistic premises, in particular the intrinsic goodness of

God. One of the compelling reasons for raising the issue of divine racism is to force a discussion of traditional concepts of God as possible props for oppression.

The major point can now be made: From a *de novo* perspective, the rival claims, God is a white racist and God is a soul brother, stand on equal footing. Accordingly, the black theologian cannot avoid the issue of divine racism. In fact it can be argued that he contradicts himself methodologically if he emphasizes black suffering and calls for a comprehensive scrutiny of the tradition but fails to raise the question of divine racism.

The presuppositions of the black theologians, in summary, force the conclusion that the foundation for their systems must be a theodicy that effectively rebuts the charge that God is a white racist. Whether they provide the requisite rebuttal can only be determined by critical inspection of their thought.

I would insist at the outset that the black theologian cannot simply assume the falsity of the charge. His own norm makes this plain. Black suffering must be analyzed from an existential and not an abstract or theoretical perspective. The question of divine racism emerges because of the blood and guts of black suffering. The black theologian, accordingly, must utilize evidential materials drawn from the actual black experience, past, present—and if he dares—the future. What is to be rejected are mere rational and theoretical formulations that are not substantiated by the actual history of blacks. In this connection I will contend that the liberation of non-blacks, e.g. the Jews in the Exodus account, can never count decisively against the charge that God is a white racist. . . .

⚜⚜⚜⚜⚜⚜

James Cone
God, Champion of the Oppressed

Cone's theodicy provides an illuminating comparison and contrast to [Joseph R.] Washington's. On the one hand he unconditionally rejects Washington's primary model of vicarious suffering and substitutes what, for him, is a more central biblical pattern. Here the two stand at opposite poles of the theological spectrum. On the other hand, the logical structure of Cone's theodicy is in fact identical to Washington's, and the same fatal flaws that infected Washington's reasoning are also present in Cone's.

Like Washington, Cone fails to corroborate the event of black liberation that the validity and soundness of his position require. Cone's refutation of the theodicy of deserved punishment is ineffectual, and again like Washington, the consistency of his viewpoint is seriously endangered. At the heart of Cone's theodicy, too, is a question-begging component—the concept of blacks as the oppressed.

The validity of Cone's theodicy can be more accurately appraised and its more subtle shortcomings pinpointed if we discuss first the specific theodicies he rejects and the grounds for the rejection.[1] This is of critical importance, for this taking of a position through the process of eliminating indefensible theodicies establishes the logical and theological boundaries within which he must operate—if he is to be consistent. It is at this point that what is peculiar to his own thinking might be expected to emerge and assume command of his system.

Every criticism or refutation presupposes a critical apparatus or norm on the basis of which the object under analysis is said to be acceptable or not. For Cone, any theodicy that "reconciles the oppressed to unjust treatment committed against them"[2] must be rejected. Stated positively, whatever advances the goal of black liberation, which is to say, the liberation of the oppressed, is suitable for a black theodicy. Thus the pro-liberation quotient of the theodicy in question appears to be his functional norm. If this is not the case, it is difficult to account for the summary manner in which he discards well-known theodicies with an impeccable biblical ancestry, such as the theodicy of vicarious suffering and the theodicy of deserved punishment.

The Refutation of the Theodicy of Vicarious Suffering

God, Cone maintains, has not chosen blacks "for redemptive suffering but for freedom." They are not "elected to be Yahweh's suffering people." Rather, they are elected because they are oppressed[3] "against [their] will and God has decided to make [their] liberation his own."[4]

Two different claims can be extracted from his statements here, and Cone appears to endorse both. Blacks are not chosen to suffer for the other, that is, the white oppressor. The other-directed impulse of the suffering servant is replaced with a self-sacrificing love for oneself and the black nation. There is no hint of the duality of black suffering in Cone's analysis. In fact, suffering for the other, in his understanding, can only be regarded as a feature of God's disfavor.

The statements also yield the interpretation that blacks are not chosen to suffer. Rather, the exact opposite must be affirmed: their election signifies their eventual liberation from the suffering that defines oppression. Indeed it would appear that the continued suffering of blacks, from Cone's perspective, is tantamount to the claim that God is a white racist. "God cannot be the God of black people and also will their suffering,"[5] be it redemptive or not. For this reason, then, substantiating the exaltation-liberation event for blacks, i.e. that which terminates black oppression, is mandatory for Cone.

It appears, however, that the suffering implicit in vicarious suffering is not what Cone finds abhorrent, for he explicitly allows that God's election of blacks for eventual liberation entails unavoidable suffering. He admits that the suffering involved in "the struggle for liberation" is inescapable. Moreover, he acknowledges that this type of suffering is central to the biblical perspective and the Church's account of the earthly ministry of Jesus:

> The relationship between freedom and suffering is . . . evident in the biblical tradition. The election of Israel is a call to share in Yahweh's liberation. . . . To be Yahweh's people, Israel must be willing to fight against everything that is against this liberation. . . . This involves suffering, because liberation means a confrontation between evil and the will of him who directs history. The existence of Jesus also discloses that freedom is bound up with suffering. It is not possible to be for him and not realize that one has chosen an existence in suffering.[6]

Thus it appears that the real object of Cone's theological scorn is suffering for the other when the other is the *oppressor.* Indeed to affirm vicarious suffering for the oppressor would contradict his doctrine of God. Moreover, it would mean that the work of God and the activity of the Christian would be at cross purposes. This can be affirmed because God intends the destruction of the oppressor, not his salvation. And God can do no other, in Cone's scheme, because His essence is to be against oppression. Cone expresses God's annihilating wrath against oppression and the oppressor at several key points:

> Black theology will accept only a love of God which participates in the destruction of the white enemy.[7]

> What we need is the divine love as expressed in Black Power, which is the power of black people to destroy their oppressors here and now by any means at their disposal. Unless God is participating in this holy activity, we must reject his love.[8]

It would be necessary to reject God's love, because to permit oppression to remain would signify that God's nature is not to be for the oppressed; rather, it would reveal that God is a God of racism. Thus Cone's rejection of vicarious suffering, based on God's nature and purpose, requires that he substantiate the definitive liberation event for blacks.[9]

To make the same point in another way: Cone must repudiate a theodicy of vicarious suffering, because God's love is restricted to the oppressed. It is worth noting that the black theologians who endorse vicarious suffering also affirm God's universal love, His concern for the salvation and well-being of both the oppressor and the oppressed. The explicit universalism of Washington has been documented. J. Deotis Roberts' emphasis upon liberation and reconciliation as the twin purposes of God moves in the same direction. A similar accent illustrates the thought of Major Jones.

But, for Cone and Albert Cleage, God is not for all; they replace His universal love with a radical particularity of concern:

> In the New Testament, Jesus is not for all, but for the oppressed, the poor and unwanted of society, and against oppressors. . . . Either God is for black people in their fight for liberation and against the white oppressors, or he is not. He cannot be both for us and for the white oppressors at the same time.[10]

In sum, to assert God's universal love for both the oppressed and the oppressor is to make God a monstrously immoral Dr. Jekyll and Mr. Hyde.

Cone's argument for the essential unity of God's love and God's wrath, God's love and God's righteousness goes hand in hand with his rejection of the theodicy of vicarious suffering. It is necessary to elevate God's wrath to co-ordinate rank with his love, because of the actual and potential theological abuse that comes from an exclusive emphasis upon God's love, especially self-sacrificing love. Once God's wrath is divorced from His love, the oppressed must submit to the oppressor's dehumanizing activity without reprisal, with only verbal condemnation or, as it were, a slap on the wrist. "A God without wrath does not plan to do much liberating, for the two concepts belong together."[11]

However, there are several ways of interpreting the unity of God's love and His wrath, and it is not always clear which of them Cone intends. But it is unmistakable which of the two interpretations is mandatory for the inner consistency of his position. One can argue that God's love for X requires His opposition to non-X. This approach appeals to the principle that every affirmation involves a negation, expressed here as all those persons who frustrate God's plan for X. This view informs Cone's claim that God's love for the oppressed dictates His destruction of the white oppressor. The consequence of his theological stance is to push God's wrath in the direction of retributive punishment; His wrath aims at the ultimate destruction of the oppressor, and not his salvation.

The connection between divine love and divine righteousness can be interpreted in yet another way: In this context God's wrath is remedial and redemptive. This view corresponds roughly to the position already considered where suffering or punishment is a sign of God's favor; suffering indicates what He sanctions and what He opposes, and thus serves as a guide to the straight and narrow path of salvation.

This redemptive, in contrast to the retributive, interpretation does not appear to be Cone's view, for to advance it would push him much closer to Roberts. It would require that he, like Roberts, must advance both liberation and reconciliation as the core of the gospel, rather than emphasizing almost exclusively the theme of liberation as Cone does. Cone would also have to argue that the "destruction" of the white oppressor is in fact related to his eventual salvation.

Several crucial consequences follow from Cone's claims that God has elected blacks not for vicarious suffering but liberation and that God's wrath involves the destruction of the white oppressor. If he adopts the retributive interpretation—and this is my understanding—it becomes all the more imperative for him to substantiate the definitive event of black liberation. If he does not do this, he will be in this curious and embarrassing situation: Having rejected vicarious suffering, which allows for a surplus of suffering for the elect, he is forced to define the white oppressor as the object of God's scorn, though it is the oppressive situation of blacks that corresponds, perhaps more closely, to that status. Cone is now pushed to prove his point by shifting the surplus of suffering from blacks to whites. There must be a reversal of roles, with whites now the primary sufferer. A cursory reading of history and the actual black experience, past and future, seems to contradict this position.

By emphasizing God's wrath as destruction, Cone inadvertently affirms the theodicy of deserved punishment as the explanation for certain occurrences of suffering. Having made this allowance, it becomes a possible explanation for black suffering as well. Accordingly it becomes all the more crucial for him to show that black suffering is not deserved punishment. Indeed, having repudiated the theodicy of deserved punishment, the refutation of deserved punishment is even more imperative for Cone than for Washington. Strictly speaking, the real mystery of mysteries in

Cone's system is the *origin* of black suffering. For if God is for blacks, if their suffering is neither vicarious nor merited punishment, whence their suffering in the first place?

The Refutation of the Theodicy of Deserved Punishment

In addition to the theodicy of vicarious suffering, Cone also dismisses the theodicy of deserved punishment—but on radically different grounds. It hardly needs saying that the validity of his treatment of black suffering requires an unmistakable demonstration that the suffering he connects with oppression is not punishment for prior sin. What he actually establishes are some dubious epistemological canons, and these are totally incommensurate to the logical demands of his theodicy.

His first epistemological claim is that whites cannot make any valid judgment about black sin; they therefore cannot legitimately judge whether black suffering is the result of prior sin. "The oppressors are in no position to speak about the sinfulness of the oppressed. Black theology rejects categorically white statements about the sins of black people, suggesting that we are partly responsible for our plight."[12] And again in the same vein: "White people are not permitted to speak about what blacks have done to contribute to their condition."[13]

This conclusion about the perceptive judgment of whites is joined with a second epistemological claim about blacks, namely that sin is a "community concept" and accordingly "only black people can speak about sin in a black perspective."[14]

My purpose here is not to challenge the adequacy of the foregoing claims; rather, I wish to question the validity of Cone's refutation of the theodicy of deserved punishment. I contend that the aforementioned epistemological claims do not rebut the view that black suffering is the consequence of prior sin.

Let us grant for the sake of argument that whites cannot legitimately talk about black sin and consequently are without grounds for describing black suffering as merited punishment. All that Cone can establish by this claim is who is not competent to decide if black suffering is deserved punishment. Granted that an answer from the white side is neither legitimate nor possible, this simply means that the answer must be given by blacks. It does not mean, as Cone appears to conclude, that the question need not be answered at all.

As a matter of fact, once the issue of divine racism is raised, as Cone himself raises it, it is necessary to show that the suffering at issue is not deserved or a sign of divine disfavor. To be sure, the special epistemolog-ical status he assigns to blacks is undermined as long as the interpretation of deserved punishment is not decisively rebutted. For until Cone con-firms that punishment for sin is not the case, he cannot establish the major plank of his theodicy: blacks are the oppressed, a group with a special and favored relation to God.

Note the core of Cone's argument here. It is by virtue of their status as the oppressed that blacks occupy the unique epistemological position that makes them sole judge of the character of their sin and its relation to their suffering. However, without a persuasive refutation of the theodicy of deserved punishment, the classification of blacks as oppressed clearly begs the question, and Cone's theodicy is invalid until this flaw is eliminated.

Other Defective Theodicies

Cone's eventual statement of theodicy is shaped also by his refutation of other classical theodicies. He repudiates any treatment of black suffering that appeals to God's inscrutable will or transports the rationale for black oppression to a sphere beyond human comprehension. He also rejects any appeal to an eschatological compensation for earthly suffering, though there may be an inconsistency on this point.[15] Two concerns motivate Cone here: One is to rebut divine racism. The other is to avoid those theodicies which are conceptual props for oppression, in particular quietism.

It is now necessary to indicate the general theological viewpoint that, for Cone, provides support for the ideology of oppression. The specific position he attacks is Emil Brunner's concept of divine providence. Brun-ner's position, according to Cone, reduces to the following propositions:

> All that is, and all that happens, takes place within the knowledge and the will of God. . . . All that happens is connected with the divine pur-pose; all is ordered in accordance with, and in subordination to, the divine plan and the final divine purpose.[16]

Over against this position Cone wants to affirm the concept of God that must inform an authentic black theodicy: "Black theology cannot accept any view of God that even *indirectly* places divine approval on human suffering."[17]

To clarify the issues introduced by Brunner's statement and Cone's counterstatement it is helpful to compare and contrast the respective theodicies of Cone and Rabbi Richard Rubenstein. Rubenstein would agree with Cone that Brunner's concept of divine providence leads to the "theological obscenity" of making Hitler God's redemptive agent and the slaughter of six million Jews His will. He also, like Cone, wants to avoid the conclusion that God is demonic, an anti-Semite, or responsible for the crimes of human history. Rubenstein concludes that the only way to steer clear of this conclusion is to abandon the theological hypothesis of God's activity within and God's sovereignty over human history or both. It is for this reason that Rubenstein introduces a concept of God with only minimal connection to human history.

Cone, however, wants to retain the sovereignty of God over human history and His activity within it and yet avoid the damaging consequences of this affirmation in Brunner's thought. Cone seeks to accomplish this theological sleight of hand by restricting God's sovereignty or activity to selected events of human history, those areas in which the oppressed are liberated.

Cone's instincts are surely understandable from a pragmatic viewpoint and even from a psychological perspective. But theologically, and especially logically, his position is not tenable. This becomes clear if we isolate the two opposing demands he tries unsuccessfully to honor: One demand of a black theology of liberation is to insure that blacks will assign only a negative quality to their oppressive suffering and thus provide the necessary motivation for its elimination. A second demand is to hold fast to God's sovereignty at all costs, for to deny His omnipotence is to annihilate black hope and to plunge blacks into the quicksand of defeatism. In point of fact, the same conclusion would follow from the conviction that God is a white racist, and it is for this reason that the refutation of divine racism becomes a primary enterprise for the black theologian.

Cone's argument for a belief "in the future reality of life after death" explains his reason for clinging to God's sovereignty as an indispensable cornerstone for black theology. "Blacks can fight against overwhelming odds," because they believe that the future is in fact the future of God, the liberator of the oppressed. Accordingly victory over oppression, evil, and death is assured. But, once the belief in immortality is challenged, then

> All is despair. The guns . . . and every conceivable weapon of destruction are in the hands of the enemy. By these standards all seems lost. But there is another way of evaluating history. . . . If we really believe that death is not the last word, then we can fight, risking death for the freedom of man, knowing that man's ultimate destiny is in the hands of him who has called us into being.[18]

This view of sovereignty creates special problems for Cone. He agrees that God's controlling or overruling sovereignty must be affirmed relative to human history or the eschaton. But this conclusion automatically raises the question of why God's overruling and controlling sovereignty does not operate where the crimes of human history are involved. Cone is now required to answer how white racism thrives within the larger freedom and sovereignty of God. If white racism runs rampant while God is allegedly "in control," where then is the basis for black hope?

Cone's actual position is obscure regarding these issues. Strictly speaking, he equivocates between two different and opposed concepts of divine transcendence, utilizing one or the other where it most easily fits the particular argument at hand. The passage just cited suggests God's overruling and controlling sovereignty, and accordingly, His plan for the liberation of the oppressed will never be frustrated.[19] Other passages affirming the same point may be readily cited. But this line of argument pushes him directly into Brunner's theological camp, which he rejects with such vehemence.

Dr. Cone also employs a concept of divine transcendence that appears to be identical to essential features of humanocentric theism. At the primal level of reality, at the ontological level, God is sovereign. But, at the level of human history, He exercises his omnipotence by making man a codetermining partner, thus giving man, as it were, functional control over human history. God retains His sovereignty at both the ontological and the historical levels, but He refuses to exert his power in an overruling fashion in human history out of respect for man's freedom. Thus God's sovereignty is not functionally ultimate relative to human history, but this, as we will see, negates the view that His plan of liberation for the oppressed will necessarily come to fruition.

Let us take the argument one step further. Recognize that the issue of divine transcendence raises the question of God's knowledge and will relative to human suffering in general and black suffering in particular. With this understanding, several features of Cone's argument fall into place. We understand his reason for affirming that God does not "even indirectly" approve of human suffering, and we understand how various parts of his position feed into that assertion. If he argues that God approves of some instances of human suffering but not all, he is forced to provide the criterion to differentiate between what is approved and what is unapproved suffering. Merely to state the problem identifies its difficulty.

His more universal claim, namely that God does not approve of human suffering even indirectly, has several advantages: It does not necessitate the criteriology just cited. It also serves admirably another demand of a theology of liberation: to give a negative quality to the suffering implicit in oppression. But it runs afoul of Cone's affirmation regarding God's controlling sovereignty. If God abhors human suffering, then how are we to account for its actual presence? The fact of suffering calls into question the sovereignty of God, or else it suggests that He is not exercising His transcendence for the good of black liberation.

Cone's desire to restrict God's activity and God's sovereignty in history to the liberation of the oppressed, while tracing the oppression itself to other causes, such as white racism, is understandable. In this way he establishes that God does not approve of black suffering; hence, an implicit refutation of divine racism. But is his theological strategy successful here? I think not. If his approach is not to be offensively arbitrary, if it is to avoid a self-serving strategy that permits him to choose the events that fit his theory and simply dismiss the contrary evidence, he is bound to provide specific arguments for his case.

His strategy is not possible without the unwarranted presupposition of God's intrinsic goodness relative to blacks or at least a citation of the mighty acts of God relative to black liberation. Cone's strategy also presupposes that where the biblical God of history is active in human affairs, He is pursuing a benevolent purpose for the oppressed. But once Cone has defined the issue as he did initially—a God of racism or a God of liberation—he cannot begin his analysis with these two presuppositions. Rather, they must be conclusions demonstrated. In sum, Cone must first refute one of the two interpretive options he outlines, before he can reasonably affirm the other. He is required to disprove the charge of divine racism, to identify what he regards as the definitive event(s) of black liberation, and also to refute the theodicy of deserved punishment.

Cone faces similar methodological demands because of his rejection of specific theodicies and the grounds for those rejections. Having discarded the theodicy of deserved punishment and denied that God is a white racist, Cone effectively precludes any interpretation of black suffering as a sign of divine disfavor. Hence he is forced to operate in the framework of suffering as a sign of divine favor. But this, too, pushes the necessity of an event of black liberation to the forefront.

In sum, Cone's rejection of the defective theodicies makes it difficult for him to account for the maldistribution and the very origin of suffering, which is the starting point of his theological construction. The position he assumes relative to these theodicies also obliges him to identify the definitive event of liberation for blacks. The discussion of these issues as they relate to divine racism must now be discussed.

Are Blacks Oppressed?

The core of Washington's theodicy was summarized in the following syllogism:

> If Blacks are the suffering servant / chosen people, then God is not a white racist.
> Blacks are in fact the suffering servant / chosen people.
> ___
> Therefore God is not a white racist.

Cone's theodicy can also be reduced to syllogistic form:

> If blacks are the oppressed, then God is not a white racist.
> Blacks are obviously the oppressed.
> ___
> Therefore God is not a white racist.

A comparison of these syllogisms indicates that Cone's theodicy has the same logical structure. Cone puts forward a class that *by virtue of his stipulative definition* involves a favored and specialized relation to God. Whereas Washington posited the class of suffering servant, Cone advances the class of the oppressed. Thus the soundness of Cone's argument stands or falls on the demonstration of the second premise: blacks are oppressed. In this connection the reader must recognize that Cone adds a defining element to the concept of the oppressed that is question-begging in light of the issue of divine racism that he raises. Essential to his meaning of "oppressed" is the claim that they are the object of God's special concern and love. This stipulative meaning of "oppressed" thus constitutes an implicit "refutation" of the charge of divine racism. Consequently the real effect of Cone's arbitrary definition of "oppressed" is to eliminate, but only by definition, all the subclasses of divine disfavor, such as divine racism and deserved punishment. But this point cannot be emphasized too strongly; the refutation is the consequence of the classification and stipulative definition, and only that. In this context, then, the real issue for Cone reduces to this crucial question: Has he substantiated that blacks are in fact the oppressed? It is necessary to translate the last statement into the language of Cone's definition and thus identify the specific proposition he must validate. Has he substantiated that blacks are in fact *the object of God's favor?* Because of the common tendency to classify blacks as oppressed, and because common usage does not include Cone's stipulative property, namely that God is favorably inclined toward the oppressed, it is necessary to phrase the question as just stated to avoid begging the question. Because it is commonly held that blacks are oppressed, Cone's affirmation of the same proposition seems self-evidently certain, and the syllogistic statement of his theodicy appears logically impeccable. His argument accordingly presents itself with a logical certitude that it does not actually possess. For this reason, too, Cone's special and personalized definition of "oppressed" must be pinpointed.

Looked at from another perspective, Cone's theodicy and its implicit refutation of divine racism rest finally upon a doctrine of God's nature: "The liberation of the oppressed is a part of the innermost activity of God himself. This means that liberation is not an afterthought, but the essence of divine activity."[20] This is Cone's way of stating the classical theistic principle that goodness is intrinsic to God. It must also be indicated that the divine activity of liberation incorporates, as well, the work of Jesus Christ, especially the Resurrection.

It goes without saying that if liberation of the oppressed is in fact the essence of God's nature and action, divine racism is clearly excluded. It is not possible for a divine racist and a liberator of oppressed blacks to coexist in the same divine person. To appraise the validity of Cone's theodicy, then, demands that we examine his exposition for this specific description of God. He seeks to validate this description of God's nature through three primary demonstrations, but they turn out to be different ways of saying the same thing. That the liberation of the oppressed is the core of the biblical message and of Israelite history is his first claim: "It is indeed the biblical witness that says that God is a God of liberation, who calls to himself the oppressed and abused . . . and assures them that his righteousness will vindicate their suffering."[21]

The second demonstration appeals to Jesus' personhood and work:

> In the New Testament, the Old Testament theme of liberation is reaffirmed by Jesus himself. The conflict with Satan and the powers, the condemnation of the rich, the insistence that the Kingdom is for the poor, and the locating of his ministry among the poor—these and other features of the career of Jesus show that his work was directed to the oppressed for the purpose of their liberation.[22]

Because of the biblical emphasis upon liberation, revelation must also center around the liberation of the oppressed. This is the third demonstration in his approach. It is necessary here, for the sake of a subsequent criticism, to call attention to Cone's emphasis upon revelation as grounded in concrete, i.e., actual, events in which the community of the faithful detect the liberating hand of God:

> In the Bible revelation is inseparable from history and faith. History is the arena in which God's revelation takes place. . . . The God of the Bible makes his will and purpose known through his participation in human history. . . . Christianity . . . is a religion which affirms that we know who God is by what he does in the historical events of man.[23] In fact, there is no revelation of God without history. The two are inseparable.[24]

A second passage must be cited in detail as background for the claim that Cone's own doctrine of revelation, as well as other essentials of his system, force him to identify the definitive event(s) of black liberation:

> God chose to make himself known to an oppressed people, and the nature of his revelatory activity was synonymous with their emancipation. The Exodus of Israel from Egypt meant that God's revelation was an act of liberation. In this revelatory event, Israel not only came to know God as the liberator of the oppressed, but she also realized that her being as a people was inseparable from divine activity. Thus Yahweh was known primarily for what he did for Israel when other political powers threatened her existence as a community. . . . God's revelation means political emancipation, which involves the destruction of the enemy. . . . The entire history of Israel is a history of what God has done, is doing and will do in moments of oppression.[25]

The foregoing account of revelation forces the conclusion, as Cone acknowledges, "There is no revelation of God without a condition of oppression which develops into a situation of liberation."[26] Only one meaning can be extracted from this statement in particular and Cone's doctrine of revelation in general: Revelation involves two necessary conditions. There is (1) the event of suffering or oppression, which is replaced by its opposite (2) liberation or exaltation. It should be noted that these conditions are the same two elements already identified as central to the concept of suffering servant. Can we avoid the conclusion here that Cone's own doctrine of revelation affirms that in the absence of the liberation event there is no revelation? And this is to say that there is no accurate knowledge of God's nature. Can we avoid the conclusion that knowledge of God's nature as liberator—and it must be remembered that for Cone this is His essence—presupposes concrete instances of liberation? In like manner, can we affirm that black liberation is part of God's innermost nature except on the basis of the actual liberation of blacks?

Cone's concern to establish the nature of God as the primary category for theodicy and his conclusion that revelation of God's nature is mediated only through events of liberation oblige him to adopt a particular theological method—if circularity is to be avoided. I would identify the following methodological requirements:

(1) The description of God's nature as favoring the oppressed cannot legitimately be part of the presuppositional baggage the theologian brings to his analysis. Rather, God's nature as favoring the oppressed must be validated. It also means that the theologian cannot use this description at the outset to dismiss the alleged counterevidence; rather, this description can stand only after the counterevidence has been refuted or shown not to be decisive.

(2) It also means that this view of God must be confirmed by the mighty acts of God, by an inspection of human history and the citation of those events in which God's liberating activity is claimed to be present, as, for example, in the Exodus. This is another way of saying that the theologian must identify actual events of liberation, concrete instances where the oppression in fact ceases, where, to use a metaphor of Cone's, "the last become first."

(3) The event of liberation must involve the liberation of the particular group in question; that is, an event of *Jewish* liberation cannot corroborate the claim that *black* liberation is part of God's innermost nature. The meaning of these last two methodological consequences will be clarified after the analysis below has exposed the question-begging features of Cone's concept of "oppressed."

(4) The final consequence to be identified has already been discussed in terms of the principle that God is the sum of His acts. The concern now is to show that Cone's controlling theological categories presuppose the same principle. Consider for instance his concept of revelation when he says: "There is no revelation without a condition of oppression which develops into a situation of liberation." Does not this claim entail that whatever character we assign to God must be substantiated by reference to His past and/or present acts? This especially appears to be the case because Cone has rejected any appeal to an eschatological compensation for suffering passed through here and now. Consequently it appears that

the only option for Cone is to speak of God as for the oppressed only on the basis of events of liberation in the past, the present, or in the process of actualization.

Consider some of the decisive statements from Cone himself that support this interpretation:

> Black theology rejects the tendency of classical Christianity to appeal to divine providence. To suggest that black suffering is consistent with the knowledge and will of God and that in the end everything will happen for the good of those who love God is unacceptable to black people. The eschatological promise of heaven is insufficient to account for the earthly pain of black suffering. . . .[27] Providence is not a statement about the future. It is . . . a statement about present reality—the reality of the liberation of the oppressed.[28]

Cone's doctrine of God's immanence leads to the same conclusion: "The immanence of God . . . forces man to look for God . . . and make decisions about the ultimate in terms of present historical reality. Man cannot postpone his decision about God or condition it in terms of a future reality. The finality of God is his involvement in man's now experiences."[29]

Cone's claims that God does not indirectly approve of human suffering and that God is totally identified with black liberation also force him to identify the past or contemporary events of black liberation. How can blacks know that God disapproves of black suffering except by His elimination of it, except by His bringing it to an immediate halt?

Yet other statements by Cone demand a similar demonstration: "If God is truly the God of and for the oppressed for the purpose of their liberation, then . . . our movement in the world cannot be a meaningless thrust towards an unrealizable future, but a certainty grounded in the past and present reality of God."[30]

The same methodology must question Cone's use of the category "the oppressed" to describe blacks in America. When the meaning of oppressed in Cone's usage is laid bare, it is clear that Cone has not substantiated his claim that blacks are the oppressed. In this connection the reader must recall that Cone's own scaffolding requires the demonstration that blacks are the object of God's favor and that their liberation is central to His will.

Before the category of the oppressed can be used legitimately and accurately to describe blacks, it is necessary to demonstrate that the suffering they experience is not deserved punishment. Blacks can be indexed as oppressed only after it has been substantiated that their suffering is not merited. It is precisely at this point that the weakness of his refutation of the theodicy of deserved punishment returns to haunt Cone's system and render dubious his classification of blacks as oppressed.

If the conclusion is correct that the cessation of suffering, i.e., the liberation event, must occur to establish that suffering is undeserved, then Cone must identify what he regards as the definitive event of black liberation. Otherwise, there is no way to decide if black suffering is deserved punishment or unmerited suffering.

It must also be noted here that the positions Cone assumed to dismiss other theodicies severely hamper his theological maneuverability. His rejection of eschatological compensation, for instance, forces him to identify a contemporary or past event of black liberation. That the situation of blacks still requires radical correction indicates his classification is premature if not gratuitous.

Other problems confront Cone in his effort to identify the precise liberation event his position requires. To say that blacks are the oppressed is to say that God is or has been active in behalf of their liberation. This also means that Cone must show that the liberation of blacks is part of God's innermost nature. This cannot be accomplished by appealing to God's liberating activity for mankind in general or for non-blacks, such as the Exodus of the Jews. The Exodus may refute the charge of divine anti-Semitism, but it is irrelevant to the accusation of divine racism. What is demanded, then, is for Cone to specify concrete and definitive events of black liberation.

Other claims of Cone demand the same conclusion: He argues that we cannot know God "independently of his liberating work"[31] and, further, that knowledge of God as He is in Himself is not possible: "We can only know God in his relation to man, or more particularly in his liberating activity on behalf of oppressed man."[32] These twin claims allow us to speak of God as liberator only in terms of the concrete groups of the oppressed that he in fact liberates. Any other claim would be to talk of God "independently of his liberating acts." It would be similar to the argument that because Huey Long aided oppressed whites, he can be said to be the champion of oppressed blacks as well.

Albert Cleage clarifies the criticism here. He correctly recognizes the theological issue at stake: it is the scandal of particularity which is introduced by the character of black suffering and the accusation of divine racism. And the scandal of the particularity of black suffering can be answered only by an appeal to the particularity of God's liberating activity—an Exodus-type event for blacks. With this understanding, Cleage establishes God's liberating activity for blacks at the outset by arguing for the blackness of God, Jesus, and the Jews. The physical blackness of God and Jesus insures their identification with and participation in the struggle for black liberation. The blackness of the Jews guarantees that the Exodus is an authentic event of *black* liberation, the liberation of the particular group at issue.

Cone himself also recognizes that the Exodus is the liberation of a particular oppressed group and that a more universal event of liberation is required to accommodate the oppressed non-Jews. Is this not the import of the following passage, in which the Resurrection of Jesus is introduced as the universal event of liberation?

> If the history of Israel and the New Testament description of the historical Jesus reveal that God is a God who is identified with Israel because she is an oppressed community, the resurrection of Christ means that all oppressed people become his people. Herein lies the universal note implied in the gospel message of Jesus. The resurrection event means that God's liberating work is not only for the house of Israel but for all who are enslaved by principalities and powers.[33]

But this confession is fatal to Cone's approach, for he is actually acknowledging that the biblical Exodus lacks any decisive import for the claim that the liberation of *blacks* is part of God's innermost nature. Unless he is willing, like Cleage, to make the Exodus an event of black liberation on the grounds that Jews are black, the Exodus is not available as evidence for his position. Indeed it would appear that the whole history of the Israelite nation as the object of God's liberating work is not relevant for his argument that God is involved in *black* liberation.

Thus he is left with the Resurrection as the crucial event for establishing that black liberation is part of God's nature. But even here one can question Cone's success in making the Resurrection a *universal* event of liberation and, by implication, an event of black liberation. Strictly speaking, is not the movement here, from the universal to the particular, to misunderstand the real issue of the charge of divine racism? He affirms the universal import of the Resurrection, but at no point does he indicate which of its features warrants its designation as an event of black liberation or of universal liberation. It would appear that Cone can speak of the Resurrection as a universal event only to the extent that particular groups are in fact liberated and only to the degree that liberation actually becomes or is in fact universal. Moreover, if we honor the suggestion that we can know God only in relation to man and in terms of His liberating acts, then we can speak of God as for *all* oppressed people only on the basis of the liberation of *all* oppressed people.

In point of fact, does not the continued suffering of blacks *after* the Resurrection raise the essential question all over again: Is God for blacks? We must not forget that black misery, slavery, and oppression—the very facts that make black liberation necessary—are all post-Resurrection events. Must not the fact of black oppression after the Resurrection raise the most serious questions about Cone's designation of the Resurrection as the event of universal liberation? It is closer to the truth, it seems, to say that Cone is affirming liberation in an unliberated world!

Still another claim of Cone makes problematical his classification of blacks as the oppressed. "Black theology," he argues, "cannot accept a view of God which does not represent him as being for blacks and thus against whites. . . . We must know where God is and what he is doing in the revolution. There is no use for a God who loves whites the same as blacks."[34] In the light of this assertion and the affirmation that God is only for the oppressed, can Cone show that God is on the side of blacks except by marshaling evidence for God's opposition to whites? It is embarrassing when we have to note that whites have been on top for aeons, apparently somewhat longer than Cone's purview of history permits. Moreover, the manner in which Cone structures the argument here makes it impossible to point to a progressive improvement for blacks and identify this as the liberation event if the status of blacks relative to whites has not significantly improved.

One final observation about Cone's theodicy is in order: If for the sake of argument we should allow his theodicy a gratuitous validity, a troublesome question would still remain unanswered. Indeed the greater his success in establishing that black liberation is essential to God's nature, the more troublesome this question would become: Whence comes the suffering of the oppressed in the first place if God is for the oppressed? How is the origin of black oppression to be accounted for? How is black slavery now to be squared with the claim that God has been and is on the side of blacks? The crucial issue in Cone's system is not the more traditional issue of original sin, but the original oppression of blacks.

On the basis of the foregoing arguments, I conclude that Cone has not certified the single proposition he himself affirms must be established if God is not a murderer: viz., black liberation is central to God's essence. In the absence of this demonstration, the remainder of the system totters for want of a convincing structural validity.

Notes

Divine Racism

1. James Cone, *A Black Theology of Liberation* (New York: Lippincott, 1970), pp. 120–21.
2. *Liberation*, pp. 59–60.
3. *Liberation*, p. 115.
4. J. Deotis Roberts, *Liberation and Reconciliation: A Black Theology* (Philadelphia: Westminster Press, 1971), p. 83.
5. One point will establish that the multievidentiality of suffering is acknowledged by the black theologians, however inadvertently. Once the black theologian allows that deserved punishment is a possible interpretation of human suffering, and also denies that all suffering is deserved punishment, he cannot avoid the conclusion that suffering is multievidential.
6. *Liberation*, pp. 26–27.
7. *Liberation*, pp. 113–14.

James Cone: God, Champion of the Oppressed

1. It has already been established that Cone advances the issue of divine racism as an inevitable question for black theology. Consequently it is not necessary to demonstrate this point.
2. *Liberation*, p. 241.
3. Cone defines "oppressed" in a way that departs radically from common usage. An essential feature of his definition is that the oppressed are the object of God's special concern and favor.
4. *Liberation*, pp. 108–9.
5. *Liberation*, p. 149.
6. *Liberation*, p. 181.
7. *Liberation*, p. 136.
8. *Liberation*, p. 132.
9. Several aspects of Cone's thought, as will be shown, necessitate the substantiation of the definitive event of liberation for blacks.
10. *Liberation*, pp. 25–26.
11. *Liberation*, p. 131.
12. *Liberation*, p. 100.
13. *Liberation*, p. 194.
14. *Liberation*, p. 100.
15. "Cone rejects the concept of eschatological compensation for this-worldly suffering, but, curiously, introduces something strikingly similar in content and intent: He finds it necessary to postulate 'the future reality of life after death' for various reasons: to substantiate that God is on the side of blacks, to insure that fear of death will not lead to defeatism and thus diminish one's total commitment to the struggle, to assure that the death of the black freedom fighter is not meaningless, etc. One wonders, however, what the real difference is between the eschatological perspective he accepts and the one he rejects. The slave eschatology promised compensation for those who suffer patiently here, while Cone's eschatology guarantees reward and meaning for those who die valiantly here. Though the difference reflects a much-needed corrective for black ethics, is it an improvement on black theodicy? I raise this question because the following pos-

sibility sticks in my mind. Consider: the promise of a future reality after death motivates blacks to make the ultimate sacrifice for liberation, and this is the means by which a racist God beckons blacks to suicidal efforts and thus accomplishes black genocide." William Jones, "Theodicy and Methodology in Black Theology: A Critique of Washington, Cone and Cleage," *Harvard Theological Review*, 64:4 (October 1971), p. 553.

16. Emil Brunner, *The Christian Doctrine of Creation and Redemption* (Philadelphia: Westminster Press, 1952), p. 155.
17. *Liberation*, p. 149. Emphasis in the original.
18. *Liberation*, p. 248.
19. Consider also the following passage: "The future of God belongs to the future of the poor, the people who are assured that God's present righteousness will not be defeated by those who seek to usurp divine authority. The poor need not worry about the evil of this world; they will see the glory of Yahweh in their own fight against injustice." *Liberation*, pp. 243–44.
20. *Liberation*, p. 121.
21. *Liberation*, p. 66.
22. *Liberation*, pp. 19–20.
23. Note that the principle that God is the sum of his acts is affirmed here as well as in the next citation. Moreover, this principle is said to be a central biblical motif.
24. *Liberation*, p. 93.
25. *Liberation*, pp. 93–94.
26. *Liberation*, p. 91.
27. *Liberation*, p. 44.
28. *Liberation*, p. 149.
29. *Liberation*, p. 142.
30. *Liberation*, pp. 247–48.
31. *Liberation*, p. 133.
32. *Liberation*, p. 133.
33. *Liberation*, p. 21.
34. *Liberation*, pp. 131–32.

Chapter 37

Black Theology and Marxist Thought

Cornel West

B lack theologians and Marxist thinkers are strangers. They steer clear of one another, each content to express concerns to their respective audiences. Needless to say, their concerns overlap. Both focus on the plight of the exploited, oppressed and degraded peoples of the world, their relative powerlessness and possible empowerment. I believe this common focus warrants a serious dialogue between Black theologians and Marxist thinkers. This dialogue should not be a mere academic chat that separates religionists and secularists, theists and atheists. Instead it ought to be an earnest encounter that specifies clearly the different sources of their praxis of faith, yet accents the possibility of mutually arrived-at political action.

The aim of this encounter is to change the world, not each other's faith; to put both groups on the offensive for structural social change, not put Black Christians on the defensive; and to enhance the quality of life of the dispossessed, not expose the empty Marxist meaning of death. In short, Black theologians and Marxist thinkers must preserve their own existential and intellectual integrity and explore the possibility of promoting fundamental social amelioration together.

Black theology and Marxist thought are not monolithic bodies of thought; each contains different perspectives, distinct viewpoints and diverse conclusions. Therefore it is necessary to identify the particular claims put forward by Black Theology and Marxist thought, those claims that distinguish both as discernible schools of thought. Black Theology claims that (1) the historical experience of Black people and the readings of the biblical texts that emerge from there are the centers around which reflection about God evolves; and that (2) this reflection is related, in some way, to the liberation of Black people, to the creation of a more abundant life definable in existential, economic, social and political terms.

Marxist thought contains two specific elements: a theory of history and an understanding of capitalism. Both are inextricably interlinked, but it may be helpful to characterize them separately.

The *Marxist theory of history* claims: (1) The history of human societies is the history of their transitional stages. (2) The transitional stages of human societies are discernible owing to their systems of production, or their organizational arrangements in which people produce goods and services for their survival. (3) Conflict within systems of production of human societies ultimately results in fundamental social change, or transitions from one historical stage to another. (4) Conflict within systems of production of human societies consists of cleavages between social classes (in those systems of production). (5) Social classes are historically transient, rooted in a particular set of socioeconomic conditions. (6) Therefore, the history of all hitherto existing society is the history of class struggles.

The *Marxist theory of capitalist society* claims: Capitalism is a historically transient system of production which requires human beings to produce commodities for the purpose of maximizing surplus value (profits). This production presupposes a fundamental social relation between the purchasers and sellers of a particular commodity, namely the labor-power (time, skill and expertise) of producers. This crucial commodity is bought by capitalists who own the land, instruments and capital necessary for production; it is sold by producers, whose labor-power is needed for production. The aim of the former is to maximize profits; that of the latter, to insure their own survival.

I shall claim that Black Theology and Marxist thought share three characteristics. (1) Both adhere to a similar methodology, the same way of approaching their respective subject matter and arriving at conclusions. (2) Both link some notion of liberation to the future socioeconomic conditions of the downtrodden. (3) And this is most important, both attempt to put forward trenchant critiques of liberal capitalist America. I will try to show that these three traits provide a springboard for a meaningful dialogue between Black theologians and Marxist thinkers and possibly spearhead a unifying effort for structural social change in liberal capitalist America.

Dialectical Methodology: Unmasking Falsehoods

Black theologians have either consciously or unconsciously employed a dialectical methodology in approaching their subject matter. This methodology consists of a three-step procedure of negation, preservation, and transformation; their subject matter, of White interpretations of the Christian gospel and their own circumstances. Dialectical methodology is critical in character and hermeneutic in content.[1] For Black theologians it is highly critical of dogmatic viewpoints of the gospel, questioning whether certain unjustifiable prejudgments are operative. It is hermeneutic in that it is concerned with unearthing assumptions of particular interpretations and presenting an understanding of the gospel that extends and expands its ever unfolding truth.

Black theologians have, for the most part, been compelled to adopt a dialectical methodology. They have refused to accept what has been given to them by White theologians: they have claimed that all reflection about God by Whites must be digested, decoded and deciphered. The first theological formulations by Afro-Americans based on biblical texts tried to come to terms with their White owners' viewpoints and their own servitude. Since its inception, Black theologians have been forced to reduce White deception and distortion of the gospel and make the Christian story meaningful in light of their oppressive conditions.

Black theological reflection begins by negating White interpretations of the gospel, continues by preserving its own perceived truths of the biblical texts, and ends by transforming past understandings of the gospel into new and novel ones. These three steps embody an awareness of the social context of theologizing, the need to accent the historical experience of Black people and the insights of the Bible, and the ever evolving task of recovering, regaining and repeating the gospel.

Black theologians underscore the importance of the social context of theological reflection.[2] Their dialectical methodology makes them sensitive to the hidden agendas of theological formulations they negate, agendas often guided by social interests. Their penchant for revealing distortions leads them to adopt a sociology of knowledge-approach that stresses the way in which particular viewpoints endorse and encourage ulterior aims.

An interpretation of the Black historical experience and the readings of the biblical texts that emerge out of this experience constitute the raw ingredients for the second step of Black theological reflection. By trying to understand the plight of Black people in light of the Bible, Black theologians claim to preserve the biblical truth that God sides with the oppressed and acts on their behalf.[3] Subsequently, the Black historical experience and the biblical texts form a symbiotic relationship, each illuminating the other.

Since Black theologians believe in the living presence of God and the work of the Holy Spirit, they acknowledge the constant unfolding process of the gospel. Paradoxically, the gospel is unchanging, yet it is deepened by embracing and encompassing new human realities and experiences. The gospel must speak to every age. Therefore it must be recovered and repeated, often sounding different, but, in substance, remaining the same. For Black theologians, it sounds different because it addresses various contexts of oppression; it remains the same because it is essentially a gospel of liberation.

Marxist thinkers, like Black theologians, employ a dialectical methodology in approaching their subject matter. But they do so consciously and their subject matter is bourgeois theories about capitalist society. The primary theoretical task of Marxist thinkers is to uncover the systematic misunderstanding of capitalist society by bourgeois thinkers; to show how this misunderstanding, whether deliberate or not, supports and sanctions exploitation and oppression in this society; and to put forward the correct understanding of this society in order to change it.

Marxist social theory is first and foremost a critique of inadequate theories of capitalist society and subsequently a critique of capitalist society itself. The subtitle of Marx's magnum opus, *Capital*, is "A Critique of Political Economy," not "A Critique of Capitalism." This work takes bourgeois economists to task for perpetuating falsehoods, and results in revealing the internal dynamics of capitalism and their inhumane consequences. For Marx, a correct understanding of capitalist society is possible only by overcoming present mystifications of it; and this correct understanding is requisite for a propitious political praxis.

Marxist thought stresses the conflict-laden unfolding of history, the conflict-producing nature of social processes. Therefore it is not surprising that Marxist thinkers employ a dialectical methodology, a methodology deeply suspicious of stasis and stability, and highly skeptical of equilibrium and equipoise. This methodology, like that of Black theologians, is critical in character and hermeneutic in content. It is critical of perspectives presented by bourgeois social scientists, questioning whether certain ideological biases are operative. It is hermeneutic in that it is obsessed with discovering correct understanding underneath wrong interpretations, disclosing latent truths behind manifest distortions. For Marx, to be scientific is to be dialectical and to be dialectical is to unmask, unearth, bring to light.[4]

This conception of science, derived from Hegel, attempts to discern the hidden kernel of an evolving truth becoming manifest by bursting through a visible husk. The husk, once a hidden kernel, dissolves, leaving its indelible imprint upon the new emerging kernel. This idea of inquiry highlights the moments of negation, preservation and transformation. By presenting his theory of history and society from this perspective, Marx provided the most powerful and penetrating social criticism in modern times. Dialectical methodology enabled him to create a whole mode of inquiry distinctively his own, though often appearing hermetic and rigid to the untutored and fanatic.

Despite the similar procedure Black theologians and Marxist thinkers share, there has been little discussion about it between them. This is so primarily because a dialectical methodology is implicit, undeveloped and often unnoticed in Black Theology. This failure to examine the methodological stance embodied in Black theological reflection obscures its similarity with that of Marxist thought.

Liberation: Its Constitutive Elements

Black theologians all agree that Black liberation has something to do with ameliorating the socioeconomic conditions of Black people. But it is not clear what this amelioration amounts to. There is little discussion in their writings about what the liberating society will look like. The notion and process of liberation is often mentioned, but, surprisingly, one is hard put to find a sketch of what liberation would actually mean in the everyday lives of Black people, what power they would possess, and what resources they would have access to.

There are two main reasons for this neglect among Black theologians. First, a dialectical methodology discourages discussions about the ideal society and simply what ought to be. Instead, it encourages criticizing and overcoming existing society, negating and opposing what is.

The second reason, the one with which we shall be concerned in this section, is the failure of Black theologians to talk specifically about the way in which the existing system of production and social structure relates to Black oppression and exploitation. Without focusing on this relation, it becomes extremely difficult to present an idea of liberation with socioeconomic content. In short, the lack of a clear-cut social theory prevents the emergence of any substantive political program or social vision.

Except for the latest writings of James Cone, Black theologians remain uncritical of America's imperialist presence in Third World countries, its capitalist system of production, and its grossly unequal distribution of wealth. Therefore we may assume they find this acceptable. If this is so, then the political and socioeconomic components of Black liberation amount to racial equality before the law; equal opportunities in employment, education and business; and economic parity with Whites in median income.

Surely this situation would be better than the current dismal one. But it hardly can be viewed as Black liberation. It roughly equates liberation with American middle-class status, leaving the unequal distribution of wealth relatively untouched and the capitalist system of production, along with its imperialist ventures, intact. Liberation would consist of including Black people within the mainstream of liberal capitalist America. If this is the social vision of Black theologians, they should drop the meretricious and flamboyant term "liberation" and adopt the more accurate and sober word "inclusion."

Marxist thought, like Black Theology, does not elaborate on the ideal society. As we noted earlier, a dialectical methodology does not permit this elaboration. But the brief sketch Marxist thinkers provide requires a particular system of production and political arrangement: namely, participatory democracy in each. Human liberation occurs only when people participate substantively in the decision-making processes in the major institutions that regulate their lives. Democratic control over the institutions in the productive and political processes in order for them to satisfy human needs and protect personal liberties of the populace constitutes human liberation.

Marxist thinkers are able to present this sketch of human liberation primarily because they stress what people must liberate themselves *from*. They suggest what liberation is for only after understanding the internal dynamics of the society people must be liberated from. Without this clear-cut social theory about what *is*, it is difficult to say anything significant about what can *be*. The possibility of liberation is found only within the depths of the actuality of oppression. Without an adequate social theory, this possibility is precluded.

Social Criticism: Class, Race, and Culture

Black Theology puts forward a vehement, often vociferous, critique of liberal capitalist America. One of its most attractive and alluring characteristics is its theological indictment of racist American society. An undisputable claim of Black Theology is America's unfair treatment of Black people. What is less apparent is the way in which Black theologians understand the internal dynamics of liberal capitalist America, how it functions, why it operates the way it does, who possesses substantive power, and where it is headed. As noted earlier, Black theologians do not utilize a social theory that relates the oppression of Black people to the overall make-up of America's system of production, foreign policy, political arrangement, and cultural practices.

Black theologians hardly mention the wealth, power, and influence of multinational corporations that monopolize production in the marketplace and prosper partially owing to their dependence on public support in the form of government subsidies, free technological equipment, lucrative contracts and sometimes even direct-transfer payments. Black theologians do not stress the way in which corporate interests and the government intermesh, usually resulting in policies favorable to the former. Black theologians fail to highlight the fact that in liberal capitalist America one-half of 1 percent own 22 percent of the wealth, 1 percent own 33 percent of the wealth, the lower 61 percent own only 7 percent of the wealth, and the bottom 45 percent own only 2 percent of the wealth.[5] Lastly, Black theologians do not emphasize sufficiently the way in which the racist interpretations of the gospel they reject encourage and support the capitalist system of production, its grossly unequal distribution of wealth and its closely connected political arrangements.

Instead of focusing on these matters, Black theologians draw attention to the racist practices in American society. Since these practices constitute the most visible and vicious form of oppression in America, Black theologians justifiably do so. Like the Black Power proponents of the sixties, they call for the empowerment of Black people, the need for Black people to gain significant control over their lives. But neither Black Power proponents nor Black theologians have made it sufficiently clear as to what constitutes this Black control, the real power to direct institutions such that Black people can live free of excessive exploitation and oppression. The tendency is to assume that middle-class status is equivalent to such control, that a well-paying job amounts to such power. And surely this assumption is fallacious.

The important point here is not that racist practices should be stressed less by Black theologians, for such practices deeply affect Black people and shape their perceptions of American society. What is crucial is that these practices must be linked to the role they play in buttressing the current mode of production, concealing the unequal distribution of wealth, and portraying the lethargy of the political system. Black theologians are correct to relate racist practices to degrees of Black powerlessness, but they obscure this relation by failing to provide a lucid definition of what power is in American society. Subsequently, they often fall into the trap of assuming power in American society to be synonymous with receiving high wages.

Marxist social criticism can be quite helpful at this point. For Marx, power in modern industrial society consists of a group's participation in the decision-making processes of the major institutions that affect their destinies. Since institutions of production, such as multinational corporations, play an important role in people's lives, these institutions should be significantly accountable to the populace. In short, they should be democratically controlled by the citizenry; people should participate in their decision-making processes. Only collective control over the major institutions of society constitutes genuine power on behalf of the people.

For Marx, power in modern industrial society is closely related to a group's say over what happens to products produced in the work situation, to a group's input into decisions that direct the production flow of goods and services. The most powerful group in society has the most say and input into decisions over this production flow; the least powerful group does not participate at all in such decisions. In liberal capitalist America, the former consists of multiple corporate owners who dictate policies concerning the mass production of a variety of products produced by white- and blue-collar workers who receive wages in return. The latter consists of the so-called underclass, the perennially unemployed, who are totally removed from the work situation, precluded from any kind of input affecting the production flow, including negotiation and strikes available to white- and blue-collar workers.

Racist practices intensify the degree of powerlessness among Black people. This is illustrated by the high rates of Black unemployment, the heavy Black concentration in low-paying jobs, and inferior housing, education, police protection and health care. But it is important to note that this powerlessness differs from that of white- and blue-collar workers in degree, not in kind. In human terms, this difference is immense, incalculable; in structural terms, this difference is negligible, trifling. In other words, most Americans are, to a significant degree, powerless. They have no substantive control over their lives, little participation in the decision-making process of the major institutions that regulate their lives. Among Afro-Americans, this powerlessness is exacerbated, creating an apparent qualitative difference in oppression.

This contrast of the social criticism of Black theologians and Marxist thinkers raises the age-old question as to whether class position or racial status is the major determinant of Black oppression in America. This question should be formulated in the following way: Does class position or racial status contribute more to the fundamental form of powerlessness in America?

Racial status contributes greatly to Black oppression. But Black middle-class people are essentially well-paid white- or blue-collar workers who have little control over their lives primarily owing to their class position, not racial status. This is so because the same limited control is held by White middle-class people, despite the fact that a higher percentage of Whites are well-paid white- and blue-collar workers than Blacks. Significant degrees of powerlessness pertain to most Americans and this could be so only if class position determines such powerlessness. Therefore, class position contributes more than racial status to the basic form of powerlessness in America.

I am suggesting that the more Black theologians discard or overlook Marxist social criticism, the further they distance themselves from the fundamental determinant of Black oppression and any effective strategy to alleviate it.[6] This distancing also obscures the direct relation of Black oppression in America to Black and Brown oppression in Third World countries. The most powerful group in America, those multiple corporate owners who dictate crucial corporate policies over a variety of production flows, are intimately and inextricably linked (through their highly paid American and Third World white-collar workers and grossly underpaid Third World blue-collar workers) to the economies and governments of Third World countries, including the most repressive ones. Marxist social criticism permits this relation to come to light in an extremely clear and convincing way.

The social criticism of Black theologians reflects the peculiar phenomenon of American liberal and radical criticism. This criticism rarely has viewed class position as a major determinant of oppression primarily owing to America's lack of a feudal past, the heterogeneity of its population, the many and disparate regions of its geography, and the ever increasing levels of productivity and growth. These facts make it difficult to see class divisions; indeed, along with other forms of oppression, they make it almost impossible to see the divisions. But, like protons leaving vapor trails in a cloud chamber, one is forced to posit these class divisions in light of the overwhelming evidence for their existence. Only class divisions can explain the gross disparity between rich and poor, the immense benefits accruing to the former and the depravity of the latter.

Region, sex, age, ethnicity, and race often have been considered the only worthy candidates as determinants of oppression. This has been so primarily because American liberal and radical criticism usually has presupposed the existing system of production, assumed class divisions and attempted to include only marginal groups in the mainstream of liberal capitalist America. This criticism has fostered a petit-bourgeois viewpoint that clamors for a bigger piece of the ever growing American pie, rarely asking fundamental questions such as why it never gets recut more equally or how it gets baked in the first place. In short, this criticism remains silent about class divisions, the crucial role they play in maintaining the unequal distribution of goods and services, and how they undergird discrimination against regions, impose ceilings on upward social mobility and foster racism, sexism and ageism. With the exception of the most recent writings of James Cone, contemporary Black theologians suffer from this general myopia of American liberal and radical criticism.

Despite this shortsightedness, Black theologians have performed an important service for Marxist thinkers, namely emphasizing the ways in which culture and religion resist oppression. They have been admirably sensitive to the Black cultural buffers against oppression, especially the Black religious sources of struggle and strength, vitality and vigor. They also have stressed the indispensable contribution the Black churches have made toward the survival, dignity and self-worth of Black people.

Contrary to Marxist thinkers, Black theologians recognize that cultural and religious attitudes, values, and sensibilities have a life and logic of their own, not fully accountable in terms of a class analysis. Subsequently, racist practices are not reducible to a mere clever and successful strategy of divide-and-conquer promoted by the ruling class to prevent proletarian unity. Rather, racism is an integral element within the very fabric of American culture and society. It is embedded in the country's first collective self-definition; enunciated in its subsequent laws; and imbued in its dominant way of life.

The orthodox Marxist analysis of culture and religion that simply relates racist practices to misconceived material interests is only partially true, hence deceptive and misleading. These practices are fully comprehensible only if one conceives of culture, not as a mere hoax played by the ruling class on workers, but as the tradition that informs one's conception of tradition, as social practices that shape one's idea of social practice.

The major objection to the orthodox Marxist analysis of culture and religion is not that it is wrong, but that it is too narrow, rigid and dogmatic. It views popular culture and religion only as instruments of domination, vehicles of pacification. It sees only their negative and repressive elements. On this view, only enlightenment, reason, or clarity imposed from the outside can break through the cultural layers of popular false consciousness.[7] Therefore, the orthodox Marxist analysis refuses to acknowledge the positive, liberating aspects of popular culture and religion, and their potential for fostering structural social change.

This issue is at the heart of the heated debate over the adequacy of a Marxist analysis between Black theologians and Latin American liberation theologians. The latter tend to adopt the orthodox Marxist view, paying little attention to the positive, liberating aspects of popular culture and religion.[8] They display a contempt for popular culture and religion, a kind of tacit condescension that reeks of paternalism and elitism. They often speak of the poor possessing a privileged access to truth and reality, but rarely do they take seriously the prevailing beliefs, values or outlooks of the poor. Instead, Latin American liberation theologians stress the discontinuity and radical rupture of progressive consciousness with popular culture and religion, suggesting a desire to wipe the cultural slate clean and begin anew.

To the contrary, Black theologians recognize the positive and negative elements, the liberating and repressive possibilities, of popular culture and religion. To no one's surprise, they devote much attention to the armors of survival, forms of reaction, and products of response created by Black people in order to preserve their dignity and self-respect.[9] Black theologians view themselves as working within a tradition of political struggle and cultural and religious resistance to oppression. They emphasize their continuity with this tradition.

It is possible to account for this important difference between Black theologians and Latin American liberation theologians by appealing to the different histories of the particular countries about which they theorize. But there is possibly a deeper reason for this disagreement. It relates directly to the composition of the two groups of theologians.

For the most part, Latin American liberation theologians belong to the dominant cultural group in their respective countries. As intellectuals educated in either European schools or Europeanized Latin American universities and seminaries, they adopt cosmopolitan habits and outlooks.[10] Like their theoretical master, Karl Marx, a true cosmopolitan far removed from his indigenous Jewish culture, they tend to see popular culture and religion as provincial and parochial. It is something to be shed and ultimately discarded, replaced by something qualitatively different and better. They do not seem to have encountered frequently situations in which they were forced to rely on their own indigenous cultural and religious resources in an alien and hostile environment. So their own experiences often limit their capacity to see the existential richness and radical potential of popular culture and religion.

In contrast to this, Black theologians belong to the degraded cultural group in the United States. As intellectuals trained in American colleges, universities and seminaries, they have first-hand experiences of cultural condescension, arrogance and haughtiness. They know what it is like to be a part of a culture considered to be provincial and parochial. Hence they view Black culture and religion as something to be preserved and promoted, improved and enhanced, not erased and replaced. In short, Black theologians acknowledge their personal debts to Black culture and religion, and incorporate its fecundity and fertility in their understanding of American society.

Latin American liberation theologians and Black theologians can learn from each other on this matter. The former must be more sensitive to the complexities and ambiguities of popular culture and religion; the latter should more closely relate their view of Black culture and religion to a sophisticated notion of power in liberal capitalist America. And both can learn from the most penetrating Marxist theorist of culture in this century, Antonio Gramsci.[11]

Gramsci provides a valuable framework in which to understand culture, its autonomous activity and status, while preserving its indirect yet crucial link with power in society. Unlike the Latin American liberation theologians, he does not downplay the importance of popular culture; unlike the Black theologians, he does not minimize the significance of class. Instead, he views the systems of production and culture in a symbiotic relationship with one another, each containing intense tension, struggle and even warfare. Class struggle is not simply the battle between capitalists and proletariat, owners and producers, in the work situation. It also takes the form of cultural and religious conflict over which attitudes, values and beliefs will dominate the thought and behavior of people. For Gramsci, this incessant conflict is crucial. It contains the key to structural social change; it is the springboard for a revolutionary political praxis.

According to Gramsci, no state and society can be sustained by force alone. It must put forward convincing and persuasive reasons, arguments, ideologies or propaganda for its continued existence. A state and society require not only military protection, but also principled legitimation. This legitimation takes place in the cultural and religious spheres, in those arenas where the immediacy of everyday life is felt, outlooks are formed, and self-images adopted.

Gramsci deepens Marx's understanding of the legitimation process by replacing the notion of ideology with his central concept of hegemony. For Marx, ideology is the set of formal ideas and beliefs promoted by the ruling class for the purpose of preserving its privileged position in society; for Gramsci, hegemony is the set of formal ideas and beliefs and informal modes of behavior, habits, manners, sensibilities and outlooks that support and sanction the existing order.

In Gramsci's view, culture is both tradition and current practices. Tradition is understood, not as the mere remnants of the past or the lingering, inert elements in the present but, rather, as active formative and transformative modalities of a society. Current practices are viewed as actualizations of particular modalities, creating new habits, sensibilities and world-views against the pressures and limits of the dominant ones.

A hegemonic culture subtly and effectively encourages people to identify themselves with the habits, sensibilities, and world-views supportive of the status quo and the class interests that dominate it. It is a culture successful in persuading people to "consent" to their oppression and exploitation. A hegemonic culture survives and thrives as long as it convinces people to adopt its preferred formative modality, its favored socialization process. It begins to crumble when people start to opt for a transformative modality, a socialization process that opposes the dominant one. The latter constitutes a counter-hegemonic culture, the deeply embedded oppositional elements within a society. It is these elements that the hegemonic culture seeks to contain and control.

Based on the insights of Gramsci, along with those of the distinguished English cultural critic Raymond Williams, I shall present a theoretical framework that may be quite serviceable to Black theologians, Latin American liberation theologians, and Marxist thinkers.[12] Cultural processes can be understood in light of four categories: hegemonic, pre-hegemonic, neo-hegemonic, and counter-hegemonic.

Hegemonic culture is to be viewed as the effectively operative dominant world-views, sensibilities, and habits that sanction the established order. Pre-hegemonic culture consists of those residual elements of the past which continue to shape and mold thought and behavior in the present; it often criticizes hegemonic culture, harking back to a golden age in the pristine past. Neo-hegemonic culture constitutes a new phase of hegemonic culture; it postures as an oppositional force, but, in substance, is a new manifestation of people's allegiance and loyalty to the status quo. Counter-hegemonic culture represents genuine opposition to hegemonic culture; it fosters an alternative set of habits, sensibilities, and world-views that cannot possibly be realized within the perimeters of the established order.

This framework presupposes three major points. First, it accents the equivocal character of culture and religion, their capacity to be instruments of freedom or domination, vehicles of liberation or pacification. Second, it focuses on the ideological function of culture and religion, the necessity of their being either forces for freedom or forces for domination, for liberation or for pacification. Third, it views the struggle between these two forces as open-ended. The only guarantee of freedom rests upon the contingencies of human practice; the only assurance of liberation relies on the transformative modalities of a society. No matter how wide the scope of hegemonic culture may be, it never encompasses or exhausts all human practice or every transformative modality in a society. Human struggle is always a possibility in any society and culture.

In order to clarify further my four categories, I shall identify them crudely with particular elements in contemporary American society. Hegemonic culture can be seen as the prevailing Horatio Alger mystique, the widespread hopes and dreams for social upward mobility among Americans. This mystique nourishes the values, outlooks, and lifestyles of achievement, careerism, leisurism, and consumerism that pervade American culture. Pre-hegemonic culture is negligible owing to the country's peculiar inception, namely, that it was "born liberal." Subsequently, American conservatives and reactionaries find themselves in the ironic position of quarreling with liberals by defending early versions of liberalism. Neo-hegemonic culture is best illustrated by the counter-cultural movement of the sixties, specifically the protests of White middle-class youth (spin-offs of the Black political struggles) which, with few exceptions, was effectively absorbed by the mainstream of liberal capitalist America. The continuous creation of a counter-hegemonic culture is manifest in the multifarious, though disparate, radical grass-roots organizations; elements of the socialist feminist groups; and aspects of Afro-American culture and religion.

A present challenge confronting Black theologians is to discover and discern what aspects of Afro-American culture and religion can contribute to a counter-hegemonic culture in American society. They may find Gramsci's conception of organic intellectuals helpful on this matter.[13] Gramsci views organic intellectuals as leaders and thinkers directly tied to a particular cultural group primarily by means of institutional affiliations. Organic intellectuals combine theory and action, and relate popular culture and religion to structural social change.

Black religious leadership can make an enormous contribution to a counter-hegemonic culture and structural social change in American society. Black preachers and pastors are in charge of the most numerous and continuous gatherings of Black people, those who are the worst victims of liberal capitalist America and whose churches are financially, culturally and politically independent of corporate influence.[14] This freedom of Black preachers and pastors, unlike that of most Black professionals, is immense. They are the leaders of the only major institutions in the Black community that are not accountable to the status quo. Needless to say, many abuse this freedom. But what is important to note is that the contribution of Black religious leaders can be prodigious, as exemplified by the great luminaries of the past, including Nat Turner, Martin Delany, Martin Luther King, Jr., and Malcolm X.

An Alliance of Black Theology and Marxist Thought: The Case of Reverend George Washington Woodbey

The best example of a Black religious thinker and leader who combined the insights of Black theological reflection and Marxist social theory was the Rev. George Washington Woodbey.[15] He devoted his life to promoting structural social change and creating a counter-hegemonic culture in liberal capitalist America.

Rev. Mr. Woodbey was a Baptist preacher, for many years pastor of Mt. Zion Baptist Church in San Diego, California, and a major socialist leader in the first few decades of this century. He was uncompromising in his religious faith, unyielding in his confidence in the radical potential of Black culture and religion, and unrelenting in his devotion to fundamental social change. Widely known in California during his day as "The Great Negro Socialist Orator," Woodbey delivered poignant yet incisive lectures across the country, including his famous reply to Booker T. Washington's "Capitalist Argument for the Negro." Woodbey also wrote books such as *The Bible and Socialism: A Conversation between Two Preachers* (1904) and *The Distribution of Wealth* (1910), and such essays as "Why the Negro Should Vote the Socialist Ticket" (1908) and "Why the Socialists Must Reach the Churches with Their Message" (1915).[16]

Woodbey's most influential work, *What to Do and How to Do It or Socialism vs. Capitalism* (1903) was translated into three languages. It was often compared to Robert Blatchford's *Merrie England*, the most widely read Socialist educational publication at the turn of the century.

Woodbey's important work consists of a conversation between himself and his mother, taking place after a long separation. She begins with the question, "Have you given up the Bible and the ministry and gone into politics?" He replies that he became a Socialist precisely because of his strict adherence to principles put forward in the Bible. She then points out that many of his comrades do not believe in God or in biblical truths. He reminds her that other political parties, such as the Republican and Democratic parties, have their equal portion of nonbelievers. He assures her that he does not fully agree with some of his comrades on religious matters, but since Socialism is "a scheme for bettering things here first," he can be a Socialist without giving up his religious beliefs. He then states that, under Socialism, religious freedom will be guaranteed.

Later on, the mother asks, "like all other women, I want to know where are we to come in?" He answers that it is in the interest of "the women, more than the men, if possible, to be Socialists because they suffer more from capitalism than anyone else." Under Socialism, each woman will receive her own income and be an equal shareholder in the industries of the country. Under these conditions, there will be no need for a woman to "sell herself through a so-called marriage to someone she did not love, in order to get a living"; instead, she could marry for genuine love. In capitalist society, a working man is a slave, "and his wife is the slave of a slave." Therefore liberation of both would enhance the position of women more than that of men. This conversation ends with the mother's conversion to Socialism, and she comments,

> Well, you have convinced me that I am about as much a slave now as I was in the south, and I am ready to accept any way out of this drudgery.

Rev. Mr. Woodbey was the only Black delegate to the Socialist Party conventions of 1904 and 1908. In the latter convention, he was nominated as Eugene Debs's running mate in the presidential election of 1908. He was once described as "the greatest living negro in America . . . his style is simple and his logic invincible. He knows the race question, and one of his most popular lectures relates to the settlement of this vexed question under Socialism."

Jailed frequently, hospitalized more than once owing to police brutality, barely escaping murder during the famous 1912 Free Speech fight in San Diego, Rev. Mr. Woodbey was a devoted Christian who sacrificed greatly for fostering a counter-hegemonic culture and promoting structural social change in liberal capitalist America. He was a man of inexorable Christian faith, anchored deep in the best of Black culture and religion, and of intransigent Socialist conviction. His life and writings best exemplify the point at which Black theologians and Marxist thinkers are no longer strangers.

Notes

1. Dialectical methodology is a complex procedure useful for grasping, comprehending, interpreting, explaining or predicting phenomena. Aside from the foundation laid by Plato, this procedure was first fully developed by Hegel and deepened by Marx. Hegel's most succinct discussions of this approach can be found in his *Logic* (Part 1, *Encyclopedia of Philosophical Sciences*) trans. William Wallace (Oxford, 1975), no. 81, pp. 115–119, and *The Phenomenology of Mind*, trans. J. B. Baillie (New York, 1967), pp. 80 ff. For Marx's brief formal presentation of this approach as it relates to his social theory, see *The Grundrisse*, trans. Martin Nicolaus (New York, 1973), pp. 83–111.

2. The most explicit and extensive treatment of this matter by a Black theologian is found in James Cone's *God of the Oppressed* (New York, 1975), chap. 3, pp. 39–61.

3. The most sophisticated dialogue among Black theologians has focused on the status of this biblical truth. William Jones has claimed that Black theologians do not provide sufficient empirical evidence to warrant this truth. He suggests that Black theologians have not taken seriously the possibility of a malevolent deity. For Jones, an acceptable Black Theology must deal adequately with the problem of theodicy. James Cone has responded to Jones's argument by claiming that Jesus' victory over suffering and death constitutes the necessary and sufficient evidence for the belief that God sides with the oppressed and acts on their behalf. In short, Cone holds that empirical evidence is never a reliable basis of a biblical truth; the problem of theodicy is never solved in a theoretical manner, only defeated by one's faith in Jesus Christ. For Jones's incisive and insightful discussion, see his *Is God a White Racist?* (Garden City, N.Y., 1973). For Cone's reply, see his *God of the Oppressed*, op. cit., pp. 187–194.

4. This conception of science pervades Marx's mature writings. For example, he states, "But all science would be superfluous if the outward appearance and the essence of things directly coincided," *Capital*, ed. Friedrich Engels (New York, 1967), vol. 3, p. 817. Notice also the demystifying aim of theory in the first few paragraphs of the famous section 4, entitled, "The Fetishism of Commodities and the Secret Thereof" of chap. 1 in *Capital*, vol. 1, pp. 71 ff.

5. These figures come from the nearest thing to an official survey on the maldistribution of wealth in America, conducted by the Federal Reserve Board in 1962. As one of its authors, Herman Miller, noted, "the figures were so striking as to obviate the need to search for trends." For further exposition and elaboration on this study, see "The Other Economy: America's Working Poor," Gus Tyler, *The New Leader* (Special Issue), May 8, 1978, pp. 20–24.

6. I have tried to give persuasive reasons as to why this is so for any viewpoint which overlooks class oppression, in my paper, "Institutional Racism, Liberalism, and Self-Determination" (published in the Fall 1979 issue of *The Journal of Religious Ethics*).

7. This point illustrates the undeniable link of the orthodox Marxist view to the Enlightenment. More specifically, it portrays the inherent elitism and paternalism of such a view. We need only recall Lenin's well-known claim (in *What Is to Be Done?*) that the working class can achieve only trade-union consciousness on its own, thereby requiring a vanguard party to elevate it to revolutionary consciousness. For Lenin, this party brings enlightenment to the benighted proletariat.

8. This view is illustrated clearly in an essay by José Míguez Bonino, a leading Latin American liberation theologian, entitled "Popular Piety in Latin America," in which he states, "From a theological as well as a political perspective the popular piety that used to exist

and that still predominates in Latin America can only be considered as a profoundly alienated and alienating piety, a manifestation of an enslaved consciousness and, at the same time, a ready instrument for the continuation and consolidation of oppression. The intent to transform the mobilizing power of that piety to goals of transformation without radically altering the very content of the religious consciousness seems psychologically impossible and theologically unacceptable." This essay appeared in *Cristianismo y Sociedad* (Buenos Aires), no. 47 (first issue, 1976), pp. 31–38, trans. James and Margaret Goff. Gustavo Gutiérrez, another prominent Latin American liberation theologian, understands popular culture and religion in a more subtle and sophisticated way. I base this judgment on my cordial and provocative discussions with him during his visiting professorship at Union Theological Seminary in the fall of 1977. It seems to me his own cultural roots and his serious study of cultural Marxist thinkers, especially Antonio Gramsci and José Carlos Mariátegui (the father of Latin American Marxism) principally account for his sensitivity to popular culture and religion.

9. This serious concern of Black theologians and religious scholars is exemplifed best by Charles H. Long's highly suggestive essay, "Perspectives for a Study of Afro-American Religion in the United States," *History of Religions*, vol. 2, no. 1 (August 1977), pp. 54–66; Gayraud S. Wilmore's solid study, *Black Religion and Black Radicalism* (Garden City, N.Y., 1972), esp. pp. 298–306; and James Cone's speculative work, *The Spirituals and the Blues* (New York, 1972). The "armors, forms, and products" of Afro-American culture I have in mind here are the spirituals, blues, gospels, jazz, folktales and sermons. What is not sufficiently emphasized by Black theologians, religious scholars or cultural critics is the radical potential embedded within the style of these art-forms. The most important aspect of them is not what is conveyed, but *how* this "what" is conveyed. It is this "how" which bears the imprint of struggle and constitutes the distinctive imposition of order on chaos by Black people. It is this "how," or style, that contains the real message or genuine content of these works of art. To my knowledge, only the essays of Ralph Ellison and Albert Murray explore this frontier of Afro-American art-forms.

10. This point is best illustrated by the words of Hugo Assmann, one of the most radical Latin American theologians. "In my opening address I was sometimes aggressive because, as a Westernized Latin American, I don't feel at ease with my colour, my 'gringo' face, my German origin. I don't feel happy with the fact that my theological dissertation was written in German. I have a psychological necessity to say to you in Western language that I am not Western. We Latin Americans are still in the early stages of our search for a Latin American identity. If you look in my library you will find books by German authors, French authors, Italian authors, Marx, Moltmann, etc. There is something false in this, . . . something which is not Latin American." This quote is from the publication *Risk*, which is based on the Symposium on Black Theology and Latin American Theology of Liberation, May 1973 at the Ecumenical Center in Geneva, Switzerland, p. 62.

11. It is not surprising that Gramsci comes from a degraded cultural region in Italy, namely Sardinia, and had intense experiences of ostracism owing to his hunchback, poor health and short height (he was barely five feet tall). A sample of his writings can be found in *Selections from the Prison Notebooks*, trans. and ed. Quintin Hoare and Geoffrey Nowell Smith (New York, 1971).

12. The book by Raymond Williams I have in mind is his *Marxism and Literature* (London, 1977), esp. chap. 2, pp. 75–141.

13. Gramsci discusses this conception in his seminal essay, "The Intellectuals," *Selections from the Prison Notebooks*, op. cit., pp. 5–23. Although he completely misunderstands the nature of the radical potential of Afro-American culture and Afro-American intellectuals, this does not harm his theoretical formulation of the notion of organic intellectuals.

14. I should add that this also holds to an important degree for White poor and Hispanic Pentecostal churches.

15. My information about this fascinating Black preacher comes directly from Philip Foner's timely essay, "Reverend George Washington Woodbey: Early Twentieth Century California Black Socialist," *The Journal of Negro History*, vol. 61, no. 2 (April 1976). For Foner's treatment of Woodbey along with other Black Socialist preachers in the United States, including the Reverends George W. Slater, Jr., S. C. Garrison and George Frazier Miller, see his monumental work, *American Socialism and Black Americans: From the Age of Jackson to World War II* (Westport, Conn., 1977), chap. 7, pp. 151–181.

16. It is interesting to note that the first book mentioned here was dedicated to "the Preachers and Members of the Churches, and all others who are interested in knowing what the Bible teaches on the question at issue between the Socialists and the Capitalists, by one who began preaching twenty-nine years ago, and still continues."

Chapter 38

Ontological Blackness in Theology

Victor Anderson

In 1969, a revolutionary moment in black American culture, James H. Cone wrote: "What is needed is not integration but a sense of worth in being black, and only black people can teach that. Black consciousness is the key to the Black man's emancipation from his distorted self-image" (1989, 19). The juxtaposition of black revolutionary consciousness (as the subject of liberation) and hope (as the ground motive of liberation) frame the argument of this chapter. The black theology project was born out of the chaos of deferred cultural fulfillment. A new revolutionary racial consciousness was ascending among an emergent educated class of black intellectuals, and black theology sought to defend this revolutionary agenda.

Black theology would take its point of departure from black life and experience, which constitute the exceptional social location for a theology of black power. If white theology was viewed as an ideology of oppression, then black theology would become the ideology of liberation (127). Black theology's method is correlational. The task of the black theologian is to show the critical correlations existing between black life/experience and traditional theological categories (God, humanity, Christ, eschatology, and so forth), between black religion and black radicalism (Wilmore, 1983), and the correlations between the black church and black theology. The sources of black theology are black history, black faith, and black cultural activities. And the ultimate end of black theology is the construction of a "new black being" (134).

The argument of this chapter is that black theology constructs its new being on the dialectical structures that categorical racism and white racial ideology bequeathed to African American intellectuals (notwithstanding its claims for privileging black sources). However, the new being of black

893

theology remains an alienated being whose mode of existence is determined by crisis, struggle, resistance, and survival—not thriving, flourishing, or fulfillment. Its self-identity is always bound by white racism and the culture of survival. The motive of transcendence from this unresolved matrix of struggle and survival recedes into the background as oppression is required for the self-disclosure of the oppressed. I suggest that as long as black theology remains determined by ontological blackness, it remains not only a crisis theology but also a theology in a crisis of legitimation.

The Black Theology Project

The expressive elements of black heroic genius in African American theology peaked in 1969 and the '70s in the black theology project. James H. Cone is its unsurpassed representative. In the preface to his 1986 edition of *A Black Theology of Liberation* (1991), first published in 1970, Cone framed his discourse under the idea of ontological blackness. Cone suggests that the theological problem for blacks as well as the entire problem of American culture is subsumed under white racism. And in the matrix of black existence and white racism, Cone explicates the meaning of ontological blackness in terms of an emergent collective black revolutionary consciousness (23). The critical task of black theologians is to disclose the "essential religious and theological meaning" of this new black collective consciousness in light of the black experience, black history, and black culture. Black experience is a "totality of black existence in a white world where babies are tortured, women are raped, and men are shot. . . . The black experience is existence in a system of white racism" (24). Such an experiential matrix is symbolized by Cone as a *Symbolic Blackness* (7). It expresses itself in:

> The power to love oneself precisely because one is black and a readiness to die if whites try to make one behave otherwise. It is the sound of James Brown singing, "I'm Black and I'm Proud" and Aretha Franklin demanding "respect." The black experience is catching the spirit of blackness and loving it. It is hearing black preachers speak of God's love in spite of the filthy ghetto, and black congregations responding Amen, which means that they realize that ghetto existence is not the result of divine decree but of white inhumanity. (25)

The black theology project seeks to disclose the essential meanings of black faith in the black God revealed in the black Christ from the perspective of the black experience. Cone writes in a later work:

When I speak of black faith, I am referring only secondarily to organized religion and primarily to black people's collective acknowledgment of the spirit of liberation in their midst, a Spirit who empowers
them to struggle for freedom even though the odds are against them.
This is the historical matrix out of which my hermeneutical perspective has been formed. (1986, 43)

The essential meaning of the black collective consciousness (ontological
blackness) is the resolve of two cultural motifs, both of which are recon-
figurations of the classical black aesthetic: black survivalist culture and
black revolutionary self-assertion.

Survival "is a way of life for the black community," says Cone. And C.
Eric Lincoln and Lawrence Mamiya would write twenty years after Cone,
in their monumental work on the black church, that black "culture is the
sum of the options for creative survival" (1990, 3). "Black theology is a theology of survival," Cone argued, "because it seeks to interpret the theological significance of the being of a community whose existence is threatened
by the power of non-being" (1991, 16). Moreover, it seeks to elicit the
essential theological meaning of black self-assertion as "an event of liberation taking place in the black community in which blacks recognize that it
is incumbent upon them to throw off the chains of white oppression by
whatever means they regard as necessary" (5). And, for Cone, any means
necessary might mean "attacking the enemy of black humanity by throwing a Molotov cocktail into a white-owned building and watching it go up
in flames" (25). Although such a position seems revolutionary enough, such
an act of racial frustration is not likely to transact cultural fulfillment.

It is only insofar as Cone extends these essentialized meanings of the
new black revolutionary consciousness to black cultural productions
themselves that ontological blackness climaxes in the absurdity that "the
black experience is possible only for black persons":

[The black experience] means having natural hair cuts, wearing
African dashikis, and dancing to the sound of Johnny Lee Hooker or
B. B. King, knowing that no matter how hard whitey tries there can
be no real duplication of black "soul." Black soul is not learned; *it comes
from the totality of black experience*, the experience of carving out an existence in a society that says you do not belong. (25; emphasis mine)

For Cone, the essential theological meanings of black experience, black
history, and black culture—all of which represent the black collective

consciousness—emerge in a symbolic expressive play of the heroic survivalist culture of the black community, the pain and joy it derives from
"reacting to whiteness and affirming blackness" and "the mythic power
inherent in [its historical] symbols for the present revolution against white
racism" (28). When the theological meaning of ontological blackness is
accented, black theology approaches an identification of black culture
with the Christ event in which "God's revelation comes to us in and
through the cultural situation of the oppressed" (28). And black culture
(art, music, literature, and theology) is the expressive vehicle of black liberation by the black messiah.

A number of problems plagued Cone's project from the beginning.
These problems centered around the relation of black theology to the black
churches. Early critics, particularly those who pressed internal criticisms as
black church theologians, asked how black theology could be a theology of
the black churches if it fundamentally disentangles itself from the creeds
and confessions, as well as the liturgical practices that structure the black
churches. To some, black theology appeared to posit within itself a revolutionary consciousness that looked more like the mirror of white racism and
less like an expression of the evangelical gospel that characterized most
black churches. Was black theology, then, an academic project in theology
rather than an ecclesiastical project? Others asked, in what sense could
black theology be black since its theological method was derived from white
European theologians, notably Karl Barth and Paul Tillich, and European
philosophers such as Albert Camus and Jean Paul Sartre?

In subsequent writings throughout the '70s and '80s, Cone tried to
answer many of the problems that center around the relation of black theology to the black churches and to black culture in books such as *A Black
Theology of Liberation* (1970), *The Spirituals and the Blues* (1972), *God of the
Oppressed* (1975), and *Speaking the Truth* (1986). The fundamental difficulty lies in Cone's call for the radical disentanglement of black theology
from white theology and European religious sources.

Cone's radically oppositional rhetoric leaves him with this dilemma: he
could either capitulate his claims for exceptionalism in the production of
black theology by acknowledging the indebtedness of black theology to
the west European manuscript tradition in the theological formation of
the black churches, or he might insist on the radical disjunction of black
theology from European sources and remain a theologian alienated from
the theology of the churches and their evangelical roots. Cone chose the
latter. He attempted to overcome his academic alienation from the black
churches by emphasizing the necessity of black sources for the construc-

tion of black theology. But this apologetic preoccupation with black sources creates more contradictions in the project than it solves.

Most of Cone's problems center around the category of symbolic blackness. Cone's problems are matters of internal contradiction. First, black theology, as Cone formulated it, risks self-referential inconsistency when it sees itself as radically oppositional to white racism and white theology. Because Cone collapses metaphysics into ontology, blackness is reified into a totality or a unity of black experience. At the same time, blackness is regarded as symbolic, so that anyone who can participate in its meaning can also be said to be black (1991, 9). However, black theology exceptionally circumscribes the meaning of symbolic blackness in terms of black oppression and suffering.

The difficulty arises here: (a) blackness is a signification of ontology and corresponds to black experience. (b) Black experience is defined as the experience of suffering and rebellion against whiteness. Yet (c) both black suffering and rebellion are ontologically created and provoked by whiteness as a necessary condition of blackness. (d) Whiteness appears to be the ground of black experience, and hence of black theology and its new black being. Therefore, while black theology justifies itself as radically oppositional to whiteness, it nevertheless requires whiteness, white racism, and white theology for the self-disclosure of its new black being and its legitimacy. In this way, black theology effectively renders whiteness identifiable with what is of ultimate concern. "Our ultimate concern is that which determines our being or not being," says Tillich (1967, 14).

The cogency of black theology, in its classical formulation, also appears performatively contradictory. Cone defined blackness in terms of Tillich's semiotics (1991, 7). On Tillich's terms, then, symbolic blackness must point to something other than itself. According to Tillich, revelatory word-symbols have a basic correlation to the ultimate mystery signified by the symbol. However, the symbolic correlation of our ordinary language and ultimate mystery is asymptotic. Thus, while theological words are not identifiable with ultimate mystery, they nevertheless may have "a denotative power that points through the ordinary meaning to us." They also have an "expressive power which points through ordinary expressive possibilities of language to the unexpressible and its relations to us," says Tillich (1967, 124).

Whether denotatively or expressively, on Tillich's account, revelatory word-symbols reflexively point beyond their ordinary meanings to the unexpressible. Therefore, theological symbols approximate what is of ultimate concern but are not identifiable with ultimate concern. "When speaking of the ultimate, of being and meaning, ordinary language brings it down to the level of the preliminary, the conditioned, the finite, thus muffling its revelatory power," says Tillich (124). Theological symbols are idolatrous when they are taken for the ground of being or nonbeing.

In black theology, blackness has become a totality of meaning. It cannot point to any transcendent meaning beyond itself without also fragmenting. Because black life is fundamentally determined by black suffering and resistance to whiteness (the power of nonbeing), black existence is without the possibility of transcendence from the blackness that whiteness created. Without transcendence from the determinancy of whiteness, black theology's promise of liberation remains existentially a function of black self-consciousness (to see oneself as black, free, and self-determined). However, since as Cone argues it is whiteness, white racism, and white theology that threatens the nonbeing of blacks, the promise of black liberation remains bracketed both existentially and politically.

Existentially, the new black being remains bound by whiteness. Politically, it remains unfulfilled because blackness is ontologically defined as the experience of suffering and survival. Any amelioration of these essential marks of blackness performatively contradicts ontological blackness in black theology. Insofar as it is predicated ontologically on symbolic blackness, black theology remains alienated from black interests in not only surviving against suffering but also thriving, flourishing, and obtaining cultural fulfillment.

Subsequent projects of thinkers such as Dwight Hopkins, James Evans, and womanist thinkers, such as Katie Cannon, Jacquelyn Grant, and Delores Williams, have tried to reassure the ecclesiastical and public relevancy of black theology. In the remaining pages of this chapter, I make clear how these subsequent formulations of the black theology project differ from the classical formulation but, at the same time, remain under the burden of ontological blackness. The decisive turn occurs in these later theologians' intentions to reassure the exceptional and essential sources legitimizing the project under *the hermeneutics of return* to black sources and the expansion of experiential matrices for rethinking ontological blackness in light of black women's experience.

"The hermeneutics of return," as I retrieve the idea from Said (1993, xii–xiii), is a narrative return to distinctively black sources for the purpose of establishing and reassuring the legitimacy of black theology in a postrevolutionary context. The theological gaze here returns to African traditional religions and slave narratives, autobiography, and folklore in order to assure the vitality of the black church (church theology) and the cultural solidarities that transcend the individualism that drives our market culture and morality, and rob the black community of moral vitality. The hermeneutics of return is a decisive element of African American fundamental theology. As a function of fundamental theology, hermeneutics is therefore prolegomenon to African American constructive theology.

Dwight N. Hopkins has been at the forefront of this fundamental theology. In his recent book, *Shoes That Fit Our Feet: Sources for a Constructive Black Theology* (1993), Hopkins attempts to play out the systematic implications of *slave theology* for the black theology project. Hopkins gives several significations for the sort of return he proposes for constructive black theology. The return is at once to *slave theology* and *bush arbor theology*. Yet as I shall show presently, both sources are attributive to black theology in such a way that it is not clear whether they are *sources* for a constructive black theology or the *product* of constructive black theology. Slave theology and African American religious experience are hybrids. Slave theology is the synthesis of "white Christianity with the remains of African religions under slavery," says Hopkins (1993, 15). As his argument goes, African slaves maintained enough residual aspects, or what Hopkins calls *remains*, of their former religions to establish a historically effective slave religion. This religion was preserved and transmitted in an invisible institution, among bushes and trees away from the eyes and ears of white and black guardians. In that institution, these *remains* achieved some measure of coherence and a regulative content. However, one of the problems in understanding Hopkins's argument is that while slave theology is fundamentally a religious hybrid, the individuated elements (African traditional religions, on the one side, and white Christianity, on the other side) are unidentifiable from the theological content of black theology.

Let us look more closely at Hopkins's argument. Hopkins argues that "enslaved Africans, the majority coming from the African West Coast, brought a distinct perception of God to North America" (16). And "African traditional religions described their ultimate divinity as the High God" (16). Hopkins then suggests that there is a correlation between the High God (who has no name in Hopkins's discourse) and Western "theological" notions of omnipresence, omnipotence, transcendence, and immanence. However, the correlation Hopkins proposes turns out to be one between the High God of African traditional religions and Israel's God.

Hopkins sees other correlations between African traditional religions and the Hebrew God when he compares cosmologies in which the earth and human flourishing are regarded as actions of the compassion and care of the High God and Yahweh:

African indigenous religions believe in a God who cares; some call God "the Compassionate One"; others see "the God of Pity," who rescues victims in need. Even more, God is kind and "looks after the case of the poor man." In fact, God is the main hope of the poor in society. As Guardian and Keeper, God is named "the protector of the poor" by some African traditional religions. They further specify that "there is a Saviour and only he can keep our lives." As judge, God metes out justice, punishment, and retribution. Similarly, God displays protectiveness by avenging injustice. God is a divinity of partiality to the victim; God sides with the political powerlessness of society's injured. (17)

A third correlation is also proposed in what Hopkins regards as a theological anthropology. These religions are shown to share a "dynamic and interdependent relation between the individual and the community" (17). And this correlation justifies the opposition of black theology to *individualism.*

African religions gave rise to a dynamic interplay between community and individual. Whatever happened to the communal gathering affected the individual; whatever happened to the individual had an impact on the community. Such a theological view of humanity cuts across bourgeois notions of white Christianity's individualism and "me-first-ism." It seeks to forge a group solidarity and identity, beginning with God, proceeding through the ancestors to the community and immediate family and continuing even to the unborn. One cannot be a human being unless one becomes a part of, feels a responsibility to, and serves the community. To preserve the community's well-being (through liberation) in African religions is to preserve the individual's well-being (through salvation). Thus salvation and liberation become a holistic individual-collective and personal-systemic ultimate concern. (17)

Hopkins argues that there are possible correlations between the High God of African traditional religions and the Hebrew God at the levels of both formal and moral utterances. And there are possible correlations between the formal and moral utterances concerning humanity at the level of theological anthropology. However, Hopkins has the burden of showing that there is a correlation between the *remains* of African traditional religions, *Africanism(s)* and *slave religion.* He must also show that the elements in correspondence are genetically independent for a successful argument for hybridity. He argues that the biblical faith of the slaves effects the synthesis:

> Enslaved Africans took the remnant of their traditional religious structures and meshed them together with their interpretation of the Bible. All of this occurred in the "Invisible Institution," far away from the watchful eyes of white people. Only in their own cultural idiom and political space could black slaves truly worship God. (18)

Bush arbor theology (the theology slaves created hidden among bushes and trees away from the eyes and ears of their masters) signifies a distinctive discursive site for the formation of a slave theology. Hopkins argues that among trees and bushes, slaves achieved "a remarkable clarity concerning the cultural dimension of their theology" (19). And the distinctive formation of their religious experience was materially manifest in ecstatic religious expressions and a political space from which they defined their humanity and established creative forms of resistance (19). Slave theology defines the content of its faith in terms of the egalitarian principle, absolute justice, and divine preference for the poor. Its content echoes both incarnational and resurrection triumphalism; and the mark of authenticity in religious experience is religious immediacy.

When I examine the claims that Hopkins makes for slave religion as a hybrid religion, I am left asking whether the hermeneutics of narrative return does not introduce more ambiguities and contradictions into Hopkins's project than it solves. Two lines of argument seem warranted: an examination of whether the coherence of Hopkins's project is compromised by committing a performative contradiction, and an examination of whether the project's legitimacy depends on a viciously circular mode of reasoning that commits hermeneutical violence not only to the African sources but also to the narrative sources. On the first charge, for all of Hopkins's talk about privileging African sources as an effective means for reassuring the legitimacy of black theology, these sources seem to fall out of or are simply consumed into Hebraic-Christian utterances. That is, so-called Africanisms are unidentifiable from the biblical utterances of Christian slaves. And instead of slave religion manifesting a hybridity, Hopkins's African slaves baptize the African gods into Hebrew faith. Therefore, Hopkins violates his principle of correlation by collapsing correlation into identification, since African religions collapse into biblical faith.

In order to explicate the biblical faith of the slaves, Hopkins has to show how the High God(s) of African traditional religions, tending to be *deus otiosus*, is identifiable with the Hebrew God of slave religions without also committing violence against the former God(s). Failure to demonstrate correlation constitutes a performative contradiction. Hopkins's argument for hybridity collapses in a performative contradiction for several reasons. Hopkins begs the question of whether the belief systems of African traditional religions are translatable (notwithstanding whatever family resemblances may exist between them and slave religion) into the languages of Hebrew/Christian faith without also committing violence against traditional religions.

Hopkins also does not show how the differences already signaled in the notion of African traditional *religions* (plural) are reducible to the sort of categorical simplicities which he calls *Africanisms*. Hopkins calls these categories *remains*. But the misnomer seems ironically quite appropriate. For in the interest of forcing not only a correlation but also an identification of African traditional religions with slave religion, Hopkins has his slave theologians carrying the *remains* of their African gods into their invisible institution and disposing of the *remains* in the inauguration of slave religion. The performative contradiction renders the return to African traditional religions a moot point if, in the end, there are no recognizable differences that would count as independent sources for black theology.

This brings me to my second criticism: that Hopkins's hermeneutics of narrative return ends up justifying the black theology project by a vicious circularity of reasoning that renders the legitimacy of slave religion coterminous with black theology and the legitimacy of black liberation theology coterminous with slave religion. When comparing the utterances properly ascribed to the slave narratives with those characteristic of the black theology project, there appears to be no significant differences that would suggest that the latter (black theology) is effectively indebted to the former sources (African traditional religion and slave theology). Both antecedent sources tend to be identified as liberation utterances. This is to say that there appears to be no difference between a source (antecedent) and its effect (consequent).

The slave narratives are rendered as just so much *proto-black liberation theology*. At its best, this is an anachronism, and at its worst, this is hermeneutical violence for the sake of reassuring the identity of the black theology project by grounding it in authentic African American religious experience. By identifying the legitimacy of black theology with that of slave religion (authentic African American religious experience and practices), Hopkins *connotatively* overcomes one of the problems that has plagued the black theology project from its inception: How is black theology an authentic expression of the black churches and their theology, and not the ideological invention of black middle-class academic theologians (mostly heterosexual males) seeking to come to terms with their alienation from the everyday, routinized functions of the churches and their members?

My criticisms try to disclose intentions in the hermeneutics of return that distinguish the recent emphasis in the black theology project from its classical formulation in the '70s. I contend that the controlling intention is to reassure, in contemporary African American public life, the ideological position of the black theology project. In other words, the return to black sources is attributive to an ideological function that is culturally apologetic. It is apologetic insofar as black theology must assure its relevance for African American public life as a project that effectively contributes to the formation of a contemporary black cultural consciousness. Its cultural relevance is not self-evident. The *return* is also an attempt to place the black theology project in solidarity with the pressing problems of the urban underclass and its culture of poverty, and to construct a position that can effectively speak to the crisis of black nihilism and its culture of violence.

The hermeneutics of return projects a grand narrative that evokes a great cloud of witnesses whose heroic legacy of survival, resistance, and hope can mediate the fragility of African American public life today and bind together our alienated generation that is so much in need of a heroic black faith. But the consequence of such a hermeneutic is that whatever claims are made for African American identity in terms of black subjectivity, these are subsumed under a black collective consciousness definable in terms of black faith. So not only are the *remains* of the African gods disposed of under the totalizing hermeneutics of black theology, but black subjectivity itself is also subjugated under the totality of black faith.

The recent systematic theology by James H. Evans, Jr., *We Have Been Believers: An African American Systematic Theology* (1992), is another attempt to reassure the project of black theology in our postmodern context of African American cultural life. Like Hopkins, Evans also continues to legitimize the project of black academic theology almost singularly in terms of ontological blackness and a cult of black heroic genius. Evans's project is also fundamentally justified in terms of a hermeneutic of return in which theology is primarily a church-dependent discourse that "is essentially the church's response to the autobiographical impulse, and it grows out of the need to proclaim with authority and commitment the identity and mission of the church in the world" (1992, 1).

However, a problem of academic black theology is its tendency toward alienation from the existential pathos and crises of the church as a community. The primary directive of Evans's book is to suggest ways in which the alienation of professional black theologians from church members can be overcome and how their mutual relation can be "strengthened so that it becomes clear that black theology is rooted in the faith of the church and that the faith of the church is given intellectual clarity and expression in black theology" (1).

Such clarity is predicated on hermeneutics more than on ritual performances, which are routinized in the everyday practices of the church. African American theology "requires a praxeological commitment to the community of faith" (1). And the faith that occupies the black theologian's tasks is that which African Americans *constructed* out of their unprecedented experience of African chattel slavery. In this context,

> They created distinctive ways of conceptualizing and speaking about ultimate concerns. Black theology is a continuation of that discursive tradition. Therefore, African-American theological development can be best understood as the convergence of an African-derived world view, the complexities of the experience of slavery, oppression, survival, rebellion, and adjustment in the New World, and the encounter with the biblical text. These realities shaped the African-American intellect and spirit. (2)

African American theology is grounded both by the theologian's recognition that his or her project is historically derivative from the economy of slavery and also expressive of the passions, feelings, and rationality that constitutes African-American Christianity.

Already some of the marks of the classical black aesthetic begin to resurface as the creative matrix from which black theology's self-understanding occurs. Through ecstatic reason, black theology correlates the economy of slavery and the heroic impetuses of survival, rebellion, and adjustment with Christian faith. Ecstatic reason is privileged as a distinctive mark of black rationality. It connects the project of black theology with the classical black aesthetics. As Evans puts it, an authentic African American theology must be "in touch with the 'guts' of Black religion. Without this quality, it would forfeit its claim to authenticity" (2). While black theology must have some occupation with "formal, self-conscious, systematic attempt[s] to interpret that faith," its mode of conceptualization is regarded as oppositional, nonlinear, and non-Western. The black theology project is not only epistemologically oppositional in its Afro-centric ideology. As an Afrocentric discourse, black theology is ontologi-cally oppositional. The marks of Western ontology are the devaluing of community, the idolization of individuality, and "private property and individual rights as the basis of social and political organization." In dis-tinction from these essential marks, Evans says that:

> The cultural matrix of the African tended to affirm the infinite worth of the African as a human being in relation to other human beings and under the auspices of a benevolent creator God. The community (the no longer living, the living, and the yet to be born) was affirmed as the basic social unit and the social framework in which the indi-vidual was defined. All creation, including nature, was seen as infused with the spiritual presence of God. (5)

What fundamentally guides the "hermeneutics of return" to black sources among the recent black theologians? Evans wants black theology to speak to the problems of contemporary black Christianity—namely, the threat of black cultural fragility and nihilism. On the one side, African Americans are caught in a crisis of faith in which they "struggle with the pull of a secular materialistic, hedonistic, narcissistic, and pessimistic cul-ture." And on the other side, they also struggle to "experience, to varying degrees, the magnetic hold of a spiritual, integrated, communal, and hope-ful, counter-culture" of black faith (6). The oppositional tension between nihilism and faith tends to push Evans normatively to affirm and reassure the communal focus in black theology and to minimize individuality.

The legitimacy for such a focus is found in the hermeneutics of narra-tive return. The kernel beliefs that identify African American religious faith involve a selective retrieval of the *canonical story* of God's divine inter-ventions into the affairs of oppressors in order to effect the liberation of the oppressed in both the exodus and the Christ events. But there is also a selective reception of "folk stories" that drives black theologians to the slave narratives. The heart of these stories centers on their "fears, frus-trations and struggle as well as the determination for freedom from exis-tential anxiety, political oppression, and cultural exploitation that constitutes our experience" (7). The theologian as storyteller has a diffi-cult task of overcoming the vicious circularity between oppression and lib-eration. The black theologian has to reassure the canonical gospel story as an effective liberating story in the context of black suffering. One would hope therefore that suffering can be ameliorated or transcended. At the same time, liberation is the correlate of black experience, but black experience is essentially the experience of unrelenting crisis. The oppression-liberation circle remains viciously closed to cultural transcendence.

Although Hopkins and Evans try to reassure the black theology project in terms of an Afrocentric narrative return, it remains a crisis theology in two senses. First, it is a theology of crisis insofar as it identifies ontological blackness with *black experience* and black experience as the experience of suffering and black rebellion. Where either term (suffering or rebellion) is existentially mitigated or ameliorated so that suffering and rebellion are no longer the *way of life* for black people, then the ontological matrix of such a theology must enter into a crisis of legitimacy. This is the second sense in which black theology is a theology in a crisis of legitimation. It is a theology in crisis insofar as social and cultural elements of differentiation genuinely occur among African Americans, which are sufficient to call into question any reasonable assent to such ideological totalities as *the black church, the black faith,* or *the black sacred cosmos.*

Where radical differentiation occurs among African Americans, such ideological totalities are relativized by a pluralism of quasi-religious and not so religious organizations (street gangs, black gay and lesbian clubs, military service, fraternities and sororities). They are relativized by a multitude of faith traditions including non-Christian ones (Judaism, traditional orthodox Islam, African traditional religions, and new religions). And they are relativized by the plurality of world and life views held by African Americans who occupy varying social positions of class, gender, sex, and ethnicity. Under such differentiations, suffering, rebellion, and survival cannot be categorically descriptive of black experience. Many African Americans experience privileges and benefits of social mobilization within black culture itself. To make suffering, rebellion, and survival essential marks of black existence, it seems to me, trivializes the nature of oppression many blacks genuinely experience by the absurdity that anyone who is black is also oppressed.

Both Hopkins and Evans remain honest in their intentions to reassure the viability of the black faith in our market culture by privileging black community over black subjectivity. As a community of resistance, survival, and rebellion, however, the black community subjugates black subjectivity under ontological blackness. Since ontological blackness is identifiable with black experience, it is defined by and coterminous with black resistance and black suffering. Black theology—both in its classical and Afrocentric varieties—fails to show how cultural transcendence over white racism is possible. It also fails to disclose what forms existential amelioration of black suffering and resistance will take. If suffering and resistance and white racism are ontologically constitutive of black life, faith, and theology, then transcendence from ontological blackness puts at risk the cogency of black theology.

The Challenge of Womanist Theology

One of the greatest challenges facing the integrity of the black theology project is womanist theology. Themes presented in the work of theologians such as Katie Cannon (1988), Jacquelyn Grant (1989), and Delores Williams (1993) not only form shared rhetorical matrices for the production of future womanist theologies, they also form a constellation of values. In the end, we shall have to consider whether these values are successful in mitigating the aporias of black theology, which are created by black theologians' commitments to ontological blackness. Womanist theology poses several challenges for rethinking black theology.

Womanist theology attempts to negotiate the legitimation crisis of black theology both in its classical and Afrocentric variety. When it makes gender along with race and class a constitutive category of criticism, womanist theology makes regulative a womanist consciousness that includes within itself the privilege of difference. Therefore, theoretically, it can mediate the impasses of binary oppositions that often subjugate black women's experience. Such oppositions are those between whiteness/blackness, oppressors/oppressed, and community/personality.

Delores Williams sees mediatorial possibilities as constitutive of what Alice Walker means by *womanist*. Williams is worth quoting at length:

> Walker identifies a womanist as Black or of other color. Cone has shown well enough how Black people's color has been the basis upon which many white Americans have judged Black people to be subhuman. Walker lifts up Black women involved in the single-parenting act of passing on advice to the female child. The relationship between mother and child in a single-parent household is not valued as the proper circumstance out of which "normal" and psychologically healthy children can come. These kinds of relationships and family life are devalued. Needless to say, American culture does not value the advice women give. Walker, in her description of a womanist, challenges stereotypical ideas devaluating Black women. She describes a womanist as "responsible . . . in charge . . . serious." This challenges the stigma of "childlike," "girlish," and "frivolous," which

patriarchal and demonarchial social attitudes assign to Black women. According to Walker, a womanist loves men and women sexually or nonsexually. This challenges those who devalue the humanity of lesbian women. A womanist defines universality in terms of an array of skin colors. This gives intrinsic value to all skin colors: "brown, pink, and yellow" as well as "white, beige, and black." Walker describes Black women's love in terms of dance, the moon, the spirit, love, food, roundness, struggle, the folks, and love of themselves as women. This affirms the cultural elements through which black women express their humanity. To devalue any of this understanding of a womanist is to devalue Black women's womanhood, to devalue their humanity, to be guilty of sin—the sin that denies that Black women's humanity is in the image of God as is all humanity. (1993, 145–46)

Williams sees in the promise of womanist prose an inclusive vision for reinscribing black women's consciousness beyond the ontological categories of black theology. So the promise of racial and cultural mediation seems included in the womanist definition. Williams rightly sees that womanist theologians add not only challenges to the hegemony of black, male clergy over legitimacy claims in African American religion and theology. But the question remains whether their gender challenges contextually and hermeneutically transcend the fundamental orientations of ontological blackness that structure the black theology project without at the same time vitiating their real interests.

Contextually, womanist theology makes regulative a comprehensive experiential matrix for the analysis of African American life. This experiential matrix is a tri-modal configuration of black oppression: racism, sexism, and classism. Therefore, womanist theology poses a challenge to the binary matrices that have driven prior racial discourse in African American religion and theology. However, it is evident that womanist theology contextually remains bound by ontological blackness, since the defining category is black oppression.

At the contextual level, womanist theologians tend to accent themes of cultural domination and alienation as vitiating cultural fulfillment. Black women's *womanhood* is devalued by white racism and sexism. The hegemony of white, male cultural elitism and black, male elitism remain hegemonic. Domination is not the only attending sign of black women's experience. In addition, there is also alienation. The general context for womanist theological writings tends to be not only that of pervasive racism and its discriminatory effects resulting in the domination of white over black. But the context is also one of alienation from the goods of democratic society.

Katie Cannon puts it in these terms:

> I first began pondering the relationship between faith and ethics as a schoolgirl while listening to my grandfather teach the central affirmations of Christianity within the context of a racially segregated society. My community of faith taught me that the principles of God's universal parenthood which engendered a social, intellectual and cultural ethos, embracing the equal humanity of all people. Yet, my city, state, and nation declared it a punishable offense against the laws and mores for Blacks and whites to travel, eat, defecate, wait, be buried, make love, play, relax, and even speak together, except in the stereotyped context of master and servant interaction. (1988, 1)

While Cannon stresses the ways that white racism determines black women's experience, Jacquelyn Grant emphasizes the internal duplicity that is signified by white racism. She attends to the complicity of white-female privilege and its legitimation of black women's oppression. In *White Women's Christ and Black Women's Jesus* (1989), Grant tends to emphasize the triple oppression of black women as a fundamental differentiating precedent for constructive womanist theology. This triple cluster allows Grant to press charges of white women's complicity in black women's oppression. Grant argues that "feminist theology is inadequate for two reasons: it is White and racist" (1989, 195). Therefore, it cannot be a viable source of womanist discourse, because it cannot disentangle itself from the determinants of biological pedigree. Neither can it disentangle itself from the legacy of the white manuscript tradition in theology (195). "Although there are sharp differences among feminist theologians," Grant nevertheless argues that "they are *all* of the *same* race and the influence of their race has led them to similar sources for the definition of their perspectives on the faith" (195; Grant's emphasis). Grant's critique of feminist theology is that it is not only white but also racist. This identification of whiteness and racism is for her categorical. Therefore, it is a matter of definition.

Grant's argument depends on her accepting a definition of racism that is categorically predicated on the supremacist action of a dominant racial group on a minor and subjugated racial group (199 ff.). The logic of Grant's argument is that racism is categorically a function of the systemic behavior of the dominant racial group—namely, whites. Since white women are entailed in the privileges of white racism, white feminist theology is by definition also racist.

What is at stake in Grant's categorical argument in distinction from Cannon's relative silence about white feminist complicity in black women's oppression? For Grant, the issue is black women allowing whites, in this case white women, to define black women's experience in terms of white women's racial and class interests.

Grant holds that whatever interests black women may share with white women in terms of gender identification, the privileges that attend to whiteness at racial and class levels negate white feminists' genuine interest in the liberation of black women from black women's tri-modal oppression. The historic disparities between white and black women sexually under the economy of slavery and segregation, Grant argues, "have created a gulf between these women, that White feminists' common assumptions that all women are in the same situation with respect to sexism is difficult to understand when history so clearly tells us a different story" (196).

At the contextual level, their triple experience of oppression in terms of race, gender, and class provides womanist theologians an angle of vision that anticipates some promise of transcendence over the burdens of ontological blackness. Black existence, whether male or female, is bound by unprecedented suffering and survival. Yet it appears, at least on Grant's argument, that womanists' demands and claims for exceptionalism require the stability of ontological blackness for the legitimacy of their project. In the case of Grant, ontological blackness results in a categorical racial reductionism that morally diminishes her capacity to distinguish friends from enemies.

By making racism categorical and identifiable with whiteness, Grant effectively reduces the logic of womanist exceptionalism formally to the reductio ad absurdum that every black woman is also a womanist. Presently, we shall see how one African American theologian, Cheryl J. Sanders, challenges the logic of Grant's racial reductionism. Womanist claims for contextual exceptionalism are defective when they are based on ontological blackness. More importantly, such racial reasoning also lessens the possibilities of transcendence promised experientially in Walker's womanist connotations. In this regard, Grant appears to be a mitigated womanist theologian.

At the hermeneutical level of womanist theological criticism, womanist theology tends to privilege not only traditional biblical/theological manuscript sources but also narratives, autobiographies, and black women's writings as primary sources for theology. By giving centrality to black women's writings, however, womanist theologians make a significant advancement on the black theology project by adding not merely a neglected dimension of discourse but adding discourse that has been subjugated under black-male elitism. Womanist hermeneutics takes its defining materials from black women's literature and slave narratives to disclose ancestral wisdom. For womanist theologians, these sources function as black women's wisdom literature.

Like the hermeneutical return of classical black theology and its recent Afrocentric variety, womanist narrativism inevitably ends up reassuring its project in terms of ontological blackness. The ironic consequence is that a discourse predicated on self-definition and black women's difference remains bound by the specter of black masculinity and its cult of black heroic genius. Their stress lies on the unprecedented evidence of black women's capacities for survival under unprecedented suffering. Black women's sources tend to be used toward disclosing the heroic, survivalist genius of black women.

The turn to black women's literature tends to serve the apologetic intentions of buttressing the exceptionalist claims made for womanist theology. A few representational passages must suffice here rather than close readings. "Black women have created and cultivated a set of ethical values that allow them to prevail against the odds, with moral integrity, in their ongoing participation in the white-male-capitalist value system," says Katie Cannon (1988, 75 ff.). She continues: "The best available literary repository for this underground treasury of values is the Black women's literary tradition" (75). This literary treasure ought not to be identified strictly with black women's novels or poetry. But the womanist narrative return includes writings drawn from autobiographers, ex-slave interviewers, journalists, and black women essayists. Although there are many available sources from which womanist theologians draw for their project, their historical retrievals are governed by survivalist intentions.

From these various sources, womanist theologians engage in a selective retrieval of materials which in turn reinforce a constellation of values that identify them with the womanist project. The following represents a typical constellation of figures: Maria Stewart, Harriet Tubman, Sojourner Truth, Harriet Jacobs, Mary Prince, Louisa Picuet, Mattie Jackson, Zora Hurston, Alice Walker, and Toni Morrison. They form a constellation of *sassy* witnesses whose stories of suffering and whose accounts of survival and resistance are representational of womanist consciousness.

Clarice Martin sees in the strategy of reiterative hermeneutics a theological methodology that is intricately expressive of black women's spiritual autobiography. Reiterative hermeneutics is a strategy that involves "a declarative rehearsal, a reiteration of the ways in which God has delivered, rescued, transformed, and re-empowered the self or the community in the face of suffering and calamity," says Martin (1993, 28):

> African-American autobiographies typically include expressed desires for full and uninhibited self-actualization, a critique of external national conditions, and an interweaving of individual and communal consciousness. It is the African American "spiritual" autobiography that contains some of the most poignantly stirring recitations and reiterations of the conviction that God sustains life as it exists in a whirlwind of chaos. God rescues, delivers, and succors the sufferer and besieged sojourner on the road to life. (28)

Black women's autobiographies are representational of "radical uses of traditional forms of spirituality," says Martin. Such a radicalism led black women "to question fearlessly what they perceived to be illegitimate authority to wage war against an intemperate, sexist, and slave holding society" (29).

Womanist hermeneutics aims at reassuring the humanity of black women by disclosing forms of false and illusionary consciousness among black women and in the black community. "Only by attending to Black women's feelings and experiences, understanding and reflection, judgement and evaluation about their situation," M. Shawn Copeland argues, "can we adequately challenge the stereotypes about Black women—especially stereotypes that coalesce around that most popular social convention of female sexuality, the 'cult of true womanhood'" (1993, 111). Positively stated, the existential import of womanist hermeneutics is to disclose an authentic consciousness of black womanhood that speaks to "black women's accounts of pain and anguish, of their individual and collective struggle to grasp and manage, rather than be managed by their suffering" (111, 118).

There is much that is commendable about womanist theology. It reminds us that black women's experience is complex and often neglected in the interest of racial criticism. It is useful for disclosing forms of consciousness that subjugate black women's subjectivity and personality under the totality of race and black masculinity. Yet in its hermeneutics, womanist theology suffers the contradictions of ontological blackness. It proposes the privilege of self-definition. Yet ontological blackness binds the discourse almost exclusively and exceptionally to suffering and resistance.

If suffering and resistance continue to have a totalizing function in womanist theological discourse as they do in classical black theology and

Afrocentric theologies, on what does transcendence depend? At what point do thriving and flourishing enter the equation of suffering and resistance? An existence that is bound existentially only by the dimensions of struggle and resistance or survival, it seems to me, constitutes a less than fulfilling human existence. We all want more than to survive: that is a minimal requirement of a fulfilled life. We also want to thrive and flourish.

Womanist theology understands itself to be a liberation theology. However, liberation appears to be existential more than political. It appears related to the construction of a positive self-consciousness that is fundamentally defined by the heroic qualities of black women's genius (strength and creative resistance against racism, sexism, and classism). Still, the womanist consciousness, proposed in this theology, tends to mirror those qualities of authentic black consciousness that were defined in the revolutionary discourse of the black theology project—a male-dominated discourse that is indebted to European nationalistic impulses and philosophical existentialism for its legitimacy.

The womanist theologian has become, it seems, the mirror of black masculinity: strong and rebellious, surviving and resisting, heroic and epochal. As the mirror of black heroic genius, womanist theology remains devoted to ontological blackness. However, the promise of cultural transcendence proffered by the womanist theologian's self-defining nomenclature, *womanist*, appears subjugated under ontological blackness.

Cheryl J. Sanders (1989), an African American Christian ethicist at Howard University, makes problematic the womanist theologian's ability to transcend the aporias of ontological blackness. In order to suggest how it is an improper basis for constructive womanist theology, Sanders highlights the ways that Alice Walker's construal of a *womanist* transcends ontological blackness by affirming black lesbian love and relativizing race or color. Sanders worries that if Walker's womanist connotations are made regulative in black women's consciousness, the womanist theologian renders herself an alienated theologian, cut off from the *real interests* that structure black life. Therefore, it is possible that the real interests of black life and those of black women's subjectivity can be at odds. Sanders wonders in what sense womanist theology can be womanist, if not all of the connotative marks Walker commends are retrieved by the theologian.

Sanders charges her womanist theological colleagues as having bought into a highly loaded definition of *womanism*. It is a definition that is at its core anti-Christian and anti-black. Womanism is anti-Christian insofar as it is categorically secular. That is, as Sanders see it, womanism is the extension of the modernist moral impulses that are driven by individualism and moral autonomy, and are religiously antinomian. Womanism is anti-black insofar as its openness to homosexual love devalues the real interests of black life, which are the sustaining of black families and the wholeness of the black community.

If I read Sanders's essay correctly, she charges her womanist colleagues with making a categorical error. The error is their identifying the freedoms and transcendence Walker anticipates in her womanist connotations with ontological blackness. "I suspect that it is Christianity and not womanism," Sanders says, "that forms the primary ground of theological and ethical identity with our audacious, serious foremothers" (91).

Sanders understands *womanism* as a secular category that black women theologians have good warrants for rejecting:

> Walker's definition comprises an implicit ethics of moral autonomy, liberation, sexuality and love that is not contingent upon the idea of God or revelation. In any case, to be authentically "womanist" a theological or ethical statement should embrace the full complement of womanist criteria without omissions or additions intended to sanctify, defeminize or otherwise alter the perspective Walker intended the word womanist to convey. (87)

According to Sanders, the inclusion of womanism into the construction of black women's theology is defective because black women's experience is categorically based on theistic principles, biblical faith, and a moral tradition that eschews the radical claims to sexual autonomy that Walker commends.

Sanders casts the womanist theological debate in terms of an ontological dilemma. If womanist theologians affirm the privilege of self-definition and the racial and cultural transcendence promised by Walker's womanist connotations, then they risk alienating themselves from the real interests of black life. On the other hand, if they mitigate their claims for womanism, then they risk self-referential inconsistency as womanists. She writes:

> In my view there is a fundamental discrepancy between the womanist criteria that would affirm and/or advocate homosexual practice, and the ethical norms the black church might employ to promote the survival and wholeness of black families. It is problematic for those of us who claim connectedness to and concern for the black family and church to engage these criteria authoritatively and/or uncritically in the formulation of theological-ethical discourse for the two institutions. If black

women's ethics is to be pertinent to the needs of our community, then at least some of us must be in a position to offer intellectual guidance to the church as the principal (and perhaps only remaining) advocate for marriage and family in the black community. There is a need for the black churches to promote a positive sexual ethics within the black community as one means of responding to the growing normalization of the single-parent family, and the attendant increases in poverty, welfare dependency, and a host of other problems. (90)

Sanders's internal critique of womanist theology is provocative but flawed on several points. First, Sanders's insistence that in order to qualify as an authentic or *real* womanist, one must buy all of Walker's connotations, begs the question as to whether one might legitimately be resigned to a mitigated version of Walker's womanism. Jacquelyn Grant may well be an instance of a mitigated womanist. Grant's categorical rejection of whiteness does not require that she reject all other connotations of womanism, neither does it prevent her from adding a few other connotations of her own among the existing ones Walker proposes. A mitigated womanism is possible because the various connotations signified by *womanism* are not themselves logically dependent. Therefore, by insisting that womanist consciousness be ultimately bound by Walker's connotations, Sanders mistakes connotative utterances (the meanings of which are extrinsic and conventional) for denotative ones (the meanings of which are intrinsic and essential). In Grant's case, her racial conclusions only make her a mitigated womanist, they do not make her an inconsistent one. Sanders's proposed womanist theological dilemma is unsuccessful.

Second, Sanders would have done better to avoid the argument from secularism in her internal critique of womanist theology. The argument leads her to an untenable disjunction (either/or) between womanism and Christianity. It is clear that for Sanders the word *secular,* in her critique of womanist ethics, is pejorative. *Secular* is used by Sanders to connote a modernist orientation in morals that privileges radical autonomy expressed as the power of self-definition and that ethically affirms monistic forms of spirituality as Walker does. If these characteristics are expressive of womanism's moral and spiritual dispositions, then womanists stand in good company among Christian humanists for whom autonomous moral action is constitutive of the moral life and for whom the unity of all beings coheres in radical monotheistic faith. Such a religious humanism makes possible a *secular* theology. This is a possibility that Sanders's disjunctive opposition between secularism and Christianity does not admit.

Sanders misconstrues the womanist theological debate when she casts it in terms of secularism versus Christianity. Rather, the conflicts are more accurately internal ones among black women who hold incommensurable Christian sensibilities and theologies. That is, the conflict may be between women whose moral and religious sensibilities are commensurable with a secular theology if not a biblical or evangelical one. This point is emphasized in the roundtable responses to Sanders by her womanist colleagues, Cannon, Townes, Copeland, hooks, and Gilkes.

Kelly Brown Douglas casts the debate in its sharpest terms when she suggests that what was missed in the roundtable debate was an opportunity for womanist theologians to make clear their unambiguous no to heterosexism and homophobia in womanist theology (1994, 100–101).

For Sanders, the criteria of legitimacy in African American religion and theology is ontological blackness. And black women theologians' legitimacy is determined by their identifications with black crises. This places black women theologians in a dilemma, according to Sanders. They may choose either the power of self-definition and the actualization of interests that support the celebration of personality and risk alienation from the real interests of black life. Or they may choose to act on the real interests of black life and sacrifice their claims to self-defining personality. In either case, ontological blackness renders black women's consciousness an alienated consciousness. And that is a tragic choice predicated on a false dichotomy between personality and community.

Sanders's disjunctive reasoning renders her critique of womanist theology unpersuasive. Nevertheless, her argument crystalizes the problem facing the womanist theological project. Can womanist theology transcend the aporias of ontological blackness and, at the same time, hold to the transcending openings that Walker's womanist connotations commend?

This is not a question peculiar to womanist theology. It is a question posed to other African American theologies where ontological blackness determines the exceptional and existential meanings connected with black life and experience. When black life is fundamentally determined by the totality of a binary racial dialectic that admits no possibility of cultural transcendence, then African American theologians hold few prospects for effectively ameliorating the social and existential crises that bind black life. Talk about liberation becomes hard to justify where freedom appears as nothing more than defiant self-assertion of a revolutionary racial consciousness that requires for its legitimacy the opposition of white racism. Where there exists no possibility of transcending the blackness that whiteness created, African American theologies of liberation must be seen not only as crisis theologies; they remain theologies in a crisis of legitimation.

To press beyond ontological blackness, African American theology needs a public theology that is informed by the enlightening and emancipatory aspects of postmodern African American cultural criticism. It also needs the iconoclastic rigor and utopian dimensions of postmodern African American religious criticism.

Works Cited

Cannon, Katie.
  1988. *Black Womanist Ethics*. Atlanta: Scholars Press.
Cone, James H.
  1986. *Speaking the Truth*. Grand Rapids: Eerdmans.
  1989. *Black Theology and Black Power*. New York: Harper/Collins.
  1991. *A Black Theology of Liberation*. Maryknoll: Orbis.
Copeland, M. Shawn.
  1993. "Wading Through Many Sorrows." Emilie Townes, ed. *A Troubling in My Soul: Womanist Perspectives on Evil and Suffering*. Maryknoll: Orbis, 109–29.
Douglas, Kelly Brown.
  1994. *The Black Christ*. Maryknoll: Orbis.
Evans, James H.
  1992. *We Have Been Believers: An African American Systematic Theology*. Minneapolis: Fortress.
Grant, Jacquelyn.
  1989. *White Women's Christ and Black Women's Jesus*. Atlanta: Scholars Press.
Hopkins, Dwight.
  1993. *Shoes that Fit Our Feet: Sources for a Constructive Black Theology*. Maryknoll: Orbis.
Lincoln, C. Eric, and Mamiya, Lawrence.
  1990. *The Black Church in the African American Experience*. Durham: Duke University Press.
Martin, Clarice.
  1993. "Black Women's Spiritual Autobiography." *A Troubling in My Soul: Womanist Perspectives on Evil and Suffering*. Maryknoll: Orbis, 13–36.
Said, Edward.
  1993. *Culture and Imperialism*. New York: Knopf.
Sanders, Cheryl J.
  1989. "Roundtable Discussion: Christian Ethics and Theology in Womanist Perspective." *Journal of Feminist Studies in Religion*, 5:83–91.
Tillich, Paul.
  1967. *Systematic Theology*. Chicago: University of Chicago Press.
Williams, Delores.
  1993. "A Womanist Perspective on Sin." *A Troubling in My Soul: Womanist Perspectives on Evil and Suffering*. Maryknoll: Orbis, 130–50.
Wilmore, Gayraud.
  1983. *Black Religion and Black Radicalism*. Maryknoll: Orbis.

Part 8

African American Religion and Cultural Criticism

Chapter 39

Jesse Jackson and the Symbolic Politics of Black Christendom

James Melvin Washington

The 1984 campaign of the Reverend Jesse Louis Jackson for the Democratic party's presidential nomination was perhaps the most historic development in an otherwise uneventful public ritual. If politics involves, at its most primal level, the rhetorical manipulation of basic public symbols and beliefs to legitimate maintenance or change in the social order, surely, Jackson's extraordinary communication skills proved more than equal to the task. But Jackson lacked a genuine feel for the tribal signals of white America. Furthermore, his own commitment to the folk style of black Christianity exacerbated the cultural cleavage between black and white America.

This article seeks to explain why Jackson's rainbow coalition did not win the support of the white majority, and why even some black leaders eschewed Jackson's intriguing attempt to renovate some semblance of a pluralistic vision of American politics. First, I contend that Jesse Jackson is the leader of the black church movement's latest and most effective response to the unjust politics of white supremacists. It is a serious misreading to see Jesse Jackson as a lone, charismatic politico. On the contrary, his primary constituency is the black church movement. In order to ascertain why Jesse Jackson's rainbow coalition was unsuccessful, I shall offer a historical profile of a religious black political ethos. Second, I disagree with the claim that the black church is apolitical and I describe its political styles. Third, I shall examine the relation between the rise of a culture of consumption in American society and the ineffectiveness of moral suasion in black politics. Then I shall examine the role of political revivalism in what I call the symbolic poetics of black Christendom.

What is Black Christendom?

I consider all of the predominantly black religious bodies in the United States to be part of the black church movement. I use the word "church" here to mean essentially local groups or congregations organized around various Islamic, Protestant, Catholic, and Jewish beliefs. Black Protestants are by far the largest of black religious groups in the United States. But if one considers the entire Western Hemisphere, black Catholics certainly are the dominant group.

The focus here, however, is upon black Protestants in the United States. They are so diffuse and varied in their theologies that it would be futile to define them according to doctrine. But there are amazing similarities in their worship styles, which differ more according to class differentiation than according to denominational affiliation. At any rate, I use Paul Tillich's accent on the prophetic political significance of Protestantism in general as the major distinction of black Protestantism. According to Tillich, "the most important contribution of Protestantism to the world in the past, present, and future is the principle of prophetic protest against every power which claims divine character for itself—whether it be the church or state, party or leader."[1] The powerful presence of this prophetic criticism is the central theme in the formation of practically every black religious movement. Indeed, this political praxis, be it symbolic or emphatic, joins forces with different liturgical nuances to form a holistic coterie of beliefs and rituals that constitute the black church movement.[2]

The ideology and political praxis of this distinctive religious culture championed the progressive liberal tradition in American history as the moral expression most favorable to black aspirations. Identification with this tradition does not, however, exhaust the possibilities available to the black community.

Indeed, there have been three cultural strands and one highly diverse prophetic political response constituting the symbolic capital of the largely unexamined political ethos that is black Christendom. The three cultural strands are folk, bourgeois, and urban. And borrowing Cornel West's designation, I refer to the major counter-hegemonic black political tradition as prophetic African American Christianity.[3] These cultural strata have three historical counterpoints in the form of revivalistic, pastoral, and prophetic political praxes, which function as different strategies for resisting white supremacy. A brief historical review of these political praxes in relation to the three cultural strata will show how they have interacted.

The major historical black denominations include the African Methodist Episcopal church, incorporated in 1816; the African Methodist Episcopal Zion church, in 1821; the National Baptist Convention, U.S.A., Inc., in 1840;[4] and the Christian Methodist Episcopal church, in 1870. Practically all other black religious movements originated in congregations once affiliated with these denominations. In fact the black church movement itself began among black urban dwellers in the late eighteenth century who belonged to congregations within these denominations. Out of what began as ecclesiastical injustice among the Methodists and indifference among the Baptists, the black church movement immediately thrived wherever possible. Moreover, it became the chief engine that pulled and supported many black social reform movements such as the abolitionist movement before the Civil War and the civil rights movement of the 1960s. The black church movement accumulated what Pierre Bourdieu calls "cultural capital" sufficient to nurture its own political ethic and ethos to resist the hegemony of white supremacists.

The ideology of white supremacy is the stepchild of modern Western Christianity. A white tribal aesthetic began to erode the Christian doctrine of the universal Christ in the High Middle Ages by employing what Roger Bastide calls the progressive Aryanization of Christ, which, he believes, "is in strict accordance with the logic of the color symbolism" of the Western world. Indeed, "it did not start, however, until Christianity came into close contact with the other races—with the African race, in particular. Christian artists began to avoid the darker tints in depicting Christ its order to remove as much as possible of their evil suggestion."[5] It would be quite easy and woefully redundant to recast the findings of recent genealogists of modern racism such as David Brion Davis, Winthrop Jordan, and Cornel West. In short, the darker the hue, the more akin to evil the thing or person came to be conceived.

Besides resistance to all forms of thingification, the black church movement fought against moral and political cynicism within black America. The movement's attachment to the rather shortsighted moralisms of eighteenth- and nineteenth-century Evangelicalism, its parent religious impulse, often eclipsed the different cultural and psychological application of its innovative form of Christian spirituality. The progressive leaders of black Christianity continuously warned against the boomerang effect of moral laxity, political apathy, and racial divisiveness. They argued that blacks must develop psychic and spiritual callosity against white racism, yet simultaneously seek to influence public opinion. Despite this counsel, however, black political sarcasm continued to grow without much abatement until the huge turnout for Jesse Jackson in the 1984 Democratic primaries. Jackson's use of the techniques of political revivalism proved to be historic.

The Political Strategies of Black Christendom

Black political revivalism includes the use of sermonic folk discourse and a complex of cultural praxes that are all rooted in the distinctive spirituality of black Christianity. It is comparable to what Anthony F. C. Wallace calls revitalization movements.[6] The ancient processes of spiritual renewal involve the psychic fortification of an entire social grouping. When an essentially religious group consists of persons in an inherently politically oppressive situation—for example, slavery, being colonized, or perverse racist practices such as Jim Crowism, tragic political inequalities, lynchings, burnings, and bombings—it must find ways of maintaining its sense of community.

Revivals function as planned events that intentionally try to reclaim some idyllic moment of group cohesion for communities whose identities are under seige. The black church has been the major practitioner and proponent of revivalism as a means of rejuvenating a community gripped by psychic and economic depression. It uses liturgies forged in the crucible of the slave regime, segregation, depressed urban ghettos, and rural shanties to fight assaults upon the psychic well-being of black people.[7] Despite continuous and powerful white attempts to control the black church movement, much internal struggle, and, most certainly, much struggle with secular black competitors, the black church has maintained political and spiritual brokerage.

From its inception in the late eighteenth century, the black church movement took advantage of the historic liberty that the Bill of Rights granted religious bodies. Although white church leaders expressed cultural disdain for black spirituality, they sometimes offered support and protection. Some of them would even express admiration for the spiritual integrity of black people. But they were also protecting their own investments in religious liberty by taking this benevolent approach despite their suspicion that something profoundly revolutionary was occurring among these enslaved Christians. They did not know what to do about this revolutionary activity, however, without running the risk of losing their own religious liberty.

A New Prophetic Form of Christianity

The slave revolts of Gabriel Prosser, Denmark Vesey, and Nat Turner, all fomented in the clandestine wombs of religious fellowship among the slaves, forced the various states to pass strict laws for the regulation of the religious life of the slaves. This was especially true after Nat Turner's Revolt in 1831.

Meanwhile, between 1829 and 1843, northern blacks and their liberal white compatriots began to raise a mighty prophetic outcry against the American Colonization Society's racist project of returning blacks to Africa. There was certainly a latent bourgeois cultural chauvinism toward Africa in the resistance to the return, but the historical significance of this development was that it became the first united political stance of African Americans. They reached the conclusion that racism was a national, not a southern, problem, and that it would not be eradicated by escaping to the North. Many of them, such as David Walker, Frederick Douglass, Sojourner Truth, and the Reverends Henry Highland Garnet, Samuel H. Davis, Jermain Wesley Loguen, and James William Charles Pennington, helped to form the tradition of prophetic black politics by their fiery denunciations of slavery. Like their white comrades, such as Sarah and Angelina Grimké, Theodore Weld, William Lloyd Garrison, Beriah Green, and Gerrit Smith, they came to the conclusion that slavery was part of a systematic social and economic cancer that left no part of American culture unscathed.

These allies for freedom forged a progressive political alliance, which has had its ups and downs.[8] Although strained, the alliance remains intact today despite the constant defections of some white progressives from the cause of racial and economic justice and despite Jesse Jackson's embarrassing "hymie" *faux pas* and Louis Farrakhan's unfortunate anti-Jewish rhetoric.

Progressive Pastoral Resistance

Blacks did not form organizations exclusively for protest until the twentieth century, however. The first one was, of course, the National Association for the Advancement of Colored People (NAACP), established in 1909. The other important ones were the National Urban League, founded in 1910; the Congress of Racial Equality, founded in 1942; the Southern Christian Leadership Conference (SCLC), founded its 1957; and People United to Save Humanity (PUSH), founded in 1971. Of these major protest organizations, the NAACP, SCLC, and PUSH have always had significant religious bases and often equally powerful religious leadership. Black religious leaders have had far more power in the NAACP than was recognized before the Reverend Benjamin E. Hooks became its executive director. For example, the Reverend Dr. Channing Tobias, the powerful national executive director of the Colored Young Men's Christian Association and a member of Roosevelt's Black Cabinet, served for years as the chairman of the NAACP's board of directors.

Although we cannot review the full history of the leadership struggle here, it must be noted that we are currently in the midst of a major leadership power struggle that began immediately after the deaths of Malcolm X in 1965 and the Reverend Dr. Martin Luther King, Jr., in 1968.

After King's assassination on 4 April 1968, black leaders reverted to the more traditional procedure of dividing leadership responsibilities. The tough persistence of this leadership style had even challenged King's unquestionable reign between 1963 and 1968. The division of labor went along the lines of religious, social, political, and economic leadership. Only the ministers were able to prevail, from time to time, in all of these areas. In fact it might be helpful to see the 1960s as an attempt on the part of lesser-known black leaders such as Whitney Young, Roy Wilkins, James Farmer, and Malcolm X to usurp, if not secularize, the rhetoric of black leaders.

But this disorganized strategy did not work. The ministers simply reverted to their traditional division of labor. Some went into politics. Andrew Young, a minister in the United Church of Christ, became a congressman representing the state of Georgia. Walter Fauntroy, a Baptist pastor and former head of SCLC's office in the District of Columbia, became an at-large U.S. congressional representative for the District. Others, including the Reverend Wyatt Tee Walker, returned to the pastorates of local congregations, where they engaged in major social uplift endeavors such as the reform of public education and the construction of publicly financed housing.

The ministers' social reform projects would have been untenable without Lyndon Baines Johnson's Great Society programs, which Richard Nixon began to eliminate. Nixon urged the creation of programs to stimulate black capitalism. A number of Martin Luther King, Jr.'s disciples denounced Nixon's renunciation of the welfare state. They sensed that a more enduring national move toward conservatism was inevitable.

Nixon's black capitalism became the conservative economic philosophy of quasi-revolutionary black nationalism. Jesse Jackson was the most prominent King disciple to embrace this ironic philosophical partnership between a neoclassical economic philosophy and a liberal social philosophy. The national government failed, however, to stimulate black capitalism, and Jackson therefore returned to the progressive fold and then even moved to the left of it.

By the 1976 presidential campaign Jackson had succeeded in broadening his programmatic base. He embraced the consumers' rights tactics of Ralph Nader, and he aided several black business executives in becoming millionaires. But this tangential support for black capitalism did little to help the deprived.

The Culture of Consumption and Political Cynicism

As a result of the depression that stubbornly gripped the black community, Jackson, like other notable leaders of black America, had to ask some fundamental questions. For example, What recourse should the victims of injustice in America take? Better yet, What strategies have they employed to resist systemic unfairness? Since it is obvious from even a superficial knowledge of American history that violent revolution has not been a common strategy, we must look elsewhere. The answer is simple and yet complex: they resorted to individual and group protests against and criticisms of the status quo. But this response proved to be ineffectual in the 1970s and 1980s. America itself had undergone in the 1960s and 1970s what Sydney E. Ahlstrom called a moral and cultural revolution. As we view it now, however, the resistance to an economic restructuring that would be more reflective of a just society proved to be the broken cog in the wheel of this glorious revolution.

Amazing technological advancements certainly pushed America, which still clung stubbornly to its Victorian values, into this tremendous watershed period. Richard Nixon's silent majority was gladly seduced, however, by the simplisms of Jerry Falwell's Moral Majority, and by Falwell's fellow television evangelists who sent daily pleas across the airwaves for America to turn back the clock. This powerful conservative reaction retreated into the arms of the lapsed moralism of the profit motive. Many—even erstwhile liberals—felt that the American myth of the right to practice what Thorstein Veblen called conspicuous consumption was unfairly under assault.

America had embraced a new order,[9] according to Rifkin and Howard, that was characterized by the demise of liberalism and the rise of a more disciplined entrepreneurial spirit. They believed American religious conservatives would be in the forefront of this new capitalist phalanx. Progressive black Christian leaders have been slow to decipher the meaning and consequences of the rise of this new righteous culture of consumption. But perhaps the presidential campaign experience of Jesse Jackson and the reelection of Ronald Reagan might awaken all progressive religious leaders to the shortcomings of the politics of moral suasion, political revivalism, and prophetic pronouncement without a tough-minded, yet compassionate, political praxis determined to reorient an often unjust American political economy.

Another important issue is at stake here also. That is, blacks who identified with liberalism in both its political and moral expressions overlooked the nihilistic potential of public opinion. The *modus operandi* of classical liberalism's moral adjudications is based on utilitarianism. Alexis de Tocqueville warned about this danger in the 1840s:

> Not only is common opinion the only guide which private judgement retains among a democratic people, but among such a people it possesses a power infinitely beyond what it has elsewhere. At periods of equality men have no faith in one another, by reason of their common resemblance; but this very resemblance gives them almost unbounded confidence in the judgement of the public; for it would seem probable that, as they are all endowed with equal means of judging, the greater truth should go with the greater number.[10]

The founders of the United States believed the Bill of Rights would protect Americans from the nihilistic pragmatism of utilitarianism. They suspected that the success of this form of reaching political compromise depended heavily upon as much social and cultural homogeneity as possible. That is why several of them feared the black presence. And they were correct. James Rawley summarized the challenge presented by the racial factor in American political life and discourse:

> Race relations have rarely been treated rationally by Americans. Discussions of them usually turn to inanities, culminating in the question "Do you want your daughter to marry a Negro?" Race is the one thing in our history that has defied the political genius of the American people.[11]

American political ingenuity has also failed to meet the negative challenge that white supremacy poses to its democratic political idealism. Amidst the perennial social amnesia of many white Americans, especially as it regards racial justice, the politics of black Christendom offers a restorationist ideology and political praxis. It levels stinging moral judgments that expose the gilded cage of white suburbia and the fortified townhouses of affluent urban neighborhoods that seemingly remain oblivious to the moral outrage of their impoverished neighbors at home and abroad.

The Pastoral Power of the Jackson Campaign

Although the tradition of black ministers as community activists is an old tradition, it has undergone important changes since the death of Martin Luther King, Jr. *Time* magazine referred to the dispersion of King's phase of the civil rights movement as the creation of leadership in the form of localism.[12] But in truth the strong secondary local leadership had been there all the time. After 1968 it received a new impetus with the return and infusion of talented black clerical leadership.

Clearly, Jesse Jackson rose to the top of this list of leaders. Blessed with photogenic pizzazz, a rich—although often grating—poetic jingoism, adroit political savvy, and the prophetic, pastoral, and priestly responsibility—customary of black ministers, especially after Dr. King's death—to be a community leader, Jackson became one of the prime foci of the hungry cameras of the news media age. But it would be a mistake to conclude that Jesse Jackson is a creation of the news media. His roots are planted deeply within the black church's rich tradition of social, political, and economic activism. He builds upon the tradition of prophetic politics that I outlined previously. Jackson's political ingenuity, however, lies in his ability to reform the techniques of black political revivalism. Jackson, unlike Martin Luther King, Jr., has been able to translate the southern agrarian ethos of the civil rights movements into the language and ethos of urban black America without losing the southern tenor of the movement.

Jackson achieved this transformation by using his gifts as a publicist, prophetic politico, and political revivalist. Moreover, the presidential campaign in effect bestowed upon Jackson the presidency of black America, a de facto office held by such notables as Frederick Douglass, Booker T. Washington, Adam Clayton Powell, Jr., and Martin Luther King, Jr. Undoubtedly, Jackson has become a national and international spokesperson for the downtrodden. In fact, Jackson is the most influential black man in America since Booker T. Washington. The key for understanding both how he rose to power and how he continues to acquire it at such an amazing rate lies not with his ability but with his willingness to take advantage of his religious roots.

The PUSH Revival

The power of political revivalism rallied black Americans during their three major historic campaigns for civil and human rights in the abolitionist movement, and in the civil rights movements between 1865 and 1914 and those between 1953 and 1965. The use of black religious rituals in social movements came under intense criticism, however, from the black power movement, a secularist impulse, after the rise of this movement in 1965. Actually, those who were embarrassed by the use of black hymns, spirituals, prayers, and preaching in the civil rights movements were oftentimes secular-minded black college students who crassly, often with shadowy verve, appropriated Karl Marx's dictum that "religion is the opium of the people." They were willing to romanticize practically every aspect of black culture except its distinguished great-grandparent, the black church movement.

The abandonment of the black church movement was not universal, however. In fact, a cadre of bright, courageous black college students and seminarians, such as Robert Moses, James Lawson, C. T. Vivian, Diane Nash, Marion Barry—who is now mayor of Washington, D.C.—John Lewis, Julian Bond, Courtland Cox, and the untempered—although exceptionally bright—Stokely Carmichael, actually radicalized King's movement. This was especially true of the Student Nonviolent Coordinating Committee (SNCC), which was formed under the leadership of the ubiquitous Ella Baker after the Greensboro, North Carolina, sit-ins started by four local black students from the Agricultural and Technical College of North Carolina. Even though some of the major leaders of SNCC, such as Stokely Carmichael, later refused to use the exorcisms of black religiosity, many of them were primarily attracted to the movement partly because of its religious fervor for justice. Indeed, as one Protestant minister reported in the *San Francisco Sunday Chronicle* as late as 21 March 1965, the religiosity of the civil rights movement had not waned. It was a sterling, and probably consummate, illustration of black political revivalism: "this movement to procure civil rights is distinctly a religious movement," said the Reverend Andrew Juvinall,

> rooted in the conviction that God has "made of one blood all the nations of mankind" and it is His will that all should stand erect in their full manhood. The movement of the Southern Christian Leadership Conference has political and economic aspects but it is most of all a profound spiritual movement.[13]

One of the bright college students who understood this historic alliance between religion and social change was Jesse Jackson. Jackson was the president of the student body at the Agricultural and Technical College of North Carolina when four of his classmates started the sit-in movement. Jackson graduated from the college in 1963 after successfully assuming leadership of the sit-in demonstrations. In the fall of 1963 he enrolled at Chicago Theological Seminary.

Even as a young seminarian, Jackson was able to organize and mobilize the black community in preparation for Martin Luther King's initial effort to move the civil rights movement to the stubborn Northern urban frontier. Jackson's charisma won the confidence of many of the local black ministers of Chicago. Even then he fervently stressed the need to relate ministry to social and political change.

Of course one could argue that Jackson received his greatest inspiration from Martin Luther King, Jr. That is true. But without his own charismatic gifts, he could have never won the support of stalwart and able colleagues such as the Reverends David Wallace, George Riddick, Willie Barrows, Wilbur Reid, and Calvin Morris. They were all very charismatic figures in their own right. But there was an energy and contagion about Jackson and certainly about the movement itself that elicited their best efforts.

Jesse Jackson's charisma attracted and held the allegiance of several of his early Operation Breadbasket colleagues long enough to make it a forceful movement of national and international stature.[14] But not even his great charismatic powers could retain them past 1971, when Operation Breadbasket became Operation PUSH. PUSH both revived and expanded the Breadbasket program. As such PUSH became a national urban religious movement for social, economic, and political change. It sought to revitalize the moral, psychic, economic, and political health of depressed urban black communities across the United States.

Although Jackson now has formed and heads an openly political alliance called the rainbow coalition, this organization, as well as the earlier ones he has headed, should be seen as part of his deep commitment to an activist understanding of Christian ministry. His primary base, however, is still his Chicago-based Operation PUSH. PUSH gained a major portion of its fervor and its resources as a result of the tough, yet eloquent, prophetic pastoral style of Jackson's leadership of the PUSH congregation, which meets every Saturday for at least two or three hours. This activistic religious assembly numbers well over 5000. With the help of several other ministers, especially the Reverend Mrs. Willie Barrows, Jackson formed a prophetic local bridgehead in black Chicago and was instrumental in the election of Harold Washington as the city's first black mayor. Indeed, between 1968 and 1983, Jackson solidified his contacts with the wider black church movement through his own hectic speaking tours and through close associates in different denominations, such as Bishop H. H. Brookins of the African Methodist Episcopal church. Within the National Baptist Convention, U.S.A., Inc., Jackson drew the major portion of his national support from the ministerial network. In fact this collegium provided basic psychic and financial support for Jackson's rainbow coalition.

Black Baptist Roots

Although Jesse Jackson enjoys friendships that cross denominational lines, his primary religious constituency is the black National Baptist Convention, U.S.A., Inc. But maintaining his relationship with the usually conservative leadership of this denominational movement has not been easy for one so single-mindedly committed to social and political activism.

For 29 years, until 1982, the president of that convention was the conservative Reverend Dr. Joseph Harrison Jackson. He was also pastor of the powerful Olivet Baptist Church of Chicago and one of the late Mayor Richard Daley's faithful cronies. The causes Jesse Jackson favored J. H. Jackson did not: the latter attacked Dr. King's Operation Breadbasket, which the former headed for SCLC; J. H. Jackson opposed the protest strategies of the civil rights movement; and he was part of the Daley machine, which Jesse Jackson courageously opposed.

Despite Jesse's fierce ideological disagreements with Reverend Joseph Harrison Jackson, he never left the National Baptist Convention. One explanation for this is Jackson's basically conservative evangelical theology, which was evident, for example, in his initial opposition to abortion and homosexual rights. The convention's powerful black folk spirituality, its traditional evangelical theology, and, from a historical viewpoint, its atypical political conservatism—thanks to Joseph Jackson—vied successfully for Jesse Jackson's allegiance.

Jesse Jackson was not indifferent to the convention's tentative turn toward political conservatism. He correctly interpreted it more as a by-product of the convention's affection for the spiritual persona of Joseph Jackson than as a result of an inherent conservative bent.

Joseph Jackson is actually a rather consistent anti-communist who earnestly believes that the civil rights movement was a Communist front. With consistent political acumen, he learned how to manage the convention's black populist ethos in order to accommodate his own conservative beliefs. Although he is the pastor of a large urban congregation, he always ran on the platform that he was the defender of the little preachers and the small congregations that constitute the bulk of this denomination.

Jesse Jackson also understood and accepted the convention's powerful populist impulse. Thus his description of himself as a country preacher is both genuine and politically astute.

Because the convention has the capacity to change its political mood, as long as its populist and black cultural nationalist commitments are not violated, its various factions have a history of competing to control the leadership of the convention. The most significant recent melee occurred in 1961. As a consequence of this embarrassingly turbulent meeting, the convention sustained a significant split. The primary issue ostensibly was how long the president should hold office. But the most powerful undercurrent was the issue of whether or not the convention should officially support King's civil disobedience campaign. This issue infused the heated annual campaigns for the convention's presidency. After J. H. Jackson's defeat of Dr. Gardner C. Taylor, pastor of the 14,000 members of the Concord Baptist Church of Christ in Brooklyn, New York, for the presidency, many of the convention's prominent urban churches banded together to form the more activistic Progressive National Baptist Convention. It seems that Jesse Jackson could also have left for the new convention.

Jesse Jackson remained with the National Baptist Convention, U.S.A., not only because he is theologically conservative, but also because he has strong personal ties to key ministers belonging to that convention. For instance, when Jackson came to Chicago in 1963 as a student at the Chicago Theological Seminary, he was hired almost immediately as the assistant pastor of Fellowship Baptist Church. The Reverend Clay Evans, the pastor of Fellowship, became quite instrumental in establishing Jackson as a powerful presence in Chicago. In fact, Evans's church is one of the largest black churches in Chicago. He has significant local and national friends, such as the late Reverend C. L. Franklin of Detroit, the father of Aretha Franklin, the renowned black recording artist. Jackson's friendship with these powerful stalwarts of the National Baptist Convention is so close that Evans and Franklin both sponsored Jackson's ordination into the Baptist ministry in June 1968, nearly two months after the assassination of Dr. King. Despite a few political disagreements, Clay Evans still serves as the honorary chairman of PUSH's board of directors.

In September 1982, the Reverend Dr. Theodore J. Jemison ran for the presidency of the National Baptist Convention, U.S.A., against

J. H. Jackson and defeated him. One consequence of J. H. Jackson's defeat was that Jesse Jackson acquired the influential position of chairman of the convention's Civil Rights Commission. This was not only an important recognition of Jackson's influential assistance in helping Dr. Jemison acquire the presidency; it also gave tacit convention recognition to Jackson's status within the civil rights movement and eventually to his bid for the U.S. presidency.

The influential network of black Baptist ministers that Jackson knows both within the National Baptist Convention and in the other Baptist conventions provides powerful local roots and sustenance to Jackson's role as a minister in the forefront of the civil rights movement. But Jackson could not maintain these links on notoriety alone. He also projects the image of a conscientious pastor of a great movement. He is the confidant of black artists and professionals of national and international repute. This pastoral skill is nurtured by a charisma that is legendary among black Baptist preachers. One could also point to the Reverend Benjamin E. Hooks, executive director of the NAACP, as another example of this special type of black religious and social leader. Hooks also maintains his standing among black preachers because he continues to be the nominal and effective pastor of two independent black Baptist congregations in Detroit and Memphis.

Ministers and leaders such as Hooks and Jackson belong to a strong activist tradition within their own denominations and within the black church movement as a whole. They practice a domineering pastoral style that is in accordance with their religious tradition. Black pastors are independent, set their own agendas, and are deeply admired by their people. The people's admiration, if not love and respect, is based upon reverence for the pastoral office as the most sacrificial and generous vocation a black person can hold. Being on the margin of society, black people have not fully developed a trust and respect for the integrity of other professionals. In fact they have too often been victimized by incompetent professionals and entrepreneurs. It is their pastor who visits the sick, buries the dead, and does innumerable personal favors such as getting them jobs and getting them out of jail. Above all, the pastor defends the poor and attacks injustice. Black people trust their pastor, who is seen as a friend and a prophet.

They admire the Reverend Mr. Jackson because he stands tall in this proud tradition. But he is fast earning himself a distinctiveness comparable only to that of Booker T. Washington. He is amassing a huge black patronage system. Similar to King, but only from the materialistic vantage point, he is more like a cardinal who is a prime candidate for a new kind of black American papacy in which the world itself can become his parish.

Fusion Politics

Despite his strong religious base, in order to expand his influence Jackson must continue to use fusion politics to survive politically. Besides divisiveness within the black community, Jackson must lead black America in a movement against a new form of racism. As John Hope Franklin notes, "The chief barriers to racial justice today are subtle and much less conducive to media coverage."[15]

The general mode of domination in American society is, as it always has been, more a matter of cultural than of social relations. There has been a change in American cultural relations, however, that increases the subtlety of obstacles to racial justice. After a long, arduous struggle, America no longer needs to mimic European society. For better or worse, America is now the major standard-bearer of Western culture. However, the reality of an expanding black and Hispanic underclass accents the depth of the racist classism that beguiles a republic that has lost sight of its original moral social vision.

Jesse Jackson was the only candidate in the 1984 presidential campaign who pinpointed this critical relation between the breakdown of democratic values and the demise of a just political vision. He said repeatedly that "the rainbow coalition is, first, a moral cause, not just a political campaign" and that the nation's "genius must not be in how much we consume, but in how much we share." But in the minds of white America, he is a black man trying to demonstrate his worth. As they used to say on the streets of the black ghetto, "The Negro is an insanity which overtakes the white man." Martin Luther King, Jr., said the same thing in far more eloquent terms:

> Ever since the founding fathers of our nation dreamed this noble dream, America has been something of a schizophrenic personality, tragically divided against herself. On the one hand we have proudly professed the principles of democracy, and on the other hand we have sadly practiced the very antithesis of those principles. Indeed slavery and segregation have been strange paradoxes in a nation founded on the principle that all men are created equal.[16]

Jesse Jackson's very presence in the presidential campaign represented a new threat to white supremacy. He had the audacity to act as if his race did not disqualify him from becoming the president of the United States. Black Americans generally viewed Jackson's self-confident presence as a refreshing assertion of group pride. White Americans, on the other hand, read Jackson's political style as a brazenly cocky demeanor that threatened the political and psychic space that white male hegemony has traditionally claimed in American society. America's majority people viewed his participation as a symbolic attack against the racist cultural grid that constitutes the psychic infrastructure of the central public ritual of the United States.

Although he did not win the Democratic primary, the Jackson campaign demonstrated that the right black candidate can indeed muster significant support. Jackson won over 3.5 million popular votes; he won over 60 congressional districts, with half of them in the South. Jackson was victorious in most of the largest urban centers in the North as well as in the South. In fact, he captured the popular vote in Louisiana, South Carolina, Mississippi, Virginia, and the District of Columbia. But as Jackson says himself, "Most of all, we have gained a new confidence relative to our politics."[17]

Jackson's woefully misunderstood and maligned alliance with Louis Farrakhan was one large part of that new corporate political self-esteem. Lu Palmer, the leader of the important political action group called Chicago Black United Communities, has observed that "the joining of Jesse Jackson and Louis Farrakhan represents a new dimension of unity in the Black community. Those two symbolize the coming together of different thoughts, ideology and religions around one common cause: Black empowerment."[18] We forget how deep the public division was between Martin Luther King, Jr.'s southern crusade and Malcolm X's northern urban militancy. Jackson and Farrakhan were trying to heal this wound.

Maulana Karenga correctly pinpoints the nature and depth of the opposition to Jackson's campaign from the American Jewish community, Israel, the news media, the black political establishment, even from most of the white Left, and of course the old-line Democratic party stalwarts. Jackson's urban victories probably could not have been achieved without Farrakhan. While Farrakhan's untempered anti-Jewish rhetoric embarrassed Jackson and his black and white progressive cohorts, the alliance between the two men was more political than religious or philosophical. Jackson's enemies, with the assistance of the black *Washington Post* reporter Milton Coleman, unjustifiably maligned either Jackson's character or his political savvy. Jackson finally had to sever his ties with Farrakhan. He learned the hard way, as did Martin Luther King, Jr., that the news media, the eyes and ears of the great white American middle class, expect and demand moral perfection.

With the pressures inside and outside the black community, black leaders had to understand that great psychic and spiritual fortitude is part of their unwritten job description. Thus strong black religious leaders have usually been at the forefront of black protest because only the strong ones could deal with the pressure.

Nevertheless, Jackson, like most astute leaders of the black religious community, understood that successful politicians are priests who know how to manage the core narratives, symbols, and beliefs of a people. The more social trust exists, the more likely it is that these rituals can solidify public opinion. Yet every social network has a gnosis. Access to the collective memory, interaction rituals, and private interests of different social configurations, especially if they have political power, is difficult. In fact the ability to manipulate the collective gnosis of the powerful depends greatly upon how well those who seek it understand the nature of what Michel Foucault calls pastoral power: "This form of power cannot be exercised without knowing the inside of the people's minds, without exploring their souls, without making them reveal their innermost secrets. It implies a knowledge of the conscience and an ability to direct it."[19]

If this description is true, then Ronald Reagan is undoubtedly the most effective manager of pastoral power in America. He has demonstrated his ability both to acquire and to manage the symbols and the dynamics of power. But he also has that rare priestly gift of knowing the gnosis of his flock, available only from the oracle at Delphi.

Merely acquiring pastoral power is not enough. The major leaders of the black church movement have always understood how to acquire and administer pastoral power. But when they tried to translate that into a larger following beyond their own racial boundaries, they usually did not succeed. This is not their failure, however. It illustrates the sad failure of American pluralism.

The Political Future of Black Christendom

Progressive African American Christians, such as Jesse Jackson, have drawn on the spiritual and practical wisdom of the conventicles of a political culture that is older than the United States. In the crucible of slavery and free black denizenship, blacks sought to devise various means of resisting oppression.[20] Some of these forms of resistance have been far more subtle and effective than many observers and scholars realize. The task before progressive black religious scholars now is to describe and analyze this phenomenon so that we can learn from its successes and failures. We need to determine when each form coalesced to respond to major threats to the black body politic and what the representative views and advocates of each phase were. With this information in hand, we can be better prepared to address the pressing issues not just of the 1980s, but, more important, those of the twenty-first century.

A large part of this reorientation of the scholarly world and the black church itself has already been advocated by the leaders of the black theology movement that began in 1969 upon the publication of James Hal Cone's *Black Theology and Black Power*. Unlike an earlier generation of black religious scholars and church leaders, Cone argues for the cultural distinctiveness and political necessity of black Christianity. He disagrees with earlier black religious leaders who argued that black Christianity is a Jim Crow arrangement. Cone also believes that black Christianity has now, as in the past, a revolutionary as well as therapeutic role to play in the advancement of black America and oppressed peoples throughout the world. In other words, despite black Christianity's seemingly "ambiguous politics"[21] and apparently "deficient political wisdom,"[22] it moves with integrity toward where Paul Lehmann argues "the empirical church points." According to Lehmann, the church points, "despite its ambiguity, to the fact that there is in the world a *laboratory of the living word*, or, to change the metaphor, a *bridgehead of maturity*, namely, the Christian *koinonia*."[23]

It is true that Jesse Jackson's aspirations for political office were frustrated. But beyond simply indicating the blatant role of white tribalism, other factors need to be considered, such as the following: (1) distrust of Jackson's identification with the persona of a black Southern country preacher; (2) the demise of what John Diggins calls the lost soul of American politics and the concomitant, unquestionable dominance of a culture of consumption; and (3) bourgeois cultural disdain for the moralistic and agrarian political revivalism of black Southern culture, the primary *modus operandi* of the symbolic political aspirations of black Christendom.

Despite the unrelenting criticisms, whether constructive or destructive, of the symbolic struggle waged by the black church movement, Jesse has steered progressive black Christians into new, uncharted waters. He helped us to see that the politics of black Christendom are the ethical exorcisms that oppressed African American Christians can use to defend their collective egos against the callousness of white supremacy. The project of black Christendom is the maximum realization of human freedom. The pedagogy of black Christendom seeks to train black people to acquire symbolic capital in order to continue "the acquisition of a reputation for competence and an image of respectability and honourability that are easily converted into political positions as a local or national *notable*."[24]

Black Christians have always found it difficult to justify the direct accumulation of economic capital because of a prior commitment to a biblical eschatology that looks with suspicion upon all attempts to idolize material things. But perhaps the recent attempt of the historic black denominations to form a Congress on Black Churches augurs well for building solidarity across congregational, denominational, class, and even economic lines, a necessary development if these churches intend to have an impact on a highly organized society with a new, highly refined form of racism.

The most subtle and effective aspect of the politics of black Christendom, however, is the spiritual praxis that nurtures and supports the psychic infrastructure of black America. The positivistic obsession of the social sciences, however, has often ignored both the reality and the importance of what William Stringfellow rightly calls the politics of spirituality.[25] Indeed, I agree with Ida Rousseau Mukenge's salient assessment of the indispensability of this central praxis to the future direction of the black church movement:

> As we move through the last decades of the twentieth century, the special role of the church in maintaining mental health and psychological stability is pre-eminent. In fact, the present interpretation of the historical and contemporary church suggests that this is the role the black urban church *must* perform.[26]

While we need not embrace intellectual suicide, it is imperative that prophetic self-criticisms of the black church be heard.[27] The politics of black spirituality, which are inherently symbolic and psychological, must be embodied in church programs that recognize and resist the systemic nature of injustice lest they fall prey to the pitfalls of undisciplined subjectivism.

Certainly the symbolic politics of black Christendom are not vacuous. This set of political praxes consists of ideologies and strategies embraced by the oppressed to defend themselves against the crushing sincerity[28] of the powerful whose benevolence is a false love that represents the postponement of justice and that is an arduous attempt to soothe the conscience without making the sacrifices genuine penance demands. But as Jackson has shown, the black church movement itself can and must refine its politics to meet the new challenge. Indeed, it seems that a cadre of anointed martyrs will be needed before this powerful, yet infantile, culture of consumption sees the wisdom of the ancient need for reciprocity and responds institutionally to the religious call for justice, love, and mercy.

Notes

1. Paul Tillich, *The Protestant Era*, trans. James Luther Adams (Chicago: University of Chicago Press, 1948), p. 230.
2. I shall use interchangeably the terms "black church movement," "black Christianity," "black Christendom," and "black Protestantism." These terms all signify this general phenomenon that is simultaneously both religious and political. I believe it indeed constitutes a religious political culture in its own right.
3. Cornel West, *Prophesy Deliverance! An Afro-American Revolutionary Christianity* (Philadelphia: Westminster Press, 1982), esp. chap. 4. The best discussion of the idea and development of political revivalism is John L. Hammond, *The Politics of Benevolence: Revival Religion and American Voting Behavior* (Norwood, NJ: Ablex, 1979), esp. pp. 1–19.
4. The usual date given for the founding of this convention, 1880, is erroneous. The first incorporated black Baptist convention with a national constituency was the American Baptist Missionary Convention, which was incorporated in New York State in 1840. See James Melvin Washington, *The Origins and Emergence of Black Baptist Separatism, 1863–1897* (Ph.D. diss., Yale University, 1979), pp. 35–42.
5. Roger Bastide, "Color, Racism, and Christianity" in *Color and Race*, ed. John Hope Franklin (Boston: Beacon Press, 1969), pp. 37–38.
6. Anthony F. C. Wallace, *Religion: An Anthropological View* (New York: Random House, 1966), esp. pp. 30–39.
7. See an extensive discussion of the meaning and goals of black spirituality in James Melvin Washington, *Afro-American Protestant Spirituality* (Ramsey, NJ: Paulist Press, 1987).
8. The progress of this alliance in the post–Civil War era is shown in James McPherson, *The Abolitionist Legacy: From Reconstruction to the NAACP* (Princeton, NJ: Princeton University Press, 1975).
9. See Jeremy Rifkin and Ted Howard, *The Emergence of a New Order: God in the Age of Scarcity* (New York: G. P. Putnam, 1979).
10. Alexis de Tocqueville, *Democracy in America* (New York: Vintage Books, 1945), 2:11.
11. James Rawley, *Race and Politics: "Bleeding Kansas" and the Coming of the Civil War* (Philadelphia: J. B. Lippincott, 1969), p. ix.
12. *Time*, 6 Apr. 1970.
13. Quoted in Daniel Day Williams, *The Spirit and the Forms of Love* (Lanham, MD: University Press of America, 1981), p. 269.
14. The best account of the history of Operation Breadbasket is the excellent master of divinity thesis by Gary Massoni, "Perspective on Operation Breadbasket" (Thesis, Chicago Theological Seminary, 1971).
15. Quoted in Susan Bloch, "A Continuing Climate of Racism," *Duke*, 71(2):14 (Nov–Dec. 1984).
16. Martin Luther King, Jr., "The American Dream," a speech given at Lincoln University, 6 June 1961, in Philip S. Foner, ed., *The Voice of Black America: Major Speeches by Negroes in the United States, 1797–1971* (New York: Simon & Schuster, 1972), p. 934.
17. Jesse Jackson, "The Rainbow Coalition Is Here to Stay," *Black Scholar*, 15(5):72 (Sept.–Oct. 1984).
18. Maulana Karenga, "Jesse Jackson and the Presidential Campaign: The Invitation and the Oppositions of History," *Black Scholar*, 15(5):62 (Sept.–Oct. 1984).
19. Hubert L. Dreyfus and Paul Rabinow, *Michel Foucault: Beyond Structuralism and Hermeneutics*, 2nd ed. (Chicago: University of Chicago Press, 1983), p. 214.

20. Northern and southern antebellum free blacks often had an unclear legal status because jurists could not agree on whether or not they had the rights of natural or naturalized citizens. According to James H. Kettner, "free Negroes appeared to occupy a middle ground in terms of the rights they were allowed to claim in practice, a status that could not be described in the traditional language of slave, alien, or citizen." James H. Kettner, *The Development of American Citizenship, 1608–1870* (Chapel Hill: University of North Carolina Press, 1970), p. 319. The word "denizenship" was often used to describe this status. And although there was much disagreement about the appropriateness of using this designation, it is a useful word for capturing the complexity of the free blacks' legal status. See ibid., pp. 287–333, for an excellent summary of the juridical discussion. See also Leon F. Litwack, *North of Slavery: The Negro in the Free States, 1790–1860* (Chicago: University of Chicago Press, 1961); and Ira Berlin, *Slaves without Masters: The Free Negro in the Antebellum South* (New York: Pantheon Books, 1974).

21. Manning Marable, *How Capitalism Underdeveloped Black America: Problems in Race, Political Economy and Society* (Boston: South End Press, 1983), pp. 195–214.

22. Peter J. Paris, *The Social Teaching of the Black Churches* (Philadelphia: Fortress Press, 1985), pp. 83–105.

23. Paul L. Lehmann, *Ethics in a Christian Context* (New York: Harper & Row, 1960), p. 131.

24. Pierre Bourdieu, *Distinction: A Social Critique of the Judgement of Taste*, trans. Richard Nice (Cambridge, MA: Harvard University Press, 1984), p. 231.

25. William Stringfellow, *The Politics of Spirituality* (Philadelphia: Westminster Press, 1984).

26. Ida Rousseau Mukenge, *The Black Church in Urban America: A Case Study in Political Economy* (Lanham, MD: University Press of America, 1983), p. 204; see also Cheryl Townsend Gilkes's excellent article, "The Black Church as a Therapeutic Community: Suggested Areas for Research into the Black Religious Experience," *Journal of the Interdenominational Theological Center* 8: 29–43 (Fall 1980).

27. An example of such criticism is James H. Cone, "Black Theology and the Black Church," in his *My Soul Looks Back* (Nashville, TN: Abingdon, 1982), pp. 64–92; and West, *Prophesy Deliverance!*

28. Lionel Trilling, *Sincerity and Authenticity* (Cambridge, MA: Harvard University Press, 1972), pp. 1–25.

Chapter 40

The Madonna of 115th Street Revisited

Vodou and Haitian Catholicism in the Age of Transnationalism

Elizabeth McAlister

Reclaimed by the Virgin

Every year on the fifteenth of July, the tall, wrought-iron gates of the big, brick Church of Our Lady of Mount Carmel in East Harlem swing open to welcome thousands of religious pilgrims. Women and men, children and the elderly, throng to the church for evening Mass, after which they follow a larger-than-life statue of the Virgin Mary through the New York City streets in a long, night-time procession. After a midnight Mass they spend the night in the church, or go home and come back early the next day, dressed in the Madonna's colors of blue and white and carrying flowers, letters, rosaries, and money. In this way, the faithful celebrate the feast day of Our Lady and perform devotions for one of the many appellations of the Blessed Mother.

In 1995, ten-year-old Marie-Carmel wore a puffy, sky-blue satin dress whose many layers and petticoats made her look as though she were the topmost decoration on a multitiered cake. She sat patiently through the Mass, listening to the priest while she wrestled with her squirming baby brother on her lap. Her long, dark hair was carefully oiled and braided, each braid ending in a shiny blue and gold ribbon tied in a bow. As she rose with her family to join the line to receive Holy Communion, she faltered and tripped, and her mother had to catch her by the arm and help her up. Marie-Carmel looked down in embarrassment and studied her patent-leather Mary Janes as she approached the priest.

---

*In this essay, I capitalize the term Black American to refer to the specific national group that is regularly designated as a category separate from other Americans.

When Marie-Carmel lifted her head to receive the Host, her knees buckled and she staggered backward, wheeling into an aunt standing behind her. After she took communion, the family helped Marie-Carmel out of the church for some fresh air in the courtyard. They smiled and waved away the concern of the deacon who approached them about the little girl. "She'll be fine, thank you," said her mother, "it's just that she hasn't eaten today."

She turned to her sister and to me, as I was a friend of the family and had come to join them. Beginning in French, she finished in her mother tongue, Haitian Creole: *"C'est la Vierge. Li vin manifeste nan tèt ti-moun nan"* (It's the Virgin. She manifested herself in the child's head). To indicate her continuing protection over the little girl, Notre Dame du Mont Carmel (Our Lady of Mount Carmel) had, briefly, possessed her namesake, Marie-Carmel.

The little girl's fall inside the church yielded two different interpretations, delivered in three languages. The family explained to the deacon, in English, that the girl was simply hungry.[1] But the deeper reality for the family had to do with their long relationship with the Virgin. That meaning was expressed in Haitian Creole, with, as a nod to me, a *blan* (foreigner), a translation in French.[2] This ten-minute drama at the church in East Harlem was only a small part of a much larger story about the involvement of Notre Dame du Mont Carmel in the life of a new immigrant family from the island nation of Haiti. It is a story about migration and religious expression, production, and performance, and like language itself, it contains multiple levels of meaning for various audiences.

Thousands of Haitian people have been making the yearly pilgrimage to the Church of Our Lady of Mount Carmel in East Harlem for the last two decades. It is surely the largest annual religious gathering of Haitians in North America. It takes place at the same moment when thousands in Haiti flock to a mountainside waterfall at a village called Sodo (pronounced "So-DOE"), for the Fèt Vièj Mirak (Feast of the Miracle Virgin). Temporarily relaxing class, color, and political boundaries during the pilgrimage, the feast day of the "Miracle Virgin" also brings Haitian people in New York together for two days to pray, sing, and socialize in a particularly Haitian style. In this sense, Marie-Carmel's small drama in church was also part of an even wider story about Haitian religiosity in the United States.

For several years I have been following that story through the words and actions of the Haitian people who come to visit Our Lady of Mount Carmel. The stories here will not only feature individual women and men expressing their devotion, but will also consider the role of social forces in their religious lives. These social forces extend back to the legacies of

French colonization and the lasting effects of slavery, and the ways that Afro-Haitian religion appropriated Roman Catholicism to form what Haitians call "le mélange" (the mixing) and what anthropologists call "religious syncretism." Another shaping factor is the postcolonial or, more properly put, the neocolonial relationship between Haiti and the United States. This relationship has contributed to the creation of the Haitian *djaspora*, or "diaspora," which, since the fall of Jean-Claude Duvalier in 1986, has been increasingly shaped by the phenomenon of transnational migration—the frequent movement back and forth of migrants from home countries to host countries.

What, then, can this pilgrimage tell us about immigrant religiosity? What do Roman Catholic devotions mean in the ritual vocabulary of Afro-Haitian religious culture? What meanings do these same devotions acquire in the United States? This chapter tries to answer these questions by focusing on the Haitian experience of the feast.

I offer four central points. First, religious culture in Haiti is a creolized system, wherein actors have learned to "code-switch" between performances of Catholicism and Vodou. Second, it is in Vodou that the feminine divine spiritually enfranchises Haitian women. Third, in the United States, Catholic codes themselves become part of a strategy of Haitian disaffiliation from African Americans, in an attempt to contest and renegotiate United States systems of racialization.

Fourth and finally, West Indians and Latin Americans actively use religion to articulate American identities, and in so doing they continue a long-standing strategy used by previous immigrant groups. Unlike older immigrants from Europe, however, Haitian religious articulations are bound up with the realities of transnational movement. Religious sites in the United States become added to the American landscape; they multiply, rather than replace, spiritual centers of the home country.

Revisiting 115th Street: Religious Borderlands

The story of the Haitian devotion at the Church of Our Lady of Mount Carmel in East Harlem is only the latest chapter in the ongoing history of that feast. Although the annual July feast at 115th Street now attracts thousands of Haitians, the church was built in 1884 by the Roman Catholic Pallottine order as a mission church to minister to the Italian immigrant population of that era. Italian Harlem nourished itself with the love and protection of La Madonna del Carmine, continuing a tradition they had known back in Italy. Robert Anthony Orsi's book *The Madonna of 115th*

Street: Faith and Community in Italian Harlem, 1880–1950, paints a lyrical and sensitive portrait of the ways the *festa* for the Madonna shaped people's lives—especially the mothers, wives, daughters, and sisters in the community for whom the Blessed Virgin was mother, goddess, protector, and role model. Her feast day, July 16, grew to be a major ritual marker in Italian New York, helping Italians forge an American identity based largely on their Catholicism (Orsi 1985). Although the mission of the church officially remains the same—to minister to Italian immigrants—now only 750 Italian Americans are left in its neighborhood (Laurino 1995).[3]

The ethnic flavor of the area began to change when Puerto Ricans started migrating into East Harlem just before World War II. By 1963, eleven public housing projects were built in the vicinity of the Church of Our Lady of Mount Carmel for twelve thousand low-income black and Latino families (Orsi 1992, 326; Bourgois 1995, 51). The neighborhood transformed into Spanish Harlem, the strong "Nuyorican" community affectionately known as "El Barrio" that now shares its territory with Mexicans, Dominicans, and West Africans.

The Italian immigrant families that moved to East Harlem between the 1880s and the 1920s had prospered by the 1950s, and as the Puerto Rican families moved in, the Italians emigrated to middle-class suburban communities with lawns and fences. Many of them still come back to the church to organize the feast, to attend the novena still prayed in Italian beforehand, to celebrate a special Mass for the dead, or to bless a bride or groom the day before their wedding. But these days, the majority of the pilgrims form a sea of coffee-, mahogany-, and cinnamon-colored bodies; clad in sky blue and white, praying and singing in French and Haitian Creole. The Haitians' presence at the feast is actually part of a larger social drama that is playing itself out among the Virgin, the Pallottine order, the Italian Americans who organize the event, their Puerto Rican (and other Latino) neighbors, and the Haitian pilgrims. Haitians have become actors on a multiethnic social stage that is vastly more diverse than their relatively homogeneous home ground.[4]

This Catholic church and its surrounding neighborhood have become a religious borderland of sorts. During the feast for Our Lady, Masses are said every hour in Latin, Italian, Spanish, English, French, or Haitian Creole. There are a very few Latino pilgrims in attendance, and only a handful of Irish Americans who search out the Tridentine Mass still said there. But this feast, which is sponsored and produced by Italian Americans, has come to be peopled by new immigrants, who turn the space of the large church into a site of Haitian religious activity.

Haitians at East 115th Street

Most Haitians in New York know where the Church of Our Lady of Mount Carmel is and have visited it—or know someone who has. By attending what they call the "Fête du Notre Dame du Mont Carmel" by the thousands, the New York Haitian population has collectively placed the church on an invisible community map. Stepping onto the public stage of this Catholic feast, they orient themselves within the shifting "ethnoscape" of New York City (Appadurai 1990). They make sense of the confusing complexity of this ethnic landscape by locating the church as a center of spiritual power where they will be welcome.

Haitians come in pilgrimage to East Harlem from diverse places in Haitian New York—Queens, Brooklyn, Manhattan, Long Island—and New Jersey, and from as far away as Atlanta, Chicago, and Montreal. Although they could attend feasts at other churches for Our Lady of Mount Carmel, like the one in Brooklyn's Williamsburg, thousands choose instead to cross the East River to Harlem.

Some say the Haitians come en masse to 115th Street because the church is a shrine, an official sanctuary for the Blessed Mother. It received this special status in 1903 from Pope Leo XIII, who thereupon donated two emeralds from the Vatican to adorn the golden crown of the parish's statue of the Madonna.[5] Others say that the statue's hair—real human hair—makes her the most powerful Virgin in the area. Some Haitians are attracted to 115th Street because of the French Mass said there on the first Saturday of every month in support of the canonization of Pierre Toussaint, a Haitian slave who emigrated to colonial New York with his master. There may be another factor as well: as *teledjol* (word of mouth) began to bring Haitians to the shrine, others came to be able to worship La Vierge (the Virgin) in the presence of their countrymen and -women. While they cannot possibly re-create the busy, celebratory atmosphere of the Sodo pilgrimage in the Haitian mountains, they can nevertheless find friends, reunite with long-lost neighbors, speak and sing in Creole and French, and perform spiritual work for the Vièj Mirak.

The Haitian community, as did (and do) the Italians, begins to celebrate the feast nine days before July 16 with a novena—a series of daily prayers to the Virgin at the 115th Street church. Their numbers increase until the two days the feast is celebrated, the fifteenth and sixteenth of July. The activity at the church begins to build throughout the day of the fifteenth. The Italian American ladies who form the religious articles committee unpack the goods they sell on behalf of the church: statues, medallions, scapulars, prayer cards, crosses, and crucifixes. Soon pilgrims pull up in cars, step down from buses, and climb the stairs leading from the subway. For the two days of the feast the sidewalks leading from the Lexington Avenue IRT trains become rivers of people wearing "Sunday best" outfits of the light blue associated with the Blessed Mother (and with ritual begging in Vodou), or white, a color of ritual purity for Catholic and Vodouist alike. They stroll on the arms of husbands, children, old people, and friends. Boys dressed in little suits and ties gallop ahead, racing little girls wearing dresses of satin tiers of sugary-looking cloth.

Notre Dame du Mont Carmel is especially known for the miracles she bestows on her followers, particularly those related to marriage and childbirth. I stop to talk to one young family and learn that their little girl—another Marie-Carmel—has ritually dressed in blue all of her life. She is *an ve* (in French, *en voeu*, or "in the condition of wishing"). At birth her mother dedicated her to Mont Carmel because she was born with an illness. To repay the Vièj Mirak for her recovery and continued protection, she will wear only blue or white clothing until the day of her First Holy Communion.

Pilgrims arrive throughout the day, and by nine o'clock that evening the huge church is filled to capacity for the Latin Mass; more than two thousand are in attendance. Hundreds more gather together in the courtyard and spill out into the sidewalk for the candlelight procession behind the larger-than-life statue of Our Lady of Mount Carmel.

Soon a great popping can be heard; this is the fireworks that announce and salute the Virgin at various places on the procession route. The smell of gunpowder fills the air, and the Haitian ladies, candles in their hands, lift their hands upward in a posture learned from Charismatic Catholicism.[6] The noise and smell of the firecrackers "heat up" the prayers, as each pilgrim hopes that the fireworks will carry his or her message to the Virgin. But the sound of bursting gunpowder is also an aural semiotic sign for Ezili Dantò, the goddess who "walks behind" the Vièj Mirak. In Vodou services for Dantò and the rest of the spirits in the Petwo rite to which she belongs, whips are cracked and gunpowder is lit to create the slaps and pops that Petwo spirits like. When the fireworks go off in front of the Madonna on 115th Street, not a few women falter and clutch at those around them, fighting off spirit possession.

Each July fifteenth, the statue of Our Lady is brought out thus, and she is paraded along a route designated by the church priests. Past Second Avenue after a left to Saint Ann's Church on 110th Street, more fireworks are lit, and more prayers launched heavenward: Some pilgrims take the opportunity to go inside and visit Saint Ann. Just as she is the mother of Mary in Roman Catholicism, in Vodou cosmology she is Grann Ezili, an older form of Ezili. A few Haitian pilgrims have come to East Harlem specifically to see her. "The power starts with the mother," confided one woman. "Me, I come to the *fèt* to *pran woulib* [take a ride] on the procession." She uses the mystical power of the feast day to strengthen her request to the older feminine powers, Grann Ezili/Saint Ann.

The procession winds down Second Avenue from Saint Ann's back up First Avenue, past 116th to 118th Street, pausing at various points along the way to light firecrackers. Many of these stopping places are homes of the Italian American families still in the neighborhood, who contribute time and money to the feast. They have decorated their brownstones, some in the old style of hanging linens from the windows, others by placing blue candles and statues along their steps. The fireworks are a sort of salute to patronage that the Haitian community understands from their own Carnival and Rara celebrations, where music is played for the contributions of local *gwo nèg*, or "big men" (McAlister 1995a).

During the procession some families walk together and sing hymns like "Ave Maria," "Louange a Toi," and "Chez Nous Soyez Reine," or the Lord's Prayer in French. Others crowd toward the float bearing the Madonna, touching the blue and white plastic fringe as they walk. Candles in hand, the pilgrims wear the brown scapulars of Our Lady of Mount Carmel. Bearing a brown scapular when she originally appeared, the Blessed Virgin promised that whosoever wore her scapular at the moment of death would escape the fires of eternal damnation.

When the procession reaches the church, every seat is filled for the midnight Mass. The courtyard is a scene of another sort, one closer in mood to the mountain celebrations at Sodo. Each year several women bring food, which they ritually distribute among the pilgrims. Standing in the vicinity you may be handed delicious *soup joumou* (pumpkin soup), rice and beans, *griyo* (fried pork, the ritual food of Ezili Dantò), soda, and black, sugary Haitian coffee. The women who bring the food explain that they are continuing a tradition they kept at Sodo, inherited from their mothers, a form of ritual feeding of the poor. In late-night New York there are no homeless or needy people around this church, so other Haitian pilgrims stand in for the poor and consume the food with gusto. The menfolk stand around drinking rum or whiskey, talking politics among themselves. Manbo Miracia, a priestess of Vodou who is a pilgrim here, nudges me and nods to a knot of middle-aged gentlemen. "The majority of them are married to Ezili Dantò," she said. "I know because I performed the services."[7]

On the day of the sixteenth, the feast day proper, a 9:00 A.M. Mass is followed by another procession. Throughout the day, a quick Mass is said every half-hour in a different language, as hundreds of people arrive at the church, hand flowers to the workers in the sacristy, light candles, pray to the saints, attend Mass, and receive communion. Pilgrims pass in front of the various statues, praying out loud in the Haitian style, asking for the intercession of the Blessed Mother.

Some pilgrims bring a practical orientation born out of their Afro-Creole religious culture. "Never come into the church through the back door from the courtyard," one woman instructs me. "You should not approach the saint from her back—she has to see you walking in." Other pilgrims come to perform spiritual work that is meaningful in the ritual logic of Vodou. They leave money near the statues, either dollar bills or ritual amounts of coins. A few leave candles or sprinkle Florida Water, the cologne commonly used in Vodou for its sweet, spiced scent. Occasionally the priests have found plates of food as offerings to the *lwa*, the spirits of Vodou. Many leave notes and letters stuffed in Jesus' hands, on Saint Lucy's plate of eyes, and in the folds of the gowns of Saint Damien and Cosmos. The priests walk the length of the church from time to time, collecting the money and sweeping up the letters into piles (which they later throw away). Some of the letters are written to the Virgin for help in a specific problem, related to good health, jobs, or love. Other letters are formulas for spiritual work with *lwa*. One, with name written seven times with three *X*s and the word *Jistis*, is asking Ezili Dantò for justice. Another name, written repeatedly on one side of a scrap of paper, is echoed by a name listed on its reverse. Here Ezili is asked to reconcile two enemies, or two lovers.

Every once in a while at the shrine in East Harlem, I have seen newly born *ounsi*, or "initiate," arrive with their godmother or godfather in Vodou. A *ounsi* must dress in white for a period of time designated by the *lwa*, usually forty-two days. In the first week after the week-long *kouche kanzo*, or "formal initiation," each *ounsi* must go to a new church each day and speak to the saints and the *zanj*, or "angels," of Vodou that "walk with them." For anyone initiated around July sixteenth, a trip to the Fèt Vièj Mirak is a special opportunity. These pilgrims arrive dressed entirely in the whitest white from head to toe, with white head ties and straw hats. By performing the spiritual work of Vodou in a Catholic sacred space, they illustrate how Afro-Haitian religion uses and incorporates Catholicism.

The new *ounsi* is a rare sight in East Harlem, but not because people are not initiated in the summer. On the contrary, the summer season is the best time for those who are *reklame* (reclaimed) by the spirits to undergo the long religious ordeal of ritual worldly death and the joy of spiritual rebirth, instruction, and fortification. But just as churches are sites of spiritual power, physical space is very important in Vodou. Whenever possible Haitians will return to Haiti for initiation at the place of their *demambre*, or "ancestral spiritual homes." If these places in the country-side have been sold or stolen by the *tonton makout* (destroyed), then people will be initiated into the formal temple system in Port-au-Prince. After the fall of Duvalier in 1986 allowed the Haitian population abroad to return home, the geography of spiritual work changed. As a result, the United States has become chiefly a place to perform healings and interventions in crisis. Sickness, work-related problems, and love are the most pressing issues brought to *oungan* (priest) and *manbo* (priestess) here. The more serious works—initiations, funerary rituals, or becoming a priest or priestess—are all carefully planned for trips back to Haiti (Brown 1991, McAlister 1992–93).

Religious Culture, Diaspora, and Transnational Migration

In many ways, Haitians' experience of the Mount Carmel feast is similar to that of their Italian predecessors at the church. In fact, their general positions as immigrant populations run parallel. Like Italians fleeing from *la miseria* (poverty) at the end of the last century, Haitians have come to the United States to escape the structural violence of *la mizè*, the poverty of the poorest country in the Western Hemisphere. Both agricultural peoples, arriving Italians and Haitians were (and are) similarly independent, family-centered, and devoted to local religious forms. The Italian emphasis on *rispetto* (respect) and dependence on *padroni* (patrons) (Orsi 1985) is similar to the Haitians' social hierarchies, articulated through patronage and loyalty to a *patron*, or *gwo nèg*.

There are, however, major differences between the experiences of these two communities that visit this shrine for the Madonna. For example, compared to the Haitians, Italian immigrants fit better the classic pattern of nineteenth-century migration. "Uprooting" themselves from the home country, they were "transplanted" to the United States and gradually created a new, Italian American national identity (Handlin 1951, Orsi 1992, 316). In contrast, many Haitians in the contemporary United States perceive themselves to be living *nan djaspora*, "in the diaspora," defined against Haiti as an essential location of its own, regardless of whether they live in Miami, Montreal, Paris, or Senegal. Haiti itself is real, tangible, and, in fact, often a place of partial residence. From local points "in the diaspora," Haitians live transnational lives. That is, they live embedded in international networks, sustaining social relations that link their societies of origin with their new settlement (Basch et al. 1994). Haitian transmigrants typically work jobs in New York to support homes in Haiti, keeping their children in Haitian schools until they are young teens. They return to Haiti during periods of illness or unemployment; for vacations; for important family events like baptisms, marriages, or funerals; and sometimes for national celebrations like the inauguration of a president, the yearly Carnival or Rara, or the pilgrimage to Sodo for Fèt Vièj Mirak. After decades in the United States, the elderly may return to spend their last years at home. Family roles shift between the two countries, so that children come of age and migrate north, and old folks retire and return southward to home. Both opportunity and tragedy can be the occasion to *janbe dlo*, or "cross over the water."[8]

It is the U.S. Immigration Act of 1965 and its liberalizing entrance policies that allowed for the legal immigration of large numbers of non-European peoples. We can look to this moment as a pivotal occasion that heralds the vast increase in migrants from developing countries, many of whom have brought new religious traditions—Hinduism, Buddhism, Islam, and numerous local, "traditional" spiritualities—to the United States. But this legislation cannot be the sole explanation for the increase of Caribbean (and other) immigrants. It does not explain, for one thing, why so many thousands of people would want to leave their homelands and cultures and come live in the *djaspora* in cold and hostile environments.

Such drastic movement of people is linked to economic conditions. The past several decades can be characterized in terms of new levels of capital penetrations into "Third World" economies, the development of export processing, and the increased migration of people from the peripheries to the centers (Wallerstein 1974, 229–231; Nash 1983, 3–69; Sassen-Koob 1982). Individual actors who maintain lives in two nation-states at once are engaging in a creative strategy that maximizes their position in the present configuration of global capital. It is more practical, for example, for many women to work as nurses in New York and send remittances back to Haiti to raise small children so that they will become *kretyen vivan* (good people, or literally "living Christians") and not *gate* (ruined) by the harshness of New York life. In this way we can see that economic conditions are affecting both the flows of transmigrant activities and "the manner in which they come to understand who they are and what they are doing" (Basch et al. 1994, 12).

It is increasingly true that in order to understand religious life for some new immigrants, we must also understand their continued relationship with the religious world of their home countries (Levitt 1998). Unlike the earlier Italian immigrants of East Harlem, who shifted their religious focus from the churches of the old country to East 115th Street, Haitians join congregations and undertake pilgrimages *nan djaspora*, and also continue religious activities when they go to Haiti. They often plan business or vacation trips to coincide with opportunities to perform religious work at one of the many important spiritual sites at home. When they arrive, they are labeled *djaspora* by the townspeople who could not afford to leave.

As spaces where other Haitians congregate, religious sites in diasporic locations become inflected with meanings that span both home and host nations. Working with Cubans at a shrine church in Miami, Thomas Tweed (1997) suggests that we can usefully understand diasporic religious communities as translocative (moving symbolically between the homeland and the new land) and transtemporal (relating to a constructed past and an imagined future). In Latin America the saints, with their feast days on the calendar and their churches in different villages, already have both temporal and territorialized identities, and become an organizational principle in the countryside. Each saint governs a day of the week, and the market days correspond to the saints' days. In Capotille, Haiti, for example, the church is dedicated to Notre Dame du Mont Carmel, and Tuesday is her day. Tuesday is also market day in Capotille.

The pilgrimage to Our Lady of Mount Carmel in East Harlem expands the saint's influence in the Haitian world. Rather than substituting the New York feast for the ones they left behind in Haiti, they add the Harlem location as another site of spiritual work. In this way East Harlem is opened up as one more place in the expanding "religioscape" of transnational Haitian religious culture.[9] During the pilgrimage to the Vièj Mirak in New York, the Haitian population reterritorializes spiritual practice, reinscribing sacred, translocative space onto their new landscape of settlement.[10] Haitians in diaspora reach out to Mont Carmel and Ezili Dantò, powerful nationalist symbols, extending prayers for family and friends throughout the *djaspora* and in Haiti. Temporally they include concern for the dead and departed in Haiti as well as the hoped-for children of the future. Insofar as the Haitian population is able to return to Haiti— unlike the Cuban community at the time of this writing—the activities at the shrine are those of an actively transnational religious culture.

In 1993, commercial air travel was suspended during the U.S. embargo against Haiti after the 1991 coup d'état that had ousted Haitian president Jean-Bertrand Aristide. Many Haitians who had come to New York for brief visits were delayed in the United States for months, and some who came to the feast that year told me they regretted not being back in Haiti. Their prayers on behalf of their beleaguered home nation were especially poignant. They were praying not for a remote ancestral homeland but for an embattled place of (partial) residence. Thus the feast in New York is not an isolated enclave of Haitian festivity focused solely on life in the United States. The movements, religious practices and ideologies of pilgrim actors mirror the realities of Haitian transnational migrants.

Vièj Mirak: Mont Carmel in Haiti

Many of the pilgrims at the New York Church of Our Lady of Mount Carmel, if they are in Haiti in July, would go to one of the pilgrimage sites for the Vièj Mirak back home. The biggest one, at Sodo in Ville Bonheur, attracts thousands of pilgrims who come for summer vacation and stay for weeks around the time of the July sixteenth feast. This small village is located high in the mountain range between Mirebalais and Saint Marc, with a population that is probably under three thousand (Laguerre 1989, 84). During the month of the feast, the town swells with pilgrims and vacationers, who rent rooms and houses from the villagers.

It is for the Fèt Vièj Mirak that many *djaspora* are willing to plan their international travel, don the light blue clothing of the ritual beggar pilgrim or the burlap sacks of penitence, and ride for seven hours on a *bourik* (donkey) into the mountainous Haitian countryside. Although Notre Dame du Perpetuel Secours (Our Lady of Perpetual Help) is the official patron saint of Haiti, the chapel for Notre Dame du Mont Carmel at Sodo is the most popular pilgrimage of the country.

"Sodo" is the Creole spelling of "Saut d'Eau," which in French means "waterfall." The great waterfall of Sodo was created during an earthquake on May 7, 1842 (Rouzier 1891, 262; cited in Laguerre 1989, 86). Farmers in the region understood "sodo" to be a natural dwelling place of various water spirits in Afro-Haitian cosmology: the serpent Danbala Wèdo and his rainbow wife Ayida Wèdo, Simbi Dlo (Simbi of the water), and others. It is indeed a beautiful place. White, frothy mineral water falls hundreds of feet, bounces off boulders, and runs through twisting tree roots into pools below. As the cool spray splashes off the rocks, tiny rainbows glisten in the air. Pilgrims, hot from the seven-hour ride through the mountains, step under the falls and are sometimes possessed by the spirits. Their faltering steps and wide-eyed expressions become the visual currency of the ubiquitous foreign photographers who ring the falls, fighting for the best spots for their tripods in the undergrowth.[11]

In July 1849, some time after the creation of the waterfall, rumors began to circulate that a peasant farmer had sighted the Virgin Mary in a nearby palm tree. President Faustin Soulouque, Haiti's ruler from 1847 to 1859, appointed members of his legislative cabinet to study the apparition. After satisfying himself with their report, he ordered the (now) lemon-yellow chapel built in honor of Notre Dame du Mont Carmel (Laguerre 1989, 87).[12]

Since the apparition, the pilgrimage at Sodo has been not only a center of spiritual power but also a place of celebration. Haitians of all classes travel to Sodo in July with their families. Struggling entrepreneurs arrive early to set up food stalls, market stands, and gambling houses. Rich vacationers build or rent houses and arrive in private cars with the family to spend a few weeks enjoying the festivities. Among these, the *djaspora* from the United States are easily recognizable. They arrive wearing the latest fashions from Brooklyn or Miami, the women in shorts and halter tops with blonde streaks in their permed hair and long acrylic nails painted with designs. Young men likewise adopt the styles of Black American popular culture, often crossed with a Jamaican sensibility they learn through their contact with the Jamaican youth in their own West Indian neighborhoods. They wear athletic shoes, baseball hats, and the red, green, and gold belts of the Rastafari looped through their baggy jeans.[13] This small mountain village turns into a crossroads of the global Haitian diaspora each July, as returning pilgrims also come from Zaire, Martinique, Guadeloupe, the Bahamas, Boston, and Montreal.

Nights in Ville Bonheur before and after the feast are a series of ongoing parties by all the classes that come together in the village. The town is without electricity, like the rest of the Haitian countryside. The wealthy sit on their porches, enjoying whiskey, telling jokes, listening to Haitian *konpa* dance music on portable radios they power with batteries. Young sons may go out into the night in search of the many *bouzen* (prostitutes) who come into the town especially for the feast.

The less well-to-do stroll through the streets, tend their businesses, or stop in at one of the many Vodou ceremonies that enliven the village during the month of July. Traveling Vodou societies may bring their entire personnel, who set up their drums and call out the songs of the *lwa*, who are sometimes called *zanj* (angels) of Vodou. Street life is full and lively. By the light of the *tèt gridap* (kerosene lamps) or the burning torches set around the town, people recognize old friends, acquire new ones, make economic transactions, and perform the spiritual work they need to do in order to effect change in their lives.

The Haitian Religious Continuum

The chapel and the waterfall at Sodo are both important and impressive. However, *manbo* and *oungan* who serve the spirits of Vodou insist that the most powerful spot is the actual place where the Madonna appeared. Called *Nan Palm* (In the Palm Grove), this site stands near the entrance to the village. It is here that the Virgin dwells with her counterpart Ezili Dantò, the powerful Afro-Haitian goddess. Dantò's co-existence with the Vièj Mirak is an example of the great mystery of *le mélange*, or the syncretism of African and Catholic symbolisms. Like Mexico's Virgin of Guadalupe, who appeared to an Indian man at the shrine of an Aztec goddess, Notre Dame du Mont Carmel at Sodo is a powerful national figure resonant with multiple layers of meaning. When pilgrims make the trip through the mountains to Sodo, they visit the church, the waterfall, and the palm grove—a three-fold spiritual site.[14]

The *manbo* I have worked with tell me that Notre Dame du Mont Carmel "walks a path" with Ezili Dantò, a *lwa* or *mistè* "mystery" who has become one of the most important divinities in the culture.[15] While she can be represented by Mont Carmel, Ezili Dantò is most often represented in popular Haitian iconography as Notre Dame du Czestochowa, the Black Virgin of Poland, whose face bears two scars running down her cheek. Like both Czestochowa and Mont Carmel, Ezili Dantò carries a baby in her arms. Dantò's baby is not the infant Jesus but, interestingly, a daughter. Some call her "Anayiz," others "Ti-Gungun." Dantò is known as single mother, a hard-working black woman, and a powerful warrior and fighter. A symbol of nationalist pride, she is said to have been a leader in the slaves' victorious war of independence against Napoleon's army, when she earned the scars she carries (Brown 1991, 229).

Sometimes Dantò is described as a lesbian, and she is thought to choose which men will live as effeminate homosexuals. When she possesses people (for she can "ride" both women and men), she drinks *kleren* cane liquor and demands to eat pork, often the ears and feet of the roasted pig. In her incarnation as Ezili Ge Wouj (Red Eyed Ezili), she speaks without the use of the front of her tongue, saying only "ke ke ke ke," and pantomiming her meanings. Some say her tongue was cut out during the Haitian revolution so she would not betray her side's secrets (Brown 1991, 229).

When pilgrims go to the East Harlem shrine or to *Nan Palm* at Sodo and light a candle, sing to the Virgin, and *fè demann* (make requests), they are addressing Notre Dame du Mont Carmel and Ezili Dantò *at the same time*. This overlapping, simultaneous practice of Catholicism and Vodou has puzzled outsiders—both Haitian intellectuals and foreigners—for generations. Within anthropology, "syncretism" was the theoretical concept developed by Melville Herskovits (1941) and then Roger Bastide (1960) to understand the processes of change that arose with culture contact. Syncretism came to describe an "impure" religious tradition, saturated with local, unorthodox strains. Recent terms used to describe cultural mixings have included "creolization," "symbiosis," and "interculture" (Stewart and Shaw 1994, Desmangles 1992).

The received way of thinking about Vodou and Catholicism is to imagine them as a pair of binary opposites. It is true that Haitian Catholics have affirmed their own status by stressing their apartness from Vodou. A Catholic who is not at all involved in serving the *lwa* identifies as a *fran katolik* (straight Catholic), and there are some in the Haitian upper classes who know nothing of Afro-Haitian religion. The upper classes were (and are) generally literate, French-speaking, politically enfranchised, light-skinned, and emphatically Catholic. On the stage of cultural politics, Vodou was (and is) held up as the pagan, Satanic superstition of the poor, dark, nonliterate, and disenfranchised majority. Politically, then, Catholicism has always positioned itself in opposition to Vodou.[16]

In practice, it may be more helpful to imagine these two traditions occupying either end of a continuum, with Roman Catholicism on one end and Vodou on the other.[17] Any given actor in Haiti falls somewhere along the continuum, some as Catholics, some as Vodouists, and the vast majority living their lives in the middle, going through the rites of passage of the Catholic church while simultaneously maintaining contact with Vodou healers and the *lwa*, especially in times of crisis.

Even this continuum model must be complicated with further qualifications. Elsewhere, I have written that both the Afro-Haitian religion and the Catholicism that evolved in Haiti were constructed in dialectical relation to the other in a process of creolization. In this sense there is simply no "pure Catholicism" or "pure Vodou" in Haiti. To a degree that some advocates in each tradition might not like to admit, each has incorporated the other into its philosophies and practices. Each tradition is therefore constitutive and revealing of the other (McAlister 1995a, 179).[18]

While one tradition may be bound up in the other, the Haitian cultural politics that divides the enfranchised from the disenfranchised insists on seeing each as a separate religion. This same politics governs the behavior of actors in public space. It can be useful to understand the Haitian majority as being "bicultural" or "bireligious," a population able to speak both of the religious languages operating within the culture (Murphy

1988, 124). People strategically employ "religious code-switching" to translate the logics of Catholicism and Vodou back and forth to suit the social situation at hand. For this reason it may make sense to view the religious worldview of the vast majority as "Haitian religious culture," a term that "reflects a religion in two-way communication with the structures of authority around it" (Davis 1982). It is a religious culture that contains within it shifting sets of possible elements, complicated yet bounded by the theologies and practices of both Roman Catholicism and Vodou.

Catholics throughout Latin America make *promesas* (promises) to the saints, in which they ask for a favor and in return make a sacrificial promise. Some promise to return to a church on its feast day each year, others make pilgrimages barefoot, and still others donate family treasures to the saint's shrine. In Haiti, people will also make a request (*fè demann*) and tell the saint what they will give in return. Often the requests to the saints are governed by the logic of Vodou.

Madame Luc, an older woman who grew up in a small village in northern Haiti and who now goes to the East Harlem pilgrimage each year, explained to me that her family was Catholic and did not serve the spirits. But although she considers herself Catholic, she "thinks in Vodou" (Murphy 1988, 124). In keeping with a worldview focused on the family, she maintains that the Virgins of Mont Carmel, Altagrace, and La Merci are sisters.

For Catholics, the Virgin Mary and the saints are intercessors; they carry our prayers to God. If they grace us with our wish, we are blessed, but if they do not, we must accept things as they are as God's will. For Vodouist Catholics, things are slightly different. If one saint does not give us what we want, we may berate it, argue with it, and ultimately turn to a different saint with the same wish. Just as we can punish them by turning away, they can punish us if we do not live up to our promise. Madame Luc told me that making promises to the saints is tricky: "Watch out, because if you promise something to them and then you forget, you're in trouble." She told me that if you promise to give the saint a cow, for example, you had better make good on your word. "How do you bring a cow to the church?" I asked her. "No, you don't give it to the church; the church isn't involved in that sort of thing," she said. "You make your request at the church. But you are dealing with the spirit behind the saint." She explained that if you promise a cow to the saint and your request is granted, you must give the cow to "the people who serve the *zanj* [angels]," a Vodou society. Madame Luc therefore places herself in an intermediary space where her actions are performed in the Catholic church, but her dealings are with the *zanj* of Vodou. Thus it is possible to situate her toward the Catholic end of a continuum between Catholicism and Vodou, themselves intertwined in Haitian culture.

The fact that people do the spiritual work of Afro-Haitian religion in church settings does not mean that they are not also fully participating Catholics. For the Haitians, the pilgrimage at 115th Street is very much respected as a Catholic event, and any spiritual work that is done explicitly for the *lwa* is done discreetly. Vodou remains an unspoken presence at the feast in New York, and each sign that carries meaning within Vodou can also be read as a form of Catholic devotion. Wearing light blue clothing, saying prayers during fireworks, distributing pork in the churchyard, writing letters to the Virgin—all these things have a place in the ritual vocabulary of Catholicism, even if they are seen by the priests at the church as the quaint expressions of the "folk."

The spiritual works of Vodouist Catholics are achieved in a process of religious code-switching through the subtle use of language, the nuanced use of color, and discreet offerings of spiritual significance. It is possible, then, to communicate with Ezili Dantò through Mont Carmel on the public stage without detection, even by fellow community-members standing at one's side. Devotions to Our Lady that are also spiritual work for Ezili Dantò are masked with a discretion that has come from generations of experience with colonial and postcolonial repression from France and Rome. Because of the historical circumstances involving the church's repression of Vodou, then, it is quite possible to serve Ezili Dantò through the coded performance of Catholicism.

Anthropologist Initiate–Outsider Insider: A Word on Position and Method

The first time I went to Haiti, I traveled with a group of friends "back" to that country with a master drummer of Vodou music. We went as musical apprentices, and not as anthropologists. Rather than choosing a site for field research and then going to it, my trip mirrored patterns of transmigration, as I went "home" with an immigrant who had settled in my area.

Because we were traveling in July, our host insisted that we go to Sodo for the Fèt Vièj Mirak to receive good luck from the spirits. The trip was in 1984, two years before the fall of Jean-Claude Duvalier. Since then much has happened between us as a result of that trip, which was launched under the auspices of Notre Dame du Mont Carmel. The stories are too long and too complex to tell here. Some of us married Haitians. Five children have been born, and two doctoral dissertations on Haitian culture were written (Wilcken 1991; McAlister 1995a, 1995b). Three of us were initiated together as *marasa* (twins) in the Afro-Haitian spiritual system.

Anthropologists are supposed to go off to the field by themselves (or with a spouse, who is briefly mentioned in the final academic work), and to conduct fieldwork and interviews alone. This has rarely been the case for me working in Haiti or in Haitian New York. Starting with that first visit to Haiti with a group of friends, I have always seemed to work with others, be they friends, family, photographers, assistants, or colleagues.

By the same token, I have never been to the pilgrimage to Mont Carmel in Haiti or in New York by myself. To arrive somewhere by oneself in the Haitian context is to signal unimportance, or worse, unconnectedness; it implies that *ou pa gen moun,* "you have no people." I have visited the site with other scholars, with Haitian friends, and with a group of women in a Brooklyn Vodou society. This is not to say that because I am with companions I am not doing field research, not taking notes, not making audio recordings, and not acutely observing the ritual around me. In a sense I am in my own mental universe, while others are in theirs.

The methodologies I have used in this study have ranged from the casual visit to Haiti with friends in 1984 to the formal interviewing of pilgrims in New York in the early 1990s. Much of my knowledge of Afro-Haitian spirituality comes from being a partial "insider" as a Vodou initiate, although I recognize myself fundamentally as an "outsider" to Haitian culture. My own research and writing have been ongoing, and the period of my doctoral fieldwork let me taste the experience of transnational migration as I went back and forth to Haiti seven times in five years (McAlister 1992–93, McAlister 1995a).

To research and articulate the inherent realities of new migrants means following the movements of immigrants and retracing circuits of transnational migration. It entails working in immigrant enclaves in American cities and returning to home countries with recent immigrants. As one becomes embedded in these networks, field research involves working in proximity with others in new ways. This may well become the predominant field model in sociology and anthropology as scholars increasingly understand their own neighborhoods as places of globalizing cultural contact and cultural change.

A Household Reception for the Vièj Mirak

One evening in New York, as the candlelight procession for the Blessed Mother returned to the church courtyard, I noticed a ring of ladies in

Creole dresses of the dark blue colors associated with Ezili Dantò. They were sitting in a semicircle atop bags of dresses and spices they had come to sell at the feast. I recognized them as *manbo* of Vodou. They were, in fact, the core initiates of a small Vodou society in Brooklyn. They would sleep in the church and after Mass in the morning set up their wares in a makeshift market on the church sidewalk.

Karen McCarthy Brown's 1991 book *Mama Lola: A Vodou Priestess in Brooklyn* recounts the spiritual biography of a Brooklyn *manbo* with great insight and sensitivity, showing the many relationships Mama Lola maintains with the spirits of Vodou. Like Mama Lola, Manbo Miracia, the spiritual mother of the society I encountered, has had a long-standing relationship with Notre Dame du Mont Carmel. Her own mother was born on July sixteenth, the Virgin's feast day. Miracia was born a twin, and her mother named her "Miracia" to tie her to the "miracle Virgin." To her sister she gave the name "Lamèsi," for "Notre Dame de la Merci," another Virgin represented by a statue in the Ville Bonheur chapel. "Ever since we were in the womb, my mother brought us to Sodo each year," said Miracia proudly with an emphatic nod. "And my daughter Carmel went with me in *my* belly."

Manbo Miracia grew up to fall in love with a man also born on July sixteenth, dedicated to Mont Carmel by virtue of his birth. When she was pregnant with their daughter, she had a vision of a dark-skinned woman with two scars running down her cheek. It was the same face as the Polish Virgin of Czestochowa, the image Haitians know also to be Ezili Dantò. "The lady was carrying my daughter in her arms," she confided. When her daughter was born on the feast day for Czestochowa, September 2, she dedicated her to Ezili Dantò and the Virgins of Czestochowa and Mont Carmel, naming her "Marie-Carmel." Thus Miracia is linked to Notre Dame du Mont Carmel in various ways through the significant dates in her family.

Manbo Miracia invited me to a reception in her home for the Virgin. Every year she holds this event to honor their special relationship. The reception would not be a Vodou ceremony where drums, antiphonal singing, and dancers would call the spirits. Rather, it would be a series of Catholic prayers said in honor of the Vièj Mirak in the presence of family and friends. By sponsoring the service in her own home, Miracia positioned herself as a producer of her own religious work, sustaining a direct relationship with the saints and the spirits, outside of the direction of male, possibly non-Haitian, Catholic priests.

Manbo Miracia lives in a small apartment in the Crown Heights section of Brooklyn with her daughter Carmel and Carmel's two children.

She had rearranged her house for the prayer service by pushing her furniture to the walls and setting up chairs in the living room. A simple altar table was set up under a large poster depicting Notre Dame du Mont Carmel. Flowers fashioned from blue crepe paper framed the image to create a baroque effect. On the lace-covered table sat a homemade oil lamp used on altars in Haiti, made of a metal star supporting a cotton wick suspended in oil by four corks. Two deep-blue, seven-day candles flanked the lamp, near a bouquet of flowers.

A number of people were assembled, dressed nicely and sitting on chairs against the three walls not taken up with the altar. I recognized in their number one of Brooklyn's busiest and most popular *oungan* (priest of Vodou), dressed in a white dashiki and surrounded by his entourage. But it was not he who would lead the service. That honor was reserved for the *prèt savann* (bush priest).

A *prèt savann* holds a distinct rank in Vodou. Specialists in the Catholic rites of baptism, marriage, and last rites, these officials are always men proficient in Latin. A number of *prèt savann* make the main cemetery in Port-au-Prince their daily place of business, singing in Latin and French the memorial masses that Vodouists perform a year and a week after death.

As I fell into a conversation with the priest, I learned that he had joined an order of brothers in his youth, intending to be a monk. On the eve of the fourth and final vow, he was rejected for candidacy The *zanj* in his family appeared to him in a dream and told him that they had adopted him; he was *reklame*, or "reclaimed," by the spirits (see also McAlister 1992–93). Three years later he underwent the *kouche kanzo*, or initiation into a Vodou society. On his finger he wore both gold and silver wedding rings; he confided to me that he was married to both Ezili Dantò and Ezili Freda, her light-skinned counterpart. Many Haitian men accept marriage to these two powerful goddesses; they must both be "served" to achieve the correct balance.

Formally schooled in the Latin and French texts of the church, he now lends his services to say novenas in the home, to officiate over marriages between people and the *zanj* during a Vodou ceremony, or to preside at the sort of reception that Manbo Miracia had decided to hold. He had brought a black leather bag with him, out of which he extracted several prayer books, a chalice, a brass censer, and a small bucket of holy water. When the proper time came, he selected a white lace chasuble and donned it, adding to it a necklace bearing a large wooden cross.

Like many Catholic events requested by the *lwa*, the event was full of coded signs meaningful in the logic of Vodou. The priest began, for example, by purifying the room, scattering the four cardinal directions with Florida Water. Then he lit a bundle of charcoal topped with frankincense in the incense burner and moved through the congregation for all to be touched by rich, pungent fingers of smoke. He disappeared into the kitchen and returned for a dramatic entrance, singing loudly and formally in Latin. Taking up his small bucket and sprinkler, he scattered holy water on all of us. He motioned to Miracia to light the two big, blue candles on the altar.

The priest moved to a *ti chèz ba* (little low chair), the kind of small wooden chair used by Vodou priests for the long series of Catholic prayers sung in French before a Vodou ceremony. He proceeded to lead the small congregation in a Mass drawn from photocopied pages and prayer books he had brought. The assembled guests knew most of the songs and prayers. After a while he stopped the prayers and introduced himself by name, saying that we were saying our Hail Marys for Miracia's family, for the homeless, for the children who live in the streets, and for Haiti.

The service featured none of the songs or invocations for the *lwa*, and none appeared in possession. But as in the end of a Vodou ceremony for Ezili Dantò, Manbo Miracia distributed plates filled with rice and beans and fried pork. We bit gratefully into the meat, deliciously greasy and spiced with garlic and *piman*, the hot scotchbonnet pepper of Caribbean cuisine. She set aside the remainder of the enormous pot of meat. This dish would "sleep" on the floor under the altar table, a practice called "feeding the spirits" that would nourish Ezili Dantò with Miracia's symbolic sacrifice. On the altar itself would "sleep" a big cake with blue frosting, a sweet dessert for Ezili to consume. We returned the next day to enjoy a slice of the cake after it had slept. By then Manbo Miracia had put her apartment back in its usual state, with the altar table replaced by television and stereo. She was tired but pleased to have received the saints into her home with her family and friends.

Domestic prayer services like this one are not uncommon in the Haitian context. The home is transformed into sacred space by rearranging furniture, constructing an altar, and assembling a familial community in prayer. Susana Gallardo (1994) illustrates the ways in which the institutional ritual of the church is not central to Catholicism as it is practiced in many Chicano/a communities. Like the Chicana/o case, the Haitian home altar can be seen as an alternative sacred space controlled primarily by women. Prayer is offered according to the codes of Haitian religious culture, and dedicated to the spiritual work necessary to maintain relationships with the spiritual energy of both the saints *and* the *lwa*.

The Roman Catholic Church
and the Haitian Community in New York

The current population of an estimated four hundred thousand Haitians in the New York area has brought an increase in Catholics to the region. The Catholic church's response to this Haitian migration has followed the pattern it established with other ethnic groups of encouraging the creation of separate ethnic congregations within the local parish. In this way the church has joined other institutions in promoting ethnic group formation and the maintenance of ethnic identity (Glick-Schiller 1975, Buchanan 1980).[19]

The head of the Haitian Apostolate for Brooklyn and Queens, Father Guy Sansariqc, is effectively the leader of the Haitian Catholic church in the New York metropolitan area. He leads a thriving Haitian congregation at the church of Saint Jerome in Brooklyn, which he estimates one thousand four hundred parishioners attend each Sunday. As the coordinator of the National Office of Haitian American Catholics, he is also a national and transnational figure. He travels to Haiti frequently for conferences, always looking for Creole-speaking priests who might be able to serve the New York community. He also organizes pilgrimages to Our Lady of Perpetual Help in Bay Ridge, Brooklyn, and to Our Lady of Fatima in New Jersey. He terms the pilgrimage in East Harlem "without guidance," since it was not initiated by the church but rather by the pilgrims themselves.

Besides Saint Jerome's, there are various other Catholic churches serving the Haitian community. A French Mass for Haitians in New York was said by a Haitian priest as early as 1966, and by 1970 eight hundred people regularly attended. In the early 1970s ten other parishes instituted French Masses, and the Brooklyn diocese created the Haitian Apostolate of Brooklyn (Glick-Schiller 1975, Buchanan 1980).

Today, there are fourteen churches with French or Creole Masses to serve the Haitian community in Brooklyn and Queens, and another four or five in Manhattan and Rockland County.[20] The Haitian Apostolate struggles to maintain service centers for Haitian refugees and immigrants, many of whom are traumatized in various ways from their experiences of military repression and flight from Haiti.[21] Father Sansariqc identifies other issues to be more critical for the Haitian population in the New York area than the question of syncretism. The legal issues that revolve around immigration status are his most pressing concerns.

The Haitian presence at the shrine for Our Lady of Mount Carmel began as a spontaneous devotion; no church institution initiated or invited the Haitian participation. Not even the sponsoring Pallottine order ministers to the Haitians as a group, except for holding a monthly Mass in French. Part of this has to do with diocesan politics and the territorial jurisdictions of the church. The Haitian leadership is located in Brooklyn and Queens, in the Brooklyn diocese. The feast in East Harlem falls into the New York archdiocese, covering Manhattan, Rockland, and Westchester. With only thirty-five priests of Haitian descent living and serving in the United States, there is a shortage of priests with Haitian cultural fluency. Yet the pilgrims at Mount Carmel do not seem to be concerned.

A small, informal group of committed Haitians prints the text of the Mass in French and distributes it during the feast. The priests at Mount Carmel explain that they offer two Masses in French out of the eight that are said that day "as a courtesy." They have also appointed a Haitian man quasideacon, endowing him with some, but not all, of the responsibilities of that position. Yet the pilgrims who come to the feast have not played a great role in organizing it. The pilgrimage is, for the Haitians, a matter apart from their regular church activities. It is an affair between themselves and the Virgin.

The community of Haitians at the Church for Our Lady of Mount Carmel is what makes this site a translocative one—symbolically engaged with both home and host countries. The image of the festivities back in Haiti at Sodo is a quietly spoken reference. Ezili Dantò, the powerful feminine divinity who fought for Haitian independence, forms the backdrop for prayers and conversation about the various transmutations of Haitian national politics—the fall of Duvalier, the election of Aristide, the coup d'état, and the U.S. military "intervasion"—as well as U.S. elections and immigration legislation. People can see old friends, be seen by new friends, and ritually distribute their Haitian foods to enthusiastic recipients. By sharing this important date with one another, actors build a religious community of sorts, maintaining the nostalgia for Haiti and reaffirming the dream of eventual return. As they would at Sodo, they can stay up late to *bay blag* (tell jokes) and sleep in groups in the church on the night before the feast. They can pray the rosary together in French and relax into the common codes of their culture. In one of the few times of liminal community solidarity, they can enjoy the deeply satisfying company of their sisters and brothers from Haiti around them as they pray, sing, and speak to their common mother, the Vièj Mirak.

Catholicism and the Haitian Strategy of Alterity

bell hooks (1989) has noted that scholars may be more comfortable focusing on international or postcolonial issues than addressing race and class differences at home. She points out that language that diasporizes and internationalizes U.S. minorities can obscure understandings of structured inequalities of class and race in the national arena. While they are dubbed "*djaspora*" when they return to Haiti, in the United States the Haitian population is engaged in a struggle over questions of identity and definition that are inseparable from American processes of racialization.

Immigrants who establish themselves in the United States enter an increasingly plural society, where ethnic identity is structured through various processes that include race, class, religion, language, and gender as well as the politics of nationalism. Recent scholarship by David Mittelberg and Mary C. Waters (1992) suggests that immigrants' identities in the United States will be formed out of a dialectic of sorts. Identity will be made up of the category into which the receiving society assigns them on one hand and the "cognitive map" of the immigrants themselves on the other. Mittelberg and Waters offer the hypothetical case of a Polish immigrant. Americans, familiar with other Polish Americans, assign him or her to the category "Polish." The Polish American population becomes what is referred to as the "proximal host," the group to which the receiving society would assign the immigrant. The newly arrived Pole is different, of course, from Polish Americans, but most likely perceives a series of historical similarities and begins to develop a Polish American self-understanding and identity (ibid., 416).

But what if the receiving society assigns the new immigrant to a proximal host that the immigrant does not recognize? Afro-Caribbean immigrants are caught in this problematic position. As black immigrants they are offered the label "African American." But here the proximal host to which the dominant society assigns them is not the identity that they understand themselves to have. They understand themselves to be historically and culturally distinct from Black Americans. Yet social scientists have shown that groups defined through race will have the least amount of choice in self-identification. Groups of black African descent will inevitably be labeled "black." In contrast, "white ethnics" like Irish Americans or Italian Americans have a considerable amount of choice in the ways they may cast their identity (ibid.).

Scholars of race have demonstrated that there is no such thing, really, as "race," but rather that racializations and racisms are processes in historical evolution, changing through time and across space (Hall 1978). We can see the ways in which the former slaveholding societies of Latin America, the West Indies, and the United States have all developed differently racialized configurations. When Haitians arrive in the United States, they carry cognitive maps charting a complex sense of Caribbean racialization in which people are located along a color continuum, mitigated by class and family lineage. Race in the United States has been constructed along a color line, making people either black or white. Haitian Americans' identity and subjective positions of racialization must be seen as being superimposed onto their new experience of United States constructions of race. Part of the challenge people of color face when they emigrate is in assessing and renegotiating a newly found racial status in North America.

Unpacking the complexities of Haitian American identity, Carolle Charles (1990) argues that the categories of race, class, and ethnicity by which Haitians identify themselves are expressions of their social consciousness, and are part of a process of rejection and redefinition of categories of race and ethnicity ascribed in the United States. Charles's work reveals Haitians' tendency to disaffiliate with African Americans. Haitians are acutely aware that Black Americans have been assigned again and again to the lowest status position in the United States. Haitian immigrants see that meanings of blackness in the United States are subordinated, that blacks represent the bottom of United States society. Haitians reject this placement and tend to dismiss U.S. meanings of blackness, while affirming their own race and culture.

Although Haitians self-identify as black, they link their blackness through Haitian history to Africa and not via the United States. Haitian racial identity is closely connected to pride in the Haitian revolution of 1791–1804, which created the first black-ruled nation in the Americas. The revolution was fought by slaves said to be inspired by Vodou and fortified by magical weapons. Blackness and militarism became key tropes of Haitian nationalism, along with allusions to Afro-Creole spiritual power. Citizens of the black nation that defeated Napoleon's army, Haitians carry a deep sense of national pride that is linked to blackness and independence (Charles 1990; see also McAlister 1995a).

The paths that they chart reveal Haitians in the United States to be actors constructing their own identity as a population. Two important performative elements they have available to use in carving out their own identities are language and religion. A common Haitian American tactic is to display, use, and value their Francophone (and Creolophone) abilities. By referring to themselves as "Frenchies" and speaking French in public, Haitians display a foreign-born status that is at once an upper-class marker in Haitian society (Charles 1990, Mittelberg and Waters 1992). By continuing to participate in Catholic congregations and public feasts, Haitian Americans distinguish themselves further from African Americans, whom they generally view as members of the black Protestant church establishment.[22]

It is thus possible to view the Haitian devotion at the Church of Our Lady of Mount Carmel and at other pilgrimages to the Blessed Mother in the United States as a partial strategy in the Haitian American struggle to create an American identity, "a self-constitution through the strategy of alterity within the broader context of American racial semiotics" (Orsi 1992, 321). By maintaining Frenchness, Creoleness, and Catholicism, and by dressing in conservative, French-influenced fashions and hair styles, Haitians broadcast their difference from African Americans. By displaying and practicing their Catholic culture with its Latin and French linguistic attributes, Haitians can underscore to themselves, their children, and the larger society that they are fully Haitian, Afro-Caribbean, Catholic, immigrant—and not African American. In a sense, Haitian Americans can be said to be struggling to create a new black ethnicity in the United States.

While this conservative Francophile strategy is a long-standing one for Haitians throughout the diaspora, it is worth noting that this is not the only stance possible for Haitian American identity. Since the fall of Duvalier in 1986, the *racine* (roots) movement has created an alternative Haitianized identity. This politically progressive movement cultivates a peasant, "folksy" style and an explicitly pro-Vodou ethos. There are also many important political and social alliances between African American and Haitian American groups, each working out of a pro-black consciousness (McAlister 1995a).

Nevertheless, while the pilgrimage is a place to perform spiritual work, it is also an occasion to perform Catholicism on the public stage, regardless of where each person stands on the Catholic-Vodou continuum in Haitian religious culture. Catholicism becomes one ritual performance among others in the larger cultural repertoire. This performance is a continuation of a stance developed in slavery and throughout the postcolonial history of Haiti in the face of church repression of African-based spirituality. In the U.S. context, the performance becomes one element in the Haitian strategy to redefine American categories of race and ethnicity.

Italians and Haitians: Race and Religious Symbiosis

The arrival of both Italians and Puerto Ricans into the United States has been racially charged, each in a specific way. Robert Orsi (1985, 160) writes of the "racial inbetweenness" of late-nineteenth-century Italian immigrants, arguing that Italians were initially viewed as unassimilable "African racial stock." Tallulah, Louisiana, became the bloody scene of race hatred when five Sicilian men (targets of a terrorism historically reserved for African Americans) were lynched "because they had violated the protocols of racial interaction." Italian Americans created an identity in reaction to early racism against them and in turn, larger issues about their position with respect to other dark-skinned peoples. Immigrants from Italy learned that "achievement in their new environment meant successfully differentiating themselves from the dark-skinned other" (Orsi 1992, 314–317).

In New York Puerto Rican people have also been met with a racialized hatred (Orsi 1992, Díaz-Stevens 1993, Bourgois 1995). When Puerto Rican migrants moved into Italian Harlem in the pre–World War II period, the Italians reacted with hostility to this "other dark-skinned other," and three-way violence broke out between African Americans, Italian Americans, and Puerto Ricans. Insofar as organized crime syndicates held sway in the Italian community, they forced local landlords to maintain white-only segregated buildings (Bourgois 1995, 60).[23] They could not, however, stop the public housing projects being built in the neighborhood, which were replacing Italian families with black and Latino ones. "We had to leave when the 'goombas' moved in," an Italian American pilgrim returning to Our Lady of Mount Carmel told me. Italians spoke with disdain of the "so-called Puerto Ricans" who as Latins were culturally and linguistically similar, yet whose arrival threatened Italian control of East Harlem and soon turned *cara Harlem* into *el barrio* (Orsi 1992, 326).

Despite the important place reserved for Our Lady of Mount Carmel in their devotions, Puerto Ricans quickly sensed that they would find no welcome at the feast on 115th Street. "Puerto Ricans knew to stay away, because on these days and nights Italian Americans were in the grip of a profound experience of their own power and identity (conflicted and polysemous as this was) and would not tolerate the appearance of 'outsiders' among them, especially those 'outsiders' who lived in the neighborhood" (ibid., 330). The Italians were determined to maintain the Italian ethnic flavor of the feast, ensuring that the *festa* not become a *fiesta*. Even at the present writing, few Puerto Rican pilgrims attend the July sixteenth festivities.

By the time Haitian immigrants began to attend the feast in large numbers in the 1970s, the Italian battle for territory was over. Most Italian American families had moved out of East Harlem, and for them the July feast had become another sort of pilgrimage—a nostalgic visit to the old neighborhood where their parents' American journey began (ibid.). Today Italian American families return to the feast with video cameras; after Mass they line the sidewalks to film the old neighborhood for posterity. The feast is still produced and controlled by the Pallottine order, and the Italian American old guard organizes the feast committees. But the fact is that without hundreds of Haitian bodies at the processions and thousands of Haitians who come to Mass, the feast of Our Lady would not be possible.

The Italians producing the feast receive the Haitians very differently from the way they did the Puerto Ricans a generation ago. The Haitians' arrival from outside the neighborhood and their departure afterward makes their yearly "invasion" less threatening than that of the Puerto Ricans who overtook East Harlem as residents (see also McGreevy 1996). The Italians make gestures welcoming the Haitians, adding a French Mass "as a courtesy," and flying the Haitian flag next to the Italian one in the parade. They comment on how prayerful and devoted the Haitians are. "Look how they pray, the beautiful way they dress, they come from all over, they are so devoted to the Blessed Mother," said one lay worker approvingly. They sense *rispetto* (respect) for the Blessed Mother in the little suits and "wedding-cake dresses" that make up the Haitian "Sunday best."

The Italians express hostility toward Puerto Rican *santeros* (priests in the Yoruba-based religion called *La Regla de Ocha*) when they come to do spiritual work at the church. They describe *Ocha* as "satanism" while at the same time denying that the Haitians are involved in Vodou. Florida Water, candles, and fried pork set near the altars are left only by "a few crazy ones" (Orsi 1992, 334). The elderly Italian American women are nevertheless anxious about the new influx and express fears to one another about the statue's safety in the midst of the newest pilgrims. Some advocate restricting Haitian access to the nave of the church (Bourgois 1995, 347).

Despite Italian anxieties, the Haitians are accommodated and even respected at the church. Language has been an important marker shaping the respect the Italians have for the Haitians. Well versed in the Tridentine Mass, the Haitians chant the prayers in Latin along with the priests, which impresses the Italians. In the respect and prayerfulness of the Haitians, the Italian Americans recognize a conservative, pre–Vatican II religiosity, and identify them as "traditional Catholics" (Orsi 1992, 333). The Haitians' Creole impresses the Italians, on whom the difference between French and Creole is lost. The Italian Americans recognize the Haitian strategies of racial alterity and emphatically assert that "Haitians are not considered as black people" (Orsi 1992, 334). In a sense, the two communities find sympathetic reflection in one another.

For the days of the feast, Haitians and Italians form a sort of symbiosis, each allowing the other to extend once again a cherished event from their past into the future. Italians and Haitians engage in a kind of pact, and each community fills the needs of the other. While the Italian Americans produce the feast, they maintain control over their old neighborhood and the shrine church, one of the three most important Marian sites in all the Americas. Meanwhile, the Haitians are consumers at the shrine. They arrive with flowers, make donations, and buy religious articles—scapulars, statues, and prayer cards. They sing the Mass in Latin and French, and their presence fills the streets in the procession. Without having to organize and produce it, they use the feast as a public stage upon which to serve the Virgin and perform their ethnicity. When it is all over the Haitians retreat, leaving the Italian community to itself. In the often racially tense landscape of New York, this week represents a smooth collaboration that suits everybody involved. For one week each year, the Italian American community of East Harlem becomes a sort of "religious host," welcoming Haitians from near and far. Each community allows the other to preserve their myths, their hopes, and their own deep sense of identity.

Conclusions

Let us return for a moment to little Marie-Carmel, who was touched by the Virgin at the opening of the chapter. This ten-year-old Haitian American girl had never seen Haiti, yet her life story was intimately tied to both the symbols of Haitian religious culture and to social networks of migrants moving back and forth to the island. Her mother, years earlier, was diagnosed with cancer just after she migrated to New York. Like many immigrants of little means in her position, she gathered her things to return to Haiti to die. When she arrived, as she tells it, she dreamed her own mother came to her with a message. "Nothing is wrong. You're just pregnant. When you deliver your baby, call her Marie-Carmel." Convinced that the Vièj Mirak removed her cancer and gave her a child, she attends her *fèt*—whether in Haiti or in the *djaspora*—each year in gratitude.

When little Marie-Carmel fainted at the communion rail, she experienced a profound religious crisis, common in narratives about the spirits in Afro-Haitian culture. Marie-Carmel's mother saw clearly that the Vièj Mirak, with Ezili Dantò next to her, had reclaimed (*reklame*) the little girl. Usually beginning in adolescence as a series of fits, fainting spells, or full-fledged spirit possessions, the process of learning to serve the spirits is initiated when the spirits themselves choose and adopt the children who will become mediums and healer-priests. Having once made Marie-Carmel's life possible, the Vièj Mirak was continuing to bestow her grace on the family through this "reclaiming" spirit possession (McAlister 1992–93).

The fact that this important moment of spiritual contact came to pass at a Catholic church is not out of the ordinary in Haitian religious culture, nor is it uncommon for people to discreetly conceal such events. Catholics who also serve the spirits of Vodou have learned to practice a form of religious code-switching by performing one ritual practice through the codes of another when socially appropriate. One story is switched for another, and both become true. Language here reveals levels of intimacy: to respond to the concern of the priest, the family used English to report that Marie-Carmel fainted for lack of food. For insiders—family and others in Vodou societies—an interpretation emerged in French and then Creole that Marie-Carmel had been "touched," briefly, by the Virgin, and thus "reclaimed" by Ezili.

The deft and quick response of Marie-Carmel's mother to the priest comes out of a historical tradition of religious code-switching developed in Haiti in the face of dominant Catholic pressures. I have argued in this chapter that Vodou and Haitian Catholicism are at once opposed politically and intertwined historically, two religions on either end of a continuum of Haitian religious culture that contains within it multiple and shifting symbols and practices. Individual actors live their lives at various points on the continuum, here going through Catholic sacraments, and there making contact with the spirit world of the angels. It is possible to be a fully practicing Catholic who, through Catholicism, also receives the spiritual calls and blessings of the Vodou spirits. In church spaces, work for the spirits is switched into subtly coded Catholic ritual language.

The New York pilgrimage, I have argued, becomes the site for a second kind of code-switching, where Haitian actors respond to a new cultural politics of race. Haitians are assigned by the dominant society to the African American proximal host niche, yet they do not understand themselves to be African American. Haitian Americans' identities are in tension as the immigrant population struggles to define itself on its own terms. One tactic (among others) of the Haitian American community is to develop French-inflected identities, stressing their French and Creole language, French style of dress, and Roman Catholicism. By attending Roman Catholic churches, schools, and pilgrimages, Haitians broadcast their distinctive language, culture, and religion. Through this "strategy of alterity," Haitians broadcast cultural difference from African Americans and contest U.S. systems of racialization.

Roman Catholicism is, for Haitians, one ritual performance among others in a larger cultural repertoire. It is a religious "code" that in the United States can stand in public for all of Haitian religious culture, Vodou and Catholicism alike. Catholic churches are familiar spaces that host the saints intimately known to many Haitian Catholics. And whether one is praying to Ezili or to the Virgin Mary, stepping into a Catholic church is also stepping into a legitimate modern American identity. In a process quite similar to that undergone by the Italian American community before them, Haitians find an aspect of their public face in the church. Perhaps the Italian Americans who host the feast for the Blessed Mother at 115th Street recognize themselves in the new immigrants praying before them.

In this chapter I set out to illustrate that in order to understand religious life for some new immigrants, we must understand their continuing relationships with the religious cultures of their home countries. The Haitian diaspora represents an actively transnational population, embedded in social, political, and financial networks that span home and host countries. The Fèt Vièj Mirak on East 115th Street is a religious event whose meaning also spans New York and Haiti. But rather than substituting the New York feast for the one they left behind at Sodo, Haitians add the Harlem location as another possible site of spiritual work. In this way East 115th Street is opened up as one more site in the expanding "religioscape" of transnational Haitian religious culture. During the pilgrimage for Notre Dame du Mont Carmel in New York, the Haitian population reterritorializes spiritual practice, reinscribing sacred space onto their new landscape of settlement.

The pilgrimage to Mount Carmel in East Harlem expands the saint's influence in the Haitian world. Haitians in diaspora reach out to Mont Carmel and Ezili Dantò, both nationalist divinities, extending prayers for family and friends throughout the *djaspora* and in Haiti. By attending the feast by the thousands, the New York Haitian population has collectively placed the Church of Our Lady of Mount Carmel on an invisible community map. In stepping onto the public stage of the Catholic feast, they orient themselves within the shifting "ethnoscape" of New York City. They make sense of the confusing complexity of this ethnic landscape by locating the church as a center of spiritual power where they will be welcome.

Most Latin American countries have national shrines that use religion to connect tropes about the nation to other symbolisms about gender and sexuality.[24] Mexicans make pilgrimages to the shrine of Nuestra Señora de Guadalupe, Puerto Ricans to Nuestra Señora de la Monserrate,

Cubans to Nuestra Señora de Caridad del Cobre, Colombians to La Virgen de Las Lajas, Brazilians to Bom Jesus da Lapa, and Dominicans to Nuestra Señora de Altagracia del Higuey (Laguerre 1989, 83; Díaz-Stevens 1993, 47). When national populations spread through migration to new localities, they bring their divinities with them, re-territorializing their religious practices. The supernatural world assents, and comes to bear up communities in transition.

Notes

1. Before the Second Vatican Council of the 1960s, it was customary to fast until taking communion. While this particular family no longer observed that tradition, it did serve as an implicit, legitimating explanation for Marie-Carmel's fainting.
2. Although I speak Creole fluently, older Haitians often address me in French, as they might any non-Haitian, for French is more widely spoken worldwide and is also a marker of prestige. In Haitian Creole, foreigners are always called *blan*, implying "whiteness." An Anglo-American woman like me is a *fanm blan*, while an African American woman would be a *nègès blan*, a "black white/foreigner." In Creole, blackness is normative, hence the word for "man" is *nèg*, connoting "black man." A Haitian man is always a *nèg*, even if he is of European descent, in which case he is a *nèg blan*, a "white black man" or a *nèg milat*, a "mulatto black man." Much has been written on Haitian codes of racialization, which are different from those in both the United States and other parts of Latin America and the Caribbean (see Nicholls 1979, Dupuy 1989).
3. Robert Orsi (personal communication, New York, July 1992) notes that the last Italian religious supply shop closed in 1990.
4. The vast majority of Haitians are black people of African descent. There is also a small minority of *Ayisyen blanc*, or "European Haitians," *milat*, or "mulatto Haitians," and a tiny but economically significant sector of *Siryen*, a gloss for the Lebanese, Palestinian, Syrian, and Israeli diaspora merchant community in Port-au-Prince.
5. Only a few hundred other statues of the Virgin share this special shrine status worldwide, and of these the church at 115th Street was only the third in all the Americas. The two others were designated by the same pope. Our Lady of Perpetual Help in the Ursuline Convent in New Orleans was erected in 1727. Our Lady of Guadalupe, now in the Basilica in Mexico City, was erected on an Aztec site in 1532 (Orsi 1985, 60; Pistella 1954, 76–88).
6. Interview, Father Guy Sansariqc, head of the Haitian Apostolate, Brooklyn, June 1996.
7. Spiritual marriage to the spirits, or *lwa*, of Vodou is common in Haitian religious culture (see Brown 1991).
8. Tragedy can include forced deportation, for example. Increasingly the United States and weaker nations are collaborating in an institutionalized transnational policy whereby persons convicted of crimes are deported to their home country after serving their sentences in U.S. jails. This policy was made possible by Title 3 of the Illegal Immigration Reform and Immigrant Responsibility Act of 1996, and represents a new era in international relations.
9. Arjun Appadurai (1990, 6) writes of the disjoined flows that are set in motion with increased globalization: "ethnoscapes, mediascapes, technoscapes, financescapes and

ideoscapes." It is possible here to think of "religioscapes" as the subjective religious maps (and attendant theologies) of diasporic communities who are also in global flow and flux.

10. Important religious sites dot the New York landscape, and include intersections where offerings can be made to Papa Legba, *lwa* of the crossroads; public parks where trees and rocks are used for their spiritual power; cemeteries where the recently dead can be honored; and churches housing the saints, where Creole Mass is spoken. Other pilgrimages are also mapped onto the metropolitan area as well: for example, thousands of Haitians take chartered buses to the Church of Czestochowa in Pennsylvania for the Feast of the Assumption. For a treatment of sacred urban landscape in Afro-Cuban tradition, see David Hilary Brown (1989, 353–357).

11. See, for example, Carole Devillers (1985) and the Winter 1992 issue of *Aperture* (vol. 126) that focused on Haiti.

12. He was subsequently crowned emperor of the Haitian Republic and the de facto head of its Roman Catholic church (see n. 18 below). Sodo is still a site of political manipulations. During the period after the fall of Jean-Claude Duvalier, the ruling junta members built cinder-block vacation houses among the wooden and straw houses right next to the falls in order to maintain a visible public presence at the site.

13. For the only ethnographic work to date on Rastafari in New York City, see the essay by Randal L. Hepner in *Gatherings in Diaspora*, ed. R. Stephen Warner and Judith G. Wittner (Philadelphia: Temple University Press), chap. 6.

14. Another spot, called Fey Sen Jan, was the site of a ritual the night before the Mont Carmel feast in Ville Bonheur, but it has virtually disappeared (Laguerre 1989, 84; interview with Manbo Gislene, New York City, July 1994).

15. In French her name was written "Erzulie Dantor," and it appears that way often in Vodou flags, songs, and other works of art, as well as in priests' notebooks and other sacred writings. The etymological history of her name merits future research.

16. Throughout Haitian history, the Catholic church has launched waves of repression against Vodou practitioners in "anti-superstition campaigns" (see Desmangles 1992).

17. This understanding applies to religion the theories on Creole linguistics worked out by Lee Drummond (1980).

18. Although the history is too lengthy to elaborate here, it is important to note that with Haitian Independence in 1804, ties were officially cut to the Vatican, and a Catholicism in Haiti evolved with its own national flavor. In 1860 a concordat was signed reopening the relationship with Rome. By that time, Afro-Haitian spirituality had established itself as the worldview of the vast majority of Haitians.

19. Although Haiti has historically been a Catholic country, evangelical Protestantism is now enjoying enormous success. On the Haitian American membership in the Southern Baptist Convention, see Carolle Charles (1990, 262–280).

20. Interview, Father Guy Sansariqc, Brooklyn, June 1996.

21. In the three devastating years after the coup d'état against Aristide, the Haitian military run by General Raoul Cedras embarked on a terrorist campaign of rape unprecedented in Haitian history. Many people who fled the country by sea ended up in the U.S. naval base in Cuba, Guantánamo, to be further traumatized by human rights abuses there (see Americas Watch et al. 1991).

22. Haitians also tend to send their children to Catholic schools in relatively high numbers (see Lawrence 1997).

23. In his ethnography *In Search of Respect: Selling Crack in El Barrio*, Philippe Bourgois (1995, 48–76) chronicles the largely Puerto Rican–controlled drug trade that ravaged the neighborhood around the Church of Our Lady in the 1980s. He argues that this area of Manhattan has long been a site of "crime, violence and substance abuse," from the early Dutch tobacco farms to the heroin and cocaine trades of Italian crime families to the Latino crack dealers. While it is dangerous to attempt to describe drug-dealing networks because of the potential for stereotyping, it is important to be conscious of the realities of both legal and extralegal economic spheres and subcultures and their influence on wider communities.

24. See Andrew Parker et al. (1992).

References

Americas Watch, Physicians for Human Rights, and National Coalition for Haitian Refugees. 1991. *Return to the Darkest Days: Human Rights in Haiti Since the Coup.* New York: Americas Watch.

Aperture. 1992. 126 (Winter): 40–47.

Appadurai, Arjun. 1990. "Disjuncture and Difference in the Global Cultural Economy." *Public Culture* 2 (2): 1–24.

Basch, Linda, Nina Glick-Schiller, and Cristina Szanton Blanc. 1994. *Nations Unbound: Transnational Projects, Postcolonial Predicaments, and Deterritorialized Nation-States.* Langhorne, Pa.: Gordon and Breach.

Bastide, Roger. 1960. *The African Religions of Brazil: Towards a Sociology of the Interpenetration of Civilizations.* Baltimore: Johns Hopkins University Press.

Bourgois, Philippe. 1995. *In Search of Respect: Selling Crack in El Barrio.* New York and Cambridge: Cambridge University Press.

Brown, David Hilary. 1989. "Garden in the Machine: Afro-Cuban Sacred Art and Performance in New Jersey and New York." Ph.D. dissertation, Yale University.

Brown, Karen McCarthy. 1991. *Mama Lola: A Vodou Priestess in Brooklyn.* Berkeley: University of California Press.

Buchanan, Susan. 1980. "Scattered Seeds: The Meaning of the Migration for Haitians in New York City." Ph.D. dissertation, New York University.

Cabon, Adolphe. 1933. *Notes sur l'Histoire Religieuse d'Haiti: De la Révolution au Concordad (1789–1860).* Port-au-Prince: Petit Seminaire College Saint-Martial.

Charles, Carolle. 1990. "Distinct Meanings of Blackness: Haitian Migrants in New York City." *Cimarron* 2 (3): 129–138.

———. 1991. "A Transnational Dialectic of Race, Class, and Ethnicity: Patterns of Identities and Forms of Consciousness Among Haitian Migrants in New York City." Ph.D. dissertation, SUNY Binghamton.

Clifford, James. 1994. "Diasporas." *Cultural Anthropology* 9 (3): 302–338.

Davis, Nathalie Z. 1982. "From 'Popular Religion' to Religious Cultures." Pp. 312–343 in *Reformation Europe: A Guide to Research*, edited by Steven Ozment. St. Louis: Center for Reformation Research.

Desmangles, Leslie G. 1992. *The Faces of the Gods: Vodou and Roman Catholicism in Haiti.* Chapel Hill: University of North Carolina Press.

Devillers, Carole. 1985. "Haiti's Voodoo Pilgrimages of Spirits and Saints." *National Geographic* 167 (March): 394–408.

Díaz-Stevens, Ana-María. 1993. *Oxcart Catholicism on Fifth Avenue: The Impact of the Puerto Rican Migration upon the Archdiocese of New York.* Notre Dame, Ind.: University of Notre Dame Press.

Dolan, Jay. 1985. *The American Catholic Experience: A History from Colonial Times to the Present.* New York: Doubleday and Company.

Drummond, Lee. 1980. "The Cultural Continuum: A Theory of Intersystems." *Man* 15: 352–374.

Dupuy, Alex. 1989. *Haiti in the World Economy: Class, Race, and Underdevelopment Since 1700.* Boulder, Colo.: Westview Press.

Gallardo, Susana. 1994. Proposal to the New Ethnic and Immigrant Congregations Project. Unpublished manuscript, Stanford University.

Glick-Schiller, Nina. 1975. "The Formation of an Haitian Ethnic Group." Ph.D. dissertation, Columbia University.

Hall, Stuart, ed. 1978. *Policing the Crisis: Mugging, the State, and Law and Order.* New York: Holmes and Meier.

Handlin, Oscar. 1951. *The Uprooted.* New York: Grosset and Dunlap.

Herskovits, Melville. 1941. *The Myth of the Negro Past.* Boston: Beacon, 1958.

hooks, bell. 1989. "Critical Interrogation: Talking Race, Resisting Racism." *Inscriptions* 5: 159–164.

Jolibois, Gerard. 1970. "Notre Principal Pelerinage Marial." *Le Nouveau Monde,* no. 1299, July 30.

Laguerre, Michel. 1989. *Voodoo and Politics in Haiti.* New York: St. Martin's Press.

Laurino, Maria. 1995. "Sharing a Saint: The Two Worlds of Our Lady of Mount Carmel." *New York Times,* July 23, sect. 13, p. 5, col. 3.

Lawrence, Stewart. 1997. "U.S. Immigrants in the Catholic Schools: A Preliminary Assessment." Unpublished paper, Catholic University of America, Washington, D.C.

Levitt, Peggy. 1998. "Local-Level Global Religion: The Case of U.S-Dominican Migration." *Journal for the Scientific Study of Religion.*

McAlister, Elizabeth. 1992–93. "Sacred Stories from the Haitian Diaspora: A Collective Biography of Seven Vodou Priestesses in New York City." *Journal of Caribbean Studies,* 9 (1–2, Winter 1992–Spring 1993): 10–27.

———. 1995a. "'Men Moun Yo; Here Are the People: Rara Festivals and Transnational Popular Culture in New York City." Ph.D. dissertation, Yale University.

———. 1995b. "A Sorcerer's Bottle: The Art of Magic in Haiti." Pp. 304–321 in *The Sacred Arts of Haitian Vodou,* edited by Donald J. Cosentino. Los Angeles: Fowler Museum of Cultural History.

McGreevy, John. 1996. *Parish Boundaries: The Catholic Encounter with Race in the Twentieth-Century Urban North.* Chicago: University of Chicago Press.

Mittelberg, David, and Mary C. Waters. 1992. "The Process of Ethnogenesis Among Haitian and Israeli Immigrants in the United States." *Ethnic and Racial Studies* 15 (3): 412–435.

Murphy, Joseph. 1988. *Santeria: An African Religion in America.* Boston: Beacon Press.

Nash, June. 1983. "The Impact of the Changing International Division of Labor on Different Sectors of the Labor Force." Pp. 3–69. In *Women, Men, and the International Division of Labor,* edited by June Nash and Patricia Fernandez-Kelly. Albany: SUNY Press.

Nicholls, David. 1979. *From Dessalines to Duvalier: Race, Color, and National Independence in Haiti.* New York: Cambridge University Press.

Orsi, Robert Anthony. 1985. *The Madonna of 115th Street: Faith and Community in Italian Harlem, 1880–1950*. New Haven: Yale University Press.

———. 1992. "The Religious Boundaries of an Inbetween People: Street Feste and the Problem of the Dark-Skinned Other in Italian Harlem, 1920–1990." *American Quarterly* 44 (3): 313–341.

Parker, Andrew, Mary Russo, Doris Sommer, and Patricia Yaeger, eds. 1992. *Nationalisms and Sexualities*. New York: Routledge.

Pistella, Domenico. 1954. *The Crowning of a Queen*, translated by Peter Rofrano. New York: Shrine of Our Lady of Mount Carmel.

Price-Mars, Jean. 1983. *So Spoke the Uncle*, translated by Magdaline W. Shannon. Originally published 1928. Washington, D.C.: Three Continents Press.

Rouzier, Sémexan. 1891. *Dictionnaire Géographique d'Haiti*. Paris: Charles Blot.

Sassen-Koob, Saskia. 1982. "Recomposition and Peripherialization at the Core." *Contemporary Marxism* 5: 88–100.

Stewart, Charles, and Rosalind Shaw. 1994. *Syncretism/Anti-Syncretism: The Politics of Religious Synthesis*. New York: Routledge.

Tweed, Thomas A. 1997. *Our Lady of the Exile: Diasporic Religion at a Cuban Catholic Shrine in Miami*. New York and Oxford: Oxford University Press.

Wallerstein, Emmanuel. 1974. *The Modern World System*. New York: Academic Press.

Wilcken, Lois. 1991. "Music, Folklore, and Haitians in New York: Stage Representations and the Negotiation of Identity." Ph.D. dissertation, Columbia University.

Chapter 41

Rethinking Vernacular Culture

Black Religion and Race Records in the 1920s and 1930s

Evelyn Brooks Higginbotham

If black religious culture in its varied beliefs and practices has fostered bright and shining stars such as Martin Luther King, Jr., Malcolm X, Marian Anderson, Aretha Franklin, Jesse Jackson, and Cornel West, then as this list of names suggests, black religious culture has played a signifi-cant role in the contestation of ideologies in African-American commu-nities. This contestation occurs between the middle class and working class, and it also occurs within the working class itself. Unfortunately, the trend in recent scholarship has not given the religious culture of the work-ing class the attention it deserves. Some of the most imaginative and ana-lytically sophisticated studies tend to privilege the secular life of black working-class communities. Such studies often draw upon the "race records" of the 1920s and 1930s, linking blues records with socioeco-nomic processes of migration and urbanization. They focus on the lyrics of the blues and the lives of blues singers as emblematic of sexual freedom, iconoclastic values, and an overall culture of resistance to the hegemony of middle-class ideology.[1] Implicitly, if not explicitly, the blues is deemed the "authentic" signifier of African-American culture.[2] Blues culture, working-class culture, and "blackness" become virtually synonymous. The religious culture of the working poor, when visible at all, appears as an anomaly or false consciousness. The blues and church are thus coun-terposed as cultural icons of class division. Perhaps this representation of working-class religion stems from the belief that African-American Christianity is white-derived, middle-class in orientation, and thus less authentically black. Or conversely, perhaps religion among the poor is not taken seriously because it is perceived as otherworldly, lower-class

978

escapism, having no ideological implications and playing no strategic role in struggles over moral and cultural authority.

The race records of the 1920s and 1930s are useful for analysis, since they included not only the blues but also the explicitly religious articulations of the black working class.[3] Companies such as Okeh, Victor, Vocalion, and Paramount recorded vernacular discourses of religion in the form of sermons and gospel music, called gospel blues, as eagerly as they recorded the raunchiest blues lyrics.[4] The religious records tapped into the cultural repertoire of storefront Baptist churches and the rising numbers of Holiness and Pentecostal churches in urban ghettos. Langston Hughes recalled his impressions of the Holiness churches in Chicago around the time of World War I: "I was entranced by their stepped-up rhythms, tambourines, hand clapping, and uninhibited dynamics, rivaled only by Ma Rainey singing the blues at the old Monogram Theater."[5] Just as Hughes had juxtaposed the songs of the church with the blues, this odd coupling of the sacred and profane appeared regularly in newspaper advertisements for race records. Paramount Records informed the readers of the *Chicago Defender* that they could "get these Red-Hot Blues and Inspiring Spirituals" through mail order. Okeh included in a single advertisement blues singer Lonnie Johnson and gospel singer Jessie May Hill. Featuring Johnson's "Mean Old Bed Bug Blues," the advertisement read: "Bedbugs big as a jackass bite you and stand and grin. Then drink a bottle of bed bug poison and come and bite you again. The Hottest Blues You Ever Heard." Yet the same advertisement listed "Sister Jessie May Hill and Sisters of the Congregation singing 'Earth Is No Resting Place.'"[6]

If, as some scholars suggest, advertising's juxtaposition of religious and blues records served as an affront to the pious, the coupling nonetheless offers an analytical rubric for disentangling the working class from its exclusive identification with blues culture. Clearly, the church was just as indigenous to the working poor as was the blues. On one level the popularity of the sermons and gospel songs speaks to an emotional folk orality that contested the ethics and aesthetics of the black middle class. Not through the counterculture of the blues, but rather through vernacular discourses of religion, the black poor waged a struggle over cultural authority that ultimately subverted the hegemonic values and aesthetic standards of the traditional Protestantism of the black middle class. On another level the religious race records speak to the existence of multiple and conflicting subcultures within the black working class, indicating differences of consciousness, values, and lifestyle even among the most poor. The religious culture of the poor, as evidenced in the Pentecostal and Holiness churches, for example, embraced a strict moral code that denounced the fast and free lifestyle of blues culture.[7] In the dialect, imagery, and rhythms of the black poor, the religious race records repudiate sexual freedom, gambling, drinking, womanizing, and general defiance of the law. Nina Simone reminisced about her working-class family: "Mama and them were so religious that they wouldn't allow you to play boogie-woogie in the house, but would allow you to use the same boogie-woogie beat to play a gospel tune."[8]

The religious race records of the 1920s gave a new public dimension to black religion and especially to the working-class churches. The records validated the creative energies of the rural folk, turned urban proletariat, as an alternate, competing voice within African-American communities. At the most prosaic levels, the ascendant voice of southern folk culture challenged the middle-class ideology of racial uplift as pronounced by educated religious leaders of the late nineteenth century. The latter group had defined racial progress not merely in the context of black-white relations but also in the context of a class-based contestation over group beliefs and practices. Educated religious leaders emphasized written texts and rational discourses in the struggle for the advancement of their people.[9] These religious leaders articulated sentiments similar to W.E.B. Du Bois's viewpoint that the black colleges brought African Americans "in contact with modern civilization."[10] Commitment to collegiate education figured prominently in their belief in an intellectual and professional vanguard—the Talented Tenth as Du Bois characterized the black elite at the turn of the century.

As time and schooling distanced African Americans further and further from their slave past, many became self-conscious, conflicted, even critical of the culture of their forebears. From gentle persuasion to ridicule and punishment, white and black missionary teachers sought the demise of the older forms of singing and worship. In 1870, Elizabeth Kilham, a white northern teacher among the freedman, acknowledged the impact of education on the younger generation:

> The distinctive features of negro hymnology are gradually disappearing, and with another generation will probably be obliterated entirely. The cause for this lies in the education of the younger people. . . . Already they have learned to ridicule the extravagant preaching, the meaningless hymns, and the noisy singing of their elders.

Not perhaps as yet, to any great extent in the country; changes come always more slowly there, but in the cities, the young people have, in many cases, taken the matter into their own hands, formed choirs, adopted the hymns and tunes in use in the white churches. . . .[11]

It is interesting that Kilham, while praising the shift to white hymns, conceded the slowness with which blacks in the countryside assimilated. Bishop Daniel Alexander Payne of the African Methodist Episcopal Church recalled his frustrating experience in a rural church in South Carolina:

After the sermon they formed a ring, and with coats off sung, clapped their hands and stamped their feet in a most ridiculous and heathenish way. I requested the pastor to go and stop their dancing. At his request they stopped their dancing and clapping of hands, but remained singing and rocking their bodies to and fro. This they did for about fifteen minutes. I then went, and taking their leader by the arm requested him to desist and to sit down and sing in a *rational* manner. I told him also that it was a heathenish way to worship and disgraceful to themselves, the race, and the Christian name.[12] (my emphasis)

Payne's plea for a "rational manner" of singing formed part of the larger assimilationist project of ridding the black community of sensuality, intemperance, "superstition," and the emotional style of worship practiced in the hush harbors of the slave era. His emphasis on a calm, intellectually oriented religious expression signaled the growing class and cultural differences that would surface prominently as rural southern migrants poured into the northern cities. For Bishop Payne, loud and emotive behavior constituted more than an individual's impropriety or doctrinal error. It marked the retrogression of the entire racial group. In the midst of heightened racial discrimination and social Darwinist thought, educated leaders decried the moaning and bodily movements of black worship.[13] Educated African Americans such as James Trotter posited that vocal and instrumental music in the form of the "noble organ . . . sacred chant, the prayer or thanksgiving, uttered in melodious song by the choir or by all the congregation" served as an antidote to "the cares and wild passions" of the world. For Trotter music functioned as a civilizing force, a "source of refinement and pleasure . . . to the possessor himself, and by which he may add to the tranquility, the joys, of his own and the home life of his neighbors and friends."[14]

Literacy and published texts came to be linked increasingly to the expression of religious culture. The Reverend Sutton Griggs, a college-educated Baptist minister and novelist, typified the black middle class in its preference for print discourse, thus implicitly devaluing the interpretative authority of illiterate leaders. He proclaimed, "To succeed as a race, we must move up out of the age of the voice. . . ."[15] Educated leaders perceived the medium of print as a source of communication and power. They made continual appeals for the publication of texts that would present the African-American side of history and instill pride in their people. They commonly used the term "distinctive literature," referring to any text that was written and/or published by African Americans.[16] Yet the phenomenal rise in literacy among African Americans in the decades after the Civil War occurred with unsettling consequences for traditions of black worship. Calling attention to the clash between literate and oral traditions in the postbellum South, Elsa Barkley Brown describes the conflict surrounding the introduction of printed songbooks in the First African Baptist Church in Richmond. The adoption of hymnals superseded the older practice of "lining out hymns," a practice increasingly labeled "unrefined" and a vestige of slave culture by educated blacks and whites. Lining out had not required literacy, but only an able song leader to introduce each verse of song, which in turn was followed by the congregation's repetition of the verse. The introduction of hymnals, however, disadvantaged the illiterate, since it reconfigured the collective voice to include the literate only. For the illiterate, asserts Elsa Barkley Brown, "it was the equivalent of being deprived of a voice, all the more significant in an oral culture."[17] Efforts to supplant the oral culture by a literate one were depicted by the black poet Daniel Webster Davis in the 1890s. In "De Linin' ub de Hymns," Davis employs dialect in order to voice the critique of uneducated African Americans against the cultural transformations taking place:

> Dar's a mighty row in Zion, an' de debbil's gettin' high,
> . . . .
> 'Twuz 'bout a bery leetle thing—de linin' ub a hymn.
> De Young folks say 'tain't stylish to lin' um out no mo';
> Dat dey's got edikashun, an' dey wants us all to know
> Dey likes to hab dar singin'-books a-holin' fore dar eyes,
> An' sing de hymns right straight along 'to manshuns in de skies.'
> . . . .
> An' ef de ol' folks will kumplain 'cause dey is ol' an' blind,

An' slabry's chain don' kep' dem back frum larnin' how to read—
Dat dey mus' take a corner seat, an' let de young folks lead.
. . . .
De ol'-time groans an' shouts an' moans am passin' out ub sight—
Edikashun changed all dat, an' we belebe it right,
We should serb God wid 'telligence; fur dis one thing I plead:
Jes' lebe a leetle place in church fur dem ez kin not read.[18]

An entire genre of race literature arose in the late nineteenth century for the purpose of "uplifting" the black masses culturally, politically, and economically. The rise of literacy had been foundational to the evolution of a black reading public, and it was this very readership that constituted the race market so crucial to the success of church-based entrepreneurship. Many local religious presses as well as the large denominational ones (the A.M.E. Book Concern, the A.M.E. Sunday School Union Press, the A.M.E. Zion Book Concern, the A.M.E. Zion Publication House, the National Baptist Publishing Board, and the Sunday School Publishing Board of the National Baptist Convention, U.S.A., Inc.) figured significantly in the production of hymnals, church literature, newspapers, and to a lesser extent works of fiction. For example, the earliest novels of Frances Ellen Watkins Harper appeared in syndicated form in the *Christian Recorder* of the A.M.E. Church.[19] Literature produced by African Americans strove to negate the pejorative racial images prevalent in film, media, art and scholarly and popular books. Photographs in black-owned periodicals often depicted middle-class men and women in the act of reading. Captions to such photographs made reference to the cultivation of the "higher arts" and sought to convey images of refinement and civility, material comfort and respectability. The conflation of musical taste and literature culture is apparent in the 1904 issue of the *Voice of the Negro*, which featured a photographic series of "representative" black men and women. A caption to a photograph of a young black woman read: "An admirer of Fine Art, a performer on the violin and the piano, a sweet singer, a writer—mostly given to essays, a lover of good books, and a home making girl."[20]

It is no small irony, then, that the newly urbanized southern folk ushered in the "age of the voice" at the height of the renaissance of the black literati.[21] During the 1920s and 1930s the black working class effected the shift to an emotional folk orality that challenged the cultural authority of the black middle class. The migrants built storefront churches, established sects and cults, and "infiltrated" and transformed many of the "old-line" Baptist and Methodist churches with the gospel blues, a twentieth-century musical innovation with roots in the slave past. Historian Lawrence Levine conveys this blend of old and new in the religious culture of the migrants:

> While many churches within the black community sought respectability by turning their backs on the past, banning the shout, discouraging enthusiastic religion, and adopting more sedate hymns and refined concertized versions of the spirituals, the Holiness churches constituted a revitalization movement with their emphasis upon healing, gifts of prophecy, speaking in tongues, spirit possession, and religious dance. Musically, they reached back to the traditions of the slave past and out to the rhythms of the secular black musical world around them. They brought into the church not only the sounds of ragtime, blues and jazz but also the instruments.[22]

The public emergence of a folk orality can be attributed to both the massive migration of southern blacks to northern cities and to a triumphant American commercialism, which during the 1920s turned its gaze upon black consumers. Through advertising, department stores, catalog shopping, and installment buying, the new commercial culture made its impact on the Great Migration. The recently arrived migrants soon became a consuming public, hungry for their own musical styles and for an array of products with a racial appeal.[23] They swelled the ranks of the race market and reconfigured black supply and demand well beyond the small entrepreneur and communities of readership at the turn of the century. Historian Jackson Lears describes the commercial culture of America in the 1920s as quite different from the past: "the older culture was suited to a production-oriented society of small entrepreneurs; the new culture epitomized a consumption-oriented society dominated by bureaucratic corporations."[24]

Race-consciousness, creative expression, and the black church itself became implicated in America's growing corporate capitalism. Nowhere is this more evident than in the nexus between working-class religion and the record industry. The record industry tapped into the cultural repertoire of the black working-class churches, drawing upon and promoting the very folk traditions that the middle class had sought to eradicate. While the commodification of black religious culture and the attendant reality of white-controlled profits speak to the problematic aspects of the race records industry,[25] it cannot be denied that this commodification was made possible by the matrix of exchange inherent in the black working-class church.

The church was and is at once the producer of musicians and music forms as well as a consumer market with changing tastes. Technological advancement and the consequent rise of the record and broadcast industries, along with mass advertising in the national black press, e.g., the *Chicago Defender*, all worked together to effect the commodification of the religious experience. This process of religious commodification calls to mind philosopher Kwame Anthony Appiah's analysis of modernity in regard to Max Weber's characterization of charismatic versus rational authority.

> What we can see . . . is not the triumph of Enlightenment capital-R Reason—which would have entailed exactly the end of charisma and the universalization of the secular—not even the penetration of a narrower instrumental reason into all spheres of life, but what Weber mistook for that: namely, the incorporation of all areas of the world and all areas of even formerly "private" life into the money economy. Modernity has turned every element of the real into a sign, and the sign reads "for sale"; this is true even in domains like religion. . . .[26]

If African-American religion succumbed to the commercialism and consumerism of the 1920s, it did so while harnessing new venues for working-class cultural production. A new public voice, indeed a charismatic authority, rivaled the authority of the educated black leadership. The nineteenth century had witnessed the ascendancy of the middle class as the literate public voice of the race. The twentieth century witnessed the ascendancy of the black working class as the oral narrator of modernity.[27] Growing working-class consumerism, coupled with black middle-class disdain for the cultural styles of the poor, had initiated this important shift to working-class orality within the black public sphere. Even the Reverend Sutton Griggs, who had earlier admonished his people to "move up out of the age of the voice," recorded sermons on the Victor label during the 1920s.[28] However, the rise of race records should not imply a false dichotomy between reading and oral/aural constituencies. More often than not, the two constituencies were one and the same, since record consumers looked primarily to black newspapers for the advertisement of new record releases and for coverage on the personal lives and public appearances of recording stars.

Blues scholar Paul Oliver notes that religious records enjoyed a popularity equal to that of the blues, and possibly greater.[29] Produced in three-minute and six-minute sound bites, these records attempt to re-create the black worship experience, presenting highly emotional preaching, moaning, ecstatic audience response, vocal and instrumental accompaniment. Oliver recounts their unrestrained quality: "The preacher develops his subject, often speaking in a direct address at first and moving to a singing tone as he warms to his theme . . . . Urged on by the murmurs, cries, shouts of approval and encouragement from the congregation, he might struggle for the right words, 'straining' with constricted throat . . . 'moaning,' 'mourning,' 'whooping.'"[30]

Building on patterns from the folk tradition and thus rejecting a rational, dispassionate style, the recorded sermons and religious songs were especially appealing to the waves of rural migrants who poured into northern cities, uprooted and in search of cultural continuity.[31] Record companies catered to the migrants' preference for a "down-home," i.e., more rural, southern style by adopting such phrases as "old-fashioned," "real Southern style" and "old-time" in their record titles and advertisements. Paramount proudly announced its "latest new electric method" of record production in its advertisement for *Old Time Baptism* by the Reverend P. M. Massey. Okeh Records invoked similar images of an immediate and authentic black religious experience in its advertisement of two sermons by the Reverend F. W. McGee and his congregation: "They make you feel as if you're right in the church. You hear it all just as it actually happens. The preacher's burning words . . . spontaneous shouts from the congregation . . . and the low-pitched hum of musical instruments."[32] Musical accompaniment in recorded sermons often included the moaning sounds of women in the background, a boogie-woogie piano or the sounds of cornet, guitar and drums. The sermons met with instant success. The Reverend J. C. Burnett's sermon, the *Downfall of Nebuchadnezzar*, sold eighty thousand records within months of its release in November 1926. Interestingly, the sermon begins in the tradition of the slaves with the lining out of the hymn *I Heard the Voice of Jesus Say*.[33] The sale of Burnett's record quadrupled the normal sale of a Bessie Smith record. By the end of the 1930s, the number of black preachers, male and female, on record had soared from six to seventy, while more than 750 sermons had been recorded.[34]

Also popular during the 1920s and early 1930s were the religious records of male and female singers, especially those identified with the storefront Baptist, Holiness, and Pentecostal churches. The strictly musical records outlived the sermons in their appeal to consumers.[35] Arizona Dranes, the blind vocalist, who sang for Okeh Records, played in a piano style reminiscent of ragtime and boogie-woogie as she rendered the songs of black Pentecostalism to record consumers across the nation. The records of Sanctified singers (Paul Oliver's term for female singers in the Pentecostal and Holiness churches) such as Jessie May Hill, Leora Ross, Bessie Johnson, Melinda Taylor, and Rosetta Tharpe with her gospel hybridization of jazz and swing, were widely distributed in black communities.[36] Sanctified singers did not limit themselves to the piano, but employed secular accompaniment—guitars, jug bands, and tambourines. Oliver notes that blues singers even cut religious records, after record promoters convinced them of the lucrative nature of the religious market. Classic blues queens, such as Bessie Smith, Sara Martin, Clara Smith, and Leola Manning claimed at least one sacred song in their repertoire of otherwise secular recordings.[37]

The standard hymn, with its implicit connotations of order and respectability, yielded ineluctably to improvisation and earthy rhythms. The capitulation of middle-class notions of assimilation and respectability to the new "gospel blues" occurred most glaringly in the black Baptist church.[38] This shifting emphasis is epitomized by the musical styles of Marian Anderson and Mahalia Jackson, both of whose musical talents were discovered and nurtured in the church. During the first two decades of the twentieth century, the talents of the future opera star Marian Anderson grew to maturity under the influence of the musical traditions of Philadelphia's Union Baptist Church. By age thirteen she was promoted to the adult choir, having sung in the junior choir since she was six. Her sense of music and its cultural meaning was informed by traditional hymnody and orchestral performances. Black hymnody in this setting is reminiscent of Houston Baker's discussion of the "mastery of form." Baker identifies such mastery as a strategy efficaciously adopted in the name of group advancement, but clearly based upon the acknowledgment of an appeal to white America's hegemonic cultural styles and values, i.e., the nation's *standards*.[39] The church's annual concerts frequently engaged tenor Roland Hayes who "sang old Italian airs, German Lieder, and French songs exquisitely." Anderson recalls in her autobiography that "even people with little understanding of music knew it was beautiful singing, and they were proud Mr. Hayes was one of their own and world famous."[40]

Mahalia Jackson's talents were cultivated in the musical traditions of the southern black church. She began her singing career in New Orleans, the birthplace of jazz. She performed in an up-tempo rhythm expressive of what Michael W. Harris terms "indigenous black religious song in a down-home manner."[41] Her singing group, while popular in the South, met with initial disfavor after she migrated to Chicago in 1927 at the age of sixteen. In his study of the rise of gospel blues, Harris notes that

Jackson was once thrown out of a church—the minister shouting, "Get that twisting and jazz out of the church."[42] Similar views are expressed in the poem "When Mahalia Sings" by Quandra Prettyman. Although the poem tells of Prettyman's eventual respect for the emotional religiosity of the working poor, the excerpt below emphasizes her initial mockery of the "holiness rhythms" of the storefront churches:

> We used to gather at the high window
> of the holiness church and, on tip-toe
> look in and laugh at the dresses, too small
> on the ladies, and how wretched they all
> looked—an old garage for a church, for pews,
> old wooden chairs. It seemed a lame excuse
> for a church. Not solemn or grand,
> with no real robed choir, but a loose jazz band,
> or so it sounded to our mocking ears.
> So we responded to their hymns with jeers.[43]

Mahalia Jackson's gospel blues appealed greatly to the swelling numbers of poor, Deep South migrants to Chicago. Jackson gave new voice to an old spirituality as she regularly performed at storefront churches. By 1932 she was receiving invitations from the established, old-line churches and would soon sing at the annual meetings of the National Baptist Convention.[44] The gospel blues had subverted the central, if not hegemonic position of standard hymnody even in these churches. Far less concerned about the gaze of white America in the projection of an African-American image, the gospel blues evoked the call and response of blacks themselves.

Nor did church leaders continue to link inextricably racial progress with their congregants' mastery of Western expressivity and styles of decorum. At issue here is more than the contestation between middle-class and working-class cultures; it is rather the interpenetration of the two. While both Marian Anderson and Mahalia Jackson enjoyed enormous fame throughout their lives, the musical repertoire of urban black Baptist churches came increasingly to identify (although not without contestation) the old-line voice with European hymns, while associating the modern with the more spontaneous, emotive style of down-home religious culture.[45] The transition of black church discourses symbolized the responsive soundings of a people in transition from an old to a new order. The commodification of black religious culture roared along with the 1920s as a marker of the decade's preoccupation with the black vernacular.[46]

Yet the contestation of cultures occurred not merely between the working class and the middle class. Division and dispute occurred within the working class itself. While the musical form of gospel blues incorporated the rhythmic patterns and sounds of secular blues, ragtime, and jazz, the lyrical content of gospel blues was embedded in institutions and belief structures that repudiated secular blues themes. Enjoying a prominence that was not confined to a particular congregation or region, men such as the Reverends E. D. Campbell, A. W. Nix, J. M. Gates and women such as the Reverends Leora Ross and Mary Nelson brought messages of doom and salvation to African Americans throughout the nation. Through recorded sermons and songs they drew upon biblical passages in their denunciation of crime, liquor, dancing, women's fashions, gambling, and fast living in general.[47] In *Better Get Ready for Judgement* the Reverend Mary Nelson sings in a strong a capella voice, condemning the hypocrites, drunkards, liars, and adulterers.[48] The recordings constituted vernacular discourses of religion, calling attention to the conditions of ghetto life in the everyday language of the poor and uneducated.

The railroad train figures prominently in the religious race records, just as it does in the blues. In discussing the blues, literary scholars Houston Baker and Hazel Carby point to the train's varied meanings of freedom and loneliness for male and female migrants.[49] However, in the religious race records, the train symbolizes a vehicle of judgment—an image altogether different from its metaphorical usage in the secular blues. For example, the Reverend J. M. Gates's sermon, *Death's Black Train Is Coming*, portrays the train as an instrument of retribution for fast living. The most popular use of the train motif was Reverend A. W. Nix's *Black Diamond Express to Hell*.[50] The Vocalion advertisement announced: "Here she comes! The 'Black Diamond Express to Hell' with Sin, the Engineer, holding the throttle wide open; Pleasure is the Headlight, and the Devil is the Conductor. You can feel the roaring of the Express and the moanin' of the Drunkards, Liars, Gamblers and other folk who have got aboard. They are hell-bound and they don't want to go. The train makes eleven stops but nobody can get off." The route of the train included stops at "Liars's Ave., Dance Hall Depot, and Stealing Town."[51]

Themes of justice to the wicked and proud abound in the recorded sermons. Against the background of moaning voices and cries of amen, Reverend Burnett began his blockbuster hit, the *Downfall of Nebuchadnezzar*, by prophesying the inevitable ruin of people who hold themselves in high estimation and manipulate the weak. Burnett's message serves as a promise to the oppressed: God will bring down the liars, backsliders, and rich men.[52] A similar theme can be found in Reverend J. M. Gates's record, *Samson and the Woman*. Despite the title, the sermon focuses not on gender but on class and race relations. Gates, like Burnett, targets those people who think that their positions of strength, privilege, and power over others will last forever. Those on top will be leveled in time, he proclaims repeatedly in the sermon.[53] Gates was one of the most popular of the recorded preachers, holding contracts with five different record companies during the 1920s. Titles of his recorded sermons reveal concern about rising crime, e.g., *The First Born Was a Murderer, Did You Spend Christmas in Jail?, Death Might Be Your Santa Claus, No Room in the Jail-house*, and *Dying Gambler*. Whether sung or preached, the religious race records condemned the growing disorder, alienation, and criminal elements in the urban setting, but they did so in the common, everyday language of the black working class.[54] The vernacular discourses of religion constituted a moral idiom for distinguishing the personal and collective identity of the "righteous" from other working-class identities (e.g., blues people). The messages in the recorded sermons and songs articulated shared meanings and constraints for evaluating and interpreting social reality. They sought to establish boundaries around the lives of the black poor in the effort to shield them from dangers that were perceived as emanating from both outside and inside their own communities.

At issue here are not only conflicting value systems but internally generated norms. This latter point is often overlooked by scholars who too readily attribute efforts to restore "moral order" to the intentionality, ideology, and disciplinary mechanisms of the middle class. The middle class certainly played a role in disciplining the poor and in policing black women's bodies, as Hazel Carby perceptively discusses, but so, too, did Pentecostal churches.[55] Nor were notions of "moral panic" situated solely within a 1920s bourgeois ideology. The quest for moral order is replete in the sermons, gospel songs, and religious institutions of the working class. The storefront Baptist, Pentecostal, and Holiness churches along with a variety of urban sects and cults, e.g., Father Divine's Peace Mission movement and Daddy Grace's United House of Prayer, were doubtless more effective than middle-class reformers in policing the black woman's body and demanding conformity to strict guidelines of gender roles and sexual conduct.[56] Within these religious traditions, an impassioned embrace of outward emotion and bodily movement went hand-in-hand with the rejection of sexual contact outside of marriage, secular dancing, and worldly indulgence.

In conclusion, I offer these comments on religion and race records in order to ponder competing values and moral discourses within the black working class. Juxtaposing the sacred and profane forces a rethinking of the oft-rendered image of a working class that is the monolithic and coherent bearer of an "authentic" black consciousness. Black working-class culture, as the generative site of the blues and the zoot suit, produced as well Pentecostalism and the Nation of Islam.[57] Religious culture, like the blues, found expression in the black vernacular.

Notes

1. See, for example, Houston A. Baker Jr., *Blues, Ideology, and Afro-American Literature: A Vernacular Theory* (Chicago: University of Chicago Press, 1984); Hazel V. Carby, "Policing the Black Woman's Body in an Urban Context," *Critical Inquiry* 18 (Summer 1992): 738–55; Carby, "'It Jus Be's Dat Way Sometime': The Sexual Politics of Women's Blues," in *Unequal Sisters: A Multi-cultural Reader in U.S. Women's History*, ed. Vicki L. Ruiz and Ellen Carol DuBois, 2nd ed. (New York: Routledge, 1994), 330–41.

2. See Ann duCille's important critique that this emphasis has caused the blues to be thought of as a "metonym for authentic blackness." Ann duCille, "Blues Notes on Black Sexuality: Sex and the Texts of Jessie Fauset and Nella Larsen," *Journal of the History of Sexuality* 3 (January 1993): 418–44, esp. 419–20. Published since the presentation of this paper at the Race Matters Conference in April 1994 is Farah Griffin's rich interdisciplinary study of the migration narrative. See Farah Jasmine Griffin, *"Who Set You Flowin'?": The African-American Migration Narrative* (New York: Oxford University Press, 1995), 61–63. Griffin draws some of her analysis of working-class religion from an earlier version of this paper, in particular Evelyn Brooks Higginbotham, "'Out of the Age of the Voice': The Black Church and Discourses of Modernity" (paper delivered at the Conference on the Black Public Sphere in the Era of Reagan and Bush, University of Chicago, October 14, 1993).

3. I am focusing on religious records in contradistinction to the interesting work of scholars of religion who locate religious inflections (theology and theodicy) in blues and rap. For example, Jon Michael Spencer finds in the blues and Michael Dyson finds in rap and in the songs of Michael Jackson moral reflections on evil, hypocrisy, suffering, justice, and biblical lore. See Jon Michael Spencer, *Blues and Evil* (Knoxville: University of Tennessee Press, 1993), xxviii, 35, 43–53. Michael Eric Dyson, *Reflecting Black: African-American Cultural Criticism* (Minneapolis: University of Minnesota Press, 1993), 35–60.

4. I am indebted to the following scholars for their pioneering work on race records in both the blues and religious traditions: Paul Oliver, *Songsters and Saints: Vocal Traditions on Race Records* (Cambridge: Cambridge University Press, 1984); Robert M. W. Dixon and John Godrich, *Recording the Blues* (New York: Stein & Day, 1970); Jeff Todd Titon, *Early Downhome Blues: A Musical and Cultural Analysis* (Urbana: University of Illinois Press, 1977); Tony Heilbut, *The Gospel Sound: Good News and Bad Times* (New York: Simon & Schuster, 1971).

5. Hughes is quoted in Lawrence Levine, *Black Culture and Black Consciousness: Afro-American Folk Thought from Slavery to Freedom* (New York: Oxford University Press, 1978), 180.

6. The advertisement appeared in the *Chicago Defender*, October 8, 1927, 8.

7. See the following: Cheryl Townsend Gilkes, "'Together and in Harness': Women's Traditions in the Sanctified Church," *Signs: Journal of Women in Culture and Society* 10 (Summer 1985): 679; Arthur Huff Fauset, *Black Gods of the Metropolis: Negro Religious Cults of the Urban North* (Philadelphia: University of Pennsylvania Press, 1944); Melvin D. Williams, *Community in a Black Pentecostal Church: An Anthropological Study* (University of Pittsburgh Press, 1974); Arthur E. Paris, *Black Pentecostalism: Southern Religion in an Urban World* (Amherst: University of Massachusetts Press, 1982).

8. Levine, *Black Culture*, 200.

9. Evelyn Brooks Higginbotham, *Righteous Discontent: The Women's Movement in the Black Baptist Church, 1880–1920* (Cambridge, Mass.: Harvard University Press, 1993), 42–46.

10. W. E. Burghardt Du Bois, "The Talented Tenth," in Booker T. Washington et al., *The Negro Problem: A Series of Articles by Representative Negroes of Today* (New York: James Pott, 1903), 54–55.

11. Elizabeth Kilham, "Sketches in Color," is quoted in Dena J. Epstein, *Sinful Tunes and Spirituals: Black Folk Music to the Civil War* (Urbana: University of Illinois Press, 1977), 277.

12. Daniel Alexander Payne, *Recollections of Seventy Years* (New York: Arno Press and the *New York Times*, 1969), 253–54.

13. Levine, *Black Culture*, 162–66; also see analysis of the "politics of respectability" in Higginbotham, *Righteous Discontent*, 187–99.

14. James M. Trotter, *Music and Some Highly Musical People* (Chicago: Afro-American Press, 1969; reprint of 1880 ed.), 58–59, 285.

15. Sutton Griggs is quoted and discussed in Wilson Jeremiah Moses, *The Golden Age of Black Nationalism, 1850–1925* (New York: Oxford University Press, 1978), 170–93.

16. Virginia W. Broughton, "Need of Distinctive Literature," *National Baptist Union* 13 (December 1902).

17. Elsa Barkley Brown, "Negotiating and Transforming the Public Sphere: African American Political Life in the Transition from Slavery to Freedom," *Public Culture* 7 (November 1994): 135–36; Levine, *Black Culture*, 24.

18. Daniel Webster Davis, *'Weh Down Souf and Other Poems* (Cleveland: Helman-Taylor Co., 1897), 54–56, as quoted in Brown, "Negotiating and Transforming the Public Sphere," 136.

19. Frances Smith Foster, ed., *Minnie's Sacrifice; Sowing and Reaping; Trial and Triumph: Three Rediscovered Novels by Frances E. W. Harper* (Boston: Beacon Press, 1994), xxiv–xxvi.

20. For a discussion of the role of photographic imagery in racial reconstruction, see Henry Louis Gates, Jr., "The Trope of a New Negro and the Reconstruction of the Image of the Black," *Representations* 24 (Fall 1988): 141.

21. For discussion of the literati during the Harlem Renaissance, see David Levering Lewis, *When Harlem Was in Vogue* (New York: Oxford University Press, 1989; originally published by Knopf, 1981), 119–55.

22. Levine, *Black Culture*, 179–80.

23. For a discussion of black consumerism during the 1920s and 1930s, see Liz Cohen, *Making a New Deal: Industrial Workers in Chicago, 1919–1939* (New York: Cambridge University Press, 1990), 147–58.

24. Richard Wightman Fox and T. J. Jackson Lears, eds., *The Culture of Consumption: Critical Essays in American History, 1880–1980* (New York: Pantheon, 1983), 3, also ix–xiii.

25. For a discussion of the inability of a black-owned record company, the Black Swan Com-

pany, to compete successfully against the large white corporations, such as Victor and Paramount, see Dixon and Godrich, *Recording the Blues*, 13, 21–32, 44.

26. Kwame Anthony Appiah, *In My Father's House: Africa in the Philosophy of Culture* (New York: Oxford University Press, 1992), 145.

27. Here I am reminded of Houston Baker's brilliant discussion of the "blending . . . of class and mass—*poetic* mastery discovered as a function of deformative [subversive] *folk* sound—constitutes the essence of black discursive modernism." Baker, *Modernism and the Harlem Renaissance*, 93; the oral narrative in literature is described by Henry Louis Gates, Jr., as the "speakerly text." See Gates, *The Signifying Monkey: A Theory of African-American Literary Criticism* (New York: Oxford University Press, 1988), xxv–xxvi, 181.

28. Sutton Griggs, *A Hero Closes a War*, Victor 21706-B (1928), and *A Surprise Answer to Prayer*, Victor 21706-A (1928); Oliver, *Songsters and Saints*, 146–47.

29. Paul Oliver discusses the popular appeal of the recorded sermons of black Baptist, Holiness, and Pentecostal preachers in Oliver, *Songsters and Saints*, 140–228; Dixon and Godrich, *Recording the Blues*, 38, 56–57.

30. Oliver, *Songsters and Saints*, 155.

31. Record companies began to scour southern cities and hamlets in the mid-1920s in search of down-home religious and secular talent. Jeff Titon argues, however, that part of the return to the old-time was part of a "folk" vogue that swept American culture in the post–World War I period as a counter-voice to the increasing sophistication and slickness of urbanity and the Jazz Age of the 1920s. Titon argues that race records must be seen as a part of this larger vogue, which also included "hillbilly" music, Broadway plays about mountain life in North Carolina and Kentucky during the 1923–24 season, and a general romanticization of a simpler, agrarian society. Titon, *Early Downhome Blues*, 215–16, 243–45.

32. *Chicago Defender*, October 1, 1927, and May 12, 1928.

33. See the analysis of recorded sermons in Michael Harris's biography of Thomas A. Dorsey: Michael W. Harris, *Rise of Gospel Blues: The Music of Thomas Andrew Dorsey in the Urban Church* (New York: Oxford University Press, 1992), 156–63.

34. Oliver, *Songsters and Saints*, 140–45, 155, 159.

35. Recorded sermons seem to have enjoyed the greatest popularity between 1926 and 1931. The onset of the Great Depression caused a precipitous decline in the release of sermonic records. Gospel music records continue to be popular to this day. Moreover, gospel queens outlasted the classic blues singers of the 1920s in popularity. Dixon and Godrich, *Recording the Blues*, 85; Oliver, *Songsters and Saints*, 188–98, 203–5; Heilbut, *The Gospel Sound*, 9–35.

36. Oliver, *Songsters and Saints*, 183–87. See advertisements for Rev. Leora Ross's *Dry Bones in the Valley* and *A Gambler Broke in a Strange Land*, Okeh 8486, and Jessie May Hill's *The Crucifixion of Christ* and *God Rode in the Windstorm*, Okeh 8490, in the *Chicago Defender*, August 27, 1927, and September 24, 1927; also Jerma Jackson, "Testifying at the Cross: Thomas Andrew Dorsey, Sister Rosetta Tharpe, and the Politics of African-American Sacred and Secular Music" (Ph.D. diss., Rutgers University, 1995), 157–80, 263–71.

37. Oliver, *Songsters and Saints*, 203–5.

38. Harris, *Rise of Gospel Blues*, 182–208.

39. Houston A. Baker, Jr., *Modernism and the Harlem Renaissance* (Chicago: University of Chicago Press, 1987), 93.

40. Anderson notes that her church made possible her initial training at the studio of Giuseppe Boghetti by helping to pay the costs for instruction. Marian Anderson, *My Lord, What a Morning* (New York: Viking Press, 1956), 7, 23–38, 49.

41. Michael Harris notes that Mahalia Jackson received voice training from gospel-blues songwriter Thomas Dorsey, then music director at Pilgrim Baptist Church in Chicago but formerly a blues lyricist and piano accompanist to Ma Rainey, Bessie Smith, and other blues queens. Harris, *Rise of Gospel Blues*, 259–60.

42. Quoted in ibid., 258; Mahalia Jackson noted in her autobiography: "In those days the big colored churches didn't want me and they didn't let me in. I had to make it my business to pack the little basement-hall congregations and store-front churches and get their respect that way. When they began to see the crowds I drew, the big churches began to sit up and take notice." Mahalia Jackson, *Movin' On Up* (New York: Hawthorn Books, 1966).

43. I am indebted to Quandra Prettyman for permission to reprint this poem, which is found in its entirety in Arnold Adoff, comp., *The Poetry of Black America: Anthology of the Twentieth Century* (New York: Harper & Row, 1973).

44. Harris, Rise of Gospel Blues, 258–71.

45. Ibid., 269–70.

46. The new urban context of the 1920s unleashed strivings for "authentic" racial expression in music (blues and jazz), in literature (Harlem Renaissance writers such as Zora Neale Hurston and Langston Hughes), and in political movements such as Marcus Garvey's Universal Negro Improvement Association. Black church culture must be situated in this historical context.

47. Oliver, *Songsters and Saints*, 145, 155, 159.

48. Ibid., 146; Rev. Mary Nelson, *Better Get Ready for Judgement*, Vocalion 1109-B.

49. Baker argues that the train represents the migrants' perceptions of freedom and mobility. However, Carby argues that the train imagery holds distinctively gendered connotations, since male blues singers more frequently associate the train with freedom and mobility than women. For blues women, train images often convey meanings of desertion and loneliness. See Baker, *Blues, Ideology, and Afro-American Literature*, 11–12; Carby, "'It Jus Be's Dat Way Sometime,'" 335.

50. In the religious race records, the train represents the vehicle of punishment to the wicked and salvation to the righteous. See Rev. J. M. Gates, *Death's Black Train Is Coming*, Victor 20211 (1926); Rev. A. W. Nix, *Black Diamond Express to Hell*, which was issued in six parts. Parts 1 and 2 appeared on Vocalion 1098 in May 1927, parts 3 and 4 on Vocalion 1421, released in November 1929, and parts 5 and 6 on Vocalion 1486 in June 1930. Nix also recorded *White Flyer to Heaven*, Vocalion 1170 (1927). Dixon and Godrich, *Recording the Blues*, 57; Paul Oliver, Max Harrison, and William Bolcom, *The New Grove Gospel, Blues, and Jazz with Spirituals and Ragtime* (New York: Norton, 1986), 194–95.

51. Dixon and Godrich, *Recording the Blues*, 39, 57.

52. Rev. J. C. Burnett, *The Downfall of Nebuchadnezzar*, Columbia 14166 (1926).

53. Gates, *Samson and the Woman*, Victor 21125 (1927).

54. Gates, *The First Born Was a Murderer*, Victor 21125 (1927); *Death Might Be Your Santa Claus*, Okeh 8413 (1926); *Did You Spend Christmas in Jail?*, Okeh 8753-A; *No Room in the Jailhouse*, Okeh 8753-B (1929); and *Dying Gambler*, Okeh 8387 (1926); Oliver, Harrison, and Bolcom, *The New Grove Gospel*, 194–95.

55. Carby, "Policing the Black Woman's Body," 739–55.

56. Hans A. Baer and Merrill Singer, *African-American Religion in the Twentieth Century: Varieties of Protest and Accommodation* (Knoxville: University of Tennessee Press, 1992), 147–78, 215–21; Jill Watts, *God, Harlem, U.S.A.: The Father Divine Story* (Berkeley: University of California Press, 1992), 161–62.

57. "I knew that our strict moral code and discipline was what repelled them most," stated Malcolm X in reference to the fact that many blacks came to hear him but far fewer joined the Muslims. He continued: "No Muslim who followed Elijah Muhammad could dance, gamble, date, attend movies, or sports, or take long vacations from work." Malcolm X with the assistance of Alex Haley, *The Autobiography of Malcolm X* (New York: Ballantine, 1973), 221; for a brilliant analysis of the zoot suit culture that attracted the young Malcolm, see Robin D. G. Kelley, "The Riddle of the Zoot: Malcolm Little and Black Cultural Politics During World War II," in *Malcolm X: In Our Own Image*, ed. Joe Wood (New York: St. Martin's Press, 1992), 155–82.

Chapter 42

Homophobia and Heterosexism in the Black Church and Community

Kelly Brown Douglas

- I can love the sinner, but not the sin.
- Homosexuality is an abomination.
- To be gay goes against nature.
- If we were supposed to be homosexual, God would have created Adam and Steve, not Adam and Eve.
- I don't mind gay people, but why do they have to be so vocal and pushy about their rights?
- Homosexuality is a White thing.
- Africa did not have homosexuals before Europeans went there.
- Homosexuality is detrimental to the Black family.

I often hear students pronounce these assertions and similar ones in my classes anytime we address the issue of homophobia in the Black church and community. In my ten years of teaching at the Howard University School of Divinity, no topic has seemed to touch more of a raw nerve than homosexuality. During classroom discussions, many students seem to have no inhibitions in expressing their disgust with gay and lesbian sexuality. They speak about gay and lesbian persons as sinners, abominations, perverts, and diseased. They often carry on their tirades as if gay and lesbian people do not deserve love and respect as human beings, although they paradoxically proclaim that as Christians they love everybody. Many of the students express themselves with little regard for whether or not they are inflicting deep pain on other students, gay or nongay, in the class. Because the discussion surrounding homophobia is frequently so venomous, I find myself questioning the wisdom of including it in my syllabus. But year after year I do, convinced that homophobia is a subject that the Black community must confront. And, as will become clearer, I am also increasingly convinced that this is an issue that no Christian theologian, especially a womanist theologian, can avoid with integrity.

Yet virtual silence—beyond moral invectives and self-righteous assertions—has characterized the Black community's consideration of gay and lesbian sexuality. Why is the Black community so averse to reflecting seriously on issues surrounding gay and lesbian sexuality? Why is the subject so particularly burdensome? Why does the mention of homosexuality often create acrimonious debate? How is it that a church community so committed to racial justice can be so intransigent about gay and lesbian rights? The answers to these questions seem submerged in the reasoning behind Black homophobic attitudes and practices, which, in turn, stem from the complexity of Black people's oppression at the hands of White culture.

Given the intensity of feelings toward homosexuality in the Black community, many have suggested that homophobia is more virulent and rampant among Black people than in the wider heterosexist American society. Though the rhetoric surrounding Black homophobia may suggest that this is the case, the facts do not bear this out. On the one hand, there have been no persons more ardently homophobic than White televangelists Pat Robertson and Jerry Falwell or political commentator Pat Buchanan. More recently, Senate Majority Leader Trent Lott's remarks comparing homosexuals to alcoholics, kleptomaniacs, and sex addicts has ignited a vigorous campaign by the religious right urging homosexuals to "be cured."

On the other hand, while homophobia is certainly pervasive in the Black community, there have been significant Black voices that have forthrightly supported gay and lesbian rights. Civil rights leaders such as Jesse Jackson, Joseph Lowery, Coretta Scott King, and Benjamin Chavis have all publicly decried discriminatory policies or behaviors toward gay and lesbian persons. At the same time they have supported agendas promoting gay and lesbian rights. In addition, the Congressional Black Caucus as a body, as well as its individual members, has consistently rejected legislation that would discriminate against gay and lesbian persons, and it has openly supported gay and lesbian rights.

If the Black community is not more homophobic than the wider heterosexist society of which it is a part, then why do both Whites and Blacks often assert that the Black community is hyperhomophobic? Why does it often appear from casual observation that the Black community is much more rigid and zealous than other communities about its antigay and antilesbian sentiments? Again, the answer to these questions is found in the history of Black people's oppression. While the Black church and community share the logic of others who denounce homosexuality, their particular history of White racist oppression and sexual exploitation makes Black homophobia appear even more passionate, trenchant, and unyielding. Angela Davis acknowledges the role of White culture in shaping the Black church's response to homosexuality:

> The fear of homosexuality perpetuated by the church is related to a generalized fear of sexuality. This fear of sexuality takes on new meaning when considered in light of the fact that the freedom to choose sexual partners was one of the most powerful distinctions between the condition of slavery and the postemancipation status of African Americans.[1]

Essentially, Black people's views toward homosexuality must be understood in light of their responses to sexuality in general, particularly as those responses have been refracted by White culture. Given that, it is important to understand that the complexity of Black homophobia cannot be adequately covered in a single chapter. It is a topic that warrants extensive study, as homophobia is manifested in various ways throughout the Black community, from the church to popular hip-hop and gangsta culture. Most recently, for instance, Angie and Debbie Winans created controversy throughout the Black community when they released a song that denounced homosexuality, "It's Not Natural." A comprehensive analysis of the nature of Black homophobia, as well as the reality that gives birth to a song like "It's Not Natural," deserves its own book. This chapter, therefore, does not propose to provide a complete analysis of Black homophobia; instead, it will outline the general contours of this analysis as it seeks to understand the relationship between Black homophobia and Black oppression, particularly the exploitation of Black sexuality. This chapter will also explore the role of a sexual discourse of resistance in addressing Black homophobia.

The Bible and Homosexuality

Not unlike others who condemn homosexuality, the Black community appeals to the Bible. On numerous occasions when discussing the issue of homophobia, my Black interlocutors have ended their arguments with some version of "The bottom line is that the Bible says homosexuality is wrong." Whether they are churchgoers or not, Black people often argue that the Bible makes clear that homosexuality is a sin. By invoking biblical authority they place a sacred canopy, a divine sanction, over their views toward gay and lesbian persons. This canopy renders homophobia practically intractable. The Bible becomes, then, a tool for censoring a group of people, in this case, gay men and lesbians.

The irony is, however, that the Bible does not present as clear a position on homosexuality as is often self-righteously asserted. The meaning of the biblical stories customarily referred to as proof against homosexual practices has generally been misconstrued or distorted. Biblical scholars have painstakingly shown that the Leviticus Holiness Codes (Lev. 18:22; 20:13), the story of Sodom and Gomorrah (Gen. 19:1–9), and Paul's Epistle to the Romans (1:26–27) do not present a compelling case against homoeroticism.[2] These scholars have also pointed out that neither the words nor the actions of Jesus, as recorded in the Gospels, suggest an antigay or antilesbian stance. In fact, the New Testament shows Jesus to be virtually indifferent about matters of sexuality. When Jesus discussed sexual issues, he was typically making a wider point. For example, Jesus used the example of committing adultery "in one's heart" to point to the role of intention in committing sin. When confronted with actual adulterers, Jesus recommended no apparent punishment but, instead, suggested that self-examination was of equal concern (John 8:3–11). The only sexual issue that seemed of grave importance to Jesus was fidelity, in that he prohibited divorce except in cases of infidelity. Jesus made no pronouncement and certainly no condemnation concerning homosexuality. As John Boswell accurately points out, "No effort is made to elaborate a comprehensive sexual ethic: Jesus and his followers simply responded to situations and questions requiring immediate attention."[3] Therefore, as is the case with the Old Testament, the New Testament provides no indisputable position on homosexuality.

Given the Bible's unclear view, to use the Bible to support a position on homosexuality would seem untenable. Yet scripture is often the cornerstone of homophobia in the Black community. Why is this the case? It is probably safe to say that homophobic prejudice has driven our reading of the Bible, as opposed to the Bible shaping homophobia. Biased eyes often turn to the biblical witness in support of the bias, particularly when communities attempt to justify their oppression of other human beings. The Bible then becomes a tool of oppression and is taken up as a weapon to censor the behavior and restrict the life possibilities of others. This has been true for White exploitation of Black people. The White slaveholding class interpreted the Bible in such a way to suggest that God ordained slavery and that blackness was a curse. Fortunately, Black people were able to hear the Bible for themselves and to realize that such an interpretation was more reflective of the White slaveholders' desire for privilege than of what was found in the Bible.

With such a history of the Bible being used against them, it seems abhorrent for Black people to be so steadfast in their use of the Bible against other Black persons, in this case, gay men and lesbians. How can a community that has suffered under an oppression covered with a sacred canopy inflict the same oppression upon others? How can such a community be so unwilling to reevaluate its use of biblical authority? How can it remain so closed to new understandings of problematic texts?

While there is certainly no excuse for placing a sacred canopy over any type of injustice or human misery, Black people's utilization of the Bible to damn homosexuality is somewhat understandable in light of their history of oppression. It is not simply a matter of a bigoted refusal to be "enlightened" by biblical scholarship or of a narrow-minded literalism. Black biblical scholars are beginning to discern that Black people's approaches to biblical texts bespeak a judicious sense of biblical authority born during the period of enslavement and honed throughout their history of struggle in America. Two well-known Black biblical scholars, Vincent Wimbush and Renita Weems, provide extended explications of how the Bible functions in the Black community. Their understanding of biblical authority as conceived in the Black community has important implications for Black people's use of the Bible in supporting homophobia.

The Black Biblical Tradition

Wimbush postulates that "a history of African Americans' historical readings of the Bible is likely to reflect their historical self-understandings—as Africans in America."[4] He explains that the Bible provided African Americans with a "language world" that helped them to negotiate their "strange existence." "In short," he argues, "the Bible became a 'world' into which African Americans could retreat, a 'world' they could identify with, draw strength from, and in fact manipulate for self-affirmation."[5]

Renita Weems looks specifically at the way in which African American women have appropriated biblical texts in light of their use to support both racial and gender inequity. She challenges biblical scholars to realize that the influence of the Bible in African American lives, especially in the lives of African American women, "involves more than the reader's lack of sophistication, or a slavish dogmatic devotion to the Bible."[6]

Both Wimbush and Weems recognize that the use of the Bible to justify Africans' enslavement has clearly impacted Black people's approach to biblical texts. Wimbush says that the enslaved men and women initially reacted to such usage with an "admixture of rejection, suspicion, and awe."[7] They rejected any notion of "book religion" because of the way their enslavers utilized this particular book and, most notably, because of their "well-established and elaborate" oral traditions. Yet "the fact that those who were conquering the New World were 'Bible Christians' was not at all lost on the Africans,"[8] says Wimbush. They were very cognizant of the power found in the Bible. Despite the fact that they were not permitted to learn to read or write or to encounter the Bible independently from their enslavers, the enslaved Africans found a way to know this "powerful" book for themselves. Rendered basically illiterate in terms of English by their slavery, they did this primarily through an oral/aural tradition of sermons, songs, and public readings. Weems points out, "What the slavemasters did not foresee, however, was that the very material they forbade the slaves from touching and studying with their hands and eyes, the slaves learned to claim and study through the powers of listening and memory."[9] A distinct understanding of biblical authority emerged as part of this oral/aural tradition of transmission, and it determined two things: the stories that would be transmitted and how they would be interpreted.

The oral/aural tradition is selective about which biblical texts are passed on. Stories from scripture that seemed to support enslavement and that were most used by the enslavers held little significance for the enslaved men and women and did not survive in the oral/aural tradition. The stories that did survive were those that were compatible with Black life and freedom, and, in time, they comprised the oral/aural Black biblical tradition. Weems clarifies, "Where the Bible has been able to capture the imagination of African American women [and men], it has been and continues to be able to do so because significant portions speak to the deepest aspirations of oppressed people for freedom, dignity, justice, and vindication."[10]

Essentially the oral/aural tradition attests to the creation of a "canon within the canon" for the Black community. Certain texts and stories became favorites and thus have been most often recited in song, prayer, and testimony. Wimbush explains how "the occurrence of certain clusters of biblical materials over and over [is] significant especially in terms of the development of a 'canon.'"[11] He continues:

> [The enslaved Africans] were attracted primarily to the narratives of the Hebrew Bible dealing with the adventures of the Hebrews in

bondage and escaping from bondage, to the oracles of the eighteenth-century prophets and their denunciation of social injustice and visions of social justice, and to the New Testament texts concerning the compassion, passion, and resurrection of Jesus. With these and other texts, the African American Christians laid the foundations for what can be seen as an emerging "canon."[12]

Indeed, the canon that initially emerged in the oral/aural tradition of the enslaved community appears to be germane today. Black spirituals, prayers, and testimony continue to reflect Black people's allegiance to particular texts that express the concern for the weak over the strong, or where the oppressed are set free and the despised are preferred. Most notably, the events and heroes of the Exodus story remain as central to contemporary Black faith as they were to enslaved religion. Repeatedly, and in various forms, Black church people refer to the victory of the Hebrew children over the mighty army of Pharaoh. They also give consistent jubilant and vivid testimony to David's humbling of the great Goliath, to Daniel being freed from the lions' den, to Jonah's release from the belly of the whale, and to the Hebrew children escaping from the fiery furnace.

Not only did the oral/aural tradition reflect a precise canon, but it also signaled a definite principle of interpretation. Weems says of this, "[T]he transmitters of the Bible in a slave culture rehearsed and interpreted the contents of the Bible as they saw fit."[13] To interpret as "they saw fit" typically meant that the enslaved men and women appropriated particular scriptural texts through the lens of their own experience. They interpreted the biblical stories in a manner that might shed light on their particular struggles for survival and freedom and that affirmed their faith in a God who was for them, not against them. As Wimbush puts it:

> The interpretation was not controlled by the literal words of the texts, but by social experience. The texts were heard more than read; they were engaged as stories that seized and freed the imagination. Interpretation was therefore controlled by the freeing of the collective consciousness and imagination of the African slaves as they heard the biblical stories and retold them to reflect their actual social situation, as well as their visions for something different.[14]

To recapitulate, the way Black people have historically approached the Bible reveals an understanding of biblical authority that emerged out of and maintains an oral/aural tradition of biblical transmission. Those texts with authority in this tradition are ones that Black people consider compatible with their own struggle for life and freedom. This legacy of biblical authority has several implications that impact Black people's use of the Bible in relation to homosexuality.

Black Biblical Authority and Homosexuality

First, the prevalence of the oral/aural tradition suggests that the Bible to which Black people attest is the Bible that has been handed down to them in this tradition. Even though contemporary Black people may have more access to the written Bible than did their enslaved forebears, they do not necessarily embrace all texts as equally authoritative. This is evidenced by the stories Black people most commonly refer to in sermon, song, prayer, and testimony. The stories that had significance and authority in the past continue to have significance and authority today. As mentioned earlier, the Exodus event as well as the stories of David, Daniel, and others continue to be primary to Black faith. So while the oral/aural canon is not strictly closed, it is defined.

Black people's allegiance to this particular biblical tradition does not reflect a recalcitrant refusal to learn new things; rather, it is a testament to a faith and stories of faith that have served Black people well in their struggle for life and freedom. Any adjustments to this tradition need to emerge, therefore, from Black people's continuing experiences of struggle. These adjustments must resonate with Black people's faith in a God that nurtures Black well-being as it is defined by them.

Second, biblical stories continue to be understood in the way they have been handed down and interpreted. Thus, when questioned about a Bible story, it is not uncommon to hear a Black person reply, "Well, I only know what I was taught, and that is good enough for me." It is difficult to alter an interpretative biblical tradition that has served Black people so well.

Finally, the existence of the oral/aural tradition signifies that the Black community gives virtually no credence to White interpretations of the Bible, and for good reason. The way in which the enslavers used the Bible and the history of White biblical scholarship have caused many Black people to be suspicious of most biblical scholarship, of "book religion." In the minds of many Black people, biblical scholarship in general has been painted by the broad brush of European and Euro-American bias. Such bias is even reflected in the historical-critical approach to the Bible, which tends to "exalt a White cultural world view over other world views."[15] Black biblical scholar William Myers explains:

The approach tends to lock the interpretative task in the past (e.g., in debates over authorial intent) while evading key contemporary issues like racism or intercultural dialogue. Although many of these works suggest that they cover the entire history of interpretation or that they address the full range of contemporary hermeneutical developments, in them one rarely finds any discussion of an African American interpretation of the Scriptures.[16]

Black people continue to rely more on their oral/aural tradition for appropriating the Bible than on what may come out of books about the Bible. Evidence of this is heard in numerous statements often made by Black men and women to the effect that "all that book learning [in relation to the Bible] has nothing to do with God."

What does this Black mistrust of White interpretation and the centrality of the oral/aural Black biblical tradition mean for the discussion of homosexuality in the Black community? It suggests that it is going to take more than "traditional" (White) biblical scholarship to persuade many in the Black community that homosexuality is not condemned by scripture. The mistrust of White people's handling of the Bible runs too deep for Black people, who, as a result, find it hard to accept White renderings of biblical texts on any matter, including sexuality. This means that the interpretation of certain texts (such as Lev. 18:22; 20:13; Gen. 19:1–9; and Rom. 1:26–27) will more likely reflect the homophobic understandings handed down in the Black oral/aural tradition than the exegetical findings of biblical scholars, especially since these traditional understandings seem to have served Black people well. (More will be said about this later.) So what does this suggest for the possibility of arresting Black people's use of the Bible as a sacred canopy for their homophobia? For it must not be thought that an understanding of the complexity of the Black biblical tradition that supports homophobia makes using the Bible to support human oppression any more tolerable.

In order to mitigate biblically based Black homophobia, a meaningful discussion of the Bible and sexuality, specifically homosexuality, will have to emerge from the Black community itself. It is a discussion that must take place within the wider context of Black people's own struggle for life and wholeness. It goes without saying that Black biblical scholars have particular responsibility in this area.

First, they are compelled to identify for Black people what has been a "biblical tradition of terror." This tradition is characterized by the use of various biblical texts to justify slavery, one of the most vile atrocities against humanity. In drawing attention to this "tradition of terror," these scholars must prompt Black people to make the connections between the way the Bible was used by Whites to terrorize them and the manner in which Black people use it to terrorize gay and lesbian persons. It must be made clear that participation in a biblical tradition of terror and allegiance to a biblical tradition that supports freedom are absolutely incompatible and hypocritical.

Next, Black biblical scholars must urge Black people to adopt a consistent "hermeneutic of suspicion" in relation to the way they use and interpret the biblical witness. This hermeneutic should be based on what has typically been the measure of biblical authority for Black people: Does the text support the life and freedom of all Black people? If Black men and women find themselves utilizing the Bible in a way that terrorizes other human beings, then they should disavow such usage. Most importantly, they should critically reevaluate the particular text that has led to such terror. It may be that certain offending texts will lose authority in the Black faith. Just as certain writings of Paul (especially those from Ephesians) have lost authority for many Black people, perhaps those that too easily lend themselves to the oppression of gay and lesbian persons should also be dismissed.

In light of the need for the Black faith community to reevaluate its understanding of certain texts, Black biblical scholars are obligated to find ways to communicate the complex and rich message of the scriptural witness on issues surrounding sexuality to Black people in a language and manner that maintains the integrity of the Black biblical oral/aural tradition. Black biblical scholars are challenged to advance the discussion of the Bible and homosexuality by employing the canon that has become authoritative for Black people. The Exodus event, for example, will have to be interpreted and understood in light of the experience of Black gay and lesbian persons.

Correspondingly, Black biblical scholars will have to confront the most significant component of Black biblical authority: biblical texts and interpretations of those texts that have gained authority in the Black community are those that resonate with the quest for Black survival and freedom. This principle of authority presents a special problem to the discussion of homosexuality, since homosexuality has long been viewed by many in the Black community as antithetical to Black well-being. Therefore any texts or interpretations of texts that would presume to support homoerotic behavior would more than likely remain nonauthoritative for the Black community and receive little hearing—unless homosexuality can be shown not to have a deleterious effect on Black life.

Homosexuality and the Well-Being of the Black Community
Homosexuality: A White Thing

The fact that homosexuality can be considered harmful to Black well-being is inextricably related to the sexual exploitation and denigration of Black people by White culture. Because White culture racialized sex and "sexuated" race by equating blackness with sexual deviance, the Black community has been diligent in its efforts to sever the link between such deviance and blackness. Recognizing Black homophobia in part as a response to White sexual exploitation, Barbara Smith observes:

> One of the reasons that I have thought for homophobic attitudes among Black women is the whole sexual stereotyping used against Black people anyway, but especially women in relation to homosexuality—you know, the "Black bulldagger" image. Lesbianism is definitely about something sexual, a so-called deviant sexuality. So the way most Black women deal with it is to be just as rigid and closed about it as possible. White people don't have a sexual image that another oppressor community has put on them.[17]

Essentially, given a heterosexist society that considers homosexuality at best abnormal and at worse perverted, Black people have various ways to denounce homosexual practices in the Black community. There has been a vocal contingent, especially among nationalists and/or Afrocentrists, that has done this by asserting that homosexuality is a White thing. They argue that if Black people are indeed homosexual it is because they have come under the corrupting influence of White culture and values. In *The Isis Papers*, a popular book in the Black community, Frances Cress Welsing says: "Black male passivity, effeminization, bisexuality and homosexuality are being encountered increasingly by Black psychiatrists working with Black patient populations . . . , although [these conditions were] an almost nonexistent behavioral phenomenon amongst indigenous Blacks in Africa."[18]

Popular Afrocentrist Molefi Kete Asante shares Welsing's opinion, as he asserts that homosexuality is antagonistic to a commitment to the Black community since homosexuality reflects European decadence. He counsels male homosexuals: "We can no longer allow our social lives to be controlled by European decadence. The time has come for us to redeem our manhood through planned Afrocentric action. All brothers who are homosexuals should know that they too can become committed to the collective will."[19]

Yet these arguments that imply that homosexuality is anathema to African culture ignore numerous findings that suggest otherwise. In his movingly poignant account of being Black and gay in America, Keith Boykin provides an excellent summary of these findings:

> Modern anthropological evidence suggests the existence of homosexuality in virtually all human cultures, including those of Africa. . . . Scholars such as Warren Johansson, Geoff Puterbaugh, Stephen Murray, and Melville Herskovits have documented the reports of various sexual practices and family structures in black cultures. For example Portuguese sources indicate that homosexuality was common among the people of Angola at the time when colonists were scouting for slaves. Members of Nubian and Zulu cultures were known to assume alternative gender roles, women taking on important duties and men engaging in transvestite homosexuality. In 1937, Herskovits found that homosexuality was practiced by adolescents in Dahomey, and that some same-sex pairing persisted for life. S. F. Nadel reported having found "widespread homosexuality and transvestism" among the Otoro people in Sudan, as well as among the Moro, Nyima, and Tira. In his book *The Nuba* (1947), Nadel also documented marriages of Krongo *londo* and Masakin *tubele*. In a different example, he revealed that attractive prepubescent boys served as pages to the chiefs of the Mossi people and assumed some female gender roles, including their style of dress. In Mombassa, Kenya, a dance known as *lelemama* served to identify and recruit married women into the lesbian subculture.[20]

In recognizing the close bonds that women have often formed, Audre Lorde cites the following story of a ninety-two-year-old Efik-Ibibio woman of Nigeria: "I had a woman friend to whom I revealed my secrets. She was very fond of keeping secrets to herself. We acted as husband and wife. We always moved hand in glove and my husband and hers knew about our relationship. The villagers nicknamed us twin sisters."[21]

The egregious claims that homosexuality is a White disease thus not only ignore the facts but also carelessly deny the humanity of many Black women and men. Barbara Smith puts it this way: "So often lesbianism and male homosexuality [are] talked about as a White disease within the Black community. It is just so negating of our lives."[22] Yet, regardless of the pain inflicted upon Black people, many persons alleging commitment to the life and freedom of the Black community continue to relinquish responsibility for their life-negating homophobic attitudes and practices with the easy excuse that homosexuality is a White thing.

Homosexuality: A Threat to the Black Family

Buttressing the belief that homosexuality is hostile to Black life is the argument that it erodes the Black family and concomitantly threatens Black masculinity. These arguments again appear viable in light of White cultural manipulation of Black sexuality. As noted above, one of the primary ways in which White culture has created an image of Black people as sexually deviant has been through its attacks on the Black family. Not only has the Black family been undermined by the structures of White racism in ways that have made it extremely difficult, if not at times impossible, for Black families (meaning, parents and children) to occupy the same households, but White culture has also attacked the models of family that Black people have erected to foster their survival. The Moynihan Report is a prime example of such an attack.

Recognizing the manipulation of the Black family by White culture, Rhonda Williams says:

> Black families have long functioned as markers in the public imagination: they generally signify and manifest a morally problematic sexually [*sic*] agency, a cultural degeneracy. The conventional social scientific wisdom is clear: "the problem" is that so much black sexuality and kinship formation transgresses the boundaries of married (and therefore healthy) heterosexuality.[23]

One of the Black community's responses to this attack upon Black sexuality has been to advocate White family norms—that is, to espouse a family model more acceptable within a White patriarchal and heterosexist society. This model allows Black men to enjoy male privilege within the family structure. This becomes even more crucial in the Black community, perhaps, since the Black male is stripped of such privilege—by virtue of his blackness—in wider society. Though highly critical of this logic, activist and literary artist Cheryl Clarke recognizes the significance for the Black community of advocating White family norms:

> The concept of the black family has been exploited since the publication of the infamous Moynihan report. . . . Because the insular, privatized nuclear family is upheld as the model of Western family stability, all other forms—for example, the extended family, the

female-headed family, the lesbian family—are devalued. Many black people, especially middle-class black people, have accepted the male-dominated nuclear family model, though we have had to modify it because black women usually must work outside the home.[24]

Recognizing the relationship between "protecting" the Black family and homophobia, Rhonda Williams bluntly says:

> Like Sapphire, black queers betray the quest for healthy black families, a regulated and normalized black sexuality. Whether viewed as the products of broken families or betrayers of family life together, black gays and lesbians are a potential anathema to straight African Americans whose resistance to racist narratives inspires them to "clean up" images of black sexuality.[25]

Nonheterosexual coupling has also been attacked for being nonproductive, and, as a result, homosexuality has been deemed genocidal for the Black race. Again, such an argument can appear feasible simply because of the fragility of Black life in a White racist society that is so hostile to blackness. Clarke, however, speaks to the problematic assumptions of such an argument:

> Homosexuality is viewed as a threat to the continued existence of the heterosexual family, because homosexual unions do not, in and of themselves, produce offspring—as if one's only function within a family, within a relationship, or in sex were to produce offspring. Black family lifestyles and homosexual lifestyles are not antithetical. Most black lesbians and gay men grew up in families and are still critically involved with their families. Many black lesbians and gay men are raising children. Why must the black family be so strictly viewed as the result of a heterosexual dyad?[26]

Audre Lorde also denounces the connection between homosexuality and Black genocide:

> At a recent Black literary conference, a heterosexual Black woman stated that to endorse lesbianism was to endorse the death of our race. This position reflects acute fright or a faulty reasoning. . . . This position supposes that if we do not eradicate lesbianism in the Black community, all Black women will become lesbians. It also supposes that lesbians do not have children. Both suppositions are patently false.[27]

Despite the falsity of these types of claims, Black thinkers have made them with relative impunity. For instance, Black sociologists Nathan and Julia Hare argued in their 1984 book, *The Endangered Black Family: Coping with the Unisexualization and Coming Extinction of the Black Race*, that homosexuality was a sign of "family disintegration" and a "decaying and decadent society." The Hares presume that "homosexuality does not promote black family stability and that it historically has been a product largely of the Europeanized society."[28]

Black female ethicist Cheryl Sanders places a "sacred canopy" over such rhetoric. In arguing against the use of a womanist nomenclature by Christian religious scholars, since a womanist stance implies an acceptance of gay and lesbian sexuality, Sanders says:

> In my view there is a discrepancy between the womanist criteria that would affirm and/or advocate homosexual practice, and the ethical norms the black church might employ to promote the survival and wholeness of black families. It is problematic for those of us who claim connectedness to and concern for the black family and church to engage these criteria authoritatively and/or uncritically in the formulation of theological-ethical discourse for those two institutions. If black women's ethics is to be pertinent to the needs of our community, then at least some of us must be in a position to offer intellectual guidance to the church as the principal (and perhaps only remaining) advocate for marriage and family in the black community. There is a great need for the black churches to promote a positive sexual ethics within the black community as one means of responding to the growing normalization of a single-parent family, and the attendant increases in poverty, welfare dependency, and a host of other problems. Moreover, it is indisputably in the best interest of black children for the church not only to strengthen and support existing families, but also to educate them ethically for marriage and parenthood.[29]

Homosexuality: A Threat to Black Manhood

Even as homosexuality is seen as a threat to Black families, Black families have been held responsible for causing homosexuality, especially among males. Following the logic of the Moynihan Report, many Black homophobic arguments stress the importance of a male-dominated family model. They suggest that the absence of such a model leaves young Black males woefully susceptible to the "disease" of homosexuality. This argument, which is an indirect accusation against the Black woman, is based on the false assumption that male homosexuality is equated with effeminate behavior. In the minds of various Black thinkers, homosexuality indicates a defect in the development of Black masculinity and is a perversion of manhood. Jawanza Kunjufu argues, for example, that young males who do not experience enough male companionship are "prime candidates for homosexuality."[30] Asante sharpens this perspective:

> The rise of homosexuality in the African-American male's psyche is real and complicated. An Afrocentric perspective recognizes its existence but homosexuality cannot be condoned or accepted as good for the national development of a strong people. It can be and must be tolerated until such time as our families and schools are engaged in Afrocentric instructions for males. . . . The time has come for us to redeem our manhood through planned Afrocentric action.[31]

Again reflective of patriarchal/sexist norms, manhood in the Black community is inextricably related to physical strength, independence, and dominance. Given such a notion, nowhere does the image of manhood, and the desire to protect it, come into more conflict with homosexuality than in the world of sports. The Black athlete is portrayed as the quintessence of masculinity. It is therefore no surprise that anything that would impugn the "manhood" of the Black male athlete is quickly dismissed or denied. Such is the case with homosexuality.

While the shared kiss between Isiah Thomas and Magic Johnson prior to the 1988 NBA championship games was acceptable as a part of the on-court rituals of male bonding, that Magic Johnson contracted HIV was not all right. Because the disease was so wrongly associated with gay men, the world of Black athletes quickly disassociated itself from Magic by voicing unwarranted fear over becoming infected by him and by creating an image of Black athletes as heterosexual family men. The players often made references to their wives or to their need to rethink their promiscuous heterosexual behavior. As for Magic Johnson, he quickly and fervently denounced any speculation that he may be gay. Shortly after his announcement that he was HIV positive, he appeared on the *Arsenio Hall Show* and proclaimed that "I'm far from being homosexual." He followed this announcement with assurances that he was infected as a result of unprotected sex with a woman. As if to eradicate any lingering doubt concerning his sexuality (meaning his masculinity), Magic made very public his extremely promiscuous heterosexual lifestyle. It seemed to matter more to him that the public knew he was a "man" than to protect his wife from humiliating references to his lack of fidelity during their long courtship. As if to cement his "manly" sexuality, Magic also made not-too-subtle references in public interviews to the fact that despite his HIV infection he and his wife still enjoyed an active sex life.

Finally, it cannot be overemphasized that Black sexism is clearly manifest in this protection of masculinity and manhood. As seen earlier, homosexuality is often wrongly associated with effeminate behaviors. It is no surprise then that the strong Black mother is blamed for creating the gay male. But nowhere does the sexism of homophobia make itself more manifest than in the responses to lesbians.

The Lesbian Threat

Lesbians are often thought of as a betrayal of manhood by simple virtue of who they are. Malicious references to "dykes" or "bulldaggers" insinuate that they are some deviant form of a wanna-be man. In actuality, there is perhaps no individual perceived as more challenging to male prerogatives than a lesbian. Barbara Christian explains: "By being sexually independent of men, lesbians by their very existence call into question society's definition of woman at its deepest levels."[32] Thus, in a society that grants privilege to White heterosexual males, Black lesbians suffer under a tremendous burden within the society at large as well as in the Black community. This is in part due to the fact that the Black man's quest for manhood, according to White patriarchal definitions, is threatened by the presence of Black lesbians. Clarke explains: "The black man may view the lesbian—who cannot be manipulated or seduced sexually by him—in much the same way the white slave master once viewed the black male, viz, as some perverse caricature of manhood threatening his position of dominance over the female body."[33]

Indeed, some Black people's desire to maintain a degree of privilege in a White patriarchal society makes homophobia even more formidable in the Black community. In a society where privilege is accorded on the basis of race (namely, whiteness), gender (maleness), and sexual preference (heterosexuality), heterosexual privilege is virtually the only privilege that Black people—especially Black women—can claim in order to move to the center. In the words of Cheryl Clarke, "heterosexuality was one of [black people's] only means of power over [their] condition as slaves."[34]

Barbara Smith speaks specifically of the heterosexual privilege accorded many Black women: "Heterosexual privilege is usually the only privilege that Black women have. None of us have racial or sexual privilege, almost none of us have class privilege, maintaining 'straightness' is our last resort."[35] Patricia Hill Collins also recognizes this point of privilege:

> In the same way that the white feminists identify with their victimization as women yet ignore the privilege that racism grants them, and that Black men decry racism yet see sexism as less objectionable, African American women may perceive their own race and gender oppression, yet victimize someone else by invoking the benefits of heterosexual privilege.[36]

Collins further points out that homophobic stances, like silence, also shield Black women from becoming a part of the "ultimate other" in relation to the heterosexual White male norm upheld by White culture. Silence ostensibly protects them from being labeled as lesbians. Collins clarifies, "For Black women who have already been labeled the other by virtue of our race and gender, the threat of being labeled a lesbian can have a chilling effect on Black women's ideas and on our relationships with one another."[37] Karen Baker-Fletcher admits that a fear of being "labeled" or ostracized is perhaps a significant factor in womanist theological silence surrounding issues of homophobia. She says of womanist silence, "I suspect that for many it is for the same reason that many gays and lesbians hesitate to come out of the closet: fear of losing a job, of being thrown out of church, ostracized in community."[38]

It has also been pointed out, and rightly so, that many Black women are rendered silent or are even vocal homophobes because of their fears concerning their own feelings for women. Audre Lorde recognizes this when she says, "[T]he Black lesbian is an emotional threat only to those Black women whose feelings of kinship and love for other Black women are problematic in some way."[39] Barbara Smith pointedly says, "I think the reason that Black women are so homophobic is the attraction-repulsion thing. They have to speak out vociferously against lesbianism because if they don't they may have to deal with their own deep feelings for women."[40]

So what does all of this mean in the Black community? The first general conclusion to be drawn is that the discussion of homosexuality in the Black community is not a simple matter. Homophobia does not reflect merely a close-minded sexual bigotry by Black men and women. This is a phobia and prejudice nurtured in large part by a history of White sexual exploitation. The case supporting homophobia in the Black community reveals homophobia almost as a misguided strategy for protecting Black lives and the integrity of Black sexuality, as a necessary position to safeguard Black life and freedom. Homosexuality is seen as threatening Black well-being. The passion that often surrounds homophobic attitudes is perhaps best understood in light of Black people's mistaken efforts to protect "authentic blackness" rather than as a sign of a community more intensely homophobic than other communities.

Yet while appreciating the history of oppression that shapes Black homophobia certainly makes it easier to understand the intransigence of homophobia in the Black community, it does not make it any more acceptable. Black homophobia cannot be excused. Regardless of the reasons for it, it is wrong because it negates the unique richness, value, and worth of human beings. As Cheryl Clarke rightly puts it, "[black people] cannot rationalize the disease of homophobia among black people as the white man's fault, for to do so is to absolve ourselves of our responsibility to transform ourselves."[41] How can this transformation begin?

Homophobia and a Sexual Discourse of Resistance

Such transformation cannot take place apart from a sexual discourse of resistance. This discourse is the first step toward helping Black men and women to understand that homophobia threatens Black well-being instead of protecting it. A discourse of resistance must expose how the sexual politics of White culture, with its varied attacks on Black sexuality, has made it appear that homophobia is compatible with Black life and freedom, even though this is not so. By exposing the relationships among race, sex, and power, a discourse of resistance will show that homophobia plays into the hands of White culture and racism. Homophobia does this by creating discord among Black people. Audre Lorde would no doubt describe Black homophobia as "horizontal hostility" because it causes Black people to fight one another instead of the structures of oppression that truly threaten Black life.[42]

And what is most significant, homophobia destroys Black life because it impairs the Black community's ability to respond to HIV/AIDS, a disease that has devastated the Black community. Though Black people constitute only 12 to 13 percent of the U.S. population, they account for at least 57 percent of all HIV/AIDS cases. Regardless of the disproportionate numbers of Black people affected by HIV/AIDS, the Black community has been slow in responding to this illness. As pointed out earlier, clearly one of the reasons for such a slow response has been the homophobic association of this illness with homosexuality. Homophobia mimics White culture in the way it destroys Black lives. Keith Boykin says it incisively:

> With all the efforts being made to divide minorities, it is important to remember that the real enemy is injustice, not each other. Homophobia, not homosexuality, leads some lesbians and gays to engage in risky and self-destructive behaviors. Homophobia, not homosexuality, leads many of them away from their families, their communities and their places of worship. And when closeted black lesbians and gays continue to deceive themselves with unsuccessful marriages and families, it is homophobia, not homosexuality, that threatens the survival of the African-American family.
>
> The enemy within us is often more threatening than the enemies surrounding us. But that internal enemy is not homosexuality but, rather, the hurtful way we treat one another. Physically, spiritually, and intellectually, blacks are warring against each other instead of supporting each other.[43]

It is perhaps in revealing that homophobia is actually *contrary* to the well-being of Black life that Black people might arrive at a more liberating view of the biblical tradition in matters of sexuality. It might allow the Black community to lift the sacred canopy that it has placed over homophobia. To reiterate, the authority of scripture is in large measure determined by whether or not a text supports the life and freedom of the Black community. A sexual discourse of resistance should clarify that homophobia is antithetical to Black life and freedom and thus disrupt the terrorizing manner in which Black people have used biblical texts in regard to homosexuality.

Finally, a sexual discourse of resistance should help Black people understand how they are using the very tools of power that have been used against them to oppress gay and lesbian persons. They take up these tools when they construct sexual discourse against gay and lesbian persons and shelter it under a biblical sacred canopy, suggesting that such sexuality is an abomination to God and that it endangers Black existence. This discourse serves to denigrate and destroy a significant segment of Black humanity, in much the same way that White sexual discourse seeks to destroy Black people.

The Black community's sexual discourse against homosexuality does not save Black lives, but rather helps White culture to destroy them. In this regard Lorde is right: "The master's tools will never dismantle the

1016 *Kelly Brown Douglas*

master's house."[44] A discourse of resistance will stress that Black well-being is not fostered by adopting the oppressive, destructive, life-negating tools of White culture. The community must be constrained in its dialogue and action by its concern for the flourishing of Black life. A sexual discourse of resistance could nurture the kind of discussion that promotes acceptance and appreciation of the rich diversity—even sexual diversity—within the Black community. It would empower, if not compel, Black men and women to disavow and dismantle any structures, systems, or ways of behaving or thinking that in any way foster homophobia.

Conclusions

This chapter has shown the significance of a sexual discourse of resistance for the Black community. Without such a discourse homophobia can exist with relative impunity because it masquerades as a defender of Black life and freedom. At the same time a sacred canopy remains intact and serves as a divine affirmation of Black homophobia. A sexual discourse of resistance may help to dismantle this homophobic sacred canopy by exposing the links between the exploitation of Black sexuality and the intensity of Black homophobia. Ultimately, it will reveal that homophobia actually betrays Black self-interest and Black life.

In the end, what does this discussion of sexuality have to do with theology, more specifically with the Black theological tradition? While the ability to foster and nurture Black life and wholeness is a compelling enough reason for theologians, especially womanist theologians, to engage in sexual discourse, there are even more compelling reasons for doing so. As we will discover, the core belief of Black faith in a God who came down to earth in Jesus Christ demands a sexual discourse of resistance.

Notes

1. Angela Davis, *Blues Legacies and Black Feminism* (New York: Pantheon, 1998), 131.
2. See, for instance, Robin Scroggs, *The New Testament and Homosexuality* (Philadelphia: Fortress Press, 1983); John McNeil, *The Church and the Homosexual* (Kansas City: Sheed, Andrews and McMeel, 1976); L. D. Scanzoni and V. R. Mollencott, *Is the Homosexual My Neighbor? A Positive Christian Response*, rev. ed. (San Francisco: Harper and Row, 1994).
3. John Boswell, *Christianity, Social Tolerance, and Homosexuality* (Chicago: University of Chicago Press, 1980), 117.
4. Vincent Wimbush, "The Bible and African Americans: An Outline of an Interpretative History," in *Stony the Road We Trod: African American Biblical Interpretation*, ed. Cain Hope Felder (Minneapolis: Fortress Press, 1991), 82.

5. Ibid., 83.
6. Renita Weems, "Reading Her Way through the Struggle: African American Women and the Bible," in *Stony the Road We Trod*, 57–58.
7. Wimbush, "The Bible and African Americans," 85.
8. Ibid., 85.
9. Weems, "Reading Her Way," 61.
10. Ibid., 70.
11. Wimbush, "The Bible and African Americans," 84.
12. Ibid., 86.
13. Weems, "Reading Her Way," 60–61.
14. Wimbush, "The Bible and African Americans," 88.
15. William H. Myers, "The Hermeneutical Dilemma of the African American Biblical Student," in *Stony the Road We Trod*, 41.
16. Ibid.
17. Barbara Smith and Beverly Smith, "Across the Kitchen Table: A Sister to Sister Dialogue," in *This Bridge Called My Back: Writing by Radical Women of Color*, ed. Cherríe Moraga and Gloria Anzaldúa (New York: Kitchen Table/Women of Color Press, 1983), 124.
18. Frances Cress Welsing, *The Isis Papers: The Keys to the Colors* (Chicago: Third World Press, 1991), 81.
19. Molefi Kete Asante, *Afrocentricity* (Trenton, N.J.: African World Press, 1988), 57.
20. Keith Boykin, *One More River to Cross: Black and Gay in America* (New York: Anchor Books/Doubleday, 1996), 194. See also Colin Spencer, *Homosexuality in History* (New York: Harcourt Brace and Company, 1995).
21. Audre Lorde, "Scratching the Surface: Some Notes on Barriers to Women and Loving," in *Sister Outsider* (Freedom, Calif.: The Crossing Press, 1984), 49–50.
22. Smith and Smith, "Across the Kitchen Table," 125.
23. Rhonda Williams, "Living at the Crossroads: Explorations in Race, Nationality, Sexuality, and Gender," in *The House That Race Built: Black American, U.S. Terrain*, ed. Wahneema Lubiano (New York: Pantheon, 1997), 140.
24. Cheryl Clarke, "The Failure to Transform: Homophobia in the Black Community," in *Home Girls: A Black Feminist Anthology*, ed. Barbara Smith (New York: Kitchen Table/Women of Color Press, 1983), 200.
25. Williams, "Living at the Crossroads," 144.
26. Clarke, "Failure to Transform," 200.
27. Lorde, "Scratching the Surface," 51–52.
28. Nathan Hare and Julia Hare, *The Endangered Black Family: Coping with the Unisexualization and Coming Extinction of the Black Race* (San Francisco: Black Think Tank, 1984), 65.
29. Cheryl Sanders, "Christian Ethics and Theology in Womanist Perspective," in *Journal of Feminist Studies in Religion* 5, no. 2 (fall 1989): 90.
30. Jawanza Kunjufu, *Countering the Conspiracy to Destroy Black Boys* (Chicago: African American Images, 1985), 21.
31. Asante, *Afrocentricity*, 57.
32. Barbara Christian, *Black Feminist Criticism: Perspectives on Black Women Writers* (New York: Pergamon, 1985), 199.
33. Cheryl Clarke, "Lesbianism: An Act of Resistance," in *This Bridge Called My Back*, 131–32.

34. Ibid.
35. Barbara Smith, "Toward a Black Feminist Criticism," in *But Some of Us Are Brave*, ed. Gloria T. Hull, Patricia Bell Scott, and Barbara Smith (Old Westbury, N.Y.: Feminist Press, 1982), 171.
36. Patricia Hill Collins, *Black Feminist Thought: Knowledge, Consciousness, and the Politics of Empowerment* (Boston: Unwin Hyman, 1990), 194.
37. Ibid., 195.
38. Karen Baker-Fletcher and Garth Kasimu Baker-Fletcher, *My Sister, My Brother: Womanist and Xodus God-Talk* (Maryknoll, N.Y.: Orbis Books, 1997), 259.
39. Lorde, "Scratching the Surface," 49.
40. Smith and Smith, "Across the Kitchen Table," 124.
41. Clarke, "Failure to Transform," 197.
42. See Lorde, "Scratching the Surface," 48.
43. Boykin, *One More River*, 270–71.
44. Lorde, *Sister Outsider*, 110.

Chapter 43

For Rent, "Cabin in the Sky"

Race, Religion, and Representational Quagmires in American Film

Judith Weisenfeld

> In our image of the Negro breathes the past we deny, not dead but living yet and powerful, the beast in our jungle of statistics. It is this which defeats us, which continues to defeat us. . . . Wherever the problem touches there is confusion, there is danger. Wherever the Negro face appears a tension is created, the tension of a silence filled with things unutterable.
>
> James Baldwin, *Notes of a Native Son*

In 1941 when African-American filmmaker Spencer Williams released *The Blood of Jesus*, black audiences' cinematic choices also included Gary Cooper in *Sergeant York*, Maureen O'Hara and Roddy McDowell in *How Green Was My Valley*, Cary Grant and Joan Fontaine in *Suspicion*, and Orson Welles' *Citizen Kane*. In segregated theatres, in church basements and in community centers, African-American audiences participated in the Hollywood process of making American identity through the viewing of films. For them, however, constructions of African-American identity proved a complex and disturbing process. Preston Sturges' film *Sullivan's Travels*, also released that year, made telling use of the image of black audiences of Hollywood films. Sturges sends his main character, film director John Sullivan, on an odyssey through American poverty in search of material for his next film. What begins as a tourist's view ultimately leads Sullivan to prison, sentenced to six years at hard labor. One evening the prisoners, treated to a picture show in a local black church, enter at the end of the service and find the congregation singing "Go Down, Moses . . . let my people go." The prisoners and the congregation then watch the films together. In the course of viewing the Disney cartoon before the feature and hearing the laughter about him, Sullivan has an epiphany and comes to "understand" the role that humor and comedy play in the lives of the poor. Finally rescued from prison by the studio heads, he determines to make comedies rather than political advocacy films in order to reach the masses more effectively. That Sturges chose to set the climactic scene of the film in the physical space of a black church provides particular insight into the questions I take up here. Sullivan's epiphany, that popular culture serves primarily as an escape for the masses, rather than as a tool for educating and promoting social change, applies most especially to African-Americans as religious beings, for Sturges. In this presentation, the black church becomes the ultimate diversion from social and political problems for the most downtrodden of Americans who seek nothing more than their "cabin in the sky" (to borrow the title of a 1943 Vincente Minnelli film).

The issue of representations of people of color in American film has long interested me, a voracious consumer of old movies from the days of my childhood. As a child of color I could not help, in seeking to place myself in the images framed on the screen, but notice the literal marginalization of African-Americans in particular in this body of work. At the same time that the romantic travails of Ingrid Bergman or Ava Gardner compelled me and the dangerous situation in which Humphrey Bogart or Barbara Stanwyck found themselves moved me to the edge of my seat, the African-American maid, butler, or porter in the background drew my eye as well. What were *they* thinking? What were *their* lives like? Finding black characters in any context in which they appeared as multidimensional human beings in these films indeed proves a daunting task. Nurturing mammys, contented slaves, bowing uncles, dancing children, and lazy and corrupt black leaders abound at the edges of the stories of white heroes and heroines. Certainly, similar issues face viewers examining the presence of other people of color in American films.[1]

Representations of African-Americans as religious—generally within the context of Christianity—proved to be an important key to finding those often fleeting moments in which black characters emerged as complex subjects in Hollywood films. Time after time in these movies, the shuffling, bowing butler or porter suddenly stands up straight and a depth of emotion and personality emerges from the normally silent maid or cook when he or she utters a prayer in the background. And, indeed, I found these characters often praying. For example, after having viewed Alfred Hitchcock's 1944 *Lifeboat* many times and having consigned the African-American ship's porter who joins the passengers in the lifeboat to a "yessah" role, I recently noticed another aspect of this character. When the baby of a passenger, whom the porter had struggled so desperately to save, finally dies, the group aboard the lifeboat bury the child at sea. Some of the men look out on the water and search for the words to the 23rd Psalm, but falter. The porter appears in the frame with his head held high, filling in the words and completing the recitation of the psalm. As I have discovered in many of these Hollywood films, black characters often appear as most fully drawn when pictured as participating in Christianity. Certainly, representations of African traditional and African-derived religions rarely move beyond depictions of savage cannibalism; but in American film, African-American Christians present an unusual opening.

Many years later, I became exposed to black independent cinema, now garnering increasing attention from scholars in many fields, and have come to see African-American religious subjectivity occupying an important place in this body of work. The struggle for a black independent cinema is nearly as old as commercial film in America, beginning with such early films as the 1919 *Birth of a Race*, made in response to D. W. Griffith's 1915 *Birth of a Nation*. Griffith's film, so innovative in its use of the medium, proved wildly popular among white viewers and, through that popularity, projected established literary representations onto a new level. Responses to the potential of film to operate as a means of reinforcing white supremacy took a number of approaches. In addition to protests against the film mounted by the National Association for the Advancement of Colored People, black producers like George and Noble Johnson of the Lincoln Motion Picture Company and directors like Oscar Micheaux and Spencer Williams strove in the years following to use film to present a range of images of African-American life. This process of "framing blackness," as Ed Guerrero (1993) has termed it, never took place entirely outside the context of the larger, white-controlled film industry, and rarely did it *not* involve the participation of whites. Thomas Cripps' work on the genre of black film emphasizes that it is not defined by an aesthetic, authentic "blackness," to the exclusion of white, but, rather, by what it has to say about black life. Cripps writes, "No other genre, except perhaps the American western, spoke so directly to the meaning and importance of shared values embraced by its audience" (1978: 12). These films, collectively known as "race movies," produced over a period of thirty-six years, may be marked by the boundaries of the 1912 film *The Railroad Porter* and the 1948 *Souls of Sin* (Bowser).

These early films elucidate a significant struggle over images of African-Americans in the evolving medium. In this essay I will explore some of the ways in which African-American religious practices became a playing field on which both white and black filmmakers worked out the potentials of film with regard to issues of race and representation. My contention that, in early American film, some white filmmakers used film in ways that sometimes generated and often perpetuated racist stereotypes of African-Americans is admittedly not a novel one, nor that African-American filmmakers mounted responses to such images. Yet the ways in which a constructed African-American religious subject position figures as a multivalent trope in both Hollywood and black independent cinema has not been fully explored. Moreover, I argue that this trope occupies a central place in the ongoing struggle over race and representation in American film through World War II. As a preliminary venture in this area, this essay examines three films that provide productive readings of some of the contours of this struggle: *Within Our Gates* (1919), a silent film by African-American filmmaker Oscar Micheaux; *Hallelujah!* (1929), by white Hollywood director King Vidor; and *The Blood of Jesus* (1941), by African-American filmmaker Spencer Williams.

While I see religious subjectivity as figuring largely in a contest over representations of African-Americans, I explicitly reject an interpretation of this contest in which white Hollywood directors emerge with the scale tipped irredeemably against them in weighing "positive" and "negative" representations over time. I hope, here, to complicate considerably the definitions of these terms in order to interrogate notions of a normative cinematic image of African-American people. In addition, I resist the desire to measure these representations of African-American religious life in American film against something called "real" African-American religious experience. Rather than presupposing the existence of a univalent African-American religious experience, these films, perhaps, provide a window on a process of constructing, bounding, controlling, and/or expanding that experience. In the same way, rather than merely enter a battle over cinematic successes and failures in putting forth positive and negative images, I choose, instead, to view a complex of representations that, in their very conflicted natures, reveal the power and potential of the filmic trope of African-American religious subjectivity.

The three filmmakers whose films I examine here had varied relationships with the filmmaking industry that influenced, to some degree, their approach to their work. Black filmmaker Oscar Micheaux (1884–1951), who wrote, produced, and directed at least forty-five films between 1919 and 1948, remained, throughout the era of the silent film, the most doggedly independent of white financial or artistic control. Financial difficulties after 1928 did force Micheaux to seek support from white investors. Spencer Williams (1893–1969), also an African-American filmmaker, who wrote and directed nine films between 1941 and 1947, had a much closer working relationship both with the Hollywood machine and with white-owned production companies. Beginning in the late 1920s, Williams worked for Hollywood studios in the capacities of screenwriter, assistant director, and actor, becoming best known in this period for his roles in a group of popular black westerns, including *The Bronze Buckaroo, Harlem Rides the Range, Two-Gun Man from Harlem,* and *Harlem on the Prairie,* as well as the 1937 first all-black horror film, *Son of Ingagi,* for which Williams also wrote the script. His productive working relationship in these years with white producer Alfred Sack led to Sack's funding of Williams' independent films in the 1940s. King Vidor (1894–1982) was one of the white directors who helped to make Hollywood, with a career spanning forty years and three major studios—MGM, Universal, and United Artists (Lloyd and Fuller; Finler). The three filmmakers, then, represent a variety of possibilities on a spectrum of the relationship between institutionalized, white-controlled mechanisms dominating the production of American films and questions of race, religion, and representation. I will begin with brief summaries of the plot lines of the films, as well as some of the major themes related to our topic, and then turn to a comparative discussion.

Within Our Gates (1919)

While neither religious institutions, nor religious subjectivity occupy center stage in Micheaux's *Within Our Gates,* images of African-Americans as religious beings provide a significant undercurrent in the plot. The film tells the story of Sylvia Landry, an African-American teacher in a Southern school for black children, founded by Rev. Wilson Jacobs, "an apostle of education for the black race."[2] Rev. Jacobs and his sister, Constance, oversee the school which serves the nearby community of poor African-Americans and has come upon serious financial difficulties. Moved by the need and sincerity of her students, Sylvia spends sleepless nights during which she can "think of nothing but the eternal struggle of her race and how she could uplift it." She finally volunteers to go north and help raise funds to save the school. Sylvia announces to Rev. Jacobs, "It is my duty and the duty of each member of our race to help destroy ignorance and superstition. I'm going up north where I'll try to raise the money we need. May God be with us!"

In Boston, Sylvia meets Mrs. Elena Warwick, a white philanthropist who agrees to consider donating the money the school needs to survive.

Warwick calls on Mrs. Geraldine Stratton, a rich white Southern woman visiting Boston, to advise her on the best way to help African-Americans in the South. Stratton unleashes a tirade in response to Warwick's queries about the needs of Southern blacks. "Lumber-jacks and field hands. Let me tell you—it is an error to try and educate them. Besides, they don't want an education. Can't you see that thinking would only give them a headache? Their ambition is to belong to a dozen lodges, consume religion without restraint, and, when they die, go straight up to Heaven. Wasting $5000 on a school is plain silly when you could give $100 to old Ned, the best colored preacher in the world who will do more to keep Negroes in their place than all your schools put together."

The scene fades and the title introduces: "Old Ned as He Is" (his only appearance in the film), preaching a sermon on "Abraham and the Fatted Calf." Ned preaches, "Behold, I see that black people will be the first and will be the last. While the white folk, with all their schooling, all their wealth, all their sins, will all fall into the everlasting inferno! While our race, lacking these vices and whose souls are most pure, most all will ascend into Heaven! Hallelujah!" Old Ned jumps and points and shouts, and the congregation becomes increasingly involved in the sermon, some jumping out of their seats and shouting, participating in the sermon. Ned quickly takes advantage of their attention to coerce a large offering from the members of the church.

The next day Ned visits "his white friends," who ask his "opinion" on a newspaper article on African-American voting. Ned tells them, "Y'all knows what I always preach. This is a land for the white man and black folk got ta know their place. Let the white man go to Hell with his politics, wealth, and sins. Give me Jesus!" The white men applaud as Ned continues, "Leave it to me gen'men. I always preach that the vices and sins of the white folk will end them up in Hell. When the Judgement Day comes, more Negroes than white will rise up to Heaven." As Ned prepares to leave, one of the white men kicks him in the rear and Ned leaves with a smile, saying, "Yessir, white folks is mighty fine." Once outside the room, Ned's anger shows on his face and we read his thoughts (in the titles), "Again I've sold my birthright, all for a miserable 'mess of pottage.' Negroes and whites— all are equal. As for me, miserable sinner, Hell is my destiny." Returning to Warwick and Stratton, Stratton concludes, "And so, my dear, you needn't trouble yourself over this illusion of educating the Negro. Leave it to those of us who know them—and who know just what they need."

By the film's end, Mrs. Warwick gives, not $5000, but $50,000 to save the school, having been convinced by Sylvia's presentation and horrified by

Stratton's attitudes. The climax of the story comes, not with Warwick's assistance to the school, but with the revelation of Sylvia's life story as she tries to escape blackmail by her cousin's criminal friend, Larry, who believes that Sylvia had had an affair with a white man. We learn that Sylvia, adopted by a poor, sharecropping family, became the center of the family's hopes, because her education allowed her to keep her father's books, a direct threat to the sharecropping system that kept farmers in perpetual debt. When Jasper Landry, Sylvia's father, is wrongly accused of the murder of Philip Gridlestone, the landowner, the entire family flees. Sylvia's parents and brother do not escape the mob of whites seeking Gridlestone's killer and, in a terrifying sequence, a member of the mob shoots the young brother and the group lynches the Landry parents. Sylvia, hiding in an empty house, is pursued by Gridlestone's brother, who finds her and attempts to rape her. When he sees the scar on her chest, Gridlestone realizes that Sylvia is his daughter and he sends her north to be educated. This is the white man with whom Larry mistakenly believes that Sylvia has become involved. The film closes with the audience assured that Sylvia will marry the successful, educated, and politically active Dr. V. Vivian of Boston.

Micheaux's chilling depiction of the lynching of a family generally receives the attention of contemporary scholars, particularly because Micheaux released the film in 1919, known as "Red Summer" (because of heightened violence against African-Americans following the return of black soldiers from the war in Europe). The potential for additional urban race riots as a result of the showing of Micheaux's film aroused great controversy and forced him, at times, to remove part or all of the lynching scenes. While this scene represents an important moment in black independent film history, we leave it aside, and turn instead to Micheaux's attention to aspects of African-American religiosity.

In *Within Our Gates*, as well as in other of his films, Micheaux continually questions institutionalized forms of Christianity in African-American communities, particularly those institutions that do not explicitly engage in projects aimed at improving the political, social, and economic conditions of all African-Americans. Thus, Micheaux promotes Rev. Jacobs as a model because his school does not foster class conflict, but seeks to "uplift the race" through education. Nevertheless, Micheaux's work does rely on a vision of African-Americans as "naturally" religious and, therefore, susceptible to the desires of any unscrupulous con artist. Old Ned, then, appears as a particular incarnation of a character who makes his way into many of Micheaux's films and whom he develops most fully in *Body and Soul*, a 1924 film in which Paul Robeson plays a con man/preacher who wreaks havoc in a small community. Indeed, the similarities in the set, the stock characters in the church pews and the sequence of shots in Old Ned's scene in *Within Our Gates* and the central preaching scene in *Body and Soul* indicate related concerns. In both cases, Micheaux presents an African-American religious community that blindly follows its unscrupulous minister to its own detriment.

Micheaux does not present the possibility for deception as the "essence" of Christianity, however, and his films do not reject Christianity—the dominant religious orientation of African-Americans. In one example in which Micheaux makes a particular claim for Christianity, we see Dr. V. Vivian engaged in study. He reads a text that we also see on the screen: "The Negro is a human being. His nature is not different from other human nature. Thus, we must recognize his rights as a human being. Such is the teaching of Christianity." We are to assume, because of the linguistic distance placed between the author and "the Negro," that the author of this text is white and that Micheaux not only sees positive possibilities in Christianity for African-Americans, but also sees it as having the potential to bridge white and black communities of a particular social strata. Thus, Micheaux sets Old Ned's religious belief and practice against Dr. V. Vivian's and Rev. Jacobs', with *Old* Ned markedly representing a past in which Christianity among African-Americans functioned to benefit racist whites. Vivian and Jacobs point to a future in which African-Americans embrace Christianity for the benefit of their own communities.

King Vidor's *Hallelujah!* (1929)

King Vidor's *Hallelujah!*, an all–black cast film made for Metro-Goldwyn-Mayer, concerns itself with the relationship between religion and sexuality for African-Americans. Reflecting on his motivations for making this film at a time when Hollywood studios feared producing movies that would be perceived as targeting black audiences, Vidor, a white Southerner, wrote, "For several years I had nurtured a secret hope. I wanted to make a film about Negroes, using only Negroes in the cast. The sincerity and fervor of their religious expression intrigued me, as did the honest simplicity of their sexual drives. In many instances the intermingling of these two activities seemed to offer strikingly dramatic content" (Kisch and Mapp: xx; Cripps, 1977: 237).

Zeke Johnson, the film's main character, is the eldest son in an extremely large family of cotton sharecroppers who, although engaged in back-breaking labor all day in the hot sun, all still have energy to sing and tap dance in the evenings. Zeke, sent to town to sell the crop, becomes entranced by a woman, called "High Yella," who enters into a scheme with "Hot Shot," a local gambler; both trick Zeke into gambling his family's earnings away. The fight that ensues once he realizes what has happened leads to the death of Zeke's younger brother, sent along to assist him in the selling of the crop. Zeke returns home devastated by the consequences of his actions and, at his brother's funeral, has a transforming experience in which God "shows him the light."

The next time we see Zeke, he is a well-known preacher travelling with his family (all now neatly dressed and scrubbed) conducting camp meetings under the name "Ezekiel the Prophet." High Yella and Hot Shot stand with the crowd and realize that the preacher is the same country bumpkin they had tricked in another town. High Yella goes to the camp meeting to heckle Zeke, but instead becomes converted by the power of his preaching. The lure of sexuality, however, remains too strong for Zeke who, becoming aware that "the devil is on him," tries to rid himself of his problems by proposing to Rose, the plain and virtuous family friend travelling with them. Still, that evening at another service, when Zeke sees High Yella, he runs off with her and the two move in together. The drudgery of everyday life does not suit High Yella, and, when Hot Shot returns to find her, she leaves with him. Zeke follows and murders Hot Shot after High Yella is killed in a fall from their wagon. After serving a sentence in the penitentiary, Zeke returns to the bosom of his loving family and to Rose, who still loves him. Mrs. Johnson's offer of chitterlings and spare ribs signals the resolution of all Zeke's problems.

On one level, Vidor makes a grossly simplistic connection between the impulses that drive religious fervor and sexual desire that, in his own reflections on the film, hold especially true for African-Americans—always stereotyped as "nature's people," to use Nell Painter's term—*naturally* religious and *naturally* sexual in ways over which we have no control. Zeke cannot check his sexuality, not just where High Yella is concerned, but also around Rose who, nevertheless, appears as a more appropriate mate for Zeke. In another example, early in the film, a neighboring couple, accompanied by their many children, interrupts the Johnson family's evening revelry to ask Zeke's father, who we are to assume is some sort of religious official, to marry them. Amused by the lateness of the wedding—given the large number of children the couple already have—Mr. Johnson nevertheless performs the ceremony. In the context of the wedding, Vidor edits in a scene in which Zeke attempts to rape Rose. Vidor, then, moves from the image and words of a religious ceremony to the image of Zeke, with the face and body posture of an uncontrolled animal, advancing on Rose shrinking in terror. Beyond merely indicating the simultaneity of the action of the wedding and the attempted assault, Vidor's editing decisions also underscore for the viewer the association between religion and sexuality for African-Americans and what religious fervor camouflages.

For High Yella, her drive for gambling, for money, for men, for dancing, for drinking, and for religion emerge as deeply interrelated passions. After Zeke baptises her, along with the other camp meeting converts, High Yella collapses and Zeke carries her into a tent. Both Zeke and High Yella, now aroused with religious emotion, succumb to the pull of sexual expression, and Mrs. Johnson discovers them kissing. Mrs. Johnson chastises High Yella, telling her to get up because she's "got more religion than is good for her." Too much of anything for African-Americans, even religion, leads to dissipation in the world of this film.

Vidor does present the possibility within religious leadership of conferring "manhood" on African-American men. Only when Zeke sings religious songs or preaches does he appear neither as a grinning clown nor a mesmerized hypersexual animal. At those moments his face calms, his voice deepens, and his posture straightens, and, as preacher, he inspires confidence in people and moves them to conversion. On the level of African-American communities, Vidor poses religion as that force which has the ability to help black folk resist vice by channelling sexual energy away from sex. The faith of the Johnson family, expressed in communal reading of the Bible and family prayer, keeps them together. Furthermore, we are meant to interpret Zeke's difficulties as resulting from his contact with the evils of the nearby town. Thus, in order to resist vice successfully, black folk must know that their place remains on the plantation, One reviewer in *Variety* emphasized the centrality of this theme to the film, writing,

> Whites will accept [*Hallelujah!*] as a camera reproduction of the typical southland with its wide open cotton spaces, where the good natured, singing negro continues to eke out a bare existence; where he lives untrammeled by city ways unless he invades their riotous precincts; where he has his moments of joy, passion and religion. It brings realistically to the screen how he lives in nondescript surroundings, with continual evidence of illiteracy that even remains unpolished when becoming hysterically religious; of the happier side of plantation life, the carefree, syncopating singing and dancing cotton pickers whose lives run uneventful until death stalks in their midst or sordid tragedy drops into their gayety. (August 28, 1929)

Thus, for this reviewer, death and sordid tragedy of their own making, rather than lynching, segregation, economic discrimination, and the withholding of civil rights, constitute the primary difficulties in the lives of carefree, rural African-Americans.

It becomes clear that Vidor's characterizations apply specifically to African-Americans, and his work rests on the interarticulation of religion and constructions of race. The religious practices of the African-Americans that Vidor presents function differently than religion does for white Americans because, for Vidor, race necessarily mediates religious experience and possibility. For Vidor, in his own words, even "the polished Negro . . . possesses, under the surface, the rhythm and abandon, the love song and laughter of those in a primitive state" (Cripps, 1977: 243), and therefore every African-American's experience of Christianity becomes filtered through this primitive state, just as this primitivism propels African-American religiosity. Despite Zeke's valiant attempts to re-create himself as a mature, responsible, and thoughtfully religious man, his underlying, racially marked nature continually emerges. A reviewer in *Literary Digest* noted Vidor's success in conveying race as a mediating element in religious experience when he wrote that the film affirmed that "the Negro is as different from the rest of us as we are from the Russians, the Germans, or the French" (October 5, 1929). Another *Vanity Fair* reviewer put it simply, "If the picture is limited, its boundaries are inherent to the subject" (August 28, 1929).

The Blood of Jesus (1941)

Spencer Williams' film, *The Blood of Jesus*, opens with the image of an African-American man plowing a field, followed by rural images to set the scene, with a soundtrack by Rev. R. L. Robertson's Heavenly Choir singing "Good News, the Chariot's Coming," and "Go Down, Moses." A voice-over begins:

> Almost gone are the days when peace ruled the earth with a firm and gentle hand, when fear of God dwelt in the hearts of men and women and children, when the ten original commandments were the accepted laws of every civilized country and nation on the face of the globe, when those who went to church on Sunday did not go back home to prey on their neighbors the remaining six days of the week, when religion was practiced with unfalse solemnity and honest sincerity and when soul salvation was a heritage from heaven for not

merely a few thousand, but for many millions. Those days are almost gone from the earth . . . almost.

The main action begins with the central character, Martha Jackson, about to be baptised. We learn from the gossiping church women on the banks of the river that Martha's husband, Ras, has not been baptised, does not belong to the church, and has, in fact, gone off hunting for the day. One of the gossips, Sister Jenkins, accompanies Martha home and they find Ras sitting on the porch with a sack of stolen hogs that, when discovered by Jenkins, he argues that he stole only to feed his family. Later Martha encourages Ras to pray and "get religion" because this would make them much happier, and he agrees to try. As Ras sets his shotgun down it falls and discharges, shooting Martha as she gazes lovingly at a picture of Jesus on the wall near the bed.

As members of Martha's church pray over her and sing, Ras sits in the corner crying and praying himself. Then, as Martha's body remains on the bed, we see her spirit respond to a beckoning angel and rise from the bed. They leave the house and walk along the road, coming to a point where shadowy figures pace back and forth. Martha asks the why these people remain in mourning. The angel replies, "They mourn because their efforts are yet unrewarded, because the unjust have struck down the good and the unselfish, because sin is enthroned in the seat of power." But, she informs Martha, her time has not yet come and, thus, Martha must make the journey home. The angel points her to the highway of life, warning of the choice she must make at the crossroads—to the right, life, and to the left, death, hell and destruction. Significantly, the highway of life leads through "the city," and Martha must avoid the temptations therein.

Satan appears at the side of the road, dressed in a shiny red suit and, through his agent, Judas Green, successfully distracts Martha by presenting her with a dress and matching shoes and accompanying her to a nightclub. There Judas introduces Martha to Rufus Brown, who offers her a job. The three then go to Rufus' small juke joint where Martha realizes that Rufus expects her to work as a prostitute. Martha flees, followed by a group of male patrons from the juke joint who have mistaken her for another woman who picked the pocket of one of the customers. She comes to the crossroads where a sign before her points the way: "Hell" to the left and "Zion" to the right. Satan makes one last attempt to distract her, but this time Jesus, through a voice-over, intervenes and frightens him away. When the men reach Martha, Jesus again intervenes, and the biblical incident of the attempt to stone the prostitute is recapitulated. Collapsing from exhaustion, she lies under the crossroad sign, now a crucifix. As

Martha prays, the blood of Jesus begins to drip in large, thick globules from the crucifix, falling on her face. The scene dissolves, and the film ends with Martha in bed again, waking up. Ras and the church members gather and Martha's guiding angel reappears.

In one sense *The Blood of Jesus* may be interpreted as depicting the decline of an idyllic rural past into the decay and alienation of urbanization. One of the messages of the film is indeed that, like Martha Jackson, African-Americans as a community have been lured from the enveloping safety of the small town and the community church. Williams seems to be telling his audience that it is God's wish, even God's plan, that African-Americans reclaim or cling to the rural past. Martha's path is one that, significantly, passes *through* the city and, with the aid of Jesus and the angel, brings her back to her family and community. From this perspective, Thomas Cripps' assertion, in *Black Film as Genre*, that Williams' message is a "fundamentalist" one and exists only on the surface has some merit, as the film is grounded in belief in the redemptive power of the crucifixion and in the reality of miracles in the lives of good Christians. Yet the proclamation on the lobby cards and posters for the film that this is "a mighty epic of modern morals," contains within it a key to a deeper interpretation. It is a story of *modern* morals for the community from Williams' perspective, and thus much more than a plea for a return to an idyllic past.

At every juncture, Williams problematizes the rural contexts and insistently refuses to romanticize the Southern black folk as maintaining a pure and authentic traditional life. In keeping with many films of the period that investigate the future of small towns in an industrial age (Levine, 1993), Williams' work evidences some degree of nostalgia for rural life. It seems unlikely, however, that African-Americans at the end of the Depression—an era that followed a heightened period of urban race riots and Southern lynchings, following the period in which segregation developed, following the failures of Reconstruction, following slavery—would identify the glorious past that the voice-over describes in the opening of the film with any point in their own history. Did any moment in the history of the American South correspond to the narrator's time "when the ten original commandments were the accepted laws for every civilized country and nation on the face of the globe"? While Williams affirms some aspects of rural life by juxtaposing rural images with the opening narrative, the disjuncture between the idyllic fantasy and the realities of sharecropping, perpetual debt, scarce access to education, and the spectre of terrorism by whites calls into question an interpretation according to which the film asserts that in this Southern setting the black folk maintain a pure and authentic traditional life untroubled by any outside concerns.

In addition, the use of the spiritual, "Go Down, Moses," with its refrain of "let my people go" against the scenes of a man engaged in back-breaking agricultural labor suggests a call for a rethinking of the traditional connection between African-Americans and the rural South.

Williams also refuses to romanticize the folk of the community. When, for example, the members of the church observe Martha's baptism, they gossip, and they continue to gossip every time they appear, even when they are engaged in prayer. Importantly, the black church itself does not escape unscathed in Williams' story. The minister of this church community appears as ineffectual and largely absent, particularly from the community's watch over Martha's bedside. The real spiritual center of the congregation's life is not the minister, but Sister Jenkins, one of the women attending Martha at her baptism, a strong woman and a multidimensional personality who leads the community in prayer. The frictions evident within the community, as well as between the rural and the urban become clear in the ever-present tension between the spirituals and the blues on the film's soundtrack.

In *The Blood of Jesus*, Williams presents a story larger than that of one woman's spiritual journey. As viewers of the film we do not, for one moment, think that Martha will not successfully come through her trials in "the city." Indeed Martha's experience in the city hardly seems beyond her powers of comprehension, but, instead, figures as an almost inevitable experience that must be processed by all. Martha's experience serves instead as a vehicle for the transformation of both Ras and the church community. While this text functions on one level as a cautionary tale against certain elements of urban life, Martha journeys back not to a preserved community, but to one that came together and evaluated itself in the face of their experiences and of her "trip" to the city. Williams' prescription for African-Americans at this time calls for uniting as a Christian community that is emphatically not fundamentalist to the degree that it excludes its own members, but rather as one that can embrace varieties of experience. As the tension between the spirituals and the blues ultimately gave rise to gospel music, a form that integrates aspects of both, so too African-American Christians are called to bring together seemingly incompatible and disparate elements into an organic whole in order to advance the community.

Further Reflections

Although produced in substantially different historical moments, each film addresses questions of African-American identities and the relation of these communities to the nation. Micheaux positions black Americans, emerging from the experience of the First World War, as fully American and as a group within the national body with as much complexity and potential—religious and otherwise—as any other group. Vidor's film sits at the cusp of the Depression era, and he offers the support of black families and communal effort as a means of withstanding the hard times ahead. In Williams' work, a strong communal ethos also functions to build hope for the future as America faces war in Europe.

In addition to addressing broad questions of national identity, religious experience and practice emerge as a central means of constructing a range of racialized identities for African-Americans in each of these films. Although the practice of Christianity by African-Americans holds within it the possibility of bridging the gap between white and black Americans for both Micheaux and Vidor, they differ on the question of how wide the gap and who controls the bridge. In Vidor's *Hallelujah!* the self-contained black world he constructs exists merely as a shadow of an absent, yet strongly implied white world that sets a standard for "true" religiosity unreachable by Zeke and his family. What we are led to admire is their constant attempt to approximate that standard of Christian experience and expression despite the inescapable mediating factor of race. Micheaux's approach differs considerably in that he presents African-Americans as able to construct a bridge between themselves and sympathetic white Americans through the *practice* of Christianity. Through the characters of Sylvia, Rev. Jacobs, and Dr. V. Vivian, Micheaux rejects attempts by some whites to use Christianity as a means of controlling the potential of African-Americans to challenge the prevailing social order. Micheaux's work stands out among both race films and Hollywood all–black cast films in that he refuses to exclude white people from the world of his films and insists on portraying them as a social group filled with complexities and issues of identity construction and maintenance, just as he depicts African-Americans. Significantly, Micheaux can envision cooperation between black and white Americans on ground and terms set by African-Americans and chooses to emphasize this possibility in *Within Our Gates*.

The films also present a variety of perspectives on the role of the Bible in constructing African-American religious subjects. Micheaux's character of Old Ned illustrates the dangers of an illiterate minister and congregation. Despite Ned's conflation of Bible stories into a sermon on "Abraham and the fatted calf," his congregation seems neither surprised nor dismayed at his mangling of the Bible, nor does his error interfere with their ability to engage the sermon with high emotions. In the end,

Ned uses the fervor of his congregation and their biblical illiteracy to his financial benefit. Micheaux holds up literacy as the key to the advancement of African-Americans in spiritual terms as well as political and economic. In *Hallelujah!* Vidor presents a poor but not uneducated family, at its best when gathered around the Bible in the evening. We come to understand that Zeke's situation has become too much for him when we witness his sermon at the camp meeting, one that seems to lack a grounding in the Biblical text. His return to the family and the Bible mark the resolution of his difficulties. In contrast to Micheaux and Vidor's use of biblical literacy as an important marker, the Bible as text remains conspicuously absent in Williams' *The Blood of Jesus*. The religious ethos of the film relies heavily on African-American folk religious traditions established through the period of slavery and transformed thereafter. The ubiquitous presence of slave spirituals as the musical setting underscores the ground in slave religion. As Lawrence Levine's (1977) work on slave culture emphasizes, spirituals functioned, in part, to expand the boundaries of time and space, both backward and forward, and allow enslaved African-Americans to bring the biblical past into the present time and to project themselves into a future in which justice prevails. In addition, through spirituals, biblical figures became real and active in the world. In Williams' film, instead of reading the text of the Bible, the characters interact with Satan, with Judas, and other figures made real, and thus evidence a biblical literacy not dependent on the ability to read.

All three films make use of images of African-American religious excess and all counsel moderation in religious expression, but each puts these images to different uses. For Vidor, excess is the "natural" mode of African-American expression, whether in sexuality, joy, religion, or general vice, and should not be encouraged and, indeed, should be limited wherever possible. Thus, Zeke's role as public, popularly supported evangelist finally becomes more than he can handle with integrity. The resolution that Vidor provides for Zeke requires that he no longer be in the public spotlight, that he no longer have the access to material goods that the profession of preaching afforded him, that he no longer have access to a woman he finds attractive, and that he no longer look outside the bounds of his own family for anything. In Williams' *The Blood of Jesus*, moderation in religious expression becomes a means for broadening the boundaries of Christian community. Those on whom Williams calls to moderate their expression of Christianity are those who create a rigid behavioral standard for admission into the community of Christians and yet themselves behave in ways that impugn those standards through gossip, jealousy, suspicion, or selfishness. Micheaux's religious prescription for African-American communities calls for an approach to religious practice that is more intellectual than emotional but does not, however, rest on class distinctions among African-Americans. Although educated and elite African-Americans appear at the center of Micheaux's narrative, they do not retain exclusive control of the characteristics that Micheaux seeks to promote. He presents hard-working, steadfast, intelligent although poor and uneducated people as individuals with as much access to Micheaux's advocated religious subject position as the elite. Similarly, members of the privileged class of African-Americans are equally likely to engage in vice in Micheaux's film world.

I have meant for this essay to be primarily suggestive of the possibilities of exploring cinematic representations of African-Americans as religious subjects in American film. Each film provides a simple and superficial reading which renders African-American people as religious in transparently sincere ways that, for better or worse, ground them in an all-black world that always "pales" in comparison with white worlds. I hope that this examination of these three films, albeit brief, serves to point the way to more complex readings that accord African-American religious life an important place in examining ways in which American film functioned to negotiate a complex and ongoing process of constructing African-American and American identities.

Notes

1. I do not use the example of African-Americans in American film as a simple stand-in for a discussion of "race" in these works. My work makes use of a growing body of literature that deals with race as a socially constructed discourse concerned with the fluid nature of categories of race and their relation to the structuring of community boundaries and levels of power within communities. In this examination of the ways in which films participate in the process of formulating ideas about race, I make use of the specific case of images of African-Americans as part of a larger project on race, religion, and film in which I also address other racialized groups (Appiah; Fields; Higginbotham).
2. All quotations from *Within Our Gates* are taken from the titles, reconstructed by Scott Simmon, for the Library of Congress Video Collection edition of the film. The film had been "lost" until the late 1970s when Thomas Cripps identified a print of the film in Spain under the title *La Negra*. Scott Simmon and the Library of Congress restored the film and reconstructed the titles by translating the Spanish-language titles in the Spanish print, through the use of four surviving English-language titles from the film, by using the model of another of Micheaux's extant silent films, and through readings of Micheaux's novels. See Scott Simmon, information booklet for The Library of Congress Video Collection, Volume I: "The African-American Cinema I: Oscar Micheaux's *Within Our Gates* (1919)."

Works Consulted

Appiah, Anthony. 1986. "The Uncompleted Argument: Du Bois and the Illusion of Race." Pp. 21–37 in *"Race," Writing, and Difference.* Ed. Henry Louis Gates. Chicago: University of Chicago Press.

Bogle, Donald. 1973. *Toms, Coons, Mulattoes, Mammies, and Bucks.* New York: Bantam.

Bowser, Pearl. 1990. "From Harlem to Hollywood." Program Notes, American Museum of the Moving Image, New York City.

Cripps, Thomas. 1977. *Slow Fade to Black: The Negro in American Film, 1900–1942.* New York: Oxford University Press.

————. 1978. *Black Film as Genre.* Bloomington: Indiana University Press.

Fields, Barbara J. 1982. "Ideology and Race in American History." Pp. 134–47 in *Region, Race and Reconstruction: Essays in Honor of C. Vann Woodward.* Ed. J. Morgan Kousser and James M. McPherson. New York: Oxford University Press.

Finler, Joel W. 1988. *The Hollywood Story.* New York: Crown.

Gaines, Jane. 1993. "Fire and Desire: Race, Melodrama, and Oscar Micheaux." Pp. 49–70 in *Black American Cinema.* Ed. Manthia Diawara. New York: Routledge.

Guerrero, Ed. 1993. *Framing Blackness: The African-American Image in Film.* Philadelphia: Temple University Press.

Higginbotham, Evelyn Brooks. 1992. "African-American Women's History and the Metalanguage of Race." *Signs* 17: 251–74.

Kisch, John, and Edward Mapp. 1992. *A Separate Cinema: Fifty Years of Black Cast Posters.* New York: The Noonday Press.

Levine, Lawrence W. 1977. *Black Culture and Black Consciousness: Afro-American Folk Thought From Slavery to Freedom.* New York: Oxford University Press.

————. 1993. *The Unpredictable Past: Explorations in American Cultural History.* New York: Oxford University Press.

Lloyd, Ann, and Graham Fuller. 1987. *The Illustrated Who's Who of the Cinema.* New York: Portland House.

Turner, Patricia A. 1994. *Ceramic Uncles and Celluloid Mammies: Black Images and Their Influence on Culture.* New York: Anchor.

Chapter 44

The Prophetic Tradition in Afro-America

Cornel West

P rophetic modes of thought and action are dotted across the landscape of Afro-American history. I understand these modes to consist of protracted and principled struggles against forms of personal despair, intellectual dogmatism, and socioeconomic oppression that foster communities of hope. Therefore the distinctive features of prophetic activity are Pascalian leaps of faith in the capacity of human beings to transform their circumstances, engage in relentless criticism and self-criticism, and project visions, analyses, and practices of social freedom. In this chapter I shall attempt to characterize and criticize—hence try to reactivate—the prophetic tradition in Afro-America.

The American Terrain

It is impossible to characterize adequately prophetic activity among Afro-Americans without understanding the specific circumstances under which these practices occur. So it is necessary to put forward a brief sketch of the specificity of American society and culture—highlighting the ideological, political, and economic spheres.

The most crucial brute fact about the American terrain is that the USA began as a liberal capitalist nation permeated with patriarchal oppression and based, in large part, upon a slave economy. Born modern, born liberal, and born bourgeois, the USA's relative absence of a feudal past gave way in the northern states to an agrarian utopia of free independent farmers on "free" land. In the southern states, the thriving economy of slavery underscored an aristocratic ethos and an entrepreneurial ethic. These beginnings facilitated the ideological predominance of an American-style liberalism which, on the one hand, promoted the sanctity of private property, the virtue of capital accumulation, and the subordination of women; and, on the other hand, encouraged the flowering of a slave-based society principally upon the ideological pillar of the inferiority of non-Europeans, especially Africans.

This native form of liberalism was engendered not by opposition to feudalism as in Europe but rather by securing property-owning white male consensus in order to maintain social stability. Motivated by notions of new beginnings, Edenic innocence, and exemplary performance, the anticolonial sentiments of the nation entailed an abiding distrust of institutional power, bureaucracy, and, above all, the state. Despite unprecedented proliferation of voluntary associations, American political discourse placed great emphasis on the welfare of propertied persons as atomistic individuals rather than as community dwellers or citizens of a republic.

This liberal ideology of Americanism embodied the ideals of bourgeois freedom (such as the freedom to own property, accumulate capital, speak one's mind, and organize to worship) and formal equality (equal treatment under the law)—circumscribed by racist, sexist, and class constraints. These ideological viewpoints indeed have undergone change over time, yet their traces strongly persist in contemporary American life. To put it crudely, most Americans even now—be they of the right or the left—are highly individualistic, libertarian, and antistatist as well as racist and sexist.

The ideals of bourgeois freedom and formal equality became a beacon to oppressed social classes and ethnic groups around the world. Widespread immigration to the USA contributed to the first ecumenical, multiethnic, and multiracial working class in the world and the most complex heterogeneous population in modernity. In addition, the boomtown character of American industrialization—urban centers which appeared virtually overnight—set the context for the flourishing of nativism, jingoism, anti-Semitism, the already entrenched sexism, and, above all, racism.

In the political sphere, the infamous "gift of suffrage" to the white male component of the working class without the need for organized proletarian organization—in fact prior to widespread industrialization hence substantive modern class formation—yielded deep allegiance of the white male populace to the existing political order. The political arrangement of coalitional politics and political machines within the framework of a two-party system channeled organizational efforts of class, race, and gender into practical interest group struggles and thereby relegated oppositional movements to either ill-fated third parties or political oblivion. Furthermore, harsh state repression has been exercised against perceived extremists who threaten the tenuous consensus which the liberal ideology of Americanism reinforces.

This ingenious political setup encourages diverse modes of interest group articulation and permits incremental social change; it also domesticates oppositional movements, dilutes credible wholesale programs of social change, and discourages sustained organizational efforts at undermining the liberal consensus. The political predicament of all prophetic practices in the USA has been and remains that of ideological purity and political irrelevance or ideological compromise and political marginality. Extraordinary American productivity principally owing to tremendous technological innovation (motivated, in part, by labor shortages), abundant natural resources (secured by imperialist domination of indigenous and Mexican peoples), and cheap labor (usually imported from various parts of the globe) has enabled social upward mobility unknown in the modern world. The availability of goods, luxuries, and conveniences— which has made comfort an American obsession—to significant segments of the population gives the appearance of a widely fluid social structure. This perception provides credence to the Horatio Alger dimension of the liberal ideology of Americanism: the possibility of rags-to-riches success for all. Even the lower classes remain enchanted by this seductive ideological drama.

High levels of productivity, with uneven expressions across various regions of the country, have made the commitment to economic growth an unquestioned national dogma. From the far right (for whom growth is a symptom of liberty) to the sophisticated left (for whom growth makes easier redistribution), Americans remain captive to the notion of economic expansion. This dogma undergirds the consensus of American-style liberalism and thereby views *as natural necessity* the close partnership of the state, banks, and large corporations and their coordinated expansionist activities abroad—often with repressive consequences for the native populations. This partnership, along with its imperialist extension, is the linchpin of the American terrain.

On Black Prophetic Practices

These distinctively American circumstances have produced *truncated* prophetic practices especially among Afro-Americans. Such practices—be they populist, feminist, trade-unionist, socialist, or Red, Green, and Black politics—are truncated in that they are rendered relatively impotent if they fall outside the liberal consensus and irreparably innocuous if they function within this consensus. In other words, if prophetic practices radically call into question the orthodoxy of American-style liberalism they are either repudiated or repressed; and if they accept the perimeters of this orthodoxy they are effectively domesticated and absorbed by the powers that be. This clever American way of dealing with prophetic critiques has produced a marvelously stable society; it also has reduced the capacity of this society to grow and develop. In fact, it can be said with confidence that American society is one of the few to move from innocence to corruption without a mediating stage of maturity. In short, American society has been and remains unable to face its systemic and structural problems.

A major problem perennially facing black prophetic practices is that only in brief historical moments have basic black concerns—such as institutional racism—gained a foothold in American public discourse. Hence, most black prophetic practices have had minimal impact on American society and culture. This is ironic in that a strong case can be made that black Americans are the most American of all Americans; that is, they not only cling most deeply to the ideals of Americanism as enunciated in the Declaration of Independence and the Constitution but they also are the most hybrid of Americans in blood, colors, and cultural creations.

Black prophetic practices best exemplify the truncated content and character of American prophetic practices; they reveal the strengths and shortcomings, the importance and impotence, of prophetic activities in recalcitrant America. Black prophetic practices can be generally characterized by three basic features: *a deep-seated moralism, an inescapable opportunism*, and *an aggressive pessimism*. This deep-seated moralism flows from the pervasive influence of Protestant Christianity—unmatched among other modern industrial and postindustrial nations. Afro-American prophetic practices have been and, for the most part, remain ensconced in a moralistic mood: that is, they are grounded in a moralistic conception of the world in which the rightness or wrongness of human actions—be they individually or collectively understood—are measured by ethical ideals or moral standards. Like the Puritans, the first European Americans, black prophetic Americans have tended to assume that such ideals and standards ought to make a difference in regard to how individuals act and how institutions operate. In short, black prophetic practices assume that—after the most intense scrutiny—some ultimate sense of a morally grounded sense of justice ought to prevail in personal and societal affairs.

The inescapable opportunism—or the unprincipled scrambling for crumbs—of black prophetic practices is largely a function of both the unmet needs of black Americans and, more importantly, the design and operation of the American social system. The needs of black Americans are similar to those of most Americans: more control over their lives and destinies, better living conditions, health care, education, and the extension of liberties for the effective exercise of their unique capacities and potentialities. The satisfaction of these needs are rooted in the quest for more democratic arrangements—in the political, economic, and cultural spheres—which facilitate more self-realization.

The design and operation of the American social system requires that this quest for democracy and self-realization be channeled into unfair competitive circumstances such that opportunistic results are unavoidable. In fact, in an ironic way, opportunistic practices become requisite to sustain the very sense of prophetic sensibilities and values in the USA. This is so primarily because deliverance is the common denominator in American society and culture—and a set of practices of whatever sort cannot be sustained or legitimated over time and space without some kind of delivery-system or some way of showing that crucial consequences and effects (such as goods and services) flow from one's project. This "delivery prerequisite" usually forces even prophetic critiques and actions to adopt opportunistic strategies and tactics in order to justify themselves to a disadvantaged and downtrodden constituency.

This situation often results in a profound pessimism among prophetic black Americans regarding the possibilities of fundamental transformation of American society and culture. The odds seem so overwhelming, the incorporative strategies of the status quo so effective—and the racism so deeply entrenched in American life. Yet most prophetic practices among black Americans have given this pessimism an aggressiveness such that it becomes sobering rather than disenabling, a stumbling block rather than a dead end, a challenge to meet rather than a conclusion to accept.

In the remainder of this discussion, I shall try to defend my general characterization of black prophetic practices by presenting persuasive interpretations of three central sets of these practices in Afro-America: prophetic black Christian practices, prophetic black womanist practices, and prophetic black socialist practices. Although I may highlight certain individuals within each set of practices, I intend to view these individuals as but embodiments of the set they best represent.

Prophetic Black Christian Practices

The institutional roots of the prophetic tradition in Afro-America lie in black churches. Although never acquiring a majority of black people within its walls, black churches have had a disproportionate amount of influence in Afro-America. These institutions were the unique products of a courageous and creative people who struggled under excruciating conditions of economic exploitation, political oppression, and cultural degradation. Owing to a lower ratio of African to European Americans— as well as laboring in smaller plantations with much less absentee owner- ship—than that of Latin America, black people in the USA interacted more intensely and frequently with white Americans. And with an inhu- mane stress on slave *reproduction*—as opposed to slave *importation* in the Caribbean and Latin America—it was more difficult for young genera- tions of Afro-Americans to preserve their ties to African customs and rit- uals. It is important to keep in mind that only 4.5 percent of all Africans imported to the New World—427,000 out of 9.5 million—came to North America. In stark contrast, 3.7 million Africans were imported to Brazil, 748,000 to Jamaica, and 702,000 to Cuba.

The African appropriation of Euro-American Christianity was, in part, the result of the black encounter with the absurd; that is, an attempt to make sense out of a meaningless and senseless predicament. With the generational distancing from African culture—hence the waning of African traditional religions among the new progeny of slaves—Afro- Americans became more and more attracted to religious dissenters in American culture. White Methodists and especially white Baptists seized the imagination of many black slaves for a variety of reasons. First, black people found themselves locked into what Orlando Patterson has coined "natal alienation"; that is, the loss of ties at birth in both ascending and descending generations. Hence, they experienced a form of social death as dishonored persons with no public worth, only economic value. Dis- senting Protestant Christianity provided many black slaves with a sense of somebodiness, a personal and egalitarian God who gave them an iden- tity and dignity not found in American society. It also yielded a deep sense of the tragic—not accented in West African religions—while holding out the possibility of ultimate triumph.

The Baptist polity—adopted by a majority of black Christian slaves— provided a precious historical possession not found among other groups of oppressed black people in the New World: control over their own ecclesiastical institutions. The uncomplicated requirements for member- ship, open and easy access to the clergy and congregation-centered mode of church governance set the cultural context for the flowering of African- isms, invaluable fellowship, and political discourse. In fact, this setting served as the crucible for not simply distinctive Afro-American cultural products but also for much of the unique American cultural contributions to the world—including the spirituals, blues, and jazz.

Black churches permitted and promoted the kinetic orality of Afro-Americans—the fluid and protean power of the Word in speech and song along with the rich Africanisms such as antiphonality (call-and-response), polyrhythms, syncopation, and repetition; the passionate physicality, including the bodily participation in liturgical and everyday expressions; and the combative spirituality which accents a supernatural and subversive joy, an oppositional perseverance and patience. Some of these churches served as the places where slave insurrections were planned—such as those of Gabriel Prosser, Denmark Vesey, and Nat Turner. And legal sanctions against black people worshiping God without white supervision were pervasive throughout the southern USA. In short, black churches were the major public spheres in Afro-America where strategies of survival and visions of liberation, tactics of reform and dreams of emancipation were put forward. Black Christian discourse became the predominant language wherein subversive desires and utopian energies of Afro-Americans were garnered, cultivated, and expressed.

Yet, as it has been noted, Afro-American Christianity did not produce a militant millennialist tradition. This does not mean that there was no prophetic tradition among Afro-American Christians; only that this prophetic tradition did not promote explicitly revolutionary action on a broad scale. This was so for three basic reasons. First, the American status quo, especially in the South, was too entrenched, too solid. A Black Christian millennialist revolt would only result in communal or personal suicide—as evidenced in the executions of Prosser, Vesey, Turner, and those who followed them. Second, the Afro-American Christian accent on the tragic sense of life and history precluded perfectionistic conceptions of the kingdom of God on earth—conceptions which often fuel millennial movements. Third, militant millennial movements usually result from the complex tension generated from a clash of two distinct ways of life in which an exemplary prophet calls for a return and recovery of pristine origins that yield ascetic sensibilities and revolutionary action. Afro-American Christian slaves—despite harsh domination—shared too much in common with Euro-American slaveholders in regard to culture and civilization. Notwithstanding deep dissimilarities, these differences were not deep enough to give cultural credence and existential authenticity to claims about Afro-Americans and Euro-Americans inhabiting two distinct and different ways of life. Subsequent black nationalist movements have attempted to authenticate such claims—but usually to no avail in regard to revolutionary action. In fact, most black nationalist movements have been Zionist, as with Chief Sam or Marcus Garvey, or explicitly apolitical as with Elijah Muhammad's Nation of Islam. Maulana Karenga's US—owing to his creative leadership and openness to criticism—is the major black nationalist organization which serves as an exception.

The inability of Afro-American Christianity to produce a millennialist tradition is a tribute to black Christians—for as great and heroic as it may sound in books, it would have resulted, more than likely, in either wholesale genocide for black people or disenabling despair and overwhelming self-destruction among black people. In fact, the latter has been in process since the sixties among young poor black people given the high, almost millennial, expectations generated by the civil rights and Black Power movements and the inadequate response of the American powers that be. In stark contrast, the Afro-American prophetic tradition has remained more pessimistic—and realistic—regarding America's will to justice and thereby preserved a more tempered disposition toward quick change. Such a disposition indeed may buttress the status quo, yet it also resists suicidal efforts to revolt prematurely against it.

Martin Luther King, Jr., is a unique figure in Afro-American Christianity in that he represents both a heroic effort to reform and a suicidal effort to revolutionize American society and culture. In the early years of his prophetic Christian leadership of the civil rights movement, King attempted to bring oppressed black southerners into the mainstream of American life. In a crypto-fascist, underindustrialized racist American South, even these efforts at minimal reform could cost one's life. Yet as King moved into the urban North, reassessed U.S. presence in the Dominican Republic, South Africa, and South Vietnam, he concluded that only a fundamental transformation of American society and culture—a democratic socialist USA which promoted nonracist life-styles—could provide black freedom. This latter conclusion moved King far out of the mainstream of Afro-American Christianity and of American public discourse. Such a prophetic vision of America proved too threatening to America from one whose prophecy was not simply words but, more importantly, action. In this regard, King and his ability to mobilize people of different races and groups was far more dangerous than a library full of black liberation theology texts or a room full of black liberation theologians who remain distant from peoples' resistance movements. Yet King's deep moralism rooted in his black Christian convictions, his inescapable opportunism as enacted in his deal with President Johnson to exclude Fannie Lou Hamer and the black Mississippi Democrats at the Democratic National

Convention (1964) in Atlantic City and his aggressive pessimism, as seen in his later depiction of American society as "sicker" than he ever imagined, bear out the predicament of black prophetic practices in the USA.

Prophetic Black Womanist Practices

The first national articulation of black prophetic practices in the USA rests with black women. The first nationwide protest organization among Afro-Americans was created by black women. Predating the National Urban League (1900) and the National Association for the Advancement of Colored People (1909), the National Federation of Afro-American Women (1895) brought together black women across denominational, ideological, and political lines. Inspired by the militant anti-lynching and womanist spokeswoman, Ida Wells-Barnett, black women's clubs around the country came together in order to focus on two major issues: the humiliating conditions of black women's work, especially the sexual abuse and degrading images of black women in domestic service (in which a majority of black women were employed) and the debilitating effects of Jim Crowism, especially the unique American institution (literally invented here) of lynching—which victimized two black persons a week from 1885 to 1922. Furthermore, the black women accented the subtle connection between black sexuality and white violence by acknowledging the fact that lynching was justified often as a way of protecting white women against rape by black men.

Building upon the heroic action of the underground railroad revolutionary Harriet Tubman, the outspoken abolitionist Marie W. Stuart, the exemplary nineteenth-century womanist Sojourner Truth, and the Sorbonne-educated teacher and writer Anna Cooper, the national organizations of black women raised their voices in unison against institutional racism in the country and institutional sexism in the country and in the black community. In her texts, *Southern Horrors* (1892) and *A Red Record* (1895), Ida Wells-Barnett delineated, in excruciating detail, the figures and facts of southern lynchings—including the white male and female victims—as well as put forward a broad account of why the lynchings systematically occurred—an account that acknowledged the sexual and economic motivations for lynching. And in Anna Cooper's important yet neglected book, *A Voice from the South* (1892), a sophisticated case was made linking again both racism in American society and sexism in Afro-America.

The long and winding career of Ida Wells-Barnett is illuminating for an understanding of the power and pitfalls of black prophetic practices.

Beginning as editor of *Free Speech and Headlight,* a Baptist weekly in Memphis, Tennessee, Wells-Barnett was run out of town by racist whites after an article of hers presented a scathing critique of the city's silence concerning the lynching of her three close friends. She served briefly as a columnist for T. Thomas Fortune's renowned *New York Age* and then moved to Chicago where she founded and edited (along with her militant lawyer-husband, Ferdinand Barnett) the *Chicago Conservator.* Famous for her devastating criticisms of accommodationist black clergy and her bold support of black self-defense, Wells-Barnett engaged in a lifelong battle with Booker T. Washington and his ubiquitous machine. Recent works on Washington have disclosed the extent to which he controlled, connived, spied on, and manipulated the major black institutions and movements of his day. And his opposition to Wells-Barnett—principally owing to her militancy—exemplifies such behavior. For example, Washington's wife, Margaret, not only headed the first national black women's organization, she also joined the other major leader, Mary Church Terrell, in blocking Wells-Barnett from holding high office. Furthermore, Washington's control of the Chicago NAACP branch cut off valuable funding for Wells-Barnett's settlement house. Even W.E.B. Du Bois curtailed Wells-Barnett's presence on the national level of the NAACP—an organization she, along with Du Bois and others (mostly white liberals and socialists), founded—by excluding her from the board of directors. In short, Wells-Barnett employed a moral standard and found the black male clergy wanting, fell victim many times to Booker T. Washington's rapacious opportunism, and found herself abandoned by the very organizations she helped found and build. Her career ended with a similar aggressive pessimism to that of Martin Luther King, Jr.—yet hers was directed not only at the "sickness" of American society but also at the sexism of Afro-America.

This sense of aggressive pessimism can be seen in subsequent prophetic practices of black women. It is apparent in the efforts of Bonita Williams, Eloise and Audley Moore—all black women members of the Communist Party USA in the thirties—who in the midst of the least racist organization in the USA during the depression still objected to its subtle racism. In their attempt to promote a ban on the rampant interracial marriages in the party they were forced to ask a black male comrade from Kansas City, Abner Berry, to make the motion at the Central Committee meeting only to discover later that he was married to a white woman. Similar experiences of marginality in the labor movement can be seen in the gallant struggles of Victoria Garvin—the first black woman to hold a high elected office in American trade-unionism, as vice president of the Distributing,

Processing and Office Workers (DPOWA-CIO)—and Octavia Hawkins, the leader of UAW Local 453 in Chicago—both of whom were major figures in the National Negro Labor Council, the foremost black protest group in the early fifties which was soon crushed by McCarthyism.

In the recent black freedom struggle, the list goes on and on. From the legendary Fannie Lou Hamer of the National Welfare Rights Organization, Miranda Smith of the Tobacco Workers Union, Frances Beale of SNCC (now of Line of March), Ericka Huggins of the Black Panther Party to Angela Davis of the Communist Party USA. Although each case is quite different, the common denominator is protracted struggle against the effects of race, class, and gender oppression in the USA and those of class and gender combination in Afro-America. The contemporary writings of Gayl Jones, Toni Cade Bambara, Alice Walker, Toni Morrison, Sonia Sanchez, Lucille Clifton, and Audre Lorde—though constituting both a grand literary upsurge and a dim hope for black women's enhancement—repeat the cycle of black prophetic practices: initial moralism, inescapable opportunism, and combative pessimism.

Prophetic Black Socialist Practices and the Future

Black prophetic practices as manifest in black socialist thought and action, though in my view the most important set for political purposes, requires less attention and scrutiny than the black prophetic church and black womanism. This is so, in part, because socialism as a modern tradition is less indigenous to black prophetic practices than the other two. Socialism—different from African communalism or agrarian cooperativism—is preeminently a European discourse and practice which remains far removed from both Afro-American and American life. Unlike Euro-American Christianity and white feminism, socialism has not been seriously appropriated by black people and rearticulated within an Afro-American context and language. This does not mean that there have been no noteworthy black socialists—yet none have had the will, vision, and imagination to *Afro-Americanize* socialist thought and practice. Yet, recently, rudimentary efforts have been made—such as Manning Marable's *Blackwater*, Maulana Karenga's *Kawaida Theory*, my own *Prophesy Deliverance!* and Cedric Robinson's *Black Marxism*.

The cultural distance from socialist thought and action have forced most black socialists to shun the very riches and resources of Afro-American culture, especially its deep moralism, combative spirituality and aggressive pessimism. The results have been mere emulations and bland imitations of Euro-American socialists, who themselves possess a weak tradition of theory and practice. It is no accident that the disproportionate number of black socialist intellectuals in the USA since WW II have yet to produce a major black socialist theorist (I consider neither Du Bois nor Oliver Cox major theoretical thinkers). Or that there has been but one serious black socialist leader in this century—and he, a Baptist preacher during the Debsian phase of American socialism, Rev. George Washington Woodbey.

The major challenge of the prophetic tradition in Afro-America in the last decades of this century is to build upon the best of the black prophetic church, to promote the further flowering of black womanist practices, and to indigenize socialist thought and practice in conjunction with ecological concerns. This latter endeavor consists of reinscribing and rearticulating the specific forms of class exploitation and imperialist oppression *and* the violent destruction of the biosphere, nature, and potentially the planet within the context of the Afro-American past and present.

This challenge is both intellectual and practical. It is intellectual in that it requires new forms of theoretical activity from black thinkers who are in close dialogue with European, Asian, African, Latin American, and Native American intellectuals yet rooted in the best of the Afro-American intellectual past. These new forms of theoretical activity must learn from Marxism (class and imperialist oppression), populism (local peoples' empowerment), civic republicanism (decentralized democratic control), liberalism (individual liberties, due process of law, separation of church and state, and checks and balances), and womanism (women's control of their bodies and destinies) as well as ecologism (communion with rather than domination of nature) and elements of Garveyism (dignity of African peoples). Similarly, it is a practical challenge in that it must be feasible and credible to a majority of the populace; that is, it must have organizational expressions with enough support, potency and power to transform fundamentally the present order. In this regard, black prophetic practices are not simply inseparable from prophetic practices of other peoples: they also hold a crucial key to the widespread impact of prophetic practices upon prevailing retarding ones.

Therefore black prophetic practices will remain truncated—as with all other American prophetic practices—unless the struggles against forms of despair, dogmatisms, and oppressions are cast on a new plane—a higher moral plane, a more sophisticated and open-ended theoretical plane, and a more culturally grounded political plane. The higher moral standard must make the all-inclusive ideals of individuality and socialist democracy the center of a prophetic vision. The more sophisticated and open-ended theoretical activity must reject unidimensional analyses and master discourses yet preserve intellectual rigor and complexity. And the more culturally grounded political plane must be deeply rooted in the everyday lives of ordinary people—people who have the ability and capacity to change the world and govern themselves under circumstances not of their own choosing.

Permissions Acknowledgments

ism," from *African-American Religion in the Twentieth Century: Varieties of Protest and Accommodation.* Copyright © 1992 by The University of Tennessee Press.

"Chosen Peoples of the Metropolis: Black Muslims, Black Jews, and Others" by Wilson Jeremiah Moses is from *Black Messiahs and Uncle Toms.* Published in University Park, Pennsylvania, by The Pennsylvania State University Press, 1982, pp. 183–195. Copyright 1982 by The Pennsylvania State University. Reproduced by permission of the publisher.

"Religious Ethos of the UNIA" is reprinted from *Garveyism as a Religious Movement: The Institutionalization of Black Civil Religion* by Randall K. Burkett and published by Scarecrow Press and The American Theological Library Association. Used by permission of Scarecrow Press and The American Theological Library Association.

"Marcus Garvey, Father Divine, and the Gender Politics of Race Difference and Race Neutrality" by Beryl Satter is reprinted from "Marcus Garvey, Father Divine and the Gender Politics of Race Neutrality." *American Quarterly* 48:1 (1996), 43–76. © The American Studies Association. Reprinted with permission of the Johns Hopkins University Press.

"Charles Manuel 'Sweet Daddy' Grace" by John O. Hodges is reprinted from *Twentieth-Century Shapers of American Popular Religion* (ed. Charles H. Lippy). Copyright © by Greenwood Publishing Group. Reproduced by permission of Greenwood Publishing Group, Inc., Westport, CT.

"The Black Roots of Pentecostalism" by Iain MacRobert is reprinted from *Pentecost, Mission, and Ecumenism: Essays on Intercultural Theology* edited by Jan A. B. Jongeneel and published in 1992 by Peter Lang Publishing Group. Used by permission of the Peter Lang Publishing Group.

"'Together and in Harness': Women's Traditions in the Sanctified Church" by Cheryl Townsend Gilkes is from *Signs* 10, 4, summer 1985, and published by The University of Chicago Press. Used by permission of Cheryl Townsend Gilkes and The University of Chicago Press.

"Reverend George Washington Woodbey: Early Twentieth-Century California Black Socialist" by Philip S. Foner is reprinted from *The Journal of Negro History*, vol. 61, no. 2, (April 1976), pages 136–157, and published by The Association for the Study of African-American Life and History, Inc. Used by permission of The Association for the Study of African-American Life and History.

The excerpt from *The Luminous Darkness* is from *A Strange Freedom: The Best of Howard Thurman on Religious Experience and Public Life* by Howard Thurman (Walter Earl Fluker and Catherine Tumber, eds.) and published in 1998 by Beacon Press. Used by permission of Friends University Press.

"Martin Luther King, Jr., and the African-American Social Gospel" by Clayborne Carson is reprinted from *African American Christianity: Essays in History* and published by the University of California Press. Used by permission of the University of California Press.

"The Religion of Black Power" by Vincent Harding is reprinted from *The Religious Situation: 1968* (Donald R. Cutler, ed.) and published in 1968 by Beacon Press. Used by permission of Vincent Harding and Beacon Press.

"Integrationism and Nationalism in African-American Intellectual History" is reprinted from *Martin and Malcolm and America* by James H. Cone and published in 1991 by Orbis Books. Used by permission of Orbis Books.